MW00358590

137 -151
276-283

SUMMARY OF CONTENTS

CONTENTS

IV

DEFINITIONAL AND TRACING ISSUES   137

V

EVIDENTIARY PRESUMPTIONS IN CALIFORNIA
COMMUNITY PROPERTY LAW   153

VI

CLASSIFICATION OF PROPERTY   217

VII

MANAGEMENT AND CREDITORS' RIGHTS   379

VIII

INCEPTION AND TERMINATION OF THE ECONOMIC COMMUNITY

IX

PROPERTY DISTRIBUTION AT DIVORCE 485

X

PROPERTY DISTRIBUTION AT DEATH   543

XI

CHOICE OF LAW AT DIVORCE AND DEATH   565

XII

FEDERAL PREEMPTION OF STATE MARITAL
PROPERTY LAW 609

CALIFORNIA STATUTORY APPENDIX 623

PREFACE

Now in its fourth edition, this book is intended to work on several levels. Most basically, it provides comprehensive coverage of California community property law, with a view toward preparation for the California bar examination and California practice, particularly in the areas of divorce, decedents' estates, and creditors' rights. Additionally, the scope and usefulness of the book extend beyond the borders of California. Every state now has some form of marital property system. California community property law, once viewed as an exotic and obscure area of local law, is now considered one of the leading systems of marital property law. The book uses California law to examine the issues that face any marital property system. Because California community property law is more extensively developed than the marital property law of many other jurisdictions, it is a valuable aid for attorneys and legislators in sister states. Moreover, choice-of-law principles often require that sister-state probate and divorce practitioners have some familiarity with California community property law in order to serve clients formerly domiciled in California.

The introductory chapter locates California community property law in the international and national landscape of marital property law. Throughout the book, the notes makes comparative reference to the law of other jurisdictions, the Uniform Marital Property Act, and, especially, the marital property chapter of the American Law Institute's recently published Principles of the Law of Family Dissolution. The book also locates marital property law within the larger domain of family law. The introductory chapter explores the relationship between marital property law and support law, and surveys different approaches to family wealth allocation at the dissolution of a marriage.

The development of California community property law provides abundant illustration of the interplay of social and legal change. Although the 1849 California Constitutional Convention adopted Spanish community propety law principles in order to protect the interests of married women, the California legislature and courts initially constructed a marital property system as oppressive as the common law regime explicitly rejected by the constitutional convention. Women's progress toward formal, or de jure, sexual equality is reflected in a series of amendments from 1872 to 1975. Later, attention shifted from de jure equality to de facto equality, and the legislature sought to remedy de facto spousal inequality in a series of community property enactments that define the fiduciary responsibilities of a managing spouse and allow a nonmanaging spouse access to the community property.

Some of the most difficult marital property issues concern the classification of human capital and career assets. When community property law initially developed, personal wealth consisted largely of physical capital, usually agricultural land, which was made productive by relatively unskilled labor. Under such circumstances, a system that differentiated between earnings during marriage (community property) and earnings after dissolution (an earner's separate property) was conceptually sound and easy to administer. In our century, however, we tend increasingly to invest in ourselves and to rely on our human capital, usually in the form of education and vocational experience, to produce an ever-growing stream of income. To the extent that earnings after dissolution represent, in part, a return on human capital acquired during marriage (as contrasted with a return on post-dissolution labor), the traditional classification rubric may seem inadequate. The issue is presented when, for example, a person acquires a professional education or business goodwill during marriage, but reaps the rewards of that acquisition after divorce. Closely related are the deferred compensation issues raised by pensions, disability benefits, severance pay, employee stock options, bonuses, and merit-based salary increases. The book closely and comprehensively examines the classification of career-related assets because they represent the primary source of wealth for many persons and they pose a significant conceptual challenge for marital property law.

The study of community property affords us an extended view of the most intimate relationship in American culture, the conjugal relationship. It is a subject to which we all bring personal experience, whether our own or that of our parents and friends. Community property may cause us to reflect on how we might structure or restructure our present or future relationships. It also invites us to consider how we can best serve clients when their intimate relationships are terminated by separation, divorce, or death.

Readers familiar with prior editions of the book will find that the fourth edition introduces or substantially reworks a number of topics.

- This edition includes excerpts from the American Law Institute's Principles of the Law of Family Dissolution: Analysis and Recommendations, published in 2002 after a decade of consideration and revision. Throughout the book, the ALI Principles are presented and discussed in the textual notes in order to shed comparative light on the content of California law.
- The treatment of premarital agreements (Chapter III) has been extensively revised to cover Marriage of Pendleton & Fireman and Marriage of Bonds, and the response of the California legislature to the holdings of those cases. Like the debate between the judiciary and the legislature about the treatment of separate property contributions to the acquisition of jointly titled property (Chapter V), the developments concerning premarital agreements provide an opportunity to examine a spirited encounter between the judiciary and the legislature.
- The chapter on marriage (Chapter VIII) has been expanded to cover domestic partnerships. In 1999, the California legislature created a new legal status called "domestic partnership," which is primarily intended for same-sex couples. Subse-

quent legislation has expanded the marriage-like rights of registered domestic partners. The casebook discussion of domestic partnership puts the California legislation in national and worldwide perspective.

- Debt allocation at the death of a spouse (Chapter X) has been revised to include the 2001 amendment of Probate Code section 11444. Repealing prior treatment, which applied the rules concerning liability for debts during marriage, the 2001 legislation instead applies the rules controlling the assignment of outstanding debts at divorce.
- Continuing to explore the fiduciary duties of a managing spouse, this edition adds Marriage of Rossi, which applies the penalty provision of Family Code section 1101(h) to award concealed community property entirely to the wronged spouse.

Grace Ganz Blumberg

December 2002

ACKNOWLEDGMENTS

I gratefully acknowledge the contributions of my UCLA students, my secretary Margaret Kiever, and the staff at Aspen.

I acknowledge the permissions kindly granted to reproduce excerpts from the materials indicated below:

American Law Institute, Principles of the Law of Family Dissolution: Analysis and Recommendations (2002). Copyright © 2002 by the American Law Institute. Reprinted with permission. All rights reserved. The complete text of the Principles of the Law of Family Dissolution: Analysis and Recommendations is now available on the ALI website at www.ali.org or by calling ALI at 1-800-253-6397.

Fred M. Adams, Is Professional Goodwill Divisible Community Property?, 6 Community Property Journal 61, 61-63, 70-72 (1979). Copyright © 1979. Reprinted with permission of Aspen Law & Business Publishers.

Grace Blumberg, Additional Thoughts on Lezine. Originally published in 1997 California Family Law Monthly 60-61 (February 1997). Copyright © 1997. Reprinted with permission of Matthew Bender & Co., Inc.

June Carbone and Margaret F. Brinig, Rethinking Marriage: Feminist Ideology, Economic Change, and Divorce Reform. Originally published in 65 Tul. L. Rev. 953-1010. Copyright © 1991. Reprinted with permission of Tulane Law Review.

Richard E. Denner, Nonmarital Cohabitation After Marvin: In Search of a Standard. Originally published in 2 California Family Law Monthly, No. 7, 229, 232-235 (February 1986). Copyright © 1986. Reprinted with permission of Matthew Bender & Co., Inc.

William de Funiak and Michael Vaughn, Principles of Community Property (2d ed.). Reprinted with permission of University of Arizona Press, Tucson, Arizona. Copyright © 1971.

Linda Gach, The Mix-Hicks Mix: Tracing Troubles under California's Community Property System. Originally published in 26 UCLA L. Rev. 1232. Copyright © 1979, The Regents of the University of California. All rights reserved.

Joan Krauskopf, Recompense for Financing Spouse's Education: Legal Protec-

tion for the Marital Investor in Human Capital, 28 Kan. L. Rev. 379. Copyright ©
1980. Reprinted with permission of the Kansas Law Review. University of Kansas.

Susan Westerberg Prager, The Persistence of Separate Property Concepts in
California's Community Property System, 1849-1975. Originally published in 24
UCLA L. Rev. 1. Copyright © 1976, The Regents of the University of California.
All rights reserved.

COMMUNITY PROPERTY IN CALIFORNIA

I

INTRODUCTION

Some property interests arise by operation of law rather than by agreement of the parties. They include ownership by adverse possession, statutory tenancy, and dower. California community property also arises by operation of law. In California, unless the parties agree otherwise, marriage brings with it a complex and intricate system of marital property. This introduction places the California system in international and national perspective.

A. THE RELATIONSHIP BETWEEN THE FAMILY AND PROPERTY OWNERSHIP: A COMPARATIVE OVERVIEW

In many cultures, the family or some component of it is designated the owner of property acquired by its members. In prerevolutionary China, for example, the household unit, or chia, generally consisting of some dozen or so adult members related by blood or marriage, was the owner of all wealth acquired by its members.[1] In the western world, the basic ownership unit has been the conjugal, or husband-wife, dyad. Apparently rooted in Germanic and Visigothic law, community property principles spread over Europe and many of the areas colonized by Europeans, such as South Africa and Latin America.

When the Normans invaded England in 1066, they had not yet adopted community property law. Instead they brought to England what we now call the *common law* system of ownership. This system endured, essentially unchanged, for centuries and was exported by the English to their American colonies, where it experienced substantial alteration in the Married Women's Property Acts of the nineteenth century. Louisiana, settled by the French, adopted a community property system derived from Spanish law. Later, seven western states, all late admittees to the Union, declined for

COMMON LAW v. CP

1. M. J. Meijer, Marriage Law and Policy in the Chinese People's Republic 5-22 (1971).

1

various reasons to adopt the common law system and chose instead the Spanish community property law extant in the western territories wrested from Mexico.[2]

The Spanish community property system, because of its adoption by other countries and the Spanish colonization of Latin America, has become the dominant form of community property in the western world. It is not, however, the exclusive form. The most salient characteristic of Spanish community property is its distinction between marital property — that is, property earned during marriage by the labor of the parties — and separate property — that is, property acquired before marriage by any means and property acquired during marriage by gift, bequest, devise, or descent. Thus the Spanish community property system appropriates to the conjugal unit the fruits of all labor during marriage. In contrast, the Roman-Dutch system creates a universal marital community of all property whenever and however acquired. The Roman-Dutch system now exists in the Netherlands, South Africa, Brazil, Denmark, Norway, and Iceland.[3] A second prominent characteristic of the Spanish community property system is its creation of present interests. Under modern law, the nonearning spouse's interest attaches as soon as the property is acquired. In contrast, a number of Northern European countries have adopted a system characterized as "deferred community property." In Germany, Sweden, Norway, and Denmark, property is owned individually during marriage but at divorce or death is essentially treated as though it were community property.[4]

B. MARITAL PROPERTY IN THE UNITED STATES

The distinctions between modern common law and community property jurisdictions are often overstated. This section will explore the differences and show that the similarities are more frequent and important than the differences.

1. The Modern American Common Law Marital Property System: The Elective Share and Equitable Distribution

In order to understand the modern common law marital property system, it is necessary to pay some brief attention to its history. Before the nineteenth century, marriage brought about a single unified property interest with most of the incidents of ownership and all control residing in the husband. Upon marriage, a woman's

---

2. For comparative and historical background, see Comparative Law of Matrimonial Property (A. Kiralfy ed. 1972); W. de Funiak and M. Vaughn, Principles of Community Property 1-91 (2d ed. 1971); G. McKay, A Treatise on the Law of Community Property 1-63 (2d ed. 1925); Vaughn, The Policy of Community Property and Inter-Spousal Transactions. 19 Baylor L. Rev. 20 (1967); Kirkwood, Historical Background and Objectives of the Law of Community Property in the Pacific Coast States. 11 Wash. L. Rev. 1 (1936); McMurray, The Beginnings of the Community Property System in California and the Adoption of the Common Law, 3 Calif. L. Rev. 359 (1915): Loewy, The Spanish Community of Acquests and Gains and Its Adoption and Modification by the State of California, 1 Calif. L. Rev. 32 (1912). See also Bibliography, 68 Marq. L. Rev. 519 (1985).

3. Rheinstein and Glendon, Interspousal Relations (ch. 4) at 49-77, 139, in 4 Int. Encyclopedia of Comp. L. (A. Chloros ed. 1980).

4. Id.

property became for most purposes her husband's and he was entitled to her earnings during marriage. Blackstone's often quoted description of the common law as merging all of the spouses' interests into one person, the husband,[5] was in most respects correct.

During the nineteenth century, this system was radically reformed. The major thrust of the reform was to treat married women, for purposes of property ownership, as though they were still single. Enacted in all common law states by the end of the century, the Married Women's Property Acts regard the married woman as the separate and individual owner of all property that would have been hers but for the marriage. A married woman owns and controls all property that she brings to the marriage from whatever source and all property that she acquires or earns during marriage. Thus, in the modern common law system property belongs either to the husband or to the wife. Property is held jointly only when one or both spouses elect to take title jointly. The modern common law separation of interests contrasts with the unity of interest implicit in both the community property and pre-nineteenth century common law systems.

Yet the enactment of legal equality for married women did not establish their economic equality. Interspousal economic inequality does not generally present serious problems during marriage, when husband and wife substantially share their resources. However, when marriage is dissolved by death or divorce, the economically inferior spouse may experience material hardship. In the past hundred years or so, modern common law jurisdictions have developed two redistributional mechanisms at marital termination: the elective share and equitable distribution. The elective share takes effect at death, and equitable distribution operates at divorce.

The elective share, whose historical antecedent is the surviving spouse's dower or curtesy right in certain freehold interests, ensures that the surviving spouse receives a substantial portion of the decedent's entire estate, both real and personal. This portion is generally one-third. To guarantee the survivor's share, many states make it difficult to defeat a surviving spouse's share by pre-death gift transfers.[6]

The elective share comes into play only when the decedent has left a will or otherwise disposed of his estate in derogation of the survivor's elective portion. If the decedent dies without a will or other dispositive instrument, the survivor takes under state intestacy law. In modern common law jurisdictions, the surviving spouse is an heir and, depending on the existence of other heirs, generally takes one-third, one-half, or all of the decedent's intestate estate.

Equitable distribution doctrine empowers the divorce court to assign property without regard to predivorce legal ownership. Although equitable distribution originated in the nineteenth century, it has experienced dramatic development within the last several decades. This growth accompanied widespread adoption of no-fault divorce, which was in turn spurred by rising divorce rates. Equitable distribution took hold of divorce law in three ways. First, as recently as 1975, many prominent

---

5. By marriage, the husband, and wife are one person in law; that is, the very being or legal existence of the woman is suspended during the marriage, or at least is incorporated and consolidated into that of the husband; under whose wing, protection, and cover, she performs everything. . . . [E]ven the disabilities which the wife lies under, are for the most part intended for her protection and benefit. So great a favourite is the female sex in the laws of England.

William Blackstone, 1 Commentaries on the Laws of England 455-457 (3d ed. 1862).

6. See, e.g., N.Y. Est. Powers & Trusts Law §5-1.1(b) (2002); Uniform Probate Code art. II, pt. II, 8 U.L.A. 73 (1983 and Supp. 1992).

states, including New York, Pennsylvania, Maryland, and Virginia, did not have equitable distribution. Such states were called *title* jurisdictions. For purposes of divorce, they had no marital property system at all. Yet by 1986, every common law state had adopted equitable distribution.[7] Second, as equitable distribution has been widely legislated, its content has been transformed to more fully embrace the concept of marriage as a sharing partnership.[8] Finally, and not entirely separated from the last point, a doctrine that began as a means to register highly discretionary judicial response to unusual situations has become a routine economic reallocation between the spouses. Though the doctrine initially contained no proportional norms, presumptive norms of 50-50 contribution or distribution are becoming more frequent.[9] As the doctrine has progressed from occasional to routine application, case law has developed apace. What, exactly, is *property* for purposes of an equitable distribution? A pension? An unvested pension? The goodwill from a professional practice? The increased earning potential due to a professional degree? To answer these questions, common law courts often look to already-developed community property case law.

With respect to the definition of property subject to the court's equitable distribution, the common law possibilities parallel the community property choices. The Roman-Dutch universal community of all property whenever and however acquired has its analog in the *hotchpot* approach of the substantial minority of American common law states that empower the divorce court to redistribute all property owned by either spouse. In contrast, the remaining common law jurisdictions, like the Spanish community property system, distinguish between property acquired before marriage and property acquired during marriage.[10] In some of these states, however, a portion of property acquired before marriage may also be subject to equitable distribution.[11] Even those states that do distinguish between nonmarital and marital

7. Mississippi was the last state to adopt equitable distribution. In a series of cases decided during 1985 and 1986, the Mississippi Supreme Court announced the principle that jointly accumulated property of both married and unmarried cohabitants should be equitably divided according to the market and nonmarket economic contributions of each partner. Pickens v. Pickens, 490 So. 2d 872 (1986); Maxcy v. Estate of Maxcy, 485 So. 2d 1077 (1986); Watts v. Watts, 466 So. 2d 889 (1985). See also Dudley v. Light, 586 So. 2d 155 (1991) and Jones v. Jones, 532 So. 2d 574 (1988).

8. Compare, e.g., Anderson v. Anderson, 68 N.W.2d 849 (N.D. 1955) ($2,000 equitable distribution award to *W* reversed because she had contributed no extraordinary services, that is, no services beyond those of an ordinary housewife) with recent case law and legislation requiring that homemaking services be taken into account in property distribution. See, e.g., Ark. Code Ann. 9-12-315 (2002); Ind. Code Ann. §31-15-7-5 (2002); Neb. Rev. Stat. §42-365 (2002); Wis. Stat. Ann. §767.255 (2002).

9. See, e.g., Ark. Code Ann. §9-12-315 (2002) ("All marital property shall be distributed one-half to each party unless the court finds such a division to be inequitable. . . . [T]he court must state its basis and reasons for not dividing the marital property equally . . ."). See cases and statutes collected in Blumberg, Marital Property Treatment of Pensions, Disability Pay, Workers' Compensation and Other Wage Substitutes: An Insurance, or Replacement, Analysis, 34 UCLA L. Rev. 1250, 1251, n.7 (1986). For discussion of the distinction between equal contribution and equal distribution, see pages 24-26 infra.

10. Freed and Walker, Family Law in the Fifty States: An Overview, 23 Fam. L.Q. 309, 332-340 (1991).

11. See, e.g., Minn. Stat. Ann. §518.58 (2002):

> [T]he court shall make a just and equitable disposition of the marital property of the parties without regard to marital misconduct. . . . The course may also award to either spouse the household goods and furniture of the parties, whether or not acquired during marriage. . . .
>
> If the course finds that either spouse's resources or property, including the spouse's portion of the marital property . . . are so inadequate as to work an unfair hardship, considering all relevant circumstances, the court may, in addition to the marital property, apportion up to one-half [of the other spouse's separate property] . . . to prevent the unfair hardship.

acquisitions may not follow the Spanish distinction between property acquired by labor and property acquired by gift or bequest. Delaware, for example, classifies as marital property gifts received by either spouse during marriage, Husband R.T.G. v. Wife R.T.G., 410 A.2d 155 (Del. Super. Ct. 1979). See also Gregg v. Gregg, 510 A.2d 474 (Del. 1986).

2. Community Property

Community property has traditionally been associated with eight contiguous American states. Moving geographically from northwest to southeast, they are: Washington, Idaho, Nevada, California, Arizona, New Mexico, Texas, and Louisiana. American community property law, patterned on the Spanish system, establishes two categories of marital property: community property and separate property. Community property is all property produced by the labor of either spouse during marriage. Community property is owned equally by the spouses from the moment of acquisition. Absent an agreement of the spouses, there is ordinarily no right to partition the community property during marriage. On termination of the marriage by death, the surviving spouse and the decedent's estate each own one-half of the community property. Although 50-50 distribution at divorce is the rule in California, New Mexico, and Louisiana, the other five community property states empower their courts to make, incident to divorce, an equitable distribution of the community property.[12] Community property jurisdictions in the United States have typically defined *separate* property as all property owned before marriage and acquired thereafter by gift, bequest, devise, or descent. The American community property systems emphasize common ownership but at the same time provide for separation of certain of the spouses' property interests.

3. Contrast between Modern Common Law and Community Property Systems

With respect to the ongoing marriage, modern common law and community property regimes take different positions on the desirability of unifying the property interests of husband and wife. In a common law jurisdiction, joint ownership is possible only by explicit choice. The spouses are regarded, for property ownership purposes, as though they were two unmarried persons. In contrast, community property law assumes joint ownership unless the parties demonstrate otherwise, either by showing that the property is by definition separate or that the parties explicitly agreed to a separate classification. Thus, insofar as the two systems characterize property during the ongoing marriage, they manifest quite different judgments about the nature of the marital relationship and the assumptions and expectations of the individuals who enter it.

Issues of property ownership rarely arise, however, during an ongoing marriage; instead, they become prominent at dissolution. Here, as we have seen, the

---

12. Cal. Fam. Code §2550 (2002); Bustos v. Bustos, 100 N.M. 556, 558, 673 P.2d 1289 (1983); La. Civ. Code art. 2336 (2002); Ariz. Rev. Stat. Ann. §25-318 (2002); Idaho Code §32-712 (2002); Nev. Rev. Stat. §125.150 (2002); Tex. Fam. Code Ann. §7.001 (2002); Wash. Rev. Code Ann. §26.09.080 (2002). The Washington statute allows the divorce court to equitably distribute the parties' separate property as well.

lines between modern common law and community property blur. In community property states, the divorced spouse is entitled to a portion of the community property; in five of the eight states, this portion is variable and subject to the court's equitable distribution. In modern common law states, the divorced spouse is entitled to a portion of the marital property and perhaps to a portion of the other spouse's separate property as well. In modern common law states, variable distribution is the norm although there is some movement toward 50-50 distribution. At death, community property distribution has its counterpart for the surviving spouse in the modern common law elective share of the decedent's estate.[13]

Nevertheless, the notion of a spouse's present equal interest in marital property has considerable symbolic force. It clearly announces that spouses are understood to contribute equally to the family without regard to actual division of labor. It dignifies the work of the homemaker, tends to rectify sex-related inequality of employment opportunity, and recognizes that the couple may make unequal human capital investment in the spouses.[14] The community property view may also affect the manner in which courts equitably distribute property at divorce, that is, the way that courts allocate property at divorce may be influenced by predivorce legal ownership of that property.

In 1979, the National Conference of Commissioners on Uniform State Laws began to promulgate a uniform marital property act. After carefully considering the possibility of deferred community property derived from Northern European models, the drafters selected a full-blown community property regime, largely for its symbolic and normative value: "It is a law that translates the emotional and perceived concept of 'ours' into a verified legal reality."[15] The Uniform Marital Property Act was approved by the National Conference of Commissioners on August 1, 1983. It has been enacted in Wisconsin.

In 1989, the American Law Institute undertook a project entitled Principles of the Law of Family Dissolution: Analysis and Recommendations, which covers all aspects of divorce and nonmarital cohabitation. The project was called Principles rather than Restatement, because the purpose was to rethink and, where desirable, recast the law of family dissolution. By mid-2000, the major chapters had been approved by the membership of the American Law Institute. The final version of the Principles was published in 2002. The chapter on property division adopts many of the basic principles of California community property law.

California community property law, once perceived as a local and exotic subject, now occupies a central position in the rapidly developing field of American marital property law. California cases are frequently considered by sister-state courts when they add content to their own less developed law. Similarly, the Uniform Marital Property Act (UMPA) and the American Law Institute's Principles of the Law of Family Dissolution (ALI Principles) provide critical mirrors for California law. They adopt many California rules, but reject others as unwieldy, unworkable, or unwise. This book comparatively notes sister-state, UMPA, and ALI treatment of particular marital property issues.

---

13. There is, however, a significant distinction from the perspective of the spouse who dies first. The elective share only operates in favor of the surviving spouse. Thus, the spouse who dies first has no power to will away any interest in the survivor's property. In contrast, either spouse may exercise testamentary power over his one-half of the community property. Under what circumstances might this difference matter to the predeceased spouse?

14. See pages 47-49 infra.

15. Introduction to the 1982 Draft.

C.   MARITAL PROPERTY AS A FORM OF DIVORCE-RELATED WEALTH DISTRIBUTION: THE RELATIONSHIP BETWEEN PROPERTY DISTRIBUTION AND SPOUSAL AND CHILD SUPPORT

Marital property law may be studied as a discrete subject, as is customary in many California law schools. Yet at divorce, community property law may also be understood, in theory and in practice, as simply one component of a more comprehensive treatment of the spouses' economic relationship and their continuing economic claims against each other on behalf of themselves and the children of their marriage. The other two components are child support and spousal support.

Although support and property distribution may be economically interchangeable for the divorcing litigants, they do have different legal attributes. Unless the parties agree otherwise, spousal support is judicially modifiable and generally terminates at the death of the support obligor or obligee, at the obligee's remarriage, and, in many jurisdictions, upon the obligee's marriage-like cohabitation with a third party. See, for example, California Family Code sections 3591, 3651, 4323, and 4337, reprinted at pages 683-698 infra. Property distribution is unaffected by these events and is nonmodifiable. Property distribution obligations may be dischargeable in bankruptcy, but support obligations are not.[16] Federal income tax law makes certain divorce-related periodic payments taxable to the payee and deductible by the payor;[17] no such consequences attach to an immediate property distribution.

1.   Child Support

In the past decade, child support has been regularized and rationalized in the United States. As required by federal welfare law, all states have now formulated mathematical guidelines generally based upon the percentage of income that parents at various income levels spend on children in intact families.[18] In the United States, child support is generally intended to support only children. It is not designed to provide for their custodial caretaker. The current California child support guideline is codified at Family Code sections 4050-4073, reprinted at pages 686-693 infra.

2.   Spousal Support (also known as alimony or maintenance)*

At traditional common law, the quid pro quo for the husband's control of the wife's property was his duty to support her. This duty persisted even when the parties

---

16. 11 U.S.C. §523(a)(5) and (15) (2002).
17. 26 U.S.C. §§71, 215, and 1041 (2002).
18. See generally Garfinkel and Melli, The Use of Normative Standards in Family Law Decisions: Developing Mathematical Standards for Child Support, 24 Fam. L.Q. 157 (1990).

* Copyright © 1997, 2002, Matthew Bender & Co., Inc. All rights reserved. Adapted from 2 Valuation and Distribution of Marital Property, 41-8–41-12, with permission of the publisher.

were legally separated (divorce *a mensa et thoro,* that is, from bed and board). Although absolute divorce provisions were not legislated until the mid-nineteenth century in England, many of the American colonies enacted absolute divorce statutes earlier. These enactments maintained the possibility of a support duty that survived not only legal separation but divorce as well.

In its doctrinally most expansive formulation, alimony was conceived as permanent, that is, as payable until death or remarriage obviated the recipient's need for support. The traditional measure of alimony was the marital standard of living insofar as it was maintainable in two postdivorce households. Yet alimony, even in its doctrinal heyday, was neither generously nor frequently granted.[19] Moreover, alimony has always been difficult to collect.[20]

Beginning in the 1970s, coextensive with rising divorce rates, the nominal liberalization of divorce, and the expansion of marital property law, a number of American states experienced doctrinal constriction of alimony. In some jurisdictions, statutes were rewritten to promote short term, or rehabilitative, alimony.[21] In other jurisdictions appellate case law promoted the same outcome.[22] In still other jurisdictions, trial court judges, acting on their own and purporting to apply "new principles of sexual equality," declined to order long-term alimony where existing state legal norms still seemed to require it.[23]

The most principled and influential expression of this position appeared in the Uniform Marriage and Divorce Act (UMDA), promulgated in 1974.[24] The UMDA vigorously promoted property division as an alternative to spousal support.[25] It proposed that all assets, whenever and however acquired by the parties, be distributed according to principles of need and contribution, with homemaking contributions explicitly taken into account.[26] The economic quid pro quo for this expansive property division was abandonment of the traditional alimony formulation, which had nominally contemplated maintenance of the wife's marital standard of living, subject to the husband's ability to pay. Instead the UMDA established a threshold requirement: A spouse is eligible for support only if she is unable to meet her *reasonable needs* from property, including that distributed to her at divorce, and earnings from her own gainful employment, unless the presence of young children or her own incapacity makes such employment infeasible.[27] If a spouse is able to meet the threshold eligibility requirement, that is, if her resources are inadequate to meet her reasonable

19. H. Clark, The Law of Domestic Relations in the United States §16.4 and sources cited therein (2d ed. 1988).

20. Id.

21. See, e.g., The Uniform Marriage and Divorce Act, §308, 9A U.L.A. 446 (1998).

22. See, e.g., Contogeorgos v. Contogeorgos, 482 So. 2d 590 (Fla. App. 1986); Herring v. Herring, 335 S.E.2d 366 (S.C. 1985).

23. For California experience, see Kay, An Appraisal of California's No-Fault Divorce Law, 75 Cal. L. Rev. 291, 300-302 (1987).

24. 9A U.L.A. 159 (1998). National Conference of Commissioners on Uniform State Laws, Uniform Marriage and Divorce Act (recommended by the National Conference of Commissioners in 1970, amended in 1971, and approved by the House of Delegates of the American Bar Association in 1974). The UMDA has been enacted in eight states: Arizona, Colorado, Illinois, Kentucky, Minnesota, Missouri, Montana, and Washington.

25. Prefatory Note, Uniform Marriage and Divorce Act, 9A U.L.A. 161 (1998) and Comment to §308, id. at 447.

26. §307, UMDA, 9A U.L.A. 288 (1998).

27. §308(a), UMDA, 9A U.L.A. 446 (1998).

needs, then the court is instructed to apply the traditional criteria[28] to establish the level of support. The Act also contemplates that spousal support may be time-limited. In setting the duration of the award, it instructs the court to consider "the time necessary to acquire sufficient education or training to enable the party seeking maintenance to find appropriate employment."[29] Although only eight states adopted the Act[30] and one of them, Arizona, moderated the support provision,[31] the content of the UMDA support provision was judicially and legislatively expressed in other jurisdictions as well.[32] In some jurisdictions, "reasonable needs" replaced "marital standard of living" as a measure both of threshold eligibility and level of support,[33] and short-term awards supplanted alimony of indefinite duration. In practice, this often meant a bare bones, time-limited payment until the divorced spouse could find employment to provide for her basic needs. Although often optimistically labeled "rehabilitative" alimony, such awards rarely included funds for education or training. In many cases "minimal and short term" would have been a more accurate descriptive label.[34] In 1988, Professor Krauskopf conducted a national survey from which she concluded that legislatures and courts have been expressing increasing disenchantment with this constricted notion of spousal support.[35]

The legislatures of several states, including New York and California, have amended their divorce statutes to revive traditional concepts of spousal support. In 1986, the New York legislature amended its support law to emphasize that courts "may award permanent maintenance." Deleting "reasonable needs," the legislature substituted "standard of living of the parties established during the marriage" as the benchmark for a spousal support award.[36]

In 1988, California amended its spousal support law to require that the divorce court make specific findings about the parties' standard of living during their marriage and, in making the award, consider the parties' marital standard of living and the extent to which the earning capacity of each spouse is sufficient to maintain that standard of living. The court is further instructed to assess the *needs* of each party "based on the standard of living established during the marriage."[37] The current California spousal support provisions, Family Code sections 4300-4360, are reprinted at pages 694-698 infra. Less dramatically, but significantly in California, where the divorce court must generally retain jurisdiction in order to award spousal support at some future date, in 1987 California legislated that the divorce court

---

28. The traditional criteria include the parties' needs, the marital standard of living, and the duration of the marriage. §308(b), UMDA, 9A U.L.A. 348 (1998). Note the disjunctive nature of the level of support criteria. The spouse seeking support must be unable to satisfy her *reasonable needs* in order to cross the eligibility threshold, but once she does, support may be calculated in terms of the *marital standard of living*.

29. Id. §308(b)(2).

30. See jurisdictions listed in note 24 supra.

31. Ariz. Rev. Stat. Ann. §25-319 (2002).

32. See Clark, supra note 19.

33. Contrast Uniform Marriage and Divorce Act §308, discussed immediately supra. Inability to meet reasonable needs is a threshold requirement; if it is met, marital standard of living is a benchmark for support.

34. Krauskopf, Rehabilitative Alimony: Uses and Abuses of Limited Duration Alimony, 21 Fam. L.Q. 573, 581 (1988).

35. Id.

36. 1986 N.Y. Laws, ch. 884, §4, amending N.Y. Dom. Rel. Law §236, Part B(6)(a), (c) (2002).

37. 1988 Cal. Stat., ch. 407, amending Cal. Civ. Code §4801 (West 1992), now codified at Cal. Fam. Code §4320(d) (2002).

retains jurisdiction indefinitely when the marriage has been of long duration. A marriage of more than 10 years is presumptively of long duration, but a marriage of fewer than 10 years may also be considered of long duration.[38]

Professor Krauskopf's national survey of appellate cases from the 1980s reveals a "phenomenal" number of appellate reversals of trial court awards of time-limited spousal support. The incidence of reversal is particularly noteworthy in an area where the standard of review has traditionally been "abuse of discretion."[39] Professor Krauskopf notes two distinct case law trends. With respect to time-limited spousal support, appellate courts increasingly require that there be evidence in the record showing that termination will be justified at the expiration of the limited time.[40] In lengthy traditional marriages where the former homemaker's earnings are modest or meager, the trend is to continue spousal support indefinitely.[41] Recent appellate decisions tend to treat marriages of 15 years or longer as lengthy marriages.[42]

The ALI Principles abandon spousal support (alimony) in favor of "compensatory spousal payments," which are intended to distribute fairly between the spouses the economic losses caused by the dissolution of marriage. The degree and duration of redistribution from a higher income spouse to a lower income spouse is determined by uniform rules, which take into account the length of the marriage and the amount of time a spouse took primary responsibility for the care of the parties' children. Although the decision-maker is given some bounded discretion, the ALI formulation would produce awards that are both more predictable and more consistent than those currently generated under the rubric of spousal support.[43]

During the last several decades many academic commentators, ranging from neoclassical economists to feminist activists, have addressed the theoretical dimensions of spousal support and, more broadly, wealth distribution at divorce. Some of their work is surveyed at pages 22-43 infra.

D. THE COMMON LAW TITLE SYSTEM

Wirth v. Wirth was decided before New York's 1980 adoption of equitable distribution,[44] that is, when New York had no divorce-related marital property law.

---

38. 1987 Cal. Stat., ch. 1086, §2, amending Cal. Civ. Code §4801(d) (West 1992), now codified at Cal. Fam. Code §4336.

39. Krauskopf, supra note 34, at 575.

40. Krauskopf, supra note 34, at 577. See, e.g., Doerflinger v. Doerflinger, 646 S.W.2d 798, 802 (Mo. 1983) (en banc); Lepis v. Lepis, 83 N.J. 139, 416 A.2d 45, 53, n. 9 (1980); Herring v. Herring, 286 S.C. 447, 335 S.E.2d 366, 368-369 (1985); Molnar v. Molnar, 314 S.E.2d 73, 77 (W. Va. 1984).

41. Id. at 579. See, e.g., Rosenberg v. Rosenberg, 64 Md. App. 487, 497 A.2d 485 (1985); Zorich v. Zorich, 63 Md. App. 710, 493 A.2d 1096 (1985); Weir v. Weir, 374 N.W. 2d 858 (N.D. 1985); Pacella v. Pacella, 341 Pa. Super. 178, 492 A.2d 707 (1985); Crim v. Crim, 289 S.C. 360, 345 S.E.2d 515 (1986); Herring v. Herring, 286 S.C. 447, 335 S.E. 2d 366 (1985); Stubbe v. Stubbe, 376 N.W.2d 807 (S.D. 1985); Olson v. Olson, 704 P.2d 564 (Utah 1985); Jones v. Jones, 700 P.2d 1072 (Utah 1985); Molnar v. Molnar, 314 S.E.2d 73 (W. Va. 1984).

42. Id. at 580. Compare Cal. Fam. Code §4336, discussed in the text immediately supra.

43. The American Law Institute, Principles of the Law of Family Dissolution: Analysis and Recommendations §§5.01–5.14 (2002).

44. 1980 N.Y. Laws, chs. 281, 645, eff. July 19, 1980, now codified at N.Y. Dom. Rel. Law §236 (2002).

WIRTH v. WIRTH
38 A.D.2d 611, 326 N.Y.S.2d 308 (1971)

Appeal from an order . . . which granted defendant's motion to dismiss the complaint, and from the judgment entered thereon.

In 1970, the appellant obtained a foreign divorce. Thereafter, the parties stipulated that her pending New York divorce action would abate insofar as the divorce was concerned but continue with respect to the property claims. This appeal results from the trial court's decision on the property claims.

In her complaint, appellant seeks judgment declaring that she is half owner of real and personal property held by her former husband in his own name and purchased with his own earnings. She claims that he was able to acquire these assets because his legal obligation to support her and their two children was fulfilled out of her earnings, not his.

Appellant's theory is constructive trust. A constructive trust may be found by a court when a party, because of a confidential relationship, relies upon a promise of another which is later breached resulting in unjust enrichment to the other. . . . The essential ingredients to support the action are that the person damaged must be induced to act to his detriment and the other's unjust benefit because of an abuse of the relationship of trust existing between the two. The language customarily used is that there is "actual or constructive fraud" in the transaction. . . .

For 22 years of marriage, the respondent delivered all his earnings to appellant, who handled the finances, to be pooled with her earnings to support the family. She paid the bills and made the investments. In 1956, he started a "crash" savings program telling appellant it was "for our latter days." She says he told her it was "for the two of us." From then on, appellant's earnings, supplemented by rental from an upstairs apartment and part of respondent's income, were used for family expenses and respondent's remaining salary was invested. This invested money has always been respondent's. It is not property appellant transferred to him. His enrichment, it is claimed, arose because she spent her salary to meet the costs of maintaining the family, while the respondent accumulated his earnings in his own name. Appellant's argument is that she parted with her property just as surely as if she delivered her check to her husband because her earnings fulfilled his support obligations.

A legal cause of action cannot be spelled out of her assumption of the family expenses after 1956. There is no doubt that a husband has the duty to support his wife and children within the limit of his means. . . . But a wife who uses her own money to pay household expenses may obtain reimbursement from her husband only when her husband either impliedly or expressly has promised he would repay her. (Manufacturers Trust Co. v. Gray, 278 N.Y. 380, 16 N.E.2d 373; Nostrand v. Ditmis, 127 N.Y. 355, 360, 28 N.E. 27.) That promise does not appear in the evidence.

What appellant really seeks is a community property division under the guise of equitable relief. She premises her claimed right to equitable relief on the brief discussions between the parties in 1956 when respondent said he intended to save money for "the two of them." There was no promise or "arrangement" born either from that incident or the parties' course of conduct thereafter. Respondent did not agree that the property would be held in joint names. . . .

The elements of concealment or misrepresentation usually found in fraudulent transactions are missing. The facts are that appellant acquiesced in the original suggestion and she has known for many years that the property was in her husband's name alone.

Respondent's statement that he intended to save for later years may well have expressed an intent that there be a joint future benefit, but it did not give appellant a vested interest in any specific portion of his assets, come what might. Indeed, although appellant complained of lack of funds from time to time, she apparently evidenced no interest in the title to the investments or savings funds until 1967.

With respect to their home, the title to it was acquired in respondent's name alone in 1949 with the down payment of $6,500 being supplied by his mother. It clearly was not subject to any supposed agreement or "arrangement." Similarly, his life insurance and retirement antedated the discussions in 1956 and the only arguable issue concerns the investments and savings.

A constructive trust is a vehicle for "fraud rectifying." . . . There may be a moral judgment that can be made on the basis of respondent's conduct and the imperfectly expressed intention of some possible future benefit to appellant, but that is not enough to set the court in motion. . . .

Order and judgment affirmed, without costs.

Notes and Questions

1. What, exactly, is the defect in Mrs. Wirth's constructive trust theory?

2. Is there ever likely to be actual fraud, or misrepresentation, in the happier days of a marriage when the relied-upon promise or statement was made? Surely Mr. Wirth meant what he said when he said it; he simply changed his mind later.

3. *Wirth* shows that even a spouse employed outside the home might be unfairly treated under the common law *title* approach to property acquired by married persons. Yet Mrs. Wirth, with her employment history, did generate market earnings. Her problem was that she relinquished control of them. The homemaker's plight could not be cured by her own behavior. Even if she carefully managed the household allowance her husband provided in order to put aside a little for her old age, at divorce her husband could impose a constructive trust on these savings titled in her name. He, after all, had intended to provide her only with household expense money. Any remaining funds were his. Marks v. Marks, 250 A.D. 289, 294 N.Y.S. 70 (1937) (dictum).

4. For further illustration of the difficulty of using constructive trust theory as a substitute for marital property law, see Saff v. Saff, 61 A.D.2d 452, 402 N.Y.S.2d 690 (1978), *appeal dismissed,* 46 N.Y.2d 969, 389 N.E.2d 142, 415 N.Y.S.2d 829 (1979). At the dissolution of their 30-year marriage, Mrs. Saff unsuccessfully sought to impose a constructive trust on a business established and developed with the funds and labor of both spouses but "owned" by her husband.

E.   EQUITABLE DISTRIBUTION

In some common law states, equitable property distribution at divorce is of relatively recent origin. Equitable distribution often accompanied other divorce reform measures, such as liberalized divorce rules and the introduction of no-fault grounds. Painter v. Painter, immediately below, is illustrative. From the content of the 1971 New Jersey reform provisions, you can infer the substance of pre-1971 law. Can you reconstruct the content of divorce negotiation under pre-1971 law? How would you explain the linkage of equitable distribution and other divorce reforms? What social factors have contributed to this recent rapid spread of equitable distribution?

PAINTER v. PAINTER
65 N.J. 196, 320 A.2d 484 (1974)

MOUNTAIN, J. The parties to this suit were divorced by judgment entered March 14, 1972 upon the ground, urged in defendant's counterclaim, that they had lived separate and apart for at least 18 or more consecutive months and that there was no reasonable prospect of reconciliation. N.J.S.A. 2A:34-2(d).[1] Thereafter, in accordance with the authority contained in N.J.S.A. 2A:34-23—as amended by the 1971 enactment—the trial court made an equitable distribution of the marital property. 118 N.J. Super. 332, 287 A.2d 467 (Ch. Div. 1972). We granted certification, 62 N.J. 192, 299 A.2d 726 (1972), as we did simultaneously in several companion cases, in order to consider the questions these cases raise and that are generally presented by this important legislation.

Stephen and Joan Painter were married October 17, 1953, and lived together as husband and wife until January 23, 1967. Three children were born of the marriage and at the time of the institution of this suit, in October, 1970, they were 15, 12 and 7 years of age. They have always been, and remain, in the custody of the mother.

At the trial it was determined that the total assets of plaintiff, Stephen Painter, had a value of $230,309 and those of defendant, Joan Painter, a value of $99,709. However, in determining the value of property subject to equitable distribution pursuant to N.J.S.A. 2A:34-23, the court excluded assets which were acquired by gift or inheritance during marriage as well as property owned prior to marriage. Pursuant to this formula, the court determined the plaintiff's and defendant's assets available for distribution, as being $82,571 and $58,199, respectively. In addition, plaintiff's income in 1971 was found to have been $32,218.

The court then entered an order directing plaintiff to pay (a) alimony and support in the sum of $12,000 per year, allocated $500 per month as alimony and $166.66 per month as support for each of the three children; (b) all reasonable medical and dental care for the three children and all medical care for the defendant; (c) "twenty per cent (20%) of the difference between plaintiff's and defendant's *available* assets—$4,874." (emphasis added).

The issues presented to the Court on this appeal concern both the constitutionality and the interpretation of L.1971, c.212. . . .

Pursuant to L.1967, c.57 . . . the Legislature created a Divorce Law Study Commission ". . . to study and review the statutes and court decisions concerning divorce

---

1. This is the so-called "no fault" ground for divorce, introduced for the first time into our law by L.1971, c.212, which became effective September 13, 1971.

and nullity of marriage and related matters . . ." L.1967, c.57, 144-145. In the preamble to this enactment it was noted that not since 1907 had there been any general revision of the statutes of the State relating to divorce, nullity of marriage or other phases of the law of domestic relations. Consequently, it went on to point out, except for the Blackwell Act (L.1923, c.187), which added extreme cruelty as a ground for divorce, there had been no significant legislation during this period pertaining to this general subject matter, although during the same interval concepts of marriage and divorce had been drastically altered. Legislative investigation and study were deemed essential as a necessary prerequisite to the drafting of a law that would adequately respond to the felt needs of our present day society in this area. On May 11, 1970 the Final Report of the Commission was submitted to the Governor and the Legislature. In very large part, but not entirely, the resulting statute, L.1971, c.212, was based upon the proposed Divorce Reform Bill which accompanied and was made part of this Report.

The most significant changes in our matrimonial law that have resulted from the adoption of this act are the following:

1. In addition to the pre-existing statutory causes for divorce, i.e., (1) adultery, (2) desertion and (3) extreme cruelty, the act includes as additional grounds: (4) separation for at least 18 months where there is no reasonable prospect of reconciliation; (5) voluntarily induced addiction to a narcotic drug, or habitual drunkenness, for a period of 12 months; (6) institutionalization because of mental illness for a period of 24 months; (7) imprisonment of the defendant for 18 months; and (8) deviant sexual conduct voluntarily performed by the defendant without the consent of the plaintiff. N.J.S.A. 2A:34-2.

2. Obstinacy need no longer be proven in order to establish a cause of action for desertion, which now accrues after twelve months willful and continued desertion rather than after two years as had previously been the case. Id.

3. Extreme cruelty, as a ground for divorce, is now defined by statute to include "any physical or mental cruelty which endangers the safety or health of the plaintiff or makes it improper or unreasonable to expect the plaintiff to continue to cohabit with the defendant . . ." Id.

4. A plaintiff seeking a divorce on the ground of extreme cruelty may now file a complaint three months after the date of the last act of cruelty complained of, instead of being required to wait six months as was formerly the case. Id.

5. Divorce from bed and board [judicial separation], which may be adjudged for the same causes as divorce from the bonds of matrimony, may now be had only upon the consent of both parties. Either party may thereafter at any time apply to have such divorce converted to a divorce from the bonds of matrimony, which application shall be granted as a matter of right. N.J.S.A. 2A:34-3.

6. Recrimination, condonation and the clean hands doctrine are no longer available as defenses. N.J.S.A. 8A:34-7.

7. If both parties make out grounds for divorce, judgment may run in favor of each. Id.

8. The durational residence requirement to initiate an action for divorce, except for adultery as to which there is no such requirement, has been shortened from two years to one year. N.J.S.A. 2A:34-10.

9. Issue of an annulled marriage shall be deemed legitimate even if — as was not heretofore the case — the annulled marriage was a nonceremonial, bigamous union. N.J.S.A. 2A:34-20.

10. Alimony may be awarded to either spouse. Except where the judgment for divorce is granted on the no-fault ground of separation, the court may, in awarding alimony, consider the proofs submitted in support of the ground upon which the judgment of divorce is made to rest. N.J.S.A. 2A:34-23.

11. Incident to the grant of divorce ". . . the court may make . . . [an] award or awards to the parties in addition to alimony and maintenance, to effectuate an equitable distribution of the property, both real and personal, which was legally and beneficially acquired by them or either of them during the marriage." Id.

An effort has been made, as is apparent from the Commission Report, to move away from the concept of fault on the part of one spouse as having been solely responsible for the marital breakdown, toward a recognition that in all probability each party has in some way and to some extent been to blame. One objective of the Commission was to make it possible to terminate dead marriages regardless of where the responsibility for the failure lay. Final Report, Divorce Law Study Commission 6. The Legislature accepted this recommendation and provided, as we have noted above, that separation for at least 18 months where there is no reasonable prospect of reconciliation shall be a ground for divorce. At the same time the Legislature concurred in the Commission's recommendation that fault grounds for divorce be retained, although somewhat liberalizing the requisites for their availability.

We turn then to the constitutional contentions which have been advanced. . . .

The second basis of constitutional challenge is that the section of the act providing for equitable distribution is impermissibly vague and uncertain. The argument here is two-pronged. It is first urged that the term "equitable" is insufficiently precise as a guide to a matrimonial judge in effecting distribution of marital property; secondly, it is contended that there is lacking any sufficient legislative statement as to what property shall be eligible for apportionment between the spouses.

The doctrine that a statute may be declared invalid because of indefiniteness is well settled, but the rationale upon which it rests has not been very clearly formulated. It has been suggested that there are two important statutory functions which may be significantly affected by indefiniteness. "One of these functions is to guide the adjudication of rights and duties; the other is to guide the individual in planning his own future conduct." Note, Due Process Requirements of Definiteness in Statutes, 62 Harv. L. Rev. 77 (1948). In other words due process requires that the adjudication of a litigant's rights and duties be governed by rules sufficiently clear and objective to guard against an arbitrary result, and that such rules be sufficiently precise to enable a lawyer to advise a client intelligently as to the probable results of a proposed course of conduct.

Judged by these criteria the words, "equitable distribution" set forth a standard which is not unduly vague. This phrase simply directs and requires that the matrimonial judge apportion the marital assets in such manner as will be just to the parties concerned, under all of the circumstances of the particular case. That a judge shall do equity is a notion understood by lawyer and litigant alike. It was the realization that certain matters must be disposed of "equitably" that led to the creation and rapid rise in influence of the Court of Chancery in the fifteenth and sixteenth centuries. Maitland, Equity (Chaytor & Whittaker ed. 1920) 3-10. The great body of equity jurisprudence that has since developed is a response to the continuing insistence that this need be met. . . .

Today in the laws of many other states, in words very similar to those found in our statute, provision is made for the fair and equitable distribution of marital assets in the event of divorce. . . . Counsel have cited no case, nor have we found any, in which legislation of this sort has been successfully attacked as affording insufficient guidelines to the judge charged with the responsibility of allocating marital assets upon the dissolution of a marriage. As Justice Peters observed in Addison v. Addison, 62 Cal. 2d 558, 43 Cal. Rptr. 97, 399 P.2d 897 (1965),

> . . . many common-law jurisdictions have provided for the division of the separate property of the respective spouses in a manner which is "just and reasonable" and none of these statutes have been overturned on a constitutional basis.

We hold that the statute before us is free from any constitutional insufficiency upon this score.

It seems appropriate at this point to suggest some of the criteria which may properly be taken into account by a matrimonial judge in determining in a given case how the distribution may most fairly be made. In his opinion in the trial court Judge Consodine, after examining authorities in other jurisdictions, compiled a list of such factors, which we here quote with approval.

> Guideline criteria over the broad spectrum of litigation in this area include: (1) respective age, background and earning ability of the parties; (2) duration of the marriage; (3) the standard of living of the parties during the marriage; (4) what money or property each brought into the marriage; (5) the present income of the parties; (6) the property acquired during the marriage by either or both parties; (7) the source of acquisition; (8) the current value and income producing capacity of the property; (9) the debts and liabilities of the parties to the marriage; (10) the present mental and physical health of the parties; (11) the probability of continuing present employment at present earnings or better in the future; (12) effect of distribution of assets on the ability to pay alimony and support; and (13) gifts from one spouse to the other during marriage. [118 N.J. Super. at 335, 287 A.2d at 469]

. . . These factors are obviously intended to be illustrative and not exhaustive. The trial judge must in each case regard all of the particular circumstances of the individuals before the court, and having weighed and evaluated them reach a determination as to how best to fulfill the mandate of the statute. As is made clear in Chalmers v. Chalmers, 65 N.J. 186, 320 A.2d 478 (1974), decided this day, fault of a marital nature is not an appropriate criterion for consideration in effecting an equitable distribution of marital assets. The judicial task may upon occasion be a difficult one but it will hardly be novel. Seeking just and equitable results is and has always been inherent in the judicial function; it has been a chief concern of the courts for many centuries. . . .

It is finally contended that the enactment must fall because there is a fatal lack of specificity as to what property shall be eligible for equitable distribution. It will be recalled that the statute authorizes "[an] award or awards to the parties, in addition to alimony and maintenance, to effectuate an equitable distribution of the property, both real and personal, which was legally and beneficially acquired by them or either of them during the marriage." N.J.S.A. 2A:34-23. The general purpose of the legislation is clear. The courts are now empowered to allocate marital assets between the spouses, regardless of ownership. This was not the case before the enactment of the statute. In Calame v. Calame, 25 N.J. Eq. 548 (E. & A. 1874) Chief Justice Beasley, writing for a unanimous court, held that the statute permitting the payment of alimony and maintenance to a wife, incident to the grant of a divorce, could not be read to permit the assignment to her of a portion of the husband's real estate in fee or of a sum of money in gross. It was held that the statute comprehended only the grant of power "to give the wife an allowance of money in periodical installments." 25 N.J. Eq. at 549. There was, however, no suggestion in the opinion that the Legislature might not, if it saw fit, authorize the allocation of a husband's property by way of provision for a wife who had successfully sought a divorce. The Legislature simply had not chosen to do so. This rule, limiting the court's power to dispose of marital assets, continued unchanged until the passage of the present statute. Parmly v. Parmly, 125 N.J. Eq. 545, 5 A.2d 789 (E. & A. 1939). While the grant of power in the present enactment is expressed in rather comprehensive and general terms, this will not, in itself, in any way derogate from its constitutional validity if judicial interpretation, rendered on a case by case basis if need be, can supply specific guidelines to govern particular situations. This, we conclude, can readily be done.

Clearly any property owned by a husband or wife at the time of marriage will remain the separate property of such spouse and in the event of divorce will not qualify as an asset eligible for distribution. As to this the statute is explicit. We also hold that if such property, owned at the time of the marriage, later increases in value, such increment enjoys a like immunity.[4] Furthermore the income or other usufruct derived from such property, as well as any asset for which the original property may be exchanged or into which it, or the proceeds of its sale, may be traceable shall similarly be considered the separate property of the particular spouse. The burden of establishing such immunity as to any particular asset will rest upon the spouse who asserts it. In reaching these latter conclusions we admittedly pass beyond the words of the statute. These determinations are, we conceive, those most consonant with presumed legislative intent.

A further question is presented when we consider assets that have come into the ownership of a spouse, or of both spouses jointly, during coverture. To the extent that such property is attributable to the expenditure of effort by either spouse, it clearly qualifies for distribution. Here we have principally in mind the earnings of husband or wife; such assets are certainly comprehended by the statute. But what of property secured by gift, bequest, devise, descent, or in some other way? The trial court found that such property was not available for distribution. We reach a contrary conclusion essentially for the reasons given below.

In the first place we read the statute on its face to express an intent to include such property as eligible for distribution. In the second place, we believe that the exclusion of such assets would result in importing into our law of property, to a significant extent at least, doctrines of community property law. We discern no intent on the part of the Legislature to do this, and we do not think that such a result, with all that it might portend, should be allowed to come about indirectly or without due deliberation.

---

4. The immunity of incremental value to which we refer is not necessarily intended to include elements of value contributed by the other spouse, nor those for which husband and wife are jointly responsible.

The court is authorized to distribute equitably ". . . the property, both real and personal, which was legally and beneficially *acquired* by them [the spouses] or either of them during the marriage." [Emphasis added.] It will be seen that "acquired" is the key word. The trial court accepted a definition to be found in Webster's Third New International Dictionary (1965) that the word "acquired" means "attained by the individual by his own efforts." We think the Legislature used the word in a more comprehensive sense to include not only property title to which is the direct or indirect result of an expenditure of effort on the part of a spouse, but also, assets title to which is received by gift or inheritance, or indeed in any other way. Had the former, more restricted meaning been intended, we believe that some confining language would have been employed to manifest this purpose. It is certainly a commonplace to say that property has been acquired by gift or that an asset has been acquired by inheritance. In fact the thought is probably most often expressed in this fashion. We think the word should be given this more inclusive meaning in the statute, absent any indication to the contrary. . . .

We therefore hold the legislature intent to be that *all* property, regardless of its source, in which a spouse acquires an interest during the marriage shall be eligible for distribution in the event of divorce.

Finally we think it necessary to consider and determine exactly what span of time is intended by the words, "during the marriage." While apparently clear on its face, the phrase may, in its application, present difficulties. Obviously the period commences as soon as the marriage ceremony has taken place. But when, for the purposes of this statute, does it end? Reading the act literally, the terminal point would seem to be the day the judgment of divorce is granted. Such an interpretation, however, presents practical obstacles. If that date were to be adopted a bifurcated trial would be required in most cases. It would normally not be practicable to introduce at the trial, evidence as to the value of assets determined as of that day. Such a rule, resulting in duplicitous hearings, should be avoided if possible. Conversely, it might be argued that for equitable reasons or for some conceived purpose of public policy no assets should be included that were acquired after it could be shown that there was an irretrievable breakdown of the marriage or after a cause of action for divorce had arisen. But such a rule would be unworkable. How is one to establish with any reasonable precision when a breakdown of the marital relationship has become irretrievable, or, in many cases at least, when a cause of action for divorce first arises?

We think the better rule to be that for purposes of determining what property will be eligible for distribution the period of acquisition should be deemed to terminate the day the complaint is filed. In adopting this interpretation of the statute, we also have in mind the probable necessity in many cases of providing a period for discovery both as to the available marital assets of the other spouse, as well as to their value.

The only portions of the judgment below that are before us on this appeal relate to the disposition of property. The cause is remanded for the reconsideration of this issue in the light of what has been said above in this opinion. Because of the interrelationship of property distribution and the award of alimony and maintenance, the provision of the judgment touching upon the latter will also be considered reopened for such review, if any, as the trial court may deem appropriate.

For remandment: Chief Justice HUGHES, and Justices HALL, MOUNTAIN, SULLIVAN, PASHMAN and CLIFFORD — 6.

Opposed: None.

Notes and Questions

Property classification issues

1. *Gifts. Painter* does not adopt the community property view that gifts to one spouse during marriage are that spouse's separate property. How should such gifts be characterized? Who is the source of most gifts to married persons? What is the likely motivation for such gifts? What is the likely intent of the donor? Ought the intent of the donor be the determinative factor?

In 1980, the New Jersey legislature rejected the *Painter* treatment of gifts and bequests. The legislature adopted the community property view and amended the equitable distribution statute accordingly:

> However, all such property, real and personal or otherwise, legally or benefi-cially acquired during the marriage by either party by way of gift, devise or bequest shall not be subject to equitable distribution, except that interspousal gifts shall be subject to equitable distribution. [1980 N.J. Laws ch. 181 §1, eff. Dec. 31, 1980, *amending* N.J.S.A. 2A:34-23.]

Consider the last phrase of the 1980 amendment: "except that interspousal gifts shall be subject to equitable distribution." Do you agree? If a husband uses his earnings to buy his wife a diamond ring for her birthday, should that ring be treated as marital property? Compare California Family Code section 852, reprinted at page 646 infra.

2. *The end of the economic community. Painter* holds that the marital economic community terminates at the filing of the complaint. Would you choose this event as the appropriate termination point? Compare California law discussed at pages 480-483 infra.

Distributional issues

3. *Distributional criteria.* In *Painter,* the trial court used 13 factors to determine how the distribution should be made. Do you find them sound? Are there any appropriate factors that are missing? Virtually all the 13 factors may be sorted into two criteria: (i) relative contribution of the parties to the acquisition of the marital assets and (ii) relative postdivorce economic needs of the parties. Which criterion predominates in terms of the frequency with which it is mentioned?

Is this listing of factors likely to help a decision-maker distribute property? In most marriages, the spouse who makes the lesser cash contribution to the acquisition of marital assets is likely to have the greater postdivorce need. *Painter* is illustrative.

4. *The* Painter *distribution.* What, in fact, was the *Painter* distribution? How does it compare to a California community property distribution? Do you have any diffi-culty making such a comparison?

5. *Comparing equitable distribution and California 50-50 distribution.* Apart from the gift issue, *Painter* seems to approve the trial court's equitable distribution, which appears, by California standards, remarkably unredistributive. *Painter* presents a husband who has greater assets and far greater earning capacity than his wife. Yet the trial court awarded the wife only 20 percent of the difference between the hus-band's and wife's distributable assets. Although have-not spouses seem to be doing

somewhat better more recently, eastern and midwestern commentators have shown that *contribution* often overwhelms *need* as a distributional criterion. Thus, under contemporary equitable distribution practice, the higher earner, usually the husband, may take substantially more than half the distributable property. See, for example, Reynolds, The Relationship of Property Division and Alimony: The Division of Property to Address Need, 56 Fordham L. Rev. 827 (1988); Divorce Law is Called Unfair by Bar and Women's Groups, N.Y. Times, Aug. 5, 1985, at 1 (in sample of 70 cases, women received, on average, only 30 percent of marital assets).

Comparison with prominent eastern equitable distribution states, such as New York and New Jersey, tends to make Californians complacent about California community property law. Although some may believe that California distributive equality does not always achieve perfect justice, as when it forces the sale of a community property home in which the parties' children reside, nevertheless they tend to conclude that California law does compare favorably to equitable distribution regimes that generally award substantially *less* than half to the economically inferior spouse.

Yet the comparison may be inapt. California probably should not be compared to eastern equitable distribution states, which have no community property tradition. It should not be surprising that eastern and midwestern states, which have no tradition that the spouses equally *own* marital property, should tend to consider contribution to the detriment of need in distributing marital property at divorce. Because the earner-spouse owns his individually titled property up to the moment of divorce distribution, any displacement of his ownership implicitly requires that his spouse establish an ownership-entitlement claim. See, for example, Fratangelo v. Fratangelo, 520 A.2d 1195, 1200 (Pa. Super. 1987), rejecting a 50-50 starting point for the distribution of *marital* property under the Pennsylvania equitable distribution statute because a 50-50 starting point would unconstitutionally deprive the title-holder of property in violation of due process by "bestow[ing] the separate property of one spouse on the other." *Fratangelo* takes the position that "record ownership of assets remains significant and *the court must find that equity requires a transfer of ownership from one party to the other*" (emphasis in original).

A more apt comparison for California 50-50 distribution may be found in the five community property jurisdictions that practice equitable distribution at divorce as well as in the western common law equitable distribution states, like Oregon and Montana, that strongly presume equal spousal *contribution* to the acquisition of marital property.

In these western community property and common law states, equitable distribution differs markedly from its eastern counterpart. In both statute and case law, the spouses are strongly, even conclusively, presumed to contribute equally to the acquisition of marital property. Hence equality is the *distributive* starting point and is appropriate when the parties are equally situated with respect to postdivorce income. In most such states there is only one justification for unequal distribution: disparity in projected postdivorce earnings or needs. Thus substantially unequal distributions are frequent and invariably favor the needier spouse.[45]

---

45. See Wash. Rev. Code Ann. 26.09.080 (2002), which makes no mention of contribution as a distributional criterion and instead proposes only need-based criteria, including:

> The economic circumstances of each spouse at the time the division of property is to become effective, including the desirability of awarding the family home or the right to live therein for reasonable periods to a spouse with whom the children reside the majority of time.

6. *Relative need as a distributional criterion.* Are you surprised to see *need*-based criteria used for *property* distribution? Californians often perceive the inclusion of need as "confused" or "anomalous." For Californians, *need* is a factor in spousal support, but not in property division, where our inexorable 50-50 divorce distribution rule exactly mirrors our 50-50 community property ownership rule.

As suggested above, the California perspective is relatively unusual. Five of the other seven traditional community property states have 50-50 ownership rules for community property, but they nevertheless make unequal need-based distributions at divorce.[46] Unlike California, these states do not conflate property ownership and divorce distribution.

Because California conceptualizes divorce-related property distribution as the realization, or vindication, of property *rights,* Californians are infrequently required to ask *why* we have a marital property system, and what ends it does or ought to serve. In states that practice equitable distribution, each distribution implicitly raises these questions. In California, in contrast, we are only required to confront these questions when we address a new substantive issue. Should professional education, for example, be treated as community property? It is difficult to think about this issue without considering the purposes of a marital property system.

Jurisdictions that use *need* as a property distribution criterion also tend to understand property distribution as merely one component of a divorce-engendered economic "package" that may include spousal and child support as well. Indeed, western equitable distribution states, community property and common law alike, tend to use the same criteria for property division and spousal support.[47] California, contradistinctively, balkanizes property division and spousal support, dividing property "as of right" and often appearing to give short shrift to the "weaker" non-right-based support claim. In contrast, the western states that look to postdivorce income disparity for purposes of both support and property distribution seem to give more generous support as well as more generous property awards to the economically weaker spouse.

7. California Family Code section 2550 requires equal division of the community estate at divorce. In 1994, California Assemblymember Bornstein introduced Assembly Bill 3061, which would have added the following amendment to Section 2550:

Compare Idaho Code Ann. 32-712 (2002), which requires substantially equal division absent "compelling reasons otherwise" and enumerates factors that may warrant unequal distribution, all of which assess the relative postdivorce economic needs of the parties. For a similar approach, see Ariz. Rev. Stat. Ann. §25-318 (2002), discussed in Hatch v. Hatch, 113 Ariz. 130, 547 P.2d 1044 (in banc 1976). See also Nev. Rev. Stat. 125.150 (2002), as interpreted in McNabney v. McNabney, 105 Nev. 652, 782 P.2d 1291 (1989) and Anderson v. Anderson, 816 P.2d 463 (1991).

For western common law states that presume equal *contribution* but make unequal need-based *distribution,* see, for example, Or. Rev. Stat. Ann. §107.105(1)(f) (2002), as interpreted in Marriage of Stice and Stice, 308 Or. 316, 779 P.2d 1020 (1989); Marriage of Pierson, 294 Or. 117, 653 P.2d 1258 (in banc 1982); Marriage of Dull, 104 Or. App. 275, 800 P.2d 306 (1990); Marriage of Crislip and Crislip, 86 Or. App. 146, 738 P.2d 602 (1987). See also Mont. Code Ann. 40-4-202 (2002), as interpreted in Marriage of Hurley, 222 Mont. 287, 721 P.2d 1279 (1986) (dictum); Marriage of King, 216 Mont. 92, 700 P.2d 591 (1985); Eschenburg v. Eschenburg, 171 Mont. 247, 557 P.2d 1014 (1977). For discussion of this western alternative to both California equal division and eastern contribution-focused distribution, see generally Blumberg, Fineman's The Illusion of Equality: A Review Essay, 2 UCLA Women's L.J. 309 (1992).

46. Id. and note 12 supra.

47. Id.

However, the court may award more than one-half of the community estate
to one of the parties after considering both of the following factors: (a) The
relative earning capacity of each party. (b) Whether either party has custody
of any children of the marriage.

Assembly Bill 3061 was narrowly drawn. It would not reach all cases of economic
inequality. It would not, for example, reach a marriage in which the spouses' earnings are relatively equal, but one spouse's income is disproportionally consumed
by medical expenses. Nor would it reach a marriage in which the spouses' earning
capacities, although equal, are limited, and one spouse has great separate property
wealth. Yet the narrowness of the statute is also a virtue. By limiting the divorce
court's inquiry to the two most significant causes of spousal economic inequality,
earning capacity and the custody of children, the bill avoids the often unhelpfully
circular presentation of competing budgets, which inevitably occurs when "need"
is explicitly and generally addressed, as it is, for example, in spousal support. This
seemingly modest proposal was poorly received by the state bench and bar. See
1994 California Family Law Monthly 139-140 (June 1994). It died in the Assembly.

F.   WHY DO WE HAVE A MARITAL PROPERTY SYSTEM? OR, MORE BROADLY, HOW MIGHT WE THINK ABOUT INTERSPOUSAL WEALTH ALLOCATION?

As you read this section, identify and consider the various rationales for a marital property system. The following problem may help anchor your thoughts.

Harry and Wanda Simon are getting divorced today after a 14-year marriage.
Harry is 42 and Wanda is 40. They married when Harry was 28 and Wanda was 26.
It was the first marriage for both. Harry was then an engineer with a B.S. in chemical
engineering. He was earning $30,000 a year. Wanda was a public grade school
teacher holding a B.A. with joint majors in English and education. She was earning
$15,000 a year. Both are UCLA graduates.

During their marriage, they had 2 children, now age 8 and 10. They are healthy
and attend public school. Wanda is primarily responsible for their well-being.
Wanda took some, but not a lot, of unpaid maternity leave to have the children,
so her current salary is only about $2,000 a year less than it would be had she not
taken any maternity leave. Before the children were born, she took night courses
that added a few thousand dollars to her salary. Her current salary is $30,000 a year.
There is little opportunity for salary growth in her field.

For two years, Harry went to night school to earn an M.B.A. He continued to
work full-time as an engineer so that his acquisition of an M.B.A. did not impose
any apparent opportunity cost on the family. With an M.B.A., he was able to advance
to a managerial position in his firm, where he now earns $85,000 (gross) a year.
He would be making about $55,000 without the M.B.A. His income is likely to grow
in the future.

The parties agree that Wanda shall have primary custody of the two children
and that Harry shall have generous visitation. Under current California child support guidelines, Harry will pay $19,825 child support a year for the two children.

Harry's child support obligation to each child will end when the child reaches 18. Under California law, Harry has no obligation to contribute to his children's college education.

	Harry		*Wanda*
$65,000	net after-tax income	$25,000	net after-tax income
−19,825	child support	+19,825	child support
$45,175	net for Harry	$44,825	net for Wanda + 2 children

The Simons own a substantially appreciated home. They bought it at marriage for $150,000. It is now worth $400,000 and they have paid off the mortgage. They have about $100,000 in savings. Each has a pension plan that will pay out retirement benefits as a percentage of his or her final preretirement salary. The value of their other assets is insignificant. Ignoring property distribution and considering income alone, Harry will have $45,175 net annual income ($3,765 monthly), and Wanda will share $44,825 net annual income ($3,735 monthly) with their two children. Clearly, there is some inequality here, but you may be wondering how much. Using the Bureau of Labor Statistics Household Equivalence Scale[48] and taking into account Harry's expenditure for child visitation as well as Wanda's expenditure to maintain a home for the children, Harry will experience a 26 percent increase in standard of living, while Wanda and the children experience a 35 percent decline in standard of living. For further treatment of household equivalence scales, see the American Law Institute, Principles of the Law of Family Dissolution: Analysis and Recommendations, Tentative Draft No. 3, Part II, Chapter 3, Child Support, 150-168 (April 8, 1998), approved by the membership of the ALI on May 14, 1998.

Economically, what should be the outcome at divorce? What should our goals be? Why? What is the likely result in California? How would each of the scholars in the Carbone and Brinig article (at pages 26-40) set the economic terms of the Harry-Wanda divorce?

This section will sketch the different ways that we customarily do or might think about marital property law and other interspousal wealth distribution mechanisms. The various possibilities are not mutually exclusive. Some or all may cumulate and many may overlap. On the other hand, some may have differing distributional implications. The purpose of this section is to offer possibilities for your consideration and to aid you in formulating your own views about the legitimate ends of marital property law.

1. *Marital property as simply a property system.* Although few states share this perspective, California's long experience with community property as a property *ownership* system enables Californians to take community property as a legal given needing no special justification. In the early years of statehood, Anglo-American California judges, trying to make sense of California's constitutionally required Spanish community property system (see Chapter 2), described spouses as "matrimonial partners" and marriage as a "matrimonial copartnership." Ord v. De La Guerra, 18 Cal. 67, 74 (1861). For similar discussion, see Lynam v. Vorwerk, at page 159 infra. Yet with time, as community property law became embedded in the fabric

---

48. Bureau of Labor Statistics, U.S. Department of Labor, Revised Equivalence Scale for Estimating Equivalent Incomes or Budget Costs by Family Type 4 (Table 1), Bulletin No. 1570-2 (1968).

of California law, it assumed the legitimacy usually accorded venerable rules of property and is generally no longer thought to require any explanatory justification.

There are at least two implications of treating community property as an unexamined embedded property right. The first is the tendency, demonstrated in California law, to conflate ownership and distribution, in other words, to believe that because the spouses equally own the community property, the only just resolution at divorce is 50-50 distribution of the community property. In The Divorce Revolution (1985), sociologist Lenore Weitzman, a longtime resident of California, strongly criticized the unequal economic outcomes incident to California's 50-50 distribution. Professor Weitzman reported that one year after divorce, men's standard of living had substantially increased while that of women had sharply declined. Id. at 339. Yet she recommended retention of 50-50 divorce distribution because she and her California survey respondents believed that it is the only just rule.

> There is widespread approval of the California rule that requires an equal division of all property acquired during marriage. All categories of our respondents — judges, lawyers, men and women — support the equal division rule in principle, and consider it fair and just. The vast majority believe that each spouse is *entitled* to one-half of the property acquired during the marriage. . . . (emphasis in original).

Id. at 384.

The second effect of an unexamined embedded property entitlement is the dichotomization of property and support claims. Each is regulated by different principles, and the strength of the property entitlement tends to minimize, by comparison, the nonentitlement-based support claim.

The ALI Principles of the Law of Family Dissolution also adopt a mandatory rule of 50-50 property distribution at divorce. As in California, the ALI equal distribution principle is founded on a property-based notion of "entitlement" to assets acquired during marriage.[49] Although both California and the ALI have the same distribution rule, the ALI rule was formulated in a somewhat different context. Many of the results accomplished by those western equitable distribution states that often distribute more than half the community property to the economically weaker spouse (see page 20 supra) are accomplished by ALI compensatory spousal payments, the regularized and routinized ALI substitute for spousal support (see page 10 supra). Thus, to be fully comprehended, the property distribution rules of any jurisdiction must be considered together with the jurisdiction's other means and practices of wealth redistribution at and after family dissolution.

2. *The partnership view of marriage.* Just as early Anglo-American judges in California invoked partnership imagery to explain California community property law, so partnership notions have been used by judges during the last several decades to

---

49. The ALI adoption of the California rule may, in part, reflect the background of the three ALI reporters. Two are graduates of the University of California at Berkeley Law School (Boalt Hall): Professor Ira Ellman of Arizona State Law School, author of the ALI chapters on marital property and compensatory spousal payments, and co-author of the chapters on cohabitation and agreements; and Professor Katharine Bartlett of Duke Law School, author of the chapter on child custody. The third reporter is Professor Grace Blumberg of UCLA Law School, author of the chapter on child support and co-author of the chapters on cohabitation and agreements. On the other hand, the ALI advisers (judges, practitioners, and law professors) are broadly representative of the entire nation, and there was general support for a 50-50 distribution rule, at least in combination with the ALI concept of "compensatory spousal payments."

rationalize the introduction and growth of equitable distribution principles in the common law states. Partnership theory posits that both spouses contribute to the marriage and thus both have an earned entitlement to the assets acquired by either spouse during marriage. Partnership theory does not posit that husbands and wives make qualitatively equal contributions. On the contrary, statutory emphasis on homemaker as well as market contribution suggests that the spouses may contribute differently along gendered lines.[50]

The attractiveness of the notion that marriage is, inter alia, an economic partnership may be explained in a number of ways. Professor Susan Prager suggests that, empirically, spouses make choices and sacrifices for the good of the marital unit, and partnership sharing at divorce or death thus vindicates reasonable expectations arising from spousal behavior and understanding during marriage. She asserts that marriage itself promotes sharing behavior, that sharing behavior tends to perpetuate and preserve marriages, and thus that even the attainment of sexual equality would not lessen the vitality and desirability of marital property partnership, or sharing, principles. Prager, Sharing Principles and the Future of Marital Property Law, 25 UCLA L. Rev. 1 (1977). Alternatively, we may understand partnership as a normative construct. Whether or not spouses follow the sharing patterns described by Professor Prager, we would like to encourage them to do so, or at least not discourage them from doing so. The partnership construct may also have a mythic dimension. It tells us a story we like to hear about ourselves. It acts as a mirror that casts back flattering images of American marriage and family life.

Yet partnership and contribution rhetoric has been strongly criticized by Professor Martha Fineman, who claims that it deflects our attention from the proper goal of property distribution at divorce, which is the achievement of substantively equal postdivorce economic outcomes for divorcing husbands and wives. Professor Fineman argues that substantive equality often requires that divorcing wives receive substantially more than half the marital property. M. Fineman, The Illusion of Equality: The Rhetoric and Reality of Divorce Reform 36-52 (1991). Professor Fineman's analysis, like California law, seems to conflate *contribution* and *distribution*. The experience of the western equitable distribution states (see pages 20-21 supra) suggests that states with strongly developed contribution and partnership constructs have nevertheless been able to distinguish between equality of spousal *ownership* (based on principles of equal contribution) and unequal *distribution* (based on rela-

---

50. See Diamond & Prinsell, Note, New York's Equitable Distribution Law: A Sweeping Reform, 47 Brook. L. Rev. 67, 81 n.53 (1980), listing 20 common law equitable distribution jurisdictions that have homemaker provisions. See, e.g., Me. Rev. Stat. Ann., tit. 19 §722-A(1) (West 1981 & Supp. 1991), which provides that the divorce court "shall divide the marital property in such proportions as the court deems just after considering all relevant factors, including . . . the contribution of each spouse to the acquisition of marital property, including the contribution of a spouse as homemaker." The Maine provision tracks §307 of the Uniform Marriage and Divorce Act, 9A U.L.A. 288 (1998).

Community property laws never refer to market or homemaker contribution because they effectively presume that the spouses contribute equally to the acquisition of community property.

> Special "homemaker" provisions should be irrelevant in community property states, since those states do not start with the common law premise that there is some connection between a spouse's relative earnings and her claim on property acquired during the marriage. The community property system has embedded within it the alternative premise that both spouses have contributed equally to the acquisition of all assets. There is no doubt that the trend in common law states is toward this approach, but there remains a great variation in the nature and extent of the common law marital property reforms.

I. Ellman, P. Kurtz, and K. Bartlett, Family Law 235 (2d ed. 1991).

tive postdivorce income inequality). For further discussion, see Blumberg, Review-Essay, Fineman's The Illusion of Equality, 2 UCLA Women's L.J. 309, 313-318 (1992).

3. *Family wealth redistribution.* Wealth redistribution is an important economic function of the family. The intact nuclear family redistributes wealth from parents to children and, generally, from husbands to wives, avoiding what might otherwise be socially intolerable wealth inequality between adults and children and between men and women. When families are broken by divorce, property distribution and continuing support obligations may be understood to maintain, to some extent, the wealth redistribution function of the intact family. See generally Blumberg, Reworking the Past, Imagining the Future: On Jacob's Silent Revolution, 16 Law and Social Inquiry 115, 149-152 (1991). When marriage persists until the death of one of the spouses, property distribution is often the only available redistributional mechanism because a spouse's support obligations generally do not survive his death.

Postdissolution wealth redistribution also serves an important public welfare function. Postdissolution redistribution makes it less likely that family members will become public charges.

4. *Marital property as a mechanism to adjust sex-related economic inequality.* Although legal rules ultimately must be articulated in sex-neutral form,[51] it is not unconstitutional to observe that most men and women are not similarly situated in marriage and the labor market, and that divorce thus poses different and unequal risks for men and women.

The following article surveys and critically evaluates a substantial portion of the economic and legal literature addressing the relationship between sex-related inequality and wealth distribution at divorce. Although some of the scholars, particularly the economists, focus on spousal support rather than property distribution, their analysis may equally be applied to property distribution. As you read this article, evaluate both the underlying theories and the authors' critique of those theories.

JUNE CARBONE AND MARGARET F. BRINIG, RETHINKING MARRIAGE: FEMINIST IDEOLOGY, ECONOMIC CHANGE, AND DIVORCE REFORM
65 Tulane L. Rev. 953 (1991)

. . . In analyzing marriage as a form of civil obligation, and in identifying the policies that are served by modern divorce law,[2] the most striking observation is the identification of the interests that are not protected. Marriage historically in-

---

51. Orr v. Orr, 440 U.S. 268, 99 S. Ct. 1102, 59 L. Ed. 2d 306 (1979), requires that divorce-related economic rules be facially sex-neutral. *Orr* disapproved an Alabama law allowing spousal support for wives only.

[2.] See generally M. Glendon, [The New Family and the New Property 13-46 (1981)]; M. Rheinstein, [Marriage Stability, Divorce and the Law (1972)]; Ellman, The Theory of Alimony, 77 Calif. L. Rev. 3, 13-23 (1989); O'Connell, Alimony After No-Fault: A Practice in Search of a Theory, 23 New Eng. L. Rev. 437, 444-454 (1988); Schneider, Moral Discourse and the Transformation of American Family Law, 83 Mich. L. Rev. 1803, 1809-1811 (1985); Scott, Rational Decisionmaking About Marriage and Divorce, 76 Va. L. Rev. 9, 10 (1990).

volved the life-long exchange of the husband's support for the wife's services in a union consecrated by God and unalterable by the parties. Fault — the requirement that one party, and only one party, egregiously violate the canons of marriage — served to identify those cases in which one party had so flouted his or her marital obligations that the other party deserved to be released from the obligations of a relationship that had effectively ceased to exist. As a prerequisite for divorce, fault became obsolete once society recognized the right of an unhappy couple to terminate its union. But the recognition of no-fault grounds for ending the marriage did not necessarily mean that either party could choose to leave with impunity. The law could still recognize marriage as a contract whose breach gave rise to liability.

Most states, however, have not done so. In adopting no-fault grounds for divorce, many states have precluded consideration of marital misconduct altogether. Without identification of the party responsible for the end of the marriage, the commitment to remain married becomes unenforceable. In traditional civil terms, neither the expectation interest (the standard of living made possible by the marriage) nor the reliance interest (sacrifices made in the belief the marriage will last) can be protected.[24] Economists would argue that such a result makes sense only to the degree that the costs imposed by a determination that marital obligations have been breached exceed the interests to be protected by an expectation or reliance standard.

Such an analysis has never been undertaken with any rigor. While the costs of a fault determination are deemed self-evident by anyone familiar with the older system, the costs of a no-fault system have not been weighed against the possible benefits of a more expansive system of divorce awards. The benefits are those traditionally identified with civil obligation — deterring breach and encouraging reliance over the life of the relationship. Within marriage, deterring breach translates into lower divorce rates. Encouraging reliance primarily means encouraging the career sacrifices women have traditionally made in the interests of their families. A decision to preclude consideration of marital misconduct could be justified, therefore, either on the ground that the cost of the determination has increased or because . . . the interests to be served by such a determination (primarily the interests associated with perpetuating traditional marital roles) are not as important as they once were.[29] Either way, the interests sacrificed must be considered along with the costs. . . .

Once a state has precluded consideration of marital misconduct, the law of civil obligation also helps to define the interests that remain. Again, application of

---

24. The Restatement (Second) of Contracts §344 (1981) adopts the following definitions:

> (a) his "expectation interest," which is his interest in having the benefit of his bargain by being put in as good a position as he would have been in had the contract been performed,
> (b) his "reliance interest," which is his interest in being reimbursed for loss caused by reliance on the contract by being put in as good a position as he would have been in had the contract not been made. . . .

29. . . . [T]here are two important justifications for precluding consideration of fault that are independent of the difficulty of making the determination. First, tying the financial consequences of divorce to a determination that marital obligations have been breached serves to reinforce traditional gender roles, encouraging women to think in terms of marriage rather than the market for their financial well-being. . . . Second, a fault system makes it more difficult for the lower earning, rather than the higher earning, spouse to decide to end a marriage. See sources cited infra notes 196-98 and accompanying text; see also Rutherford, Duty in Divorce: Shared Income as a Path to Equality, 58 Fordham L. Rev. 539, 541 (1990).

traditional civil terms leads to the conclusion that, while contract and tort remedies depend on a determination of breach of contract or breach of duty, restitution does not. Contract and tort require such a determination in order to justify imposition of one party's loss upon the other. Restitution requires only that one party gain at the other's expense in circumstances in which it would be unjust to allow retention of the gain without payment.[30] Within marriage, restitution is therefore possible whenever the divorce separates gains and losses that would otherwise be shared.[31] Economists observe that the decision to provide compensation—that is, to reach a legal conclusion that retention of the benefit is unjust rather than a conclusion that the benefit has been gratuitously rendered—involves a decision to encourage these forms of exchange.[32]

Translated into the language of civil obligation, the existing divorce system has largely rejected contract and tort, expectation and reliance, in favor of restitution.[33] Marriage as a lifelong commitment is gone, with expanding protection for particular exchanges made while the marriage lasted.[34] . . .

. . . In this . . . section, we examine the possibilities for reform, analyzing the alternative agendas in terms of the nature of marriage that the advocates wish to encourage.

In considering the different visions of the family, it is useful to start with what we will call the "traditionalist" view, that is, a defense of the relatively traditional pattern of gender responsibilities that prevailed during the latter part of the nineteenth and first half of the twentieth century.[155] The traditionalists argue that men

30. G. Palmer, The Law of Restitution §1.7 (1978). For a discussion of the role of restitution in marriage, see Carbone, [Economics, Feminism and the Reinvention of Alimony or Why the Desire to Remove Distorting Incentives Does Not a Theory Make, 43 Vand. L. Rev. 1463 (1990)]; Casad, Unmarried Couples and Unjust Enrichment: From Status to Contract and Back Again?, 77 Mich. L. Rev. 47 (1978); Krauskopf, Recompense for Financing Spouse's Education: Legal Protection for the Marital Investor in Human Capital, 28 Kan. L. Rev. 379, 386 (1980).

31. If husband and wife decide, for example, to have the wife quit her job rather than hire a nanny, both parents will share the benefit from the care provided for the children, but only the wife will bear the continuing loss. Similarly, to take an equally stereotyped example, if the wife contributes to the husband's medical education, and the divorce occurs shortly after he graduates, he will have the sole benefit from an investment the couple jointly undertook and paid for. . . .

32. . . . Restitution recoveries are narrower than expectation or reliance recoveries in part because they focus on selected transactions, not on the marriage as a whole. A reliance standard, for example, would ask the question: what would the wife's earning capacity have been had she not relied primarily on her husband's income for her wellbeing? A restitution standard asks the question, "To what extent is the wife bearing a disproportionate share of the cost of having children?"

33. In discussing divorce awards in terms of civil obligation, this analysis is limited to a discussion of adjustments made after the initial division of property between the spouses. Such adjustments usually take the form of spousal support. . . .

34. See generally M. Glendon, supra note [2], at 9-96. The degree of protection provided is limited by the theory of liability. To the extent that the husband's otherwise incalculable benefit from the children is measured by the cost necessary to raise them, that cost involves the wife's foregone earning potential from the particular decisions the couple made as they raised the children. The wife's overall potential, however, is the sum of a series of decisions—to complete college, to accept a transfer, to enter a training program, to switch to a job with more flexible hours—all of which may have been made in the anticipation that her marital role would be more important than her career development. An expectation measure (the standard of living made possible by the marriage) or a reliance measure (the position she would have been in had she not married) would allow a larger part of that lost potential to be taken into account. Restitution limits consideration of lost earning potential to that potential lost at the time a particular exchange was made.

155. In examining the traditionalist perspective, we have focused primarily on those influenced by Gary Becker and the use of economic analysis because they have received the greatest attention in the legal literature. There are certainly other traditionalist perspectives, however. See, e.g., F. Cancian, Love in America: Gender and Self-Development 122-33 (1987); Gedlicks & Hendrix, Democracy, Autonomy and Values: Some Thoughts on Religion and Law in Modern America, 60 S. Cal. L. Rev. 1579 (1987);

and women *should* continue to perform different roles within marriage, that these gender differences make women more economically vulnerable to divorce than men, and that, when divorce is common, women will continue to devote their energies to childrearing and homemaking only if these contributions are protected.[156] The traditionalists favor a contract approach that protects the expectation interest of the non-breaching party in order to encourage specialization within the family and to deter breaches or "shirking" of marital obligations.[157] They therefore decry the elimination of fault from divorce, and favor relatively generous financial settlements for non-breaching wives.[158]

Gary Becker, a University of Chicago economist who pioneered the application of economic analysis to the family, is the traditionalists' leading proponent. He justifies a division of labor between paid employment and domestic work on efficiency grounds. He argues that the theory of comparative advantage demonstrates that specialization will result in greater productivity; that, for biological reasons, women are better suited than men for childrearing; and that women will sacrifice their own earning capacity for household-specific investments, such as childrearing, only if their financial sacrifices are protected by enforceable long-term contracts.[159] On that basis, Becker's associate, Elisabeth Landes, has argued for retention of fault as a basis for divorce awards and for the use of alimony to compensate for the opportunity costs women incur in entering into traditional marriages.[160]

Lloyd Cohen has reached similar conclusions on somewhat different grounds. Citing statistics demonstrating that divorced women enjoy lesser opportunities for remarriage than divorced men, Cohen argues that "women in general are of relatively higher value as wives at younger ages and depreciate much more rapidly than do men."[161] Cohen attributes the differences to different mortality rates, the presence of children, and the nature of sexual attraction.[162] He observes that, because of these factors, gains from the marriage are not distributed symmetrically. Rather, he suggests that

> men tend to obtain gains early in the relationship when their own contributions to the marriage are relatively low and that of their wives relatively great.

Hafen, The Family as an Entity, 22 U.C. Davis L. Rev. 865 (1989); Hafen, The Constitutional Status of Marriage, Kinship and Sexual Privacy—Balancing the Individual and Social Interest, 81 Mich. L. Rev. 463 (1983). . . .

156. See G. Becker, [A Treatise on the Family 16 (1981)].

157. For an economic critique of Becker, see P. England & G. Farkas, [Households, Employment and Gender 88-89 (1986)].

158. See, e.g., Landes, [Economics of Alimony, 7 J. Legal Stud. 35 (1978)]; see also Haas, The Rationality and Enforceability of Contractual Restrictions on Divorce, 66 N.C.L. Rev. 879 (1988). None of these writers has fully explained what such a divorce system would look like or what definition of breach of marital obligations would apply.

159. G. Becker, supra note [156], at 14-37. . . .

160. Landes, in particular, argues that

> an efficient alimony system would penalize the party more at fault in contributing to a divorce. Such a penalty would reduce the incentive of both spouses to cheat within marriage, since the gain from cheating would be reduced by the expected alimony penalty should the marriage dissolve. Hence, penalizing the party more at fault in contributing to a divorce economizes on the costs of enforcing the terms of the marriage and increases the expected gain from investment in the marriage.

Landes, supra note [158], at 48-49; see also Haas, supra note 158, at 889.

161. Cohen, [Marriage, Divorce, and Quasi Rents: Or, "I Gave Him the Best Years of My Life," 16 J. Legal Stud. 267, 278 (1987)].

162. Id. at 278-87.

> Similarly, later on in the marriage women tend as a general rule to obtain
> more from the contract than do men. The creation of this long-term imbal-
> ance provides the opportunity for strategic behavior whereby one of the par-
> ties, generally the man, might find it in his interest to breach the contract
> unless otherwise constrained.[163]

Cohen concludes that the failure of the legal system to deal with the problem contributes to fewer marriages, fewer middle-class children, and fewer women specializing in homemaking — producing "an inefficient allocation of resources."[164] While
Cohen declines to embrace any of the possible solutions he critiques, he acknowledges that the most effective legal response would require a determination of who
breached the marriage contract and of the resulting loss to the non-breaching
party, in short, the traditional elements of a contract approach.

Becker and Cohen thus present two different justifications for a contract model
of divorce. Becker uses the language of economics to re-invent the separate spheres
that were the hallmark of the nineteenth-century ideal of complementarity. He
describes gender roles in terms of a choice between either shared responsibilities,
or female specialization in the home combined with male specialization in the market. His analysis dictates a contract approach designed to protect expectation because of his depiction of female specialization in terms of a lifetime commitment
to homemaking at the expense of career development. . . . [However,] the large
scale entry of married mothers into the labor force has been marked far more by
increasing specialization among women than by any decreasing specialization
within the family. Women may devote more of their energies to their careers than to
homemaking, while still remaining primarily responsible for the family's domestic
affairs.[168] Because Becker addresses only "the sharp sexual division of labor in all
societies between the market and household sectors,"[169] he offers no basis for the
modern choice between contract — and protection of the standard of living made
possible by the other spouse's higher income — and restitution, which compensates
only for specific sacrifices made in the interests of the children. Becker's conclusion
that specialization within the family is "efficient" begs the question of whether
greater specialization among women in the provision of domestic services is not
"efficient" as well.

Conversely, Cohen's analysis, at least at the point at which it is farthest from
Becker's, provides a justification for a contract approach that is independent of the
existence of economic inequality between husbands and wives. In line with Cohen's
analysis, even if men and women enjoyed equal career opportunities, and even if

---

163. Id. at 287.

164. Id. at 295-98. Cohen acknowledges that a variety of societal trends have contributed to these
changes and that the legal system provides only one, and not necessarily the most effective, of the restraints that have traditionally been used to police marital contracts.

168. Indeed, if the nineteenth-century shift from farm to factory can be described in terms of
increasing specialization among men, the twentieth-century movement of mothers from home to office
can be described in terms of increasing specialization among women. Most studies show that as married
women have increased their participation in the labor force, they have hired other women to assist
them. Their husbands assume only slightly more responsibility for housework than they did when their
wives stayed home. See V. Fuchs, [Women's Quest for Economic Equality 78, 103 (1988)] . . . Stafford,
Backman & Dibona, The Division of Labor Among Cohabitating and Married Couples, 39 J. Marriage &
Fam. 43 (1977); Vanek, Time Spent in Housework, 231 Sci. Am. 116, 118 (1974). . . .

169. G. Becker, supra note [156], at 21.

they shared child-care responsibilities equally, women would still enjoy fewer opportunities for remarriage than men because of differences in mortality and the nature of sexual attraction. Accordingly, even in an era of economic equality, men would have greater incentives than women to breach their marital obligations, and women would have less of an incentive to enter into marriage if they could not enforce marital commitments.[174]

Separating Cohen's analysis from its economic underpinnings, however, raises other problems with use of the analysis as a justification for a contract approach. First, England and Farkas suggest that "the nature of sexual attraction," which Cohen describes as eternal and unchanging, may itself be a function of the traditional division of gender roles. They predict that age differences between spouses will decline over time.[175] Second, as Cohen points out, calculating the value of marriage in terms of companionship is problematic at best.[176] So long as marriage was viewed as an economic relationship, the expectation interest in marriage could be valued in terms of the standard of living made possible by the other spouse's income, that is, in terms of the traditional standard for spousal support. To the extent the marital relationship is characterized as a primarily romantic one, neither specific performance nor damages provide an appropriate remedy. Finally, even if these problems could be overcome, Cohen provides no basis for evaluating the wisdom of such an approach. The "losses" Cohen attributes to the failure to deter male strategic behavior are the losses Becker attributes to decreasing specialization — "underinvestment" in marriage, children, and homemaking. Yet, Cohen, like Becker, makes no attempt to weigh those losses against the benefits from increasing workforce participation by married women. Accordingly, while Cohen's analysis raises issues of equity between men and women, it is significant in the efficiency terms he addresses only when coupled with Becker's advocacy of traditional gender roles.

Herma Hill Kay, writing from a "liberal feminist" perspective, takes the position most diametrically opposed to that of the Chicago School economists. Concerned about equality rather than efficiency,[179] Kay argues that women will never be equal with men so long as they continue to "make choices that will be economically disabling for women, thereby perpetuating their traditional financial dependence

---

174. This is another way of saying that the lost opportunity to have married another is more significant for women than for men because men are better able to recoup those lost opportunities through remarriage. Moreover, since the loss in this case is the companionship from the marriage, compensation for lost career opportunities and other restitution style awards would be inadequate. Only a contract measure defined in terms of expectation — as a surrogate for the opportunities lost in the form of other opportunities to marry — would appropriately compensate for this loss. . . .

175. England and Farkas argue that the tendency of older men to marry younger women is at least in part a result of the traditional exchange of economic security (better provided by older than younger men) for domestic services (with childbearing and sexual attractiveness more associated with younger than older women). P. England & G. Farkas, supra note [157], at 57.

176. Cohen, supra note [161], at 303.

179. Kay would almost certainly reject Becker's definition of efficiency as well. While Kay, drawing on the work of Kathleen Gough, observes that the "lengthy period of dependence of the human infant serves as the basis for an efficient division of labor within the family by function, if not by sex, even today," she concludes that a "strategy for childrearing that will bind both fathers and mothers to the nurturance of the child seems better suited to its growth and development under modern conditions in which the child's natal family is less frequently the unit in which it reaches maturity." Kay, [Equality and Difference: A Perspective on No-Fault Divorce and its Aftermath, 56 U. Cinn. L. Rev. 1, 80, 82-84 (1987).]

upon men and contributing to their inequality with men at divorce.''[180] Kay further observes that:

> since . . . Anglo-American family law has traditionally reflected the social division of function by sex within marriage, it will be necessary to withdraw existing legal supports for that arrangement as a cultural norm. No sweeping new legal reforms of marriage and divorce will be required, however, to achieve this end. It will be enough, I think, to continue the present trend begun in the nineteenth century toward the emancipation of married women, and implemented more recently by gender-neutral family laws, as well as the current emphasis on sharing principles in marital property law.[181]

Kay concludes that the law, far from encouraging specialization in gender roles, should discourage it. She agrees with Becker and Cohen that the most effective way to encourage women's economic independence is to fail to compensate choices that lead to economic marginalization. She therefore opposes the reintroduction of fault in any form, and by implication, contract-based awards, both because she wishes to discourage women from pursuing the traditional homemaking role and because of concern that even if fault-based awards produced higher settlements for women, that outcome might not be ''worth the cost of perpetuating the blackmail and other abuses that accompanied the fault system.''[182] Kay is equivocal on the subject of restitution-based awards, favoring compensation for the lost career opportunities of older dependent homemakers while opposing support for women who make ''economically disabling'' choices in the future.[183] Identifying child-care responsibilities as the major source of continued sexual inequality, Kay believes that men should be encouraged to share responsibility for the rearing of their children, receiving joint custody upon divorce and remaining emotionally and financially involved thereafter. She believes that if this is accomplished, the ''large disparity between men's and women's household standard of living that Weitzman discovered . . . should be greatly reduced'' and ''the trend begun in California toward eliminating fault from all aspects of marital dissolution can continue to work itself out without the risk of financial harm to dependent women and children.''[184]

Taken to its logical conclusion, Kay's analysis suggests that the appropriate response to women's dependence on their husbands' incomes is less, not more, financial support upon divorce. In order to dismantle the gendered division of labor within the family, Kay argues that the marital bargain, at least the traditional one that exchanges male support for female services, should not be enforceable.[185] Her analysis further implies that compensation for lost career opportunities, at least for modern women who make choices that are ''economically disabling,'' should

180. Id. at 80.
181. Id. at 86.
182. Id. at 76-77. Kay also questions whether fault-based awards would in fact be higher. The data she cites, however, compares awards in the states that continue to list fault as a potential ground for divorce with states that have abolished fault as a consideration in granting divorces. Id. at 67. Kay is certainly correct that the adoption of no-fault grounds for divorce is not itself the cause of low divorce awards, but a truer test of the role of fault in the new era would be a comparison of awards in states that require consideration of marital misconduct in the financial allocation made upon divorce with awards in states that bar such consideration. . . .
183. See Kay, supra note [179], at 79-80. . . .
184. Kay, supra note [179], at 86-87.
185. To Kay, therefore, fault *is* irrelevant.

also be limited.[186] In states that preclude consideration of fault, lost career opportunities are emerging as the primary basis for spousal support.[187] Compensation for those lost opportunities, however, sanctions the very choices of which Kay so strongly disapproves: namely, decisions by modern women to forego substantial career opportunities in order to contribute to the care of their children or their husband's careers.[188] Kay issues no call for a reduction in divorce awards, but such a call is unnecessary. Her endorsement, albeit qualified,[189] of the present divorce system, which Lenore Weitzman depicts as a system of transitional awards that falls far short of compensating the career sacrifices modern women are continuing to make,[190] has much the same effect.[191]

Kay's central premise is that in order to achieve equality, men and women need to make the same choices. Women need to join men in the pursuit of careers; men need to join women in caring for their children. "Cultural feminists" or "feminists of difference," influenced by the ideology of Carol Gilligan and the sociology of Lenore Weitzman, question whether women *should* make the same decisions as men and oppose laws that penalize women's different choices.[192] Mary O'Connell . . . poses the challenge directly:

---

186. See Kay, supra note [179], at 80.

187. See Ellman, supra note 2, at 53-65; Krauskopf, [Maintenance: A Decade of Development, 50 Mo. L. Rev. 259, 265-68 (1985)]. . . .

188. As we noted above, Kay is equivocal as to the extent to which she supports compensation for lost career opportunities. She specifically embraces such an analysis only for the two groups in which it is least at issue: (1) the older wife, divorced after a lengthy marriage in which she forewent "her own economic self-development in order to devote herself to the role of a full-time homemaker and mother . . . in the context of strong cultural expectations that such choices were proper ones for married women," namely women who, because of the pervasive sex discrimination of the time, enjoyed limited career prospects in the first place; and (2) the younger spouse, contributing to the mate's acquisition of a professional degree, where lost career opportunities may be one aspect of a larger contribution. Kay, [An Appraisal of California's No-Fault Divorce Law, 75 Calif. L. Rev. 291, 310-319 (1987)]. . . .

189. For Kay's proposals for reform, see Kay, supra note [188], at 310-19.

190. Kay describes an important objective of the existing divorce system as permitting the couple to rebuild their own lives after divorce. She observes:

> Divorce, after all, is a legal declaration that frees both spouses to seek new relationships. The financial consequences of divorce may have a more severe immediate impact on women than on men, but over time women are more likely to experience an improved quality of life following divorce than are men. . . . The financial settlement should have as its goal not only security for children, but also opportunity for growth for their parents.

Id. at 318.

191. See Kay, supra note [179], at 85; Kay, supra note [188], at 318. See generally L. Weitzman, [The Divorce Revolution (1985)]. Kay acknowledges that "[a]s Weitzman has shown in such dramatic detail, women and children have borne the brunt of the transition that took place in California's legal regulation of the family between 1970 and 1987." Kay, supra note [188], at 319. While Kay describes this as "unfortunate and unnecessary," presumably because she believes traditional homemakers should have been treated more generously under existing law, some transitional impact is inevitable under Kay's analysis. If women are to be persuaded to make different choices by "withdraw[ing] existing legal supports for that arrangement [the social division of function by sex within marriage]," then presumably they will be persuaded by the adverse economic consequences that they suffer or that they see other women suffering. Kay, supra note [179], at 85.

192. Joan Williams observes:

> In the 1980's two phenomena have shifted feminists' attention from assimilationists' focus on how individual women are *like* men to a focus on gender *differences*, on how women as a group differ from men as a group. The first is the feminization of poverty, which dramatizes the chronic and increasing economic vulnerability of women. Feminists now realize that the assimilationists' traditional focus on gender-neutrality may have rendered women more vulnerable to certain gender-related disabilities that have important economic consequences. The second phenomenon that plays a central role

> [The] issue is this: the vast majority of American women live what can only be fairly described as a feminine lifestyle. They undertake the major—and sometimes sole—responsibility for rearing children, and interrupt or scale down their participation in the paid labor force in order to do so. At divorce, however, this lifestyle choice is either minimized (equality theory) or treated as deviant (victim theory). A woman is either told that she must accept the consequences of her choice and go on, or her husband is ordered to "repair" part of the "damage" his wife has suffered, so that she can be fully self-supporting (that is, function like a man) in the future.[193]

O'Connell further notes:

> If our model for the correct post divorce result is equal lifestyles, and if we begin to recognize that it is not only years absent from the labor force but also the presence of children which compromise one's ability to earn a living at paid work, we may begin to move toward a model which insists that the parent who devotes herself to childrearing must not end up in a worse position than the one who devotes himself to the labor force. . . . We need a new model, a model which does not treat the uncompensated rearing of children as aberrant, a model which sees women as women, but does not rush either to protect or to penalize them on that basis.[194]

O'Connell reaches the "unpopular conclusion" that women will continue to be more likely than men to compromise labor force participation in order to rear their children and that, rather than dissuade them, the childrearing role must be made "less economically perilous."[195] To do so, O'Connell advocates "an augmented role for alimony in the middle-class divorces of the future."[196]

While O'Connell may disagree with Kay about the desired extent of women's contributions to childrearing, she shares her rejection of a fault standard as a way to secure greater economic security for women. O'Connell, like other feminists of difference, wishes to encourage greater appreciation for "feminine" values without a return to economic dependence on men or marriage. The traditional marital exchange of lifelong support for lifelong services locked women into a relationship in which they were dependent on their husbands' income to maintain their standard of living. Fault served to restrain men from leaving or flouting their marital obligations too egregiously, but it also left women with little bargaining power within the relationship.[197] Women dissatisfied with their mates or their mates' behavior could not leave—or effectively threaten to leave—without facing financial ruin.[198]

> in the current feminist imagination is that of career women "choosing" to abandon or subordinate their careers so they can spend more time with their small children. These phenomena highlight the fact that deep-seated social differences continue to encourage men and women to make different choices with respect to work and family.

Williams, [Deconstructing Gender, 87 Mich. L. Rev. 797, 798-99 (1989)].
   193. O'Connell, supra note 2, at 500.
   194. Id. at 507-08 (footnotes omitted).
   195. Id. at 507.
   196. Id. at 506. . . .
   197. See generally P. England & G. Farkas, supra note [157].
   198. Victor Fuchs observes:

> Consider a couple who are *bargaining* (explicitly or implicitly) over how the household's income will be spent and how household chores will be allocated. *Game theory* assumes that, other things being held constant, the strength of each participant in the bargaining situation will depend on how well off each would be if they fail to reach

To be effective in achieving O'Connell's objectives, any new system must encourage women's economic independence without penalizing their devotion to their children. O'Connell herself sets forth no specific suggestions, but other writers propose two broad categories of reform. The first, which we will call restitution based, would formalize and expand the existing trend toward basing divorce awards on the gains and losses of the marriage. This approach, pioneered by Joan Krauskopf[199] and recently set forth in a different form by Ira Ellman,[200] declares that compensation is due any time a marriage ends with one spouse retaining a benefit at the other spouse's expense. If, for example, the wife accepts a lower paying job to be able to spend more time with the children, the couple has, in effect, decided to finance their childrearing efforts through the wife's foregone income. At divorce, both parents will retain the benefit of having had children or of having raised them in a particular way, but only the wife will bear the cost. Similarly, if one spouse finances the other's medical education and the divorce occurs shortly after graduation, the doctor will reap the entire benefit of an investment the couple jointly undertook and paid for.[201] In both cases, an adjustment will be due that goes beyond more conventional provisions for property division or spousal support.[202] Krauskopf identifies

---

agreement—in this case, if they divorce. (Game theory is a theoretical approach to interactive decision making, used in economics to analyze situations where prices and quantities are the outcome of bargaining by individual participants, rather than the automatic result of a competitive market.) The stronger the individual's situation outside marriage, the stronger his or her bargaining position within marriage. . . . When her alternative as a divorced woman is better, her bargaining position—and her well-being—as a married woman is also improved.

V. Fuchs, [Women's Quest for Economic Equality 71 (1988)] (emphasis in original).

199. Krauskopf's work was heavily influenced by the econonmics-of-the-family literature. See Krauskopf, supra note 30, at 386; see also Krauskopf, supra note [187], at 299; Krauskopf, [Theories of Property Division/Spousal Support: Searching for Solutions to the Mystery, 23 Fam. L.Q. 253, 260-68 (1989)].

200. This is not to say that Krauskopf would necessarily agree with Ellman's proposals, only that they are both examples of a restitution approach. See Krauskopf, supra note [199, 23 Fam. L.Q.], at 273 n.72, 274 n.76. Moreover, Ellman advances a justification for his proposals very similar to Becker's without recognizing either the restitution nature of his proposals or the fact that they cannot advance the interests he identifies. Compare Becker, [Landes & Michael, An Economic Analysis of Marital Instability, 85 J. Pol. Econ. 1141, 1151-77 (1977)] with Ellman, supra note 2, at 24-28, 40-53.

201. There is a complex relationship between the loss foregone and the resulting gain described in the economic literature on restitution. Basically, we take the position that the loss may be compensated on a restitution rather than a reliance basis so long as it corresponds to a resulting gain. Economists argue that there will be such a correspondence to the extent that we can assume that a rational couple, in choosing to have the mother care for the children, values the benefit from the mother's services at least as much as the foregone income. While the benefit from the children and the mother's particular childrearing practices will always be intangible, the income foregone becomes a surrogate measure of the gain once we assume that the benefit must be at least as great as the loss. Accordingly, the principle at the core of these proposals is compensation for the enrichment even though much of the discussion is cast in terms of the loss. . . .

202. The distinction between property divisions and spousal support has been blurred by the conflation of what should be two separate questions: (1) whose property is it? and (2) for what purposes shall the property be used? At common law, the courts determined property ownership in accordance with title or with the spouse's respective financial contributions. Alimony served as a continuation of the husband's duty of support and as a liquidated form of property distribution in a system in which the husband was awarded the bulk, indeed often all, of the family property. . . .

Contemporaneously with the enactment of no-fault grounds for divorce, divorce reformers fought for greater recognition of homemakers' contributions. As Herma Hill Kay explains, the reformers argued that the courts should start with a presumption favoring an equal division of the property in recognition of the homemaker's independent economic contribution to the acquisition of the family property (that is, a theory that says the property belongs to both of them because they equally contributed to its acquisition), not as compensation for the services rendered (that is, not a theory that the property is really

a strong trend toward the adoption of this rationale as the primary purpose of support awards.[203]

O'Connell, while viewing these proposals as improvements over the earlier reforms, is nonetheless dissatisfied because restitution awards still place a premium on labor market investments rather than domestic investments. She observes that such proposals reserve their greatest benefits for women who abandon established careers[205] and concludes:

> The theory seems incapable of capturing the subtler effects of the adoption of a feminine lifestyle. It does not, for example, address the fact that the wife may well have chosen her earlier work with an eye to interrupted or reduced labor force participation during her childrearing years. Flexibility may have outweighed remuneration or potential for advancement as a value to be maximized in choosing a job. No formulation of human capital theory captures the impact of this choice. Yet, by ignoring it, the model is, in effect, applying a masculine template to a feminine lifestyle, the contours of which it does not even begin to discern.[206]

While O'Connell's feminine lifestyle does not involve the lifelong separation of home and market, it does embrace decisions, with lifelong consequences, to value family above individual advancement. O'Connell insists on protection not just for well-educated women who delay childrearing long enough to establish careers, but for women who marry young and invest less in their education and in the acquisition of marketable skills than in their search for a suitable mate. She objects not to these choices, but to the economic powerlessness that comes with them.[207]

O'Connell accordingly sees more promise in the recent efforts to use a partner-

---

his because he paid for it, but that he should give some to her in compensation for the services she performed for his benefit during the marriage). Kay, supra note [179], at 50-51. The reformers also argued that property, rather than alimony, should be used whenever possible to address a dependent spouse's financial need. Id. at 47. In theory, such a practice requires the two determinations described above: (1) whose property is it? (presuming a 50/50 division of the property acquired during the marriage), and (2) will the divorce (including the property division) leave one of the spouses in need? If so, the courts should adjust the division of property beyond a 50/50 split to provide for that need or, if there is insufficient property to do so, award maintenance. Few observers believe that the property division has ever been handled in this matter, and most also believe that a need standard, at least one designed to insure only that divorced spouses stay off the welfare rolls, is inadequate. See Krauskopf, supra note [199, 23 Fam. L.Q.] at 273-75. Reynolds, in particular, argues that property division has rarely been used to address need, and that it ordinarily reflects contribution alone. Reynolds, The Relationship of Property Division and Alimony: The Division of Property to Address Need, 56 Fordham L. Rev. 827, 840-41 (1988); cf. Krauskopf, supra note [199, 23 Fam. L.Q.] at 274 (arguing that courts probably do consider need, but value contributions unequally).

Dissatisfaction with the need standard and with the paucity of property accumulated in most marriages has prompted greater interest in the concept of lost career opportunities as a justification for divorce awards. Id. at 263. . . .

203. Krauskopf, supra note [199, 23 Fam. L.Q.] at 265.

205. Ellman's proposals are an excellent case in point. He would base alimony awards primarily on a spouse's ability to demonstrate lost earning potential. See Ellman, supra note 2, at 78-80. Other writers who favor basing awards on lost earning capacity would nonetheless allow a more relaxed burden of proof. . . . To the extent that such awards compensate women for premarital decisions to forego college or to become a school teacher rather than a machinist because of the more flexible hours, however, it is harder to establish a restitution basis for such compensation.

206. O'Connell, supra note 2, at 503.

207. Id. at 507. Radical feminists are likely to agree with much of O'Connell's critique without necessarily concluding that women, freed from a patriarchal structure, would continue to make the choices in the same way. See, e.g., C. MacKinnon, [Toward a Feminist Theory of the State 220-22 (1989)].

ship model to equalize post-divorce standards of living.[208] Jana Singer, writing after O'Connell, proposes that

> each ex-spouse would be entitled to an equal share of the couple's combined income for a set number of years after the formal dissolution of their marriage. The time period for this post-divorce sharing would depend upon the length of the marriage. I would propose, as a starting point, one year of post-divorce income sharing for each two years of marriage.[209]

Singer's justification for these proposals, like the earlier use of property division to address need,[210] conflates two separate determinations. First, whose income is it? In invoking the concept of economic partnership, Singer suggests that the post-divorce disparity in earning power is a reflection of the couple's investment decisions and that the higher earning spouse's income is at least to some degree theirs, not just his or hers.[212] Second, for what purposes will income adjustments be made? Singer emphasizes the ability of her proposal to provide compensation for lost career opportunities, to advance the purposes of rehabilitative alimony, and to address need without explaining the relationship between these purposes and the determination of whose income it is in the first place.[213] The partnership model, in short, embraces the existing justifications for expanded property divisions and spousal support, while eschewing any effort to achieve precise calculations.

While the justifications advanced for the partnership model are conventional

---

208. O'Connell, supra note 2, at 507-08.

209. Singer, [Divorce Reform and Gender Justice, 67 N.C.L. Rev. 1103, 1117-18 (1989)]; see also Rutherford, supra note 29, at 577-84; Sugarman, Dividing Financial Interests Upon Divorce, in Divorce Reform at the Crossroads 130-65 (S. Sugarman & H. Kay eds. 1990). Although Singer suggests this standard as "a starting point," she strongly argues for limiting judicial discretion. Singer, supra, at 1119.

210. See discussion supra note 202.

212. Singer, supra note [209], at 1117-18. Indeed, some commentators have argued for expanded definitions of property to include career assets, but, with the exception of New York, such efforts have largely failed. For a review of these developments, see Krauskopf, supra note [199, 23 Fam. L.Q.], at 260-61. In discussing proposals similar to Singer's, Sugarman discusses the comingling of the parties' income-producing interests rather than the need to adjust for lost career opportunities as the basis for the proposals. Sugarman, supra note 209. Rutherford, in proposing what she terms "income sharing," rejects the idea of adjustment for prior contributions, stating instead

> Income sharing is not based on need, pre-divorce standard of living, prior contributions or fault. Instead, it represents a conscious effort to achieve equality between spouses who have divided their labors during marriage. If spouses have not divided the labor, either because they were not married long enough, or because they did not have children, then income sharing should not apply.

Rutherford, supra note 29, at 578.

213. Singer, supra note [209], at 1118-19. If a partnership proposal were to address these issues directly, it would resemble the restitution model described above in the most stereotypical cases. Consider the following example:

> Two M.B.A.'s marry shortly after graduation from business schools and have comparable jobs during the early years of their marriage. He is soon working 60 hour weeks in positions that take him up the corporate ladder. She scales back her hours after the children are born, taking less demanding, parttime positions that offer little promise of advancement. They divorce after 15 years of marriage. He is making $200,000 a year. She is making $60,000 and has custody of the children.

In this case, it is reasonable to assume that most of the income disparity is explained by her childrearing responsibilities. Accordingly, the result is the same whether the case is analyzed in terms of her lost earning potential (she would be making $200,000 a year but for the children); his gain (he could have his 60-hour-a-week executive position and well-cared for children only because of her efforts); or a sharing of post-divorce income. . . .

ones, the symbolic consequences are quite different from those of the other models. Partnership proponents will not satisfy the traditionalists because they refuse to embrace what Becker calls "the sharp sexual division of labor in all societies between the market and the household sectors" or the lifetime commitment necessary, in Becker's view, to make that division possible. At the same time, the partnership approach eschews the liberals' insistence that women be encouraged to look to their own careers rather than to their husbands as the primary source of financial security. Rather, because these models reserve their greatest benefits for the marriages with the greatest income disparity and do so independently of any actual contribution made, the proposals validate not just decisions to value children over individual advancement, but marriage over career, and the search for a financially attractive mate over investment in one's own earning capacity.[217] Partnership models, in their effort to make women's choices less disabling, also make the traditional role more comfortable.

V. CONCLUSION

A. BREAKING THE IMPASSE: THE ROLE OF CHILDREN

Both Herma Hill Kay and Mary O'Connell discuss legal proposals that, at most, involve incremental changes in the family order. Underlying their respective visions, however, are potentially dramatic implications for the nature of human relationships.

The central premise of the liberal feminist critique of the relationships between men and women is that women's childrearing role stands in the way of full equality.[218] Victor Fuchs argues, however, that it is not the fact that women raise children, but the fact "that, on average, women have a stronger demand for children than men do, and have more concern for children after they are born," that creates the disadvantage.[219] Fuchs observes:

> Suppose women were better than men at producing and caring for children but had no particular desire to do so, while it was the men who wanted the children and cared more about their welfare. We would probably still see the same division of labor we see now, but men would have to pay dearly for women's services. The present hierarchy of power would be reversed.[220]

Instead, women, on average, are more willing than men to sacrifice their own well-being to have children and to protect the interests of their children.[221] The result is that men individually and society generally are able to have children at a lower

217. Ironically, Singer justifies this model on the ground that it insists "on substantial post-divorce sharing of income without invoking the harmful stereotypes that underlie traditional alimony doctrine." She then argues that the proposal is appropriate because it "affirms the social value of childrearing and other domestic labor" and "equalize[s] the financial consequences of these gender-linked marital investment decisions." Singer, supra note [209], at 1118.

218. See, e.g., Kay, supra note [179], at 80-81.

219. V. Fuchs, supra note [198], at 68. Women also assume greater responsibility for the care of other relatives. See, e.g., Trading Places: The Daughter Track, Newsweek, July 16, 1990, at 48.

220. V. Fuchs, supra note [198], at 68.

221. Id. at 68-73; Weiss & Willis, Children as Collective Goods in Divorce Settlements, 3 J. Lab. Econ. 268, 276 (1985).

price than the price they would have to pay if women's preferences were the same as men's.

The liberal feminist strategy of withdrawing support for the maternal childrearing role is aimed at changing these preferences.[222] While the liberal ideal may be shared parenting,[223] the immediate effect of higher divorce rates and low divorce awards is to convince women that they make sacrifices for their children at their own peril. Later marriages and fewer middle-class children are predictable consequences of that strategy. . . .

If the result of this strategy is to persuade women to value children less, then men who want children of their own may have to give up more to have them. Or there may simply be fewer children. At that point, society generally should have a greater interest in encouraging investment in children, mandating more generous parental leave, subsidizing child care, providing tax breaks, increasing educational resources, and otherwise assisting childcare providers.[227] Or the United States could meet its labor force demands by selectively increasing immigration.

Whichever result occurs, the price for children will be higher. But women will no longer pay such a disproportionate share of the price. In the interim, however, women and their children will bear the major burden of the transition.[228] For the liberal strategy to succeed, the disparity between men and women's preferences for children must change. They are more likely to change if society withdraws its support for the traditional maternal role. The economic consequences Lenore Weitzman chronicles are therefore a prerequisite for liberal success.[229]

Cultural feminists, however much they may agree that the greater value women place on children is the source of women's lack of power, applaud such values.[230] They are unwilling to encourage women to value children less or to pay a penalty for refusing to do so. For cultural feminists, therefore, greater protection for the childrearing role is essential. The challenge for these feminists is to persuade society to do so without perpetuating women's dependence, economic or psychological, on men.[232]

These divisions in feminist theory . . . are unnecessarily accentuated by the exclusive focus on divorcing husbands and wives. The historical source of protection for childrearing has been marriages that lock women into unequal relationships with their husbands. To the extent that modern proposals continue to tie support for the childrearing role to the husband's income and the length of the marriage,

---

222. Kay, supra note [179], at 85.

223. Id. at 80-85.

227. As Victor Fuchs points out, such policies would benefit women more than men so long as women cared more about children than men did. V. Fuchs, supra note [198], at 71-72.

228. Herma Hill Kay recognizes the problems and voices her greatest support for older wives who chose to devote themselves "to the role of full-time homemaker and mother . . . in the context of strong cultural expectations that such choices were proper ones for married women." Kay, supra note [188], at 316. Kay would not, however, provide such support for modern women who make the same choices.

229. See L. Weitzman, supra note [191], at 164. . . . This is not to say that Herma Hill Kay or other liberal feminists embrace the conclusions in this analysis. We mean to say only that such conclusions are implicit in this line of analysis. Individual writers may disagree with all or part of these proposals.

230. See, e.g., O'Connell, supra note 2, at 507-08.

232. Radical feminists are likely to agree with liberal feminists in identifying differences, including differences in the childrearing role, as a source of disparities in power, and they are likely to agree with the cultural feminists in seeking to change those power relationships without necessarily making women more like men. Radical feminists are likely, however, to attribute less importance to motherhood and to give higher priority to redressing the power relationship than are the cultural feminists. For a discussion of the differences in perspective, see West, [The Jurisprudence of Gender, 55 U. Chi. L. Rev. 1, 13-15 (1988)].

they risk perpetuating women's dependence.[235] A more radical strategy may be a child-centered approach that separates support for childrearing from marital roles and insists on greater recognition of both the societal and the individual responsibility for children. Such a strategy would emphasize: (1) increased societal support for day care, parental leave, education, nutrition, medical care, and other subsidies that directly benefit children and their primary caretakers;[236] (2) allocation of property and post-divorce income for the children's benefit before the spouse's individual claims are considered;[237] and (3) recognition of the parents' continuing responsibility for, and benefit from, children as a primary basis for divorce adjustments.[238] While these principles can be combined with other approaches,[239] and while they cannot and should not provide the exclusive basis for the financial allocations made upon divorce,[240] we believe that emphasis on children and childrearing will do more to advance a feminist perspective than any examination limited to the relationship between husband and wife.

Notes

1. *Distinguishing economic behavior during marriage from the propensity to divorce.* June Carbone and Margaret Brinig, as well as some of the theorists they study, generally evaluate alternative economic outcomes at divorce in terms of the behav-

---

235. They do so partly because, as we noted above, they continue to validate the choice of marital partner as a source of financial security and partly because of the potential effect on bargaining power within the marriage. Under Singer's partnership model, for example, the higher earning spouse would have an incentive to terminate the marriage earlier rather than later, while the lower earning spouse would have a financial incentive to stay in the marriage as long as possible.

236. See V. Fuchs, supra note [198], at 72.

237. See Glendon, Family Law Reform in the 1980's, 44 La. L. Rev. 1553, 1555-65 (1984). See also Rutherford's proposals which advocate income sharing on a per capita basis in order to take children's interests into account. Rutherford, supra note 29, at 578. Better enforcement of such obligations is also essential.

238. In describing what we call the restitution approach, and what others have described in terms of lost career opportunities, human capital, enhanced earning power, rehabilitative alimony, and other terms, we believe the emphasis should be on the fact that, in many divorces, one parent is able to retain the benefit involved from having had children or having had them raised in a particular way without bearing a full share of the cost. That the cost may be measured in terms of lost career opportunities should not obscure the fact that the basis for compensation is retention of the benefit, not existence of the loss. We would similarly insist on recognition that when the gain is the husband's ability to combine parenthood with the professional success that comes with being able to devote 60 hours a week to the job, the primary benefit is the children, not the enhanced income. . . .

To the extent that partnership proposals are similarly based on either contributions to the higher earning spouse's career or the lower earning spouse's lost career opportunities, we believe that the rationales should be recast in terms of parental benefits and obligations arising from children.

239. The first two parts of this proposal are compatible with a liberal strategy because they do not necessarily provide support for women who curtail their labor force involvement because of parenthood. The insistence that the benefits from children be a basis for adjustment at divorce does encourage career sacrifices made for the benefit of the children.

Incorporation of these principles in a partnership approach would probably require limiting the equal division of post-divorce income to marriage in which there were children and in which the lower earning spouse bore more than half of the responsibility for childrearing. Glendon observes that "childless and child-rearing marriages involve different social, political and moral issues and should therefore be analyzed separately." Glendon, supra note 237, at 1560.

240. The other two major considerations in divorce adjustments will be the determination of what part of marital property and post-divorce income is joint as opposed to separate property and the identification of benefits, such as professional degrees and other forms of enhanced income or lifestyles, that will trigger compensation independently of the presence of children. See discussion supra notes 201, 212.

iors that they are likely to promote. In the language of contract, Professors Carbone and Brinig identify two prominent goals: encouraging reliance (primarily career sacrifices that women have traditionally made for their families) and deterring breach (divorce or, at least, "unwarranted" divorce).

Are these two goals equally sensitive to divorce-related economic rules? To what extent is economic behavior during marriage likely to be shaped (i) by the possibility of divorce and (ii) by the content of the economic rules that might apply at divorce? Consider a Virginia study described by Professor Ira Ellman:

> One study confirms the widely held intuition that people have unrealistically optimistic expectations of the durability of their marriage. [R]andomly selected . . . marriage license applicants in Virginia were surprisingly accurate in their estimate, about 50 percent, of the proportion of new marriages that now end in divorce. But when asked their estimate of the chance that their marriage would end in divorce, the median response was zero. Lynn A. Baker & Robert E. Emery, When Every Relationship is Above Average: Perceptions and Expectations of Divorce at the Time of Marriage, 17 Law and Human Behavior 439 (1993). This result suggests it may be pointless to ask about the parties' expectations at the time of their marriage as to the disposition of their property should they divorce, for they probably have no expectation at all because they do not expect to divorce. The data suggest that economic decisions made during marriage are largely premised on the assumption that the marriage will continue. . . .

American Law Institute, Principles of the Law of Family Dissolution: Analysis and Recommendations §4.12, Reporter's Note to Comment a. As you read the three professional education cases in the next section, consider whether and how the wives might have altered their marital behavior in response to the three different rules established in their respective cases.

Yet highly redistributive economic rules are likely to discourage the higher earning spouse from seeking a divorce. This insight antedates economists Gary Becker and Lloyd Cohen by several millennia. For a contemporary illustration of this ancient wisdom, see Marriage of Noghrey, at page 88 infra. Yet a divorce disincentive for the higher earning spouse would seem to be equally a divorce incentive for the lower earning spouse. How might Professors Cohen and Fuchs respond?

2. *Distinguishing economic behavior during marriage from premarital behavior.* The contractarian focus of their initial discussion limits Professors Carbone and Brinig to the marriage contract goals of reliance and breach deterrence, that is, to aspects of the spouses' behavior *after* they marry.

Dean Herma Hill Kay expresses equal concern about the economic behavior of young women *before* marriage, about the educational and career choices that they make. It would seem plausible that a young, as yet unmarried woman contemplating divorce statistics and a law of divorce that does not favor divorced homemakers would prepare herself for a lifetime of gainful employment. Yet this thoughtful young woman would also contemplate the likelihood that she will marry and bear children, a probability far greater even than divorce. As she considers the constraints and limitations that marriage and motherhood may impose upon her labor market participation, she may understandably choose an occupation that offers easy entry and reentry, flexible and controllable hours, and geographic mobility. She may choose, for example, primary or secondary education, nursing, or social work. She might understandably pause as she considers the "jealous mistress" professions of law, medicine, and university teaching, professions that, as constructed, generally require single-minded dedication and inordinate hours during the years that our young woman will start and raise her family. Ought our divorce law, as Dean Kay suggests, encourage this young woman to focus exclusively on her career potential and thus make the same career choices that a man would? Even if we answer this question affirmatively, should we reasonably expect that the content of divorce law will weigh heavily in the calculus as our young woman contemplates her career choices? In other words, should we distinguish between the power of divorce statistics to encourage young women to prepare for gainful employment and the potential of ungenerous divorce law to encourage young women to make occupational choices unconstrained by the prospect of future family roles?

3. *Efficiency or fairness?* If you find yourself unpersuaded that divorce rules will shape marital behavior, as opposed to divorce propensity, you may wish to reject theories that rely upon considerations of efficiency. Yet some of these theories were not formulated in terms of economic efficiency, and all of them may be cast or recast in terms of fairness at divorce. Do they hold up as theories of marital justice? Do considerations of fairness argue for greater or lesser redistribution than do considerations of efficiency?

4. *The marriage market.* Only Professor Cohen considers sex-related differences in opportunities for remarriage. Are men and women equally situated in terms of their opportunities for marriage at *any* age? In terms of the "deal" they strike for and during marriage? Economist Victor Fuchs shows that "women have a stronger demand for children than men do, and have more concern for children after they are born." Women's Quest for Economic Equality 68 (1988). Does this demand and concern affect their relative opportunities and bargaining positions at all ages? Do relaxed sexual mores and sex-related economic inequality also affect women's opportunities for marriage and remarriage? Should divorce law take into account such sex-related differences?

5. *The elusive goal of equality.* Dean Kay would seem to place equality above efficiency or fairness. She is, perhaps, as concerned about women's premarital behavior as their marital behavior. The law's insensitivity to sex-related economic inequality at divorce may send some young women the cautionary message that they must develop their own earning capacity. Nevertheless, the demands of marriage and children may prove inconsistent with full exercise of that earning capacity. Does Dean Kay's approach adequately account for the realities of women's lives? See generally A. Hochschild, The Second Shift (1989) (how women accommodate their market labor to the needs and demands of children and husbands). Does Dean Kay's approach adequately account for the prescient choices of young women who select careers that do not fully develop their market potential *because* such careers are more readily reconcilable with motherhood and homemaking? Should divorce law account for such *pre*marital choices? Would it be fair to the other spouse? Would it undermine Dean Kay's vision of equality?

Professor Martha Fineman vigorously argues for another form of equality, equality of economic outcomes at divorce. She takes the view that women's commitment to childrearing should be sanctioned and rewarded by a guarantee of equal economic outcomes at divorce. The Illusion of Equality: The Rhetoric and Reality of Divorce Reform 3-4, 21-23 (1991).

6. *Distinguishing between property division and spousal support.* Although Professors Carbone and Brinig may be read to imply a bright line between property division and spousal support, most commentators find it increasingly difficult to distinguish

the two either in terms of rationale or substantive reach. Marital property claims to career assets, which can only be measured and realized in future postdivorce income, tend to confuse the traditional borders between property division and spousal support. The next three cases are illustrative.

G. PROFESSIONAL EDUCATION: THE CUTTING EDGE OF SEVERAL MAJOR MARITAL PROPERTY ISSUES

The following materials are designed to be read on a number of levels. They pose a basic question of marital property classification that should be of considerable interest to you: If you are married, will your law degree be community property? Although you should think about this question now, keep your conclusions tentative until you study the treatment of unvested pensions and professional goodwill at pages 283-324 infra. These materials also pose questions about the capacity of various systems to provide some response to an arguably deserving claim. How much flexibility does a system need in order to be adequately responsive? Again, what is the relationship between spousal support and property division? To what extent are the two interchangeable? Most important, these materials are intended to pique your interest and to involve you personally in this subject.

MARRIAGE OF GRAHAM
194 Colo. 429, 574 P.2d 75 (1978)

LEE, Justice: This case presents the novel question of whether in a marriage dissolution proceeding a master's degree in business administration (M.B.A.) constitutes marital property which is subject to division by the court. In its opinion in Graham v. Graham, 38 Colo. App. 130, 555 P.2d 527, the Colorado Court of Appeals held that it was not. We affirm the judgment.

The Uniform Dissolution of Marriage Act requires that a court shall divide marital property, without regard to marital misconduct, in such proportions as the court deems just after considering all relevant factors. The Act defines marital property as follows:

> For purposes of this article only, "marital property" means all property acquired by either spouse subsequent to the marriage except:
> (a) Property acquired by gift, bequest, devise, or descent;
> (b) Property acquired in exchange for property acquired prior to the marriage or in exchange for property acquired by gift, bequest, devise, or descent;
> (c) Property acquired by a spouse after a decree of legal separation; and
> (d) Property excluded by valid agreement of the parties.

Section 14-10-113(2), C.R.S. 1973.

The parties to this proceeding were married on August 5, 1968, in Denver, Colorado. Throughout the six-year marriage, Anne P. Graham, wife and petitioner here, was employed full-time as an airline stewardess. She is still so employed. Her husband, Dennis J. Graham, respondent, worked part-time for most of the marriage, although his main pursuit was his education. He attended school for approximately three and one-half years of the marriage, acquiring both a bachelor of science degree in engineering physics and a master's degree in business administration at the University of Colorado. Following graduation, he obtained a job as an executive assistant with a large corporation at a starting salary of $14,000 per year.

The trial court determined that during the marriage petitioner contributed seventy percent of the financial support, which was used both for family expenses and for her husband's education. No marital assets were accumulated during the marriage. In addition, the Grahams together managed an apartment house and petitioner did the majority of housework and cooked most of the meals for the couple. No children were born during the marriage.

The parties jointly filed a petition for dissolution, on February 4, 1974, in the Boulder County District Court. Petitioner did not make a claim for maintenance or for attorney fees. After a hearing on October 24, 1974, the trial court found, as a matter of law, that an education obtained by one spouse during a marriage is jointly-owned property to which the other spouse has a property right. The future earnings value of the M.B.A. to respondent was evaluated at $82,836 and petitioner was awarded $33,134 of this amount, payable in monthly installments of $100.

The court of appeals reversed, holding that an education is not itself "property" subject to division under the Act, although it was one factor to be considered in determining maintenance or in arriving at an equitable property division.

The purpose of the division of marital property is to allocate to each spouse what equitably belongs to him or her. See H. Clark, Domestic Relations §14.8. The division is committed to the sound discretion of the trial court and there is no rigid mathematical formula that the court must adhere to. Carlson v. Carlson, 178 Colo. 283, 497 P.2d 1006; Greer v. Greer, 32 Colo. App. 196, 510 P.2d 905. An appellate court will alter a division of property only if the trial court abuses its discretion. This court, however, is empowered at all times to interpret Colorado statutes.

The legislature intended the term "property" to be broadly inclusive, as indicated by its use of the qualifying adjective "all" in section 14-10-113(2). Previous Colorado cases have given "property" a comprehensive meaning, as typified by the following definition: "In short it embraces anything and everything which may belong to a man and in the ownership of which he has a right to be protected by law." Las Animas County High School District v. Raye, 144 Colo. 367, 356 P.2d 237.

Nonetheless, there are necessary limits upon what may be considered "property," and we do not find any indication in the Act that the concept as used by the legislature is other than that usually understood to be embodied within the term. One helpful definition is "everything that has an exchangeable value or which goes to make up wealth or estate." Black's Law Dictionary 1382 (rev. 4th ed. 1968). In Ellis v. Ellis, 191 Colo. 317, 552 P.2d 506, this court held that military retirement pay was not property for the reason that it did not have any of the elements of cash surrender value, loan value, redemption value, lump sum value, or value realizable after death. The court of appeals has considered other factors as well in deciding whether something falls within the concept, particularly whether it can be assigned, sold, transferred, conveyed, or pledged, or whether it terminates on the death of the owner. . . .

An educational degree, such as an M.B.A., is simply not encompassed even by the broad views of the concept of "property." It does not have an exchange value or any objective transferable value on an open market. It is personal to the holder. It terminates on death of the holder and is not inheritable. It cannot be assigned, sold, transferred, conveyed or pledged. An advanced degree is a cumulative product of many years of previous education, combined with diligence and hard work. It may not be acquired by the mere expenditure of money. It is simply an intellectual achievement that may potentially assist in the future acquisition of property. In our view, it has none of the attributes of property in the usual sense of that term. . . .

A spouse who provides financial support while the other spouse acquires an education is not without a remedy. Where there is marital property to be divided, such contribution to the education of the other spouse may be taken into consideration by the court. . . . Here, we again note that no marital property had been accumulated by the parties. Further, if maintenance is sought and a need is demonstrated, the trial court may make an award based on all relevant factors. Section 14-10-114(2). Certainly, among the relevant factors to be considered is the contribution of the spouse seeking maintenance to the education of the other spouse from whom the maintenance is sought. Again, we note that in this case petitioner sought no maintenance from respondent.

The judgment is affirmed.

Mr. Justice CARRIGAN dissenting: I respectfully dissent.

As a matter of economic reality the most valuable asset acquired by either party during this six-year marriage was the husband's increased earning capacity. There is no dispute that this asset resulted from his having obtained Bachelor of Science and Master of Business Administration degrees while married. These degrees, in turn, resulted in large part from the wife's employment which contributed about 70% of the couple's total income. Her earnings not only provided her husband's support but also were "invested" in his education in the sense that she assumed the role of breadwinner so that he would have the time and funds necessary to obtain his education.

The case presents the not-unfamiliar pattern of the wife who, willing to sacrifice for a more secure family financial future, works to educate her husband, only to be awarded a divorce decree shortly after he is awarded his degree. The issue here is whether traditional, narrow concepts of what constitutes "property" render the courts impotent to provide a remedy for an obvious injustice.

In cases such as this, equity demands that courts seek extraordinary remedies to prevent extraordinary injustice. If the parties had remained married long enough after the husband had completed his postgraduate education so that they could have accumulated substantial property, there would have been no problem. In that situation abundant precedent authorizes the trial court, in determining how much of the marital property to allocate to the wife, to take into account her contributions to her husband's earning capacity. Greer v. Greer, 32 Colo. App. 196, 510 P.2d 905 (1973) (wife supported husband through medical school); In re Marriage of Vanet, 544 S.W.2d 236 (Mo. App. 1976) (wife was breadwinner while husband was in law school).

A husband's future income earning potential, sometimes as indicated by the goodwill value of a professional practice, may be considered in deciding property division or alimony matters, and the wife's award may be increased on the ground that the husband probably will have substantial future earnings. Todd v. Todd, 272

Cal. App. 2d 786, 78 Cal. Rptr. 131 (1969) (goodwill of husband's law practice); Golden v. Golden, 270 Cal. App. 2d 401, 75 Cal. Rptr. 735 (1969) (goodwill of husband's medical practice); Mueller v. Mueller, 144 Cal. App. 2d 245, 301 P.2d 90 (1956) (goodwill of husband's dental lab); In re Marriage of Goger, 27 Or. App. 729, 557 P.2d 46 (1976) (potential earnings of husband's dental practice); In re Marriage of Lukens, 16 Wash. App. 481, 558 P.2d 279 (1976) (goodwill of husband's medical practice indicated future earning capacity).

Similarly, the wife's contributions to enhancing the husband's financial status or earning capacity have been considered in awarding alimony and maintenance. Kraus v. Kraus, 159 Colo. 331, 411 P.2d 240 (1966); Shapiro v. Shapiro, 115 Colo. 505, 176 P.2d 363 (1946). The majority opinion emphasizes that in this case no maintenance was requested. However, the Colorado statute would seem to preclude an award of maintenance here, for it restricts the court's power to award maintenance to cases where the spouse seeking it is unable to support himself or herself. Section 14-10-114, C.R.S. 1973.

While the majority opinion focuses on whether the husband's master's degree is marital "property" subject to division, it is not the degree itself which constitutes the asset in question. Rather it is the increase in the husband's earning power concomitant to that degree which is the asset conferred on him by his wife's efforts. That increased earning capacity was the asset appraised in the economist's expert opinion testimony as having a discounted present value of $82,000.

Unquestionably the law, in other contexts, recognizes future earning capacity as an asset whose wrongful deprivation is compensable. Thus one who tortiously destroys or impairs another's future earning capacity must pay as damages the amount the injured party has lost in anticipated future earnings. Nemer v. Anderson, 151 Colo. 411, 378 P.2d 841 (1963); Abram, Personal Injury Damages in Colorado, 35 Colo. L. Rev. 332, 338 (1963).

Where a husband is killed, his widow is entitled to recover for loss of his future support damages based in part on the present value of his anticipated future earnings, which may be computed by taking into account probable future increases in his earning capacity. See United States v. Sommers, 351 F.2d 354 (10th Cir. 1965); Good v. Chance, 39 Colo. App. 70, 565 P.2d 217 (1977). See also Colo. J.I. (Civil) 10:3.

The day before the divorce the wife had a legally recognized interest in her husband's earning capacity. Perhaps the wife might have a remedy in a separate action based on implied debt, quasi-contract, unjust enrichment, or some similar theory. See, e.g., Dass v. Epplen, 162 Colo. 60, 424 P.2d 779 (1967). Nevertheless, the law favors settling all aspects of a dispute in a single action where that is possible. Therefore I would affirm the trial court's award.

I am authorized to state that Mr. Chief Justice PRINGLE and Mr. Justice GROVES join in this dissent.

JOAN KRAUSKOPF, RECOMPENSE FOR FINANCING SPOUSE'S EDUCATION: LEGAL PROTECTION FOR THE MARITAL INVESTOR IN HUMAN CAPITAL
28 Kan. L. Rev. 379 (1980)

1. Theory of Investment in Human Capital

According to the concept of human capital, human skills, talents, and knowledge that increase productivity are a form of wealth. Expenditures to acquire or to increase a person's skills or knowledge that lead to increased future productivity are an investment in human capital. . . .

The rebirth of this concept has been attributed to the 1979 Nobel Prize winner Theodore W. Schultz, particularly to his presidential address at the 1969 meeting of the American Economic Association in St. Louis, Missouri. Schultz pointed out that, although it was obvious that people acquired useful skills and knowledge, it had not been obvious to economists that these skills and knowledge, which were largely the product of deliberate investment, were a form of capital, and the growth of this capital had occurred in Western societies much faster than the growth of conventional or nonhuman capital. Schultz maintained that the rise in economic output during this century, which is unaccounted for by the growth in traditionally recognized wealth, is attributable to a real growth in productivity per unit of labor as a result of the steadily growing amount of human capital per worker.

A consensus has developed among economists that human capital is a form of wealth in which investments are made that must be accounted for in economic analyses. Although some economists are opposed to the human capital concept because they do not like to consider people as land or machines, most economists recognize that it is not the human being that constitutes the capital, but rather, his skills and knowledge. Schultz observed that

> the productive capacity of human beings is now vastly larger than all other forms of wealth taken together. What economists have not stressed is the simple truth that people invest in themselves and that these investments are very large. . . . This knowledge and skill are in great part the product of investment and, combined with other human investment, predominantly account for the productive superiority of the technically advanced countries. . . .

B. The "Family as Firm" Concept

The human capital concept had encouraged further analysis by economists of the importance of human time, and this analysis led to a recognition of the importance of the allocation of human resources within the family unit.[35] In economic analysis, the family is a decision making unit that operates to maximize the unit's utility in consumption and also in the allocation of human time and production

---

35. A recognized subgroup of family economics came into existence with the publication of Economics of the Family (T. Schultz ed. 1974) [hereinafter cited as Economics]. This book compiled studies on the family as an economic unit.

activities.[36] This view of the family is an application of the traditional economic theory of the firm. Under this theory, the family makes decisions in order to maximize the utility of the family as a whole, and thus the welfare of each member is integrated into a unified family welfare function.[37] Consequently, the family makes decisions that do not necessarily maximize the utility for a particular individual, but maximize the utility for the family firm.[38]

A pattern of individual sacrifice for the greater good of the family is exhibited by both the traditional family, in which the husband is the primary wage earner and the wife remains in the home during all or a large portion of their married life, and the nontraditional family, in which the wife works to support the family while the husband obtains a higher education. The traditional family situation has been analyzed by economists as an efficient allocation of time for maximizing the utility of the family firm.[39] Because of this allocation of time, both the husband's earning capacity and his general welfare are increased by being a member of the firm.[40] Empirical studies, however, confirm that the gains to the marriage firm from the time spent by the housewife in the home are achieved at a cost far beyond the wages that she foregoes while remaining in the home.[41] A homemaker who drops out of the employment market, as most married women do for half of their adult married life,[42] causes a depreciation in her own earning capacity in two ways: first, she is not in the labor market and thus does not enjoy increases in income, fringe benefits, and seniority that the normal continuous employee achieves; and second, she foregoes the opportunity to continually reinvest in her human capital, which ordinarily occurs as an employee becomes more skillful and thus, a more valuable employee. . . .

The employed spouse/student spouse marriage is a more complex firm. The first consideration in the husband and wife decision concerning further investment through education involves the decision in whom to invest in order to achieve the maximum utility for the family. Traditionally, many women contemplate dropping out of the labor market when children are young, which means a large decrease in the woman's earning capacity because of the period of time in which she is not

---

36. A premium currently attaches to optimizing allocation of the ability and time of both men and women in managing households and in investing in themselves. The increase in the total body of knowledge in the world has led to an increased demand for human time to apply that knowledge and to make it useful, and as a result the market place is willing to pay more for human time.

37. Benham, Benefits of Women's Education Within Marriage, in Economics, supra note 35, at 376; Landes, Economics of Alimony, 7 J. Legal Stud. 35, 36 (1978).

38. Even though economists use a monetary model when they conceive of the family as a firm, they are concerned with total utility. This model is an analytical tool for determining the relative importance of monetary factors in a broader context that is also influenced by nonmonetary factors. In economic analysis, "gain from marriage" includes not only physical goods, but encompasses all the utilities of a family relationship, including love, companionship, care, child bearing, and recreation—the total flow of satisfaction from the family unit. Becker, A Theory of Marriage, in Economics, supra note 35, at 304; Landes, supra note 37, at 40. One commentator has suggested that economic analysis is enlarging and enriching the role of the family by its assumption that the family integrates the welfare of its members into an internally consistent family utility function. Schultz, Fertility and Economic Values, in Economics, supra note 35, at 11. The author believes that the economic model should enhance our ability to analyze the dynamics of a family relationship, and consequently, criticism that the use of an economic analysis would be destructive to the family is hardly justified.

39. Becker, A Theory of Marriage, in Economics, supra note 35, at 301.

40. Becker, Landes & Michael, An Economic Analysis of Marital Instability, 85 J. Political Econ. 1141, 1146 (1977); Landes, supra note 37, at 49.

41. See, e.g., Mincer & Polachek, Family Investments in Human Capital: Earnings of Women, in Economics, supra note 35, at 397.

42. Id. at 401.

in the labor force. Consequently, when a husband and a wife, even though they have equal abilities and ambitions, realize that they can afford only the costs of further education for one of them, the probabilities are that they will choose to invest in the husband's earning ability.

The second factor in this decision is that the husband may not be able to continue to invest in education without the funds supplied from his wife's earnings, particularly if he is working on a postgraduate or professional degree and is foregoing substantial earnings. . . . The husband . . . has a free market for funds in the wife's earnings: no loan must be repaid and no interest accrues.

The wife who is employed in order to enable her husband to obtain postgraduate education not only provides the funds that are invested to increase the husband's human capital, but she may sacrifice the opportunity to increase her own human capital through education. During the education period, she sacrifices with him his foregone earnings. From the wife's perspective the fact that the family operates as a firm explains why she is willing to sacrifice and to invest her own valuable time in order to increase the human capital of another individual. She expects that the return he obtains on his investment will be shared by them equally in the later years of the marriage.

The development of earning capacity through education of one spouse, however, . . . is valuable to both partners only if the marriage continues. Economists have recognized that the marriage period investment in the development of one spouse's earning capacity is made for a *prospective* utilization of that human capital; the couple determines its current allocation of time by considering the prospective effects of that allocation. The wife is willing to invest in her husband's earning capacity at a cost to herself because she expects to share jointly with her husband in the future earnings generated by her investment. Therefore, although the total value of the husband's earnings would not be at risk if the couple obtained a divorce — the partner whose earning capacity was increased will, of course, possess that earning capacity wholly to himself — the wife's claim as a result of her investment is very much at risk.

No economists have yet dealt with the dissolution of an employed spouse/ student spouse marriage. Economic analysis of the dissolution of the traditional marriage, however, is especially pertinent. According to Landes' study of the marriage of the traditional housewife who foregoes the opportunity to develop her earning capacity because she has maximized family utility by allocating her time to the household, "alimony" should recompense her for her foregone opportunities when divorce cuts off her returns from the husband's increased earning capacity. Landes contends that if "alimony" is a payment of money to recompense for foregone opportunities, it will serve as an incentive for the most efficient allocation of time and resources for the couple jointly during marriage. Alimony would encourage investment in the earning capacity of one of the spouses while allocating the other spouse's time to the household to the extent that the couple achieved maximum utility.

The homemaker who does not remain in the home, but remains employed, perhaps at a relatively low level job in order to enable her husband to attend a graduate or a professional school, fits clearly into these analyses. As a partner in the family firm she has invested her opportunities for educational and career advancement and her standard of living in the human capital of her spouse. Unless the courts protect her investment at divorce, the incentive for the wife to invest her time in increasing her husband's human capital will be reduced. . . .

B. Theories of Economic Settlement at Marriage Dissolution

1. Fault Regimes

Until the early 1970s two apparently unrelated theories controlled economic disposition at divorce: a court should grant a divorce only to an individual who was innocent against a party who was at fault and each party should retain assets titled separately in his or her name. Since the Married Women's Property Acts allowed a married woman to hold property in her own name, the common law marital property regime involved "separation of assets" with little power and less theoretical basis for a divorce court to allocate property between the parties. The only economic disposition that many courts could order was a payment of money by the husband to the wife in the form of alimony. The homemaker, who had not had the opportunity to earn money or to acquire any property, ordinarily did not wish to be divorced because she needed the economic security of marriage. Her strongest bargaining tool for economic settlement was the threat of preventing divorce by showing fault by the husband. Consequently, most divorces were ultimately noncontested after negotiation and settlement, and a great many property transfers and agreements for alimony occurred without any court action. Courts awarded alimony only after an apparent contest had established the husband's fault. The courts indicated that the purpose of alimony was for the support of a dependent wife, to award damages for breach of the marriage contract, or occasionally to effect a monetary form of division of property. Courts engaged in little in-depth analysis of why payment and receipt of alimony should serve these purposes, perhaps because the social dimensions of the issues were relatively minor: there were few divorces, the parties settled the economic consequences of most divorces, and often an extended family could care for the divorced wife.

2. "No-Fault" Regimes

Pressure for "no-fault" marriage dissolutions occurred simultaneously with a significant increase in the breakdown of marriages. Because "no-fault" dissolution removed the economic bargaining tool of the fault regimes, it was essential that the law assure a fair economic settlement in other ways.[96] . . . [T]he nationwide trend has been for legislation that empowers courts to divide property and to award "maintenance" instead of alimony.

The theoretical basis of property division at dissolution is that marriage is an economic partnership akin to a business partnership and that at dissolution the courts should divide the assets acquired during the marriage on a basis other than their technical title. These laws recognize the economist's "firm theory" of marriage — both partners contribute toward maximum family welfare, including accu-

---

96. The Archbishop's group that studied divorce reform in England stated:

> As matters now stand, divorce as such is apt to affect the economic and financial position of wives more adversely than that of their husbands . . . it would be unjust to allow the principle of breakdown to operate freely . . . unless the legislature has first taken steps to insure that unoffending respondents and children would not be penalized economically and socially by the grant of decrees. This we regard as another necessary condition of reforming the divorce law.

Group Appointed by Lord Archbishop of Canterbury, Putting Asunder: A Divorce Law for Contemporary Society (1990), at 47.

mulation of assets. These statutes also allow division of property to perform a function of maintenance. . . . The 1970 Uniform Marriage and Divorce Act specifically provides that courts are to consider the economic circumstances of the parties in dividing the property, and that courts are to divide property before considering maintenance. . . .

The justification for utilizing property to fulfill the purpose of maintenance is that division of property is final and nonmodifiable, which increases certainty of payment and thus minimizes future contact between the parties.[104]

Under the no-fault regimes, which permit dissolution without regard to fault and authorize division of property, maintenance has a more limited function than alimony under the fault regimes. One of the reasons for divorce without the establishment of fault was to eliminate the bitterness of litigation concerning fault, and therefore, it would be anomalous to award damages for breach of the marital contract. Because courts have power to divide property in kind or by money awards, no need should exist for maintenance or alimony payments as a substitute for division of property.

There are two primary justifications for maintenance under the new laws: recompense for lost earning capacity and recompense for contribution to the welfare of the family.[105] Recompense for lost earning capacity is a legitimate function for maintenance because the homemaker who has devoted all or a portion of her employable time to the home has lost or reduced the opportunity to develop her earning capacity.[106] The longer the marriage has lasted and the older the individual is, the more severe is this lost opportunity; the dependent homemaker may or may not be able to achieve any degree of self-sufficiency. In this respect, the award of maintenance should be modifiable because if the woman becomes self-sufficient or if she remarries, those previous lost opportunities would no longer be disadvantageous to her. . . . [Landes'] economic analysis of alimony is in accord with this theory of the function of maintenance. Landes concluded that the social justification for alimony is to recompense an individual for lost opportunities during the marriage. If the law does not provide recompense at divorce for those lost opportunities, according to this analysis, the homemaker will not contribute to the family to the extent that would best maximize utility for the family as a firm, and thus, alimony serves as an incentive toward the optimal maximization of utility for the married couple. This is the classic "need for support" purpose of alimony. Although seldom articulated in that matter, it has traditionally been a major function of modifiable periodic alimony, and it continues to be a major function for modifiable periodic maintenance under the new "no-fault" laws.

The second theoretical justification for modern maintenance is to compensate the spouse for her contribution to the welfare of the family, which presumably has not been otherwise compensated by division of property. The award would provide a "return" for benefits contributed to the family, as distinguished from merely

---

104. Moss v. Moss, 531 P.2d 635, 638 (Colo. App. 1974); Rothman v. Rothman, 65 N.J. 219, 228-29, 320 A.2d 496, 498-501 (1974); Rheinstein, Division of Marital Property, 12 Willamette L.J. 413, 425 (1976).

105. R. Levy, Uniform Marriage and Divorce Legislation (1968), at 153; Krauskopf, Applying the Maintenance Statute, 33 J. Mo. B. 93, 100 (1977); Krauskopf, [Maintenance: Theory and Negotiation, 33 J. Mo. B. 24 (1977)].

106. In recent years, legal literature has widely recognized this more sophisticated basis for the "need for support." Perhaps the clearest evidence of statutory purpose is in the 1977 Wisconsin divorce law. Wis. Stat. Ann. §247.26(l)(c) (West Supp. 1978).

preventing suffering due to lost opportunities. Unlike recompense for lost opportunities to develop one's own earning power, recompense for contribution should be made whether or not the investing spouse remarries or becomes self-sufficient. Nonmodifiable . . . maintenance would be an appropriate method of making this award. Maintenance as compensation is likely to be rare, however. Under the partnership theory of marriage, contributions to the welfare of the family through routine household tasks are indirect contributions to the accumulation of assets and, therefore, like monetary contributions to assets, can be adequately accounted for in the division of property. In certain situations, however, maintenance is essential to achieve a just economic settlement. . . .

MAHONEY v. MAHONEY
91 N.J. 488, 453 A.2d 527 (1982)

PASHMAN, J. Once again the Court must interpret this state's law regarding the distribution of marital property upon divorce. The question here is whether the defendant has the right to share the value of a professional business (M.B.A.) degree earned by her former husband during their marriage. The Court must decide whether the plaintiff's degree is "property" for purposes of N.J.S.A. 2A:34-23, which requires equitable distribution of "the property, both real and personal, which was legally and beneficially acquired . . . during the marriage." If the M.B.A. degree is not property, we must still decide whether the defendant can nonetheless recover the money she contributed to her husband's support while he pursued his professional education. For the reasons stated below, we hold that the plaintiff's professional degree is not property and therefore reject the defendant's claim that the degree is subject to equitable distribution. To this extent, we concur in the reasoning of the Appellate Division. Notwithstanding this concurrence, we reverse the judgment of the Appellate Division, which had the effect of denying the defendant any remedial relief for her contributions toward her husband's professional education and remand for further proceedings.

I

When the parties married in Indiana in 1971, plaintiff, Melvin Mahoney, had an engineering degree and defendant, June Lee Mahoney, had a bachelor of science degree. From that time until the parties separated in October 1978 they generally shared all household expenses. The sole exception was the period between September 1975 and January 1977, when the plaintiff attended the Wharton School of the University of Pennsylvania and received an M.B.A. degree.

During the 16-month period in which the plaintiff attended school, June Lee Mahoney contributed about $24,000 to the household. Her husband made no financial contribution while he was a student. Melvin's educational expenses of about $6,500 were paid for by a combination of veterans' benefits and a payment from the Air Force. After receiving his degree, the plaintiff went to work as a commercial lending officer for Chase Manhattan Bank.

Meanwhile, in 1976 the defendant began a part-time graduate program at Rutgers University, paid for by her employer, that led to a master's degree in micro-

biology one year after the parties had separated. June Lee worked full-time throughout the course of her graduate schooling.

In March 1979, Melvin Mahoney sued for divorce; his wife filed a counterclaim
also seeking a divorce. In May 1980, the trial court granted dual judgments of divorce on the ground of 18 months continuous separation.

At the time of trial, plaintiff's annual income was $25,600 and defendant's
income was $21,000. No claim for alimony was made. The parties owned no real
property and divided the small amount of their personal property by agreement.

The only issue at trial was the defendant's claim for reimbursement of the
amount of support she gave her husband while he obtained his M.B.A. degree.
Defendant sought 50% of the $24,000 she had contributed to the household during
that time, plus one-half of the $6,500 cost of her husband's tuition.

The trial court decided that defendant should be reimbursed, 175 N.J. Super.
443, 419 A.2d 1149 (Ch. Div. 1980), holding that "the education and degree obtained by plaintiff, under the circumstances of this case, constitute a property right.
. . ." Id. at 447, 419 A.2d 1149. However, the court did not attempt to determine
the value of plaintiff's M.B.A. degree. Instead, finding that in this case "[t]o ignore
the contributions of the sacrificing spouse would be . . . an unjust enrichment of
the educated spouse," id. at 446, 419 A.2d 1149, the court ordered the award of a
"reasonable sum as a credit [for] . . . the maintenance of the household and the
support of plaintiff during the educational period." Id. at 447, 419 A.2d 1149. Plaintiff was ordered to reimburse his wife in the amount of $5,000, to be paid at the
rate of $100 per month. The court did not explain why it chose this amount.

Plaintiff appealed to the Appellate Division, which reversed the award. 182
N.J. Super. 598, 442 A.2d 1062 (1982). It not only rejected defendant's claim for
reimbursement but also held that neither a professional license nor an educational
degree is "property" for the purposes of the equitable distribution statute, N.J.S.A.
2A:34-23. In so holding, the Appellate Division stated that it was bound by Stern
v. Stern, 66 N.J. 340, 345, 331 A.2d 257 (1975), where the Court held that "a person's earning capacity . . . should not be recognized as a separate, particular item
of property within the meaning of N.J.S.A. 2A:34-23" (footnote omitted). The Appellate Division noted that if enhanced earning capacity is not property, then "neither is the license or degree, which is merely the memorialization of the attainment
of the skill, qualification and educational background which is the prerequisite of
the enhanced earning capacity. . . ." 182 N.J. Super. at 605, 442 A.2d 1062. The
court noted that degrees and licenses lack many of the attributes of most property
rights, id. at 605, 442 A.2d 1062, and that their value is not only speculative, id. at
609, 442 A.2d 1062, but also may be fully accounted for by way of alimony and
equitable division of the other assets. Id. at 607, 442 A.2d 1062.

In rejecting defendant's claim for reimbursement, the Appellate Division disapproved of the attempt to measure the contributions of the parties to one another
or to their marriage. The court cited with approval Wisner v. Wisner, 129 Ariz. 333,
631 P.2d 115, 123 (Ct. App. 1981), where an Arizona appeals court stated:

> [I]t is improper for a court to treat a marriage as an arm's length transaction
> by allowing a spouse to come into court *after* the fact and make legal argu-
> ments regarding unjust enrichment. . . .
>   [C]ourts should assume, in the absence of contrary proof, that the deci-
> sion [to obtain a professional degree] was mutual and took into account what
> sacrifices the community [of husband and wife] needed to make in the fur-
> therance of that decision. [emphasis in original]

The Appellate Division saw no need to distinguish contributions made toward a spouse's attainment of a license or degree from other contributions, calling such special treatment "a kind of elitism which inappropriately depreciates the value of all the other types of contributions made to each other by other spouses. . . ." 182 N.J. Super. at 613, 442 A.2d 1062. Finally, the court noted that in this case each spouse left the marriage "with comparable earning capacity and comparable educational achievements." Id. at 615, 442 A.2d 1062. The court did not order a remand.

We granted certification, 91 N.J. 191, 450 A.2d 526 (1982).

II

This case first involves a question of statutory interpretation. The Court must decide whether the Legislature intended an M.B.A. degree to be "property" so that, if acquired by either spouse during a marriage, its value must be equitably distributed upon divorce. In determining whether the Legislature intended to treat an M.B.A. degree as property under N.J.S.A. 2A:34-23, the Court gains little guidance from traditional rules of statutory construction. There is no legislative history on the meaning of the word "property" in the equitable distribution statute, L.1971, c.212, N.J.S.A. 2A:34-23, and the statute itself offers no guidance. Therefore, statutory construction in this case means little more than an inquiry into the extent to which professional degrees and licenses share the qualities of other things that the Legislature and courts have treated as property.

Regarding equitable distribution, this Court has frequently held that an "expansive interpretation [is] to be given to the word 'property,'" Gauger v. Gauger, 73 N.J. 538, 544, 376 A.2d 523 (1977). . . . New Jersey courts have subjected a broad range of assets and interests to equitable distribution including vested but unmatured private pensions, Kikkert v. Kikkert, 88 N.J. 4, 438 A.2d 317 (1981); military retirement pay and disability benefits, Kruger v. Kruger [73 N.J. 464, 375 A.2d 659 (1977)]; unliquidated claims for benefits under workers' compensation, Hughes v. Hughes, 132 N.J. Super. 559, 334 A.2d 379 (Ch. Div. 1975); and personal injury claims, DiTolvo v. DiTolvo, 131 N.J. Super. 72, 80-82, 328 A.2d 625 (App. Div. 1974). . . .

This Court, however, has never subjected to equitable distribution an asset whose future monetary value is as uncertain and unquantifiable as a professional degree or license. . . .

A professional license or degree is a personal achievement of the holder. It cannot be sold and its value cannot readily be determined. A professional license or degree represents the opportunity to obtain an amount of money only upon the occurrence of highly uncertain future events. By contrast, the vested but unmatured pension at issue in Kikkert, supra, entitled the owner to a definite amount of money at a certain future date.

The value of a professional degree for purposes of property distribution is nothing more than the possibility of enhanced earnings that the particular academic credential will provide. In Stern v. Stern, 66 N.J. 340, 345, 331 A.2d 257 (1975), we held that a lawyer's

> earning capacity, even where its development has been aided and enhanced
> by the other spouse . . . should not be recognized as a separate, particular

> item of property within the meaning of N.J.S.A. 2A:34-23. Potential earning
> capacity . . . should not be deemed property as such within the meaning of
> the statute.[3]

Equitable distribution of a professional degree would similarly require distribution
of "earning capacity"—income that the degree holder might never acquire. The
amount of future earnings would be entirely speculative. Moreover, any assets resulting from income for professional services would be property acquired *after* the
marriage; the statute restricts equitable distribution to property acquired *during* the
marriage. N.J.S.A. 2A:34-23. . . .

Valuing a professional degree in the hands of any particular individual at the
start of his or her career would involve a gamut of calculations that reduces to little
more than guesswork. As the Appellate Division noted, courts would be required
to determine far more than what the degree holder could earn in the new career.
The admittedly speculative dollar amount of

> earnings in the "enhanced" career [must] be reduced by the . . . income the
> spouse should be assumed to have been able to earn if otherwise employed. In
> our view [this] is ordinarily nothing but speculation, particularly when it is
> fair to assume that a person with the ability and motivation to complete pro-
> fessional training or higher education would probably utilize those attributes
> in concomitantly productive alternative endeavors. [182 N.J. Super. at 609,
> 442 A.2d 1062]

Even if such estimates could be made, however, there would remain a world
of unforeseen events that could affect the earning potential—not to mention the
actual earnings—of any particular degree holder.

> A person qualified by education for a given profession may choose not to
> practice it, may fail at it, or may practice in a speciality, location or manner
> which generates less than the average income enjoyed by fellow professionals.
> The potential worth of the education may never be realized for these or many
> other reasons. An award based upon the prediction of the degree holder's
> success at the chosen field may bear no relationship to the reality he or she
> faces after the divorce. [DeWitt v. DeWitt, 98 Wis. 2d 44, 296 N.W.2d 761,
> 768 (Ct. App. 1980)]

Moreover, the likelihood that an equitable distribution will prove to be unfair
is increased in those cases where the court miscalculates the value of the license
or degree.

> The potential for inequity to the failed professional or one who changes ca-
> reers is at once apparent; his or her spouse will have been awarded a share
> of something which never existed in any real sense. [Id.]

The finality of property distribution precludes any remedy for such unfairness. "Unlike an award of alimony, which can be adjusted after divorce to reflect unantici-

---

3. A professional degree should not be equated with goodwill which, as we noted in *Stern*, may, in
a given case, add economic worth to a property interest. Stern v. Stern, 66 N.J. at 346-47 n.5, 331 A.2d
257 (1975).

pated changes in the parties' circumstances, a property division may not [be adjusted]." Id.

Because of these problems, most courts that have faced the issue have declined to treat professional degrees and licenses as marital property subject to distribution upon divorce. . . . Several courts, while not treating educational degrees as property, have awarded the supporting spouse an amount based on the cost to the supporting spouse of obtaining the degree. In effect, the supporting spouse was reimbursed for her financial contributions used by the supported spouse in obtaining a degree. See, e.g., DeLa Rosa v. DeLa Rosa, 309 N.W.2d 755, 759 (Minn. 1981) (medical degree); Hubbard v. Hubbard, 603 P.2d 747, 751 (Okla. 1979) (medical degree); In re Marriage of Horstmann, 263 N.W.2d 885, 891 (Iowa 1978) (law degree). Cf. Inman v. Inman, 578 S.W.2d 266, 269 (Ky. Ct. App. 1979) (dental license held to be property but measure of wife's interest was amount of investment in husband's education).

Even if it were marital property, valuing educational assets in terms of their cost would be an erroneous application of equitable distribution law. As the Appellate Division explained, the cost of a professional degree "has little to do with any real value of the degree and fails to consider at all the nonfinancial efforts made by the degree holder in completing his course of study." 182 N.J. Super. at 610, 442 A.2d 1062. See also DeWitt, supra, 296 N.W.2d at 767. Once a degree candidate has earned his or her degree, the amount that a spouse — or anyone else — paid towards its attainment has no bearing whatever on its value. The cost of a spouse's financial contributions has no logical connection to the value of that degree.

As the Appellate Division correctly noted, "the cost approach [to equitable distribution] is plainly not conceptually predicated on a property theory at all but rather represents a general notion of how to do equity in this one special situation." 182 N.J. Super. at 610, 442 A.2d 1062. Equitable distribution in these cases derives from the proposition that the supporting spouse should be reimbursed for contributions to the marital unit that, because of the divorce, did not bear its expected fruit for the supporting spouse.

The trial court recognized that the theoretical basis for the amount of its award was not equitable distribution, but rather reimbursement. It held that "the education and degree obtained by plaintiff, under the circumstances of this case, constitute a property right *subject to equitable offset* upon the dissolution of the marriage." 175 N.J. Super. at 447, 419 A.2d 1149 (emphasis added). The court allowed a "reasonable sum as a credit . . . on behalf of the maintenance of the household and the support of the plaintiff during the educational period." Id. Although the court found that the degree was distributable property, it actually reimbursed the defendant without attempting to give her part of the *value* of the degree.

This Court does not support reimbursement between former spouses in alimony proceedings as a general principle. Marriage is not a business arrangement in which the parties keep track of debits and credits, their accounts to be settled upon divorce. Rather, as we have said, "marriage is a shared enterprise, a joint undertaking . . . in many ways it is akin to a partnership." Rothman v. Rothman, 65 N.J. 219, 229, 320 A.2d 496 (1974). . . . But every joint undertaking has its bounds of fairness. Where a partner to marriage takes the benefits of his spouse's support in obtaining a professional degree or license with the understanding that future benefits will accrue and inure to both of them, and the marriage is then terminated without the supported spouse giving anything in return, an unfairness has occurred that calls for a remedy.

In this case, the supporting spouse made financial contributions towards her husband's professional education with the expectation that both parties would enjoy material benefits flowing from the professional license or degree. It is therefore patently unfair that the supporting spouse be denied the mutually anticipated benefit while the supported spouse keeps not only the degree, but also all of the financial and material rewards flowing from it.

Furthermore, it is realistic to recognize that in this case, a supporting spouse has contributed more than mere earnings to her husband with the mutual expectation that both of them — she as well as he — will realize and enjoy material improvements in their marriage as a result of his increased earning capacity. Also, the wife has presumably made personal financial sacrifices, resulting in a reduced or lowered standard of living. Additionally, her husband, by pursuing preparations for a future career, has foregone gainful employment and financial contributions to the marriage that would have been forthcoming had he been employed. He thereby has further reduced the level of support his wife might otherwise have received, as well as the standard of living both of them would have otherwise enjoyed. In effect, through her contributions, the supporting spouse has consented to live at a lower material level while her husband has prepared for another career. She has postponed, as it were, present consumption and a higher standard of living, for the future prospect of greater support and material benefits. The supporting spouse's sacrifices would have been rewarded had the marriage endured and the mutual expectations of both of them been fulfilled. The unredressed sacrifices — loss of support and reduction of the standard of living — coupled with the unfairness attendant upon the defeat of the supporting spouse's shared expectation of future advantages, further justify a remedial reward. In this sense, an award that is referable to the spouse's monetary contributions to her partner's education significantly implicates basic considerations of marital support and standard of living — factors that are clearly relevant in the determination and award of conventional alimony.

To provide a fair and effective means of compensating a supporting spouse who has suffered a loss or reduction of support, or has incurred a lower standard of living, or has been deprived of a better standard of living in the future, the Court now introduces the concept of reimbursement alimony into divorce proceedings. The concept properly accords with the Court's belief that regardless of the appropriateness of permanent alimony or the presence or absence of marital property to be equitably distributed, there will be circumstances where a supporting spouse should be reimbursed for the financial contributions he or she made to the spouse's successful professional training. Such reimbursement alimony should cover *all* financial contributions towards the former spouse's education, including household expenses, educational costs, school travel expenses and any other contributions used by the supported spouse in obtaining his or her degree or license. . . .

The Court does not hold that every spouse who contributes toward his or her partner's education or professional training is entitled to reimbursement alimony. Only monetary contributions made with the mutual and shared expectation that both parties to the marriage will derive increased income and material benefits should be a basis for such an award. For example, it is unlikely that a financially successful executive's spouse who, after many years of homemaking, returns to school would upon divorce be required to reimburse her husband for his contributions toward her degree. Reimbursement alimony should not subvert the basic goals of traditional alimony and equitable distribution.

In proper circumstances, however, courts should not hesitate to award reimbursement alimony. Marriage should not be a free ticket to professional education and training without subsequent obligations. This Court should not ignore the scenario of the young professional who after being supported through graduate school leaves his mate for supposedly greener pastures. One spouse ought not to receive a divorce complaint when the other receives a diploma. Those spouses supported through professional school should recognize that they may be called upon to reimburse the supporting spouses for the financial contributions they received in pursuit of their professional training. And they cannot deny the basic fairness of this result.[5]

As we have stated, reimbursement alimony will not always be appropriate or necessary to compensate a spouse who has contributed financially to the partner's professional education or training. "Rehabilitative alimony" may be more appropriate in cases where a spouse who gave up or postponed her own education to support the household requires a lump sum or a short-term award to achieve economic self-sufficiency. . . . However, rehabilitative alimony would not be appropriate where the supporting spouse is unable to return to the job market, or has already attained economic self-sufficiency.

Similarly, where the parties to a divorce have accumulated substantial assets during a lengthy marriage, courts should compensate for any unfairness to one party who sacrificed for the other's education, not by reimbursement alimony but by an equitable distribution of the assets to reflect the parties' different circumstances and earning capacities. . . . If the degree-holding spouse has already put his professional education to use, the degree's value in enhanced earning potential will have been realized in the form of property, such as a partnership interest or other asset, that is subject to equitable distribution. . . .

The degree holder's earning capacity can also be considered in an award of permanent alimony.[6] Alimony awards under N.J.S.A. 2A:34-23 must take into account the supporting spouse's ability to pay; earning capacity is certainly relevant to this determination. Our courts have recognized that a primary purpose of alimony, besides preventing either spouse from requiring public assistance, is "to permit the wife, who contributed during marriage to the accumulation of the marital assets, to share therein." Lynn v. Lynn, 153 N.J. Super. 377, 382, 379 A.2d 1046 (Ch. Div. 1977), *rev'd on other grounds,* 165 N.J. Super. 328, 398 A.2d 141 (App. Div. 1979). . . . Even though the enhanced earning potential provided by a degree or license is not "property" for purposes of N.J.S.A. 2A:34-23, it clearly should be a factor

5. This decision recognizes the fairness of an award of reimbursement alimony for past contributions to a spouse's professional education that were made with the expectation of mutual economic benefit. We need not in the present posture of this case determine the degree of finality or permanency that should be accorded an award of reimbursement alimony as compared to conventional alimony. As noted, an award of reimbursement alimony combines elements relating to the support, standard of living and financial expectations of the parties with notions of marital fairness and avoidance of unjust enrichment. We must also recognize that, while these cases frequently illustrate common patterns of human behavior and experience among married couples, circumstances vary among cases. Consequently, it would be unwise to attempt to anticipate all of the ramifications that flow from our present recognition of a right to reimbursement alimony. We therefore leave for future cases questions as to whether and under what changed circumstances such awards may be modified or adjusted.

6. It should be noted that alimony is not generally available for a self-supporting spouse under the laws of Minnesota, see DeLa Rosa, supra, 309 N.W.2d at 758, or Kentucky, see Inman, supra, 578 S.W.2d at 270, two states that have treated professional licenses as property. Those states are thus handicapped in their ability to do equity in situations where little or no marital property has been accumulated and the supporting spouse does not qualify for maintenance unless they treat professional licenses as property.

considered by the trial judge in determining a proper amount of alimony. If the degree holder's actual earnings turn out to diverge greatly from the court's estimate, making the amount of alimony unfair to either party, the alimony award can be adjusted accordingly.

III

We stated in *Stern*, supra, that while earning potential should not be treated as a separate item of property,

> [p]otential earning capacity is doubtless a factor to be considered by a trial judge in determining what distribution will be "equitable" and it is even more obviously relevant upon the issue of alimony. [66 N.J. at 345, 331 A.2d 257]

We believe that *Stern* presents the best approach for achieving fairness when one spouse has acquired a professional degree or license during the marriage. Courts may not make any permanent distribution of the value of professional degrees and licenses, whether based upon estimated worth or cost. However, where a spouse has received from his or her partner financial contributions used in obtaining a professional degree or license with the expectation of deriving material benefits for both marriage partners, that spouse may be called upon to reimburse the supporting spouse for the amount of contributions received.

In the present case, the defendant's financial support helped her husband to obtain his M.B.A. degree, which assistance was undertaken with the expectation of deriving material benefits for both spouses. Although the trial court awarded the defendant a sum as "equitable offset" for her contributions, the trial court's approach was not consistent with the guidelines we have announced in this opinion. Therefore, we are remanding the case so the trial court can determine whether reimbursement alimony should be awarded in this case and, if so, what amount is appropriate.

The judgment of the Appellate Division is reversed and the cause remanded for further proceedings not inconsistent with this opinion.

For reversal and remandment — Chief Justice WILENTZ and Justices PASHMAN, CLIFFORD, SCHREIBER, HANDLER, POLLOCK and O'HERN — 7.

For affirmance — None.

O'BRIEN v. O'BRIEN
66 N.Y.2d 576, 489 N.E.2d 712, 498 N.Y.S.2d 743 (1985)

SIMONS, J. In this divorce action, the parties' only asset of any consequence is the husband's newly acquired license to practice medicine. The principal issue presented is whether that license, acquired during their marriage, is marital property subject to equitable distribution under Domestic Relations Law §236(B)(5). Supreme Court held that it was and accordingly made a distributive award in defendant's favor. . . . On appeal to the Appellate Division, a majority of that court held that plaintiff's medical license is not marital property. . . . We now hold that plaintiff's medical license constitutes "marital property" within the meaning of Domestic Relations Law §236(B)(1)(c) and that it is therefore subject to equitable distribution pursuant to subdivision 5 of that part. . . .

I

Plaintiff and defendant married on April 3, 1971. At the time both were employed as teachers at the same private school. Defendant had a bachelor's degree and a temporary teaching certificate but required 18 months of postgraduate classes at an approximate cost of $3,000, excluding living expenses, to obtain permanent certification in New York. She claimed, and the trial court found, that she had relinquished the opportunity to obtain permanent certification while plaintiff pursued his education. At the time of the marriage, plaintiff had completed only three and one-half years of college but shortly afterward he returned to school at night to earn his bachelor's degree and to complete sufficient premedical courses to enter medical school. In September 1973 the parties moved to Guadalajara, Mexico, where plaintiff became a full-time medical student. While he pursued his studies defendant held several teaching and tutorial positions and contributed her earnings to their joint expenses. The parties returned to New York in December 1976 so that plaintiff could complete the last two semesters of medical school and internship training here. After they returned, defendant resumed her former teaching position and she remained in it at the time this action was commenced. Plaintiff was licensed to practice medicine in October 1980. He commenced this action for divorce two months later. At the time of trial, he was a resident in general surgery.

During the marriage both parties contributed to paying the living and educational expenses and they received additional help from both of their families. They disagreed on the amounts of their respective contributions but it is undisputed that in addition to performing household work and managing the family finances defendant was gainfully employed throughout the marriage, that she contributed all of her earnings to their living and educational expenses and that her financial contributions exceeded those of plaintiff. The trial court found that she had contributed 76% of the parties' income exclusive of a $10,000 student loan obtained by defendant. Finding that plaintiff's medical degree and license are marital property, the court received evidence of its value and ordered a distributive award to defendant.

Defendant presented expert testimony that the present value of plaintiff's medical license was $472,000. Her expert testified that he arrived at this figure by comparing the average income of a college graduate and that of a general surgeon between 1985, when plaintiff's residency would end, and 2012, when he would reach age 65. After considering Federal income taxes, an inflation rate of 10% and a real interest rate of 3% he capitalized the difference in average earnings and reduced the amount to present value. He also gave his opinion that the present value of defendant's contribution to plaintiff's medical education was $103,390. Plaintiff offered no expert testimony on the subject.

The court, after considering the life-style that plaintiff would enjoy from the enhanced earning potential his medical license would bring and defendant's contributions and efforts toward attainment of it, made a distributive award to her of $188,800, representing 40% of the value of the license, and ordered it paid in 11 annual installments of various amounts beginning November 1, 1982 and ending

November 1, 1992. The court also directed plaintiff to maintain a life insurance policy on his life for defendant's benefit for the unpaid balance of the award and it ordered plaintiff to pay defendant's counsel fees of $7,000 and her expert witness fee of $1,000. It did not award defendant maintenance.

A divided Appellate Division, relying on its prior decision in Conner v. Conner (97 A.D.2d 88) and the decision of the Fourth Department in Lesman v. Lesman (88 A.D.2d 153, *appeal dismissed* 57 N.Y.2d 956), concluded that a professional license acquired during marriage is not marital property subject to distribution. . . .

II

The Equitable Distribution Law contemplates only two classes of property: marital property and separate property (Domestic Relations Law §236[B][c], [d]). The former, which is subject to equitable distribution, is defined broadly as "*all* property acquired by either or both spouses during the marriage and before the execution of a separation agreement or the commencement of a matrimonial action, *regardless of the form in which title is held*" (Domestic Relations Law §236[B][1][c] [emphasis added]; see, §236[B][5][b], [c]). Plaintiff does not contend that his license is excluded from distribution because it is separate property; rather, he claims that it is not property at all but represents a personal attainment in acquiring knowledge. He rests his argument on decisions in similar cases from other jurisdictions and on his view that a license does not satisfy common-law concepts of property. Neither contention is controlling because decisions in other States rely principally on their own statutes, and the legislative history underlying them, and because the New York Legislature deliberately went beyond traditional property concepts when it formulated the Equitable Distribution Law (see generally, 2 Foster-Freed-Bandes, Law and the Family—New York ch. 33, at 917 et seq. [1985 Cum. Supp.]). Instead, our statute recognizes that spouses have an equitable claim to things of value arising out of the marital relationship and classifies them as subject to distribution by focusing on the marital status of the parties at the time of acquisition. Those things acquired during marriage and subject to distribution have been classified as "marital property" although, as one commentator has observed, they hardly fall within the traditional property concepts because there is no common-law property interest remotely resembling marital property.

> It is a statutory creature, is of no meaning whatsoever during the normal course of a marriage and arises full-grown, like Athena, upon the signing of a separation agreement or the commencement of a matrimonial action. [Thus] [i]t is hardly surprising, and not at all relevant, that traditional common law property concepts do not fit in parsing the meaning of "marital property" (Florescue, Market Value, Professional Licenses and Marital Property: A Dilemma in Search of a Horn, 1982 N.Y. St. Bar Assn. Fam. L. Rev. 13 [Dec.]).

Having classified the "property" subject to distribution, the Legislature did not attempt to go further and define it but left it to the courts to determine what interests come within the terms of section 236(B)(1)(c).

We made such a determination in Majauskas v. Majauskas (61 N.Y.2d 481), holding there that vested but unmatured pension rights are marital property subject to equitable distribution. Because pension benefits are not specifically identified as marital property in the statute, we looked to the express reference to pension rights contained in section 236(B)(5)(d)(4), which deals with equitable distribution of marital property, to other provisions of the equitable distribution statute and to the legislative intent behind its enactment to determine whether pension rights are marital property or separate property. A similar analysis is appropriate here and leads to the conclusion that marital property encompasses a license to practice medicine to the extent that the license is acquired during marriage.

Section 236 provides that in making an equitable distribution of marital property,

> the court shall consider: . . . (6) any equitable claim to, interest in, or direct or indirect contribution made to the acquisition of such marital property by the party not having title, including joint efforts or expenditures and contributions and services as a spouse, parent, wage earner and homemaker, and *to the career or career potential* of the other party [and] . . . (9) the impossibility or difficulty of evaluating any component asset or any interest in a business, corporation or *profession* (Domestic Relations Law §236[B][5][d][6], [9] [emphasis added]).

Where equitable distribution of marital property is appropriate but "the distribution of an interest in a business, corporation or *profession* would be contrary to law" the court shall make a distributive award in lieu of an actual distribution of the property (Domestic Relations Law §236[B][5][e] [emphasis added]). The words mean exactly what they say: that an interest in a profession or professional career potential is marital property which may be represented by direct or indirect contributions of the non-title-holding spouse, including financial contributions and non-financial contributions made by caring for the home and family.

The history which preceded enactment of the statute confirms this interpretation. Reform of section 236 was advocated because experience had proven that application of the traditional common-law title theory of property had caused inequities upon dissolution of a marriage. The Legislature replaced the existing system with equitable distribution of marital property, an entirely new theory which considered all the circumstances of the case and of the respective parties to the marriage (Assembly Memorandum, 1980 N.Y. Legis. Ann., at 129-130). Equitable distribution was based on the premise that a marriage is, among other things, an economic partnership to which both parties contribute as spouse, parent, wage earner or homemaker (id., at 130; see, Governor's Memorandum of Approval, 1980 McKinney's Session Laws of N.Y., at 1863). Consistent with this purpose, and implicit in the statutory scheme as a whole, is the view that upon dissolution of the marriage there should be a winding up of the parties' economic affairs and a severance of their economic ties by an equitable distribution of the marital assets. Thus, the concept of alimony, which often served as a means of lifetime support and dependence for one spouse upon the other long after the marriage was over, was replaced with the concept of maintenance which seeks to allow "the recipient spouse an opportunity to achieve [economic] independence" (Assembly Memorandum, 1980 N.Y. Legis. Ann., at 130).

The determination that a professional license is marital property is also consistent with the conceptual base upon which the statute rests. As this case demonstrates, few undertakings during a marriage better qualify as the type of joint effort that the statute's economic partnership theory is intended to address than contributions toward one spouse's acquisition of a professional license. Working spouses are often required to contribute substantial income as wage earners, sacrifice their own educational or career goals and opportunities for child rearing, perform the bulk of household duties and responsibilities and forego the acquisition of marital assets that could have been accumulated if the professional spouse had been employed rather than occupied with the study and training necessary to acquire a professional license. In this case, nearly all of the parties' nine-year marriage was devoted to the acquisition of plaintiff's medical license and defendant played a major role in that project. She worked continuously during the marriage and contributed all of her earnings to their joint effort, she sacrificed her own educational and career opportunities, and she traveled with plaintiff to Mexico for three and one-half years while he attended medical school there. The Legislature has decided, by its explicit reference in the statute to the contributions of one spouse to the other's profession or career (see, Domestic Relations Law §236[B][5][d][6], [9]; [e]), that these contributions represent investments in the economic partnership of the marriage and that the product of the parties' joint efforts, the professional license, should be considered marital property.

The majority at the Appellate Division held that the cited statutory provisions do not refer to the license held by a professional who has yet to establish a practice but only to a going professional practice (see, e.g., Arvantides v. Arvantides, 64 N.Y.2d 1033; Litman v. Litman, 61 N.Y.2d 918). There is no reason in law or logic to restrict the plain language of the statute to existing practices, however, for it is of little consequence in making an award of marital property, except for the purpose of valuation, whether the professional spouse has already established a practice or whether he or she has yet to do so. An established practice merely represents the exercise of the privileges conferred upon the professional spouse by the license and the income flowing from that practice represents the receipt of the enhanced earning capacity that licensure allows. That being so, it would be unfair not to consider the license a marital asset.

Plaintiff's principal argument, adopted by the majority below, is that a professional license is not marital property because it does not fit within the traditional view of property as something which has an exchange value on the open market and is capable of sale, assignment or transfer. The position does not withstand analysis for at least two reasons. First, as we have observed, it ignores the fact that whether a professional license constitutes marital property is to be judged by the language of the statute which created this new species of property previously unknown at common law or under prior statutes. Thus, whether the license fits within traditional property concepts is of no consequence. Second, it is an overstatement to assert that a professional license could not be considered property even outside the context of section 236(B). A professional license is a valuable property right, reflected in the money, effort and lost opportunity for employment expended in its acquisition, and also in the enhanced earning capacity it affords its holder, which may not be revoked without due process of law (see, Matter of Bender v. Board of Regents, 262 App. Div. 627, 631; People ex rel. Greenberg v. Reid, 151 App. Div. 324, 326). That a professional license has no market value is irrelevant. Obviously, a license may not be alienated as may other property and for that reason the working spouse's interest in it is limited. The Legislature has recognized that limitation, however, and has provided for an award in lieu of its actual distribution (see, Domestic Relations Law §236[B][5][e]).

Plaintiff also contends that alternative remedies should be employed, such as an award of rehabilitative maintenance or reimbursement for direct financial contributions. . . . The statute does not expressly authorize retrospective maintenance or rehabilitative awards and we have no occasion to decide in this case whether the authority to do so may ever be implied from its provisions (but see, Cappiello v. Cappiello, 66 N.Y.2d 107). It is sufficient to observe that normally a working spouse should not be restricted to that relief because to do so frustrates the purposes underlying the Equitable Distribution Law. Limiting a working spouse to a maintenance award, either general or rehabilitative, not only is contrary to the economic partnership concept underlying the statute but also retains the uncertain and inequitable economic ties of dependence that the Legislature sought to extinguish by equitable distribution. Maintenance is subject to termination upon the recipient's remarriage and a working spouse may never receive adequate consideration for his or her contribution and may even be penalized for the decision to remarry if that is the only method of compensating the contribution. As one court said so well,

> [t]he function of equitable distribution is to recognize that when a marriage ends, each of the spouses, based on the totality of the contributions made to it, has a stake in and right to a share of the marital assets accumulated while it endured, not because that share is needed, but because those assets represent the capital product of what was essentially a partnership entity (Wood v. Wood, 119 Misc. 2d 1076, 1079).

The Legislature stated its intention to eliminate such inequities by providing that a supporting spouse's "direct or indirect contribution" be recognized, considered and rewarded (Domestic Relations Law §236[B][5][d][6]).

Turning to the question of valuation, it has been suggested that even if a professional license is considered marital property, the working spouse is entitled only to reimbursement of his or her direct financial contributions. . . . By parity of reasoning, a spouse's down payment on real estate or contribution to the purchase of securities would be limited to the money contributed, without any remuneration for any incremental value in the asset because of price appreciation. Such a result is completely at odds with the statute's requirement that the court give full consideration to both direct and indirect contributions "made to the acquisition of such marital property by the party not having title, including joint *efforts* or expenditures and *contributions and services as a spouse, parent*, wage earner *and homemaker*" (Domestic Relations Law §236[B][5][d][6] [emphasis added]). If the license is marital property, then the working spouse is entitled to an equitable portion of it, not a return of funds advanced. Its value is the enhanced earning capacity it affords the holder and although fixing the present value of that enhanced earning capacity may present problems, the problems are not insurmountable. Certainly they are no more difficult than computing tort damages for wrongful death or diminished earning capacity resulting from injury and they differ only in degree from the problems presented when valuing a professional practice for purposes of a distributive award, something the courts have not hesitated to do. . . . The trial court retains the flexibility and discretion to structure the distributive award equitably, taking into consideration factors such as the working spouse's need for immediate payment, the licensed spouse's current ability to pay and the income tax consequences of prolonging the period of payment (see, Internal Revenue Code [26 U.S.C.] §71[a][1]; [c][2]; Treas. Reg. [26 C.F.R.] §1.71-1[d][4]) and, once it has received evidence of the present value of the license and the working spouse's contributions toward its acquisition and considered the remaining factors mandated by the statute (see, Domestic Relations Law §236[B][5] [d][1]-[10]), it may then make an appropriate distribution of the marital property including a distributive award for the professional license if such an award is warranted. When other marital assets are of sufficient value to provide for the supporting spouse's equitable portion of the marital property, including his or her contributions to the acquisition of the professional license, however, the court retains the discretion to distribute these other marital assets or to make a distributive award in lieu of an actual distribution of the value of the professional spouse's license (see, Majauskas v. Majauskas, 61 N.Y.2d 481, 493, supra). . . .

Accordingly, in view of our holding that plaintiff's license to practice medicine is marital property, the order of the Appellate Division should be modified . . . by reinstating the judgment. . . .

MEYER, J. (concurring). I concur in Judge Simons' opinion but write separately to point up for consideration by the Legislature the potential for unfairness involved in distributive awards based upon a license of a professional still in training.

An equity court normally has power to "'change its decrees where there has been a change of circumstances'" (People v. Scanlon, 11 N.Y.2d 459, 462, *on second appeal* 13 N.Y.2d 982). The implication of Domestic Relations Law §236(B)(9)(b), which deals with modification of an order or decree as to maintenance or child support, is, however, that a distributive award pursuant to section 236(B)(5)(e), once made, is not subject to change. Yet a professional in training who is not finally committed to a career choice when the distributive award is made may be locked into a particular kind of practice simply because the monetary obligations imposed by the distributive award made on the basis of the trial judge's conclusion (prophecy may be a better word) as to what the career choice will be leaves him or her no alternative.

The present case points up the problem. A medical license is but a step toward the practice ultimately engaged in by its holder, which follows after internship, residency and, for particular specialties, board certification. Here it is undisputed that plaintiff was in a residency for general surgery at the time of the trial, but had the previous year done a residency in internal medicine. Defendant's expert based his opinion on the difference between the average income of a general surgeon and that of a college graduate of plaintiff's age and life expectancy, which the trial judge utilized, impliedly finding that plaintiff would engage in a surgical practice despite plaintiff's testimony that he was dissatisfied with the general surgery program he was in and was attempting to return to the internal medicine training he had been in the previous year. The trial judge had the right, of course, to discredit that testimony, but the point is that equitable distribution was not intended to permit a judge to make a career decision for a licensed spouse still in training. Yet the degree of speculation involved in the award made is emphasized by the testimony of the expert on which it was based. Asked whether his assumptions and calculations were in any way speculative, he replied:

> Yes. They're speculative to the extent of, will Dr. O'Brien practice medicine? Will Dr. O'Brien earn more or less than the average surgeon earns? Will Dr. O'Brien live to age sixty-five? Will Dr. O'Brien have a heart attack or will he be injured in an automobile accident? Will he be disabled? I mean, there is a degree of speculation. That speculative aspect is no more to be taken into

account, cannot be taken into account, and it's a question, again, Mr. Emanu-
elli, not for the expert but for the courts to decide. It's not my function nor
could it be.

The equitable distribution provisions of the Domestic Relations Law were intended to provide flexibility so that equity could be done. But if the assumption as
to career choice on which a distributive award payable over a number of years is
based turns out not to be the fact (as, for example, should a general surgery trainee
accidentally lose the use of his hand), it should be possible for the court to revise
the distributive award to conform to the fact. And there will be no unfairness in
so doing if either spouse can seek reconsideration, for the licensed spouse is more
likely to seek reconsideration based on real, rather than imagined, cause if he or
she knows that the nonlicensed spouse can seek not only reinstatement of the original award, but counsel fees in addition, should the purported circumstances on
which a change is made turn out to have been feigned or to be illusory.

Chief Judge WACHTLER and Judges JASEN, MEYER, KAYE, ALEXANDER and
TITONE concur with Judge SIMONS; Judges MEYER and TITONE concur in separate
concurring opinions.

Notes and Questions

1. *Organizing the issues.* The question "Should professional education acquired
during marriage be treated as a distributable asset at divorce?" poses many issues,
some of which are recurrent in marital property law and theory. The question may
be broken down into two smaller questions: Can we do it? and Should we do it?
The first question asks how we might go about valuing and distributing professional
education, and the second question assumes technical capacity to accomplish the
task, but asks whether, as a matter of policy, we ought to do it. Although the two
questions are not unrelated, they are useful organizing categories.

2. *The value of a professional education.* How might we measure the value of a
professional education? How do you calculate the potential value of your legal education? Did you consider the question before deciding to attend law school? If so,
reconstruct your thinking.

In the principal cases, the trial courts that undertook the task of placing a
present value on a spouse's professional degree made a serious accounting error.
In *Graham,* the trial court estimated the discounted present value of the degree at
$82,836, awarded the other spouse $33,134 of this amount, payable in monthly
installments of $100. (At this rate, the entire payout would take almost 28 years.)
Similarly, the trial court in *O'Brien* determined that the present value of the husband's medical license was $472,000, and awarded the wife $188,800 of that amount,
payable in 11 annual installments. Do you see the error in both cases? If you do
not, estimate what you would pay now for the right to receive $100 a month for 28
years. (In estimating what you would pay, assume the availability of safe investments
annually yielding 10 percent, the California legal interest rate.) How might the trial
courts have avoided their error?

3. *The cost of a professional education.* Although marital property law normally
inquires about the value of a distributable asset, as opposed to its cost, some case
law treatment of professional education has focused instead on its cost. What are
the true costs of a professional education? What costs would you include in a full

accounting of the costs of attending law school? What expenditures would you exclude?

4. *The relationship between cost and value.* Do you agree with *Mahoney,* at page 56 supra, that "the cost of a professional degree 'has little to do with any real value of the degree'"? Are cost and value generally unrelated? Economists observe that the relationship between the cost and the value of human capital (professional education) is not significantly different from the relationship between the cost and value of other forms of capital. The value of any asset is its capacity to generate future income. The cost of any asset is the discounted present value of that future income. In the case of professional education, the equality of cost and value is merely approximate, because there are various "market imperfections," such as monopoly advantages of the professions.

5. *Is a professional education "property"?* As the three principal cases illustrate, many courts have posed and considered this question at great length. But is it a meaningful question? At most, what sort of answer can it yield? How would you refine and contextualize the question in order to frame the inquiry in a way that will allow a full consideration of the issues you would like to see addressed?

6. *The policy issues.* What policy issues are raised by the question whether a professional degree earned during marriage should be treated as a distributable asset at divorce? Identify all the issues that seem important to you, on both sides of the question. How do they weigh in the balance? What position would likely be taken by each of the academic figures in the Carbone and Brinig article, at page 26 supra? Do you prefer the *Graham* result (nonrecognition), the *Mahoney* result (reimbursement of certain expenditures), the *O'Brien* result (full recognition as marital property), or some other result? Would you find the *O'Brien* result more problematic in California than in New York, which allows the divorce court considerable discretion in equitably distributing the marital property?

II

THE HISTORY OF CALIFORNIA COMMUNITY PROPERTY

A. MAJOR DEVELOPMENTS IN CALIFORNIA COMMUNITY PROPERTY LAW

1849   California constitutional convention provides guarantee of separate property to wife:

> All property, both real and personal, of the wife, owned or claimed by her before marriage, and that acquired afterwards by gift, devise or descent, shall be her separate property; and laws shall be passed more clearly defining the rights of the wife, in relation as well to her separate property, as to that held in common with her husband. Laws shall also be passed providing for the registration of the wife's separate property. [Cal. Const. art. XI, §14 (1849).]

(This provision was taken directly from the Texas constitutional provision of 1845, Tex. Const. art. 7, §19, and is identical to it.)

1850   The first California legislature establishes marital property law in accord with Spanish civil law, creating two categories, separate property and common property. The husband is given unlimited managerial control of the community property: "The husband shall have the entire management and control of the common property, with the like absolute power of disposition as of his own separate estate." Act of Apr. 17, 1850, ch. 103, §9, 1849-50 Cal. Stat. 254. The husband is given managerial control of his wife's *separate* property as well, except that he cannot convey or encumber it without her consent, id. §6. The wife cannot make a valid will without her husband's consent, Act of Apr. 10, 1850, ch. 72, §2, 1849-50 Cal. Stat. 177. Thus,

69

the wife has no inter vivos or testamentary power to manage or dispose of her separate property.

1860 — Chief Justice Field characterizes the wife's interest in community property as a "mere expectancy." Van Maren v. Johnson, 15 Cal. 308, 311.

1860 — George v. Ranson, 15 Cal. 322, declares unconstitutional the 1850 act adopting the Spanish rule that the rents and profits received from separate property during marriage are community property. The 1850 act is found inconsistent with the California constitutional requirement that the legislature maintain a distinction between the wife's separate property and the community property. "We think the Legislature has not the Constitutional power to say that the fruits of the property of the wife shall be taken from her, and given to the husband or his creditors." Henceforth rents and profits from separate property are separate property in California. (The Texas Supreme Court reached the opposite conclusion when it interpreted an identically worded constitutional provision; it invalidated a Texas statute that had repealed the Spanish rule and had effectively enacted George v. Ransom. Arnold v. Leonard, 114 Tex. 535, 273 S.W. 799 (1925). Which approach do you favor? Which approach is more likely to protect the property interests of married women?)

1866 — Statute eliminates the need for wife to obtain her husband's consent to make a will, thus enabling her to will her separate property. Act of Mar. 20, 1866, ch. 285, §1, 1865-66 Cal. Stat. 316.

1872 — The Field Code of 1872 grants the wife management of her separate property. 1 Codes and Statutes of California §5162, at 595 (T. Hittel ed. 1876).

1889 — Enactment of the special presumption governing titles in the name of a married woman. Act of Mar. 19, 1889, ch. 219, 1889 Cal. Stat. 328.

1891 — Enactment of restrictions on the husband's power to make gifts of community property without the consent of his wife. Act of Mar. 31, 1891, ch. 220, 1891 Cal. Stat. 425.

1901 — Enactment of restrictions on the husband's power to convey or encumber home furnishings or wearing apparel without the consent of his wife. Act of Mar. 23, 1901, ch. 190, 1901 Cal. Stat. 598.

1917 — Enactment of real property joint consent provisions to limit the husband's management of community realty. Act of May 23, 1917, ch. 583, 1917 Cal. Stat. 829-830.

1923 — Legislature grants the wife testamentary power over her half of the community property when she pre-deceases her husband. Act of Apr. 16, 1923, ch. 18, 1923 Cal. Stat. 29. Prior to 1923, if the wife died first, her husband received all the community property.

1927   Legislature declares the spouses' interests in community property to be "present, existing and equal," under the management and control of the husband. Act of Apr. 28, 1927, ch. 265, §1, 1927 Cal. Stat. 484. (This action was designed to eliminate the "mere expectancy" doctrine and secure the advantages of federal income tax income-splitting for California couples.)

1951   Legislature grants wife power to manage her own community property earnings, provided they are not commingled with community property managed by the husband. Act of June 16, 1951, ch. 1102, 1951 Cal. Stat. 2860-2861.

1970   No-fault divorce statute establishes irreconcilable differences as the primary ground for divorce, eliminates fault as a consideration in community property division, and mandates 50-50 division of community property. The Family Law Act of 1969, 1969 Cal. Stat. ch. 1608, effective Jan. 1, 1970.

1975   Legislature provides for equal management of community property by husband and wife. Act of Oct. 1, 1973, ch. 987, 1973 Cal. Stat. 1897-1905, effective Jan. 1, 1975.

1940-   Case law expansion of the definition of divisible *property* and legisla-
present   tion to provide managerial equality.

B.   THE 1849 CONSTITUTIONAL CONVENTION

J. ROSS BROWNE, REPORT OF THE DEBATES IN THE CONVENTION OF CALIFORNIA ON THE FORMATION OF THE STATE CONSTITUTION IN SEPTEMBER AND OCTOBER 1849
257-269 (1850)

The thirteenth section of the report being under consideration as follows:

Sec. 13. All property, both real and personal, of the wife, owned or claimed by her before marriage, and that acquired afterwards by gift, devise, or descent, shall be her separate property, and laws shall be passed more clearly defining the rights of the wife, in relation as well to her separate property as that held in common with her husband. Laws shall also be passed providing for the registration of the wife's separate property.

Mr. Lippitt.   . . . I think that we tread upon dangerous ground when we make an invasion upon that system [common law] that has prevailed among ourselves and our ancestors for hundreds and hundreds of years. . . .

Mr. Tefft.   . . . It was said this evening that this was an attempt to insert in our
Constitution a provision of the civil law. Very well — suppose it is; there are
gentlemen in this House wedded to the common law; I am myself greatly
attached to it; but that does not prevent me from seeing many very excellent
provisions in the civil law. . . . I think that to strike this section out would be
a very decided invasion upon the people of California. . . . It would be an
unheard of invasion, not to secure and guarantee the rights of the wife to her
separate property; and of all classes in California, where the civil law is the law
of the land, where families have lived and died under it, where the rights of
the wife are as necessary to be cared for as those of the husband, we must take
into consideration the feelings of the native Californians, who have always lived
under this law. . . .

Mr. Halleck.   . . . I am not wedded either to the common law or the civil law, nor
as yet, to a woman; but having some hopes that some time or other I may be
wedded, . . . I shall advocate this section in the Constitution, and I would call
upon all the bachelors in this Convention to vote for it. I do not think we can
offer a greater inducement for women of fortune to come to California. . . .

Mr. Botts.   . . . I think it is radically wrong. In my opinion, there is no provision so
beautiful in the common law, so admirable and beneficial, as that which regulates this sacred contract between man and wife. Sir, the God of nature made
woman frail, lovely, and dependent; and such the common law pronounces
her. Nature did what the common law has done — put her under the protection of man; and it is the object of this clause to withdraw her from that protection, and put her under the protection of the law. I say, sir; the husband will
take better care of the wife, provide for her better and protect her better, than
the law. . . . When she trusts him with her happiness, she may well trust him
with her gold. You lose the substance in the shadow; by this provision you risk
her happiness forever, whilst you protect her property. . . . This proposition,
I believe, is calculated to produce dissention and strife in families. The only
despotism on earth that I would advocate, is the despotism of the husband.
There must be a head and there must be a master in every household; and I
believe this plan by which you propose to make the wife independent of the
husband, is contrary to the law and provisions of nature — contrary to all the
wisdom which we have derived from experience. This doctrine of women's
rights, is the doctrine of those mental hermaphrodites. Abby Folsom, Fanny
Wright, and the rest of that tribe. . . . It is often the case that the union takes
place between a man of little or no property, and a woman of immense landed
estate. But do you mean to say that, under such circumstances, the husband
must remain a dependent upon his wife? A dependent upon her bounty?
Would you, in short make Prince Alberts of us all? . . .

Mr. Lippitt.   . . . I am inclined to think that all wives may be divided into two classes:
those who wear the breeches and those who do not. . . . [E]very wife who
habitually yields to her husband, will yield to him in all cases relative to the
disposition of . . . [her] property, and the husband will have the control of it,
just as if no such enactment existed. If, on the other hand, the wife is of that
class which does not yield, I think it is evidence that the very existence of such
a right would only tend to increase and foment every dissension, no matter
how trifling the cause may have been in the first place. . . . I have lived in Paris,
and I was assured by respectable inhabitants there, that it was an ascertained
fact, that two-thirds of the married couples in Paris were living separately.

. . . If there is any country in the world which presents the spectacle of domestic disunion more than another, it is France, where this principle is carried most completely into effect. . . . We must also look to the rights of the creditor in this matter. . . . If the husband is a dishonest man, gets in debt, and cannot or will not pay his debts, he has only to pretend, when a bill or execution is sent against his property, that it belongs to his wife—that it is her separate property. There is a lawsuit to ensue. It is throwing impediments against the collection of debts. . . .

Mr. Dimmick. . . . Women now possess in this country [California] the right which is proposed to be introduced in the Constitution. Blot it out, and introduce the common law, and what do you do? The wife who owns her separate property loses it the moment the common law prevails. . . . At the time the common law was introduced, woman occupied a position far inferior to that which she now occupies. As the world has advanced in civilization, her social position has been the subject of increased consideration, and by general consent of all intelligent men, she is now regarded as entitled to many of the rights in her peculiar sphere which were formerly considered as belonging only to man. This part of the common law is one of those portions belonging to the dark ages, which has not yet been expunged by the advance of civilization. . . . We are told, Mr. Chairman, that woman is a frail being; that she is formed by nature to obey and ought to be protected by her husband, who is her natural protector. That is true, sir, but is there anything in all this to impair her right of property which she possessed previous to entering into the marriage contract? I contend not. In justice to her and to her family, who may become dependent upon her, these rights should not be impaired.

Mr. Jones. . . . Are we to adopt laws which make man a despot of woman, and give woman no right because she has no representation? . . . Sir, the marriage contract is a civil contract—not a sacrament. . . . The law must prescribe the rights of the contracting parties. You cannot say that one party consents to have all its rights annihilated, all its property lost, by this contract of marriage. . . .

Mr. Norton. . . . [I]t is necessary if we attempt at all to provide for the security of the wife, that we should adopt some such article as this. I believe, sir, that we should do this as a matter of necessity. Every one here can relate to you instance after instance where the property of the wife has been sacrificed through the idle habits, carelessness or dissipation of the husband; and is it not necessary, forming a new State as we are about to do, that we should protect the wife against such contingencies as this? . . .

Mr. Botts. . . . "By marriage" says Blackstone, "the husband and wife are one person in law." . . . This is but another mode of repeating the declaration of the Holy Book, that they are flesh of one flesh, and bone of bone. That is the principle of the common law, and it is the principle of the [B]ible. It is a principle, Mr. Chairman, not only of poetry, but of wisdom, of truth, and of justice. Sir, it is supposed by the common law that the woman says to the man in the beautiful language of Ruth: "Whither thou goest I will go; and where thou lodgest, I will lodge; thy people shall be my people, and thy God my God." This, sir, is the character of that holy ceremony which gentlemen have considered as a mere money copartnership. Sir, it is this view of that contract that has produced that peculiar and lovely English word *home,* which it has been said no other people on the face of the earth know. It arises from the very peculiar light in which the English law looks upon this social relation.

Bear that in mind, you who love your homes. . . .

I want to know to whose benefit is this provision to ensure? . . . [T]he husband and wife together may enjoy my property and yours, and become possessed of thousands and thousands, leaving us beggars. . . . I ask you, sir, what honest woman could avail herself of this cause? I ask you what honest woman could see the creditor knocking at the door appealing for the payment of what is justly due to him [for her husband's debts], and send him away? Who is it then that it benefits? The fraudulent husband and the colluding wife. . . . But sir, you cannot make an honest woman dishonest if you would; you may seek to do it by constitutional provision, or by legislative enactment, but her great spirit will burst through all your bonds, and she will come to the husband's rescue, and so long as she has a single cent she will pay his debts. Thank God you cannot by any of your laws crush that spirit of integrity which abides in the breast of woman. . . .

The thirteenth section was then adopted.

Notes and Questions

1. What lobby did Mr. Botts represent? Who would you cast to play him? To whom did Ruth address her much-quoted pledge? See Book of Ruth 1:16-17. From the context, we can infer that the widowed Ruth had never spoken these words to her deceased husband.

2. Note how the delegates refer to the evils of the common law system. By 1849, a number of eastern states had already enacted married woman's property acts. Yet the delegates seem ignorant of this development. See generally McMurray, The Beginnings of the Community Property System in California and the Adoption of the Common Law, 3 Calif. L. Rev. 360 (1915).

C.   A NARRATIVE HISTORY

The California constitutional convention met in Monterey in 1849, and elevated to constitutional status one element of the civil law that prevailed in California during the period of Spanish and Mexican control. This element was the basic principle of Spanish community property law. The adoption of community property law was motivated by a spirit of conciliation toward the Spanish-speaking minority and a desire to improve the legal status of married women. The choice was also the product of considerable ignorance. The delegates lacked knowledge of both the recent common law reforms and the Spanish community property system. Had they been more fully informed, they might well have chosen to enact a common law regime with a married woman's property act.

Carefully examine the language of the 1849 constitutional provision:

> All property, both real and personal, of the wife, owned or claimed by her
> before marriage, and that acquired afterwards by gift, devise or descent, shall
> be her separate property; and laws shall be passed more clearly defining the
> rights of the wife, in relation as well to her separate property, as to that held

in common with her husband. Laws shall also be passed providing for the registration of the wife's separate property. [Cal. Const. art. XI, §14 (1849).]

Note how the provision focuses on the rights of the wife and the separate property of the wife. The only reference to community property comes in the last phrase of the first sentence: "laws shall be passed more clearly defining the rights of the wife . . . to [property] held in common with her husband."

Obedient to the constitutional mandate, the legislature promptly passed community property laws. This 1850 legislation codified the Spanish system of two categories of property: separate property, that property owned before the marriage or acquired afterward by gift, bequest, devise, or descent,[1] and "common" property, that acquired other than by gift or inheritance by either spouse during marriage.[2]

The 1850 legislation gave the husband the power to manage and control his wife's *separate* property. There were two limitations on this power. The husband could encumber or transfer the wife's separate property only with her consent.[3] If she had cause to fear her husband's waste or mismanagement, she could petition a court to appoint a trustee to manage her property.[4] Yet she could not exercise control herself. Her testamentary power over her separate property was similarly limited: She could not write a valid will without her husband's consent.[5]

With respect to *community* property, the husband had full managerial power. There were no restraints on his control and no checks on his exercise of judgment: "The husband shall have the entire management and control of the common property, with the like absolute power of disposition as of his own separate estate."[6] Thus, during marriage, the common ownership principle had no significance: The husband could treat the common property as though it were his separate property. The wife's rights materialized only at termination of the marriage. At death, one-half of the community property passed to the surviving spouse; the other half passed to the decedent's lineal descendants. If there were no lineal descendants, the surviving spouse received all the community property.[7] At divorce, each spouse received one-half of the community property.[8] (The mandatory equal division at divorce lasted only seven years: In 1857, the legislature provided for unequal division if the divorce ground were adultery or extreme cruelty.[9] More than a century later, the

---

1. Act of Apr. 17, 1850, ch. 103, §1.
2. Id. §2.
3. Id. §6.
4. Id. §8.
5. Act of Apr. 10, 1850, ch. 72, §2.
6. Act of Apr. 17, 1850, ch. 103, §9.
7. Id. §11. The sexual equality expressed in this 1850 provision was short-lived. An 1861 amendment provided that at the wife's death, the entire community property vested in the husband without any administration. The wife had no testamentary power over her share of the community property. If the husband predeceased the wife, his one-half interest in the community continued to pass to his lineal descendants. If, however, he were not survived by lineal descendants, he could exercise testamentary power over his one-half interest. If he were survived neither by lineal descendants nor by a will, his one-half interest passed according to the general intestacy law. Act of May 8, 1861, ch. 323, §1, 1860-61 Cal. Stat. 310. The 1872 Field Code incorporated the 1861 statute, but reversed the order of disposition for a predeceased husband's one-half of the community property. His half was subject to his testamentary disposition and, in the absence of such disposition, passed to his lineal descendants. If he left neither a will nor descendants, his property passed by intestacy, in which case his surviving wife received a portion as one of his intestate heirs. 1 Code and Statutes of California §§6401, 6402, at 734 (T. Hittel ed. 1876). This death treatment of community property remained essentially unchanged until 1923. Act of Apr. 16, 1923, ch. 18.
8. Act of Apr. 17, 1850, ch. 103, §12.
9. Act of Apr. 14, 1857, ch. 176.

1969 enactment of a no-fault divorce law was accompanied by the restoration of mandatory equal division.[10])

The 1850 scheme inspired Chief Justice Field to characterize the wife's interest during the marriage as a "mere expectancy":

> [T]he title to [common] property rests in the husband. He can dispose of the same absolutely, as if it were his own separate property. The interest of the wife is a mere expectancy, like the interest which an heir may possess in the property of his ancestor. [Van Maren v. Johnson, 15 Cal. 308, 311 (1860).]

Although the 1850 legislation may have deviated from Spanish civil law in some details of management, it followed Spanish law exactly with respect to its characterization of ownership of property as separate or community. One basic principle of Spanish law is that the income, rents, and profits derived during marriage from separate property are community property. Appreciation, in contrast, remains separate property. If, for example, the husband owns separate rental property worth $100,000 at marriage, under Spanish law the rental income received during marriage is community property. If at divorce the market value of the property is $300,000, the $200,000 appreciation remains the husband's separate property. (In this illustration, assume an increase due to rising land values rather than marital investment of labor or capital. Do you see why this assumption is necessary?)

In George v. Ransom, 15 Cal. 322 (1860), the California Supreme Court invalidated the California legislation embodying this element of Spanish law. A creditor of the husband sought to reach stock dividends earned on the wife's separate property. The dividends were reachable only if they were characterized as community property, as they were under Spanish law and the 1850 legislation. The court held that this aspect of the 1850 legislation violated the 1849 constitutional guarantee that the wife would be the owner of her separate property:

> We think the Legislature has not the Constitutional power to say that the fruits of the property of the wife shall be taken from her, and given to the husband or his creditors. . . .
> It has been seen that the provision of the Constitution is, that the property acquired by the wife by devise, bequest, etc., shall be her separate property. This term "separate property" has a fixed meaning in the common law, and had in the minds of those who framed the Constitution, the large majority of whom were familiar with, and had lived under that system. By the common law, the idea attached to separate property in the wife, and which forms a portion of its definition, is, that it is an estate, held as well in its use as in its title, for the exclusive benefit and advantage of the wife. The common law recognized no such solecism as a right in the wife to the estate, and a right in someone else to use it as he pleased, and to enjoy all the advantages of its use. It is not perceived that property can be in one, in full and separate ownership, with a right in another to control it, and enjoy all of its benefits. The sole value of property is in its use; to dissociate the right of property from the use . . . would be to preserve the name — the mere shadow — and destroy the thing itself — the substance. It would be to make the wife the trustee for the husband, holding the legal title, while he held the fruits of that title. This [cannot] be done. [15 Cal. at 323-324.]

10. The Family Law Act of 1969, Act of Sept. 4, 1969, ch. 1608, §8, 1969 Cal. Stat. 3324, Cal. Civ. Code §4800 (West 1992), now codified at Cal. Fam. Code §2550.

George v. Ransom is a significant case for a variety of reasons. What do you think of the court's methodology? If you were deciding this issue in 1860, would you look to the common law? Is there a more appropriate guide to constitutional interpretation? In any event, the California judges, schooled in the common law, ignored Spanish law sources. In this respect, George v. Ransom is typical.

On the substantive common law issue, George v. Ransom is doubly wrong. "Separate property," being a community property term unknown to the common law, could hardly have, as the court asserts, "a fixed meaning in the common law." Moreover, the common law provides a persuasive example of the separation of title and profits. At common law, upon marriage the husband acquired possession and managerial control of the wife's real property. During marriage he had a right to all the profits. At dissolution, however, she regained title and control of her real property.

With respect to the basic issue whether the income during marriage from separate property ought to be treated as community property or separate property, the answer depends on the underlying goal of the 1849 constitutional provision. If the primary purpose of the 1849 provision was to protect the wife's separate property, and the language of the provision supports this view, then George v. Ransom gives substance to that protection. If, on the other hand, the basic purpose of that provision was to protect married women by enacting a community property regime, George v. Ransom undercuts this goal because it sharply limits the scope of the community. In the generality of cases, do you think that married women have profited from George v. Ransom?

Let us digress briefly from this historical narrative to consider the origins of the Spanish rule and to evaluate its application today. Under traditional Spanish community property law, income received from separate property during marriage is community property but appreciation to separate property remains separate property.[11] Community property law was codified in Spain from the seventh to the sixteenth centuries, when the dominant form of wealth was land.[12] The Spanish system flows inexorably from its two basic premises: Ancestral land should remain in the bloodline, that is, should pass to a decedent's lineal descendants, and the married couple should enjoy all the fruits of marital labor. Ancestral land was either brought into marriage or received during marriage by gift, devise, or inheritance. Hence the definition of separate property. But land produces income only if it is worked. Given that the fruit of all marital labor belongs to the community, it made sense as a general rule to treat all income as community property. Appreciation, on the other hand, was inseparable from the land. To separate out appreciation and call it "community" would have required the division of hereditary land and allowed its departure from the bloodline.

Writing in 1983, the drafters of the Uniform Marital Property Act adopted the Spanish distinction between income (community) and appreciation (separate).[13] William Cantwell, the chief drafter, explained this adoption as a "rough compromise" between the community and separate estates. But our modern forms of wealth make such a distinction illusory. If a spouse decides to invest his separate property in growth stock for its appreciation, he preserves the separate nature of that property. If, instead, he buys a bond for its interest, the bond generates community p.

11. W. de Funiak and M. Vaughn, Principles of Community Property 160-163 (2d ed. 1971).
12. Id. at 40.
13. §4(d) and (g)(3), 9A U.L.A. 116 (1998).

nity income. Moreover, with stock the choice between interest and appreciation may not even be in the owner's hands. If the company decides to issue a dividend, it is community property. If the company declares no dividend, the stock appreciates in value and that appreciation remains separate property. If all couples kept balanced portfolios, the "compromise" might work rough justice. But many couples favor one type of investment over another as a matter of personal preference or because of market conditions. In the 1970s, for example, many individual investors left the stock market and invested in interest-bearing instruments. In the 1980s, they returned to the stock market. Should this investment behavior affect marital property distributions? Furthermore, in the individual business, partnership, or closely held corporation, the allocation between appreciation and income is in the hands of the managing spouse, who decides whether and how much to draw out of the business. Unless we develop some notion of imputed income when separate property business income is reinvested rather than withdrawn, the decision to reinvest will deprive the marital community of is proper share. But if we do develop some notion of imputed income for small businesses, it would seem equally applicable when a publicly-held corporation decides to reinvest rather than declare a full dividend. The nub of the problem is that appreciation and income are economically indistinguishable. Are there any modern noneconomic reasons to distinguish between the two? If not, we ought to treat them equally, either as separate property or community property. Which approach do you prefer? What are the drawbacks of treating both as community property? As separate property?

Resuming the historical narrative, the development of California community property law since 1866 has largely consisted of efforts to mitigate the sexual inequality of the early legislation. For approximately a century, most legislation took the direction of giving the married woman control over her separate property, expanding the definition of her separate property, and subjecting certain community property to her joint or unilateral control. In the last three decades, however, the goal has shifted from mitigation to elimination of sexual inequality,[14] and the means have been expansion of the scope of community property and establishment of the spouses as equal managers.

In 1866, the married woman was given full testamentary power over her separate property.[15] In 1872, the Field Code gave her complete managerial power over her separate property.[16] In 1889, a special married woman's title presumption was enacted. Carving out an exception to the general presumption that property acquired during marriage is community property, this provision created a presumption that property conveyed to a married woman in a written instrument is her separate property.[17] This presumption was in effect until 1975 and still applies to property acquired before 1975.[18] In 1951, the legislature granted the wife power to

---

14. In fact, serious legislative efforts began much earlier, but the legislature was far in advance of the citizenry. After World War I, shortly before ratification of the women's suffrage amendment to the federal Constitution, the 1919 California legislature enacted, and the governor signed, a series of measures that would have created sex neutral inter vivos and testamentary management rights. 1919 Cal. Stat. ch. 611, p. 1274. Public reaction was unfavorable. A referendum petition placed the matter on the ballot of the Nov. 2, 1920, election. A great public debate ensued and, despite women's suffrage, the legislation was defeated by more than 2 to 1. See generally P. T. Conmy, The Historic Spanish Origin of California's Property Law and Its Development and Adaptation to Meet the Needs of an American State (1957); Kidd, The Proposed Community Property Bills, 7 Calif. L. Rev. 166, 173 (1919).

15. Act of Mar. 20, 1866, ch. 285, §1.

16. 1 Codes and Statutes of California §5162, at 595 (T. Hittel ed. 1876).

17. Act of Mar. 19, 1889, ch. 219.

18. Act of Oct. 1, 1973, ch. 987, eff. Jan. 1, 1975, now codified at Family Code §803.

manage her own earnings, provided they were not commingled with other community property managed by her husband.[19] (Her earnings remained, of course, *community* property.) By 1951, in terms of management, as opposed to ownership, California closely resembled the common law states: The wife managed her separate property and that property to which she had legal title or had earned herself.[20] With respect to underlying ownership, California largely maintained its distinctive system.

As the legislature increased the wife's control of her separate property and her community earnings, it restricted the husband's control over the community property. An 1891 provision required the written consent of the wife in order for the husband to make an effective gift of community property.[21] In 1901, the legislature extended the written consent requirement to a husband's sale, conveyance, or encumbrance of household furnishings and the clothing of the wife and minor children.[22] In 1917, the legislature required that the husband secure the wife's consent "in executing any instrument by which . . . community real property or any interest therein is leased for a longer period than one year, or is sold, conveyed or encumbered."[23]

Prior to 1923, the wife had no testamentary power over her half of the community property.[24] Beginning in 1923, she could will her half.[25] One must say "her half" guardedly because at that time she still had a "mere expectancy" until death or divorce. It was not until 1927 that the legislature enacted the provision that is now California Family Code section 751: "The respective interests of the husband and wife in community property during continuance of the marriage relation are present, existing and equal interests." The creation of a present interest was not intended to advance the legal status of married women; it was instead designed to secure beneficial federal income tax treatment of California residents. Under then-existing Treasury Department regulations, a couple residing in a community property state could enjoy the income tax benefit of income-splitting so long as state law gave the wife an immediate vested one-half interest. The California legislature enacted conforming legislation.[26]

It was not until 1975 that the legislature repealed the general male management provisions.[27] By this time, they were of doubtful constitutionality. The United States Supreme Court had already decided Reed v. Reed, 404 U.S. 71 (1971), and the California Supreme Court had decided Sail 'er Inn, Inc. v. Kirby, 5 Cal. 3d 1, 485 P.2d 529, 95 Cal. Rptr. 329 (1971), which indicated that both courts were willing to use the Fourteenth Amendment's equal protection clause to invalidate statutory sexual inequality that disadvantaged women. *Sail 'er Inn* was especially significant because it purported to classify sex as a "suspect classification." The legislature was well aware of the import of these decisions.[28]

The legislature essentially had two choices: to extend the separation of func-

19. Act of June 16, 1851, ch. 1102.

20. Prager, The Persistence of Separate Property Concepts in California's Community Property System 1849-1975, 24 UCLA L. Rev. 1 (1976).

21. Act of Mar. 31, 1891, ch. 220.

22. Act of Mar. 23, 1901, ch. 190.

23. Act of May 23, 1917, ch. 583.

24. See note 7 supra.

25. Act of Apr. 16, 1923, ch. 18.

26. See generally Bittker, Federal Income Taxation and the Family, 27 Stan. L. Rev. 1389 (1975).

27. Act of Oct. 1, 1973, ch. 987, eff. Jan. 1, 1975, now codified at Family Code §1100(a).

28. Hearings on Community Property Before the California Legislature's Jt. Interim Comm. on the Judiciary 1972, at 69, 88-96, 136.

tions by making each spouse sole manager of his or her earnings and having joint management only for commingled funds, if any; or to make the spouses equal managers of all community property. Texas had taken the first path; Washington had taken the second. California and, eventually, all the remaining community property states chose the Washington model: Either spouse acting alone may manage the community property but both spouses must join together for certain important events, such as gifts and real property transactions. While the basic principle is clearcut, there are a number of practical impediments to a spouse's exercise of equal rights. They will be explored in the chapter on managerial rights.

The history of the ownership and management provisions of California community property law[29] is of practical as welll as scholarly interest. The California Supreme Court has held that due process considerations require that most of the reforms be given prospective effect only. Thus, one may encounter in practice today property that is controlled by prior legislation.

In addition to legislative alteration of managerial rights, California community property law has experienced substantial case law expansion of the scope of the community and enlargement of the definition of *property* subject to division. Wealth earlier denominated entirely separate, such as a personally operated business brought into marriage by one spouse, may now be divided into separate and community components. Sources of income previously disregarded as *intangible* or *inchoate,* such as unvested pensions, are now designated *property subject to division.* These and other such developments constitute a substantial portion of this casebook.

---

29. For a more extended treatment of the general subject, see Prager, The Persistence of Separate Property Concepts in California's Community Property System 1849-1975, 24 UCLA L. Rev. 1 (1976).

III

TRANSMUTATION: CONTRACTS AND GIFTS

A. CONTRACTUAL VARIATION OF THE STATUTORY SCHEME: GENERAL BACKGROUND AND THE CALIFORNIA CASE LAW TRADITION

Introductory Note

Historically, premarital agreements have served many purposes. Customary Jewish and Islamic agreements have long required a husband to transfer property to his wife in the event of divorce, in order to discourage the husband from exercising his otherwise unfettered right of divorce and, should deterrence fail, to provide for the wife after divorce. See Marriage of Noghrey, at page 88 infra. At English common law, upon marriage a husband assumed control of his wife's property. To insulate daughters from the operation of the common law, wealthy English families created trusts for the wife's separate benefit and negotiated premarital contracts that gave the wife control of her property during marriage. Those trusts and contracts were enforced by English courts of equity.[1]

More recently, premarital agreements have served the needs of older persons, often widows and widowers, who wish to remarry but also to safeguard the family patrimony for the children of a prior marriage. Originally, such contracts regulated the disposition of property upon the death of one of the parties. Typically, each spouse waived all death rights in the other's estate. See Estate of Sheldon at page 110 infra. In principle, these agreements were enforceable in most American jurisdictions, although states varied in their willingness to enforce particular agreements. Some common law states were, in practice, quite restrictive. By contrast, California followed the civil law tradition, which freely permits contractual variation of the community property regime. Thus California has routinely enforced premarital waivers of property rights that might otherwise arise at the death of a spouse.

---

1. Jesse Dukeminier and James E. Krier, Property 324-325 (2d ed. 1988).

As the frequency of divorce increased, attorneys began to insert divorce provisions in premarital ageements. In time, courts expressed willingness to enforce provisions regulating the disposition of property at divorce, as well as at death. More recently, attorneys enlarged the scope of premarital agreements by adding spousal support waivers. In combination, these contract terms, if enforceable, would allow persons to marry without any of the legal rights and obligations to each other that would otherwise ensue at divorce or at the death of a spouse.

MARRIAGE OF DAWLEY
17 CAL. 3D 342, 551 P.2D 323, 131 Cal. Rptr. 3 (1976)

TOBRINER, J. The present case involves the validity of an antenuptial contract in which the parties agreed that their earnings and other property acquired during the marriage would be held as separate property. At the time they entered the agreement, the parties anticipated the early dissolution of their marriage. Relying on In re Marriage of Higgason (1973) 10 Cal. 3d 476 [110 Cal. Rptr. 897, 516 P.2d 289], which stated in dictum that an antenuptial agreement "must be made in contemplation that the marriage relation will continue until the parties are separated by death" (p.485), the wife contends that the agreement violates public policy.

We shall point out that the quoted language from *Higgason* does not accurately state California law. Our decisions, including *Higgason* itself, do not hold an agreement void if the parties contemplated dissolution; they hold it void only insofar as the terms of the agreement itself promote the dissolution of the marriage. The test of the validity of the contract thus does not turn on the subjective contemplation of the parties — a standard which would make it impossible to rely on any antenuptial agreement — but upon the objective language of the contract itself. Applying that test, we conclude that the agreement at bar, which provides that the parties will hold their earnings as separate property, does not offend public policy. . . .

Betty Johnson, a tenured elementary school teacher, and James Dawley, an engineer, met in 1961 and maintained an intimate relationship until March of 1964. On May 11, 1964, Betty went to James' residence to pick up her belongings, but following a long and emotional discussion they agreed to resume their relationship. Two weeks later Betty discovered that she was pregnant.

Betty told James that she feared a nonmarital pregnancy would result in her losing her teaching job. An acrimonious exchange ensued, during which Betty claims James refused to help her, and James claims she threatened him with a paternity suit accompanied by publicity intended to imperil James' employment. Finally, both agreed to a temporary marriage as a solution to their dilemma.

James insisted on an antenuptial agreement to protect his property and earnings from Betty's claims; she insisted that he agree to support Carolyn, her daughter from a previous relationship, and herself for the period of her pregnancy and thereafter until she could resume teaching duties. James and Betty agreed to ask Michael diLeonardo, James' attorney, to draft the agreement. Betty reviewed the contract with her attorney, and accepted its provisions. They signed the agreement on June 11, 1964, and married two days later.

The antenuptial agreement, the complete text of which appears in footnote,[1] provided in paragraphs V and VI that all property, including earnings, belonging to either spouse at the commencement of marriage or acquired by him through purchase, gift or inheritance during marriage would be owned by that spouse as his separate property. Each spouse disclaimed all rights, including community property rights, in the property of the other spouse. James agreed in paragraph VIII to support Betty and Carolyn "for the minimum period of fourteen calendar months following said marriage, in order that [Betty] may take a leave of absence from the teaching profession for said period"; in paragraph IX he agreed to support any child born to Betty in the next ten months until the child reached majority.

1. The antenuptial agreement reads as follows: "This Agreement is entered into on the 11 day of June 4, 1964, by and between James R. Dawley and Betty Jean Calvert Johnson. [¶] This agreement is made with reference to the following facts: [¶] James R. Dawley and Betty Jean Calvert Johnson are contemplating marriage. [¶] II James R. Dawley is the owner of real and personal property set forth and described in Exhibit "A" attached to this agreement and by this reference thereto made a part hereof as though fully set forth. [¶] III Betty Jean Calvert Johnson is the owner of real and personal property set forth and described in exhibit "B" attached [to] this agreement and by this reference thereto made a part hereof as though fully set forth. [¶] IV James R. Dawley has two children of a former marriage, whose names are: Katherine June Dawley and James R. Dawley. [¶] V The parties desire to define the respective rights of each in the property of the other after marriage, and the parties desire that all property owned by either of them at the time of the marriage and property purchased by either of them from their own earnings during the marriage, shall be their respective separate property. [¶] VI (a) Betty Jean Calvert Johnson agrees that all property of any nature or in any place, including but not being limited to the earnings and income resulting from his personal services, skill, effort, and work, belonging to James R. Dawley at the commencement of the marriage or acquired by or coming to James R. Dawley by purchase, gift or inheritance during the marriage, shall be his separate property, and shall be enjoyed by him and shall be subject to his disposition as his separate property in the same manner as though the proposed marriage had never been entered into. Betty Jean Calvert Johnson acknowledges that she understands that, except for this agreement, the earnings and income resulting from the personal services, skill, effort, and work of James R. Dawley after the marriage would be community property, but that by this agreement such earnings and income are made his separate property. [¶] (b) James R. Dawley agrees that all property of any nature or in any place, including but not being limited to the earnings and income resulting from her personal services, skill, effort, and work, belonging to Betty Jean Calvert Johnson at the commencement of the marriage or acquired by or coming to Betty Jean Calvert Johnson by purchase, gifts or inheritance during the marriage, shall be her separate property and shall be enjoyed by her and shall be subject to her disposition as her separate property in the same manner as though the proposed marriage had never been entered into. James R. Dawley acknowledges that he understands that, except for this agreement, the earnings and income resulting from the personal services, skill, effort, and work of Betty Jean Calvert Johnson after the marriage would be community property, but that by this agreement such earnings and income are made her separate property. [¶] VII (a) Betty Jean Calvert Johnson hereby relinquishes, disclaims, releases, and forever gives up any and all right, claim, or interest in or to the property of James R. Dawley including but without being limited to community property rights, rights as an heir or widow, rights to family allowance, rights in case of death, or right to act as administratrix of the estate of James R. Dawley. [¶] (b) James R. Dawley hereby relinquishes, disclaims, releases, and forever gives up any and all right, claim, or interest in or to the property of Betty Jean Calvert Johnson including but without being limited to community property rights, rights as an heir or widower, rights of family allowance, rights in case of death, or right to act as administrator of the estate of Betty Jean Calvert Johnson. [¶] VIII James R. Dawley agrees, that at all events, if he and Betty Jean Calvert Johnson are married, he will support Betty Jean Calvert Johnson and her daughter, Carolyn Kaye, in the same manner to which they are now accustomed, for the minimum period of fourteen calendar months following said marriage, in order that Betty Jean Calvert Johnson may take a leave of absence from the teaching profession for said period. [¶] IX James R. Dawley further agrees that in the event that a child or children is or are born to Betty Jean Calvert Johnson during the next ten calendar months, he will pay to said Betty Jean Calvert Johnson or to a legally appointed guardian or trustee for such child or children, a reasonable amount each month during the minority of said child or children for the support and education thereof. It is understood that except for the fourteen months above described James R. Dawley has no legal or financial responsibility for Carolyn Kaye Johnson unless he so chooses. [¶] X It is expressly agreed by and between the parties hereto that the various provisions contained in this agreement are severable. If any provision of this agreement is held to be invalid or unenforceable all other provisions shall continue in full force and effect." . . .

Lisa Dawley, the parties' daughter, was born in January of 1965. The 14-month period mentioned in the agreement expired in September of 1965 when Betty resumed her teaching duties. The parties, however, did not separate at that time, but continued to live together until July of 1972.

In April of 1973, James filed for dissolution of the marriage. The trial court granted the dissolution, and awarded Betty spousal support of $1 per year, custody of Lisa with support of $300 per month, and $1,000 in attorney's fees. Relying on the antenuptial agreement, the court found no community property subject to division in the dissolution action, and awarded James all property purchased with his separate income. Betty appeals from the court's failure to find the existence of and to divide community property.

Pursuant to Civil Code sections 5133 through 5137 [Family Code sections 1500 through 1502], " '[p]arties contemplating marriage may validly contract as to their property rights, both as to property then owned by them and as to property, including earnings, which may be acquired by them after marriage.' " (In re Marriage of Higgason, supra, 10 Cal. 3d 476, 486, quoting Barker v. Barker (1956) 139 Cal. App. 2d 206, 212 [293 P.2d 85]). Betty concedes that the agreement between James and herself conforms to the statutory requirements governing antenuptial agreements.

Betty contends, however, that the agreement is entirely invalid because uncontradicted evidence shows that it was not entered into in contemplation of a marriage to last until death. She relies for this proposition upon a sentence taken from our opinion in Marriage of Higgason, supra, in which we stated that an antenuptial agreement "must be made in contemplation that the marriage relation will continue until the parties are separated by death." (10 Cal. 3d 476, 485.) We shall explain, however, that the quoted language from *Higgason* does not accurately reflect California law. Enforcement of the state policy to foster and protect marriage (see Hill v. Hill (1943) 23 Cal. 2d 82, 93 [142 P.2d 417]) does not require the invalidation of entire agreements based upon the subjective contemplation of the parties; it requires only that the courts refuse to enforce specific contractual provisions which by their terms seek to promote the dissolution of a marriage.

From Loveren v. Loveren (1895) 106 Cal. 509 [39 P. 801] to the most recent decision of this court on the matter, Glickman v. Collins (1975) 13 Cal. 3d 852 [120 Cal. Rptr. 76, 533 P.2d 204], California courts have uniformly held that contracts offend the state policy favoring marriage only insofar as the terms of the contract "facilitate," "encourage," or "promote" divorce or dissolution.[5]

Apart from *Higgason,* no case has distinguished, in terms of the policy favoring marriage, between antenuptial agreements and those executed during a viable mar-

---

5. See Glickman v. Collins, supra, 13 Cal. 3d 852, 857; Barham v. Barham (1949) 33 Cal. 2d 416, 428 [202 P.2d 289]; Pereira v. Pereira (1909) 156 Cal. 1, 4-5 [103 P. 488]; Newman v. Freitas (1900) 129 Cal. 283, 289 [61 P. 907]; Loveren v. Loveren, supra, 106 Cal. 509, 512; Estate of Nelson (1964) 224 Cal. App. 2d 138, 142 [36 Cal. Rptr. 352]; Whiting v. Whiting (1923) 62 Cal. App. 157, 165 [216 P. 92]; McCahan v. McCahan (1920) 47 Cal. App. 173, 175 [190 P. 458].

Although the cited cases assert that an agreement which "facilitates" dissolution violates public policy, this terminology is misleading. In a literal sense, any contract which delimits the property rights of the spouses might "facilitate" dissolution by making possible a shorter and less expensive dissolution hearing. But public policy does not render property agreements unenforceable merely because such agreements simplify the division of marital property; it is only when the agreement encourages or promotes dissolution that it offends the public policy to foster and protect marriage.

riage,[6] and none have asserted that only agreements made in contemplation of a lifelong marriage are valid. The cases have uniformly directed their inquiry not to the subjective contemplation of the parties, but to the objective terms of the contract, and the effect of those terms in promoting the dissolution of the marriage.

Indeed *Higgason* itself exemplifies this objective approach to ascertaining the validity of agreements. In *Higgason* a wealthy 73-year-old woman married a man, age 48, without financial resources. Prior to the marriage they executed an agreement under which each waived all interest in the property of the other and all right to support. In the subsequent dissolution action the husband challenged the validity of the agreement.

Although our opinion in *Higgason* asserted that a valid antenuptial agreement must be made in contemplation of a marriage lasting until death, we did not attempt to determine what the parties actually contemplated at the time of the execution of the agreement. Instead, the opinion proceeds directly to examine the *terms* of the contract. Upholding the husband's waiver of property rights, we stated that "Insofar as an antenuptial agreement relates to the disposition of the property of the respective parties, and does not seek to alter support obligations imposed by law, it will be upheld. . . . Accordingly, the provisions relating to property rights in the antenuptial agreement entered into between the husband and the wife herein are valid." (10 Cal. 3d 476, 485.) Relying, however, on decisions invalidating a wife's waiver of support rights because it promoted divorce, we held the same principle barred enforcement of the husband's waiver of support rights.

Turning to the cases preceding *Higgason,* we find no decision which struck down a contract which merely provided that the earnings and accumulations of each spouse will be held as separate property. On two occasions courts held invalid as promotive of divorce provisions which waived or limited rights of spousal support, yet enforced property divisions contained in the same agreement. (Barham v. Barham, supra, 33 Cal. 2d 416, 428; Whiting v. Whiting, supra, 62 Cal. App. 157; see discussion in Barker v. Barker, supra, 139 Cal. App. 2d 206, 212.) The few decisions striking down property provisions have all involved contracts in which those provisions were inseverably linked to other terms which waived or limited rights to support or attorney's fees. (Pereira v. Pereira, supra, 156 Cal. 1 ($10,000 consideration in settlement of support and alimony claims); Estate of Nelson, supra, 224 Cal. App. 2d 138 (waiver of all property and support rights in contract procured by undue influence).)

Our disagreement with *Higgason*'s dictum that parties to an antenuptial agreement must contemplate a lifelong marriage, however, is not merely a matter of adherence to precedent. A rule measuring the validity of antenuptial agreements by the subjective contemplation of the parties hazards the validity of all antenuptial agreements. No agreement would be safe against the risk that a spouse might later testify that he or she anticipated a marriage of short duration when he or she executed the agreement. Disputes concerning the validity of the agreement may arise, moreover, many years after its execution, perhaps even after the death of the par-

---

6. Married couples may freely contract to alter the separate or community status of their property (see Civ. Code, §5103 [Fam. Code §721]), but unless the marriage relationship has irreparably broken down, so that the legitimate objects of matrimony have been utterly destroyed, an agreement which promotes divorce violates public policy. (Glickman v. Collins, supra, 13 Cal. 3d 852, 857; Hill v. Hill, supra, 23 Cal. 2d 82, 93.)

ties, thus rendering any attempt to reconstruct the subjective anticipation of the parties fruitless. In consequence, under a test based upon the subjective contemplation of the parties, neither persons dealing with the parties nor even the parties themselves could rely on the terms of an antenuptial agreement.

Further uncertainties arise from the inherent vagueness of any test based on the subjective contemplation of the parties. A man and woman entering into marriage may pledge their faith "til death do us part," but the unromantic statistics show that many marriages end in separation or dissolution. Spouses who enter into an antenuptial agreement cannot forecast the future; they must, as a realistic matter, take into account both the possibility of lifelong marriage and the possibility of dissolution. In consequence, a dichotomous test which insists that the contracting parties must contemplate either a marriage until death or an earlier termination is utterly unworkable. Such a test might invalidate virtually all antenuptial agreements on the ground that the parties contemplated dissolution, or it might uphold all on the ground that the parties also contemplated the possibility of a lifelong relationship, but it provides no principled basis for determining which antenuptial agreements offend public policy and which do not.

We conclude that an antenuptial agreement violates the state policy favoring marriage only insofar as its terms encourage or promote dissolution. The dictum in *Higgason* that such agreements are invalid unless the parties contemplated a marriage lasting until death is hereby disapproved.

In view of our conclusion that the validity of an antenuptial agreement does not turn on whether the parties contemplated a lifelong marriage, Betty's claim that uncontradicted evidence establishes that both parties contemplated that the marriage relationship would be eventually terminated by separation and dissolution does not frame an issue relevant to the validity of the agreement. The testimony on which Betty relies does not relate to the meaning or interpretation of the agreement, but to the supposed invalidity of the agreement under *Higgason*'s dictum that valid antenuptial agreements must be made in contemplation of a lifelong marriage; in disapproving that dictum, we expose and demonstrate the irrelevancy of the offered testimony.

Under the principles we have explained, Betty can succeed in overturning the trial court's order enforcing the agreement only if she can show that the *terms* of the agreement promote or encourage the dissolution of their marriage. An examination of the Dawleys' antenuptial contract, however, reveals no provision which on its face might promote or encourage dissolution, and Betty presented no evidence to show that any provision is reasonably susceptible of an interpretation which might promote or encourage dissolution. . . .

Betty contends that the antenuptial agreement is tainted by undue influence. . . . From the trial court's conclusion that Betty freely and voluntarily entered into the antenuptial agreement we . . . imply a finding that her consent was not procured by undue influence.

Substantial evidence supports the implied finding negating undue influence. Parties who are not yet married are not presumed to share a confidential relationship (Handley v. Handley (1952) 113 Cal. App. 2d 280, 285, [248 p.2d 59] . . .); the record demonstrates that Betty did not rely on the advice and integrity of James in entering into the antenuptial agreement.

Betty points out that even in the absence of a confidential relationship, a contract may be tainted by undue influence if one party takes "a grossly oppressive and unfair advantage of another's necessities or distress." (Civ. Code, §1575.) We appreciate that Betty was compelled to enter into the antenuptial agreement by her unplanned pregnancy and her fear that she would lose her job, but James, threatened with a paternity suit and likely loss of his position, was in no position to take advantage of her distress. Perhaps reflecting this rough equality of bargaining power, the Dawleys' antenuptial agreement was in no way "oppressive or unfair." Both James and Betty secured their earnings and property acquired with those earnings as separate property, and James agreed to support both Betty and her daughter during the period when Betty would not be working.[8]

We therefore conclude that substantial evidence supports the trial court's finding that the agreement was not procured by undue influence. . . .

In times past antenuptial agreements were most often used by wealthy men and women who feared that less wealthy fiances might be marrying for money. In recent years, however, an increasing number of couples have executed antenuptial agreements in order to structure their legal relationship in a manner more suited to their needs and values. (See generally Weitzman, Legal Regulation of Marriage: Tradition and Change (1974) 62 Cal. L. Rev. 1169.) Neither the reordering of property rights to fit the needs and desires of the couple, nor realistic planning that takes account of the possibility of dissolution, offends the public policy favoring and protecting marriage. It is only when the terms of an agreement go further — when they promote and encourage dissolution, and thereby threaten to induce the destruction of a marriage that might otherwise endure — that such terms offend public policy.

For the reasons we have explained, the agreement at bar does not fall within this ban. Having freely contracted that the earnings of each, and property derived from those earnings, will be the separate property of the earning spouse, the parties are bound by their agreement.

The judgment is affirmed.

WRIGHT, C.J., McCOMB, J., MOSK, J., SULLIVAN, J., CLARK, J., AND RICHARDSON, J., CONCURRED.

Notes and Questions

1. Having created a partnership model of marriage in its community property system, why does California allow people to opt out? What sort of people are likely to wish to opt out?

2. Read the Dawleys' premarital agreement carefully. This is a typical *separation of property* contract. What are its essential terms? Can you infer the legal requirements for an enforceable contract from the content of the Dawleys' largely standard-form contract?

---

8. Estate of Nelson, supra, 224 Cal. App. 2d 138, on which Betty bases her contention, is factually distinguishable. In *Nelson* a 50-year-old real estate broker, before marrying his 22-year-old secretary, obtained from her an agreement in which she waived all community property rights, and agreed that in the event of divorce Nelson would neither pay spousal support nor be responsible for more than $150 in attorney's fees and costs. Stating that the consideration to the wife was so small as to shock the conscience of the court, the Court of Appeal upheld the trial court's determination that the agreement was procured by fraud and undue influence.

In contrast to *Nelson,* in the case at bar both husband and wife were educated and experienced professionals. Betty did not rely on James' advice, but consulted her personal counsel before executing the agreement. Finally, the terms of the Dawleys' antenuptial agreement do not shock the conscience, but provide significant benefits for both parties. . . .

3. Note the distinction at page 85 supra between property division and support. How does a support provision promote divorce in a way that a property provision does not? Is there an alternative rationale for the distinction between property rights and support rights?

4. Reread the paragraph beginning "In view of our conclusion . . ." at page 86 supra. Does this "uncontradicted evidence" have a bearing on "the meaning or interpretation" of the agreement? Frame an argument for Betty.

5. *Dawley* concludes "that an antenuptial agreement violates the state policy favoring marriage only insofar as its terms encourage or promote dissolution." Under what circumstances might the property distribution terms of a premarital agreement encourage or promote dissolution?

MARRIAGE OF NOGHREY
169 Cal. App. 3d 326, 215 Cal. Rptr. 153 (1985)

FOLEY, J. — Kambiz Noghrey appeals from a decision finding valid a premarital agreement. We reverse.

Kambiz and Farima were married for seven and one-half months when Farima filed for divorce. Her petition alleged the existence of an antenuptial agreement setting forth the property rights of the parties. The issue of the existence and validity of the agreement was bifurcated from the dissolution proceeding and heard first.

Frances and Charles Kandel had known Farima for several years prior to her marriage. Farima lived with the Kandels for the two years preceding the wedding.

Mrs. Kandel testified that when she and her family arrived for the Noghrey wedding Farima and Kambiz were not yet present, nor were Farima's parents. As she entered the hotel where the wedding was to take place, Mrs. Kandel was met by Kambiz' brother, Jamshid, who asked Mrs. Kandel and her husband to step aside. He handed Mrs. Kandel a piece of paper and a pen and then began, with Kambiz' cousin, dictating terms of a premarital agreement.

Mrs. Kandel remembered writing "I, Kambiz Noghrey, agree to settle on Farima Human, the house . . . [i]n Sunnyvale, . . . [a]nd $500,000.00 or one-half of my assets, whichever is greater, in the event of a divorce." The agreement was written on the reverse side of the ceremonial wedding certificate which Mrs. Kandel believes was given to the rabbi.[1]

Mrs. Kandel then brought the completed document to Kambiz for his signature. Kambiz indicated he knew what the document was and that he wanted to sign the agreement. Mrs. Kandel testified she cautioned Kambiz to be very careful and to read the document because he would be giving his wife half of everything he had. She inquired whether Kambiz wanted to sign the document. According to Mrs. Kandel, Kambiz indicated he would gladly give the property to his bride-to-be and he appeared serious when making the statement. Kambiz and Farima then signed the document, with Mr. Kandel and Kambiz' cousin signing as witnesses.

Farima testified that she signed the document because a husband has to give some protection to a new wife in case of divorce. She explained that it is hard for

---

1. Kambiz and his brother testified that the document was given to Farima's father. In any event, the document could not be found for trial.

an Iranian woman to remarry after a divorce because she is no longer a virgin. In return for the premarital agreement, Farima gave Kambiz assurances that she was a virgin and was medically examined for that purpose. . . .

Of the many issues raised by Kambiz in this appeal, we find the first dispositive. We are in accord with his view that the antenuptial agreement on which this case centers encourages and promotes divorce. It is hence contrary to the public policy of this state and unenforceable.

As previously noted, the issues of the agreement's existence and validity were bifurcated from the remaining issues in the case and tried separately. Following trial of these issues the trial court filed the following Memorandum of Decision: "It is the opinion of the Court that the petitioner and respondent entered into a written antenuptial agreement, also known as 'Katuba' [sic], prior to their marriage.[2] The terms of the agreement were as follows: 'I, Kambiz Noghrey, agree to settle on Farima Human the house in Sunnyvale and $500,000 or one-half my assets, whichever is greater, in the event of a divorce. The said agreement should be found to be a valid, binding, and enforceable agreement.'"

An antenuptial agreement, the terms of which encourage or promote divorce, is against public policy and is unenforceable. . . .

We wish it understood that not all antenuptial agreements violate public policy. Such agreements by which the parties provide for their property rights are not *ipso facto*, illegal and void. Antenuptial agreements dealing with property owned prior to marriage and property and earnings accumulated subsequent to marriage are generally valid. (In re Marriage of Dawley (1976) 17 Cal. 3d 342, 351 [131 Cal. Rptr. 3, 551 P.2d 32].) *Dawley*, nevertheless, reaffirmed the rule that such contracts are offensive to the public policy of this state if the "terms of the contract 'facilitate,' 'encourage,' or 'promote' divorce or dissolution." (Id., at p.350.) The court further pointed out that the term "facilitate" should not be misconstrued so as to render illegal agreements that merely define the property rights of spouses, thereby simplifying the issues and reducing the costs of a dissolution proceeding. "[P]ublic policy does not render property agreements unenforceable merely because such agreements simplify the division of marital property; it is only when the agreement encourages or promotes dissolution that if offends the public policy to foster and protect marriage." (Id., at p.350, fn. 5.)

The agreement before us, however, is not of the type that seeks to define the character of property acquired after marriage nor does it seek to ensure the separate character of property acquired prior to marriage. This agreement is surely different and speaks to a wholly unrelated subject. It constitutes a promise by the husband to give the wife a very substantial amount of money and property, *but only upon the occurrence of a divorce*. No one could reasonably contend this agreement encourages the husband to seek a dissolution. Common sense and fiscal prudence

2. The *kethuba* is a marriage document which represents the obligation of the husband under the Jewish faith to, inter alia, provide for his wife upon divorcing her. Since the husband could apparently divorce his wife at will, the *kethuba* was a device created to provide economic security for the wife, but was also intended to discourage divorce by making it costly and undesirable for the husband. The wife, on the other hand, was not as free to divorce and was subject to loss or reduction of her rights should she divorce her husband on certain grounds. ("Kethuba" by Rachel Bernstein Wischnitzer, The Universal Jewish Encyclopedia (1942) Vol. 6, pp.367-372.)

Although the very roots of the *kethuba* are embedded in religious doctrine, we do not reach the issue of whether a civil court, applying neutral principles of law, could interpret and construe such a document and resolve the property issues in question without running afoul of the Establishment clauses of the federal and state Constitutions.

dictate the opposite. Such is not the case with the wife. She, for her part, is encouraged by the very terms of the agreement to seek a dissolution, and with all deliberate speed, lest the husband suffer an untimely demise, nullifying the contract, and the wife's right to the money and property. . . .

Farima did testify that neither she nor her parents possessed a great wealth. The prospect of receiving a house and a minimum of $500,000 by obtaining the no-fault divorce available in California would menace the marriage of the best intentioned spouse.

The judgment of the trial court is reversed.

PANELLI, P.J., and AGLIANO, J., concurred.

Respondent's petition for review by the Supreme Court was denied September 18, 1985. BIRD, C.J., was of the opinion that the petition should be granted.

Notes and Questions

1. Might Farima's contract claim have been denied as a matter of contract interpretation: The contract did not contemplate a civil divorce, that is, a divorce in which Farima, the *wife*, was the moving party? Marriage of Noghrey was followed in Marriage of Dajani, 204 Cal. App. 3d 1387, 251 Cal. Rptr. 871 (1988). Nabil, a United States resident, married Awatef by proxy in Jordan in 1982. Their Islamic marriage contract provided that Nabil would pay his wife Awatef 5,000 Jordanian dinars (about $1,666) at divorce or Nabil's death. Awatef joined Nabil in California. Two years later, she moved for divorce and sought enforcement of the marriage contract. There was a conflict of expert testimony on whether the sum was due Awatef in the event that *she* moved for divorce, but the court of appeal found it unnecessary to reach that issue. Citing *Noghrey*, it held that the provision was in any event unenforceable because it encouraged divorce and hence violated public policy.

2. Does *Noghrey* effectively hold that all kethuba provisions for the wife in the event of divorce are legally unenforceable? Would the Noghreys' contract have been equally unenforceable if Kambiz, the husband, had initiated a civil divorce action or had divorced Farima according to Jewish law? On the other hand, does the kethuba arguably encourage divorce even if Kambiz is understood to be the only person with the power to obtain a divorce? In other words, is the moving party invariably the true initiator of a divorce? In Neilson v. Neilson, 780 P.2d 1264 (Utah App. 1989), one provision of the parties' civil premarital agreement provided that the husband would transfer specified property to the wife only in the event that he divorced her. Some months after the wedding, the husband moved to end the marriage. The Utah Court of Appeals, purporting to follow *Noghrey*, held the provision unenforceable because it might encourage the wife to goad the husband to seek a divorce. For similar reasoning, see Matthews v. Matthews, 2 N.C. App. 143, 147, 162 S.E.2d 697 (1968).

3. Even though the kethuba may occasionally encourage divorce, its purpose and probably its principal effect is to discourage divorce by imposing a heavy tax on divorce initiators. Should contracts discouraging divorce in this manner be enforced by California courts?

4. Can you redraft the *Noghrey* premarital agreement so that it is legally enforceable but still maintains the economic and power relations embodied in the

traditional kethuba? In other words, can you draft an enforceable contract insuring Farima against divorce in a manner acceptable to Kambiz?

5. What is the combined effect of the *Dawley/Noghrey* doctrine in terms of the economic positions and power relations of the spouses? Does the doctrine tend to favor have or have-not spouses?

6. In Borelli v. Brusseau, 12 Cal. App. 4th 647, 16 Cal. Rptr. 2d (1993), *review denied*, the husband and wife made an agreement *during* marriage. The husband was gravely ill and did not want to be cared for in a nursing home. He and his wife agreed that she would provide him with round-the-clock home nursing care and that, in exchange, he would leave her specified property at his death. She performed her promise: she cared for him until his death. However, he did not perform his promise. After his death, the wife sought specific performance of the husband's promise. The court of appeal held the husband's promise unenforceable for two reasons. First, there was no consideration because of the pre-existing duty rule: The wife had a pre-existing duty to provide her husband with nursing care. Second, the court considered the contract "void as against public policy" on the ground that "sickbed bargaining . . . [is] antithetical to the institution of marriage. . . . We therefore adhere to the longstanding rule that a spouse is not entitled to compensation for support, aside from rights to community property and the like that arise from the marital relation itself." Although *premarital* agreements do not require consideration, the public policy objection would seem equally applicable to marital and premarital agreements.

It is noteworthy, as dissenting Justice Poché pointed out, that before marriage Mr. Borelli required that his wife-to-be sign an enforceable premarital agreement waiving her community property rights in his earnings. Thus, the combined effect of *Dawley* and *Borelli* left Mrs. Borelli entirely without recompense for performance of her marital duties.

B.   THE CALIFORNIA PREMARITAL AGREEMENT ACT [CPAA]

1.   *The CPAA, as Enacted in 1985*

In 1983, the Uniform Premarital Agreement Act (UPAA) was approved by the National Conference of Commissioners on Uniform State Laws. The UPAA was designed to remedy "substantial uncertainty as to the enforceability . . . of the provisions of [premarital] agreements and a significant lack of uniformity of treatment of these agreements among the states." Prefatory Note, 9B U.L.A. 369 (1987). In American and comparative law, the UPAA embodies extreme positions on the permissible subject matter and enforceability of premarital agreements. The UPAA specifically allows waivers of spousal support, as well as property rights. Uniform Premarital Agreement Act, §3, 9B U.L.A. 373 (1987). (Compare *Dawley* supra.) The UPAA requires the party resisting enforcement to prove that (a) he or she did not execute the agreement voluntarily or (b) the agreement was unconscionable when executed and he or she (1) was not provided fair and reasonable disclosure of the property rights and financial obligations of the other party, (2) did not waive the right to disclosure, and (3) did not have, or reasonably could not have had, an adequate knowledge of the property and financial obligations of the other party. Id. §6(a), 9B U.L.A. 376 (1987). To allay the public fisc concerns of state legislatures, the UPAA provides:

Don't want spouse on welfare, so will require spouse to support.

> If a provision of a premarital agreement modifies or eliminates spousal support and that modification or elimination causes one party to the agreement to be eligible for support under a program of public assistance at the time of the separation or marital dissolution, a court, notwithstanding the terms of the agreement, may require the other party to provide support to the extent necessary to avoid that eligibility.

Id. §6(b), 9B U.L.A. 376 (1987).

In 1985, California enacted a modified version of the UPAA. The California Premarital Agreement Act (CPAA) included the UPAA procedural provisions tending to ensure contract enforceability but omitted the UPAA provision allowing spousal support waivers and, consequently, the corresponding public assistance provision. Attorneys and commentators believed that the text and legislative history of the CPAA evidenced legislative intention to continue the California ban on premarital support waivers. As modified, the CPAA was generally believed to have little effect on California law, which had always readily enforced property, as opposed to support, waivers. As enacted in 1985, the CPAA included the following provisions:

§1601.   Application of chapter

This chapter is effective on and after January 1, 1986, and applies to any premarital agreement executed on or after that date.

§1610.   Definitions

As used in this chapter:

(a) "Premarital agreement" means an agreement between prospective spouses made in contemplation of marriage and to be effective upon marriage.

(b) "Property" means an interest, present or future, legal or equitable, vested or contingent, in real or personal property, including income and earnings.

§1611.   Formalities; consideration

A premarital agreement shall be in writing and signed by both parties. It is enforceable without consideration.

§1612.   Subject matter of premarital agreement

(a) Parties to a premarital agreement may contract with respect to all of the following:

(1) The rights and obligations of each of the parties in any of the property of either or both of them whenever and wherever acquired or located.

(2) The right to buy, sell, use, transfer, exchange, abandon, lease, consume, expend, assign, create a security interest in, mortgage, encumber, dispose of, or otherwise manage and control property. *Relinquish*

(3) The disposition of property upon separation, marital dissolution, death, or the occurrence or nonoccurrence of any other event.

(4) The making of a <u>will</u>, trust, or other arrangement to carry out the provisions of the agreement.

(5) The ownership rights in and disposition of the death benefit from a <u>life insurance policy.</u>

(6) The choice of law governing the construction of the agreement.

(7) Any other matter, including their personal rights and obligations, not in violation of public policy or a statute imposing a criminal penalty.

[handwritten margin note: Kennard was referring to spousal support being public policy.]

(b) <u>The right of a child to support may not be adversely affected by a pre-marital agreement.</u>

§1613. Agreement becomes effective upon marriage

A premarital agreement becomes effective upon marriage.

§1614. Amendment; revocation

After marriage, a premarital agreement may be amended or revoked only by a written agreement signed by the parties. The amended agreement or the revocation is enforceable without consideration.

§1615. Enforcement

(a) A premarital agreement is not enforceable if the party against whom enforcement is sought proves either of the following:

(1) That party did not execute the agreement voluntarily.

(2) The agreement was unconscionable when it was executed and, before execution of the agreement, all of the following applied to that party:

(A) That party was not provided a fair and reasonable disclosure of the property or financial obligations of the other party.

(B) That party did not voluntarily and expressly <u>waive</u>, in writing, any right to disclosure of the property or financial obligations of the other party beyond the disclosure provided.

[handwritten margin note: Q: I waive my rt to know about your $?]

(C) That party did not have, or reasonably could not have had, an <u>adequate knowledge</u> of the property or financial obligations of the other party.

(b) An issue of unconscionability of a premarital agreement shall be decided by the court as a matter of law.

§1616. Effect of void marriage

If a marriage is determined to be void, an agreement that would otherwise have been a premarital agreement is enforceable only to the extent necessary to avoid an inequitable result.

§1617. Limitation of actions

Any statute of limitations applicable to an action asserting a claim for relief under a premarital agreement is tolled during the marriage of the parties to the agreement. However, equitable defenses limiting the time for enforcement, including laches and estoppel, are available to either party.

Question

Does Noghrey *survive enactment of the California Premarital Agreement Act?* With respect to premarital agreements made after 1985, does Family Code section 1612 alter the *Noghrey* principle that property provisions encouraging or promoting divorce violate public policy and are therefore unenforceable? Compare subsection (a)(3) with subsection (a)(7). Which subsection should control?

2. The CPAA, as Interpreted by the California Supreme Court in 2000: Marriage of Pendleton & Fireman and Marriage of Bonds

a. Spousal Support Waivers

In Marriage of Pendleton & Fireman, 24 Cal. 4th 39, 5 P.3d 839, 99 Cal. Rptr. 2d 278 (2000), the California Supreme Court held that premarital spousal support waivers are not per se unenforceable. The court disagreed with the prevailing view that the California Premarital Agreement Act banned spousal support waivers. The court observed that the ban on support waivers was historically a judge-made rule, and interpreted the California Act and its legislative history merely to evidence legislative intention to leave the enforceability of support waivers to the wisdom of the California judiciary. In exercising that wisdom, the court repudiated the case law ban because its historic rationale was no longer meaningful: "No basis appears on which to distinguish premarital waivers of spousal support from agreements governing property rights insofar as either has a potential for promoting dissolution." 24 Cal. 4th at 53. In dissent, Justice Kennard argued that there are, however, other reasons for banning spousal support waivers, and those reasons were expressed in the legislative history of the adoption of the California Premarital Agreement Act:

> Such waivers do not allow for changed circumstances between execution of the premarital agreement and separation or dissolution of the marriage. An agreement equitable at the time of marriage may later become inequitable and unjust. For example, the health, earning capacity, or financial resources of a spouse may change markedly during the marriage, especially one that is lengthy. An elderly spouse or one in poor health may be left destitute. The earning capacity of a spouse may be impaired by the obligations of caring for children produced by a marriage of short duration. After the marriage one spouse may elect to give up his or her career to raise the children of the marriage or to move to another location in the interest of furthering the career of the other spouse. And a spouse may substantially deplete his or her financial resources to advance the other spouse's education, training, or career during marriage.
>
> These considerations are reflected in the Legislature's enactment of Family Code section 4320, which sets forth spousal support guidelines for the trial courts. They are also reflected in the Legislature's express declarations that spousal support is a "serious legal obligation" (Fam. Code, §4250,

subd.(a)) and that it "is the policy of the State of California" to "ensure fair and sufficient" spousal support awards (id., §2100, subd. (a)). In rejecting the proposed provision [of the UPAA] to allow premarital waivers of spousal support, the Legislature must have recognized the serious potential for injustice at the time of dissolution of marriage.

Id. at 57. The majority responded to Justice Kennard's dissent by tailoring its holding to avoid the injustices she foresaw:

> We need not decide here whether circumstances existing at the time enforcement of a waiver of spousal support is sought might make enforcement unjust. It is enough to conclude here [on the facts of *Pendleton*] that no public policy is violated by permitting enforcement of a waiver of spousal support executed by intelligent, well-educated persons, each of whom appears to be self-sufficient in property and earning ability, and both of whom have the advice of counsel regarding their rights and obligations as marital partners at the time they execute the waiver. Such a waiver does not violate public policy and is not per se unenforceable. . . .

Id. at 52-53.

Notes and Questions

1. Pendleton *and the California Premarital Agreement Act.* The supreme court suggests that, depending on the facts of each case, enforcement of some premarital spousal support waivers might violate public policy while enforcement of others would not. As a matter of statutory interpretation, can the California Premarital Agreement Act, as originally enacted, be read to allow a court to enforce some but not all spousal support waivers? Reread the Act, with special attention to section 1612. Under what section of the Act could a court reasonably conclude that enforcement of a particular support waiver would violate public policy? What is the functional role of the section 1612(a)(7) public policy limitation? If that limitation will not allow a court to discriminate among spousal support waivers, will any other section of the Act enable a court to do so?

2. *The weight of authority.* In ruling that support waivers are not per se unenforceable, *Pendleton* observed:

> Some 41 jurisdictions have already abandoned the common law restrictions on premarital waivers of spousal support. In 21 jurisdictions, premarital waivers of spousal support are authorized by statutes that either adopt all or substantially all of the provisions of the UPAA . . . and in another 18 the right to enforce a premarital waiver of spousal support exists pursuant to judicial decision.

24 Cal. 4th at 49. However, the 18 judicial decisions cited by *Pendleton* reveal a highly qualified rule of enforceability. Premarital agreements are enforceable only if they are, variously, "fair in result," "fair and reasonable," "just and reasonable," "not . . . unconscionable at the time enforcement [is] sought," reviewed "for unconscionability at time enforcement is sought," and "changed circumstances [do not] make enforcement unfair and unreasonable." Id. at 49-50, n. 11. Moreover, a number of jurisdictions nominally adopting the UPAA have rewritten the unconsciona-

bility provision to refer to the time of enforcement. See, for example, Conn. Gen. Stat. §46b-36g ("[a] premarital agreement . . . shall not be enforceable . . . if [t]he agreement was unconscionable when it was executed or when enforcement is sought") and N.J. Stat. Ann. §37:2-28 ("[a] premarital agreement shall not be enforceable if . . . [t]he agreement was unconscionable at the time enforcement was sought"). In these jurisdictions, courts take a "second look" at divorce to determine whether an agreement unobjectionable when made may nevertheless be unenforceable at divorce. Does the CPAA, as originally enacted, allow a second look?

3. *The application of* Pendleton *to agreements made before* Pendleton *was decided.* Mrs. Pendleton, the party resisting enforcement of the spousal support waiver, was represented by Ronald Anteau, a prominent Beverly Hills attorney. After interviewing him, the Los Angeles Times reported:

> Previously, many lawyers advised clients that they did not have to be concerned about alimony [spousal support] waivers because courts would never enforce them. "Now almost every prenup out there is going to end up in a legal malpractice lawsuit," Anteau said.

Los Angeles Times, August 22, 2000, at A1.

b.   The Meaning of "Voluntarily"

Section 1615(a) states that a premarital agreement is not enforceable if the party resisting enforcement shows that he or she did not execute the agreement *voluntarily.* In Marriage of Bonds, 24 Cal. 4th 1, 5 P.3d 815, 99 Cal. Rptr. 2d 252 (2000), a companion case to *Pendleton,* the California Supreme Court addressed the meaning of "voluntarily." *Bonds* did not involve a spousal support waiver. The question was whether the wife's consent to a premarital property waiver was voluntary.

Giants outfielder Barry Bonds was 23 when he met his future wife, Sun, a 23-year-old Swedish immigrant working as a bartender and studying to be a cosmetologist. After living together for some time, they decided to get married. Barry's financial adviser referred him to attorneys who drafted an agreement by which Sun would waive her rights to community property. At that time Barry was earning $106,000 a year as a player for the Pittsburgh Pirates.

The court of appeal opinion, 83 Cal. Rptr. 2d 783 (1999), reports that just before the parties' scheduled flight to Las Vegas, where they planned to wed two days later, Barry's attorneys presented Sun and Barry with copies of the premarital agreement, which neither had previously had an opportunity to review. The attorneys read the agreement, which contained numerous errors and omissions, to Sun and Barry, and attempted to explain its many provisions to them. Sun signed the agreement, and the parties were married as planned.

Sun was not represented by independent counsel and, although the evidence was mixed, there was substantial evidence that neither party grasped the import of the agreement. Barry testified:

> Sun said she didn't want a lawyer. Sun didn't have anything. I paid for everything. Sun said, what do I need a lawyer for? I don't have anything. I mean, I know exactly what she said in that conversation.

Sun testified:

> My recollection is that we were there together, and the attorneys were there
> just to help us out with this. . . . I didn't think that I needed to have somebody
> else there. . . . [T]hey were there to help us out with this agreement, and
> then we were going to get married.

When asked why she did not believe that she needed her own attorney, Sun testified:

> Because Barry—Barry and I were there together, and they were attorneys.
> And they didn't come out and, you know, in the sense that they were not
> here for you. I don't recall them ever coming out to me that way. I didn't
> know anything about attorneys. I didn't know how it with worked with attor-
> neys, that you have one and I have one.

83 Cal. Rptr. 2d 788-789. The parties were living in California when, six years and
two children later, Barry filed for dissolution. Sun responded by seeking child custody, child support, spousal support, and property division. At separation, Barry
was earning $8,000,000 a year. The trial court enforced the premarital agreement,
granted Sun custody of the children, and awarded her child support and two and
one-half years of spousal support.

The court of appeal reversed and remanded, with elaborate instructions for
retrial on the enforceability of the agreement. The court of appeal was troubled
by the facts (was Sun's consent "knowing" and "free from duress"?), the attorneys'
conduct in the drafting and signing of the premarital agreement, and the character
and content of their communication with Sun about seeking independent legal
counsel. The result was a long opinion intended as a primer for attorneys, and an
ostensible holding that reached beyond the requirements of the case:

> We hold that when a party challenging a premarital agreement establishes
> that he or she did not have legal counsel while the other party had such
> assistance, and the unrepresented party did not have the opportunity to ob-
> tain legal counsel or did not knowingly refuse legal counsel, the court must
> strictly scrutinize the totality of the circumstances involved in the execution
> of the contract.

Id. at 787. The court of appeal proceeded to strictly scrutinize all the circumstances
and effectively concluded, on the basis of the facts before it, that the premarital
agreement was unenforceable because of defects in its execution. However, the
court remanded to give the parties the opportunity to develop facts responsive to
its ruling. Id. at 812.

The court of appeal opinion was superseded and depublished by the California
Supreme Court's decision to grant review. The supreme court determined, inter
alia, that the court of appeal's holding was inconsistent with Family Code section
1615:

> We conclude that [the Court of Appeal] erred in holding that a premarital
> agreement in which one party is not represented by independent counsel
> should be subjected to strict scrutiny for voluntariness. Such a holding is in-
> consistent with Family Code section 1615, which governs the enforceability
> of premarital agreements. . . . [M]ost significantly, the rule created by the

Court of Appeal would have the effect of shifting the burden of proof on the question of voluntariness to the party seeking enforcement of the premarital agreement, even though the statute expressly places the burden upon the party challenging the voluntariness of the agreement. Because the commissioners and our Legislature placed the burden of proof of involuntariness upon the party challenging a premarital agreement, it seems obvious that the party seeking enforcement should not be required to prove that the absence of any factor tending to establish voluntariness did not render the agreement involuntary—the inevitable result were we to adopt the strict scrutiny standard suggested by the Court of Appeal.

24 Cal. 4th at 12-24. The supreme court concluded that, although the evidence was conflicting, the necessary quantum of evidence, "substantial evidence," supported the trial court's determination that Sun *voluntarily* consented to the agreement. The trial court had found that Sun understood what she was giving up in the way of property rights, her consent was not coerced, and she had reasonable opportunity to obtain counsel. In terms of the canons of statutory interpretation and appellate review, *Bonds* was an easy case for the California Supreme Court. Nevertheless, the court wrestled at length with the meaning of "voluntary" in the context of premarital agreements and, more broadly, with the issues raised by premarital agreements:

> There is nothing novel about statutory provisions recognizing the ability of parties to enter into premarital agreements regarding property, because such agreements long were common and legally enforceable under English law, and have enjoyed a lengthy history in this country. In California, a premarital agreement generally has been considered to be enforceable as a contract, although when there is proof of fraud, constructive fraud, duress, or undue influence, the contract is not enforceable. . . . [T]he only issue we face concerns the trial court's determination that Sun entered into the agreement voluntarily.
>
> Neither the article of the Family Code in which section 1615 is located, nor the Uniform Act, defines the term "voluntarily." . . . To the extent it is unclear on the face of the statute what was intended by the Legislature in employing the term "voluntarily," we consult the history of the statute and consider its general intent in order to determine the sense in which the Legislature used the term. . . . The debate that preceded the adoption of the Uniform Act indicated a basic disagreement between those commissioners at the National Conference of Commissioners on Uniform State Laws who placed the highest value on certainty in enforcement of premarital agreements and the vocal minority of commissioners who urged that such contracts routinely should be evaluated for substantive fairness at the time of enforcement. . . . Indeed, over sharp and repeated objection from commissioners of the minority view, eventually it was settled that the party against whom enforcement of a premarital agreement was sought only could raise the issue of unconscionability, that is, the substantive unfairness of an agreement [at the time it was made], if he or she also could demonstrate lack of disclosure of assets, lack of waiver of disclosure, and lack of imputed knowledge of assets. The language adopted was intended to enhance the enforceability of premarital agreements and to convey the sense that an agreement voluntarily entered into would be enforced without regard to the apparent unfairness of its terms, as long as the objecting party knew or should have known of the other party's assets, or voluntarily had waived disclosure. . . . The commissioners, however, did

conditions

she has to act first b/4 he acts.

not supply a definition of the term "voluntarily," nor was there much discussion of the term.

We find an indication of the commissioners' understanding of the term in their official comment to the enforcement provision of the Uniform Act, stating that the conditions to enforcement "are comparable to concepts which are expressed in the statutory and decisional law of many jurisdictions." . . . In the majority of these cases . . . the question is viewed as one involving such ordinary contract defenses as fraud, undue influence, or duress, along with some examination of the parties' knowledge of the rights being waived, or at least knowledge of the intent of the agreement. . . . [I]t is clear from the cases cited in the comment to the enforcement section of the Uniform Act that the Commission intended that the party seeking to avoid a premarital agreement may prevail by establishing that the agreement was involuntary, and that evidence of lack of capacity, duress, fraud, and undue influence, as demonstrated by a number of factors uniquely probative of coercion in the premarital context, would be relevant in establishing the involuntariness of the agreement.

Not only did the commissioners intend that the above factors be considered in determining whether a premarital agreement was entered into voluntarily, but the same intention safely may be attributed to the California Legislature, because an examination of the history of the enactment of Family Code section 1615 in California indicates that the Legislature adopted the views of the Commission in all respects relevant to the present discussion. . . .

Although we agree with Barry that the lack of independent counsel for each party cannot alter the burden of proof that, by operation of statute, rests upon the party challenging the validity of the premarital agreement, we also agree with the Court of Appeal majority that considerations applicable to commercial contexts do not necessarily govern the determination whether a premarital agreement was entered into voluntarily.

Some of the commissioners debating the Uniform Act appeared to equate a premarital agreement with a commercial contract, and one court has emphasized that both parties contemplating marriage possess freedom of contract, which should not be restricted except as it would be in the context of a commercial contract. (Simeone v. Simeone (Pa. 1990) 525 Pa. 392, 581 A.2d 162, 165-166 [not interpreting the Uniform Act].) Apart from the circumstance that there is no statutory requirement that commercial contracts be entered into voluntarily as that term is used in Family Code section 1615, we observe some significant distinctions between the two types of contracts. A commercial contract most frequently constitutes a private regulatory agreement intended to ensure the successful outcome of the business between the contracting parties—in essence, to guide their relationship so that the object of the contract may be achieved. Normally, the execution of the contract ushers in the applicability of the regulatory scheme contemplated by the contract, and the endeavor that is the object of the contract. As for a premarital agreement (or clause of such an agreement) providing solely for the division of property upon marital dissolution, the parties generally enter into the agreement anticipating that it never will be invoked, and the agreement, far from regulating the relationship of the contracting parties and providing the method for attaining their joint objectives, exists to provide for eventualities that will arise only if the relationship founders, possibly in the distant future under greatly changed and unforeseeable circumstances.

Furthermore, marriage itself is a highly regulated institution of undisputed social value, and there are many limitations on the ability of persons to contract with respect to it, or to vary its statutory terms, that have nothing to do with maximizing the satisfaction of the parties or carrying out their intent. Such limitations are inconsistent with the freedom-of-contract analysis espoused, for example, by the Pennsylvania Supreme Court. (See Simeone v. Simeone, supra, 581 A.2d at p.165.) We refer to rules establishing a duty of mutual financial support during the marriage (Fam. Code, §720) and prohibiting agreements in derogation of the duty to support a child of the marriage (Fam. Code, §§1612, subd. (b), 3900-3901 . . .); the unenforceability of a promise to marry (Civ. Code, §43.5, subd. (d); Askew v. Askew (1994) 22 Cal. App. 4th 942 [tracing the history of the rule that breach of a promise to marry does not give rise to an action in contract or tort]); the circumstance that a party may abandon the marriage unilaterally under this state's no-fault laws; and the pervasive state involvement in the dissolution of marital status, the marriage contract, and the arrangements to be made for the children of the marriage even without consideration of the circumstance that marriage normally lacks a predominantly commercial object. . . . We note, too, that there is authority as conceded by the commissioners who considered the Uniform Act to the effect that a contract to pay a spouse for personal services such as nursing cannot be enforced, despite the undoubted economic value of the services (see Borelli v. Brusseau (1993) 12 Cal. App. 4th 647, 651-654; see also Silbaugh, Marriage Contracts and the Family Economy (1998) 93 Nw. U. L. Rev. 65, 123 [most jurisdictions will not enforce agreements with respect to personal services rendered during marriage] . . .). These limitations demonstrate further that freedom of contract with respect to marital arrangements is tempered with statutory requirements and case law expressing social policy with respect to marriage.

There also are obvious differences between the remedies that realistically may be awarded with respect to commercial contracts and premarital agreements. Although a party seeking rescission of a commercial contract, for example, may be required to restore the status quo ante by restoring the consideration received, and a party in breach may be required to pay damages, the status quo ante for spouses cannot be restored to either party, nor are damages contemplated for breach of the marital contract. In any event, the suggestion that commercial contracts are strictly enforced without regard to the fairness or oppressiveness of the terms or the inequality of the bargaining power of the parties is anachronistic and inaccurate, in that claims such as duress, unconscionability, and undue influence turn upon the specific context in which the contract is formed. . . .

We also . . . believe the reference to voluntariness in the Uniform Act was intended to convey an element of knowing waiver that is not a consistent feature of commercial contract enforcement. Further, although the Uniform Act contemplated that contract defenses should apply, in the sense that an agreement should be free from fraud (including constructive fraud), duress, or undue influence, it is clear from the debate of the commissioners who adopted the Uniform Act and the cases cited in support of the enforcement provision of the Uniform Act that subtle coercion that would not be considered in challenges to ordinary commercial contracts may be considered in the context of the premarital agreement. (See, e.g., Lutgert v. Lutgert [(Fla. Dist. Ct. App. 1976)], 338 So. 2d [1111] 1113-1116 [agreement presented too close to the wedding, with passage booked on an expensive cruise].) The obvious distinctions between premarital agreements and ordinary commercial contracts lead us to conclude that factual circumstances relating to contract defenses . . . that would not necessarily support the rescission of a commercial contract may suffice to render a premarital agreement unenforceable. The question of voluntariness must be examined in the unique context of the marital relationship. . . .

On the other hand, we do not agree with Sun and the Court of Appeal majority that a premarital agreement should be interpreted and enforced under the same standards applicable to marital settlement agreements. First, although persons, once they are married, are in a fiduciary relationship to one another (Fam. Code, §721, subd. (b)), so that whenever the parties enter into an agreement in which one party gains an advantage, the advantaged party bears the burden of demonstrating that the agreement was not obtained through undue influence (In re Marriage of Haines (1995) 33 Cal. App. 4th 277, 293), a different burden applies under the Uniform Act in the premarital setting. Even when the premarital agreement clearly advantages one of the parties, the party challenging the agreement bears the burden of demonstrating that the agreement was not entered into voluntarily. Further, under the Uniform Act, even when there has been a failure of disclosure, the statute still places the burden upon the party challenging the agreement to prove that the terms of the agreement were unconscionable when executed, rather than placing the burden on the advantaged party to demonstrate that the agreement was not unconscionable. Thus the terms of the act itself do not support the Court of Appeal's conclusion that the Legislature intended that premarital agreements should be interpreted in the same manner as agreements entered into during marriage.

In particular, we believe that both the Court of Appeal majority and Sun err to the extent they suggest that the Uniform Act or its California analog established that persons who enter into premarital agreements must be presumed to be in a confidential relationship, a status that would give rise to the fiduciary duties between spouses expressly established by section 721 of the Family Code. California law prior to the enactment of the Uniform Act was to the contrary (see In re Marriage of Dawley 17 Cal. 3d [342], 355 [persons entering into prenuptial agreement are not presumed to be in a confidential relationship]), and we discern nothing in the Uniform Act suggesting that its adoption in California was intended to overrule our earlier decision. The primary consequences of designating a relationship as fiduciary in nature are that the parties owe a duty of full disclosure, and that a presumption arises that a party who owes a fiduciary duty, and who secures a benefit through an agreement, has done so through undue influence. . . .

Because the Uniform Act was intended to enhance the enforceability of premarital agreements, because it expressly places the burden of proof upon the person challenging the agreement, and finally because the California statute imposing fiduciary duties in the family law setting applies only to spouses, we do not believe that the commissioners or our Legislature contemplated that the voluntariness of a premarital agreement would be examined in light of the strict fiduciary duties . . . imposed expressly by statute upon persons who are married. (See Fam. Code, §721.) Nor do we find any indication that the California Legislature intended to overrule our *Dawley* decision. Although we certainly agree that persons contemplating marriage morally owe each other a duty of fair dealing and obviously are not embarking upon a purely commercial contract, we do not believe that these circumstances permit us to interpret our statute as imposing a presumption of undue influence or as requiring the kind of strict scrutiny that is conducted when a lawyer or other fiduciary engages in self-dealing. On the contrary, it is evident that the Uniform Act was intended to enhance the enforceability of premarital agreements, a goal that would be undermined by presuming the existence of a confidential or fiduciary relationship.

Finally, the reference by the Court of Appeal majority to the state's interest in an equal division of marital property appears misplaced in the premarital context, and its claim that the same policy interests apply to premarital agreements is flawed. We have not been directed to relevant authority establishing that the Legislature intended that premarital agreements should be examined for fairness or enforceability on the same basis as marital settlement agreements. Instead, multiple differences in the statutes regulating each type of agreement suggest that the Legislature contemplated different standards for each type of agreement. Although community property law expresses a strong state interest in the equal division of property obtained during a marriage, so that any agreement [entered during marriage or at separation] in derogation of equal distribution should be subject to searching scrutiny for fairness, the substantive fairness of a premarital agreement is not open to examination unless the party objecting to enforcement meets the demands of Family Code section 1615, subdivision (a)(2). As explained above, with respect to division of property during marriage and upon dissolution of marriage, the Family Code provides that the parties stand in a confidential, fiduciary relationship to one another (Fam. Code, §721, subd. (b)), but such a proviso does not appear in the California Uniform Act regulating premarital agreements. Marital settlement [separation] agreements must be preceded by rather elaborate disclosure of assets and liabilities, as well as income and expenses, and strict rules govern the waiver of disclosure. (Fam. Code, §§2100-2110; In re Marriage of Fell (1997) 55 Cal. App. 4th 1058, 1064-1066.) Such detailed requirements do not apply to premarital agreements. We are not persuaded that the policy of equal division of assets at the time of dissolution is intended to apply to premarital agreements. In sum, the Court of Appeal majority erred in suggesting that the voluntariness of a premarital agreement should be assessed on the assumption that the parties were in a confidential relationship and in pursuit of the policy favoring equal division of assets upon dissolution. . . .

Id. at 13-29.

Notes and Questions

1. *Text and subtext. Bonds* advances the goals of the Act that it interprets. It protects the Act against those who would dilute its provisions. Yet the supreme court's ruminations on the nature of premarital agreements may be read to call into question the essential soundness of the Act. What implications do you draw from the court's discussion?

With the court's discussion, compare the American Law Institute's commentary on the same set of issues:

Special circumstances applicable to agreements about family dissolution. While there are good reasons to respect contracts relating to the consequences of family dissolution, the family context requires some departure from the rules that govern the commercial arena. First, the relationship between contracting parties who are married, or about to marry, is different than the usual commercial relationship in ways that matter to the law's treatment of their agreements. Persons planning to marry usually assume that they share with their intended spouse a mutual and deep concern for one another's welfare. Business people negotiating a commercial agreement do not usually have such expectations of one another. . . . The distinctive expectations that persons planning to marry usually have about one another can disarm their capacity for self-protective judgment, or their inclination to exercise it, as compared to parties negotiating commercial agreements. This difference justifies legal rules designed to strengthen parties' ability and inclination to consider how a proposed agreement affects their own interest, such as rules that require transparency in the agreement's language and that encourage parties to seek independent legal counsel.

Second, even though the terms of agreements made before . . . an ongoing family relationship address the consequences of its dissolution, the parties ordinarily do not expect the family unit to dissolve. Even if the possibility of dissolution is considered, it is necessarily imagined as arising at some indefinite time in the future. The remoteness of dissolution in both likelihood and timing, as well as the difficulty of anticipating other life changes that might occur during the course of the marriage, further impedes the ability of persons to evaluate the impact that the contract terms will have on them in the future when its enforcement is sought. . . .

The two concerns just identified describe distinctive limits on the cognitive capacity with which persons may enter family contracts, as contrasted with commercial agreements. There is, in addition, the point that the rights and obligations that parties might seek to waive through private agreements are designed to protect the interests of persons who enter into family relationships, and the interests of their children. Enforcement of agreements about the consequences of family dissolution therefore present a different policy question than enforcement of commercial agreements between persons who otherwise have no claims on one another's property or income. Family contracts set aside otherwise applicable public policies while commercial agreements do not. Two implications of this difference are noted here. First, when a contract departs from otherwise applicable public policies that are designed to protect parties, the law can reasonably require greater assurance that the parties understand and appreciate what they are doing, than when the contract does not. Second, vindication of the public policies may require rules that limit the enforcement of private agreements that significantly infringe upon them. These policy concerns thus suggest a rationale for special rules for family contracts that is additional to the rationale based upon the cognitive limitations that are likely to impinge upon persons entering into family contracts. In short, while the [ALI] provisions are necessarily concerned with contractual integrity, they are also informed by concerns of family-law policy.

Provisions . . . requiring distinctive rules for [premarital] contracts . . . are justified on at least one, and often both, of these two basic rationales. Indeed, the cases in which the parties are most likely to make errors of cognition overlap considerably with those in which significant public policies are most likely implicated: long marriages and marriages producing children. . . .

In providing some limits to the enforceability of agreements made before or during an ongoing family relationship, [the law] can play a useful role in encouraging parties to draft agreements that are more reasonable than the agreements they might otherwise negotiate. Faced with the possibility that an agreement might be set aside if various procedural and substantive limits are transgressed, the parties have an incentive to deal more openly and fairly with one another.

Principles of the Law of Family Dissolution, §7.02, cmt. c (2002).

2. *The law in other English-speaking countries.* The excerpt from *Bonds* begins with the court's observation that "premarital agreements regarding property . . . were common and legally enforceable under English law." However, current English law grants the divorce court unfettered power to ignore the terms of a premarital or marital agreement. It allows the court to make:

> an order varying[,] for the benefit of the parties to the marriage and of the children of the family or either or any of them[,] any ante-nuptial or post-nuptial settlement . . . notwithstanding that there are no children of the family.

English Matrimonial Causes Act of 1973, §24. Similarly, the Canadian province of British Columbia allows "judicial reapportionment on the basis of fairness" when "the provisions for division of property between spouses under their marriage [premarital or marital] agreement . . . would be unfair" having regard to a wide variety of equitable factors. Family Relations Act of British Columbia [R.S.B.C. 1996], ch. 128, §65.

The English and the British Columbia provisions, by implication, limit enforceability to the property terms of a premarital or marital agreement. Terms relating spousal or child support are unmentioned and, presumably, unenforceable. Compare the Uniform Premarital Agreement Act (UPAA), which enforces waivers of spousal support, as well as property rights, without any consideration of "fairness" at dissolution. For discussion of state law adoption and modification of these UPAA provisions, see Principles of the Law of Family Dissolution, §7.04, Reporter's Note to Comment g; and §7.05, Reporter's Note to Comment b. For criticism of the UPAA generally, see id.

3. *Premarital agreements in the American Law Institute's Principles of the Law of Family Dissolution: Analysis and Recommendations (2002).* Chapter 7 of the Principles covers agreements, including premarital, marital, and separation agreements. The Principles begin with the premise that the law of premarital agreements should reflect a balancing of, on the one hand, the values of contractual freedom and contractual integrity, and on the other, the interests expressed in the generally applicable default rules of family law, that is, the equitable and human welfare concerns that underlie the rules that apply at dissolution in the absence of any contract. In comparison with the UPAA, the Principles adopt more demanding standards for enforcement of premarital agreements. In its execution, a premarital agreement must satisfy certain procedural formalities (§7.04) and, even when it does, may still be subject to a "second look" at dissolution (§7.05).

Section 7.04 reverses the UPAA burden of proof by generally providing that "a party seeking to enforce [a premarital] agreement must show that the other party's consent to it was informed and not obtained under duress." However, section 7.04 also provides a "safe harbor," the satisfaction of which effectively reverses the burden of proof. The safe-harbor provision raises a presumption that consent was informed and not obtained under duress when the party seeking enforcement shows that: (1) the agreement was executed at least 30 days before the marriage; (2) both parties were advised to obtain independent legal counsel and had reasonable opportunity to do so before the agreement's execution; and (3) in the case of agreements concluded without the assistance of independent legal counsel for each party, the agreement states, in language easily understandable by an adult of ordinary intelligence with no legal training (a) the nature of any rights or claims otherwise arising at dissolution that are altered by the contract, and the nature of that alteration and (b) that the interests of the spouses with respect to the agreement may be adverse.

Even when an agreement survives section 7.04 of the Principles, it may founder on section 7.05, the "second look" provision. Section 7.05 subjects agreements to a substantive review at dissolution only in certain types of marriages: (1) long marriages; (2) marriages in which a child has been born to or adopted by the parties; and (3) marriages in which the circumstances of the parties have significantly changed in ways unforeseeable when the agreement was made. The party resisting enforcement bears the burden of demonstrating that enforcement of a term of the agreement "would work a substantial injustice," according to specified criteria. If the party discharges that burden, the term in unenforceable.

The rationale of section 7.05 is twofold. First, the enforceability of contracts is based, inter alia, on the premise that persons know what is best for them and the law therefore ought not second-guess their agreements. However, long-term agreements generally strain the limits of human cognition, and the cognitive difficulties with premarital agreements are considerably more severe than with long-term business contracts. Parties about to be married often are unable to imagine a distant future under changed circumstances. In particular, prospective spouses often do not foresee the changes that children will bring to their lives. Second, long marriages and marriages to which children are born are those marriages that are of the greatest concern to divorce law. Thus, the Principles take the view that a balancing is required between the values expressed in contract law and those expressed in divorce law. The Principles' resolution of this tension is that, even in those cases categorically qualifying for a second look, the premarital contract is nevertheless enforceable unless its enforcement would work a substantial injustice at dissolution.

3. The CPAA, as Amended by the Legislature in 2001

In 2001, the legislature responded pointedly to *Pendleton* and *Bonds* in Senate Bill 78. The chaptered version (chapter 286) of that bill provides (with amendments italicized):

> *The people of the State of California do enact as follows:*
> SECTION 1. Section 1612 of the Family Code is amended to read:

1612. (a) Parties to a premarital agreement may contract with respect to all of the following:

(1) The rights and obligations of each of the parties in any of the property of either or both of them whenever and wherever acquired or located.

(2) The right to buy, sell, use, transfer, exchange, abandon, lease, consume, expend, assign, create a security interest in, mortgage, encumber, dispose of, or otherwise manage and control property.

(3) The disposition of property upon separation, marital dissolution, death, or the occurrence or nonoccurrence of any other event.

(4) The making of a will, trust, or other arrangement to carry out the provisions of the agreement.

(5) The ownership rights in and disposition of the death benefit from a life insurance policy.

(6) The choice of law governing the construction of the agreement.

(7) Any other matter, including their personal rights and obligations, not in violation of public policy or a statute imposing a criminal penalty.

(b) The right of a child to support may not be adversely affected by a premarital agreement.

(c) Any provision in a premarital agreement regarding spousal support, including, but not limited to, a waiver of it, is not enforceable if the party against whom enforcement of the spousal support provision is sought was not represented by independent counsel at the time the agreement containing the provision was signed, or if the provision regarding spousal support is unconscionable at the time of enforcement. An otherwise unenforceable provision in a premarital agreement regarding spousal support may not become enforceable solely because the party against whom enforcement is sought was represented by independent counsel.

SECTION 2. Section 1615 of the Family Code is amended to read:

1615. (a) A premarital agreement is not enforceable if the party against whom enforcement is sought proves either of the following:

(1) That party did not execute the agreement voluntarily.

(2) The agreement was unconscionable when it was executed and, before execution of the agreement, all of the following applied to that party:

(A) That party was not provided a fair, reasonable, and *full* disclosure of the property or financial obligations of the other party.

(B) That party did not voluntarily and expressly waive, in writing, any right to disclosure of the property or financial obligations of the other party beyond the disclosure provided.

• (C) That party did not have, or reasonably could not have had, an adequate knowledge of the property or financial obligations of the other party.

(b) An issue of unconscionability of a premarital agreement shall be decided by the court as a matter of law.

• *(c) For the purposes of subdivision (a), it shall be deemed that a premarital agreement was not executed voluntarily unless the court finds in writing or on the record all of the following:*

(1) The party against whom enforcement is sought was represented by independent legal counsel at the time of signing the agreement or, after being advised to seek independent legal counsel, expressly waived, in a separate writing, representation by independent legal counsel.

(2) The party against whom enforcement is sought had not less than seven calendar days between the time that party was first presented with the agreement and advised to seek independent legal counsel and the time the agreement was signed.

(3) The party against whom enforcement is sought, if unrepresented by legal counsel, was fully informed of the terms and basic effect of the agreement as well as the rights and obligations he or she was giving up by signing the agreement, and was proficient in the language in which the explanation of the party's rights was conducted and in which the agreement was written. The explanation of the rights and obligations relinquished shall be memorialized in writing and delivered to the party prior to signing the agreement. The

unrepresented party shall, on or before the signing of the premarital agreement, execute a document declaring that he or she received the information required by this paragraph and indicating who provided that information.

(4) The agreement and the writings executed pursuant to paragraphs (1) and (3) were not executed under duress, fraud, or undue influence, and the parties did not lack capacity to enter into the agreement.

(5) Any other factors the court deems relevant.

Notes and Questions

1. *The history of S.B. 78.* As originally introduced on January 11, 2001, S.B. 78 would have reversed *Pendleton* by explicitly excluding spousal support from the list of subjects about which parties may contract. It would have amended Family Code section 1612(b) to read: "The right of a child *or a spouse* to support may not be adversely affected by a premarital agreement." 2001 Cal. S.B. 78, Jan. 11, 2001. Blanket exclusion was later abandoned in favor of making spousal support waivers unenforceable under certain circumstances. Additionally, the first version of the bill would have extended the fiduciary duties of spouses to prospective spouses negotiating a premarital agreement. Id. This provision was later abandoned entirely.

2. *Waivers and limitations of spousal support.* S.B. 78 provides that a premarital contract term concerning spousal support is unenforceable if the party resisting enforcement was not represented by independent counsel or the provision is unconscionable at the time of enforcement. With the second condition, California joins the jurisdictions allowing a "second look" at dissolution. However, unlike most second-look jurisdictions, California limits its second look to spousal support, in contrast to property distribution.

Who has the burden of proof on whether (a) the resisting party was represented by independent counsel and (b) the provision is unconscionable at the time of enforcement?

3. *"If the provision . . . is unconscionable at the time of enforcement."* Strictly speaking, unconscionability refers to the time of execution, not the time of enforcement. Moreover, it is not the provision itself that is unconscionable, but rather its enforcement at dissolution. (For these reasons, section 7.05 of the ALI Principles requires the divorce court to determine that enforcement of an otherwise enforceable term of a premarital agreement "would not work a substantial injustice.") Nevertheless, other second-look states have employed the language of S.B. 78, and thus there is considerable guidance for California courts as they interpret S.B. 78. For example, New Jersey's modification of the UPAA provides that an agreement is unenforceable if it is unconscionable at the time enforcement is sought (N.J. Stat. Ann. §37:2-38) and defines unconscionability as follows:

> "Unconscionable premarital agreement" means an agreement, either due to lack of property or unemployability:
> (1) Which would render a spouse without a means of reasonable support;
> (2) Which would make a spouse a public charge; or
> (3) Which would provide a standard of living far below that which was enjoyed before the marriage.

N.J. Stat. Ann. §37:2-32. For further discussion of the New Jersey "unconscionability at divorce" standard, see Charlotte K. Goldberg, "If It Ain't Broke, Don't Fix It": Premarital Agreements and Spousal Support Waivers in California, 33 Loy. L.A. L.Rev 1245, 1261-1270 (2000) (arguing for retention of the California ban on spousal support waivers or, as second best, a "second look" at divorce).

4. *The meaning of "not executed voluntarily."* S.B. 78 provides that execution was *not* voluntary unless a court determines that certain procedural requirements were met and the agreement was not executed under duress, fraud, undue influence, incapacity, or any other taint. Under section 1615(c), which party has the burden of proof? Compare section 1615(a). Which subsection is controlling?

S.B. 78 may curtail judicial propensity to find that a premarital agreement was executed voluntarily. In Marriage of Iverson, 11 Cal. App. 4th 1495, 15 Cal. Rptr. 2d 70 (1992), the trial judge expected that his decision would be appealed and said, "I want whoever reviews this to be able to have the benefit of my reasoning." Thus, in his oral statement of decision he was remarkably candid in explaining why he concluded that the wife's execution of the premarital agreement was voluntary. His exceptional candor was rewarded by appellate reversal, the court of appeal finding that the statement of decision was "so replete with gender bias that we are forced to conclude [the wife] could not have received a fair trial." Id. at 1496. Nevertheless, the trial court's colorful analysis illuminates the relative bargaining positions of the parties to a premarital agreement and how those positions may influence a trial court's finding on whether the party resisting the agreement executed it voluntarily.

5. *Application of S.B. 78.* As enacted in 1985, section 1601 provides that the CPAA "is effective on and after January 1, 1986, and applies to any premarital agreement executed on or after that date." S.B. 78 contains no effective date. It was signed into law by the governor on September 10, 2001. Article 4, section 8 of the California Constitution provides that "a statute enacted at a regular session shall go into effect on January 1 next following a 90-day period from the date of enactment of the statute." Should S.B. 78 apply only to agreements entered after its effective date, January 1, 2002?

At a pre-enactment hearing, opponents of S.B. 78 expressed concern about retroactive application of the bill to spousal support waivers executed before 2002, in reliance on *Pendleton*. The sponsors of the S.B. 78 responded:

> This bill contains no provision for retroactive application. As a general rule, laws operate prospectively unless retroactive application is provided for specifically, or unless the new legislation clarifies existing law.

S.B. 78 Bill Analysis, Senate Judiciary Committee, Apr. 24, 2001. Did the sponsors answer yes or no to the question of retroactive application?

Retroactive application is not solely a question of legislative intent. Even if legislation purports to apply to contracts entered before its effective date, retroactive application may violate the due process clause. See pages 192–210 infra. By contrast, judicial decisions are routinely applied retroactively. *Pendleton* is illustrative. When the Pendleton premarital agreement was executed, spousal support waivers were not enforceable. Nevertheless, the Pendleton waiver was enforced after the supreme court reformulated the spousal support rule in *Pendleton*. Is the distinction between judge-made law and legislation justifiable?

C. PREMARITAL AGREEMENTS: THE STATUTE OF FRAUDS AND AVOIDANCE TECHNIQUES

CALIFORNIA FAMILY CODE SECTION 1611

§1611. Formalities; consideration

A premarital agreement shall be in writing and signed by both parties. It is enforceable without consideration.

1. *Executed Oral Agreements*

FREITAS v. FREITAS
31 Cal. App. 16, 159 P. 611 (1916)

THE COURT. — The plaintiff in this case is the widow of Manuel T. Freitas, deceased. The defendants, Manuel F. Freitas, Jr., Mary Freitas Lopez, Francisco Freitas, and Anna Freitas Nula are the children of said deceased by a former marriage. The defendant Unica Portugueza de Estada da California is a beneficiary corporation. The complaint in substance alleged, and the trial court in effect found, that the plaintiff was induced to marry Manuel T. Freitas, since deceased, by an antenuptial agreement, wherein he promised the plaintiff that if she would marry him he would make her the beneficiary of a policy of life insurance in the sum of one thousand dollars which he then held and which had been issued to him by the corporation defendant. Upon his marriage to the plaintiff Freitas, with the intent and purpose of performing his antenuptial promise, caused the plaintiff to be named as the beneficiary in the policy of insurance, and thereupon delivered the same to her. Subsequently he secured possession of the policy and, without the consent or knowledge of the plaintiff, caused the children above mentioned to be substituted as beneficiaries, and they were the beneficiaries named in the policy at the time of his death.

The corporation defendant did not defend against the action, but deposited in court the amount called for in the policy subject to a determination of the conflicting claims of the plaintiff and the other defendants.

Judgment was rendered for the plaintiff, from which the individual defendants alone have appealed. . . .

The evidence supports the findings, and the findings support the judgment. While the evidence shows, and the court in effect found, that the antenuptial agreement was not expressed in writing, nevertheless the evidence further shows, and the court found, that in keeping with his agreement and the consideration of the plaintiff's marriage to him, Freitas, the insured, procured her to be designated as the beneficiary of the sum secured by the policy of insurance. The antenuptial contract thereby became fully executed (Supreme Lodge v. Ferrell, 83 Kan. 491, [33 L.R.A. (N. S.) 777, 112 Pac. 155]) and it is settled law that the statute of frauds has no application to an executed oral agreement (Bates v. Babcock, 95 Cal. 479, 488, [29 Am. St. Rep. 133, 16 L.R.A. 745, 30 Pac. 605]).

The judgment appealed from is affirmed.

A petition to have the cause heard in the supreme court, after judgment in the district court of appeal, was denied by the supreme court on August 25, 1916.

2. *Estoppel to Assert the Statute of Frauds*

ESTATE OF SHELDON
75 Cal. App. 3d 364, 142 Cal. Rptr. 119 (1977)

[Estate of Sheldon involves the interplay of an antenuptial mutual waiver of death rights and former Probate Code section 70, which provided that a will written by a decedent *before* marriage was revoked as to the surviving spouse unless certain conditions were satisfied. When the will was revoked as to the surviving spouse under section 70, the surviving spouse took an intestate share under former sections 220 and 221. Sections 70 and 220 are reprinted in footnotes 1 and 2 of the opinion. Current Probate Code sections 21610, 21611, and 21612 reach the same result in a slightly different manner.]

BROWN (G. A.), P.J. — In January 1974 the decedent, 80-year-old Florence Sheldon, married 78-year-old Al Sheldon. About eight months later, on September 14, 1974, Florence died testate, she having drawn a valid holographic will on April 19, 1972, which, aside from some conditional specific gifts to her grandchildren, left her estate in equal shares to her two children by a prior marriage. They are petitioner and appellant. Oscar Marion Huffman (hereinafter Marion), and contestant and appellant, Helen Peterson (hereinafter Helen). No provision was made in the premarriage will for her surviving husband, Al, nor was he mentioned in the will.

On September 19, 1974, and January 3, 1975, Al assigned his interest in decedent's estate to Helen and her husband, Duane Peterson.

Thereafter Marion filed a petition to determine heirship and Helen and her husband filed a statement of claim of interest in the estate based upon the assignments from Al. Since Helen's and her husband's claim (other than to what Helen is entitled as a named devisee and legatee under the will) is grounded on the assignments from Al, the ultimate issue herein is whether Al has a claim to one-third of the estate (see Prob. Code, §221 [now Prob. Code §6401(c)(3)]) by virtue of the provisions of probate Code section 70[1] and, assuming Probate Code section 70 operates to revoke the will as to Al, the effect of Probate Code section 220.[2]

---

1. Probate Code section 70 provides: "If a person marries after making a will, and the spouse survives the maker, the will is revoked as to the spouse, unless provision has been made for the spouse by marriage contract, or unless the spouse is provided for in the will, or in such way mentioned therein as to show an intention not to make such provision; and no other evidence to rebut the presumption of revocation can be received."

2. Probate Code section 220 provides: "The separate property of a person who dies without disposing of it by will is succeeded to and must be distributed as hereinafter provided, *subject to the limitation of any marriage or other contract. . . .*" (Italics added.)

Marion contends that there was an antenuptial oral contract between the decedent and Al by the terms of which the decedent and Al agreed that neither would share in the other's estate; that the oral contract qualifies under Probate Code section 70 as a marriage contract under which provision is made for Al, thus preventing the revocation of the will as to him. Marion further agrees that if it does not so qualify under Probate Code section 70 . . . then the contract does qualify under the provisions of Probate Code section 220 which makes intestate succession under Probate Code section 221 "subject to the limitation of any marriage or other contract. . . ."

The case was submitted to the jury for its advisory verdict; the jury found that Al had no right to inherit any of the property of the decedent. By a special verdict the jury also found that there was a contract between the decedent and Al by which he agreed not to accept any inheritance from her estate and that decedent relied on the contract and changed her position to her detriment. The court entered findings of fact and conclusions of law which followed the special verdict and also found and concluded that, though oral, the contract was legally binding and enforceable because it was an executed and fully performed oral agreement, and that Helen and her husband were estopped to insist that the contract be in writing because decedent changed her position to her detriment in reliance upon the oral contract. . . .

Marion relies upon a line of cases holding that a fully executed prenuptial agreement does not have to be in writing to be enforceable. . . .

All of the cases are distinguishable. The principal ones relied upon are Estate of Dokoozlian (1963) 219 Cal. App. 2d 531 [33 Cal. Rptr. 151], Estate of Piatt (1947) 81 Cal. App. 2d 348 [183 P.2d 919], and Freitas v. Freitas (1916) 31 Cal. App. 16 [159 P. 611]. In Dokoozlian the court held that the trial court erred in rejecting an offer of proof that there was an oral prenuptial agreement between the decedent husband and the surviving wife under which the husband agreed to and in fact did convey certain property and bank accounts to both of them in satisfaction of any claim of the wife to the husband's estate. The court held the testimony was admissible to show a fully performed oral antenuptial agreement which would not be barred by [Family Code section 1611]. . . .

Freitas v. Freitas . . . held the statute of frauds had no application to an executed oral agreement whereby a deceased husband induced the surviving wife to marry him upon the representation that if she would do so he would make her beneficiary of a life insurance policy. After marriage he designated her as the beneficiary pursuant to the agreement and delivered the policy to her. Later, without her knowledge, he named others as the beneficiaries. The court held the oral agreement was enforceable notwithstanding . . . [Family Code section 1611]. (See also Higgins v. Jennings (1920) 46 Cal. App. 135 [188 P. 847].)

These cases are distinguishable from the case sub judice. First, the cause at bench is not concerned with the changing of the character of the ownership of property between husband and wife by oral agreement. Secondly, insofar as any of the above cases refer to full execution of the agreement they involved affirmative acts pursuant to the agreement, such as the transfer of title to assets, whereas in this cause the decedent's activities were wholly passive, that is, a refraining from action. However, it is unnecessary for us to decide whether purely passive conduct can amount to performance of an oral contract so as to take it out of the requirement for a writing because we decide the case on other grounds. . . .

Marion . . . argues that Helen is estopped to assert the statute of frauds. Marion can rely upon this theory even though neither he nor Helen was a party to the original contract. (Monarco v. Lo Greco (1950) 35 Cal. 2d 621, 627 [220 P.2d 737].)

> In those cases . . . where either an unconscionable injury or unjust enrich-
> ment would result from refusal to enforce the contract, the doctrine of estop-
> pel has been applied. . . .

The jury and the court found that decedent relied upon Al's oral promise not to share in her estate to her detriment, she having forgone any claim to Al's estate should he [sic] have survived her [sic], having not comingled her assets with his and she having not changed her will. (See Monarco v. Lo Greco, supra, 35 Cal. 2d 621, 622 — change of position can consist of act of dying without changing will to provide for heirs.)

[In an omitted portion of the opinion, the court also noted Florence's "state-ment to her granddaughter that the agreement removed her 'reluctance' to marry Al."]

However, following the precise holding in Estate of Tassi (1961) 196 Cal. App. 2d 494, 504-505 [16 Cal. Rptr. 616], we hold proof of an estoppel would violate the specific terms of section 70 providing that "no other evidence to rebut the presumption of revocation can be received." That case stated: "It is apparent to us that, under this statute, the presumption of revocation which arises when a testator marries after making a will can be rebutted *only* by evidence in support of the spe-cific defenses set forth within the section itself. Since the statute makes no mention of estoppel as a permissible defense, we conclude that claimant's offer of proof was properly denied pursuant to the express wording of the section that "no other evidence to rebut the presumption of revocation can be received." (196 Cal. App. 2d at p.505.) As was said in Estate of Turney (1951) 101 Cal. App. 2d 720, 722 [226 P.2d 80], referring to section 70, "A party seeking to rebut the statutory presump-tion of revocation must bring himself within the literal terms of one of the excep-tions." . . .

Clearly, though, no such restriction is contained in Probate Code section 220. Therefore, the theory of estoppel to assert that the contract should be in writing furnishes a legal basis for the court's findings and conclusions that Al (and thus Helen and her husband) was not entitled to inherit an intestate share of the dece-dent's estate. Accordingly, the decision was not against the law.

HOPPER, J., and HANSON (P. D.), J., concurred.

Notes and Questions

1. Probate Code sections 70 and 220 did not work smoothly in the face of an enforceable premarital waiver of death rights. Under section 70, the will was re-voked as to the surviving spouse because the waiver did not furnish the statutorily required "provision . . . for the spouse by marriage contract," but the surviving spouse could not take in intestacy under section 220 because the premarital agree-ment was effective to waive this right. It was clear that the surviving spouse took nothing, but not clear whether the revoked portion of the estate should pass to decedent's will beneficiaries or to her intestate heirs. The current successor provis-ions to sections 70 and 220 are Probate Code sections 21610-21612. The current

provisions contemplate the possibility of a premarital waiver of death rights and provide a clear resolution of this issue.

2. Which facts, if any, support the conclusion that Florence relied to her detriment on Al's oral promise that he would not make any claim against her estate? Evaluate the trial court finding of detrimental reliance.

3. Suppose that you had interviewed Florence at her wedding reception. If you had asked her whether and how she had relied, or would rely, on Al's premarital waiver, what do you imagine she would have responded?

4. Should marriage alone work an estoppel to assert the statute of frauds? Cf. Hall v. Hall, 222 Cal. App. 3d 578, 586, 271 Cal. Rptr. 773 (1990): "It [is] well established that marriage itself . . . [is] not sufficient performance to take an oral prenuptial agreement out of the writing requirement of the statute. . . ." Why is marriage insufficient as performance and insufficient to raise an estoppel?

5. Was the parties' oral contract executed after marriage? Can you frame an argument for Florence that does more than simply restate her estoppel argument?

6. *Enactment of the California Premarital Agreement Act.* In 1985, California adopted a modified version of the Uniform Premarital Agreement Act (UPAA), which applies to agreements *made* after 1985. The California Premarital Agreement Act (CPAA) is codified at Family Code sections 1600 to 1617.

The CPAA has been judicially interpreted to preserve case law exceptions to the statute of frauds, namely, the execution and estoppel exceptions illustrated in *Freitas* and *Sheldon,* supra. Hall v. Hall, 222 Cal. App. 3d 578, 587, 271 Cal. Rptr. 773 (1990).

D. TRANSMUTATION DURING MARRIAGE

1. Pre-1985 Transmutation

Prior to 1985, there were no formal requirements for property agreements made *during,* as opposed to *before,* marriage. California Civil Code section 5103 (now Family Code section 721) simply stated: ". . . either husband or wife may enter into any transaction with the other, or with any other person, respecting property, which either might if unmarried." What considerations support a distinction between premarital agreements and agreements made during marriage?

DISTINCTION BTWN AGREEMENTS DURING & B/4 MARRIAGE.

ESTATE OF RAPHAEL
91 Cal. App. 2d 931, 206 P.2d 391 (1949)

WARD, J. — As administrator and as brother and heir at law of the deceased, Harry Raphael appeals from the judgment and modified judgment decreeing "that all of the estate of Raymond Theodore Raphael, both real and personal, on the date of the death of said deceased was the community property of Raymond Theodore Raphael and his widow, Bertha Rado Raphael." . . .

The lower court made the following findings: . . . that at the time of the marriage of the . . . decedent, Raymond Theodore Raphael, and his . . . widow, Bertha Rado Raphael, . . . all of the estate owned or possessed by Raymond Theodore Raphael was his own separate property; that subsequent to the date of said marriage . . . Raymond Theodore Raphael transmuted all of his property, both real and personal, from its previous separate character to the community property of . . . Raymond Theodore Raphael and Bertha Rado Raphael, his wife, by an oral agreement which was fully executed and corroborated by documentary evidence including income tax returns filed by or on behalf of Raymond Theodore Raphael and his . . . wife, Bertha Rado Raphael. . . .

The basic contention made on this appeal is that . . . the findings are not supported by the record. In disposing of such a contention, this court's power begins and ends with a determination as to whether there is any substantial evidence to support the findings. (Estate of Bristol, 23 Cal. 2d 21 [143 P.2d 689]; Estate of Meister, 77 Cal. App. 2d 487 [175 P.2d 574].)

. . . Respondent testified that she and the deceased, a cripple, were married in August, 1939 — about nine months before he inherited the property from his mother. Death occurred on February 20, 1946. Over appellant's objections that income tax returns would not prove title to the property, respondent was shown certain certified copies of income tax returns for the years 1940 through 1945. These were subsequently received by the trial court. She identified that 1940 return as a joint return for her husband and herself, whereas the 1941 through 1944 returns were her returns in which she reported half of the total earnings of her husband and herself. She related various conversations with the deceased. The weight of such testimony as to the statements of her deceased husband was for the trial court to determine. (Estate of Henderson, 128 Cal. App. 397 [17 P.2d 786].) It was for the court to believe or disbelieve her when she testified that in February, 1940, "He told me that now that we were married, that we were partners, and marriage is a partnership, and we had to file taxes, and he said that everything he had was mine, and everything I had was his; that we were partners in everything, and everything was fifty-fifty"; that at about the time the 1941 income tax return was prepared he told her, "Now we are partners, and, dear, everything is fifty-fifty, and you have half and I have half; we are partners in everything"; and that when the 1942 return was filed, "he said that we were making some money, and that we were partners in everything . . . that everything we had, we had with each other.". . .

An examination of other cases in which testimony of an oral agreement was held to constitute sufficient proof to support a finding that separate property had been transmuted into community property, indicates that the conclusion reached by the trial court in the present case must be upheld. In Kenney v. Kenney, 220 Cal. 134 [30 P.2d 398], the husband testified that the parties had orally agreed, both before and after marriage, that all property then owned by them or subsequently acquired was to belong to them equally or "fifty-fifty." The appellate court observed in Stice v. Stice, 81 Cal. App. 2d 72, 798 [185 P.2d 402], that "the wife testified that the husband 'always said that everything we had was community property — belonged to both of us,' and that 'he said it hundreds of times.' The weight and effect of these items of evidence was, of course, a matter for the trial court to determine." In Durrell v. Bacon, 138 Cal. App. 396, 398 [32 P.2d 644], the husband testified that his wife — who had separate property — told him "what is mine is yours and what is yours is mine . . . this money will go into a home for us; it is just as much yours as mine.". . .

This is not the first case in which income tax returns showing that community income was split between the spouses have been found to constitute proof of the transmutation of property. In Heck v. Heck, 63 Cal. App. 2d 470, 475 [147 P.2d 110], the appellate court upheld the trial court's construction of "the income tax returns as evidencing an agreement between plaintiff and defendant converting one-half of plaintiff's separate interest in the partnership profits into community property." (Followed in Stice v. Stice, supra.) All that is required to show an executed oral agreement of transmutation is proof of the parties' acts and conduct in dealing with their property. (Kenney v. Kenney, supra.) In an executory contract some act remains to be done, while in an executed contract everything is completed at the time of the agreement without any outstanding promise calling for fulfillment by the further act of either party. (Mather v. Mather, 25 Cal. 2d 582 [154 P.2d 684].) The object of the oral agreement of transmutation was fully performed when the agreement was made for it immediately transmuted and converted the separate property of each spouse into community property, and nothing further remained to be done. (See Martin v. Pritchard, 52 Cal. App. 720 [199 P. 846].) The income tax returns for 1941 through 1944 constitute evidence of the fact that the parties regarded their property as community property. . . .

— TEST

There is no merit to appellant's contention that the executed oral agreement found by the trial court lacks all the necessary requisites of a valid contract in that it is indefinite and uncertain and therefore unenforceable. The authorities previously cited indicate that the agreement of transmutation may be of the most informal character. (Kenney v. Kenney, supra; Stice v. Stice, supra; Estate of Sill, 121 Cal. App. 202 [9 P.2d 243]; and see cases cited, 3 Cal. Jur. 10-Yr. Supp. 641.) The "change in the *status* of the property may be shown by the very nature of the transaction or appear from the surrounding circumstances." (Marvin v. Marvin, 46 Cal. App. 2d 551, 556 [116 P.2d 151], quoting Title Insurance etc. Co. v. Ingersoll, 153 Cal. 1, 5 [94 P. 94].)

Similarly, there is no merit to appellant's contention that the oral agreement was one of partnership only. In Martin v. Pritchard, supra, the husband testified that he and his wife had a "matrimonial partnership." The court held, at page 724, that this evidence was "not such as to require the court to find that [the wife's] interest was joint, or in common or a partnership interest rather than that of community property." The use of the term "partner" in the popular sense does not necessarily import or imply an intention that a legal partership should result. (Kloke v. Pongratz, 38 Cal. App. 2d 395 [101 P.2d 522].) . . .

The judgment is affirmed.

PETERS, P.J., and BRAY, J., concurred.

Appellant's petition for a hearing by the Supreme Court was denied July 14, 1949. SCHAUER, J., voted for a hearing.

Notes and Questions

1. When did Raymond Raphael's separate property become the community property of his marriage to Bertha? When Raymond married Bertha? When Raymond said, after marriage, that he and Bertha were "fifty-fifty . . . partners"? When they filed their 1941 tax returns?

2. Raymond's oral transmutation affected all his property, both real and personal. The statute of frauds, which covers most realty transfers, is generally inappli-

cable to pre-1985 spousal transmutation. A writing may be required, however, to transmute separate or community property into joint tenancy. Cal. Civ. Code §683. Estate of Harris, 9 Cal. 2d 649, 662, 72 P.2d 873 (1937). Why should a writing be required to effect a transmutation into joint tenancy, but not into community property? Cf. Estate of Baglione, 65 Cal. 2d 192, 197, 417 P.2d 683, 53 Cal. Rptr. 139 (1996).

MARRIAGE OF JAFEMAN
29 Cal. App. 3d 244, 105 Cal. Rptr. 483 (1972)

[When Edward married Mary, he already owned the house that is the subject of this dispute in a divorce proceeding.]

. . . It is apparent that the trial court's finding that the residence is community property may be upheld only if the record presents substantial evidence of an implied agreement between the parties to alter the character of Edward's initial equity in the home. It is true that Mary and Edward lived in the home during their marriage. However, mere use of property in the marital relationship does not alter its character. (Mears v. Mears, 180 Cal. App. 2d 484, 498 [4 Cal. Rptr. 618]; Kenney v. Kenney, 128 Cal. App. 2d 128, 135 [274 P.2d 951].) It is also true that during the first 12 years of marriage, Mary managed the family finances and applied community funds toward meeting the house payments and maintaining and improving the property. However, [Mary's] use of community funds to improve the separate property of [her] spouse does not effect a change in the character of the separate property.[2] (Spreng v. Spreng, 119 Cal. App. 155, 159 [6 P.2d 104].) Moreover, the possession and management by one spouse of the separate property of another does not in and of itself demonstrate that the spouse to whom the property belonged intended to relinquish it to the community. However, such an intent may be shown by the nature of the transaction or by the surrounding circumstances. (Title Insurance, etc. Co. v. Ingersoll, 153 Cal. 1, 5 [94 P. 94].) In addition, the acts of the parties and their dealing with the property may establish that they intended a community interest. (Estate of Nelson, 224 Cal. App. 2d 138, 143 [36 Cal. Rptr. 352]; Lawatch v. Lawatch, 161 Cal. App. 2d 780, 789 [327 P.2d 603].) The trial court apparently felt that these principles were applicable for it found that "upon the basis that after fourteen years of the aforesaid application of community funds, the clear import of the husband's conduct refutes his contention and affirms that of wife."

Turning to the record, the only evidence of conduct by Edward which related to the character of the property was testimony concerning the manner in which he referred to the residence. The testimony on this point was in conflict. Mary testified, without objection, that they always referred to the residence as "our home." Edward contended that they always distinguished between his house and Mary's house. The trial court was entitled to resolve this conflict by crediting Mary's

---

2. Note that the issue in this excerpt is whether there was "an implied agreement between the parties to alter the character of Edward's initial equity in the home." The use of community funds to reduce the principal of the purchase-money debt and to improve the property may give rise to other narrower claims for partial community ownership and for reimbursement of community funds expended on improvements. See casebook infra at 211-215, 259-269. — Ed.

testimony. Nevertheless, the mere fact that Edward referred to the residence as "our home" does not constitute substantial evidence of an intent to relinquish his separate interest in the property. (Cf. Long v. Long, 88 Cal. App. 2d 544, 549 [199 P.2d 47] [other comments by husband respecting the community character of other property]; Lawatch v. Lawatch, supra, 161 Cal. App. 2d 780, 790 [commingling of funds and filing joint tax returns with respect to income from the property]; Estate of Nelson, supra, 224 Cal. App. 2d 138, 143-144 [filing joint tax returns].)

NO JOINT TAX RETURNS

The record does not contain any other evidence tending to show an implied agreement to alter the character of Edward's interest. Edward never had the title to the property put in both parties' names.

The only evidence on this issue adduced by Mary was her testimony that "I thought it was our property." Apparently, on the basis of this testimony, the court found "that although the question of title to 133 Hickory Lane . . . was never discussed, it was the belief of [Mary] that said property was community property of the marriage. [Mary] did not learn that title was not in their joint names . . . until shortly before filing the within action for divorce in October, 1968."

It has been held that testimony of the hidden beliefs of a party is ineffective to show that a joint tenancy deed is not reflective of the character of the property. (Machado v. Machado, 58 Cal. 2d 501, 506 [25 Cal. Rptr. 87, 375 P.2d 55]; Gudelj v. Gudelj, 41 Cal. 2d 202, 212 [259 P.2d 656]; Socol v. King, 36 Cal. 2d 342, 346 [223 P.2d 627]; Watson v. Peyton, 10 Cal. 2d 156, 158 [73 P.2d 906].) An analogous conclusion is warranted by the facts of the instant case. Although it might be found that testimony by a husband as to his undisclosed intent to transmute his separate property to community property has probative value, the same cannot be said of testimony by a wife as to her undisclosed beliefs respecting her husband's property. Such testimony has no probative value as to the intent of the husband and it is not effective to show an implied agreement between the parties to alter the character of the husband's property. . . .

SPOUSE BELIEVING IT WAS CP IS NOT ENOUGH

As the finding of the trial court that the residence at 133 Hickory Lane is community property is not supported by the evidence, that portion of the judgment awarding each party an undivided one-half interest in the property must be reversed, and the matter must be remanded for further proceedings in order that the proportionate interests of the community and of Edward in the property may be ascertained. . . .

Notes and Questions

1. Compare Estate of Nelson, 224 Cal. App. 2d 138, 36 Cal. Rptr. 352 (1964):

CA: DISTINCTION BASED ON TAX RETURNS

> . . . The appellant argues that the trial court erred in finding that the apartment house was community property. The court found that, at the time of the marriage, the property was the separate property of the deceased but had subsequently been transmuted into community property by an executed oral agreement. The separate property of one spouse can be converted into community property by a mere oral agreement. . . . This transmutation may be proved by the acts of the parties and their conduct in dealing with the property (Estate of Raphael, 91 Cal. App. 2d 931, 939 [206 P.2d 391]). No express or formal agreement is required (Long v. Long, 88 Cal. App. 2d 544, 549 [199 P.2d 47]) if it may be fairly inferred from all the circumstances and

evidence that a community interest was intended by the parties (Linville v. Linville, 132 Cal. App. 2d 800, 802 [283 P.2d 34]). Nelson not only referred to the property as the mutual property of the parties but also frequently expressed a desire to provide for his wife. Furthermore, Mrs. Nelson's management of the property, the conduct of the parties during the marriage, the joint state income tax returns filed from 1949 to 1952, at a time when the state did not permit such joint returns unless the income reported was community property, were additional evidence of an executed oral agreement. Whether the statements and conduct of Nelson indicated an intent to transmute his separate property into a community interest was a question for the trier of fact (Linville v. Linville, supra) and we conclude that there is clearly sufficient evidence to support the court's finding in this regard. . . .

Can you reconcile *Jafeman* and *Nelson*?

2. In *Raphael,* the couple's 1941-1944 federal income tax returns provided corroborative evidence of Mr. Raphael's oral transmutation of his separate property into the couple's community property because the Raphaels could not lawfully have split their income unless it came from community sources. In 1948, however, the federal government enacted optional nationwide income-splitting for all married couples without regard to ownership of the income-producing property. See Bittker, Federal Income Taxation and the Family, 27 Stan. L. Rev. 1389, 1404-1414 (1975). Thus joint federal filing (income-splitting) after 1947 does not provide any evidence of transmutation from separate to community property. As *Nelson* indicates, California maintained the pre-1948 federal rules until 1952, that is, California allowed state income tax payers to split income only with respect to jointly owned property. Thus, California income tax returns for years prior to 1953 may provide corroborative evidence of transmutation.

3. California case law was uniquely liberal in recognizing transmutation during marriage. See generally W. Reppy, Jr., and C. Samuel, Community Property in the United States 24-49 (2d. ed. 1982).

4. Do you approve the California courts' liberal treatment of transmutation? Does it matter whether the issue is raised in a death or a divorce case? Does it matter whether the alleged transmutation is from separate to community or vice versa? Might it be appropriate to treat separate to community transmutation liberally but use stricter standards with community to separate transmutation? California law makes no such distinction. In view of this, what policies were furthered by the California courts' liberal treatment of transmutation?

2.   *Post-1984 Transmutation*

— MOST MUST BE IN WRITING SIGNED OR ACCEPTED BY ADVERSLY AFFECTED PARTY.

In 1984, the legislature enacted provisions requiring that most post-1984 transmutations be supported by a writing signed or accepted by the spouse whose ownership interest in the property is adversely affected. 1984 Cal. Stat., ch. 1733, enacting Civil Code sections 5110.710-5110.730. These provisions have been recodified as California Family Code sections 850-853.

§850.   Transmutation of property by agreement or
transfer

Subject to Sections 851 to 853, inclusive, married persons may by agreement or transfer, with or without consideration, do any of the following:

(a) Transmute community property to separate property of either spouse.

(b) Transmute separate property of either spouse to community property.

(c) Transmute separate property of one spouse to separate property of the other spouse.

§851. Fraudulent transfers laws apply

A transmutation is subject to the laws governing fraudulent transfers.

§852. Form of transmutation

(a) A transmutation of real or personal property is not valid unless made in writing by an express declaration that is made, joined in, consented to, or accepted by the spouse whose interest in the property is adversely affected.

· (b) A transmutation of real property is not effective as to third parties without notice thereof unless recorded.

(c) This section does not apply to a gift between the spouses of clothing, wearing apparel, jewelry, or other tangible articles of a personal nature that is used solely or principally by the spouse to whom the gift is made and that is not substantial in value taking into account the circumstances of the marriage.

(d) Nothing in this section affects the law governing characterization of property in which separate property and community property are commingled or otherwise combined.

(e) This section does not apply to or affect a transmutation of property made before January 1, 1985, and the law that would otherwise be applicable to that transmutation shall continue to apply.

§853. Effect of will

A statement in a will of the character of property is not admissible as evidence of a transmutation of the property in a proceeding commenced before the death of the person who made the will.

Notes and Questions

1. What is the purpose of Family Code section 853? Suppose that last year Henry wrote a will reciting: "All the property of which I am possessed is the community property of my marriage to Wilma." This year Henry brings a divorce action to dissolve his marriage to Wilma, and Henry claims certain property he brought into marriage as his separate property. Wilma would like to introduce Henry's will as evidence that he transmuted his separate property into the couple's community property. May she? — ▷ No!.

Section 853 reverses prior case law. See, for example, Marriage of Lotz, 120 Cal. App. 3d 379, 386, 174 Cal. Rptr. 618 (1981). Do you approve its enactment?

2. *Fraudulent transfers.* The law of fraudulent transfers, incorporated by reference in section 851, is intended to protect the interests of creditors. Civil Code section 3439.04 provides that a transfer is fraudulent as to a creditor if it is made "[w]ith actual intent to hinder, delay, or defraud any creditor of the debtor." In State Board of Equalization v. Woo, 82 Cal. App. 4th 481, 98 Cal. Rptr. 2d 206

(2000), the wife asserted that her wages could not be garnished to satisfy her husband's tax liability because the parties had entered a formally adequate agreement transmuting her future wages into her separate property. The transmutation was ineffective as to the tax creditor because it was made after the couple learned that the creditor intended to garnish the wife's wages to satisfy a debt for which community property was liable. Query whether the transmutation was nevertheless effective as between the husband and wife.

In Mejia v. Reed, 118 Cal. Rptr. 2d 415 (2002), the husband was ordered to pay support for a child he fathered outside of marriage. Soon thereafter he and his wife obtained a divorce, and their marital settlement agreement, merged into their dissolution judgment, assigned the husband's medical practice to him and assigned all the other community property to the wife, with the effect that the property assigned to the wife was no longer liable for the husband's child support obligations (see Family Code §916(a)(2)). The former husband subsequently abandoned his medical practice and earned no income. The child's mother sought to subject the property distribution to the Uniform Fraudulent Transfer Act (UFTA), Civil Code §3429 et seq., which includes as "fraudulent" any transfer for less than "a reasonably equivalent value in exchange for the transfer and the debtor . . . became insolvent as a result of the transfer" (Civil Code §3439.05). The child's mother also claimed that the property distribution worked a transmutation and hence was subject to Family Code §851. The court of appeal held that a divorce-related property transfer between husband and wife at dissolution is not a transmutation for purposes of the transmutation sections of the Family Code, but that a marital settlement agreement is nevertheless subject to UFTA. The latter holding directly conflicts with Gagan v. Gouyd, 73 Cal. App. 4th 835 (1999), which holds that divorce settlements are not subject to UFTA. On June 12, 2002, the California Supreme Court granted review to *Mejia,* thus depublishing the judgment of the court of appeal.

3. How firm is the section 852 writing requirement? Recall that the statute of frauds for premarital agreements may be avoided by the doctrines of estoppel and execution. (See *Freitas* and *Sheldon* supra.) Should these exceptions apply equally to section 852? If not, greater formality is required for a post-1984 transmutation during marriage than for a prenuptial agreement. Is this result appropriate?

On the other hand, does Estate of MacDonald, which follows, invariably require a writing for post-1984 *marital* transmutation and thus rule out recourse to the estoppel and execution exceptions to the statute of frauds, which exceptions nevertheless remain available to enforce oral *premarital* agreements altering the character of the spouses' property?

In Marriage of Campbell, 74 Cal. App. 4th 1058, 88 Cal. Rptr. 2d 580 (1999), the wife claimed that during marriage the parties transmuted the husband's separate property home into community property. The wife sought to introduce extrinsic evidence in order to (1) estop the husband from asserting the section 852 statute of frauds (she allegedly spent $60,000 of her separate property funds to improve the husband's real property, in reliance on his promise to add her name to the title of the home) and (2) then prove that during marriage, by agreement, the parties orally transmuted the home into community property. Cf. Estate of Sheldon (supra at page 110), where the decedent's estate successfully followed this route to avoid the statute of frauds requirement for premarital agreements. *Campbell* declined to follow the ordinary statute of frauds exceptions applicable to *premarital* agreements and instead held that, with respect to *marital* transmutations, section 852 bars the admission of extrinsic evidence in order to raise an estoppel and allow proof of an oral transmutation of property between spouses. The California Supreme Court denied review.

THE CONTENT OF THE EXPRESS DECLARATION

ESTATE OF MACDONALD
51 Cal. 3d 262, 794 P.2d 911, 272 Cal. Rptr. 153 (1990)

PANELLI, J. — Civil Code section 5110.730, subdivision (a) [Family Code section 852(a)] provides: "A transmutation of real or personal property is not valid unless made in writing by an express declaration that is made, joined in, consented to, or accepted by the spouse whose interest in the property is adversely affected."

In this case we are asked to decide what type of writing is necessary to satisfy the statute's requirements. In our view, section [852(a)] must be construed to preclude reference to extrinsic evidence in the proof of transmutations. Accordingly, we conclude a writing is not an "express declaration" for the purposes of section [852(a)] unless it contains language which expressly states that a change in the characterization or ownership of the property is being made. Thus, we affirm the judgment of the Court of Appeal.

Decedent Margery M. MacDonald (Margery or decedent) married respondent Robert F. MacDonald (Robert) in 1973. Both had been married previously, and each had children by a previous spouse. Robert was president of R. F. MacDonald Company (the company), where he participated in a defined benefit pension plan.

In August 1984, Margery learned that she had terminal cancer, and she and Robert made plans to divide their property into separate estates. Wishing to leave her property to her own four children, Margery divided the couple's jointly held stock, sold her half, and placed the proceeds in her separate account. The MacDonalds thereafter consulted with their personal accountant and attorney regarding the division of their jointly held real property. These properties were appraised and divided; Robert paid Margery $33,000 to equalize the division.

Robert was covered by a company defined benefit pension plan which came into existence on January 1, 1977. The designated beneficiary of Robert's interest in the pension plan was a revocable living trust he had established in 1982. The terms of the trust left the bulk of the corpus to Robert's children. In November, 1984 Robert turned 65 and his defined pension plan was terminated. On March 21, 1985, Robert received a disbursement of $266,557.90 from the plan. It is undisputed that Margery possessed a community property interest in the plan's benefit. The pension funds were not divided or otherwise accounted for at the time of the couple's previous division of their jointly held assets. These community funds were deposited into IRA accounts at three separate financial institutions.

The IRA accounts were opened solely in Robert's name, the designated beneficiary of each being the revocable living trust which had been designated as beneficiary of the pension plan. The three form documents prepared by the financial institutions for signature by IRA account holders, each entitled "Adoption Agreement and Designation of Beneficiary" (adoption agreements), provided space for the signature of a spouse not designated as the sole primary beneficiary to indicate consent to the designation.[2] Robert signed the adoption agreements, indicating his agreement to the terms of the IRA account agreements and designating his trust as beneficiary; Margery signed the consent portions of the adoption agreements (consent paragraphs).

Margery died on June 17, 1985, bequeathing the residue of her estate to her four children. Executrix Judith Bolton filed a petition to determine title to personal property (Prob. Code, §851.5), seeking to establish decedent's community property interest in the funds held in the IRA accounts. The trial court found that, in signing the consent paragraphs of the adoption agreements, decedent intended to waive any community property interest in the pension funds and to transmute her community property share of those funds into Robert's separate property. The court denied Bolton's petition, ruling that decedent had either waived her community property interest in the pension funds or, alternatively, transmuted it to Robert's separate property.

The Court of Appeal reversed, holding that the adoption agreements did not satisfy section [852(a)]. . . . A dissenting justice argued that because decedent, in signing the consent paragraphs, had taken "specific, clear and final [action to] accomplish both [a] transfer and a subsequent transmutation[, t]he language and purpose of the statutory requirement were fully satisfied."

We grant review to construe section [852(a)].

It is undisputed that Margery possessed a community property interest in Robert's pension funds at the time they were disbursed to him. However, in California, married persons may by agreement or transfer, with or without consideration, transmute community property to separate property of either spouse.[3]

In this case, the trial court made a *factual finding* that "[d]ecedent, in executing the Adoption Agreement[s] for the three IRA's, intended to waive any community right she had in those IRA's and in fact to transmute her share of that community property asset to the separate property of Respondent." However, we defer to a trial court's factual findings only when they are supported by substantial evidence. (Crawford v. Southern Pacific Co. (1935) 3 Cal. 2d 427, 429 [45 P.2d 183].)

Our close review of the record reveals that no substantial evidence supported the finding that Margery intended a transmutation. . . . In fact, there is absolutely no record evidence relating to Margery's intentions or state of mind when she signed the adoption agreements. The only testimony presented as to her state of mind during her estate planning activities relates to when she and her husband arranged an equal division of their jointly held real properties. The couple's accountant testified that she did not assist them in the division of any other assets.

---

2. The adoption agreements are one page long. They provide space for the entry of "General Information" (where Robert entered his name, address, and other personal data), for "Designation of Beneficiary," for "Consent of Spouse," for "General Provisions" (relating to payout procedures upon the participant's death) and for "Adoption of Plan" (which Robert signed, agreeing to participate in the particular financial institutions' retirement account plans). The consent portions of the adoption agreements each provided in full: "If participant's spouse is not designated as the sole primary beneficiary, spouse must sign consent. Consent of Spouse: Being the participant's spouse, I hereby consent to the above designation."

3. [Family] Code section, [850] provides: "Subject to Sections [851] to [853], inclusive, married persons may by agreement or transfer, with or without consideration, do any of the following: [¶] (a) Transmute community property to separate property of either spouse. [¶] (b) Transmute separate property of either spouse to community property. [¶] (c) Transmute the separate property of one spouse to separate property of the other spouse."

Even if the trial court's findings as to Margery's intent were supported by substantial evidence, however, they would not support a finding of transmutation in this case. The statute providing for transmutation by transfer is by its own terms "[s]ubject to Sections [851] to [853], inclusive" [Family Code §850], including, obviously, section [852(a)]. Section [852(a)] invalidates attempts to transmute real or personal property unless certain conditions are met. We must therefore determine whether Margery's actions, whether or not they were *intended* to transfer her interest in the pension funds, were effective under section [852(a)] to transmute those funds from community property to Robert's separate property. We are of the opinion that they were not.⑤

Section [852(a)] requires that a valid transmutation be made, not just in writing, but in "writing by an *express declaration* that is made, joined in, consented to, or accepted by the spouse whose interest in the property is adversely affected." (§[852(a)], italics added.) There is no dispute that the consent paragraphs in the adoption agreements, and decedent's signatures thereon, are "made in writing." These writings are manifestly "made, joined in, consented to or accepted by the spouse whose interest in the property is adversely affected," viz., decedent. Thus, the sole remaining issue to be decided is whether they constitute "an express declaration" for the purposes of section [852(a)]. . . .

[handwritten margin note: WRITING BUT NOT AN EXPRESS DECLARATION]

It is not immediately evident from a reading of section [852(a)] what is meant by the phrase "an express declaration." . . . The statute does not state what words such an "express declaration" must include, what information it must convey, or even what topics it should discuss.

Since the words of section [852(a)] themselves, including the phrase "an express declaration," are unclear and ambiguous, it is necessary to resort to other indicia of the intent of the Legislature to determine what meaning that statute should be given. . . .

[handwritten margin note: INTENT OF LEG.]

Section [852(a)] was adopted in 1984. (Stats. 1984, ch. 1733, §3, p. 6302.) Both parties refer to a 1983 report of the California Law Revision Commission (Commission) to ascertain the intent of the Legislature in enacting section [852(a)]. In recommending that the Legislature enact that statute, the Commission described "[s]ection [852] [as] impos[ing] formalities on interspousal transmutations for the purpose of increasing certainty in the determination whether a transmutation has in fact occurred." (Recommendation Relating to Marital Property Presumptions and Transmutations, 17 Cal. Law Revision Com. Rep. (1984) (Commission report) pp.224-225.) The Commission report goes on to state that section [852] overrules existing case law that permitted oral transmutation of personal property. (Commission report, supra, at pp.224-225.)

In its discussion of the law then governing transmutations (Commission report, supra, at pp. 213-215), the Commission observed that "[u]nder California law it is quite easy for spouses to transmute both real and personal property; a transmutation can be found based on oral statements or implications from the conduct of the spouses." (Id., at p.213.)

---

⑤. We decline to treat respondent's IRA accounts as decedent's will substitute, as urged by respondents. Respondent has argued that Civil Code section [852(a)] does not apply to testamentary dispositions and/or to dispositions made by will substitutes. He further alleges that the IRA consent forms signed by Margery were a will substitute. We disagree. The record contains no substantial evidence that Margery or Robert intended that the IRA accounts would be so regarded. Moreover, consideration of respondent's will-substitute theory, advanced for the first time in this court, would be contrary to our established policy. (see Cal. Rules of Court, rule 29(b).)

The Commission further observed that "the rule of easy transmutation has also generated extensive litigation in dissolution proceedings. It encourages a spouse, after the marriage has ended, to transform a passing comment into an 'agreement' or even to commit perjury by manufacturing an oral or implied transmutation." (Commission report, supra, at p.214.) The Commission concluded its discussion of transmutation law by saying that "California law should continue to recognize informal transmutations for certain personal property gifts between the spouses, but should require a writing for a transmutation of real property or other personal property." (Ibid.) Unfortunately, the Commission did not explicitly expand upon the question of what such a writing should be required to contain. . . .

There is no question that the Legislature intended, by enacting section [852(a)], to invalidate all solely oral transmutations. (Commission report, supra, at pp.224-225.) By definition, *any* writing requirement would accomplish this limited goal. It is equally clear, however, that the Legislature intended that section [852(a)] would invalidate some transmutations which, under then-prevailing case law, would have been upheld on the basis of evidence other than oral statements. (Commission report, supra, at p.214 [". . . easy transmutation . . . encourages a spouse . . . to commit perjury by manufacturing an oral *or* implied transmutation. . . ." (Italics added.)].)

In our view, the Legislature cannot have intended that *any* signed writing whatsoever by the adversely affected spouse would suffice to meet the requirements of section [852(a)]. First, to so construe that statute would render mere surplusage all the language following the words "unless made in writing," including the phrase "an express declaration." A construction rendering some words surplusage is to be avoided. . . . Second, as respondent acknowledges, some of the "easy transmutation" cases which section [852] was intended to overturn involved nonoral conduct or signed writings.[6] Therefore, it seems reasonable to assume that the Legislature intended section [852(a)] to invalidate some claimed transmutations even though some form of writing existed.

Thus, to construe section [852(a)] so that it does not contain mere surplusage, as well as to effect legislative intent, we must fashion a test by which courts may judge the adequacy of particular writings for section [852(a)] purposes.

We have previously construed a statutory writing requirement similar to section

---

6. For a detailed analysis of existing transmutation law, the Commission referred the Legislature to Reppy, Debt Collection from Married Californians: Problems Caused by Transmutations, Single-Spouse Management, and Invalid Marriage (1981) 18 San Diego L. Rev. 143 (Reppy article). (Commission report, supra, at p.213, fn. 20.) Examples of objectionable transmutation cases discussed in the Reppy article include Nevins v. Nevins (1954) 129 Cal. App. 2d 150 [276 P.2d 655]. There, a husband filed his separate federal income tax return (which at that time called for him to report half the community income) without including half of his wife's income. Since he was aware of the existence of his wife's income, the court found that the husband's signed tax return, which did not include it, was highly probative of the husband having transmuted his community property interest in his wife's income to his wife's separate property. Another example discussed in the Reppy article is In re Marriage of Lucas (1980) 27 Cal. 3d 808 [166 Cal. Rptr. 853, 614 P.2d 285]. There, a motor home purchased by a couple during marriage was declared to have been transmuted to the wife's separate property when a purchase contract was made out in the husband's name only, but title and registration were made out in the wife's name only. (27 Cal. 3d at pp. 817-818; Reppy article, supra at pp. 156-157, fns. 48-53.) See also Pacific Mut. Life Ins. Co. v. Cleverdon (1940) 16 Cal. 2d 788, 791 [108 P.2d 405] [transmutation of wife's community earnings when husband "borrowed" and repaid some of them] and O'Connor v. Traveler's Ins. Co. (1959) 169 Cal. App. 2d 763 [337 P.2d 893] [transmutation of wife's community earnings when husband made no objection to her giving some of them to her son], both discussed in the Reppy article.

[852(a)]. In doing so we elucidated a principle of construction which is of fundamental importance for this case. In California Trust Co. **v.** Bennett (1949) 33 Cal. 2d 694 [204 P.2d 324] (*Bennett*), we concluded that a rental agreement respecting a bank safe-deposit box, printed on a card and signed by a husband and wife, which by its terms related only to rights of possession and access, did not satisfy a writing requirement for the creation of joint tenancies found in Civil Code section 683 (section 683).

Section 683 defines joint tenancy and states the methods by which a joint tenancy may be created. Pursuant to section 683, a joint tenancy may be created by certain transfers, including one "from a husband and wife, when holding title as community property or otherwise to themselves and others or to one of them and to another or others, *when expressely declared in the transfer to be joint tenancy.* . . . A joint tenancy in personal property may be created by a written transfer, instrument or agreement." (Civ. Code, §683, subd. (a), italics added.) We held in *Bennett* that section 683 is mandatory, and that under it joint tenancies can be created only by a writing. (*Bennett*, supra, 33 Cal. 2d at p.697.)

More importantly, the defendant in *Bennett* contended that evidence of the decedent's declarations and the circumstances surrounding the renting of the safe-deposit box should be admitted to interpret the rental card, and that, when interpreted with this extrinsic evidence, the card was sufficient to satisfy the statutory requirement of a writing. (*Bennett*, supra, 33 Cal. 2d at p.699.)

We found that the rental agreement card in *Bennett* was "clear" and did "not purport to affect the title to the contents of the box," because it used neither the words "title" nor "ownership" but expressly referred only to rights of possession and access. We further observed that "it is well settled that where a statute requires the formality of a writing for the creation of an interest in property, it must contain words indicating an intent to transfer such interest, and in the absence of words which could be interpreted to show such intent, no parol evidence will be admitted." (*Bennett*, supra, 33 Cal. 2d at p.699.) Accordingly, we refused to allow parol evidence to supplement the words of the written agreement on the card so as to satisfy the writing requirement of section 683. (33 Cal. 2d at pp.698-699.)

Thus, just as section [852(a)] requires an "express declaration" for a valid transmutation, section 683 requires that the creation of a joint tenancy be "expressly declared." Unlike section [852(a)], however, section 683 explains what the express declaration it calls for must include. Specifically, section 683 requires that an express declaration creating a joint tenancy must, "in the transfer," declare the interest being transferred "to be a joint tenancy." (Civ. Code, §683, subd. (a).) Section 683 thus ensures that a court need not look beyond the face of a proffered writing to determine whether its writer intended to create a joint tenancy. (*Bennett*, supra, 33 Cal. 2d at p.699.)

Following the approach elucidated in *Bennett*, we conclude that a writing signed by the adversely affected spouse is not an "express declaration" for the purpose of section [852(a)] *unless* it contains language which expressly states that the characterization of ownership of the property is being changed.

Our conclusion honors each of the principles of statutory construction we have discussed. First, it interprets "express declaration," so as to give significance to all the words of section [852(a)]. Second, it effects the intent of the Legislature to create a writing requirement which enables courts to validate transmutations without resort to extrinsic evidence and, thus, without encouraging perjury and the proliferation of litigation. Third, it is consistent with our interpretation of the similar requirement in section 683.[8]

We must now consider whether the writing involved in this case satisfies section [852(a)]. Decedent signed paragraphs consenting to the designation of a beneficiary on three standard bank-form adoption agreements. These paragraphs read in full: "If participant's spouse is not designated as the sole primary beneficiary, spouse must sign consent. Consent of spouse: Being the participant's spouse, I hereby consent to the above-designation. [Signature.]"

Obviously, the consent paragraphs contain no language which characterizes the property assertedly being transmuted, viz., the pension funds which had been deposited in the account. It is not possible to tell from the face of the consent paragraphs, or even from the face of the adoption agreements as a whole, whether decedent was aware that the legal effect of her signature might be to alter the character or ownership of her interest in the pension funds. There is certainly no language in the consent paragraphs, or the adoption agreements as a whole, expressly stating that decedent was effecting a change in the character or ownership of her interest. Thus, we agree with the Court of Appeal that these writings fail to satisfy the "express declaration" requirement of section [852(a)].

We do not hold that section [852(a)] requires use of the term "transmutation" or any other particular locution. Although a writing sufficient to satisfy the "express declaration" requirement of section [852(a)] might very well contain the words "transmutation," "community property," or "separate property," it need not. For example, the paragraph signed by decedent here would have been sufficient if it had included an additional sentence reading: "I give to the account holder any interest I have in the funds deposited in this account."[9]

We are aware that section [852(a)], construed as we have construed it today, may preclude the finding of a transmutation in some cases, where some extrinsic evidence of an intent to transmute exists. But, as previously discussed, it is just such reliance on extrinsic evidence for the proof of transmutations which the Legislature intended to eliminate in enacting the writing requirement of section [852(a)].

Manifestly, there are policy considerations weighing both in favor of and against any type of transmutation proof requirement. On the one hand, honoring the intentions of the parties involving in a purported transmutation may suggest that weight should be given to *any* indication of these intentions. On the other hand, the desirability of assuring that a spouse's community property entitlements are not improperly undermined, as well as concern for judicial economy and efficiency, support somewhat more restrictive proof requirements. The Legislature, in

8. Following the filing of his petition for review, Robert submitted a letter to court asking to amend his petition for review to include the issue of whether the adoption agreements constituted a valid written consent to the disposal of a community property asset under [Family] Code section [1100], subdivision (b). Apparently, respondent's request amounted to a reformulation of his alternative argument in the Court of Appeal that decedent "waived" her interest in the IRA funds. The Court of Appeal found this argument to be "merely another means of circumventing the requirements of section [852] . . . allowing transmutations by oral agreement or conduct." We agree with the view of the Court of Appeal and, for the same reasons, reject Robert's waiver contention. In any event, Robert's letter seeking to amend his petition was never filed or approved by the court and, accordingly, our grant of review was limited to the issue of construing [852(a)].

9. Married persons who decide to open IRA accounts with community funds, of course, may or may not, in individual cases, wish to transmute those funds. Thus we do not assume that drafters of IRA account adoption agreements will want to revise their standard forms so that a spouse's signature consenting to a designation of beneficiary will always effect a transmutation.

enacting section [852(a)], apparently thought it unwise to rely on some kinds of evidence to effect transmutations. It is not for us to question that legislative conclusion. Accordingly, the judgment of the Court of Appeal is affirmed.

Lucas, C. J., Broussard, J., Eagleson J., and Kennard, J., concurred. . . .

Arabian, J., Dissenting. —

If the decedent in extremis had in her last breath uttered the question, "Oh death, where is thy sting?," the majority garbed in grim shrouds would have whispered, "At probate."

It has been said that no good deed goes unpunished. Unhappily, there is a kernel of truth in this otherwise cynical aphorism, perfectly illustrated in the majority opinion, which begins its journey attempting to protect spouses against questionable transmutations of community property, and ends by negating the estate plan of the decedent herein, and of others who, like decedent, can no longer dictate their intentions. Worse, in exalting form over substance, the majority impose unnecessarily rigid requirements on the drafting and interpretation of future transfers between spouses. In the process, they undermine the deference that trial courts deserve and merit on review. Therefore, I must respectfully dissent. . . .

Notes and Questions

1. *The applicability of the transmutation statute.* Footnotes 5 and 8 indicate that Robert's appellate attorneys persistently attempted to recast the case in order to avoid the transmutation statute. Should they have been allowed to do so? Reread the transmutation provisions. What sorts of transactions do they contemplate? Are spousal consents to nonprobate beneficiary designations within their purview? The primary beneficiaries of Robert's trust were his children. Suppose that instead of designating his trust, Robert had named his children as the direct beneficiaries of his IRA accounts. In such case, could Margery's executrix have invoked the transmutation statute? What does Family Code section 850 say? Would section 1100(b) apply instead?

Yet even with the ostensibly less demanding section 1100(b), there remains the problem of *knowing* consent. Does Margery's signature on the spousal consent form adequately demonstrate (i) that she intended to give up *her* community property interest in the IRA funds or (ii) that she even knew that she had any interest in the IRA funds? What should we require by way of knowing consent when one spouse passively acquiesces to the other spouse's beneficiary-designation disposition of community property? Does *MacDonald's* application and interpretation of the section 852 *express declaration* requirement tend to insure knowing consent?

2. *The reasoning of* MacDonald. Is the joint tenancy provision an appropriate model for a transmutation statute of frauds? There is a constructional preference against the joint tenancy because its right of survivorship imposes a variety of forfeiture on the nonsurvivor. Moreover, failure to satisfy the express declaration requirement of the joint tenancy statute does not negate the attempted conveyance; instead the transfer simply creates another form of co-tenancy, generally a tenancy in common. Yet the analogy may seem apt because Margery MacDonald, a nonsurvivor, would have lost her community property interest in the IRA funds had the court accepted her consent signature as an adequate transmutation. The court's concluding discussion suggests that it may have adopted this perspective. The court justified

its holding in terms of "the desirability of assuring that a spouse's community property entitlements are not improperly undermined." Yet California transmutation may work in either direction. Thus strict transmutation rules equally preclude claims that one or both spouses transmuted separate property into the community property of their marriage. Is the joint tenancy statute an appropriate model for separate-to-community transmutation?

On the other hand, the court may be correct in perceiving that, as a practical matter, the *express declaration* issue predominantly involves community-to-separate transmutation. This is because the section 852 writing requirement alone undermines post-1984 informal separate-to-community transmutation, and written separate-to-community transmutation is likely to satisfy the express declaration requirement by explicitly placing the property in some form of co-ownership. In contrast, ambiguity and uncertainty are more likely to appear in writings that purport to effect community-to-separate transmutation, such as the *MacDonald* spousal consent to the other spouse's beneficiary designation. Thus the holding of *MacDonald* may tend to assure "that a spouse's community property entitlements are not undermined" and yet not have any significant impact upon formal, or written, separate-to-community transmutation.

3. *Individual Retirement Accounts.* The Individual Retirement Account (IRA)[3] is widely used for old-age savings and investments. It is more attractive than an ordinary savings or investment account in that interest and earnings are not subject to income tax until they are withdrawn by the depositor. In exchange for tax deferral, the depositor accepts some limitation on his access to the funds: There is a 10 percent penalty on withdrawals before the depositor has reached age 59½. As in *MacDonald,* an IRA may also be used as a repository for pension plan distributions so that income tax liability will be deferred until the IRA funds are withdrawn or distributed to the depositor or his beneficiaries.

4. *The IRA adoption agreement.* The IRA adoption agreement used in *MacDonald* is a uniform instrument drafted by the California League of Savings Institutions, a savings bank association located in Los Angeles. In response to *MacDonald,* the League altered its IRA adoption agreement, adding the language suggested by the majority opinion to provide:

> CONSENT OF SPOUSE: BEING THE PARTICIPANT'S SPOUSE, I HEREBY CONSENT TO THE ABOVE DESIGNATION, *GIVING TO THE ACCOUNTHOLDER ANY INTEREST I HAVE IN THE FUNDS DEPOSITED IN THIS ACCOUNT.* [new language italicized]

The League neglected the court's cautionary footnote 9:

> Married persons who decide to open IRA accounts with community funds, of course, may or may not, in individual cases, wish to transmute those funds. Thus we do not assume that drafters of IRA account adoption agreements

---

3. The Individual Retirement Account is authorized by Internal Revenue Code §408(c): "[For purposes of this section] the term IRA means a trust created or organized in the United States *for the exclusive benefit of an individual or his beneficiaries. . . .*" May the italicized language be understood to preempt California community property law? In other words, does an IRA deposit effectively transmute community funds into the depositor's separate property? On the other hand, the Code provision seems to contemplate marital property distribution of IRA funds at divorce. Id. at §408(d)(6) (2002). For discussion of federal preemption of state community property law, see Chapter 12 infra.

will want to revise their standard forms so that a spouse's signature consenting to a designation of beneficiary will always effect a transmutation.

5. The IRA *adoption agreement as a will substitute and intestacy replacement.* Nonwaivable provisions of the IRA adoption agreement also provide that if the depositor fails to designate a beneficiary or the beneficiary is no longer living at the depositor's death, all remaining funds shall be distributed to the depositor's surviving spouse, if none, to his surviving issue, if none, to his estate. Why does the IRA agreement effectively create its own order of succession in disregard of the depositor's will, state intestacy law, and the separate or community character of the IRA funds?

6. *The uncertain effect of a spouse's refusal to sign the consent provision.* The IRA adoption agreement provides: "If participant's spouse is not designated as the sole beneficiary, spouse must sign consent." Suppose that the depositor designates his child by a prior marriage as the beneficiary, and his spouse refuses to sign the consent. Should the beneficiary designation form be read to render the designation entirely ineffective without the spouse's signature? In such case, do all the funds go to the depositor's uncooperative surviving spouse via the IRA default provision? Or, should the depositor's beneficiary designation be treated as an effective nonprobate death transfer of the deceased depositor's interest in the funds? The question presents a mixed issue of the interpretation of the terms of the IRA adoption agreement and the content of state law. If, for example, the "spouse must sign" language of the IRA adoption agreement is interpreted to render the attempted beneficiary designation *entirely* ineffective, then state law cannot plausibly treat it as a nonprobate transfer of the deceased depositor's interest in the funds, and the IRA default provision would seem to control. If, on the other hand, the "spouse must sign" language of the beneficiary designation is not given literal effect, then state law may treat the depositor's beneficiary designation as a nonprobate death transfer of *his* interest in the IRA funds.

7. *Legislative response to* MacDonald. In addition to amending the spousal consent provision of the IRA adoption agreement, savings institutions also sought legislative reform.

The California Law Revision Commission drafted Probate Code provisions that relieve nonprobate beneficiary designations and spousal consents from the rigorous transmutation requirements of Family Code section 852(a). A spousal consent to a nonprobate beneficiary designation that fails to satisfy section 852(a) and hence fails to effect a present transmutation, is nevertheless effective consent to a beneficiary designation, which consent remains revocable while both spouses are still living. At the death of either spouse after the effective date of the statute, January 1, 1993, such spousal consent becomes irrevocable. 1992 Cal. Stat., ch. 51, codified at Family Code section 853 and Probate Code sections 5002-5032. Thus, if Margery MacDonald had died after January 1, 1993, her consent, although not satisfying section 852(a), might nevertheless have been effective and have become irrevocable at her death. Is the new law an appropriate response to the facts and holding of *MacDonald*? Does the problem presented by *MacDonald* lie primarily in the IRA adoption agreement or in state law?

8. *The meaning of* MacDonald: *What sort of language is required to signify that a spouse intended to alter the character or ownership of his interest in the property?* In Marriage of Barneson, 69 Cal. App. 4th 583, 81 Cal. Rptr. 2d 726 (1999), the 66-year-old husband had a stroke and subsequently instructed various brokerage houses, in

writing, to "transfer" his stock certificates to his 37-year-old wife. The court of appeal concluded that the husband's written instructions failed to satisfy the section 852 "express declaration" requirement because the word "transfer" fails to expressly state that the characterization or ownership of property is being changed.

> "Transfer" is not a word with a single meaning. The term "transfer" . . . is defined in Black's Law Dictionary . . . as follows: "To convey or remove from one place, person, etc., to another; pass or hand over from one to another; specifically, to change over the possession or control of (as, to transfer a title to land. To sell or to give." . . . [W]hile the term "transfer" could refer to a change in ownership, it does not necessarily do so. The fact that the term "transfer" carries multiple definitions demonstrates the ambiguity in Barneson's direction to "transfer" stock. . . . *MacDonald* does not speak in terms of "transfers" but requires "language which expressly states that the characterization or ownership of the property is being changed." (51 Cal.3d at p. 272. . . .) "Transfer" is clearly not synonymous with "transmutation." . . . A transmutation may be effected by means of a transfer, but a transfer is not necessarily a transmutation. . . . The point is simply that a direction by a spouse to transfer stock into his spouse's name does not unambiguously indicate the ownership of the stock is being changed.

Id. at 590-591.

Barneson was unconcerned that "the securities transfers met the procedural requirements of the Securities and Exchange Commission." Id. at 586. Are you? What might go wrong if routine transfers in writing between husband and wife, which meet the requirements of federal securities law, are found years later at death or divorce to fail the rigorous test of section 852 and its case law interpretation? Is there a federal preemption issue? You will be in a better position to evaluate this possibility after you have read Chapter 12. See particularly Free v. Bland, discussed at page 620.

Estate of Bibb, 87 Cal. App. 4th 461, 104 Cal. Rptr. 2d 415 (2001), held that a grant deed signed by the husband transferring his separate interest in real property to himself and his wife as joint tenants satisfied the "express declaration" requirement of section 852(a), but that an unsigned computer printout of Department of Motor Vehicles (DMV) Vehicle Registration Information, which showed that a Rolls Royce previously registered in the husband's name alone had been reregistered in the names of husband *or* wife, did not satisfy the "express declaration" requirement for transmutation. Although the form of title (A or B) creates a presumptive joint tenancy under the Vehicle Code, *Bibb* reasoned that the printout did not satisfy section 852(a) because there was no evidence that the reregistration was "made, joined in, consented to, or accepted by" the husband, nor did the printout evidence a clear and unambiguous expression of the husband's intent to transfer an interest in the automobile. Who has power to effect a vehicular title change? Do you agree with *Bibb*'s treatment of the DMV printout?

9. *The meaning of* MacDonald: *the parol evidence rule*. Having determined that "transfer" is ambiguous, *Barneson* also states, in dictum, that the meaning of "transfer" may not be clarified by extrinsic evidence because "the determination whether the MacDonald test has been met must be made without resort to parol evidence (51 Cal. 3d at pp. 271-272.)" Is this an accurate reading of *MacDonald*? Does *MacDonald* contemplate that parol evidence may never be used? Should parol evidence be admissible on the facts of *Barneson*?

10. *The ultimate reach of the transmutation statutes.* To what extent do the transmutation statutes, as interpreted by *MacDonald*, threaten the stability of written titles? Do they govern when one or both spouses apply funds to purchase an asset, but take title to that asset in a form that differs from the character of the purchase funds? Marriage of Lucas, discussed in footnote 6 of *MacDonald*, was one of the "easy transmutation" cases considered by the Law Revision Commission. In *Lucas*, reprinted infra at page 182, the court found that the husband consented to a transmutation of community property funds (giving up his one-half interest in the community property down payment) when he made no objection to his wife's demand that the seller place title to a mobile home in her name alone. The *writing* in *Lucas* was the mobile home certificate of title naming his wife as the owner. Would section 852(a) compel a different result if the *Lucas* transaction had occurred after 1984? If so, how?

Alternatively, suppose that a husband, acting alone, uses community property purchase funds and requests that the seller put title to a vehicle in his wife's name alone, or in his wife's name alone "as her separate property." Has the husband effectively relinquished his one-half interest in the community funds under section 852(a)? In terms of the language of section 852(a), has the certificate of title been "made, joined in, consented to, or accepted by the spouse whose interest in the property is adversely affected"? Is the certificate of title an "express declaration" within the meaning of *MacDonald*?

Even more commonly, spouses use community funds to purchase a family home to which they take title in joint tenancy. Typically, the deed accepted by the spouses (as well as the purchase contract signed by the spouses) does not specify that the purchase funds are community property or that the parties intend to transmute their community property into joint tenancy. Do such joint tenancy titles run afoul of *MacDonald*'s interpretation of the "express declaration" requirement? This issue has never been directly addressed in a reported California decision. However, the application of California law in such circumstances has been addressed by the U.S. Ninth Circuit Bankruptcy Appellate Panel.

IN RE SUMMERS
278 B.R. 808 (9th Cir. BAP (California) 2002)

PERRIS, Bankruptcy Judge.

The bankruptcy court in this case declared that certain real property owned jointly by debtor and her husband, Eugene Summers (husband), is held in a joint tenancy and that husband's interest in that property is his separate property. Debtor's chapter 7[1] trustee appeals, arguing that the property is community property, and therefore is property of debtor's bankruptcy estate. The questions are whether property acquired in California by spouses through a deed that shows the spouses as joint tenants is joint tenancy or community property and whether use of community funds to acquire property as joint tenants is a transmutation. We conclude that

---

1. Unless otherwise indicated, all chapters and section references are to the Bankruptcy Code, 11 U.S.C. §§101-1330.

JT
↓
V
NO
TRANSMUTATION

the bankruptcy court correctly determined that the debtor and husband hold the property as joint tenants and that there was no transmutation. Therefore, we affirm.

The facts are not in dispute. Debtor and husband were married at the time they purchased a parcel of real property in 1994. They made a $10,000 down payment, which came from their savings and a personal injury award husband had received, and signed a note for the remainder of the $116,000 purchase price. The parties took title to the property as joint tenants with their adult daughter. Both debtor and husband signed the deed, which recited that the seller granted the property

> TO EUGENE SUMMERS AND ANN MARIE SUMMERS, HUSBAND AND WIFE AND AURORA SUMMERS, AN UNMARRIED WOMAN, ALL AS JOINT TENANTS. EUGENE SUMMERS AND ANN MARIE SUMMERS, HUSBAND AND WIFE, HEREBY ACCEPT THE INTEREST HEREIN CONVEYED TO THEM AS JOINT TENANTS WITH AURORA SUMMERS, AN UNMARRIED WOMAN.

Plaintiff's Trial Brief at 3.

Debtor, husband and Aurora Summers have each filed separate bankruptcy petitions. The trustee in debtor's case took the position that the interest debtor and husband have in the property is community property, which became property of debtor's estate under §541(a)(2). Husband claims that he holds a joint tenancy interest with debtor and Aurora, which interest does not become property of debtor's estate. Husband brought this action to determine the respective interests of the parties in the property.

After a trial, the bankruptcy court concluded that debtor and husband hold the property as joint tenants, and therefore husband's interest is not property of debtor's bankruptcy estate. The trustee appeals. . . .

Property of the estate includes all legal and equitable interests of the debtor in property as of the date of the petition. §541(a). It also includes:

> All interests of the debtor and the debtor's spouse in community property as of the commencement of the case. . . .

§541(a)(2). Although federal law determines what is property of the bankruptcy estate, state law determines what interest the debtor has in property as of the commencement of the case. In re Mantle, 153 F.3d 1082, 1084 (9th Cir. 1998).

DEBTOR:

The trustee argues that the property at issue in this case is community property and therefore property of debtor's estate because (1) Cal. Fam. Code §760 provides that, "except as otherwise provided by statute," property acquired by married persons during marriage is community property, this property was acquired during the marriage, and there is no statute to the contrary; or (2) the property was acquired with community property funds and is therefore presumed to be community property.

Although §760 provides that property is community property unless otherwise provided by statute, that section only provides for a rebuttable presumption that property acquired during marriage is community property. See Haines v. Haines, 33 Cal. App. 4th 277, 39 Cal. Rptr. 2d 673, 681 (Cal. Ct. App. 1995). This presumption can be overcome by evidence that the parties agreed to hold the property as joint tenants, such as a deed showing that the spouses took title to property as joint tenants. *Haines*, 39 Cal. Rptr. 2d at 682. . . .

Further, there are other statutes that are relevant here. Cal. Fam. Code §750 recognizes that married persons in California may hold property "as joint tenants or tenants in common, or as community property, or as community property with a right of survivorship." Cal. Civ. Code §683(a) provides that a joint tenancy is created "by a title created by a single will or transfer, when expressly declared in the will or transfer to be a joint tenancy. . . ." Those two statutes allow married persons to agree to take title to property as joint tenants.

The trustee also argues that the property is community property because it was acquired with community property funds. He is correct that, ordinarily, property acquired with community property is also community property. Tischhauser v. Tischhauser, 142 Cal. App. 2d 252, 298 P.2d 551, 554 (Cal. Ct. App. 1956). However, "when the husband and wife with community funds take title to property as joint tenants, the form of conveyance destroys the presumption that the property is community and that, consequently, the joint tenancy stands as such, the interest of each spouse being separate property, unless the spouses intended that it should remain community property." 15A Am. Jur. 2d Community Property §56 (2000) (footnote omitted). Accord Siberell v. Siberell, 214 Cal. 767, 7 P.2d 1003 (Cal. 1932) (property taken by deed showing spouses as joint tenants, purchased with community funds, characterized as joint tenancy). The presumption that the title reflects the parties' intent cannot be overcome simply by evidence of the source of the funds used to purchase the property. Blankenship v. Blankenship, 212 Cal. App. 2d 736, 28 Cal. Rptr. 176, 178-79 (Cal. Ct. App. 1963).

In this case, debtor and husband took $10,000 of community funds and used it as a down payment on a parcel of real property that had a purchase price of $116,000. The property was acquired during the marriage. Thus, it was subject to the rebuttable presumption that it was community property. However, the deed by which they acquired the property recited that they took the property with their adult daughter as "joint tenants." Thus, the presumption that the property was community property was overcome by the fact that they took the property by a deed that showed them as joint tenants.[3] The title presumption cannot be overcome simply by showing that the funds used to purchase the property were community funds. Therefore, the property was acquired as joint tenancy property.

The trustee argues that the presumption of title does not apply, because the use of community property funds as a down payment on the real property was an attempt to transmute community property to separate property, which was ineffective because it did not comply with the requirements for transmutation set out in Cal. Fam. Code §852(a). Husband argues that the title presumption controls over the transmutation requirements, and that if the transmutation requirements control, they were met here.

The requirements for transmutation set out in §852(a) apply only to interspousal transactions or agreements. Marriage of Barneson, 69 Cal. App. 4th 583, 81 Cal. Rptr. 2d 726, 733 (Cal. Ct. App. 1999); Haines v. Haines, 39 Cal. Rptr. 2d 673, 683 (Cal. Ct. App. 1995); 1 William W. Bassett, California Property Law §4:37 (3d ed. 2001) (Fam. Code §852 "brought about a radical change in the law of interspousal

---

3. There is no evidence in this case to rebut the presumption that the title accurately reflects [the] parties' intent to hold the property as joint tenants. See In re Rhoads, 130 B.R. 565, 567 (Bankr. C.D. Cal. 1991).

agreements and transmutations"). A transmutation is "an interspousal transaction or agreement which works a change in the character of the property. . . ." *Haines,* 39 Cal. Rptr. 2d at 683.

Acquisitions of property are not necessarily transmutations. "Spouses can indicate their intent with respect to the character of the property *initially* by specifying the form of title in which it is held, or spouses can *later transmute* the character of the property as between each other." Id. at 682 (emphasis supplied). Thus, where spouses acquire property initially, they can specify in the title how that property is intended to be held. Once spouses own property, the character of ownership can be effectively transmutted only by following the requirements of §852(a).

There are no California cases specifically addressing when transmutation occurs or when the requirements of §852(a) must be met. However, application of §852(a) only to interspousal transactions, rather than to acquisitions of property from third parties, is consistent with the legislative purpose of the statute. Before §852(a) was enacted, California law allowed for conversion of separate property into community property and vice versa "at any time by oral agreement between the spouses." Woods v. Security First Nat'l Bank of Los Angeles, 46 Cal. 2d 697, 299 P.2d 657, 659 (Cal. 1956). The purpose of §852(a) was to "increase certainty in the determination whether a transmutation has in fact occurred." Law Revision Commission Comment.

> The new law has as its primary purpose the elimination of ex-post facto disagreements, misunderstandings, and uncertainties. The law overrules all law previously allowing oral or informal transmutations of personal property. Real property *transfers between spouses* now should be executed following all the usual rules and formalities of transfers of real property between any other persons or entities.

1 William W. Bassett, California Community Property Law §4:37 (3d ed. 2001) (emphasis supplied). There is nothing in the legislative history that indicates an intent to change the rule that, in acquiring property during a marriage, spouses can show their agreement to take the property as joint tenants by explicitly taking title as joint tenants. See 32 Cal. Jur. 3d Family Law §406 (1994) (character of property fixed at time it is acquired; that character continues until changed in manner recognized by law, such as by agreement between spouses to transmute it).

Further, this interpretation makes sense in the context of transactions by which spouses acquire property from third parties. If the trustee's theory were correct, then nearly every property transaction involving acquisitions of property during a marriage would require compliance with §852(a) in order to give effect to an intent of the parties that the acquired property should be held in some form other than community property. Thus, whenever spouses bought an automobile, the title would have to comply with the specificity requirements of §852(a), if the spouses intended the automobile to be held other than as community property. There is no indication in the statute or the case law for such a broad application of §852(a).

It also makes sense when one considers the requirement of §852(a) that the writing evidencing the transmutation be "made, joined in, consented to, or accepted" by the spouse whose interest is "adversely affected." §852(a). Where spouses use community property funds to acquire new property that they desire to hold in a joint tenancy, it is not apparent whose interest is being adversely affected.

The cases discussing §852(a) involve interspousal transfers. For example, in Estate of Bibb, 87 Cal. App. 4th 461, 104 Cal. Rptr. 2d 415 (Cal. Ct. App. 2001), the court held that the requirements of §852(a) were met where the husband had signed a grant deed transferring his separate property interest in real property to himself and his wife as joint tenants. In Marriage of Barneson, 69 Cal. App. 4th 583, 81 Cal. Rptr. 2d 726 (Cal. Ct. App. 1999), a husband's attempted transfer of his separately owned stock to his wife was held not to meet the specificity requirements of §852(a). The court in that case stressed that the requirements of §852(a) "necessarily arise only in the context of transfers of property between spouses." 81 Cal. Rptr. 2d at 733. Accord In re Roosevelt, 87 F.3d 311 (9th Cir. 1996), overruled on other grounds, In re Bammer, 131 F.3d 788 (9th Cir. 1997) (spouses acquired real property during marriage and took title as joint tenants; later marital agreement under which the husband and wife agreed that property would be the wife's separate property was sufficient to effect transmutation under §852(a)).

The spouses in Estate of MacDonald, 51 Cal. 3d 262, 794 P.2d 911, 272 Cal. Rptr. 153 (Cal. 1990), also engaged in an interspousal transfer. In that case, the husband had a retirement fund in which his wife had a community property interest. 794 P.2d at 914. Thereafter, the community funds were deposited into individual retirement accounts (IRAs) titled solely in the husband's name. 794 P.2d at 913. This was a transmutation, subject to the requirements of §852(a), because the parties did not acquire new property from a third party but instead merely changed the form of the pension fund into IRA accounts. The change of title to the husband's name was an attempt to transmute the pension fund from community property to a pension fund belonging solely to the husband.

There was no interspousal transfer in this case. Debtor and husband took $10,000 of community property and applied it toward the $116,000 purchase price of real property. This was not a change in form of the property; it was the acquisition of entirely new property from a third party. That does not constitute a transmutation, and the transaction was therefore not subject to the requirements of §852(a).

The trustee makes bankruptcy policy arguments for why §852(a) should apply in this case. However, because property interests in bankruptcy are determined according to state law, we must look to state law to determine those interests. Bankruptcy policy cannot change state law requirements, absent some specific Bankruptcy Code provision. The trustee does not point to any such provision here.

Because the acquisition of the real property in this case was not an attempted transmutation, §852(a) does not apply. The bankruptcy court did not err in so holding.

California law recognizes that spouses can acquire property as joint tenants rather than as community property. Husband and debtor acquired the property at issue as joint tenants. The fact that they used community property funds for the acquisition and the general presumption under California law that property acquired during marriage is community property are not sufficient to defeat the creation of a joint tenancy under Cal. Civ. Code §683(a), when spouses agree to acquire property in joint tenancy and the property is conveyed to them in joint tenancy.

The acquisition of the real property in this case was not an attempted interspousal transmutation of community property into joint tenancy property, and therefore the requirements of §852(a) do not apply. Thus, the bankruptcy court did not err in concluding that the property is joint tenancy property. Accordingly, we affirm.

Question

Is *Summers* correctly decided on its facts? Does the reasoning of *Summers* apply equally to all the transactions described in note 10 above? Assuming, for the purpose of discussion, that the transmutation statutes do not apply to any of the note 10 transactions, how would you define the parties' ownership rights in each of those situations?

IV

DEFINITIONAL AND TRACING ISSUES

A. INTRODUCTION

Like most other community property states, California defines separate property and specifies that all *other* property acquired during marriage is community property. The California Family Code provides:

§760. Community property

> Except as otherwise provided by statute, all property, real or personal, wherever situated, acquired by a married person during the marriage while domiciled in this state is community property.

§770. Separate property of married person

(a) Separate property of a married person includes all of the following:
(1) All property owned by the person before marriage.
(2) All property acquired by the person after marriage by gift, bequest, devise, or descent.
(3) The rents, issues, and profits of the property described in this section.
(b) A married person may, without the consent of the person's spouse, convey the person's separate property.

§771. Earnings and accumulations while living separate and apart

> The earnings and accumulations of a spouse and the minor children living with, or in the custody of, the spouse, while living separate and apart from the other spouse, are the separate property of the spouse.

These statutes have proven problematic in that they define community property by a process of exclusion: If an asset does not fit within the definition of separate property, then it must be community property. Yet the statutes do not tell us what community property *is;* they give us inadequate guidance when we are required to classify equivocal assets.

B. DEFINING COMMUNITY PROPERTY AND SEPARATE PROPERTY: ONEROUS OR LUCRATIVE ACQUISITION?

WILLIAM W. DE FUNIAK AND MICHAEL J. VAUGHN, PRINCIPLES OF COMMUNITY PROPERTY
114-115, 127-128 (2d ed. 1971).

Our system is that inherited from Spain, which is a community of the acquests and gains by the spouses during the marriage while they are living as husband and wife. The phrase "community of acquests and gains" is sufficiently clear in itself. Indeed, the practice of the Spanish law from which our community system comes was to define the community property first and then indicate the property which was excluded therefrom and was separate property. The first provision of the group of statutes of the Novisima Recopilacion of 1805 relating to the community starts out by saying: "Everything the husband and wife may earn or purchase during union, let them both have it by halves; and if it is a gift of the King or other person, and given to both, let husband and wife have it." . . . [I]t is necessary at this point to distinguish between property and goods acquired by onerous title and property and goods acquired by lucrative title. These were important definitive elements in the Spanish community property law and are no less so in our community property law although too frequently ignored in the decisions of our courts.

That property acquired by husband and wife during the marriage through their labor or industry or other valuable consideration is said to be acquired by onerous title. Other valuable consideration might consist of payment of money, rendition of services, performance of conditions, payment of charges to which the property was subject, and the like. With the exception that property acquired through valuable consideration which is wholly the separate property of one spouse naturally retains the character of separate property, property acquired by onerous title is always community property. This is so because it is acquired by the labor and industry of members of a form of partnership, that is, a marital partnership, or is acquired for valuable consideration which had previously been acquired by the industry and labor of the marital partnership, and whatever is earned or gained by one marital partner during the existence of the marital partnership must accrue to the benefit of both marital partners, who share equally in such earnings and gains. . . .

Property acquired by lucrative title is that acquired through gift, succession, inheritance, or the like.[82] It has its basis in pure donation on the part of the donor.

---

82. Escriche, Diccionario, "Lucrativo."

"An onerous title, as defined by the Mexican law authorities, was that which was created by the payment or the rendering of a valuable consideration for the property acquired. A lucrative title, by the same law, was that which was created by donation, inheritance or devise." Fuller v. Ferguson, 26 Cal. 546, 566.

It may or may not be community property, depending on whether the donor intends it to be for the benefit of both spouses or to be for one of them alone. While on occasion it is difficult to interpret the intent of the donor, usually the instrument or terms by which the donation is made clearly indicate whether the donation is for both spouses, and thus community property, or whether it is intended for one spouse alone, and thus his or her separate property.

One of the difficulties arising in considering the question of onerous and lucrative titles has been whether a so-called reward, gift, or the like is actually a pure donation given to one spouse alone in recognition, for example, of that spouse's peculiar or individual merits, and thus that spouse's separate property, or whether it is given in remuneration of certain services rendered by the spouse, and thus actually acquired by onerous title and coming within the earnings and gains which constitute community property. This has been a matter which has resulted in many conflicting decisions by our courts because of their frequent failure to distinguish between property acquired by onerous or lucrative title and their frequent inability to differentiate between a pure donation and one actually remunerative in nature.

In addition, our courts have been extremely prone to be misled by a literal interpretation of their local statutes providing that all property acquired during marriage, except that acquired by gift, bequest, devise, or inheritance, is community property. Overlooking or not comprehending the fact that one of the basic principles of community property law is that by "property acquired during marriage" is primarily meant property acquired by onerous title, they have frequently tended, without adequate analysis, to hold any property acquired during marriage to be community property, just so long as it was not acquired by gift, bequest, devise, or inheritance. This has been true of rights of action for personal injury to a spouse, money or property obtained upon the personal credit or security of a spouse, and other instances of property not actually acquired by onerous title.

ESTATE OF CLARK
94 Cal. App. 453, 271 P. 542 (1928)

CRAIL, J., pro tem. — This is an appeal from a judgment . . . by which a large part of the estate of the decedent, Dillard H. Clark, was distributed under the terms of his will, as separate property, to his two children, Dillard H. Clark, Jr., and Alice Clark Myers. . . .

The question for decision is whether certain moneys and property in the estate were community property, or were the separate property of the decedent.

The question arose in the trial court upon the petition of the children for partial distribution of the estate under the will, and the answer or response of the widow, the latter alleging that a large part of the estate belonged to the community, and that she was entitled to one-half of all such community property. . . .

The decedent, Dillard H. Clark . . . was by his first marriage the father of three children, Edwin Howard Clark, Dillard H. Clark, Jr., and Alice Clark Myers. On July 29, 1923, his son, Edwin Howard Clark, died, but his other two children survived him. On August 11, 1923, or about two weeks after the death of Edwin Howard Clark, Major Clark was married to Eliza Simpson Clark; and thereafter, on February 12, 1926, he died . . . leaving her as his widow.

During or about the year 1922 oil was discovered on a tract of land in Noble County, Oklahoma, then belonging to Major Clark. After enjoying the revenue for a time, he conveyed his mineral right in said land to his three children, all of whom were then living, so that each became the owner of one-third of such rights. These mineral rights continued to yield large revenues and, to a considerable though diminishing degree, still do so.

Major Clark would have inherited the entire estate of his son, Edwin Howard Clark, had the latter died intestate. Said estate consisted chiefly of such mineral rights as Major Clark had conveyed to his son, and the revenues from the same, which were and are of large value. Edwin Howard Clark, however, left a document, purporting to be a will, which was offered for probate as an original proceeding both in Noble County, Oklahoma, and in San Diego. In this document nothing of consequence was left by the decedent to his father, . . . Major Clark, the entire estate . . . being bequeathed to other persons. . . . Probate of this writing was contested by Major Clark, both in the county court of Noble County, Oklahoma, and in the superior court of San Diego County. It was denied probate in the county court of Noble County, Oklahoma, and an appeal was taken by the proponents to the district court of said county, where the law provides for trial de novo in such cases. In the superior court at San Diego, on the other hand, said will was, over the protest of Major Clark, admitted to probate, from which action Major Clark took an appeal to the supreme court which appeal has never been formally determined.

Such proceedings were in due time had in the district court of Noble County, Oklahoma, that the contest there was about to be tried by the district court, or was in fact partially tried, when a compromise was reached between Major Clark and the proponents of his son's will [by which Major Clark received one-half his son's estate. Before his death, Major Clark received more than $150,000 from the settlement and this money constituted part of Major Clark's estate on his death, which occurred about two and a half years after his son Edwin's death and the Major's second marriage.].

Major Clark himself left a will . . . the terms of which make provision for his wife, as follows: A trust fund for her benefit whereby she is to receive during her life the income from securities of the approximate value of $40,000, leaving the bulk of his property to his surviving children.

By proper instruments Mrs. Eliza S. Winn Clark waived and relinquished all rights under the will of her husband, and elected to take that portion of his estate to which under the law she might be entitled.

All of the property of the estate, except that received by Major Clark as the result of the compromise of the will contest, as hereinbefore explained, was property or the proceeds of property owned by him prior to his marriage with appellant, and was his separate property. . . .

Separate property and community property are defined in the Civil Code as follows:

Sec. 163. "All property owned by the husband before marriage, and that acquired afterwards by gift, bequest devise or descent, with the rents, issues and profits thereof, is his separate property."

Sec. 164. "All other property acquired after marriage by either husband or wife, or both, including real property situated in this state, and personal property wherever situated, . . . is community property. . . ."

The supreme court has construed the definition of separate property contained in section 163 of the Civil Code to include "property taken in exchange for, or in the investment, or as the price of the property so originally owned or acquired." (Meyer v. Kinzer, 12 Cal. 247 [73 Am. Dec. 538]; Smith v. Smith, 12 Cal. 216 [73 Am. Dec. 533].)

In case the will was held to be invalid, Major Clark was the sole heir of his son, and his right to contest the will was cast upon him immediately upon the death of his son. He claimed that his son's will was not a valid will. In this contention he had been sustained by the county court of Noble County, Oklahoma. By way of compromise, however, he consented to the dismissal of his contest and to the admission of the will to probate. The terms of the compromise contemplated, however, that in consideration of withdrawing his contest, Major Clark should receive the half of his son's estate. It is this property and the profits thereof which are involved in this litigation. Had the will been rejected, he would have received all of his son's estate, and beyond doubt it would have been his separate property. The question is whether what he did receive is any the less his separate property because it came to him through the compromise that was effected. It would not be questioned that if, instead of acquiring a clear title to half of his son's estate by withdrawing his contest to the will, Major Clark had adopted the method of having the appeal dismissed and the will denied probate, and then transferring to the legatees and devisees one-half of the property, this property would be his separate property. . . .

The right of an heir to transfer his inheritance, even though there is a will or purported will in existence, is recognized by our courts. At the instant of his son's death Major Clark had a property right which he could assign or transfer or surrender for a consideration acceptable to him, and also the statutory right, which of itself is a property right, to contest his son's will. (Estate of Baker, 170 Cal. 578 [150 Pac. 989].) This right was a right vested in him prior to his marriage, and therefore was his separate property. The property involved in this litigation came to Major Clark in exchange or in payment for such property, and was likewise his separate property.

It is the contention of appellant that the right of action to contest a will is not assignable, nor the subject of conveyance, and that it is not property. Such is not the law of California. Our law specifically provides that "any person interested" may appear and contest a will and includes "heirs" as among those interested. (Code Civ. Proc., sec. 1307.) "Broadly speaking, a contest of a will is in its essence an action for the recovery of property unlawfully taken or about to be taken from the ownership of the contestant." (Estate of Baker, supra.) While the mere expectancy of an heir is not usually regarded as property, the moment the ancestor has died, that expectancy is changed into a vested interest in property. It becomes thus vested by virtue of the death. The contest of a will therefore goes to establish upon the part of the contestant that his right to property has been violated. This right is such as the Civil Code, section 954, declares upon: "A thing in action, arising out of the violation of a right of property . . . may be transferred by the owner." (Estate of Baker, supra.)

Much reliance is placed by appellant upon the case of Pancoast v. Pancoast, 57 Cal. 320. This case involved a situation where a man before his marriage intruded, *without any right*, on certain land, and after his marriage made a deed and gave up possession of a portion of the same to the rightful owner, in consideration whereof the owner conveyed to the trespasser the rest of the tract in fee. In this case the court held that as the trespasser had nothing before marriage except the mere ability to give trouble and cause expense to the true owners, the title which the latter conveyed to him after his marriage was something wholly new and did not fall within any of the classes of new acquisitions enumerated in the statute as being separate property, and was in law community property. There are some features of the case which are similar to the instant case; but there is this difference: that in the Pancoast case the occupation does not appear to have been founded on any claim of right at all, but was a naked trespass, and the court refused to recognize a mere trespass as property; whereas Major Clark's claim to his son's estate was made in good faith on a bona fide contention that his son's will was invalid, and the Oklahoma court approved the settlement and found that it was free from fraud and duress and was for the best interests of the proponents of the will. In other words, that the contest was brought on probable cause. But above the good faith and above the probable cause, as steadfast as the rock of Gibraltar, stands out this element of differentiation that his contest was the assertion of a statutory right amounting to property. . . .

When a suit is brought bona fide on probable cause, a promise to compromise it is a valuable consideration, even though the suit should be held to be unfounded.

It is true that the property in litigation was acquired by Major Clark during the time he was married to appellant, but it was acquired by way of the compromise of a statutory right which was in itself property and which he owned prior to his marriage. Property acquired by compromise is separate property if the right compromised is separate. The right compromised is the consideration for the property obtained by the compromise, and the principle is the same as where property is purchased with separate funds. (31 Cor. Jur., p.24, sec. 1099.)

Judgment affirmed.

Notes and Questions

1. Why did the court conclude that the oil rights Major Clark acquired during marriage were the major's separate property?

2. Major Clark's son Edwin, the author of the contested will, died two weeks before the major married Eliza Simpson. After the major's death, Eliza asserted that the oil rights were community property in which she had a 50 percent interest. Would Eliza have prevailed if Edwin had lived to attend her wedding and had expired shortly thereafter?

3. Should proceeds from the settlement of a will contest be classified the same way as an uncontested inheritance or distribution under a will? What would Professors de Funiak and Vaughn say?

ANDREWS v. ANDREWS
116 Wash. 513, 199 P. 981 (1921)

BRIDGES, J. — A. D. Andrews brought this suit for the purpose of establishing and enforcing an alleged oral contract with his father, Joshua Andrews, to the effect that the latter would, by will or otherwise, at the time of his death, give to the plaintiff all property then owned by him. Upon a trial on the merits, the lower court dismissed the action, and the plaintiff has appealed.

The direct and surrounding facts are as follows: Joshua and Harriet Andrews were, respectively the father and mother of the appellant. . . . Mrs. Andrews, senior, was afflicted with cancer, and for many months the wife of the son, A. D. Andrews, daily at times, and at other times less frequently, went to the home of Mrs. Andrews, senior, and nursed her and took care of her wants. After some months of this manner of care, it was agreed between the two families that Joshua and his wife should move to West Seattle and live in the home of their son and his family. . . . The mother continued to reside in the home of her son until her death, and the father lived there much longer. Mrs. Andrews, senior, seems to have felt herself much indebted to her son and his family for their services to her in her long and serious sickness, and it was her desire that they should be compensated. During January, 1904, she made a will giving all of her property to her husband, but in the will expressed the desire that, at the death of her husband, the property should go to their son, the appellant. . . . Mrs. Andrews, senior, died within a month or two after making her will. The appellant alleges that, at the time Mrs. Andrews, senior, made her will, . . . it was orally agreed between Joshua Andrews and the appellant that the former should continue to live with the latter and receive his care and attention for such length of time as Joshua should desire to live with him, in consideration of which Joshua orally agreed that, at the time of his death, he would will all of his property to his son.

After the death of his wife, Mr. Andrews, senior, continued to abide with the son and his family until the son, for business reasons, went to Nome, Alaska. . . . When the son's family went to Nome they solicited the father to go with them and agreed to give him a home there. In fact, the testimony shows that arrangements at Nome had already been made by the son for the proper care of his father. The latter, however, deemed himself too old to make the trip or to live in the rigorous climate of the far north, and refused to accompany the family thence. He continued, however, to live at the son's home in West Seattle, but took care of himself and paid his own living expenses, until 1908, when he was married to the respondent. Shortly thereafter he and his wife took up their residence in the city of Seattle, where they continued to reside until his death several years after. Long after the appellant and his family moved to Nome, and on November 20, 1907, Joshua undertook to make his will. That instrument, however, was void as a will because it had but one witness instead of two, as required by statute. This purported will gave certain small sums to the children of appellant, and all remaining of the estate to the appellant. Still later, and long after he was remarried, and on August 20, 1918, Joshua attached a codicil to the previous will, modifying it to the extent of giving his wife $500 in cash, the household furniture, and the use of the homestead for a period of five years. Except as indicated in the codicil, the will was left as originally written. This codicil was also illegal because it had but one witness. . . . [W]e take it that the trial court found as a fact that the oral contract was made substantially as contended for by the appellant, but that the latter breached it by moving to Nome.

This court has more than once held that an oral contract of the character here mentioned is enforceable notwithstanding the statute of frauds, if there has been full or partial performance. . . .

The first question we must discuss is whether the original contract was made. It is a well settled principle of law that contracts of this character must be established by clear and convincing evidence. The appellant undertook to establish the existence of this contract by the testimony of his wife. At the trial the respondent objected to her testifying concerning any conversations on this subject had between Joshua Andrews and the appellant, for the reason that the appellant's wife was a

party in interest. The respondent's objections were overruled. The appellant neither in his brief nor in his oral argument touched the question as to the competency
of his wife to testify concerning the contract, and the respondent makes no further
argument on the subject than that his "objections of all of her testimony should
have been sustained. She was the wife of the plaintiff and therefore vitally interested.
She will surely be benefited if he prevails in this action." The question, however,
is foremost in the case and must be decided.While the judgment of the lower court
ran in favor of the respondent, against whom this witness testified, and respondent
has not appealed, yet this is an equity case and we must hear it de novo; consequently, we must consider only such testimony as is competent. Section 1211, Rem.
Code, is as follows:

> No person offered as a witness shall be excluded from giving evidence
> by reason of his interest in the event of an action, as a party thereto or other-
> wise; but such interest may be shown to affect his credibility: *Provided, however,*
> That in an action or proceeding where the adverse party sues or defends as
> executor, administrator, or legal representative of any deceased person, or
> as deriving right or title by, through, or from any deceased person, or as the
> guardian or conservator of the estate of any insane person or of any minor
> under the age of fourteen years, then a party in interest or to the record shall
> not be admitted to testify in his own behalf as to any transaction had by him
> with or statement made to him by any such deceased or insane person, or
> by such minor under the age of fourteen years. . . .

The whole question here, then, resolves itself into the proposition whether the
property which the appellant sought to recover would have been, had he succeeded
in recovering it, community property or his separate property. If it would have been
community property, then the wife was a party in interest and could not testify, and
the objection of the respondent should have been sustained.

We are convinced that the property sought to be acquired by this action would
have been community property had it been acquired. Section 5915, Rem. Code,
defines the separate property of the husband as follows:

> Property and pecuniary rights owned by the husband before marriage
> and that acquired by him afterwards by gift, bequest, devise or descent, with
> the rents, issues and profits thereof, shall not be subject to the debts and
> contracts of his wife, and he may manage, lease, sell, convey, encumber or
> devise by will, such property without the wife joining in such management,
> alienation or encumbrance, as freely and to the same extent as though he
> were unmarried.

Section 5916, Rem. Code, defines in substantially the same words the separate
property of the wife. Section 5917, Rem. Code, defines community property as follows:

> Property, not acquired or owned as prescribed in the next two preceding
> sections, acquired after marriage by either husband or wife, or both, is com-
> munity property.

The main question is, was the property sought to be obtained by this suit acquired by "gift, bequest, devise, or descent," within the spirit of the statute?

We are satisfied that it would not have been so acquired. It would have been acquired by contract. There is no element of gift, bequest or devise involved in this case. Joshua Andrews, according to the alleged agreement, was to will his property to his son for a consideration, and that consideration was that the latter was to maintain and support him during the remainder of his life, or such portion thereof as he might elect to accept such maintenance and support. The testimony was that the services to be performed in payment of the property to be acquired were performed by the appellant and his wife. It was their community property which housed and sheltered Joshua Andrews; it was the community money of the appellant and his wife which furnished, and was to furnish, the table from which Mr. Andrews, senior, was to eat. The testimony shows that the appellant's wife did the housework and cooked the food, and did the other usual duties in the maintenance of the home, and in the care and attention given to Mr. Andrews, senior. Everything that went into his maintenance was the joint effort of the appellant and his wife. In no true sense was the appellant to acquire this property by gift. He was to acquire it by virtue of a contract which was to be performed on the one side by himself and his wife. Bouvier's Law Dictionary defines "Gift" as a "voluntary conveyance or transfer of property; that is, one not founded on the consideration of money or love. A voluntary, immediate, absolute transfer of property without consideration." The "gift, bequest, devise or descent" contemplated by the statute as constituting separate property is not based upon contract or consideration, and property willed by one to another in compliance with a contract between the parties is not a gift or bequest in contemplation of the statute. If the appellant had alleged and shown that the contract was a personal one between his father and himself and was to be performed, and was performed, by means of his separate property and his individual endeavors, then the property to have been acquired might have been his separate property, and his wife might have testified as to the terms of the contract. But this situation is not before us and we do not decide it. But, even in that instance, it would be his separate property by purchase and it would not have been his by gift, devise or descent within the spirit of the statute. If the alleged contract had been made by the appellant with a stranger and not with his blood relation, then it would seem to us that everyone must say that the property to be acquired under it would be community property, because we have always held that property acquired by the joint efforts of the husband and wife is presumed to be community property. The mere fact that it is alleged that the contract here was made with the appellant's father could not change the legal situation, and the legal effect must be the same as if the contract had been made with entire strangers.

Without the testimony of the appellant's wife, there is not sufficient evidence upon which to base any contract. While the self-sacrifice made by the appellant, and particularly by his wife, is to be highly commended, the rules of law forbid them any compensation.

The judgment must be affirmed. PARKER, C.J., MACKINTOSH, FULLERTON, and HOLCOMB, J.J., concur.

Notes and Questions

1. Why, exactly, would the son's recovery on his father's promise to make a will be community property? What does the court mean by the son's "individual endeavors" in the third-to-last paragraph of the opinion?

2. If the father had written a valid will leaving all his property to his son, would the will proceeds be community property? If you were representing the son in a subsequent divorce, what arguments would you make?

3. *Mixed motivations.* Contemplating the content and spirit of the family's transactions, *Andrews* asserts: "There is no element of gift, bequest or devise involved in this case." With equal confidence in the polarity and unambiguousness of human motivation and behavior, de Funiak and Vaughn supra, opine that gifts and bequests have their "basis in pure donation on the part of the donor" and inquire whether a "so-called . . . gift" is "actually a pure donation given to one spouse alone in recognition . . . of that spouse's peculiar or individual merits . . . or whether it is given in remuneration of certain services rendered by the spouse, and thus actually acquired by onerous title." Do gifts and bequests, particularly from parents and other family members, fall like manna from heaven? On the other hand, would Mr. Andrews have promised all his property to someone who was not his child?

DOWNER v. BRAMET
152 Cal. App. 3d 837, 199 Cal. Rptr. 830 (1984)

KAUFMAN, J. — Plaintiff Gloria Alice Bramet Downer (hereinafter referred to as former wife) appeals from a judgment of nonsuit on her complaint for the determination of her rights in certain property. . . . She claims a community property interest in the proceeds of sale of a one-third interest in a ranch conveyed to her former husband George Keith Bramet by his employer after the parties separated. At the close of former wife's case, former husband moved for nonsuit. The motion was granted and judgment entered accordingly.

The parties were married in 1953, and separated in 1971. Former husband was an accountant and a tax expert. He worked for Chilcott Enterprises before, during and after the marriage, beginning in 1943. Chilcott Enterprises consisted of several businesses and corporations owned and operated by Edward Chilcott and his wife. Former husband was an officer of several of the corporations and acted as secretary-treasurer, accountant and recordkeeper for all of the Chilcotts' operations. Mr. Chilcott considered former husband his "righthand man."

Chilcott Enterprises had no retirement program of any kind for its employees. According to former wife's testimony, sometime in the mid-1960's former husband told her that Mr. Chilcott was going to give to him and two other employees a ranch in Oregon in lieu of retirement benefits. Nothing further was thereafter said about the ranch.

The parties separated in November 1971. In December 1972, after some exchange of drafts between the parties and their counsel, a marital settlement agreement was executed. The agreement, which was later incorporated in the judgment of dissolution, . . . contained a warranty "that neither party is now possessed of any property of any kind or description whatsoever, other than the property specifically mentioned in this Agreement" and a provision reading: "If it shall hereafter be determined by a Court of competent jurisdiction that one party is now possessed of any community property not set forth herein . . . such party hereby

[handwritten margin note: Worked for co. for 10 yrs b/4 marriage]

[handwritten note at bottom: Warranty that stated that any future CP would be divided equally.]

covenants and agrees to pay to . . . the other on demand an amount equal to one-half of the then . . . or present fair market value of such property, whichever is greater."

In August 1972, before the parties executed the agreement, . . . the Chilcotts deeded the W-4 Ranch in Oregon to former husband and two other employees.[3] Former husband did not mention his interest in the ranch at the time he executed the settlement agreement in December 1972.

Former husband continued working for Chilcott Enterprises after the dissolution until he became disabled after suffering a stroke in 1976. In 1978, the ranch was sold for over $1.35 million and former husband's interest in the sale proceeds was turned over to his conservator. This action was instituted in 1980 shortly after former wife learned of the conveyance of the ranch to former husband and the other employees.

Mr. Chilcott testified in essence that the conveyance to the three employees was a gift—the reason he deeded the ranch to the three employees was that he did not need the money and he just felt like giving it away.

Gift?

Additional facts will be included in the discussion of the propriety of the nonsuit. . . .

A nonsuit may be granted only when, "'. . . disregarding conflicting evidence and giving to plaintiff's evidence all the value to which it is legally entitled, herein indulging in every legitimate inference which may be drawn from that evidence, the result is a determination that there is no evidence of sufficient substantiality to support a verdict in favor of the plaintiff if such a verdict were given.'" (Estate of Lances (1932) 216 Cal. 397, 400 [14 P.2d 768].) The question is thus whether there was substantial evidence that would have supported a verdict in favor of former wife on the issue of her interest in the ranch (or, more correctly, the proceeds from the sale of the ranch).

Former wife contends there was substantial evidence the transfer of the ranch interest to former husband was in lieu of pension benefits, and is therefore community property. Former husband contends there is no substantial evidence the ranch constituted a retirement benefit and argues the transfer of the ranch interest was a gift, and thus, separate property pursuant to Civil Code section 5108 [now Family Code section 770].[4] The trial court agreed with former husband that the transfer of the interest in the ranch to him was a gift and concluded therefore that it was his separate property.

We agree with the trial court and former husband that the Chilcotts' transfer of a one-third interest in the ranch to former husband was legally in the form of a gift. Civil Code section 1146 defines a gift as "a transfer of personal property, made voluntarily, and without consideration." The evidence establishes that that is precisely what was done in the case at bench. There is no evidence the ranch was transferred pursuant to a legal obligation to do so on the part of the Chilcotts.

Gift b/c there was no moral obligation

---

3. Apparently for the purpose of minimizing gift tax consequences, the transaction was cast in the form of a sale with an $18,000 cash down payment and a note and deed of trust in the amount of $254,000 calling for payments of $18,000 a year. However, the Chilcotts gave each of the three employees $6,000 for the down payment and were to give them annually an additional $6,000 each to make the annual trust deed payments.

4. Civil Code section 5108 [Family Code section 770] reads in pertinent part: "All property owned by the husband before marriage, and that acquired afterwards by *gift*, bequest, devise, or descent, with the rents, issues, and profits thereof, is his separate property." (Italics added.)

There is no evidence of any bargained-for contractual obligation nor of any detrimental reliance by former husband sufficient to invoke the doctrine of promissory estoppel. There is nothing to show, for example, that former husband was induced to stay in the Chilcotts' employ by the statement assertedly made by Mr. Chilcott that the ranch was going to be conveyed to the three employees in lieu of a pension program. There being no evidence of any legal obligation to convey the ranch, its conveyance can only have been a gift.

However, the conclusion the conveyance was legally a gift does not resolve the ultimate question of the characterization of the ranch interest or the proceeds of its sale as community or separate. Although [Family] Code section [770] provides that property acquired by the husband after marriage by gift is his separate property, the language of section [770] must be read in the context of the entire marital property scheme. Earnings or property attributable to or acquired as a result of the labor, skill and effort of a spouse during marriage are community property. . . . Even though the transfer of the ranch interest was legally a gift, there is substantial, indeed strong, evidence the gift was made by former husband's employer in recognition of former husband's devoted and skillful services during his lifelong employment at Chilcott Enterprises.

The evidence shows former husband began working for Chilcott Enterprises in 1943. He became Mr. Chilcott's righthand man, did all the accounting for the various Chilcott operations, was responsible for all the tax planning, advice, and filing of returns, handled sales contracts and record-keeping, served as officer in several of the corporate entities and supervised the ranch operations in California, Arizona and Oregon. For over 30 years, he was the Chilcotts' loyal and trusted employee. By contrast, there was no evidence of any social or personal relationship between former husband and the Chilcotts. The Bramets never went out socially with the Chilcotts, and former husband never played golf or other sports with Mr. Chilcott, never took a social trip, played cards or anything of that sort with the Chilcotts. The Bramets went to the Chilcotts' house once to attend the wedding of the Chilcotts' oldest daughter, and one time former husband took care of the Chilcotts' home while they were away on vacation. Otherwise, former husband never went to the Chilcotts' home socially. Mr. Chilcott testified that, except for their business relationship, he had practically no contact with former husband.

Thus, although the conveyance of the ranch interest to former husband was in the form of a gift, the evidence would support, indeed strongly suggests, that it was in whole or part a remuneratory gift in recognition of former husband's loyal and skilled efforts for and services to his employer. (Holby v. Holby (1981) 131 Ariz. 113 [638 P.2d 1359, 1360]; de Funiak and Vaughn, Principles of Community Property (2d ed. 1971) §70, pp.157-160.) To the extent it was and to the extent the efforts and services were rendered during the marriage (see In re Marriage of Poppe (1979) 97 Cal. App. 3d 1, 8-9 [158 Cal. Rptr. 500]; In re Marriage of Judd (1977) 68 Cal. App. 3d 515, 522-523 [137 Cal. Rptr. 318]), the ranch interest conveyed to former husband and the proceeds of its sale were community property. (Holby v. Holby, supra, 131 Ariz. 113) [638 P.2d 1359, 1360]; de Funiak and Vaughn, Principles of Community Property (2d ed. 1971) §70, pp.157-160.)

It was error therefore to grant the nonsuit as to the cause of action to establish former wife's interest in the proceeds of sale of the ranch interest. . . .

The judgment of nonsuit is reversed as to the cause of action to establish plaintiff's interest in the proceeds of sale of the interest in the ranch property. . . .

MORRIS, P.J., and RICKLES, J., concurred.

A petition for a rehearing was denied March 29, 1984, and respondents' petition for a hearing by the Supreme Court was denied May 2, 1984.

Notes and Questions

1. *The significance of the evidence.* Why does the court emphasize the absence of any social or personal relationship between the husband and his employer? Would it matter if the husband were the employer's nephew or son? In such event, would the employer's relationship with the other two donee-employees be material?

2. *The purpose of the inquiry.* Compare the methodology of the trial court and the court of appeal. Both address the same issue: Was the ranch interest a gift to the husband? The trial court responded formally and acontextually: The ranch interest must have been a gift because the husband had no legally enforceable claim to it. In contrast, the court of appeal recognized that although the ranch deed was formally a legal gift, that is, "a transfer of . . . property, made voluntarily, and without consideration," and although the transfer might be a gift for other legal purposes, nevertheless for purposes of Family Code 760, the ranch interest appeared to be property attributable to the efforts of a spouse during marriage and hence to be community property.

Even within community property law, a gift for one purpose may not be a gift for another. For example, in California community property law, a spouse may neither make a gift of community property nor dispose of community property "for less than fair and reasonable value, without the written consent of the other spouse." Section 1100(b). A nonconsenting spouse may seek compensation from the donor spouse. Section 1101(a). Suppose that the employer, Edward Chilcott, had transferred the ranch interests without his wife's consent. If you were representing Mrs. Chilcott, the *employer's* wife, at her subsequent divorce proceeding, would you be controlled by the Downer v. Bramet "no-gift" determination? Could you argue that although George's interest in the ranch might be an onerous acquisition as between George and Gloria Bramet, as between Edward Chilcott and his wife, the ranch deed to Edward's three employees was an unauthorized 1100(b) gift because it was not supported by legally adequate consideration? With Downer v. Bramet, compare Estate of Bray, infra at page 409.

3. *Sufficiency of the evidence.* Assuming that the facts developed in the subsequent hearing remain those presented in the appellate nonsuit opinion you have just read, would a trial court conclusion that the ranch is the separate property of the husband be sustainable on appeal?

4. *Other definitional issues. Clark, Andrews,* and Downer v. Bramet do not exhaust the definitional problems explicitly identified by de Funiak and Vaughn, supra at page 138. Personal injury recoveries and credit purchases, for example, are neither onerously nor lucratively acquired. Their characterization is treated in Chapter 6 infra.

C. TRACING

1. The General Principle

ESTATE OF CLARK
94 Cal. App. 453, 271 P. 542 (1928)

[See text of *Clark* at page 139 supra.]

Note

Although Family Code section 760 characterizes as community property any asset *acquired* during marriage, *Clark* explains that section 770 has been judicially construed to allow tracing to the source of acquisition in order to demonstrate that the asset in question, although acquired during marriage, is wholly or partially separate property because it was acquired with (i) premarital separate property or (ii) the income from such separate property or (iii) property acquired by one spouse by gift, bequest, devise, or descent. In *Clark,* the oil rights acquired by the major during marriage were traced to a source that was doubly separate because it was both premarital and a substitute for his rights as an heir.

Similarly, property that is ostensibly section 771 separate property because it was acquired after separation may be traced back to marital labor to be characterized as the parties' community property. In Downer v. Bramet, supra page 146, the husband received his interest in the ranch after the parties' permanent separation. Nevertheless his wife could claim the ranch interest as community property on the ground that it was compensation for the husband's preseparation marital labor.

2. Tracing Assets to Mixed Sources

An asset may be acquired with both community and separate funds. When an asset is untitled or titled in the purchasing spouse's name alone, it may be traced to the sources of its acquisition.[1] Thus, as between the spouses, a single asset may be owned by as many as three estates: the community, the wife's separate, and the husband's separate estate. This topic is developed infra at pages 182-215 and 259-269. Frequently, assets are purchased with separate and community funds that have been commingled in a single account. In such case, tracing conventions have been devised to determine whether and the extent to which community and separate funds have contributed to the acquisition of the asset. This topic is developed infra at pages 215-234.

Admixture of community and separate imputs may occur not only with mone-

---

1. Some forms of title may support an inference of gift or agreement of the parties to hold according to the form of title. Such gifts or agreements may logically preclude tracing to the acquisition funds. The transmutational implications of title are considered infra at pages 000-000. Yet when assets are untitled or titled on the purchaser's name alone, there can be no title implication of gift or agreement, and hence tracing to the sources of acquisition is always permitted.

tary contributions; labor may combine with cash or physical capital to produce assets that require characterization. For example, a spouse may bring a separate property business into marriage and then devote her community property labor to the management of that business during marriage. At her death or divorce, it may be necessary to characterize the business and the assets that have been purchased with business profits. This topic is explored infra at pages 234-249.

3. Conceptual Tracing Difficulties

In the instances discussed above, the conceptual principles are clear and straightforward even though the details of their execution may be complex and problematic. Yet with some assets, there may appear to be alternative sources and we may have difficulty deciding which should be the legally determinative source. For example, if a wife uses community earnings to insure her separate property automobile, how should we characterize insurance proceeds compensating for casualty damage to the car? Both imputs, the insurance policy and the insurable car, are necessary but neither alone is sufficient for recovery. Yet there is no rational basis for apportioning between the separate and community imputs. This topic is developed infra at pages 277-278. Similarly, what is the source of the proceeds of a term life insurance policy that was funded with community premiums for 10 years of marriage and then with the decedent's separate property premiums for the 10 years following separation and ending in his death? Should the separate property source of the last premium be determinative, or should the proceeds be equally divided between the estates because each estate paid half of all the premiums? Or would you take yet another approach? See text infra at pages 278-283.

With some assets, there may be tension between the section 760 principle that all assets acquired by marital labor belong to the community and the section 771 principle that postseparation earnings are the earner's separate property. What should we do with employment benefits earned during marriage that are intended as substitutes for postseparation earnings? How should we treat, for example, pension benefits earned during marriage but received after separation and divorce? Disability benefits? Workers' compensation? Are there conceptual or policy reasons for separate or community characterization? These topics are developed infra at pages 283-297 and 350-366.

V

EVIDENTIARY PRESUMPTIONS IN CALIFORNIA COMMUNITY PROPERTY LAW

INTRODUCTORY PROBLEM

As you were reading the preceding chapter, you may have noticed that it carefully skirted an often outcome-determinative question: *Who* has to prove *what?* To dramatize the question and to guide you through the first two sections of this chapter, consider the following problem. Philip Stone, an unmarried physician, rented a safe deposit box in his local San Francisco bank when he began his medical practice in 1945. He remained a bachelor until he married Amanda Bell in 1960. Last month, shortly after his retirement, Philip died. His executor was surprised to discover that the box contained undated assets worth $200,000. Philip always enjoyed substantial earnings as a physician and, during marriage, received substantial bequests from relatives and grateful patients. He left no records that would shed any light on the character of the undated assets. Philip's duly executed will leaves all his interest in the community property to his widow, Amanda, and all his separate property to his disabled sister, Lilly. How should the assets in the safe deposit box be characterized?

A. THE FRAMEWORK OF THE CALIFORNIA EVIDENCE CODE

Presumptions play a central role in California marital property law. These presumptions should be considered within the analytic framework of the California Evidence Code. As you read the Code and Comments, focus on the various purposes of presumptions so that you will be ready to evaluate the community property presumptions.

CALIFORNIA EVIDENCE CODE
SECTIONS 500, 600, 601, 603-606
(West 1966 & Supp. 1992)

§500. Party who has the burden of proof.   Except as otherwise provided by law, a party has the burden of proof as to each fact the existence or nonexistence of which is essential to the claim for relief or defense that he is asserting.

[Is this method of allocating the burden of proof at all helpful in a proceeding to distribute a couple's property? Who is the plaintiff? Who is the defendant?]

§600. Presumption and inference defined.   (a) A presumption is an assumption of fact that the law requires to be made from another fact or group of facts found or otherwise established in the action. A presumption is not evidence.

(b) An inference is a deduction of fact that may logically and reasonably be drawn from another fact or group of facts found or otherwise established in the action.

Comment—Assembly Committee on Judiciary

. . . Presumptions . . . are not "evidence" but are conclusions that the law requires to be drawn (in the absence of a sufficient contrary showing) when some other fact is proved or otherwise established in the action. . . .

§601. Classification of presumptions.   A presumption is either conclusive or rebuttable. Every rebuttable presumption is either (a) a presumption affecting the burden of producing evidence or (b) a presumption affecting the burden of proof.

Comment—Law Revision Commission

Under existing law, some presumptions are conclusive. The court or jury is required to find the existence of the presumed fact regardless of the strength of the opposing evidence. . . .

Under existing law, too, all presumptions that are not conclusive are rebuttable presumptions. . . .

For several decades, courts and legal scholars have wrangled over the purpose and function of presumptions. The view espoused by Professors Thayer (Thayer, Preliminary Treatise on Evidence 313-352 (1898)) and Wigmore (9 Wigmore, Evidence §§2485-2491 (3d ed. 1940)), accepted by most courts . . . , and adopted by the American Law Institute's Model Code of Evidence, is that a presumption is a preliminary assumption of fact that disappears from the case upon the introduction of evidence sufficient to sustain a finding of the nonexistence of the presumed fact. In Professor Thayer's view, a presumption merely reflects the judicial determination that the same conclusionary fact exists so frequently when the preliminary fact exists that, once the preliminary fact is established, proof of the conclusionary fact may be dispensed with unless there is actually some contrary evidence:

> Many facts and groups of facts often recur, and when a body of men with a
> continuous tradition has carried on for some length of time this process of

> reasoning upon facts that often repeat themselves, they cut short the process and lay down a rule. To such facts they affix, by a general declaration, the character and operation which common experience has assigned to them. [Thayer, Preliminary Treatise on Evidence 326 (1898).]

Professors Morgan and McCormick argue that a presumption should shift the burden of proof to the adverse party. Morgan, Some Problems of Proof 81 (1956); McCormick, Evidence §317 at 671-672 (1954). They believe that presumptions are created for reasons of policy and argue that, if the policy underlying a presumption is of sufficient weight to require a finding of the presumed fact when there is no contrary evidence, it should be of sufficient weight to require a finding when the mind of the trier of fact is in equilibrium, and, a fortiori, it should be of sufficient weight to require a finding if the trier of fact does not believe the contrary evidence.

what?

The classification of presumptions in the Evidence Code is based on a third view suggested by Professor Bohlen in 1920. Bohlen, The Effect of Rebuttable Presumptions of Law Upon the Burden of Proof, 68 U. Pa. L. Rev. 307 (1920). Underlying the presumptions provisions of the Evidence Code is the conclusion that the Thayer view is correct as to some presumptions, but that the Morgan view is right as to others. The fact is that presumptions are created for a variety of reasons, and no single theory or rationale of presumptions can deal adequately with all of them. Hence, the Evidence Code classifies all rebuttable presumptions as either (1) presumptions affecting the burden of producing evidence (essentially Thayer presumptions), or (2) presumptions affecting the burden of proof (essentially Morgan presumptions). . . .

Articles 3 and 4 (Sections 630-668) classify many presumptions found in California law; but many other presumptions, both statutory and common law, must await classification by the courts in accordance with the criteria contained in Sections 603 and 605.

The classification scheme contained in the Evidence Code follows a distinction that appears in the California cases. Thus, for example, the courts have at times held that presumptions do not affect the burden of proof. Estate of Eakle, 33 Cal. App. 2d 379, 91 P.2d 954 (1939) (presumption of undue influence); Valentine v. Provident Mut. Life Ins. Co., 12 Cal. App. 2d 616, 55 P.2d 1243 (1936) (presumption of death from seven years' absence). And at other times the courts have held that certain presumptions do affect the burden of proof. . . . Estate of Walker, 180 Cal. 478, 181 Pac. 792 (1919) ("clear and satisfactory proof" required to overcome presumption of legitimacy). The cases have not, however, explicitly recognized the distinction, nor have they applied it consistently. . . .

The Evidence Code clarifies the law relating to presumptions by identifying the distinguishing factors, and it provides a measure of certainty by classifying a number of specific presumptions.

§603. Presumption affecting the burden of producing evidence defined. A presumption affecting the burden of producing evidence is a presumption established to implement no public policy other than to facilitate the determination of the particular action in which the presumption is applied.

Comment — Law Revision Commission

Sections 603 and 605 set forth the criteria for determining whether a particular presumption is a presumption affecting the burden of producing evidence or a presumption affecting the burden of proof. Many presumptions are classified in Articles 3 and 4 (Sections 630-668) of this chapter. In the absence of specific statutory classification, the courts may determine whether a presumption is a presumption affecting the burden of producing evidence or a presumption affecting the burden of proof by applying the standards contained in Sections 603 and 605.

Section 603 describes those presumptions that are not based on any public policy extrinsic to the action in which they are invoked. These presumptions are designed to dispense with unnecessary proof of facts that are likely to be true if not disputed. Typically, such presumptions are based on an underlying logical inference. In some cases, the presumed fact is so likely to be true and so little likely to be disputed that the law requires it to be assumed in the absence of contrary evidence. In other cases, evidence of the nonexistence of the presumed fact, if there is any, is so much more readily available to the party against whom the presumption operates that he is not permitted to argue that the presumed fact does not exist unless he is willing to produce such evidence. In still other cases, there may be no direct evidence of the existence or nonexistence of the presumed fact; but, because the case must be decided, the law requires a determination that the presumed fact exists in light of common experience indicating that it usually exists in such cases. . . .

Typical of such presumptions are the presumption that a mailed letter was received (Section 641) and presumptions relating to the authenticity of documents (Sections 643-645).

The presumptions described in Section 603 are not expressions of policy; they are expressions of experience. They are intended solely to eliminate the need for the trier of fact to reason from the proven or established fact to the presumed fact and to forestall argument over the existence of the presumed fact when there is no evidence tending to prove the nonexistence of the presumed fact.

§604. Effect of presumption affecting burden of producing evidence. The effect of a presumption affecting the burden of producing evidence is to require the trier of fact to assume the existence of the presumed fact unless and until evidence is introduced which would support a finding of its nonexistence, in which case the trier of fact shall determine the existence or nonexistence of the presumed fact from the evidence and without regard to the presumption. Nothing in this section shall be construed to prevent the drawing of any inference that may be appropriate.

Comment — Assembly Committee on Judiciary

Section 604 describes the manner in which a presumption affecting the burden of producing evidence operates. Such a presumption is merely a preliminary assumption in the absence of contrary evidence, i.e., evidence sufficient to sustain a finding of the nonexistence of the presumed fact. If contrary evidence is introduced, the trier of fact must weigh the inferences arising from the facts that gave rise to the presumption against the contrary evidence and resolve the conflict. For example, if a party proves that a letter was mailed, the trier of fact is required to find that the letter was received in the absence of any believable contrary evidence. However, if the adverse party denies receipt, the presumption is gone from the case. The trier of fact must then weigh the denial of receipt against the inference of receipt arising from proof of mailing and decide whether or not the letter was received. . . .

§605. Presumption affecting the burden of proof defined. A presumption affecting the burden of proof is a presumption established to implement some public policy other than to facilitate the determination of the particular action in which the presumption is applied, such as the policy in favor of establishment of a parent and child relationship, the validity of marriage, the stability of titles to property, or the security of those who entrust themselves or their property to the administration of others.

Comment — Law Revision Commission

Section 605 describes a presumption affecting the burden of proof. Such presumptions are established in order to carry out or to effectuate some public policy other than or in addition to the policy of facilitating the trial of actions.

Frequently, presumptions affecting the burden of proof are designed to facilitate determination of the action in which they are applied. Superficially, therefore, such presumptions may appear merely to be presumptions affecting the burden of producing evidence. What makes a presumption one affecting the burden of proof is the fact that there is always some further reason of policy for the establishment of the presumption. It is the existence of this further basis in policy that distinguishes a presumption affecting the burden of proof from a presumption affecting the burden of producing evidence. For example, the presumption of death from seven years' absence (Section 667) exists in part to facilitate the disposition of actions by supplying a rule of thumb to govern certain cases in which there is likely to be no direct evidence of the presumed fact. But the policy in favor of distributing estates, of settling titles, and of permitting life to proceed normally at some time prior to the expiration of the absentee's normal life expectancy (perhaps 30 or 40 years) that underlies the presumption indicates that it should be a presumption affecting the burden of proof.

Frequently, too, a presumption affecting the burden of proof will have an underlying basis in probability and logical inference. For example, the presumption of the validity of a ceremonial marriage may be based in part on the probability that most marriages are valid. However, an underlying logical inference is not essential. In fact, the lack of an underlying inference is a strong indication that the presumption affects the burden of proof. Only the needs of public policy can justify the direction of a particular assumption that is not warranted by the application of probability and common experience to the known facts. Thus, the total lack of any inference underlying the presumption of the negligence of an employer that arises from his failure to secure the payment of workmen's compensation (Labor Code §3708) is a clear indication that the presumption is based on public policy and affects the burden of proof. Similarly, the fact that the presumption of death from seven years' absence may conflict directly with the logical inference that life continues for its normal expectancy is an indication that the presumption is based on public policy and, hence, affects the burden of proof.

§606. Effect of presumption affecting burden of proof. The effect of a presumption affecting the burden of proof is to impose upon the party against whom it operates the burden of proof as to the nonexistence of the presumed fact.

Comment — Assembly Committee on Judiciary

Section 606 describes the manner in which a presumption affecting the burden of proof operates. In the ordinary case, the party against whom it is invoked will have the burden of proving the nonexistence of the presumed fact by a preponderance of the evidence. Certain presumptions affecting the burden of proof may be overcome only by clear and convincing proof. When such a presumption is relied on, the party against whom the presumption operates will have a heavier burden of proof and will be required to persuade the trier of fact of the nonexistence of the presumed fact by proof " 'sufficiently strong to command the unhesitating assent of every reasonable mind.' " Sheehan v. Sullivan, 126 Cal. 189, 193, 58 Pac. 543, 544 (1899). . . .

Notes and Questions

1. As the California Evidence Code and Comments suggest, legal presumptions generally serve one or more of three distinct functions: They reflect probability, the parties' relative access to the evidence, and the strength of the public interest in finding one way rather than the other. Considerations of probability and access to the evidence generate burdens affecting the production of evidence; public policy considerations generate presumptions affecting the burden of proof and rules concerning the quantum of proof necessary to overcome those presumptions. Compelling public policy concerns have, on occasion, given rise to irrebuttable presumptions. See, for example, Kusior v. Silver, 54 Cal. 2d 603, 354 P.2d 657 (1960) (discussing a former California statute providing that "the issue of a wife cohabiting with her husband, who is not impotent, is indisputably presumed to be legitimate"). This provision, now weakened, is embodied in California Family Code sections 7540 and 7541. Does an irrebuttable presumption of paternity that is contrary to a fact now conclusively ascertainable by genetic tests violate the husband's due process rights? See Marriage of Stephen and Sharyne B., 124 Cal. App. 3d 524, 177 Cal. Rptr. 429 (1981); cf. Michelle W. v. Ronald W., 39 Cal. 3d 358, 703 P.2d 88, 216 Cal. Rptr. 748 (1985).

2. The California Evidence Code does not specifically address community property presumptions and hence does not specify whether they are section 603 or section 605 presumptions. Nor does the California Family Code.

Compare the Uniform Marital Property Act, which provides:

> "Presumption" or a "presumed" fact means the imposition on the person against whom the presumption or presumed fact is directed of the burden of proving that the nonexistence of the presumed fact is more probable than its existence.

Uniform Marital Property Act §1(14), 9A U.L.A. 112 (1998).

B. THE PRESUMPTION THAT PROPERTY ACQUIRED OR POSSESSED DURING MARRIAGE IS COMMUNITY PROPERTY

The next two cases illustrate the wide variation in judicial articulation of the presumption that property acquired or possessed during marriage is community property. As you read these cases, keep in mind the classification scheme of the California Evidence Code.

LYNAM v. VORWERK
13 Cal. App. 507, 110 P. 355 (1910)

COOPER, P.J. — This is an appeal from the judgment in favor of plaintiff for $1,646.20, with interest, and from the order denying defendant's motion for a new trial.

The plaintiff is the administratrix of the estate of Gottlieb Damkroeger, deceased, and the defendant is the executor of the will of Karolina Damkroeger, deceased. The facts of the case are undisputed, and raise a question of law as to the title to the money for which judgment was given.

On September 29, 1899, Gottlieb and Karolina Damkroeger were and for several years prior thereto had been husband and wife, and had money on deposit with the German Savings and Loan Society in their joint names. In connection with the said deposit account there appears the following:

7850.   San Francisco, September 29, 1899.

The German Savings and Loan Society, pay all or any sum or sums that are now or may hereafter be deposited with you by us, and entered in pass-book numbered 124,097, to whichever of us, the undersigned, shall demand and receipt for the same and produce said book.

> *Karolina Damkroeger.*
> *Gottlieb Damkroeger.*

It was admitted that the writing contained the correct signatures of both husband and wife.

There was no evidence other than as herein stated as to the source from which the money came, or as to its being the common, joint or separate property of either husband or wife.

Gottlieb, the husband, died in April, 1903, leaving Karolina surviving him. After her husband's death Karolina withdrew the deposit. She qualified as administratrix of the estate of her deceased husband, but never accounted for the moneys so withdrawn by her as any part of the assets of his estate.

In January, 1907, she died, and this action was afterward brought against the executor of her last will and testament.

The plaintiff relied upon the provisions of section 164 of the Civil Code, which declares that all property acquired after marriage by either husband or wife, except that acquired by gift, bequest, devise or descent (Civil Code, section 163), is community property. The section expressly provides that all property acquired by either husband or wife after marriage is community property. The property (money) was in the possession of the husband and wife long after their marriage, and was by them jointly deposited in the bank. Does the fact that the husband and wife are in possession of money after their marriage raise a presumption that it was acquired after such marriage? In our opinion it does. The relation of husband and wife as to their property is somewhat in the nature of a partnership, where there is usually partnership property and the separate property of the copartners. If the copartners should jointly go to a bank and deposit money in their joint names, it seems, in the absence of other evidence, that the most reasonable inference would be that the money was the joint money of such copartners, and that being in their possession as such copartners, it would be presumed to have been acquired by the copartnership. In fact, usually and in most cases where money or property is in the possession of the husband or wife or both after marriage, it has been acquired after marriage. This is a matter of common knowledge. Of course, such possession raises only a presumption, which may be overcome by evidence as to the facts; but in the absence of such evidence the presumption is sufficient. It has been held that the possession of money by either or both husband and wife after marriage, in the absence of other evidence, raises a presumption that it is community property. In Fennell v. Drinkhouse, 131 Cal. 447, [82 Am. St. Rep. 361, 63 Pac. 734], it was so held. The court there said:

> All of the money found in the bank and received by the said administrator was deposited after the marriage of plaintiff and Mrs. Fennell, and the presumption therefore was, in the absence of other evidence, that all of it was community property, and the burden of proof was upon appellant. This presumption can be overcome by evidence of a clear, certain and convincing character establishing the contrary, and the burden of this showing rested with the parties claiming the separate character of the property. In the absence of such proof the presumption as to the community character was absolute and conclusive.

. . . The appellant contends that the writing given to the bank had the effect to create a joint tenancy in the husband and wife, with the right of survivorship. In our opinion such contention is not plausible. It is provided in the Civil Code (section 683): "A joint interest is one owned by several persons in equal shares, by a title created by a single will or transfer, when expressly declared in the will or transfer to be a joint tenancy, or when granted or devised to executors or trustees as joint tenants." The writing given to the German Savings and Loan Society was merely an authority to the bank to pay the amount entered in the passbook to either of the parties in whose name the deposit was made. . . .

The judgment and order are affirmed.

FIDELITY & CASUALTY COMPANY v. MAHONEY
71 Cal. App. 2d 65, 161 P.2d 944 (1945)

WOOD (Parker), J. — On June 28, 1943, in Louisville, Kentucky, J. B. Mahoney, Sr., a resident of Los Angeles, purchased an airplane-travel accident insurance policy from the plaintiff insurance company and mailed it to the beneficiary named therein, J. B. Mahoney, Jr., of Los Angeles, his sixteen-year-old son by a former marriage. Soon after the policy was purchased, the insured boarded an airplane for the purpose of going to Los Angeles, and within an hour thereafter the airplane fell in Kentucky and as a result thereof he was killed.

Patricia Mahoney and the insured had been married about two months preceding the airplane accident, and at all times during their marriage they were domiciled in California. She made a demand on the insurance company for one-half the proceeds of the policy on the ground that the policy was purchased with community property.

The insurance company filed this action in interpleader, and upon stipulation an interlocutory decree was entered wherein it was ordered that upon deposit in court by the insurance company of $4,989.50 (being the amount of the policy less $10.50 for costs) it would be released from liability under the policy, and it was further ordered that J. B. Mahoney, Jr., and Patricia Mahoney litigate between themselves to determine who was entitled to receive the amount so deposited. The insurance company made the deposit.

Defendant Patricia Mahoney alleged, among other things, that she was the widow of J. B. Mahoney, deceased; that the premium on said policy was paid by J. B. Mahoney from community property funds owned by him and her; and that as his widow she was entitled to one-half of said $5,000.

Defendant J. B. Mahoney, Jr., alleged, among other things, that he was the beneficiary named in the policy; that the $5,000 was not community property; that Patricia Mahoney had no right, title or interest in said $5,000; and that the policy was purchased with the separate property of the deceased J. B. Mahoney.

The court found that the $5,000 was not community property; that Patricia Mahoney had no right, title or interest therein; and that the policy was purchased with the separate property of deceased J. B. Mahoney. . . .

Defendant Patricia Mahoney appeals from the judgment, and contends that the findings of fact are not supported by the evidence.

In the statement on appeal it is recited:

> There is no evidence as to the nature or extent of the decedent's estate, whether separate or community, except that it is shown the decedent earned a gross monthly salary in an undetermined amount during the period of his second marriage and that he had a bank account in his own name. There was no evidence on behalf of either of the defendants as to whether or not the premium paid for said policy of insurance came from the separate estate or the community estate of the decedent.

The record does not show what amount was paid for the policy, but since it was stated in the written opinion of the trial judge and in the briefs that the amount was $1.00, it will be assumed herein that $1.00 was the amount of the premium.

Appellant's theory is that the insurance premium was paid by the insured from community funds, that such payment was a gift by the husband of community funds, and that such gift, being without her written consent, was a nullity under the provisions of section 172 of the Civil Code as to her one-half interest in the premium money, and therefore she is entitled to one-half the proceeds of the policy.

Section 172 of the Civil Code provides: "The husband has the management and control of the community personal property, with like absolute power of disposition, other than testamentary, as he has of his separate estate; provided, however, that he cannot make a gift of such community personal property . . . without the written consent of the wife." If the insurance premium was paid from the husband's separate funds the wife was not entitled to any part of the proceeds of the policy, it being provided in section 157 of the Civil Code that "Neither husband nor wife has any interest in the property of the other. . . ." In Mundt v. Connecticut Gen. Life Ins. Co., (1939), 35 Cal. App. 2d 416 [95 P.2d 966], wherein the husband had paid the premiums on his life insurance policy from community funds without the wife's consent, the question was whether the wife, who was not the named beneficiary, was entitled to one-half the proceeds of the policy. In that case the court said at page 421: ". . . the only test applied to this problem has been whether the premiums (on a policy issued on the life of a husband after coverture) are paid entirely from community funds. If so, the policy becomes a community asset and the non-consenting wife may recover an undivided one-half thereof. . . ." (See, also, Bazzell v. Endriss (1940), 41 Cal. App. 2d 463 [107 P.2d 49].) The court was required to find whether the money used in paying the premium was paid from community funds. As above shown, there was no oral or documentary evidence as to whether the money used in paying the premium was community property or separate property. As to appellant's contention that the findings were not supported by the evidence, she argues that, since there was no evidence to the contrary, the presumption, under section 164 of the Civil Code that property acquired after marriage (other than by gift, devise, or descent) is community property, is determinative that the money used to pay the insurance premium was community property. There is a presumption that property acquired after marriage, other than by gift, devise, or descent, is community property. (Estate of Duncan, 9 Cal. 2d 207, 217 [70 P.2d 174].) Where the marriage relation has existed a short period of time the presumption that property acquired after marriage is community property is of less weight than in the case of a long-continued marriage relation. (Estate of Duncan, supra, 217; Falk v. Falk, 48 Cal. App. 2d 762, 767 [120 P.2d 714]; 41 C.J.S. 1031.) There is no presumption, however, as to when property was acquired. (Scott v. Austin, 57 Cal. App. 553, 556 [207 P. 710]; 3 Cal. Jur. Supp. 554.) The marriage relation had existed about two months. The husband had a bank account in his own name. It was not shown at the trial whether his bank account was large or small or whether the bank account had been in existence a long or short time, and it was not shown whether his monthly salary was large or small. It would seem that proof of such matters was available. Such proof would have been of material assistance to the trial court in determining whether the $1.00 used in paying the premium was acquired before or after the marriage, especially in view of the short time of marriage and in view of the small amount of the premium. . . . The appellant was not entitled to a portion of the $5,000 unless, as above stated, the premium was paid from community funds. . . . It was necessary therefore to determine the source of the $1.00 used in paying the premium. The burden was upon appellant to prove that the $1.00 premium was paid from community funds. . . . She failed to carry the burden. . . .

The judgment is affirmed. DESMOND, P.J., and SHINN, J., concurred.

Notes and Questions

1. Is it significant that Karolina and Gottlieb Damkroeger were both owners of the account containing the disputed funds? Would the result be different if the account were in Gottlieb's name alone? Or in Karolina's? What does the court say? Do you agree?

2. Despite frequent case law suggestion to the contrary, California *statutes* do not embody any presumptions in favor of community property. (For good discussion of this point, see Marriage of Lusk, 86 Cal. App. 3d 228, 150 Cal. Rptr. 63 (1978).) Family Code section 760 defines community property as "property . . . acquired by a married person during the marriage." Section 770 limits this definition to onerous acquisition by providing that property acquired during marriage by gift, bequest, devise, or descent (so-called lucrative acquisition) is a married

person's separate property. Section 770 further provides that property owned by a spouse before marriage is his or her separate property. The statutes do not address either of the following burden of proof questions.

(a) Who has the burden of proving whether a given asset was acquired during marriage? Does the community property proponent have to show that it was acquired during marriage or must the separate property proponent show that it was not acquired during marriage?

(b.) Assuming that one party has demonstrated acquisition during marriage, which estate must demonstrate the facts that establish whether the asset is community or separate property? In other words, must the community property proponent show that the asset was earned by community labor, or must the separate property proponent show that acquisition during marriage was either lucrative or traceable to a separate property source, such as premarital earnings?

The second question is answered by the case law presumption in favor of community property, which is variously claimed to attach to property "acquired" or "possessed" during marriage. Thus, the separate property proponent must show that acquisition was lucrative or traceable to a separate property source.

A number of early supreme court opinions used the terms *acquisition* and *possession* interchangeably. See, for example, Smith v. Smith, 12 Cal. 216, 224 (1859), and Meyer v. Kinzer and Wife, 12 Cal. 247, 251 (1859). Is there a difference between *possession* and *acquisition*? Which formulation was used in Lynam v. Vorwerk? Which was used in Fidelity & Casualty Co. v. Mahoney?

The "acquired during marriage" formulation contains a burden of proof issue that is avoided by the "possessed during marriage" standard. If the question is whether an asset was *possessed* during marriage, it is generally unnecessary to allocate the burden of demonstrating possession. That the asset is possessed at the end of marriage, that is, at death or divorce, is normally conclusive evidence that the asset was possessed during marriage.[1] In contrast, possession at death or divorce is not, without more, strongly probative of *acquisition* during marriage.

In *Mahoney*, the court acknowledges that "[t]here is a presumption that property acquired after marriage . . . is community property," but observes that "[t]here is no presumption, however, as to when property was acquired." The court then effectively assigns to the community property proponent the burden of showing that the $1 used to pay the insurance premium was acquired during marriage. The court suggests that Mrs. Mahoney simply failed to prove her case and chides her for having neglected to adduce adequate evidence. Could Mrs. Mahoney, in fact, have proven her case? Would proof on the issues identified by the appellate court "have been of material assistance to the trial court"?

Why did *Mahoney* assign the community property proponent the burden of showing that an asset possessed at the end of the marriage was acquired during marriage? Was it because the statute (now California Family Code section 760) defines community property as property "acquired during marriage," and the court concluded that the community property proponent must prove all the elements

---

1. There may be some question with respect to assets acquired during the interval between the termination of the economic community by permanent separation and the property division at divorce. Proof with respect to such recent acquisitions is, however, likely to be readily available.

that would bring an asset within the statutory definition? Is this an unavoidable conclusion? Suppose that the court had begun its analysis with section 770, which defines separate property as "all property owned by the person before marriage." Might the court, with equal plausibility, have assigned the separate property proponent the burden of demonstrating that the $1 was owned by Mr. Mahoney before his marriage to Patricia? How should the court have resolved this burden of proof dilemma? Consider the California Evidence Code provisions reprinted above and notes 4 and 5 below.

If, instead, the court had assigned to the separate estate the burden of showing that the asset was owned before marriage, there would be no meaningful difference between the *acquisition* and *possession* formulations. With either, the separate estate would have to prove that the asset was acquired before marriage.

3. Compare the draft and final versions of the Uniform Marital Property Act:

> All property *owned* by spouses during marriage is presumed to be marital property. [Emphasis added.] [1/1/82 Draft §6(a).]

> All property of spouses is presumed to be marital property. [Uniform Marital Property Act §4(b), 9A U.L.A. 116 (1998).]

The final version of the Uniform Act follows the Spanish-Mexican law from which the California community property system was derived. Robbins, Community Property Law 16 (1940), quoting Matienzo's commentary on the Nueva Recopilacion. Is there any significant difference between the Uniform Act presumption and the "possession during marriage" formulation?

Louisiana and Texas have codified the "possession" formulation. La. Civ. Code Ann. art. 2340 (2002); Tex. Fam. Code Ann. §3.003 (2002). New Mexico has codified the "acquired during marriage" standard. New Mex. Stat. Ann. §40-3-12 (2002). Even in those states, as well as in states such as California that have not codified any standard, case law is inconsistent. See cases collected in W. Reppy, Jr., and C. Samuel, Community Property in the United States 4-3-4-4 (3d ed. 1991). Of all the formulations, which do you prefer? Which is most favorable to the community? To the separate estate? Which is most simple to administer?

4. Why do we have a presumption that property acquired or possessed during marriage is community property? What rationale does Lynam v. Vorwerk give for the presumption? How do you imagine the court in *Mahoney* would explain the presumption?

Consider the supreme court's discussion in Meyer v. Kinzer and Wife, 12 Cal. 247, 252-254 (1859):

> This invariable presumption which attends the possession of property by either spouse during the existence of the community, can only be overcome by clear and certain proof that it was owned by the claimant before marriage or acquired afterwards in one of the particular ways specified in the statute, or that it is property taken in exchange for, or in the investment, or as the price of the property so originally owned or acquired. The burden of proof must rest with the claimant of the separate estate. Any other rule would lead to infinite embarrassment, confusion, and fraud. In vain would creditors or purchasers attempt to show that the particular property seized or bought was *not* owned by the claimant before marriage and was *not* acquired by gift, be-

quest, devise or descent, or was not such property under a new form consequent upon some exchange, sale or investment. In vain would they essay to
trace through its various changes the disposition of any separate estate of the
wife, so as to exclude any blending of it with the particular property which
might be the subject of consideration.

Meyer v. Kinzer and Wife was a creditors' rights case and, arguably, represents a
correct allocation of the burden of proof between a married couple and its creditors. Is the analysis persuasive, however, when applied to the more frequent inter
se dispute between husband and wife? Ought burden of proof allocation be identical in inter se and third party disputes? (By way of analogy, several California community property statutes insulate third party bona fide purchasers from claims that
one spouse might have against the other. See, for example, California Family Code
section 803 with respect to the treatment of property acquired in a married woman's
name before 1975.) On the other hand, are the spouses equally situated in terms
of access to the evidence? Is the separate property or community property proponent more likely to have access to relevant evidence?

5. In terms of the California Evidence Code classifications, do you think the
community property presumption ought to shift the burden of proof or merely
the burden of producing evidence? California courts have generally treated marital
property presumptions as presumptions affecting the burden of proof. See, for example, Baron v. Baron, 9 Cal. App. 3d 933, 939, 88 Cal. Rptr. 404 (1970) (presumption at divorce that joint tenancy is community property); Ashodian v. Ashodian,
96 Cal. App. 3d 43, 46-47, 157 Cal. Rptr. 555 (1979) (separate property presumption
when married woman acquired property in her name before 1975).

6. *Quantum of proof required to overcome the presumption.* The Meyer v. Kinzer and
Wife dictum that "clear and certain proof" is required to overcome the community
property presumption has been repeated in recent intermediate appellate decisions. See, for example, *Ashodian,* supra, and Bank of California v. Connolly, 36
Cal. App. 3d 350, 111 Cal. Rptr. 468 (1973). Yet the supreme court repudiated the
Meyer v. Kinzer and Wife dictum in Freese v. Hibernia Savings and Loan Society,
139 Cal. 392, 73 P. 172 (1903) (rejecting the heightened standard and holding that
a mere preponderance of the evidence suffices to overcome the community property presumption).

7. *Standard of review on appeal.* Although *preponderance of the evidence* and *clear
and convincing evidence* are the two competing evidentiary standards prescribed by
appellate courts for use at trial, they are not the standards applied in California
appellate review. On appellate review, the issue is whether the trial court's finding
is supported by *substantial* evidence, or whether a party has presented *sufficient* evidence to rebut the presumption that property acquired during marriage is community property. For the "substantial evidence" standard, see Estate of Raphael at
page 114 supra; Marriage of Mix, at page 223 infra; Ford v. Ford, at page 254 infra;
and Marriage of Frick, at page 233 infra. For the "sufficient evidence to rebut the
presumption" formulation, see Gudelj v. Gudelj, at page 251 infra, and Marriage
of Grinius, at page 259 infra. Marriage of Knickerbocker, 43 Cal. App. 3d 1039,
1042, 118 Cal. Rptr. 232 (1974), explains:

The rules governing the determination of the character of marital property are well settled. A finding that property owned by a married person is

separate property is a finding of ultimate fact. (In re Marriage of Jafeman (1972) 29 Cal. App. 3d 244, 254 [105 Cal. Rptr. 483].) Whether the evidence adduced to overcome the presumption of community property is sufficient for the purpose is a question of fact for the trial court (Thomasset v. Thomasset (1953) 122 Cal. App. 2d 116, 123 [264 P.2d 626] (disapproved on other grounds in See v. See (1966) 64 Cal. 2d 778, 785-786 [51 Cal. Rptr. 888, 415 P.2d 776].) Such a finding is binding upon an appellate court if it is supported by sufficient evidence or if it is drawn from evidence which is conflicting or subject to differing inferences. If the trial court has concluded that a presumption has been overcome, this determination will not be disturbed upon appeal if the evidence is in substantial conflict or is subject to varying inferences. (In re Marriage of Jafeman, supra, pp.254-255.) Only where the evidence to rebut the presumption is so weak and improbable that the finding is without substantial support may the appellate court set aside the decision of the trier of fact. (In re Marriage of Wall (1973) 30 Cal. App. 3d 1042, 1048 [106 Cal. Rptr. 690].)

Why do courts use a lesser standard on review? Do you see why a lower standard is necessary when the appellate court is not empowered to exercise *de novo* review? Some states do direct their appellate courts to exercise *de novo* review in family law cases. See, for example, Marriage of Latimer and Latimer, 103 Or. App. 43, 795 P.2d 1102 (1990). California appellate courts, in contrast, exercise conventional appellate review.

Thus, California cases frequently present factual issues that could be decided either way at trial insofar as either result would be sustained upon appeal, each being adequately supported by *substantial,* or *sufficient,* evidence. See, for example, Bowman v. Bowman, infra at page 179, and Marriage of Fortier, infra at page 309. Such cases are underrepresented in casebooks because attorneys generally do not appeal them and, even when appealed, they may be pedagogically unattractive to casebook editors.

8. Identification of the "property" in question may be vital to the ultimate result. What property was the subject of the court's classification in *Mahoney*? The insurance policy or the dollar? Did it matter? Rethink *Mahoney* with the premise that the *insurance policy* was the asset acquired during marriage. Do you see the court's error? How would you explain the error in terms of the methodology of California community property law?

9. Community property that is not divided at divorce becomes tenancy in common and patiently awaits future division. See Henn v. Henn, reprinted at page 516 infra. In 1965, the legislature enacted what is now California Family Code section 802:

> The presumption that property acquired during marriage is community property does not apply to any property . . . held by a person at the time of the person's death if the marriage during which the property was acquired was terminated by [divorce] . . . more than four years before the death.

How does this statute alter the usual burden of proof allocation? Assume that a surviving divorced wife has just discovered that her deceased former husband acquired certain bonds shortly before the couple separated in 1986. The bonds were not listed in the pleadings or divided in their 1987 divorce. The husband died in 1993. What must the former wife show to establish her claim?

C. THE ROLE OF TITLE GENERALLY

It is sometimes suggested that title is immaterial in community property law.[2] This is an overstatement derived from the observation that title in one spouse's name does not defeat the presumption that property acquired or possessed during marriage is owned by the community.[3] Thus, for example, if the husband purchases a new car during marriage and places title in his name alone, the car is still presumptively community property. It is necessarily a basic principle of community property law that a spouse may not appropriate community property to himself by placing title in his name alone. Thus title in one spouse's name alone, without more, is insufficient to overcome the presumption that property acquired during marriage is community property. Simply stated, a spouse may not make a gift of community property to himself.

On the other hand, the form of title may be some evidence that one spouse has made a gift of his separate or community interest to the other spouse or that the parties have joined together to transform ownership from separate to community or from community to separate. Suppose, for example, that the husband who purchased the car placed title in his wife's name alone and gave her the keys when they went out to dinner on her birthday. An observer might reasonably infer from the state of title and the surrounding circumstances that the husband intended to give up any interest he might otherwise have in the car. Similarly, suppose that a couple used community funds to purchase a home in joint tenancy. That both parties accepted the joint tenancy deed would logically support an inference that the parties agreed to hold their home as joint tenancy, with a right of survivorship, rather than as community property, which has no right of survivorship.[4]

Because most California litigation has involved property held in joint title, a state of title from which spousal agreement may reasonably be inferred, case law dictum sometimes makes the excessively broad assertion "that the form of title by which property is held gives rise to a rebuttable presumption of its character."[5] Yet upon closer examination, the citations for this proposition invariably involve forms of joint title, that is, forms of ownership that on their face appear to evidence an *agreement of the parties* to hold in that form.

Thus, the truth lies somewhere in between the antithetical claims that title is invariably immaterial and that title is presumptively controlling. A more accurate, albeit less definitive, generalization is that title is sometimes immaterial and sometimes presumptively controlling. The following materials deal with forms of title that have been given some presumptive effect. These materials, part case law and part statute, consist of a disparate group of presumptions for which gift and/or transmutation analysis provides a convenient organizing principle. As you consider

2. See, e.g., W. de Funiak and M. Vaughn, Principles of Community Property 119-120 (2d ed. 1971).

3. See, e.g., Burdick v. Pope, 90 Nev. 28, 518 P.2d 146 (Nev. 1974) (title to property acquired during marriage in one spouse's name as that spouse's "sole and separate" property did not, standing alone, overcome the presumption that property acquired during marriage is community property). But see the presumption below (in Section D) that property acquired before 1975 by a married woman in her name is her separate property.

4. But query, for post-1984 transactions, whether the transmutation statute, Family Code section 852, has been satisfied in either of the two examples.

5. Marriage of Buol, 159 Cal. App. 3d 174, 180 (1984), depublished when the California Supreme Court accepted review. For the supreme court opinion, see page 192 infra.

these presumptions, ask yourself whether each presumption is designed to serve as an evidentiary aid to ascertain the parties' original intentions, or to effectuate substantive policy preferences, or to protect by means of burden of proof allocation parties who have lesser access to essential evidence. Moreover, in each instance, insofar as the presumption is primarily intended to ascertain party intent, ought spousal intent be the critical issue? Does a determination based on spousal intent during the ongoing marriage necessarily produce a just result at the termination of the marriage? Instead of using presumptions as a method of divining the original intent of one or both spouses, ought we ask instead what should be done at divorce? Such a normative analysis would not cast out all presumptions and individual spousal agreements; instead it would establish normative presumptions — for example, persons contributing separate property to jointly held property are entitled at divorce to reimbursement of the contribution and a pro rata share of the appreciation. Such presumptions could be overcome by, inter alia, a showing of some agreement to the contrary. Finally, are you persuaded that the parties in these cases ever had an ascertainable intent of any sort?

D.   FORMS OF TITLE THAT RAISE PRESUMPTIONS OF GIFT OR AGREEMENT TO TRANSMUTE

1.   The Married Woman's Special Presumption

§803.   Property acquired by married woman before January 1, 1975

Notwithstanding any other provision of this part, whenever any real or personal property, or any interest therein or encumbrance thereon, was acquired before January 1, 1975, by a married woman by an instrument in writing, the following presumptions apply, and are conclusive in favor of any person dealing in good faith and for a valuable consideration with the married woman or her legal representatives or successors in interest, regardless of any change in her marital status after acquisition of the property:

(a) If acquired by the married woman, the presumption is that the property is the married woman's separate property.

(b) If acquired by the married woman and any other person, the presumption is that the married woman takes the part acquired by her as tenant in common, unless a different intention is expressed in the instrument.

(c) If acquired by husband and wife by an instrument in which they are described as husband and wife, the presumption is that the property is the community property of the husband and wife, unless a different intention is expressed in the instrument.

This presumption, first enacted in 1889, was repealed (but only with respect to post-1974 *acquisitions*) with the 1975 initiation of sex-neutral equal management. For title acquired during the pre-1975 period of male management, is this presumption a good measure of spousal intent and other material evidence? How might a married woman obtain property in her name? What reasonable inferences could one draw from the fact that a wife, under the male management regime, acquired property in her name? Note that the presumption is conclusive in favor of good faith third party purchasers from the wife (why?) but is, by implication, rebuttable by the husband and his privies with respect to property still held by the wife or her donees. What evidence should suffice to overcome the presumption?

HOLMES v. HOLMES
27 Cal. App. 546, 150 P. 793 (1915)

SHAW, J.—Plaintiff appeals from the judgment, in support of which she presents a bill of exceptions.

The action was brought by plaintiff to obtain a decree against defendant quieting her title to certain real estate. . . .

Title to the property described as parcels 2 and 3 was, by an instrument in writing . . . , vested in plaintiff [wife], and by virtue of the provision of section [803] . . . , is presumed to be her separate estate. This presumption, however, is disputable and may be controverted by any competent evidence tending to overcome it. (Killian v. Killian, 10 Cal. App. 312, [101 Pac. 806]; Fanning v. Green, 156 Cal. 279, [104 Pac. 308].) The record, however, is silent as to any evidence tending in any degree to overcome such presumption, other than the fact that the purchase price thereof was paid from the joint earnings of plaintiff and her husband. Defendant insists that such fact, as to which there was a conflict of evidence, justifies the finding that said real estate was community property. The judgment as to parcels of property designated as 2 and 3 rests upon this finding.

Conceding the purchase made from the joint earnings of the husband and wife, such fact, standing alone and in the absence of any other showing, is not sufficient to rebut the presumption that the property was the separate estate of plaintiff. Community funds may be the subject of a gift from husband to wife (Fanning v. Green [supra]; Alferitz v. Arrivillaga, 143 Cal. 646, [77 Pac. 657]); and where property deeded to the wife is purchased with community funds a presumption, since it is essential to the theory that the property is, as provided in said section [803], the separate property of the wife, arises that the husband, knowing the effect of such transaction, intended, in the absence of any evidence to the contrary, to give it to the wife. (Hamilton v. Hubbard, 134 Cal. 603, [65 Pac. 621, 66 Pac. 860]; Fanning v. Green [supra].

. . . [I]n so far as it affects the property described in parcels 2 and 3, the judgment is reversed. CONREY, P.J., and JAMES, J., concurred.

LOUKNITSKY v. LOUKNITSKY
123 Cal. App. 2d 406, 266 P.2d 910 (1954)

WOOD (Fred B.), J. — Plaintiff Olga Louknitsky has appealed from an interlocutory decree which awarded her a divorce upon the ground of extreme cruelty. She asserts error in . . . the finding that all the property belonged to the community. . . .

There is substantial evidence that the major portion of the funds available for investment in the property described were derived from the earnings and the proceeds of the earnings of the husband, defendant Vladimir Louknitsky, while the parties resided in Shanghai, China, before coming to California.

There being no evidence concerning the applicable laws of China or of Hong-kong (where they resided for a short time before coming to California), those laws are presumed to be the same as the laws of California. (Christ v. Superior Court, 211 Cal. 593, 598 [296 P. 612].) Accordingly, the funds acquired in China, under the circumstances indicated, are deemed community property. Olga came to this country, directly to California, some little time ahead of Vladimir, who joined her here. Each has resided here ever since arrival.

The only other source of funds since they took up residence in this state has been the compensation received by either of them when gainfully employed. For a period of about 10 months after her arrival here, he sent her $70 a month from his earnings. There is evidence that since his arrival he has been paying the install-ments on the purchase price mortgages which she executed upon acquiring the house and lot in San Francisco. . . .

The . . . factor which might cast a doubt upon the community character of the house and lot acquired in San Francisco, inheres in the fact that the deed of convey-ance ran to Olga only, not to Olga and Vladimir as grantees. Normally, in such a case, there arises a disputable presumption that land thus conveyed is the separate property of the wife; in this case, Olga. ([Family Code, §803].)

However, the purchase was made and the deed executed and delivered before Vladimir's arrival here. He testified that he did not know until some time after the event, that she took the property in her name only; also, that after his arrival here he paid all the installment payments on the mortgage until he was "vacated" by the court from the house, some time prior to the trial. These circumstances, particu-larly the husband's lack of knowledge at the time of the purchase that Olga was the sole grantee and the absence of any agreement that the money, already held to be community property, should be converted into separate property by the wife's investing it in her name, tend to rebut the presumption. There is thus ample sup-port for the trial court's finding that the home property belongs to the commu-nity. . . .

The judgment is affirmed.

The section 803 presumption works a sex-based discrimination that disadvan-tages men. A pre-1975 acquisition held by a married woman in her name alone is presumptively her separate property, whereas a pre-1975 acquisition held by a mar-ried man in his name alone is presumptively community property. As the following case illustrates, the presumption may work perverse results when the husband and wife took pre-1975 title jointly.

DUNN v. MULLAN
211 Cal. 583, 296 P. 604 (1931)

THE COURT. — Action to quiet title. Plaintiff, as administrator . . . to the estate of Patrick J. Lyons, deceased, sought to quiet title to . . . sixty-eight acres located in the San Joaquin Valley. Patrick J. Lyons and Margaret Lyons were husband and wife, their marriage occurring in the year 1913, and continuing up to the time of the death of Patrick J. Lyons on the ninth day of June, 1924. His wife, Margaret Lyons, died the following day. . . . The property in controversy at the time of their death stood in the name of both Patrick J. Lyons and Margaret Lyons; thirty-eight acres of it having been conveyed to them by deed dated June 28, 1917, and the remaining thirty acres having been conveyed to them by deed dated November 28, 1917. It appears without dispute that in each deed of conveyance Patrick J. Lyons and Margaret Lyons were named the grantees as husband and wife. . . .

The suit to quiet title was opposed by the joint administratrices of the estate of Margaret Lyons and the findings were in accordance with the answer filed by one of the administratrices in which she alleged that one-half of the property involved was the separate property of the deceased wife and the remaining one-half interest was the community property of the deceased wife and her deceased husband.

The judgment of the trial court, based on said findings, was to the effect that on the date of the death of Patrick J. Lyons, his wife, Margaret Lyons, was the absolute owner of an undivided one-half interest in and to all of the real property described in the complaint as her separate property; that the remaining one-half undivided interest in said real property was the community property of Patrick J. Lyons and his wife, Margaret Lyons. . . .

It was further ordered, adjudged and decreed that the heirs of Patrick J. Lyons were entitled to a one-half interest in the community property [which interest was, therefore, a one-fourth interest in the entire property in controversy], and that the heirs of Margaret Lyons were entitled to a one-half interest in the community property and to the whole of the separate property of Margaret Lyons [which interest was, therefore, a three-fourths interest in the entire property in controversy]. From this judgment, the administrator of the husband's estate has appealed. . . .

No evidence was offered as to the source of the funds used for the purchase price of the two parcels of land. The deeds in which the wife was named as one of the grantees were offered in evidence, and the presumption expressed in section 164 of the Civil Code that "in case the conveyance is to such married woman and her husband, . . . the presumption is that the married woman takes the part conveyed to her, as tenant in common, unless a different intention is expressed in the instrument" was relied upon in support of the claim that an undivided one-half interest in the property belonged to the wife as her separate property. . . .

Appellant contends, first, that if under the presumption set forth in section 164 of the Civil Code, the wife is to be deemed to hold her share of the property as her separate property as a tenant in common, it must necessarily follow that the husband holds his share of the property as his separate property as a tenant in common and not as community property. . . . Although we may concede that there appears to be some merit in this contention, nevertheless in view of the fact that it is definitely and distinctly held in Miller v. Brode, 186 Cal. 409, 414 [199 Pac. 531], and Estate of Regnart, 102 Cal. App. 643 [283 Pac. 860], that deeds naming as grantees both husband and wife presumptively vest property in spouses as tenants in common, the interest conveyed to the wife being presumed under section 164 of the Civil Code to be her separate property and that conveyed to her husband the community property of the marriage, we think this question is no longer open to controversy. . . .

It follows that in so far as this objection is concerned, the findings of the trial court that Margaret Lyons at the date of the death of her husband was the owner of an undivided one-half interest in said property as her separate property, and that the remaining undivided one-half interest in said property was held by the husband as community property was correct, and the judgment based thereon must be affirmed. . . .

Notes and Problems

1. It may initially be difficult to understand how one co-tenant may hold an interest as her separate property and another co-tenant may own his interest as community property. Quite apart from the married woman's special presumption, suppose that Bill, married to Margaret, joins together with his married sister Sue to purchase property as tenants in common. Sue's purchase funds come from her separate premarital savings; Bill's purchase money comes from his marital savings. Sue owns her one-half interest as her separate property; Bill owns his one-half interest as the community property of his marriage to Margaret. Similarly, in Dunn v. Mullan, the husband's interest was presumptively community property because the property was acquired by purchase during marriage. The wife's interest was presumptively her separate property by virtue of the married woman's special presumption.

2. After Dunn v. Mullan, the married woman's special presumption statute was amended to provide that when property is "acquired by husband and wife by an instrument in which they are described as husband and wife, the presumption is that the property is the community property of the husband and wife, unless a different intention is expressed in the instrument." Additionally, the California Supreme Court held that a husband-wife *joint tenancy* expresses "a different intention" within the meaning of section 803(b) and hence avoids the lopsided Dunn v. Mullan result. Siberell v. Siberell, 214 Cal. 767, 7 P.2d 1003 (1932). Thus, the only pre-1975 husband-wife co-ownership interest apparently still subject to Dunn v. Mullan treatment is the tenancy in common, that is husband-wife co-ownership that is neither joint tenancy nor community property. Cardew v. Cardew, 192 Cal. App. 2d 502, 514, 13 Cal. Rptr. 620 (1961).

3. *The wording of co-ownership instruments of title.* A husband and wife may hold title as joint tenants, tenants in common, or as community property. Family Code §750. To create a joint tenancy, the governing instrument must expressly declare that the owners hold in joint tenancy. Civ. Code §683. (See discussion supra at page 160.) Concurrent ownership that is not held in joint tenancy is held as tenancy in common or as community property. Civ. Code §686. To explicitly create community property title, the governing instrument may either specify that the property is held *as community property* or that the co-owners are husband and wife.

What is the effect of a deed to "John Jenkins and Jennifer Jenkins, husband and wife, in joint tenancy"? Cf. Family Code section 803.

Less certain is the effect of spouses taking post-1974 title simply as "Bernard Burton and Betty Burton." When such title was taken before 1975, the section 803 married woman's special presumption specifies that the parties took as tenants in common. The prospective abolition of the married woman's special presumption eliminates the statutory basis for this result with respect to post-1974 title. In common law property theory, the tenancy in common is a residual, or catch-all, category for interests not specifically titled otherwise. Yet community property is not part of the common law, and California property statutes (Civil Code sections 682-687) do not address the question. Does the general section 760 principle that property acquired during marriage is community property argue in favor of interpreting post-1974 title in both spouses' names as community property *title?* Cf. Probate Code section 5305: "[I]f parties to . . . [a bank] account are married to each other, whether or not they are so described in the deposit agreement, their net contribution to the account is presumed to be . . . their community property."

4. *Specific presumptions arising from the form of title compared to the general presumption arising from acquisition during marriage.* As *Holmes* and *Louknitsky* indicate, presumptions arising from the form of title are stronger than the general presumption (arising solely from acquisition during marriage), and they may not be overcome merely by tracing to funds of a different character. This is because title is given presumptive effect *only* when the form of title itself is understood to evidence a gift or agreement of the parties to hold as indicated in the title. Hence rebuttal evidence must counter whatever inference arises from the particular form of title. Thus, in the case of the married woman's special presumption, the husband effectively must show "no gift" in order to rebut the presumption that arises from pre-1975 title in a married woman's name.

In contrast, the presumption of community property that arises *solely* from acquisition during marriage may always be overcome by tracing the acquisition to a separate property source. Because acquisition during marriage alone does not evidence any gift or agreement of the parties, tracing to a separate source is all that is required.

5. To test your mastery of the married woman's special presumption, determine the divorce distribution of the following assets.

a. Harry purchased a family home in 1970 with community funds. He had title put in Wanda's name because he was engaged in several risky business ventures and wished to shield the family home from the claims of his creditors.

b. Harold and Wilma were expecting their first child in 1972. In anticipation of the event, Harold's widowed mother moved into an apartment and sold them her single family residence, deeding it "to Harold Carter and Wilma Carter." Does it matter that Harold's mother is willing to testify for her son in his divorce proceeding?

c. Would your response vary if Harold's mother had instead made a *gift* of the residence to "Harold Carter and Wilma Carter"?

d. Assuming that Harold and his mother intended equal co-ownership interests for Harold and Wilma, how should the grantees have been designated in the 1972 deed?

6. Suppose that Hiram, now deceased, used community funds to purchase a family vacation home in 1980 (yes, *after* 1974) and put title in Wilhemina's name alone. Hiram recently died and, by will, left all his separate property and his half of the community property to his son by a prior marriage. All of Hiram's survivors were surprised to learn that Hiram had taken title to the vacation house in Wilhemina's name alone. No one could shed any light on the matter. Who owns the house?

7. The special presumption was enacted in 1889 to facilitate the wife's management of property. Armed with this presumption, third parties could deal with a married woman so long as title was in her name. Despite its historical justification, the continued force of the special presumption for pre-1975 titles presents serious problems.

Insofar as it continues to characterize ownership of pre-1975 property, does the sex-based presumption violate the Fourteenth Amendment equal protection clause or the more stringent standards articulated by the California Supreme Court? Craig v. Boren, 429 U.S. 190, 50 L. Ed. 2d 397, 97 S. Ct. 451 (1976), states that "classifications by gender must serve important governmental objectives and must be substantially related to achievement of those objectives." In Sail'er Inn, Inc. v. Kirby, 5 Cal. 3d 1, 485 P.2d 529, 95 Cal. Rptr. 329 (1971), the California Supreme Court announced that gender classifications are "suspect," and hence will survive constitutional challenge only if their proponent successfully demonstrates a compelling state interest, a close nexus between the legislative goal and the legislative means, and the absence of any alternative means of effecting the legislative goal. What is the legislative goal now with respect to pre-1975 acquisitions? Can it be achieved by alternative means?

On the other hand, would retroactive application of the repeal of the married woman's special presumption unconstitutionally impair vested property rights? In other words, if title vested in the wife in 1970 as her sole and separate property, may the legislature now retrospectively reinterpret that title in a way that would diminish the wife's ownership rights? See cases and discussion at pages 192-211 and 578-584 infra.

2. Property Held in Joint Title

a. Introduction

Joint title may present a variety of vexing issues, and the nature of those issues has evolved with the changing legal content of divorce law. Under pre-1970 fault divorce law, the prominent issue was whether title to property had been taken in joint tenancy or community property. Under fault divorce, the "innocent" spouse was entitled to more than half the community property. In contrast, the parties continued to own joint tenancy interests equally. Thus under fault divorce, whether an asset was held as joint tenancy or community property was a frequently litigated issue. (See *Schindler* and *Bowman* infra.) With no-fault divorce and 50-50 community property distribution, the prominent issues are: (i) whether and how a spouse may go behind *any* form of apparent co-ownership in order to show that true ownership is not as stated in the deed (Marriage of Buol infra) and (ii) the treatment of separate property contributions to jointly titled property (Marriage of Lucas infra).

b. Joint Tenancy

The presumption that property acquired during marriage is community property may be overcome by title evidence that the husband and wife hold the property as joint tenants. As you may remember from basic property, a joint tenancy creates equal fractional interests in an undivided parcel of property. If, for example, there are two owners, each owns a one-half interest in the undivided whole. Equality of ownership is an essential feature of a joint tenancy; if two persons hold unequal interests, there can be no joint tenancy. Cal. Civ. Code §683. (In contrast, the tenancy in common does not require proportional equality of ownership.) The major distinction between the joint tenancy and the tenancy in common is the right of survivorship: In a joint tenancy, the survivor takes all. For this reason the joint tenancy is much favored by married couples, as is the similar but more indestructible tenancy by the entirety used in 22 noncommunity property states.

Joint tenancy represents a form of *separate* property ownership: Each spouse owns a *separate* one-half interest in the joint tenancy. Unlike a spouse's one-half interest in community property, one spouse's interest in a joint tenancy can be unilaterally transferred. This transfer not only alienates that spouse's one-half interest but also destroys the survivorship incident of the joint tenancy and transforms it into a tenancy in common. In contrast, a spouse cannot sever community property. He cannot, for example, apportion one-half to himself as his separate property and the other half to his spouse as her separate property. Nor can one spouse generally transfer or encumber community realty without the consent of the other. Family Code §1102. While the postmarital creditors of one spouse can reach all the community property (Family Code §910), they generally cannot reach the nondebtor spouse's separate property (Family Code §913(b)(1)). Thus, the nondebtor spouse's one-half interest in a joint tenancy may be immune from his or her spouse's creditors. See, for example, In re Rauer's Collection Co., 87 Cal. App. 2d 248, 196 P.2d 803 (1948).

California's treatment of joint tenancies has a long and tortuous history and is still the subject of considerable legal concern and disagreement. Knowledge of this history is necessary to understand current issues.

SCHINDLER v. SCHINDLER
126 Cal. App. 2d 597, 272 P.2d 566 (1954)

Mosk, J., pro tem. — Declaring that it was impossible to continue to live together as husband and wife, respondent commenced an action against appellant for divorce on October 1, 1952. In her complaint she alleged that certain real property known as 14041 Roblar Road, Sherman Oaks, California, was community property.

Her specific averment in that regard was "that the title to said property stands of record in the names of the parties hereto as joint tenants for the purpose of convenience only and for no other reason, and said property was intended between the parties hereto to be at all times and now is their bona fide community property." Appellant answered that "it was at all times since the acquisition of the said property and is now the intention of the parties that the said property be held by them as joint tenants."

After trial held on June 23, 1953, the court found "That it is true that the real property hereinabove described stands of record in the names of plaintiff/cross-defendant and defendant/cross-complainant as joint tenants, but that in truth and in fact, said property is the bona fide community property of the parties hereto." Pursuant to the foregoing finding that it was community, the trial court awarded the property to respondent, to whom it granted an interlocutory decree of divorce on the ground of extreme and habitual cruelty. From that portion of the decree relating to the real property, appellant has appealed, maintaining the realty is in fact joint tenancy.

Testimony at the trial revealed that the parties were married in Connecticut and during their marriage acquired a home in Pennsylvania, that residence having been sold when they moved to California in about 1949, at which time the Sherman Oaks residence was purchased. . . . Testimony of the respondent was in essence that she did not understand the meaning of joint tenancy, that no one explained its nature or effect to her, that she signed the papers in connection with the transaction, that she thought the property "belonged to both of us" and that it was community property, and that all payments made on the property came from appellant's earnings. She further stated on cross-examination that there had been no discussion between her and appellant as to how title should be taken. She also admitted that she did not know anything about community property at that time.

I: The sole question presented on this appeal is whether the trial court properly determined that the real property was in fact community property and therefore subject to disposition in the divorce proceedings.

It is common knowledge that innumerable husbands and wives with little or no information about estates in real property acquiesce without reflection in the suggestion that they place purchased property in joint tenancy. This estate, of course, has certain advantages. Usually not until marital discord reaches the critical stage of dividing community assets does one of the spouses—generally the one found to be innocent of wrong-doing and therefore entitled to more than half of the community property—first learn of the disadvantages of joint tenancy. At that point the issue of lack of comprehension, or absence of consent to the creation of the joint tenancy estate inevitably arises. Rare indeed is the contested divorce case today in which the trial court is not concerned with this issue.

The basic law applicable to this problem is reasonably well settled. It is in some of the refinements that we find what appears at first blush to be a conflict in the cases.

From the very nature of the estate, as between husband and wife, a community estate and a joint tenancy estate cannot exist at the same time in the same property. (Tomaier v. Tomaier, 23 Cal. 2d 754, 758 [146 P.2d 905].) This was established in Siberell v. Siberell, 214 Cal. 767 [7 P.2d 1003], the court there further holding (p.773) that "use of community funds to purchase the property and the taking of title thereto in the name of the spouses as joint tenants is tantamount to a binding agreement between them that the same shall not thereafter be held as community property but instead as a joint tenancy with all the characteristics of such an estate."

The statutory presumption that property acquired after marriage except by gift, bequest, devise, or descent is community property . . . is successfully rebutted by evidence that the property was taken in joint tenancy. (Edwards v. Deitrich, 118 Cal. App. 2d 254, 260 [257 P.2d 750].) The fact that a deed was taken in joint tenancy establishes a prima facie case that the property is in fact held in joint tenancy. (King v. King, 107 Cal. App. 2d 257, 259 [236 P.2d 912].) There is actually a presumption that the property is as described in the deed and the burden is on the party who seeks to rebut the presumption. (Edwards v. Deitrich, supra.) The form of the deed cannot be lightly disregarded. Even with evidence of contrary intent, the deed alone creates a conflict of fact. (Cox v. Cox, 82 Cal. App. 2d 867, 870-871 [187 P.2d 23].) As stated in In re Rauer's Collection Co., 87 Cal. App. 2d 248, 257 [196 P.2d 803], "The form of the conveyance is itself some evidence of the intent to change it from community property, and creates a rebuttable presumption to that effect."

On the other hand, a conveyance of property to a husband and wife as joint tenants does not necessarily, and under all circumstances, preclude the idea of their holding the same as community property. (Cummins v. Cummins, 7 Cal. App. 2d 294, 304 [46 P.2d 284].) It is clear that a husband and wife may convert community into separate property, and vice versa, by agreement between themselves, and that persuasive evidence of such an understanding will rebut the presumption created by the form of the deed. (Edwards v. Deitrich, supra.) . . .

The purchase of property with community funds is insufficient standing alone to establish that property is community property. (In re Rauer's Collection Co., supra, at p.257.) The presumption arising from the form of the deed may not be rebutted solely by evidence as to the source of the funds used to purchase the property. (Gudelj v. Gudelj, 41 Cal. 2d 202, 212 [259 P.2d 656].) However, it may be controverted by testimony indicating the "intention, understanding or agreement of the parties." (Socol v. King, 36 Cal. 2d 342, 345 [223 P.2d 627].) Respondent has emphasized the disjunctive character of the foregoing phrase, and maintains her intention alone will suffice to establish the property held in joint tenancy to be actually community. Neither the facts nor the outcome of *Socol,* however, lend her much comfort. For the unanimous court there determined that the unrevealed intention of one party alone for the property to remain a part of the community is not effective.

At this point we reach [a case] . . . upon which respondent heavily relies. Superficially [it appears] . . . to conflict with the foregoing rules, but we believe [it] . . . can be reconciled.

In Palazuelos v. Palazuelos, 103 Cal. App. 2d 826 [230 P.2d 431], the court affirmed a holding that property was community although the only evidence mentioned indicated the wife did not intend the property to be purchased in joint tenancy. Apparently there was no finding as to the husband's or their mutual intention. . . .

In *Socol, Edwards, Tomaier, Cox* and other cases herein discussed, the wife joined in the transaction by which the property was converted into joint tenancy. . . . In *Palazuelos,* however, she did not consent and that element apparently influenced the result. . . .

In the instant case, the wife signed the papers involved in the purchase of the property. In so doing, and in the absence of fraud or misrepresentation, she clearly participated in the transaction and thereby consented in writing to the transfer of community funds to joint tenancy property. Respondent further testified in response to interrogation that she "just thought it belonged to both of us" and believed that it was community property. There is no testimony in the record that she revealed those evanescent thoughts to appellant or to anyone else. On cross-examination she conceded she had not discussed the manner of taking title with appellant.

This, then, is a precise duplicate of the unilateral and uncommunicated intention that existed in Walker v. Walker, 108 Cal. App. 2d 605 [239 P.2d 106], the court there holding it utterly insufficient to meet the burden of establishing the property to be community. The wife having consented in writing to "the execution of the joint tenancy deed, she cannot defeat her act by testimony of a hidden intention not disclosed to the other party at the time of the execution of the document," said the court in Watson v. Peyton [10 Cal. 2d 156, 158, 73 P.2d 206 (1937)].

It is of no significance that the respondent stated she was unaware of or mistaken about the legal effect of the deed. Nor is it material that the home was purchased primarily from community funds. Those facts, taken together, provide no basis for an inference of a mutual understanding or agreement between the husband and wife that the community nature of the property was to be preserved regardless of the form of the deed. (Gudelj v. Gudelj, supra.) The evidence falls far short of supporting the allegation of the complaint that "said property was intended between the parties hereto to be at all times and now is their bona fide community property." In fact, there was no evidence of an agreement, nor any evidence from which it can be inferred that the parties, as distinguished from one party alone, intended the parcel to be community property. (Walker v. Walker, supra, p.609].) Therefore, the trial court was in error in attempting to dispose of the property in the divorce action. It is well settled that unless real property held in joint tenancy is in fact a community asset, the court in an action for divorce is without power to make disposition of such property. (Walker v. Walker, supra.)

Therefore that part of the interlocutory decree of divorce purporting to award the real property to respondent is reversed. . . .

WHITE, P.J., and DRAPEAU, J., concurred.

BOWMAN v. BOWMAN
149 Cal. App. 2d 773, 308 P.2d 906 (1957)

BRAY, J.—After 13 years of marriage plaintiff sued defendant for divorce on the grounds of extreme cruelty, asking for custody of the three children of the parties and a division of the community property, which allegedly included the family home. Defendant cross-complained on similar grounds asking for the custody of the children and alleged the home to be in joint tenancy. The court granted plaintiff the divorce, found the home to be community property, awarded it and the household furnishings to plaintiff. . . . Defendant appeals from the portion of the decree finding the home to be community property and awarding it to plaintiff. . . .

The deed to the property was taken in joint tenancy. This fact raises a rebuttable presumption that the property was in fact held in joint tenancy, and places on the party claiming it to be community property the burden of overcoming the presumption. . . . The fact that the property was purchased with community funds, standing alone, is insufficient to rebut the presumption created by the form of the deed. . . . Parol evidence of an oral agreement by, or intention of, the parties to hold it as community property is admissible. (Tomaier v. Tomaier (1944), 23 Cal. 2d 754 [146 P.2d 905].) While the presumption cannot be rebutted by an understanding of one party uncommunicated to the other (Gudelj v. Gudelj, supra), an understanding to hold it as community property, in spite of the form of the deed, may be shown by the conduct and declarations of the parties. . . . Here there was admittedly no express agreement that the property was to be held other than as shown by the deed. Defendant claims there was no evidence of any mutual understanding or intention of the parties to hold the property as community property and that, therefore, the presumption was not overcome.

Our task, then, is to determine whether there is substantial evidence of such understanding or intention. The home was purchased shortly after marriage, with moneys loaned by plaintiff's parents to make the down payment. This was repaid and the other payments on the property, from defendant's salary. Plaintiff did not remember discussing the purchase with her husband and the realtor. She did not know how the deed was made out, although she signed some papers at the realtor's office at the time of purchase. She and defendant never discussed the deed nor how it was to be made out. She thought it was community property as she thought that when persons were married, everything was community property. Defendant testified that at the time of the purchase he, plaintiff and a realtor had a conversation as to how the property was to be deeded. Plaintiff's parents advised that it be deeded in joint tenancy. The realtor agreed on the theory that should anything happen to one spouse, the other spouse would automatically get the home without probate. It was always defendant's understanding that it was held in joint tenancy and not as community property. In explaining his idea of the difference between the two, he stated that there would be no difference except that if one should die, the other would automatically obtain the property without probate, but in "ordinary everyday living there would be no difference. . . ." The property was bought with the intent that it should be a home for him, his wife and children. He was asked, "and that was your intention, it was to be community property and the home for them all, didn't you?" He answered "It was to be ours." Again he stated: "It is joint tenancy. It belongs to us." The fact that the original down payment came from the wife's parents and that community funds paid for the property, although by no means conclusive on the question, is of some significance. In his questionnaire defendant listed the home under "community property" although he added "joint tenancy."

While the court could have found to the contrary, there is substantial evidence to overcome the presumption and to show that both parties considered the property as community property and never intended it to have any of the attributes of joint tenancy except to avoid probate.[6] Defendant considered the property "ours," belonging "to us," not separate. The only reason given for taking the deed in joint tenancy form was to dispense with probate. Defendant never mentioned the right of survivorship. Even today, he appears not to know the characteristics of a joint tenancy. The intent to avoid probate is not inconsistent with the intent to have the property as community property. As said in Jenkins v. Jenkins, 147 Cal. App. 2d 527 [305 P.2d 289], where the circumstances were almost identical with those here, the evidence was clearly sufficient to justify a finding that the sole purpose the parties had in following the realtor's advice that the property should be put in joint tenancy was as a matter of convenience to avoid probate. A somewhat similar situation occurred in Mademann v. Sexauer, 117 Cal. App. 2d 400 [256 P.2d 34], where the property was purchased with the husband's money and the deed was taken in joint tenancy primarily because the parties believed thereby they would avoid probate and where it was contended that the presumption was not overcome, and it was held to be community property. Applicable here is the following (p.403):

> In this connection it may be observed that the intricacies of the law and the subtle distinctions in respect to real estate titles, community property in particular, are not generally understood by the layman. Certainly the real nature of a particular transaction rather than the verbal form in which it is cast, must always be the decisive factor in cases of this nature.

The record herein discloses substantial evidence that Mr. and Mrs. Made-

---

6. What does "to avoid probate" mean? How would a lay person be likely to explain the characteristics of a property interest that avoids probate? Do you agree that "[t]he intent to avoid probate is not inconsistent with the intent to have the property as community property"? — ED.

mann intended the real estate, whatever its source, to be community property, and that the joint tenancy deed was executed because of certain advice given by a person not a lawyer, and under the belief that this procedure would simplify the steps necessary to be taken upon the death of one spouse.

Our case is distinguishable from Schindler v. Schindler, . . . 126 Cal. App. 2d 597, in that there while the wife thought the property deeded in joint tenancy was community property, there was no evidence that the husband ever considered it anything but joint tenancy. The wife was relying solely on her own intention. In our case, the evidence supports the conclusion that the husband, as well as the wife, considered it, in effect, community property. . . .

Judgment affirmed. . . .

Appellant's petition for a hearing by the Supreme Court was denied May 29, 1957.

Notes and Questions

1. In *Schindler* and *Bowman,* what were the consequences of finding a joint tenancy at divorce? Of finding instead that the property was community property? How would the result change if the marriage were dissolved by death rather than divorce?

2. *Stepped-up basis at death.* In death cases, the different income tax treatment accorded community property and joint tenancy property has prompted surviving spouses to claim that property held in joint tenancy was instead intended by the parties to be held as community property. The federal estate tax consequences of the two forms of ownership are the same: The decedent's 50 percent interest is taxed in his or her estate. There is, however, a significant income tax distinction. When the surviving spouse sells the property, the basis of property held as community property is *stepped up* to the value of the entire asset at the date of the decedent's death. In contrast, joint tenancy property receives a step-up only for *decedent's* one-half interest.

To illustrate, suppose that a couple bought property for $200,000 in 1960. Last month, when the wife died, her one-half interest passed to her surviving husband, and the fair market value of the property was $2,000,000. After his wife's death, the husband sold the property for $2,000,000. If the property was held as community property, the husband realized no taxable gain upon the sale because his basis, that is, his allowable offset against the income from the sale, was the fair market value of the property at his wife's death, the so-called stepped-up basis and *not* the historic cost of $200,000. In contrast, if the property was held in joint tenancy, the husband gained a stepped-up basis only in the decedent's one-half interest. Thus he would realize no gain on the one-half interest received from his wife but would be subject to income tax on the sale of *his* one-half interest. In this case, his gain would be $900,000 (one-half the sales price less one-half the historic cost: $1,000,000 less $100,000). Int. Rev. Code of 1954, §1014(b)(6).

How would you advise a couple holding appreciated joint tenancy property today? How might they most simply achieve optimal stepped-up basis treatment? Would you also be concerned about the content of their wills?

3. *Repeal of the estate tax in 2010 and the consequences for stepped-up basis.* The income tax basis of property acquired from a decedent dying after December 31,

2009, will generally be the decedent's basis. In other words, stepped-up basis will generally be eliminated with the repeal of the estate tax. However, as a partial replacement for the current step-up, executors will be allowed to increase the basis of estate property by up to $1,300,000 for property passing to any recipient (*the general basis increase*) and by an additional $3,000,000 for property passing to a surviving spouse (*the spousal property basis increase*). Internal Revenue Code §1022(b) and (c), added by the Economic Growth and Tax Relief Reconciliation Act of 2001, Pub. L. 107-16.

4. Under *Schindler* and *Bowman,* if a spouse acquired a new car during marriage and put title in his name alone, the general community property presumption was still operative. But if the couple took title in joint tenancy, the general community property presumption was overcome and there arose a rebuttable presumption of joint tenancy. Why the difference in treatment? Does the rationale of the joint tenancy cases apply equally to tenancies in common?

5. Why do married couples so frequently take title to the family home in joint tenancy rather than as community property? Who advises them to take this form of ownership? What, if anything, are they trying to accomplish? In *Bowman,* what did the court think the couple was attempting to achieve? Suppose the Bowmans did mean to create a right of survivorship. Is such intention inconsistent with an intention to maintain the property as community property? How would a legally sophisticated person express a simultaneous intention to maintain the property as community property for purposes of divorce and to ensure that the survivor takes all in the event of death?

6. *Schindler* illustrates the pre-1965 result of a divorce finding that the property in question was held in joint tenancy rather than as community property. How did the trial court dispose of the family home? What was the result when the case was reversed by the court of appeal? In 1965, the legislature disapproved the result in cases like *Schindler* when it added the following provision to Civil Code section 164, later recodified as section 5110:

> [W]hen a single family residence of a husband and wife is acquired by them during marriage as joint tenants, *for the purpose of the division of such property upon divorce* or separate maintenance *only,* the presumption is that such single family residence is the community property of said husband and wife. [Emphasis added.] [1965 Cal. Stat. ch. 1710, p.3843.]

Section 5110 covered only single-family residences at divorce or separation. It effectively created for such residences a hybrid property interest that combined the virtues of community property and joint tenancy. At divorce, the property was subject to the court's jurisdiction and would be included in the community property distribution, but if the marriage continued until the death of one partner, the surviving spouse took all.

Compare the Uniform Marital Property Act. Explicitly recognizing that spouses may desire a hybrid form of ownership, the Act created a form of property called *survivorship marital property.*

> If the words "survivorship marital property" are used instead of the words "marital property". . . , property so held is survivorship marital property. On the death of a spouse, the ownership rights of that spouse in survivorship marital property vest solely in the surviving spouse by nontestamentary

disposition at death. The first deceased spouse does not have a right of disposition at death of any interest in survivorship marital property.

Uniform Marital Property Act, §11e, 9A U.L.A. 135 (1998).

7. *California survivorship community property.* In 2000, the legislature enacted Civil Code § 682.1, which provides:

> (a) Community property of a husband and wife, when expressly declared in the transfer document to be community property with right of survivorship, and which may be accepted in writing on the face of the document by a statement signed or initialed by the grantees, shall, upon the death of one of the spouses, pass to the survivor, without administration, pursuant to the terms of the instrument, subject to the same procedures, as property held in joint tenancy. Prior to the death of either spouse, the right of survivorship may be terminated pursuant to the same procedures by which a joint tenancy may be severed. . . .
>
> (b) This section does not apply to a joint account in a financial institution to which Part 2 (commencing with Section 5100) of Division 5 of the Probate Code applies.
>
> (c) This section shall become operative on July 1, 2001, and shall apply to instruments created on or after that date.

Civil Code section 682.1 seems to contemplate that survivorship community property may only be created by a "transfer document." Does "transfer document" include a transmutation agreement? Compare Family Code section 850, which provides that married persons may transmute property by "agreement *or* transfer." With respect to the advisability of taking title as community property with a right of survivorship, what is the $3,000,000 question? See note 3 supra.

c. Separate Property Contributions to the Purchase Price of Jointly Titled Property

Frequently spouses contribute both separate and community funds to the purchase of a substantial asset, often the family home, and they take title in some joint and equal form, generally joint tenancy or community property. Resolving a conflict among several courts of appeal regarding the treatment of separate property contributions, the California Supreme Court adopted an extreme, although plausible, position in Marriage of Lucas. The legislature reacted negatively, passing so-called anti-*Lucas* legislation, Civil Code sections 4800.1 and 4800.2, reprinted below.

Despite legislative intent to overrule *Lucas,* the holding of *Lucas* has survived for two reasons that will be explored in this section: The anti-*Lucas* legislation does not fully cover the field occupied by *Lucas,* and the California Supreme Court has held that retroactive application of the anti-*Lucas* legislation would unconstitutionally impair vested property rights.

Q: what are the
   ♂ agreements?

MARRIAGE OF LUCAS
27 Cal. 3d 808, 614 P.2d 285, 166 Cal. Rptr. 853 (1980)

MANUEL, J. — Gerald E. Lucas appeals from an interlocutory judgment dissolving his marriage to Brenda G. Lucas, awarding child custody, fixing spousal and child support and dividing property. Gerald contests only the trial court's determination of the parties' ownership interests in their residence and in a vehicle, both of which were purchased with a combination of community and separate funds. In this case we must resolve a conflict among the Courts of Appeal regarding the proper method of determining separate and community property interests in a single family dwelling acquired during the marriage with both separate property and community property funds.

Brenda and Gerald were married in March 1964 and lived together continuously until their separation in December 1976. At the time of their marriage Brenda was beneficiary of a trust. The trust corpus was distributed to her free of the trust in September 1964. She immediately established a revocable inter vivos trust of which she was trustor and beneficiary. The trust, conceded by Gerald to be Brenda's separate property, had a value of approximately $44,000 at the time of trial.

In November 1968, Brenda and Gerald bought a house for $23,300. Brenda used $6,351.57 from her trust for the down payment, and they assumed a loan of $16,948.43 for the balance of the purchase price. Title to the house was taken as "Gerald E. Lucas and Brenda G. Lucas, Husband and Wife as Joint Tenants." Brenda paid $2,962 from her trust funds for improvements to the property; the remainder of the expenses on the property was paid for with community funds. At the time of trial the residence had a fair market value of approximately $56,250 and a loan balance of approximately $14,600, leaving a net equity of approximately $41,650. The community had reduced the principal by $2,052.32 and paid $6,801.14 in interest and $5,146.20 for taxes.

The trial court findings describe the parties' intent regarding ownership of the residence as follows:

> The only discussions with regard to taking joint tenancy title to the property related to wife's understanding that title would pass to husband upon her death and that the children would benefit from this result; further, the parties contemplated that taking title in this manner would result in favorable tax consequences due to husband's veterans status. Wife did not intend to make a gift to the husband of any interest in the home purchased with her separate funds, nor did she know of any other legal significance of taking title to real property in the manner it was taken. Neither did husband intend to make a gift to wife of the payments made on the home from community funds during the period of ownership.

Brenda testified that she and Gerald did not discuss where the down payment would come from except to the extent that the payments would be higher if they did not use her trust fund and instead took a second trust deed on the house. Brenda said they had no agreement regarding the manner in which she would be disposing of the trust funds and that they did not discuss keeping the funds separate or using them to exhaust community debts. Brenda also testified that it was her intention at the time of the purchase to acquire the house for herself but that she did not discuss this with her husband.

In the interlocutory judgment entered in April 1978, the trial court deducted Brenda's $2,962 payment for improvements from the equity of $41,650.50 and then awarded a community property interest in the residence of 24.42 percent with a value of $9,477.50. A separate property interest of 75.58 percent with a value of $29,241 was confirmed to Brenda.

The Courts of Appeal have taken conflicting approaches to the question of the proper method for determining the ownership interests in a residence purchased during the parties' marriage with both separate and community funds. In *In re Marriage of Bjornestad* (1974) 38 Cal. App. 3d 801 [113 Cal. Rptr. 576], the Court of Appeal allowed only reimbursement for separate property contributions to the down payment on the purchase of the parties' residence. In In re Marriage of Aufmuth (1979) 89 Cal. App. 3d 446 [152 Cal. Rptr. 668], the Court of Appeal developed a scheme of pro rata apportionment of the equity appreciation between the separate and community property contributions to the purchase price. The Court of Appeal in In re Marriage of Trantafello (1979) 94 Cal. App. 3d 533 [156 Cal. Rptr. 556], however, held that the residence was entirely community in nature in the absence of any evidence of an agreement or understanding between the parties to the contrary.

The beginning point of analysis in each case was the nature of title taken by the parties. In *Bjornestad* and *Trantafello,* title was taken by husband and wife as joint tenants; in *Aufmuth,* it was taken as community property. Until modified by statute in 1965, there was a rebuttable presumption that the ownership interest in property was as stated in the title to it. (Machado v. Machado (1962) 58 Cal. 2d 501 [25 Cal. Rptr. 87, 375 P.2d 55]; Gudelj v. Gudelj (1953) 41 Cal. 2d 202 [259 P.2d 656]; Socol v. King (1950) 36 Cal. 2d 342 [223 P.2d 627]; Tomaier v. Tomaier (1944) 23 Cal. 2d 754 [146 P.2d 905].) Thus a residence purchased with community funds, but held by a husband and wife as joint tenants, was presumed to be separate property in which each spouse had a half interest. (See Socol v. King, supra, 36 Cal. 2d at pp.345-347.) The presumption arising from the form of title could be overcome by evidence of an agreement or understanding between the parties that the interests were to be otherwise. (Ibid.; Gudelj v. Gudelj, supra, 41 Cal. 2d at p.212; Machado v. Machado, supra, 58 Cal. 2d at p.506.) It could not be overcome, however, "solely by evidence as to the source of the funds used to purchase the property." (Gudelj v. Gudelj, supra, 41 Cal. 2d at p.212.) Nor could it "be overcome by testimony of a hidden intention not disclosed to the other grantee at the time of the execution of the conveyance." (Ibid.; Socol v. King, supra, 36 Cal. 2d at p.346; Machado v. Machado, supra, 58 Cal. 2d at p.506.)

The presumption arising from the form of title created problems upon divorce or separation when title to the parties' residence was held in joint tenancy. (Review of Selected 1965 Code Legislation (Cont. Ed. Bar) p.40; Final Rep. of Assem. Interim Com. on Judiciary Relating to Domestic Relations (1965) pp.121-122, 2 Appen. to Assem. J. (1965 Reg. Sess.) hereafter referred to as Domestic Relations Rep.) Unless the presumption of separate property created by the form of title could be overcome by evidence of a common understanding or agreement to the contrary, a house so held could not be awarded to the wife as a family residence for her and the children. (Ibid.) In 1965 the Legislature considered various proposals to remedy this problem. The Legislature also noted that

> husbands and wives take property in joint tenancy without legal counsel but primarily because deeds prepared by real estate brokers, escrow companies and by title companies are usually presented to the parties in joint tenancy form. The result is that they don't know what joint tenancy is, that they think it is community property, and then find out upon death or divorce that they didn't have what they thought they had all along and instead have something else which isn't what they had intended. (Domestic Relations Rep., p.124.)

In 1965, in an attempt to solve these problems, the Legislature added the following provision to Civil Code section 164: "[W]hen a single family residence of a husband and wife is acquired by them during marriage as joint tenants, for the purpose of the division of such property upon divorce or separate maintenance only, the presumption is that such single family residence is the community property of said husband and wife." (Stats. 1965, ch. 1710, p.3843; see now Civ. Code §5110.) The effect of this provision was to change the presumptive form of ownership to that more closely matching the intent and assumptions of most spouses who acquire and hold their residence in joint tenancy. . . . There is no indication that the Legislature intended in any way to change the rules regarding the strength and type of evidence necessary to overcome the presumption arising from the form of title. (See Domestic Relations Rep., p.124.)

The presumption arising from the form of title is to be distinguished from the general presumption . . . that property acquired during marriage is community property. It is the affirmative act of specifying a form of ownership in the conveyance of title that removes such property from the more general presumption. (See Socol v. King, supra, 36 Cal. 2d at p.346.) It is because of this express designation of ownership that a greater showing is necessary to overcome the presumption arising therefrom than is necessary to overcome the more general presumption that property acquired during marriage is community property. In the latter situation, where there is no written indication of ownership interests as between the spouses, the general presumption of community property may be overcome simply by tracing the source of funds used to acquire the property to separate property. (See In re Marriage of Mix (1975) 14 Cal. 3d 604, 608-612 [122 Cal. Rptr. 79, 536 P.2d 479]; Estate of Murphy (1976) 15 Cal. 3d 907, 917-919 [126 Cal. Rptr. 820, 544 P.2d 956]; See v. See (1966) 64 Cal. 2d 778, 783 [51 Cal. Rptr. 888, 415 P.2d 776].) It is not necessary to show that the spouses understood or intended that property traceable to separate property should remain separate.

The rule requiring an understanding or agreement comes into play when the issue is whether the presumption arising from the form of title has been overcome. It is supported by sound policy considerations, and we decline to depart from it. To allow a lesser showing could result in unfairness to the spouse who has not made the separate property contribution. Unless the latter knows that the spouse contributing the separate property expects to be reimbursed or to acquire a separate property interest, he or she has no opportunity to attempt to preserve the joint ownership of the property by making other financing arrangements. The act of taking title in a joint and equal ownership form is inconsistent with an intention to preserve a separate property interest. Accordingly, the expectations of parties who take title jointly are best protected by presuming that the specified ownership interest is intended in the absence of an agreement or understanding to the contrary. We therefore resolve the conflict in Court of Appeal opinions by following *Trantafello* and disapproving *Aufmuth* and *Bjornestad* to the extent they are inconsistent with this opinion.

In the present case there is no evidence of an agreement or understanding that Brenda was to retain a separate property interest in the house. Nor is there any finding by the trial court on the question. The only findings in this regard are that neither party intended a gift to the other. Such evidence and findings are insufficient to rebut the presumption arising from title set forth in Civil Code section 5110. The trial court's determination must therefore be reversed.

Neither the parties nor the court applied the correct rules to this case, and it is possible that had they done so the proof might have been different. In the interest of justice, therefore, the matter of the community or separate property character of the residence must be remanded for reconsideration in light of these rules.

If on reconsideration the house is found to be entirely community in nature, Brenda would also be barred from reimbursement for the separate property funds she contributed in the absence of an agreement therefor. It is a well-settled rule that a "party who uses his separate property for community purposes is entitled to reimbursement from the community or separate property of the other only if there is an agreement between the parties to that effect." (See v. See, supra, 64 Cal. 2d at p.785. . . .) While the parties are married and living together it is presumed that, "unless an agreement between the parties specifies that the contributing party be reimbursed, a party who utilizes his separate property for community purposes intends a gift to the community." (In re Marriage of Epstein [24 Cal. 3d 76, 82, 154 Cal. Rptr. 413, 592 P.2d 1165 (1979)].)

CALCULATING
SP & CP

For guidance in the event that on reconsideration the court finds there was an understanding or agreement that Brenda was to retain a separate property interest in the residence, we discuss briefly the question of the proper method of calculating the community and separate interests. In these inflationary times when residential housing is undergoing enormous and rapid appreciation in value, we believe that the most equitable method of calculating the separate and community interests when the down payment was made with separate funds and the loan was based on a community or joint obligation is that set forth by Justice McGuire in In re Marriage of Aufmuth, supra, 89 Cal. App. 3d at pages 456-457. In brief, the *Aufmuth* formula gives the spouse who made the separate property down payment a separate property interest in the residence in the proportion that the down payment bears to the purchase price; the community acquires that percentage of the residence which the community loan bears to the purchase price.[5]

If the trial court finds no agreement or understanding that Brenda was to retain a separate property interest in the residence, Brenda's contribution of $2,962 of separate funds for improvements should have no effect on the determination of the parties' interests, and the presumption of section 5110 is controlling. (See v. See, supra, 64 Cal. 2d at p.783.) If there was an understanding that Brenda's separate interest should be maintained, but no separate understanding with respect to improvements, Brenda should receive no additional credit for her expenditure for

---

3. The value of those interests is computed by first determining the amount of capital appreciation, which is computed by subtracting the purchase price from the fair market value of the residence. The separate property interest would be determined by adding the amount of capital appreciation attributable to separate funds to the amount of equity paid by separate funds. The community interest would be the amount of capital appreciation attributable to community funds plus the amount of equity paid by community funds; the amount of equity paid by community funds is represented by the amount by which the principal balance on the loan has been reduced.

These principles may be exemplified by considering a house purchased for $100,000, with the wife paying the entire down payment of $20,000 from separate property funds and the community contributing the rest of the purchase price in the amount of a loan for $80,000. There would be a 20 percent separate property interest and an 80 percent community property interest in the house. Assume that the fair market value of the house at the time of trial is $175,000, resulting in a capital appreciation of $75,000, and the mortgage balance at the time of separation was $78,000. The value of the separate property interest would be $35,000, which represents the amount of capital appreciation attributable to the separate funds (20 percent of $75,000) added to the amount of equity paid by separate funds ($20,000). The net value of the community property interest would be $62,000, which represents the amount of capital appreciation attributable to community funds (80 percent of $75,000) added to the amount of equity paid by community funds ($80,000 minus $78,000).

improvements, for it may be presumed that she intended that they redound to both the community and her separate interest in the property. (Cf., See v. See, supra, 64 Cal. 2d at p.785.)

Gerald also challenges the trial court's determination that a 1976 Harvest Mini-Motorhome, purchased in January 1976 for a cash price of $10,388, was Brenda's separate property. A community property vehicle was traded in on the purchase for an allowance of $2,567. An additional cash payment of $100 was made on the purchase from community funds. The cost of insurance and license fees ($474) added to the cash price of the motorhome, less the trade-in allowance and cash down payment, left a total unpaid balance of $8,195. That sum was paid by check drawn on Brenda's separate checking account. The community contributed 24.6 percent of the cost and Brenda contributed 75.4 percent of the cost of the vehicle. The fair market value of it at the time of trial was $9,000.

The purchase contract was made out in the name of Gerald alone, but title and registration were taken in Brenda's name only. Brenda wished to have title in her name alone, and Gerald did not object. The motorhome was purchased for family use and was referred to and used by the parties as a "family vehicle."

The trial court confirmed the motorhome to Brenda as her separate property. The interlocutory judgment stated that Gerald "had a de minimus community property interest therein which was made a gift to respondent [Brenda] at the time of the purchase."

Contrary to Gerald's contention, the trial court's determination that he made a gift of his interest is supported by substantial evidence. Title was taken in Brenda's name alone. Gerald was aware of this and did not object. This evidence constitutes substantial support for the trial court's conclusion that Gerald was making a gift to Brenda of his community property interest in the motorhome. (See In re Marriage of Frapwell (1975) 49 Cal. App. 3d 597, 600-601 [122 Cal. Rptr. 718].)

The judgment is reversed insofar as it determines the respective interests of the parties in the residence and divides the community property.

It is affirmed in all other respects. BIRD, C.J., TOBRINER, J., MOSK, J., CLARK, J., RICHARDSON, J., and NEWMAN, J., concurred.

Notes and Questions

1. Is Justice Manuel correct in his assertion that "[u]ntil modified by statute in 1965, there was a rebuttable presumption that the ownership interest in property was as stated in the title to it"? How would you rephrase this point?

2. The court discusses at length the portion of section 5110 that directed trial courts to treat single-family residences held in joint tenancy as community property at divorce. How, if at all, is this discussion relevant to the court's conclusion that "[i]t is the affirmative act of specifying a form of ownership . . . that removes such property from the more general presumption [that property acquired during marriage is community property]"? Does the affirmative act of specifying that title be taken as *community property* also create a presumption that it is *community property* unless the proponent of a separate property contribution can show an agreement to preserve that separate property contribution?

What, exactly, is the holding of *Lucas*? Does *Lucas* apply only to single-family residences held in joint tenancy at divorce? See In re Marriage of Cademartori, 119 Cal. App. 3d 970, 174 Cal. Rptr. 292 (1981) (applying *Lucas* to a warehouse), and

Marriage of Hayden, 124 Cal. App. 3d 72, 177 Cal. Rptr. 183 (1981) (applying *Lucas* to a bank account). For further discussion of Marriage of Hayden and jointly titled bank accounts, see page 223 infra.

3. Did the court effectively presume a gift of the separate property down payment when title was taken jointly? If Brenda Lucas had consulted you before she and Gerald took title to the house, how would you have advised her to take title? Is there any form of title that would simultaneously preserve Brenda's separate property down payment and also reflect the community contribution to monthly payments? Could it possibly be a joint tenancy, that is, a form of title that would pass ownership to Gerald at Brenda's death?

4. Why is it unfair to the community to recognize one spouse's separate property contribution? It is true that the community might have made alternative financing arrangements to ensure complete community ownership, but the fact is that it did not and thereby saved the money that the separate property spouse contributed to the purchase.

5. Note that *Lucas* creates a marked distinction between (1) property explicitly designated "joint tenancy" or "community property" in written title and (2) property acquired during marriage for which there is no written title or for which title is not "in a joint and equal ownership form." In the first instance an agreement is required to overcome the form of title; in the second instance, tracing to the purchase funds suffices to establish the character of the property.

6. The community lost its 25 percent contribution to the 1976 purchase of the Mini-Motorhome because Brenda insisted on title in her name and Gerald did not object. (Presumably Brenda was feeling less charitable eleven months before the couple's separation than she had been eight years earlier when they purchased the house.) How could Gerald have objected? They had already traded in their community property vehicle. Brenda had the checkbook for her separate account. To whom would the seller have listened? What do you imagine Gerald thought? (Compare *Provost*, decided during the pre-1975 era of male management: "[C]onsent cannot be presumed from the wife's mere silence, for the law has given her no right to say 'no.' " *Provost* is discussed in *Warren*, at page 212 infra.)

To what extent is the community property system designed to equalize interspousal power inequality? Does the court's treatment of the Mini-Motorhome diminish the principle that title taken by one spouse in his name alone does not change the character of community property? Should the principle be abandoned for post-1974 transactions because of the equal management provisions? With respect to post-1984 transmutation, would the Mini-Motorhome transaction satisfy Family Code section 852 requirements?

7. If, on remand, Brenda could prove an "agreement or understanding that Brenda was to retain a separate property interest in the house," *Lucas* instructs the trial court to make a pro rata apportionment of the current market value of the house. The house appreciated $32,950 (current market value less purchase price) and Brenda's separate estate furnished $6,352 of the $23,300 purchase price, entitling her separate estate to 6,352/23,300 of the $32,950 appreciation (32,950 × 6,352/23,300 = $8,983), plus the return of her original contribution, for a grand total of $15,335 ($8,983 plus $6,352). The community is entitled to 16,948/23,300 of the appreciation (16,948/23,300 × 32,950 = $23,967), plus the amount of principal indebtedness actually paid off by the community ($16,948 less $14,600 = $2,348), for a grand total of $26,315. Add it all up. It balances. The couple sells the house for $56,250, pays the bank $14,600, pays Brenda's separate estate $15,335,

and pays the community $26,315. Try to work through the figures. Don't be concerned if it does not come easily. We will review the mechanics of pro rata apportionment again in Chapter 6.

What is important to see here is that if Brenda could establish an agreement to preserve her separate interest, her separate estate would be treated as an owner. Her separate estate would share in the appreciation of the asset. Pro rata apportionment has long been the characteristic California case law response when both separate property and community property have been contributed to the purchase price. (Note that assumption of debt, or credit acquisition, here the $16,948 mortgage, is treated as a community contribution even when the community paid nothing out-of-pocket. Credit acquisition is further discussed in Chapter 6.)

The "Anti-Lucas" Law: Sections 4800.1 and 4800.2   1/1/84 ⟶▷

In 1983, the legislature enacted California Civil Code sections 4800.1 and 4800.2, effective January 1, 1984.[7]

Section 4800.1 extended the single family residence principle of section 5110 to *all* property acquired in joint tenancy during marriage:

Section 4800.1

> For the purpose of division of property upon [divorce], property acquired by the parties during marriage in joint tenancy form is presumed to be community property. This presumption is a presumption affecting the burden of proof and may be rebutted by either of the following:
>
> (a) A clear statement in the deed or other documentary evidence of title by which the property is acquired that the property is separate property and not community property.
>
> (b) Proof that the parties have made a written agreement that the property is separate property.

Note that section 4800.1, unlike section 5110, which was silent on the issue, specifies the proof required to rebut the presumption that property titled in joint tenancy is, for purposes of divorce, community property.

Section 4800.2   *REIMBURSEMENTS*

> In the division of community property under this part unless a party has made a written waiver of the right to reimbursement or signed a writing that has the effect of a waiver, the party shall be reimbursed for his or her contributions to the acquisition of the property to the extent the party traces the contributions to a separate property source. The amount reimbursed shall be without interest or adjustment for change in monetary values and shall not exceed the net value of the property at the time of the division. As used in this section, "contributions to the acquisition of the property" include downpayments, payments for improvements, and payments that reduce the principal of a loan used to finance the purchase or improvement of the property but do not include payments of interest on the loan or payments made for maintenance, insurance, or taxation of the property.

---

7. These provisions, now substantially rewritten, have been recodified as California Family Code sections 2580, 2581, and 2640.

Section 4800.2 made two significant changes. First, it reversed the gift presumption. A nongift is now presumed. Unless the spouse who contributes separate property relinquishes any separate claim in writing, the separate estate preserves an interest. Second, the statute appears to change the nature of the separate estate's interest. It now has a simple reimbursement claim. The separate estate is no longer the owner of a pro rata share of the asset but is merely a creditor recalling an interest-free loan. Moreover, repayment of the interest free loan is limited to the "net value of the property at the time of the division." The separate estate is thus assigned the risk of depreciation but not the benefit of appreciation.

This is what, on first reading, the statute appeared to do and, indeed, what the Law Revision Commission believed it did.

> Section 4800.2 overrules the case of In re Marriage of Lucas, 27 Cal. 3d 808, 614 P.2d 285, 166 Cal. Rptr. 853 (1980) (and cases following it), which precluded recognition of the separate property contribution of one of the parties to the acquisition of community property, unless the party could show an agreement between the spouses to the effect that the contribution was not intended to be a gift. Under Section 4800.2, a party making a separate property contribution to the acquisition of the property is not presumed to have made a gift, unless it is shown that the parties agreed it was a gift, but is entitled to reimbursement for the separate property contribution at dissolution of marriage. The separate property contribution is measured by the value of the contribution at the time the contribution is made. Under this rule, if the property has since appreciated in value, the community is entitled to the appreciation. If the property has since depreciated in value, reimbursement may not exceed the value of the property; if both parties are entitled to reimbursement and the property has insufficient value to permit full reimbursement of both, reimbursement should be on a proportionate basis. [16 Cal. L. Rev. Commn. Reports 2165 (1982); 1983-84 Sen. J. 4866.]

Quite apart from its wisdom, the articulation of the initial anti-*Lucas* legislation was fundamentally flawed. The statutes reflect a misreading of *Lucas* and a critical misunderstanding of California community property doctrine. The statutes were intended to work as a unit: At divorce, joint tenancy property that could not satisfy the section 4800.1 writing requirement would be treated as community property that would pour over into section 4800.2, where any separate property contribution would be reimbursed without interest to the separate property contributor. Thus, assuming Brenda Lucas did not have the necessary collateral written agreement, she would get her separate property contributions back, and the Lucas home would otherwise belong to the community. But suppose that Brenda and Gerald Lucas had initially taken title in community property form, that is, "as community property" or "as husband and wife." What would Brenda have been required to show to establish a proportional separate property ownership in the home? Does section 4800.1 address community property title? This drafting error seems to have been the result of reading *Lucas* too narrowly and concluding that its holding applied to joint tenancies only. Thus the result of section 4800.1, as originally enacted, was to make joint tenancy a more inescapable form of community property than community property itself. Despite its intention to repeal *Lucas*, section 4800.1 left *Lucas* the controlling law for any co-ownership property not held in joint tenancy, that is, for property held as community property or tenancy in common. Under

Lucas, an oral agreement or understanding would suffice to establish a separate property ownership interest.

Nor did section 4800.2 operate as apparently intended. The difficulty arose from the failure to define *community property* for the purpose of this provision. Under California doctrine, unless title indicates otherwise, the admixture of community and separate property contributions to the purchase price gives rise to an asset that is both community and separate in nature. In view of existing apportionment doctrine, to what does section 4800.2 "division of *community property*" refer?

To grasp the difficulty, how would you apply, if at all, section 4800.2 to a husband's purchase during marriage of a vacation home in his name alone with $50,000 from an inheritance and $40,000 in community earnings? The home, purchased for $90,000, now has a fair market value of $300,000. In other words, how do we determine whether an asset is community property for section 4800.2 purposes?

Since the statute's enactment, California courts have uniformly construed section 4800.2 *community property* to include only assets or portions of assets that may not otherwise be proven separate property under existing principles of California community property law. See Marriage of Buol infra at 196. Thus the vacation home purchased during marriage is ⁵⁄₉ the husband's separate property and ⁴⁄₉ community property. Because the husband took title in a form that does not imply any gift to the community, he is free to trace his ⁵⁄₉ contribution to the purchase price and to claim a resultant ⁵⁄₉ separate property ownership interest.

If you initially reached a different conclusion, awarding the house to the community and giving the husband $50,000 reimbursement, you probably gave *community property* a broader meaning, perhaps *any property acquired during marriage,* that is, any asset for which the general community property presumption arises. Yet that definition is unworkably broad. It would apply equally if the husband had purchased the home during marriage entirely with his separate funds and had put title in his name alone. Under this broader reading, he would get $90,000 back and the community would otherwise own the home. Because this clearly would be an incorrect result,[8] we must equally allow him to claim a proportional ownership interest based on his separate property contribution, and unless explicitly directed otherwise, we must give a narrower meaning to *community property* for purposes of section 4800.2. This conclusion was reached, largely without discussion, by all courts considering the issue. See, for example, Marriage of Buol, infra page 196. To repeat, *community property,* for purposes of section 4800.2, has been judicially construed to include only *property that cannot otherwise be proven separate property.*

Finally, to the extent that section 4800.2 does control, it tends to disrupt the fabric of California community property law. It creates a narrow reimbursement remedy within the context of a system in which tracing to purchase funds, *when permissible,* generally warrants pro rata ownership. Section 4800.2 contemplates only the "division of community property." Yet it is often the other way around, as when one spouse purchases a house before marriage and always maintains title in her name alone. It is clear that the house is dominantly separate property but the community asserts a claim to partial ownership based on community mortgage payments

---

8. It clearly would be incorrect because it would effectively establish a rule that the passive appreciation of separate property acquired during marriage is community property. Although such a rule is conceptually conceivable, it would represent such a marked departure from existing California community property law (cf. George v. Ransom, supra at 76) that a court would properly avoid such a result unless it were unavoidable or explicitly required by the governing statute.

(see Marriage of Moore, at page 264 infra). Section 4800.2 clearly has no application to such a case and pro rata apportionment continues to apply. Thus, one effect of section 4800.2 is to treat separate contributions to community assets (interest-free loans) differently from community contributions to the purchase of separate property (pro rata ownership).

Given the conceptual incoherence of the anti-*Lucas* measures it is not surprising that the California Supreme Court responded inhospitably to the legislation.

RETROACTIVITY

MARRIAGE OF BUOL
39 Cal. 3d 751, 705 P.2d 354, 218 Cal. Rptr. 31 (1985)

REYNOSO, JUSTICE. — May legislation requiring a writing to prove, upon dissolution of marriage, that property taken in joint tenancy form is the separate property of one spouse constitutionally be applied to cases pending before its effective date? We conclude that it may not. Applied retroactively, the statute impairs vested property rights without due process of law.

Esther and Robert Buol married in 1943 and separated in 1977. The Buols had three children together and Esther had one child from a previous marriage.

Robert worked as a laborer until 1970 when he was fired, at least in part, due to alcoholism. He began receiving Social Security total disability payments in 1973. Esther began working in 1954 as a housekeeper, a babysitter and an attendant to elderly women. Since 1959 she has been employed as a nursing attendant at a local hospital.

Home -1963
Title: JT
payments & improvements : SP

With Robert's knowledge and consent, Esther put her earnings in a separate bank account. Esther used the money to support the family, and in 1963, purchased a home in San Rafael. Although title was taken in joint tenancy on the advice of the realtor handling the sale, Esther made all mortgage, tax, insurance and maintenance payments out of her separate account. Robert contributed nothing. The original purchase price was $17,500. The home is now valued at approximately $167,500.

I: SP or CP?

The sole issue at trial was the status of the home as separate or community property. Esther testified that she purchased the home with her earnings which Robert had emphasized numerous times were hers to do with what she pleased. She also testified that she never would have gone to work without such an agreement because "that would be more money for him to put into gambling and drinking." In addition, she testified that he had always maintained that the house was hers and that he wanted no responsibility for it, until after he moved out and started demanding that she sell it so that he could have a share of the proceeds.

TESTIMONY

Esther's testimony was corroborated by two of the Buols' children, Roy and Judith, Judith's husband, and Esther's brother-in-law. Each remembered many conversations with Robert, alone or in family gatherings, in which he confirmed that the house was Esther's. Robert offered conflicting testimony, but conceded that he considered Esther's earnings to be hers alone, that he borrowed from her occasionally and that she made all the house payments out of her separate account.

Finding that the parties had an enforceable oral agreement (In re Marriage of Lucas (1980) 27 Cal. 3d 808, 166 Cal. Rptr. 853, 614 P.2d 285) that the earnings and the home were Esther's separate property, the court entered judgment awarding the home to Esther. Robert appealed, contending that there was insufficient evidence to support the finding of an oral agreement.

While the appeal was pending, Civil Code section 4800.1 was enacted. Under that section the only means of rebutting the presumption that property acquired during marriage in joint tenancy is community property is by providing evidence of a written agreement that the property is separate property. No writing exists in the instant case.

[handwritten: Under 4800.1, in order for W to rebut the presumption that JT = CP, the presumption must be rebutted in writing]

I

We must determine whether section 4800.1 may be given retroactive effect without offending the state Constitution. It appears that the Legislature intended section 4800.1 to apply retroactively to cases such as the one at bench. Section 4 of Assembly Bill No. 26 states, "This act applies to the following proceedings: [¶] (a) Proceedings commenced on or after January 1, 1984. [¶] (b) Proceedings commenced before January 1, 1984, to the extent proceedings as to the division of property are not yet final on January 1, 1984." (Stats. 1983, ch. 342, §4.) As the trial court's judgment awarding the $167,500 residence to Esther as her separate property was on appeal as of section 4800.1's January 1, 1984, effective date, the division of property was not yet final. . . . Presumably, therefore, section 4800.1 would operate to defeat Esther's separate property interest to the extent it is unprotected by section 4800.2's formula for reimbursing separate property contributions to community assets. Under section 4800.2, only $17,500 would be credited as Esther's separate property; the remaining $150,000 would be attributed to the community.

Legislative intent, however, is only one prerequisite to retroactive application of a statute. Having identified such intent, it remains for us to determine whether retroactivity is barred by constitutional constraints. We have long held that the retrospective application of a statute may be unconstitutional if it is an ex post facto law, if it deprives a person of a vested right without due process of law, or if it impairs the obligation of a contract. . . . See In re Marriage of Bouquet (1976) 16 Cal. 3d 583, 592, 128 Cal. Rptr. 427, 546 P.2d 1371. . . .

[handwritten right margin: DEPRIVATION w/out DP.]

Retroactive application of section 4800.1 would operate to deprive Esther of a vested[6] property right without due process of law. (Cal. Const., art. I, §7.) At the time of trial, Esther had a vested property interest in the residence as her separate property. (Cf. *Bouquet*, supra, 16 Cal. 3d at p.591, 128 Cal. Rptr. 427, 546 P.2d 1371; Addison v. Addison (1965) 62 Cal. 2d 558, 566, 43 Cal. Rptr. 97, 399 P.2d 897.) The law had long recognized that "separate property . . . [might] be converted into community property or *vice versa* at any time by oral agreement between the spouses." (Woods v. Security-First National Bank (1956) 46 Cal. 2d 697, 701, 299 P.2d 657. . . .)

The Buols had such an agreement as to Esther's earnings and the home she purchased and maintained with those earnings. "The status of property as community or separate is normally determined at the time of its acquisition." (*Bouquet*, supra, 16 Cal. 3d at p.591, 128 Cal. Rptr. 427, 546 P.2d 1371. . . .) . . .

At all relevant times — when Esther purchased the home, during trial and when

---

6. "The word vested assumes different meanings in different contexts. We use the word vested here to describe property rights that are not subject to a condition precedent." (*Bouquet*, supra, 16 Cal. 3d at p.591, fn. 7, 128 Cal. Rptr. 427, 546 P.2d 1371.)

the trial court entered judgment for Esther — proof of an oral agreement was all that was required to protect Esther's vested separate property interest. (See *Lucas*, supra, 27 Cal. 3d 808, 166 Cal. Rptr. 853, 614 P.2d 285; *Machado*, supra, 58 Cal. 2d 501, 25 Cal. Rptr. 87, 375 P.2d 55.) Section 4800.1's requirement of a writing evidencing the parties' intent to maintain the joint tenancy asset as separate property operates to substantially impair that interest.

Two Courts of Appeal have summarily rejected the contention that section 4800.1 directly impairs vested property rights, finding instead that the measure "merely alters the evidentiary burden of proof when a husband and wife take property by a joint tenancy deed." (In re Marriage of Martinez (1984) 156 Cal. App. 3d 20, 30, 202 Cal. Rptr. 646; see also In re Marriage of Taylor (1984) 160 Cal. App. 3d 471, 474, 206 Cal. Rptr. 557; In re Marriage of Benart (1984) 160 Cal. App. 3d 183, 188, fn. 2, 206 Cal. Rptr. 495.) This literal reading of the statute without due consideration for its practical application to proceedings initiated prior to its effective date, unnecessarily exalts form over substance, substantially impairing vested property rights along the way.

While the Legislature generally is free to apply changes in rules of evidence or procedure retroactively when no vested rights are involved, it is not so unrestrained when these changes directly affect such rights. . . .

The answer to the question whether a particular statute is "merely evidentiary" or "purely procedural" is not always to be found in the statutory language. " 'Alteration of a substantial right . . . is not merely procedural, even if the statute takes a seemingly procedural form.' " (People v. Smith (1983) 34 Cal. 3d 251, 260, 193 Cal. Rptr. 692, 667 P.2d 149, quoting Weaver v. Graham (1981) 450 U.S. 24, 29, fn. 12, 101 S. Ct. 960, 964, fn. 12, 67 L. Ed. 2d 17.) . . . We must, therefore, extend our analysis beyond the Legislature's chosen evidentiary language — "this presumption is a presumption affecting the burden of proof" — and focus upon the realities of retroactive application of the statute.

Applied retroactively, section 4800.1 unquestionably is substantive. A statute is substantive in effect when it "imposes a new or additional liability and substantially affects existing rights and obligations." (Aetna Cas. & Surety Co. v. Ind. Acc. Com. (1947) 30 Cal. 2d 388, 395, 182 P.2d 159.) Section 4800.1 imposes a statute of frauds where there was none before, penalizing the unwary for relying upon the law as it existed at the time the property rights were created rather than at the time dissolution proceedings were already underway. This paradoxical approach is aptly illustrated by the *Martinez* court's gratuitous offer to remand that case "in fairness to [the husband] . . . for a hearing at which he shall have the opportunity to prove a written agreement in accordance with section 4800.1." (Id., 156 Cal. App. 3d at p.30, 202 Cal. Rptr. 646.) Understandably, the court refrains from suggesting just how the husband might go about creating the document that is missing solely because it was never required to prove a separate property interest under former law.

The statute does much more than simply articulate the means by which the community property presumption might be rebutted. Insofar as it applies retroactively, the statute imposes an irrebuttable presumption barring recognition of the vested separate property interest. In the case at bar, and all similar proceedings instituted prior to January 1, 1984, the time for executing a written agreement as to the character of joint tenancy marital property has long passed. By eliminating the means by which one might prove the existence of the vested property right, imposing instead an evidentiary requirement with which it is impossible to comply, section 4800.1 affects the vested property right itself. . . .

Section 4800.2's provision for reimbursement of the separate property contributions to what now is conclusively presumed to be community property regardless of the parties' intent, does little to neutralize section 4800.1's adverse effect on vested property rights. In the instant case, the trial court ruled that the $167,500 home was Esther's separate property. Retroactive application of the new statutory scheme would decrease that separate property interest to only $17,500. Esther would not be reimbursed for interest payments on the mortgage (which would have constituted virtually all of her monthly payments during the early years of the loan), taxes, insurance payments or maintenance costs. The remaining $150,000 would be credited to the community, an interest which arose only after judgment was entered by the trial court. Robert would thus receive a windfall of $75,000. Moreover, because the house represents the full extent of Esther's property, she would be forced to sell it to satisfy Robert's claim. As this case all too painfully demonstrates, section 4800.2 may provide only superficial protection against section 4800.1's potentially devastating impact upon vested property rights.

II

We turn to the question whether impairment of Esther's vested property right violates due process of law. Vested rights are not immutable; the state, exercising its police power may impair such rights when considered reasonably necessary to protect the health, safety, morals and general welfare of the people. (*Bouquet,* supra, 16 Cal. 3d at p.592, 128 Cal. Rptr. 427, 546 P.2d 1371.) In determining whether a given provision contravenes the due process clause we look to

> the significance of the state interest served by the law, the importance of the retroactive application of the law to the effectuation of that interest, the extent of reliance upon the former law, the legitimacy of that reliance, the extent of actions taken on the basis of that reliance, and the extent to which the retroactive application of the new law would disrupt those actions. (Ibid.)

Where "retroactive application is necessary to subserve a sufficiently important state interest" (*Bouquet,* supra, 16 Cal. 3d at p.593, 128 Cal. Rptr. 427, 546 P.2d 1371), the inquiry need proceed no further. (See *Addison,* supra, 62 Cal. 2d at p.567, 43 Cal. Rptr. 97, 399 P.2d 897.) In *Bouquet,* where we validated retroactive application of an amendment to Civil Code section 5118 [Family Code section 771] making the postseparation earnings of both spouses, not just those of the wife, separate property, we emphasized that "[t]he state's interest in the equitable dissolution of the marital relationship supports this use of the police power to abrogate rights in marital property that derived from the patently unfair former law." (*Bouquet,* supra, 16 Cal. 3d at p.594, 128 Cal. Rptr. 427, 546 P.2d 1371.) As noted in *Bouquet,* we reached the same conclusion in *Addison,* supra, 62 Cal. 2d 558, 43 Cal. Rptr. 97, 399 P.2d 897, wherein we upheld the constitutionality of retroactive application of quasi-community property legislation despite its interference with the husband's vested property rights.

In both *Bouquet* and *Addison* we identified an important state interest in the "equitable dissolution of the marital relationship" and stressed that retroactive application was necessary to remedy "the rank injustice of the former law." (*Bouquet,* supra, 16 Cal. 3d at p.594, 128 Cal. Rptr. 427, 546 P.2d 137; *Addison,* supra, 62 Cal.

2d at p.567, 43 Cal. Rptr. 97, 399 P.2d 897.) Thus, these cases support the proposition that the state's paramount interest in the equitable dissolution of the marital partnership justifies legislative action abrogating rights in marital property where those rights derive from manifestly unfair laws. No such compelling reason exists for applying section 4800.1 retroactively. Section 4800.1 cures no "rank injustice" in the law and, in the retroactivity context, only minimally serves the state interest in equitable division of marital property, at tremendous cost to the separate property owner.

As evidence of legislative intent, the Senate reprinted the California Law Revision Commission's Report Concerning Assembly Bill No. 26 in the Senate Journal. (See Sen. Com. on Judiciary Rep. on Assembly Bill No. 26 (July 14, 1983) 3 Sen. J. (1983 Reg. Sess.) pages 4865-4867.) While the report sheds no light on the Legislature's decision to give the measure retrospective effect, it does elucidate the reasoning behind enactment of section 4800.1. The Senate was concerned that because marital partners often use community property funds to acquire assets taken in joint tenancy without knowledge of the legal distinctions between the two, and the courts are without jurisdiction to divide joint tenancy property upon dissolution, absent section 4800.1's community property presumption, the courts may be precluded from making "the most sensible disposition of all the assets of the parties." (Id., at p.4865.) Although section 5110 already contained such a presumption for the single-family residence, the Senate wanted to extend the presumption to all marital property taken in joint tenancy because "spouses frequently hold substantial amounts of their wealth in joint tenancy form, including bank accounts, stocks, and other real property." (Ibid.) In addition, the report states that a writing satisfying the statute of frauds is necessary to rebut the community property presumption, but fails to set forth the reasoning underlying that conclusion. (Id., at pp.4865-4866.)

From this statement of intent we can infer that the Legislature's primary motivation in enacting section 4800.1 was to promote the state's interest in equitable distribution of marital property upon dissolution. We are at a loss to explain, however, how retroactive application of the statute is "necessary to subserve" that interest.

Retroactive application of the writing requirement does not advance the goal of insuring equitable division of community property where, as here, the asset in question is the separate property of one spouse. Moreover, because the writing requirement only applies to joint tenancy property, it fails to achieve uniformity in the division of marital property. The presumption that property taken as "husband and wife" is community property [Family Code §803] may still be rebutted by evidence of a contrary oral agreement. (See *Lucas*, supra, 27 Cal. 3d at p.816, 166 Cal. Rptr. 853, 614 P.2d 285.) Nontitle property acquired during marriage is presumed to be community property [Family Code §760], but may be proved otherwise by tracing alone. (In re Marriage of Mix (1975) 14 Cal. 3d 604, 608-612, 122 Cal. Rptr. 79, 536 P.2d 479.)

Thus, whether or not a spouse will be able to prove that certain property is separate may well depend on happenstance alone.[9] The Legislature and the courts

---

9. For example, in *Neal* [In re Marriage of Neal, 153 Cal. App. 3d 117, 200 Cal. Rptr. 341 (1984)], the wife converted the form of title to her home to joint tenancy at the insistence of the lending institution refinancing the property. After the trial court ruled that the home, and a car and some furnishings purchased with the loan proceeds were the wife's separate property, section 4800.1 was enacted and

have long been aware that " 'husbands and wives take property in joint tenancy without legal counsel but primarily because deeds prepared by real estate brokers, escrow companies and by title companies are usually presented to the parties in joint tenancy form.' " (*Lucas,* supra, 27 Cal. 3d at p.814, 166 Cal. Rptr. 853, 614 P.2d 285.) Given the lack of uniformity in treatment of marital property presumptions, it seems manifestly unfair to apply section 4800.1 to penalize one marital partner after all is said and done, for making an uninformed legal decision at the insistence of a real estate agent, where retroactivity of the statute advances no sufficiently compelling state interest.

The extent and legitimacy of Esther's reliance on former law is, of course, difficult to gauge with certainty. However, the record is clear that Esther and Robert considered the house to be her property despite the joint tenancy form of title. The decision to take the property as joint tenants was made solely at the suggestion of a realtor. Had existing law required the parties to execute a writing as proof that the property was to remain separate, the likelihood that Esther and Robert would have done so appears great. As it stands, retroactive application of section 4800.1 vitiates Esther and Robert's oral agreement, which the trial court found to be valid and enforceable under existing law, and imposes a new writing requirement with which Esther cannot possibly comply. The parties' legitimate expectations, therefore, are substantially disregarded in favor of needless retroactivity.

Two other policy considerations work against retroactive application of section 4800.1. First ". . . to the extent the statute furthers a policy of evidentiary convenience, that policy is not served by application of the statute to cases already tried." (*Taylor,* supra, 160 Cal. App. 3d 471, 478, 206 Cal. Rptr. 557 (SIMS, J. dis.).) This is particularly true in cases, such as the one at bench, where the trial court correctly applied existing law in determining the asset to be separate property. Second, the manifest interest in finality pervading this sensitive area of the law is thwarted by retroactive application of the statute. "The net effect of retroactive legislation is that parties to marital dissolution actions cannot intelligently plan a settlement of their affairs nor even conclude their affairs with certainty after a trial based on then-applicable law." (Id., at p.479, 206 Cal. Rptr. 557 (SIMS, J. dis.).)

We conclude that retroactive application of section 4800.1 would substantially impair Esther's vested property right without due process of law. The state interest in equitable dissolution of the marital partnership is not furthered by retroactive effect. Retroactivity only serves to destroy Esther's legitimate separate property expectations as a penalty for lack of prescience of changes in the law occurring after trial. Due process cannot tolerate such a result.

The judgment is affirmed. BIRD, C.J., and MOSK, KAUS, BROUSSARD, GRODIN and LUCAS, J.J., concur.

Notes and Questions

1. The supreme court assumed without discussion that section 4800.1 required a writing to prove that the Buol home was neither joint tenancy nor community

---

the Court of Appeal reversed. . . . Without access to the vehicle registration, . . . the court was uncertain whether the car was separate property. If the registration reads "Patricia *or* Henry" then the car would be deemed to be held in joint tenancy (Veh. Code, §§4150.5, 5600.5) and section 4800.1 would apply. If, on the other hand, it reads "Patricia *and* Henry," then section 4800.1 would not apply and the parties' oral agreement would control.

property. Was this an unnecessarily broad reading of the statute? Might section 4800.1 alternatively have been read to prescribe, at divorce, that property titled in joint tenancy be treated as community property absent a writing to the contrary, and then, absent such a writing, to require that the property be treated as though it were titled as community property? In such case presumptive community property title could be rebutted by whatever means would suffice to overcome community property title, in this case the parties' oral agreement or understanding to the contrary. (See Marriage of Lucas supra.) This reading is consistent with the proof requirements of section 4800.1(a) and (b), which go only to the issue of whether the asset is held in joint tenancy or community property, and not to whether the asset is held, in whole or in part, as neither.

2. What, exactly, is the holding of *Buol*? Assume the facts of *Buol*, except that the parties' marriage endured a bit longer and Esther did not initiate a divorce action until February 1984. Does *Buol* apply?

3. In Marriage of Fabian, 41 Cal. 3d 440, 715 P.2d 253, 224 Cal. Rptr. 333 (1986), decided a year after *Buol*, the supreme court addressed the constitutionality of retroactive application of section 4800.2. In *Fabian*, the parties purchased a motel in 1972, taking title as community property. A few years later the husband used $275,000 of his separate property for motel improvements. In 1983, while the Fabian divorce was pending appeal, section 4800.2 was enacted. Although the husband was unable to assert a proportional separate property interest in the motel because he had no *Lucas understanding or agreement*, he nevertheless invoked section 4800.2 to obtain reimbursement of his $275,000 separate property contribution. Rejecting the husband's claim, the supreme court held retroactive application constitutionally impermissible. As in *Buol*, the court's rationale was considerably broader than its precise holding.

4. Responding to Marriage of Buol and recognizing that section 4800.1 was inadequately drafted, in 1986 the legislature amended section 4800.1, effective January 1, 1987:

> 4800.1. (a) The Legislature hereby finds and declares as follows:
>
> (1) It is the public policy of this state to provide uniformly and consistently for the standard of proof in establishing the character of property acquired by spouses during marriage in joint title form, and for the allocation of community and separate interests in that property between the spouses.
>
> (2) The methods provided by case and statutory law have not resulted in consistency in the treatment of spouses' interests in property which they hold in joint title, but rather, have created confusion as to which law applies at a particular point in time to property, depending on the form of title, and, as a result, spouses cannot have reliable expectations as to the characterization of their property and the allocation of the interests therein, and attorneys cannot reliably advise their clients regarding applicable law.
>
> (3) Therefore, the Legislature finds that a compelling state interest exists to provide for uniform treatment of property; thus the Legislature intends that the forms of this section and Section 4800.2, operative on January 1, 1987, shall apply to all property held in joint title regardless of the date of acquisition of the property or the date of any agreement affecting the character of the property. . . .
>
> (b) For the purpose of division of property upon dissolution of marriage or legal separation, property acquired by the parties during marriage in joint form, *including property held in tenancy in common, joint tenancy, tenancy by the entirety, or as community property* is presumed to be community property. This presumption is a presumption affecting the burden of proof and may be rebutted by either of the following:

(1) A clear statement in the deed or other documentary evidence of title by which the property is acquired that the property is separate property and not community property.

(2) Proof that the parties have made a written agreement that the property is separate property.

Were it not for the constitutional impediments imposed by *Buol* and *Fabian*, the 1986 revision of section 4800.1 would have provided much-needed simplification and uniformity in the treatment of jointly titled property. Yet the courts did not relinquish their due process objections in the face of the improved and now rationally defensible section 4800.1.

MARRIAGE OF HEIKES
10 Cal. 4th 1211, 899 P.2d 1349, 44 Cal. Rptr. 2d 155 (1995)

WERDEGAR, J. — Former Civil Code section 4800.2 (hereafter section 4800.2), now Family Code section 2640, provides that when community property is divided upon dissolution of the marriage, either spouse shall be reimbursed for his or her contributions of separate property to the acquisition of any property being divided as community property, unless the contributing spouse has waived the right of reimbursement in writing. That right was newly created on January 1, 1984, the effective date of section 4800.2. Before then, a spouse was entitled to reimbursement only if the parties had so agreed; otherwise, any contribution of separate property to the property being divided as community property was deemed an outright gift. (In re Marriage of Lucas (1980) 27 Cal. 3d 808, 816, 166 Cal. Rptr. 853, 614 P.2d 285.)

In In re Marriage of Fabian (1986) 41 Cal. 3d 440, 224 Cal. Rptr. 333, 715 P.2d 253 (*Fabian*), we held that in dissolution proceedings commenced before January 1, 1984, to apply section 4800.2 retroactively, by reimbursing a spouse for making a separate property contribution to the acquisition of community property, would deprive the other spouse of a vested property right without due process of law in violation of article I, section 7, of the California Constitution. Soon after *Fabian* was filed, the Legislature amended the statutory scheme to provide expressly that section 4800.2 would apply in dissolution proceedings commenced after January 1, 1984, regardless of the date on which the community property was acquired. (Former Civ. Code, §4800.1 (hereafter section 4800.1), subd. (a)(3), now Fam. Code, §2580, subd. (c).)

The issue in this post-1984 dissolution proceeding is whether the Constitution permits the statutorily authorized reimbursement of a husband for separate property contributions he made in 1976 to the property divided as community property in 1992. We conclude that, for the reasons stated in *Fabian*, supra, 41 Cal. 3d 440, 224 Cal. Rptr. 333, 715 P.2d 253, such reimbursement would unconstitutionally deprive the wife of a vested property right without due process of law. The only material factual distinction between this case and *Fabian* is that here, during the interval between the enactment of section 4800.2 and the commencement of the dissolution proceeding, the wife theoretically could have attempted to protect her property right by requesting the husband to execute a written waiver of his new right of reimbursement. The unlikelihood that any such attempt could succeed in this or any other marriage makes its availability too insubstantial a factor to overcome the constitutional barriers to retroactivity set forth in *Fabian*.[1]

I. FACTS AND PROCEDURAL BACKGROUND

Norman Heikes (husband) owned a home in Santa Barbara and a vacant lot near Boron, California, as his separate property. In January 1976, while married to Rose H. Heikes (wife), he conveyed both parcels to wife and himself as joint tenants. The trial court found there was no oral or written agreement preserving any interest of husband in the parcels other than the interests created by the deeds themselves.

Conveyance

The present dissolution proceeding appears to have been commenced in 1990. The judgment, filed December 11, 1992, classified both parcels as community property. On December 17, 1992, six days after the judgment, this court filed In re Marriage of Hilke (1992) 4 Cal. 4th 215, 14 Cal. Rptr. 2d 371, 841 P.2d 891, which gave retroactive effect to the presumption, applicable on dissolution of marriage, that property acquired in joint tenancy is community property (§4800.1) so as to defeat Mr. Hilke's claim of a nonvested survivorship interest in real property acquired in 1969. On December 30, 1992, the present husband moved for a partial new trial, arguing that *Hilke* manifested a change of this court's views of the constitutional restrictions on retroactive application of sections 4800.1 and 4800.2 previously set forth in *Fabian,* supra, 41 Cal. 3d 440, 224 Cal. Rptr. 333, 715 P.2d 253, and In re Marriage of Buol (1985) 39 Cal. 3d 751, 218 Cal. Rptr. 31, 705 P.2d 354.[4] The trial court accepted that argument and ordered a new trial as to the parties' respective interests in the two parcels. The Court of Appeal agreed with the trial court and affirmed the new-trial order. We granted wife's petition for review.

II. CLASSIFICATION OF PARCELS AS COMMUNITY PROPERTY

Husband claims a right of reimbursement under section 4800.2, which applies in "the division of community property." Since the two parcels in question were conveyed by husband in 1976 to himself and his wife as joint tenants, we first examine the basis for treating them as community property. The operative principles applicable to the residence and to the unimproved parcel differ.

A. RESIDENCE

"Until modified by statute in 1965, there was a rebuttable presumption that the ownership interest in property was as stated in the title to it. . . . Thus a residence

---

1. Because the trial court's judgment in the present case was entered before January 1, 1994, the operative date of the Family Code, its validity is governed by statutory provisions then in force, including sections 4800.1 and 4800.2. (Fam. Code, §4, subd. (e).) Sections 4800.1 and 4800.2 are continued in Family Code sections 2580, 2581, and 2640 without substantive change.

4. *Buol* struck down the retroactive application of section 4800.1's provision requiring a writing to rebut the presumption, applicable on dissolution of marriage, that a residence acquired in joint tenancy with the wife's separate funds is community property.

purchased with community funds, but held by a husband and wife as joint tenants, was presumed to be separate property in which each spouse had a half interest. . . . The presumption arising from the form of title could be overcome by evidence of an agreement or understanding between the parties that the interests were to be otherwise. . . ." (In re Marriage of Lucas, supra, 27 Cal. 3d 808, 813, 166 Cal. Rptr. 853, 614 P.2d 285 (hereafter *Lucas*).)

The presumption arising from the form of title created difficulties upon divorce or separation when a court saw fit to award a house held in joint tenancy to one spouse for use as a family residence. . . . Legislation intended to overcome those difficulties was added to former Civil Code section 164 in 1965 . . . , and its substance was moved in 1969 to former Civil Code section 5110 (hereafter section 5110) as part of the Family Law Act. . . . Section 5110 provided in pertinent part: "[W]hen a single family residence of a husband and wife is acquired by them during marriage as joint tenants, for the purpose of the division of such property upon dissolution of marriage or legal separation only, the presumption is that such single family residence is the community property of said husband and wife." (Stats. 1969, ch. 1608, §8, p.3339.)

The substance of section 5110's provision was again moved, in 1983, to the then new section 4800.1, where it was enlarged in two respects. First, the presumption that joint tenancy property acquired during marriage is community property was extended to all kinds of property, not just single-family residences. Second, the presumption could be rebutted only by a statement in the joint tenancy deed or a written agreement of the parties. The 1983 statute purported to make section 4800.1 applicable in all cases "to the extent proceedings as to the division of the property are not yet final on January 1, 1984." (Stats. 1983, ch. 342, §4, p.1539.)

The retroactive effect of section 4800.1 was limited, however, by this court's holding in In re Marriage of Buol, supra, 39 Cal. 3d 751, 218 Cal. Rptr. 31, 705 P.2d 354 (hereafter *Buol*), where judgment dividing the community property had been entered but was not yet final on January 1, 1984. Although title to the family home had been taken during the marriage in joint tenancy, the trial court, pursuant to the holding of *Lucas*, supra, 27 Cal. 3d 808, 166 Cal. Rptr. 853, 614 P.2d 285, had awarded the home to the wife as her separate property in accordance with the parties' oral agreement. Husband claimed a community interest in the home on the ground that under section 4800.1, enacted while the appeal was pending, the presumption that the property acquired in joint tenancy is community property could be overcome only by proof of a written instrument. This court in *Buol* unanimously rejected the claim, holding that such retroactive application of section 4800.1 would deprive the wife of a vested property right without due process of law. The following year, in 1986, the Legislature amended section 4800.1 to provide for its application to all proceedings that (unlike the proceeding in *Buol*) are commenced after January 1, 1984, except for property settlements executed, or judgments entered, before January 1, 1987. (See post, fn. 8.)

In the present case, the trial court found there was no agreement, oral or written, that either of the parcels in dispute was husband's separate property. Accordingly, application of either section 5110's presumption for single-family homes (explained in *Lucas*), or the broader presumption of section 4800.1, requires a finding that the residence is community property. Husband does not contend otherwise.

B. UNIMPROVED PARCEL

When husband conveyed the unimproved parcel to himself and wife as joint tenants in 1976, the only statutory provision for treating joint tenancy property as community property for purposes of division upon marital dissolution was section 5110, which applied only to a "single family residence." No such presumption was applicable at that time to unimproved land. The presumption of section 4800.1, however, enacted seven years later in 1983, applies to all joint tenancy property, including unimproved land. (See ante, fn. 6.)

In *Buol,* supra, 39 Cal. 3d 751, 218 Cal. Rptr. 31, 705 P.2d 354, we held that the provision of section 4800.1 requiring a writing to rebut the presumption that property acquired in joint tenancy is community property could not constitutionally be applied to deprive Mrs. Buol of her vested property interest without due process of law. Here, however, *Buol* does not preclude retroactive application of section 4800.1's presumption that the unimproved parcel conveyed by husband to himself and wife in joint tenancy is community property, because husband held no vested property right, as a joint tenant of the parcel, that he would not also have held as owner of a community property interest while both spouses were still alive. (See In re Marriage of Hilke, supra, 4 Cal. 4th at p.222, 14 Cal. Rptr. 2d 371, 841 P.2d 891 [joint tenant's survivorship interest, contingent upon surviving other joint tenant, not a vested right].) We conclude that, in accordance with section 4800.1, the trial court properly treated the unimproved lot as community property.

III. RIGHT OF REIMBURSEMENT

Husband claims reimbursement under section 4800.2 for his conveyances of the two parcels he owned separately to his wife and himself in joint tenancy, thereby making both parcels presumptively community property for purposes of dissolution. Section 4800.2 provided: "In the division of community property under this part unless a party has made a written waiver of the right to reimbursement or signed a writing that has the effect of a waiver, the party shall be reimbursed for his or her contributions to the acquisition of the property to the extent the party traces the contributions to a separate property source. . . ." The statute that originally added sections 4800.1 and 4800.2 to the Civil Code purported to make both sections applicable in all cases "to the extent proceedings as to the division of property are not yet final on January 1, 1984." (Stats. 1983, ch. 342, §4, p.1539.)

In *Fabian,* supra, 41 Cal. 3d 440, 224 Cal. Rptr. 333, 715 P.2d 253, however, we held that "retroactive application of section 4800.2 to cases pending on January 1, 1984, impairs vested property interests without due process of law" (id. at p.451, 224 Cal. Rptr. 333, 715 P.2d 253). On appeal from a judgment entered in April 1982, Mr. Fabian challenged a finding that a motel acquired by the couple was community property. Enactment of section 4800.2 while the appeal was pending raised the additional question whether he should be reimbursed for the $275,000 he had invested in the motel out of his separate property.

Affirming the judgment, we denied reimbursement, noting that "for more than 20 years prior to the enactment of section 4800.2, it was well established that, absent an agreement to the contrary, separate property contributions to a community asset were deemed gifts to the community. . . ." (*Fabian,* supra, 41 Cal. 3d at p.446, 224 Cal. Rptr. 333, 715 P.2d 253.) During that period, it was "[t]he basic rule . . . that the party who uses his separate property for community purposes is entitled to reimbursement from the community or separate property of the other only if there is an agreement between the parties to that effect.'' (See v. See (1966) 64 Cal. 2d 778, 785, 51 Cal. Rptr. 888, 415 P.2d 776, *accord, Lucas,* supra, 27 Cal. 3d at p.816, 166 Cal. Rptr. 853, 614 P.2d 285.) Because the Fabians had no such agreement for reimbursement, we concluded that retroactive application of the reimbursement requirement of section 4800.2 would have impaired Mrs. Fabian's vested property interest. (*Fabian,* supra, 41 Cal. 3d at p.448, 224 Cal. Rptr. 333, 715 P.2d 253.)

We next pointed out, however, that impairment of a vested property interest does not necessarily invalidate a statute's retroactive application if the impairment does not violate due process of law. . . . As in *Buol,* supra, 39 Cal. 3d at p.761, 218 Cal. Rptr. 31, 705 P.2d 354, we focused on the considerations material to such violation, which are outlined in In re Marriage of Bouquet (1976) 16 Cal. 3d 583, 128 Cal. Rptr. 427, 546 P.2d 1371 (*Bouquet*). These naturally divide themselves into two groups, as follows: First: ''[T]he significance of the state interest served by the law [and] the importance of the retroactive application of the law to the effectuation of that interest.'' (Id. at p.592, 128 Cal. Rptr. 427, 546 P.2d 1371.) Second: ''[T]he extent of reliance upon the former law, the legitimacy of that reliance, the extent of actions taken on the basis of that reliance, and the extent to which the retroactive application of the new law would disrupt those actions.'' (Ibid.)

With respect to the relevant state interest, we concluded in *Fabian* that the need perceived by the Legislature to enhance fairness by complementing the strengthened presumption of community property (§4800.1) with a right of reimbursement for separate property contributions (§4800.2) ''does not . . . represent a sufficiently significant state interest to mandate retroactivity.'' (*Fabian,* supra, 41 Cal. 3d at p.449, 224 Cal. Rptr. 333, 715 P.2d 253.) Because the former law was not patently unfair, retroactivity was not needed to effectuate the state's interest in equitable dissolution of the marital partnership. (Ibid.)

We next addressed the considerations pertaining to reliance. Even though ''[t]he extent of [Mrs. Fabian's] reliance on former law is difficult to pinpoint . . . , the legitimacy of such reliance is clear.'' (*Fabian,* supra, 41 Cal. 3d at p.449, 224 Cal. Rptr. 333, 715 P.2d 253.) From 1966 until ''long after the couple separated and judgment of dissolution was entered by the trial court, the law was clear and straightforward: unrestricted separate property contributions to community assets were gifts to the community'' (id. at p.450, 224 Cal. Rptr. 333, 715 P.2d 253). As to disruptive effect, ''[i]t is difficult to imagine greater disruption than retroactive application of an about-face in the law, which directly alters substantial property rights, to parties who are completely incapable of complying with the dictates of the new law. . . . By the time the Legislature created the new right to separate property reimbursement which could be waived only by a writing, the parties' marriage had been terminated by a final judgment of dissolution. The spouse who asserted a separate property right adverse to the community could hardly be expected to then execute a writing waiving his right to the property he claimed.'' (Ibid.) The scope of *Fabian*'s ultimate holding is explained in a footnote: ''We hold only that application of the statute [section 4800.2] to cases pending on January 1, 1984, impairs vested rights without due process of law.'' (Id. at p.451, fn. 12, 224 Cal. Rptr. 333, 715 P.2d 253.)

The Legislature promptly reacted to this court's pronouncements in *Buol,* supra, 39 Cal. 3d 751, 218 Cal. Rptr. 31, 705 P.2d 354, and *Fabian,* supra, 41 Cal. 3d

440, 224 Cal. Rptr. 333, 715 P.2d 253, of the constitutional limitations on retroactive application of sections 4800.1 and 4800.2. In April 1986, within a month after the filing of *Fabian,* the Governor signed urgency legislation declaring that sections 4800.1 and 4800.2 "appl[y] to proceedings commenced on or after January 1, 1984, regardless of the date of acquisition of property subject to the proceedings or the date of any agreement affecting the property" (Stats. 1986, ch. 49, §1, p.115, . . .). The urgency statute explained that sections 4800.1 and 4800.2, as enacted in 1983, had been made applicable "immediately to all family law proceedings not yet final on January 1, 1984, [their] effective date, in order to cure a serious problem in the law governing division of assets at dissolution of marriage. . . . The *Buol* decision [*Buol,* supra, 39 Cal. 3d 751, 218 Cal. Rptr. 31, 705 P.2d 354] has caused confusion among family law judges and lawyers as to what law governs in a heavily litigated area in which important property rights are affected. The decision also frustrates the intent of the Legislature to correct a serious problem in the law that is causing inequitable treatment of many parties. This act is intended to resolve the confusion created by *Buol* and to reaffirm the need for immediately applicable legislation, to the extent constitutionally permissible, in order to assure all litigants of equitable treatment upon dissolution of marriage. Any further delay will accentuate unreasonably the current confusion and problems in this area of the law." (Stats. 1986, ch. 49, §2 p.115. . . .)

Two Court of Appeal decisions soon thereafter held that the urgency statute's mandate to apply the reimbursement requirement of section 4800.2 to community property acquired before January 1, 1984, was unconstitutional. In re Marriage of Griffis, 187 Cal. App. 3d 156, 231 Cal. Rptr. 510, explained that the statute failed to declare any state interest in retroactive application that *Fabian* . . . had not already found insufficient to satisfy due process. "We must presume the Supreme Court considered every possible state interest in *Buol* and *Fabian,* including those stated by the Legislature in the new law." (In re Marriage of Griffis, supra, 187 Cal. App. 3d at p.167, 231 Cal. Rptr. 510.) In re Marriage of Hopkins & Axene (1987) 199 Cal. App. 3d 288, 245 Cal. Rptr. 433 (*review denied and publication ordered*) quoted and followed Griffis and also invoked considerations of reliance. "Here, as in Griffis, Wife acquired a community property interest at a time when the only method of defeating or diminishing that right was by proof of an agreement to the contrary. By the time section 4800.2 was enacted, Husband and Wife were already separated. Wife, therefore, had little, if any, opportunity to obtain a written waiver of Husband's right to reimbursement for his separate property contribution." (In re Marriage of Hopkins & Axene, supra, 199 Cal. App. 3d at p.293, 245 Cal. Rptr. 433.)

Meanwhile, the Legislature amended section 4800.1, as of January 1, 1987, by adding a new subdivision (a), codifying expanded recitals of "a compelling state interest . . . to provide for uniform treatment of property" and providing that, regardless of the date of the property's acquisition, or of any agreement affecting title, sections 4800.1 and 4800.2 were "applicable in all proceedings commenced on or after January 1, 1984," except "property settlement agreements executed prior to January 1, 1987, or proceedings in which judgments were rendered prior to January 1, 1987" (§4800.1, subd. (a)(3)). The Courts of Appeal, however, held that even the expanded legislative recitals in the new version of section 4800.1 were insufficient to demonstrate the compelling state interest found lacking in Fabian. . . . Accordingly, they continued to reject claims for reimbursement under section 4800.2 for contributions to community property made from separate property before January 1, 1984, as violative of due process, even in proceedings that had commenced after that date and had not culminated in any judgment before January 1, 1987. (In re Marriage of Bankovich (1988) 203 Cal. App. 3d 49, 249 Cal. Rptr. 713; In re Marriage of Cairo (1988) 204 Cal. App. 3d 1255, 251 Cal. Rptr. 731; In re Marriage of Lockman (1988) 204 Cal. App. 3d 782, 251 Cal. Rptr. 434; In re Marriage of Craig (1990) 219 Cal. App. 3d 683, 268 Cal. Rptr. 396 [quasi-community property].)

Apart from the case now under review, the foregoing six published decisions appear to be the only ones that have considered the constitutionality of requiring reimbursement of pre-1984 separate property contributions to community property under the post-*Fabian* modifications of section 4800.2. All six hold that retroactive application of the reimbursement requirement would violate due process. Yet, the present Court of Appeal refused to follow those decisions because of what it correctly characterized as "dictum" by this court in In re Marriage of Hilke, supra, 4 Cal. 4th 215, 14 Cal. Rptr. 2d 371, 841 P.2d 891 (hereafter *Hilke*).

Mrs. Hilke died during dissolution proceedings that had been commenced in 1989, and Mr. Hilke claimed ownership of the family residence (acquired in 1969) as surviving joint tenant. Relying on *Buol* . . . and *Fabian,* . . . he contended that the application to his claim of section 4800.1's presumption, that property held in joint tenancy is community property in the absence of a contrary written instrument, would deprive him of a vested property right without due process of law. We held that Mr. Hilke's claim "fails at the threshold" because in 1983, when section 4800.1 was enacted, his survivorship interest in the residence was subject to the condition precedent of his surviving his wife and therefore was not a vested property right. (*Hilke,* supra, 4 Cal. 4th at p.222, 14 Cal. Rptr. 2d 371, 841 P.2d 891.) We went on to point out that *Buol* and *Fabian* were factually distinguishable not only because they involved impairment of vested property rights, but also because the judgments in those cases were already on appeal when sections 4800.1 and 4800.2 were first enacted, whereas in *Hilke,* the dissolution proceeding commenced after that enactment.

The present Court of Appeal declared that "the statements in *Hilke* concerning the limited holding of *Fabian* are significant. They suggest our Supreme Court would apply Civil Code sections 4800.1 and 4800.2 to dissolution actions brought after the January 1, 1984, effective date of those sections, regardless of the date of the property transfers. The reliance on former law by the parties in *Fabian* and *Buol* is not present here."

In fact, however, the import of our "statements in *Hilke*" was more limited. The pertinent statements simply recognized that *Fabian*'s holding was confined to cases already pending on January 1, 1984 (*Fabian,* supra, 41 Cal. 3d at p.451, fn. 12, 224 Cal. Rptr. 333, 715 P.2d 253), and that the constitutionality of impairing vested property rights acquired before that date by retroactively applying section 4800.2 in proceedings commenced after that date was still an open question in this court. To that question we now turn.

The only material difference between the facts of the present case and those of *Fabian* is the date on which the dissolution proceeding was commenced. As in *Fabian,* husband here made a contribution to the community property well before January 1, 1984, (the effective date of section 4800.2), by conveying his separate property to wife and himself as joint tenants in 1976, thereby conferring upon wife a vested property right. The issue here, as in *Fabian,* is whether the impairment of that right through enforcement of reimbursement under section 4800.2 would violate due process in light of the factors outlined in *Bouquet*, supra, 16 Cal. 3d 583, 128 Cal. Rptr. 427, 546 P.2d 1371, pertaining to the state interest served by the law and to reliance upon the former law.

As to the relevant state interest, we concluded in *Fabian* that the perceived unfairness section 4800.2 was intended to correct did not amount to the kind of rank, patent injustice that might justify retroactive impairment of a vested property right. In the urgency statute . . . and in the statute adding subdivision (a) to section 4800.1 . . . , the Legislature explicitly declared that application of section 4800.2 "regardless of the date of acquisition of the property" (§4800.1, subd. (a) (3)) was necessary to alleviate confusion and provide for uniform treatment of property. We agree with the Courts of Appeal that have considered the matter . . . that the legislative declarations in those statutes do not manifest state interests any more compelling than the interests *Fabian* found insufficient to justify retroactive impairment of a vested right.

The considerations pertaining to "reliance upon the former law" are "the extent . . . [and] legitimacy of that reliance, the extent of actions taken on the basis of that reliance, and the extent to which the retroactive application of the new law would disrupt those actions." (*Bouquet*, supra, 16 Cal. 3d at p.592, 128 Cal. Rptr. 427, 546 P.2d 1371.) . . .

In both *Fabian* and this case, the legitimacy of the parties' reliance upon the prior law (which denied reimbursement for separate property contributions to community property in the absence of a specific agreement to the contrary) was unmistakably clear, at least from the time the property was acquired until the enactment of section 4800.2. In *Fabian*, however, "[b]y the time the Legislature created the new right to separate property reimbursement which could be waived only by a writing, the [Fabians'] marriage had been terminated by a final judgment of dissolution. The spouse who asserted a separate property right adverse to the community could hardly be expected to then execute a writing waiving his right to the property he claimed." (*Fabian*, supra, 41 Cal. 3d at p.450, 224 Cal. Rptr. 333, 715 P.2d 253.) "It is difficult to imagine greater disruption than retroactive application of an about-face in the law, which directly alters substantial property rights, to parties who are completely incapable of complying with the dictates of the new law." (Ibid.)

Here, in contrast, the dissolution proceeding was commenced five or six years after section 4800.2 took effect. . . . Accordingly, there was an interval, prior to wife's petition for dissolution, during which the parties were on notice of the existence of a statute entitling husband to reimbursement for his contribution of separate property to the parties' joint acquisition of the two parcels unless he waived reimbursement in writing. The theoretical possibility of wife's obtaining husband's written waiver during that interval, however, is too insubstantial to offset the other factors that, as in *Fabian*, call for protection of her vested property right against retroactive enforcement of husband's claim to reimbursement.

Husband's deeds of his separate property to wife and himself as joint tenants, when executed in 1976, constituted unconditional gifts. As of January 1, 1984, section 4800.2 introduced into the law a new right of reimbursement of separate property contributions to the community in the event the community property was divided upon dissolution of the marriage. Whatever the motives of generosity or otherwise that may have prompted husband to give wife her one-half interest in the property while they were married, he "could hardly be expected" (*Fabian*, supra, 41 Cal. 3d at p.450, 224 Cal. Rptr. 333, 715 P.2d 253) to waive his newly created right to be reimbursed for his contribution in the event the marriage should break up. Short of extracting such magnanimity from her husband, there was nothing wife could do to protect her vested property right from a reimbursement claim.

Moreover, to let the retroactive application of section 4800.2 depend upon factual variations in particular parties' actual reliance on prior law would unacceptably undermine the public interest in establishing uniform, predictable rules for the division of marital property. In In re Marriage of Craig, supra, 219 Cal. App. 3d 683, 268 Cal. Rptr. 396, the husband contributed his separate property to the parties' purchase of a residence in 1979 in the State of Washington. The parties lived there through December 1983, then moved to California. Dissolution proceedings were commenced in 1987. The husband sought reimbursement for his 1979 contribution to the residence, which was divisible on dissolution as quasi-community property. He contended that retroactive application of section 4800.2 was proper because neither party could have relied on California law while they were living out of state. Rejecting the contention, the Court of Appeal said that the "result husband seeks would undermine the uniformity the quasi-community property laws were enacted to establish. Actual reliance on the prior law was not the only factor cited by *Fabian* against retroactive application of section 4800.2. The opinion conceded that the extent of the wife's reliance on former law was 'difficult to pinpoint.' (In re Marriage of Fabian, supra, 41 Cal. 3d at p.449 [224 Cal. Rptr. 333, 715 P.2d 253.]) The court then noted that '[i]n the interest of finality, uniformity and predictability, retroactivity of marital property statutes should be reserved for those rare instances when such disruption is necessary to promote a significantly important state interest.' (Id., at p.450 [224 Cal. Rptr. 333, 715 P.2d 253.])" (In re Marriage of Craig, supra, 219 Cal. App. 3d at p.686, 268 Cal. Rptr. 396.) The reference in *Fabian* to the importance of "uniformity and predictability" has since been underscored by the Legislature's declaration of "a compelling state interest" to provide "uniformly and consistently" for "the allocation of community and separate interests" in marital property. (§4800.1, subd. (a); see ante, fn. 8.)

Section 4800.2 requires reimbursement for separate property contributions to the acquisition of any property that the court divides as community property.[9] We hold that the applicability of that requirement is limited by the due process clause to property acquired on or after January 1, 1984.

IV. CONCLUSION

Husband's transfer in 1976 of his separate real property to the joint ownership of his wife and himself gave wife a vested property interest that cannot constitutionally be impaired through retroactive application of the reimbursement provisions of section 4800.2 that first took effect on January 1, 1984. The trial court's ruling to the contrary, affirmed by the Court of Appeal, was in error. Accordingly, the judgment of the Court of Appeal is reversed.

LUCAS, C.J., and MOSK, KENNARD, ARABIAN, BAXTER and GEORGE, J.J., concur.

---

9. The acquisition may be of any property in joint form, whether tenancy in common, joint tenancy, tenancy by the entirety, or community property (see §4800.1, subd. (b); ante, fn. 6), so long as the acquired property is eventually divided as community property upon dissolution of marriage or legal separation.

Notes and Questions

1. *The impairment of vested interests. Heikes* discusses Marriage of Hilke, 4 Cal. 4th 215, 841 P.2d 891, 14 Cal. Rptr. 2d 371 (1992), decided by the California Supreme Court three years earlier. *Hilke* established two important principles. First, retroactive application of Family Code section 2581 (Civil Code section 4800.1) is unconstitutional only when a *vested* interest would thereby be impaired. Thus, in the garden variety case where a joint tenancy has been purchased entirely with community property funds, there is no constitutional barrier to retroactive application of section 2581 at divorce because, as between living persons, a right of survivorship is not a vested interest.

2. *Application of section 2581 in bifurcated divorces when a divorced spouse dies before the property distribution. Hilke* involved a bifurcated divorce, in which the court divorced the parties (terminated their marital status) and reserved jurisdiction to distribute their community property at a later date. The parties held their home in joint tenancy. Before the property distribution proceeding, the wife died. In the subsequent property distribution proceeding, the issue was whether the home had passed entirely to the husband by virtue of the joint tenancy right of survivorship, or whether section 2581 applied and the home was therefore community property, with the wife's half interest passing into her estate. The supreme court held that section 2581 applies in a bifurcated proceeding when one spouse has died after the divorce, but before the property distribution proceeding. Effectively, *Hilke* applied section 2581 *nunc pro tunc,* that is, it related the property distribution back to the date of the divorce. In 2001, the holding of *Hilke* was augmented by Probate Code section 5601, which provides that, subject to several exceptions, "a joint tenancy between a decedent and the decedent's former spouse, created before or during marriage, is severed as to the decedent's interest if, at the time of the decedent's death, the former spouse is not the decedent's surviving spouse. . . ."

However, when one of the parties dies *before* a divorce is entered, the divorce proceeding abates entirely, because the marriage has already been terminated by the death of a spouse. In such case, the joint tenancy right of survivorship controls. Estate of Blair, 199 Cal. App. 3d 161, 244 Cal. Rptr. 627 (1988), cited with approval in *Hilke.*

3. *The meaning of retroactivity.* A decade after *Buol, Heikes* finally issued a definitive holding on the meaning of retroactivity for purposes of applying sections 2581 and 2640. In the case of a separate property down payment on the purchase price of a home, the determinative date is the date of purchase. If separate funds are later applied to reduce the principal debt, with respect to those separate funds, should the determinative date be the date of initial purchase or the later date on which the funds were so applied?

4. *A closer look at Norman Heikes' claim.* Norman's claim to reimbursement arises from two parcels of property that he owned before marriage. During marriage, Norman conveyed the two separate property parcels to his wife Rose and himself as joint tenants. Like the California Supreme Court in *Heikes,* the courts of appeal have assumed without discussion that, absent constitutional problems of retroactive application, section 2640 applies and allows Norman to claim, as reimbursement from the community, the fair market value of the property at the time he conveyed it into joint tenancy. Is that a fair reading of section 2640(a)?

When Norman deeded, as sole grantor, his separate property to grantees Norman and Rose, as joint tenants, he seems to have satisfied the strict transmutation requirements (see §§850-853). Should he still, under section 2640, have a right of reimbursement? In other words, what does a person have to do to make an absolute gift to a spouse in California? Is transfer of title never enough?

Should section 2640 be read more narrowly to encompass only separate property *cash* contributions to the purchase price of jointly titled property? Does it distend section 2640 to apply it to cases where the "contribution" is the voluntary act of transferring title of separate property into joint property, an act that itself looks distinctly like a gift? See Mary Charles McRae, Contribution or Transmutation? The Conflicting Provisions of Sections 852 and 2640 of the California Family Code, 49 UCLA L. Rev. 1187 (2002) (proposing that section 2640 should apply only to separate property cash contributions to the acquisition of community property, and when separate property has been transmuted into community property under section 852(a), there should be no reimbursement to the separate estate under section 2640).

5. *Putting it all together: summary and problems.* After *Heikes*, the rules are clear, but their application is complex. When property is jointly titled and a vested interest is at stake, the constitutional overlay requires, according to the facts of the case, the application of either pre-1984 law, 1984-1986 law, or post-1986 law.

An asset or some portion thereof, is *community estate* property within the meaning of Family Code section 2640 only when a party cannot otherwise show that it is separate property. To the extent that a party is able to demonstrate its separate character (by whatever means are permissible in light of the form of title, if any, and the date of the transaction), the asset or, more probably, some portion thereof is analyzed according to pre-existing and generally applicable pro rata apportionment rules. (After the ownership of an asset has been apportioned between two or more estates, the application of section 2640 should yield a zero result, that is, a finding that no separate property was contributed to the acquisition of community estate property.) Whether a party will be able to make the necessary demonstration will turn on whether the property is held in joint tenancy (writing required after 1983) or community property (evidence of oral agreement or understanding sufficient until 1987; writing required thereafter) or is titled in the buyer's name alone (simple tracing) or is untitled (simple tracing).

To test your understanding of these intricate rules, distribute the following assets at divorce:

[handwritten margin note: ACQUISTION — PRE-1984 — Btwn 84-86 — As of 1987]

[handwritten margin note: Does it matter when occurred]

a. An untitled Tiffany lamp now worth $40,000 purchased for $4,000 by *W* during marriage with $2,000 of community funds and $2,000 of *W*'s separate property funds. (Does it matter when the purchase occurred?)

b. A vacation house now worth $200,000 titled in *H*'s name and purchased during marriage by *H* for $90,000 with $40,000 of community funds and a $50,000 inheritance received by *H*. (Does it matter when the purchase occurred?)

c. A home now worth $400,000 titled in joint tenancy and purchased during marriage for $100,000 with $30,000 of *W*'s separate property and $70,000 of community property if:

   i.   the parties made no collateral agreement about *W*'s separate property contribution; or

   ii. the parties made an oral agreement that *W* is to maintain a separate property interest; or

   iii. the parties made a signed written agreement that *W* is to maintain a separate property interest.

   (Does it matter when the purchase occurred?)

d.   A home now worth $400,000 titled as community property and purchased during marriage for $100,000 with $30,000 of *H*'s separate property and $70,000 of community property if:

   i.   the parties made no collateral agreement about *H*'s separate property contribution; or

   ii.   the parties made an oral agreement that *H* is to maintain a separate property interest; or

   iii.   the parties made a signed written agreement that *H* is to maintain a separate property interest.

   (Does it matter when the purchase occurred?)

6. *Joint tenancies at death.* The volume of judicial and legislative activity surrounding the treatment of joint tenancies at *divorce* has tended to obscure questions about the treatment of joint tenancies at death. Dorn v. Solomon, 57 Cal. App. 4th 650, 67 Cal. Rptr. 2d 311 (1998), holds that Family Code section 2581 (Civil Code section 4800.1) has no application when a marriage is terminated by the death of one of the spouses. In such case, property held by spouses in joint tenancy passes entirely to the surviving spouse by means of the joint tenancy right of survivorship.

7. *Parties affected by section 2581.* Although, as between husband and wife, an asset held in joint tenancy is treated as community property at divorce, the asset nevertheless remains a joint tenancy for purposes of creditor access to satisfy the debts of one spouse. Abbett Electric Corp. v. Storek, 22 Cal. App. 4th 1460, 27 Cal. Rptr. 2d 845 (1994), *review denied.*

8. *Tracing separate property contributions for purposes of section 2640 reimbursement.* In Marriage of Walrath, 17 Cal. 4th 907, 952 P.2d 1124, 72 Cal. Rptr. 2d 856 (1998), the husband sought section 2640 reimbursement for a $146,000 separate property contribution made to a community property home. The home was later refinanced with a $180,000 home equity loan, the proceeds of which were used to purchase other community property assets. The husband sought to trace his separate property contribution to the new assets, but the lower courts held that he could not trace his contribution beyond the initial asset. The supreme court reversed, holding that upon dissolution a spouse's right of reimbursement for a separate property contribution to a community property acquisition carries through to other community property assets later acquired with proceeds from the sale or hypothecation of the original acquisition.

Walrath also prescribes a tracing methodology. The separate property contributor must first establish the equity in the initial property at the time of refinancing. The percentage of separate property funds obtained from the refinancing is determined by a fraction, in which the equity is the denominator and the separate property contribution is the numerator. As the refinancing funds are applied to new acquisitions, the separate property contributor is credited with a proportional contribution. Assume, for example, that a wife contributed $50,000 of separate funds to retire the debt on a community property home. Later, when the equity in the home was $300,000, the parties refinanced, obtaining a $250,000 home equity loan. They used those funds to purchase a vacation home for $250,000. At their divorce, the vacation home is worth $400,000, but their primary home has declined in value to less than $250,000. Given the refinancing debt, there is no equity in the primary home. Thus, the wife seeks to trace her separate property contribution to the purchase price of the vacation home. The fraction is $50,000/$300,000 (the wife's contribution over the equity at the time of refinancing), so one-sixth of $250,000 (the purchase price of the vacation home), or $41,667, is traceable to the wife's initial $50,000 separate contribution to the first acquisition. She recovers $41,667 from the value of the vacation house. Two justices agreed with the general principle, but thought the court's tracing rubric unfair to the separate property contributor as well as unnecessarily complex. Justice Baxter, dissenting, would have aggregated the acquisitions to which a separate property contribution was traceable and, at divorce, have allowed separate property recovery up to the aggregate equity of the acquisitions.

E. IMPROVEMENTS: GIFT PRESUMPTIONS AND STATUTORY TREATMENT

One spouse may use community property to improve either spouse's separate property. This situation is unaffected by Family Code section 2640, which addresses only separate contributions to the improvement of community property. (When, after 1983, a spouse uses his separate property to improve community property, section 2640 controls and provides for interest-free reimbursement.)

As you read the cases, carefully evaluate the decisive evidence. Is it invariably consistent with the general principles that the courts enunciate?

MARRIAGE OF WARREN
28 Cal. App. 3d 777, 104 Cal. Rptr. 860 (1972)

ASHBY, J. — This appeal is taken by the appellant-husband . . . from an interlocutory judgment of dissolution of marriage granted to the respondent-wife. . . . He objects to determinations of the trial court relating to . . . the amount of reimbursement to the community for improvement of the respondent's separate real property. . . .

The parties entered into a stipulation that $38,000 of community funds were used to improve respondent's separate real property located at 8313-17 Firestone Boulevard in Downey, California. During the trial, appellant testified that the building was worth $33,952. The trial court found as a fact: "That 8313-17 Firestone Boulevard, Downey, California, was improved during the course of the marriage by the construction of a building thereon in connection with which building, community funds . . . were used. That neither of the parties intended that said community funds be a gift to the petitioner." [The trial court then ordered that the wife reimburse the community $33,952.] . . .

Respondent [wife] concedes that $38,000 was the amount expended, but argues as follows that the sum of $33,952 was the correct amount for community reimbursement: "Again, the issue before the court was not the community contribution in the early 1950's but what benefit was derived as measured at the time of trial."

It is only by the light of the distinction to be drawn between improvement of the separate property of the wife as opposed to that of the husband that the issue of amount of reimbursement can be made clear. Where the husband improves his own real property a form of the doctrine of tracing applies in order to prevent him from profiting from a constructive breach of his fiduciary duty to his wife. However, where the husband improves the wife's separate property, there is no tracing and any reimbursement is made solely on the basis of the agreement to reimburse. Whereas tracing results in an equity interest in the property obtained, an agreement to reimburse results in a debt interest for a specific amount expended.

When the manager of community personal property uses it to improve separate real property and a claim to the property is made on behalf of the community, there occurs an apparent conflict resulting from the tracing requirement of community property law and the merger doctrine of the law of real property fixtures. Where the husband uses community funds to improve the wife's separate real property, in the absence of any specific agreement, the law gives no right to reimbursement. (Shaw v. Bernal, 163 Cal. 262, 267-268 [124 P. 1012]; Peck v. Brummagim, 31 Cal. 440, 448-449; Carlson v. Carlson, 10 Cal. App. 300, 303 [101 P. 923].)

The rationale is that since the husband is the manager of the community, his use of it to improve the wife's separate property, in the absence of an agreement to reimburse, constitutes a presumed gift. Although this rationale made the fixtures rule of merger unnecessary, that rule is nevertheless cited in support of the decision not to trace to the source.

In Provost v. Provost, 102 Cal. App. 775, 781 [283 P. 842], the husband used the community to improve his own separate real property. The court realized that where the husband improved his own separate land "consent cannot be presumed from the wife's mere silence, for the law has given her no right to say 'no.' " With regard to the other rationale in support of not tracing — the fixture rule — the court noted that the merger doctrine would result in at least a constructive fraud and "permit the authority of the husband in controlling the community property, given him in the interest of greater freedom in its use and for its transfer for the benefit of both himself and his wife, to become a weapon to be used by him to rob her of every vestige of interest in the community property with which the law has expressly invested her."

Provost, supra, then harmonized the tracing-fixtures conflict. It concluded that, although the doctrine of fixtures precluded any title to the real property from being in the marital community, nevertheless, the doctrine of tracing as well as the husband's fiduciary duty required that the marital community be reimbursed. . . .

Thus, when the husband attempted to improve his own land with community funds the court refused to blindly apply the annexation rule of fixtures, and gave the wife a reimbursement right based upon the source doctrine of tracing and upon the husband's constructive breach of fiduciary duty. Since reimbursement is based upon commingling constituting a constructive breach of trust and upon an equity interest gained from tracing, the injured wife is entitled to either the amount expended or the value added — whichever is greater, so that there will be no benefit from the breach of trust. . . .

[By contrast, it] . . . is clear that the amount of reimbursement in the case of an agreement must be the amount expended. Therefore, the figure should have been $38,000, in accordance with the stipulation. . . .

The findings of fact and conclusions of law are ordered modified to provide for a community credit of $38,000 rather than $33,952. . . .

MARRIAGE OF JAFEMAN
29 Cal. App. 3d 244, 105 Cal. Rptr. 483 (1972)

[In a portion of Marriage of Jafeman, reprinted at page 116 supra, the court of appeal held that, despite the wife's belief to the contrary, the husband had not transmuted his separate property home into community property. In this portion of the case, the court considers the treatment of community funds that were variously spent by the husband and wife to improve the husband's separate property home.]

The use of community funds to improve the separate property of one spouse does not alter the separate character of the property. (Spreng v. Spreng, 119 Cal. App. 155, 159 [6 P.2d 104].) In the absence of a contrary agreement, the improvements have the character of the separate property and belong to its owner. (Wheeland v. Rodgers, 20 Cal. 2d 218, 222 [124 P.2d 816].) If the husband expends community funds for the improvement of his wife's separate property, it is presumed that he has made a gift of the community funds. However, if the husband expends community funds, without the consent of his wife, for the improvement of his separate property, the community is entitled to reimbursement. (Dunn v. Mullan, 211 Cal. 583, 590 [296 P. 604, 77 A.L.R. 1015].) These rules are both premised on the fact that the husband is the manager of the community funds. . . . It is reasoned that when the husband exercises this power so as to effect the improvement of his separate property, recoupment by the community is necessary in order to avoid constructive fraud against the wife. (Dunn v. Mullan, supra, at p.590; Wheeland v. Rodgers, supra, at p.222.) This reasoning is inapplicable when the wife consents to the use of community funds for the improvement of the husband's separate property. If the wife's consent is established, the community is not entitled to reimbursement. (Estate of La Belle, 93 Cal. App. 2d 538, 544-545 [209 P.2d 432]; Estate of Wooten, 64 Cal. App. 2d 96, 101 [148 P.2d 33].) . . .

As the finding of the trial court that the residence at 133 Hickory Lane is community property is not supported by the evidence, that portion of the judgment awarding each party an undivided one-half interest in the property must be reversed, and the matter must be remanded for further proceedings in order that the proportionate interests of the community and of Edward in the property may be ascertained.

In order to facilitate this determination it is appropriate to comment upon the effect of the expenditure of community funds for the improvement of the property. When community funds are expended for improvement of a husband's separate property, the community is entitled to be reimbursed only if the expenditure was made without the wife's consent. . . . The record in the instant case is devoid of any finding as to whether Mary consented to expenditure of community funds for the improvement of the entire residence. The absence of such a finding is understandable in view of the posture in which the ownership and community character of 133 Hickory Lane was presented to the trial judge. Upon the remand the trial court is directed to make findings on the issue of consent, and if further evidence on this issue is necessary, in the trial court's discretion, to reopen the case for this purpose. . . .

Notes and Questions

1. *The evidence.* In *Warren,* what was the evidentiary basis for finding a reimbursement agreement? Does it satisfy *Lucas* standards? Should it have to satisfy *Lucas* standards?

2. *The meaning of "consent."* In *Jafeman,* the trial court found that Mrs. Jafeman believed that the residence her husband brought into marriage was their community property, and that her husband called it "*our* home." The court of appeal held that this evidence was insufficient to prove a transmutation to community property. See the excerpts from *Jafeman* reprinted at page 116 supra. Suppose that the trial court, on remand, finds that the wife consented to the expenditure of community funds to improve the husband's separate property residence. In light of her erroneous belief about the true state of title, does a finding that she consented to the expenditure of community funds support the conclusion that she made a gift of her interest in the community funds? But see Marriage of Camire, 105 Cal. App. 3d 859, 164 Cal. Rptr. 667 (1980) (applying no-reimbursement rule when husband spent community funds to improve residence titled in joint tenancy but later determined by trial court to be solely the wife's separate property).

3. *Under equal management.* *Warren* and *Jafeman* are pre-1975 cases. Under post-1974 equal management, how should we view a wife's use of community property to improve her separate property? A wife's use of community property to improve her husband's separate property? Considering these questions, Marriage of Frick says:

> Beginning in 1975, both spouses were granted equal management and control of the community real and personal property, with limited exceptions. . . . However, we do not believe that this change in the law should alter the basic principles. . . . Indeed, we believe the effect of this change should be to place each spouse in the same position as the husband was before 1975. If either spouse appropriates community funds for his or her own benefit, *without the consent of the other spouse,* the community should be reimbursed. Even if in theory both spouses have an equal right to management and control, if one spouse acts in his or her self-interest to the detriment of the community interest, the community should be entitled to restitution.

181 Cal. App. 3d 997, 1019-1020, 226 Cal. Rptr. 766 (1986) (dictum) (emphasis in original).

4. *Expenditure to preserve separate property.* Similar reimbursement claims have been recognized when a husband has used his community property earnings to pay real property taxes on his separate property. See, for example, Marriage of Avril, 57 Cal. App. 3d 802, 129 Cal. Rptr. 351 (1976) (taxes), and Estate of Turner, 35 Cal. App. 2d 576, 96 P.2d 363 (1939) (taxes and special assessments).

5. *The presumption of gift.* The improvement cases have long presumed a gift when a spouse uses separate or community property to improve the other spouse's separate property. However, there is tension between that presumption of gift and the more recent rejection of gift presumptions expressed in Family Code section

2640 reimbursement, Family Code section 852 transmutation requirements, and *Moore/Marsden* pro rata purchase-price accounting (at pages 264-269). Two courts have recently declined to apply a gift presumption in improvement cases: Marriage of Wolfe, 91 Cal. App. 4th 962, 110 Cal. Rptr. 2d 921 (2001) (refusing to presume a gift and requiring the husband to reimburse the community for its improvement of his separate property: "The rule we discard—that is, the presumption of a gift in those circumstances—is . . . outside the mainstream of community property principles applied in other American jurisdictions. It is a California invention, though not one in which we should take pride, cobbled together from misunderstood doctrine and miscited cases."); Marriage of Allen, 96 Cal. App. 4th 497, 116 Cal. Rptr. 2d 887 (2002) (when wife consented to use of community property funds to improve husband's separate property, a gift should not be presumed; instead the community is entitled either to reimbursement or a pro rata interest). But see Marriage of Cross, 94 Cal. App. 4th 1143, 114 Cal. Rptr. 2d 839 (2001) (presuming gifts and declining to reimburse the community or the husband's separate property for their improvements to the wife's separate property).

F.   THE FAMILY EXPENSE PRESUMPTION

Frequently one or both spouses commingle community and separate property funds in a single account. At divorce or death the owner of separate funds may attempt to trace these funds in order to claim them as separate property. The subject of tracing will be covered in considerable detail in Chapter 6. For our present purposes, however, there are two important rules that accompany tracing efforts:

(1) Available community property funds are presumed to have been used to pay family expenses. Separate property funds are deemed to have been used to meet family expenses only when community funds are exhausted.

(2) When separate property funds are used to pay family expenses, the separate estate has no right to reimbursement unless the parties have agreed otherwise.

SEE v. SEE
64 Cal. 2d 778, 415 P.2d 776, 51 Cal. Rptr. 888 (1966)

. . . The trial court . . . followed the theory that a husband who expends his separate property for community expenses is entitled to reimbursement from community assets. This theory . . . lacks support in the statutory or case law of this state. A husband is required to support his wife and family. [See current Family Code §720.] Indeed, husband and wife assume mutual obligations of support upon marriage. These obligations are not conditioned on the existence of community property or income. The duty to support . . . requires the use of separate property of the parties when there is no community property. There is no right to reimbursement under the statutes.

Likewise a husband who elects to use his separate property instead of community property to meet community expenses cannot claim reimbursement. In the absence of an agreement to the contrary, the use of his separate property by a husband for community purposes is a gift to the community. The considerations that underlie the rule denying reimbursement to either the community or the husband's separate estate for funds expended to improve a wife's separate property . . . apply with equal force here. The husband has both management and control of the community property . . . along with the right to select the place and mode of living. . . . His use of separate property to maintain a standard of living that cannot be maintained with community resources alone no more entitles him to reimbursement from after-acquired community assets than it would from existing community assets.

Nor can we approve the recognition of an exception, a right to reimbursement of separate funds expended for community purposes at a time when a community bank account is exhausted. (Kenney v. Kenney, 128 Cal. App. 2d 128, 136 [274 P.2d 951]; Thomasset v. Thomasset, 122 Cal. App. 2d 116, 126; Hill v. Hill, 82 Cal. App. 2d 682, 698 [187 P.2d 28]; cf. Mears v. Mears, 180 Cal. App. 2d 484, 508.) Although this exception was restricted to recovery from the same community account when replenished, there is no statutory basis for it, and the court that first declared it cited no authority to support it. Such an exception conflicts with the long-standing rule that a wife who uses her separate funds in payment of family expenses without agreement regarding repayment cannot require her husband to reimburse her. (Ives v. Connacher, 162 Cal. 174, 177 [121 P.394]. . . .) Nor is a wife required to reimburse her husband in the converse situation, particularly since the husband has the control and management of community expenses and resources. The basic rule is that the party who uses his separate property for community purposes is entitled to reimbursement from the community or separate property of the other only if there is an agreement between the parties to that effect. To the extent that they conflict with this rule Mears v. Mears, supra, 180 Cal. App. 2d 484; Kenney v. Kenney, supra, 128 Cal. App. 2d 128; Thomasset v. Thomasset, supra, 122 Cal. App. 2d 116; and Hill v. Hill, 82 Cal. App. 2d 682 [187 P.2d 28], are disapproved. . . .

Note and Problem

1. *See* offers several rationales for the no-reimbursement rule. Are they persuasive? Do any survive the 1975 reform, which gives the spouses equal managerial power over community property?

2. To test your understanding of *See*, trace the following transactions involving a single checking account. How much of the money remaining on 3/2/03 is the wife's separate property?

1/1/03	*H* and *W* marry and *W* opens a new checking account.
2/1/03	*W* deposits her January pay check: $2,000. *CP*
	W deposits her AT&T stock dividends: $500. (She owned the stock prior to 1/1/03.) *SP*
2/5/03	*W* writes a rent check for $1,000.
	W withdraws $500 for monthly food and other household expenses.
2/15/03	*W* writes a check for *H*'s medical expenses: $900.
3/1/03	*W* deposits February paycheck: $2,000.

VI

CLASSIFICATION OF PROPERTY

[handwritten annotations: Funds (SP), risk, salary (Trac), $risk (CP), SECURITY ACCOUNT (SP) most, (CP) Annual salary, Personal Acct #13]

A. TRACING PROPERTY PURCHASED FROM A COMMINGLED FUND

SEE v. SEE
64 Cal. 2d 778, 415 P.2d 776, 51 Cal. Rptr. 888 (1966)

TRAYNOR, C.J.—Plaintiff Laurance A. See and cross-complainant Elizabeth Lee See appeal from an interlocutory judgment that grants each a divorce. Laurance attacks the finding that he was guilty of extreme cruelty, the granting of a divorce to Elizabeth, and the award to her of permanent alimony of $5,400 per month. Elizabeth attacks the finding that there was no community property at the time of the divorce. Neither party contests the provisions regarding custody and support of the three minor children.

The parties were married on October 17, 1941, and they separated about May 10, 1962. Throughout the marriage they were residents of California, and Laurance was employed by a family-controlled corporation, See's Candies, Inc. For most of that period he also served as president of its wholly owned subsidiary, See's Candy Shops, Inc. In the twenty-one years of the marriage he received more than $1,000,000 in salaries from the two corporations. . . .

Laurance had a personal account on the books of See's Candies, Inc., denominated Account 13. Throughout the marriage his annual salary from See's Candies, Inc., which was $60,000 at the time of the divorce, was credited to this account and many family expenses were paid by checks drawn on it. To maintain a credit balance in Account 13, Laurance from time to time transferred funds to it from an account at the Security First National Bank, hereafter called the Security Account.

The funds deposited in the Security Account came primarily from Laurance's separate property. On occasion he deposited his annual $15,000 salary from See's Candy Shops, Inc. in that account as a "reserve against taxes" on that salary. Thus there was a commingling of community property and separate property in both the Security Account and Account 13. Funds from the Security Account were sometimes

217

used to pay community expenses and also to purchase some of the assets held in Laurance's name at the time of the divorce proceedings.

Over Elizabeth's objection, the trial court followed a theory advanced by Laurance that a proven excess of community expenses over community income during the marriage establishes that there has been no acquisition of property with community funds.

Such a theory, without support in either statutory or case law of this state, would disrupt the California community property system. It would transform a wife's interest in the community property from a "present, existing and equal interest" as specified by [Family Code §751], into an inchoate expectancy to be realized only if upon termination of the marriage the community income fortuitously exceeded community expenditures. It would engender uncertainties as to testamentary and inter vivos dispositions, income, estate and gift taxation, and claims against property.

The character of property as separate or community is determined at the time of its acquisition. (In re Miller, 31 Cal. 2d 191, 197 [187 P.2d 722]; Siberell v. Siberell, 214 Cal. 767, 770 [7 P.2d 1003]; Bias v. Reed, 169 Cal. 33, 42 [145 P. 516].) If it is community property when acquired, it remains so throughout the marriage unless the spouses agree to change its nature or the spouse charged with its management makes a gift of it to the other. (Odone v. Marzocchi, 34 Cal. 2d 431, 435 [211 P.2d 297, 212 P.2d 233, 17 A.L.R.2d 1109]; Mears v. Mears, 180 Cal. App. 2d 484, 499 [4 Cal. Rptr. 618].)

Property acquired by purchase during a marriage is presumed to be community property, and the burden is on the spouse asserting its separate character to overcome the presumption. (Estate of Niccolls, 164 Cal. 368 [129 P. 278]; Thomasset v. Thomasset, 122 Cal. App. 2d 116, 123 [264 P.2d 626].) The presumption applies when a husband purchases property during the marriage with funds from an undisclosed or disputed source, such as an account or fund in which he has commingled his separate funds with community funds. (Estate of Neilson, 57 Cal. 2d 733, 742 [22 Cal. Rptr. 1, 371 P.2d 745].) He may trace the source of the property to his separate funds and overcome the presumption with evidence that community expenses exceeded community income at the time of acquisition. If he proves that at that time all community income was exhausted by family expenses, he establishes that the property was purchased with separate funds. (Estate of Neilson, supra, at p.742; Thomasset v. Thomasset, supra, at p.127.) Only when, through no fault of the husband, it is not possible to ascertain the balance of income and expenditures at the time property was acquired, can recapitulation of the total community expenses and income throughout the marriage be used to establish the character of the property. . . .

A husband who commingles the property of the community with his separate property, but fails to keep adequate records cannot invoke the burden of record keeping as a justification for a recapitulation of income and expenses at the termination of the marriage that disregards any acquisitions that may have been made during the marriage with community funds. If funds used for acquisitions during marriage cannot otherwise be traced to their source and the husband who has commingled property is unable to establish that there was a deficit in the community accounts when the assets were purchased, the presumption controls that property acquired by purchase during marriage is community property. The husband may protect his separate property by not commingling community and separate assets and income. Once he commingles, he assumes the burden of keeping records adequate to establish the balance of community income and expenditures at the time an asset is acquired with commingled property. . . .

[Next the court concluded that the husband could not claim reimbursement for separate property funds used to pay family expenses unless there was an agreement for reimbursement. This portion of the opinion is reproduced supra at page 215.]

Plaintiff has not met his burden of proving an excess of community expenses over community income at the times the other assets purchased during the marriage were acquired. The part of the judgment finding them to be his separate property is therefore reversed. Since the property issues were tried on the theory that the nature of the property could be determined by proving total community income and expenditures and since the parties may have additional evidence that would otherwise have been presented, plaintiff's failure to overcome the presumption that the assets are community property is not conclusive. We therefore remand the case for retrial of the property issues. Since the court considered the lack of community property a significant factor in determining the amount of the alimony award, that part of the judgment is also reversed.

The judgment is affirmed in all other respects. Elizabeth shall recover her costs on both appeals.

McComb, J., Peters, J., Tobriner, J., Peek, J., Mosk, J., and Burke, J., concurred.

Notes and Problems

1. Laurance See persuaded the trial court to make a recapitulative accounting, that is, to ascertain the amount of community property at the end of a marriage by subtracting total family expenses during marriage from total community property earnings during marriage. The supreme court rejected this approach. What sort of accounting would have satisfied the court?

Consider these facts. In January 2002, Wanda, a screenwriter, opened a money market account and made the following deposits and withdrawals during marriage:

	Deposits		Withdrawals
1/02	$50,000 community income		
		6/02	$20,000 family expenses (redecoration of community home)
		8/02	$20,000 purchase of AT&T
10/02	$10,000 community income		stock → CP
11/02	* $30,000 (from sale of Wanda's separate property bonds)		
		12/02	$50,000 family expenses (H's triple bypass operation)
1/03	$10,000 community income		

How would you classify the stock purchased in August 2002? The cash remaining when the couple separated in February 2003? Apply Laurance See's recapitulation accounting. Contrast the supreme court's exhaustion analysis.

2. The *See* court speaks in terms of the manager's duty to keep records, but indicates that the rigorous tracing requirements set forth in the case will not apply if, through no fault of the manager, there are no records. What circumstances might fall within the exception?

- $70 CP   - $30 SP, thus all left is SP. → rejected

$70 CP
expenses

3. How much of the rationale of *See* is dependent on the male management power over community property that prevailed in California until 1975?

MARRIAGE OF MIX
14 Cal. 3d 604, 536 P.2d 479, 122 Cal. Rptr. 79 (1975)

SULLIVAN, Justice. In this action for dissolution of marriage, appellant Richard Mix (Richard) appeals from an interlocutory judgment of dissolution declaring that appellant and respondent Esther Mix (Esther) are entitled to have their marriage dissolved, awarding custody of the minor child of the parties to Esther, and dividing their community property. Richard attacks the finding that, except for the property specifically found to be community, all property both real and personal standing in Esther's name or being in her possession at the time of the separation was her separate property.

Richard and Esther were married on September 4, 1958, and separated on December 14, 1968. There is one child of the marriage, a boy born February 24, 1960. At the time of marriage Esther was an attorney admitted to practice in California and Richard a musician and part-time teacher. Thereafter, they continued to pursue their respective careers. At the start, Esther was an associate in a law firm earning approximately $400 a month; by the time of her separation, she had become a 40 percent partner in the firm and earned about $25,000 annually. Richard's career as a musician, including regular employment with the Sacramento Symphony Orchestra, proved to be a good deal less remunerative; his annual income was generally between $1,000 and $3,000.

At the time of her marriage Esther owned considerable property. This included interests in income producing real property, a residence, a life insurance policy and bank accounts of indeterminate amounts. At that time Richard closed his savings account and the parties changed his checking account at the Bank of America into their joint account. In this new checking account, the parties deposited all their earnings as well as Esther's income from her separate property. This practice continued until 1963 when Esther opened an account in her name alone at the California Bank. In this account she deposited most of her income both from her law practice and her various investments.

The trial court found, so far as is here pertinent, that specific items of property were community property and, on the basis that it would effectuate a substantially equal division, awarded them as follows: (1) to Esther, the equity in the home of the parties, an Oldsmobile automobile, the interest in Esther's law partnership, an undivided one-sixth interest in 10 acres of real property, the household furniture and furnishings, and a tennis club membership; (2) to Richard, two sailboats, a Volkswagen automobile and the sum of $6,137. As previously stated, the court found that all other property, both real and personal, standing in Esther's name or being in her possession was her separate property. This is the finding upon which the present controversy centers. . . .

[The property, largely investment realty, that the trial court found to be Esther's separate property was purchased by Esther during marriage with funds from several bank accounts containing her commingled community earnings and separate property income.]

"The mere commingling of separate with community funds in a bank account does not destroy the character of the former if the amount thereof can be ascertained." (Hicks v. Hicks (1962) 211 Cal. App. 2d 144, 154, 27 Cal. Rptr. 307, 314. . . .) . . ."If the property, or the source of funds with which it is acquired, can be traced, its separate property character remains unchanged. . . . But if separate and community property or funds are commingled in such a manner that it is impossible to trace the source of the property or funds, the whole will be treated as community property. . . ." (Patterson v. Patterson, 242 Cal. App. 2d at p.341, 51 Cal. Rptr. at p.345 [1966].)

During the marriage of Richard and Esther the law bestowed on Richard the management and control of the community personal property other than Esther's earnings and on Esther the management and control of her community property earnings and separate property rents, issues and profits, with other exceptions not here applicable. . . . Thus under the law and the undisputed facts Esther had the management and control of the commingled bank accounts at the California Bank. Because the presumption in section 5110 that any interest in property acquired by a married woman in writing is her separate property will have no further effect after the wife acquires joint management of all community property on January 1, 1975 . . . , it should likewise not apply when the wife had management and control of the bank account in question. Otherwise, the wife managing a commingled account could by this device insulate herself from the rules applicable to commingling. We conclude therefore that the controlling presumption in this case is the one that property acquired during marriage is community property. . . .

Generally speaking such post-marital property can be established to be separate property by two independent methods of tracing. The first method involves direct tracing. As the court explained in *Hicks:* "[S]eparate funds do not lose their character as such when commingled with community funds in a bank account so long as the amount thereof can be ascertained. Whether separate funds so deposited continue to be on deposit when a withdrawal is made from such a bank account for the purpose of purchasing specific property, and whether the intention of the drawer is to withdraw such funds therefrom, are questions of fact for determination by the trial court." (Hicks v. Hicks, supra, 211 Cal. App. 2d 144, 157, 27 Cal. Rptr. 307, 315; 7 Witkin, Summary of Cal. Law (8th ed.) §33, pp.5126-5127). The second method involves a consideration of family expenses. It is based upon the presumption that family expenses are paid from community funds. . . . If at the time of the acquisition of the property in dispute, it can be shown that all community income in the commingled account has been exhausted by family expenses, then all funds remaining in the account at the time the property was purchased were necessarily separate funds. (See v. See, 64 Cal. 2d 778, 783 [415 P.2d 776, 51 Cal. Rptr. 888 (1966)].)

The effect of the presumption and the two methods of overcoming it are succinctly summarized in *See:* "If funds used for acquisitions during marriage cannot otherwise be traced to their source and the husband who has commingled property is unable to establish that there was a deficit in the community accounts when the assets were purchased, the presumption controls that property acquired by purchase during marriage is community property." (Id. at p.784, 51 Cal. Rptr. at p.892, 415 P.2d at p.780.) Throughout the marriage Esther commingled her community property earnings from her law practice with the rents, issues and proceeds from her separate property in several bank accounts. She concedes that she made no attempt to trace the source of the property by resorting to the "family expense method." We are satisfied from our review of the evidence that Esther failed to keep adequate records to show that family expenses had exhausted community funds at the time of the acquisition of any of the property here in dispute.

Esther contends, however, that she introduced sufficient evidence to trace the source of the funds used to acquire each item of disputed property to her separate property in accordance with the "direct tracing test" described in Hicks v. Hicks, supra, . . . and that therefore the trial court's finding to that effect is supported by substantial evidence. In *Hicks* the husband introduced evidence of separate property deposits amounting to $267,580.81, consisting of $91,610.90 from dividends, $66,266.70 in proceeds from sales of separate property assets, and $109,703.21 from loans secured by the credit of his separate property. He also introduced evidence of separate property withdrawals in the amount of $172,931.80 and an excess of total separate property deposits over separate property withdrawals in the amount of $94,649.01. The court held that this evidence in combination with evidence showing that the questioned withdrawals were intended to purchase the disputed property as separate property, supported the trial court's finding of separate property.

Esther introduced into evidence a schedule compiled by herself and her accountant from her records which itemized chronologically each source of separate funds, each expenditure for separate property purposes, and the balance of separate property funds remaining after each such expenditure. She received $99,632.02 attributable to her separate property; expended $42,213.79 for separate property purposes, leaving an excess of separate property receipts over separate property expenditures in the amount of $57,418.23 throughout the course of the marriage. Each year from 1958 to 1968, excepting the year 1961, there was an excess of separate property receipts over separate property expenditures, leaving a balance of separate funds. The 1961 deficit did not, however, exhaust the balance of separate funds carried forward from prior years. The schedule demonstrated that Esther's expenditures for separate property purposes closely paralleled in time and amount separate property receipts and thus established her intention to use only her separate property funds for separate property expenditures.

Richard contends that the schedule contains a fatal flaw in that the entries of receipts and expenditures are not tied to any bank account or bank accounts. Therefore, he argues, the schedule shows merely the availability of separate funds on the given dates but fails utterly to demonstrate the actual expenditures of those funds for the enumerated separate purposes. Esther concedes that she was unable to support the schedule by correlating each itemized deposit and withdrawal on the schedule with an entry in a particular bank account due to the unavailability of various bank records as well as to the lack of such records of her own. Richard urges that this state of the evidence demonstrates that Esther has failed to meet her burden, that she has therefore not overcome the community property presumption, and that her claims to specific property as being her separate property must fall.

We agree that the schedule by itself is wholly inadequate to meet the test prescribed by Hicks v. Hicks, supra, . . . and to support the trial court's finding that Esther "identified and traced" the separate property. However, the schedule was not the only evidence introduced by Esther to effect the tracing. She personally testified that the schedule was a true and accurate record, that it accurately reflected the receipts and expenditures as accomplished through various bank accounts, although she could not in all instances correlate the items of the schedule with a particular bank account, and that it accurately corroborated her intention throughout her marriage to make these expenditures for separate property purposes, notwithstanding her use of the balance of her separate property receipts for family expenses.

The trial court evidently believed Esther. "The testimony of a witness, even the party himself, may be sufficient." (6 Witkin, Cal. Procedure (2d ed.) §248, p.4240.) Viewing this evidence in the light most favorable to Esther, giving her the benefit of every reasonable inference, and resolving all conflicts in her favor, as we must under the rules of appellate review . . . , we conclude that there is substantial evidence to support the trial court's finding that Esther traced and identified the source and funds of her separate property. We are satisfied that the trial court was warranted in inferring from this evidence that the bank records if introduced would fully verify the schedule as supported by Esther's testimony to the effect that "separate funds . . . continue[d] to be on deposit when a withdrawal [was] made . . . for the purpose of purchasing specific property, and , . . [that] the intention of the drawer . . . [was] to withdraw such funds therefrom. . . ." (Hicks v. Hicks, supra, 211 Cal. App. 2d 144, 157, 27 Cal. Rptr. 307, 315.) . . .

. . . [W]e conclude that the judgment can be upheld on the basis of an adequate tracing of Esther's separate property. . . .

The judgment is affirmed. WRIGHT, C.J., and McCOMB, TOBRINER, MOSK, CLARK and BURKE, JJ., concur.

Notes and Questions

1. Since all the Mix transactions occurred before 1975, why did Esther not get the benefit of the Family Code section 803 married woman's presumption that title to property taken in her name alone is her separate property?

2. Marriage of Mix demonstrates that taking title in one's name alone during marriage does not create any presumption that the asset is the title holder's separate property. Instead, the general community property presumption (arising from acquisition during marriage) applies, and Esther Mix must overcome the presumption by tracing the acquisitions to her separate property.

3. What did Esther show to overcome the presumption that property acquired during marriage is community property? Did she use the exhaustion method discussed by the supreme court in See? What did her accountant's schedule show? What other evidence did Esther offer? Are you satisfied that the assets acquired by Esther during marriage and awarded to her as her separate property were in fact purchased with her separate funds? Can you formulate supplementary hypothetical facts that would show that the assets were community property?

4. Do Lucas *and the anti-*Lucas *legislation have any bearing at divorce on jointly titled bank accounts?* In *Mix,* several of the disputed parcels of real property were purchased with funds from the spouses' joint Bank of America account. In Marriage of Hayden, 124 Cal. App. 3d 72, 77-78, 177 Cal. Rptr. 183 (1981), decided shortly after *Lucas,* the wife sold her separate property condominium and put the proceeds into a bank account titled in her name alone. Later, she added her husband's name to the account title, making it a joint tenancy. At divorce, she sought to claim the clearly identifiable condominium sale proceeds as her separate property. The court held that tracing alone was insufficient: *Lucas* required that she show an agreement that the condominium proceeds were not to be held in joint tenancy. In 1983, the legislature enacted Probate Code section 5305 to reject *Lucas/Hayden* treatment of funds held by married couples in joint bank accounts. The legislature later amended section 5305 to provide that Family Code sections 2581 and 2640 also have no bearing on such funds. Probate Code section 5305 now reads:

(a) [I]f parties to [a bank] account are married to each other, whether or not they are so described in the deposit agreement, their net contribution to the account is presumed to be and remain their community property.

(b) Notwithstanding Sections 2581 and 2640 of the Family Code, the presumption established by this section is a presumption affecting the burden of proof and may be rebutted by either of the following:

(1) The sums on deposit that are claimed to be separate property can be traced from separate property unless it is proved that the married persons made a written agreement that expressed their clear intent that such sums be their community property.

(2) The married persons made a written agreement, separate from the deposit agreement, that expressly provided that the sums on deposit, claimed not to be community property, were not to be community property.

(c) Except as provided in Section 5307, a right of survivorship arising from the express terms of the account or under Section 5302, a beneficiary designation in a Totten trust account, or a P.O.D. [payable on death] payee designation, may not be changed by will. . . .

In light of *Buol* and *Fabian* supra, may Probate Code section 5305 constitutionally permit tracing of separate funds deposited in jointly titled accounts before the amendment's effective date?

5. *Treatment of joint accounts at the death of a spouse.* Probate Code section 5130 defines a "joint account" as "an account payable on request to one or more of two or more parties whether or not mention is made of any right of survivorship." Probate Code section 5302(a) provides that "[s]ums remaining on deposit at the death of a party to a joint account belong to the surviving party . . . as against the estate of the decedent unless there is clear and convincing evidence of a different intent." Thus, section 5302(a) creates a right of survivorship in a joint account, whether or not it is described as a joint tenancy or mentions a right of survivorship. (By contrast, if an account is described as a "tenancy in common," there is no right of survivorship unless the account or deposit agreement expressly provides for survivorship. Probate Code §5306. Similarly, if the parties to an account are married to each other and the account is expressly described as "community property," at death the property passes according to community property rules; that is, there is no right of survivorship, unless the terms of the account or deposit agreement explicitly provide otherwise. Probate Code §5307.)

When read alone, subsection (a) of section 5305 seems to apply in all circumstances to joint accounts held by married persons. The content of the account is presumed to be community property. However, subsection (c), which incorporates the death rules of section 5302, implies that subsection (a) operates only so long as both spouses are living, with the result that the community property presumption of subsection (a) may be asserted at divorce, but at death the contents of the joint account pass to the survivor under section 5302. Admittedly, the statute is awkwardly drafted. Subsections (a) and (b) should not have been added to the Probate Code because they have no bearing at the death of a spouse. Instead, the content of subsections (a) and (b) should have been appended to Family Code section 2581.

ESTATE OF MURPHY
15 Cal. 3d 907, 544 P.2d 956,
126 Cal. Rptr. 820 (1976)

WRIGHT, C.J. . . . [T]he Murphy legatees contend that the property which the trial court found to be community was acquired with the income from two farms in Kansas and certain stock that were conceded to be Murphy's separate property. As we shall explain, the separate income was not traced as a source of the assets in question and the trial court properly concluded that Murphy's legatees had failed to overcome the presumption that assets acquired by purchase during the marriage are community property. . . .

The . . . disputed assets were acquired by purchase during the marriage at times when adequate community funds were available for such acquisition. Murphy also had separate income during these times but there was no evidence from which that income could be directly traced to any of the assets in dispute.

"Property acquired by purchase during a marriage is presumed to be community property, and the burden is on the spouse asserting its separate character to overcome the presumption. . . ." (See v. See (1966) 64 Cal. 2d 778, 783 [51 Cal. Rptr. 888, 415 P.2d 776]. . . .)

The mere fact that Murphy received substantial separate income concurrently with the receipt of substantial community income does not dispel the presumption. Generally speaking there are two methods of carrying the burden of showing property purchased during the marriage to be separate: (1) direct tracing to a separate property source or (2) proof that at the time of purchase all community income was exhausted by family expenses. (In re Marriage of Mix (1975) 14 Cal. 3d 604, 611-612, 122 Cal. Rptr. 79, 536 P.2d 479; See v. See, supra, 64 Cal. 2d at p.783, 51 Cal. Rptr. 888, 415 P.2d 776.) In the present case there was no proof by either method requiring the trial court to find any of the disputed assets to be other than community property.

None of the separate income was directly traced into any particular bank account or other asset. Evidence which merely establishes the availability of separate funds on particular dates without also showing any disposition of the funds is not sufficient proof of tracing to overcome the presumption in favor of community property. (See In re Marriage of Mix, supra, 14 Cal. 3d at pp.613-614, 122 Cal. Rptr. 79, 536 P.2d 479.) Moreover, the trial court found that Murphy's separate income had been commingled with community funds in checking and savings accounts in his own name and in the joint names of himself and his wife and that there were no records adequate to identify any particular portions of such commingled funds as derived from community or separate property sources. Under these circumstances the commingled accounts and any assets acquired with funds withdrawn from them were properly treated as community property. . . .

Family living expenses are relevant to the issue of the community or separate nature of property acquired during marriage because of the presumption that such expenses are paid out of community rather than separate funds (Beam v. Bank of America (1971) 6 Cal. 3d 12, 20, 98 Cal. Rptr. 137, 490 P.2d 257; Estate of Neilson (1962) 57 Cal. 2d 733, 742, 22 Cal. Rptr. 1, 371 P.2d 745). Reliance upon such expenses to establish the separate nature of an asset purchased at any time during the marriage requires proof "that *at that time* all community income was exhausted by family expenses." (See v. See, supra, 64 Cal. 2d at p.783, 51 Cal. Rptr. at p.892, 415 P.2d at p.780; italics supplied.) In the present case there was no proof of the amount of Murphy's and Royene's living expenses except evidence of general circumstances such as their living in a house that was fully paid for by 1943 and having no dependents except Murphy's son for seven years of his minority during which he attended military school for two years. Moreover, it could be inferred from the evidence that during each year of the marriage there was more than enough community income to cover the married couple's living expenses.

The Murphy legatees contend that decisions placing the burden upon a spouse of establishing his or her ownership of separate property in a divorce or dissolution proceeding should not be fully applicable to the present probate proceeding where the prior deaths of both spouses precluded their testimony. It is true that in a dissolution proceeding testimony of the spouse claiming separate property may be crucial in overcoming the presumption that assets are community property. (See, e.g., In re Marriage of Mix, supra, 14 Cal. 3d at p.614, 122 Cal. Rptr. 79, 536 P.2d 479.) However, the burden of establishing a spouse's separate interest in presumptive community property is not simply that of presenting proof at the time of litigation but also one of keeping adequate records. "The husband may protect his separate property by not commingling community and separate assets and income. Once he commingles, he assumes the burden of keeping records adequate to establish the balance of community income and expenditures at the time an asset is acquired with commingled property." (See v. See, supra, 64 Cal. 2d at p.784, 51 Cal. Rptr. at p.892, 415 P.2d at p.780; accord, White v. White (1938) 26 Cal. App. 2d 524, 529, 79 P.2d 759.) Murphy had the opportunity during his lifetime to maintain records adequate for tracing the disposition of his separate income. His legatees are bound by the consequences of his declining to do so.

The judgment is affirmed. McComb, Tobriner, Mosk, Sullivan, Clark and Richardson, JJ., concurred.

Problem

Apply *See* exhaustion analysis and *Mix-Murphy* direct tracing in order to characterize the Columbia and Xerox stock, which has substantially appreciated in value since the date of purchase.

At the beginning of his marriage in January 2000, Harry had a savings account that contained only his $20,000 inheritance from his aunt. After marriage he made the following deposits and withdrawals:

Year	Deposits	Withdrawals
	$20,000 separate property on deposit	
2000		$1,000 rent (6/00) *[+19K SP]*
		$2,000 *W*'s medical expenses (9/00) *[17K SP]*
	$2,000 salary (10/00) *CP*	
2001	$1,000 salary (1/01) *CP*	
	$1,000 salary (8/01) *CP*	
2002	*(Total: $4K CP)*	$1,000 to pay for new suits for *H* (1/02) *[3K CP]*
		Columbia stock purchased for $3,000 (3/02) *[1K CP]*
	$2,000 salary (5/02)	
2003	*$3K CP*	$1,000 to pay for trip for *H* and *W* (1/03) *[2K CP]*
	$2,000 salary (2/03)	
	$4K CP	Xerox stock purchased for $6,000 (6/03)

All
COLUMBIA → CP

XEROX —

—$4K CP
$2K SP

LINDA GACH, THE *MIX-HICKS* MIX: TRACING TROUBLES UNDER CALIFORNIA'S COMMUNITY PROPERTY SYSTEM
26 UCLA L. Rev. 1232 (1979)

INTRODUCTION

California's community property system requires that, upon termination of marriage by death or dissolution, the community or separate character of the spouses' assets be ascertained. The effectuation of this mandate becomes complicated when the spouses have engaged in the common practice of pooling their separate funds with their community earnings in a single bank account. Unless contemporaneous records have been maintained, it becomes difficult to allocate the funds properly to the individuals and the community and to identify the character of assets purchased with proceeds from such a commingled account.

In the face of such uncertainty, a rebuttable presumption arises which dictates that disputed assets be deemed community property. This presumption may be overcome by proof that disputed assets were purchased with separate funds with the intention of retaining a separate property classification. These facts can be demonstrated through contemporaneous records or by evidence produced under either of two established tracing formulas: the direct method or the exhaustion method. These formulas seek to reconstruct the transactions that have affected the commingled account in order to ascertain the status of community and separate funds as of the date of each purchase in question. In theory, the direct method focuses on the availability of separate funds on the date of purchase, while the exhaustion formula looks to the unavailability of community funds on that date.

In the early 1960s, the California Court of Appeal, in Hicks v. Hicks, sought to invoke these tracing formulas. However, instead of focusing on the status of the commingled account on the dates when disputed assets were purchased, the court was satisfied with evidence based on a summary aggregation of all deposits and withdrawals made over the course of the entire eight year marriage. This approach, termed "recapitulation," remained viable until 1966, when the California Supreme Court, in See v. See, recognized that the cursory review produced by recapitulation was inadequate, since it failed to elicit facts from which the specific character of an asset's source could be identified.

The decision in *See* was rendered within the context of the exhaustion tracing formula. Subsequently, the use of that tracing method has effectively necessitated maintenance of contemporaneous or time-specific records. In view of the supreme court's silence, commentators assumed that *See*'s rationale discredited recapitulative *direct* tracing as well. However, in In re Marriage of Mix, decided in 1975, the court confounded the commentators by permitting the application of the recapitulative approach in a direct tracing context. The juxtaposition of *See* and *Mix* has resulted in confusion and consternation. It is the position of this Comment that *Mix* should be interpreted as an aberration and that the considerations supporting the rejection of recapitulation recognized in *See* should apply with equal force in the realm of direct tracing.

A. The Two Methods of Tracing

The first method, usually referred to as "direct tracing," requires that the party asserting separate ownership establish that separate funds sufficient to cover the amount withdrawn to purchase the asset in question were on deposit in the commingled account on the specific date of the withdrawal. It is also incumbent upon this spouse to prove that at the time of acquisition, he or she intended that separate funds be used for the purchase.

The alternative means of overcoming the community property presumption is the "exhaustion" method,[54] which is based upon the well-settled principle that all family living expenses are to be charged against community funds. Under this method, the separate character of an asset may be established by showing that, on the date of a particular withdrawal, the commingled account contained only separate funds because, prior to that time, family living expenses had completely exhausted community funds. . . .

B. The Effects of Recapitulation

Recapitulation is inherently inconsistent with the ideal tracing analyses. Both the direct and the exhaustion formulas, in their ideal forms, focus on the availability of certain funds on the date that a particular asset was purchased. Only by isolating the status of the commingled funds on that date can a dispute over property character be resolved reliably. The recapitulative approach, which merely aggregates transactions over a period of time, is thus incompatible with the objectives of the tracing formulas.

Despite its apparently narrow focus, the time-specific approach involves more than merely observing an isolated transaction at a single point in time. Rather, it requires that a cumulative, chronological evaluation be undertaken, taking into consideration all transactions that affected the commingled account prior to the date a disputed asset was purchased. In addition, proof of deposits and withdrawals of only one character, even if time-specific, is inadequate since it cannot reveal the impact of expenditures and deposits of funds of the other character. Therefore, the ideal approach to the tracing formulas requires keeping an on-going account of deposits and withdrawals of both community and separate funds in a time-specific manner.

The damaging effect which recapitulation has on any tracing analysis is best demonstrated by highlighting the inaccurate results produced under either tracing formula when such an approach is employed. Recapitulative tracing fails to consider the possibility that, as of the date of an assertedly separate purchase, separate funds may have been depleted by prior community expenses. Assume, for example, that on January 1, $500 of separate funds are deposited into a commingled account. On February 1, community funds being unavailable, the separate funds are withdrawn to cover a community expense. Two weeks later, $500 of community earnings are deposited into the account. Finally, in April, an asset is purchased with these

54. This alternative method of tracing, here labeled the "exhaustion" method, is often referred to in terms of the "family living expense presumption" or the "family expense method." See In re Marriage of Mix, 14 Cal. 3d 604. 612. 536 P.2d 479, 484, 122 Cal. Rptr. 79, 84 (1975). . . .

community funds. Under a proper tracing analysis, a court would conclude that the asset purchased in April was community property since it was purchased with community funds.

Under a scheme of recapitulative direct tracing, however, the party asserting separate ownership of the asset will prevail, since over the course of the marriage assertedly separate withdrawals did not exceed separate deposits. This result obviously flies in the face of the well-established rule that, absent an agreement otherwise, an asset acquired during marriage with community funds is community property.

Recapitulative exhaustion suffers from a similar defect. In the above illustration, a court employing such an approach would reason that the $500 of community expenses and deposits had cancelled one another out, leaving only separate funds to cover the purchase of the disputed asset. The fact that the asset was, in fact, purchased with community monies becomes irrelevant.

The two approaches above incorporate an automatic reimbursement theory. Both presume that separate funds expended for community purposes merely constitute a loan, which is repaid when subsequent deposits of community funds are made. In the previous example, this constructive loan-reimbursement principle operated when, on February 1st, the community expense required dipping into separate deposits and after-acquired community monies were then used for a separate purpose. The converse of the illustration occurs when an assertedly separate property purchase is made from community funds, followed by a deposit of separate monies. The reimbursement notion operates so that the subsequent separate deposits are automatically transformed into community funds, and the asset purchased is deemed to be separate property.

Although the reimbursement principle was, at one time, recognized in California, it was rejected by the state's highest court in 1966, in See v. See. . . .

C. See v. See — Rejection of Recapitulation and Reimbursement under the Exhaustion Method of Tracing

In See v. See, the California Supreme Court recognized that correctly ascertaining property character by the exhaustion tracing alternative is virtually impossible when a recapitulative method of accounting is employed. In that case, the husband maintained two bank accounts into which he deposited varying combinations of community and separate monies. Upon dissolution he argued, and the trial court agreed, that because community expenses over the duration of the marriage were proven to have exceeded the community income earned during the same period, it necessarily followed that the assets purchased during marriage and any remaining funds were his separate property. The California Supreme Court rejected this approach:

> It would transform a wife's interest in the community property from a "present, existing and equal interest" . . . into an inchoate expectancy to be realized only if upon termination of the marriage the community income fortuitously exceeded community expenditures. It would engender uncertainties as to testamentary and inter vivos dispositions, income . . . and claims against property.

The court held that, since the character of property is determined as of the time it is acquired, a separate property asserter who seeks to overcome the community property presumption by resort to the exhaustion method must present "evidence that community expenses exceeded community income *at the time of acquisition.*" As part of this time-specific requirement, the court stated that the party responsible for commingling is under a duty to maintain records adequate to establish the balance of community income and expenditures at the time any assertedly separate property is acquired with commingled funds. Thus, it was held that a spouse who commingles "property of the community with . . . separate property but fails to keep adequate records cannot invoke the burden of record keeping as a justification for a recapitulation of income and expenses at the termination of the marriage that disregards any acquisition that may have been made . . . with community funds."

The court also expressly disapproved the notion that a spouse whose separate property funds had previously been depleted for community purposes can automatically obtain reimbursement from acquired community funds. To eliminate this reimbursement notion, the court announced the rule that, in the absence of a contrary agreement, the use of separate property for community purposes constitutes a gift to the community.

Thus, within the context of an exhaustion tracing analysis recapitulative accounting and reimbursement were rejected by the *See* court. Nowhere in the *See* opinion, however, did the court expressly turn its attention to the direct tracing method. Yet, when direct tracing is applied in a recapitulative manner, it similarly fails to focus on the character of the specific funds used for assertedly separate property purchases and relies upon the reimbursement principle as one of its underlying assumptions. Therefore, commentators have assumed that the *See* holding and rationale also precluded the use of recapitulative direct tracing.

D.   In re Marriage of Mix: A Direct Tracing Diversion

1.   Recapitulation Reappears behind a Direct Tracing Mask

The California Supreme Court took many by surprise when it authorized recapitulative direct tracing in In re Marriage of Mix. During the ten years of their marriage, Mrs. Mix earned a substantial salary as an attorney, while her husband pursued a musical career that was "a good deal less remunerative." Additionally, Mrs. Mix entered into the marriage owning considerable separate property. Both her community property earnings from her law practice and the rents and profits from her separate property were commingled in several bank accounts. Predictably, a number of assets which Mrs. Mix asserted to be separate property were purchased from these accounts.

Although she conceded that she was unable to comply with the time-specific proof standards required under the exhaustion method as established in *See,* she nonetheless claimed that she had sufficient evidence to meet her burden under the direct tracing alternative. The evidence presented consisted of a chronological schedule compiled in anticipation of trial. The schedule itemized the sources of Mrs. Mix's separate deposits and listed each expenditure made for what she con-

tended to be a "separate property purpose." Although she testified that she was
unable to tie the itemized deposits and withdrawals to any particular bank accounts,
she nevertheless supplied information on the schedule purporting to indicate the
balance of separate funds remaining after each assertedly separate property expenditure. Moreover, she testified that it was her intent to use the proceeds of each
itemized withdrawal to purchase separate property.

The trial court agreed with Mrs. Mix's contention that she was the sole and
separate owner of the disputed properties. The California Supreme Court affirmed,
concluding that the schedule and testimony constituted substantial evidence supporting the lower court's finding that Mrs. Mix "traced and identified the source
and funds of her separate property."

The supreme court reached this conclusion through a recapitulative analysis.
Although the court initially engaged in total recapitulation, positing all of Mrs.
Mix's assertedly separate expenditures against the separate property deposits
made over the course of the marriage, it ultimately reduced the temporal scope
of its recapitulation to a year-to-year analysis. In this respect, the court seems to
have made an effort toward simulating a time-specific inquiry. However, its summary analysis was inadequate for the two reasons noted in the preceding section: recapitulation, even on a reduced scale, fails to reveal the precise character
of funds used to purchase assertedly separate assets, and reliance on Mrs. Mix's
schedule provided a skewed portrayal of available funds, since it focused solely on
the separate side of the account without considering the impact of community transactions.

To characterize the funds remaining in a commingled account accurately at
any given time, it is crucial that a court determine what impact the interplay of
prior separate and community deposits and expenditures has had. Particularly in
cases like *Mix*, where it is found that separate monies have been expended for
community purposes, a showing of separate vis-à-vis community fund activity is essential.

Thus, the result reached in *Mix* is inconsistent with *See* for a variety of reasons.
The *See* court disapproved of recapitulative exhaustion because of its inherent inability to ascertain the precise character of funds used to purchase assertedly separate property assets. As has been shown, recapitulative direct tracing suffers from
the same deficiency. The *See* court also disapproved of recapitulative exhaustion
because of its reliance on the reimbursement principle. It is anomalous for the
court subsequently to endorse recapitulative direct tracing, since the latter method
also relies upon the reimbursement principle. . . .

Only by focusing consistently on the chronological interplay of community
and separate deposits and expenditures can the precise character of funds in a
commingled account be ascertained accurately. The court's objectives in . . . *See*
. . . seem to have been to upgrade the quality, in terms of accuracy and trustworthi-
ness, of the evidence submitted to a trial court on the issue of property source and
character. In accordance with this objective, the court's record keeping mandate
should be construed to incorporate this dual requirement. To achieve these aims,
any tracing analysis must, as a prerequisite, require resort to time-specific, non-
recapitulative accounting practices. Accomplishment of this objective will eliminate
the happenstance of cases being decided on the basis of pure inference and conjec-
ture. Furthermore, the imposition of this more comprehensive record keeping obligation will provide a mechanism by which courts can effectively monitor and prevent financial overreaching by a managing spouse. . . .

MARRIAGE OF FRICK
181 Cal. App. 3d 997, 226 Cal. Rptr. 766 (1986)

[Before his marriage to Hiroko, Jerome owned the real property on which he operated the Mikado Hotel and Restaurant. The parcel was encumbered by a debt to Transamerica. The trial court found that during marriage Jerome used community funds to reduce the principal balance of the debt. Jerome appeals, contending that he adequately traced the principal payments to separate property sources.]

JOHNSON, J.—. . . Jerome incorporated the Mikado Hotel and Restaurant in September 1978. On October 1, 1978, Jerome entered into a lease between himself as lessor/landlord and the Mikado as lessee/tenant. The original lease called for payment to Jerome of $9,166 per month. The payments were reduced to $6,666 per month at the end of 1979. He deposited this amount into his personal account. Each month he made trust deed payments on the Mikado to Transamerica out of his personal account. In 1978, these payments were $5,000 per month. By the time of trial, these payments were $5,700 per month. Jerome contends the payments to Transamerica should not have been credited to the community since they were made contemporaneously or reasonably contemporaneously with his deposit of the monthly rental charge and, as such, the payments were traceable to a separate property souce. We disagree.

While it is true [that] rents which are received from a separate property source are considered separate property ([Family Code §770]), Jerome commingled these funds with community property funds.[5] As Jerome testified, the Mikado Hotels, Inc. has two accounts, a general account and a payroll account. He also has a personal account. The income from the operation of the hotel and the restaurant is first deposited into the general account. He then takes some of the money from this account and puts it into the payroll account to meet his corporate payroll needs. He deposits his salary, community property, into his personal account. It is also into this account that he deposits the rent he receives from the corporation and it is from this account that Jerome makes payments to Transamerica.[6]

Where funds are paid from a commingled account, the presumption is that the funds are community funds. (In re Marriage of Mix (1975) 14 Cal. 3d 604, 610-611 [122 Cal. Rptr. 79, 536 P.2d 479); In re Marriage of Marsden, supra, 130 Cal. App. 3d at p.441.) In order to overcome this presumption, a party must trace the funds expended to a separate property source. (Ibid.) This issue presents a question

---

5. We note this is not the typical case in which separate property is producing rent payments. In the case at bar, Jerome essentially paid himself rent. He was the owner of the corporation which paid the rent and the owner of the land, the recipient of the payments. He thus had complete control over the amount of rent payments that he required. Rent was originally $9,166 per month. He later reduced the rent to $6,666 per month since allegedly the corporation could not afford to pay the higher rate. It was thus very easy for Jerome unilaterally to manipulate that which he received as income payments and that which he received as rents. Thus, although we need not reach the issue because of the commingling in his account, we question whether such rent payments should indeed be treated as Jerome's separate property.

6. The record is unclear as to what other deposits were made into this account and what other expenditures were made with funds from this account. Although in response to this court's inquiry, Jerome's counsel cited other possible sources of money which Jerome deposited into his personal account, we do not believe the record demonstrates these deposits were indeed made into this account. . . .

of fact for the trial court and its finding will be upheld if supported by substantial evidence.

There are essentially two methods for tracing expended funds to a separate property source. The first method, relied upon by Jerome, is direct tracing. When separate funds deposited with community funds continue to be on deposit when the withdrawal is made and it is the intention of the drawer to withdraw separate funds specifically, the separate property status of the withdrawn funds is established. Jerome contends he satisfied this test. He received rent payments each month of either $9,166 or $6,666 per month. He paid Transamerica $5,000 or $5,700 per month out of this account. Thus, he concludes, these payments have been traced to a separate property source. However, this testimony is not enough to satisfy the requirements in this context. "[T]he burden of establishing a spouse's separate interest in presumptive community property is not simply that of presenting proof at the time of litigation but also one of keeping adequate records. 'The husband may protect his separate property by not commingling community and separate assets and income. Once he commingles, he assumes the burden of keeping records adequate to establish the balance of community income and expenditure at the time an asset is aquired with commingled property.' (See v. See, supra, 64 Cal. 2d at p.784 [51 Cal. Rptr. 888, 415 P.2d 776].)" (Estate of Murphy, supra, 15 Cal. 3d at p.919.) . . .

In the case at bar, Jerome provided evidence he received a specific amount of separate property income each month which he deposited in a particular personal account. He also made loan payments from this account. However, he made no other showing of the activity that occurred in this account during this month. We are merely provided an isolated portion of the account's activity. For instance, Jerome provided no evidence of what other expenditures were made from this account, the nature of the funds used, and the time in which they were expended. (Compare In re Marriage of Mix, supra, 14 Cal. 3d at pp.613-614; see Comment, The Mix-Hicks Mix: Tracing Troubles Under California's Community Property System (1979) 26 UCLA L. Rev. 1231, 1244-1245.) We are left in the dark as to the precise status and amount of separate property in Jerome's personal account at the time of these payments. As the court properly found, ". . . petitioner [Jerome] commingled community and separate funds so that no separate property funds could be found to be the source of the payments on the real estate after marriage." Moreover, we are not satisfied Jerome presented sufficient evidence to demonstrate it was his intent to use only separate property funds to make loan payments. As such, Jerome did not meet his burden of tracing the monthly loan payments to his separate property income, . . . [T]he judgment is affirmed. . . .

A petition for a rehearing was denied June 24, 1986, and the petition of appellant Husband for review by the Supreme Court was denied August 28, 1986.

Note

Is *Frick* consistent with *Mix*? Was Jerome Frick's documentary evidence more or less persuasive than that of Esther Mix? How could Jerome have failed to present "sufficient evidence to demonstrate his intent to use only separate funds to make loan payments"? How do you explain the different outcomes in *Mix* and *Frick*? See Marriage of Higinbotham, 203 Cal. App. 3d 322, 249 Cal. Rptr. 798 (1988).

B. APPORTIONMENT OF BUSINESS GROWTH AND PROFITS

This section examines the classification issues that arise when one of the spouses has a separate property business in which he or she works during marriage. In view of the George v. Ransom rule that income from separate property is separate property, the entire value of the business was initially classified as separate. In 1909, Pereira v. Pereira, 156 Cal. 1, 103 P. 488, held that marital labor should be regarded as a community contribution to the business and growth in the value of the business during marriage should be apportioned between the community and separate estates. Since then, California law has produced two competing formulas for apportionment of business growth and profits.

BEAM v. BANK OF AMERICA
6 Cal. 3d 12, 490 P.2d 257, 98 Cal. Rptr. 137 (1971)

TOBRINER, J. — Mrs. Mary Beam, defendant in this divorce action, appeals from an interlocutory judgment awarding a divorce to both husband and wife on grounds of extreme cruelty. The trial court determined that the only community property existing at the time of trial was a promissory note for $38,000, and, upon the husband's stipulation, awarded this note to the wife; the court found all other property to be the separate property of the party possessing it. The court additionally awarded Mrs. Beam $1,500 per month as alimony and granted custody of the Beam's two minor children to both parents, instructing the husband to pay $250 per month for the support of each child so long as the child remained within the wife's care.

On this appeal, Mrs. Beam attacks the judgment primarily on the grounds that the trial court (1) failed adequately to compensate the community for income attributable to the husband's skill, efforts and labors expended in the handling of his sizable separate estate during the marriage, and (2) erred in suggesting that community living expenses, paid from the income of the husband's separate estate, should be charged against community income in determining the balance of community funds. . . . For the reasons discussed below, we have concluded that substantial precedent and evidence support the various conclusions under attack; thus we conclude that the judgment must be affirmed.

Mr. and Mrs. Beam were married on January 31, 1939; the instant divorce was granted in 1968, after 29 years of marriage. Prior to and during the early years of the marriage, Mr. Beam inherited a total of $1,629,129 in cash and securities, and, except for brief and insignificant intervals in the early 1940's, he was not employed at all during the marriage but instead devoted his time to handling the separate estate and engaging in private ventures with his own capital. Mr. Beam spent the major part of his time studying the stock market and actively trading in stocks and bonds; he also undertook several real estate ventures, including the construction of two hotel resorts, Cabana Holiday I at Piercy, California, and Cabana Holiday II at Prunedale, California. Apparently, Mr. Beam was not particularly successful in these efforts, however, for, according to Mrs. Beam's own calculations, over the lengthy marriage her husband's total estate enjoyed only a very modest increase to $1,850,507.33.

Evidence introduced at trial clearly demonstrated that the only moneys received and spent by the parties during their marriage were derived from the husband's separate estate; throughout the 29 years of marriage Mrs. Beam's sole occupation was that of housewife and mother (the Beams have four children). According to the testimony of both parties, the ordinary living expenses of the family throughout the marriage amounted to $2,000 per month and, in addition, after 1960, the family incurred extraordinary expenses (for travel, weddings, gifts) of $22,000 per year. Since the family's income derived solely from Mr. Beam's separate estate, all of these household and extraordinary expenses were naturally paid from that source. . . .

[T]he wife contends that the trial court erred in failing to find any community property resulting from the industry, efforts and skill expended by her husband over the 29 years of marriage. . . .

Section 5108 of the Civil Code [Family Code section 770] provides generally that the profits accruing from a husband's separate property are also separate property.[2]

Nevertheless, long ago our courts recognized that, since income arising from the husband's skill, efforts and industry is community property, the community should receive a fair share of the profits which derive from the husband's devotion of more than minimal time and effort to the handling of his separate property. . . . Furthermore, while this principle first took root in cases involving a husband's efforts expended in connection with a separately owned farm or business . . . our courts now uniformly hold that "[a]n apportionment of profits is required not only when the husband conducts a commercial enterprise but also when he invests separate funds in real estate or securities." . . . Without question, Mr. Beam's efforts in managing his separate property throughout the marriage were more than minimal . . . and thus the trial court was compelled to determine what proportion of the total profits should properly be apportioned as community income.

Over the years our courts have evolved two quite distinct, alternative approaches to allocating earnings between separate and community income in such cases. One method of apportionment, first applied in Pereira v. Pereira (1909) 156 Cal. 1, 7 [103 P. 488] and commonly referred to as the *Pereira* approach, "is to allocate a fair return on the [husband's separate property] investment [as separate income] and to allocate any excess to the community property as arising from the husband's efforts." . . . The alternative apportionment approach, which traces its derivation to Van Camp v. Van Camp (1921) 53 Cal. App. 17, 27-28 [199 P. 885], is "to determine the reasonable value of the husband's services . . . , allocate that amount as community property, and treat the balance as separate property attributable to the normal earnings of the [separate estate]." (Tassi v. Tassi (1958) 160 Cal. App. 2d 680, 690 [325 P.2d 872].)

> In making such apportionment between separate and community property our courts have developed no precise criterion or fixed standard, but have endeavored to adopt that yardstick which is most appropriate and equi-

---

2. Section 5108 . . . provides in relevant part: "All property owned by the husband before marriage and that acquired afterwards by gift, bequest, devise or descent, with the rents, issues and profits thereof, is his separate property."

table in a particular situation . . . depending on whether the character of the capital investment in the separate property or the personal activity, ability, and capacity of the spouse is the chief contributing factor in the realization of income and profits. . . .

In applying this principle of apportionment the court is not bound either to adopt a predetermined percentage as a fair return on business capital which is separate property [the *Pereira* approach] nor need it limit the community interest only to [a] salary fixed as the reward for a spouse's service [the *Van Camp* method] but may select [whichever] formula will achieve substantial justice between the parties. . . .

Tassi v. Tassi (1958) 160 Cal. App. 2d 680, 691 [325 P.2d 872].

The trial court in the instant case was well aware of these apportionment formulas and concluded from all the circumstances that the *Pereira* approach should be utilized. As stated above, under the *Pereira* test, community income is defined as the amount by which the actual income of the separate estate exceeds the return which the initial capital investment could have been expected to earn absent the spouse's personal management. In applying the *Pereira* formula the trial court adopted the legal interest rate of 7 percent simple interest as the "reasonable rate of return" on Mr. Beam's separate property; although the wife now attacks this 7 percent simple interest figure as unrealistically high, at trial she introduced no evidence in support of any other more "realistic" rate of return and, as we stated explicitly in Weinberg v. Weinberg (1967) 67 Cal. 2d 557, 565 [63 Cal. Rptr. 13, 432 P.2d 709], in the absence of such evidence "the trial court correctly adopted the rate of legal interest." . . .

Testimony at trial indicated that, based upon this 7 percent simple interest growth factor, Mr. Beam's separate property would have been worth approximately 4.2 million dollars at the time of trial if no expenditures had been made during the marriage. Since Mrs. Beam's own calculations indicate that the present estate, plus all expenditures during marriage, would not amount to even 4 million dollars,[5] it appears that, under *Pereira,* the entire increase in the estate's value over the 29-year period would be attributable to the normal growth factor of the property itself and, thus, using this formula, all income would be designated as separate property. . . . In other words, under the *Pereira* analysis, none of the increased valuation of the husband's separate property during the marriage would be attributable to Mr. Beam's efforts, time or skill and, as a result, no community income would have been received and, consequently, no community property could presently be in existence.

The wife concedes that the use of the *Pereira* formula does sustain the trial court's conclusion that the present remainder of the husband's estate is entirely his separate property, but she contends that, under the circumstances, the *Pereira* test cannot be said to "achieve substantial justice between the parties" (Logan v. Forester (1952) 114 Cal. App. 2d 587, 600 [250 P.2d 730]) and thus that the trial court erred in not utilizing the *Van Camp* approach. Although the trial judge did not explicitly articulate his reasons for employing the *Pereira* rather than the *Van Camp* analysis, we cannot under the facts before us condemn as unreasonable the

5. According to defendant's figures, the value of Mr. Beam's estate at the time of trial was $1,850,507.33, ordinary living expenses over the marriage totalled $672,000, extraordinary expenses during this period equalled $176,000, and $610,126.93 was expended on "gifts." These calculations produce a gross total of $3,308,634.26.

judge's implicit decision that the modest increment of Mr. Beam's estate was more probably attributable to the "character of the capital investment" than to the "personal activity, ability and capacity of the spouse." . . . In any event, however, we need not decide whether the court erred in applying the *Pereira* test because we conclude, as did the trial court, that even under the *Van Camp* approach, the evidence sufficiently demonstrates that all the remaining assets in the estate constitute separate property.

Under the *Van Camp* test community income is determined by designating a reasonable value to the services performed by the husband in connection with his separate property. At trial Mrs. Beam introduced evidence that a professional investment manager, performing similar functions as those undertaken by Mr. Beam during the marriage, would have charged an annual fee of 1 percent of the corpus of the funds he was managing; Mrs. Beam contends that such a fee would amount to $17,000 per year (1 percent of the 1.7 million dollar corpus) and that, computed over the full term of their marriage, this annual "salary" would amount to $357,000 of community income. Mrs. Beam asserts that under the *Van Camp* approach she is now entitled to one-half of this $357,000.

Mrs. Beam's contention, however, overlooks the fundamental distinction between the total community *income* of the marriage, i.e., the figure derived from the *Van Camp* formula, and the community *estate* existing at the dissolution of the marriage. The resulting community estate is not equivalent to total community income so long as there are any community *expenditures* to be charged against the community income. A long line of California decisions has established that "it is presumed that the expenses of the family are paid from community rather than separate funds . . . [and] thus, in the absence of any evidence showing a different practice, the community earnings are chargeable with these expenses." . . . This "family expense presumption" has been universally invoked by prior California decisions applying either the *Pereira* or *Van Camp* formula. . . . Under these precedents, once a court ascertains the amount of community income, through either the *Pereira* or the *Van Camp* approach, it deducts the community's living expenses from community income to determine the balance of the community property.

If the "family expense" presumption is applied in the present case, clearly no part of the remaining estate can be considered to be community property. Both parties testified at trial that the family's *normal* living expenses were $2,000 per month, or $24,000 per year, and if those expenditures are charged against the annual community income, $17,000 under the *Van Camp* accounting approach, quite obviously there was never any positive balance of community property which could have been built up throughout the marriage.[6]

---

6. The trial court determined that no net community property could be established under the *Van Camp* formula by deducting total community expenses *over the course of the entire marriage* from total community income, i.e., by using a "total recapitulation" approach. Although Mrs. Beam has not challenged this total recapitulation approach on appeal, some suggestion has arisen that the trial court's resort to this accounting method is contrary to this court's decision in See v, See (1966) 64 Cal. 2d 778 [51 Cal. Rptr. 888, 415 P.2d 776]. Given the facts of the instant case, however, we need not decide whether the *See* decision, barring a husband's resort to a total recapitulation accounting in a case in which he has *voluntarily commingled separate and community income in a single account,* would also preclude total recapitulation under the instant circumstances, involving no conscious commingling. In the present case, so long as the family expense presumption is applicable, there could be no positive balance in the community estate even if the accounting procedures prescribed by *See* were utilized. The uncontradicted evidence of both parties establishes that even if the balance of the community estate were determined on a yearly, or indeed monthly, basis, rather than over the entire marriage, there was never a positive balance in the estate since community living expenses regularly exceeded the community earnings as

When a husband devotes his services to and invests his separate property in an economic enterprise, the part of the profits or increment in value attributable to the husband's services must be apportioned to the community. If the amount apportioned to the community is less than the amount expended for family purposes, and if the presumption that family expenses are paid from community funds applies, all assets traceable to the investment are deemed to be the husband's separate property. (Estate of Neilson (1962) 57 Cal. 2d 733, 742 [22 Cal. Rptr. 1, 371 P.2d 745].) . . .

[The court next considered Mrs. Beam's argument that *See* abolished the family expense presumption.] [I]n *See,* unlike the instant case, . . . a husband *chose* to pay community living expenses from existing separate funds rather than from existing community property; the husband later claimed that he was entitled to *reimbursement* for such expenditures from after-acquired community assets. Under those circumstances, we held that "a husband who *elects* to use his separate property instead of community property to meet community expenses cannot claim reimbursement. . . . The basic rule is that the party who uses his separate property for community purposes is entitled to reimbursement from the community or separate property of the other only if there is an agreement between the parties to that effect." (Italics added.) (64 Cal. 2d at p.785.)

The discussion in *See* in no way constitutes a rejection of the rule that, in the absence of other evidence, living expenses are presumed to have been paid out of community property rather than separate property, as Mrs. Beam suggests. Instead *See* merely concludes that if a spouse *does* "elect" to expend his separate property on community expenses, such expenditure "is a gift to the community" (id.) for which the spouse is not entitled to reimbursement. The cited portion of the *See* opinion thus does not involve the question of determining which assets, community or separate, have been paid out for living expenses — the subject of the family expense presumption — but instead deals with the distinct issue of the effect of a husband's voluntary decision to expend his separate property, rather than community property, on the community's living expenses.

In the instant case, of course, Mr. Beam made no conscious choice to spend his separate property, rather than the "imputed" community property on the family's living expenses. Only by means of a formula now applied by the court do we divide Mr. Beam's income into theoretical "community" and "separate" portions; Beam could hardly draw upon a fictionalized separate source to pay family expenses. Thus our decision in *See* is simply not in point. . . .

Mrs. Beam further contends, however, that even if the "family expense" presumption remains intact, the presumption was rebutted in the instant case because Mr. Beam testified at trial that family expenses were paid from his separate property. If Mr. Beam's actions demonstrated that he had made a conscious choice to use separate property, as opposed to available community property, to pay living expenses, such use of his separate property would of course constitute a gift to the community for which he would be entitled to no reimbursement. (See v. See (1966) 64 Cal. 2d 778, 785 [51 Cal. Rptr. 888, 415 P.2d 776].) The record clearly shows, however, that Mr. Beam's testimony rested totally on his assumption that *all* of his funds were his separate property; we cannot realistically characterize the husband's

which ?
assets ?

v.

Effect of
SP on
CP expenses

---

computed under *Van Camp.* Thus, on this record, the application of *See*'s accounting procedure would not alter the trial court's conclusion.

testimony as indicating that he consciously chose to pay for community expenses out of income which we now deem purely separate income, rather than from the income which, theoretically under the *Van Camp* formula, may now be designated community income.

If Mrs. Beam is to receive the benefit of the "community income" imputed by virtue of the *Pereira* or *Van Camp* tests, that income in the absence of evidence that Mr. Beam consciously declined to use available community funds, must be charged with the expenses that have been incurred by the community over the marriage: the income cannot fairly be isolated from the correlative expenses. (Cf. 1 de Funiak, Principles of Community Property (1943) §159, p.445.) Therefore we cannot conclude on this record that the trial court erred in finding that the "living expense" presumption had not been rebutted.

In sum, even if the trial court had utilized the *Van Camp* approach in determining community income, as the wife suggests, the court would still have properly concluded that there was no resulting community property from the earnings of her husband's separate property. We therefore conclude that the wife's initial contention is without merit. . . .

The judgment is affirmed. WRIGHT, C.J., McCOMB, J., PETERS, J., BURKE, J., and SULLIVAN, J., concurred. . . .

GILMORE v. GILMORE
45 Cal. 2d 142, 287 P.2d 769 (1955)

TRAYNOR, J. — Plaintiff and defendant were married in 1946 and lived together for approximately six years before this action for divorce was filed in 1952. There were no children of the marriage. . . .

Plaintiff contends that the trial court erred in finding that there was no community property. She bases this contention on the fact that during the marriage defendant's net worth representing his interests in three incorporated automobile dealerships increased from $182,010.46 to $786,045.52. During this period defendant received salaries from his dealerships ranging from a total of $22,250 in 1946 to a total of $66,799.92 in 1952. The trial court found that the salaries paid defendant by the corporations for his services "rendered to and on behalf of said corporations during the married life of the parties hereto, were and are sufficient to fully compensate said defendant and the community for all of the services rendered to and on behalf of said corporations by defendant during said period of marriage, all of which said salaries have been used and expended for community purposes during said marriage." In Huber v. Huber, 27 Cal. 2d 784, 792 [167 P.2d 708], the court stated that "In regard to earnings, the rule is that where the husband is operating a business which is his separate property, income from such business is allocated to community or separate property in accordance with the extent to which it is allocable to the husband's efforts or his capital investment." It has frequently been held that a proper method of making such allocation is to deduct from the total earnings of the business the value of the husband's services to it. The remainder, if any, represents the earnings attributable to the separate property invested in the business. . . .

This method was followed by the trial court in this case, and the evidence

sustains its findings. Defendant's corporations were staffed by well-trained personnel who were capable of carrying on the businesses unassisted. Defendant worked
relatively short hours and took many extended vacations. There was expert testimony that the salaries he received, which were found to constitute community income, were more than ample compensation for the services he rendered. Moreover,
during the period involved there was a tremendous increase in automobile business
that was accompanied by an increase in the value of dealer franchises.

Plaintiff contends, however, that the proper method for determining what part
of the increase in value of the businesses was community property is to subtract
from the total increase a reasonable return on the value at the time of the marriage
and treat the remainder as community property. She relies on Pereira v. Pereira,
156 Cal. 1, 7 [103 P. 488, 134 Am. St. Rep. 107, 23 L.R.A.N.S. 880], in which the
court stated:

> In the absence of circumstances showing a different result, it is to be pre-
> sumed that some of the profits were justly due to the capital invested. There
> is nothing to show that all of it was due to defendant's efforts alone. The
> probable contribution of the capital to the income should have been deter-
> mined from the circumstances of the case, and as the business was profitable
> it would amount at least to the usual interest on a long investment well se-
> cured.

If this method were followed in the present case it would be necessary to allocate
to the community a large part of the increase in defendant's net worth during the
marriage. The rule of the Pereira case is not, however, in conflict with the rule of
the cases cited above and followed by the trial court in this case. It is to be applied
only "In the absence of circumstances showing a different result," and the court
clearly recognized that if the husband could prove that a larger return on his capital
had in fact been realized the allocation should be made differently. (156 Cal. at
11-12.) In the present case defendant introduced substantial evidence that the salaries he received were a proper measure of the community interest in the earnings
of the businesses, and the trial court's finding based thereon cannot be disturbed
on appeal. . . .

The judgment is affirmed. GIBSON, C.J., CARTER, J., and SCHAUER, J., concurred.

SHENK, J., EDMONDS, J., and SPENCE, J., concurred in the judgment.

TASSI v. TASSI
160 Cal. App. 2d 680, 325 P.2d 872 (1958)

DOOLING, J. — Plaintiff Marjorie and decedent Harold Tassi were married on
January 31, 1942, and lived together until Harold died on February 19, 1953. At
the time of the marriage decedent owned a wholesale meat business. . . .

During the marriage in 1947 and 1948 decedent opened seven trustee accounts, three for his wife, totaling $73,962.49, and four for his brother totaling
$122,514.26. Three days before the decedent's death, Edwin wrote himself a
$20,000 check on decedent's bank account. In 1951 decedent gave to Edwin five
$1,000 United States Bearer Bonds, and in 1946 purchased for him 300 shares of

corporate stock. All of these transactions were without appellant's knowledge or consent. . . .

The trial court found "(t)hat the source of the funds which set up the accounts and purchased the securities and bonds . . . was the earnings and profits of a whole-sale meat business known as Associated Meat Company." It found that the decedent set up the trustee bank accounts with the intention of passing the money to the beneficiaries with a minimum of expense and delay in the event of his death. The court found . . . that the earnings and profits from the business "are allocable 27% to the community property of decedent and plaintiff and 73% to the separate property of decedent." It was also found that the transfers to defendant Edwin Tassi "were the community property of decedent and plaintiff to the extent of 27% thereof. . . ." . . .

Plaintiff-appellant's main attack is on the sufficiency of the evidence to support the allocation of earnings from the business in the ratio of 73 percent separate property and 27 percent community property. It is the duty of the court to allocate earnings from a business which is the separate property of a husband and in which the husband is actively employed, finding as separate property the portion of the earnings properly attributable to the business, and as community property the por-tion of the earnings properly attributable to the husband's efforts. The evidence showed that during the marriage decedent withdrew $447,805.75 from the business and paid living expenses of $44,093.16. No attempt was made by decedent to allo-cate these withdrawals between salary and business earnings. Decedent devoted full time to the management of the business.

Two approaches have ordinarily been made to the allocation of earnings in such cases: 1. to allow interest on the capital investment of the business, allocate such interest as separate property, and treat the balance as community earnings attributable to the efforts of the husband (Pereira v. Pereira, 156 Cal. 1 [103 P. 488, 13 Am. St. Rep. 107, 23 L.R.A.N.S. 880]); 2. to determine the reasonable value of the husband's services in the business, allocate that amount as community prop-erty, and treat the balance as separate property attributable to the normal earnings of the business. (Huber v. Huber, 27 Cal. 2d 784 [167 P.2d 708].) The court adopted the latter formula.

There was evidence of witnesses familiar with the wholesale meat business that the reasonable salary for the general manager of such a business was from $10,000 to $15,000 per year. Plaintiff-appellant argues that the hypothetical questions on which this testimony was based were not based upon the evidence, particularly in that they did not include the factors that this was a small, wholly owned business. The court has a wide discretion in the admission of expert testimony . . . and the salary customarily paid to general managers of wholesale meat businesses is relevant and competent evidence of the reasonable value of such services in a particular business of that character. The difficulty of obtaining evidence limited to small, wholly owned businesses is obvious. The salary allowed by such owners to themselves lies entirely in their own discretion and the surest standard would not be what such owners were accustomed to allow to themselves but rather what independent employers were in the habit of paying others for similar services in the free give and take of the open market. We find no error in the admission of this evidence.

The evidence is sufficient to support the trial court's conclusion that the rea-sonable value of decedent's services did not exceed $15,000 per year. Plaintiff-appel-lant argues that only where the husband has in fact allocated a portion of earnings to salary is the formula adopted by the court allowable. It is true that in Gilmore

v. Gilmore, 45 Cal. 2d 142, 150 [287 P.2d 769] . . ., there had been a fixed amount drawn by the husband-owner as salary. But in Huber v. Huber, supra, 27 Cal. 2d 784, in which case the husband had drawn $150 from the business every two weeks, without allocating any part to salary, and there was testimony "that the business would warrant a salary of $150 per month to defendant" the court said (p.792): "Under these circumstances the court was justified in reaching the conclusion that the earnings allocable to community property consisted of $1,800 per year. . . . " . . .

There was testimony that the period of World War II and the Korean War which followed it were years of high profits in the meat business, and an analysis of the customers' accounts showed that almost one-third of the total sales volume during the entire marriage was to purchasers who were already customers of the business when the parties were married. From this evidence the court was justified in finding that the business earnings were chiefly attributable to the business as such rather than to decedent's services. Plaintiff-appellant points to the scarcity of meat and rationing as offsetting factors to the high wartime profits but the balancing of these factors is the appropriate function of the trial court and not of this court on appeal.

Plaintiff-appellant complains that the trial court should not have deducted living expenses from the portion of business earnings attributable to community property, but "(i)t is presumed that the expenses of the family are paid from community earnings" (Huber v. Huber, supra, 27 Cal. 2d 784, 792; Thomasset v. Thomasset, 122 Cal. App. 2d 116, 126) and the court would therefore be justified in making such deduction. . . .

Since earnings were not allowed to accumulate in the business, and the business investment was the separate property of decedent we find no substance in the complaint that some part of the increase in the value of the business should have been allocated to community property.

Judgment affirmed. KAUFMAN, P.J., and DRAPER, J., concurred.

A petition for a rehearing was denied June 20, 1958, and the petitions of plaintiff and appellant and defendants and appellants for a hearing by the Supreme Court were denied July 16, 1958. SCHAUER, J., was of the opinion that the petition should be granted.

Notes and Questions

1. *Beam* approves two ostensibly different methods of apportioning gains from community labor and separate capital. What is the difference between *Van Camp* and *Pereira* apportionment? Which method was used in *Gilmore?* In *Tassi?*

2. *Van Camp* identifies the community component of a business that one spouse brought into marriage by valuing that spouse's employment in the business during marriage. Any remaining value is the business spouse's separate property. *Beam* additionally applies the family expense presumption: The value of community labor during marriage must be reduced by family expenses. (Here, apparently, recapitulative accounting is acceptable. Why?)

What facts in *Beam* suggest that the value of Mr. Beam's community labor should be reduced by the family's living expenses? Is this treatment of family expenses appropriate for most divorcing couples today? What are the critical factual issues in dealing with family expenses under a *Van Camp* accounting?

3. *Pereira,* in contrast, identifies the separate contribution by valuing the busi-

ness at the beginning of the marriage and adding a fair rate of return for the life of the marriage. If the current value of the business exceeds the original value plus imputed interest, the excess is attributed to community labor and hence belongs to the community.

Beam instructs the lower courts to account for family expenses and to subtract such expenses from the community component in *Pereira*, as well as *Van Camp*, accounting. However, subtracting family expenses in *Pereira* accounting would improperly double charge the community for family expenses. Marriage of Frick explains:

> [T]he trial court applied the *Pereira* method to apportion the profits of Jerome's business between Jerome and the community. Pursuant to this method, the court allocated a fair return on Jerome's investment in the separate property and allocated the excess profits to the community property. . . . The court determined that the community was entitled to $59,150. . . . However, the court then determined [that] all the community income was exhausted due to the community expenses incurred over the course of the marriage. As such, the community was not entitled to any of the profit from the business. We believe the court erred in this latter respect. During the course of the marriage, Jerome took out of the business whatever income he needed to meet the expenses of the community, i.e., disbursements from the business covered the community living expenses. These disbursements represented community income since had these disbursements not been made, the value of the corporation would have increased, and under the *Pereira* formula, all of this increased value would have been community property. As such, we are at a loss to understand why the community should be charged with community expenses twice. . . . A second family expense deduction is unwarranted and unfair to the community.

181 Cal. App. 3d 997, 1018-1019, 226 Cal. Rptr. 766 (1986). *Frick* recognizes the supreme court's assertion to the contrary in *Beam*, but characterizes it as dicta that does not bind the lower courts. Id. at fn. 12.

4. *Applying Van Camp and Pereira: problem.* In applying *Van Camp* and *Pereira* to the following two fact patterns, assume: (i) an annual average legal interest rate of 8 percent simple interest during the relevant period (1963-2003); (ii) an average annual managing pharmacist's salary of $15,000 during the relevant period; and (iii) average annual family expenses of $10,000 for the Smith and Jones families during the relevant period.

a. Jack Smith, a pharmacist, owned a drugstore worth $10,000 at his marriage in 1963. In 2003, the year of his divorce, the drugstore is appraised at $300,000.

b. Phil Jones, a pharmacist, owned a drugstore worth $10,000 at his marriage in 1963. In 2003, the year of his divorce, he owns a chain of drugstores worth $10,000,000.

5. What factors determine whether *Van Camp* or *Pereira* should apply in any particular case? *Beam* suggests that the *Pereira* formula was correctly applied to Mr. Beam and hence that the *Van Camp* method would be appropriate when "the personal activity, ability, and capacity of the spouse is the chief contributing factor in the realization of income and profits." (Clearly, this was not the case in *Beam*.) Do

you agree with the court? What do *Gilmore* and *Tassi* say? Would you apply *Van Camp* or *Pereira* to the Phil Jones case? Which would you apply to the Jack Smith case? Why?

6. *The American Law Institute treatment of mixed inputs of labor and capital.* Having considered California treatment of the issue, the American Law Institute adopted the following black letter rules and commentary:

§4.05.   Enhancement of Separate Property by Marital Labor

(1) A portion of any increase in the value of separate property is marital property whenever either spouse has devoted substantial time during marriage to the property's management or preservation.

(2) The increase in value of separate property over the course of the marriage is measured by the difference between the market value of the property when acquired, or at the beginning of the marriage, if later, and the market value of the property when sold, or at the end of the marriage, if sooner.

(3) The portion of the increase in value that is marital property under Paragraph (1) is the difference between the actual amount by which the property has increased in value, and the amount by which capital of the same value would have increased over the same time period if invested in assets of relative safety requiring little management.

Comment:

a. *General.* A fundamental principle of community property law followed today in most common-law jurisdictions is that the fruits of labor performed during marriage by either spouse ("marital labor") belong to the marital community, and are not the separate property of the laboring spouse. See §4.08 (1). When marital labor is applied to separate capital, and the separate capital appreciates, the principles of marital-property law require an apportionment between the appreciation attributable to the marital labor, which is marital property, and the appreciation attributable to the separate capital itself, which remains the separate property of the spousal owner of the capital. Such an apportionment is required, for example, when the separate-property owner of a business works in that business during the marriage, and the business appreciates in value. Apportionment is also required when the labor of one spouse yields appreciation in the separate property of the other spouse. In both cases the appreciation attributable to marital labor is shared by both spouses. . . .

b. *Allocation method.* Existing cases generally divide between two allocation methods. One method, akin to a *quantum meruit* approach, values the labor input by reference to prevailing compensation rates, and attributes all remaining gain to capital. The other method values the capital input by reference to ordinary rates of return, and attributes all the remaining gain to labor. If all the gain were properly allocable to either labor or capital alone, then it would not matter which was deducted from the total to find the other. Both methods would yield the same result. But in many cases, the total gain is greater than the sum of the separate gains assigned to labor and capital under these methods. This discrepancy is not surprising. A truck and a driver can haul much more together than the sum of what each can haul alone. Combining inputs may produce a synergy that enhances their yield. In that case one must allocate this surplus. Objective principles of accounting or economics offer no basis for preferring either of the commonly used allocation methods. The choice of method must therefore be made on another basis.

Paragraph (3) follows the cases that value the capital's contribution to the gain by reference to prevailing rates of return, attributing all remaining gain to marital labor. This classification rule allocates any surplus that may arise to the marital community, rather than to the separate estate. The rule is consistent with the commonly accepted principle that when separate and marital property are irreversibly commingled, the entire amount is treated as marital rather than separate. When the marital property is divided equally between the spouses, this rule divides the surplus equally between them as well.

Implementation of this section requires selecting a rate of return to apply to the separate capital. Under Paragraph (3) the gain allocated to marital labor is determined by comparing the actual increase in the separate capital's value with the return that could have been earned by investing the same amount in "assets of relative safety requiring little management." This standard follows from the decision to allocate to the marital community the surplus generated by the interaction between labor and capital. One way to estimate that surplus, articulated by this standard, is to compare the investment's total return to the return that would be earned by an investment in which the labor input is minimal. The specification of an investment "of relative safety" is based on similar reasoning. Higher-risk investments may yield a higher return. Success in higher-risk investments may be derived, however, from insights or information gained through the application of the investor's labor or talent, rendering them an inappropriate measure of the return one might expect from capital that is unaided by significant spousal labor. The standard adopted in Paragraph (3) is generally consistent with authorities that allocate to the marital community any increase in the value of the capital that exceeds its "ordinary" rate of return. The actual rate of return that is applied will necessarily vary with changing economic conditions. Interest rates fluctuate. Nor does the standard specify a particular benchmark investment. On this question the cases also vary. No fundamental principle compels the choice between intermediate term Treasury bonds and an indexed mutual fund. The standard does, however, set bounds. The returns on capital invested in comparable businesses, or in aggressive growth funds, would not be appropriate because these are not assets "of relative safety requiring little management."

Principles of the Law of Family Dissolution: Analysis and Recommendations §4.05 (2002).

What do you think of the ALI treatment? Is the fact that the gain in the value of the business is greater than the sum of the values assigned to labor and capital under the *Van Camp* and *Pereira* allocation methods primarily attributable to the "synergy" of capital and labor, or to other causes? Does the allocation rule expressed in §4.05 (3) adequately respond to cases like *Gilmore* at page 239 supra? Comment b invokes the strict tracing rules that apply when a spouse commingles separate property and community property funds. Are these rules aptly invoked?

7. *Obviating the need for apportionment.* Whatever the shortcomings of the ALI apportionment method, another provision of the ALI Principles eliminates the need for apportionment in long marriages. The Principles introduce the concept of "transmutation over time," by which separate property brought into marriage

and separate property acquired by gift during marriage become, over the course of a long marriage, marital property. The transmutation is gradual, but becomes complete after a specified number of years. The basic rule, qualified by a number of equitable exceptions, provides:

§4.12   Recharacterization of Separate Property as Marital Property at the Dissolution of Long-Term Marriage

(1) In marriages that exceed a minimum duration specified in a rule of statewide application, a portion of the separate property that each spouse held at the time of their marriage should be recharacterized at dissolution as marital property.

(a) The percentage of separate property that is recharacterized as marital property under Paragraph (1) should be determined by the duration of the marriage, according to a formula specified in a rule of statewide application.

(b) The formula should specify a marital duration at which the full value of the separate property held by the spouses at the time of their marriage is recharacterized at dissolution as marital property.

Principles of the Law of Family Dissolution: Analysis and Recommendations §4.12 (2002).

CORD v. NEUHOFF
94 Nev. 21, 573 P.2d 1170 (1978)

THOMPSON, J. . . . The Cords were married January 3, 1931, and were husband and wife until Errett's death on January 2, 1974. He died testate leaving an estate valued at $39,251,149.85. His Last Will declared the entire estate to be his separate property. His widow Virginia commenced this action asserting the estate to be community property and her entitlement to one half thereof. . . .

Since we have concluded that this action should not have been dismissed it becomes necessary to comment upon a problem which will face the district court upon remand, that is, the method to be utilized in determining whether any of Errett's estate should be apportioned to the community.

The Cords did not live in a community property jurisdiction, California, until 1937. They continued to live there, and subsequently in Nevada, also a community property state, until Errett's death in 1974. Errett's wealth in 1937 was about eight million dollars and was his separate property. When he died in 1974 the value of that estate had increased almost five fold.

The law of California and Nevada is that rents and profits from a spouse's separate property is separate property. However, it also is true that the earnings of either spouse during coverture are allocable to the community. It is evident that these concepts come into conflict when a spouse devotes his time, labor, and skill to the production of income from separate property, or to the enhancement in value of that separate property.

It is now settled in each jurisdiction that in such circumstance there must be an apportionment of any increment in value between the separate estate of the owner and the community [Pereira v. Pereira, 103 P. 488 (Cal. 1909); Johnson v. Johnson, 89 Nev. 244, 510 P.2d 625 (1973)], unless the increment is due solely to a natural enhancement of the property, or the owner of the separate estate expended only minimal effort and there was no evidence presented attributing a value to his services. There is no suggestion that the increased value of Errett's estate was due to a natural enhancement, or that he expended only minimal effort. The evidence is otherwise and establishes that he devoted great time and energy to the management of his wealth.

The methods of apportionment are expressed in the California cases of Pereira v. Pereira, supra, and Van Camp v. Van Camp, 199 P. 885 (Cal. App. 1921), which we have approved.

The Pereira method of apportionment is to allocate a fair return on the investment to the separate property and to allocate any excess to the community property as arising from the husband's efforts. In the absence of evidence of a "fair return" the court will adopt the rate of legal interest, 7 percent per annum. Beam v. Bank of America, 490 P.2d 256 (Cal. 1971).

The Van Camp method allocates to the community an annual sum equal to the salary which would have to be paid an employee rendering services proportionate to the husband's, and treats the balance as separate property attributable to the normal earnings of the separate estate.

The preferred method appears to be that suggested in *Pereira* unless the owner of the separate estate can establish that a different method of allocation is more likely to accomplish justice. In re Neilson's Estate, 317 P.2d 745 (Cal. 1962); Weinberg v. Weinberg, 432 P.2d 709 (Cal. 1967). Here, we find nothing to suggest that a different method of allocation would be more appropriate.

The financial records of Errett's wealth, income, capital gains, etc., from 1937 to 1953 were introduced in evidence. We assume that the coexecutors can produce similar records from 1953 to the year of Errett's death, 1974. If such complete financial information is available, a yearly analysis of the income generated by Errett's activities should be made, and a yearly allocation to separate and community estates accomplished. This method is preferable to an overall recapitulation for the reasons expressed by Justice Traynor in See v. See, 415 P.2d 776 (Cal. 1966). There, in a different evidentiary setting, the court rejected a tracing methodology under which the total community income over 21 years of marriage was balanced against the total community expenses for the same period. In doing so the court wrote: "It would transform a wife's interest in the community property from a 'present, existing and equal interest' as specified by Civil Code sec. 161a, into an inchoate expectancy to be realized only if upon termination of the marriage the community income fortuitously exceeded community expenditures." Id. at 779.

The same reasoning with respect to a proper recognition of the wife's "present, existing and equal interest" [NRS 123.225] applies with equal force to the case at hand. Since there must be an apportionment of the increment in value between the separate and community estates, the "present, existing and equal community interest" of Virginia arises the very moment the increment in value is large enough to require allocation. It is evident that this end can best be realized by utilizing a year-by-year analysis.[4]

_____

4. The financial records before the court, 1937 to 1953, are revealing in this regard. A year-by-year *Pereira* analysis discloses that between 1937 and 1946, Virginia acquired no community property, because

For the reasons expressed we reverse the judgment dismissing this action and remand for trial to determine the extent of Virginia's community interest in the Estate of Errett Cord.

BATJER, C.J., and MOWBRAY, GUNDERSON, and MANOUKIAN, JJ., concur.

Notes and Questions

1. *Cord* rejects recapitulation accounting in favor of an ostensibly more refined annual accounting. Professor Reppy has predicted that the approach taken by the Nevada Supreme Court in *Cord* will ultimately be adopted in California. Community Property in California 141 (1st ed. 1980).

Examine footnote 4 carefully. Is the accounting method used fair to Mr. Cord's separate estate? Is it appropriate to apply a generalized 7 percent interest rate to each year in question? Seven percent represents an average annual rate of return. In years that fall below this average, the community gains nothing, nor does it lose anything. In years that exceed the average, the community gains. The *Cord* combination produces a "heads you win, tails you lose nothing" result for the community. To be fair to the separate estate, use of an annual accounting system should probably be coupled with annual, not average, interest rates. Even this refinement may not cure the unfairness to the separate estate because the investor who generally equals average market return is likely to exceed average return in some years and fall below it in others. *Cord* accounting would appropriate the good years to the community and ignore the other years.

Cord accounting also creates difficulties in dealing with family expenses. Assuming that corpus is maintained intact, that income is applied to family expenses, and that income in excess of family expenses is reinvested in the corpus, in low return years family living expenses may exceed community income. In this event, separate income will be applied to family expenses. According to *See*, in an annual accounting system the use of separate income to defray family living expenses is a gift to the community absent a reimbursement agreement. Was the *See* principle applied in footnote 4? Should it be applied in business apportionment cases?

2. In Marriage of Denney, 115 Cal. App. 3d 543, 171 Cal. Rptr. 440 (1981), the husband owned a doughnut shop before marriage. During the marriage the husband was increasingly disabled by alcoholism and, by the time of divorce, the wife was fully responsible for the management of the shop. Although the business

---

the yearly income generated by the preceding year's net worth was always less than 7 percent. In 1947, however, income exceeded 7 percent, thus generating community income which, when decreased by 1947 community expenses, constituted 3.5 percent of the 1947 year-end net worth. Again in 1948, the income generated by the 96.5 percent of the corpus remaining separate property exceeded a normal 7 percent return, resulting in an allocation of the excess to the community estate. This excess, when added to the income *directly* generated by the 3.5 percent of the corpus constituting community property and decreased by 1948 expenses, increased the community interest in the entire corpus to approximately 15.8 percent. In all years between 1949 and 1952, community expenses exceeded community income, thus causing a decrease in residual community holdings. Thus on December 31, 1952, approximately 11.6 percent of the holdings constituted community property.

On the other hand, a total recapitulation analysis conducted from the vantage point of 1953 would reflect that Virginia had no community property in 1953. As noted in respondents' brief: "[c]ompounding $8,356,673 at 7% per year through December 31, 1952, would increase E. L. Cord's sole and separate property to $24,473,219, before there could be any community property. E. L. Cord's net worth on December 31, 1952, was $8,346,720. Therefore, obviously under the *Pereira* formula, there was no community property as of [December 31, 1952]."

was worth no more at the end of the marriage than at its beginning, Mrs. Denney theorized that the business had become valueless and she had rebuilt it. Rejecting her argument, *Denney* distinguished Marriage of Winn, 98 Cal. App. 3d 363, 159 Cal. Rptr. 445 (1979), where a bankruptcy proceeding during marriage established that the business was valueless, and its value at separation was traceable to the husband's postbankruptcy efforts to re-establish it:

> Neither the holding in *Beam* nor the result in *Winn* require the ruling sought here. The *Winn* decision must be limited to its facts; otherwise we can envision lengthy trials consumed by the introduction of exceedingly complex testimony concerning month-to-month fluctuations in the value of an ongoing business. The *Beam* court placed upon trial courts the burden of determining the fair market value of a separate business at the time of marriage and again at the time of separation. It did not anticipate that the trier of fact would be required to track the oscillations in growth or decline of a business throughout the marriage. [Marriage of Denney, supra at 550.]

3. In applying the *Pereira* formula, *Beam* assumes a simple interest rate, but *Cord* suggests that interest should be compounded. Under what circumstances is each approach correct? Is it significant whether business earnings were withdrawn or reinvested in the business?

4. Suppose that one spouse develops a community property business during marriage. For the three years between separation and divorce, the managing spouse continues to devote all his efforts to the business. How should postseparation business appreciation and income be treated at divorce? Marriage of Imperato, 45 Cal. App. 3d 432, 119 Cal. Rptr. 590 (1975), prescribes *reverse Van Camp/Pereira* analysis.

C. CREDIT ACQUISITIONS

Many major consumer purchases are made on credit or with borrowed money. At divorce, the family home, which is generally the couple's major asset, has often substantially appreciated because of market conditions even though very little of the mortgage debt has been paid off. (This ought not be surprising because the median duration of first marriages that end in divorce is 7 years while the standard mortgage has a 30-year term. Moreover, there is relatively little principal reduction in the early years of a mortgage. See page 263 infra.)

How should the credit component of a purchase be treated in terms of ownership? Does it matter that the debt has not been paid off? If the credit component is accorded a proportional ownership share, should the community or separate estate of the debtor be credited? To make these questions concrete, consider these illustrative problems:

(1) In 1985, before marriage, the husband purchased a Porsche. He took title in his name alone, paid $4,000 down, and agreed to pay the remaining $12,000 in 36 monthly installments of $333.33 plus 12 percent interest on the outstanding balance. A month later he married. He made the last payment in 1988. He and his wife now seek a divorce. The Porsche is in excellent condition and has a market value of $15,000. Who owns it?

(2) In 1980, after one year of marriage, the husband and wife decided to pur-
     chase a family residence. While the husband was away on a Fulbright lec-
     ture tour in France, the wife purchased a house in Santa Monica for
     $125,000. She took title in her name alone. The source of the $25,000
     down payment was accumulated income from a trust the wife's father had
     created for her many years before her marriage. The remaining $100,000
     was obtained from a 30-year bank loan (mortgage). The principal debt has
     been reduced by $40,000. The market value of the house is now $600,000.
     At divorce, who owns the house?

(3) A single woman purchased a Palo Alto home for $100,000 in 1980. She
     put down $20,000 and acquired a 30-year $80,000 bank loan (mortgage).
     Two years later, she married. Shortly after marriage, she became pregnant,
     quit her job, and has remained home ever since to raise the couple's chil-
     dren, of whom there are now four. The husband has made all postmarital
     mortgage payments from his earnings. Annual average mortgage pay-
     ments, including repayment of principal, interest, taxes, and insurance
     (known to mortgagees as PITI), have been $10,800 or $900 per month.
     The principal debt of $80,000 has now been reduced to $50,000. The cur-
     rent market value of the house is $500,000. The couple is getting divorced.
     Who owns the house?

(4) Husband and wife married in 1980. In 1985, the wife purchased a business
     in east Los Angeles. She financed it under a special federal program for
     small business acquisition. She was not required to make any down pay-
     ment. The government lender required security, so she gave a secured
     interest in the purchased business. She hired a manager for the business
     and did not devote any substantial effort to it. She paid back the govern-
     ment loan with receipts from the business. At divorce, who owns the busi-
     ness?

These illustrative problems present three discrete questions. First, how do we
treat credit acquisitions? Next, assuming that there are two estates that have some
claim to ownership, how do we measure their respective contributions? In the third
problem, for example, how do we calculate the community contribution in the form
of mortgage payments? Then, having ascertained the community contribution, is
the community merely entitled to reimbursement or does the community become
an owner pro tanto, that is, an owner entitled to its share of the appreciation? In
this section we shall address the first issue: how we classify credit acquisitions. In
the next section we shall examine the second and third issues.

GUDELJ v. GUDELJ
41 Cal. 2d 202, 259 P.2d 656 (1953)

EDMONDS, J. — Catherine Gudelj was awarded an interlocutory decree of divorce from John Gudelj on the ground of extreme cruelty. She has appealed from
those portions of the decree relating to . . . the disposition of the property of the
spouses.

The parties were married in 1938. Prior to that time, John was owner and operator of the Pacific Avenue Cleaners. He continued this business until 1943. In 1946, after his discharge from military service, he operated the Owl Cleaners in partnership with one Grinton. They dissolved the partnership in the following year, and John purchased a one-fourth interest in the Helene French Cleaners, where he began to work as a "benzine man." . . .

The court found that an undivided one-fourth interest in the Helene French Cleaners was the separate property of John. . . .

According to the record, the undivided one-fourth interest in the Helene French Cleaners was purchased by John for $11,500. John paid $1,500 of that amount in cash and executed a note for $10,000. No specific finding was made concerning the status of the note, but the trial court found that the cash payment was made from John's separate funds and concluded that the entire partnership interest is his separate property. Catherine contends that the evidence does not support these findings.

The evidence concerning the source of the $1,500, although confused and conflicting, is sufficient to support a finding that it was derived from John's separate property. John testified that the money came from the Owl Cleaners and, although he further stated that the equipment and fixtures of the business had been sold at a loss, apparently at least $1,500 was obtained from that source. Catherine claims that the Owl Cleaners must be presumed to have been community property because the business was acquired during the existence of the marriage. ([Family Code §760].) But that presumption is controlling only when it is impossible to trace the source of specific property. . . . Here the presumption is rebutted by the testimony of John that the Owl Cleaners was purchased with funds acquired from the sale of the equipment of the Pacific Avenue Cleaners, admittedly his separate property, and from a bank account held jointly by John with his mother in which was deposited the proceeds from the sale of real property owned by them prior to John's marriage.

However, the record does not support the conclusion that the balance of the purchase price of the partnership interest was made from John's separate property. That part of the payment was represented by a note signed by John. There is a rebuttable presumption that property acquired on credit during marriage is community property. ([Family Code §760]; Hogevoll v. Hogevoll, 59 Cal. App. 2d 188, 193-194. . . .) In accordance with this general principle, the character of property acquired by a sale upon credit is determined according to the intent of the seller to rely upon the separate property of the purchaser or upon a community asset. (Estate of Ellis, supra, 203 Cal. 414, 416; Hogevoll v. Hogevoll, supra, 59 Cal. App. 2d 188, 193-194. . . .) In the absence of evidence tending to prove that the seller primarily relied upon the purchaser's separate property in extending credit, the trial court must find in accordance with the presumption. . . .

No testimony was offered concerning the intent of the seller in extending credit to John. John asserts, however, that shortly before the credit transaction, he and his mother sold real property for some $30,000, and the seller must have relied upon John's interest in the proceeds. Furthermore, he contends, his previous failures in attempts to operate cleaning businesses demonstrate that the basis for credit could not have been his personal ability and capacity. However, even if these facts be accepted as true, there is no evidence that the seller had knowledge of their existence. There being no satisfactory evidence to contradict the presumption, it must prevail. . . .

There being no evidence as to the present value of the one-fourth interest, it must be presumed that at the commencement of the suit it was worth $11,500, the amount he paid for it. John, having contributed $1,500 or 3/23 of the purchase price, is entitled to [3/23 of its value]. . . . The community must be credited with the balance. . . .

Notes and Questions

1. Why is the intent of the seller or lender material? What other criteria could be used to characterize credit acquisitions? Texas looks instead to the liability of the community. A credit acquisition during marriage may be separate property only if the loan is so structured that, if the borrower defaults, the creditor can reach only the borrower's separate property. Dillard v. Dillard, 341 S.W.2d 668 (Tex. Civ. App. 1960). See also McElyea v. McElyea, 49 N.M. 322, 163 P.2d 635 (1945).

The Texas view avoids the potentially unjust California result that property purchased on credit during marriage may be one spouse's separate property under the intent-of-the-lender test, but all the parties' community property is nevertheless liable for any debt incurred by either spouse during marriage. Cal. Family Code §910(a).

The early California cases adopting the intent-of-the-lender rule did not contemplate this anomalous result. Most of the early cases involved purported separate credit purchases by married women. See, for example, Dyment v. Nelson, 166 Cal. 38, 134 P. 988 (1913); Flournoy v. Flournoy, 86 Cal. 286, 24 P. 1012 (1890); Schuyler v. Broughton, 70 Cal. 282, 11 P. 719 (1886). Under pre-1975 male management principles, debt liability followed managerial control. Thus, the community property was liable for the debts incurred by the husband, but not for those incurred by the wife. (See Grolemund v. Cafferata, reprinted infra at page 423.) The one early case considering a *husband's* purported separate property credit purchase effectively applied the Texas rule by holding that the credit purchase generated community property because "[t]here was nothing to show that the borrower intended to allow a debt to be created other than one of the ordinary character, for which the whole estate was *liable* according to law, as in [the] case of other debts." Estate of Holbert, 57 Cal. 257, 259 (1881) (emphasis added).

Nevertheless, as *Gudelj* indicates, later application of the intent-of-the-lender test ignored the issue of community liability for a husband's credit purchases during marriage. Post-1974 equal management principles extend the potential injustice to the wife's credit purchases as well because the community property is liable for the debts of either spouse incurred during marriage. Cal. Family Code §910(a).

2. According to *Gudelj*, the factual issue is whether the lender relied *primarily* on the borrower's separate property. If the lender relied on both separate and community property, there is no apportionment. The unitary owner *of the credit component* is the estate upon which the lender predominantly relied.

3. Does the "primarily relied" formulation provide a workable standard? Suppose a lender relies both on a married borrower's future wages and on a secured interest in her separate property collateral. Can we reasonably conclude that he relied *primarily* on either source of repayment?

Upon what do lenders generally rely? How does a bank decide whether to grant a loan to a prospective homeowner? If you do not know, ask a friend who has purchased a home.

4. California has an anti-deficiency statute, enacted during the Depression, which provides:

> No deficiency judgment shall lie in any event after a sale of real property
> . . . for failure of the purchaser to complete his contract of sale . . . or under
> a deed of trust or mortgage on a dwelling for not more than four families
> given to a lender to secure repayment of a loan which was in fact used to pay
> all or part of the purchase price of that dwelling occupied, entirely or in part,
> by the purchaser. [Cal. Code Civ. Pro. §580-b.]

This means that an owner can effectively "walk away" from his residence. The lender may foreclose and satisfy the debt, insofar as possible, from the proceeds of the foreclosure sale, but he may not obtain a personal judgment against the debtor for the difference between the debt and the foreclosure proceeds. What bearing should this statute have on application of the intent-of-the-lender rule? If you were a banker, what effect would the anti-deficiency provision have on your lending practices?

FORD v. FORD
276 Cal. App. 2d 9, 80 Cal. Rptr. 435 (1969)

CHRISTIAN, J. — Kenneth A. Ford appeals from the property provisions of an interlocutory decree of divorce awarded to his wife, Rosalind. He contends, on several grounds, that the court erred in treating as community property a farm located in the State of Illinois, and certain funds accumulated from income produced by the farm.

Before the marriage, Kenneth owned (as tenant in common with his brother John) two farms in Illinois which we shall identify as the Ohio Township farm and the Walnut Township farm. . . . About four years later, Kenneth traded his one-half interest in the Walnut Township farm for John's one-half interest in the Ohio Township farm. At the same time John sold the Walnut Township farm to Kenneth for $105,000. Kenneth obtained a $113,685 loan from the Federal Land Bank to cover the purchase price and incidentals, including a required $5,685 purchase of stock in the Federal Land Bank. The note to the Federal Land Bank was signed by both Kenneth and Rosalind; it was secured by a mortgage upon both farms, also signed by both parties.

Payments on the note between the date of Kenneth's acquisition of the Walnut Township farm and the parties' divorce were made from farm income. The farms were operated by tenants under the supervision of a professional farm manager; there was no substantial evidence that Kenneth contributed his time, energy or talent to the operation of the farms.

By terms of the judgment, Kenneth was ordered to pay to Rosalind the sum of $20,000 as her share of the community property (less the actual cash value of Rosalind's interest in her retirement fund). This provision depends upon the court's finding that the Walnut farm, as well as all bank balances and other assets traced to farm income, was to be treated as community property.

Appellant first contends that treatment of the Walnut farm as community property was incorrect because the California community property system may not be applied to Illinois real property. . . . But California courts have long applied community property rules to out-of-state realty acquired with community funds. . . .

The trial judge found that the equity in the Walnut farm (worth approximately $33,500 including $5,700 in Federal Land Bank stock) was community property. The judge also found that the community interest in other assets derived from farm income totaled $3,350. Thus a determination of the character of the farm itself controls the disposition of the other assets derived from farm income.

The trial court's finding as to the community or separate character of property is binding upon us if supported by substantial evidence; although clear and convincing evidence must be presented in order to rebut the presumption, created by [Family Code section 760], that postnuptial acquisitions are community property, that standard is to be applied by the trial court; it does not affect our review of the trial court's determination. . . . Respondent cites four items of evidence to support these findings: the wife's signature on the mortgage and promissory note; the lender's supposed reliance upon respondent's income as security for the loan; references to the Walnut property as "our farm" by appellant; and pictures taken of respondent and appellant at the farm.

Respondent does not contend that the parties entered into any agreement to change the character of the farm property after its purchase. But if money for the purchase of property is obtained on the credit of the community estate, the result is a community purchase. The *intent of the lender* with respect to the credit upon which the loan was made is determinative. (Gudelj v. Gudelj (1953) 41 Cal. 2d 202, 210-211 [259 P.2d 656]; Somps v. Somps, 250 Cal. App. 2d 328, 336-337 [1967].) Therefore the evidence pointed to by respondent must be evaluated for any bearing it may have on the Federal Land Bank's intentions in extending credit.

The photographs of the parties at the Walnut and Ohio farms throw no light upon the intention of the lender of the purchase price. The references to "our farm" by respondent likewise do not refer to the credit decision of the Federal Land Bank. Respondent argues that "[i]t is quite probable that the bank did know of respondent's occupation and income and this was one of the strong considerations in making the loan"; but the only evidence cited to support this contention is the claimed fact that appellant's attorney prepared income tax returns which showed the occupation and income of respondent. This evidence has no tendency to show knowledge and intent on the part of the loan officer at the Federal Land Bank.

The single item of evidence which gives any support to the finding is respondent's signature upon the mortgage and promissory note. No one from the Federal Land Bank testified as to the intention of that institution in making the loan. There was a suggestion that respondent's signature on the note and mortgage was obtained in order to satisfy the lender that the encumbrance would prevail over any right of common law dower which respondent might have under Illinois law. But the objective of subjecting any interest of the wife to the mortgage could as well have been met by an instrument waiving dower, or by respondent's signing the mortgage alone. (Matthews v. Hinton (1965) 234 Cal. App. 2d 736, 741-742 [44 Cal. Rptr. 692]. . . .) When she signed the note she assumed personal liability for payment of the debt.

Although proceeds of a loan obtained upon the hypothecation of separate property are themselves separate property (Gudelj v. Gudelj, supra, 41 Cal. 2d 202, 210-211 . . .), the proceeds of a loan made on the personal credit of either spouse are regarded as community property (4 Witkin, Summary of Cal. Law (7th ed. 1960)

Community Property, §20, p.2727). The property hypothecated in the present transaction was the Ohio Township farm (separate property) and the Walnut Township farm (character determined by the character of the loan proceeds). The question is whether the signature of the wife on the note and mortgage is sufficient to support the implied finding that the lender relied upon the credit of the community. Many cases indicate that such a signature does not *compel* a finding in favor of the community. . . . These cases are consistent with the idea that the community or separate character of property purchased on credit is determined, as declared by the Supreme Court in Gudelj v. Gudelj, supra, 41 Cal. 2d 202, 210, "according to the intent of the seller to rely upon the separate property of the purchaser or upon a community asset."

The state of mind of the seller (or, as in this case, the lender) is of course a question of fact. The circumstance that in this case the lender required respondent's signature on the note and mortgage raises an inference that if she had not been willing to execute the documents credit would not have been extended. That inference is not unreasonable even though the substantial value of the two farms made subject to the mortgage, as compared with the modest community estate and earning capacity, might indicate that the security given on appellant's separate property was the more weighty factor in inducing the Federal Land Bank to grant a loan. Nevertheless, it might seem that these considerations all properly fell within the province of the trial court in determining the question of fact which we have identified.

Appellant, however, points to two early decisions of the Supreme Court (Flournoy v. Flournoy (1890) 86 Cal. 286 [24 P. 1012, 21 Am. St. Rep. 39], and Martin v. Martin (1877) 52 Cal. 235) which hold that the signature of one spouse on a note and purchase money mortgage encumbering separate property of the other spouse "cannot affect the rights of the parties" (52 Cal. at p.237) as to the community or separate character of the proceeds. (Cf. Estate of Neilson (1962) 57 Cal. 2d 733, 746 [22 Cal. Rptr. 1, 371 P.2d 745].) It is difficult to reconcile the *Flournoy* and *Martin* decisions with the *Gudelj* idea that the character of loan proceeds may be determined according to the intent of the party extending credit. We note also that the *Flournoy* and *Martin* decisions do not mention the generally applicable presumption, created by the statutory definition of community property, that property acquired during the marriage is community (4 Witkin, Summary of Cal. Law (1960) supra, §25, p.2731). But it is not our function to overrule decisions of the Supreme Court even if they are old. It is our duty to follow and apply the law as expounded in the decisions of higher courts until change has been lawfully accomplished by legislation or by later decision. We therefore hold, under compulsion of the *Flournoy* and *Martin* decisions, that respondent's execution of the note and mortgage could not affect the rights of the parties. According to the evidence, the only other inducement to the Federal Land Bank's extension of credit was the security given upon appellant's separate property. Accordingly, the Walnut Township farm and the rents and profits it produced appear to have been separate property. But a further showing may be attempted by respondent on retrial. . . .

The judgment is reversed with directions to the trial court to enter a new . . . decree of divorce . . . after taking further proceedings, consistent with the views expressed herein. . . .

DEVINE, P.J., and RATTIGAN, J., concurred.

A petition for a rehearing was denied October 3, 1969, and respondent's petition for a hearing by the Supreme Court was denied October 29, 1969.

Notes and Questions

1. Suppose, on remand, that the evidence is unchanged and the trial court finds that the Walnut farm is the husband's separate property. Would *this* conclusion be sustainable on appeal? Has the husband presented sufficient evidence to overcome the presumption that property acquired during marriage is community property? Has he demonstrated that the bank relied *primarily* on his separate property?

2. Can you characterize the Federal Land Bank loan as separate or community before you characterize the ownership of Walnut Farm? But then, can you characterize the ownership of Walnut Farm before you decide whether the loan was community or separate? Is the analysis necessarily circular? Reconsider the fourth introductory problem at page 250 supra.

3. Marriage of Grinius, which follows, reflects dissatisfaction with the intent-of-the-lender rule.

MARRIAGE OF GRINIUS
166 Cal. App. 3d 1179, 212 Cal. Rptr. 803 (1985)

WORK, J. — Joyce M. Grinius appeals an interlocutory judgment of dissolution awarding restaurant real property to her husband Victor as his separate property. . . . Joyce contends [that] . . . the purchase money loans were acquired or obtained with a view toward community assets and contributions and therefore are community property. . . . We hold the restaurant real property is community property, reversing that part of the judgment effecting the property division. . . .

Shortly after marriage Victor resigned his job so he and Joyce could open a restaurant. Joyce apparently had worked in a restaurant for a number of years before marriage. They located a suitable building, costing $60,000. The purchase money was obtained from two sources: (1) a $20,000 downpayment from an $80,000 Small Business Administration (SBA) loan guaranty lent by California First Bank (hereafter referred to as SBA loan) and (2) $40,000 loaned by Home Federal Savings and Loan. Although only Victor signed the SBA loan guaranty, both Victor and Joyce signed the promissory note from California First Bank. Victor alone signed the Home Federal Savings and Loan promissory note. The SBA loan was secured by both community and separate property. Both Victor and Joyce negotiated the original purchase offer. However, without Joyce's knowledge, Victor placed title to the property in his name alone.

Victor and Joyce used the remaining $60,000 of the SBA loan to remodel the building, buy equipment, and pay their living and restaurant expenses. These funds were disbursed through the restaurant's checking account on which Victor and Joyce were the signators. Indeed, during the course of the marriage all personal and restaurant expenses were paid from this joint account.

Victor and Joyce both worked in the restaurant in several different capacities and continued to do so during the course of their marriage. Their community earnings were placed in the restaurant checking account; however, from time to time Victor also deposited funds received from his separate property into the account to prevent overdrafts.

Monthly payments on the purchase money loans were made from the joint restaurant checking account. In 1975 Victor also used . . . his separate property

funds to pay on the SBA and Home Federal loans. . . . Again, in 1978 Victor paid
$33,818 of separate property funds to retire the SBA loan. That same year, Victor
and Joyce signed a $63,000 installment note in favor of San Diego Trust and Savings,
secured by a trust deed on the restaurant property. From these proceeds, $42,000
was used to pay the outstanding balance on the Home Federal promissory note.

Victor and Joyce separated in April of 1980. Before trial, Victor stipulated the
restaurant business was community property and the business was sold. Victor and
Joyce and their respective counsels were each granted $5,000 from the sale pro-
ceeds. The trial court found all of the contested assets, except the restaurant real
property, to be community property. The restaurant real property, worth $340,000,
was determined to be Victor's separate property.

A trial court's findings regarding a property's separate or community character
is binding and conclusive on review when supported by substantial evidence (Beam
v. Bank of America (1971) 6 Cal. 3d 12, 25 [98 Cal. Rptr. 357, 490 P.2d 257] . . .),
even though evidence conflicts or supports contrary inferences. (Beam v. Bank of
America, supra, at p.25. . . .) However, substantial evidence is not synonymous with
"any" evidence. (Hall v. Department of Adoptions (1975) 47 Cal. App. 3d 898, 906
[121 Cal. Rptr. 223].) It must have ponderable legal significance and "'must be reasonable in nature, credible, and of solid value; it must actually be "substantial" proof
of the essentials which the law requires in a particular case.' [Citation.]" (Ibid.)

We review the evidence supporting the trial court's characterization of the restaurant property as Victor's separate property.

Property bought during marriage by either spouse is rebuttably presumed to
be community property ([Family Code, §760] . . . and . . . the spouse asserting its
separate character must overcome this presumption. . . .

Victor . . . traces the source of payments for the restaurant property to overcome
the fundamental community presumption. Specifically, he argues the purchase
money loans were separate property and the restaurant real property, thus acquired,
maintains the same character. . . . Here, the restaurant property was acquired shortly
after marriage and is presumed to be community property. . . . However, the character
of credit acquisitions during marriage is "determined according to the intent of the
lender to rely upon the separate property of the purchaser or upon a community
asset. . . ." (In re Marriage of Aufmuth, 89 Cal. App. 3d 446, 455 [1979].)

While the California courts have consistently and uncritically applied the intent-of-the-lender rule, they have inconsistently espoused the applicable test. . . .
In early cases, the Supreme Court required a showing the lender relied *entirely* on
the existing separate property of a spouse in extending the loan to characterize the
loan proceeds as separate property. (Estate of Holbert (1881) 57 Cal. 257, 259;
Estate of Ellis (1928) 203 Cal. 414, 416 [264 P. 743].) The more modern and oft-
cited formulation found in Gudelj v. Gudelj (1953) 41 Cal. 2d 202 [259 P. 656],
apparently relaxes the standard: "In the absence of evidence tending to prove that
the seller *primarily* relied upon the purchaser's separate property in extending
credit, the trial court must find in accordance with the [section 760] presumption."
(Id., at p.210; italics added.) The *Gudelj* opinion cited no authority for this apparent
change and had no opportunity to apply the standard since no evidence of lender
reliance on separate property was proffered. Later cases have been decided on
seemingly different standards. Courts have found evidence of lender's intent in:
(1) reliance on or hypothecation of separate property (Bank of California v. Connolly (1973) 36 Cal. App. 3d 350, 375 [111 Cal. Rptr. 468]; Ford v. Ford (1969)
276 Cal. App. 2d 9, 13-14 [80 Cal. Rptr. 435] . . . ; (2) sole reliance on separate

property (Howard v. Howard (1954) 128 Cal. App. 2d 180, 186 [275 P.2d 88]); and (3) extension of the loan on the faith of existing property belonging to the acquiring spouse (In re Marriage of Aufmuth, supra, 89 Cal. App. 3d 446, 455-456; In re Marriage of Stoner (1983) 147 Cal. App. 3d 858, 863-864 [195 Cal. Rptr. 351]). Nonetheless, in all of the above cases, loan proceeds were characterized as a spouse's separate property *only* when direct or circumstantial evidence indicated the lender relied solely on separate property in offering the loan.

With the above review in mind, we restate the applicable standard: Loan proceeds acquired during marriage are presumptively community property; however, this presumption may be overcome by showing the lender intended to rely solely upon a spouse's separate property and did in fact do so. Without satisfactory evidence of the lender's intent, the general presumption prevails.

Victor presented no direct evidence of lender intent and instead offered circumstantial evidence to prove lender reliance on his separate property. . . . He argues the "SBA loan guaranty was premised solely on [his] posting of collateral consisting of his entire separate property." However, a review of the SBA loan conditions outlined on the loan guaranty authorization refutes this contention. The SBA required nine separate conditions, only two of which necessitated hypothecation of Victor's separate property. Specifically, loan approval required: (1) a second deed of trust on the restaurant property and improvements, (2) Joyce's signature on the promissory note and all instruments of hypothecation, (3) a first lien on the restaurant machinery, equipment, furniture and fixtures presently owned and later acquired with the loan proceeds, (4) acquisition and assignment of an $80,000 life insurance policy on Victor, (5) purchase of hazard insurance on the restaurant property, (6) a third deed of trust on Victor's improved real property in San Diego, already subject to prior liens totalling $107,000, (7) assignment of 3100 shares of Victor's separate property stock, (8) the furnishing of the restaurant's quarterly balance sheets and profit and loss statements, and (9) the use of the SBA's management assistant services "as deemed necessary by SBA or Bank."

The primary collateral for the loan was the restaurant property. Alone, this hypothecation provides no inference of lender intent; to argue otherwise is to rely on circular reasoning. The requiring of Joyce's signature on the note and instruments of hypothecation does suggest the lender did look toward community assets for security. However, Joyce's signing of the documents, without more, does not compel a finding in favor of the community. (Ford v. Ford, supra, 276 Cal. App. 2d 9, 13-14. . . .) . . . Conditions three through five clearly suggest reliance on community interests. Both insurance policies and the restaurant equipment were purchased from the joint restaurant account and were presumptively community property. Indeed, Victor stipulated to the community nature of the restaurant business. Yet, some of the same loan proceeds challenged here were used for operating capital for the restaurant and were specifically earmarked for the purchase of trade fixtures and the liquor license, assets unquestioningly found to belong to the community. This inconsistency clearly contradicts Victor's contention. . . .

Loan conditions eight and nine demonstrate the SBA's concern about the operation and management of the restaurant business. . . . In granting these small business loans, the SBA is constrained by statute and policy considerations. Many of these loan guidelines are outlined in Chapter 1 of Title 13 of the Code Federal Regulations. Section 120.2(c)(1) of Chapter 1 specifically provides:

> No financial assistance shall be extended unless there exists reasonable assurance the loan can and will be repaid pursuant to its terms. Reasonable assur-

> ance of repayment will exist *only* where the past earnings record and *future prospects indicate ability to repay the loan and other obligations.* It will be deemed not to exist when the proposed loan is to accomplish an expansion which is unwarranted in light of the applicant's past experience and management ability, or when the effect of making the loan is to subsidize inferior management.

(Italics added.) Accordingly, in the absence of evidence the SBA acted contrary to their official duties in this instance (Evid. Code, §664), we find the loan was extended on both the ability of the community to repay the note and to manage the restaurant. Therefore, the SBA loan funds are a community asset, not Victor's separate property.

The second purchase money loan from Home Federal Savings and Loan was secured by a first deed of trust on the restaurant property. Victor presents no evidence to rebut the community presumption and, indeed, concedes the Home Federal Loan was likely extended in reliance on the interest in the restaurant property already acquired with the SBA loan funds. Thus, this loan must also be seen as an asset of the community. . . .

In sum, Victor has failed to present sufficient evidence to rebut the presumption property acquired during marriage is community property. Therefore, the restaurant property and all rents, issues and profits thereof are properly characterized as community property. . . .

BROWN (Gerald), P.J., and WIENER, J., concurred.

Notes and Questions

1. Does the *Grinius* reformulation of the intent-of-the-lender standard make it a more workable rule? How would the *Grinius* panel have decided *Ford?* Does *Grinius* address the potential injustice that arises from community property liability for all debts incurred by either spouse during marriage?

2. For further discussion of the intent-of-the-lender rule, see Perlman, A Reappraisal of California's Intent of the Lender Rule, 37 UCLA L. Rev. 389 (1989); Paris, Credit Acquisitions During Marriage, 9 L.A. Lawyer, no. 3 at 11 (1986); Comment, The Division of Property Purchases on Credit under California Community Property Law: A Proposal for Reform, 17 Pac. L.J. 129 (1985).

D. APPORTIONMENT OF OWNERSHIP VS. REIMBURSEMENT BY THE TITLED ESTATE

VIEUX v. VIEUX
80 Cal. App. 222, 251 P. 640 (1926)

HOUSER, J. — This is an appeal from a part of the judgment rendered in a suit for divorce.

The facts material to this inquiry are set forth in the findings by the trial court as follows:

> That shortly prior to the marriage . . . plaintiff and defendant discussed and considered the purchase of lot 24, and together viewed said property, and it was agreed between them that said property would be a desirable pur-

chase. That prior to said marriage the plaintiff entered into a contract for
the purchase of said property . . . and the plaintiff did, at the time of entering
into said contract, pay the sum of $280.00 on account of the purchase price
thereof, and immediately took possession of said property. That thereafter
plaintiff and defendant married, and after their marriage, the plaintiff and
defendant expended on said real estate from community funds for payment
on account of principal, interest and taxes, the sum of $553.68. That subse-
quent to the marriage of plaintiff and defendant, to-wit, on or about the 25th
day of November, 1921, the plaintiff received the sum of $2200.00 as payment
for a bonus for the execution of an oil lease covering said property, and that
said sum of $2200.00 was paid by the plaintiff on account of the balance of
the purchase price on said property: that subsequent to the payment of said
sum of $2200 the plaintiff executed and delivered a deed of conveyance to
said property to his parents, Aristide Vieux and Stephanus Vieux. That the
plaintiff received no consideration from his parents for the execution and
delivery of said deed, but said conveyance was made by the plaintiff for the
purpose of getting the property out of his name and avoiding any claim or
right which the defendant might have in said property. . . .

That during the married life of the plaintiff and defendant, they accumulated community property to the amount and value of $713.60; that of said sum
$553.68 was expended in and upon the hereinabove described real property.

From said findings it was adjudged and decreed that the defendant Coralyn
A. Vieux had no right, title, or interest in and to the real property to which reference
was made in the findings, but that said defendant "have and recover from said
plaintiff the sum of $713.60, the value of the community property in the possession
of said plaintiff. . . ."

It is appellant's contention that . . . the judgment . . . that the defendant Coralyn A. Vieux had no right, title, or interest in and to the property in question, is
not supported by the findings for the reason that the findings show that . . . defendant had some right, title or interest therein.

The ultimate question presented to this court for its determination is whether
in the circumstances as set forth in the foregoing findings of fact the property
therein referred to was the separate property of the husband. Although the findings
do not specifically so state, it may be inferred therefrom that the total purchase
price of the property was in the neighborhood of $3,000 — the sum of $280 having
been paid by the husband prior to the marriage, the sum of $553.68 thereafter
having been paid out of the community funds, and the further sum of $2,200, de-
rived from the bonus for an oil lease on the property, having been used to complete
the purchase price. It is therefore apparent that, so far as outlay on the part of the
husband from his separate property was concerned in acquiring the property in
question, he actually expended the sum of $280, or somewhat less than one-tenth
of the purchase price; while the sum of $553.68, or approximately one-fifth of the
purchase price, was contributed from funds belonging to the community.

Section 163 of the Civil Code provides that "All property owned by the husband
before marriage, . . . with the rents, issues, and profits thereof, is his separate property." . . .

For purposes affecting strangers, the acquisition through an installment contract of the right to purchase real property may be considered as ownership of such
property in that such holding may entitle the intending purchaser to the possession
and the use of the property to the exclusion of others; but as between husband

and wife, where community funds are used to a considerable extent in the payment of the purchase price, the meaning of the statute relating to the definition of separate and community property of spouses cannot be so limited. The confidential relationship existing between husband and wife forbids such a strict construction to be placed upon the statute as will destroy the probable intent of the husband and wife with reference to the manner in which the ownership of the property is enjoyed. Any other construction in these days of liberal terms with reference to installment purchase price contracts for the sale of real property, including the possible provision of "a dollar down and a dollar per week," would permit a husband, or a prospective husband, to buy or to agree to buy any reasonable quantity of lots or lands on the payment by him from his separate funds of a comparatively insignificant sum and thereafter to pay practically the entire purchase price from the community funds, and yet successfully maintain that because in its inception the naked right to purchase, carrying with it the right of use and possession, was his separate property, it so remained. It would seem improbable that through general definitions of terms, the intention of the lawmakers was to bring about a result which, in many if not a majority of instances, would be of so disastrous and unjust a consequence. Rather should it be assumed that when the legislature undertook to define separate property as that owned by the husband before marriage, even though in other statutes the right of exclusive possession and use was specified as the *indicia* of ownership, the "ownership" in the husband through and by virtue of which the wife's interest would be entirely excluded, would necessarily be an absolute ownership, as distinguished from a limited ownership, and that, so far as community funds might participate in the acquisition or protection of vested rights, to that extent proportionally should the property be considered as "community." . . .

Cases from other jurisdictions, particularly Guye v. Guye, 63 Wash. 340 [37 L.R.A. (N. S.) 186, 115 Pac. 731], Barrett v. Franke, 46 Nev. 170 [208 Pac. 435], and Heintz v. Brown, 46 Wash. 387 [123 Am. St. Rep. 937, 90 Pac. 211], in effect hold that in circumstances analogous to those indicated in the findings herein to which reference has been had, a part of property involved may be regarded as community and a part as separate — depending upon conditions, not essentially on the manner in which the contract for the purchase of the property was entered into or ostensibly acquired, but rather upon the manner in which the payments were made; and while the principle announced in such decisions has been subjected to some criticism, the administration of strict justice to the parties concerned, rather than the application to the facts of the hard rules of law, lends an appealing force to the conclusions reached in the cases to which reference has been had. The governing rule is indicated in 5 Ruling Case Law, page 834, as follows:

> Thus property purchased by one spouse before marriage is separate property though the deed therefor is not executed and delivered until after marriage, and this is true though a part of the purchase price is not paid until after marriage, in the absence of a showing that any part of the balance was paid with community funds. In any event it would be community property only to the extent and in the proportion that the purchase price is contributed by the community.

In the instant case, the husband having acquired an inchoate right, on compliance with certain conditions, to become an absolute owner of the property in question, and the facts showing that the required conditions were met with funds furnished by the community, aided by other funds issuing directly from the property agreed to be purchased, justice demands that the rights of the parties should be measured by the direct contributions made by the respective parties to the purchase price of the property. Accordingly, the judgment of the trial court herein should have indicated that the community interest was entitled to share in the title to the property in the same proportion as the amount contributed to the purchase price by the community, to wit, $553.68, bore to the sum of $833.86 — the total amount paid by the respective parties therefor.

It is ordered that that part of the judgment from which the appeal herein is taken be . . . reversed; and the trial court be . . . directed to enter a new judgment on its findings of fact in accordance with the law as indicated by the opinion herein.

CONREY, P.J., and YORK, J., concurred.

A petition by respondents to have the cause heard in the supreme court, after judgment in the district court of appeal, was denied by the supreme court on February 7, 1927.

Notes and Questions

1. California courts have long rejected the view, adopted by most other community property states, that classification is determined by the character of the *initial* contributions. The majority of community property states have, in most circumstances, adopted either an "inception of right" or a "time of vesting" analysis. Under the first variation, ownership rights are fixed at the moment the right to title originates. Under the second variation, ownership rights are determined when title vests. Consider an installment purchase contract entered by a single woman on the eve of her marriage. Payments are made entirely from community property and, under the sales contract, possession passes immediately but title does not pass to her until she has made the last payment. According to "inception of right" analysis, the property is the wife's separate property; under the "time of vesting" approach, the asset is community property. Under either analysis, contributions to the purchase price *after* the determinative moment of ownership characterization only give rise, at most, to a claim for reimbursement. Potthoff v. Potthoff, 128 Ariz. 557, 561-563, 627 P.2d 708, 712-714 (Ct. App. 1981); Fisher v. Fisher, 86 Idaho 131, 136, 383 P.2d 840, 842-843 (1963); Harris v. Harris, 160 So. 2d 359, 360-361 (La. Ct. App. 1964); Laughlin v. Laughlin, 49 N.M. 20, 155 P.2d 1010, 1020-1021 (1944); Dakan v. Dakan, 83 S.W.2d 620, 628 (Tex. 1935). See generally W. Reppy, Jr., and C. Samuel, Community Property in the United States, 77-83 (2d ed. 1982). California courts, in contrast, have long apportioned title to an asset according to the relative contributions of each estate. Each estate thus shares in the appreciation of the asset.

Family Code section 2640 may be read to supplant apportionment and to introduce the reimbursement remedy associated with "inception of right" and "time of vesting" analysis to those cases that it controls. This is not to suggest that section 2640 embodies an "inception of right" or "vesting of title" theory (since the separate contribution reimbursed by this section may have been made before or after the inception of right or the vesting of title); rather, the only extant legal sources for mere reimbursement are these two title-oriented theories. Section 2640 adopts the remedy without the supporting rationale.

Section 2640 is also anomalous because most other states recently reconsidering the question or, in some cases, considering it for the first time, have adopted apportionment of title with its concomitant sharing of appreciation and have explicitly rejected the alternative title theories with their reimbursement remedy. See, for example, Hoffman v. Hoffman, 676 S.W.2d 817, 823-825 (Mo. 1984) (en banc), and sources cited therein; Harper v. Harper, 448 A.2d 916, 929 (Md. Ct. App. 1982); Tibbetts v. Tibbetts, 406 A.2d 70, 76 (Me. 1979). Equitable distribution states refer to apportionment as the "source of the funds theory." See also Jensen v. Jensen, 644 S.W.2d 455 (Tex. 1983) (holding that community labor contribution to appreciation of separate property stock warrants award to the community of appreciation of the stock due to marital labor; rejects reimbursement for value of services remedy).

Moreover, section 2640 clearly does not cover the field. It has no application, for example, when community property is used to pay off the purchase price of separately titled property purchased by one spouse before marriage. Thus apportionment lives on in California, albeit in diminished circumstances.

2. While *Vieux* is generally cited as one of the earliest California cases that clearly adopts the apportionment approach, *Vieux*, because of the nature of installment land sales contracts, is somewhat ambiguous on this point. Subsequent case law, however, has made it clear that apportionment principles are unaffected by the timing of passage of title.

In an installment sales contract, title generally passes after the last payment has been made. Hence it might be said that in *Vieux* both the separate and community estates contributed to the acquisition of title. Today residential property is not generally purchased by an installment sales contract. Instead the buyer pays the seller the full purchase price, much of which the buyer has generally obtained from a lending institution, and title passes immediately to the buyer, who pays off the note, secured by a lien on the purchased property, over a period of many years.[1] As *Moore*, immediately below, indicates, modern California law makes no distinction between the *Vieux* installment sales agreement and the currently more common purchase-mortgage arrangement.

3. In the installment sales purchase, as in the modern mortgage purchase, payments include more than the initial purchase price. Note that the community payment of $553.68 in *Vieux* included principal, interest, and taxes. Most mortgage payments today include insurance as well. (See discussion of PITI supra at page 250.) At recent interest rates, principal reduction constitutes a small portion of the global mortgage payment for all but the final years of the mortgage term.

There is little principal reduction during the early years of a long-term mortgage because most of the principal-interest payment is required to cover the interest due on the outstanding loan balance. Significant annual reduction of the principal debt occurs only after the debt balance has been substantially reduced, that is, in the later years of the mortgage. The higher the interest rate, the more exaggerated the effect.[2]

---

1. At early common law, the lender (mortgagee) acquired title until the purchaser (mortgagor) repaid the entire loan. California has, however, like many other western states, adopted the "lien theory" of mortgages: The mortgagor retains legal title and the mortgagee obtains only a lien on the property.

2. For example, on a $1,000 level-payment 30-year fixed-rate loan at 14 percent annual interest, the principal debt will be reduced by $2 during the first year, $3 during the second year, $3 during the third year, $4 during the fourth year, and $4 during the fifth year. By the sixteenth year, annual principal reduction is $19. By the twenty-fifth year, it is $66 and in the final year $132. In contrast, at 7 percent annual interest, the $1,000 debt is reduced by $10 during the first year, $14 during the fifth year, and $77 in the final year.

A recent condominium purchase is illustrative. In mid-1996, Harold bought a two-bedroom condominium and took title in his name alone. The purchase price was $87,000. Harold put $7,000 down and took a 9 percent 30-year mortgage for the remaining $80,000. The global monthly payment, including PITI and condominium maintenance fees, was, and still is, $805. One month later Harold married Wilma. All mortgage payments were made from the couple's earnings during marriage. When the couple separated in mid-2003, the condominium was valued at $180,000. The bank's escrow statements for the 1996-2003 period show the following total payments:

Interest	$48,720
Principal reduction	5,376
Taxes	5,040
Insurance	2,520
Condominium maintenance fees	5,964
Total home payments in seven-year period 1996-2003	$67,620

Do all components of the global payment buy into title? Marriage of Moore addresses this question.

MARRIAGE OF MOORE
28 Cal. 3d 366, 618 P.2d 208, 168 Cal. Rptr. 662 (1980)

MANUEL, J. — David E. Moore appeals from an interlocutory judgment dissolving his marriage to Lydie D. Moore. He contests . . . the trial court's determination of the community property interest in the residence located at 121 Mira Way, Menlo Park. . . .

The principal issue to be decided in this case is the proper method of calculating the interest obtained by the community as a result of payments made during marriage on the indebtedness secured by a deed of trust on a residence which had been purchased by one of the parties before marriage.

Lydie purchased the house at 121 Mira Way in Menlo Park in April 1966, about eight months before the parties' marriage. The purchase price was $56,640.57. Lydie made a down payment of $16,640.57 and secured a loan for the balance of the purchase price. She took title in her name alone as "Lydie S. Doak, a single woman." Prior to the marriage she made seven monthly payments and reduced the principal loan balance by $245.18.

The parties lived in the house during their marriage and until their separation in June 1977. They made payment during this time with community funds and reduced the loan principal by $5,986.20. Lydie remained in the house and continued to make payments, reducing the principal by an additional $581.07 up to the time of trial. At that time the total principal paid on the purchase price was $23,453.02, the balance owing was $33,187.55, the market value of the house was $160,000, and the equity therein $126,812.45.

The trial court concluded that the residence was Lydie's separate property but that the community had an interest in it by virtue of the community property payments made during the course of the parties' marriage. The trial court further concluded that the community interest was to be determined according to the ratio that the reduction of principal resulting from community funds bears to the reduction of principal from separate funds. No credit was given for the amount paid for interest, taxes and insurance.

The community interest was calculated by multiplying the equity value of the house by the ratio of the community's reduction of principal to the total amount of principal reduction by both community and separate property ($5,986.20 divided by $23,453.02 equals 25.5242 percent). The amount of the community interest was thus determined to be $32,367.86. Lydie's separate property interest was calculated by multiplying the equity value of the house by the ratio of the separate property reduction of principal to the total amount of principal reduction ($17,466.82 divided by $23,453.02 equals 74.4758 percent). Lydie's separate property interest was thus determined to be $94,444.59.

The parties agree that the community has acquired an interest in the house by virtue of the community funds used to make the payments.[1] They disagree, however, as to how the interest is to be determined. Appellant contends that the community property interest should be based upon the full amount of the payments made, which includes interest, taxes and insurance, rather than only on the amount by which the payments reduce the principal. He relies on Vieux v. Vieux (1926) 80 Cal. App. 222 [251 P. 64].

In *Vieux,* the husband contracted before marriage to buy certain property and paid $280 on account of the purchase price. After the parties' marriage they spent $553.68 of community funds for payment of principal, interest and taxes. The Court of Appeal held that the trial court erred in finding the property to be solely the husband's separate property and stated the rule as follows: "Thus property purchased by one spouse before marriage is separate property . . . , and this is true though a part of the purchase price is not paid until after marriage, in the absence of a showing that any part of the balance was paid with community funds. In any event it would be community property only to the extent and in the proportion that the purchase price is contributed by the community." (80 Cal. App. at p.229.) The court concluded that "the community interest was entitled to share in the title to the property in the same proportion as the amount contributed to the purchase price by the community, to wit, $553.68 bore to the sum of $833.86 [*sic*] — the total amount paid by the respective parties therefor." (Ibid.)

Although the *Vieux* court included interest and taxes in its calculation, there is no indication that the issue of the propriety of doing so was presented to the court. The concern in that case was with the question of whether there should be any community interest at all. Since the *Vieux* court did not expressly consider the question of including interest and taxes in the community's interest in the property, we do not consider it to be persuasive authority on that issue.

Where community funds are used to make payments on property purchased by one of the spouses before marriage "the rule developed through decisions in California gives to the community a pro tanto community property interest in such property in the ratio that the payments on the purchase price with community

---

1. Although the trial court designated the community's interest as an "equitable charge on right," it is clear under California law that the interest is properly characterized as a community property interest in the house. (See Forbes v. Forbes (1953) 118 Cal. App. 2d 324, 325 [257 P.2d 721]; Estate of Neilson (1962) 57 Cal. 2d 733, 744 [22 Cal. Rptr. 1, 371 P.2d 745].)

funds bear to the payments made with separate funds." (Forbes v. Forbes, 118 Cal. App. 2d 324, 325 [257 P.2d 721 (1953)]; see also Bare v. Bare (1967) 256 Cal. App. 2d 684, 690 [64 Cal. Rptr. 335]; In re Marriage of Jafeman (1972) 29 Cal. App. 3d 244, 257 [105 Cal. Rptr. 483]; Estate of Neilson (1962) 57 Cal. 2d 733, 744 [22 Cal. Rptr. 1, 371 P.2d 745].) This rule has been commonly understood as excluding payments for interest and taxes. For example in Bare v. Bare, the Court of Appeal directed the trial court to determine the increase in equity in the house during marriage and the fair market value of it before and after the marriage, stating: "the community is entitled to a minimum interest in the property represented by the ratio of the community investment to the total separate and community investment in the property. In the event the fair market value has increased disproportionately to the increase in equity the wife is entitled to participate in that increment in a similar proportion." (256 Cal. App. 2d at p.690; accord In re Marriage of Jafeman, supra, 29 Cal. App. 3d at pp.256-257.) Decisions of other community property jurisdictions are in accord (see, e.g. Hanrahan v. Sims (1973) 20 Ariz. App. 313 [512 P.2d 617, 621]; Gapsch v. Gapsch (1954) 76 Idaho 44 [277 P.2d 278, 283, 54 A.L.R.2d 416]; Merkel v. Merkel (1951) 39 Wn. 2d 102 [234 P.2d 857, 864]), and *Vieux* apparently stands alone in suggesting a contrary rule.

Appellant argues, however, that interest and taxes should be included in the computation because they often represent a substantial part of current home purchase payments. We do not agree. Since such expenditures do not increase the equity value of the property, they should not be considered in its division upon dissolution of marriage. The value of real property is generally represented by the owners' equity in it, and the equity value does not include finance charges or other expenses incurred to maintain the investment. Amounts paid for interest, taxes and insurance do not contribute to the capital investment and are not considered part of it. A variety of expenses may be incurred in the maintenance of investment property, but such expenses are not considered in the valuation of the property except to the extent they may be relevant in determining its market value from which in turn the owners' equity is derived by subtracting the outstanding obligation. Upon dissolution, it is the court's duty to account for and divide the assets and the debts of the community. Payments previously made for interest, taxes and insurance are neither. Moreover, if these items were considered to be part of the community's interest, fairness would also require that the community be charged for its use of the property.

In summary, we find no basis for departing from the present rule which excludes amounts paid for interest, taxes, and insurance from the calculation of the respective separate and community interests. We turn to that calculation in this case.

Although many formulae have been suggested, we are not persuaded that any of them would be an improvement over a formula based on the reasoning of In re Marriage of Aufmuth (1979) 89 Cal. App. 3d 446 [152 Cal. Rptr. 668], which was approved in In re Marriage of Lucas (1980) 27 Cal. 3d 808 [166 Cal. Rptr. 853, 614 P.2d 285]. [See casebook at page 186 supra.] We were there concerned with determining the respective community and separate interests in a residence purchased during marriage with a combination of community and separate funds where the community contributed the loan and subsequent payments on it and there was an agreement or understanding that the party contributing the separate property down payment was to retain a pro rata separate property interest. (Id., at pp.816-817.) The formula we used there recognized the economic value of the loan taken to purchase the property. In the formula postulated in *Lucas* the proceeds of the loan were treated as a community property contribution on the assumption that the loan was made on the strength of the community assets. (Id., at pp.816-817, fn. 3.)

In the present situation, the loan was based on separate assets and was thus a separate property contribution; the down payment was also a separate property contribution. Therefore under the *Lucas/Aufmuth* formula the proceeds of the loan must be treated as a separate property contribution. Accordingly, the formula would be applied as follows: The separate property percentage interest is determined by crediting the separate property with the down payment and the full amount of the loan less the amount by which the community property payments reduced the principal balance of the loan ($16,640.57 plus ($40,000 minus $5,986.20) equals $50,654.37). This sum is divided by the purchase price for the separate property percentage share ($50,654.37 divided by $56,640.57 equals 89.43 percent). The separate property interest would be $109,901.16, which represents the amount of capital appreciation attributable to the separate funds (89.43 percent of $103,359.43) added to the amount of equity paid by separate funds ($17,466.82). The community property percentage interest is found by dividing the amount by which community property payments reduced the principal by the purchase price ($5,986.20 divided by $56,640.57 equals 10.57 percent). The community property share would be $16,911.29, which represents the amount of capital appreciation attributable to community funds (10.57 percent of $103,359.43) added to the amount of equity paid by community funds ($5,986.20).

In this case the trial court used a different formula which appears to have been based upon a statement in In re Marriage of Jafeman, supra, 29 Cal. App. 3d 244, 256, that might be interpreted to mean that the interests are to be determined according to the proportionate equity contributions only, with no credit given for the loan contribution. This formula might be appropriate when the obligation on the property has been fully paid. To apply it in the present situation, however, when the purchase price of the amount owing on the loan has not been fully paid ignores the role of the loan and produces inconsistencies with the principles of the *Lucas/Aufmuth* formula.

Although the trial court erred in determining the parties' interests in the residence, the error was in David's favor. Since he was not prejudiced by the error and Lydie did not appeal, reversal of this portion of the judgment is unwarranted. . . .

The judgment is affirmed. . . . BIRD, C.J., TOBRINER, J., MOSK, J., CLARK, J., RICHARDSON, J., and NEWMAN, J., concurred.

Notes and Problems

1. Lydie Moore bought the house eight months before marriage. How would the result have differed if she had purchased the couple's residence one month after marriage? If she took title with David in some form of joint ownership? (See pages 182-211 supra.) If she took title in her name alone?

2. *Aufmuth/Moore* proportional accounting applies to separately titled property acquired before marriage when community funds have paid off the remaining purchase-money debt. It also applies when an asset acquired with mixed funds during marriage is either untitled or titled in the purchaser's name alone. Finally, it applies to jointly titled property when there is legally adequate proof of an agreement of the

parties to preserve proportional interests based upon contributions to the purchase price.

3. The Moores married soon after Lydie purchased the house. Presumably, the market value of the home had not risen significantly during the brief intervening period. When the market value of an asset has risen between purchase and marriage, *Aufmuth/Moore* accounting must be refined to take premarital appreciation into account. Clearly, any premarital appreciation must be attributed entirely to the purchasing spouse's separate estate. Marriage of Marsden, 130 Cal. App. 3d 426, 436-439, 181 Cal. Rptr. 910 (1982); accord Marriage of Frick, 181 Cal. App. 3d 997, 1007-1009, 226 Cal. Rptr. 766 (1986). To determine the various estates' proportional interests in appreciation *during* marriage, *Marsden* and *Frick* require that the historic purchase price be used. In other words, the denominator of each estate's proportional fraction must be the historic purchase price. *Frick* rejected the purchasing spouse's argument that the appreciated fair market value at marriage would be a more appropriate denominator. The court reasoned that this figure would improperly give the purchasing spouse "*double* credit for premarital appreciation." Id. at 1009. Do you agree?

4. To test your understanding of the *Aufmuth, Moore,* and *Marsden* formulas, apply them, as appropriate, to the following problems:

a.   Hal and Wendy, married two years, purchased a house for $100,000 in 1980. Hal used a bequest from his late father to make the $20,000 down payment. Hal, a prosperous young attorney, borrowed $80,000 from California Savings for a 30-year term. The note was secured by a mortgage. Hal took title in his name alone. Last week Hal and Wendy decided to seek a divorce. The market value of the house is now $300,000. The principal debt has been reduced to $48,000. How would you calculate each spouse's share of the family home?

b.   One month before she met Herbert in 1980, Winnie purchased a home for $100,000. She paid $20,000 down and assumed an $80,000 30-year mortgage. Winnie took title in her name alone. Two months later, she married Herbert. Winnie continued to make mortgage payments from her earnings. Last week Herbert and Winnie decided to seek a divorce. The market value of the house is now $400,000. Since their marriage, the principal debt has been reduced to $48,000. (Assume that the principal reduction attributable to Winnie's first two mortgage payments is de minimis.) Calculate each spouse's share of the home.

c.   In 1980, Harry, a single man, purchased a home for $100,000. He put $20,000 down and financed the remainder of the purchase price with an $80,000 30-year mortgage. In 1985, Harry married Wyona, at which time the fair market value of the home was $180,000. Last month he and Wyona decided to seek a divorce. The house is now worth $400,000. Since 1980, the mortgage debt has been reduced by a total of $32,000. The debt reduction during marriage was $30,000. Calculate each spouse's share of the family home.

5. Do you agree with Justice Manuel in *Moore* that only principal reduction should be recognized as purchasing an ownership interest? What is the relationship between appreciation and interest rates? Is there any connection between the inter-

est component of the global mortgage payment and the ultimate appreciation of the house?

On the other hand, in constant terms, is the house really worth any more than when it was purchased? If so, how would you calculate the real increase in worth?

6. Do you think that capital preservation expenses, such as taxes, repairs, and insurance, should be included in the pro tanto buy-in to title? Do you agree with Justice Manuel that if such expenses were included, "fairness would also require that the community be charged for its use of the property"? If interest were included, would fairness also require that the resulting tax benefit to the community be calculated? (For federal income tax purposes, home-purchase interest is generally a deduction from income.)

7. Examine the trial court's calculations in *Moore*. This approach was often used by trial courts before *Moore* concluded the issue. What is the essential difference between the trial court's and the supreme court's calculations in *Moore?* Which do you prefer?

8. Is *Moore* susceptible to gift analysis; that is, could Lydie have argued that the community, by paying off the mortgage, was making a gift to her separate estate? (Apparently, the issue was never raised. "The parties agree that the community has acquired an interest in the house by virtue of the community funds used to make the payments. They disagree, however, as to how the interest is to be determined." *Moore,* at page 265 supra.) Since Family Code section 2640 has no application, should the *Lucas* gift rationale apply to *Moore?* Does *Warren,* supra page 211, suggest that gift analysis is appropriate?

The gift issue reserved by *Moore* was directly presented in Marriage of Gowdy, 178 Cal. App. 3d 1228, 224 Cal. Rptr. 400 (1986). The husband brought a separate-property home into marriage, and the wife made 33 monthly mortgage payments from the couple's joint checking account. The trial court used gift analysis to conclude that there was no community property interest in the home. Observing that there is considerable tension between *Moore* apportionment and section 2640 reimbursement, on the one hand, and the gift presumption cases, including *Lucas,* on the other, the court of appeal reversed, holding "that the payment of community funds to reduce the encumbrance on husband's separate property, even though done with knowledge and apparent consent of the wife, gave the community a pro tanto interest in that separate property. . . ." Id. at 1234. Do you agree that there is conceptual tension between *Lucas* and *Moore?* Between section 2640 and the gift presumption cases?

E. SPECIAL CLASSIFICATION PROBLEMS: TORT RECOVERIES AND INSURANCE PROCEEDS

[You may find it useful to review pages 138-139 and 150-151 before beginning this section.]

1. *Personal Injury Awards*

California's treatment of personal injury awards is anomalous and confusing. In order to present and evaluate California law, this section will describe current law and its history and then examine a different approach taken by the seven other traditional community property states. Such comparative analysis is not merely academic. It is possible to argue that the majority view expressed by the Arizona Supreme Court in Jurek v. Jurek, below, can be incorporated into the current California statutory treatment.

Initially, California statutes did not classify personal injury recoveries. The California courts, without discussion, treated personal injury recoveries during marriage as community property. This treatment was apparently based on a literal reading of the community property statutes: Because the recovery accrued during marriage and was acquired other than by gift, bequest, devise, or descent, it must be community property. McFadden v. The Santa Ana, Orange, and Tustin Street Railway Co., 87 Cal. 464, 467-468, 25 P. 681 (1891). This literal reading was roundly criticized by Justice Carter in his dissent to Zaragosa v. Craven, 33 Cal. 2d 315, 322, 202 P.2d 73 (1949):

> The community property laws in California provide that all property acquired by the spouses during marriage, other than that acquired by gift, bequest, devise or descent, is property belonging to the community.
>
> From these provisions — a patchwork of statutes — we arrive at the erroneous conclusion that all other property, no matter how acquired, is therefore community property. The fallacy in the assumption, as applied to the present case, is apparent when one considers that the person of every living human being is his or her own property. Property is uniformly protected by the law. It is provided that one who owns property, unless he has been at fault in some way, may sue for, and receive compensation in a court of law. If the property injured is the separate property of either the husband or wife, presumably the damages recovered would also be separate property under [Family Code section 770] wherein it is said that the rents, issues and profits of separate property shall be separate property. But when we are faced with an injury to the human body we then follow the law blindly, letter for letter, and declare that this money, given to compensate for pain, suffering and disfigurement, does not come to the particular spouse by "gift, bequest, devise, or descent," so therefore it *must* be community! After all, what else could it be? Franklin v. Franklin, 67 Cal. App. 2d 719, at page 721 [155 P.2d 637]. As an illustration of just how absurd this attitude is, one need only note that property owned by either spouse *before marriage* is considered his or her separate property. And yet, when the undeniably separate property of the wife's person is disfigured, or she suffers pain because of an injury to that property, any damages recovered are community property.
>
> Presumably, the Legislature intended, while putting into effect the community property laws of California, to get away from the old common law under whose provisions the wife was a chattel with a varying monetary worth. The theory back of the community property laws appears to be that marriage is a partnership, to which each spouse contributes. If it is necessary that the wife work for salary or wages in order that the family may prosper, or if the husband is unable to support the family, then her earnings are, and should be, community property. The wife also contributes her share to the partnership by her very presence in the home. It has been held, too, that the husband may relinquish any right or interest he, as manager of the community, and as the other partner, may have in the wife's earnings. But aside from this, if the wife's earning power has been lessened or diminished through an injury received by the fault of another, then to that extent, the community has suffered and the recovery should be community property. But the wife has also

suffered pain and suffering, and possibly disfigurement, which belongs to her alone, and the recovery for these injuries to her person as her separate property should also be her separate property. It is not necessary that any court should blindly try to put *any* property received during a marriage, other than by descent, bequest, devise or gift, into the pigeonhole marked "community." Indeed, in this situation, it is an erroneous application of the law to do so as her person was hers prior to marriage.

The problem is well explained in "Principles of Community Property" (1943) by William Quinby de Funiak, as follows, at page 225:

> Their (Courts) usual decision to consider the property received in exchange for separate property as taking the character of separate property is a fortunate triumph of common sense over a lack of understanding of the principles of community property. But apparently the courts are inclined to apply a similar reasoning to the right of action for personal injuries and to the compensation received; that is, it is property acquired during marriage and is not acquired by gift, etc., therefore it must be community property. But this overlooks the principles of onerous and lucrative titles and other pertinent principles. Except for gifts clearly made to the marital community, community property only consists of that which is acquired by onerous title, that is, by labor or industry of the spouses, or which is acquired in exchange for community property (which, of course, was acquired itself by onerous title, again with the exception as to the gift). It must be plainly evident that a right of action for injuries to person, reputation, property, or the like, or the compensation received therefor, is not property acquired by onerous title. The labor and industry of the spouses did not bring it into being. For that matter, it is not property acquired by lucrative title either. . . . Since the right of action for injury to the person . . . is intended to repair or make whole the injury, so far as is possible in such a case, the compensation partakes of the same character as that which has been injured or suffered loss.

In Fredrickson & Watson Const. Co. v. Boyd, 60 Nev. 117 [102 P.2d 627], the Nevada Supreme Court said that the compensation to a married woman for personal injuries takes the place of the right of personal security which was violated and belongs to the wife.

Mr. de Funiak points out that in reality when the wife has suffered an injury, both the marital community and the separate individuality of the spouse are injured.

> The only logical conclusion, therefore, is that a personal injury to a spouse, or for that matter an injury to reputation or the like, may give rise to a cause of action in the injured spouse and also in the marital community. This should be so without the necessity of statutory intervention. Indeed, it is probable that such statutes as have been enacted in some of the states result from a hazy idea of the true state of affairs. (Principles of Community Property, de Funiak, p.230.)

Injury to the husband and injury to the community from the same act has been recognized as ground for two separate actions in Lindsay v. Oregon Short Line R. Co., 13 Idaho 477 [90 P.984, 12 L.R.A.N.S. 184]. . . .

Justice Carter's vigorous criticism of California's unitary community property classification of personal injury recoveries was motivated by more than concern that such recoveries be rationally classified. The community classification meant that one spouse's claim was barred by the other's contributory negligence. Frequently, one spouse, generally the wife, was an injured passenger when the automobile her spouse was driving struck another vehicle. When the injured spouse's recovery was classified as community property, the driving spouse's contributory negligence was attributed to the community and hence operated as a bar to the passenger spouse's recovery. (See generally Reppy, The Effect of the Adoption of Comparative Negligence on California Community Property Law: Has Imputed Negligence Been Revived?, 28 Hastings L.J. 1359, 1362-1372 (1977).) If Justice Carter's view had prevailed, at least a portion of the award would have been characterized as the injured spouse's separate property and would not have been barred by the driver spouse's contributory negligence. However, his approach was never adopted. Instead, in 1957 the legislature attempted to avoid entirely the contributory negligence defense by reclassifying the recovery:

> All damages, special and general, awarded a married person in a civil action for personal injuries, are the *separate* property of such married person. [1957 Cal. Stat., ch. 2334, §3.] [Emphasis added.]

This solution proved unsatisfactory too. At dissolution of the community by divorce or death, the separate classification deprived the community of clearly community components of the award, such as recovery for lost wages and medical expenses paid by the community. Moreover, the separate classification had adverse estate and inheritance tax consequences. See 8 Cal. Law Revision Commn., Damages for Personal Injuries to a Married Person as Separate or Community Property 1389, 1390-1393 (1967).

Upon the recommendation of the California Law Revision Commission, supra, in 1968 the legislature repealed the 1957 provision and enacted what is now Family Code section 783:

> If a married person is injured by the negligent or wrongful act or omission of a person other than the married person's spouse, the fact that the negligent or wrongful act or omission of the spouse of the injured person was a concurring cause of the injury *is not a defense* in an action brought by the injured person to recover damages for the injury except in cases where the concurring negligent or wrongful act or omission would be a defense if the marriage did not exist. [Emphasis added.]

The legislature apparently believed that repeal of its 1957 separate property provision would reinstate the prior judge-made community property classification so roundly criticized by Justice Carter in Zaragosa v. Craven. This seems to have been the result desired by the legislature, at least with respect to ongoing marriages and death cases, although the legislature was silent on this subject. It was not until the enactment of the Family Code, effective January 1, 1994, that the legislature explicitly articulated a general rule in section 780.

§780.   Damages for personal injury to married person as community property

> Except as provided in Section 781 and subject to the rules of allocation set forth in Section 2603, money and other property received or to be received by a married person in satisfaction of a judgment for damages for

personal injuries, or pursuant to an agreement for the settlement or compromise of a claim for such damages, is community property if the cause of action for the damages arose during the marriage.

In contrast, with respect to *divorce*, in 1968 the legislature took a new tack and enacted what is now Family Code section 2603.

§2603.   Community estate personal injury damages

(a) "Community estate personal injury damages" as used in this section means all money or other property received or to be received by a person in satisfaction of a judgment for damages for the person's personal injuries or pursuant to an agreement for the settlement or compromise of a claim for the damages, if the cause of action for the damages arose during the marriage but is not separate property as described in Section 781, unless the money or other property has been commingled with other assets of the community estate.

(b) Community estate personal injury damages shall be assigned [at divorce] to the party who suffered the injuries unless the court, after taking into account the economic condition and needs of each party, the time that has elapsed since the recovery of the damages or the accrual of the cause of action, and all other facts of the case, determines that the interests of justice require another disposition. In such a case, the community estate personal injury damages shall be assigned to the respective parties in such proportions as the court determines to be just, except that at least one-half of the damages shall be assigned to the party who suffered the injuries.

The effect of Family Code section 2603 at divorce is nominally to characterize personal injury recoveries as "community estate" property, but to assign them entirely to the injured spouse unless certain enumerated factors persuade the court to assign up to one-half the award to the other spouse. Consideration of the economic conditions and needs of the parties is anomalous in a marital property system that otherwise purports to recognize, as a matter of property right, each spouse's 50 percent claim to wealth acquired during marriage. Does the particular context warrant a need-based deviation from the norm of equal division? Of what significance is "the time that has elapsed since the recovery of the damages"? Most important, what "other facts of the case" are material? Is this a back-door entrance for the majority community property view that a personal injury award should be broken down into its components, some of which are community property and others of which are separate property? It is true that California case law and legislative history suggest that the ostensibly unitary view of section 2603 was meant to reject the more searching analysis espoused by dissenting Justice Carter and adopted by other jurisdictions. Nevertheless, the "other facts of the case" language is vague and malleable. Moreover, in the last several decades, the unitary California approach has lost ground in the community property states. Arizona, Louisiana, Texas, Idaho, and Washington have joined Nevada and New Mexico in breaking down a personal injury award into its component parts. See Marriage of Brown, 100 Wash. 2d 729, 675 P.2d 1207 (1984); Jurek v. Jurek, 124 Ariz. 596, 606 P.2d 812 (1980) (en banc); La. Civ. Code Ann. art. 2344 (2002); Rogers v. Yellowstone Park Co., 97 Idaho 14, 539 P.2d 566 (1975); Graham v. Franco, 488 S.W.2d 390 (Tex. 1972); Soto v. Vandeventer, 56 N.M. 483, 245 P.2d 826, 829 (1952); Fredrickson & Watson Construction

Co. v. Boyd, 60 Nev. 117, 122-123, 102 P.2d 627 (1940). See also Nev. Rev. Stat. §§123.121 and 123.30 (2002). California is now the only community property state that takes a unitary approach to personal injury awards.

In Jurek v. Jurek, reproduced below, the Supreme Court of Arizona, sitting en banc, reviews the comparative history of community property treatment of personal injury damages and reverses Arizona's 54-year-old rule in order to adopt the current majority rule.

JUREK v. JUREK
124 Ariz. 596, 606 P.2d 812 (1980) (en banc)

HOLOHAN, Vice Chief Justice. James T. Jurek filed an appeal challenging the disposition of property made by the superior court in its degree of dissolution of the marriage of the parties. The sole question raised on appeal is whether the superior court erred in awarding the wife one-half of any recovery which the husband might receive for a personal injury he received two days after he filed for dissolution.

The Court of Appeals, in a memorandum decision, affirmed the judgment of the trial court. . . . We granted the appellant's petition for review. The decision of the Court of Appeals is vacated.

The parties had been living separately for approximately four months and on January 28, 1977, the appellant husband filed a petition for dissolution of the marriage. Two days later he sustained an injury which resulted in the loss of his right hand and half of his right forearm. The trial court ruled that the personal injury claim arising out of the husband's injury was a community asset; therefore the wife was entitled to one-half of any proceeds received in satisfaction of the claim.[1]

Initially we reject the husband's assertion that the filing of the dissolution action should alter the scheme of distribution of community assets acquired after the filing of the action but before the granting of the dissolution. This assertion is not supported by the applicable statutes or case law. The appellate courts of this state have consistently held that the community continues to exist, together with its rights and obligations, even when the parties may be living separate and apart. Flowers v. Flowers, 118 Ariz. 577, 578 P.2d 1006 (App. 1978); Neal v. Neal, 116 Ariz. 590, 570 P.2d 758 (1977). . . .[3]

The long-standing rule in Arizona has been that a cause of action for injury to the person of either spouse during marriage and the damages recovered therefor are community property. Pacific Construction Co. v. Cochran, 29 Ariz. 554, 243 P. 405 (1926). The rule announced in 1926 has been followed consistently ever since. . . .

The rule announced in *Pacific Construction* was based upon the general rule in community property states, particularly California. See McFadden v. Santa Ana, O. & T. St. Ry. Co., 87 Cal. 464, 25 P. 681 (1891). . . . There was no analysis in our early cases of the various component parts which make up a recovery for personal

1. Appellant was awarded benefits under Workmen's Compensation: but no claim to the amount of these benefits was made by appellee. The dispute is limited to the amount which may be recovered under a third-party tort claim.

3. Compare Cal. Fam. Code §§771 and 781. — ED.

injuries. In other jurisdictions the general rule fell into disfavor. See annotation in 35 A.L.R.2d 1199 (1954); de Funiak and Vaughn, Principles of Community Property §82 (2d ed. 1971).

The Arizona statutes applicable to the issue define the property interests as:

> All property acquired by either husband or wife during the marriage, except that which is acquired by gift, devise or descent, is the community property of the husband and wife. [A.R.S. §25-211.]

> All property, real and personal, of each spouse, owned by such spouse before marriage, and that acquired afterward by gift, devise or descent, and also the increase, rents, issues and profits thereof, is the separate property of such spouse. [A.R.S. §25-213.]

The proper interpretation of these statutes is the essence of the problem. . . .

The rule that a cause of action for personal injuries to either spouse was community property was based on a construction of the meaning of the word "acquired" as used in A.R.S. §25-211 and its predecessors. The cause of action arose during marriage; therefore it was property "acquired" during marriage, and it was not property acquired by gift, devise, or descent.

In Fredrickson & Watson Const. Co. v. Boyd. 60 Nev. 117, 102 P.2d 627 (1940) the Nevada Supreme Court declared that the word "acquired," as used in a community property statute similar to Arizona's, should not be construed to mean every known mode and manner of property acquisition. The Nevada court noted that the word should be read and interpreted in the light of the uses and purposes of community property and the establishment of community right. As thus read the court concluded that the word was not meant to apply to compensation for an injury to the person which arises from the violation of the right of personal security, which right a spouse brings to the marriage. See id., 102 P.2d at 629.

Following the decision of the Nevada Supreme Court in the *Boyd* case, the New Mexico Supreme Court in Soto v. Vandeventer, 56 N.M. 483, 245 P.2d 826 (1952) held that a cause of action for personal injuries to a wife and for the resultant pain and suffering belonged to her as her separate property. The New Mexico Supreme Court reasoned that the wife brought her body to the marriage and on its dissolution is entitled to take it away, so she should be similarly entitled to compensation from one who has wrongfully violated her right to personal security. To emphasize the point the New Mexico court pointed out:

> Under the majority doctrine, if the wife were riding a horse she had brought to the marriage and some driver of a motor vehicle negligently struck her and the horse, throwing both into a wire fence, breaking the leg of each and also disfiguring them, the cause of action for the damage to the horse would belong to the wife, but that for the injury to her would belong to the community and the husband would receive one half of the proceeds of a judgment. [Id., 245 P.2d at 832.]

If the personal injury to a spouse results in loss of wages and expenses for hospital and medical care, what is the result? Such losses and expenses are injuries to the community, and the recovery for such items belongs to the community. Soto v. Vandeventer, supra; de Funiak and Vaughn §82 pages 202 and 203.

In the case at issue the serious injuries to the appellant are personal to him.

In the same fashion as pointed out in *Soto,* the body which he brought to the marriage is certainly his separate property. The compensation for injuries to his personal well-being should belong to him as his separate property. Any expenses incurred by the community for medical care and treatment and any loss of wages resulting from the personal injury should be considered community in nature, and the community is entitled to recover for such losses.

The judgment of the superior court awarding to the appellee wife one-half of any recovery received by appellant for his personal injuries is reversed, and the cause is remanded to the trial court for further proceedings. The superior court should determine the actual loss to the community for loss of wages and medical expense and make an equitable division of any recovery for such items. The remainder of any recovery, after deduction of the community expenses and loss, shall be awarded to the appellant as his sole and separate property.

STRUCKMEYER, C.J., and HAYS, CAMERON and GORDON, JJ., concur.

Notes and Questions

1. In considering the arguments in favor of a unitary approach to personal injury recoveries, it is necessary to distinguish, for divorce cases, between the original California judge-made view that such awards were, without qualification, entirely community property, and the current statutory treatment (section 2603), which calls the recovery community estate property but directs the divorce court to award it entirely to the injured spouse unless there are extenuating circumstances. The original judge-made rule can be justified on grounds of simplicity of administration and protection of "the community interests in the elements that clearly should belong to it." Washington v. Washington, 47 Cal. 2d 249, 253, 302 P.2d 569 (1956). Does either justification support section 2603?

2. Do you agree with Jurek v. Jurek that damages for pain, suffering, and permanent physical disability ought to be characterized as the injured spouse's separate property? On the other hand, to what extent is compensation for lost wages properly characterized as community property?

3. Despite the conceptual attractiveness of a nonunitary approach to personal injury recoveries, allocation between the community and separate portions may not always be simple or even feasible. When a general, as opposed to a special, verdict has been rendered or a global settlement has been negotiated, it may be difficult for the separate property proponent to sustain his burden of proof, that is, to demonstrate that some precise portion of a personal injury award acquired during marriage is nevertheless separate property because it was intended to compensate for injury to the spouse's "separate estate." See, for example, Luxton v. Luxton, 98 N.M. 276, 278, 648 P.2d 315, 317 (1982) (injured wife failed to discharge her burden of showing what portion of the award was separate property compensation for her pain and suffering). But see Placide v. Placide, 408 So. 2d 330, 333 (La. App. 1981) (divorce court can make a rational apportionment without reference to jury allocation in the tort action).

The Uniform Marital Property Act avoids this apportionment difficulty by classifying as separate property "recovery for personal injury except for the amount of that recovery attributable to expenses paid or otherwise satisfied from marital property" (§4(g)(6)). Compare La. Civ. Code Ann. art. 2344 (2002), which provides for separate classification except insofar as the award compensates for earnings lost during marriage and medical expenses paid by the community.

4. Examine closely California Family Code section 2603(a):

> "Community estate personal injury damages" as used in this section means all money or other property received or to be received by a person in satisfaction of a judgment for damages for the person's personal injuries or pursuant to an agreement for the settlement or compromise of a claim for the damages . . . *unless the money or other property has been commingled with other assets of the community estate.* [Emphasis added.]

Should the last clause be read literally? In other words, will commingling alone turn a personal injury award into ordinary community property subject to a 50-50 split at divorce? Or, may the injured spouse trace the award according to the usual tracing rules? There is no helpful legislative history. The commingling clause does not appear in the proposal of the California Law Revision Commission, supra page 272 at 1398, and was evidently tacked on at some late point in the legislative process. The Commission clearly contemplated ordinary tracing, supra page 272 at 1397, but its proposal did not include that final perplexing clause.

5. Suppose that a couple uses a spouse's personal injury award to purchase a family home and takes title in joint tenancy or community property. Should *Lucas* and California Family Code sections 2581 and 2640 apply at divorce? See Marriage of Devlin, 138 Cal. App. 3d 804, 809-810, 189 Cal. Rptr. 1 (1982), and Marriage of Mason, 93 Cal. App. 3d 215, 222-223, 155 Cal. Rptr. 350 (1979).

6. California Family Code section 781 addresses the issue of timing. In order to be characterized as community property, must recovery be obtained before the community terminates or, more favorably to the community, need the cause of action merely arise during the subsistence of the community? Initially California took the first view: Any recovery received after divorce or separation was the injured spouse's separate property. Laws of 1969, ch. 1608. In 1979, the legislature amended the law to provide that the recovery is the injured spouse's separate property only if the cause of action arises after informal or legal separation or divorce. Laws of 1979, ch. 638. If the cause of action arises before the community is terminated by separation or divorce, recovery is Family Code section 780 community property or section 2603 community estate personal injury damages. (For further discussion of informal separation that operates to terminate the community, see pages 480-483 infra.) In the event that section 781(a) does characterize a recovery as the injured spouse's separate property, section 781(b) provides that the other spouse may seek reimbursement to the community or to his separate estate for expenses paid by reason of the personal injuries. (Note that there is no corresponding reimbursement provision in the event the award is characterized as section 2603 community estate personal injury damages. Presumably, however, such expenditures would be a "fact of the case" justifying a reimbursement award to the community or the separate estate of the noninjured spouse.)

7. So far we have been discussing personal injury recoveries against third parties. How should an *interspousal* tort recovery be characterized? See Family Code section 781(c).

2. Recovery for Damage to Property

Absent complicating circumstances, recovery for damage to property should be classified as community or separate according to the character of the damaged property. See, for example, Scoville v. Keglor, 27 Cal. App. 2d 17, 80 P.2d 162 (1938) (a wife's recovery from a third party tortfeasor for damage to her separate property automobile was classified as her separate property). Yet classification is less obvious when the source of recovery is liability insurance purchased with funds of a different character than the insured asset. Suppose, for example, that a wife owns a separate-property vacation home, and she pays home insurance premiums with her community property earnings. When the home burns down, what is the character of the insurance proceeds? Most California cases, as well as those of other community property jurisdictions, ignore the character of the premiums and instead classify insurance proceeds for property damage according to the character of the underlying property. Nilson v. Sarment, 153 Cal. 524, 529, 96 P.2d 315 (1908); Belmont v. Belmont, 188 Cal. App. 2d 33, 42, 10 Cal. Rptr. 227 (1961); Desfosses v. Desfosses, 815 P.2d 1094 (Idaho App. 1991); Thigpen v. Thigpen. 91 So. 2d 12 (La. 1956); Rolater v. Rolater, 198 S.W. 391 (Tex. Civ. App. 1917); In re Hickman's Estate, 41 Wash. 2d 519, 527, 250 P.2d 524 (1952). (*Thigpen,* supra, suggests in dictum that community payment of premiums to insure a spouse's separate property may entitle the community to reimbursement from the spouse's separate estate.)

Nevertheless, one California Court of Appeal decision has held that insurance proceeds take the character of the separate premiums rather than the insured community property. Estate of Nereson, 194 Cal. App. 3d 865, 873, 239 Cal. Rptr. 865 (1987). However, *Nereson,* citing as sole authority an inapposite life insurance case, seemed unaware of existing California property damage precedent. Id. at 873.

3. Life Insurance Proceeds

Introductory Note

There are two types of life insurance: term insurance and whole life, or cash value, insurance. Term life insurance has no cash value. The premium covers only the risk of death. When the premium period expires, there is nothing left except the right to reinsure for another premium period, usually annual periods until age 65 or 70. The right to reinsure has little or no value if the insured is still as insurable as he was at the inception of the policy.

Whole life, in contrast, is both term insurance and a savings plan. Whole life has a *face value,* the amount payable on death, and a lesser but ever-growing *cash value,* the amount for which a policy on the life of a living person may be cashed in or borrowed against. When a policy on the life of a living person has current cash value, that cash value is community property in proportion as the community funded the premiums. Cash value is simply a form of savings and exists apart from the pure insurance component of the policy. See, for example, Marriage of Holmgren, 60 Cal. App. 3d 869, 871, 130 Cal. Rptr. 440 (1976). When a person insured by whole life insurance dies, the proceeds attributable to the term component are the total death proceeds (face value) less the cash value of the policy. Thus, if the insured decedent purchased a whole life insurance policy paying $10,000 at death and the cash value before death was $3,000, then the amount attributable to the term insurance component is $7,000.

There has been a good deal of confusion and incoherence in the death and divorce cases treating *term* policy proceeds and unmatured term policies. Looking initially at death proceeds, the courts of appeal treated term life insurance proceeds as community property in proportion to the percentage of premiums paid by the community over the lifetime of the policy. Biltoft v. Wootten, 96 Cal. App. 3d 58, 157 Cal. Rptr. 581 (1979); Patillo v. Norris, 65 Cal. App. 3d 209, 135 Cal. Rptr. 210 (1976); Modern Woodmen of America v. Gray, 113 Cal. App. 729, 299 P. 754 (1931).

Yet when faced with a living insured's term policy at divorce, Marriage of Lorenz, 146 Cal. App. 3d 464, 468, 194 Cal. Rptr. 237 (1983), took a fundamentally inconsistent approach. Observing that the policy had no value at all when the current premium expired, the court held that the policy had no value at divorce. Nevertheless, in Marriage of Gonzales, 168 Cal. App. 3d 1021, 214 Cal. Rptr. 634 (1985), another court of appeal held to the contrary and remanded for a determination of the term policy's value, suggesting that the amount of premiums paid by the community might be a proper measure of its interest in the policy.

The logic of *Lorenz* undercuts application of the relative contribution rule when a spouse dies leaving term insurance proceeds, and policy premiums were paid partly by community and partly by separate funds. The logic of *Lorenz* suggests that the character of the final premium should be determinative. Four other community property states take this view. Arizona, Idaho, New Mexico, and Washington have adopted a final premium rule for term life insurance proceeds. They treat the source of the last premium as determinative and ignore prior premiums because they purchased coverage for periods that expired before the death of the insured. Gaethje v. Gaethje, 8 Ariz. App. 47, 442 P.2d 870 (1968); Travelers Ins. Co. v. Johnson, 97 Idaho 336, 344, 544 P.2d 294, 298 (1975); Estate of Schleis, 97 N.M. 561, 642 P.2d 164 (1982); Phillips v. Wellborn, 89 N.M. 340, 342, 552 P.2d 471, 473 (1976); Aetna Life Insurance Co. v. Wadsworth, 102 Wash. 2d 652, 689 P.2d 46, 49-51 (1984). See generally Comment, Community and Separate Property Interests in Life Insurance Proceeds: A Fresh Look, 51 Wash. L. Rev. 351 (1976). It is against this background that Estate of Logan arose.

ESTATE OF LOGAN
191 Cal. App. 3d 319, 236 Cal. Rptr. 368 (1987)

KING, J.—In this case we hold that a term life insurance policy upon the life of one spouse is not divisible as community property under the Family Law Act, even though premiums for the policy before separation were paid with community property funds. An exception will arise if the insured spouse becomes uninsurable during the term paid with community funds, since the right to continued coverage upon payment of future premiums is a valuable community property asset for one who is uninsurable. If the insured dies during the term paid with community funds, the proceeds of the policy are community property. When premiums for a new term have been paid from postseparation separate property earnings and the insured remains insurable, the policy must be confirmed to the insured as separate property.

Frances Jeanne Logan (now Pritchard, hereinafter Jeanne) appeals from [an order] denying her any community property interest in the proceeds of her former husband's employment-related term life insurance policy. . . .

Jeanne and William Logan married in 1947 and separated in 1966. William worked for American Airlines, which deducted premiums for a company-sponsored group term life insurance plan from his salary. Their 1968 interlocutory judgment of divorce ordered William to maintain this life insurance with the couple's minor children as beneficiaries until they reached the age of majority.

When William died in 1984, the children of his marriage to Jeanne were adults. Jeanne brought this action seeking a portion of the proceeds from William's term life insurance. She appeals the trial court's determination that she had no community property interest in these proceeds.

The trial court denied Jeanne's request for a 39.583 percent share[2] in the proceeds of William's American Airlines term life insurance policy because "I don't believe term policies are community property," explicitly rejecting contrary authority in Bowman v. Bowman (1985) 171 Cal. App. 3d 148 [217 Cal Rptr. 174] and In re Marriage of Gonzalez (1985) 168 Cal. App. 3d 1021 [214 Cal. Rptr. 634], and following the holding in In re Marriage of Lorenz (1983) 146 Cal. App. 3d 464 [194 Cal. Rptr. 237]. The two appellate court decisions actually in conflict over the issue of whether term life insurance is a community property asset are *Lorenz* and *Gonzalez,* since *Bowman,* without detailed analysis, was decided by the same division which had decided *Gonzalez* a few months earlier.

The first case to consider a closely related issue was Biltoft v. Wootten (1979) 96 Cal. App. 3d 58 [157 Cal. Rptr. 581] which involved a contributory group term life insurance policy available through the insured's employment and paid with biweekly deductions from his pay. After separation, but before dissolution, decedent had changed the beneficiary under the policy from his spouse to his children. On appeal the issue was whether the proceeds were community or separate property. The court held the proceeds were part community and part separate according to the proportion that the amount of premiums paid with community property bore to the total amount of premiums paid. The reasoning underlying the decision was that each premium payment did not purchase a new contract of insurance because, if the decedent had tried to purchase the policy after separation, "it is unlikely that he would have been able to obtain the same coverage for the same premium on the same terms of eligibility" and "The decedent's community efforts for the 20 years prior to the separation maintained the policy in force." (Id. at p.61.) The court's opinion does not indicate what evidence, if any, was presented to support the conclusion that it was "unlikely" decedent could have purchased the identical policy after separation.

Lorenz distinguished *Biltoft* as a case dealing with the right to proceeds from term insurance upon the death of the insured spouse prior to dissolution. The *Lorenz* analysis was that many fringe benefits of employment such as use of an employer's health club facilities, reduced prices at the company cafeteria or discounts on purchases of an employer's products were of value to an employee, but did not constitute community property divisible upon dissolution. *Lorenz* held that although the benefits of term life insurance have a value, until those benefits become payable, the policy itself is worthless and is not divisible as community property.

The *Gonzalez* court concluded, "*Lorenz* is simply incorrect in the assertion that assets such as term life insurance . . . have no economic value. . . ." (In re Marriage of Gonzalez, supra, 168 Cal. App. 3d at p.1024.) *Gonzalez* reasoned that the spouses had acquired rights because the policy had been obtained during marriage with

---

2. In a 1975 proceeding the trial court had amended the interlocutory judgment to provide that Jeanne's community property interest in William's pension was 39.583 percent. Jeanne claimed the same interest in his term life insurance proceeds in these proceedings.

community funds. The court concluded, with no indication what evidence existed in the record to support its conclusion, "Undoubtedly the premium rate was very favorable, and pursuant to federal statute, husband was not required to establish medical eligibility for coverage. (38 U.S.C. §777(e).) We are confident the same policy acquired today, assuming husband is still insurable, would cost considerably more." (Id., at p.1026.)

To say that "[t]he *Gonzalez* decision has been subject to criticism by members of the Bar" (Cal. Family Law Service, §23:138) is putting it mildly. . . . We believe the *Gonzalez* and *Bowman* decisions result from an erroneous analysis of the nature of term life insurance policies.

Simply stated, "Term insurance is life insurance written for a fixed or specified term. To reflect the increasing risk of death as the insured increases in age, term insurance policies either have increasing premiums from year to year or provide decreasing death benefits paid on the insured's death. At the expiration of the term of years, the policy expires without retaining cash value. One advantage of term insurance is its cost. Since it does not retain cash value, the premium cost for comparable coverage is less than it is with whole life insurance. Some forms of term insurance may be converted into permanent or whole life policies or may be automatically renewable at regular intervals at a higher premium." (5A Markey, Cal. Family Law, Practice and Procedure, §122.03[2][b].) Term life insurance policies typically contain two elements, dollar coverage payable in the event of death and a right to renewal for future terms without proof of current medical eligibility.

As to the element of dollar coverage, term life insurance simply provides for protection against the contingency of the death of the insured during the term of the policy. If the premium for the next term is not paid, the policy is not renewed. In this respect, it is the same as automobile or health insurance. Thus when the premium is paid with community funds, the policy is community property for the period covered by that premium. This is true whether the premium is paid as a fringe benefit by the insured's employer, paid for by the insured, or a combination of both. The policy provides dollar coverage only for the specific term for which the premium was paid. Thus, as to dollar coverage, term life insurance upon which premiums were paid from community funds has no value after the term has ended without the insured having become deceased.

With respect to the element of the right to renew coverage for additional terms, term life insurance has either a significant value or no value at all. The right to renewal upon payment of the premium for the next term is significant because the insured possesses the right even if he or she has become uninsurable in the meantime. Usually, as Markey points out, policies require increasing premiums and/or decreasing amounts of coverage as the insured gets older. If, as is usually the case, the insured is insurable at the end of the term purchased with community funds, the renewed policy, that is, the term policy purchased by the payment of the premium with postseparation earnings which are separate property pursuant to [Family Code] section [771], or by the employer as a postseparation fringe benefit, changes character from community to separate property.

At this time, if the insured is insurable, the community has fully received everything it bargained for, dollar protection against the contingency of death during the term paid for with community funds and the right to renew without proof of insurability for an additional term. If the insured remains insurable, the right to renew the policy has no value since the insured could obtain comparable term insurance for a comparable price in the open market. The community having re-

ceived everything it bargained for, there is no longer any community property interest in the policy and no community asset left to divide.[6]

We believe the courts in *Biltoft, Gonzalez* and *Bowman* came to incorrect conclusions because they made unsupported and erroneous assumptions about the nature
of term life insurance and the availability to the insured of other comparable insurance. In *Biltoft,* the court assumed "it is unlikely that [decedent] would have been
able to obtain the same coverage for the same premium on the same terms of
eligibility." (Biltoft v. Wootten, supra, 96 Cal. App. 3d at p.61) In *Gonzalez* the court
assumed "[u]ndoubtedly the premium rate was very favorable" and "husband was
not required to establish medical eligibility for coverage," and concluded. "We are
confident the same policy today, assuming husband is still insurable, would cost
considerably more." (In re Marriage of Gonzalez, supra, 168 Cal. App. 3d at
p.1026.) To this we ask, where was the evidence to support these assumptions? For
all we know, by the time of the appeal, Mr. Gonzalez or Mr. Bowman might well
have changed jobs and gotten new employment in the private sector which provided
greater term life insurance coverage paid for by the employer. Such coverage is
usually available even if the employed might be otherwise uninsurable, since new
employees are usually covered under the employer's group life insurance plans
without evidence of insurability. The group insurance with the former employers
would have ceased when the insured changed employment.

We believe the correct rule to be that term life insurance covering a spouse
who remains insurable is community property only for the period beyond the date
of separation for which community funds were used to pay the premium. If the
insured dies during that period the proceeds of the policy are fully community.
Otherwise, the insured remaining insurable, a term policy does not constitute a
divisible community asset since the policy is of no value and the community has
fully received what it bargained for.[7] If the insured becomes uninsurable during
the term paid with community funds, then the right to future insurance coverage
which cannot otherwise be purchased is a community asset to be divided upon
dissolution. We need not discuss how this right might be valued[8] because we deter-

---

6. Some term policies, as in the instant case, provide for a waiver of premium in the event of
disability, or for a right to convert to whole life. These options do not affect the community property
interest, if any, since they are only options in the policy upon which the premium is computed.

7. The only decision we have found in another community property state agrees with this conclusion. (See Aetna Life Ins. Co. v. Wadsworth (1984) 102 Wn. 2d 652 [689 P.2d 46].)

8. We do not minimize the difficulty of valuing the right of an insured who is no longer insurable
to obtain continued coverage. The need to value this right will rarely arise since, as here, the insured
will usually be insurable at the conclusion of the term paid with community property funds. An uninsurable person's right to continued insurance coverage is a valuable right and expert testimony can undoubtedly establish its value. It has been suggested that "in order to properly determine the value of
a term life insurance policy, the trial court might examine several factors, such as the face value of the
policy, the amount of the premium, the life expectancy of the insured, whether the policy is convertible
to whole life insurance, replacement cost, and when, if ever, the policy 'vests' and is deemed fully paid."
(In re Marriage of Gonzalez, supra, 168 Cal. App. 3d at p.1026.) We have difficulty understanding how
these factors can be used to value term insurance. Some of them would not seem relevant to establishing
value. Replacement cost would seem to be irrelevant, since for one who is uninsurable, replacement
would not be possible. The amount of the premium is a function of the age of the insured and the
amount of coverage, but again, this seems irrelevant if coverage is not available because of uninsurability.
What the *Gonzalez* court meant by "vests" is particularly puzzling since we are unaware that term life
insurance ever vests and is deemed fully paid. Convertibility, as previously discussed, is an added feature
of the policy which has been considered in fixing the premium, and is simply a right to obtain whole
life coverage without current medical eligibility, with the premium for the whole life policy being the
same as for any other insured of the same age seeking the same amount of whole life coverage. It may
be that expert testimony can utilize these factors to value the right to continued insurance coverage

mine Jeanne has no community interest in William's term life insurance policy since he was insurable when he commenced paying the premiums with his postseparation property earnings. . . .

The judgment is . . . affirmed. The parties shall bear their own costs on appeal. Low, P.J., concurred.

HANING, J. — I concur in the result. The reference to an exception in the event the insured party becomes uninsurable is not an issue before us, has not been fully briefed and is not ripe for decision under the present circumstances. Hence, I express no opinion thereon.

Notes

1. *Term insurance and the right to reinsure.* The dictum of *Logan* was partially explored in Marriage of Spengler, 5 Cal. App. 4th 288, 6 Cal. Rptr. 2d 764 (1992), reprinted infra at page 366. During marriage Daniel Spengler became uninsurable. Daniel and his wife Barbara later divorced. Daniel remarried and died shortly thereafter, having named his widow Rose as beneficiary of his employer-provided life insurance policy. Barbara asserted a community property interest in the proceeds based on Daniel's employment during their marriage and his uninsurability at their divorce. The court of appeal held that there was no community interest in the policy on the narrow ground that at divorce Daniel had no *enforceable* right to reinsure under his employment-related group insurance policy: Policy renewal depended "on the insured's continuing to work *and* on the employer's continuing to provide the group insurance plan." Id. at 770. Thus *Spengler* does not purport to address the significance of a *legally enforceable* right to reinsure when the insured is uninsurable at divorce. The narrow holding of *Spengler* will be examined infra at page 366, in connection with employment-related benefits.

2. *Beneficiary designation on community property life insurance policies.* A married person purchasing life insurance with community funds may designate as beneficiary someone other than his spouse. For discussion of the effect of such designations, see page 546 infra. See also Estate of MacDonald, supra at page 121.

F.   CLASSIFICATION OF EMPLOYMENT-RELATED INTERESTS

1.   *The Basic Pension Cases*

MARRIAGE OF BROWN
15 Cal. 3d 838, 544 P.2d 561, 126 Cal. Rptr. 633 (1976)

TOBRINER, J. — Since French v. French (1941) 17 Cal. 2d 775, 778 [112 P.2d 235, 134 A.L.R. 366], California courts have held that nonvested pension rights are

---

for one who is no longer insurable. We are not so sure, and suspect a better measure might be the actuarial present value of the proceeds payable under the policy, considering the shortened life expectancy resulting from whatever has caused the uninsurability.

not property, but a mere expectancy, and thus not a community asset subject to division upon dissolution of a marriage. . . .

Upon reconsideration of this issue, we have concluded that French v. French should be overruled and that the subsequent decisions which rely on that precedent should be disapproved. As we shall explain, the *French* rule cannot stand because nonvested pension rights are not an expectancy but a contingent interest in property; furthermore, the *French* rule compels an inequitable division of rights acquired through community effort. Pension rights, whether or not vested, represent a property interest: to the extent that such rights derive from employment during coverture, they comprise a community asset subject to division in a dissolution proceeding.

Before we turn to the facts of this appeal we must devote a few words to terminology. Some decisions that discuss pension rights, but do not involve division of marital property, describe a pension right as "vested" if the employer cannot unilaterally repudiate that right without terminating the employment relationship. (See . . . Kern v. City of Long Beach (1947) 29 Cal. 2d 848, 855 [179 P.2d 799]; Dryden v. Board of Pension Commrs. (1936) 6 Cal. 2d 575, 579 [59 P.2d 104].) As we explain later, we believe that these decisions correctly define the point at which a pension right becomes a property interest. In divorce and dissolution cases following French v. French, however, the term "vested" has acquired a special meaning; it refers to a pension right which is not subject to a condition of forfeiture if the employment relationship terminates before retirement.[1] We shall use the term "vested" in this latter sense as defining a pension right which survives the discharge or voluntary termination of the employee.

As so defined, a vested pension right must be distinguished from a "matured" or unconditional right to immediate payment. Depending upon the provisions of the retirement program, an employee's right may vest after a term of service even though it does not mature until he reaches retirement age and elects to retire. Such vested but immature rights are frequently subject to the condition, among others, that the employee survive until retirement.[2]

The issue in the present case concerns the nonvested pension rights of respondent Robert Brown. General Telephone Company, Robert's employer, maintains a noncontributory pension plan in which the rights of the employees depend upon their accumulation of "points," based upon a combination of the years of service and the age of the employee. Under this plan, an employee who is discharged before he accumulates 78 points forfeits his rights; an employee with 78 points can opt for early retirement at a lower pension, or continue to work until age 63 and retire at an increased pension.

Gloria and Robert Brown married on July 29, 1950. When they separated in November of 1973, Robert had accumulated 72 points under the pension plan, a substantial portion of which is attributable to his work during the period when the parties were married and living together. If he continues to work for General Telephone, Robert will accumulate 78 points on November 30, 1976. If he retires then, he will receive a monthly pension of $310.94; if he continues his employment until normal retirement age his pension will be $485 a month.

---

1. See Article, The Identification and Division of Intangible Community Property: Slicing the Invisible Pic (1973) 6 U.C. Davis L. Rev. 26, 29-31.

2. See, e.g., Bensing v. Bensing (1972) 25 Cal. App. 3d 889 [102 Cal. Rptr. 255], in which the vested pension rights of the employee, an Air Force major, were subject to divestment if he died or was court martialed before retirement.

Relying on the *French* rule, the trial court held that since Robert had not yet acquired a "vested" right to the retirement pension, the value of his pension rights did not become community property subject to division by the court. It divided the remaining property, awarding Gloria the larger share but directing her to pay $1,742 to Robert to equalize the value received by each spouse. The court also awarded Gloria alimony of $75 per month. Gloria appeals from the portion of the interlocutory judgment that declares that Robert's pension rights are not community property and thus not subject to division by the court.

As we have stated, the fundamental theoretical error which led to the inequitable division of marital property in the present case stems from the seminal decision of French v. French, supra, 17 Cal. 2d 775. Mrs. French claimed a community interest in the prospective retirement pay of her husband, an enlisted man in the Fleet Reserve. The court noted that "under the applicable statutes the [husband] will not be entitled to such pay until he completes a service of fourteen years in the Fleet Reserve and complies with all of the requirements of that service." (p.778.) It concluded that "At the present time, his right to retirement pay is an expectancy which is not subject to division as community property." (Ibid.) . . .

Subsequent cases, however, have limited the sweep of *French*, holding that a vested pension is community property even though it has not matured (In re Marriage of Martin (1975) 50 Cal. App. 3d 581, 584 [123 Cal. Rptr. 634]; . . . In re Marriage of Bruegl (1975) 47 Cal. App. 3d 201, 205, fn. 4 [120 Cal. Rptr. 597] . . .), or is subject to conditions within the employee's control (Waite v. Waite (1972) 6 Cal. 3d 461, 472 [99 Cal. Rptr. 325, 492 P.2d 13]; In re Marriage of Peterson (1974) 41 Cal. App. 3d 642, 650-651 [115 Cal. Rptr. 184]). But although we have frequently reiterated the *French* rule in dictum (see, e.g., In re Marriage of Jones (1975) 13 Cal. 3d 457, 461 [119 Cal. Rptr. 108, 531 P.2d 420]; In re Marriage of Fithian (1974) 10 Cal. 3d 592, 596 [111 Cal. Rptr. 369, 517 P.2d 449]; Phillipson v. Board of Administration (1970) 3 Cal. 3d 32, 40-41 [89 Cal. Rptr. 61, 473 P.2d 765] . . .), we have not previously had occasion to reexamine the merits of that rule.

Throughout our decisions we have always recognized that the community owns all pension rights attributable to employment during the marriage. . . . The *French* rule, however, rests on the theory that nonvested pension rights may be community, but that they are not property; classified as mere expectancies, such rights are not assets subject to division on dissolution of the marriage.

We have concluded, however, that the *French* court's characterization of nonvested pension rights as expectancies errs.[5] The term expectancy describes the interest of a person who merely foresees that he might receive a future beneficence, such as the interest of an heir apparent (Civ. Code, §700; see Estate of Perkins (1943) 21 Cal. 2d 561, 569 [134 P.2d 231]), or of a beneficiary designated by a living insured who has a right to change the beneficiary (see Morrison v. The Mutual L. Ins. of N.Y. (1940) 15 Cal. 2d 579, 583 [103 P.2d 963]; Mayfield v. Fidelity & Casualty Co. (1936) 16 Cal. App. 2d 611, 619 [61 P.2d 83]).[6] As these examples

5. The intermediate appellate court of the State of Washington recently reached an identical conclusion, holding that nonvested retirement benefits constitute community property under the laws of that state. (DeRevere v. DeRevere (1971) 5 Wash. App. 741 [491 P.2d 249, 251].)

6. The cases discussing the interest of an insurance beneficiary clarify the distinction between an expectancy and a contractual right. "The interest of a beneficiary designated by an insured who has the right to change the beneficiary is, like that of a legatee under a will, a mere expectancy of a gift at the time of the insured's death." (Grimm v. Grimm (1945) 26 Cal. 2d 173, 175-176 [157 P.2d 841].) But if the holder acquires a contractual right to be named as beneficiary of the policy, his interest is no longer an expectancy, but a property right. (See Page v. Washington Mut. Life Assn. (1942) 20 Cal. 2d 234, 242 [125 P.2d 20].)

demonstrate, the defining characteristic of an expectancy is that its holder has no *enforceable right* to his beneficence.

Although some jurisdictions classify retirement pensions as gratuities, it has long been settled that under California law such benefits "do not derive from the beneficence of the employer, but are properly part of the consideration earned by the employee." (In re Marriage of Fithian supra, 10 Cal. 3d 592, 596.) Since pension benefits represent a form of deferred compensation for services rendered . . . , the employee's right to such benefits is a contractual right, derived from the terms of the employment contract. Since a contractual right is not an expectancy but a chose in action, a form of property . . . , we held in Dryden v. Board of Pension Commrs., supra, 6 Cal. 2d 575, 579, that an employee acquires a property right to pension benefits when he enters upon the performance of his employment contract.

Although *Dryden* involved an employee who possessed vested pension rights, the issue of nonvested rights came before us in Kern v. City of Long Beach, supra, 29 Cal. 2d 848. There a city employee contended that the city's repeal of a pension plan unconstitutionally impaired the obligation of contract. The city defended on the ground that the employee's pension rights had not vested at the time of the abrogation of the plan.

Ruling in favor of the employee, we stated in *Kern* that:

> [T]here is little reason to make a distinction between the periods before and after the pension payments are due. It is true that an employee does not earn the right to a full pension until he has completed the prescribed period of service, but he has actually earned some pension rights as soon as he has performed substantial services for his employer. . . . He . . . has then earned certain pension benefits, the payment of which is to be made at a future date. . . . [T]he mere fact that performance is in whole or in part dependent upon certain contingencies does not prevent a contract from arising, and the employing governmental body may not deny or impair the contingent liability any more than it can refuse to make the salary payments which are immediately due. Clearly, it cannot do so after all the contingencies have happened, and in our opinion it cannot do so at any time after a contractual duty to make salary payments has arisen, since a part of the compensation which the employee has at that time earned consists of his pension rights. (29 Cal. 2d at p.855.)

Since we based our holding in *Kern* upon the constitutional prohibition against impairment of contracts, a prohibition applicable only to public entities, the private employer in Hunter v. Sparling (1948) 87 Cal. App. 2d 711 [197 P.2d 807] contended that it could repudiate an employee's nonvested pension rights without liability. Rejecting that contention, the Court of Appeal cited the language from *Kern* quoted above and concluded that once the employee performed services in reliance upon the promised pension, he could enforce his right to a pension either under traditional contract principles of offer, acceptance and consideration or under the doctrine of promissory estoppel. (87 Cal. App. 2d at p.725.) In subsequent years the courts have repeatedly reaffirmed that a nonvested pension right is nonetheless a contractual right, and thus a property right.

Although, as we have pointed out, supra, courts have previously refused to allocate this right in a nonvested pension between the spouses as community property on the ground that such pension is contingent upon continued employment,[8]

8. The fact that a contractual right is contingent upon future events does not degrade that right to an expectancy. The law has long recognized that a contingent future interest is property (see Estate

we reject this theory. In other situations when community funds or effort are expended to acquire a conditional right to future income, the courts do not hesitate to treat that right as a community asset. For example, in Waters v. Waters (1946) 75 Cal. App. 2d 265 [170 P.2d 494], the attorney husband had a contingent interest in a suit pending on appeal at the time of the divorce: the court held that his fee, when and if collected, would be a community asset. Indeed in the several recent pension cases the courts have asserted that vested but immature pensions are community assets although such pensions are commonly subject to the condition that the employee survive until retirement. (See Smith v. Lewis, 13 Cal. 3d 349, 355, fn. 4 [530 P.2d 589, 118 Cal. Rptr. 621 (1975)]; In re Marriage of Martin, supra, 50 Cal. App. 3d 581; In re Marriage of Bruegl, supra, 47 Cal. App. 3d 201, 205.)

We conclude that French v. French and subsequent cases erred in characterizing nonvested pension rights as expectancies and in denying the trial courts the authority to divide such rights as community property. This mischaracterization of pension rights has, and unless overturned, will continue to result in inequitable division of community assets. Over the past decades, pension benefits have become an increasingly significant part of the consideration earned by the employee for his services. As the date of vesting and retirement approaches, the value of the pension right grows until it often represents the most important asset of the marital community. (See Thiede, [The Community Property Interest of the Non-Employee Spouse in Private Employee Retirement Benefits, 9 U.S.F. L. Rev. 635 (1975)].) A division of community property which awards one spouse the entire value of this asset, without any offsetting award to the other spouse, does not represent that equal division of community property contemplated by [Family Code section 2550].

The present case illustrates the point. Robert's pension rights, a valuable asset built up by 24 years of community effort, under the *French* rule would escape division by the court as a community asset solely because dissolution occurred two years before the vesting date. If, as is entirely likely, Robert continues to work for General Telephone Company for the additional two years needed to acquire a vested right, he will then enjoy as his separate property an annuity created predominantly through community effort. This "potentially whimsical result," as the Court of Appeal described a similar division of community property in In re Marriage of Peterson, supra, 41 Cal. App. 3d 642, 651, cannot be reconciled with the fundamental principle that property attributable to community earnings must be divided equally when the community is dissolved.

Respondent does not deny that if nonvested pension rights are property, the *French* rule results in an inequitable division of that property. He maintains, however, that any inequity can be redressed by an award of alimony to the nonemployee spouse. Alimony, however, lies within the discretion of the trial court; the spouse "should not be dependent on the discretion of the court . . . to provide her with the equivalent of what should be hers as a matter of absolute right." (In re Marriage of Peterson, supra, 41 Cal. App. 3d 642, 651.)

Respondent and amicus further suggest that a decision repudiating the *French* rule would both impose severe practical burdens upon the courts and restrict the employee's freedom to change his place or terms of employment. We shall examine these contentions and point out why they do not justify a continued refusal by the courts to divide nonvested pension rights as a community asset.

---

of Zuber (1956) 146 Cal. App. 2d 584, 590 [304 P.2d 247]) no matter how improbable the contingency (see Civ. Code, §697): an expectancy, on the other hand, "is not to be deemed an interest of any kind." (Civ. Code, §700.)

In dividing nonvested pension rights as community property the court must take account of the possibility that death or termination of employment may destroy those rights before they mature. In some cases the trial court may be able to evaluate this risk in determining the present value of those rights. (See DeRevere v. De-Revere, supra, 491 P.2d 249; Thiede, op. cit., supra, 9 U.S.F. L. Rev. 635, 654.) But if the court concludes that because of uncertainties affecting the vesting or maturation of the pension that it should not attempt to divide the present value of pension rights, it can instead award each spouse an appropriate portion of each pension payment as it is paid. This method of dividing the community interest in the pension renders it unnecessary for the court to compute the present value of the pension rights, and divides equally the risk that the pension will fail to vest. (See Cohan & Fink, Is the Non-Employee Community Interest in Qualified Deferred Compensation a Hidden Asset or a Latent Liability? (1974) 1 Com. Prop. J. 7, 13; Note, [Retirement Pay: A Divorce in Time Saved Mine,] 24 Hastings L.J. 347, 356-357 [1973].)

As respondent points out, an award of future pension payments as they fall due will require the court to continue jurisdiction to supervise the payments of pension benefits. Yet this obligation arises whenever the court cannot equitably award all pension rights to one spouse, whether or not such rights are vested; the claim of mere administrative burden surely cannot serve as support for an inequitable substantive rule which distinguishes between vested and nonvested rights. Despite the administrative burden such an award imposes, courts in the past have successfully divided *vested* pension rights by awarding each spouse a share in future payments. (See In re Marriage of Wilson, 10 Cal. 3d 851, 855-856 [519 P.2d 165, 112 Cal. Rptr. 405 (1974)]; Bensing v. Bensing, supra, 25 Cal. App. 3d 889, 892.) Courts can divide nonvested pension rights in like fashion.

Moreover, the practical consequence of the *French* rule has been historically that the court must often award alimony to the spouse who, deprived of any share in the nonvested pension rights, lacks resources to purchase the necessities of life. (Article, op. cit., supra, 6 U.C. Davis L. Rev. 26, 32.) Judicial supervision of alimony awards, undertaken in the past, entails far more onerous a burden than supervision of future pension payment.

As to the claim that our present holding will infringe upon the employee's freedom of contract, we note that judicial recognition of the nonemployee spouse's interest in vested pension rights has not limited the employee's freedom to change or terminate his employment, to agree to a modification of the terms of his employment (including retirement benefits), or to elect between alternative retirement programs. We do not conceive that judicial recognition of spousal rights in nonvested pensions will change the law in this respect. The employee retains the right to decide, and by his decision define, the nature of the retirement benefits owned by the community.

Robert finally contends that any decision overruling French v. French, supra, 17 Cal. 2d 775 should be given purely prospective effect. Although as we explain our decision cannot be accorded complete retroactivity without upsetting final judgments of long standing, we believe the decision may properly govern any case in which no final judgment dividing the marital property has been rendered.

Although as a general rule "a decision of a court of supreme jurisdiction overruling a former decision is retrospective in its operation" . . . , we have recognized exceptions to that proposition when considerations of fairness and public policy preclude full retroactivity. . . . In Neel v. Magana, Olney, Levy, Cathcart & Gelfand (1971) 6 Cal. 3d 176, 193 [98 Cal. Rptr. 837, 491 P.2d 421], we observed that the resolution of this issue of prospective application turns primarily on two factors: "the extent of the public reliance upon the former rule, . . . [and] the ability of litigants to foresee the coming change in the law." In the present case both factors militate against a purely prospective overruling of French v. French. It is unlikely that a layman would rely upon the *French* rule, or even know of that doctrine; attorneys familiar with the decision in French v. French would also realize from our opinion in Marriage of Wilson, supra, 10 Cal. 3d 851 that the *French* rule was ripe for reconsideration. The unjust distribution of property engendered by the *French* rule should not be perpetuated by denial of *any* retrospective effect to our decision.

On the other hand, if we accord complete retroactivity to our decision today we might reopen controversies long settled by final judgment. Undoubtedly in the 35 years since the rendition of French v. French, counsel, relying on that decision, have often failed to list nonvested pension rights as among the community assets of the marriage. In some cases the inability of the nonemployee spouse to assert an interest in nonvested pension rights may have induced the court to award additional alimony. Yet under settled principles of California community property law, "property which is not mentioned in the pleadings as community property is left unadjudicated by decree of divorce, and is subject to future litigation, the parties being tenants in common meanwhile." (In re Marriage of Elkins (1972) 28 Cal. App. 3d 899, 903 [105 Cal. Rptr. 59].) Consequently full retroactivity poses the danger that a nonemployee spouse might upset a settled property distribution by a belated assertion of an interest as a tenant in common in the employee's nonvested pension rights.

We conclude that our decision today should not apply retroactively to permit a nonemployee spouse to assert an interest in nonvested pension rights when the property rights of the marriage have already been adjudicated by a decree of dissolution or separation which has become final as to such adjudication, unless the decree expressly reserved jurisdiction to divide such pension rights at a later date (see [Family Code, §2550]). Our decision will apply retroactively, however, to any case in which the property rights arising from the marriage have not yet been adjudicated, to such rights if such adjudication is still subject to appellate review, or if in such adjudication the trial court has expressly reserved jurisdiction to divide pension rights. . . .

In sum, we submit that whatever abstract terminology we impose, the joint effort that composes the community and the respective contributions of the spouses that make up its assets, are the meaningful criteria. The wife's contribution to the community is not one whit less if we declare the husband's pension rights not a contingent asset but a mere "expectancy." Fortunately we can appropriately reflect the realistic situation by recognizing that the husband's pension rights, a contingent interest, whether vested or not vested, comprise a property interest of the community and that the wife may properly share in it.

The judgment of the superior court is reversed and the cause remanded for further proceedings consistent with the views expressed herein.

Wright, C.J., McComb, J., Mosk, J., Sullivan, J., Clark, and Richardson, J., concurred.

Notes and Questions

1. *Brown* is the leading American pension case and has been followed by most community property and equitable distribution jurisdictions. See cases collected in

Blumberg, Marital Property Treatment of Pensions, Disability Pay, Workers' Compensation and Other Wage Substitutes: An Insurance, or Replacement, Analysis, 33 UCLA L. Rev. 1250, 1260-1262 (1986).

2. Is it self-evident that the right to pension benefits *after* divorce should be classified as community property? The benefits replace wages which, if earned after divorce, would be the earner's separate property. As you will soon discover, wage replacement analysis is, in fact, used to classify disability pay received after divorce as the individual spouse's separate property even when the right to such pay was earned during marriage. Are there any differences between retirement benefits and disability benefits that warrant different approaches to their classification? See Blumberg, supra note 1.

3. What, exactly, persuaded the California Supreme Court that *French* was wrongly decided? Does the observation that a pension is not an employer gratuity necessarily lead to the conclusion that *unvested* pensions should be recognized as property subject to division at divorce?

From the earner's perspective, what are the pitfalls of pension recognition and distribution at divorce? How does the court respond to these objections?

MARRIAGE OF GILLMORE
29 Cal. 3d 418, 629 P.2d 1, 174 Cal. Rptr. 493 (1981)

BIRD, C.J., — Did the trial court abuse its discretion in a dissolution action when it refused to order the immediate payment of a nonemployee spouse's interest in a retirement benefit, where the employee spouse was eligible to retire and receive the benefit but had chosen not to do so?

I

Vera and Earl Gillmore separated in 1978 after a marriage of 14 years. The trial court issued an interlocutory decree dissolving their marriage on November 27, 1978, and entered a final judgment of dissolution on January 19, 1979. The decree awarded Vera physical custody of their minor child as well as $225 per month child support and $100 per month spousal support.

The community property was divided evenly, with the exception of Earl's interest in a retirement plan managed by his employer, Pacific Telephone Company. The court found that Earl would become eligible to retire on April 11, 1979, at which time he would be entitled to a monthly benefit of $717.18. Vera's interest in that benefit was found to be approximately $177.14 per month. The court specifically reserved jurisdiction over the retirement plan.

Earl continued to work after he became eligible to retire in April 1979. He represented that he was a "healthy, active man" in his early 50's, and he intended to work for some time to come. He was not required to retire until he reached the age of 70.

In July 1979, Vera requested an order directing Earl to pay to Vera her share of the pension benefits immediately, retroactive to the date he became eligible to collect them. Earl responded with a request to modify child and spousal support.

The trial court denied both requests, retained jurisdiction over the retirement benefits, and held that it had discretion to delay distribution of the benefits until Earl actually retired.

II

Under California law, retirement benefits earned by a spouse during a marriage are community property, subject to equal division upon the dissolution of that marriage. (In re Marriage of Brown (1976) 15 Cal. 3d 838, 842; [Family Code, §2550].) This is true whether the benefits are vested or nonvested, matured or immature. (*Brown*, supra, at p.842.)[2] Vera and Earl agree that Earl's retirement benefits are community property to the extent they were earned during their marriage. The sole disagreement concerns the *timing* of the distribution of those benefits. Vera contends that the trial court abused its discretion when it refused to order Earl to begin immediate payments to her of her share. Earl claims that the trial court had discretion to postpone distribution of the benefits until he actually retired and began to receive payments from the pension plan.

Trial courts have considerable discretion to determine the value of community property and to formulate a practical way in which to divide property equally. . . . However, that discretion has been strictly circumscribed by the statutory requirement that *all* community property be divided *equally* between the parties. [Family Code §2550.] A trial court has been held to abuse its discretion when it improperly classifies community property as the separate property of one of the spouses or fails to arrive at an equal division of the community property. . . .

Under the cases and statutory law, Earl cannot time his retirement to deprive Vera of an equal share of the community's interest in his pension. It is a "settled principle that one spouse cannot, by invoking a condition wholly within his control, defeat the community interest of the other spouse." (In re Marriage of Stenquist (1978) 21 Cal. 3d 779, 786 [148 Cal. Rptr. 9, 582 P.2d 96].) . . .

Earl's retirement benefits are both vested and matured. (See ante, fn. 2.) He will not forfeit his benefits if he leaves his employment voluntarily, is terminated or retires. The only condition precedent to payment of the benefits is his retirement, a condition totally within his control. A unilateral choice to postpone retirement cannot be manipulated so as to impair a spouse's interest in those retirement benefits.

In re Marriage of Stenquist, supra, 21 Cal. 3d 779, involved a husband's election to receive disability benefits (usually separate property), rather than retirement pay (usually community property). This court held that the husband could not use this election to deprive his wife of her interest in his retirement benefits. "[T]o permit the husband, by unilateral election of a 'disability' pension, to 'transmute community property into his own separate property' (In re Marriage of Fithian, [1974,]

---

2. A "vested" benefit cannot be forfeited if employment ends. Rather, it "survives the discharge or voluntary termination of the employee." (In re Marriage of Brown, supra, 15 Cal. 3d at p.842.) A retirement benefit "matures" when the employee has an unconditional right to payment, i.e., all the "conditions precedent to the payment of the benefits have taken place or are within the control of the employee. . . ." (In re Marriage of Fithian, [1974,] 10 Cal. 3d at p.596, fn. 2: Brown, supra, 15 Cal. 3d at p.842; Smith v. Lewis, [1975,] 13 Cal. 3d at p.355, fn. 4; In re Marriage of Peterson, [1974,] 41 Cal. App. 3d at pp.649-650.) Earl's benefits have vested in that if he retires or loses his job for any reason he will be entitled to immediate benefits. They have matured in that the sole condition on his enjoyment of the benefits, his retirement, is within his control.

10 Cal. 3d 592, 602), is to negate the protective philosophy of the community property law as set out in previous decisions of this court." (Stenquist, supra, 21 Cal. 3d at p.782.)

The result of the husband's unilateral decision in *Stenquist* would have been to deprive the wife of any interest in his retirement benefits. In the present case, Vera is no less entitled to protection. The fact that the deprivation she faces is less than total is not decisive. Earl would deprive Vera of the immediate enjoyment of an asset earned by the community during the marriage. In so doing, he would subject Vera to the risk of losing the asset completely if Earl were to die while he was still employed. Although Earl has every right to choose to postpone the receipt of his pension and to run that risk, he should not be able to force Vera to do so as well.[4] . . .

[Prior] cases, however, do not preclude the employee spouse from choosing among alternative retirement plans. The employee spouse retains the right (1) to change or terminate employment; (2) to agree to a modification of the retirement benefits; or (3) to elect between alternative benefits. (In re Marriage of Brown, supra, 15 Cal. 3d at p.849.) "[T]he employee spouse retains the right to determine the nature of the benefits to be received." (In re Marriage of Stenquist, supra, 21 Cal. 3d at p.786. . . .)

The right of the employee spouse is nonetheless limited by the fact that the nonemployee spouse owns an interest in the retirement benefits. Thus, *Brown* notes that the employee spouse has a right to agree to "a reasonable, *nondetrimental* modification of the pension system" (In re Marriage of Brown, supra, 15 Cal. 3d at p.849, fn. 11, italics added), and *Stenquist* finds that the employee spouse retains the right to elect "*higher than ordinary* retirement benefits." (In re Marriage of Stenquist, supra, 21 Cal. 3d at p.786, fn. 6, italics added.) If the right to choose among alternative retirement plans is exercised in a way which impairs the nonemployee's interest in the benefits, the nonemployee spouse must be compensated.[6]

Thus, although the husband in *Stenquist* had every right to choose a disability pension rather than retirement pay, his choice did not prevent the court from ordering him to pay to the wife an amount equivalent to what her interest would have

---

4. Earl claims that the trial court's decision resulted in an equal division of the retirement benefits since he and Vera will receive their shares of the benefits at the same time—the time that he chooses to retire. However, he overlooks the fact that both the timing of receipt and the control of an asset are important aspects of its value. "Postponement, especially late in life, is often the equivalent of complete defeat. Not only are the employee spouse's chances of dying on the job increasing with each passing year (in which case the pension rights would vanish under most plans), the present value of money is much more valuable as a person enters the last years of his life." (Note, In re Marriage of Stenquist: Tracing the Community Interest in Pension Rights Altered by Spousal Election (1979) 67 Cal. L. Rev. 856, 879, In. 76.) A benefit which may be received at some unknown time in the future is of less value than one received immediately. (In re Marriage of Tammen (1976) 63 Cal. App. 3d 927, 931 [134 Cal. Rptr. 161]; see Projector, Valuation of Retirement Benefits in Marriage Dissolutions (1975) 50 L.A. Bar Bull. 229.) Further, a benefit over which an individual has no control is of less value than a benefit that can be managed personally. Thus, Earl's decision to wait to receive his pension when it will be most profitable and most convenient for him deprives Vera of both the immediate enjoyment of her benefits and the power to manage them to her own advantage. Her financial situation may involve factors significantly different from his. Both the husband and the wife should be able to make their independent decisions about how to handle their shares of the community property.

6. Trial courts can limit the employee spouse's freedom to choose to the extent necessary to protect the interests of the nonemployee spouse. For instance, In re Marriage of Lionberger (1979) 97 Cal. App. 3d 56, 67-70 [158 Cal. Rptr. 535], affirmed a trial court order precluding the husband from choosing a pension plan option that would have decreased the size of his wife's interest. In Phillipson v. Board of Administration, 3 Cal. 3d 32, 48 [1970], the court ordered the husband to choose a particular retirement benefit because such an order was the only way to protect the wife's interest. . . .

been had he chosen retirement pay. Similarly, Earl retains the right to determine what retirement benefits he will receive. He can retire now or at some time in the future. He also retains the option of choosing between the alternative pension plans offered by his employer. However, if he opts for an alternative that deprives Vera of her full share of the retirement benefits, he must compensate her for the interest she loses as a result of his decision.

Compensation is possible here because the value of Vera's interest is known to the court. Also, the only condition to the payment of the benefits, Earl's retirement, is entirely within his control. However, "if the court concludes that because of uncertainties affecting the vesting or maturation of the pension that it should not attempt to divide the present value of pension rights, it can instead award each spouse an appropriate portion of each pension payment as it is paid." (In re Marriage of Brown, supra, 15 Cal. 3d at p.848. . . .) In this case, the pension benefits have already vested and matured. There are no "uncertainties affecting . . . vesting or maturation" that could lead the trial court to conclude that distribution of the pension must be delayed. Therefore, the trial court abused its discretion when it refused to order the immediate distribution of this vested and mature retirement benefit.

Earl's claim that he is being forced to retire misses the point. He is free to continue working. However, if he does so, he must reimburse Vera for the share of the community property that she loses as a result of that decision. His claim that the court lacks jurisdiction to order him to make payments to Vera because it lacks jurisdiction over his separate property also lacks merit. Earl alone will make the decision to use separate property to reimburse Vera, when and if he decides not to retire. His situation is not unlike that faced by a couple ordered to divide a house that they own as community property. If one of the spouses chooses to keep the house, he or she is free to use separate property to purchase the other's interest. Here, Earl must divide his retirement benefits with Vera. If he does not wish to retire, he must pay her an amount equivalent to her interest.[7]

Earl's suggestion that Vera can be adequately compensated through spousal support is contrary to current law.

> As we have affirmed many times, adjustments in the amount of alimony awarded will not mitigate the hardship caused the wife by the denial of her community interest in the pension payments. Alimony lies within the discre-

---

7. One commentator argues that when an employee who is eligible to retire chooses to continue working, part of his or her salary is actually attributable to community effort.

> [F]rom an economist's perspective, the employee spouse's compensation for continued employment is not the full amount of his paycheck. Rather, his compensation is only that amount above the pension benefits that he will not receive while he continues working. For example, in the matured pension situation, if the employee can receive retirement pay in the amount of X dollars without working, then his actual compensation for services rendered is not the amount of his paycheck, Y dollars, but Y minus X dollars. This is nothing more than a reapplication of the "benefits foregone" formula of *Stenquist* [21 Cal. 3d 779]. Therefore, rather than penalizing the spouse for not retiring, the contrary is true — the community is being penalized because it is forced to subsidize the employee spouse's salary, which becomes his separate property. (Note, In re Marriage of Stenquist: Tracing the Community Interest in Pension Rights Altered by Spousal Election, supra, 67 Cal. L. Rev. 856, 879.)

Since this court does not find any taking of separate property, it is not necessary to discuss Earl's constitutional claim.

tion of the trial court and may be modified with changing circumstances: "the spouse 'should not be dependent on the discretion of the court to provide her with the equivalent of what should be hers as a matter of absolute right.'" (In re Marriage of Brown, supra, 15 Cal. 3d 838, 848.)

(In re Marriage of Stenquist, supra, 21 Cal. 3d at p.787, fn. 8.)

Earl asserts that Vera should be required to demonstrate a financial need to justify the immediate distribution of the retirement benefits. However, financial status is not relevant when dividing community property. The courts are statutorily required to divide community property equally. [Family Code §2550.] A court may consider the equities of the parties' financial situations in determining *spousal support,* but only after the community property has been equitably divided. The retirement benefit must first be divided equally. Earl may then renew his motion for a modification of spousal support in light of this new distribution of the community property.[8]

In the past, this court has encouraged trial courts, if feasible, to award all pension rights to an employee spouse, compensating the nonemployee spouse with other community property of equal value. (In re Marriage of Skaden (1977) 19 Cal. 3d 679, 688-689 [139 Cal. Rptr. 615, 566 P.2d 249]; In re Marriage of Brown, supra, 15 Cal. 3d at p.848, fn. 10; Phillipson v. Board of Administration, supra, 3 Cal. 3d at p.46.) This type of a division was not possible here since the trial court severed the issue of retirement benefits from the division of the remainder of the community property. At the time the retirement benefits were to be divided, the community property had already been distributed. As a result, there was no longer any community property which could be offset against the retirement benefits.

Frequently, parties are able to arrive at a reasonable settlement of these issues. . . . For example, the nonemployee spouse may choose to wait, preferring to receive the retirement benefits when the employee spouse actually retires. The nonemployee may thereby ensure some protection for the future and may be able to share in the increased value of the pension plan. . . .[9] However, if the nonemployee spouse chooses to receive immediate payments, as Vera does, he or she has a right to do so. Any inequities caused by the immediate distribution of retirement benefits can be resolved through adjustments in spousal support.

There are various ways in which Earl could compensate Vera. He could "buy out" her share of the retirement benefits, paying her the present value of her share of the pension plan. . . . Or, he could begin to pay her a share of the retirement payments on a monthly basis. . . . Both of these methods of payment constitute an equal distribution of the benefits. However, the parties may have preferences based on numerous factors not presently before this court, including the tax consequences of the alternative plans. Therefore, the exact method of distribution must be left to the discretion of the trial court on remand.

---

8. "Of course, the [respondent] spouse may seek a prospective modification of his or her support payments in light of any new partition of an asset not previously adjudicated." (Henn v. Henn (1980) 26 Cal. 3d 323, 332. In. 8 [161 Cal. Rptr. 502, 605 P.2d 10].)

9. The nonemployee spouse, of course, cannot have it both ways. The decision to ask for distribution of the retirement benefits before the employee spouse actually retires "constitutes an irrevocable election to give up increased payments in the future which might accrue due to increased age, longer service and a higher salary." (In re Marriage of Luciano, 104 Cal. App. 3d at p.961 [164 Cal. Rptr. 93 (1980)], citation omitted.) Thus, if Vera chooses to receive her share of the retirement benefits immediately, she will forfeit her right to share in the increased value of those benefits in the future.

That portion of the trial court's order denying Vera's request for the immediate distribution of her share of Earl's retirement benefits is reversed. The cause is remanded to the trial court for further proceedings consistent with the views expressed in this opinion.

TOBRINER, J., MOSK, J., RICHARDSON, J., NEWMAN, J., BARRY-DEAL, J., and KONGSGAARD, J., concurred.

Notes and Questions

1. In California community property terminology, how would you describe Earl Gillmore's telephone company pension? Why has Earl not yet retired?

If Vera were required to wait for distribution until Earl retires, would she receive less in actuarial terms? (Is the analysis described by the court in footnote 7 persuasive? Note that the court reports the commentator's argument in footnote 7 but does not approve or adopt it. The reasons are suggested in footnotes 4 and 9.) If Vera would not receive less actuarially, is *Stenquist* apposite? If not, what is the issue in *Gillmore?*

2. Does *Gillmore* substantially infringe Earl Gillmore's personal autonomy by treating him as though he were retired when he is not in fact? If so, is this an undesirable result? We will encounter the question of personal autonomy again when we consider professional goodwill and education.

3. Both *Brown* and *Gillmore* imply, in dictum, that a separated or divorced employee may always quit his job and, without liability, defeat his spouse's interest in an unvested pension. Does this proposition survive the holding of *Gillmore?* If the vested/nonvested distinction is dead for recognition and classification purposes and Earl Gillmore cannot postpone Vera's receipt of benefits by his voluntary, unilateral action, may an employee-spouse quit a job before his pension vests and entirely defeat the other spouse's interest?

Consider Marriage of Foster, 180 Cal. App. 3d 1068, 222 Cal. Rptr. 446 (1986). After 28 years in the Navy and Fleet Reserve, Johnnie Foster resigned from the Reserve, forfeiting his retainer pay and his right to receive retirement pay upon completing 30 years of service. In his letter of resignation, he stated that he did so "due to the State of California's obsessive desire that I share a portion of my Naval Fleet Reserve retainer pay with my ex-spouse as community property." Having been awarded 43 percent of these benefits in the divorce decree, his former wife Betty sought to impose a constructive trust upon Johnnie in order to recover her share of the value of the forgone benefits. The court of appeal agreed with Johnnie that a constructive trust was unavailable because Johnnie had "not obtained the unjust advantage or enrichment which necessarily underlies a constructive trust (Civ. Code §§2223, 2224)." Id. at 1074. The court effectively allowed Johnnie to do whatever he liked with his naval benefits so long as he was not unjustly enriched at Betty's expense. The court emphasized that Betty assumed the risk of Johnnie's perverse behavior by accepting a decree that provided her with a prospective benefit rather than an immediate distribution. The notion that Betty *chose* this risk is odd because the court acknowledged that it had no basis in the record and because a spouse does not have the power to demand as of right an immediate distribution of a pension that is not yet mature. *Foster* is difficult to reconcile with *Gillmore*. Earl Gillmore was not enriching himself at Vera's expense; she simply wanted her share now, not later. Vera was not deemed to have accepted the risk that Earl might

decline to retire when she "accepted" a postponed rather than an immediate distribution. It is not clear whether Betty's stumbling block was her substantive claim or
her choice of remedy. Could she have sought a remedy other than a constructive
trust? Cf. Marriage of Beltran, reprinted at page 419 infra. Would subsequently
amended Family Code sections 1100(e) and 1101(a), (g), and (h) have helped
Betty?

4. *Gillmore* has been followed in a number of states. See, for example, Morlan
v. Morlan, 720 P.2d 497 (Ala. 1986); Koelsch v. Koelsch, 148 Ariz. 176, 713 P.2d
1234 (1986); Wallace v. Wallace, 677 P.2d 966 (Haw. App. 1984); Dewan v. Dewan,
399 Mass. 754, 506 N.E.2d 879 (1987); Marriage of Brooks, 767 S.W.2d 358 (Mo.
App. 1989); McDermott v. McDermott, 123 Misc. 2d 355, 474 N.Y.S.2d 221 (1984).

NOTE: THE IMPACT OF FEDERAL REGULATION OF PRIVATE SECTOR PENSIONS ON STATE MARITAL PROPERTY DISTRIBUTION

The Employee Retirement Income Security Act (ERISA), 29 U.S.C. §1001 et
seq. (2002), was intended to cure two pervasive problems in American private sector
pension plans: inadequate funding and management, and unduly long vesting periods. ERISA now permits two vesting options: total vesting of accumulated employer contributions when the employee completes five years of employment, or
graduated vesting from the third through the seventh year of employment. After
a pension has vested, even if the worker subsequently quits or is discharged, he
will receive pension benefits when he reaches retirement age. (Additional years of
employment do, of course, increase the amount of the benefits.) Thus, ERISA tends
to reduce the frequency of valuable *unvested* pensions at divorce. Compare Marriage
of Brown, supra, where Robert's pension had not yet vested after more than 24
years of employment.

After enactment of ERISA, some divorcing workers argued that the Act's anti-
attachment provision preempted state law marital property divorce distribution of
private sector ERISA-regulated pensions. (For further discussion of federal preemption see Chapter 12.) Congress addressed this issue in the Retirement Equity Act
of 1984, by providing that ERISA's anti-attachment provision does not apply to a
"qualified domestic relations order" (QDRO). A QDRO is a state court order relating to marital property rights, alimony, or child support that satisfies certain formal requirements and creates or recognizes an alternate payee's right to all or a
portion of an employee's pension benefits. 29 U.S.C. §1056(d)(3) (2002).

After receiving a QDRO, the ERISA-regulated private sector pension plan administrator must distribute pension benefits according to its terms. In general, the
QDRO may not alter the amount or form of benefits payable by the pension plan.
Nevertheless, the Retirement Equity Act anticipates and resolves the *Gillmore* problem by providing that a QDRO may require a plan to pay benefits to an alternate
payee, including a spouse or former spouse, when the participant reaches the earliest retirement age even though the participant has not yet retired. Payments to the
alternate payee are to be made as though the participant had retired at the earliest
retirement age. Effectively, the plan is required to bifurcate the pension. 29 U.S.C.
§1056(d)(3)(E) (2002). ERISA does not, however, cover *public* pensions. Thus a

divorce court may not order a public pension plan to make an ERISA/*Gillmore* payout. Instead, a *Gillmore* payout order must be directed against the public employee spouse. Marriage of Jensen, 235 Cal. App. 3d 1137, 286 Cal. Rptr. 911 (1991); Marriage of Nice, 230 Cal. App. 3d 444, 281 Cal. Rptr. 415 (1991), rev. denied 9/19/91.

There are two prominent exceptions to this general rule about public pensions. In 1988, the California Government Code was amended to provide ERISA-style bifurcated *Gillmore* accounts for divorced California state employees. Cal. Gov. Code §21290 (2002). In the same year the California Education Code was similarly amended to provide ERISA-style bifurcated *Gillmore* treatment for State Teachers' Retirement System pensions. Cal. Educ. Code §22652 (2002). In discussion of *Jensen* and *Nice,* commentators suggested the desirability of some California statutory equivalent of ERISA for *all* public sector pensions. See, for example, 8 Cal. Fam. Law Monthly 238 (1992) and 7 Cal. Fam. Law Monthly 484 (1991).

In 1992, the legislature enacted chapter 431 (S.B. 2018), amending Civil Code section 4800.8, now Family Code section 2610. Chapter 431 was apparently intended as a negative response to the commentators' suggestions. It effectively provides that public pension plans shall not be required to perform ERISA-style *Gillmore* bifurcation unless they are already otherwise required to do so under state law or under the terms of the plan. As such, this legislation seemed superfluous. It did not alter existing law.

Yet chapter 431 was drafted much more broadly than necessary to affirm the status quo. It ostensibly prohibits a divorce court from making an order that will secure ERISA bifurcation of *private* sector pensions. Section (b)(2) provides: "A court shall not make any order that requires a retirement plan to . . . make the payment of benefits to any party at any time before the member retires, except as provided [for California government employees and teachers], unless the plan so provides." In section (b)(2), the California legislature inadvertently repudiated the ERISA resolution of *Gillmore* claims for private sector pensions. (But query whether ERISA preempts chapter 431 with respect to private sector ERISA-regulated pensions. See Chapter 12.) Despite the language of chapter 431, Senator Calderon, the bill's sponsor, did not intend to reach *private* sector pensions. (Telephone conversation of November 12, 1992 with Kelly Jensen, legislative aide to Senator Charles Calderon.) Senator Calderon's legislative staff planned to remedy this error by reading into the Senate record a statement of legislative intent. 9 Cal. Fam. Law Monthly 150 (1992).

2.   Business and Professional Goodwill

a.   As Property Subject to Division

Problem

After he and his wife decided to drop out of graduate school in 1994, Gene opened a San Francisco restaurant called The Golden Sutra. A skilled craftsman, Gene built all the furnishings by hand and decorated the restaurant attractively. An excellent cook, Gene developed a menu he labeled "tantric cuisine," which he taught the kitchen staff to cook. He purchased a stereo system and carefully selected albums. Located in a middle-class residential neighborhood, the restaurant was an immediate success. Many patrons dined there several evenings a week. By the fourth year, after paying all his expenses and paying himself a going managerial salary, Gene was netting $50,000 per year. Then Gene began to tire of the restaurant. He had been a classics scholar and wanted to take a long trip to Greece and Turkey. So in 1998, he and his wife decided to look into the possibility of selling out. Their accountant estimated the value of all the tangible assets at $25,000. They advertised the restaurant and within several weeks had received a firm offer of $200,000.

Notes and Questions

1. Why did the prospective buyer offer $175,000 more than "book value," that is, the value of the existing tangible assets? How did she arrive at the price of $200,000? Reconstruct her financial analysis.

2. Accountants generally apply the label *goodwill* to the difference between a buyer's offer and the substantially lower value of the assembled tangible assets. Consider the following discussion of goodwill:

FRED M. ADAMS, IS PROFESSIONAL GOODWILL DIVISIBLE COMMUNITY PROPERTY? 6 Comm. Prop. J. 61, 62-63 (1979):* . . . Although definitions of goodwill are far from uniform,[4] some general definitions may be formulated. One of the early and narrowest definitions of goodwill was expressed in 1810 by Lord Eldon.[5] He said simply that "goodwill" is the probability that old customers will resort to the old place of business.[6] This definition is similar to that announced in the California Business and Professional Code, which states, "The 'goodwill' of a business is the expectation of continued public patronage."[7] The most widely cited definition of goodwill is that of Justice Story:

> [G]oodwill may be properly enough described to be the advantage or benefit, which is acquired by an establishment, beyond the mere value of the capital stock, funds, or property employed therein, in consequence of general public patronage and encouragement, which it receives from constant or habitual customers, on account of its local position, or common celebrity, or reputation for skill or affluence, or punctuality, or from other accidental circumstances or necessities, or even from ancient partialities or prejudices.[8]

Another definition asserts that goodwill is simply the difference between book value and market value.[9] The more common definitions, however, tend to follow that of Justice Story.[10]

Finally, it should be noted that there are two concepts which must be distin-

---

*Reprinted with permission of Aspen Publishers, Inc., © 1979.

4. "Accountants, writers of accounting, economists, engineers, and courts have all tried their hands at defining goodwill. . . . The most striking characteristic of this immense amount of writing is the number and variety of disagreements reached." J. Canning, The Economics of Accountancy 28 (1929).

5. Cruttwell v. Lye, 17 Ves. R. 335, 346, 34 Eng. Rep. 129. 134 (ch. 1810).

6. Id.

7. Cal. Bus. & Prof. Code §14100 (West 1964).

8. J. Story, Commentaries on the Law of Partnerships, §99, at 170 (6th ed. 1868).

9. E. Hendricksen. Accounting Theory, 345 (8th ed. 1969): W. Meigs, C. Johnson, T. Keller, & A. Mosich. Intermediate Accounting, 442 (2d ed. 1969).

10. In re Marriage of Foster, 42 Cal. App. 3d 577, 581, 117 Cal. Rptr. 49, 51, an expert witness testified that "Goodwill is value that somebody built up . . . [i]t is part of the business; it is separate from the accounts receivable and in addition thereto."

guished: "goodwill" and "going concern value."[11] As one commentator has noted, "in discussing the problems of valuing goodwill, the courts have frequently used the terms 'goodwill' and 'going concern value' interchangeably without tendering a reasoned explanation of their difference."[12] The difference is important, however, and a distinction is essential. We have noted that "goodwill" is the built-up value of one's business beyond the value of his capital stock, funds, or property.[13] "Going concern value" has been defined as "the amount by which the value of the [tangible] assets as a whole, assembled together for the conduct of business, exceeds the aggregate of the assets taken separately."[14] Thus, when speaking of "going concern," one is dealing with the value of the assets as a whole, while when speaking of "goodwill," one is dealing with the value of the business above the value of the assets as a whole. . . .

3. Does the $175,000 goodwill component encompass all the goodwill Gene has developed? Why not? How faithful can the new owner expect Gene's patrons to be?

4. Suppose that the new owner asks Gene to stay on for six months as the manager, and the going salary for managers of similar restaurants is $3,500 per month. How much should the new owner offer Gene?

5. Assuming Gene is happy with the restaurant and does not wish to sell it, if he and his wife were to divorce, do you have any objection to recognizing the goodwill as a community asset? Are we forcing Gene to continue to work in that restaurant? (We will shortly consider how goodwill should be valued.)

6. Community property states generally recognize business and professional goodwill developed during marriage as a community asset. There has been some reluctance, however, to recognize goodwill insofar as it inheres in and is inseparable from the person of the spouse. In Nail v. Nail, 486 S.W.2d 761 (1972), the Texas Supreme Court disapproved a trial court award of goodwill in a physician's practice "payable in future monthly installments if, and as long as, the husband practiced his profession" (at 763), and held that professional goodwill is not property subject to division, at least insofar as there is no actual sale of the practice and there does not exist a professional partnership or corporation with goodwill apart from the person of the professional practitioner (at 764). With respect to the latter two exceptions, see, for example, Austin v. Austin, 619 S.W.2d 290, 292 (Tex. Civ. App. 1981) ("Once a professional practice is sold, the goodwill no longer attaches to the person of the professional man or woman. The seller's actions will no longer have significant effect on the goodwill. The value of the goodwill is fixed and it is now property that may be divided as community property"); and Geesbreght v. Geesbreght, 570 S.W.2d 427, 435-436 (Tex. Civ. App. 1978), holding that a medical corporation's goodwill that was not based on the person of the practitioner was divisible as community property:

> "Good will" is sometimes difficult to define. In a personal service enterprise such as that of a professional person or firm, there is a difference in what it means as applied to "John Doe" and as applied to "The Doe Corporation." If "John Doe" builds up a reputation for service it is personal to him. If "The Doe Company" builds up a reputation for service there may be a change in

11. 38 Am. Jur. 2d "Goodwill" §2 (1968).
12. Valuation of Professional Goodwill upon Marital Dissolution, 7 Sw. U. L. Rev. 186 at 187 n.6 (1975).
13. 17 Ves. R. 335, 346, 34 Eng. Rep. 129, 134 (ch. 1810).
14. See note 12 supra and cases cited therein.

personnel performing the service upon a sale of its business as "The Doe Company." The "good will" built up by the company would continue for a time and would last while the new management, performing the same personal services, would at least have the opportunity to justify confidence in such management while it attempted to retain the "good will" of customer clients of the former operators.

Unlike Texas, California and Washington do not limit recognition of professional goodwill. As you read the following cases, contrast the Texas and California/ Washington approaches. With which do you agree?

MARRIAGE OF LUKENS
6 Wash. App. 481, 558 P.2d 279 (1976)

REED, J.—On March 14, 1975. Roberta M. Lukens was granted a dissolution of her marriage to Dr. David L. Lukens. Dr. Lukens appeals from those portions of the Pierce County decree that pertain to: (1) the inclusion of an intangible element of professional goodwill as an asset of his medical practice; and (2) the valuation and division of this intangible as part of the property distribution. We affirm.

The parties were married in August 1965, at which time Mrs. Lukens was teaching school and Dr. Lukens was entering his final year of osteopathic school in Philadelphia. Upon completion of his education Dr. Lukens commenced a year's internship in Grand Rapids, Michigan, and Mrs. Lukens secured employment as personnel manager in a department store. In 1967 the Lukens moved to Tacoma, where they temporarily resided with her parents. Dr. Lukens obtained his license to practice in December of 1967 and immediately associated with another osteopath under a salary-bonus arrangement. Mrs. Lukens resumed school teaching in September of 1968 and remained with the University Place School District until June 1970. In 1972 Dr. Lukens established his own practice, which he still maintained and operated at the time of the dissolution. The new practice was financed with a loan, which was repaid in 1973 by withdrawing $21,000 from the parties' joint savings account. Mrs. Lukens also participated in the organization of the new practice: she maintained the personnel records, established office procedures, including a bookkeeping system, hired the office workers, and aided in the design of the office. She continued to help with the office administration until she filed for a dissolution in 1974.

Dr. Lukens enjoys a large clientele and his practice has been very successful, averaging over $50,000 net income per year. He employs a registered nurse, a full-time secretary-receptionist, and a part-time office worker. The trial court found that his practice consists of physical assets including an X-ray machine valued at $16,000, accounts receivable valued at $33,600, and cash in the amount of $6,200. The trial court also found an element of professional goodwill and valued it at $60,000, bringing the total worth of his practice to $115,800. It is the $60,000 item that is the subject of this appeal.

Dr. Lukens contends that professional goodwill has no market value and that it is therefore not subject to disposition in a dissolution proceeding. The questions presented in this appeal require consideration of the nature of goodwill, and an examination of the means by which goodwill contributes to the economic profits of the professional practice.

Goodwill is property of an intangible nature and is commonly defined as the expectation of continued public patronage. . . .

Goodwill is most often associated with commercial ventures. Nevertheless, it is recognized that the practice of an attorney, physician, or other professional person may include such an element, even though the goodwill in such instances is personal in nature and not a readily marketable commodity. See, e.g., 6A A. Corbin, Corbin on Contracts §1393 (1962); Lockhart v. Lockhart, 145 Wash. 210, 259 P. 385 (1927); In re Marriage of Lopez, 38 Cal. App. 3d 93, 113 Cal. Rptr. 58 (1974); Golden v. Golden, 270 Cal. App. 2d 401, 75 Cal. Rptr. 735 (1969). Factors contributing to professional goodwill include the practitioner's age, health, past earning power, reputation in the community for judgment, skill, and knowledge, and his comparative professional success. In re Marriage of Lopez, supra at 68.

The question of whether professional goodwill is an asset that is properly before the court in a dissolution proceeding has received limited discussion. In Nail v. Nail, 486 S.W.2d 761, 52 A.L.R.3d 1338 (Tex. 1972), it was recognized that professional goodwill is not fixed or localized, but rather attaches to the person of the professional man or woman as a result of confidence in his or her skill and ability. *Nail* found that goodwill does not possess value or constitute an asset separate and apart from the professional and his ability to practice his profession, and that in the event of his death or retirement, it would be extinguished. The Texas court went on to conclude that the goodwill of a medical practitioner was an expectancy wholly dependent upon the continuation of existing circumstances, that it was without value because there was no assurance it would prove beneficial in the future, and that it was not property subject to division under a divorce decree. Nail v. Nail, supra at 764.

A different line of authority has developed in California. In In re Marriage of Foster [42 Cal. App. 3d 577, 117 Cal. Rptr. 49 (1974)], the court did not adopt the rationale of *Nail,* but instead focused on the fact that subsequent to a marriage dissolution the professional practice continues to benefit from the same goodwill that it possessed during the marriage. Recognizing that the goodwill remains intact and is not affected by a marriage dissolution, the court found that it was an asset whose value should be accounted for in the property division. See also In re Marriage of Lopez, supra; Golden v. Golden, supra.

In the instant case, Dr. Lukens takes the position adopted in *Nail* and argues that as a sole practitioner any goodwill associated with his practice is personal, unmarketable, and without value. He emphasizes the personal nature of his goodwill by pointing out that all income produced in his practice is derived solely from his individual labor, and that if he should cease to practice, his goodwill will not generate any income on its own.

While we do not disagree with the doctor's argument that his goodwill is not readily salable, we do not think it follows a fortiori that his goodwill is without value. The fallacy of Dr. Luken's argument is demonstrated by resort to common experience. The recently graduated young professional who goes into business for himself may reasonably expect the initial years of his practice to be less profitable, this expectation being attributed in part to a lack of goodwill or "that the old customers will resort to the old place." See, e.g., In re Marriage of Foster, supra at 52. Similarly, if Dr. Lukens were to abandon his Tacoma practice and relocate as a sole practitioner in another state, he also should anticipate a shortage of business, even though his practice consists of the same physical assets and he presumably possesses the same degree of skill. Again the difference must be attributed to his not having developed in his new locale a reputation as to skill, efficiency, and the other elements comprising goodwill.

Accordingly we do not think the dispositive factor is whether Dr. Lukens can sell his goodwill. His goodwill has value despite its unmarketability, and so long as he maintains his osteopathic practice in Tacoma he will continue to receive a return on the goodwill associated with his name. The fact that professional goodwill may be elusive, intangible, and difficult to evaluate is not a proper reason to ignore its existence in a proper case, In re Marriage of Lopez, supra at 67, and once its existence and value are ascertained, professional goodwill along with the other assets of the professional practice, should be included in a property division. See Berg v. Berg, 72 Wn. 2d 532, 434 P.2d 1 (1967). . . .

The judgment is affirmed. PETRIE, C.J., and HALE, J. Pro Tem., concur.

Petition for rehearing denied January 4, 1977. Review denied by Supreme Court May 25, 1977.

b. Valuation of Professional Goodwill at Dissolution of the Community

i. Introduction

FRED M. ADAMS, IS PROFESSIONAL GOODWILL DIVISIBLE COMMUNITY PROPERTY?*
6 Comm. Prop. J. 61, 70-72 (1979)

Valuation of professional goodwill upon dissolution of the marriage generates much more uneasiness than the initial question of whether professional goodwill is community property. It has been said that, "[a]ccountants, writers on accounting, economists, engineers, and the courts have all tried their hands at . . . proposing means of valuing [goodwill]. The most striking characteristic in this immense amount of writing is the number and variety of disagreements reached."

Many methods of valuation have been proposed. These include the capitalization approach, a fair market valuation, the buy-sell agreement, and simply letting the [fact finder] treat the determination as a question of fact. . . .

The capitalization approach, which is similar to the method used by the Internal Revenue Service in valuing goodwill for tax purposes,[61] is simply a capitalization of the net earnings of the professional business.[62] . . .

The capitalization method of valuation is generally favored by the spouse of

---

* Reprinted from *Community Property Journal.* Vol. 6. pp.61-72 with permission of Aspen Publishers, Inc., © 1979.

61. A business' goodwill is measured by its net earnings. Since its value is the capitalized value of earnings in excess of a fair return on tangible assets and other invested capital, the Treasury finds this value by:

    (1) determining the average net earnings for a representative period preceding the valuation date, usually not less than a 5-year period;

    (2) deducting from these earnings an amount representing a fair return on the average tangible assets for the same period, usually from 8%-10% depending on the riskiness of the business (the greater the risk, the higher the return); and

    (3) capitalizing the difference on the basis of an appropriate percentage, usually 15%-20%, though higher percentages have been approved for higher-risk businesses and lower rates for non-fluctuating businesses.

34 Am. Jur. 2d "Valuation of Property" §8976 (1978), citing Rev. Rul. 68-609, 1968-2 CB 327.

62. U. So. Cal. Tax. Inst., 382 (1975).

the professional because he or she desires the highest valuation possible. Generally, the testimony of an accountant is the only testimony available. Even by using a low multiple one can come up with a higher valuation than the market value approach (what a willing buyer would pay for the goodwill) will produce.[65] However, it has been pointed out that this method could be counterproductive where the multiple yields such a high figure that the judge rejects the testimony entirely as calling forth too great a burden on the professional spouse. Immoderate valuation is more likely to alienate the judge and to cause him to accept the professional spouse's more conservative valuation.[66] . . .

ii. Capitalization of Excess Earnings

MARRIAGE OF FOSTER
42 Cal. App. 3d 577, 117 Cal. Rptr. 49 (1974)

MOLINARI, P.J. — In this dissolution of marriage proceeding the primary question presented on appeal is whether the trial court used a proper method of evaluating the goodwill attributable to appellant's medical practice. It is conceded by appellant that any goodwill attributable to his medical practice is community property. A determination by us that a proper evaluation method was used by the trial court requires that we decide whether the evidence is sufficient to support the lower court's evaluation.

Commencing in August 1966 appellant became associated with Dr. Smalley in a medical practice in Willits, California, at a compensation which included a monthly salary of $1,750 and an additional sum of $100 per month for car expense. This association continued for approximately nine months when appellant and Dr. Smalley formed a partnership for the practice of general medicine. On January 1, 1971, the partnership was incorporated as the "Willits Medical Group." The corporation was dissolved in August 1971 and Dr. Smalley and appellant went their separate ways, each to pursue an individual medical practice in Willits. On June 1, 1972, appellant opened a new office location. It contained 3,500 square feet occupied by four examination rooms, one baby room, one minor surgery room, one physical therapy room, one consultation room, one waiting room and a visitor's office. Appellant regularly employed 4 persons and worked between 50 and 60 hours per week. He made hospital calls every day and sometimes twice a day.

The testimony concerning the value of the goodwill of the medical practice was conflicting. Donald Heller, an accountant whose qualifications as an expert were stipulated to, testified that he had examined appellant's financial records and that in his opinion the value of the goodwill was $27,000. On direct examination Heller was asked to explain "some of the ways available to determine the fair value of goodwill of a medical practitioner." Heller stated that "One way is to take the net income for the year and subtract from that what a comparable employer [*sic*] would have as a salary in a comparable situation, and take that difference, and multiply that by a factor anywhere from, one year factor of anywhere from two to

---

65. U. So. Cal. Tax. Inst., 382, 384, 385 (1975).
66. Id.

ten." He testified further that "You can take the net earnings of the business, one year's net earnings of the business. You can take two years net earnings of the business. You can take three years net earnings of the business. You can take three months charges to accounts receivable. You can take three months receipts on accounts receivable."

Heller testified further that there is no definite method by which the value of goodwill can be determined and that it is "always just somebody's opinion." When queried as to how he arrived at the figure of $27,000 he stated he applied "these methods" and took into consideration other factors such as the facts that Willits is a small town and appellant's office was near a hospital. Finally, he stated as follows: "Mathematically I took the approximation of three months received on account, latest three months that I had, because some of the other ways I felt were resulted in a figure that was too high."

On cross-examination Heller was asked what he meant by "goodwill." He replied: "Goodwill is value that somebody has built up. . . . it is part of the business: it is separate from the accounts receivable, and is in addition thereto." When asked if he was representing to the court that appellant could find a buyer who would pay $27,000 in addition to the other assets, Heller said "not necessarily." He explained that if appellant continued in his practice, his business had a value of $27,000 in excess of tangible items, but that it depended on how long appellant let the practice "sit," whether he abandoned it, or whether he passed away. He said he had no opinion as to whether appellant could obtain $27,000 for goodwill from a buyer, but stated he would receive an amount for goodwill if he sold the practice. Heller reiterated that the $27,000 valuation for goodwill did not mean that appellant could obtain that sum by selling the medical practice and that he had no opinion as to the amount of money that could be obtained for goodwill upon a sale.

Appellant testified that the goodwill of his medical practice had no value as of July 31, 1972, the date that the parties separated. The trial court found that as of this date the goodwill of appellant's medical practice had a value of $27,000.

The specific issues tendered on this appeal are whether a proper method of evaluating goodwill was used by Heller and whether the evidence is sufficient to support a finding that the value of the goodwill of appellant's medical practice was the sum of $27,000. . . .

In a divorce case it is well established that the goodwill of a husband's professional practice as a sole practitioner is taken into consideration in determining the community property award to the wife. (In re Marriage of Fortier, 34 Cal. App. 3d 384, 388-389 [109 Cal. Rptr. 915 (1973)]; Golden v. Golden, 270 Cal. App. 2d 401, 405 [75 Cal. Rptr. 735] [1969]. . . .) Since a community interest can only be acquired during the time of the marriage the value of the goodwill must exist at the time of the dissolution and that value must be established without dependence on the potential or continuing net income of the professional spouse. (In re Marriage of Fortier, supra, 34 Cal. App. 3d 384, 388.)

Adverting to the question of valuation, we observe the rule that when goodwill attaches to a business its value is a question of fact. (Burton v. Burton, 161 Cal. App. 2d 572, 576-577 [326 P.2d 855 (1958)]; Mueller v. Mueller, 144 Cal. App. 2d 245, 251-252 [301 P.2d 90 (1956)].) The courts have not laid down rigid and unvarying rules for the determination of the value of goodwill but have indicated that each case must be determined on its own facts and circumstances and the evidence must be such as legitimately establishes value. . . . In establishing value of goodwill opinion evidence is admissible but is not conclusive. . . . The trier of fact may also take into consideration the situation of the business premises, the amount of patronage, the personality of the parties engaged in the business, the length of time the business has been established, and the habit of its customers in continuing to patronize the business. (See Burton v. Burton, supra, at pp.576-577.)

In *Fortier* we find the following statement: ". . . the value of community goodwill is simply the market value at which the goodwill could be sold upon dissolution of the marriage, taking into consideration the expectancy of the continuity of the practice." (34 Cal. App. 3d 384, 388.) This definition appears to restrict the value of goodwill in a dissolution of marriage proceeding to the value which a willing buyer would pay for the community goodwill at the dissolution of the marriage. Such a limitation would require that there be adduced evidence to this effect. We do not perceive such a rule to be the thrust of *Fortier.* In that case there was evidence that the husband had paid between $2,500 and $3,000 for goodwill when he purchased his associate's interest in 1965: that in 1969 when he took in an associate the amount of $10,963 was agreed upon as the amount the new associate would forego for a period of time before he became an equal partner; and that when the marriage was dissolved in 1971 the value of the community goodwill was testified by experts and the parties to range from nothing to $300,000. The trial court found the aforementioned amount of $10,963 to be the value of the goodwill of the business.[3] In affirming the judgment the reviewing court observed that ". . . where there has been an arm's length sale of such interest (goodwill) and there is no showing of collusion or unfair dealing to the detriment of an interested party, the price paid can be said to be *persuasive evidence* of the value of that goodwill." (Italics added.) (34 Cal. App. 3d at p.388.) Accordingly, the trial court concluded that ". . . it cannot be said that where respondent [the husband] was willing to pay, and did pay, between $2,500 and $3,000 for the goodwill in 1965 there was no evidence to support the court's conclusion that $10,963 was not reasonable." (34 Cal. App. 3d at pp.389-390.) There is nothing in *Fortier* therefore, which restricts the method of evaluating goodwill to market value.

The value of community goodwill is not necessarily the specified amount of money that a willing buyer would pay for such goodwill. In view of exigencies that are ordinarily attendant a marriage dissolution the amount obtainable in the marketplace might well be less than the true value of the goodwill. Community goodwill is a portion of the community value of the professional practice as a going concern on the date of the dissolution of the marriage. As observed in *Golden,*

> . . . in a matrimonial matter, the practice of the sole practitioner husband will continue, with the same intangible value as it had during the marriage. Under the principles of community property law, the wife, by virtue of her position of wife, made to that value the same contribution as does a wife to any of the husband's earnings and accumulations during marriage. She is as much entitled to be recompensed for that contribution as if it were represented by the increased value of stock in a family business. (270 Cal. App. 2d 401, 405.)

In sum we conclude the applicable rule in evaluating community goodwill to be that such goodwill may not be valued by any method that takes into account the

---

3. The trial court apparently treated said sum of $10,963 as being the equivalent of a price paid for goodwill.

post-marital efforts of either spouse but that a proper means of arriving at the value of such goodwill contemplates any legitimate method of evaluation that measures its present value by taking into account some past result. Insofar as the professional practice is concerned it is assumed that it will continue in the future.

In the present case respondent's expert witness testified as to the methods that could be used in computing the value of goodwill and as to some of the considerations which would enter into the valuation of appellant's medical practice. Heller stated he used one of these methods in arriving at his valuation of the goodwill. This method of valuation did not take into account the future efforts of appellant or his future earnings, but took into account past earnings and projected these into the present value of the goodwill, taking into consideration the expectancy of the continuity of the medical practice. This formula of valuation was accepted by the court and Heller's testimony provided sufficient evidence to support the sum of $27,000 as the valuation of the goodwill.

Appellant argues that the record is unclear as to the method of valuation used by Heller. We do not perceive the lack of clarity urged by appellant. In any event, assuming that it was not exactly clear which of the various methods were used by him in arriving at the $27,000 valuation, it is clear that at least one of these methods was utilized. Heller stated that the traditional methods of valuation produced a valuation higher than $27,000 and that he used a method giving a lower figure because he felt it was more appropriate.

The appeal from the order denying a new trial is dismissed; the judgment is affirmed. SIMS, J., and ELKINGTON, J., concurred.

A petition for a rehearing was denied November 14, 1974, and appellant's petition for a hearing by the Supreme Court was denied December 18, 1974.

Notes and Questions

1. What method did Heller, the accountant, use in *Foster*? A more lucid explanation is found in Mueller v. Mueller, 144 Cal. App. 2d 245, 252, 301 P.2d 90 (1956):

> The testimony of George Harbinson, a certified public accountant called as a witness by respondent, was to the effect that good will of the so-called personal services businesses can be determined . . . by ascertaining the average net income over a period of years, subtracting the portion allocable to salary and by capitalizing the difference. . . . The figure which Mr. Harbinson arrived at . . . was $34,578.15.

2. Why do courts insist that goodwill may not be valued by any method that takes into account the future earnings of either spouse? After all, what is goodwill? On the other hand, what difficulty may arise if we measure goodwill by postseparation, as opposed to marital, earnings?

iii. Market Valuation

MARRIAGE OF FORTIER
34 Cal. App. 3d 384, 109 Cal. Rptr. 915 (1973)

STEPHENS, J. — [A]ppellant wife and respondent husband were married in Michigan in 1952. At the time of the marriage, Dr. Fortier had just graduated from medical school and was resident physician in Michigan for approximately one year thereafter. Mrs. Fortier worked as a choral music supervisor in Detroit and then as a public relations personnel employee for American Blower Corporation. They moved to Colorado, where the doctor was a resident doctor at Colorado State Hospital and his spouse worked as a teacher in junior high school, and then in a real estate office. When the couple moved to Springville, California, the doctor had a residency occupation for two years and Mrs. Fortier worked as a switchboard relief operator at the hospital and did some technical typing for the director of the hospital; she also directed a junior youth group for the local church, as well as giving piano lessons. The doctor served two years in the Army Medical Corps and was stationed at the Denver Fitzsimmons Army Hospital. In 1958, the Fortiers returned to California and the doctor entered private practice as an internist in Alhambra, in association with another doctor. Mrs. Fortier worked as a bookkeeper full time in the medical office for a few months and part-time thereafter for some eight years. In about 1965, the associate relationship under which Dr. Fortier had practiced terminated due to the retirement of the other doctor, and at that time Dr. Fortier purchased all of the interest in the equipment as well as the goodwill of his associate.[1] Dr. Fortier (hereinafter, respondent) thereafter worked at his medical practice until, by a written partnership agreement dated January 17, 1969, he was joined by a Dr. Cifarelli.

On July 14, 1969, Mrs. Fortier (hereinafter, appellant) instituted proceedings for dissolution of marriage. On September 21, 1971, the trial court entered an interlocutory judgment of dissolution which, among other things, awarded to appellant the custody of the couple's three children, ordered respondent to pay certain amounts of spousal and child support, and evaluated and divided the community property. In particular, the trial court made a finding of fact that the goodwill of respondent's medical practice was a community property asset and fixed the value of that goodwill at $10,963.

On appeal, appellant's sole contention is that the trial court used an incorrect method of evaluating the goodwill of respondent's medical practice and as a consequence erroneously undervalued the couple's community property by approximately $284,000, and that there was no evidence to support the judgment as rendered. We disagree.

The trial court explained its method of evaluating the goodwill in its memorandum of intended decision:

> The medical practice involved in this case had goodwill which is a valuable asset. To the court the value of this asset is its market value; what a willing buyer would pay for it. I cannot believe the goodwill of a medical practice upon divorce means one thing, and upon a sale of the business means another. . . .
>
> In this case the court feels the value of the goodwill was established when

---

1. Dr. Fortier testified: "In asking me to buy him out, he says. 'I have all this equipment here, you know, furniture, chairs, and everything that went into this 2,200 square feet of office,' and he said, 'Give me $5,000 and the whole thing is yours,' and that is what we did. Q. In your opinion, was that the value of the physical equipment? A. It was perhaps worth a little bit less than that, I would say. Q. How much less? A. Oh, perhaps 2,500 to 3,000. Q. That is what it was worth or that is what it was worth less? A. Well, if you say $5,000, of that $5,000. I would say that the equipment in there was perhaps in the nature of $2,500 worth, perhaps $3,000. Q. What was the other $2,000 or $2,500 for? A. Well, you might say that was for the introduction, goodwill, although we didn't thrash the point. I did not argue with him. I was very pleased to have been introduced there."

Dr. Cifarelli became a partner of [respondent]. . . . They dealt at arm's length and agreed on an amount that Dr. Cifarelli would forego for a period of time before he became an equal partner.[2] That amount was $10,963 which the court finds to be the value of the goodwill of this business.

Appellant argues, however, that market value was not the correct method of evaluating the goodwill. Appellant argues that the goodwill should have been measured by any one of the following three different methods employed by her expert witness, one William Eager:(1) if respondent's net yearly income is greater than the net yearly income of like professional practices, then goodwill is: $10 \times$ (respondent's net yearly income − the net yearly income of a like professional practice); (2) goodwill is $4 \times$ (respondent's net yearly income); (3) if respondent's net yearly income is greater than the net yearly income of like professional practices, then goodwill is equivalent to an amount of principal that, when returned at 8 percent interest over a period of time equivalent to the actuarial remainder of respondent's professional career, would create monthly returns of principal and interest in an amount equivalent to the difference between respondent's net monthly income and the net monthly income of a like professional practice. Eager testified at trial that his first method showed respondent's goodwill to be $293,000, his second method showed respondent's goodwill to be $290,000, and his third method showed respondent's goodwill to be $300,000. From this, appellant argues that the actual goodwill of respondent's practice is the average of these three figures, $294,333.

In considering appellant's arguments, we note preliminarily that the goodwill of respondent's medical practice was, in fact, community property. . . .

The difficulty with each of appellant's methods of evaluating that goodwill, however, is that the future income controls in each method valuing the goodwill. Since the philosophy of the community property system is that a community interest can be acquired only during the time of the marriage, it would then be inconsistent with that philosophy to assign to any community interest the value of the post-marital efforts of either spouse.[3] It must be recognized that the value of the goodwill must exist at the time of the dissolution. That value is separate and apart from the expectation of the spouses' future earnings. As we analyze the determination of the existent value of the goodwill applicable in dissolution of marriage actions, that value must be established without dependence upon the potential or continuing net income of the selling doctor. Certainly, where there has been an arm's length sale of such interest (goodwill) and there is no showing of collusion or unfair dealing to the detriment of any interested party, the price paid can be said to be persuasive evidence of the value of that goodwill.

Therefore, since community goodwill may be evaluated by no method that is dependent upon the post-marital efforts of either spouse, then, as a consequence, the value of community goodwill is simply the market value at which the goodwill could be sold upon dissolution of the marriage, taking into consideration the expectancy of the continuity of the practice.

2. By the terms of the partnership agreement, respondent was to "participate in the profits and losses of the partnership business to the extent of 60% and Cifarelli [was to] participate to the extent of 40% until January 1, 1970, after which time the partners [were to] share equally in profits and losses."

3. Our opinion is limited to the evaluation of professional goodwill as a community property asset, and we express no opinion as to whether appellant's evaluation methods may or may not be legitimate accounting tools for evaluating professional goodwill for other, non-community-property purposes.

We have examined each of the cases cited by appellant, and though the early cases of Fritschi v. Teed, 213 Cal. App. 2d 718 [29 Cal. Rptr. 114]. Brawman v. Brawman, 199 Cal. App. 2d 876 [19 Cal. Rptr. 106 (1962)], and Mueller v. Mueller, 144 Cal. App. 2d 245 [301 P.2d 90] can be readily distinguished (as can Todd v. Todd, 272 Cal. App. 2d 786 [78 Cal. Rptr. 131 (1969)]), we feel constrained to accept the holding in Golden v. Golden, 270 Cal. App. 2d 401, 405 [75 Cal. Rptr. 735 (1969)],[4] which opinion emanated from this district and was authored by a recognized authority in the field of community property. We note, however, that in that case no formula was set forth. The problem before us, then, is not whether some formula which was suggested but not accepted by the court *could have been* accepted as a proper means of arriving at the value of the goodwill, but rather: was the formula which the court applied a proper one, and is there evidence to support the court's decision. While it is argued that there is *no* evidentiary support for the formula and figure utilized by the court in the instant case, we disagree. An examination of *Mueller,* supra, shows that the court there recognized that where the professional person "acquired" his initial interest in the business by a purchase, some or all of which was to cover "goodwill," that could establish a "purchase and sales" formula and value. The identical situation is present in the instant case. Here, respondent "purchased" his associate's interest in 1965 and paid for what he described as goodwill. It is illogical to say that in 1969, when he sold a like interest to his new partner, nothing was paid for goodwill.[6] Whether a "silent partner" reference or "sales" reference is used in the instant case, both contemplated respondent's continuing to work. The court heard the value estimates of the experts and parties, which ranged from nothing to $300,000. Certainly, it cannot be said that where respondent was willing to pay, and did pay, between $2,500 and $3,000 for the goodwill in 1965 there was no evidence to support the court's conclusion that $10,963 was not reasonable.

The judgment is affirmed. Kaus, P.J., and Hastings, J., concurred.

Appellant's petition for a hearing by the Supreme Court was denied November 21, 1973.

Notes and Questions

1. Are *Foster* and *Fortier* reconcilable, as both cases suggest? Does *Fortier* merely caution against reliance on postmarital earnings or does it entirely reject any goodwill valuation method that capitalizes marital earnings?

2. Why does the court think it significant that Dr. Fortier in 1965 paid the

---

4. "We believe the better rule is that, in a divorce case, the good will of the husband's professional practice as a sole practitioner should be taken into consideration in determining the award to the wife. Where, as in Lyon [v. Lyon. 246 Cal. App. 2d 519 (54 Cal. Rptr. 829)], the firm is being dissolved, it is understandable that a court cannot determine what, if any, of the good will of the firm will go to either partner. But, in a matrimonial matter, the practice of the sole practitioner husband will continue, with the same intangible value as it had during the marriage. Under the principles of community property law, the wife, by virtue of her position of wife, made to that value the same contribution as does a wife to any of the husband's earnings and accumulations during marriage. She is as much entitled to be recompensed for that contribution as if it were represented by the increased value of stock in a family business."

6. The testimony by respondent to the effect that in 1969 no value was placed on goodwill is not binding upon the court when the existence of goodwill at that time is acknowledged and the purchase price was over and above the physical property value.

retiring doctor $2,500 to $3,000 (but see footnote 1) in excess of the value of the equipment? What bearing does this have on the value of Dr. Fortier's goodwill?

3. How do you imagine Dr. Fortier and Dr. Cifarelli settled on $10,963? That sum aside, what did partnership promise for Dr. Cifarelli? For Dr. Fortier?

4. What does it mean to say that capitalization of excess profits produces a valuation that is "too high"? Why does capitalization usually produce a figure that is much higher than market valuation, that is, the price a buyer would pay?

5. When a court chooses market valuation or capitalization of goodwill, is it simply making a choice between alternative valuation techniques? Or does the method of valuation define the asset that the court is recognizing?

If the latter is true, goodwill recognition and goodwill valuation are synonymous: We define *what* we are valuing by the technique we use for valuation. Nevertheless, for ease of presentation this casebook has followed the usual pattern of presenting recognition and valuation as consecutive and disparate, rather than simultaneous and identical, issues.

6. Readers unfamiliar with business valuation may find the following summary account and illustration helpful. Goodwill is essentially a residual explanation of earnings that cannot otherwise be explained as a return on capital or labor. Dentist Dodge, a sole practitioner in Visalia, has net earnings of $150,000 a year. These earnings are unusually high, even for a sole practitioner, and suggest that Dodge's practice may have considerable goodwill.

How do we figure out whether there is goodwill and, if so, what it is worth? We could have Dodge put his practice on the market or we could look at comparable sales of dental practices. But such market methods tend to reflect the fact that much of Dodge's goodwill may not survive a transfer. Thus, they do not tell us what the goodwill is worth in Dodge's hands.

One way to measure the goodwill in Dodge's hands is to capitalize his excess earnings. First we find out what a person with Dodge's skill, training, and experience could command on the market. What will a dental health maintenance organization pay for Dodge's services, controlling for hours worked per week? Let us assume $80,000 a year. Then we should give Dodge a rate of return on his $100,000 investment in office equipment and furnishings. Giving him 10 percent a year on this investment will add $10,000 to the $80,000 imputed salary. The difference between his net earnings ($150,000) and his return on labor and capital ($90,000) we call "excess earnings" and characterize as a return on goodwill.

So far we have determined that Dentist Dodge has $60,000 annual excess earnings. Now we must reduce this stream of income to present value for community property division. At this point we ask what a hypothetical investor would pay now to purchase this stream of future excess earnings, taking into account the risk of nonrealization as well as the anticipated life of the stream attributable to Dentist Dodge's accumulated goodwill. In so doing, we can look for guidance to market capitalization rates used by investors purchasing comparable *transferable* goodwill. Such capitalization rates generally range from 25 to 50 percent. The choice of a capitalization rate is the most highly contested aspect of goodwill valuation. After we select a capitalization rate, we divide annual excess earnings by the capitalization rate. Suppose, for example, we choose a rate of 30 percent. This yields a present goodwill value of $200,000 ($60,000 ÷ .3).

7. Thinking about goodwill as a function of excess earnings, that is, earnings in excess of the sum of that which the professional would earn (i) in salary and (ii) as a return on the physical capital in his practice, what factors not traditionally

enumerated may contribute to this excess? The most dramatic excess earnings arise not in sole practices but instead among partners in complex professional businesses employing a substantial number of professionally subordinate salaried workers such as nurses, paramedicals, technicians, secretarial workers, paralegals, and legal associates. See, for example, Nehorayoff v. Nehorayoff, 108 Misc. 2d 311, 437 N.Y.S.2d 584 (1981), and Holbrook v. Holbrook, 103 Wis. 2d 327, 309 N.W.2d 343 (Ct. App. 1981).

iv.   Covenants Not to Compete

MARRIAGE OF CZAPAR
232 Cal. App. 3d 1308, 285 Cal. Rptr. 479 (1991)

WALLIN, Associate Justice— . . . Phyllis [appeals from the marital dissolution judgment and] contends the trial court erred in deducting the value of a future covenant not to compete from the value of the family business awarded to William. . . . We conclude the future covenant not to compete was improperly considered and remand for further proceedings. . . .

William filed a petition for marital dissolution in September 1984 to end his 22-year marriage to Phyllis. A major asset of the parties was a business called Anaheim Custom Extruders, Inc., (ACE), a plastic extruding company, which was started by them in 1977. William and Phyllis agree the business is community property.

The parties separated in January 1983. Before separation, William managed, and Phyllis had been employed by, ACE. After separation, William continued to manage ACE. Phyllis also continued to work for ACE until she was fired by William in December 1984. . . . In July and August 1988, the court held a trial on the value of ACE and other reserved issues. The final judgment was entered on May 9, 1989.

The trial court awarded ACE to William and ruled it had a cash value to the community of $494,058. ACE's actual market value was $644,058, but the court concluded that should William sell ACE he would be required to give a covenant not to compete, which diminished the value of the asset to the community. The court valued a covenant not to compete at $150,000 based upon William's prospective loss of earnings and reduced the value of ACE accordingly.

Phyllis contends the trial court erred in reducing the community property value of ACE by the value of a covenant not to compete because the existence of such a covenant is entirely speculative and, in any event, it is community property. The trial court appointed Silvan Swartz as its expert. His report is not part of the record on appeal. He testified that ACE had a market value of $637,518 and that a two-year covenant not to compete, which he valued at $50,000, would be required of William if the business was sold.

In its memorandum opinion the court concluded ACE had a value *to the community* of $494,058, that a four-year covenant not to compete was more reasonable, and that if William were to refrain from competition with ACE for four years, it would impact him financially in the amount of $150,000. Similarly, in its statement of decision, the court found ACE had a cash value of $644,058, which it reduced by $150,000, the financial impact on William of a four-year covenant not to compete.

Other than testimony regarding William's salary and what he could expect to earn in other jobs, the only information supporting the $150,000 figure is an ex parte letter written to the court by a prospective purchaser before the court appointed Swartz as its own expert to value ACE. The letter outlined a prior offer for ACE of $420,000, plus $50,000 per year to be paid to William for a three-year noncompetition agreement and a new offer of $610,000, less any "non-compete funds." However, this letter was not introduced into evidence.

The character of the proceeds of a covenant not to compete, given by a managing spouse as part of the sale of a community business, is an issue of first impression in California. Similarly, our courts have never addressed the question of whether the hypothetical value of such a covenant, given to effectuate a sale, may be considered in valuing the community property interest in the business.[2]

Other community property jurisdictions have addressed both issues. Our sister state cases, when viewed in conjunction with our own decisions valuing community assets, compel the conclusion that the consideration paid for a noncompetition agreement, or the value of that agreement, is the separate property of the covenanting spouse if such a covenant actually has been negotiated as part of the sale of the property. (Carr v. Carr (App. 1985) 108 Idaho 684, 701 P.2d 304; Dillion v. Anderson (Tex. App. 1962) 358 S.W.2d 694; Lucas v. Lucas (1980) 95 N.M. 283, 621 P.2d 500.) However, it is inappropriate when awarding the property to one spouse to reduce the value of the business by the speculative value of a hypothetical noncompetition agreement. (Mitchell v. Mitchell (App. 1986) 104 N.M. 205, 719 P.2d 432; McGehee v. McGehee (La. App. 1 Cir. 1989) 543 So. 2d 1126.)

In Lucas v. Lucas, supra, 621 P.2d 500, the husband and wife owned the stock of a funeral home which the husband operated. To divide the community property upon divorce, the husband sold the stock of the funeral home. As part of the stock sale, the husband entered into an agreement not to compete for 10 years for which he was to receive $10,000 per year as compensation. The court rejected the argument that the payments were additional compensation for the goodwill of the business. The stock had been sold for more than the value of the corporation's assets. The court stated that excess was the amount attributable to goodwill. The separate compensation for the covenant not to compete was the husband's separate property. (Id. 621 P.2d at p.502. See also Carr v. Carr, supra, 701 P.2d at p.310; Dillion v. Anderson, supra, 358 S.W.2d at p.696.)

Mitchell v. Mitchell, supra, 719 P.2d 432, is most analogous to the present case. There the trial court characterized the husband's accounting practice as community property and it was awarded to the husband. The value of the goodwill was listed at $153,968. The husband argued that the goodwill of his practice should have been characterized as a covenant not to compete and therefore, under *Lucas* should be his separate property. The appellate court affirmed, noting that goodwill is the

---

2. In re Marriage of Lotz (1981) 120 Cal. App. 3d 379, 174 Cal. Rptr. 618 raised these issues but is not dispositive. There the court valued the goodwill of a community business at $319,000 and specifically found that a covenant not to compete would be required of the husband, to whom it was awarded, if he sold it. The husband challenged the court's valuation, contending it impermissibly took into consideration his post marital efforts, i.e., his future noncompetition. While reversing on other grounds, the appellate court stated simply that there was no error in this finding because the court was not requiring the husband not to compete, but "simply evaluating the . . . goodwill by taking into account the commercial reality that such a covenant is normally included in the sale [of such a] business." (Id. at p.383, 174 Cal. Rptr. 618.) There is nothing in the opinion to suggest the court either increased or decreased the community value of the asset as a result of this finding.

value of the business in excess of its hard assets, and went on to state that unlike the goodwill of a business, a covenant not to compete cannot be valued until the business is sold. "A covenant not to compete should be viewed as an asset which is part of the value of a business *only when such a covenant is negotiated and received* by the business. . . . When a buyer insists on a noncompetition agreement, he or she is seeking to preserve the goodwill. . . . In cases such as this one, a hypothetical covenant not to compete should not be valued on divorce but should be viewed as a possible means to protect the value of the business' goodwill." (Id. 719 P.2d at pp.438-439, italics added. See also McGehee v. McGehee, supra, 543 So. 2d at p.1128.) In other words, the covenant not to compete is simply a means for protecting the value of the business goodwill. Until such a covenant has actually been negotiated, in light of the needs of the buyer and the seller, it is too speculative.

The *Lucas* and *Mitchell* cases are persuasive in view of our state's decisions rejecting speculative factors when valuing community assets. For example, it is improper to take into consideration the tax consequences of an order dividing a community asset unless the tax liability is immediate and specific and will arise in connection with the division of the community property. (See In re Marriage of Fonstein (1976) 17 Cal. 3d 738, 749, fn. 5, 131 Cal. Rptr. 873, 552 P.2d 1169. . . .) The courts have also held that the value of a community asset, such as a family home, should not be reduced by the costs of sale of the asset when the court has awarded the home to one party and there is no evidence that party intends to or is required to sell the home. (In re Marriage of Stratton (1975) 46 Cal. App. 3d 173, 119 Cal. Rptr. 924. . . .)

Here the trial court awarded the business to William. There was no evidence that a sale was required in order to meet his payment obligations to Phyllis. Neither was there evidence that a sale of ACE would occur at any time in the future. The court reasonably concluded that, as a commercial reality, a future buyer would probably require William to give a covenant not to compete. However, any number of scenarios could occur in which a sale or transfer of the business would not require such a covenant or in which the covenant would not have the value which the court placed on it. The court based the value of the covenant on what William could expect to earn for the four years following a sale, a total of $150,000. If William sold the business because he was retiring or had somehow become incapacitated, certainly the covenant would not have the same value. (See In re Marriage of Rives (1982) 130 Cal. App. 3d 138, 151, 181 Cal. Rptr. 572.)

Establishing a value for a future covenant not to compete, separate from the value of the business goodwill itself is entirely too speculative. "[O]nce having made [an] equal division [of community property], the court is not required to speculate about what either or both of the spouses may possibly do with his or her equal share and therefore to engraft on the division further adjustments reflecting situations based on theory rather than fact." (In re Marriage of Fonstein, supra, 17 Cal. 3d at p.749, 131 Cal. Rptr. 873, 552 P.2d 1169.) If ACE is ever sold it will be William's decision affecting his separate property. The true value of a possible covenant not to compete can only be determined with reference to his circumstances at that time. Reducing the community value of ACE by the covenant's speculative value was error. . . .

The judgment is reversed with respect to the valuation of ACE. . . . The matter is remanded to the trial court for further proceedings in accordance with the opinion. Phyllis is entitled to her costs of appeal.

CROSBY, Acting P.J., and MOORE, J. concur.

Notes

1. For further discussion of the *Fonstein* rule that courts may not reduce community property valuation by future tax liabilities unless the liabilities are immediate and specific, see pages 509-515 infra. Is the tax liability rule apt for covenants not to compete?.

2. More basically, is the dictum of *Czapar* persuasive? Do you agree "that the consideration paid for a noncompetition agreement, or the value of that agreement, is the separate property of the covenanting spouse if such a covenant actually has been negotiated as part of the sale of the [community] property"? Why may the purchaser of community property goodwill require a covenant not to compete? What is the purpose of the covenant? For criticism of the *Czapar* dictum, see 8 Cal. Fam. L. Monthly 81 (1991).

Cases agreeing with the dictum of *Czapar* that the value of a covenant not to compete relating to postdissolution labor of a spouse is that spouse's separate property include Marriage of Quay, 18 Cal. App. 4th 961, 22 Cal. Rptr. 2d 537 (1993), review denied; Johnston v. Johnston, 778 S.W.2d 674 (Mo. Ct. App. 1989) (trial court did not abuse discretion in excluding value of covenant not to compete in valuing dental practice); Hoeft v. Hoeft, 600 N.E.2d 746, 749 (Ohio Ct. App. 1991); Ellerbe v. Ellerbe, 473 S.E.2d 881 (S.C. Ct. App. 1996); Cutsinger v. Cutsinger, 917 S.W.2d 238 (Tenn. Ct. App. 1995); and Marriage of Monaghan, 899 P.2d 841 (Wash. App. 1995). Cases disagreeing with the dictum of *Czapar* and holding that the value of a covenant not to compete incident to the sale of a community (or marital) property business is also community property include Carr v. Carr, 701 P.2d 304, 309 (Idaho Ct. App. 1985); Reese v. Reese, 671 N.E.2d 187, 192 (Ind. Ct. App. 1997) (a restrictive covenant not to compete which is signed in conjunction with the sale of a business represents the goodwill of that business absent evidence to the contrary); McGhee v. McGhee, 543 So. 2d 1126, 1128 (La. Ct. App. 1989); Lord v. Lord, 454 A.2d 830, 834 (Me. 1983). See also Jewel Box Stores v. Morrow, 158 S.E.2d 840, 845 (N.C. 1968) (the execution of covenant not to compete, in connection with the sale of business, is essentially sale of business goodwill).

    v. Buy-out Agreements

MARRIAGE OF SLATER
100 Cal. App. 3d 241, 160 Cal. Rptr. 686 (1979)

TAYLOR, P.J. — On this appeal by the wife from an interlocutory judgment of dissolution, the contention [is] that the court erred by . . . setting a value of zero on the goodwill of the husband's group medical practice pursuant to the withdrawal provision of the partnership agreement. . . . We have concluded that the judgment must be reversed for a redetermination of the value of the husband's interest in the group medical practice. . . .

The record reveals the following pertinent facts: The parties were married in February 1958 and separated in December 1975, after 17 years, 10 months and 7 days. The wife was awarded custody of their three children, born respectively in 1960, 1962 and 1966, and husband ordered to pay child support of $250 a month per child until emancipation, majority or further order of the court. The husband, a gynecologist, had been practicing in a partnership (Hayward Medical Group) since 1954. The wife was unemployed and had no professional skills or work experience; she was attending college at the time of the judgment, studying to become a medical librarian or medical records keeper. . . .

The major contention on appeal focuses on the trial court's valuation of the husband's interest in the group medical practice at $31,350. The record indicates that the wife's accountant determined that the husband's interest in the entire medical partnership was worth over $80,000, with $44,000 specifically attributed to goodwill. The husband relied on the partnership agreement signed by both him and his wife, which specifically provided that the husband's partnership could buy back his interest upon his death, withdrawal or expulsion. The relevant portion of the agreement read:

> The purchase price shall be the . . . partner's interest in the capital account . . . plus the total of the accounts receivable less than six months old. . . . Capital account . . . shall mean supplies, inventory, equipment, fixtures, cash, securities . . . excepting accounts receivable. . . . The partners mutually agree that *a portion of the purchase price as determined above includes the sale of their interest in the goodwill of the partnership* and in the event of their withdrawal or expulsion from the partnership that they will not enter into the practice of medicine in that portion of Alameda County . . . for a period of three years (italics added).

The parties stipulated that at the time of the dissolution, the husband's share of the capital account was $6,100 and his share of the accounts receivable, less than six months old, was the sum of $25,250, or a total of $31,350. The husband and his witnesses indicated that the goodwill was nonexistent as far as the partnership was concerned. Goodwill was considered to be in the accounts receivable which a partner forfeited upon withdrawal. We reject the husband's irrelevant contention that the wife was bound by the terms of the agreement that she cosigned. The agreement was not signed for purposes of the dissolution.

As indicated above, the trial court found that the value of the husband's medical practice was $31,350. The record indicates that the court concluded that it could not value the goodwill on a different basis because "if he [husband] left the partnership . . . he would not receive that goodwill." Thus, the record indicates that the trial court felt constrained to value the husband's interest in the partnership as a withdrawal right with a goodwill of zero. However, the asset being divided in the proceeding was the husband's interest in the partnership, not his contractual withdrawal rights. His interest in the partnership was an interest in a going business analogous to pension rights (In re Marriage of Fonstein, 17 Cal. 3d 738, 745-746 [131 Cal. Rptr. 873, 552 P.2d 1169]).

The trial court's declaration is readily understandable since, as this court (Div. One) noted in In re Marriage of Foster, 42 Cal. App. 3d 577, at page 583 [117 Cal. Rptr. 49]: "The courts have not laid down rigid and unvarying rules for the determination of the value of goodwill but have indicated that each case must be determined on its own facts and circumstances and the evidence must be such as legitimately establishes value. . . ."

In *Foster,* supra, 42 Cal. App. 3d 577, this court also cautioned at page 584:

The value of community goodwill is not necessarily the specified amount of money that a willing buyer would pay for such goodwill. In view of exigencies that are ordinarily attendant a marriage dissolution the amount obtainable in the marketplace might well be less than the true value of the goodwill. *Community goodwill is a portion of the community value of the professional practice as a going concern on the date of the dissolution of the marriage.* As observed in Golden [v. Golden, 270 Cal. App. 2d 401, 405 (75 Cal. Rptr. 735)],". . . in a matrimonial matter, the practice of the sole practitioner husband will continue, with the same intangible value as it had during the marriage. Under the principles of community property law, the wife, by virtue of her position of wife, made to that value the same contribution as does a wife to any of the husband's earnings and accumulations during marriage. She is as much entitled to be recompensed for that contribution as if it were represented by the increased value of stock in a family business" (italics added).

It does not follow, however, that the trial court was required to adopt the $44,400 figure provided by the wife's accountant. The record indicates that the wife's accountant valued the goodwill of the husband's practice "as an accounting concept." For purposes of a marital dissolution, the parties are primarily concerned with the existence, value and consequences of goodwill in an economic sense, as distinguished from legal or accounting concepts. The expectancy of future earnings is not synonymous with, nor shall it be the basis for determining the value of the goodwill of a professional practice (In re Marriage of Lopez, 38 Cal. App. 3d 93, 108-109 [113 Cal. Rptr. 58]). The same is true of the future contingencies, such as withdrawal, expulsion or death. The value of the contractual withdrawal right *may provide a basis* for ascertaining the value of the community interest (cf. Marriage of Fonstein, supra, 17 Cal. 3d at p.745); however, it does not preclude a consideration of other facts.

The record also indicates that the wife's accountant erroneously included some of the husband's postdissolution earnings. As this court (Div. One) held in *Foster,* supra, 42 Cal. App. 3d, at page 584:

> In sum we conclude the applicable rule in evaluating community goodwill to be that such goodwill may not be valued by any method that takes into account the post-marital efforts of either spouse but that a proper means of arriving at the value of such goodwill contemplates any legitimate method of evaluation that measures its present value by taking into account some past result. Insofar as the professional practice is concerned it is assumed that it will continue in the future.

Thus, we can only conclude that the judgment must be reversed for a corrected evaluation of the husband's interest in the group medical practice. . . .

The trial court's decision is reversed for a reconsideration of the value of the husband's interest in his medical partnership. If necessary, the trial court may admit additional evidence on this issue.

Rouse, J. and Miller, J., concurred.

Respondent's petition for a hearing by the Supreme Court was denied February 14, 1980.

Notes and Questions

1. Accord: Marriage of Morris, 588 S.W.2d 39, 43-44 (Mo. Ct. App. 1979). See also Suther v. Suther, 28 Wash. App. 838, 627 P.2d 110, 113-114 (1981); Rogers v.

Rogers, 296 N.W.2d 849 (Minn. 1980); Marriage of Moffatt, 279 N.W.2d 15 (Iowa 1979) (buy-out agreement not dispositive in valuing closely held corporation for marital property purposes). But see Holbrook v. Holbrook, 103 Wis. 2d 327, 309 N.W.2d 343 (Ct. App. 1981).

2. Ignoring a buy-out agreement is consistent with a capitalization approach to goodwill. In contrast, if market valuation is a decision-maker's preferred approach, should an existing buy-out agreement be controlling?

MARRIAGE OF MARRON

170 Cal. App. 3d 151 (1985) (review denied and ordered depublished by the California Supreme Court on Sept. 25, 1985)

KING, J. — In this case we adopt a general rule that the date for valuation of the community property interest in a law partnership, for purposes of division of assets in a marital dissolution, is the date of separation of the parties, not a date as near as practicable to the time of trial. We also hold it is error to value the community interest based upon the value of withdrawal rights contained in the partnership agreement, even though the lawyer spouse withdraws from the law partnership between the date of separation and the time of trial, when withdrawal value does not reasonably reflect the value of the community interest in the law partnership as of the date of separation.

Nancy Marron appeals from the final judgment of dissolution of her marriage to Michael Marron filed June 10, 1981. She contends the trial court erred in valuing the community interest in Michael's law practice. We conclude that the trial court did err in its valuation of the community interest in Michael's practice.

As relevant to the issues on appeal, the facts are that Nancy and Michael separated on December 30, 1976, after a 17-year marriage. Following separation Michael remained in the former family residence while Nancy and their minor children occupied rented housing. Pursuant to court orders, Michael paid temporary and permanent child and spousal support to Nancy plus attorney fees and costs.

Michael, a 1962 graduate of Harvard Law School, joined the law firm of Steinhart, Goldberg, Feigenbaum and Ladar (hereafter Steinhart law firm) as an associate in May 1966. He became a partner on January 1, 1970, under articles of partnership providing that in the event of a partner's withdrawal from the firm, his "withdrawal rights" would be limited to the amount of his capital account plus the undrawn portion of his share of the profits for that year. At separation, Michael had no intention of leaving the Steinhart law firm, however, in 1979, he and other lawyers withdrew from the firm to open their own office. Upon withdrawal, Michael received the balance in his capital account, $26,000, and his undrawn portion of the firm's profits, $7,834, a total of $33,834. He and the other attorneys also took a number of uncompleted cases with them, which had substantial value.

The valuation of the community property interest in the Steinhart law firm is the central issue on appeal. At trial Nancy called Melvin A. Schiller, a certified public accountant, as an expert to testify to the value of Michael's law practice. As part of the basis for his valuation Schiller used the financial statements prepared for the Steinhart law firm by an accounting firm for the years 1974 through 1978. He concluded that the community's interest in the assets of the firm at the end of

December 1976 was $102,531, excluding goodwill. This included Michael's capital account, undrawn profits for 1976, and his pro rata share of unbilled work in progress and accounts receivable, less unpaid liabilities. It also included a share of the value of the physical assets of the firm, the value of the furniture, furnishings, machinery, equipment, law library, supplies and inventory. Schiller separately valued Michael's goodwill in the practice at $56,000.

Stephen Schwartz, an attorney, testified as Michael's expert. Schwartz consulted the same financial statements as Schiller, and also considered the Steinhart articles of partnership. He concluded Michael's interest in the Steinhart law firm was constrained by the statement of withdrawal rights contained in the partnership agreement and he included *only* the value of Michael's capital account, and undrawn profits in reaching his opinion of $33,834 for the community's interest in the firm.

The court found Michael received $33,834 at the time of his withdrawal from the Steinhart law firm, "which represents the community interest in the capital account and his undrawn share of the profits. [Michael] received no other monies from the community interest in said law firm." The court also found that Michael's goodwill interest in the firm at the date of separation was worth $9,982,[3] making the total value of the community's interest in the Steinhart law firm $43,726.

Nancy contends the trial court erred by failing to consider Michael's share of the firm's accounts receivable, work in process and fixed assets, including personal property and supplies inventory, in its valuation of the community interest in his law practice. We hold that the court erroneously excluded these factors.

> [I]n determining the value of a law practice or interest therein, the trial court should determine the existence and value of the following: (a) fixed assets, which we deem to include cash, furniture, equipment, supplies and law library; (b) other assets, including properly aged accounts receivable, costs advanced with due regard for their collectability; work in progress partially completed but not billed as a receivable, and work completed but not billed; (c) goodwill of the practitioner in his law business as a going concern; and (d) liabilities of the practitioner related to his business. (In re Marriage of Lopez (1974) 38 Cal. App. 3d 93, 110 [113 Cal. Rptr. 58], *disapproved on other grounds by* In re Marriage of Morrison (1978) 20 Cal. 3d 437 [143 Cal. Rptr. 139, 573 P.2d 41].)

Moreover, in reaching its valuation the trial court is not bound by the terms of a partnership agreement relating to a partner's withdrawal rights. "The value of the contractual withdrawal right *may provide a basis* for ascertaining the value of the community interest [citation]; however, it does not preclude a consideration of other facts." (In re Marriage of Slater (1979) 100 Cal. App. 3d 241, 246-247 [160 Cal. Rptr. 686]. . . .)

In both *Slater* and *Fenton* [In re Marriage of Fenton, 134 Cal. App. 3d 451, 184 Cal. Rptr. 597 (1982)] the professional spouse argued that the partnership agreement controlled on the question of existence or valuation of a professional

---

3. Since the sole basis of Michael's cross-appeal is that the court erred in finding there was any goodwill because of his withdrawal from the firm, and neither party otherwise challenges the trial court's valuation of goodwill, we need not consider how the court arrived at the figure of $9,982 for goodwill. In the unpublished portion of this opinion we do hold that there was substantial evidence to support a determination that there was goodwill.

practice. In both cases the reviewing court disagreed, stating that the asset being divided was the community interest in the partnership, *not* the professional spouse's contractual withdrawal rights. Therefore, while the court might find that goodwill did not exist under the facts of a particular case . . . , the terms of the partnership agreement were not necessarily controlling on the issue and the court must consider the factors listed in *Lopez* in order to decide the value of a professional practice. . . .

Here the court apparently found itself constrained by the terms of the partnership agreement in valuing every asset of the law partnership *except* goodwill. . . . [T]he court was somewhat ambiguous about what it considered in reaching its valuation. . . .

It appears from the record, however, that the court did fail to consider the factors listed in *Lopez*. While the court acknowledged that Michael's practice had a *goodwill* value over and above his contractual interest on withdrawal, it did *not* consider or include the value of the firm's accounts receivable, unbilled work in process, or personal property, supplies and inventory.

Accounts receivable directly attributable to services performed prior to separation are earnings of the working spouse during marriage and therefore constitute community property. (In re Marriage of House (1975) 50 Cal. App. 3d 578, 580 [123 Cal. Rptr. 451].)

The value of an attorney's unbilled work in process should be apportioned to community and separate property according to the amount of effort performed before and after separation. (Waters v. Waters (1946) 75 Cal. App. 2d 265, 269-270 [170 P.2d 494].) Fixed assets, including cash, furniture, equipment, supplies and law library, represent a portion of the value of a law practice. (In re Marriage of Lopez, supra, 38 Cal. App. 3d at p.110.)

Michael acknowledges that his share of accounts receivable and unbilled work in process existing at separation formed part of the profits he received between the date of separation and his withdrawal from the firm two-and-a-half years later.

The trial court should have considered additional factors listed in *Lopez* in its valuation of the community interest in the law practice. In addition, Michael's earnings and his share in the law practice up to the date of separation, including accounts receivable and unbilled work in process, are community property. Money attributable to services performed by him after the date of separation is his separate property pursuant to [Family Code section 771].[4]

Michael contends the trial court chose to value the practice at the time he withdrew in 1979, rather than at the parties' separation in 1976, since that represented the date "as near as practicable to the time of trial" pursuant to [Family Code section 2552]. He ignores the fact that earnings attributable to services performed after the date of separation, in a professional practice of the type in which he engaged, are separate rather than community property.

The resolution of the proper date for valuation of community interests in most law partnerships requires a reconciliation between [Family Code section 2552] (". . . the court shall value the assets and liabilities as near as practicable to the time of trial . . . ") and [Family Code section 771] (". . . earnings . . . of a spouse . . . while living separate and apart from the other spouse, are the separate property

_____

4. [Family Code section 771] provides: "The earnings and accumulations of a spouse and the minor children living with, or in the custody of, the spouse, while living separate and apart from the other spouse, are the separate property of the spouse."

of the spouse."). With "the enactment of [Family Code section 771], . . . any portion of the law practice assets including goodwill which are attributable to the earnings and accumulations of a spouse living separate and apart are the separate property of the spouse earning or accumulating the same." (In re Marriage of Lopez, supra, 38 Cal. App. 3d at p.110.)

At any given moment the major assets of most law firms are not capital assets, but are those related to the direct rendering of professional services, most particularly accounts receivable and work in process. "Many past and present distinguished California lawyers of initial humble and impecunious beginnings will attest to the fact that it is not ordinarily capital investment by a sole legal practitioner which is the chief contributing factor in the realization of income and profits." (38 Cal. App. 3d at pp.106-107.)

For these reasons we adopt a general rule that in determining the community property interest in law partnerships (including goodwill) in order to divide community property in a marital dissolution action, the proper date of valuation is the date of separation of the parties, not a date as near as practicable to the time of trial. This rule is applicable even though, as here, the lawyer spouse has withdrawn from the law partnership between the date of separation and the date of trial. After all, between those dates, as here, the lawyer spouse will usually have received any balance of accounts receivable and work in process which existed on the date of separation. Additionally, as a matter of public policy the lawyer spouse's unilateral decision after separation to withdraw from his law partnership, a decision in which his spouse has no voice, should not result in a reduction in the value of the community assets to be divided between the spouses.

This will not be a general rule without exceptions. However, exceptions will usually be related to situations where the postseparation efforts of the lawyer spouse have minimal impact upon any increase in the value of the law partnership interest. In some cases the partnership interest in a large law firm (or shareholder interest in a large professional corporation) may be so relatively small that the lawyer spouse's postseparation efforts cannot be considered a significant factor in any increase in the value of the partnership (or professional corporation) between the date of separation and time of trial. (See In re Marriage of Aufmuth, 89 Cal. App. 3d 446 [152 Cal. Rptr. 668 (1979)].) Under these circumstances, it could certainly be argued that the lawyer with a small partnership interest in a 200 member law firm, may be indistinguishable from an executive with General Motors who also owns shares of General Motors stock, and an exception to the general rule should be made to value the interest as near as practicable to the time of trial. In other cases, the formula contained in the partnership agreement for payment upon withdrawal of a partner may also be an accurate method for determining the value of the partnership as a going business as well, or the parties may not dispute the use of the withdrawal formula to determine the value of the partnership interest. (See In re Marriage of Fonstein, 17 Cal. 3d 738 [552 P.2d 1169, 131 Cal. Rptr. 873 (1976)].) . . .

We conclude that the community interest in Michael's law practice should have been determined as of the date of separation and his withdrawal rights, not having been shown to reasonably reflect the value of his partnership at the date of separation, were not controlling. . . .

We affirm the judgment in all respects except as follows: We reverse and remand for retrial the valuation of the community interest in the law partnership, other than goodwill. . . .

Low, P.J., concurred.

HANING, J.—I respectfully dissent. It should not be necessary to wrestle with the inherently defective process of evaluating the goodwill of a professional practice, since in this case there was no such asset to divide. A brief chronology of relevant events bears repeating:

Date of marriage	1959
Husband joins law firm	1966
Date of separation	1976
Dissolution petition filed	1977
Husband leaves law firm	1979
Trial commences	May 1980
Interlocutory Judgment filed	December 1980

It is obvious that by the time of trial the husband had no interest in his prior law firm, and we know exactly what he received for his interest upon his departure therefrom—a total of $33,834.[1] [Family Code section 2550] requires the court, upon dissolution of a marriage, to divide the community property equally. In my opinion that was not done by the trial court, nor will it be accomplished by the majority's decision. The *Lopez* [(1974) 38 Cal. App. 3d 93 (113 Cal. Rptr. 58)], *Fonstein* [(1976) 17 Cal. 3d 738 (131 Cal. Rptr. 873, 552 P.2d 1169)], *Slater* and *Fenton* [(1982) 134 Cal. App. 3d 451 (184 Cal. Rptr. 597)] cases cited by the majority are all readily distinguishable in that they dealt with the evaluation of goodwill in an *ongoing* professional practice. None of the professional spouses in those cases had imminent plans of terminating their practices, nor their interest in the firm, a group or corporation of which they were a member.

By contrast, the husband in the instant case had terminated his interest in his former law firm and had been *fully* compensated for that interest; the amount of that compensation is *undisputed*.[2] In short, for his *entire* partnership interest, goodwill included, the husband received from his former firm a grand total of $33,834. To award the nonprofessional spouse anything more than one-half of this amount results in an unequal division of community assets, with one party receiving hard cash and the other nothing more than, with due apologies to Marcel Proust, a remembrance of things past.

The majority states that "as a matter of public policy the lawyer spouse's unilateral decision after separation to withdraw from his law partnership, a decision in which his spouse has no voice, should not result in a reduction in the value of the community assets to be divided between the spouses." This is an interesting concept if the lawyer husband were receiving something of value not shared with his wife, but in this case he is not. To suggest, however, that a legitimate career change cannot be undertaken without spousal consent except upon payment of tribute, smacks of involuntary servitude. (U.S. Const., Amend. XIII; Cal. Const., art. I, §6.) Whether the spouses are separated or not should not matter, since the decision is or should be that of the professional practitioner alone. It seems to me that a better

---

1. I do not include any value for any uncompleted cases which the husband and the other departing attorneys took with them. No evidence was presented concerning the value of these cases. Assuming they had any value which could be properly classified as a community asset, then they should have been appraised and a finding made thereon.

2. It is important to keep in mind that, insofar as "goodwill" is concerned, we are not dealing with any "individual goodwill" attached personally to the lawyer husband. Rather, we are dealing with his alleged share of the goodwill of a law firm of which he has ceased to be a member.

public policy is to permit doctors, lawyers, accountants and other professionally self-employed individuals the unencumbered freedom to make their own career choices.[3] I would go even further and rule that such freedom is constitutionally protected.[4]

I would affirm the judgment except for that portion dealing with the division of the former partnership interest and the goodwill. As to that I would reverse and remand with instructions to evaluate it in accordance with the undisputed evidence, and award each party one-half of the $33,834 received.

Notes and Questions

1. On a simple accounting, or tracing, level, what is wrong with Michael's argument that his partnership withdrawal agreement accurately establishes the value of the community property interest in his law partnership?

2. Michael further argued that, however the court values his interest in the firm, it may not include any goodwill interest because he has left the firm and, as per the withdrawal agreement, has received no compensation for goodwill (footnote 3). Does the majority respond adequately to this argument? Has Michael, as the court suggests, effectively committed waste by withdrawing from the Steinhart law firm? How do you explain Michael's decision to withdraw, together with other members of the Steinhart firm, and set up a new partnership? Is it likely that Michael lost anything? How might Nancy's attorney have traced the missing goodwill?

3. *Rethinking goodwill.* Having studied the California treatment of goodwill, you may now yearn for the simplicity of the Texas rule, which recognizes goodwill only insofar as it is separable from the person of the spouse who manages the business or professional practice. The ALI Principles adopt the Texas rule:

§4.07   Earning Capacity and Goodwill

(1) Spousal earning capacity, spousal skills, and post-dissolution spousal labor are not marital property.

(2) Occupational licenses and educational degrees are not marital property.

(3) Business goodwill and professional goodwill earned during marriage are marital property to the extent they have value apart from the value of spousal earning capacity, spousal skills, or post-dissolution spousal labor.

(a) Evidence of an increment during marriage in the market value of business or professional goodwill establishes the existence of divisible marital property in that amount except to the extent that market value includes the value of post-dissolution spousal labor.

(b) Business or professional goodwill that is not marketable is nevertheless

3. In the interest of preserving domestic harmony, it may be prudent to obtain spousal approval before exchanging a lucrative neurosurgical practice in Carmel for a chicken ranch in Topeka or a hotdog stand in Buffalo. However, a public policy requiring such consent prior to leaving a partnership and opening one's own practice in the same community is quite another thing, particularly when the professional move is viewed as a gateway to "upward mobility," and the attendant increased earnings which are expected to accompany the move.

4. I refer only to legitimate career moves, and not to the situation where one spouse drops a promising and rewarding career for a life of meditation or wood-chopping merely to avoid lawful obligations of support. In my experience this happens infrequently, and self-interest usually motivates most professionals to continue with their careers.

marital property to the extent a value can be established for it that does not include the value of spousal earning capacity, spousal skills, or post-dissolution spousal labor.

Principles of the Law of Family Dissolution: Analysis and Recommendations §4.07
(2002).

The ALI and the Texas rules are identical, but their context differs markedly.
Texas spousal support law is among the most restrictive in the nation. (See Texas
Fam. Code §§8.001-8.061.) Nevertheless, it reflects the general reluctance of American divorce courts to order spousal support. California's expansive treatment of
goodwill may be understood as a counterpoint to an ungenerous law of spousal
support. The ALI, in contrast, replaces spousal support with potentially generous
"compensatory spousal payments." Consider Comment (a) to §4.07 of the Principles:

Comment:

   *a. Earning capacity and the relation between property and compensatory pay-
ments.* Section 4.07 provides that spousal skills and earning capacity are not
divisible property. An increment in spousal earning capacity during marriage
therefore creates no property claim. Relative earning capacity is nonetheless
relevant at divorce because it can give rise to a claim for compensatory payments. . . . Chapters 4 [property division] and 5 [compensatory spousal pay-
ments] reflect a common policy of recognizing the validity of spousal claims
on one another's earning capacity by compensatory payments rather than by
characterizing that earning capacity as marital property. The two Chapters are
thus interdependent. The rationale for each depends in part on the other's
resolution of this common policy question.
   "Earning capacity" has no meaning or existence independent of the
method used to measure it. It is generally measured by finding a present value
for all or some part of the individual's future earnings, and is thus no more
than a shorthand term for that present value. A rule characterizing earning
capacity as marital property is a rule treating future earnings as marital property, which in operation requires that those earnings be estimated at divorce
so that their present value can then be fixed and allocated between the
spouses.
   Traditionally, however, spousal claims on post-divorce earnings were
made under the rubric of alimony, an equitable remedy that Chapter 5's compensatory payments are designed to replace. A major purpose of Chapter 5
is to reconceive alimony in a form that provides a more reliable and consistent
remedy, in cases of disparate earning capacity, than is offered by the existing
law. It is likely that the historical unreliability of the alimony remedy is an
important reason why some potential alimony claimants recast their claim on
post-marital earnings into property terms. The ease with which any income
flow can be described as a property interest of equivalent value facilitates this
strategy. Responsive to the equities in the particular case, some recent decisions effectively treat earning capacity as property. Only a few, however, do
so overtly. . . .
   While property and alimony remedies are financially fungible, they have
different procedural and substantive traditions that bear on the kind of claims
best treated under each. These traditions explain why courts that confront
the question directly usually decline to treat earning capacity as property. The

approach taken by this section is thus consistent with prevailing American law, while the equitable concerns that motivate the minority view are addressed by the entitlements to compensatory payments set forth in Chapter 5.

Procedurally, alimony awards are exercises of continuing equitable authority and typically remain modifiable, while a division of marital property is an ordinary civil judgement and therefore final and nonmodifiable. The finality and nonmodifiability that are critical to adjudications of property ownership make these judgements poor instruments by which to allocate future spousal earnings. Not only may the earnings of the former spouses vary in unpredictable ways, but also spousal claims on one another's post-dissolution income are properly affected by some post-dissolution events, such as the obligee's remarriage. . . .

3.   Professional Degrees and Licenses[4]

MARRIAGE OF SULLIVAN
37 Cal. 3d 762, 691 P.2d 1020, 209 Cal. Rptr. 354 (1984)

Bird, C.J. — Is a spouse, who has made economic sacrifices to enable the other spouse to obtain a professional education, entitled to any compensation for his or her contribution upon dissolution of the marriage?

Janet and Mark Sullivan were married in September of 1967. The following year, Mark (respondent) entered medical school at Irvine and Janet (appellant) began her final year of undergraduate college at UCLA.

Appellant gives the following abbreviated account of the ensuing years. From 1968 through 1971, respondent attended medical school. Until 1969, appellant worked part-time while completing her undergraduate education. After graduation, she obtained a full-time position which she held through 1971.

In 1972, respondent began his internship at Portland, Oregon. Appellant gave up her full-time job to accompany him there. Shortly after the move, she obtained part-time employment.

The couple's daughter, Treisa, was born in May of 1974. Appellant ceased work until 1975 when she resumed part-time employment. From 1976 through 1977, she worked full-time. During this period, respondent completed his residency.

Both parties then moved back to California. Shortly afterward, they separated. In August 1978, respondent petitioned for dissolution of the marriage.

During the marriage, the couple had accumulated some used furniture and two automobiles, both with payments outstanding. This property was disposed of by agreement. Appellant received $500, some used furniture and her automobile, including the obligation to complete the payments.

At the dissolution proceeding, appellant sought to introduce evidence of the value of respondent's medical education. She argued that the education was obtained by the joint efforts and sacrifices of the couple, that it constituted the greatest asset of the marriage, and that — accordingly — both parties should share in its benefits.

4. See also Chapter 1.

The superior court rejected these arguments and granted respondent's motion . . . to exclude all evidence pertaining to the value of the education. At the same time, the court granted partial summary judgement to the effect that respondent's education did not constitute community property. The court indicated that it was barred from awarding appellant any compensation for her contribution to respondent's education by the rule of In re Marriage of Aufmuth (1979) 89 Cal. App. 3d 446, 461 [152 Cal. Rptr. 668] (professional education does not constitute community property).

In May of 1980, the court issued its interlocutory judgement of dissolution. Appellant was awarded no spousal support, but the court reserved jurisdiction for five years to modify that determination. The parties were awarded joint custody of their daughter. Respondent was ordered to pay appellant $250 per month for child support and to reimburse her for half the cost of the child's medical insurance. . . .

[JANET] appealed.

This court originally granted a hearing in this case primarily to determine whether a spouse, who has made economic sacrifices to enable the other spouse to obtain an education, is entitled to compensation upon dissolution of the marriage. While the case was pending before this court, the Legislature amended the Family Law Act to provide compensation in all cases not yet final on January 1. 1985. (Stats. 1984, ch. 1661. §§2-4, No. 8 Deering's Adv. Legis. Service, pp.717-719.)

The amendments provide for the community to be reimbursed, absent an express written agreement to the contrary, for "community contributions to education or training of a party that substantially enhances the earning capacity of the party." (Civ. Code, §4800.3 [now Family Code §2641], added by Stats. 1984, ch. 1661, §2, No. 8 Deering's Adv. Legis. Service, p.717.) The compensable community contributions are defined as "payments made with community property for education or training or for the repayment of a loan incurred for education or training." (Ibid.) The reimbursement award may be reduced or modified where an injustice would otherwise result. (Ibid.)[5]

In addition to providing for reimbursement, the amendments require the court to consider, in awarding spousal support, "the extent to which the supported spouse contributed to the attainment of an education, training, or a license by the other spouse." (Civ. Code, §4801 [now Family Code §4320], *as amended by* Stats. 1984, ch. 1661, §3, No. 8 Deering's Adv. Legis. Service, p.718.)

NEED CLARIFICATION

Since the property settlement in the present proceeding will not be final on January 1, 1985 (see Cal. Rules of Court, rule 24(a)), appellant is entitled to the benefit of the new amendments. (Stats. 1984, ch. 1661, §4, No. 8 Deering's Adv. Legis. Service, p.719.) The trial court did not, of course, make the findings necessary to determine whether and in what amount reimbursement and/or support should be awarded under these provisions since they were not in existence at that time. Accordingly, the judgment denying any compensation for contributions to education must be reversed. . . .

The judgment denying compensation for contributions to spousal education is reversed and the cause remanded for further proceedings consistent with the views expressed in this opinion. Appellant to recover costs on both appeals.

---

5. The text of the reimbursement provision (Family Code section 2641) appears in the statutory supplement, infra, at page 680.—ED.

KAUS, J., BROUSSARD, J., REYNOSO, J., and GRODIN, J., concurred.

MOSK, J. — While I agree this matter should be returned to the trial court for consideration in the light of recent legislation. I fear that inappropriate language in the majority opinion may mislead the bench and bar. Several times in the majority opinion — indeed, in framing a question at the outset — there is reference to "compensation" for contributions to education. I must assume the repetition of that term was calculated and not inadvertent.

At no place in the relevant legislation does the word "compensation" appear. With clarity and precision, the Legislature referred instead to "reimbursement." The terms are not synonymous; there is a significant distinction that extends beyond mere semantics. Reimbursement implies repayment of a debt or obligation; that is what the Legislature obviously contemplated. Compensation, on the other hand, may be payment in any sum for any lawful purpose; the Legislature also obviously did not intend to give such a blank check to trial courts.

Furthermore, the majority, in their creative reference to "compensation," fail to emphasize to whom it is to be paid. It is not to an individual spouse, in response to the initial query of the majority. The Legislature was crystal clear: reimbursement is to be made to the *community*. The community consists of both the husband and the wife, not one or the other. Thus when reimbursement is made to the community, that reclaimed community asset should be divided between the husband and wife in the same manner as all other community property.

I point out that the issue framed in this case does not involve the element of spousal support. That is to be awarded generally on the basis of the needs of one spouse and the ability of the other to pay, although a number of other factors may be considered. (Civ. Code, §4801 [Family Code §4320].) The only issue raised by the appellant in these proceedings is whether acquired knowledge and education are a species of property subject to monetary division. The Legislature has now answered that question in the negative.

To review the legislation, Civil Code section 4800.3 [Family Code section 2641], subdivision (b)(1), provides "The *community* shall be *reimbursed* for community contributions to education or training of a party that substantially enhances the earning capacity of the party. The amount *reimbursed* shall be with interest. . . ." Subdivision (c) provides "The *reimbursement* and assignment required by this section shall be reduced or modified. . . ." Subdivision (d) is even more precise: "*Reimbursement for community contributions and assignment of loans pursuant to this section is the exclusive remedy of the community or a party* for the education or training and any resulting enhancement of the earning capacity of a party." (Italics added.)

One searches in vain in the statute for a single use of the word "compensation." Thus I find it curious that the majority choose to employ that term rather than to consistently adhere to "reimbursement," the only monetary claim authorized by the Legislature. I trust that trial courts will not be misled into making awards of any sums for any purpose other than that permitted in what the Legislature described with remarkable emphasis as "the exclusive remedy."

Notes and Questions

1. In terms of recognition as property subject to distribution at divorce, does professional education differ from professional goodwill in any significant way? Janet Sullivan appealed to the California Supreme Court in order to press her claim

that Mark's professional education be treated as divisible community property. If the legislature had not intervened, how do you think the California Supreme Court, as constituted in 1984, would have ruled on Janet's claim?

2. As we have seen so far, the California legislature has, by default, generally left to the judiciary the task of determining whether any given asset ought to be characterized as property subject to division. This allocation of legislative authority has been equally characteristic of other community property and equitable distribution states. Nevertheless, professional education generated a good deal of California legislative activity. Assembly Member Alister McAlister first proposed a broad provision for community property recognition of all gains in earning power during marriage, A.B. 525 (1983-1984 Regular Session). One version of this bill (as amended June 13, 1983) was restricted to dissolution of marriages into which a child had been born or adopted. (Shades of the fee simple conditional abolished in 1285 by the Statute De Donis Conditionalibus.) The last version of A.B. 525 (as amended January 5, 1984) eliminated the procreative requirement and shifted ground from property division to a lump-sum spousal support remedy "to avoid unjust enrichment when a party has enhanced . . . his or her earning capacity during the marriage." Unless an enumerated variety of equitable factors indicated otherwise, augmentation of earning capacity was the measure of the lump-sum support award. Unlike other court-ordered support, such lump-sum awards were to be nonmodifiable except that the death of either party would terminate amounts still owing and not yet due. Why support rather than property division?

A.B. 525 did not pass. Shortly after its demise, Assembly Member Elihu Harris introduced a more modest proposal, A.B. 3000, which was enacted in 1984. It added Civil Code section 4800.3, now Family Code section 2641, which allows reimbursement to the community for community contributions to education or training that substantially enhances the earning power of a spouse. Family Code section 2641 also requires that any loan incurred during marriage for education or training be assigned to the educated party as his separate debt, thus excluding it from the equal division of assets and liabilities. Reimbursement and debt assignment are explicitly designated the exclusive property division remedies, and the court may reduce or modify either remedy according to enumerated equitable considerations. The law also amended the spousal support provision, now Family Code 4320, by adding a new factor to the list that the court shall consider in evaluating a request for spousal support: "the extent to which the supported spouse contributed to the attainment of an education, training, or a license by the other spouse."

Before you read Marriage of Watt, the next case, study section 2641 and the current version of much-amended section 4320, which are reprinted in the statutory supplement, and then consider the following questions. What does section 2641 include within the term "community contributions to education or training"? Does the term include:

(1) out-of-pocket expenses for tuition and books;
(2) out-of-pocket living expenses for the educated spouse;
(3) opportunity costs of the educated spouse;
(4) opportunity costs of the other spouse?

If you answer this question narrowly by, for example, restricting "community contributions" to out-of-pocket expenses for tuition and books, how would you treat section 2641(b)(2) loans? Is the loan section limited by the definition of "community contributions"?

What is the meaning of "the extent to which the supported party contributed to the attainment of an education" for purposes of section 4320(b) spousal support? Is it the same as the meaning of "contributions to education" for purposes of section 2641 reimbursement?

MARRIAGE OF WATT
214 Cal. App. 3d 340, 262 Cal. Rptr. 783 (1989)

ANDERSON, P.J.—In this dissolution of a career-threshold marriage, we hold that the trial court must consider the totality of one spouse's contributions to the other's attainment of an education, including contributions for living expenses, when making a spousal support award decision pursuant to Civil Code section 4801 [now Family Code section 4320]. We further determine that in applying the spousal support criterion in effect at the time of trial, the court improperly focussed exclusively on the actual marital standard of living, without taking into account the reasons for the low standard. Finally, we hold that reimbursable community expenditures for the student spouse's education under section 4800.3 [now Family Code section 2641] generally do not include ordinary living expenses.

In this marital dissolution action Elaine Watt appeals from the judgment on reserved issues denying her requests for spousal support and reimbursement to the community of funds spent on David Watt's education. . . . We affirm in part and reverse in part.

I.   BACKGROUND

The parties married on June 17, 1972, and separated nine and one-half years later on December 15, 1981. In 1974 they moved to Hawaii so David could continue his studies there. The couple had no children.

David was a full-time student for the entire nine and one-half years of the marriage, advancing from an undergraduate program to postgraduate studies and finally medical school; he received his medical degree five months after separation. Elaine worked full-time during the marriage, using all of her income for family expenses.

For the years 1975 through 1981 (exclusive of 1977, for which we have no information), the parties combined gross income was $81,779.92, of which Elaine contributed $66,923.92 in earnings and David contributed $14,856. David's student loans for the same period totalled $26,642. David used at least $3,000 in loan funds for direct educational expenses (tuition, books, fees), leaving approximately $23,642 for the couple's living expenses.

For the past 17 years Elaine has worked for Kaiser Foundation Hospital (Kaiser), first as a pharmacy clerk and, since 1979, as a pharmacy technician. Following separation, Elaine held two part-time jobs, working sometimes 60 hours per week to meet monthly living expenses. In 1986 she assumed a full-time position at Kaiser.

Elaine became interested in nutrition and culinary arts and started taking cooking classes in 1981. She testified that during their marriage, she talked with David about the possibility of attending school after he finished his education and stated, "that's when I decided I would like to go into culinary arts." Shortly after the couple separated, Elaine borrowed $500 from David's mother to pursue a junior college education in the field of nutrition. After two semesters she abandoned that effort because she could not "make it" working part-time or being on call, and had to take another job. She later repaid the loan.

At trial Elaine explained she would like to enroll in the 16-month program at the California Culinary Academy in San Francisco. Her aspiration is to start her own catering business.

David now is an anesthesiologist with the Permanente Medical Group. In 1987 his annual salary was approximately $94,000. With overtime, his actual income has been much higher.[2]

The parties' marital status was terminated June 18, 1985, with the court retaining jurisdiction over all other matters. The central issues at trial were Elaine's requests for (1) spousal support for her further education and training and also because of need, and (2) reimbursement for community funds spent on David's education. The court ordered David to pay $7,500 in attorney fees on Elaine's behalf, but did not grant her any other relief. Elaine appeals from the judgment. . . .

II.   THE TRIAL COURT DECISION

The trial court issued a detailed statement of decision which included the following findings pertinent to this appeal: (1) the extent to which Elaine contributed to David's attainment of an education, training, career position or license "was minimal to the point of 'de minimis non curat lex'"; (2) Elaine evidenced no need for spousal support, retraining or education to obtain more marketable skills/employment; and (3) the couple's standard of living during the marriage did not exceed Elaine's present standard of living.

The court also found that Elaine's gross income was higher than the income she indicated was "achievable" as a chef and concluded, "a need to change [jobs] has not been shown. . . . [Elaine is] self supporting, beyond the standard of living attained by the parties while married, and in no need of support. . . ."

On the matter of reimbursement for the expenses of David's education, the court determined there were no community contributions which should be reimbursed. Finally, the court ordered David to assume full responsibility for repayment of all student loans (nothing had been repaid during the marriage).

III.   ELAINE'S APPEAL

On appeal Elaine contends the trial court abused its discretion in denying spousal support and erred in ruling that the community made no reimbursable contributions to David's education.

2. Additional pay for the first six months of 1987 totalled $12,114.13.

Elaine's arguments concern interpretation of amendments to the Family Law Act which the Legislature enacted in 1984 to provide for (1) reimbursement of the community's contributions for the education or training of a spouse under specified circumstances and (2) consideration of the nonstudent spouse's contributions to the attainment of that education or training when awarding spousal support. Specifically, the amendments added [Family Code] section [2641], subdivision (b)(1), which mandates that absent a written agreement to the contrary, and subject to certain limitations, "[t]he community shall be reimbursed for community contributions to education or training of a party that substantially enhances the earning capacity of the party." The statute defines compensable community contributions as "payments made with community [or quasi-community] property for education or training or [the] repayment of a loan incurred for education or training." (§[2641], subd. (a).) Additionally, the amendments also amended section [4320], subdivision [(b)], to require the court to consider, when making a spousal support determination, "The extent to which the supported [party] contributed to the attainment of an education, training, a career position, or a license by the [supporting party]."

A. Spousal Support

The Family Law Act [now Family Code] vests broad discretion in the trial court to decide the property of a spousal support award. (In re Marriage of Wilson (1988) 201 Cal. App. 3d 913, 916 [247 Cal. Rptr. 522]. A reviewing court will not disturb this exercise of discretion unless "it can fairly be said that no judge would reasonably make the same order under the same circumstances." (In re Marriage of Sinks (1988) 204 Cal. App. 3d 586, 591 [251 Cal. Rptr. 379]).

Section [4320] establishes the criteria a court must follow in fashioning an appropriate support order. The court must not simply recognize these criteria, it must also apply them in arriving at its decision. (In re Marriage of Fransen (1983) 142 Cal. App. 3d 419, 425 [190 Cal. Rptr. 885].)

Elaine asserts we must reverse the judgment because the trial court based its decision on incorrect legal or factual conclusions about (1) her potential income as a chef; (2) her economic needs; (3) the contributions she made to David's career; and (4) the couple's lifestyle. We discuss each of these concerns and conclude that the lower court did err in applying the third and fourth concerns.

(1)   Retraining

In considering the specific criteria set forth in section [4320], sub-division [(a)(1)], the court concluded Elaine had no need for retraining or education to acquire more marketable skills. In connection with this conclusion the court found that her then-current income was higher than would be "achievable" as a chef. Elaine claims the evidence does not support this finding, and, in turn, the court erroneously determined she did not need retraining.

The evidence shows Elaine's gross annual income to be $26,156.00. The brochure for the California Culinary Academy indicates graduates report an average annual starting salary of $25,000. A newspaper article included in the record states that graduates attaining top executive chef status earn at least $50,000 annually plus a percentage of the business. From the record it is apparent that starting out, Elaine in fact would be no better off economically for completing the program than she is now, although her earning potential might be higher.

Elaine also argues that the court's finding is misleading because the $26,156 is pay for a 60-hour, not a 40-hour week. True, Elaine testified she worked 60 hours a week "on and off" for the last 5 years. She also testified that in 1985 or 1986 she took a full-time job at Kaiser. We do not know when she quit her second job, or how much of the $26,156 would be related to working in excess of a 40-hour week. Further, we do not know how many hours a chef works.

We think the reasonable inference from the facts presented is that the career change anticipated by Elaine would not immediately or necessarily result in a material increase in income and, thus, Elaine did not demonstrate a present need for retraining or education to attain more marketable skills. Substantial evidence supports this conclusion.

(2) Needs

Elaine next urges that the court should have awarded spousal support based on need. The trial court found her monthly net income to be between $1,400 and $1,600, with monthly expenses running approximately $1,400. Under these facts, Elaine was earning just enough to get by.

Elaine disputes the monthly expense finding. Her income and expense declaration filed July 22, 1987, listed monthly expenses of $2,409, as contrasted with $1,359 as of December 17, 1986. During cross-examination, it became apparent that certain items such as rent, transportation and incidentals, although substantially higher on the second statement, either had not changed at all, or had not changed as much. . . .

It appears the trial court in weighing the evidence and, in particular, the discrepancies brought out during cross-examination, chose to accept the earlier financial statement as more accurately reflecting Elaine's true monthly expenses. This is within the province of the trial court, and we conclude that its finding concerning Elaine's monthly expenses is supported by substantial evidence. Thus the court did not abuse its discretion in failing to award spousal support based on need.

(3) Contributions

Elaine additionally argues that the trial court erroneously found she had made a "de minimis" contribution to David's attainment of an education and career position. The evidence shows that all of David's direct, out-of-pocket educational expenses, such as tuition, books and lab fees, were paid for with proceeds from student loans and grants. However, Elaine shouldered approximately 64 percent of the community's living expenses for the period 1975-1981.[5] In dollar terms, she paid $28,426 more than David did — an amount which is not so minimal that the law does not accord it notice.

The court's conclusion is either factually wrong and, therefore, not supported by the evidence, or is based on an interpretation of section [4320] that does not take living expenses into account when examining the extent to which the nonstu-

---

5. Again, this information is exclusive of 1977. Our calculation is based on Elaine's earnings ($66,924) as matched against David's contribution of $38,498 (representing earnings, plus student loan funds available for living expenses).

dent spouse "contributed to the attainment of" the student spouse's education and career.

We begin our analysis by pointing out that the operative section [4320] language is ambiguous because the concept of "contributing to the attainment" of an education is open-ended and nowhere defined in the statutory scheme. As such, the language is subject to conflicting interpretations.

Thus, some discussion of the legislative history of section [4320] is appropriate here. In November 1983, the Assembly Committee on Judiciary held a public hearing on legislative proposals to resolve community property/career asset issues presented in the high profile case of In re Marriage of Sullivan,[6] then pending before the Supreme Court. In that case, Janet Sullivan argued that her husband obtained his medical education by virtue of the couple's joint efforts and sacrifices, it was their greatest asset, and both should share in its benefits upon dissolution. The committee inquired whether existing law allowed for adequate compensation for the spouse who assisted his or her mate in attaining an education. At the hearings, a spokesperson for the California Law Revision Commission (CLRC) discussed the commission's legislative proposal for a reimbursement solution.[7]

Assembly Bill No. 3000 was drafted after the hearings and enacted by the Legislature in August 1984; it incorporated the CLRC proposal and additionally expanded the spousal support criteria set forth in section [4320] to include consideration of the nonstudent spouse's contribution to the student spouse's education or training. Thus, the new legislative scheme afforded two remedies, as appropriate, in cases where one spouse worked to put the other through school: (1) reimbursement and (2) support.

The new spousal support guideline is a companion to, but not duplicative of, the section [2641] right of reimbursement for community contributions to the student spouse's education. (See Hogoboom & King, Cal. Practice Guide: Family Law (Rutter 1989), §§6:88.2-6.88:4, rev. no. 1, 1990.) Although section [2641], subdivision (d), specifically states that reimbursement and loan assignment is the exclusive remedy for the education or enhanced earning capacity of a spouse, it also clarifies that nothing therein "shall limit consideration of the effect of the education, training, or enhancement, or the amount reimbursed . . . , on the circumstances of the parties for the purpose of an order for support pursuant to Section [4320]." Thus Hogoboom and King suggest that a spouse might rely on section [4320] to claim a right to support while pursuing education or training for a new career or better paying job when he or she supported the other spouse through an advanced degree program. (Id., at p.6-91.)

We agree that section [4320], subdivision [(b)], should be interpreted broadly to require consideration of *all* of the working spouse's efforts to assist the student spouse in acquiring an education and enhanced earning capacity. Where the nonstudent helped the student through school and into a higher earning career position, that spouse's contributions should be given weighty consideration by the trial court in deciding the propriety and extent of a spousal support award.

Nothing in the statutory language indicates that one spouse's contribution to the attainment of the other's education or career is limited to direct education expenses. The notion of "contributing to the attainment" of an education is

6. See In re Marriage of Sullivan (1984) 37 Cal. 3d 762 [209 Cal. Rptr. 354, 691 P.2d 1020].

7. Shortly before the hearings, in September 1983, CLRC published its "Recommendation Relating to Reimbursement of Educational Expenses." (17 Cal. Law Revision Com. Rep. (1984) pp.229 et seq.)

broader than the section [2641] concept of "payments made for" education or training. Common sense tells us that more goes into contributing to the attainment of an education than the mere cost of tuition, books and supplies. Many students who seriously pursue education or training forego full-time or even part-time remunerative employment, relying instead on other sources to provide for their necessities of life. Certainly, these other sources contribute to the student's attainment of an education. We thus hold that in the case of a career-threshold marriage where the working spouse provided a far greater share of living expenses while the student spouse acquired a professional degree, section [4320] requires the trial court to consider the totality of the nonstudent's contributions and efforts toward attainment of that degree, including contributions for ordinary living expenses.

Because the trial court either misconstrued the applicability of the section [4320], subdivision [(b)], language, or made a finding contrary to the evidence concerning Elaine's contribution, we conclude the judgment must be reversed insofar as it denied Elaine spousal support.

(4)   Lifestyle

Elaine finally maintains that the trial court also erred in focussing exclusively on the parties' preseparation standard of living, which they *deliberately* maintained at a low level so that David could finish school. In this regard the trial court made a specific finding that "The parties contemplated an upward change in their financial circumstances should Petitioner obtain the necessary credentials, and licensing, in medicine, and should Petitioner thereafter practice medicine." Nevertheless, in applying the section [4320] criterion, the court ignored this finding and instead based denial of spousal support in part on the conclusion that since separation, Elaine had not experienced a lowering of that standard of living which she had attained during the marriage and, indeed, was self-supporting "beyond" that standard.

Pursuant to the language of section [4320] in effect at the time of trial, the standard of living of the parties was but one factor to weigh with other factors when deciding the propriety of an award. It is apparent from the statement of decision that in applying this factor, the trial court proceeded on a straight dollar-for-dollar comparison of marital and postseparation lifestyles. Although the phrase "standard of living of the parties" perhaps at first glance appears unambiguous, our rules of statutory construction teach us that courts should look to the substance rather than the letter of the statute if absurd or unjust results follow from a literal interpretation. (Smith v. Mt. Diablo Unified Sch. Dist. (1976) 56 Cal. App. 3d 412, 420 [128 Cal. Rptr. 572]). Further, we are mindful that whenever possible, courts should give effect to the statute as a whole, including every clause, so that no provision is rendered useless or meaningless. (Code Civ. Proc., §1858; Carleson v. Unemployment Ins. Appeals Bd. (1976) 64 Cal. App. 3d 145, 155-156 [134 Cal. Rptr. 278].)

With these principles in mind it is apparent that the trial court's application (and implied interpretation) of the standard of living factor led to absurd results. Such a dollar-for-dollar analysis ignores the fact that the parties consciously subjected themselves to a student standard of living, on the expectation of future improvement for the community's benefit.

Under these circumstances, the section [4320], subdivision [(b)] factor becomes meaningless in the very instance where it should make a difference. This is because the flip side of the working spouse's contribution to living expenses and the student spouse's attainment of an education is the student's absence from the full-time work force. And that absence, of course, directly impacts the couple's standard of living. The spouse who primarily establishes the marital standard of living by virtue of his or her earnings and continues working after separation will rarely experience a further lowering of that standard. Therefore, if the court only looks at the deliberately depressed marital standard of living in these situations, the working spouse's subdivision [(b)] contributions become irrelevant. We thus conclude that when applying the standard of living criterion to its spousal support determination, the trial court should not have denied spousal support *simply because* there was no dip in Elaine's standard of living after separation. Rather, the court should have taken into account the impact of David's absence from the full-time work force on that standard—an absence which, in reality, only benefited him.

(5) Remand

Since we hold that the trial court improperly exercised its discretion in applying and interpreting the contribution to education and standard of living factors, and since we cannot discern how these errors affected the consideration of other spousal support criteria, we must remand the cause with directions to the trial court to reexercise its discretion, consistent with the principles enunciated herein.[8] . . .

B. REIMBURSEMENT FOR CONTRIBUTION TO HIS EDUCATION

Elaine's second attack concerns the trial court's ruling that there were no reimbursable community contributions to David's education. The record reveals that direct education expenses were paid from loan and grant funds. Elaine asserts that section [2641] does not limit "payments made with community property for education or training" to direct costs, and should be construed broadly with its remedial purpose in mind to include living expenses over the nine and one-half years of marriage.

Section [2641] remedies the injustice that often occurred when a couple separated on the eve of, or shortly after, a spouse's graduation or other educational accomplishment, long before that education could benefit the community. (In re Marriage of Slivka (1986) 183 Cal. App. 3d 159, 167 [228 Cal. Rptr. 76].) Prior to its enactment, there was no right of the community to reimbursement for expenditures made for education or training. The new remedy, however, is not unlimited.

The CLRC comment to section [2641] explains that the purpose of the provi-

---

8. In August 1988 the Legislature once again amended §4801, subdivision (a) [now Family Code §4330] (effective Jan. 1, 1989), to make the standard of living established during the marriage an overreaching reference point against which the court assesses the other spousal support factors. (Stats, 1988, ch. 407, §1, p.1555.) The trial court must also make specific factual findings concerning the appropriate standard. Further, the amendments now require the trial court to generally recognize the extent to which the working spouse contributed to the student spouse's attainment of an education, rather than considering this factor only with respect to the earning capacity of each spouse. [These provisions are now codified at Family Code sections 4320-4339.]

The parties have not briefed the issue of whether the 1988 amendments would apply on remand, and consequently we express no opinion concerning their retroactive application.

sion is to authorize reimbursement of community expenditures for educational expenses that have benefited primarily one party to the marriage. It goes on to state: "Subdivision (a) does not detail the expenditures that might be included within the concept of 'community contributions.' These expenditures would at least include cost of tuition, fees, books and supplies, and transportation." (Cal. Law Revision Com. com., West's Ann. Civ. Code, §4800.3 (1989 pocket supp.) p.95 [Deering's Ann. Civ. Code, §4800.3 (1989 pocket supp.) p.102].)

From this comment, as well as the definition of community contributions to education or training, it is evident that the thrust of section [2641] is to require reimbursement for expenses that are related to the education experience itself. *"ed. experience"* The married couple would incur ordinary living expenses regardless of whether one spouse is attending school, staying home, or working.

Elaine has pursued her reimbursement claim on the theory that section [2641] entitles the community to full reimbursement for *all* its contributions to living expenses over the nine and one-half–year period. She has failed to show what expenses, if any, were specially connected to David's education. There was no evidence produced at trial that the community paid for any education-related expenses, such as tuition, fees, or special living expenses incurred because of the education experience. Based upon such a lack of evidence, we conclude the trial court correctly ruled that the community made no reimbursable contributions pursuant to section [2641]. . . .

Finally, we reject Elaine's suggestion that this court declare David's medical degree community property. Section [2641], subdivision (d), makes it abundantly clear that reimbursement is the *only* remedy in California. The CLRC comment further explains: "Although the education, degree or license or the resulting enhanced earning capacity is not 'property' subject to division, community expenditures for them are properly subject to reimbursement." (Cal. Law Revision Com. com., West's Ann. Civ. Code, §4800.3 (1989 pocket supp.) p.95 [Deering's Ann. Civ. Code. §4800.3m (1989 pocket supp.) p.102].) . . .

The judgment is affirmed in part and reversed in part, with directions to conduct further proceedings consistent with this opinion. David to pay costs on appeal.

CHANNELL, J., and PERLEY, J., concurred.

Notes and Questions

1. Under Family Code section 2641, David Watt was assigned, as his separate debt, the full amount of his outstanding student loans, $26,642. Of the $26,642, $3,000 had been used for direct educational expenses and $23,642 had been spent for the couple's living expenses. Can this result be reconciled with the *Watt* interpretation of section 2641 reimbursable "payments"? In other words, do important differences in treatment turn on whether education is financed by loan or by direct wage contribution? If so, is there any justification for such a difference?

2. If you were representing Elaine Watt, how would you explain the court of appeal opinion to her? Would you characterize it as a victory or a defeat? Would you advise her to pursue her support claim on remand? Before the same trial court judge?

3. Does the California statutory scheme, as judicially construed, respond adequately to Elaine Watt's claims? If not, what sort of response would comport with your sense of justice?

4. *The ALI treatment of professional education.* Chapter 4, Division of Property Upon Dissolution, section 4.07(2), reprinted supra at page 322, provides that "occupational licenses and educational degrees are not property divisible on divorce." However, chapter 5, Compensatory Spousal Payments, provides a reimbursement remedy:

§5.12   Compensation for Contributions to the Other Spouse's Education or Training

(1) A spouse is entitled at divorce to reimbursement for the financial contributions made to the other spouse's education or training when all of the following are shown:

(a) the claimant provided funds for the tuition or other direct costs of the other spouse's education or training, or provided the principal financial support of the family while the other spouse acquired the education or training;

(b) the education or training was completed in less than a specified number of years, set in a rule of statewide application, before the filing of the petition for dissolution;

(c) the education or training for which reimbursement is sought substantially enhanced the obligor's earning capacity. . . .

(3) If both spouses qualify for reimbursement under this section their claims are netted against one another.

(4) The award allowed under this section is calculated by

(a) adding the obligor's share of the family living expenses during the period of education or training to the obligor's direct educational costs, to determine the obligor's total education or training costs;

(b) subtracting from the total costs the income of the obligor during that period, the amount of any debts then incurred which remain outstanding at the time of divorce and which are assigned to the obligor, and expenditures made during that period from the obligor's separate property; and

(c) adjusting the difference for changes in the real value of the dollar between the time when the education was obtained and the time of divorce.

(5) An award under this section is nonmodifiable. . . .

Principles of the Law of Family Dissolution: Analysis and Recommendations §5.12 (2002). Assuming that some reimbursement remedy is appropriate, does paragraph (4) properly calculate the award?

4.   Further Discussion of Pensions and Other Wage Replacement Benefits

a.   Working It Out: The California "Time Rule"

MARRIAGE OF POPPE
97 Cal. App. 3d 1, 158 Cal. Rptr. 500 (1979)

KAUFMAN, J.— . . . Daniel G. Poppe (hereafter former husband) appeals from an order . . . granting the application of Josephine A. Poppe (former wife) for "modification" of the judgment by fixing her interest in the Naval Reserve pension being received by former husband on the basis of the "time rule" at one-half the fraction 27.25/31.50, the numerator being the number of years of reserve service during the marriage before separation and the denominator being the number of former husband's "qualifying" years of service, which amounts to $253.60 of the total of $592 per month presently being received.

Former husband entered the Navy on July 1, 1937. He served on active duty from that date until July 13, 1946, at which time he became a member of the Naval Reserve. On February 23, 1946, the parties were married. The parties separated on June 16, 1973, and their marriage was subsequently dissolved. . . . After the separation of the parties former husband continued serving in the Naval Reserve until he retired on October 31, 1977. He commenced receiving pension payments on November 30, 1977.

Retirement benefits paid to Navy personnel retiring from active duty are based on the number of years served and the amount of the retiree's salary during active service. Contrastingly, the amount of the pension paid to Naval Reserve retirees is a percentage of the base pay for the rank achieved arrived at on the basis of the number of points accumulated by the retiree during his service in the Naval Reserve. Essentially one point is earned for each drill attended. For example, 14 or 15 points would be earned during the annual two weeks' training duty. For periods of active duty, one point is credited for each day. To be eligible for retirement a Naval reservist must have been credited with a minimum number of "qualifying" years of service, that is, years in which 50 or more points were earned. However, if the minimum "qualifying" years requirement is met, all points earned are counted in the calculation of the pension notwithstanding that in some years less than 50 points were earned.

Former husband retired with a total of 5,002 points of which more than 3,000 were earned during the period he was on active duty prior to the marriage. The number of points accumulated during the marriage was 1,632. The balance of former husband's points were earned by him for his participation in the Naval Reserve after the separation of the parties. It was former husband's contention in the trial court that former wife's interest in the pension should be computed by multiplying one-half times the fraction 1632/5002 times the amount of the pension, $592 per month. Apportioning the pension in that fashion, former wife's share would amount to approximately $95.50 per month, and former husband had been paying that sum to former wife. However, the trial court determined that former husband's "qualifying" years totaled 31.50 and apportioned the pension on the basis of the "time rule" by dividing the 27.25 years between marriage and separation by the 31.5 "qualifying" years so that former wife's share amounts to $253.60 per month. . . . [W]e agree that the apportionment made by the trial court was erroneous because the basis upon which the apportionment was made, years of service during the marriage before separation compared to "qualifying" years in service, bears no substantial rational relationship to the amount of the pension.

Former wife asserts that the "time rule" is the normal basis for apportioning retirement benefits earned in part during coverture and was appropriately employed by the court in the case at bench. Although the "time rule" is not the only acceptable method for apportioning retirement benefits between the community and separate estates (see In re Marriage of Adams, 64 Cal. App. 3d 181, 186, fn. 6, 187, fn. 8 [134 Cal. Rptr. 298]), it is apparently the method most frequently employed. . . .

However, apportionment on the basis of the "time rule" is appropriate only where the amount of the retirement benefits is substantially related to the number of years of service. The rule and its rationale were aptly stated in In re Marriage of Judd, 68 Cal. App. 3d at pages 522-523 [137 Cal. Rptr. 318, 321 (1977)]:

> The most effective method of accomplishing the above result would be to determine the community interest to be that fraction of retirement assets, the numerator of which represents the length of service during the marriage but before the separation, and the denominator of which represents the total length of service by the employee-spouse. Such disposition would comport with what we have termed the "time rule."
>
> . . . The reason why California courts have accepted this manner of division as properly implementive of the "equal division" requirement of [Family Code section 2550] is apparent: *Where the total number of years served by an employee-spouse is a substantial factor in computing the amount of retirement benefits to be received* by that spouse, the community is entitled to have its share based upon the length of service performed on behalf of the community in proportion to the total length of service necessary to earn those benefits. *The relation between years of community service to total years of service provides a fair gauge of that portion of retirement benefits attributable to community effort.* (Italics added.)

Thus it is that in each and all of the cited cases the amount to be received in retirement benefits depended upon or was substantially related to the number of years of service rendered. . . .

· In the case at bench the amount of former husband's pension is not substantially related to the number of years he served in the Naval Reserve. The only relationship between the number of years of service and the pension is that to be eligible for the pension former husband must have served a minimum number of "qualifying" years, years in which he earned 50 or more points. That condition having been satisfied, all points earned, whether in a "qualifying" year or not, counted in fixing the amount of his pension. The number of points that can be earned in a year may be as high as 364 or as low as 1, depending on the nature and frequency of the service rendered, not the number of years served. Thus the amount of the pension is not a function of the number of years of service; the number of years of service during the marriage is not a fair gauge of the community contribution; and the court's apportionment of the pension on the basis of the number of "qualifying" years served as compared to the number of years of service during the marriage must be said to be unreasonable, arbitrary and an abuse of discretion.

The argument that without the reserve service during the marriage no pension at all would be received is correct, but it is of no significant help in resolving the problem. There would likewise be no pension but for former husband's service before the marriage and after the separation of the parties. To the extent service during the marriage contributed to former husband's rank and thus increased his base pay, former wife has no cause for complaint. The pension is based on the increased base pay, and she thus receives the benefit of the increased base pay. Indeed, she receives the benefit also of any increase in base pay resulting from former husband's reserve service after separation of the parties. . . . Although it is fairly obvious that apportionment on the basis of points as urged by former husband would be appropriate, we would usurp the function of the trial court by modifying the judgment to apportion the retirement benefits on that basis.

Accordingly, the order is reversed insofar as it establishes former wife's interest in the Naval Reserve pension, with directions to the trial court to redetermine the respective interests in the pension in a manner and on a basis consistent with this opinion. . . .

TAMURA, Acting P.J., and McDANIEL, J., concurred.

Notes and Questions

1. *The multiplicand of the time fraction: benefits received.* As *Poppe* indicates, the time rule is generally applied when the "amount of retirement benefits is substantially related to the number of years of service." For an immediate distribution, the time-rule fraction is applied to the present value of the pension. More frequently, distribution is deferred until pension receipt and, in California, the time-rule fraction is applied to *benefits actually received.* See, for example, Marriage of Crook, 2 Cal. App. 4th 1606, 3 Cal. Rptr. 2d 905, 908-909 (1992). As a conceptual matter, is this appropriate? Is this consistent with the usual assertion that the community ends at separation and the separated spouse has no claim to the fruits of the other spouse's postseparation labor?

2. Consider the following account. In 2003, at the age of 60, Harry is entitled to full retirement benefits (based on 40 years of employment for X Company) set at 60 percent of his preretirement salary, annually adjusted for inflation. Harry began assembly line work in 1963 at age 20. He married Wanda in 1968, and was promoted to foreman in 1973 and to supervising foreman in 1983. Harry and Wanda divorced in 1994. The court, as per *Brown,* reserved continuing jurisdiction over the pension. In 1995, Harry was promoted to plant manager. In 2001, Harry developed hypertension and ulcers. In 2003, Harry retired at the age of 60 and started collecting retirement pension benefits.

How would you apply the time rule? If you were representing Harry, what might you argue against application of the California time rule? What substitute formula would you propose? See note 1 supra and Berry v. Berry, 674 S.W.2d 945 (Tex. 1983) (setting out a different time-rule formulation). If you were representing Wanda, what would you respond?

3. Why is it, exactly, that a worker's real wages (controlling for inflation) may increase over the course of his work life? Which, if any, of the following explanations seem plausible to you?

   a. A worker, by his own effort, materially alters the nature of his work and the resultant compensation — for example, Harry's promotion from supervising foreman to plant manager.
   b. A worker in a primary labor market (often unionized) job slides along an almost inevitable upward path in terms of real wages and perhaps even position. Seniority is the key in the blue collar and white collar primary labor market. Similarly, in primary market legal practice, the movement is from associate to partner. Do partners really work harder? Are partners really more skilled or productive?
   c. Real income largely increases because of real increases in worker productivity. The same person doing the same job without earning any seniority becomes, because of improving technology, more productive.

Which explanations support the California time rule? Which undercut it?.

4. Harry's pension is a *defined benefit* pension, in which years of employment

qualify a worker for a monthly pension benefit, generally set as a percentage of average monthly salary during the several highest earning years directly preceding retirement. Even though the employee may nominally contribute to the pension fund through wage withholding, his contributions generally do not fully reflect the value of his defined benefit pension, which must be calculated in terms of expected payout rather than nominal employee contributions. A time rule is likely to be the only workable approach to defined benefit plans.

In contrast to defined benefit pensions, *defined contribution* plans allow the possibility of other valuation methods. In such plans, each employee has a separate record of contributions and a periodic statement of gains made from investment of the contributions. At retirement, the employee is merely entitled to the funds in his retirement account, or to an annuity purchased with those funds. Should the time rule also be applied to defined contribution pensions? If your answer is negative, how do you feel about having the community property result turn on the way in which the employer structured the pension plan?

5. Is the California time rule fully justified by the following case?

MARRIAGE OF GOWAN
54 Cal. App. 4th 80, 62 Cal. Rptr. 2d 453 (1997)

COTTLE, P.J.—After judgment in a marital dissolution action between James Robert Gowan, Jr., and his former wife, Ramona Helen Gowan, the trial court entered an order dividing the community property interest in James's pension plan. Because we find that the trial court had retained jurisdiction to divide the pension plan, and did not abuse its discretion in dividing the pension plan according to the "time rule," we affirm the order.

I.   FACTS

James and Ramona were married in June 1957. On May 27, 1960, James began employment with Beckman Instruments, Inc. (Beckman). He was employed there continuously until January 11, 1974, when he left Beckman. At the time his employment terminated, James was earning approximately $30,000 per year.

On October 25, 1978, an interlocutory judgment was entered dissolving the parties' marriage. The interlocutory judgment was based upon a stipulation of the parties, and reflected the parties' agreement regarding support and property division. A final judgment of dissolution was filed on February 21, 1979.

In paragraph 9 of the 1978 interlocutory judgment, the parties agreed to the following: "[Ramona] shall have confirmed to herself as her sole and separate property an undivided one-half interest in any and all retirement benefits to which [James] may be entitled from Beckman Instruments Inc. of Fullerton, California. Said retirement benefits having all been earned by [James] during the course of this marriage, they are all . . . therefore community property. This court shall retain jurisdiction over the subject matter and [James] agrees to pay to [Ramona] as and when he receives said funds her one-half thereof forthwith."

At the time of this interlocutory judgment, the Beckman Instruments, Inc. Pension Plan (Beckman Pension Plan) was not joined in the proceedings. When James left Beckman in January 1974, it was anticipated that he would receive a monthly annuity in the amount of approximately $137.16 from the Beckman Pension Plan beginning on July 1, 1999.

On May 1, 1989, James was again hired by Beckman. His salary for this employment was more than $100,000 per year. James retired from Beckman on June 3, 1994.

For purposes of benefit accrual under the Beckman Pension Plan, both of James's employment periods (1960-1974 and 1989-1994) were added together for a total service credit of more than 18 years.[1] In June 1994, James filed a payment directive with the Beckman Pension Plan electing a single life monthly payment option with a social security adjustment.

After his retirement in 1994, James began receiving a monthly pension benefit in an initial amount over $3,400. As of March 1, 1996, when James would be entitled to social security benefits, his pension benefit was to be reduced to approximately $2,500 per month for the remainder of his life. James did not commence payments to Ramona once he began receiving monthly retirement benefits.

On July 28, 1995, Ramona filed a motion seeking enforcement of pension division, the entry of a qualified domestic relations order (QDRO), and attorneys' fees and costs. . . .

In her motion seeking enforcement of the pension division, Ramona argued that because James's pension benefit was based upon over 18 years of service, approximately 14 of which were during their marriage, 72.95 percent of the pension was community property, and she was entitled to one-half of this community property interest or 36.475 percent of the pension. James argued that the 1978 judgment was res judicata, that Ramona's community property share was limited to $68.81 per month, and that the "time rule" should not be applied. After a hearing on December 14, 1995, the court took the matter under submission.

On January 5, 1996, the court filed its findings and orders after hearing. The court concluded that it had authority to divide the pension pursuant to the jurisdiction retained in the 1978 judgment, and granted Ramona's motion to enter a QDRO based upon the time rule. . . . James filed a timely appeal from the court's order. . . .

II. DISCUSSION

On appeal, James challenges the trial court's order determining the community property interests in his pension according to the time rule. His main contention . . . [is] that the time rule was improperly applied. . . .

The trial court concluded that the combined pension included both separate property and community property, and that the time rule was the appropriate method for ascertaining the community's interest. When a trial court concludes that property contains both separate and community interests, the court has very broad discretion to fashion an apportionment of interests that is equitable under the circumstances of the case. . . . Consequently, we review the trial court's utiliza-

---

1. In order to give James credit for his total service time, Beckman moved the initial hire date forward to September 27, 1975, which, according to Beckman, yielded the same total benefits service as adding the service from each employment period together.

tion of the time rule to divide the combined pension under an abuse of discretion standard. . . .

Under the time rule, the community is allocated a fraction of the benefits, the numerator representing length of service during marriage but before separation, and the denominator representing the total length of service by the employee spouse. That ratio is then multiplied by the final plan benefit to determine the community interest. (In re Marriage of Judd (1977) 68 Cal. App. 3d 515, 522, 137 Cal. Rptr. 318; In re Marriage of Cobb (1977) 68 Cal. App. 3d 855, 861, 137 Cal. Rptr. 670.)

The rationale for the use of the time rule was set forth in In re Marriage of Judd, supra, 68 Cal. App. 3d 515, 137 Cal. Rptr. 318: "Where the total number of years served by an employee-spouse is a substantial factor in computing the amount of retirement benefits to be received by that spouse, the community is entitled to have its share based upon the length of service performed on behalf of the community in proportion to the total length of service necessary to earn those benefits. The relation between years of community service to total years of service provides a fair gauge of that portion of the retirement benefits attributable to community effort." (Id. at pp.522-523, 137 Cal. Rptr. 318.) Using this rationale, courts have frequently used this method of determining the community's interest where the amount of the benefit is substantially related to the number of years of service rendered. . . .

James challenges the court's decision to apply the time rule to the combined pension on both factual and legal grounds. Factually, he argues that his pension benefit was not related in any way to his years of employment with Beckman during his marriage to Ramona. In a declaration submitted to the trial court, James stated: "[T]his [1989 employment with Beckman] was a separately negotiated contract with nothing at all to do with my prior employment with Beckman between 1960 and 1974. I only received the benefits that I did in exchange for a salary reduction. I did not receive these benefits based upon prior employment with Beckman. My job description was entirely different, . . . my compensation was entirely different, and it was based upon my experience, education, and abilities that I generated the 'perks,' including pension benefits, that I obtained." . . .

The trial court did not find this factual argument persuasive. . . . The court found that "James did not meet his burden to prove that the increase in the ultimate pension benefits was a result of post-separation negotiations and not attributable to his first employment period."

We have reviewed the entire record on appeal, and find the evidence sufficient to support this finding. Although James's declaration stated that his pension benefits were entirely unrelated to the first employment period, a letter to Ramona's counsel from the Beckman's Benefits Project Manager states that James had two employment periods with Beckman, and that "[b]oth of these employment periods are credited service for Pension Plan benefit accrual." This letter supports Ramona's argument that James's pension was based upon all of the years of his service with Beckman, including the years during his marriage to Ramona. Given the conflicting inferences possible from the evidence, the trial court was entitled to find that the pension was, in fact, related to all of James's service years with Beckman, including those during his marriage to Ramona. This factual finding will not be disturbed on appeal.

James's legal argument is that the time rule has been applied in cases in which the employment period "continues uninterrupted beyond the date the judgment of dissolution is entered," . . . and not in cases involving a "break in service" between two employment periods. James is correct that the cases employing the time rule generally involve a single, continuing period of employment. . . . The parties have cited no case in which the time rule has been applied to a pension based upon two separate employment periods. . . .

[E]ven where an employee's service is not continuous, a pension based upon total service years may be divided according to the time rule. The rationale for the time rule applies wherever the total number of years served by the employee spouse (continuous or otherwise) is a substantial factor in computing the retirement benefits. Although James had two separate employment periods with Beckman, his pension was based upon his total service years. The time rule fairly accounts for both the marital and post-marital years of service because it assigns to the community only a portion of the pension corresponding to the portion of service during marriage and before separation.

Finally, we consider the argument, made implicitly by James, that his later service years at high salaries contributed more to the value of his pension than his earlier years at lower salaries. Similar arguments in cases involving continuous employment have been repeatedly rejected by California courts. For example, in In re Marriage of Judd, the husband argued that because his annuity payments were based in part upon post-marital years of service, which would have a significantly greater dollar value than his years of service during the marriage, the community property award should not give equal weight to the different years of service. The *Judd* court, however, held that a husband and wife share the same qualitative interest in the retirement rights, and the fact that a plan reflects subsequent salary increases does not alter the community's interest in those rights. "[A]n employee's contributions in the early years of employment during the marriage, even though based on a smaller salary, may actually be worth more than contributions during the post-separation years, due to the longer period of accumulated interest and investment income prior to the commencement of benefit payments." (In re Marriage of Judd, supra, 68 Cal. App. 3d at p. 523, 137 Cal. Rptr. 318.) The court therefore gave the first service years (during the marriage) as much weight in computing total service as the last few years (after separation).

Like the court in *Judd*, we are persuaded that the community contribution to James's pension (approximately 14 years, beginning in 1960) was crucial to its final value and to the amount received by James. Under these circumstances, despite the break in service and the salary differential, the trial court acted within its discretion when it utilized the time rule to apportion the parties' interests in the pension. . . .

The trial court's order of January 5, 1996, . . . is affirmed.

Premo and Bamattre-Manoukian, JJ., concur.

Notes

1. How does *Gowan* rationalize (i) the equal weighting of each year in the application of the time rule and (ii) the use of the worker's final salary, that is, the choice of the California rather than the Texas rule (*Berry* at page 339)? Are you persuaded? What do you make of the fact that James Gowan could have gone to work in 1989 for a different company, in which case his pension from that job

would be entirely his separate property and hence unreachable by his former wife Ramona?

2. Marriage of Judd is cited as authority in *Gowan*. Although *Judd* is apt for defined contribution (annuity) plans, it seems off point for defined benefit plans, where there is no "accumulation," but rather a right upon retirement to a benefit calculated as a percentage of preretirement salary, the sort of pension apparently at issue in *Gowan*. Although *Judd* seems inapt authority for *Gowan*, the reasoning of *Gowan* does not depend on the rationale of *Judd*.

b. The Right to Reinstate a Pension

MARRIAGE OF FORREST
97 Cal. App. 3d 850, 159 Cal. Rptr. 229 (1979)

THE COURT. — Husband Lacy Laden Forrest, Jr. (Lacy) appeals portions of an interlocutory judgment of dissolution which (1) deny him a share in the right of wife Nancy Lou Forrest (Nancy) to reinstate her federal civil service retirement benefits. . . . The parties separated after a 15-year marriage.

Before the parties' separation, Nancy worked in the federal civil service system, separated from employment and withdrew her retirement contributions. She had the right to reinstate her benefits if she resumed employment with the federal government and redeposited the withdrawn contributions. The amount she must redeposit is $4,846 plus interest of $1,693. At the time of trial she had resumed federal employment and had begun reinstating by means of monthly payroll deductions.

Lacy contends Nancy's present right to purchase the retirement annuity has a value, which can be actuarially calculated, and although he does not seek a lump sum share of that present value, he does claim the trial court should retain jurisdiction so that if Nancy does reinstate all her contributions and eventually begins to draw a pension, Lacy can share in that benefit proportional to the community interest based on nine years of contributions during the marriage. In support of his position he cites cases such as In re Marriage of Brown, 15 Cal. 3d 838 [126 Cal. Rptr. 633, 544 P.2d 561], and In re Marriage of Fithian, 10 Cal. 3d 592 [111 Cal. Rptr. 369, 517 P.2d 449], holding a nonvested pension may nonetheless be a community asset subject to retained trial court jurisdiction and eventual division.

Here, however, the alleged pension asset is not only not vested, it is in fact nonexistent. Its existence is subject to the condition precedent of Nancy's ability to reinstate some $6,500 of withdrawn contributions. That contingency may not occur, since its fulfillment will depend on Nancy's continued good health, ability to work, and ability to continue reinstating contributions in the face of the inflationary cost of living increases which she undoubtedly must face, in addition to the hazards of chance ill fortune. Further, the community has not been depleted by Nancy's past contributions as would be the case if she had been contributing all along to a nonvested pension, because here she has withdrawn the contributions during the marriage and presumably used them for community purposes. Her present contributions are from her own separate property. There is no authority mandating division of so tenuous an asset as Nancy's right to reinstate a federal pension. . . .

The judgment is affirmed.

Note and Question

1. What is the value of a right to purchase reinstatement of a pension?
2. Two years later a different panel of the Fourth District Court of Appeal disapproved the result in *Forrest.* See Marriage of Lucero, immediately below.

MARRIAGE OF LUCERO
118 Cal. App. 3d 836, 173 Cal. Rptr. 680 (1981)

TAMURA, J.— . . . Husband worked for the federal government in various capacities beginning in 1942 and ending with his retirement in October 1977 at the age of 57. Husband's employment was not continuous but was interrupted several times. At the time of retirement, husband received credit for 30 years and 1 month of employment service. However, he had withdrawn his retirement contributions to date in 1966. To obtain the maximum retirement benefit, he had to redeposit these funds, in the amount of $9,373. Husband did redeposit this amount, after separation from wife, using his own separate funds. As of October 1977, the date of retirement, his monthly retirement benefit was $840 per month. If husband had not redeposited his retirement contributions, his monthly benefit would have been $474 per month. Husband had not sought any other employment after retirement up to the time of trial.

[T]he trial court determined [that] . . . the community interest extended only to the benefit husband would have received absent the redeposit of funds, or approximately 68 percent of $474, subject to periodic cost of living increases.

Wife contends . . . the trial court erred in determining that the community interest in husband's pension extended only to the benefits that would have been received absent redeposit of funds. . . .

Wife contends first that the community interest in husband's retirement benefits extends to the full amount of those benefits after redeposit of employee retirement contributions. She concedes that the community must pay its pro rata share of the redeposit and indicates that she has at all times been willing to contribute her fair share. Husband responds that the increase due to redeposit is entirely his separate property because the redeposit was made with his separate funds after separation. . . .

In the present case, husband withdrew his retirement contribution in 1966 and this money was spent for community purposes. When the parties separated in 1976, only a negligible amount (about $50) had been redeposited. Husband retired one year later, in 1977, and made the redeposit using separate funds. The advantage of the redeposit is blindingly clear. Husband's benefits immediately increased by $366 per month, so that the total redeposit amount ($9,373) was recouped in about two years. Thereafter husband, who was still not 60 years old, could expect to enjoy the extra $366 per month for many years. In effect, husband purchased a $366 per month annuity, subject to periodic cost of living increases, for $9,373. This was obviously a great bargain and was possible only as consideration for husband's service of over 30 years as a government employee.

To allow husband the sole right to decide whether to redeposit and the sole right to elect whether to redeposit with separate or community funds is to treat the redeposit right as husband's separate property. This is incorrect because the redeposit right is a pension right and "the community owns *all* pension rights attributable to employment during the marriage." (In re Marriage of Brown (1976) 15 Cal. 3d 838, 844 [126 Cal. Rptr. 633, 544 P.2d 561, 94 A.L.R.3d 164], italics supplied.)

Accordingly, we conclude that the trial court erred in failing to recognize wife's right to elect to share in the increased retirement benefits upon payment of her pro rata share of the redeposit. . . .

We have concluded, reluctantly, that *Forrest* is not compatible with the reasoning of our Supreme Court in the landmark case which recognized that nonvested pension rights are community property subject to division on dissolution of marriage. (In re Marriage of Brown, supra, 15 Cal. 3d 838, 841.) In so ruling, the court explained that "nonvested pension rights are not an expectancy but a contingent interest in property." (Ibid.) The court noted that "the defining characteristic of an expectancy is that its holder has no *enforceable right* to his beneficence." (Id., at p.845; original italics.) Pension rights, however, derive from the contract of employment and are a form of property. (Ibid.) "The fact that a contractual right is contingent upon future events does not degrade that right to an expectancy." (Id., at p.846, fn. 8.)

We fail to perceive any material difference between the ordinary nonvested pension right discussed in *Brown,* and a nonvested pension subject to the single additional contingency of redeposit of retirement contributions previously withdrawn. Both are contingent contract rights, and thus both should be treated as property subject to division on dissolution of marriage. . . .

The judgment is modified as follows:

1. Paragraph 6 of the judgment is amended to read: "6. Petitioner, having elected to participate in the redeposit of respondent's employee retirement contributions, is ordered to pay respondent $3,154 as her pro rata share ($1/2 \times 244/361 \times \$9,373 = \$3,154$).[6] Respondent is ordered to pay petitioner 122/361 of all retirement benefits received to date. Hereafter petitioner's share, 122/361 of each payment, shall be paid to her directly by the United States Office of Personnel Management.". . .

c. The Terminable Interest Doctrine

i. Introduction

Pensions provided by private employers generally come in two forms: a periodic benefit for the pensioner until his death *or* a lower periodic benefit until the pensioner's death and a further reduced benefit for the surviving spouse until her death. Often an employee and his spouse may choose between the two.[7] Monthly benefits under the single life option are higher than under the joint-and-survivor option. Yet in most plans, both options have equal actuarial value. Public pensions

---

6. Is the court's formula correct? — ED.

7. The Retirement Equity Act of 1984 (REA) amended ERISA to require that all ERISA-regulated private sector pensions offer a joint-and-survivor option and further to require the nonemployee spouse's written consent before a married employee may elect *not* to take the joint-and-survivor option. Pub. L. 98-397, 98 Stat. 1429, codified at 29 U.S.C. §1055. For further discussion of REA and ERISA, see casebook at 296 and 609.

often adopt a joint-and-survivor model for the worker and his spouse but, consistent with a more general concern for public welfare, may not allow the married worker and his spouse to opt for higher benefits for the worker's life alone.

As an introduction to the terminable interest issues, you may find it helpful to consider your intuitive response to each of the following claims. (i) Hiram earned his public joint-and-survivor pension entirely during his marriage to Ann. Upon his retirement, he divorced Ann and married Betty. A few years later Hiram died. As per the pension plan, Hiram's surviving spouse, Betty, began receiving a surviving spouse's benefit. What was Ann's claim to the pension during Hiram's lifetime? What is her claim now that Betty is receiving a surviving spouse's benefit? Will Ann have any claim after Betty's death? (ii) Harold married Wendy shortly after college graduation and worked all his life as a public school teacher. Wendy was a homemaker and volunteer community worker. A few years after Harold's retirement, Wendy died, leaving "all my interest in the community property to my disabled sister, Sally." Does Sally take one-half of Harold's monthly pension benefits?

ii. California Case Law Construction of the Terminable Interest Doctrine

In Benson v. City of Los Angeles, 60 Cal. 2d 355, 384 P.2d 649, 33 Cal. Rptr. 257 (1963), a Los Angeles fireman earned a joint-and-survivor pension during his marriage to his first wife, Teresa. He subsequently divorced Teresa and married Olive. After his death, both Teresa and Olive asserted claims to the surviving spouse's benefits. The California Supreme Court, observing that Teresa was not a surviving spouse, awarded the benefits entirely to Olive. The court's holding in *Benson* articulated the first prong of the terminable interest doctrine: A nonemployee's community property interest in her former spouse's pension does not survive the employee's death.

In Waite v. Waite, 6 Cal. 3d 461, 492 P.2d 13, 99 Cal. Rptr. 335 (1972), the California Supreme Court formulated the second prong of the terminable interest doctrine. The divorce court had awarded the plaintiff one-half her husband's monthly public pension benefits and ordered that such benefits be paid "directly to plaintiff . . . or her devisee or heirs." The California Supreme Court disapproved the award insofar as it provided that benefits be paid to the wife's devisee or heirs. The court effectively held that the nonemployee spouse's community property interest terminated at her death as well as at the death of the employee.[8]

The terminable interest doctrine is a doctrinal anomaly. Teresa Benson's claim was not based on her status as a surviving spouse, but instead on her ownership interest in *any* benefits earned by her husband during their marriage. Washington vigorously rejected the terminable interest doctrine in Farver v. Department of Retirement Systems, 97 Wash. 2d 344, 644 P.2d 1149 (1982). The California Courts of Appeal avoided the doctrine whenever possible. See, e.g., Bowman v. Bowman, 171 Cal. App. 3d 148, 217 Cal. Rptr. 174 (1985) (terminable interest doctrine inap-

---

8. This is the usual reading of *Waite*. See, e.g., Bowman v. Bowman, 171 Cal. App. 3d 148, 217 Cal. Rptr. 174 (1985); Chirmside v. Board of Administration, 143 Cal. App. 3d 205, 191 Cal. Rptr. 605 (1983). Alternatively, *Waite* may be read more narrowly to hold that the nonemployee spouse must nevertheless be compensated for the unequal division of the community pension. Waite v. Waite, 6 Cal. 3d 461, 474 n.9, 492 P.2d 13, 99 Cal. Rptr. 335 (1972).

plicable to private, as opposed to public, pensions); Chirmside v. Board of Administration, 143 Cal. App. 3d 205, 191 Cal. Rptr. 605 (1983) (doctrine inapplicable to community contributions portion of a public retirement pension).

iii. California Legislative Repeal

In 1986, the California legislature repealed the terminable interest doctrine:

1986 CAL. STAT., CH. 686

SECTION 1. Section 4800.8 is added to the Civil Code, to read:

4800.8. The court shall make whatever orders are necessary or appropriate to assure that each party receives his or her full community property share in any retirement plan, whether public or private, including all survivor and death benefits, including, but not limited to, either of the following:

(a) Order the division of any retirement benefits payable upon or after the death of either party in a manner consistent with Section 4800 [Family Code §2550].

(b) Order a party to elect a survivor benefit annuity or other similar election for the benefit of the other party, as specified by the court, in any case in which a retirement plan provides for such an election.

SECTION 2. It is the intent of the Legislature to abolish the terminable interest rule set forth in Waite v. Waite, 6 Cal. 3d 461, and Benson v. City of Los Angeles, 60 Cal. 2d 355, in order that retirement benefits shall be divided in accordance with Section 4800 [Family Code §2550].

Civil Code section 4800.8, as amended, has been recodified as Family Code section 2610. The statement of legislative intent has never been codified.

iv. California Judicial Reception of Civil Code
Section 4800.8, now Family Code Section 2610

Appellate decisions have broadly defined the scope and reach of this statute. Although the statute is located in the dissolution distribution sections of both codes, Estate of Austin, 206 Cal. App. 3d 1249, 254 Cal. Rptr. 372 (1988), holds that it applies equally to marriages that persist until the death of one of the parties. Marriage of Taylor, 189 Cal. App. 3d 435, 234 Cal. Rptr. 486 (1987), holds that the statute applies to all cases still on appeal on its effective date. Marriage of Powers, 218 Cal. App. 3d 626, 267 Cal. Rptr. 350 (1990), holds that it applies as well to all cases, *whenever decided,* in which the court has retained continuing jurisdiction over the pension. *Powers* has substantial potential for disturbing settled expectations. For commentary from the bench, bar, and academe, see 6 Cal. Fam. Law Monthly 414-418 (1990).

As broadly interpreted by California courts, a Family Code section 2610 distribution may yield surprising results, particularly with public pension plans that provide benefits for a deceased employee's surviving spouse and children. Under section 2610, a divorced nonemployee spouse may assert her community property interest in *any* benefit generated by community labor. Marriage of Carnall, 216 Cal. App. 3d 1010, 265 Cal. Rptr. 271 (1989). Moreover, a deceased divorced nonemployee's estate may make such claims. *Powers* supra. Finally, even when a marriage has persisted until death, the employee's estate or will beneficiary may seek to assert the employee's community property (and separate property) interest in his surviving spouse's benefits.

v. ERISA Partial Preemptive Revival of the Terminable Interest Doctrine for ERISA-Regulated Pensions

After the federal Employee Retirement Income Security Act (ERISA)[9] was enacted in 1974, many divorcing employee-spouses argued that ERISA's spendthrift, or anti-alienation, provision preempted state marital property division of ERISA-regulated private sector pensions at divorce. The spendthrift provision states that "benefits provided under the [retirement] plan may not be assigned or alienated." 29 U.S.C. §1056(d). Congress responded to this claim in the Retirement Equity Act of 1984, which specifically allows divorce-related state law property and support distribution to an *alternate payee* pursuant to a qualified domestic relations order (QDRO). An alternate payee may be a spouse, former spouse, child, or other dependent of the pension holder.

Nevertheless, the ERISA preemption claim was renewed in Boggs v. Boggs, 320 U.S. 833, 117 S. Ct. 1754, 138 L. Ed. 2d 45 (1997), which is reprinted at page 609 of the casebook. Isaac and Dorothy Boggs were residents of Louisiana, a community property state. Their long marriage ended at Dorothy's death in 1979. Dorothy's will left all her interest in the community property (i) as a life estate for husband Isaac and (ii) after Isaac's death, the remainder to their three sons. A year later, Isaac married Sandra.

When Isaac retired in 1985, he had an ERISA-regulated joint-and-survivor annuity that paid him monthly benefits, and would at his death pay Sandra surviving spouse's benefits. Under Louisiana community property law, the pension was the community property of Isaac's first marriage to Dorothy. Louisiana treats pensions and retirement benefits as it does any other community property asset; in other words, Louisiana has no terminable interest doctrine.

Isaac and Sandra remained married until Isaac's death in 1989, when the three sons claimed their remainder interest under their mother's will. They asserted a claim to Dorothy's community property interest in Sandra's surviving spouse's benefit. Sandra opposed the claim.

Sandra responded that now that Isaac was dead, her interest in his ERISA-regulated pension was the entire survivor's benefit of the joint and survivor annuity. This, she argued, was what Congress intended, through ERISA, to provide for a surviving spouse. And she alone was the surviving spouse. Congress did not intend that a portion of her benefit go to the three sons from her deceased husband's first marriage. The United States Supreme Court agreed, effectively reviving the *Waite* arm of the terminable interest doctrine for marriages terminated by the death of a spouse.

---

9. See discussion of ERISA at page 296 supra.

Interpreting *Boggs,* Branco v. UFCW–Northern California Employers Joint Pension Plan, 279 F.3d 1154 (9th Cir. 2002), held that ERISA preempts a California divorce court distribution of a community property pension insofar as it purports to enable a divorced wife to leave her share of the community property pension earned by her former husband to her heirs at her death. Under *Branco,* the interest of a former spouse who is an alternate payee under an ERISA QDRO expires at his or her death and reverts to the surviving employee spouse. *Branco* thus revives the *Waite* arm of the terminable interest rule for pensions distributed at divorce. (For discussion of ERISA QDROs, see pages 296-297 supra.)

d. Disability Benefits

MARRIAGE OF JONES
13 Cal. 3d 457, 531 P.2d 420, 119 Cal. Rptr. 108 (1975)

TOBRINER, J. — On this appeal, we hold that a married serviceman's right to disability pay, unlike a vested right to retirement pay, does not comprise a community asset and thus does not become subject to division upon dissolution of the marriage. Such disability pay is not a form of deferred compensation for past services. Rather, it serves to compensate the veteran for the personal anguish caused by the permanent disability as well as for the loss of earnings resulting from his compelled premature military retirement and from diminished ability to compete in the civilian job market. These losses and disabilities fall upon the disabled spouse, not on the uninjured and healthy one; hence, upon dissolution of marriage, the right of the disabled spouse to future disability payment should be his separate property.

Respondent Herschel Jones entered military service in 1957. He married petitioner Sumiko Jones in 1964. In 1969, Herschel lost a leg in combat in Vietnam, and was retired for disability, with monthly disability pay of $379.12. When Sumiko filed suit for dissolution of the marriage in 1972, she claimed her husband's right to lifetime disability payments as a community asset. The superior court rejected that claim, ruling that payments received after dissolution would be the separate property of the husband. Since we agree with the superior court that Herschel's right to disability payments subsequent to dissolution is not a community asset, we affirm the judgment.

Herschel's disability payments derive from the military retirement program enacted in title 10 of the United States Code. Section 1201 of that title provides that the secretary of the military branch concerned may retire a permanently disabled serviceman, with right to "retired pay," if either (a) he has served at least 20 years, (b) his disability rates at 30 percent or higher, and he has served at least 8 years, or (c) his disability rates at 30 percent or higher and was incurred on active duty, or in the line of duty during wartime. Permanently disabled servicemen whose length of service and degree of disability do not entitle them to retired pay receive disability severance pay. (10 U.S.C. §1212.) . . .

In the present case, Herschel, having served for only 12 years, had no vested right to a pension by reason of longevity of service; he receives a pension only because of his disability. In resolving the instant case, therefore, we do not decide whether, or to what extent, a disability pension granted *after* the serviceman has earned by longevity of service a vested right to retirement pay may constitute a community asset; we limit our decision to holding only that a serviceman's right to disability pay, acquired *before* such a serviceman has earned by longevity of service a vested right to retirement pay, is not a community asset.[4] . . .

We have recently reaffirmed the principle that under California community property law vested retirement benefits, attributable to employment during marriage, constitute a community asset subject to division upon dissolution. (Waite v. Waite (1972) 6 Cal. 3d 461 [99 Cal. Rptr. 325, 492 P.2d 13]; Phillipson v. Board of Administration (1970) 3 Cal. 3d 32 [89 Cal. Rptr. 61, 473 P.2d 765].) The principle rests upon the belief that retirement benefits are not gratuities but deferred consideration for past services rendered by the employee. . . .

Disability pay, however, does not serve primarily as a form of deferred compensation for past services. Although longevity of service plays a role, the veteran's right to disability payments, and the amount of the payments, depend primarily on the existence and extent of the disability. Such payments serve to compensate the disabled veteran for the loss of military pay caused by his premature retirement and for his diminished ability to compete for civilian employment. (See Note (1973) 27 JAG J. 392, 400.) So long as the marriage subsists, the veteran's reduced earnings works a loss to the community. But such community loss does not continue after dissolution; at that point the earnings or accumulations of each party are the separate property of such party. ([Family Code §771].) Then any diminution in earning capacity becomes the separate loss of the disabled spouse.

Disability payments serve a second purpose. We have suggested supra that they compensate the veteran for the pain, suffering, disfigurement and the misfortune caused by his disability. Pain, suffering, disfigurement or the loss of a limb, as here, is the peculiar anguish of the person who suffers it; it can never be wholly shared even by a loving spouse and surely not after the dissolution of a marriage by a departed one.

Disability pay, consequently, compares to compensation for personal injury rather than to retirement pay. . . .

Since disability pay serves primarily to compensate the disabled serviceman for current suffering and lost earning capacity, we conclude that only such payments as are received during the marriage constitute a community asset. The veteran's right to payments subsequent to dissolution is his separate and personal right.

The judgment is affirmed. WRIGHT, C.J., McCOMB, J., MOSK, J., SULLIVAN, J., CLARK, J., and BURKE, J., concurred.

Notes and Questions

1. What, exactly, is the primary justification for classifying a retirement pension earned during marriage as community property? That it is deferred compensation? Or that it was earned during marriage?

---

4. Sumiko relies upon decisions of the Texas courts holding that, under Texas community property law, a veteran's right to disability pay is a community asset. (Busby v. Busby (Tex. 1970) 457 S.W.2d 551, 553-554; Dominey v. Dominey (Tex. Civ. App. 1972) 481 S.W.2d 473, 475-476; but cf. Ramsey v. Ramsey (Tex. Civ. App. 1971) 474 S.W.2d 939 (Veterans' Administration pension held separate property).) In both *Busby* and *Dominey*, however, the veteran receiving disability pay had completed 20 years of service and thus acquired a *vested* right to retirement pay (see 10 U.S.C. §§1201, 1401), which right, a community asset, he waived in return for a disability pension.

2. Is a retirement pension really deferred compensation at all? Supposing a defined-benefit pension is payable only for the life of the worker and he dies before retirement? Supposing it is instead a joint-and-survivor pension, that is, for the lives of the worker and his spouse, and both of them die before the worker retires? If a pension were truly or solely deferred compensation, it would be paid without regard to the worker's survival or, in the case of a joint-and-survivor pension, the survival of the worker or his spouse. Is it more accurate to characterize pensions as group insurance against income loss due to superannuation, that is, survival past the age of retirement? Under this view, the right to a pension seems remarkably similar to the right to disability pay, which arises from group insurance against loss of income due to disability. Reference to social security tends to support this characterization. Old Age, Survivors, and Disability Insurance, popularly called social security, insures workers and their immediate families against income loss caused by retirement, death, and disability. (See generally Blumberg, Adult Derivative Benefits in Social Security, 32 Stan. L. Rev. 233 (1980).)

3. How and when does a worker earn his right to employer-paid disability benefits? Is there generally any *significant* distinction between the basis for his retirement and disability coverage? If not, which is questionable: California's treatment of pensions or of disability benefits?

4. What if the disability coverage was purchased by *employee* payroll deductions during marriage? See Marriage of Olhausen, 48 Cal. App. 3d 190, 121 Cal. Rptr. 444 (1975) (disability pay received after divorce still disabled worker's separate property). Should it make any difference whether an employee's group disability insurance is funded by employee or employer payroll deductions? In the final analysis, who really pays? Should it matter that the source of disability benefits received after divorce was an individual disability insurance policy purchased during marriage with community funds? See Marriage of Saslow, 40 Cal. 3d 848, 710 P.2d 346, 221 Cal. Rptr. 546 (1985), holding that postseparation disability payments received by a physician from community-funded individual policies are the physician's separate property.

5. Is personal injury recovery an apt analog for disability pay? Are there any important differences between the two? In an omitted portion of the opinion, *Jones* analogized disability pay to personal injury recovery and looked to then-existing California treatment of personal injury recovery to justify its conclusion that disability pay should be classified according to the time of its receipt. (When *Jones* was decided, California classified personal injury recovery as community or separate according to when the award or settlement was received.) After *Jones*, California Civil Code section 5126, now Family Code section 781, was rewritten to refer to the time *the cause of action arose*, as opposed to the time of receipt of the award or settlement. (See page 277 supra.) Thus, current California treatment of personal injury recovery no longer supports *Jones*. The supreme court acknowledged this in Marriage of Saslow, 40 Cal. 3d 848, 860, 710 P.2d 346, 221 Cal. Rptr. 546 (1985), but nevertheless reaffirmed the holding of *Jones* that postseparation disability benefits are the disabled spouse's separate property. The court observed:

> The primary purpose of disability benefits is to compensate the disabled spouse for lost earnings — earnings which would normally be separate property after dissolution. If postdissolution disability benefits are held to be community property, a young ablebodied ex-spouse will be able to work and retain all his or her earnings, and will in addition be entitled to half the disability benefits of the disabled ex-spouse. This might impose a grave hardship on

the disabled individual, who not only may not be able to work, but who may also require special equipment or extraordinary care.

Does the court's poignant account adequately distinguish disability benefits from retirement benefits?

6. From a comparative perspective, marital property treatment of disability pay is in disarray. Among jurisdictions, there is great diversity of result and rationale. Within jurisdictions, there is often inconsistent treatment of closely analogous assets, such as disability pay, workers' compensation, and personal injury recoveries. For a thorough survey of American law in this area, see Blumberg, Intangible Assets: Recognition and Valuation, in 2 Valuation and Distribution of Marital Property §23.03 (1995). See also In re Marriage of Smith, 84 Ill. App. 3d 466, 405 N.E.2d 884 (1980).

Those community property and equitable distribution jurisdictions that classify disability pay received after divorce as community, or marital, property when the right to such pay can be traced to community funds or labor tend to rely on one or more of the following rationales:

(1)   a mechanical reading of the classification statute (it is not separate so it must be community);
(2)   emphasis on the source of the benefit, that is, community funds or labor;
(3)   analogy to personal injury recoveries, which the jurisdiction treats as community property; or
(4)   equation with retirement pensions, which the jurisdiction classifies as community property.

See, e.g., Guy v. Guy, 98 Idaho 205, 207, 560 P.2d 876, 879 (1977) (but see Griggs v. Griggs, 107 Idaho 123, 686 P.2d 68 (1984)); Marriage of Smith, 84 Ill. App. 3d 446, 405 N.E.2d 884, 890 (1980); Kruger v. Kruger, 73 N.J. 464, 375 A.2d 659 (1977); Stroshine v. Stroshine, 98 N.M. 742, 652 P.2d 1193 (1982); Simmons v. Simmons, 568 S.W.2d 169 (Tex. Civ. App. 1978).

Jurisdictions that, in contrast, treat postdivorce disability pay as the disabled worker's separate property even though the right to such pay was funded by the community tend to focus exclusively on the replacement nature of the benefits, that is, that they are a substitute for postdivorce wages. Often they refer, by way of analogy, to personal injury awards. In addition to California law, see, for example, Villasenor v. Villasenor, 657 P.2d 889 (Ariz. Ct. App. 1982); Griggs v. Griggs, 107 Idaho 123, 686 P.2d 68 (1984) (contra Guy v. Guy, 98 Idaho 205, 207, 560 P.2d 876, 879 (1977)); Gilbert v. Gilbert, 442 So. 2d 1330 (La. Ct. App. 1983); Newell v. Newell, 121 Misc. 2d 586, 468 N.Y.S.2d 814 (1983); Leighton v. Leighton, 81 Wis. 2d 620, 261 N.W.2d 417, 464-465 (1978).

MARRIAGE OF STENQUIST
21 Cal. 3d 779, 582 P.2d 96, 148 Cal. Rptr. 9 (1978)

TOBRINER, J. . . . [T]he husband joined the Army in 1944 and married in 1950. In 1953 he suffered a service-related injury leading to amputation of his left fore-arm, for which the Army assigned him an 80 percent disability rating. If the husband had retired immediately, his maximum "disability" pay would have been 75 percent of basic pay, compared to a maximum "retirement" pay of 22½ percent of basic pay. He nevertheless continued his military service until he retired in 1970. At that time he faced the choice of taking regular "retirement" pay at the rate of 65 percent of his basic pay, or taking "disability" pay, a stipend equal to 75 percent of basic pay. Assuming the husband desired the higher amount, the Army began making "disability" payments to him.

The husband commenced proceedings for dissolution of the marriage in 1974. The trial court first determined that all pension rights attributable to the husband's military service before marriage, plus the portion of those rights earned during marriage attributable to the husband's disability, constituted his separate property. It then ruled that that portion of the pension rights earned after the marriage equivalent to an ordinary retirement pension, computed on the basis of longevity of service and rank at retirement, constituted a community asset.

The court finally divided this asset equally between the spouses. The husband appeals from the portion of the judgment awarding his wife part of his pension as community property. . . .

We begin our discussion of this issue by reviewing the procedure by which a disabled serviceman may compute the amount of "retired pay" to which he is entitled. He may elect, first, to compute his "retired pay" on the basis of his rank and disability by multiplying his monthly basic pay by his percentage of disability. Alternatively, he can compute his "retired pay" on the basis of rank and longevity of service by multiplying his monthly basic pay by 2½ percent times his years of service. (10 U.S.C.§1401.) Under either formula, he cannot receive more than 75 percent of his last monthly basic pay. The amount of retired pay the serviceman receives under either option therefore depends largely on his monthly pay at retirement, a function of longevity of service and rank; rank itself is closely related to length of service.

In In re Marriage of Jones, 13 Cal. 3d 457 [531 P.2d 420, 119 Cal. Rptr. 108 (1975)], . . . we held that a serviceman's right to "disability" pay, acquired before he had earned a "vested" right to ordinary retirement pay, was separate property. Subsequently in In re Marriage of Brown (1976) 15 Cal. 3d 838 [126 Cal. Rptr. 633, 544 P.2d 561], we held that "vested" and "nonvested" pension rights should be treated alike. Relying on those decisions, the husband contends that all military pensions based on disability are now separate property. Closer examination, however, reveals that the reasoning of *Jones* and *Brown* supports the division of the husband's pension which the present trial court ordered.

In *Jones*, we held that when a spouse is entitled to receive a pension only because he is disabled, and *has no right to a pension because of longevity of service,* the disability benefit payments are his separate property upon dissolution of the marriage. At the time *Jones* was decided, however, we deemed the community interest in a nonvested retirement pension a mere expectancy, and not a property interest. (See French v. French (1941) 17 Cal. 2d 775 [112 P.2d 235, 134 A.L.R. 366].) Since Jones retired before his right to a "retirement" pension vested, his acceptance of "disability" pay did not affect any present community asset, but merely prevented an expectancy from coming into fruition. Recognizing, however, that the principles in *Jones* might not govern a case in which the serviceman had acquired a vested right to retired pay wholly apart from his disability, we expressly limited our decision to cases involving nonvested pensions.

One year following our decision in *Jones* we overturned past precedent and held in In re Marriage of Brown, supra, 15 Cal. 3d 838, that pension rights, whether or not vested, constituted a property interest; that to the extent that such rights derive from employment during coverture, they now comprise community assets. This holding undermines the fundamental premise of *Jones:* that the award of a serviceman's "disability" pension to the serviceman as his separate property would not impair any community interest of his spouse. Under current law—in contrast to the law prevailing when *Jones* was decided—both the nonvested retirement pension in *Jones* and the husband's vested right to a "retirement" pension in the present case constitute valuable community assets deserving of judicial protection.

Our reasoning in *Brown* is particularly appropriate to the present case. As we stated there,

> [o]ver the past decades, pension benefits have become an increasingly significant part of the consideration earned by the employee for his services. As the date of vesting and retirement approaches, the value of the pension right grows until it often represents the most important asset of the marital community. . . . A division of community property which awards one spouse the entire value of this asset, without any offsetting award to the other spouse, does not represent that equal division of community property contemplated by [the Family Code]. (In re Marriage of Brown, supra, 15 Cal. 3d 838, 847.)

We cannot permit the serviceman's election of a "disability" pension to defeat the community interest in his right to a pension based on longevity. In the first place, such a result would violate the settled principle that one spouse cannot, by invoking a condition wholly within his control, defeat the community interest of the other spouse. . . .

In the second place, "only a portion of husband's pension benefit payments, though termed 'disability payments,' is properly allocable to disability. It would be unjust to deprive wife of a valuable property right simply because a misleading label has been affixed to husband's pension fund benefits." . . .

The purpose of disability benefits, as we explained in *Jones,* is primarily to compensate the disabled veteran for "the loss of earnings resulting from his compelled premature military retirement and from diminished ability to compete in the civilian job market" (13 Cal. 3d at p.459) and secondarily to compensate him for the personal suffering caused by the disability. Military retired pay based on disability, however, does not serve those purposes exclusively. Because it replaces a "retirement" pension, and is computed in part on the basis of longevity of service and rank at retirement, it also serves the objective of providing support for the serviceman and his spouse after he leaves the service. Moreover, as the veteran approaches normal retirement age, this latter purpose may become the predominate function served by the "disability" pension.

The present case illustrates the point. The husband here did not retire prematurely from military service to face the prospect of competing on the civilian labor market handicapped by his disability; he served for 26 years, retiring only after he had acquired a vested right to a "retirement" pension. He did not begin to receive his disability pension until 17 years after the injury. The value of his present "disability" pension depends largely on the high military rank he had achieved at the time of retirement and his extensive military service; it does not relate to his rank or longevity at the time of injury. Under these circumstances, the pension's function of compensating the husband for loss of earning capacity or providing recompense for personal suffering is secondary to the primary objective of providing retirement support.

The Court of Appeal in In re Marriage of Mueller, 70 Cal. App. 3d 66 [137 Cal. Rptr. 129 (1977)], explained the method of allocating a disability pension between the separate interest of the disabled spouse and the community interest in the retirement benefits. It stated that "where the employee spouse elects to receive disability benefits in lieu of a matured right to retirement benefits, only the net amount thus received over and above what would have been received as retirement benefits constitutes compensation for personal anguish and loss of earning capacity and is, thus, the employee spouse's separate property. The amount received in lieu of matured retirement benefits remains community property subject to division on dissolution." (70 Cal. App. 3d at p.71.)[9]

The trial court in the present case correctly followed this formula. It first classified as separate property that portion of the husband's pension attributable to employment before marriage. Turning to the balance of the pension, it assigned as separate property only the excess of the husband's pension over the "retirement" pension that he would have received if not disabled; the remainder of the pension it divided as community property. Finding this portion of the trial court's decision in accord with the principles stated in In re Marriage of Mueller, supra, 70 Cal. 3d 68, and adopted in this opinion, we affirm its division of the marital property. . . .

BIRD, C.J., MOSK, J., RICHARDSON, J., MANUEL, J., and JEFFERSON, J., concurred.

Note and Questions

1. Do you agree with the court's dictum that *Brown* alters the holding of *Jones*? Should *Jones* be decided any differently today in order to take into account the value of Mr. Jones' unvested military pension? Applying the *Mueller* formula, approved in *Stenquist*, to the facts of *Jones*, what result do you reach? Is footnote 9 correct? What is the value of an unvested retirement pension that we know will never vest or mature?

2. "Disability pay" that continues beyond retirement age may no longer reasonably be understood as replacement of wages lost on account of disability. How should such postretirement "disability pay" be treated? In Marriage of Saslow, 40 Cal. 3d 848, 710 P.2d 346, 221 Cal. Rptr. 546 (1985), Dr. Saslow, an allergist, purchased several disability policies during marriage with community funds. At age 59, Dr. Saslow became permanently disabled and he began to collect benefits. A few years later, he and his wife separated. The supreme court reported that the "benefits totaled $2,181 per month until the husband reached the age of 60, when one of the policies expired and the benefits were reduced to $1,881 per month. A second policy will expire and the benefits from another policy will decrease when the husband reaches age 70, reducing the monthly payments to $631. When the husband reaches age 75, a third policy will expire and the benefits will be reduced to $506 per month. That amount will be payable each month until the husband's death." The husband also held eight life insurance policies, but "did not invest in a retirement or pension plan." Id. at 85. The supreme court remanded to the trial

9. Although the quoted language from In re Marriage of Mueller speaks of "matured" retirement benefits, the court earlier in its opinion made clear that matured benefits could not be distinguished from immature but vested benefits. Indeed in light of In re Marriage of Brown, supra, 15 Cal. 3d 838, no distinction can be drawn between matured benefits and nonvested benefits.

court to determine when the disability benefits effectively became retirement benefits, and then to make a *Stenquist* allocation between the two types of benefits. If you were the trial judge, how would you make such a determination?

3. With respect to *military* disability pay elected in lieu of retirement benefits, *Stenquist* treatment is at least temporarily suspended by the United States Supreme Court federal preemption decision in Mansell v. Mansell, 490 U.S. 581, 104 L. Ed. 2d 675, 109 S. Ct. 2023 (1989), discussed at page 620 infra.

e. Severance Pay

MARRIAGE OF WRIGHT
140 Cal. App. 3d 342, 189 Cal. Rptr. 336 (1983)

ANDREEN, J. . . . The primary question raised by this appeal is whether termination pay received by a spouse after separation is community or separate property. . . .

The parties separated on June 23, 1976, after 12 years of marriage. On July 13, 1976, husband received $24,208.64 (net) from his employer, San Joaquin Community Hospital Corporation. Husband testified it was not a bonus for past work, but equaled approximately one year's pay and was given because of his termination due to harassment caused by wife and her father.

By stipulation, the deposition testimony of Joe B. Hurst, the hospital administrator, was received into evidence. It establishes that husband was employed at the hospital from 1972 until July 13, 1976, and had attained the position of assistant administrator. Wife's father was the hospital chaplain.

Hurst related that husband was paid his normal rate of pay for the first six months of 1976, and was then given a lump sum payment of $24,208.64 in July. He was paid that amount because he was leaving the hospital and in recognition that he would experience difficulty securing further employment. Hurst's testimony shows the lump sum payment was voluntary on the hospital's part and was not part of the employment contract. Hurst stated that part of the difficulties which he expected husband to encounter would be due to some actions he anticipated wife and her father, the chaplain, would take. They had threatened to ruin him financially, professionally, and personally. It was the chaplain's behavior in response to the divorce which caused Hurst, on July 13, 1976, to recommend, and husband accept, termination of husband's employment at the hospital.[1]

---

1. We quote from Hurst's testimony: "[T]here was approximately one year's compensation paid at the time Mr. Wright ended his employment, not in consideration of work for that year or his past performance — I think this is important to remember — but in consideration of the fact that he was leaving our employment in a responsible position with a number of difficulties that I was aware of that he would be facing, particularly in the securing of other positions. And as it still remains, field positions in hospital administration are difficult, at best, for a person with Mr. Wright's previous background and experience.

" . . .

"A. No, [counsel]. It was not considered a merit increase. I think that Mr. Wright was involved in some situations that I was acquainted with, and that I realized were going to affect his future ability to secure employment; that were going to give him an opportunity to experience a great deal of problems. And as a result of this, it is customary in administrative circles to grant termination pay, if you want to call it this — or not termination. Excuse me — pay for an employee when they leave a responsible position where there may be the expectation they're going to have trouble securing another position.

" . . .

Wife contends the termination payment was based on services rendered during marriage and therefore is community property. Husband contends it is separate property since the payment was made after separation. ([Family] Code, §[771].[2])

Neither party has cited relevant case law. Independent research, however, has found persuasive precedent.

This case is analogous to In re Marriage of Flockhart (1981) 119 Cal. App. 3d 240 [173 Cal. Rptr. 818]. The employee there was compensated by the United States government for loss of future earnings because his employment was affected by the expansion of Redwood National Park. He lost his job after his separation from his wife. The payment of replacement income was held to be the employee's separate property. He received the payments not because of any contractual agreement with his prior employer but because of his loss of employment in the timber industry. (At p.243.)

Similarly, the instant case is analogous to cases involving disability benefits. Such payments serve the principal purpose of compensating the disabled employee for his/her injury, including prospective loss of earnings and diminished earning capacity. (In re Marriage of Samuels (1979) 96 Cal. App. 3d 122, 128 [158 Cal. Rptr. 38].) Disability payments paid after separation consistently have been held to be the separate property of the spouse who receives them, except for that portion of the payment which is payable as a pension. . . . Likewise, workers' compensation awards paid after separation are the separate property of the injured spouse. (In re Marriage of McDonald (1975) 52 Cal. App. 3d 509, 512-513 [125 Cal. Rptr. 160].) The purpose underlying the separate property treatment of both is compensation for future loss of earnings, not payment for services previously performed. The rulings are not based on the fact that the right to the payments accrued after separation, for in each of the cases cited in this paragraph . . . , the injury giving rise to the compensation occurred during coverture.

In the case at bench the termination payment was made in recognition that husband would encounter difficulty in securing future employment which would entail prospective loss of earnings. Since it was paid after separation it is clear it was separate property.

In re Marriage of Skaden (1977) 19 Cal. 3d 679 [139 Cal. Rptr. 615, 566 P.2d 249] is distinguishable. Skaden was employed as an insurance agent. His contract provided that if he was terminated two or more years after the effective date, he would receive termination benefits consisting of specific percentages of net premiums, collected within a five-year period of termination, on policies he had sold prior to termination. It was held that since the right derived from the terms of the agent's agreement, it was a property right which was community in character. The court noted that, "Nothing in the agreement suggests that such benefits are 'consideration for termination.'" (At p.687.) The court further stated:

> We think it clear from the foregoing that the termination benefits contemplated by the subject contract were, like pension benefits, "a form of deferred

---

"... Mrs. Wright indicated to me a number of situations in Mr. Wright's and her personal relationship; her attitude about his particular situation; what she anticipated doing about it. I received the same kind of profession from her father with certain indications as to the types of difficulty that would be raised in order that Mr. Wright would be sure to pay for whatever his experience was going to be."

2. [Family] Code section [771] provides: "The earnings and accumulations of a spouse and the minor children living with, or in the custody of, the spouse, while living separate and apart from the other spouse, are the separate property of the spouse."

compensation for services rendered." The right to these benefits "derived from the terms of the employment contract" and under those terms became vested upon the expiration of two years after the date of execution. Manifestly, then, under the cases we have cited. . . . That right is property subject to division, to the extent of its community character, upon dissolution of the marriage. ([Family Code §2550].)

(At pp.687-688.)

Skaden is inapposite, since the right to a percentage of the insurance premiums earned on policies issued during coverture was a contract right payable *irrespective of continued employment.* Even though in the disability cases the payments were pursuant to a contract right, they were made because *the employment was no longer available.* The instant case is like the disability cases; the payment was made because the employee faced diminished earnings in the immediate future.

The judgment is reversed. The trial court is directed to vacate its judgment awarding wife one-half of the termination benefit and to enter a new judgment declaring the sum to be the separate property of husband.

FRANSON, Acting P.J., and WOOLPERT, J., concurred.

Notes and Questions

1. Does it matter that the severance pay was "voluntary . . . and not part of the employment contract"? Would a bonus for "a fine year's work" awarded three weeks after separation also be the worker's separate property? See Downer v. Bramet, supra at page 146.

2. Looking again at the California distinction between retirement benefits and all other forms of wage replacement received after separation (disability benefits, workers' compensation, severance pay), a replacement analysis seems to prevail with respect to all wage substitutes *except* that occasioned by superannuation, that is, retirement pensions. Only with retirement pensions do we ask: "When was the benefit earned?" With respect to all other wage replacement, we do not care when the right was earned; the only significant issue is: "What does it replace?"

This approach is consistent with marital property treatment of insurance proceeds resulting from casualty to insured property. If, for example, a husband insures his separate property boat with community funds and the boat is destroyed in a storm, how should the resulting insurance proceeds be characterized? Most cases that have directly addressed the issue treat the proceeds as the husband's separate property. See page 278 supra.

Assuming that replacement analysis is a generally sound approach to the classification of wage replacement and other insurance proceeds, our treatment of retirement benefits represents an exception to a generally applicable rule. What, if anything, justifies treating retirement pensions differently from all other wage replacement benefits? In our initial consideration of this problem, the question was not posed in this manner because retirement pensions have dominated marital property case law. We are accustomed to asking whether and how a difficult-to-classify fringe benefit resembles a retirement pension. We have not entertained the possibility that retirement pensions are sui generis and should not be treated as a model for other employment-related benefits. See Blumberg, Marital Property Treatment of Pensions, Disability Pay, Workers' Compensation and Other Wage Substitutes: An Insurance, or Replacement, Analysis, 33 UCLA L. Rev. 1250 (1986).

3. For additional severance pay cases, see Marriage of DeShurley, 207 Cal. App. 3d 992, 255 Cal. Rptr. 150 (1989); Marriage of Lawson, 208 Cal. App. 3d 466, 256 Cal. Rptr. 283 (1989); Marriage of Horn, 181 Cal. App. 3d 540, 226 Cal. Rptr. 666 (1986); Marriage of Kuzmiak, 176 Cal. App. 3d 1152, 222 Cal. Rptr. 644 (1986), cert. den. sub nom. Kuzmiak v. Kuzmiak, 479 U.S. 885 (1986). The cases reflect the tension between California's disparate treatment of employment-generated old age pensions, on the one hand, and disability benefits, on the other. When severance pay most resembles a retirement pension (for example, National Football League termination benefits in *Horn*), it is treated as a community asset to the extent that the benefit was earned during marriage. When severance pay more closely resembles disability pay, it has been classified according to its replacement function. The California severance pay cases are explored in Blumberg, California Classification of Severance Pay, Com. Prop. J., July 1987, at 14-19.

f. Early Retirement Benefits

MARRIAGE OF LEHMAN
18 Cal. 4th 169, 955 P.2d 451, 74 Cal. Rptr. 2d 825 (1998)

Mosk, J. — We granted review in this case in order to address an important question relating to the characterization of retirement benefits as community or separate property under a so-called "defined benefit retirement plan," which specifies payments in advance in accordance with a formula that comprises factors such as final compensation, age, length of service, and a per-service-year multiplier: Does a nonemployee spouse who owns a community property interest in an employee spouse's retirement benefits under such a plan own a community property interest in the retirement benefits as enhanced? As we shall explain, we conclude that the answer is: Yes.

Jack R. Lehman (Husband) was born on September 3, 1940, and Marietta Lehman was born on November 13, 1941. On June 15, 1959, he was hired by the Pacific Gas and Electric Company (PG & E). On June 11, 1960, the couple married. On May 1, 1962, he began to participate in PG & E's defined benefit retirement plan, and thereby began to accrue a right to retirement benefits thereunder. On October 29, 1977, the couple separated. On December 19, 1978, they obtained an interlocutory judgment of dissolution of marriage from the superior court, which retained jurisdiction for purposes including the division of the community property interest in his retirement benefits at the time of retirement. On February 23, 1979, they obtained a final judgment of dissolution. In March 1993, in order to avoid discharging certain employees, PG & E offered an enhanced retirement program, called the "Voluntary Retirement Incentive" (VRI). It described the VRI program as a "management tool" to "reduc[e] costs" by "bring[ing] our workforce in line with the needs of our changing business" through enhancement of retirement benefits by means of "two special improvements to the retirement benefit formula," namely, the crediting of 3 putative years of service and the waiving of the normal actuarial reduction of 18 percent for early retirement, which is designed to account for more projected payments. It stated that the "decision to participate . . . is completely voluntary." For eligibility, it required, among other things, that the employee in question had attained the age of 50, and had accumulated 15 years of service, as of December 31, 1992. Husband met the conditions. He elected to retire early at about 54⅓ years of age under the VRI program effective January 1, 1995, with enhanced retirement benefits in the amount of $3,059.30 per month—based on final compensation of $5,360.43 per month, length of service of 35.67 years, including 3 putative years, and a per-service-year multiplier of 1.6 percent. (Without the 3-year putative service credit, he would have received enhanced retirement benefits in the amount of $2,802 per month; without the waiver of the normal 18 percent early retirement actuarial reduction, he would have received enhanced retirement benefits in the amount of $2,508.63 per month.) Had he waited to retire early at 55 years of age, without the 3-year putative service credit and without the waiver of the normal 18 percent early retirement actuarial reduction, he would have received retirement benefits in the amount of $2,350.39 per month—based on (presumed) final compensation of $5,360.43 per month, length of service of 33.42 years, and a per-service-year multiplier of 1.6 percent. . . . By electing to retire early at about 54⅓ years of age under the VRI program instead of waiting to retire early at 55 years of age, he received enhanced retirement benefits in an amount of $708.91 per month.

After Husband retired, Wife made various motions in the superior court, seeking various orders together with a determination as to characterization that she owned a community property interest in his retirement benefits as enhanced. In response, Husband admitted that she owned such an interest in his retirement benefits, but denied that she owned one in them as enhanced. What was in contest was solely characterization, i.e., whether the enhancement was a community asset in any part, and not apportionment, i.e., to what extent the enhancement, if a community asset at least in some part, belonged to the community and separate estates. Generally following In re Marriage of Gram (1994) 25 Cal. App. 4th 859, 30 Cal. Rptr. 2d 792 (hereafter sometimes *Gram*), which had recently been decided, the superior court issued orders favorable to Wife, including the determination that, by owning a community property interest in Husband's retirement benefits, she owned a community property interest in his retirement benefits as enhanced. As to apportionment, it applied the so-called "time rule." . . . Under that method, the community property interest in retirement benefits is the percentage representing the fraction whose numerator is the employee spouse's length of service during marriage before separation, here 17.39 years, and whose denominator is the employee spouse's length of service in total, here 32.67 years; the separate property interest is the percentage representing the remainder of 100 percent minus the community property interest percentage. The superior court determined that the community property interest in Husband's retirement benefits as enhanced was 53.23 percent and that the separate property interest therein was 46.77 percent. It proceeded to award Wife, as her share, one-half of the community property interest, here 26.62 percent—which yielded her an amount of about $814.39 per month, including about $188.71 per month attributable to the enhancement. It declined to follow *Gram* to the extent that *Gram* suggested that it had to add any putative years credited to the employee spouse's service to the denominator of the time-rule fraction. On Husband's appeal, the Court of Appeal affirmed. . . . [T]he Court of Appeal concluded that the superior court was correct in its characterization. In this regard, it agreed with *Gram*. At the same time, it disagreed with the then-recent decision in In re Marriage of Frahm (1996) 45 Cal. App. 4th 536, 53 Cal. Rptr. 2d 31 (hereafter sometimes *Frahm*), which it read to be in conflict. . . .

On Husband's petition, we granted review. We now affirm.

The question before us is one of characterization of retirement benefits as community or separate property under a defined benefit retirement plan, specifically, whether a nonemployee spouse who owns a community property interest in an employee spouse's retirement benefits under such a plan owns a community property interest in the latter's retirement benefits as enhanced.

Generally, all property acquired by a spouse during marriage before separation is community property. (See Fam. Code, §§760, 771.)

Under the leading case of In re Marriage of Brown (1976) 15 Cal. 3d 838, 126 Cal. Rptr. 633, 544 P.2d 561 (hereafter sometimes *Brown*), and its progeny, such property may include the right to retirement benefits accrued by the employee spouse as deferred compensation for services rendered. . . . The right to retirement benefits is a right to "draw . . . from [a] stream of income that . . . begins to flow" on retirement, as that stream is then defined. . . .

The stream's volume at retirement may depend on various events or conditions after separation and even after dissolution. . . . Such events and conditions include both changes in the retirement-benefit formula . . . and also changes in the basis on which the retirement-benefit formula operates. . . . Changes in the retirement-benefit formula may be frequent. . . . Changes in the basis on which the retirement-benefit formula operates are virtually constant. (See, e.g., In re Marriage of Adams, supra, 64 Cal. App. 3d at p.186, 134 Cal. Rptr. 298 [changes in the basis on which the retirement-benefit formula operates are effected continuously through "additional years of service," "increase in earnings," and "increase in age"].)

Thus, the stream's volume at retirement may turn out to be even less than feared, as when the right to retirement benefits fails to vest or mature . . . , or when the employment itself ceases because the employer ceases to do business. By contrast, it may turn out to be even more than hoped for, as when the employer increases the per-service-year multiplier of the retirement-benefit formula . . . , or when the employee spouse lives to a greater than expected age, or serves more than expected years, or attains a higher than expected final compensation. . . . That the nonemployee spouse might happen to enjoy an increase, or suffer a decrease, in retirement benefits because of post-separation or even post-dissolution events or conditions is justified by the nature of the right to retirement benefits as a right to draw from a stream of income that begins to flow, and is defined, on retirement . . . , with the nonemployee spouse, at one and the same time, holding the chance of more . . . and bearing the risk of less . . . equally with the employee spouse. Because the nonemployee spouse is compelled to share the bad with the employee spouse . . . , he or she must be allowed to share the good as well.

Hence, if the right to retirement benefits accrues, in some part, during marriage before separation, it is a community asset and is therefore owned by the community in which the nonemployee spouse as well as the employee spouse owns an interest. . . .

It follows that a nonemployee spouse who owns a community property interest in an employee spouse's retirement benefits owns a community property interest in the latter's retirement benefits as enhanced. That is because, practically by definition, the right to retirement benefits that accrues, at least in part, during marriage before separation underlies any right to an enhancement. . . .

The fact that a nonemployee spouse who owns a community property interest in an employee spouse's retirement benefits owns a community property interest in the latter's retirement benefits as enhanced does not mean that the enhancement is a community asset in its entirety. But the question to what extent such an enhancement belongs to the community and separate estates is one of apportionment and not characterization.

At the outset, both the *Gram* court and the *Frahm* court recognized that the issue of characterization of property . . . does not turn on the motive of the employer. In any context, motive is, at best, hard to discern. . . . In this context, it is also "irrelevant.". . . That is because the employer acts for its own business reasons, and not for reasons bearing on the characterization of property for employee spouses and nonemployee spouses. . . . Beyond that point, however, the *Gram* court and the *Frahm* court diverged. . . .

On their respective facts, *Gram* and *Frahm* are each correct in its result as to characterization. *Gram* concludes that a nonemployee spouse who owns a community property interest in an employee spouse's retirement benefits owns a community property interest in the latter's retirement benefits as enhanced. For its part, *Frahm* concludes that a nonemployee spouse does not own a community property interest in an employee spouse's severance payment when the latter accrues a right thereto solely after separation. . . . As we held in *Brown*, what is determinative is the single concrete fact of time. To the extent—and only to the extent—that an employee spouse accrues a right to property during marriage before separation, the property in question is a community asset. . . .

Turning to the proceeding at bar, we now consider the decision of the Court of Appeal sustaining the superior court's determination as to characterization that, by owning a community property interest in Husband's retirement benefits under PG & E's defined benefit retirement plan, Wife owns a community property interest in his retirement benefits as enhanced by the VRI program.

[W]e . . . believe that the Court of Appeal properly concluded that the superior court's determination as to characterization was correct. . . .

Husband argues against our conclusion as to characterization. He proves unpersuasive. Husband asserts that Wife does not own a community property interest in his retirement benefits as enhanced. He concedes that, as a general matter, a nonemployee spouse who owns a community property interest in an employee spouse's retirement benefits owns a community property interest in the latter's retirement benefits as enhanced. He maintains, however, that a nonemployee spouse does not own a community property interest in the employee spouse's retirement benefits as enhanced through a post-separation "contract" between the employee spouse and the employer independent of any right to retirement benefits that accrued, in some part, during marriage before separation—whereby, for example, the employer gives the enhancement in consideration for immediate retirement, and the employee spouse immediately retires in consideration for the enhancement. Husband's retirement benefits, however, were not enhanced by a "contract" of this sort. Any such "contract" was derivative of the right to retirement benefits that accrued, in some part, during marriage before separation. Contrary to his position . . . , the "enhancement" is a "modification of an asset not the creation of a new one." (Olivo v. Olivo, . . . 82 N.Y. 2d [202], 210, 604 N.Y.S.2d 23, 624 N.E.2d 151.) By its very terms, it results from "improvements to the retirement benefit formula" under PG & E's existing defined benefit retirement plan, not from a new plan altogether. Husband's premise, viz., that he accrued a right to the enhancement solely after separation, is unsupported.

Husband then asserts, more radically, that Wife does not own a community property interest in his retirement benefits as enhanced because the enhancement amounts to a severance payment and, as such, is his separate property. The enhancement here, however, was not a severance payment either in name or in nature. It called itself, and was in fact, an increase in retirement benefits. Distinguishable, aaccordingly, is In re Marriage of Lawson, supra, 208 Cal. App. 3d 446, 256 Cal. Rptr. 283. There, the court held that a nonemployee spouse did not own a community property interest in a severance payment given to an employee spouse after separation. . . . But, unlike Husband and his retirement benefits, the employee spouse had not previously accrued any right to the payment whatsoever. . . . Distinguishable as well is In re Marriage of Nelson (1986) 177 Cal. App. 3d 150, 222 Cal. Rptr. 790. There, the court held that a nonemployee spouse did not own a community property interest in a stock option granted to an employee spouse after separation. . . . Again, unlike Husband and his retirement benefits, the employee spouse had not previously accrued any right to the option whatsoever. . . . At oral argument, Husband acknowledged that what the employer does is material and not why. It is of no consequence that PG & E enhanced his retirement benefits because it wanted him to retire immediately. Just as it would be of no consequence that he himself enhanced his retirement benefits, as by seeking and obtaining higher final compensation, because he wanted to retire comfortably. . . . Rather, it is dispositive that PG & E enhanced his retirement benefits — in which Wife admittedly owns a community property interest.

Although neither Husband nor Wife claimed in the Court of Appeal, or claims here, that the superior court erred in its determination as to apportionment of Husband's retirement benefits as enhanced between community and separate property interests through its application of the time rule, we shall address that question because their arguments about characterization may be deemed to reach apportionment by implication. . . .

We find unsound Gram's suggestion that, in applying the time rule to apportion an employee spouse's retirement benefits as enhanced between community and separate property interests, the superior court must add any putative years credited to the employee spouse's service to the denominator of the time-rule fraction. . . . Such years are fictive — they have no independent existence, but are merely a means by which the employer effects the enhancement. The employer can achieve exactly the same outcome, for example, by crediting a putative sum to the employee spouse's final compensation — in this proceeding, $492.23 to $5,360.43 per month, for a total of $5,852.66 per month. Or by increasing the per-service-year multiplier in the retirement-benefit formula that operates on the basis provided by the employee spouse — in this proceeding, from 1.6 percent to 1.74692 percent. Neither the community nor the employee spouse supplied the putative service credit as a mechanism of enhancement. The employer did. But both the community and the employee spouse supplied part of the basis on which the retirement-benefit formula operates, specifically, the years of service. And they both must share in what the putative service credit yields, because that credit amounts to a post-separation and even post-dissolution event or condition on which the volume of the stream of income that constitutes retirement benefits depends. . . . To the extent that Gram is to the contrary, it is disapproved.

For the reasons stated above, we conclude that we must affirm the judgment of the Court of Appeal.

It is so ordered.

GEORGE, C.J., and KENNARD, WERDEGAR and BROWN, JJ., concur.

Notes and Questions

1. *The distinction between early retirement benefits and severance pay.* Are you persuaded by the California Supreme Court's distinction between an early retirement package expressed entirely in terms of retirement benefits (*Gram*) and an early retirement package combining enhanced retirement benefits with lump-sum severance pay (*Frahm*) or periodic severance pay? It is certainly a "bright line" distinction, but does it make any sense? Two justices (Baxter and Chin) thought not and dissented:

> Manifestly, the increased monthly retirement benefit offered in return for participation in the VRI program was intended as consideration for the employee's post-marital agreement to retire early, and as a partial replacement of the future compensation, both in monthly salary and in continuing accrual of pension rights, that the employee would thereby give up. Pension rights under the VRI option stemmed from a separate contract between the employee and the employer, offered and accepted after the marriage ended for reasons unrelated to the former community's efforts.

74 Cal. Rptr. 2d at 841.

More basically, *Lehman* points up the difficulty of sustaining a principled distinction between a retirement pension and severance pay. Each is earned by employment, and each is intended to cushion the employee's separation from employment.

2. *The tension between Lehman and Oddino.* Dissenting in *Lehman,* Justice Baxter also pointed out the tension between the court's holding in *Lehman* and Marriage of Oddino, 16 Cal. 4th 67 (1997), decided the preceding year. In Marriage of Oddino, the husband continued working after he reached 55, the earliest age at which he was eligible to retire. As in *Gillmore* (at page 290 supra), his wife requested an immediate distribution of the pension in order to realize her community property interest. The pension was an ERISA-regulated pension, so the court's task was to frame a qualified domestic relations order (QDRO) requiring the pension plan to bifurcate the pension and begin payment to the wife. The ERISA bifurcation-for-early-payment provision requires that benefits be calculated on the basis of the "present value of benefits actually accrued and not taking into account . . . any employer subsidy for early retirement." Although the husband had not yet reached retirement age, the plan allowed early retirement without a consequential actuarial reduction in monthly benefits. The issue was whether the value of the wife's interest in the benefits should be calculated with or without actuarial reduction. The California Supreme Court held that the benefits should be actuarially reduced because the plan's waiver of actuarial reduction for early retirees was "an employee subsidy for early retirement." The issues in *Lehman* and *Oddino* are not identical. *Oddino* interprets a federal statute (ERISA), and *Lehman* interprets California community property law. Moreover, *Lehman* deals with benefits actually received, while the early retirement benefit not taken by Mr. Oddino would never otherwise be realized. Yet there remains considerable tension between the two holdings.

3. *Must a "property right" invariably accrue during marriage?* Does Justice Mosk, writing for the majority, overstate the point when he says:

> To the extent—and only to the extent—that an employee spouse accrues a right to property during marriage before separation, the property in question is a community asset.

74 Cal. Rptr. 2d at 832.

Do you think that this dictum was intended to disapprove cases like Downer v. Bramet, at page 146 supra? Should it?

g. Employment-Related Group Life and Health Insurance

i. *Life Insurance*

MARRIAGE OF SPENGLER
5 Cal. App. 4th 288, 6 Cal. Rptr. 2d 764 (1992)

SIMS, Associate Justice.

In this postjudgment marital dissolution proceeding, petitioner below, Barbara Ann Spengler (wife), filed a complaint in joinder against claimant Rose G. Spengler (beneficiary) in which wife claimed a community property interest in proceeds received by beneficiary from a term life insurance policy upon the death of wife's former husband, Daniel F. Spengler, Sr. (husband). The trial court found the policy was an omitted community asset [Family Code §2556], and entered judgment awarding half the proceeds to wife. The issue on appeal is whether an employment-related group term life insurance policy is community property subject to division in a marital dissolution. The narrower question is whether such policy's provision of a right to renewed coverage without proof of current insurability is a valuable community asset subject to division in a marital dissolution where the insured spouse becomes uninsurable during the marriage, such that the existing policy provides future coverage the insured spouse could not otherwise obtain. We will conclude the employment-related group term life insurance policy is not a community property asset beyond expiration of the term acquired with community efforts, and this result is unaffected by uninsurability if the insured employee has no enforceable right to compel the employer to renew the policy. We will therefore reverse the judgment.

Wife and husband were married in 1967.

In 1980, husband began working for Mid-Valley Dairy company. The employer provided various life insurance benefits to employees, apparently as fringe benefits. The policy at issue in this case was a group term life insurance plan that insured employees for the amount of their salary up to $180,000. The insured group was large enough so that employees were not required to undergo a physical examination or submit proof of insurability. This coverage continued, though underwritten by different insurers, until husband's death.

In 1982, husband was diagnosed with . . . cancer. According to testimony of an insurance expert, a person in husband's situation would have been "uninsurable," i.e., unable to obtain individual life insurance.

Husband and wife separated in 1986. The marriage was dissolved by bifurcated judgment from which wife appealed. . . .

After dissolution, the insurance coverage continued under a policy issued by Hartford Life Insurance Company in September 1989. That same month, husband married Rose Spengler and named her as his beneficiary under the policy.

Three months later, husband died.

Beneficiary received approximately $100,000 as designated beneficiary of the subject policy. Wife filed a complaint in joinder, seeking half the proceeds as a community asset. . . .

Following a bench trial, the trial court concluded the insurance policy was community property and was an omitted asset under [Family code section 2556]. The court entered judgment in favor of wife for one-half of the policy proceeds.

Beneficiary contends a term life insurance policy is not a community asset subject to division under the Family [Code] and does not become a community asset by virtue of the insured spouse becoming uninsurable during the marriage. We agree. . . .

The Courts of Appeal are split on the issue of whether a term life insurance policy is community property. The Second District has held that a term life insurance policy, having no cash surrender value, is not "property" within the meaning of the community property laws. (In re Marriage of Lorenz (1983) 146 Cal. App. 3d 464, 467, 194 Cal. Rptr. 237.) The Fourth District has held that, even though term life insurance lacks cash surrender value, it may have replacement value subject to community property division where insurability is lessened by advancing age or declining health of the insured spouse. (E.g., In re Marriage of Gonzalez (1985) 168 Cal. App. 3d 1021, 1025, 214 Cal. Rptr. 634.) The First District has held that, as long as the insured spouse remains insurable, term life insurance has no divisible community property value upon expiration of the term acquired with community funds/efforts. (Estate of Logan (1987) 191 Cal. App. 3d 319, 325, 236 Cal. Rptr. 368.) However, according to dictum in *Logan,* if the insured becomes uninsurable during the marriage, the policy's renewal rights to continued coverage that cannot otherwise be purchased is a community asset to be divided upon dissolution. (Id. at p.326, 236 Cal. Rptr. 368.) As will appear, we agree with *Logan's* holding but disagree with its dictum.

Logan, supra, 191 Cal. App. 3d 319, 236 Cal. Rptr. 368, was an action against an estate, in which a former wife sought a share in the proceeds of her deceased former husband's employment-related term life insurance policy, for which preseparation premium payments had been paid with community funds. [The court quotes extensively from *Logan,* which is reprinted at page 279 supra.] . . .

We agree with *Logan's* holding that an employment-related term life insurance policy is not a community property asset after expiration of the term acquired with community funds/efforts. We respectfully disagree, however, with *Logan's* dictum finding an exception where the insured spouse becomes uninsurable during the marriage.

In our view, the fallacy of classifying the renewal right in this case as community property is that it is based on the faulty premise that during the marriage husband was able to acquire a policy that could not thereafter be taken away. But that is not the case. The right to continued insurance protection under an employment-related insurance policy is not inexorably earned by the investment of community funds/efforts in acquiring the policy. It depends on the insured's continuing to work at that employment *and* on the employer's continuing to provide the group insurance plan.

In order to qualify as community property, an asset or interest must be "property" within the meaning of the community property laws. (*Lorenz,* supra, 146 Cal. App. 3d at p.467, 194 Cal. Rptr. 237.) Thus, the question is whether the isolated interest in this case — the renewal right — is "property" as opposed to a mere expectancy. (See In re Marriage of Brown (1976) 15 Cal. 3d 838, 846, fn.8, 126 Cal. Rptr. 633, 544 P.2d 461, citing §697 [contingent future interest is property] and §700 [expectancy is not to be deemed an interest of any kind].)

We recognize that "Fringe benefits are not a gift from the employer but are earned by the employee as part of the compensation for services. . . . Thus fringe benefits such as . . . employer-paid life insurance . . . are community property to the extent they are earned by the time, skill and effort of a spouse during marriage. . . . Fringe benefits consisting of *contractual rights* to future benefits after separation, though unvested and unmatured, are property subject to allocation between community and separate interests at the time of dissolution." . . .

The fact that a benefit is subject to contingencies does not preclude a finding of a divisible property interest. (In re Marriage of Brown, supra, 15 Cal. 3d at p.846, fn.8, 126 Cal. Rptr. 633, 544 P.2d 561.) A contract right, though contingent, may be a valuable property right if it is "subject only to conditions within the control of the [holder of the right]." (In re Marriage of Fonstein (1976) 17 Cal. 3d 738, 745-746, 131 Cal. Rptr. 873, 552 P.2d 1169 [right to withdraw from partnership]; . . . see also cases cited in In re Marriage of Kilbourne (1991) 232 Cal. App. 3d 1518, 1524, fn.5, 284 Cal. App. 3d 1518, 1524, fn.5, 284 Cal. Rptr. 201 [that husband's right to receive fees from law practice was contingent on future events did not negate status as community assets].)

To be distinguished from the *contract rights* referenced in the preceding paragraphs is a "mere expectancy," which does not constitute a property interest under community property laws. Thus, our Supreme Court has indicated that a benefit contingent on continued employment may or may not be "property" subject to the community property laws depending on whether it is a mere expectancy or a contract right. (In re Marriage of Brown, supra, 15 Cal. 3d 838, 126 Cal. Rptr. 633, 544 P.2d 561 [nonvested pension rights are property].) "The term expectancy describes the interest of a person who merely foresees that he might receive a future beneficence, such as the interest of an heir apparent . . . , or a beneficiary designated by a living insured who has a right to change the beneficiary. . . . [T]he defining characteristic of an expectancy is that its holder has no *enforceable right* to his beneficence." (Id. at pp.844-845, 126 Cal. Rptr. 633, 544, P.2d 561, original emphasis, fn. omitted.) . . .

Applying the above principles, we conclude that the isolated interest in this case — the renewal right — was a mere expectancy rather than a contingent property interest. We emphasize that the interest we are examining is *only* the renewal right, *not* the coverage element of the policy. The renewal right depended not only on continued employment by husband but also on continued offering of the plan by the employer. Although there was no testimony about the specifics of husband's employment terms, the insurance expert testified that any group term life insurance policy can be terminated by the employer at any time, with 30 days notice. He further testified that continued coverage for the uninsurable employee depended both on the employee continuing the employment *and* the employer continuing the policy. Wife does not dispute this evidence, nor does she contend that anything in husband's employment contract prevented the employer from discontinuing the group plan. Thus, although there is a contingent contract right to policy *proceeds* in the event of death during the term, there is no right on the part of husband to compel the employer to *renew* the coverage upon expiration of the term. In other words, the prospect of renewal of the policy by the employer was a beneficence to which husband had no enforceable right.

Thus, while the renewal right has potential value, we conclude that in the absence of a right by the insured spouse to enforce that value, the renewal right is not "property" within the meaning of the community property laws. (In re Marriage of Brown, supra, 15 Cal. 3d at pp.844-845, 126 Cal. Rptr. 633, 544 P.2d 561.) That the policy *was* renewed in this case is immaterial, because this is not a question to be answered in hindsight. As a matter of law, the renewal right aspect of an employment-related group term life insurance policy is not property subject to division in marital dissolution where the employee has no enforceable right to renewal.

This result is equitable, because the community has received the full benefit of its bargain — continued coverage protection throughout the course of the marriage. There is no carry-over right from the days of the marriage. There is no right to insurance that transcends the separation.

We conclude the trial court erred in finding the insurance policy in this case to be community property asset.

The judgment is reversed. Appellant will recover her costs on appeal.

PUGLIA, P.J., and NICHOLSON, J., concur.

Notes and Questions

1. *Spengler* identifies two requirements for continuing coverage under Daniel Spengler's employer-provided group health insurance policy: that the employee continue employment and that the employer maintain the policy. Do both or either warrant the court's conclusion that, for community property purposes, the life insurance coverage or, more narrowly, the right to reinsure is thus a noncognizable *beneficence* rather than cognizable *property*? With respect to the necessity of continued employment, is *Spengler* consistent with *Brown*, supra at page 283, and *Lucero*, supra at page 345? In terms of employer beneficence, is *Spengler* consistent with Downer v. Bramet, supra at page 146?

On the other hand, are the pension cases inapposite for term insurance?

2. Do you agree that Daniel Spengler's employer, Mid-Valley Dairy Company, is entirely free to cancel its group life insurance policy? If Mid-Valley were to announce its intention to do so, how would you counsel currently uninsurable employees who have long enjoyed life insurance under the group plan?

3. What do you make of the fact, mentioned in both *Logan* and *Spengler*, that large companies are able to offer group insurance to new employees without initial proof of insurability? For uninsurable employees and prospective employees, the availability of such group insurance, both health and life, is a powerful incentive for remaining with or joining the company.

On the other hand, does the availability of such employment-related insurance call into question the very notion of "uninsurability" and cast further doubt on the value of the opportunity to reinsure?

4. *Life insurance as wage replacement.* Ought employment-related term life insurance, or term life insurance generally, be characterized as a form of wage replacement, for which the relevant issue is not the funding source but rather the character of the wages replaced? (See disability benefits and severance pay at pages 350-360 supra.) Under this analysis, Daniel Spengler's death proceeds are his separate prop-

erty because they replace postdivorce wages he would have earned had he lived. To the extent that his former wife Barbara had some claim to those postdivorce wages in the form of *spousal support,* her interest could have been secured under Family Code section 4360. For further discussion, see Blumberg, Marital Property Treatment of Pensions, Disability Pay, Workers' Compensation and Other Wage Substitutes: An Insurance, or Replacement Analysis, 33 UCLA L. Rev. 1250, 1284-1289 (1986).

Adopting this view, the ALI Principles include disability pay, workers' compensation payments, personal injury recoveries, and life insurance proceeds in the category of "benefits received as compensation for a loss." These benefits "take their character from the asset they replace." Principles of the Law of Family Dissolution: Analysis and Recommendations, §4.08 (2) (2002).

ii. Health Insurance

In an era in which few can afford the health care costs of serious or chronic illness, adequate health insurance is a vital asset. In the United States, health insurance is predominantly employment-related. Middle and upper income employees generally receive, as part of their pay package, group health insurance for themselves and their families. Coverage for a child generally lasts until the child ceases to be dependent, as defined by the policy. Coverage for a spouse generally lasts until divorce.

Thus, at divorce there is no health insurance to divide. So long as the employee retains his job, health insurance coverage continues for the employee and his dependent children[10] but, by the terms of the group health insurance policy, his spouse loses her derivative coverage upon divorce. Because community property law only purports to divide existing rights, it cannot reform the health insurance contract to provide continuing coverage for the divorced nonemployee spouse.

Federal law provides short-term relief for persons who have lost eligibility for employer-provided group health insurance on account of certain qualifying events, including divorce. The Consolidated Omnibus Budget Reconciliation Act of 1985 (COBRA) requires that the sponsors of ERISA-regulated group health insurance plans offer an employee's divorced spouse up to 36 months of individual health insurance continuation. The sponsor may charge the divorced spouse the full premium. 29 U.S.C. §§1161-1168 (2002). Employers of fewer than 20 employees are exempted from these federal requirements. In 1997, the California legislature enacted a California equivalent of COBRA to cover the health care and group disability plans of employers with 2 to 19 eligible employees. 1997 Cal. Stat., ch. 665, codified at California Health and Safety Code §§1366.20-1366.28 and 1373.621 (2002).

Additionally, the cost of health insurance may be included within Family Code section 4330 spousal support, although there is no specific statutory authorization for health insurance as a form of spousal support. (Compare section 4360, specifying life insurance or an annuity as a form of spousal support, and section 3751, specifying health insurance as an aspect of child support.)

---

10. The employee's wife might, as in *Spengler,* supra, make some community claim to the *employee's* continuing coverage, particularly if he is currently uninsurable, but such a claim will run into the roadblocks identified in *Spengler* and the notes following *Spengler.*

5.   Reprise and Finale: Basic Conceptual Difficulties in Determining When Compensation for Labor Is Earned

MARRIAGE OF HUG
154 Cal. App. 3d 780, 201 Cal. Rptr. 676 (1984)

KING, J.—. . . Maria and Paul were married [in April] 1956, and separated on June 9, 1976. On November 6, 1972, Paul left a position with International Business Machines, Inc. (IBM) to begin employment at Amdahl. While employed at Amdahl, he was granted options to purchase 3,100 shares of Amdahl's stock. The trial court found that the stock option plan was adopted "for the purpose of attracting and retaining the services of selected directors, executives and other key employees and for the purpose of providing an incentive to encourage and stimulate increased efforts by them."

Amdahl granted the first of the disputed options on August 9, 1974, an option to purchase 1,000 shares at $1 per share. The trial court found that this option "replaced" an earlier option to purchase 1,000 shares at $20 per share which had been awarded on November 22, 1972, just two weeks after Paul commenced employment at Amdahl. Paul and Amdahl mutually rescinded the 1972 agreement in August of 1974. Amdahl also granted the second option on August 9, 1974, for 1,300 shares at $1 per share. Amdahl granted a third option for 800 shares on September 15, 1975, at $5 per share. Each of the options was exercisable over four years each in yearly increments of 30 percent, 25 percent, 25 percent, and 20 percent.

Since portions of the options were exercisable only after the parties' separation, the court sought to allocate the options to reflect the relationship between periods of Paul's community contribution in comparison to his overall contribution to earning the option rights. In other words, the trial court attempted to fairly allocate the stock options between compensation for services prior to and after the date of separation.[1]

Thus, the court found that

> [t]he community property portion of the unexercised shares is the product of a fraction whose numerator is the length of service expressed in months by respondent [Paul] with Amdahl from the date of commencement of service to the date of separation of the parties and the denominator is the length of service expressed in months from the date of commencement of service to the date when an option could be first exercised, multiplied by the number of shares that could be purchased on the date of exercise.

. . . Paul agrees that an apportionment should be accomplished according to a time rule, but contends the trial court utilized an erroneous formula.[2] Paul con-

---

1. Postseparation earnings of a spouse are the separate property of that spouse. [Family Code §771.]

2. The term "time rule" has heretofore been primarily utilized to describe a formula for determining the community interest in retirement benefits according to the ratio of the length of employment between the date of marriage (or date of commencement of employment, if later) and the date of separation to the total length of employment. (In re Marriage of Judd (1977) 68 Cal. App. 3d 515 [137 Cal. Rptr. 318]; In re Marriage of Adams (1976) 64 Cal. App. 3d 181 [134 Cal. Rptr. 298].)

tends that the proper time rule should begin as of the date of granting the option, not the date of commencement of employment, since the options were not granted [as] an incentive to become employed by Amdahl. In addition, he argues that each annual option is a separate and distinct option which is compensation for services during that year, thus it accrues after the date of separation and should be totally his separate property.

Our research leads us to conclude that the issue before us, that of determining community and separate property interests in employee stock options granted to the employee's spouse prior to the date of separation, but only exercisable thereafter, is an issue of first impression.

Treatises which describe employee stock options in the context of general corporations law strongly suggest that contractual rights to such benefits vary so widely as to preclude the accuracy of any but the most general characterization of them. Thus, there is no compelling reason to require that employee stock options must always be classified as compensation exclusively for past, present, or future services. Rather, since the purposes underlying stock options differ, reference to the facts of each particular case must be made to reveal the features and implications of a particular employee stock option.

At the most general level, employment benefits such as stock options may be classified as an alternative to fixed salaries to secure optimal tax treatment.[3] (5 Fletcher, Cyclopedia Corporations (rev. ed. 1976) §2136, p.514.) In this sense, stock options fall into the same category as, for example, fringe benefits, health and welfare benefits, incentive compensation based on company profits, deferred compensation plans, and pension and profit-sharing arrangements. (1 Washington & Rothschild, Compensating the Corporate Executive (3d ed. 1962) pp.29-30. See also Steadman, Increasing Management's Real Income Through Deferral and Stock Options (1960) 15 Bus. Law. 764.)

Along with the general goal of structuring compensation favorably, other purposes accompany various benefit plans.

> Bonus and profit-sharing arrangements may take various forms such as a stock purchase option for a certain period, a management stock-purchase plan, or an employees' stock purchase plan. The primary purpose of a company stock-option plan is the attraction and retention of executive, key or qualified personnel, and the granting of such option is considered a form of compensation. . . . The purchase of shares by the executive officers in connection with an employee stock-purchase plan which may give the privilege of obtaining shares on a large scale at less than the market price often amounts to a lucrative bonus. (5 Fletcher, op. cit. supra, §2143.1, at p.551.)

A number of factors may prompt companies to use such alternatives, among them management's wish for a direct share in company profits, the possibility of increasing management's incentive and efforts, cutting taxes and providing security for the executive. (1 Washington & Rothschild, op. cit. supra, at p.30.)

If any of the various purposes of stock option plans can be said to bear empha-

---

3. The tax benefits to an employee of qualified stock option plans can be substantial, if the employer is a company with a high potential which is achieved by the time the options are exercisable. In Paul's case, for example, if Amdahl stock is selling for $20 when his options are exercisable he will pay only $1 or $5 (his option price), yet he will receive stock worth $20 a share, with no recognizable taxable gain. . . .

sis, it is probably that of providing incentive. "One of the most widespread programs for providing employees with additional incentive and creating an identification of interest between the company and the key employees is a stock option plan." (The Lawyer's Basic Corporate Practice Manual (ALI 2d ed. 1978) §8.06, p.130.) "Share options are a form of incentive compensation based on the idea that good management results in higher prices which render the share option valuable." (Henne, Corporations (2d ed. 1970) §248, p.492. See also Steadman, Stock Options and Other Executive Incentive Arrangements (1959) 13 Vand. L. Rev. 311, 314-315.)

Consistent with the emphasis on incentive is the supposition that options are granted for future services, either primarily or exclusively. This proposition appears bolstered by the general rule that option agreements must ordinarily be supported by consideration, and that "[i]n practice, consideration will usually be supplied by the executive in the form of continued services." (2 Washington & Rothschild, op. cit. supra, at p.575.)

Nevertheless, the temptation to conclude that options are earned exclusively by future services lessens somewhat in light of the flexibility and variety of option plans, as well as the size and circumstances of the offering company. "For the smaller company, for the company without substantial cash resources, for the company in distressed circumstances, stock options may provide a means of attracting strong management willing to render its services for modest current compensation in return for substantial future rewards on a tax-favored basis." (2 Washington & Rothschild, op. cit. supra, at p.571.) Although the purpose of providing incentive remains in the latter situation (and such an arrangement may be geared to future services as well), the primary goal appears to be *deferring compensation for present services*. At the least, such a use of stock options seems consistent with providing compensation for *either* present or future services, just as would its use as a bonus, noted in the description above. . . .

Finally, stock options may be used as additional compensation, *even for past services*, so long as to meet reasonable expectations as to such compensation which existed while the employee rendered the services. (2 Washington & Rothschild, op. cit. supra, at p.578.) Also, although out of keeping with common business practice, companies frequently provide rewards or bonuses for past services. (5 Fletcher, op. cit. supra, §2143, at p.538.)

Thus, no single characterization can be given to employee stock options. Whether they can be characterized as compensation for future services, for past services, or for both, depends upon the circumstances involved in the grant of the employee stock option.

In the instant case, the trial court found that the stock option agreement arose from the standard corporate purpose of "attracting and retaining the services of selected directors, executives and other key employees and for the purpose of providing an incentive to encourage and stimulate increased efforts by them." Since the options are keyed to periods of employment after the date of each grant, Paul argues that the options constitute compensation exclusively for future services rather than past or present services. For that reason, he says the period of employment prior to the granting of the option to him contributed nothing to earning the options and should be excluded from the time frame by which the court calculated its "time rule" allocation formula. . . .

Paul challenges the trial court's judgment for lack of findings as to the basis for applying the time rule in the manner it did. Specifically, he argues that the court failed to make appropriate factual findings to justify, including his first two years of employment at Amdahl, the time used to allocate the options in issue. He further argues that insufficient evidence was adduced at trial to support such findings.

By including the two years prior to the granting of the options in question, the trial court impliedly found that period of service contributed to earning the option rights in issue. (See Elliot v. Jensen (1960) 187 Cal. App. 2d 389, 393 [9 Cal. Rptr. 642] [subsidiary findings necessary to support the judgment are implied].) Substantial evidence supports this finding. Prior to becoming employed by Amdahl, Paul had worked for IBM Corporation for nearly seven years, at which point his retirement benefits, according to Maria's testimony, would have vested. In this context, the timing of such a critical career move apparently led the court to infer that inducements offered by Amdahl to some extent replaced the benefits left behind at IBM. Additionally, as noted above, Amdahl's option plan was designed to attract as well as to retain key employees. The parties discussed the implications of Paul's jump to Amdahl, and the offer of stock in some form seems to have been a key inducement to making the move. These facts support an implied finding that the options were earned from the commencement of Paul's employment at Amdahl.

The evidence further shows that providing incentive was far from Amdahl's only purpose in granting the options. The record shows that Paul anticipated the options from the outset and that Amdahl, in part, likely granted them in lieu of present compensation during the initial period of Paul's employment, a time when Amdahl's success was limited. Assuming the evidence demonstrated to the court's satisfaction that option rights represented deferred compensation for present services, the court was justified in finding that the option rights were earned in part during the first two years.

Paul's objection to the lack of findings as to the basis for including his first two years at Amdahl in the allocation formula ignores the trial court's finding that cited his receipt "[o]n August 9, 1974, [of] one thousand (1,000) shares at a price of one dollar (1.00) per share in a nonqualified plan which replaced the 1,000 shares of the 11/22/72 grant of 1,000 shares at $20.00 per share." Paul and Amdahl mutually rescinded the 1972 agreement, the lack of increased value of Amdahl's stock having left that option worthless. As a substitute for the rescinded option, which was by any standard earned during the years 1972-1974, the 1974 agreement could be seen as the product of Paul's employment during those years. The abortive first option further demonstrates that the option rights constituted a vital part of Paul's compensation package from the very outset of employment.

Finally, Paul's claim of reversible error by the trial court's failure to fix the value of the option rights as of the date of separation seems confused in light of In re Marriage of Brown (1976) 15 Cal. 3d 838 [126 Cal. Rptr. 633, 544 P.2d 561, 94 A.L.R.3d 164]. There the court acknowledged various difficulties inherent in the present division of contingent future contractual rights, but pointed out that it is appropriate to divide benefits as they are paid. (Id., at p.848.) There is no merit to Paul's contention that where benefits cannot be valued presently they cannot be divided. The reasoning of *Brown* and subsequent decisions flatly contradict this notion. . . .

In sum, the evidence supports a finding that the options were earned from the outset of Paul's service with Amdahl. The trial court impliedly arrived at this determination by considering the compensation scheme as a whole, including the implications of Paul's move from IBM and the place option rights occupied in the entire context of his service. Additionally, another option agreement took the place of the first, indicating that options were a critical feature in the total scheme of compensation. Paul's emphasis on the fact that the options, as is usually the case, became exercisable after specific periods of service subsequent to their granting diminishes in relation to the details of the entire employment circumstance.

Nothing in the makeup of the Amdahl stock option plan requires that they be construed as compensation exclusively for future services. Further, case law suggests that the time provisions of a compensation plan not be too literally construed, at least in the context of marital property, lest courts overlook the realities of when and how compensation is earned, as well as the purposes behind it. . . .

Apart from In re Marriage of Judd, supra, 68 Cal. App. 3d at page 522, where the court found a "contingent stock account" amenable to allocation of the type effected by the time rule, no California case deals with employee stock options per se. . . .

Considering the frequency with which employee stock options are provided as part of key employee compensation packages, it is surprising that the allocation of community and separate property interests therein has not previously been addressed by California's appellate courts. Although we approve the use of the time rule fashioned by the trial court under the facts of this case, we stress that no single rule or formula is applicable to every dissolution case involving employee stock options. Trial courts should be vested with broad discretion to fashion approaches which will achieve the most equitable results under the facts of each case.

Undoubtedly there are other factual circumstances where the application of the time rule approved here would also achieve an equitable result. . . . [I]t is possible that equity could require a determination that stock options are solely the separate property of the employee spouse. An employee spouse can be expected to make this argument as to options granted after the date of separation and certainly for any granted after the dissolution of the marriage. Since the community interest in the employee options under the time rule we approve, commences with the date of employment, four years before the granting of the options, it could be argued by a nonemployee spouse that options granted to the employee spouse four years after the dissolution has occurred would contain a community interest therein. We want to make clear that by approving the time rule fixing the community interest in Paul's options beginning at a point in time four years before he and Maria separated, when his employment commenced with Amdahl, we do not mean to imply that stock options Paul may be granted after the divorce will be subject to a similar time rule and therefore possess a community interest. That issue is not before us.[4]

We mention the foregoing alternatives to emphasize that the trial court should exercise its discretion to fashion an equitable allocation of separate and community interests in employee stock options exercisable by the employee spouse after the date of separation of the parties. We recognize that were we to adopt an inflexible rule, it might help litigating spouses and their counsel settle option disputes and, at the same time, provide an easy measure to be applied by trial courts. However, to do so would be to follow the recent tendency of appellate courts and the Legisla-

---

4. Claims of a community interest in employee stock options granted to the employee spouse after the dissolution of the marriage would appear too speculative and would lack the immediacy and specificity necessary for exercise of jurisdiction over them. (See In re Marriage of Fonstein (1976) 17 Cal. 3d 738 [131 Cal. Rptr. 873, 552 P.2d 1169]; see also Weinberg v. Weinberg (1967) 67 Cal. 2d 557 [63 Cal. Rptr. 13, 432 P.2d 709].)

ture, which we decry, to adopt rules which on the surface are easy to apply and foster consistency yet, as applied, too often achieve inequitable results.[5]

In the 200 years since the formation of our country, its incredible population growth and the increasing complexity of both our society and our government have virtually eliminated the ability of the executive and legislative branches of our state and federal governments to be responsive to the problems and concerns of the individual citizen. The beauty of our system of justice is that the individual citizen still enjoys the opportunity to have the judicial branch of government, at both trial and appellate court levels, focus exclusively on his or her litigation. A special benefit of a system which allows for equitable considerations, especially in the family law field, is to afford the judge before whom the litigants appear, subject to applicable legal principles, the opportunity to fashion a remedy which achieves a just result. While critics may claim this results in inconsistency, we believe the strength of the judicial system is enhanced when the judiciary possesses the ability in family law cases to tailor a remedy to fit the circumstances of the individual litigants before the court.

Finally, by approving a time rule allocating community and separate property interests in employee stock options in this case, we reach a result which continues Paul and Maria's joint ownership interests in the community options. We do not suggest that this will always be the proper method of distribution of employee stock options. For example, some stock options are publicly traded or can otherwise be valued, even though exercisable in the future. In either case, it would appear to be most equitable to fix the value of the community interests as of the date of separation and distribute the community interests to the employee spouse, awarding other community property of equivalent value to the nonemployee spouse in order to achieve the equal division of community property required by [Family Code section 2550]. Employee stock options are normally exercisable on the condition that the employee remain with the employer and, as between the spouses, that is obviously within the control of the employee spouse. Additionally, to whatever extent an increase in the value of the company stock results from the employee's performance, or a decrease in the value of the stock occurs because of the company's poor performance or the economy, or because the employee terminates his employment, the risk of such rewards or losses is best borne by the employee spouse.

The trial court properly exercised its discretion in fashioning the time rule it utilized to equitably allocate the separate and community property interests in the Amdahl employee stock options. Paul's arguments to the contrary overlook the

---

5. A recent example of appellate courts limiting trial court discretion by developing a simple and inflexible rule is In re Marriage of Lucas (1980) 27 Cal. 3d 808 [166 Cal. Rptr. 853, 614 P.2d 285], which held that the separate property of one spouse placed in joint tenancy with the other becomes their community property, absent an agreement or understanding to the contrary. This is a simple rule, easy to apply, and inflexible. The difficulty with it is that it ignores normal human conduct in marriages and the fact that the transferring party usually acts without legal advice and with no understanding of the legal consequences while, at the same time, assuming that the marriage is going to last forever.

The apparently unforeseen inequities which resulted from this simple, inflexible rule caused the Legislature to enact anti-*Lucas* legislation only three years later. (See Civ. Code, §4800.2 [later amended and recodified as Family Code §2640].) At the present session of the Legislature efforts are being undertaken in the name of consistency to narrow and limit the discretion of trial courts in fixing child support. (See Assem. Bill No. 1527.) Such efforts, if successful, are just as certain to lead to inequitable results. The lesson to appellate courts and the Legislature should be that, subject to the application of proper legal principles, because of the variety and complexity of factual circumstances which occur in marital relationships, trial courts should have broad discretion to achieve equity for the litigants who appear before them.

community interests in contractual rights earned during the marriage as a factor of employee compensation.

The judgment is affirmed. Low, P.J., and HANING, J., concurred.

Appellant's petition for a hearing by the Supreme Court was denied June 27, 1984.

Notes and Questions

1. Following *Hug*, how would you treat a merit increase granted on the eve of separation? Is any or all of the employee's postseparation salary community property? Does the merit increase present an easier or harder case than the stock options in *Hug*? How would you treat an annual bonus granted one week before separation? Is most employee compensation both retrospective and prospective in nature? How far does *Hug* lead us away from the basic marital property principle that wages earned during marriage are community property and wages earned after separation are the earner's separate property?

2. When Paul Hug considered leaving IBM to join Amdahl, he contemplated the prospect of giving up considerable security and an almost vested pension in exchange for a much less certain opportunity. Supposing Amdahl, instead of the stock option, simply offered to double Paul's IBM salary. To what extent, if any, would Paul's postseparation salary be community property? How would you argue for the community? For Paul?

3. Justice King attempts to limit *Hug* to stock options granted before separation. Is this limitation logical?

4. *Overcoming the general community property presumption.* To what extent is *Hug* a presumption/burden of proof case? When were the stock options acquired? When they were issued (during marriage) or when they were exercisable (after separation)? Assuming they were *acquired* when they were issued and they embodied some indeterminate portions of compensation for services during marriage ("coming on board" and labor during marriage) as well as payment for postseparation services, who has the burden of proof? Indeed, did Paul fail to make his case for "future services," that is, fail to demonstrate that some determinate portion of presumptively community property was, in fact, his separate property? Would this failure have warranted a 100-percent award to the community? What sort of evidence would have helped Paul?

5. *Manner of distribution.* In the penultimate paragraph, Justice King suggests that, when possible, stock options exercisable only in the future be valued at the date of separation and that an immediate offsetting distribution of community property be made to the nonemployee spouse even before the options are exercisable. His rationale is that the risks of employment termination as well as of increase or decline in stock value due to employee or company performance and the state of the economy are "best borne by the employee spouse." Do you agree with the allocation of risk as to any or all of these factors? Why should the employee spouse exclusively be assigned the risk of factors entirely beyond his control? Does the court assume facts about Mrs. Hug that are not revealed in the opinion? (Compare Marriage of Connolly, page 531 infra. There the California Supreme Court approved a deviation from the norm of 50-50 division of *each* asset for the purpose of awarding all community property Amdahl stock to the husband: "This uncertain, non-income-producing stock might be a valuable holding for an individual who was

otherwise financially secure, but a court or counsel might well conclude that a less-risky, more assured income-producing investment such as an interest-bearing note with a fixed principal would more appropriately serve an unemployed woman with custody of two minor children." 23 Cal. 3d at 590 (1979).) If so, should the particular circumstances of Mrs. Hug or stereotypical assumptions about the sexes contribute to the formulation of generally applicable rules? Is this consistent with Justice King's plea for individualized discretionary justice?

Even though Amdahl is a publicly traded stock, apparently Mr. Hug persuasively argued that it was not possible to establish a market value for his options prior to the dates on which they were exercisable. What characteristic of employee stock options makes them unmarketable? Given this relatively uniform feature of employee stock options, valuation is unavoidably postponed until the option is exercisable. Thus, Justice King's discussion of risk allocation is largely gratuitous.

6. *Trial court competence.* Justice King makes an unusually forthright and eloquent plea for trial court discretion in marital property distribution. In footnote 5 he attacks the "simple and inflexible" *Lucas* rule, which the legislature replaced with the equally simple and inflexible Civil Code sections 4800.1 and 4800.2 (subsequently Family Code sections 2581 and 2640). Do you feel confident that most trial judges have either the time or skill to perform the sort of stock option analysis that Justice King envisages?

7. For further discussion of stock option classification, see Marriage of Nelson, 177 Cal. App. 3d 150, 222 Cal. Rptr. 790 (1986). *Nelson* approves the general principles articulated in *Hug* while affirming the trial court's decision to use a formula less favorable to the community: "the numerator was the number of months from the date of the grant of each block of options to the date of the couple's separation, while the denominator was the period from the time of each grant to its date of exercisability." Use of this formula was justified by the court's finding that the *Nelson* options were not designed to attract new employees or to reward past services. Instead they were intended only to reward future productivity. See also Marriage of Walker, 216 Cal. App. 3d 644, 265 Cal. Rptr. 32 (1989), and Marriage of Harrison, 179 Cal. App. 3d 1216, 225 Cal. Rptr. 234 (1986).

VII

MANAGEMENT AND CREDITORS' RIGHTS

A. MANAGEMENT OF COMMUNITY PROPERTY

1. Introduction

In Spanish civil law husband and wife were regarded as equal owners of the community property, and the husband was the manager of the community property. American community property states followed this basic management principle well into the twentieth century. The following excerpt discusses the history of California's movement away from the traditional pattern of male management of community property.

SUSAN WESTERBERG PRAGER, THE PERSISTENCE OF SEPARATE PROPERTY CONCEPTS IN CALIFORNIA'S COMMUNITY PROPERTY SYSTEM, 1849-1975
24 UCLA L. Rev. 1, 64-80 (1976)

. . . Early in the 1950's California law broke with traditional community property theory and accorded married women the right to manage and control their [community property] earnings.[322] Control was qualified in two important ways. Once the wife's earnings were mingled with property managed by her husband, she lost her managerial capacity. Furthermore, the husband alone could manage

---

322. Act of June 16, 1951, ch. 1102. [1951] Cal. Stat. 2860-61. The statute granted the wife management and control over "community property money earned by her, or community property money damages received by her for personal injuries suffered by her," and expressly made the prohibition on gifts applicable to her managerial acts. Id. at 2860. The legislature also provided:

> This section shall not be construed as making such money the separate property of the wife, nor as changing the respective interests of the husband and wife in such money. . . .

and control community realty;[324] consequently, if a wife translated her earnings into a real estate acquisition, her control vanished. The result of the two exceptions, continuation of predominantly male-oriented dominion over the community,[325] should not obscure the significance of the 1951 amendment. Decision-making power was to be determined according to the source of the marital income. This emphasis on the spouse who "earned" the property was in conflict with the basic community property principle that both spouses "earn" and contribute equally to each acquisition of a community character.

Recognition of direct earnings as the standard for determining managerial power over community property in part may reflect a changed economic structure. At the time community property systems developed, there were no "earnings" in the sense of wages, today's typical method of community acquisition. Property which came to the marriage through community efforts often came at the end of a particular season, or through a common enterprise to which members of the family contributed in a real and direct sense.

The modern separation of the sources of family sustenance from the home may have contributed to the view, taken by a significant number of people, that a spouse not employed for wages does not "work" and hence does not contribute to the marital community.[326] As the distinguished American historian David Potter observed: "[With] the advent of the money economy, in which income is the index of achievement . . . the housewife is the only worker who does not get paid." This aspect of modern life "in a subtle way, caused society to devalue the modern activities of women as compared with those of men. . . ." The linking of management to earnings was a manifestation of this devaluation.

The notion that women who were not employed for pay did not "work" may have made the earnings philosophy more attractive. In addition, by the early 1950's approximately one-third of the married women worked for pay. To these women, a rule of law which accorded their husbands full management of all community property seemed unfair and inappropriate. Thus, the presence of large numbers of employed married women helped produce the management change.

At first glance the earnings philosophy embodied in the 1951 amendment appears to be a sharp departure from prior law, which severely undermines the central principle that both spouses are equal contributors to community acquisitions during the marriage. This observation is correct, if the earnings standard is judged in terms of traditional community property principles. However, a traditional marital community was either never in force in California or was only operable in the period from 1849 to 1860.

When viewed in the context of the preceding century of California marital property developments, the 1951 assignment of managerial power based upon earn-

---

324. This may have been inadvertent. The management scheme was contained in two separate statutes, one governing community personal property, the other governing community realty. Only the personal property statute was changed to permit married women to manage their earnings and personal injury recoveries. The real property statute continued to read: "[T]he husband has the management and control of the community real property. . . ." . . . On the other hand, a change in real property management might have been viewed as unnecessary because the statute had, since 1917, required joinder of the spouses for important realty transactions. . . .

325. The by-product of these exceptions was the understandable reluctance of creditors to deal with a married women without also obtaining the signature of her husband. See note 335 infra.

326. Resistance to the concept of community property is usually traceable to this view. [See, e.g., Hearings on Community Property Before the California Legislature's Jt. Interim Comm. on the Judiciary 20-21 (1972).]

ings appears as yet another facet of a separate property system hiding under a community property label. In fact, the change represents the culmination of the separate property theory in the California law. . . . With the 1951 transfer of community property management, the wife's earnings became functionally more comparable to her separate property, so that the California married woman, like her counterpart in a reformed common law state, could own and manage not simply property which she owned before marriage or was given thereafter, but her earnings as well. After 1951, then, the difference between a common law jurisdiction's treatment of marital property and California's framework was the disposition of property at the death of the marriage and that difference can be seen as one of degree, not of social philosophy.

Two competing themes are represented in the development of the California community property law in the period from 1849 to 1975. One emphasizes the common interests of the spouses and the concept of sharing as partners in the gains of the marriage. The more dominant theme, however, stresses separation of the spouses' interests. These rival philosophies were to meet once again and clash in the context of the 1973 legislative changes to California's marital property law. Perhaps for the first time since California's constitutional convention, the community property policies became clearly dominant.

III. THE RECENT CHANGES

As the 1970's began, the California community property law constituted in large part a separate property system with a most peculiar set of checks and balances on managerial power over community property. The California law had established significant distinctions between the property rights of the husband and those of the wife, distinctions which appeared to have little to do with the original Spanish civil law or the economic and social needs and expectations of California married people.

In overview, it may have seemed fair and sensible to balance a husband's extensive managerial rights by according his wife special protections and rights. Yet, in detail after detail the disparate treatment of husbands and wives began to appear as nothing short of irrational.[333] Without regard to the peculiar manner in which

---

333. For example, a wife possessed managerial power over her earnings until she mingled her earnings with other community property but her husband controlled his earnings in all circumstances. . . . Property titled in the name of a husband was presumptively community property, but the same property from the same source if titled in his wife would be presumed her separate property. . . .

After a couple separated and began living apart, the wife's earnings became her separate property; her husband's earnings did not take on the character of separate property until there was court action to dissolve the marriage. This principle was introduced in the law in 1870, Act of March 9, 1870, ch. 161 §2, [1869-70] Cal. Stat. 226, and was later extended to personal injury recoveries, Act of July 3, 1868, ch. 457, §5, [1968] Cal. Stat. 1079. In 1971, in response to equal protection concerns, the statue was changed to provide that the earnings of either spouse become separate property after separation. Cal. Civ. Code §5118 (West Supp. 1976) [now Family Code §771]. See also Cal. Civ. Code §5119 (West Supp. 1976) [now Family Code §772]. For similar treatment of personal injury recoveries, see Cal. Civ. Code §5126(a) (West Supp. 1976) [now Family Code §781]. Thus the California law applies a functional rather than formal test for the termination of the community. For consideration of circumstances which constitute separation for purposes of terminating the community, see Loring v. Stuart, 79 Cal. 200, 21 P. 651 (1889); Tobin v. Galvin, 49 Cal. 34 (1874); Makeig v. United Security Bank & Trust Co., 112 Cal. App. 138, 296 P. 673 (1st Dist. 1931).

After the 1972 statute, during the pendency of dissolution actions well advised husbands began making spousal and child support payments from community funds, saving to whatever extent possible

the balance had been struck, Californians began to question the very concept of sex differentiation as an appropriate standard for balancing of power and benefits in the community property system. Criticism of the law took on differing tones. One attack proceeded on a constitutional level, arguing that the sex-based discriminations violated the equal protection clause of the fourteenth amendment and the state constitution. Another criticism proceeded on the rationale that the law represented inaccurate and unwise social judgments and ought to be changed to maximize individual merit.[335]

A. THE LEGISLATURE'S OPTIONS

Pressures rooted in constitutional and social concerns mandated some change. The goal of equality shaped a number of possible solutions.

1. Perfecting the Separate Property Philosophy

The most obvious remedy for the sex discriminatory aspects of the law was to perfect the separate property philosophy which already had considerable vitality in the California law. This would have entailed continuing to link management to earnings, and adopting a sex-neutral principle for control rather than male management once property had been commingled.[336]

Source of earnings as a managerial rule apparently reflects the judgment that managerial responsibility is more appropriately lodged in the individual directly responsible for earning the property. Community contributions of a non-earning spouse result in equal ownership but not in control, unless the earner grants control by some action such as commingling.[337] Whatever its virtues, a managerial rule centered on earnings clearly undercuts the fundamental theory of community property

---

current earnings which were separate property. This practice resulted in the depletion of community accumulations. In 1974 the legislature responded by amending section 4805 of the Civil Code to require that support payments be made first from earnings during separation. Cal. Civ. Code §4805 (West Supp. 1976) [now Family Code §4338].

335. The existing male management pattern contributed to the reluctance of third parties to transact business with married women. Because creditors could only expect to reach property managed by a spouse in satisfaction of a debt, creditors had an important economic incentive to deal with husbands or both spouses. Much of the push for change in the law came from dissatisfaction with the treatment of women in the market place.

Many people were concerned about the impact of the allocation of power over marital property on the dignity of women, particularly those who remained in the home. . . . This concern may well have been stronger in community property jurisdictions than in common law states. On the one hand, a community property law told women that they contributed to acquisitions during marriage and thus shared ownership equally with their husbands, but on the other, denied the married woman meaningful control of the property. The law seemed to conclude that unless she earned the property in a direct sense she was not qualified to manage it. One major strain of the recent movement for equal rights for women has been to emphasize the value of the traditional role of women and to argue for recognition of that value. In a community property jurisdiction it was easier to effectuate that goal in the marital property law because the equal ownership principle already existed.

336. Texas followed this direction in 1967 by providing that each spouse is to manage property which he or she "would have owned if a single person." In the event that Texas spouses combine property which would otherwise be subject to exclusive management, then both spouses become the manager. The Texas law is structured to permit third parties to rely on unilateral managerial action with respect to the mixed community property, and separately managed community property. Tex. Fam. Code §§5.22, 5.24 (1975).

337. In many marriages, control is extended by the individual arrangement of the spouses, through devices like joint accounts.

that the contributions of the spouses are regarded as equal. During the ongoing marriage, such a rule makes the non-earning spouse's ownership a matter of form only. Furthermore, community property and separate property become functionally identical except for their significance upon the termination of the relationship.

Another alternative for California would have been to move to a separate property system in a direct way. Although this was advocated by some witnesses in the public legislative hearings held in 1972, abandonment of community property principles was not seriously considered.[340]

2. *Joint Control*

Another possible approach to eliminating sex as a determinant of managerial power would have been to require the consent of both spouses for community property transactions. Certain community real property management decisions in California had required joint control through joint consent for many years. [In 1917, the legislature enacted a provision requiring consent of both spouses for sales, encumbrances, and leases for more than one year.] The major problem with making joint control generally applicable is the resulting serious burden on the spouses as well as the commercial system. No jurisdiction has taken this route.

3. *Unilateral [Control]*

The equal protection problems inherent in laws which lodge control primarily in the husband could have been addressed by permitting either spouse to fully manage all community property regardless of who earned it and without any necessity for securing the consent of the other. The 1973 amendments to the California law contain strong elements of this approach. On the theory that irrespective of actual contribution, the spouses share equally in the marital community, the new law emphasizes a meaningful shared ownership principle.

4. *Combining Unilateral and Mutual Power*

Requiring the agreement of both marital partners for some transactions while according each spouse full authority to act alone in others, irrespective of who earned the property, was also an alternative. This method requires a special approach to management for certain designated transactions. An example of this approach is the joinder requirement instituted in 1917 for major decisions involving community realty. While the 1973 amendments continue the preexisting realty management scheme, the California legislature rejected extending this philosophy.[346]

5. *Private Choice*

Another possible method of selecting community property managers would have been to require the spouses to designate a management scheme. An initial

340. There would certainly have been constitutional problems in doing so, for the spouses equally own the community property. Any retroactive change in ownership would constitute a taking of property to be judged in light of fourteenth amendment principles.

346. One version of the California legislation contained a joint consent requirement for transactions over $1,000. S.B. 569, 1973-74 Reg. Sess., as amended June 11, 1973.

choice could be made at the time of marriage, and modifications could be permitted thereafter so that changed attitudes and circumstances could be reflected in each couple's private choice. Both the initial choice and its subsequent alteration could be evidenced by a filing with the county clerk or recorder. One objection to this approach is grounded in society's reluctance to permit individual discretion in such matters.[348] A more serious objection stems from third-party reluctance to tolerate the uncertainties which result when a variety of individual management patterns are present.[349]

B. THE NEW LAW—A BRIEF SUMMARY

In 1973, the California Legislature chose to combine aspects of unilateral management and joint control of community property in a plan of management which was not linked to the source of earnings. The central principle of the new law is management of community property by either spouse. The spouses can each make managerial decisions without regard to which of them is directly responsible for earning the property. The management pattern for community personal property is considerably different from that governing real property. Personal property may be managed by either spouse *acting alone*. . . . Although either spouse is granted managerial power over community real property, the longstanding restriction which calls for the mutual consent of the spouses for certain major actions remains in the law. Thus decisions to transfer, encumber or lease for more than one year continue to be regarded as peculiarly important, calling for a joint decision on the part of the spouses.

The ability to subject property to liability is an important facet of managerial power, and the 1973 changes continue the principle that, in general, liability will follow management and control. One . . . by-product of California's version of equal management is that more marital property is subject to the reach of creditors than was previously the case.[356] A spouse can now enter into a contractual arrangement which may be satisfied from the noncontracting spouse's earnings, property previously exempt. The management and creditor provisions appear to be fully retroactive. . . .

The 1973 legislation also deletes the wife's special presumption for property titled in her name and subjects all post-1974 acquisitions made during marriage to the basic presumption of community ownership. The special presumption of separate property continues to apply to pre-1975 acquisitions.

Some amendments focus on the difficult question of managerial abuse in the context of the marital relationship. The law continues to restrain the exercise of community property management much as it did under the prior law. The restrictions on gifts of community property are carried forward and are applicable regard-

---

348. Nevertheless, for many years the California law has permitted the spouses to enter into agreements which change the character of marital property.

349. One solution is to regard the agreement as binding between the spouses, but not upon third parties who are unaware of it. Another is to place the agreement on a card carried by the spouses on which the creditor can then rely as representing an accurate picture of financial responsibility.

356. Compare former Cal. Civ. Code §§5116-17, 5120-23, 5130, 5132 (West 1970) with id. §§5116, 5121-22, 5132 (West Supp. 1976) [now Family Code §§900-1000]. It is arguable that creditors are the largest beneficiaries of the management changes. Since the California law continues to regard management as the relevant principle for determining creditors' rights, when management over almost all community property is extended to either spouse, more community property becomes available to creditors. . . .

less of whether the gift is made by husband or wife. Similarly, the restriction on transfers of home furnishings and clothing is continued and is applicable to both spouses. In addition, the legislature attempted to deal with the increased potential for abuse of managerial power which accompanies full management by either spouse by explicitly providing that "[e]ach spouse shall act in good faith with respect to the other spouse in the management and control of the community property." Although new to the statutes, for many years California courts have assumed that the spouses stand in some type of fiduciary relationship with respect to the community.

C. REJECTION OF SEPARATE PROPERTY PRINCIPLES

In eliminating the earnings criteria for management and the wife's special separate property presumption, the 1973 changes have removed from the California law the most substantial remaining elements of the separate property system. . . .

As long as management was linked to earnings, the California law functioned during the ongoing marriage in ways quite similar to the separate property system of a common law state, despite the legislature's declaration of equal ownership. For many years the California law viewed the husband's earnings as *his* property. In theory, the wife's earnings were community property, but in reality the married woman's special separate property presumption and the exemption of the wife's earnings from the reach of her husband's creditors resulted in treatment of the wife's earnings as separate property. After 1927, despite the concept that the spouses' interests in the community property were present and equal, functionally the husband's earnings were his and the wife's earnings were hers. In 1951, with the express grant of managerial power to married women over their earnings, the earnings-management philosophy became even more important. The new law has destroyed two elements of the earnings philosophy. First, earnings no longer constitute a valid criterion for management, and second, as to obligations incurred during the marriage, the liability of community property is no longer limited to the earnings of the debtor spouse.

By destroying the earnings-management link, the new management rules breathe considerable force into the community property concept. While California law once simply paid lip service to the concept of equal ownership of the fruits of community efforts, the 1973 management rules give the concept tangible meaning. The spouse who may not have contributed to the acquisition in any direct sense now has decision-making power and can bind the community. The California law has moved well beyond the Spanish concept of a marital partnership and has established a meaningful sharing of power and interests during the marital relationship as well as upon its death. . . .

2. Real Property Management

CALIFORNIA FAMILY CODE SECTION 1102

**§1102. Management and control of community real
property**

(a) Except as provided in Sections 761 and 1103, either spouse has the management and control of the community real property, whether acquired prior to or on or after January 1, 1975, but both spouses, either personally or by a duly authorized agent, must join in executing any instrument by which that community real property or any interest therein is leased for a longer period than one year, or is sold, conveyed, or encumbered.

(b) Nothing in this section shall be construed to apply to a lease, mortgage, conveyance, or transfer of real property or of any interest in real property between husband and wife.

(c) Notwithstanding subdivision (b):

(1) The sole lease, contract, mortgage, or deed of the husband, holding the record title to community real property, to a lessee, purchaser, or encumbrancer, in good faith without knowledge of the marriage relation, shall be presumed to be valid if executed prior to January 1, 1975.

(2) The sole lease, contract, mortgage, or deed of either spouse, holding the record title to community real property to a lessee, purchaser, or encumbrancer, in good faith without knowledge of the marriage relation, shall be presumed to be valid if executed on or after January 1, 1975.

(d) No action to avoid any instrument mentioned in this section, affecting any property standing of record in the name of either spouse alone, executed by the spouse alone, shall be commenced after the expiration of one year from the filing for record of that instrument in the recorder's office in the county in which the land is situated.

(e) [Subsection (e), omitted here, was added in 1992 to respond to Droeger v. Friedman, Sloan & Ross, discussed in the next principal case. Subsection (e) is printed in the Statutory Appendix.]

The predecessor to section 1102 was enacted in 1917 to restrict the husband's powers over the community realty. The 1975 reform maintained the joinder requirement for real property and made it sex-neutral.

LEZINE v. SECURITY PACIFIC FINANCIAL SERVICES, INC.
14 Cal. 4th 56, 925 P.2d 1002, 58 Cal. Rptr. 2d 76 (1996)

GEORGE, C. J.—During his marriage to plaintiff Gloria J. Lezine (plaintiff), Henry Lezine (Lezine) unilaterally transferred a security interest in community real property (the Halm Avenue property) to defendant Security Pacific Financial Services, Inc. (Security Pacific), without the knowledge or consent of plaintiff, in violation of former section 5127 of the Civil Code (hereafter former section 5127).[1] [After Gloria refused to consent to Henry's plan to obtain loans by using their community property home as security, Henry forged Gloria's signature on a quit claim deed to the home. Henry then borrowed large sums of money, giving the lender a secured interest in the home. The loan proceeds were not used for the

----

1. Effective January 1, 1994, section 5127 was repealed and reenacted without substantive change as Family Code section 1102.

benefit of the community and were not repaid. When Gloria learned of Henry's behavior, she moved for divorce.] By the present action, plaintiff sought to have the transfer of the security interest set aside in its entirety pursuant to the authority of former section 5127 and Droeger v. Friedman, Sloan & Ross (1991) 54 Cal. 3d 26, 283 Cal. Rptr. 584, 812 P.2d 931. Droeger holds that when a nonconsenting spouse, during the marriage, timely challenges a transfer made in violation of former section 5127, the transfer is voidable in its entirety. The superior court set aside the transfer of the security interest in its entirety, concurrently awarding Security Pacific a money judgment against Lezine in the amount of the formerly secured debt. Security Pacific recorded an abstract of judgment (reflecting the money judgment) in the county in which the Halm Avenue property was located.

Thereafter, as part of the division of property in the parties' marital dissolution proceeding, the Halm Avenue property was awarded to plaintiff as her sole and separate property. When plaintiff later discovered the recorded abstract of judgment, she moved for clarification of the judgment in the present action, and the trial court ruled that the abstract of judgment "shall not constitute [a lien]" on the Halm Avenue property. The issue for our determination is whether the trial court exceeded its authority in extinguishing Security Pacific's judgment lien encumbering the Halm Avenue property.

Our determination of this issue requires that we review the nature of the equitable relief that may be afforded under former section 5127, including any conditions to that relief, such as restitution of consideration paid for the transfer that is set aside. This issue also requires that we resolve the tension among competing, and facially inconsistent, principles, policies, and statutory rules governing, on the one hand, the rights of spouses who are innocent of wrongdoing under former section 5127 and, on the other hand, the liability of community real property for the satisfaction of debts incurred during the marriage. . . .

We granted review to determine whether community real property remains liable for satisfaction of a debt after the transfer of a security interest, which secured repayment of that debt, is set aside pursuant to former section 5127.

II

Before stating the various contentions of the parties and framing the legal issues presented for our determination, we shall review the statutory schemes governing the liability of community property for marital debts, as well as the liability of real property received by the nondebtor spouse following the division of property in a dissolution proceeding. We shall then turn to former section 5127 and its purpose and underlying policies.

We consider first the applicable rules governing the liability of community property for debts incurred during the marriage (such as the loan obligation incurred by Lezine owing to Security Pacific). In general, "[e]xcept as otherwise expressly provided by statute, the community estate is liable for a debt incurred by either spouse before or during marriage, regardless of which spouse has the management and control of the property and regardless of whether one or both spouses are parties to the debt or to a judgment for the debt." (Fam. Code, §910, subd. (a).) Thus, the liability of community property is not limited to debts incurred for the benefit of the community, but extends to debts incurred by one spouse alone exclusively for his or her own personal benefit. . . . Although a spouse may be required to reimburse the community for the misuse of community assets (see, e.g., Fam. Code, §§1101, 2602 . . .), the community estate remains liable to third party creditors for any debt incurred as a result of such misuse of assets. . . .

Under these rules, if a valid judgment lien in favor of Security Pacific attached to the Halm Avenue property before it was awarded to plaintiff as her sole and separate property, plaintiff received the property subject to the lien, and the property remained liable for satisfaction of the lien, even though the underlying debt was assigned to Lezine. In the event Security Pacific satisfies the judgment by enforcement of the lien, plaintiff has a right of reimbursement against Lezine to the extent of the property applied.

The question before us is whether the foregoing rules and principles governing the liability of the Halm Avenue property for the loan obligations incurred by Lezine are altered or otherwise affected by former section 5127, or the circumstance that the deed of trust that formerly secured that obligation was set aside pursuant to former section 5127.

Former section 5127 [now Family Code section 1102] provided in pertinent part that "either spouse has the management and control of the community real property . . . but both spouses either personally or by duly authorized agent, must join in executing any instrument by which such community real property or any interest therein is leased for a longer period than one year, or is sold, conveyed, or encumbered. . . ." The statutory provision requiring that both spouses join in the execution of any instrument transferring an interest in real property first appeared in former section 172a of the Civil Code (Stats. 1917, ch. 583, §2, p.829), the predecessor to former section 5127. The enactment of former section 172a reflected the evolution of community property law in recognizing the wife's equal status, and a legislative intent to protect the innocent spouse against an unauthorized transfer of community real property by the other spouse. (See Droeger v. Friedman, Sloan, & Ross, supra, 54 Cal. 3d at pp.32-33, 283 Cal. Rptr. 584, 812 P.2d 931.) . . .

In Droeger v. Friedman, Sloan, & Ross, supra, 54 Cal. 3d 26, 283 Cal. Rptr. 584, 812 P.2d 931, this court, reaffirming prior decisional law, held that under former section 5127, both spouses must consent to the transfer of an interest in community real property, regardless whether the transaction is a gift or supported by consideration. Resolving a conflict among appellate decisions as to the relief that may be afforded under former section 5127, the court . . . further held that when a nonconsenting spouse, during the marriage, timely challenges a transfer made in violation of former section 5127, the transfer is voidable in its entirety. (54 Cal. 3d at p.30, 283 Cal. Rptr. 584, 812 P.2d 931.)

In Droeger, supra, 54 Cal. 3d 26, 283 Cal. Rptr. 584, 812 P.2d 931, after husband and wife had separated, wife encumbered two parcels of community real property with deeds of trust in order to secure repayment of attorney fees incurred during the dissolution proceedings. Husband did not join in the execution of the deeds of trust and, while the dissolution proceedings were pending, he filed an action to quiet title, challenging the validity of the deeds of trust in favor of wife's attorneys. This court held that, because the husband's consent was required under former section 5127 to effect the encumbrance, he was entitled to invalidate the encumbrance in its entirely, and was not limited to setting aside the transfer only with respect to his one-half community interest. (Droeger, supra, 54 Cal. 3d at p.30, 283 Cal. Rptr. 584, 812 P.2d 931.) The court reasoned that any lesser relief would contravene principles of equal management and control of community property, and the fundamental premise that neither spouse acting alone may partition the community estate during the marriage. Allowing any part of the transfer to stand could have the effect of partitioning the community estate during marriage, whereas California law provides for such division only (i) after termination of marriage by legal proceedings or death, or (ii) during marriage with the consent of both spouses. The court further noted that the enforcement of any part of a unilateral transfer effectively would transmute community property into a tenancy in common, resulting in the nonconsenting spouse being forced to become a tenant in common with a stranger. (Id., at pp.46-47, 283 Cal. Rptr. 584, 812 P.2d 931.)

The court in *Droeger* further concluded that, although economically weak spouses are at a disadvantage in securing adequate counsel in dissolution proceedings, nothing in the language or legislative history of former section 5127 permitted the general rule against unilateral transfers to be subject to an exception for securing attorney fees in dissolution proceedings. (54 Cal. 3d at p.41, 283 Cal. Rptr. 584, 812 P.2d 931.)[7]

Significantly (with respect to the issue presented in this case), the court in *Droeger* did not address the effect of the cancellation of the deeds of trust on the underlying obligation for payment of attorney fees; in other words, the court did not hold that, as a result of the setting aside of the security for the underlying debt, the community estate no longer was liable for the payment of attorney fees, or that the attorney creditors no longer could seek to apply the community real property formerly encumbered by the deeds of trust toward satisfaction of an obligation for payment of attorney fees.

The specific issue before us is whether the trial court, in addition to setting aside Security Pacific's deed of trust encumbering the Halm Avenue property pursuant to former section 5127, had the authority to extinguish a lien that otherwise would be enforceable to satisfy a money judgment arising from the setting aside of that deed of trust. The Court of Appeal concluded that, as a result of setting aside the deed of trust pursuant to former section 5127, Security Pacific's security for the community debt was canceled but that the underlying community debt was not, and the relief afforded under former section 5127 did not alter the liability of the community real property for the underlying debt, or the enforcement of a money judgment for that debt. The Court of Appeal further concluded that, under Family Code section 916, the award of the Halm Avenue property to plaintiff as her separate property did not affect the enforceability of the judgment lien; accordingly the trial court lacked authority to extinguish the judgment lien in favor of Security Pacific.

Urging a contrary result, plaintiff maintains that when a security interest in community real property that was transferred unilaterally by a debtor spouse in violation of former section 5127 is canceled, that real property no longer is liable for satisfaction of a money judgment that previously was secured by the deed of trust. Otherwise, argues plaintiff, the nonconsenting spouse is in the same position after the security interest is set aside as he or she was in prior to the granting of

---

7. In response to the *Droeger* decision, the Legislature in 1992 enacted former sections 4372 and 4373 of the Civil Code, providing procedures for the encumbrance of a spouse's interest in community real property in order to pay attorney fees in actions under the Family Law Act. Former section 5127 also was amended to state that "[n]othing in this section shall preclude either spouse from encumbering his or her interest in community real property as provided in Section 4372." Effective January 1, 1994, former sections 4372 and 4373 of the Civil Code were repealed and replaced by Family Code sections 2033 and 2034.

relief, i.e., the property remains subject to an encumbrance in the amount of the underlying loan obligation; consequently the relief afforded under former section 5127 would be nullified, and the action to set aside the unilateral transfer will have been a futile act. Such a result, urges plaintiff, would be contrary to the legislative purpose of former section 5127.

In resolving the issue presented, we note there is scant authority pertaining to the rights and remedies, in general, of a transferee of an interest in community real property after the unauthorized transfer is set aside pursuant to former section 5127. In one early decision involving a unilateral transfer made in violation of former section 172a of the Civil Code (the predecessor to former section 5127), the court held that, although the transfer was voidable by the nonconsenting wife, the third party innocent purchaser, without knowledge of the marriage, was entitled to restoration of the purchase price from the community. (Mark v. Title Guar. & Trust Co. (1932) 122 Cal. App. 301, 9 P.2d 839.) In *Mark*, the husband had transferred to a third party the community interest in a contract for the sale of real property, without the knowledge or consent of his wife, and had retained for his own use and benefit the sale proceeds paid by the purchaser.

The court concluded that the wife was entitled to set aside the unilateral transfer, pursuant to former section 172a of the Civil Code. The court further held, however, that the bona fide purchaser, without knowledge of the marriage relationship, was entitled to restoration of the purchase price from the community. In reaching this conclusion, the court first noted "the difficulty of protecting the expectancy of the innocent wife and at the same time of safeguarding the rights of innocent purchasers. . . ." (Mark v. Title Guar. & Trust Co., supra, 122 Cal. App. at p.311, 9 P.2d 839.) Nonetheless, the court further observed that although husband had misappropriated the sale proceeds for his own personal use and benefit, the proceeds had the character of community property and had been paid into the community estate. "The fact that the wife derived no benefit from the transaction and that the husband expended the whole of the proceeds for his own sole benefit did not change the complexion of the property. Its character was not altered because the husband, instead of conserving the money, used it for his own purposes." (Id., at p.312, 9 P.2d 839.) The court accordingly concluded that the community was required to reimburse the purchaser for the consideration paid as a condition of the set-aside relief.

In Andrade Development Co. v. Martin (1982) 138 Cal. App. 3d 330, 187 Cal. Rptr. 863, the court observed, in dicta, that in the case of a contract for the sale of community real property that is voided pursuant to former section 5127, the purchaser who acquired the contractual interest in the property, in good faith and without knowledge of the marriage relationship, might be entitled to damages for breach of contract from the community estate. (138 Cal. App. 3d at pp.337-338, 187 Cal. Rptr. 863.)

Legal commentators have noted that, in the case of a unilateral transfer that is set aside pursuant to former section 5127, the third party transferee properly should be deprived of any interest in the real property itself, but should be permitted to assert rights as an unsecured creditor for repayment of whatever consideration was passed in exchange for the ineffective title. "This solution would entail no violation of community property management principles, as either spouse may unilaterally incur a debt for which the community is liable." (Bruch, Protecting the Rights of Spouses in Intact Marriages—The 1987 California Community Property Reform and Why It Was So Hard to Get (1990) Wis. L. Rev. 731, 743, fn. 35; see

Hogoboom & King, Cal. Practice Guide: Family Law (The Rutter Group 1996) ¶8:
687 p.8-166 ["Arguably . . . since set-aside relief is an equitable remedy, it should
be ordered subject to the return of consideration paid by the innocent purchaser
who entered the transaction having no knowledge and no reason to know the transferor was married."].)

The foregoing rules and principles articulated in *Mark* and *Andrade,* and by
family law commentators, are consistent with the rules generally governing the liability of community property for marital debts, as well as with equitable principles.
When these rules and principles are applied to the transfer of a security interest
in community real property, if the security interest is forfeited pursuant to former
section 5127 the community remains liable to the formerly secured creditor for the
underlying debt. The loss of the security does not extinguish the underlying debt,
or the character of that unsecured debt as one for which the community estate is
liable. . . .

Under the foregoing principles, a court in equity may require as a condition
to the granting of equitable relief under former section 5127 the restoration of any
consideration transferred by an innocent encumbrancer in exchange for the security interest, who acts without knowledge of the community status of the property.
The trial court in the present case granted such relief in the form of a money
judgment against Lezine.[8] At the time of the entry of that judgment (prior to the
property division in the separate marital dissolution proceedings), the community
property (which included the Halm Avenue property) was liable for satisfaction of
that money judgment.

The remaining question is whether former section 5127, or any policy underlying that statute, precludes a creditor such as Security Pacific from seeking to apply
community real property toward satisfaction of a debt that previously was secured
by that same real property but which security interest was voided under former
section 5127. The plain language of the current statute, requiring that "both
spouses . . . must join in executing any instrument by which such community real
property or any interest therein . . ." is transferred, reflects a legislative intent to
protect an innocent spouse against an unauthorized unilateral transfer of community real property by the other spouse. Nothing in the foregoing statutory language
refers to the liability of community real property for marital debts. In contrast,
the Legislature has enacted a variety of statutory schemes that expressly exempt or
otherwise protect the interests of a real property owner from creditor claims, such
as the provisions for declared homesteads (Code Civ. Proc., §704.910 et seq.) or
governing home equity sales contracts (Civ. Code, §1695.1). No part of former section 5127, however, indicates any similar intent to exempt community real property
from liability for marital debts, even debts incurred unilaterally by one spouse.

Instead, as reflected in Code of Civil Procedure section 695.020, the Legislature
expressly has established the liability of community real property for the satisfaction
of money judgments rendered against either spouse, including the nondebtor
spouse's one-half community interest. Indeed, because California law governing
the enforcement of judgments and debts enables a judgment creditor of one spouse
to levy execution on community real property, "[i]n effect, one spouse alone can

---

8. We have no occasion to determine the rights and remedies available to an encumbrancer that,
at the time of the creation of the encumbrance, had knowledge of the marriage relationship or knew
the transfer was in violation of former section 5127. In the present case, record title to the Halm Avenue
property stood in Lezine's name alone. . . .

indirectly alienate community realty by incurring an enforceable obligation and refusing to pay it.'' (Reppy, Debt Collection from Married Californians: Problems Caused by Transmutations, Single-Spouse Management, and Invalid Marriage (1981) 18 San Diego L. Rev. 143, 169, fn. omitted.) Thus, for example, one spouse unilaterally may incur credit card charges which, if unpaid, may be reduced to a money judgment that may be satisfied from community real property. The Legislature has not created any statutory exception — either in former section 5127 or any other statute — for money judgments reflecting a debt arising from, or formerly secured by, a unilateral transfer of community real property made in violation of former section 5127.

Thus, construing former section 5127 with reference to, and in harmony with, the various statutory schemes governing the liability of community property for marital debts, it does not appear that the purpose or effect of former section 5127 is to exempt community real property from liability for satisfaction of marital debts incurred unilaterally by one spouse, for which the community otherwise is liable. Thus, the creditor who loses its security interest under former section 5127 retains the rights of any other unsecured creditor to resort to the community real property for satisfaction of the underlying debt.

If we were to conclude, as plaintiff urges, that, after a security interest in real property is set aside pursuant to former section 5127, the formerly secured creditor no longer may resort to the property to satisfy the debt, that creditor would be placed in a position less advantageous than that of other unsecured creditors of the community estate — the formerly secured creditor, having obtained a judgment against the debtor spouse, would be precluded from establishing a judgment lien that attaches to the community real property to satisfy the judgment, while the unsecured creditor (such as the credit card issuer, for example), after obtaining a judgment against the debtor spouse, could proceed to record an abstract of judgment creating a judgment lien that attaches to the community real property. There is no principled basis for treating the formerly secured creditor, who originally obtained its security interest in good faith, less favorably than any other unsecured creditor, with respect to the ability to resort to community real property to satisfy a money judgment for which the community is liable.

For these reasons, we conclude that neither former section 5127 nor *Droeger* carve out an exception to the rules governing the liability of community real property for enforcement of a money judgment against a debtor spouse, or the enforceability of a judgment lien that has attached to community real property for satisfaction of a money judgment. Accordingly, a creditor who previously has forfeited a security interest in community real property under former section 5127 is placed in the position of any other unsecured creditor entitled to seek a judgment against the debtor spouse, and to enforce its money judgment against the community estate. Furthermore, the judgment creditor's recordation of an abstract of judgment creates a judgment lien that attaches to the community real property and that may be enforced to satisfy the lien.

We recognize that our holding effectively may nullify in substantial part the relief afforded under former section 5127 when the unilateral transfer is a security interest for the repayment of a debt. If the creditor obtains a judgment for the amount of the debt when the security interest is set aside and records an abstract of judgment, the security interest will be converted into a judgment lien encumbering the community real property. Nevertheless, the purpose of the statute is served — the unauthorized direct transfer is cancelled, and both spouses retain full management and control of the property. Moreover, as explained above, the same result could obtain had the court set aside a unilateral sale or lease of the property and rendered judgment in favor of the purchaser or lessee for the amount of the consideration paid.

Accordingly, in the present case, after Security Pacific's deed of trust was set aside pursuant to section 5127 and Security Pacific was awarded a money judgment against Lezine, it was placed in the position of any other judgment creditor entitled to enforce the judgment against the community estate. By recording an abstract of judgment in Los Angeles County, reflecting the money judgment against Lezine, Security Pacific created a judgment lien that attached to all real property in Los Angeles County that was subject to enforcement of the money judgment, including the Halm Avenue property.

The transfer of the Halm Avenue property to plaintiff in the property division as her sole and separate property, after the judgment lien of Security Pacific had attached, did not alter the liability of the property to satisfy the lien or otherwise affect the judgment lien. . . . Accordingly, the trial court in the present case lacked authority to expunge Security Pacific's judgment lien after the court in the marital dissolution proceedings awarded the Halm Avenue property to plaintiff as her separate property. . . .

We recognize that the result we reach may appear inequitable in some respects. An institutional lender such as Security Pacific may be in a far better position than the innocent nondebtor spouse to protect against forgeries and deception by a debtor spouse such as Lezine who seeks a loan to be secured by community real property. The result we reach nevertheless is dictated by existing legislation protecting the rights of creditors.

For the foregoing reasons, we conclude that the Court of Appeal properly determined that the trial court exceeded its authority in declaring the Halm Avenue property free of any judgment lien in favor of Security Pacific. Our holding is without prejudice to the right of plaintiff to seek a reallocation of the community property as to which the court in the marital dissolution proceeding retained jurisdiction.

III

The judgment of the Court of Appeal is affirmed.

MOSK, KENNARD, BAXTER, WERDEGAR, CHIN and BROWN, JJ., concur.

Notes and Questions

1. *Reflections on* Lezine.

> A lay reporter from the Los Angeles Times called to talk about *Lezine*. She was disturbed by the ultimate result, that the creditor could do by one means what it could not by another and thus render illusory the requirements and protection of Family Code Section 1102 (former Civil Code Section 5127). I explained the difference between a Section 1102 encumbrance to secure a debt and the underlying debt itself, the distinction upon which the Supreme Court relies to reach its result. As I was running through the explanation a second time, I began to think of the ironic old saw that I was told

as a first year law student, which went something like this: "If you can contemplate two things that most people would understand to be inextricably related and you can think about them separately and independently, then you have the makings of a fine lawyer." *Lezine* is a case in point.

We are so familiar with the distinction between the underlying debt and security for the debt that the result in *Lezine* seems almost inevitable. Yet for lenders, the loan and security are inextricably related. Without the security of the family home, the two net debts totaling almost $200,000, massive debt for a middle-income family, never could have been incurred. Thus it is impossible to think about the debt without thinking about its wrongful basis, the wife's deprivation of her Section 1102 right to refuse to consent to encumbrance of the community estate family home. Had she exercised this right, it is not simply that there would be no encumbrance; there would also be no debt. From this perspective, it is inappropriate to compare unsecured and secured creditors and to worry about the distinction that an alternative rule would create between the two. The unsecured creditor is differently situated because the debt owed to him was not predicated upon the wrongful deprivation of a spouse's Section 1102 rights. Thus there is nothing objectionable in allowing him recourse to Section 1102 realty to enforce a judgment for the debt owed to him, while denying such recourse to a creditor whose very loan was predicated upon the wrongfully obtained security interest.

As the Supreme Court recognizes, sound social policy would seem to support such a distinction. In *Lezine*, the trial court found that the first lender (which abandoned its appeal) ought to have recognized that the quitclaim deed was fraudulent. More generally, institutional lenders are much better situated to protect themselves from fraud than are innocent defrauded spouses. The effect of *Lezine* is to let institutional lenders off the hook entirely and to impose all costs on a spouse who, as the Supreme Court acknowledges, is entirely unable to protect herself against the violation of her Section 1102 rights.

Grace Blumberg, Additional Thoughts on *Lezine*, Cal. Fam. L. Monthly 60-61 (Feb. 1997).*

2. *Legislative response to* Droeger. In 1992, the legislature added several provisions facilitating the award and payment of attorney's fees. 1992 Cal. Stat., ch. 356 (A.B. 3399). Chapter 356 added, inter alia, Civil Code section 4372, now Family Code section 2033, providing:

> Either party may encumber his or her interest in community real property to pay reasonable attorney's fees in order to retain or maintain legal counsel in a proceeding for dissolution of marriage. . . . This encumbrance shall be known as a "family law attorney's real property lien" and attaches only to the encumbering party's interest in the community real property.

The legislature also added a new subsection (e) to Family Code section 1102. It is reprinted in the Statutory Appendix.

3. *Legislative response to* Lezine. Like *Droeger*, *Lezine* inspired a bill, but it was not enacted. Assembly Bill 1394 (1997) would have provided that community real property unilaterally transferred by a spouse to secure a debt is not liable for that debt if the transfer is later set aside and the real property is awarded to the other

spouse at dissolution. In other words, the bill would have directly and narrowly abrogated *Lezine.*

4. *The section 1102 statute of limitations.* What is the scope of the section 1102 abbreviated one-year statute of limitations? Byrd v. Blanton, 149 Cal. App. 3d 987, 993, 197 Cal. Rptr. 190 (1983), holds that the one-year limitation "only protects bona fide transferees with no knowledge of the marital relation who have no reason to suspect another signature is necessary."

3. Personal Property Management

CALIFORNIA FAMILY CODE SECTION 1100

(a) Except as provided in subdivisions (b), (c), and (d) and Sections 761 [trusts] and 1103 [where one spouse has a conservator] either spouse has the management and control of the community personal property, whether acquired prior to or on or after January 1, 1975, with like absolute power of disposition, other than testamentary, as the spouse has of the separate estate of the spouse.

(b) A spouse may not make a gift of community personal property, or dispose of community personal property for less than fair and reasonable value, without the written consent of the other spouse. This subdivision does not apply to gifts mutually given by both spouses to third parties and to gifts given by one spouse to the other spouse.

(c) A spouse may not sell, convey, or encumber community personal property used as the family dwelling, or the furniture, furnishings, or fittings of the home, or the clothing or wearing apparel of the other spouse or minor children which is community personal property, without the written consent of the other spouse.

(d) Except as provided in subdivisions (b) and (c), and in Section 1102, a spouse who is operating or managing a business or an interest in a business that is all or substantially all community personal property has the primary management and control of the business or interest. Primary management and control means that the managing spouse may act alone in all transactions but shall give prior written notice to the other spouse of any sale, lease, exchange, encumbrance, or other disposition of all or substantially all of the personal property used in the operation of the business (including personal property used for agricultural purposes), whether or not title to that property is held in the name of only one spouse. Written notice is not, however, required when prohibited by the law otherwise applicable to the transaction.

Remedies for the failure by a managing spouse to give prior written notice as required by this subdivision are only as specified in Section 1101. A failure to give prior written notice shall not adversely affect the validity of a transaction nor of any interest transferred.

(e) Each spouse shall act in good faith with respect to the other spouse in the management and control of the community property in accordance with the general rules governing fiduciary relationships which control the actions of persons having relationships of personal confidence as specified in Section 721, until such time as the property has been divided by the parties or by a court. This duty includes the obligation to make full disclosure to the other spouse of all material facts and information regarding the existence, characterization, and valuation of all assets in which the community has or may have an interest and debts for which the community is or may be liable, and to provide equal access to all information, records, and books that pertain to the value and character of those assets and debts, upon request.

a.   Either Spouse Can Act, but . . .

Section 1100(a) states that "*either* spouse has the management and control of the community personal property." Both spouses have authority to manage the community property. One spouse can take the other spouse's earnings and make effective transfers for value. The consent of the earning spouse is not required. But consider the effect of the following statute on management of community property.

CALIFORNIA FINANCIAL CODE SECTION 851

A bank account by or in the name of a married person shall be held for the exclusive right and benefit of the person, shall be free from the control or lien of any other person except a creditor, and shall be paid to the person or to the order of the person, and payment so made is a valid and sufficient release and discharge to the bank for the deposit or any part thereof.

Notes and Questions

1. What are the purposes of Financial Code section 851? Who is the intended beneficiary of the provision? Does it affect *ownership* rights? Does it affect creditors' rights? If one spouse incurs a debt during marriage, may her creditor reach a bank account titled solely in the other spouse's name and containing his community earnings? See Family Code §910.

2. Emilia seeks your advice. Her husband Tom has placed all his earnings in a bank account in his name alone. Emilia understands that she is supposed to be able to manage community property even though she has no labor market earnings. Emilia has no complaint about the quality of Tom's management of his community earnings. He is a prudent manager and is saving for the couple's retirement. Nevertheless, Emilia would like to use some of the savings for current consumption. What can you tell Emilia?

3. Is intervention during marriage desirable? Is it possible? Consider the pre-equal management decision in *Wilcox*.

WILCOX v. WILCOX
21 Cal. App. 3d 457, 98 Cal. Rptr. 319 (1971)

COUGHLIN. J.—. . . Plaintiff's complaint alleges he and defendant are husband and wife; defendant has taken, is in exclusive possession of, and has secreted

$30,000 of community funds; demand has been made upon her for this money; and she refuses to pay the same to plaintiff.

Defendant's demurrer to the complaint was upon the ground: "This Court does not have jurisdiction over the subject matter of this action, in that there is no statutory authority which allows a spouse to sue the other for mismanagement of community funds."

The court sustained the demurrer without leave to amend.

The cause of action alleged in plaintiff's complaint is not premised upon defendant's mismanagement of community funds, as stated in her demurrer, but upon defendant's violation of plaintiff's right to manage, control and dispose of community funds.

By statute a husband "has the management and control of the community personal property, with like absolute power of disposition, other than testamentary, as he has of his separate estate," subject to certain exceptions not material to the case at bench. (Civ. Code, §5125.) The right of the husband thus conferred to manage, control and dispose of community personal property is invaded by his wife when she deprives him thereof by taking, secreting and exercising exclusive control over community funds. A husband has a cause of action against his wife for such an invasion and violation of his right in the premises with attendant appropriate remedies. . . .

The right of the husband to maintain an action against his wife to protect his property rights in community funds, including the right to manage, control and dispose of such, with the incident right to possession thereof for this purpose, is not dependent upon statutory authority to sue his wife, as claimed by defendant in her demurrer. In McAlvay v. Consumer's Salt Co., 112 Cal. App. 383, 396 [297 P. 135], the court said: "[T]he right of a husband to maintain an action to quiet his title to community property against the wife has been frequently upheld. . . ." In Salveter v. Salveter, 135 Cal. App. 238, 240 [26 P.2d 836], the court upheld the right of the husband to recover and required his wife to account for community funds which were the proceeds of community property. In neither of the foregoing cases was the right of the defendant to sue premised on statutory authority. Basic to the situation at bench is the provision of Civil Code section 3523 that: "For every wrong there is a remedy."

The order sustaining the demurrer was error.

The judgment is reversed. BROWN (Gerald), P.J., and WHELAN, J., concurred.

Note

Can you bring a *Wilcox* suit on behalf of Emilia, whose problem is described in Note 2 supra? Has Tom violated the Family Code section 1100(e) requirement that he "act with respect to the other spouse in the management and control of the community property in accordance with the general rules governing fiduciary relationships"? How might Tom argue that he has not? Would a remedy for Emilia be inconsistent with the 1975 California unilateral management principle?

Professor Cross, writing about the Washington equal management law, has taken the position that suits during marriage were not intended and are inappropriate. See Cross, Equality of Spouses in Washington Community Property Law — 1972 Statutory Changes, 48 Wash. L. Rev. 527 (1973).

The Uniform Marital Property Act (see generally page 6 supra) does seem to offer Emilia a solution. First, the Act differs from California in its approach to personal property management. Either spouse may manage marital property alone only when the property is held solely in that spouse's name or is held with the other spouse in an alternative ("either . . . or . . .") form. Unif. Marital Property Act, §5(b), 9A U.L.A. 114 (1987). Thus, under UMPA, Tom may lawfully control the marital property bank account he maintains in his name alone. Nevertheless, Emilia may petition a court to add her name to the title. (This right extends to all property other than that generally included within the California section 1100(d) business exception, discussed immediately infra.) If Emilia's name is added to the account, putting title in the cumulative rather than the disjunctive, UMPA requires that she and Tom act together with respect to the account. Is this resolution problematic? Or the court may order the alternative form of title. Would you foresee any problem with an "either/or" designation? What may Tom do after the order is entered? Can the court forestall Tom's efforts to maintain sole management of his community earnings? Is the enforcement of equal management rights a distinctly more difficult problem than that presented by *Wilcox*? Finally, it is not clear from UMPA or its commentary whether the "add-a-name" remedy is generally available whenever one spouse is excluded from management, or is confined to instances in which the managing spouse has been damaging the other spouse's *ownership* interest in the property. Should Tom's history of prudent management preclude Emilia's claim to equal management rights?

In 1986, the California legislature enacted Civil Code section 5125.1(c), now Family Code section 1101(c), which adopts the UMPA add-a-name remedy. 1986 Cal. Stat., ch. 1091. On the face of the statute, it is unclear whether this remedy is available whenever title to community property is held in one spouse's name alone, or whether it may only be imposed when the nonmanaging spouse has "a claim against the other spouse for a breach of the fiduciary duty imposed by Section 1100 or 1102 that results in impairment to the claimant spouse's present undivided one-half interest in the community estate." Cal. Family Code §1101(a). Would Emilia be able to substantiate a section 1101(a) claim? Has Tom breached any section 1100 duty? If so, has such breach impaired Emilia's present undivided one-half interest in the community property?

The legislative history of section 1101 indicates that the drafters designed the first three subsections as a series of independent claims. They intended that the subsection (c) add-a-name remedy and the subsection (b) accounting remedy be available without any showing of a subsection (a) violation. Assembly Judiciary Committee, Committee Analysis (Senate Bill 1071), July 1, 1986; Letter from Senator Bill Lockyer to Assembly Member Elihu Harris, July 8, 1986.

Thus the legislature has responded to Emilia's complaint. Would you counsel Emilia to bring a section 1101(c) action? What possible problems do you foresee?

b.   The Business Exception: Family Code Section 1100(d)

Section 1100(d) states:

> . . . [A] spouse who is operating or managing a business or an interest in a business that is all or substantially all community personal property has the primary management and control of the business or interest. Primary

management and control means that the managing spouse may act alone in all transactions but shall give prior written notice to the other spouse of any sale, lease, exchange, encumbrance or other disposition of all or substantially all of the personal property used in the operation of the business (including personal property used for agricultural purposes), whether or not title to that property is held in the name of only one spouse. Written notice is not, however, required when prohibited by the law otherwise applicable to the transaction.

Remedies for the failure by a managing spouse to give prior written notice as required by this subdivision are only as specified in Section 1101. A failure to give prior written notice shall not adversely affect the validity of a transaction nor of any interest transferred.

Notes and Questions

1. What are the purposes of the business exception? Why did the legislature single out this one form of property for special treatment? In what ways is a spouse-managed business different from other community property?

2. Ought debts incurred solely by Harold encumber Wilma's section 1100(d) business? Will they? See Cal. Family Code §910(a). See further discussion at pages 431-432 infra.

3. Washington and Nevada have also subjected spousal businesses to special management rules. Washington Revised Code section 26.16.030(6) (1986) provides:

> Neither spouse shall acquire, purchase, sell, convey, or encumber the assets, including real estate, or the good will of a business where both spouses participate in its management without the consent of the other: *Provided,* That where only one spouse participates in such management the participating spouse may, in the ordinary course of such business, acquire, purchase, sell, convey or encumber the assets, including real estate, or the good will of the business without the consent of the nonparticipating spouse.

2 spouse control

v.

1 spouse control

To the same effect, see Nev. Rev. Stat. §123.230(6) (1991). How do the Washington and Nevada provisions differ from the California business exception?

c. The Personal Belongings Exception: Family Code Section 1100(c)

Section 1100(c) states: "A spouse may not sell, convey, or encumber community personal property used as the family dwelling, or the furniture, furnishings, or fittings of the home, or the clothing or wearing apparel of the other spouse or minor children which is community personal property, without the written consent of the other spouse."

The predecessor statute to section 1100(c) was enacted in 1901 as a restriction on the husband's powers over the community. At that time, during the intact marriage the wife's interest in the community property was characterized as a mere expectancy rather than a present interest.

In Duncan v. Duncan, the first decision interpreting the 1901 statute, the court's characterization of the wife's new veto power departed significantly from the generally prevailing mere expectancy view. "The provision of the law is intended for the benefit of the wife. It gives her a right in such property which she may protect." 6 Cal. App. 404, 406, 92 P. 310 (1907). By the time the statute was next considered, the mere expectancy concept of the wife's interest had been discarded and the courts gave substantial force to the prohibition on transfers of furnishings and clothing. Matthews v. Hamburger, 36 Cal. App. 2d 182, 97 P. 2d 465 (1939), followed the rationale of the unauthorized gift cases (see pages 400-413 infra) and ordered the full transfer returned to the community if action were taken during the marriage. Dynan v. Gallinatti, 87 Cal. App. 2d 553. 197 P.2d 391 (1948), held that even after the death of her husband, the wife could set aside an encumbrance of household furnishings in full, not simply to the extent of the wife's one-half interest in the community. (In contrast, when a decedent has made an unauthorized inter vivos gift of community property, the survivor may void it only to the extent of her one-half interest. See pages 543-547 infra.) The court explained the different treatment of household goods and gifts by distinguishing the quality of the property involved: "The legislature has recognized that these items are necessary for the maintenance of the surviving family — more necessary in fact after the death of the husband than during his lifetime. . . ." 87 Cal. App. 2d at 557, 197 P.2d at 393, noted in 22 S. Cal. L. Rev. 291 (1949).

B. GENERAL LIMITATIONS ON MANAGERIAL POWER

1. Gifts of Community Property

In Spanish law, the husband's powers of management over the community included the right to make reasonable gifts. A number of community property states have retained this principle. In such states, the issue is whether a particular gift is appropriate given its nature and the wealth of the parties. See generally W. Reppy, Jr., and C. Samuel, Community Property in the United States 15-21–15-28 (3d ed. 1991).

California initially followed the reasonable gift principle. Lord v. Hough, 43 Cal. 581 (1872). In 1891, the legislature set California on a different path by enacting the predecessor to current California Family Code section 1100(b): "A spouse may not make a gift of community personal property, or dispose of community personal property for less than fair and reasonable value, without the written consent of the other spouse."

The 1916 *Spreckels* decision, one of many involving the Spreckels family, is the leading gift case. The concept of the wife's interest in the community as a "mere expectancy" looms large in the court's analysis of the gift restriction. How much of *Spreckels* survives the 1927 legislative declaration that the interests of the husband and wife in the community are "present, existing and equal interests"?

SPRECKELS v. SPRECKELS
172 Cal. 775, 158 P. 537 (1916)

SHAW, J. — This is an action by Claus A. Spreckels and Rudolph Spreckels, as executors of the will of Anna C. Spreckels, and also in their capacity as executors of the will of Claus Spreckels, and by them and Emma C. Ferris, as individuals, to compel an accounting by the defendants respecting certain property received by them from the decedent, Claus Spreckels, in his lifetime, and for restitution thereof, so far as it exceeded one-half of the community property of Claus Spreckels and Anna C. Spreckels, his wife, and, if restitution cannot be made, then for judgment for the value thereof.

The court below sustained a demurrer to the second amended complaint and thereupon gave judgment for the defendants. From this judgment the plaintiffs appeal.

Claus A. Spreckels and Anna C. Spreckels intermarried on July 11, 1852, and lived together as husband and wife, residing in California, from that time until the death of Claus Spreckels on December 26, 1908. Anna C. Spreckels died on February 15, 1910. They had but five children. Three of them are the plaintiffs above named. The other two are the defendants. All the property owned by the decedent, Claus Spreckels, during his marriage and at his death, was acquired during said marriage and was community property.

In the eight years between 1896 and 1905, Claus Spreckels made gifts to John D. Spreckels and Adolph B. Spreckels of large amounts of this community property aggregating in value about twenty-five millions of dollars, according to the allegations of the complaint, leaving remaining in his possession and ownership, at the time of his death, other property not exceeding ten million dollars in value. Anna C. Spreckels did not, in her husband's lifetime, consent to the making of any of these gifts, either in writing or otherwise. The plaintiffs, by this action, seek to recover on behalf of the estate of Claus Spreckels and also on behalf of the estate of Anna C. Spreckels, and also in their own right, as legatees and devisees of the entire estate of Anna C. Spreckels, a one-half interest in the specific property so given to the defendants, or an amount equal to one-half thereof, if such property cannot be identified.

The first provision of our statutory law on the subject of the respective rights of the husband and wife in the community property during the marriage was section 9 of the act of April 17, 1850 (Stats. 1850, p.254). It was as follows: "The husband shall have the entire management and control of the common property with the like absolute power of disposition as of his own separate estate."

Construing this act, the court held that it and other statutes in force were intended to adopt the Mexican law upon the subject of community property, and decided that, during the marriage, the estate of the husband in the community property was absolute, while that of the wife was a mere expectancy, as that of an heir. But in consequence of the provisions of section 11 of the same act, declaring that on the death of either husband or wife one-half of the common property should go to the survivor and the other half to the descendants of the deceased spouse, . . . it was further held that the husband could not, by his will, prevent her from inheriting one-half thereof upon his death. . . . Section 9 of the act of 1850 remained in force until the enactment of the Civil Code in 1872, the subject being therein covered by section 172 thereof. Codifying the previous decisions regarding the testamentary power of the husband over community property, the provision was, in the code, changed to read as follows:

"The husband has the management and control of the community property, with the like absolute power of disposition (other than testamentary) as he has of his separate estate."

This section remained without alteration until 1891, when a proviso was added, making the section read as follows:

"The husband has the management and control of the community property, with the like absolute power of disposition, other than testamentary, as he has of his separate estate; provided, however, that he cannot make a gift of such community property, or convey the same without a valuable consideration, unless the wife, in writing, consent thereto.". . .

The appellants contend that the declaration of the proviso that the husband "cannot make a gift" of community property, unless the wife consent thereto in writing, limits his power in that respect absolutely, so that such a gift is absolutely void even in his own lifetime, and may be recovered by him or by the executors of his will after his death. They also contend that if not void as to the husband, such gifts are absolutely void as to the wife, if she survives him, and that she, in her lifetime, or her representatives or heirs after her death, may recover the same. Upon these theories they seek to maintain the sufficiency of the complaint.

Under the statute prior to the addition of the first proviso in 1891, it was the established doctrine in this state during the marriage the husband was the sole and exclusive owner of all of the community property, and that the wife had no title thereto, nor interest or estate therein, other than a mere expectancy as heir, if she survived him. . . .

The limitation upon the husband's testamentary power contained in the code was not understood to vest in the wife, during the marriage, any interest or estate whatever in the community property, but merely to constitute a restriction upon the husband's power. If the husband undertook to dispose of all of the community property by will, giving the wife less than one-half thereof, such disposition was not absolutely void, but had the effect of putting her to her election whether to take under the statute or under the will. If she took the latter provision, the disposition in the will of the remaining portion of the property was thereby affirmed and made valid. (Morrison v. Bowman, 29 Cal. 346; Estate of Stewart, 74 Cal. 98, 104, [15 Pac. 445]; Estate of Smith, 108 Cal. 119, [40 Pac. 1037]; Estate of Vogt, 154 Cal. 509, [98 Pac. 265].) The testamentary disposition in such a case, therefore, was voidable but not absolutely void. If it had been void, in the extreme sense, the logical result would have been that a mere election by the wife would not transfer the remainder of her statutory half to the other beneficiaries under the will, but that a conveyance by her would be necessary. It has been always understood that her election is sufficient for that purpose and that the will, in that event, operates to transfer the property. . . .

We are satisfied that the proviso of 1891 does not render a gift of community property by the husband without the consent of the wife void as to him, nor confer upon him, in his lifetime, or upon his personal representatives after his death, any right or power to revoke the gift or recover the property. There is nothing in the language to express the idea that the title does not, as before, remain wholly in him. The provision is merely for a limitation upon his power to dispose of it. He is bound by his own gift as fully as if it was of his separate estate. . . .

Neither does the proviso purport to vest in the wife, during the marriage, any present interest or estate in the community property given away by the husband without her written consent. In view of the long settled doctrine that the entire estate therein is in the husband during the marriage relation, a doctrine that had become a fixed and well understood rule of property, it is not to be supposed that the legislature would have made a change of so radical a character without plain language to that effect. We do not find in the proviso such language, nor anything that can reasonably be so construed. If it confers upon her, during the marriage, any right respecting such gifts, it is nothing more than a right to revoke the gift and, if necessary, sue to recover the property, not as her separate estate, but to reinstate it as a part of the community property, with the title vested in the husband and subject to sale by him, as before. . . .

The limitation upon the husband's power to make a gift is even less positive than that upon the testamentary power, for it depends upon two questions of fact: The absence of a valuable consideration, and the absence of her written consent, both of which may have to be proven by collateral evidence. The gift, when made, immediately vests the property in the donee subject to her right of revocation. She may give her consent at any time during her life, and if she does the gift becomes absolute with respect to her. The provision was manifestly intended solely for the benefit of the wife. If she seeks to assert such right, it is incumbent upon her to show that the facts exist upon which it depends. The conclusion seems inevitable that the gift is not absolutely void with respect to her but only voidable by her upon proof of the facts necessary to that end. . . .

We are thus brought to the question whether the wife has ratified and confirmed these gifts by her acts after his death, assuming that then, and not before, she became vested of the right to impeach or avoid them.

By the will of her husband all the property of which he died seized was declared to be community property. It purported to dispose of all of his property that was subject to his testamentary disposition at his death. As his wife survived him, the effect was that he did not, by the will, dispose of the one-half of the estate that descended to her at his death, but left it to go to her by the law. The other half he gave to certain trustees in trust, among other purposes, "to pay over the net annual income thereof to my wife during the term of her natural life." Subject to the trusts, the *corpus* of the estate was given to the three plaintiffs, Claus A. Spreckels, Rudolph Spreckels, and to Emma C. Ferris and her children, in three equal parts, to be divided between them at the death of his widow, as in the will directed. (Estate of Spreckels, 162 Cal. 559, 586, [123 Pac. 371].)

The will further declared, with regard to the two defendants herein, as follows:

"Fourth: I make no provision in this will for my sons John D. Spreckels and Adolph Spreckels for the reason that I have already given to them a large part of my estate."

This will was duly admitted to probate on January 9, 1909, and the executors named duly qualified as such on the same day, and they have ever since continued to act therein. The widow became entitled to receive the annual income of the one-half of the estate either immediately upon his death (Civ. Code, sec. 1366), or at the expiration of one year thereafter. (Civ. Code, sec. 1368.) The complaint does not aver that she received any of it in her lifetime, but as it appears that the estate was solvent, and the regular course of business is presumed to have been followed, it may perhaps be assumed that she did receive the income during her life. At all events the facts alleged show that she did have full knowledge of the provisions of her husband's will, and of the fact that it had been duly admitted to probate. It is not alleged that she did not also have full knowledge of all of the alleged gifts by her husband to the defendants. The allegations show that she did have full knowledge of a large part of them. The fourth clause of his will, above quoted, certainly put her on inquiry as to all of them. It is alleged that she caused an inquiry to be made concerning them. In this condition of her affairs she proceeded, on August 16, 1909, seven months after the probate of her deceased husband's will, to make and execute her own will. The second clause declares: "I hereby give, devise and bequeath all of my estate, of every kind and description'' to the three children, Claus A., Rudolph, and Emma C., plaintiffs herein. This would include her inherited one-half of the community property and, in addition, all the income from the other half which would accrue to her up to the time of her own death. It would also, if taken alone, carry the right she would have to avoid or acquiesce in the gifts made by her husband in his lifetime without her written consent, if such right survived, and if she did not otherwise dispose of or exercise such right. With respect to those gifts she then declared as follows:

"Fourth: I intentionally omit making any provision in this will for my sons, John D. Spreckels and Adolph B. Spreckels and I intentionally omit to make any provision therein for the issue of either of my said sons, in case either of my said sons shall die before my death, because I do not desire my said two sons or any of their issue to take any part of my estate. This I do for the reason that my deceased husband, Claus Spreckels, prior to his death, had already given and advanced to my said sons a large part of his estate, and for other reasons satisfactory to me."

The words "I hereby give all *my* estate, of every kind and description," to the three other children, excluded John and Adolph from participation in her estate. At that time, and up to her death, they held the property given to them by their father out of the community property. He had declared in his will that because of these gifts he gave them none of the remaining property. He thereby, in effect, declared, as a part of his last will, that they were to keep and hold all of the property he had given to them. Knowing this, and because of this disposition by him of a part of the community property, in effect because they already had the whole of that part, not a half interest only, she declared that she intentionally omitted to give them any share in the remainder disposable by her. The declaration is entirely inconsistent with the existence of a purpose, desire, or intention on her part that her executors or the beneficiaries under her will should have the right to recover a half of that which she says had been "given and advanced" to them. The provision, in connection with the circumstances under which it was made, precludes all idea that she regarded the property so given to the two defendants, or any part thereof or right in regard thereto, as any part of her descendible estate, or that the other three children were to receive, by her will or otherwise, any claim to that property or right to an accounting thereof. It was equivalent to an express ratification and confirmation of said gifts, and it was a consent thereto, by her, in writing, advisedly made. This will she retained unrevoked until her death, showing that notwithstanding her alleged direction to the plaintiff, Claus A. Spreckels, soon after the death of her husband, to begin an action to recover the property so given to John and Adolph, her last and final wish and will was that they should retain it all, but should receive nothing from her. . . .

Upon this view of the case it is immaterial whether the gifts to John and Adolph were or were not made to prevent the wife from receiving one-half of the community property of said marriage, or with the design of excluding the other children from ultimate participation, by will or inheritance from her, in any part thereof. It is also unnecessary to consider the question whether or not the right of the widow to attack or avoid those gifts survived her death and passed to the executors of her will, or to those to whom she devised and bequeathed her estate. During her lifetime she was the only person who had the right to gainsay these gifts. Her power in that respect was complete, so far as others were concerned, and her ratification and confirmation thereof by her will concluded all other persons, regardless of the motive that prompted the gifts or of the nature of her right to avoid them.

The judgment is affirmed. MELVIN, J., HENSHAW, J., LORIGAN, J., SLOSS, J., LAWLOR, J., and ANGELLOTTI, C.J., concurred.

Rehearing denied.

Notes and Questions

1. Do you agree with the court's conclusion that Anna Spreckels ratified her husband's gifts in her will provisions? How might she have explained her behavior? During her lifetime, would she have been acting inconsistently if she had begun a proceeding to recover her one-half interest in the gifts after she wrote her August 16, 1909, will? Why might she have preferred to leave the decision whether to bring an action to her children, Claus, Rudolph, and Emma?

2. If *Spreckels* arose for the first time today in our era of equal management and ownership rights, what considerations might impel the court to conclude, as it did in 1916, that an unauthorized gift is merely voidable and not void? Consider the testamentary impact of a contrary holding. (See generally Chapter 10 infra.)

3. Should the statute of limitations start to run as soon as the nondonor spouse discovers that an unauthorized gift has been made "or, in the exercise of reasonable diligence, should have discovered it"? Should the statute of limitations force recovery actions by one spouse against the other during an ongoing marriage? Are such actions likely to occur? Ought the statute of limitations instead be tolled during marriage? In 1986, the legislature addressed these issues by adding Civil Code section 5125.1, subsections (d) and (f), now Family Code section 1101, subsections (d) and (f).

FIELDS v. MICHAEL
91 Cal. App. 2d 443, 105 P.2d 402 (1949)

SHINN, P.J.—. . . Defendant is the duly appointed and acting executrix of the estate of W. C. Fields, who died on December 25, 1946. Plaintiff married decedent in California on April 8, 1900, and was his wife at all times thereafter until his death. At the time of the marriage decedent had no assets or estate of any kind whatsoever, and all of the estate which he acquired subsequent to marriage was from compensation for personal services rendered during marriage together with the increment thereon. Several years subsequent to their marriage, decedent deserted plaintiff. He never discussed his financial affairs with her and wilfully withheld from her all information concerning the extent of his assets and any gifts or transfers made by him out of the community property. Solely from his personal earnings for services rendered during marriage, decedent secretly and without plaintiff's knowledge or consent made extensive transfers of money by way of gifts. Ten separate gifts in stated amounts, made to named individuals are set out, all of which "were illusory and were transferred and set over by said decedent wilfully and fraudulently, secretly and clandestinely, from the community property of plaintiff and said decedent with intent to defraud plaintiff of her interest in her and his estate." The total amount of these gifts was $482,450. Upon information and belief, six additional gifts in unknown amounts to fictitiously named defendants are alleged. The complaint states that "plaintiff has not at any time consented to the making of said gifts or to any one or more of them and said gifts and each of them were made without her knowledge and approval and are all disaffirmed by plaintiff''; and alleges that plaintiff did not learn of any of the gifts until after the death of her husband.

On July 23, 1947, plaintiff duly and regularly filed her "Creditor's Claim and Disaffirmance" with defendant as executrix setting forth substantially the same facts related above and claiming the sum of $241,225 due to plaintiff as her community interest in the unauthorized gifts. The claim was rejected.

This action was thereafter brought against the estate for the reason that

> many of said donees are deceased and that those remaining alive reside at divers places, some of them away from the State of California, and that they have used up and dissipated the sums of money by way of gift transferred and set over to them as aforesaid, and would not be able to pay a judgment, if one were rendered against them for return to plaintiff of said gifts or of some part thereof. Plaintiff is without any means of collecting in full from said donees those portions of said gifts which she is entitled to.

It is also alleged that defendant executrix has possession and control of the financial records and papers of decedent; that she has refused to permit plaintiff to inspect them; and that these records disclose to a large extent detailed information concerning the alleged gifts of money as to which plaintiff is without information. The prayer for relief was twofold: (1) "By reason of plaintiff's disaffirmance of the gifts hereinbefore described, that defendant pay the plaintiff the sum of $241,225.00." (2) An accounting be had to determine the amount of any additional gifts made by decedent from community funds, and upon such accounting judgment be rendered for plaintiff to the extent of her interest therein. . . . The paramount issue presented is whether plaintiff may proceed directly against the estate of her husband to secure relief from his dissipation of the community funds through secret and unauthorized inter vivos gifts, or must seek recourse solely against the donees.

Section 574 of the Probate Code provides that "any person, or the personal representative of any person, may maintain an action against the executor or administrator of any testator or intestate who in his lifetime has wasted, destroyed, taken, or carried away, or converted to his own use, the property of any such person. . . ."

The facts alleged in the complaint are in our opinion sufficient to bring the action within these provisions. . . .

The position of the husband, in whom the management and control of the entire community estate is vested by statute (Civ. Code, §§161a, 172, 172a), has been frequently analogized to that of a partner, agent, or fiduciary. . . . Section 2219 of the Civil Code provides: "Everyone who voluntarily assumes a relation of personal confidence with another is deemed a trustee . . . as to the person who reposes such confidence. . . ." It is clear that, being a party to the confidential relationship of marriage, the husband must, for some purposes at least, be deemed a trustee for his wife in respect to their common property. . . . Fundamental principles governing trust relationships are set forth in sections 2228 and 2229 of the Civil Code: "In all matters connected with his trust, a trustee is bound to act in the highest good faith toward his beneficiary, and may not obtain any advantage therein over the latter by the slightest misrepresentation, concealment, threat, or adverse pressure of any kind. A trustee may not use or deal with the trust property for his own profit, or for any other purpose unconnected with the trust, in any manner." . . . Nine years prior to their marriage, section 172 of the Civil Code was amended to provide that the husband could not make a gift of community property without the written consent of his wife. (Stats. 1891, p.425.) Fields' disregard of this affirmative duty imposed upon him as manager of the community estate was a violation of his fiduciary obligations as defined in sections 2228 and 2229 of the Civil Code, supra. Even if good faith were to be shown, he would nevertheless be subject to personal liability for disposing of trust property in an unauthorized manner. (Civ. Code, §2238.)

It is well settled, of course, that a gift made in violation of section 172 is, as against the donee, voidable by the wife in its entirety during the husband's lifetime . . . and to the extent of one-half after his death. . . . The beneficiary of a trust, however, is not required to pursue the trust property, but may elect to hold the trustee (or after his death, his estate) personally liable (McElroy v. McElroy, 32 Cal. 2d 828, 831 [198 P.2d 683]; Lathrop v. Bampton, 31 Cal. 17, 23 [89 Am. Dec. 141]); and the latter may not escape such liability by showing that the trust property has been dissipated. (54 Am. Jur. §253, p.196.) Manifestly, a wife whose community property rights have been violated, as plaintiff alleges hers have been, is entitled to pursue whatever course is best calculated to give her effective relief. Where the amount of the gifts and identity of the donees are known, and the property can be readily reached, the former remedy may be decidedly more advantageous to the plaintiff than an action against the husband's estate, since the assets of the latter may be insufficient to satisfy a judgment. On the other hand, where recourse against the donees would be ineffective to give relief, as in the present instance, a denial of the alternative remedy would not only be in disregard of rudimentary principles applicable to persons acting in a fiduciary capacity, insofar as the husband stood in that relation, but would also amount to a concession that the law is powerless to accord to the wife's community interest the full protection which section 172 was evidently designed to ensure. We think the law is not so toothless. Whether the action is viewed as one based upon actual fraud, or as one based upon a violation of a statutory limitation upon the husband's power of control and management, is immaterial, for the dissipation of community assets by means of unauthorized gifts is in either view a conversion of the "property" of the wife such as would subject the husband's estate to suit under section 574 of the Probate Code. The statutory language is sufficiently comprehensive to include any wrongful conduct resulting in a loss of "property" to another. . . .

Wood, J., and Vallee, J., concurred.

A petition for a rehearing was denied May 19, 1949, and respondent's petition for a hearing by the Supreme Court was denied June 23, 1949.

HARRIS v. HARRIS
57 Cal. 2d 367, 369 P.2d 481, 19 Cal. Rptr. 793 (1962)

Traynor, J. — . . . Plaintiff is the son of Marshall C. Harris and Susie Almeda Harris and the father of defendant Rolland H. Harris. Marshall and Susie Harris were married in 1894. In 1945 Susie Harris made a will leaving all her property to Marshall Harris if he was living six months after her death. If he was not then living her property was to go to plaintiff. In 1948 Susie Harris was adjudged an incompetent, and Marshall Harris was appointed her guardian. He relinquished the guardianship and was replaced by plaintiff on March 28, 1957. Susie Harris died on September 26, 1957. Marshall Harris died on December 10, 1957.

Between 1950 and March 28, 1957, Marshall Harris made gifts of community property totalling $29,543.76 to defendants. After March 28, 1957, he gave defendants certain stock, to which the trial court assigned no value, and other assets valued at $26,665.89. The finding of the trial court that Susie Harris was incapable of giving her consent to any of these gifts is amply supported by the record.

Section 172 of the Civil Code provides: ". . . [T]he husband has the management and control of the community personal property, with like absolute power of disposition, other than testamentary, as he has of his separate estate; provided, however, that he cannot make a gift of such community personal property, or dispose of the same without a valuable consideration . . . without the written consent of the wife." Gifts made without the consent of the wife are not void, but are voidable at the instance of the wife. (Trimble v. Trimble, 219 Cal. 340, 344 [26 P.2d 477]; Spreckels v. Spreckels, 172 Cal. 775, 784 [158 P. 537].) If the wife acts to avoid the gift during the continuance of the community, the whole gift will be avoided. (Britton v. Hammell, 4 Cal. 2d 690, 692 [52 P.2d 221].) If she acts after the community has been dissolved, the gift will be avoided to the extent of her one-half interest in the community property transferred. (Trimble v. Trimble, supra, p.347.)

Defendant contends that plaintiff cannot maintain this action on the ground that the right to avoid gifts made in violation of section 172 is a right personal to the wife that does not survive her death and cannot be exercised by her executor. . . .

A cause of action for the violation of a property right survives the death of the owner of the right. (Civ. Code, §954.) The present interest of a wife in community property and her right to dispose of one-half by will are property rights that are invaded by a husband's gift without her consent. Thus the right to set aside such gifts survives the death of the wife and may be exercised by her personal representative.

The record establishes that the gifts made by Marshall Harris after March 28, 1957, were made without the consent of Susie Harris. The trial court found that she was incapable of giving such consent. Nor was it given by plaintiff while he was her guardian. It could not be given after her death. Therefore it is clear that plaintiff should recover one-half of the property transferred after March 28, 1957.

The gifts made between 1950 and March 28, 1957, present a more difficult question. During this period Marshall Harris was his wife's guardian. If he had power as her guardian to give the consent required by section 172 and validly gave such consent plaintiff cannot set those gifts aside.

Although "'neither the general guardian nor a court has the power to dispose of the ward's property by way of gift,' such rigid principle has its exception where allowances from the surplus income of the estate are sought as 'donations for charitable and religious purposes' and with the object of 'carrying out the presumed wishes of' the incompe[te]nt person." (Guardianship of Hall, 31 Cal. 2d 157, 168 [187 P.2d 396].) Allowances for the support of next of kin may also be approved upon a showing that the incompetent would have made them as suggested. (Prob. Code, §1558; Guardianship of Hall, supra. . . .) A guardian has no authority, however, to make such gifts without prior court permission. (Guardianship of Hall, supra.) Defendants do not claim that Marshall Harris secured such permission before, or after, making the contested gifts. Nor have they presented evidence tending to establish that Susie Harris would have approved the gifts had she been competent. The pre–March 28, 1957, gifts, as well as those made after that date, were therefore made without the consent of Susie Harris as required by Civil Code section 172. The trial court correctly determined that plaintiff should recover one-half of all gifts of community property made by Marshall Harris to defendants between 1950 and his death in 1957.

The judgment is affirmed. GIBSON, C.J., PETERS, J., WHITE, J., and DOOLING, J., concurred.

Rehearing denied; SCHAUER, J., and McCOMB, J., dissenting.

Notes and Questions

1. Is it self-evident that a spouse's right to avoid unauthorized gifts should survive her death? What considerations argue against the court's conclusion in *Harris*?

2. After Susie became incompetent, Marshall made the gifts of community property that are the subject of this action. To whom, exactly, did he make the gifts? Had Susie not been incompetent, and hence incapable of consent, do you think she would have joined in these gifts?

Approximately half the gifts were made while Marshall was her guardian; the other half were made after Marshall, growing old himself, relinquished the guardianship to his son. After he relinquished the guardianship, he had to secure the consent of his son, plaintiff in this action. In view of his son's subsequent behavior, such consent was improbable. The family conflict we see in *Harris* is not unlikely when one spouse has become incompetent and the other is aged. The couple's children are likely to be the parties' will beneficiaries and do not wish to see community resources diverted by the competent spouse's inter vivos gifts.

3. If Marshall Harris had consulted you regarding the gifts he planned to make after March 28, 1957, what would you have advised him? Could he have anticipated and headed off this litigation with a provision in *his* will?

4. The current guardianship (now called conservatorship) provisions are found at Probate Code sections 3000 et seq. They were specifically drafted for the management and disposition of community property when one spouse lacks legal capacity.

ESTATE OF BRAY
230 Cal. App. 2d 136, 40 Cal. Rptr. 750 (1964)

SALSMAN, J. — This is an appeal by Belle Bray, as co-executrix of the will of her late husband, Walter G. Bray. . . .

Appellant and decedent Walter G. Bray were married in 1919, and their marriage continued until decedent's death in 1960. At the time of marriage neither party had any substantial amount of property. It is undisputed that all property involved in the present controversy is community property.

In 1929 decedent started a food brokerage business. For a short time he had a partner, but this relationship was terminated and the business continued and was solely owned by decedent until the time of his death.

In 1938 the decedent requested his son by a former marriage, who is the respondent here, to come and work in the business. Respondent accepted the offer of employment, and from 1938 until decedent's death continued his employment in the business as a salaried employee.

In 1944, without the knowledge or consent of his wife, decedent opened a joint tenancy savings account with respondent, and each year thereafter deposited in the account funds withdrawn from his business bank account. No withdrawals were ever made from the joint account. At date of death the balance in the account, including interest additions, amounted to $74,385.88. Although respondent knew of the existence of this bank account, because he signed a form card for the bank when the account was opened, he did not know when deposits were made in the account, or in what amount, nor did he at any time before his father's death know the balance in the account. The bank book was at all times kept by the decedent.

The decedent also purchased U.S. Savings Bonds with community funds. These too were registered in the joint names of decedent and respondent, without the knowledge or consent of appellant. The value of these bonds at date of death was $10,701.94. The respondent did not know when the bonds were purchased, but he did know of their existence, because his father once asked him to make a list of the bonds, and respondent had them in his possession briefly for this purpose. After the list was prepared, respondent returned the bonds to his father, who retained possession of them until his death.

In proceedings for distribution of the decedent's estate, respondent claimed the bank account and bonds as surviving joint tenant. Appellant claimed the joint tenancies had been created by the use of community funds, without her consent and without valuable consideration, and therefore respondent should restore to the estate one-half the value of such joint tenancies. (Civ. Code, §172; Estate of McNutt, 36 Cal. App. 2d 542, 553 [98 P.2d 253].)

The probate court found that respondent had rendered valuable consideration to the decedent in return for the creation of the joint tenancies in the bank account and bonds and that no part of such joint tenancy property belonged to the estate of the decedent. The valuable consideration relied upon by the court consisted of services rendered by respondent to the decedent in the conduct of his business during decedent's lifetime. We have concluded that this finding is not supported by substantial evidence and that the order from which this appeal is taken must be reversed.

Respondent presented various witnesses in support of his contention that he rendered valuable consideration in return for the creation of the joint tenancies. He offered his own testimony thus:

Q. . . . the fact is that you paid nothing to your father for any of those deposits that went into this joint tenancy account?
A. That is debatable.
Q. Did you pay any money to him at all for that?
A. I did not hand my father money out of my pocket for him to make a deposit, but the services that I rendered, and the consideration for that, to bring money into that business for my services, my father set that aside for me for my reward for the services rendered over the period of time when my salary was not exhorbitant [sic] and the fact that I worked Saturdays and Sundays and did not take vacations was considered. . . .

Appellant testified that her husband had once told her that respondent "was a fine son and a fine boy and was doing a good job."

Grace Lillon, a niece of the decedent, testified that decedent had told her "God never blessed a man with a finer son than Dick. I could not run the business without him."

The testimony of Calvin Rossi, an employee of the bank where the joint account was maintained, was to the effect that the decedent had told him that his son had earned the money; that he did not want his son to know about the money but he "wanted him to have it at the end." Mr. Solinsky, decedent's attorney, testified that the decedent had told him "Dick was always on the job, was there, and was doing excellent work, and that he was taking care of Dick in view of all of his services."

Appellant objected to most of this testimony on the ground that it was hearsay and self-serving. . . . The trial court overruled these objections. Respondent asserts the testimony was properly admitted because it tended to show decedent's state of mind and his intentions regarding compensation for his son at the time the joint tenancies were created and as they were increased from time to time by the addition of deposits and the purchase of bonds. We think the evidence was properly admitted (Hansen v. Bear Film Co., Inc., 28 Cal. 2d 154, 173 [168 P.2d 946] . . .), but that it falls far short of substantial evidence to show that a valuable consideration was received sufficient to support the transfer of community funds.

At the time the decedent opened the joint bank account with respondent there was no promise on his part to deposit any money in it in exchange for any promise, act or service on the part of respondent. There was evidence that once or twice the decedent had said to respondent that there was too much cash in the bank account — presumably the business checking account — and that some should be transferred to savings. But there was no evidence that such excess was deposited in the joint account because of any act or promise on the part of respondent. During the entire 15-year period, respondent never knew of any amounts deposited by decedent or when the deposits were made.

In 1944, when the account was opened, respondent's salary was $225 per month and he received no bonus. His compensation was at the same rate for the year 1945. Thereafter, respondent's basic salary increased from $250 in 1946 to $375 in 1959. In all years following 1945 save one respondent received a substantial annual bonus varying from $1,800 in 1946 to $5,000 for each of the four years prior to his father's death. There is evidence that in later years respondent had greater responsibilities than he had at first, but there is no evidence to show that these duties were assumed because of any promise by his father to deposit any money in the joint bank account.

Thus, we find no substantial evidence in the record to show that respondent rendered any valuable consideration to the decedent or gave any consideration at all for the creation of the joint tenancies in either the bank account or the bonds.

Consideration may be either (1) a benefit conferred or agreed to be conferred upon the promisor or some other person; or (2) a detriment suffered or agreed to be suffered by the promisee or some other person. (Civ. Code, §1605.) It must be an act or a return promise, bargained for and given in exchange for a promise. (Simmons v. California Institute of Technology, 34 Cal. 2d 264, 272 [209 P.2d 581]. . . .) Here there is no evidence of any promise on the part of the decedent to make deposits in the joint bank account, or to buy bonds registered jointly in the names of decedent and respondent, in return for any promise on the part of respondent, or any act on respondent's part. After the joint account was opened in 1944, respondent continued to render services to decedent's business as a salaried employee, with no knowledge of what money, if any, was actually being deposited in the joint account, or how many bonds were being purchased, if any. Respondent was duty-bound to render faithful service to the decedent in return for his salary and a bonus. Under the definition of consideration in Civil Code section 1605, doing what one is already legally bound to do cannot be consideration. (Pacific Finance Corp. v. First Nat. Bank, 4 Cal. 2d 47, 49 [47 P.2d 460]. . . .)

It is undoubtedly true that, as one witness testified, decedent wished to keep the joint account secret from respondent as well as his wife and that he intended respondent should have it "at the end," that is, upon decedent's death. It is undisputed also that all deposits to the account were made from community funds. This evidence discloses only a gift, unsupported by a valuable consideration, and hence voidable in part by appellant, pursuant to Civil Code section 172.

There was some evidence received, over objection of appellant, that decedent had established joint tenancies with appellant during his lifetime, and that upon decedent's death appellant had received at least one-half of all property in which decedent had an interest at the time of his death. This evidence was immaterial to a resolution of the issue of whether a valuable consideration had been given for the creation of the joint tenancy bank account and the joint tenancies in the bonds. A wife has a vested interest in all of the community property and her interest extends to every part and parcel of the community property estate. The husband during the lifetime of the parties may not give away any portion of it. In Dargie v. Patterson, 176 Cal. 714, 721 [169 P. 360], the court said: ". . . upon the death of a husband who has attempted to convey community property . . . his nonconsenting wife may recover an undivided one-half of such property in an action brought against the grantee, and this without regard to the amount or condition of the estate remaining in his hands at the time of his death.". . .

Respondent further claims that Belle Bray ratified and confirmed the creation of the joint tenancies in the bank account and the bonds. This assertion derives from the fact that she signed the inventory and appraisement and the federal estate tax return and that both the inventory and the tax return showed the joint tenancy character of the bank account and the bonds. It does not appear however that the widow understood the significance or the legal meaning of the term "joint tenancy," or that the term was explained to her by counsel. Moreover, there is substantial evidence that she was ill at the time the documents were presented to her for signature and that she did not read them. . . .

The order is reversed, with directions to the probate court to require respondent to account to the estate for one-half of the joint tenancy bank account and for one-half of the U.S. Savings Bonds. . . .

DRAPER, P.J., and DEVINE, J., concurred.

. . . Respondent's petition for a hearing by the Supreme Court was denied December 9, 1964.

Notes and Questions

1. Does the court take too narrow a view of "valuable consideration"? Consider an annual Christmas bonus. An employer is not legally obligated to give it, but may the employer's wife sue the employee to recover the bonus on the ground that it was an unauthorized gift of community funds? Do the funds Walter put aside for his son Dick differ from a bonus in any significant respect?

2. Suppose that son Dick were now being divorced by his wife Doris. If you were

representing Doris, would you acquiesce to Dick's characterization of the funds (the one-half remaining after *Bray*) as "separate property *gifts* from Dad"? What would you argue? (Compare Downer v. Bramet at page 146 supra.) Does the definition of "gift" for purposes of avoiding community property characterization (Doris v. Dick) mean something different from "gift" for purposes of avoiding the gift consent requirement (Belle v. Dick)? How might you justify such a distinction?

3. Did Walter's estate plan effectively put Belle to an election to either assert her one-half interest in every community asset or take as the surviving tenant under the joint tenancies he had set up for her? See pages 547-555 infra.

4. If Walter had come to see you before he began his probate avoidance estate planning, how would you have advised him?

5. Note that the gift restriction is unqualified; it covers all gifts. If you were advising a charitable organization, how might you anticipate and avoid gift revocation by the nondonor spouse?

2.   *The Fiduciary Duty*

It is frequently said that the spouse who manages and controls a particular community asset acts as a fiduciary with respect to the other spouse's interest in the asset. This view is now expressed in four sections of the California Family Code: sections 721, 1100, 1101, and 2602. During the past two decades the legislature has expressed concern about spousal overreaching. The predecessor to current section 1101 was first enacted in 1986 to provide nonmanaging spouses with rights and remedies. In 1991 and 2002, current Family Code sections 721, 1100, and 1101 were amended to strengthen the position of nonmanaging spouses. S.B. 716, 1991 Cal. Stat., ch. 1026 and S.B. 1936, 2002 Cal. Stat., ch. 310. The four provisions are reprinted below, and the amendments are italicized. As you read pre-1991 cases that follow the statutes, consider whether they survive the post-1990 legislation.

California Family Code Section 721

. . . [I]n transactions between themselves, a husband and wife are subject to the general rules *governing fiduciary relationships* which control the actions of persons occupying confidential relations with each other. *This confidential relationship imposes a duty of the highest good faith and fair dealing on each spouse, and neither shall take any unfair advantage of the other. This confidential relationship is a fiduciary relationship subject to the same rights and duties of nonmarital business partners, as provided in Sections 16403, 16404, and 16503 of the Corporations Code,*[1] including, but not limited to, the following:

(1) Providing each spouse access at all times to any books kept regarding a transaction for the purposes of inspection and copying.

(2) Rendering upon request, true and full information of all things affecting any transaction which concerns the community property. Nothing in this section is intended to

---

1. Section 16403 gives partners access to the partnership books and records. Section 16503 regulates transfers of partnership interests. Section 16404 sets out the fiduciary duties that a partner owes to the partnership and the other partners. There are two duties: the duty of loyalty and the duty of care. Both are defined with specificity by Section 16404, reproduced in the Statutory Appendix at pages 642-643.

impose a duty for either spouse to keep detailed books and records of community property transactions.

(3) Accounting to the spouse, and holding as a trustee, any benefit or profit derived from any transaction by one spouse without the consent of the other spouse which concerns the community property.

California Family Code Section 1100(e)

Each spouse shall act with respect to the other spouse in the management and control of the community property in accordance with the general rules *governing fiduciary relationships* which control the actions of persons having relationships of personal confidence as specified in Section 721, until such time as the property has been divided by the parties or by a court. This duty includes the obligation to make full disclosure to the other spouse of *all material facts and information regarding* the existence, *characterization, and valuation of all* assets in which the community has *or may have* an interest and debts for which the community *is or* may be liable, *and to provide equal access to all information, records, and books that pertain to the value and character of those assets and debts*, upon request.

California Family Code Section 1101

(a) A spouse has a claim against the other spouse for any breach of the *fiduciary* duty that results in impairment to the claimant spouse's present undivided one-half interest in the community *estate, including, but not limited to, a single transaction or a pattern or series of transactions, which transaction or transactions have caused or will cause a detrimental impact to the claimant spouse's undivided one-half interest in the community* estate.

(b) A court may order an accounting of the property and obligations of the parties to a marriage and may determine the rights of ownership in, the beneficial enjoyment of, or access to, community property, and the classification of all property of the parties to a marriage.

(c) A court may order that the name of a spouse shall be added to community property held in the name of the other spouse alone or that the title of community property held in some other title form shall be reformed to reflect its community character, except with respect to any of the following:

(1) A partnership interest held by the other spouse as a general partner.

(2) An interest in a professional corporation or professional association.

(3) An asset of an unincorporated business if the other spouse is the only spouse involved in operating and managing the business.

(4) Any other property, if the revision would adversely affect the rights of a third person.

(d) (1) Except as provided in paragraph (2), any action under subdivision (a) shall be commenced within three years of the date a petitioning spouse had actual knowledge that the transaction or event for which the remedy is being sought occurred.

(2) An action may be commenced under this section upon the death of a spouse or in conjunction with an action for legal separation, dissolution of marriage, or nullity without regard to the time limitations set forth in paragraph (1).

(3) The defense of laches may be raised in any action brought under this section.

(4) Except as to actions authorized by paragraph (2), remedies under subdivision (a) apply only to transactions or events occurring on or after July 1, 1987.

(e) In any transaction affecting community property in which the consent of both spouses is required, the court may, upon the motion of a spouse, dispense with the requirement of the other spouse's consent if both of the following requirements are met:

(1) The proposed transaction is in the best interest of the community.

(2) Consent has been arbitrarily refused or cannot be obtained due to the physical incapacity, mental incapacity, or prolonged absence of the nonconsenting spouse.

(f) Any action may be brought under this section without filing an action for dissolution of marriage, legal separation, or nullity, or may be brought in conjunction with the action or upon the death of a spouse.

(g) *Remedies for breach of the fiduciary duty by one spouse, including those set out in Sections 721 and 1100, shall include, but not be limited to, an award to the other spouse of 50 percent, or an amount equal to 50 percent, of any asset undisclosed or transferred in breach of the fiduciary duty plus attorney's fees and court costs. The value of the asset shall be determined to be its highest value at the date of the breach of the fiduciary duty, the date of the sale or disposition of the asset, or the date of the award by the court.*

(h) *Remedies for the breach of the fiduciary duty by one spouse, as set forth in Sections 721 and 1100, when the breach falls within the ambit of Section 3294 of the Civil Code*[2] *shall include, but not be limited to, an award to the other spouse of 100 percent, or an amount equal to 100 percent, of any asset undisclosed or transferred in breach of the fiduciary duty.*

California Family Code Section 2602

As an additional award or offset against existing property, the court may award, from a party's share, the amount the court determines to have been deliberately misappropriated by the party to the exclusion of the interest of the other party in the community estate.

---

2. Civil Code section 3294 provides for punitive, or exemplary, damages. — ED.

§3294.   Exemplary damages; when allowable; definitions

(a) In an action for the breach of an obligation not arising from contract, where it is proven by clear and convincing evidence that the defendant has been guilty of oppression, fraud, or malice, the plaintiff, in addition to the actual damages, may recover damages for the sake of example and by way of punishing the defendant. . . .

(c) As used in this section, the following definitions shall apply:

(1) "Malice" means conduct which is intended by the defendant to cause injury to the plaintiff or despicable conduct which is carried on by the defendant with a willful and conscious disregard of the rights or safety of others.

(2) "Oppression" means despicable conduct that subjects a person to cruel and unjust hardship in conscious disregard of that person's rights.

(3) "Fraud" means an intentional misrepresentation, deceit, or concealment of a material fact known to the defendant with the intention on the part of the defendant of thereby depriving a person of property or legal rights or otherwise causing injury. . . .

Notes and Questions

Community property case law does not yield a clear definition of the fiduciary duty. This is, in part, a reflection of the myriad and disparate circumstances in which the duty may be invoked as well as the broad range of obligations that may plausibly be contained within the duty. Two relatively frequent problems typically arise at divorce: Substantial community property disappears on the eve of divorce; and, during divorce negotiations, one spouse gives the other arguably inadequate information about the existence, nature, or value of the community property. The first problem effectively asks whether there is a duty to account; the second asks whether there is a duty to disclose. Both issues have been addressed by the 1991 amendments to current Family Code section 1100(e) supra. Because these two problems are likely to originate after the marriage has already broken down, that is, when we may have altered expectations about the parties' behavior, they are examined in Chapter 9, Property Distribution at Divorce. This section treats a constellation of questions that are likely to arise throughout the intact marriage, although they are generally not presented for judicial resolution until the marriage ends by divorce or death. To what level of managerial competence is a spouse held? For what purposes may a married person permissibly spend community funds? Must a managing spouse put the community's interest before those of his separate estate?

Consider the issues raised by the following situations. With respect to situations 4 through 9, does your response vary according to whether the aggrieved spouse seeks compensatory relief at death or divorce, or instead seeks some remedy that will stop the other spouse's continuing dissipation of community funds during the marriage?

(1) Husband manages a community property business and negligently failed to collect various business debts before the statute of limitations expired.

(2) Husband, against Wife's wishes, made blue chip investments in a declining market, and lost a good deal of community money.

(3) Wife, hoping to strike it rich for the family, invested in the commodities market and lost a great deal of community money.
    (a) She did so without Husband's knowledge.
    (b) She did so with his knowledge but with his extreme disapproval.
    (c) He knew, but expressed no opinion.

(4) Despite Wife's disapproval, Husband, unable to control a compulsion to gamble, lost a large portion of the community assets in the California Lottery and at the Santa Ana racetrack.

(5) Despite Wife's strong disapproval, Husband spent substantial portions of his community earnings in the local bar and at neighborhood poker parties.

(6) Despite Husband's strong disapproval, Wife spent a large portion of her community earnings on cocaine.

(7) Husband "adjusted" to marital sexual incompatibility by having a mistress whom he "helped out" with a substantial portion of his community earnings. Wife knew nothing.

(8) Husband is a homebody, but Wife has wanderlust and spent most of her community earnings traveling the world during her summer vacations.

(9) Husband, fearful of banks and investments, kept all his community earnings in a safe deposit box. Wife disapproved and urged husband to put the money in federally insured interest-bearing bank certificates of deposit. Husband persistently refused.

(10) Wife received an excellent stock tip. Purchase opportunity was limited and, having both separate and community funds available, Wife used her separate funds. Six months later, Wife sold the greatly appreciated stock.

(11) Wife's company gave her stock options, which she exercised with separate funds even though community funds were available. She made considerable profit.

MARRIAGE OF SCHULTZ
105 Cal. App. 3d 846, 164 Cal. Rptr. 653 (1980)

JEFFERSON (Bernard), J.—. . . A debt of $4,250, owed to one Conrad Blasco, was listed in the interlocutory judgment as a debt of the community; its nature is not disputed by Alvin. Creditor Blasco became tired of awaiting voluntary payment, and sought judgment against Alvin in a municipal court action. Alvin appeared there in propria persona but apparently failed to go to court on the trial date; Blasco obtained a default judgment. The "Accounting" made by Carol's attorney lists that judgment as a debt of $5,000. The order adjusting the accounting recites: "The Court finds that the Respondent [Alvin] represented himself as pro per in suit filed against him by one, Conrad Blasco, and therefore engendered the duty of informing the Court in which said suit was filed of his new address where Notice of Trial date should have been sent." On this basis, the trial court assigned $1,500 of the indebtedness to Carol, and the remainder ($3,500, approximately) to Alvin.

Alvin [once again representing himself] argues here that his address was the family residence during this period, whether he was living there or not; implicit in his claim is that no negligence with respect to this obligation should have been attributed to him by an unequal division of the debt. We agree.

[Family] Code section [2550] mandates equal division of assets, and, [section 2602] states that, as an exception to equal division, "the court may award, from a party's share, [the amount the court] determines to have been *deliberately misappropriated* by [the] party to the exclusion of the [interest of the other party in the community estate]." (Italics added.) But nothing is said in the statute about negligence. The term "deliberate misappropriation" has reference to calculated thievery by a spouse, not the mishandling of assets.

We perceive that the same distinction should be made with respect to *debts*. There may be situations in which a spouse may be held responsible as a fiduciary for *gross* mishandling of community financial affairs which would be tantamount to fraud, but, in the case at bench, the circumstances surrounding the misdirection of a notice of trial do not warrant the imposition by the trial court upon one spouse of what amounted to a penalty, charging Alvin's share of residual assets with more than one-half of the debt. Nor does the fact that Alvin chose not to hire a lawyer to represent him in the municipal court, in and of itself, establish culpability. We find no basis for the trial court's determination that equity required an unequal division of the Blasco debt. Hence, the order containing that ruling was erroneous. . . .

The judgment (order) is reversed. . . . KINGSLEY, Acting P.J., and McCLOSKY, J., concurred.

A petition for a rehearing was denied June 5, 1980.

MARRIAGE OF MOORE
28 Cal. 3d 366, 618 P.2d 208, 168 Cal. Rptr. 662 (1980)

MANUEL, J.—. . . David . . . challenges the trial court's finding that he deliberately misappropriated items of community personal property by disposing of them without valuable consideration and without the consent of his wife in order to purchase alcoholic beverages. Based on this finding the court made a compensatory award to Lydie pursuant to [Family] Code section [2602], which allows the court to "award, from a party's share, [the amount the court] determines to have been deliberately misappropriated by [the] party to the exclusion of the [interest of the other party in the community estate]." David contends that the evidence is insufficient to support this finding. We agree.

The record discloses that a number of community property items were missing from the home at the time of separation. Both David and Lydie testified that certain community items had been disappearing during the last few years of their marriage. David said that none of these items were in his possession and that he did not know where they were. Lydie believed that David sold the items in order to purchase alcoholic beverages, but she did not know the prices he received for the items.

Under section 5125, subdivision (b) of the Civil Code, [now, as amended, Family Code section 1100(b)], "A spouse may not make a gift of community personal property, or dispose of community personal property without a valuable consideration, without the written consent of the other spouse." Lydie, however, has failed to prove that David made a gift of the missing items or disposed of them without valuable consideration. The only evidence presented on the question—Lydie's belief that he disposed of the items to buy alcoholic beverages—indicates to the contrary. David could not have purchased alcoholic beverages with the items if he had not received valuable consideration for them.

Lydie suggests that the trial court's finding of deliberate misappropriation could also be upheld on the ground that David's disposal of the items violated subdivision (c) of Civil Code section 5125 [now, as amended, Family Code section 1100(c)], which provides that "A spouse may not sell, convey, or encumber the furniture, furnishings, or fittings of the home, or the clothing or wearing apparel of the other spouse or minor children which is community personal property, without the written consent of the other spouse." The trial court made no findings regarding whether the items missing constituted "furniture, furnishings, or fittings of the home," and we are unable to make that determination on the record presented. Accordingly, we reverse that portion of the judgment.

The portion of the judgment determining the rights of the parties in and awarding the community property is reversed with directions to redetermine the amount, if any, that was deliberately misappropriated through violation of [Family] Code section [1100], subdivision (c), and to adjust the award accordingly. . . .

BIRD, C.J., TOBRINER, J., MOSK, J., CLARK, J., RICHARDSON, J., and NEWMAN, J., concurred.

Note

Compare the language of former Civil Code section 5125(b), quoted in *Moore*, with current Family Code section 1100(b). What is the difference between "valuable consideration" and "fair and reasonable value"? Do alcoholic beverages provide "fair and reasonable value" for community personal property?

MARRIAGE OF BELTRAN
183 Cal. App. 3d 292, 227 Cal. Rptr. 924 (1986)

NEWSOM, J. — The present appeal presents the question of whether a husband must reimburse the community for the amount of a military pension forfeited as part of a sentence in a military court-martial. The factual background may be summarized as follows.

Husband and wife were married October 14, 1976. They originally separated March 30, 1981, and wife filed a petition for dissolution on April 3, 1981. After a brief reconciliation from June 30, 1981, to December 16, 1982, action on the petition commenced in 1983. . . .

Husband was a colonel in the United States Army when the parties finally separated. During his tenure in the military, he earned substantial benefits, including a pension and accrued leave. The trial court found that 19.47 percent of his military pension and 31 days of his accrued leave were community property and valued such assets at $117,000 and $5,115 respectively.

While the divorce action was pending, husband was convicted of committing lewd and lascivious acts upon a child under 14 in violation of Penal Code section 288, subdivision (a). On July 13, 1983, a military tribunal convicted husband of the same crime, and, as a result, he was dismissed from the Army and stripped of all military benefits, including his pension and accrued leave.

As part of the dissolution judgment, the trial court charged husband with receipt of the forfeited military pension and accrued leave and ordered accordingly that distribution of the community property be equalized by husband's payment of one-half of such military benefits, in the amount of $59,230.50 to wife. This appeal followed.

In a somewhat analogous situation, it has long been established that the community is entitled to reimbursement when community funds are used to pay one spouse's separate debt. (E.g., In re Marriage of Epstein (1979) 24 Cal. 3d 76, 89 [154 Cal. Rptr. 413, 592 P.2d 1165] [husband used community savings to pay taxes on his postseparation separate income]; In re Marriage of Lister (1984) 152 Cal. App. 3d 411, 417-418 [199 Cal. Rptr. 321] [husband transferred community-owned house to satisfy his separate debts]; In re Marriage of Walter (1976) 57 Cal. App. 3d 802, 806-807 [129 Cal. Rptr. 351] [husband used community funds to pay taxes and make mortgage payments on his separate property]; Somps v. Somps (1967)

250 Cal. App. 2d 328, 338 [58 Cal. Rptr. 304] [husband used community funds to improve his separate property].)

Other analogies are close at hand. In the recent case of In re Marriage of Stitt (1983) 147 Cal. App. 3d 579 [195 Cal. Rptr. 172], the wife incurred an obligation of $10,989.20 in attorney fees to defend against charges of embezzlement. She personally signed a note for the debt and executed a second trust deed against the family residence. The trial court found the attorney fee obligation to be the wife's separate obligation, chargeable against her share of the community assets. On appeal, the reviewing court affirmed, holding that the wife was fully responsible for all financial consequences of her embezzlement, reasoning that, while the attorney fees were a community obligation in the sense that the attorneys were entitled to satisfy their claims from the community, as between the spouses such fees were the wife's separate obligation. "No principle of law required the innocent spouse to share the loss created by the other party. Husband had not waived his right to receive his share of the community property free from any loss attributable to wife's separate conduct. Therefore it was proper for the court to make orders which carried out the law's intention that only responsible participants in crime or tort bear the loss." (Stitt, supra, 147 Cal. App. 3d at p.588.)

Husband seeks to distinguish Stitt on the ground that the loss of his pension benefits resulted from imposed forfeiture rather than voluntary payment of a debt. But we find the distinction to be without legal significance. As we read Stitt, it was the wife's separate *conduct* which led the court to hold her personally responsible for the loss. The Stitt reasoning seems equally applicable whether the loss was incurred by contractual obligation, tort liability or criminal penalty.[1]

Here, as in Stitt, husband's criminal conduct diminished the wife's share of the community property to which the wife was otherwise entitled upon dissolution. (In re Marriage of Brown (1976) 15 Cal. 3d 838, 845-846 [126 Cal. Rptr. 633, 544 P.2d 561, 94 A.L.R.3d 164].) In our view, wife should not be made in effect to share in a penalty imposed upon husband for his criminal conduct. We accordingly conclude as a matter of equity that criminal conduct on the part of husband which directly caused forfeiture of pension benefits justified the trial court's conclusion that wife was entitled to reimbursement for her share of such lost community property.[2] . . .

Judgment is affirmed. RACANELLI, P.J., and HOLMDAHL, J., concurred. Appellant's petition for review by the Supreme Court was denied October 16, 1986.

Notes

1. *Spousal negligence.* Consider Marriage of Hirsch, 211 Cal. App. 3d 104, 259 Cal. Rptr. 39 (1989), rev. denied August 17, 1989. During marriage Clement Hirsch

---

1. The Stitt court noted that not every financial loss need be accounted for upon dissolution of marriage. "We are reminded that there is a principle that one takes a spouse 'for better or worse.' This may be so. Because of the continuing nature of the marital relationship, principles of waiver, condonation and laches would in most cases prevent any belated attempt at the time of dissolution proceedings to seek an accounting of all community property losses attributable to the independent delicts of the spouses. Here, however, the court had conclusive evidence of recently committed criminal activity which culminated in financial consequences at the time the marriage was coming to an end." (Stitt, supra, 147 Cal. App. 3d at p.588.)

2. In light of our conclusion we need not reach the question of whether the trial court's ruling can be upheld as an award or offset for sums "deliberately misappropriated" within the meaning of [Family] Code section [2602].

served as a salaried director of a corporation. During divorce proceedings, Clement learned that he had been named as a defendant in several actions arising from his marital service as a director. He settled the claims and sought reimbursement for one-half the settlement costs. Purporting to follow *Stitt* (discussed in *Beltran* at page 420 supra), the trial court held that the settlement costs "were incurred by Clement as a result of his tortious conduct and . . . should therefore not be charged against the community." Although approving the result in *Stitt, Hirsch* sharply criticizes the broad reasoning of *Stitt:* "[T]o the extent that *Stitt* holds that the negligent conduct of a spouse engaged in an activity benefiting the community provides sufficient justification to characterize a debt as a separate obligation, it is incorrect." *Hirsch* holds that spousal negligence incident to an activity that benefits the community gives rise to a community debt. In order to dispute the community characterization, Mrs. Hirsch would have to show that Clement's service on the board was designed to protect his separate property business interests.

2. *Unsound investment.* In Marriage of Duffy, 91 Cal. App. 4th 923, 111 Cal. Rptr. 4th 923 (2001), the husband invested his community property retirement funds in technology equities, which substantially declined in value. At divorce, expert witnesses testified that the investment was far too risky and undiversified, and calculated damages for the husband's alleged breach of fiduciary duty according to the difference between the highest value of the retirement account and its value at divorce. The court of appeal held that the fiduciary duty imposed by sections 721 and 1100 includes a duty of loyalty, but not a duty of care: "[A] spouse generally is not bound by the Prudent Investor Rule [now codified at Probate Code section 16047] and does not owe the other spouse the duty of care one business partner owes to another." Id. at 940. In other words, assuming good faith, one spouse is not liable to the other for the improvident investment of community property. Do you approve *Duffy*'s interpretation of the spousal fiduciary duty? The legislature did not. Stating its intention "to abrogate the ruling in In re Marriage of Duffy . . . to the extent that it is in conflict with this clarification," the legislature amended Family Code section 721 to incorporate Corporation Code section 16404, which prescribes a duty of care, as well as a duty of loyalty. 2002 Cal. Stat., ch. 310. For the text of section 16404, see pages 642-643 infra.

[handwritten margin note: overruled & amended...]

MARRIAGE OF LUCERO
118 Cal. App. 3d 836, 173 Cal. Rptr. 680 (1981)

[In the first portion of this opinion, reproduced at page 345 supra, the court of appeal held that the husband's right to reinstate a pension earned during marriage is community property subject to division at divorce. In this part of the opinion, the court of appeal responds to the husband's argument that his use of separate funds to reinstate the pension was permissible and warrants a finding that the portion of his pension benefits attributable to his separate property reinstatement contributions is his separate property.]

TAMURA, J.—Wife contends first that the community interest in husband's retirement benefits extends to the full amount of those benefits after redeposit of employee retirement contributions. She concedes that the community must pay its pro rata share of the redeposit and indicates that she has at all times been willing to contribute her fair share. Husband responds that the increase due to redeposit is entirely his separate property because the redeposit was made with his separate funds after separation.

The duties of spouses to deal fairly with each other do not terminate when they separate and obtain dissolution of their marriage. In particular, "one spouse cannot, by invoking a condition wholly within his control, defeat the community interest of the other spouse." (In re Marriage of Stenquist (1978) 21 Cal. 3d 779, 786 [148 Cal. Rptr. 9, 582 P.2d 96].) Thus a serviceman's election of a disability pension in lieu of a pension based on length of service does not defeat the community interest in the pension based on length of service (ibid.), nor will an employee spouse be permitted to defeat the other spouse's community interest in a pension by converting it to a joint and survivor annuity (In re Marriage of Lionberger (1979) 97 Cal. App. 3d 56, 67-71 [158 Cal. Rptr. 535]). The principle is clearly relevant to the issue raised by a spouse's election to use separate funds to redeposit retirement contributions.

In the present case, husband withdrew his retirement contribution in 1966 and this money was spent for community purposes. When the parties separated in 1976, only a negligible amount (about $50) had been redeposited. Husband retired one year later, in 1977, and made the redeposit using separate funds. The advantage of the redeposit is blindingly clear. Husband's benefits immediately increased by $366 per month, so that the total redeposit amount ($9,373) was recouped in about two years. Thereafter husband, who was still not 60 years old, could expect to enjoy the extra $366 per month for many years. In effect, husband purchased a $366 per month annuity, subject to periodic cost of living increases, for $9,373.[4] This was obviously a great bargain and was possible only as consideration for husband's service of over 30 years as a government employee.

To allow husband the sole right to decide whether to redeposit and the sole right to elect whether to redeposit with separate or community funds is to treat the redeposit right as husband's separate property. This is incorrect because the redeposit right is a pension right and "the community owns *all* pension rights attributable to employment during the marriage." (In re Marriage of Brown (1976) 15 Cal. 3d 838, 844 [126 Cal. Rptr. 633, 544 P.2d 561, 94 A.L.R.3d 164], italics supplied.)

Accordingly, we conclude that the trial court erred in failing to recognize wife's right to elect to share in the increased retirement benefits upon payment of her pro rata share of the redeposit. . . .

SOMPS v. SOMPS
250 Cal. App. 2d 328, 58 Cal. Rptr. 304 (1967)

[Husband's home construction partnership was a mixed separate and community asset, for which the trial court made a *Van Camp* accounting. During marriage, together with his business partner McKay, husband used his separate funds to purchase certain investment realty known as the Binkley property.]

. . . [Wife] further contends that husband breached a fiduciary relationship

---

4. At the time of trial, the size of the increase attributable to redeposit had already grown from $366 to $437 per month.

between husband and wife in that he should have purchased the property with community funds which were available. The fact that husband purchased the Binkley property with his separate funds, as the trial court found, is not evidence of taking any undue advantage nor is it a breach of a fiduciary relationship which would invoke a presumption of fraud or undue influence. There is no reason why husband should be compelled to keep his separate funds idle. Husband apparently had made many investments benefitting the community during the marriage which resulted in the substantial estate owned by the parties at the time of divorce. . . .

Notes and Questions

1. Are *Lucero* and *Somps* reconcilable?
2. To what extent do the principal cases address the 11 situations described at pages 416-417 supra? Do the amended California fiduciary provisions, discussed at pages 413-415 supra, provide any guidance?
3. Comprehensive codification of the spousal fiduciary duty has also been attempted in the Uniform Marital Property Act, 9A U.L.A. 107 (1987):

§2. Responsibility Between Spouses

> (a) Each spouse shall act in good faith with respect to the other spouse in matters involving marital property or other property of the other spouse. This obligation may not be varied by a marital property agreement.

Comment

> Spouses are not trustees or guarantors toward each other. Neither are they simple parties to a contract endeavoring to further their individual interests. The duty is between, and is one of good faith. A spouse is not bound always to succeed in matters involving marital property ventures, but while endeavoring to succeed in a venture, must proceed with an appropriate regard for the property interests of the other spouse and without taking unfair advantage of the other spouse. . . . This is one of four provisions in the Act that cannot be varied by a marital property agreement. (Section 10(c)).

To what extent does the Uniform Marital Property Act address the 11 situations described at pages 416-417 supra?

C.   CREDITORS' RIGHTS

1.   The Basic Principle

GROLEMUND v. CAFFERATA
17 Cal. 2d 679, 111 P.2d 641 (1941)

CURTIS, J.—Lena Grolemund and Caesaer Grolemund, her husband, instituted this action against Emilio Cafferata and the respective sheriffs of the city and county of San Francisco and the county of San Mateo, for the purpose of procuring a permanent injunction restraining defendants from proceeding with the sale of certain personal property in San Francisco and certain real property in San Mateo County pursuant to executions issued on a judgment in favor of defendant Emilio Cafferata and others, as plaintiffs, and against plaintiff Caesaer Grolemund, as defendant. From a final judgment in favor of defendants, plaintiff Lena Grolemund appeals. . . .

On April 17, 1935, Emilio Cafferata and others recovered a judgment in an action prosecuted in the Superior Court of San Francisco against Caesaer Grolemund because of damages sustained on August 6, 1933, in an automobile collision, wherein the defendant was adjudged negligent in the operation of his car. . . .

The principal question to be decided on this appeal is whether community property may be subjected to the satisfaction of a judgment against the husband for his tort. Fundamental to our determination of this basic issue is consideration of the change wrought in our community system by enactment in 1927 of section 161a of the Civil Code. The general rule that community property in California acquired prior to 1927, has always been held liable for the husband's debts (Cal. Jur. Supp., vol. 3, p.663, sec. 146) was given unqualified recognition by this court in the celebrated case of Spreckels v. Spreckels, 116 Cal. 339, 343 [48 Pac. 228, 58 Am. St. Rep. 170, 36 L.R.A. 497], wherein it is stated that the creditor of the husband could, at his option, sell under execution either the husband's separate property or the community property. The rule announced in that case has never been departed from by any decision of this court to which our attention has been called. Appellant claims, however, that by virtue of the enactment in 1927 of section 161a of the Civil Code, the wife now has a vested interest in the community property, of which she cannot be deprived because of the debt of the husband alone. Respondents resist this contention as contrary to the statutes and prior decisions of the courts of this state. Because of the emphasis placed by the parties on this enactment as it reflects on the instant issue, we shall consider first its effect upon the property of the Grolemunds acquired subsequent to the enactment of said section 161a. . . .

Section 172 of the Civil Code, while it does not specifically create a liability or an exemption for any particular type of community property, gives to the husband "the management and control of the community personal property, with like absolute power of disposition, other than testamentary, as he has of his separate estate." It reasonably follows from the express language above quoted that this section in effect subjects the entire community personalty . . . to any and all contracts of the husband, as well as to judgments arising out of his tort. Furthermore, since the only limitation upon the husband is to refrain from making a gift of such property without consideration, he is not prevented from paying it out in compromise or satisfaction of a tort claim, for payment of a tort claim is not payment without consideration.

Section 172a of the Civil Code gives the husband "the management and control of the community real property," subject to the proviso that in regard to conveyances the wife must join with him in executing the necessary instruments. Since this restriction concerns only *voluntary* transfers, it has no application to the instant case involving the satisfaction of a judgment by levy of execution, so that for all practical purposes herein the husband's power of management and control of the community real property involved here is as absolute and complete as it is with respect to community personal property, as outlined in section 172. That the addition in 1927 of section 161a, defining the interests of the spouses in community property, did not change the rule vesting in the husband the entire management and control of the community property is manifest by the express recognition accorded sections 172 and 172a in the later statute. . . .

With reference to California legislation on the question of liability or exemption of property of the spouses for payment of obligations arising out of the husband's tort, the sole enactments are section 168, which exempts the wife's earnings (community property) from liability for debts of the husband, and section 171, which extends the same exemption in respect to the wife's separate property. It is significant to note that nothing is said in regard to the liability of the husband's separate property, the husband's earnings, or the balance of the community property (the wife's earnings excepted by Civ. Code, sec. 168) in regard to an obligation created by the husband's tort. From this silence of the legislature it logically can be inferred that it was thereby intended that the husband, as agent of the community, should retain the power to divest the parties of their community property by his own act in the same manner that he might divest himself of his separate property, so long as he did not make a gift of the former without consideration. To hold that the husband could not subject the community property to liability for his tort would be to hold that he could not manage and control the same. To illustrate, suppose that the tort action had never been instituted by Emilio Cafferata and his co-plaintiffs, but the Caesaer Grolemund, after injuring these parties, had made a voluntary settlement of his liability. It cannot be said that the husband would be without power to use common funds to pay for the damages sustained by the injured persons because of his negligent act. Or let us suppose that the damage suit was brought and judgment had gone against Caesaer Grolemund, as here, but that no execution had been levied, it is obvious that the husband could satisfy such judgment voluntarily from a bank account under his control but which consisted of community funds. The foregoing analysis compels us to conclude that there is no logical distinction to be drawn between satisfaction of a judgment against the husband by levy of execution against the community property and satisfaction of a like judgment by the husband's voluntary payment from community funds. . . .

Appellant advances the argument that the statutes of Washington and the statutes of California regarding community property are the same, and, therefore, the rules announced in decisions of the Washington courts interpreting their code sections should be followed here. This contention is singularly devoid of merit in view of the fact that the underlying theories of the community system in the two states are entirely distinct. The Washington statutes are based on the theory of tenancy by entireties, with its fundamental concept of "community debts," and in that state the community property is not liable for the separate debts of the husband, much less of the wife, but is liable only for so-called "community debts." (Cal. Jur. Supp., vol. 3, p.665, sec. 147, and cases there cited.) For example, in Sun Life Assur. Co. v. Outler, 172 Wash. 540 [20 Pac. (2d) 1110], the Washington court said at page 544: "The test of a community obligation is: 'Was the transaction carried on for the material benefit of the community?'" Thus, in Washington where the system makes the community property responsible only for "community debts" or "community liabilities," the community property cannot be reached for the individual tort of either the husband or wife. But in California there is no like concept of "community debts," though occasionally the courts in this state refer to such, overlooking the fact that the phrase is not appropriate to the California system (Cal. Jur. Supp., vol. 3, p.666, sec. 147). A complete reading of all our code sections on community property clearly demonstrates that our community system is based upon the principle that all debts which are not specifically made the obligation of the wife are grouped together as the obligations of the husband and the community property (with the single exception of the wife's earnings, which are exempted from certain types of debt, Civ. Code, sec. 168). This proposition was confirmed in Street v. Bertolone, 193 Cal. 751, 753 [226 Pac. 913]: "The term 'the debts of the husband,' unless otherwise qualified, includes debts incurred by the husband for the benefit of the community as well as his own separate debts." Since in this state there is strictly no such thing as "community debts" in the sense in which they exist in Washington, the decisions of the latter state lose force as a precedent here. . . .

Since it is our opinion that the enactment of section 161a of the Civil Code, defining the interests of the spouses in community property, has not altered the situation with respect to the wife's interest remaining subject to the husband's power of management and control, all community property, whether acquired prior to or subsequent to July 29, 1927 (the effective date of this statute), is liable for satisfaction of the husband's debts. . . .

Our conclusion in the instant case is not only in conformity with legal principles, but is consonant with practical considerations and public policy as well, for otherwise a person injured by the separate act of the husband would fail to gain redress for his damage in such case where the only property of the spouses is community. This obviously unfair and unjust result would have a disastrous effect on the very foundation of our community system and would be entirely out of harmony with the general rule that the community property is liable for the husband's debts. The trial court properly held that respondents may proceed to levy execution upon both the community real and personal property of the Grolemunds, and sell the same in satisfaction of the tort judgment obtained against the husband alone.

The judgment appealed from is accordingly affirmed. TRAYNOR, J., and SHENK, J., concurred.

A petition for a hearing in Bank was denied April 25, 1941. EDMONDS, J., and CARTER, J., voted for a hearing.

Notes

1. *Grolemund* expresses the basic principle of debt liability under California marital property law: Liability of property for debt is coextensive with the debtor's legal power to manage and control that property. The methodology is essentially in rem: One determines whether a particular asset is subject to liability by inquiring about the debtor's relationship to the asset, namely, does the debtor have the power to manage and control that asset? Thus, under the former male management regime, the community property was liable for all the husband's debts, whenever incurred, but not for any of the wife's debts because she had no legal power to manage the community property. That she had a one-half ownership interest in the community property was immaterial; it could not be reached for her debts.

2. Nor does a creditor's access to community property turn on whether the debt was incurred for community or noncommunity purposes. That the debt did not benefit the community may affect the parties' inter se rights to, for example, reimbursement, but does not bar a creditor's claim. The particular subject at issue in *Grolemund*, a *tort* creditor's access to community property, is now further regulated by a statutory order of satisfaction, which does distinguish between tort debts according to whether the tortfeasor was performing an activity for the benefit of

the community. See Family Code §1000(b). This provision is the only instance in which, *from a creditor's perspective*, California distinguishes among debts incurred by a spouse during marriage. Note that section 1000(b) merely prescribes an order of satisfaction; it does not shield community property when no other assets are available to satisfy the tort debt. Thus, the basic principle of *Grolemund* remains unaffected.

2. The Current California Family Code Debt Liability Provisions

When the legislature enacted equal management, it maintained the management and control theory of debt liability, refashioned it to reflect equal management, and gave retroactive effect to the new provisions:

> SECTION 1. The legislature finds and declares that (1) the extension of the right to manage and control all of the community property of a marriage to both spouses entails important social and economic considerations, (2) the right to manage and control community property is not a fundamental right which may not be divested by the Legislature and is not accorded the same status as the rights of the spouses in community property during marriage which are, and remain, present, existing, and equal, and (3) the application of the right to manage and control community property to all community property of a marriage, whether acquired before or after January 1, 1975, is necessary to achieve social and economic equality and facilitate commercial transactions.
>
> The Legislature further finds and declares that (1) the liability of community property for the debts of the spouses has been coextensive with the right to manage and control community property and should remain so, (2) the extension of the liability of community property for obligations contracted prior to January 1, 1975, does not impair the rights of creditors or the interests of the spouses in the community property, and (3) the extension of the liability of community property avoids undesirable preferences among creditors of the community. [1974 Cal. Stats., ch. 1206.]

The 1975 provisions, as amended, provide:

CALIFORNIA FAMILY CODE SECTIONS 900-1000

PART 3. LIABILITY OF MARITAL PROPERTY

Chapter 1. Definitions

§900. Application of definitions

Unless the provision or context otherwise requires, the definitions in this chapter govern the construction of this part.

§902.   "Debt"

"Debt" means an obligation incurred by a married person before or during marriage, whether based on contract, tort, or otherwise.

§903.   Time debt "incurred"

A debt is "incurred" at the following time:
(a) In the case of a contract, at the time the contract is made.
(b) In the case of a tort, at the time the tort occurs.
(c) In other cases, at the time the obligation arises.

Chapter 2.   General Rules of Liability

§910.   Community estate liable for debt of either spouse

(a) Except as otherwise expressly provided by statute, the community estate is liable for a debt incurred by either spouse before or during marriage, regardless of which spouse has the management and control of the property and regardless of whether one or both spouses are parties to the debt or to a judgment for the debt.

(b) "During marriage" for purposes of this section does not include the period during which the spouses are living separate and apart before a judgment of dissolution of marriage or legal separation of the parties.

§911.   Liability of married person's earnings for premarital debt of spouse

(a) The earnings of a married person during marriage are not liable for a debt incurred by the person's spouse before marriage. After the earnings of the married person are paid, they remain not liable so long as they are held in a deposit account in which the person's spouse has no right of withdrawal and are uncommingled with other property in the community estate, except property insignificant in amount.

(b) As used in this section:
(1) "Deposit account" has the meaning prescribed in paragraph (29) of subdivision (a) of Section 9102 of the Commercial Code.[3]
(2) "Earnings" means compensation for personal services performed, whether as an employee or otherwise.

§912.   Liability of quasi-community property

For the purposes of this part, quasi-community property is liable to the same extent, and shall be treated the same in all other respects, as community property.

---

3. Paragraph (29) provides:

"Deposit account" means a demand, time, savings, passbook or like account maintained with a bank. The term does not include investment property or accounts evidenced by an instrument.

§913. Liability of separate property

(a) The separate property of a married person is liable for a debt incurred by the person before or during marriage.

(b) Except as otherwise provided by statute:

(1) The separate property of a married person is not liable for a debt incurred by the person's spouse before or during marriage.

(2) The joinder or consent of a married person to an encumbrance of community estate property to secure payment of a debt incurred by the person's spouse does not subject the person's separate property to liability for the debt unless the person also incurred the debt.

§914. Liability for necessaries

(a) Notwithstanding Section 913, a married person is personally liable for the following debts incurred by the person's spouse during marriage:

(1) A debt incurred for necessaries of life[4] of the person's spouse while the spouses are living together.

(2) Except as provided in Section 4302, a debt incurred for common necessaries of life[5] of the person's spouse while the spouses are living separately.

(b) The separate property of a married person may be applied to the satisfaction of a debt for which the person is personally liable pursuant to this section. If separate property is so applied at a time when nonexempt community estate property or separate property of the person's spouse is available but is not applied to the satisfaction of the debt, the married person is entitled to reimbursement to the extent such property was available. . . .

§915. Liability for support obligation

(a) For the purpose of this part, a child or spousal support obligation of a married person that does not arise out of the marriage shall be treated as a debt incurred before marriage, regardless of whether a court order for support is made or modified before or during marriage and regardless of whether any installment payment on the obligation accrues before or during marriage.

(b) If property in the community estate is applied to the satisfaction of a child or spousal support obligation of a married person that does not arise out of the marriage, at a time when nonexempt separate income of the person is available but is not applied to the satisfaction of the obligation, the community estate is entitled to reimbursement from the person in the amount of the separate income, not exceeding the community estate property so applied.

(c) Nothing in this section limits the matters a court may take into consideration in determining or modifying the amount of a support order, including, but not limited to, the earnings of the spouses of the parties.

---

4. *Necessaries* are living costs consistent with the parties' station in life. See, for example, Wisnom v. McCarthy, 48 Cal. App. 697, 701, 192 P. 337 (1920) ("[T]he [domestic] services were necessaries of life for persons in the economic and social position of the defendants.")

5. *Common necessaries*, in contrast, are "such things as are ordinarily required for the sustenance of *all men*." Ratzlaff v. Portillo, 14 Cal. App. 3d 1013, 1015, 92 Cal. Rptr. 722 (1971).

§916.   Liability after property division

(a) Notwithstanding any other provision of this chapter, after division of community and quasi-community property pursuant to Division 7 (commencing with Section 2500):

(1) The separate property owned by a married person at the time of the division and the property received by the person in the division is liable for a debt incurred by the person before or during marriage and the person is personally liable for the debt, whether or not the debt was assigned for payment by the person's spouse in the division.

(2) The separate property owned by a married person at the time of the division and the property received by the person in the division is not liable for a debt incurred by the person's spouse before or during marriage, and the person is not personally liable for the debt, unless the debt was assigned for payment by the person in the division of the property. Nothing in this paragraph affects the liability of property for the satisfaction of a lien on the property.

(3) The separate property owned by a married person at the time of the division and the property received by the person in the division is liable for a debt incurred by the person's spouse before or during marriage, and the person is personally liable for the debt, if the debt was assigned for payment by the person in the division of the property. If a money judgment for the debt is entered after the division, the property is not subject to enforcement of the judgment and the judgment may not be enforced against the married person, unless the person is made a party to the judgment for the purpose of this paragraph.

(b) If property of a married person is applied to the satisfaction of a money judgment pursuant to subdivision (a) for a debt incurred by the person that is assigned for payment by the person's spouse, the person has a right of reimbursement from the person's spouse to the extent of the property applied, with interest at the legal rate, and may recover reasonable attorney's fees incurred in enforcing the right of reimbursement.

Chapter 3.   Reimbursement

§920.   General provisions

A right of reimbursement provided by this part is subject to the following provisions:

(a) The right arises regardless of which spouse applies the property to the satisfaction of the debt, regardless of whether the property is applied to the satisfaction of the debt voluntarily or involuntarily, and regardless of whether the debt to which the property is applied is satisfied in whole or in part. The right is subject to an express written waiver of the right by the spouse in whose favor the right arises.

(b) The measure of reimbursement is the value of the property or interest in property at the time the right arises.

(c) The right shall be exercised not later than the earlier of the following times:

(1) Within three years after the spouse in whose favor the right arises has

actual knowledge of the application of the property to the satisfaction of the debt.

(2) In proceedings for division of community and quasi-community property pursuant to Division 7 (commencing with Section 2500) or in proceedings upon the death of a spouse.

Chapter 4. Transitional Provisions

§930. Enforcement of debts

Except as otherwise provided by statute, this part governs the liability of separate and community estate property and the personal liability of a married person for a debt enforced on or after January 1, 1985, regardless of whether the debt was incurred before, on, or after that date.

§931. Reimbursement rights

The provisions of this part that govern reimbursement apply to all debts, regardless of whether satisfied before, on, or after January 1, 1985.

Chapter 5. Liability for Death or Injury

§1000. Liability for death or injury

(a) A married person is not liable for any injury or damage caused by the other spouse except in cases where the married person would be liable therefore if the marriage did not exist.

(b) The liability of a married person for death or injury to person or property shall be satisfied as follows:

(1) If the liability of the married person is based upon an act or omission which occurred while the married person was performing an activity for the benefit of the community, the liability shall first be satisfied from the community estate property and second from the separate property of the married person.

(2) If the liability of the married person is not based upon an act or omission which occurred while the married person was performing an activity for the benefit of the community, the liability shall first be satisfied from the separate property of the married person and second from the community estate property.

(c) This section does not apply to the extent the liability is satisfied out of proceeds of insurance for the liability, whether the proceeds are community estate property or separate property. Notwithstanding Section 920, no right of reimbursement under this section shall be exercised more than seven years after the spouse in whose favor the right arises has actual knowledge of the application of the property to the satisfaction of the debt.

Notes and Problem

1. Given that the 1975 legislation was intended to maintain the principle that debt liability follows management and control, what approach is suitable for com-

munity property to which the legislature did not extend the equal management principle, namely the Family Code section 1100(d) community business managed by one spouse and the Financial Code section 851 bank account titled in one spouse's name? This issue was not addressed until the 1984 legislation, which provides that "the community property is liable for a debt incurred by either spouse before or during marriage *regardless which spouse has the management and control of the property*" (emphasis added). Does this amendment undermine the purpose of section 1100(d)? Is it consistent with the goal of Financial Code section 851?

2. This summary table is designed to help you master the statutory provisions. For each claim, indicate what property is liable for its satisfaction and whether the estate that satisfies the debt may have a statutory reimbursement claim against the community or the separate estate of one spouse, as the case may be.

SUMMARY TABLE

	a. Incurred before marriage by one spouse	b. Incurred during marriage by one spouse acting alone	c. Incurred after separation but before divorce[6]
1. Contract debt			
2. Debt for necessaries			
3. Child or spousal support obligation			
4. Tort debt			

3. *Emilia's complaint (again).* Having no access to funds with which to hire an attorney, Emilia has abandoned hope of gaining court-ordered access to Tom's bank account. (See page 398 supra.) Is there any way she can persuade a merchant or lender to extend her credit?

In the male management era, the doctrine of necessaries, now codified at California Family Code section 914(a), enabled a wife to use her husband's credit to purchase goods appropriate to her station in life. (Note that the separate property of one spouse is liable for debts contracted by the other during marriage only when

---

6. For discussion of debt allocation at divorce, see pages 506-509 infra. For creditors' rights after debt assignment at divorce, see Family Code section 916.

the debts are for necessaries. To the same effect, see section 4301.) Creditors still make use of the doctrine, but it is complex and strewn with pitfalls. See generally H. Clark, Law of Domestic Relations 189-192 (1968).

Need Emilia rely today on the doctrine of necessaries? She has equal management rights with Tom. Can she simply pledge the contents of the community bank account titled in Tom's name? Even if the creditor will not rely on a bank account alone and demands instead a current earnings record, Tom has been employed for many years by a large national corporation known for its benevolent employment policies. Many creditors have offered Tom credit on this basis alone. Can Emilia make equal use of Tom's excellent employment history?

Taking this view, the Federal Reserve Board, pursuant to the Equal Credit Opportunity Act (ECOA), 15 U.S.C. §§1691 et seq., enacted Regulation B, which states that a prospective creditor of a married community property state resident may request her spouse's signature only if "applicable state law denies the applicant power to manage or control sufficient community property for the amount of credit requested." 12 C.F.R. §202.7(d)(3). Believing that the nonearner spouse has power to subject her husband's future wages to creditors' claims in all equal-management community property states (all community property states except Texas), the government took the position that creditors must extend credit on the homemaker's signature alone and may not demand the signature of the wage-earning spouse upon whose wages the creditor relies for repayment.

Many consumer loan companies, which rely for repayment on the borrower's future earnings, did not comply with the government's interpretation of Regulation B, but continued instead to require that the wage-earning spouse join in the loan application. The attorney general brought suit against two such companies, seeking injunctive relief and civil penalties for willful violation of ECOA and Regulation B. As a matter of California law, was the government's position correct or at least defensible? Are Tom's future earnings necessarily community property? Will their characterization affect debt collection?

In United States v. ITT Consumer Financial Corp., 816 F.2d 487 (1987), a three-judge panel of the Ninth Circuit Court of Appeals disapproved the government's interpretation of Regulation B. Issue was joined on the meaning of the term "community property" within the context of Regulation B. The government argued that the term "community property" includes future earnings. The court agreed with the defendants that

> [b]ecause a spouse's future earnings may become separate property rather than community property, the characterization of future earnings cannot be made prospectively. Earnings cannot be characterized as community property until they are earned. A married applicant's equal management power over community property, therefore, does not extend to the applicant's spouse's future earnings, and the applicant cannot commit his or her spouse's future earnings to repay the loan unless the spouse signs a promissory note or some other document to accomplish this result. Accordingly, a lender is justified in requiring the spouse's signature when a married applicant relies on his or her spouse's future earnings to establish creditworthiness.

Id. at 490-491. How may a spouse's future earnings become separate property rather than community property? There are many possibilities. In terms of current California law, the Ninth Circuit panel was surely correct. Ought California law be changed? In other words, as a matter of community property law, ought Emilia be legally competent to pledge Tom's future wages?

4. *Spousal and child support obligations from prior relationships.* Frequently, one spouse enters marriage with a pre-existing spousal or child support obligation and discharges it out of current community earnings. His current spouse may feel aggrieved, particularly if their marriage ends in divorce. Prior case law sanctioned the obligor spouse's dutiful behavior but specified circumstances under which he would be required to reimburse the community. Weinberg v. Weinberg, 67 Cal. 2d 557, 432 P.2d 709, 63 Cal. Rptr. 13 (1967); Marriage of Smaltz, 82 Cal. App. 3d 568, 147 Cal. Rptr. 154 (1978). Family Code section 915, initially enacted in 1984, modifies prior case law doctrine. Does the statute strike a reasonable balance between the competing claims of the obligor's prior and current families?

The current wife might feel even more aggrieved if her husband failed to discharge his prior support obligation, and the community wealth *she* contributed to the marriage were attached to satisfy his support duties. The legislature has anticipated this possibility in Family Code sections 911 and 915. If the principle of section 911 is correct, is the statutory protection adequate? Is the principle correct?

VIII

INCEPTION AND TERMINATION OF THE ECONOMIC COMMUNITY

A. INTRODUCTION

This chapter addresses two questions. Which relationships are included within the purview of the California community property system? Then, assuming that a particular conjugal relationship is included within the system, at what point during the breakdown of the relationship does the economic community come to an end?

With respect to the first question, it should be clear by now that a lawful marriage is subject to community property law unless the parties agree otherwise. Suppose, however, that the parties went through all the motions of getting married—license, blood tests, witnessed ceremony, and recordation of the marriage certificate—but they were not legally competent to marry because of a defect unknown to one or both, such as a prior legally ineffective divorce. Does your response vary if they both knew of the defect? Or, suppose that a couple believes they are lawfully married because they have cohabited for more than seven years and have had two children. They do not know that the seven-year common law marriage is largely a matter of popular folklore and that there is no common law marriage in California. Suppose, instead, that a couple has cohabited for many years but specifically denies being married because marriage is a "suffocating bourgeois concept." Suppose that the couple has cohabited for many years and would very much like to marry, but cannot because both partners are of the same sex. Should any of these couples be subject to the community property system when separation or death brings their relationship to an end? What criteria would you select to distinguish between those who should be included and those who should be excluded from the system? As you read the next three sections of this chapter, try to identify the criteria that the California courts and legislature have chosen.

The second issue posed by this chapter—when the community ends—is not as perplexing as the first, but is sufficiently problematic to have generated frequent legislative tinkering and some scholarly comment.

B.   LAWFUL MARRIAGE

In California, as in other American jurisdictions, there are two requisites for a lawful marriage. First, both parties must have legal capacity. Neither may have a prior subsisting marriage.[1] Nor may their relationship fall within the statutorily prohibited degrees of consanguinity.[2] Bigamy and incest will generally render any attempted marriage void.[3] A number of lesser defects of legal capacity, such as non-age, fraud, coercion, sexual incapacity, and lack of consent, may make the marriage voidable at the election of an interested party.[4]

Second, the parties must satisfy the legal requirements for contracting a marriage. Historically, American jurisdictions tended to recognize both formal and informal unions. Duly formalized ceremonial unions are licensed, witnessed, and registered.[5] The essential element of a formal union is the witnessed ceremony, in which the parties unequivocally and publicly declare their marriage. (For further discussion of the irreducible minimum that will satisfy formal requirements, see Note 1 at page 445 infra.)

Informal, or common law, unions generally involve no attempt to comply with formal marriage requirements. In the late nineteenth and early twentieth centuries most states, including California, repudiated the doctrine of common law marriage. Today common law marriage survives in only a dozen American states. These states recognize informal marriages proven by direct or circumstantial evidence of the parties' agreement to marry. Most commonly, a court may infer a (usually fictive) informal agreement to marry from evidence of "habit and reputation," that is, from the parties' marriage-like cohabitation and representation to the community that they are husband and wife.[6] Even though California abolished common law marriage shortly before the turn of the century.[7] California does recognize common law marriages validly contracted elsewhere.[8] Parties may contract a marriage in any jurisdiction. Thus California domiciliaries may enter a common law marriage while sojourning in another jurisdiction.

---

1. Cal. Fam. Code §2201.
2. Cal. Fam. Code §2200.
3. Cal. Fam. Code §§2200, 2201.
4. Cal. Fam. Code §§2210, 2211.
5. See, e.g., Cal. Fam. Code §§300, 306.
6. See generally H. Clark, Law of Domestic Relations 45-55 (1968).
7. The abolition of common law marriage (1895 Cal. Stat., ch. 129) is embodied in current California Family Code section 300:

> Marriage is a personal relation arising out of a civil contract between a man and a woman, to which the consent of the parties making that contract is necessary. Consent alone does not constitute marriage. Consent must be followed by the issuance of a license and solemnization as authorized by this division. . . .

Section 306 provides:

> . . . [M]arriage must be licensed, solemnized, and authenticated, and the certificate of registry of marriage must be filed as provided in this part; but noncompliance with this part by a nonparty to a marriage does not invalidate the marriage.

8. California Family Code section 308 provides:

> A marriage contracted outside this state that would be valid by the laws of the jurisdiction in which the marriage was contracted is valid in this state.

Section 308 codifies a widely observed choice of law principle. For further discussion, see note 1 at page 445 infra.

C. PUTATIVE SPOUSES

ESTATE OF VARGAS
36 Cal. App. 3d 714, 111 Cal. Rptr. 779 (1974)

FLEMING, J.—For 24 years Juan Vargas lived a double life as husband and father to two separate families, neither of which knew of the other's existence. This terrestrial paradise came to an end in 1969 when Juan died intestate in an automobile accident. In subsequent heirship proceedings the probate court divided his estate equally between the two wives. Juan's first wife Mildred appeals, contending that the evidence did not establish Juan's second wife Josephine as a putative spouse, and that even if Josephine were considered a putative spouse an equal division of the estate was erroneous.

Mildred presented evidence that she and Juan married in 1929, raised three children, and lived together continuously in Los Angeles until Juan's death in 1969. From 1945 until his death Juan never spent more than a week or 10 days away from home. They acquired no substantial assets until after 1945.

Josephine countered with evidence that she met Juan in 1942 while employed in his exporting business. They married in Las Vegas in February 1945 and went through a second marriage ceremony in Santa Ana in May 1945. Josephine knew Juan had been previously married, but Juan assured her he had acquired a divorce. In July 1945 they moved into a home in West Los Angeles and there raised a family of four children. After 1949 Juan no longer spent his nights at home, explaining to Josephine that he spent the nights in Long Beach in order to be close to his business, but he and Josephine continued to engage in sexual relations until his death in 1969. He visited Josephine and their children every weekday for dinner, spent time with them weekends, supported the family, and exercised control over its affairs as husband and father. Throughout the years Josephine continued to perform secretarial work for Juan's business at home without pay.

The foregoing evidence amply supports the court's finding that Josephine was a putative spouse. An innocent participant who has duly solemnized a matrimonial union which is void because of some legal infirmity acquires the status of putative spouse. . . . Although Josephine's marriage was void because Juan was still married to Mildred, Josephine, according to her testimony, married Juan in the good-faith belief he was divorced from his first wife. Her testimony was not inherently improbable; her credibility was a question for determination by the trial court . . . and court acceptance of her testimony established her status as a putative spouse.

The more difficult question involves the equal division of Juan's estate between Mildred and Josephine.

California courts have relied on at least two legal theories to justify the award of an interest in a decedent's estate to a putative spouse. (Luther & Luther, Support and Property Rights of the Putative Spouse, 24 Hastings L.J. 311, 313-317; see also Annot., 31 A.L.R.2d 1255, 1271-1277.) The theory of "quasi-marital property" equates property rights acquired during a putative marriage with community property rights acquired during a legal marriage. (Blache v. Blache, 69 Cal. App. 2d 616, 624 [160 P.2d 136].) Subsequent to the time of Juan's death this theory was codified in Civil Code section 4452 [now rewritten and recodified, without substantive change, as Family Code section 2251]:

> Whenever a determination is made that a marriage is void or voidable and the court finds that either party or both parties believed in good faith that the marriage was valid, the court shall declare such party or parties to have the status of a putative spouse, and, if the division of property is in issue, shall divide, in accordance with [Civil Code] Section 4800 [now Family Code section 2550], that property acquired during the union which would have been community property or quasi-community property if the union had not been void or voidable. Such property shall be termed "quasi-marital property."

A second legal theory treats the putative marriage as a partnership:

> In effect, the innocent putative spouse was in partnership or a joint enterprise with her spouse, contributing her services—and in this case, her earnings—to the common enterprise. Thus, their accumulated property was held in effect in tenancy-in-common in equal shares. Upon death of the husband, only his half interest is considered as community property, to which the rights of the lawful spouse attach. (Sousa v. Freitas, 10 Cal. App. 3d 660, 666 [89 Cal. Rptr. 485].)

In practice, these sometimes-conflicting theories have proved no more than convenient explanations to justify reasonable results, for when the theories do not fit the facts, courts have customarily resorted to general principles of equity to effect a just disposition of property rights. . . . For example, in Brown v. Brown, 274 Cal. App. 2d 178 [79 Cal. Rptr. 257], the court found that a legal wife's acquiescence in a putative wife's 28-year marriage equitably estopped the legal wife from claiming any interest in the community property.

The present case is complicated by the fact that the laws regulating succession . . . and the disposition of marital property . . . are not designed to cope with the extraordinary circumstance of purposeful bigamy at the expense of two innocent parties.[2] The laws of marital succession assume compliance with basic law . . . and do not provide for contingencies arising during the course of felonious activity. For this reason resort to equitable principles becomes particularly appropriate here. "Equity or chancery law has its origin in the necessity for exceptions to the application of rules of law in those cases where the law, by reason of its universality, would create injustice in the affairs of men." (Estate of Lankershim, 6 Cal. 2d 568, 572-573 [58 Cal. Rptr. 1282]. . . .)

Equity acts "in order to meet the requirements of every case, and to satisfy the needs of progressive social condition, in which new primary rights and duties are constantly arising, and new kinds of wrongs are constantly committed." (Wuest v. Wuest, 53 Cal. App. 2d 339, 346 [127 P.2d 934].) Equity need not wait upon precedent "but will assert itself in those situations where right and justice would be defeated but for its intervention." (Satterfield v. Garmire, 65 Cal. 2d 638, 645 [56 Cal. Rptr. 102, 422 P.2d 990].) . . .

In the present case, depending on which statute or legal theory is applied, both Mildred, as legal spouse, and Josephine, as putative spouse, have valid or plausible claims to at least half, perhaps three-quarters, possibly all, of Juan's estate. The court found that both wives contributed in indeterminable amounts and proportions to the accumulations of the community. . . . Since statutes and judicial decisions provide no sure guidance for the resolution of the controversy, the pro-

---

2. "[I]n most, if not all, of the reported decisions involving a putative spouse, the supposed husband did in fact separate from his lawful wife." (Luther & Luther, supra, at p.318.)

bate court cut the Gordian knot of competing claims and divided the estate equally between the two wives, presumably on the theory that innocent wives of practicing bigamists are entitled to equal shares of property accumulated during the active phase of the bigamy. No injury has been visited upon third parties, and the wisdom of Solomon is not required to perceive the justice of the result.

The judgment is affirmed. ROTH, P.J., and COMPTON, J., concurred.

Notes and Questions

1. California, like most other community property states and a few common law states, follows the civil law putative spouse doctrine, which applies when parties attempt to contract a lawful marriage and one or both maintain a good faith belief that the marriage is valid. Putative spouse status lasts only as long as the good faith belief; once a putative spouse learns that her marriage is invalid, she loses her protected status with respect to subsequently acquired property. Lazzarevich v. Lazzarevich, 88 Cal. App. 2d 708, 718, 200 P.2d 49 (1948). Compare 42 U.S.C. §416(h)(1)(B) (1988), which provides that a person shall be deemed a surviving spouse for social security purposes if "such applicant in good faith went through a marriage ceremony with such [insured] individual resulting in a purported marriage between them which, but for a legal impediment not known to the applicant *at the time of such ceremony*, would have been a valid marriage . . ." (emphasis added). Which formulation do you prefer?

If Josephine had predeceased Juan, leaving substantial assets in her name earned during her putative marriage to Juan, could Juan have claimed a quasi-marital interest in the assets? The good faith requirement suggests the possibility of asymmetric results. (This question is further discussed in both Marriage of Cary and Marvin v. Marvin, reproduced later in this chapter.)

2. Putative spouse doctrine is generally understood to address a defect in legal capacity, as opposed to a failure to follow the formal requirements for contracting a lawful marriage. H. Clark, Law of Domestic Relations 54 (1968). Estate of Vargas, like most other California cases, defines a putative spouse as a person who has "*duly solemnized* a matrimonial union which is void because of some legal infirmity" (emphasis added). Nevertheless, several California cases have used the doctrine to salvage unions that are defective because the parties failed to comply with formal marriage requirements. In Santos v. Santos, 32 Cal. App. 2d 62, 89 P.2d 164 (1939), the court appeared to find a putative marriage when a non-English-speaking couple unfamiliar with California law secured a marriage license and, believing they were thereby married, began living together as husband and wife. In Sancha v. Arnold, 114 Cal. App. 2d 772, 251 P.2d 67, 252 P.2d 55 (1952), the court, without regard to the possible invalidity of the couple's common law Nevada marriage, held that the wife was a putative spouse because she entertained a good faith belief in the validity of her Nevada common law marriage, which she contracted when Nevada still permitted common law marriages. Do Santos v. Santos and Sancha v. Arnold support the court's conclusion in the following case?

[handwritten margin note: No ceremony]

WAGNER v. COUNTY OF IMPERIAL
145 Cal. App. 3d 980, 193 Cal. Rptr. 820 (1983)

BROWN (Gerald), P.J.—Plaintiff Sharon Wagner appeals a judgment favoring the County of Imperial (County) on her complaint for Clifton Wagner's wrongful death.

In October 1976, Sharon and Clifton exchanged personal marriage vows. At Clifton's request, Sharon promised to take his name, be his wife, love him, have his children and live with him all their lives in sickness and health. Sharon and Clifton began living together and held themselves out as a married couple. In May 1977, their son was born. Sharon and Clifton lived together with their son until Clifton was killed in a traffic accident in October 1978.

Alleging she was Clifton's surviving putative spouse, Sharon sued the County under Code of Civil Procedure section 377 for wrongfully causing his death by maintaining its property in a dangerous condition. . . . [T]he court ordered a separate trial on the issue whether Sharon was Clifton's putative spouse. . . . After trial the court found Sharon was dependent on Clifton and believed in good faith she was validly married to him. The court also found the relationship between Sharon and Clifton was a void or voidable common law marriage. However, the court held Sharon was not a putative spouse entitled to sue under section 377 for Clifton's wrongful death, saying: "The law does not permit recovery for wrongful death by a party to a marital agreement where no actual solemnization has occurred." The court entered judgment for the County and Sharon appeals.

Sharon contends the court erred in ruling she was not entitled to recover for Clifton's wrongful death because she and Clifton did not participate in a marital solemnization ceremony. Under section 377 an action for wrongful death may be brought by the decedent's putative spouse where such putative spouse was dependent on the decedent. Section 377, subdivision (b)(2) defines putative spouse as "the surviving spouse of a void or voidable marriage who is found by the court to have believed in good faith that the marriage to the decedent was valid." Here the court specifically found Sharon met all the elements of section 377, subdivision (b)(2)'s definition of putative spouse: Sharon's relationship with Clifton was a void or voidable common law marriage but Sharon believed in good faith they were validly married. The court further found Sharon was dependent on Clifton. Despite such findings the court said Sharon could not recover for Clifton's wrongful death because "[t]he law does not permit recovery for wrongful death by a party to a marital agreement where no actual solemnization has occurred."

Relying on Miller v. Johnson (1963) 214 Cal. App. 2d 123, 126 [29 Cal. Rptr. 251] and Estate of Krone (1948) 83 Cal. App. 2d 766, 768 [189 P.2d 741] the superior court said: "The putative marriage is one that has to be solemnized in due form and celebrated in good faith on the part of one or both of the parties, but which by reason of legal infirmity is either void or voidable. The marriage must be solemnized, authenticated with a certificate of registration of marriage filed in California." However, although the usual putative marriage situation may arise under circumstances where a marriage is duly solemnized and celebrated in good faith but suffers from a legal infirmity, lack of a solemnization ceremony does not necessarily mean bad faith precluding finding a putative marriage. (See Sancha v. Arnold (1952) 114 Cal. App. 2d 772 [251 P.2d 67, 252 P.2d 55]; Santos v. Santos (1932) 32 Cal. App. 2d 62 [89 P.2d 164].)

The Legislature specifically defined "putative spouse" in section 377, subdivision (b)(2). Nothing in section 377, subdivision (b)(2)'s clear and unambiguous definition of "putative spouse" requires a solemnization ceremony. Where, as here, a statute specifically prescribes a meaning for particular terms used by it, such meaning is generally binding on the courts. (See Urban Renewal Agency v. California Coastal Zone Conservation Com. (1975) 15 Cal. 3d 577, 584-585 [125 Cal. Rptr. 485, 542 P.2d 645].) The County contends in adopting section 377, subdivision (b)(2) the Legislature intended to codify existing case law defining "putative spouse" to require a solemnization ceremony. However, the County points to nothing in section 377, subdivision (b)(2)'s legislative history showing such intent. Indeed, the County concedes such legislative history does not clearly show what the Legislature intended to encompass in section 377, subdivision (b)(2)'s definition of "putative spouse." Under these circumstances the County's assertion the Legislature intended section 377, subdivision (b)(2) to require a solemnization ceremony is pure speculation.

To establish she was Clifton's putative spouse under section 377, Sharon was not required to show she and Clifton participated in a solemnization ceremony. Under section 377 Sharon must only prove she had a good faith belief her marriage to Clifton was valid; solemnization would be at most evidence of such good faith belief. Construing [Family] Code section [2251's] similar definition of "putative spouse," the court in In re Marriage of Monti (1982) 135 Cal. App. 3d 50, 56 [185 Cal. Rptr. 72], said "the essence of a putative spouse is a good faith belief in the existence of a valid marriage." Here the superior court specifically found Sharon believed in good faith she was validly married to Clifton. The court's legal conclusion Sharon was not Clifton's putative spouse is contrary to such express finding of good faith. The court should have held Sharon was Clifton's putative spouse. As Clifton's surviving dependent putative spouse, Sharon is entitled to sue the County for his wrongful death.

The judgment is reversed. WIENER, J., and BUTLER, J., concurred.

A petition for a rehearing was denied August 26, 1983, and respondent's petition for a hearing by the Supreme Court was denied October 5, 1983.

Notes and Questions

1. Does *Wagner* give adequate weight to California's legislative abolition of common law marriage? In light of California marriage law, was Sharon a Code of Civil Procedure section 377 "surviving spouse of a void or voidable *marriage*"? See California Family Code section 300. Do you approve the result in *Wagner*?

With *Wagner*, compare Centinela Hospital Medical Center v. Superior Court, 215 Cal. App. 3d 971, 263 Cal. Rptr. 672 (1989), review denied January 18, 1990. Interpreting the same wrongful death statute, *Centinela Hospital* rejected, as legally insufficient, putative spouse status predicated upon a purported *California common law marriage*. *Centinela Hospital* requires a *reasonable* belief that there *is* a marriage and concludes that California's 1895 abolition of common law marriage makes such a belief unreasonable as a matter of law. The California Supreme Court denied review in *Centinela Hospital*, thus declining to resolve conflicting decisions in the courts of appeal.

2. *Subjective or objective good faith belief?* A putative spouse claim poses two distinct questions. First, was there *any marriage at all*, albeit one that was void or voidable? If so, did the claimant maintain a subjective good faith belief in the validity of the putative marriage? If the marriage was a duly licensed ceremonial marriage, the only issue is the claimant's subjective good faith belief in its validity. Estate of Vargas is illustrative. However, when there was no duly licensed ceremonial marriage, the claimant must also prove that there was a marriage. In such circumstance, some recent cases, including *Centinela Hospital*, require that *the belief that there was a marriage* be objectively reasonable. See also Marriage of Vryonis, 202 Cal. App. 3d

712, 720-723, 248 Cal. Rptr. 807 (1988) (finding objectively unreasonable a foreign claimant's belief that she entered a California marriage when she neglected to inquire about or follow California marriage requirements). Compare *Wagner,* where the court required only a subjective good faith (albeit erroneous) belief that the parties had entered a marriage.

3. Unbeknown to his lawful wife Mildred, Juan Vargas led a "double life." Had Juan not chosen a life of *simultaneous* bigamy, Mildred would have taken all the community property when Juan died intestate. Cal. Prob. Code §6401(a). Instead she received only her one-half share, and the trial court awarded Juan's one-half share, which ordinarily would have passed intestate to the surviving spouse, to Josephine, Juan's putative spouse. Is this fair to Mildred? Suppose there were a second putative spouse whose claim was as strong as Josephine's. Ought all three share equally in the property acquired by Juan during the simultaneous subsistence of the three relationships? Or does Mildred's entitlement have some irreducible minimum, for example, her one-half interest in the community property?

Simultaneous bigamy is relatively rare in the United States and is the type of bigamy that is most likely to be criminally prosecuted because it violates the generally accepted norm of "one spouse at a time." In contrast, sequential bigamy is frequent but rarely prosecuted. It occurs when a spouse "remarries" without having secured an effective divorce. The putative spouse status that arises from sequential bigamy does not give rise to competing claims at dissolution of the putative marriage by inter vivos *annulment* (judgment of nullity) because the only property issue is the division of the quasi-marital property, which is treated as though it were community property by Family Code section 2251. Competing claims may arise, however, at *death* because intestacy law gives the surviving spouse rights in the decedent's separate as well as community property. See Probate Code 6401. Thus, sequential bigamy may present even more complex issues than those raised by *Vargas.* Assume, for example, that Harry lawfully marries Alice, leaves her, "marries" putative spouse Betty, leaves her, and "marries" putative spouse Carol, with whom he is living when he dies intestate with property earned during all three relationships. Property earned during his marriage to Alice is community property for Alice but separate property vis-à-vis Betty and Carol. Property earned during his relationship with Betty is quasi-marital property for Betty but separate property for Alice and Carol. And so forth for Carol. See, for example. Estate of Hafner, 184 Cal. App. 3d 1371, 229 Cal. Rptr. 676 (1986). Our next principal case, Estate of Leslie, considers whether, for purposes of intestate succession, the putative spouse's claim extends to decedent's *separate* property.

ESTATE OF LESLIE
37 Cal. 3d 186, 689 P.2d 133, 207 Cal. Rptr. 561 (1984)

BIRD, Chief Justice.—Is a surviving putative spouse entitled to succeed to a share of his or her decedent's separate property under the Probate Code?

On April 22, 1972, William Garvin and Fay Reah Leslie were married in Tijuana, Mexico. The marriage was invalid because it was never recorded as required by Mexican law.[1] However, Garvin believed that he and Leslie were validly married. The couple lived together as husband and wife for almost nine years, until Leslie's death in 1981. Throughout this period, they resided in a house in Mira Loma. The house had been purchased by Leslie, Mike Bosnich, her former husband, and respondent Alton B. Smith, a son from a prior marriage who lived next door. This case concerns the administration and distribution of Leslie's estate.

During Leslie's and Garvin's marriage, restaurant property, which had been acquired by Leslie prior to the marriage, was remodeled. As a result, it increased in value. . . . After the improvements were made, Leslie sold the restaurant and received a promissory note secured by a deed of trust in her name.

During the marriage, Leslie and Garvin acquired three parcels of real property in the Desert Hot Springs area. The manner in which title was taken varied for each parcel. The first two parcels were purchased in 1977. Title to Parcel 1 was taken in joint tenancy by "Fay Bosnich, an unmarried woman," and William A. Garvin, an unmarried man." Title to Parcel 2 was taken in the name of "Fay Bosnich, an unmarried woman," Parcel 3 was purchased approximately 16 months later, and title to it was taken as a tenancy in common by "Fay Bosnich, an unmarried woman, and William Garvin, a widower."[2] . . .

On February 6, 1981, Leslie died intestate. She was survived by Garvin, her son Smith, and three other adult children from a prior marriage.

Smith filed a petition for letters of administration in the estate of his deceased mother. Garvin objected to Smith's petition, filed his own petition for letters of administration, and sought a determination as to who was entitled to distribution of the estate. . . .

In January 1982, a court trial was held to determine the appointment of the administrator and the distribution of the property in the estate. The trial court found that a putative marriage had existed between Garvin and Leslie,[4] denied Garvin's petition for letters of administration, and determined that he was not entitled to any of decedent's separate property. The court also found that some of the property was quasi-marital[5] and some was separate. . . .

Garvin makes several contentions on appeal. First, he argues that he is entitled to an intestate share of the decedent's separate property. Second, he contends that he should have been appointed administrator of the estate. . . .

---

1. Civil Code section 4104 [now Family Code section 308] provides that "[a]ll marriages contracted without this state, which would be valid by the laws of the jurisdiction in which the same were contracted, are valid in this state."

Since the marriage was not valid under Mexican law, it was not valid in California. At trial, Garvin's attorney conceded that he could not prove the validity of the marriage because it had never been recorded.

2. Garvin had apparently been widowed once before.

4. A putative marriage is one in which at least one of the parties to an invalid marriage has a good faith belief that the marriage is valid. (Sanguinetti v. Sanguinetti (1937) 9 Cal. 2d 95, 99, 69 P.2d 845.)

Civil Code section 4452 [now Family Code section 2251] sets forth the basis for finding a putative marriage. That section provides in relevant part that "[w]henever a determination is made that a marriage is void or voidable and the court finds that either party or both parties believed in good faith that the marriage was valid, the court shall declare such party or parties to have the status of a putative spouse. . . ."

Neither of the parties contests the trial court's finding of a putative marriage in this case.

5. Quasi-marital property is property acquired during a putative marriage which would have been community property or quasi-community property had the marriage been valid. (See Civ. Code, §4452 [Family Code §2251]; Estate of Vargas (1974) 36 Cal. App. 3d 714, 717, 111 Cal. Rptr. 779.)

The principal issue presented by this case is whether a putative spouse is entitled to succeed to a share of his or her decedent's separate property. Although this court has not directly confronted this question, the conclusions of other courts on this and analogous questions are instructive. . . .

. . . California courts, as well as federal courts applying California law, have accorded surviving putative spouses the same rights as surviving legal spouses. Examples abound.

In Kunakoff v. Woods, 166 Cal. App. 2d 59, 67-68, 332 P.2d 773 [1958], a surviving putative spouse was held to be an heir for the purposes of Code of Civil Procedure section 377. As such, she was entitled to bring an action for the wrongful death of her deceased partner. The Court of Appeal noted that the term "spouse" may include a putative spouse. (Kunakoff v. Woods, supra, 166 Cal. App. 2d at p.63, 332 P.2d 59.) The court reasoned that since a putative spouse is an heir for purposes of succession, she is an heir for purposes of maintaining an action for wrongful death. (Id., 166 Cal. App. 2d at pp.67-68, 332 P.2d 773.)

A surviving putative spouse has also been held to be a surviving spouse within the meaning of Government Code section 21364. (Adduddell v. Board of Administration, supra, 8 Cal. App. 3d 243, 87 Cal. Rptr. 268.) That statute entitles a surviving spouse to special death benefits under the Public Employees' Retirement Law. . . .

A surviving putative spouse has also been held to be a "surviving widow" within the meaning of a former version of Labor Code section 4702 (Stats. 1969, ch. 65, §1, p.187), and thus entitled to recovery of workers' compensation death benefits. (Brennfleck v. Workmen's Comp. App. Bd., supra, 3 Cal. App. 3d 666, 84 Cal. Rptr. 50. . . .)

Finally, it is noteworthy that putative spouses have been awarded spousal benefits under the civil service retirement statute (5 U.S.C. §8341, Brown v. Devine (N.D. Cal. 1983) 574 F. Supp. 790, 792), under the Longshoremen's and Harbor Workers' Compensation Act (33 U.S.C. §901 et seq., Powell v. Rogers (9th Cir. 1974) 496 F.2d 1248, 1250, cert. den., 419 U.S. 1032, 95 S. Ct. 514, 42 L. Ed. 2d 307; Holland America Insurance Company v. Rogers (N.D. Cal. 1970) 313 F. Supp. 314, 317-318), and under the Social Security Act (42 U.S.C. §416, Aubrey v. Folsom (N.D. Cal. 1957) 151 F. Supp. 836, 840; Speedling v. Hobby (N.D. Cal. 1955) 132 F. Supp. 833, 836).

The foregoing authority compels but one conclusion: a surviving putative spouse is entitled to succeed to a share of his or her decedent's separate property.[11] This result is inherently fair. By definition, a putative marriage is a union in which at least one partner believes in good faith that a valid marriage exists. As in this case, the couple conducts themselves as husband and wife throughout the period of their union. Why should the right to separate property accorded to legal spouses be denied to putative spouses?

Further, to deny a putative spouse the status of surviving spouse for the purposes of succeeding to a share of the decedent's separate property would lead to anomalous and unjust results. For example, where the decedent is survived by a putative spouse and children of the putative marriage, such a rule would deny the spouse succession rights to separate property even though the children are ac-

---

11. There may be cases in which two or more surviving spouses each claim an intestate share of the decedent's separate property. However, that scenario is not before this court and need not be resolved at this time.

corded such rights.[12] Such a rule would also deny succession rights to a putative spouse who lived with the decedent for many years, while according these rights to the legal spouse, even if that spouse's partner died the day the couple were married. (Laughran & Laughran, Property and Inheritance Rights of Putative Spouses in California: Selected Problems and Suggested Solutions (1977) 11 Loy. L.A. L. Rev. 45, 68.) Surely, the Legislature never intended such results. . . .

Accordingly, the portion of the trial court's judgment denying Garvin an interest in decedent's separate property and letters of administration in decedent's estate is reversed. In all other respects, the judgment is affirmed.

MOSK, KAUS, BROUSSARD, REYNOSO, GRODIN and LUCAS, JJ., concur.

Notes and Questions

1. The formal requirements of a lawful marriage are threefold: a license, a witnessed ceremony, and public recordation. Most putative marriages are formally adequate but legally ineffective because one or both spouses are still married to another person. In contrast, William Garvin and Fay Leslie were legally competent to marry. Mexican law, like American law, requires that ceremonial marriages be recorded. The California Supreme Court treats the nonrecordation of a California couple's Mexican marriage as a fatal defect. This conclusion might have been avoided in two different ways. First, failure to observe a mandatory recordation requirement need not mean that a duly witnessed ceremonial marriage is thereby invalid. Some American jurisdictions that have specifically considered the issue have concluded that the witnessed ceremony is the legal essential, and failure to record is not a fatal defect. See, for example, N.Y. Dom. Rel. Law §25 (2002). See generally H. Clark, Law of Domestic Relations 41 (1968). Thus, the legally relevant issue was not whether Mexico requires recordation but whether Mexico takes the view that nonrecordation invalidates an otherwise valid ceremonial marriage.

Even if Mexico treats nonrecordation as a fatal defect, choice of law principles still may allow the application of the law of another jurisdiction in order to validate the marriage. California Family Code section 308 is a permissive statute: It validates "a marriage contracted outside this state that would be valid by the laws of the jurisdiction in which the marriage was contracted." The statute requires recognition of lawful out-of-state marriages that would not be lawful if contracted in California, such as informal, or common law, marriages. It does not require, as the supreme court implies in footnote 1, that California find *invalid* any out-of-state marriage that was not valid in the jurisdiction in which it was contracted. California may, for example, recognize out-of-state marriages that would have been valid if contracted in California or in the parties' domicile, if elsewhere, when they married. The Restatement, Conflict of Laws, Second (1971) provides:

§283. **Validity of marriage**

(1) The validity of a marriage will be determined by a local law of the state which, with respect to the particular issue, has the most significant relationship to the spouses and the marriage. . . .

---

12. By statute, children of a putative marriage possess the right of intestate succession to the separate property of their deceased parents. (See [Probate Code §6408; Family Code §7602].)

(2) A marriage which satisfies the requirements of the state where the marriage was contracted will everywhere be recognized as valid unless it violates the strong public policy of another state which had the most significant relationship to the spouses and the marriage at the time of the marriage. . . .

Subsections (1) and (2) are alternative validating provisions. Family Code section 308 is Restatement section 283(2) without the public policy proviso. Assuming arguendo that failure to record is not a fatal defect in California, section 283(1) may validate the marriage. At this juncture, the question is whether Mexico, the place of marriage, or California, the place of domicile, has "the most significant relationship . . . to the particular issue." Is the "issue" the validity of the marriage, in which case California easily prevails, or the recordation requirement, in which case Mexico may be understood to be more directly concerned? See generally H. Clark, Law of Domestic Relations 43-44 (1968).

Having adopted the civil law *putative spouse* doctrine and having applied it to defects of contract as well as of legal capacity, California has not been pressed to define the irreducible minimum for contracting a lawful marriage. Thus, California case law and statutes do not explicitly tell us whether the unrecorded Garvin-Leslie marriage would have been a legally sufficient and not merely a putative marriage had it been contracted in California.[9] Estate of Leslie further reduces the differences between legal and putative spouses, making moot the distinction for most persons whose marriage is legally defective but sufficient to qualify as a putative marriage. In cases, however, where there may be some issue about the initial existence or persistence of a good faith belief in the lawfulness of the marriage, the distinction between a lawful and putative marriage may be determinative. In Estate of Leslie, for example, what might one infer from the couple's persistent purchase of property as "an unmarried woman . . . and . . . an unmarried man"?

2. Why would it be "unjust and anomalous" to allow the children but not the putative spouse to succeed to decedent's separate property? Children born to unmarried cohabiting parents have rights of succession that are not shared by their parents. If, for example, their mother dies intestate, they will succeed to her property and their father will have no claim. Similarly, succession rights are denied to the unmarried cohabitant "who lived with the decedent for many years, while [accorded] . . . to the legal spouse, even if that spouse's partner died the day the couple were married."

3. As Estate of Leslie indicates, judicial decision to treat a putative spouse as though she were a lawful spouse has generally been effectuated by interpreting the term "spouse" to include the putative, as well as the lawfully wedded, spouse. This approach is still required for death cases because the Probate Code makes no spe-

---

9. But see California Family Code section 300, which may plausibly be read to indicate that failure to record is not a fatal defect so long as the marriage is licensed and property solemnized:

> Marriage is a personal relation arising out of a civil contract between a man and a woman, to which the consent of the parties capable of making that contract is necessary. Consent alone does not constitute marriage. Consent must be followed by the issuance of a license and solemnization as authorized by this division. . . .

See also Cal. Fam. Code §306. Estate of DePasse, 97 Cal. App. 4th 92, 118 Cal. Rptr. 2d 143 (2002), held that issuance of a marriage license is a mandatory requirement for a valid marriage in California. The claimed marriage found invalid in *DePasse* was a deathbed ceremony conducted by a hospital chaplain without a license, because there was insufficient time to obtain one. *DePasse* further held that the surviving spouse was not a putative spouse because he knew of the license requirement and thus had no objectively reasonable belief that he had contracted a valid marriage.

cific provision for putative spouses. The Family Code, however, now explicitly regulates the property and support rights of putative spouses in marital dissolution actions. California Family Code sections 2251 and 2254 provide that a putative spouse shall enjoy the same property and support rights as a lawful spouse.

4. In Estate of Hafner, 184 Cal. App. 3d 1371, 229 Cal. Rptr. 676 (1986), the court of appeal declined to follow the dictum of Estate of Leslie. *Hafner* determined that a surviving putative spouse is ineligible for a family allowance (Probate Code section 6540) by interpreting the statutory term "surviving spouse" to include only lawfully married persons. In contrast, Estate of Sax, 214 Cal. App. 3d 1300, 263 Cal. Rptr. 190 (1989), held that a putative spouse is a "surviving spouse" for purposes of Probate Code section 21610, the omitted spouse provision. (For discussion of section 21610, see page 112 supra.)

Putative spouses may also encounter difficulty with private benefit contracts, such as pensions. In Allen v. Western Conference of Teamsters Pension Trust Fund, 788 F.2d 648 (9th Cir. 1986), interpreting California law, a pension benefit for a "surviving spouse" was narrowly construed to include only lawfully wedded spouses. But compare Western Conference of Teamsters Pension Trust Fund v. Jones, 646 F. Supp. 228 (1986). Although a putative spouse is not a "surviving spouse" within the meaning of the pension plan, *Jones* holds that a putative spouse nevertheless may be a quasi-marital *owner* of an interest in a surviving spouse's benefit. In *Jones,* the putative spouse was "married" to the employee for the entire period during which he earned the pension. Thus she was a one-half owner of the surviving spouse's benefit. The other half went to the deceased employee's long-estranged lawful spouse, who was the "surviving spouse" within the meaning of the pension plan contract. In *Jones,* when will the putative spouse's entitlement end? With respect to ERISA-regulated private sector pensions, does *Jones* survive Boggs v. Boggs at page 609 infra?

5. If a claim to putative spouse status would fail because the claimant knew that her duly regularized marriage was invalid, the doctrine of estoppel may provide an effective substitute. When a spouse asserting the invalidity of his marriage to a claimant knew that it was invalid but nevertheless continued to enjoy the benefits of cohabitation, he may be estopped to assert the invalidity of the marriage. California courts have applied estoppel liberally. See, for example, Marriage of Recknor, 138 Cal. App. 3d 539, 187 Cal. Rptr. 887 (1982). See generally Spellens v. Spellens, 49 Cal. 2d 210, 317 P.2d 613 (1957).

6. In divorce and annulment cases, do the putative spouse and estoppel doctrines accomplish anything that could not more simply and fairly be achieved by treating valid, voidable, and void marriages equally for purposes of support and property division? This has been a fairly common pattern of reform in states that do not share California's civil law tradition. See, for example, N.Y. Dom. Rel. Law §236 (McKinney 1988). See H. Clark, Law of Domestic Relations 135-137 (1968).

Probate law reform has not, however, kept pace with divorce law reform. The putative spouse doctrine has no common law counterpart at death.

D. LICENSING SAME-SEX DOMESTIC RELATIONSHIPS

California Family Code section 300 defines marriage as "a personal relation arising out of a civil contract between a man and a woman." In 1977, the California legislature added the words "between a man and a woman" to signify that same-sex couples may not lawfully marry in California.[10] However, California courts may recognize a marriage lawfully contracted in another jurisdiction even though the marriage would not satisfy California marriage requirements if it were contracted in California. In 1993, Baehr v. Lewin, 852 P.2d 44, 875 P.2d 225 (Hawaii 1993), raised the possibility that same-sex couples domiciled in California might ultimately be able to marry in Hawaii under Hawaii law and have their valid Hawaii marriages recognized by the courts of California.

Invoking the equal protection clause of the Hawaii constitution, *Baehr* held that the state must satisfy the very highest standard of constitutional review, "the strict scrutiny standard," in order to justify restricting marriage to opposite-sex couples. Entirely avoiding discussion of sexual orientation, the Hawaii Supreme Court characterized the restriction as sex discrimination: Persons of one sex are denied the right to marry persons of the same sex, a right accorded to persons of the other sex.[11] On remand to the trial court, the state failed to meet its heavy constitutional burden, with the result that the state of Hawaii seemed destined to make marriage equally available to same-sex couples. Baehr v. Miike, 1996 WL 694235 (Haw. Cir. Ct. 1996), aff'd, 950 P.2d 1234 (Haw. 1997).

The import of *Baehr* was national. Persons may marry in any state, and, under traditional choice-of-law principles, states recognize as valid a marriage that is valid where contracted unless recognition would violate the state's strong public policy. Under this principle, California recognizes common law marriages validly contracted in other states even though common law marriage may not be contracted in California.[12] Usually, recognition of a marriage validly contracted elsewhere is withheld only when marital cohabitation of the parties would violate the state's criminal laws.[13] Same-sex relationships are not illegal in California. Thus, even

10. 1977 Cal. Stat., ch. 339, now codified as Family Code section 300. For discussion of the history of this amendment, see Hinman v. Department of Personnel Admin., 167 Cal. App. 3d 516, 524, 213 Cal. Rptr. 410 (1985) (rejecting claim for spousal benefits by employee's same-sex "family partner").

11. The court found its inspiration in Loving v. Virginia, 388 U.S. 1, 87 S. Ct. 1817, 18 L. Ed. 2d 1010 (1967), which may be understood to offer a parallel interpretation of the equal protection clause of the Fourteenth Amendment. Striking down Virginia's anti-miscegenation laws on the grounds of equal protection and substantive due process, the United States Supreme Court rejected Virginia's argument that its prohibition of interracial marriages satisfied the equal protection clause because it treated all races equally in that no person of one race was allowed to marry a person of another race.

12. In 1895, California amended its marriage statute to disallow California common law marriages. It did so by adding the words "Consent alone does not constitute marriage. Consent must be followed by the issuance of a license and solemnization as authorized by this division. . . ." This rule is currently codified in Family Code section 300. Nevertheless, California has always recognized common law marriages validly contracted elsewhere. See, for example, In re Marriage of Smyklo, 180 Cal. App. 3d 1095, 226 Cal. Rptr. 174 (1986) (recognizing Alabama common law marriage).

13. See generally pages 445-446 supra and R. Weintraub, Commentary on the Conflict of Laws 222-228 (2d ed. 1981). Although Family Code section 308 expresses the usual choice-of-law rule that a marriage validly contracted in one jurisdiction shall be recognized in every other jurisdiction, it does not contain the standard public policy proviso that recognition of such marriage must not offend the strong public policy of the state of California. California case law has implied the public policy proviso and has applied it in a rubric liberally tending to recognize the inoffensive incidents of marriages generally repugnant to California law. In re Bir's Estate, 83 Cal. App. 2d 256, 261, 188 P.2d 499 (1948), allowed intestacy claims by two "surviving spouse" polygamous wives from India, who were lawfully married in India to the California decedent, on the ground that no public policy of California is violated by such intestacy claims even though the polygamous marriage would have violated the strong public policy of California had the decedent and his two wives sought to reside together in this state during his lifetime. Thus, when a claimant seeks recognition of some incident of a marriage lawfully contracted elsewhere that would generally offend the strong public policy of California, such as a bigamous or incestuous marriage, the issue is: Would recognition of this particular *incident* offend any strong public policy of the state of California? It is unlikely that any economic incident of marriage would offend California

though California amended its marriage statute in 1977 to restrict California marriages to opposite-sex couples, under traditional choice-of-law principles California courts might hold that recognition of same-sex marriages validly contracted elsewhere—for example, in Hawaii—would not violate the strong public policy of California.

In 1996, the United States Congress enacted legislation allowing states to refuse to recognize same-sex marriages and declining to recognize them for federal law purposes. Defense of Marriage Act (DOMA), Pub. L. 104-199, 110 Stat. 2419, Sept. 21, 1996, codified at 28 U.S.C. §1738c (states are not required to recognize sister-state same-sex marriages), and 1 U.S.C. 37 (federal government does not recognize same-sex marriages). By 2000, more than 30 states had enacted legislation declining to recognize same-sex marriages. The California electorate joined this movement when it approved Proposition 22, which provides that California will not recognize same-sex marriages contracted elsewhere. Proposition 22 is codified at Family Code section 308.5 (2002).

This flurry of legislation proved unnecessary because the voters of Hawaii ultimately authorized their legislature to overrule *Baehr*. The quid pro quo, however, was Hawaii's enactment of "reciprocal beneficiary" legislation, which extends some of the benefits of marriage to any two unmarried persons who are ineligible to marry each other but who name each other as reciprocal beneficiaries. 1997 Haw. Sess. Laws, Act 383, codified at Haw. Rev. Stat. Ann. §§572C-1 to 572C-7. Reciprocal beneficiaries may be, inter alia, a brother and sister, a mother and son, and "two individuals who are of the same gender." Id., §2. In view of the broad definition of reciprocal beneficiaries, the Hawaii legislation is necessarily limited to the extension of certain social benefits, such as the right to include another on a health insurance policy. Reciprocal beneficiary legislation does not, and could not reasonably, impose the mutual obligations undertaken by married persons. Thus, a reciprocal beneficiary may terminate the relationship at any time and, upon termination, incurs no obligations. Reciprocal beneficiary status is well suited for unmarried blood relatives who, lacking any marital obligations, wish to help each other out. However, it would seem inadequate for same-sex couples whose relationship is largely indistinguishable from that of opposite-sex married couples.

The Vermont Constitution includes a *common benefit* clause, which provides that the government is "instituted for the common benefit, protection, and security of the people, nation, or community, and not for the particular emolument or advantage of any single person, family, or set of persons, who are a part only of that community." Vt. Const. ch. 1, art. 7. In Baker v. State, 744 A.2d 864 (Vt. 1999), the Vermont Supreme Court held that the common benefit clause was violated by Vermont's exclusion of same-sex couples from the benefits and protections that Vermont provides to opposite-sex married couples. The court concluded that Vermont had two options: It could extend the status of marriage to same-sex couples, or it could extend to same-sex couples the benefits and protections provided to married couples. The Vermont legislature chose the latter option, enacting legislation that extends all the state law rights and obligations of marriage to same-sex partners who enter a legally regulated "civil union." An Act Relating to Civil Unions, 1999 Vt. Acts & Resolves 91. From the point of view of family law, the

---

public policy. For more extensive discussion of this treatment of the public policy proviso, see In re Estate of Lenherr, 455 Pa. 225, 314 A.2d 255 (1974).

distinction between a Vermont civil union and a lawful marriage is merely symbolic. In law, marriage is simply the sum of its legal incidents. Of course, from the perspective of religion or social psychology, there may be other dimensions to marriage.

Although no other state's legislation has matched the scope of the Vermont civil union statute, one state and many municipalities have enacted domestic partnership legislation. California enacted modest domestic partnership legislation before the voters approved Proposition 22. (And the proponents of Proposition 22 emphasized that they did not oppose domestic partnership legislation; their goal was merely to preserve the special status of marriage for opposite-sex couples alone. David O. Coolidge, Marriage Is Not Meant for Same-Sex Couples, L.A. Times, Feb. 28, 2000, at B5.)

The initial California legislation (1999 Cal. Stat., ch. 588) was a small first step in extending some of the rights and obligations of marriage to domestic partners, defined by Family Code section 297 as "two adults who have chosen to share one another's lives in an intimate and committed relationship of mutual caring." Section 297 permits state registration of "domestic partnerships" composed of two unmarried adults either who are of the same sex or, if they are of the opposite sex, one or both of whom are over the age of 62 and qualify for social security benefits. Partners must share a common residence, agree to be jointly responsible for basic living expenses incurred by either of them during their relationship (and creditors may enforce this responsibility), and file a declaration of domestic relationship with the Secretary of State. Section 298 regulates the registration of domestic partnerships and section 299 regulates their termination.

The initial legislation created only two rights for registered domestic partners. It required health facilities to treat a domestic partner and the children of a domestic partner as family members for purposes of hospital visitation, and it authorized state and local government employers to offer health care coverage and related benefits to the domestic partners of state and local government employees. More significantly, in creating a new legal status, the legislation established a toe hold, which could be supplemented by incremental legislation. Accordingly, A.B. 25 (2001 Cal. Stat., ch. 893) was enacted two years later, in 2001. A.B. 25 treats a registered domestic partner as a spouse in claims for negligent infliction of emotional distress and wrongful death, step-parent adoption, and eligibility for group health insurance coverage. Expanding health insurance benefits for the domestic-partner households of government employees, A.B. 25 additionally authorizes health insurance coverage for a deceased employee's surviving domestic partner and the children of a domestic partner. A.B. 25 requires any employer who allows an employee to use sick leave to care for a spouse or child to equally allow the use of sick leave to care for a domestic partner or a domestic partner's child. For purposes of the creation of conservatorships and trusts, the administration of decedent's estates, and the revocation of a will, A.B. 25 treats a domestic partner as a spouse. It also revises the statutory will form to include a domestic partner among a testator's potential beneficiaries. As originally introduced, A.B. 25 would also have treated a domestic partner as a spouse for purposes of intestate succession. However, the intestacy provision was abandoned at the insistence of Governor Davis. Jenifer Warren, Capitol Gains for Gay Pols, Los Angeles Times, Dec. 10, 2001, at A1 (characterizing Governor Davis as a "go-slow moderate on gay rights" and reporting that he demanded removal of the intestacy provision before he would sign A.B. 25 into law). Nevertheless, in 2002, Governor Davis signed into law A.B. 2216 (2002 Cal. Stat., ch. 447), which amends Probate Code section 6401(c) to include a surviving registered domestic partner as an intestate heir of a deceased partner. Governor Davis said that the measure would assist family members of those who died in the September 11 attacks. One of the proponents of A.B. 2216 was Keith Bradkowski, whose registered domestic partner, Jeff Collman, was a flight attendant on one of the planes that crashed into the World Trade Center. Gay Activists Split Despite Successes, Los Angeles Times. Sept. 16, 2002, at B5.

Domestic partnership legislation has been extensive in western Europe. Some countries have introduced registered partnership for same-sex couples only (Denmark, Norway, Sweden, and Iceland). Others have introduced registered partnerships for all couples (Netherlands, France, and the Spanish provinces of Catalunya and Aragon). In most European countries, partnership registration has all of the consequences of marriage, except for rights pertaining to the adoption of children. These countries and jurisdictions are, in order of enactment, Denmark (Danish Registered Partnership Act, 1989); Norway (Norwegian Registered Partnership Act of 1993); Sweden (1995); Iceland (1996); Greenland (1996); Netherlands (1998); Catalunya, Spain (1998); Aragon, Spain (1999); and France (PACS, 1999).

For related discussion of nonmarital cohabitation, see pages 474-480 infra.

E. UNMARRIED COHABITATION

The content of the next principal case, Marriage of Cary, has been entirely repudiated by the California Supreme Court in Marvin v. Marvin, reproduced immediately after *Cary*. Nevertheless, *Cary* is noteworthy because it represents the path not taken and, as such, provides a useful foil for evaluating the *Marvin* approach to unmarried cohabitation.

MARRIAGE OF CARY
34 Cal. App. 3d 345, 109 Cal. Rptr. 862 (1973)

ELKINGTON, J.—The principal issue presented by this appeal concerns California's Family Law Act (Civ. Code §§4000-5138, inclusive, sometimes hereafter the "Act"), effective January 1, 1970, [now the California Family Code], which provides among other things that the concept of individual "fault," or "guilt," or "punishment" for such human error, shall not be considered in determining *family property rights*.

Paul Cary and Janet Forbes, never married to each other, lived together for more than eight years. During that time they held themselves out to their friends and parents, and to the world generally, as a married couple; she always used the name of Cary. They purchased a home and other property, borrowed money, obtained credit, filed joint income tax returns and otherwise conducted all business as husband and wife. Both knew that they were not married; they had talked several times about a wedding ceremony, but somehow they never got around to it. Four children were born to Paul and Janet; they were supported by Paul, who always acknowledged them as his own. Their birth certificates and school registration recorded the parents as Paul and Janet Cary. While Paul worked Janet generally stayed at home taking care of the children and the house.

The relationship between Paul, Janet, and their children must reasonably be deemed that of a *family,* coming within the broad purview of the Family Law Act. Paul makes no contention to the contrary.

While living together the parties accumulated some real and personal property through the earnings of Paul. Had they been married it would have been community property, a fact conceded by the parties.

In 1971 Paul petitioned the superior court for "Nullity of the marriage. . . ." A principal trial issue was the question of Janet's rights in the property acquired with Paul's earnings. The trial court's determination that this property should be equally divided resulted in the instant appeal by Paul.

An early day, but nevertheless still valid, rationale of California's community property law is found in Meyer v. Kinzer (1859) 12 Cal. 247, 251-252, where the state's Supreme Court said:

> The [community property law] proceeds upon the theory that the marriage, in respect to property acquired during its existence, is a community of which each spouse is a member, equally contributing by his or her industry to its prosperity, and possessing an equal right to succeed to the property after dissolution, in case of surviving the other. To the community all acquisitions by either, whether made jointly or separately, belong. . . . All property is common property, except that owned previous to marriage or subsequently acquired in a particular way. . . .

This principle is given present day expression by Civil Code section 687 which, with exceptions here inapplicable, provides: "Community property is property acquired by husband and wife, *or either,* during marriage. . . ." (Italics added.)

While ordinarily applying only to those legally wed, the community property principle has frequently been applied where one or both of the parties mistakenly, *but in good faith,* believed themselves married. . . .

In such situations the property has been treated in substantially the same manner as if the parties had been validly married. No inquiry into the respective property "contributions" was permitted. Speaking of the claim of one who in good faith, but mistakenly, believed her marriage valid, the court in Coats v. Coats (1911) 160 Cal. 671, 678-679 [118 P. 441], stated:

> [I]t is entirely immaterial that the bulk of the property was acquired between the years 1900 and 1906, and that the plaintiff's services in its accumulation were "of no monetary value." She is not suing to recover for services rendered under a contract for labor, nor to establish the value of her interest in a business partnership. What she did, she did as a wife, and her share of the joint accumulations must be measured by what a wife would receive out of community property on the termination of the marriage. "The law will not inquire . . . whether the acquisition was by the joint efforts of the husband and wife, or attempt to adjust their respective rights in proportion to the amount each contributed thereto. The law will not concern itself with such an inquiry, but will leave the parties to share in the property in the same proportion as though the marriage contract was what the wife had every reason to believe it to be, i.e., a valid marriage." . . .

But where unmarried persons knowingly lived together in a "meretricious" or "sinful" relationship the law of California had consistently shown no concern for vindication of property rights, which under a valid marriage would have been legally established. (See Keene v. Keene (1962) 57 Cal. 2d 657, 662-665 [21 Cal. Rptr. 593, 371 P.2d 329]; Vallera v. Vallera, [21 Cal. 2d 681, 134 P.2d 761 (1943)]....) "Equitable considerations" were not present, the courts held, because of the "guilt" of both of the parties. . . . The parties were denied any relief and "'the law would leave them in the position in which they placed themselves.'" (Cline v. Festersen (1954) 128 Cal. App. 2d 380, 384 [275 P.2d 149] . . .), often to the profit of one (usually the man) and to the prejudice of the other (see Keene v. Keene, supra, 57 Cal. 2d at p.662, fn. 2, and authority there cited).

Even where a marriage had been solemnized, upon its dissolution and where some moral disparity between the parties was found to exist, it was the judicial practice "'to visit punishment upon the erring spouse in the apportionment of the community property. . . .'" (Markovitz v. Markovitz (1969) 272 Cal. App. 2d 150, 153 [77 Cal. Rptr. 96]. . . .) This punishment might even result in the award of all of the community property to the "innocent" marital partner. (Barham v. Barham (1949) 33 Cal. 2d 416, 431 [202 P.2d 289]; Irish v. Irish (1966) 246 Cal. App. 2d 705, 708 [55 Cal. Rptr. 55].) In such cases a trial court's failure to punish the errant spouse was an abuse of discretion, requiring reversal of the judgment. (Rocha v. Rocha (1954) 123 Cal. App. 2d 28, 29 [266 P.2d 130]; Gaeta v. Gaeta (1951) 102 Cal. App. 2d 87, 88 [226 P.2d 619].)

. . . The "punishment and reward" concept of California's family law was widely criticized. Many believe that it was "tacit recognition of the developing public opinion that resulted in enactment of the new law [the Family Law Act]." (See Attorney's Guide to Family Law Practice (Cont. Ed. Bar 2d ed. 1972) p.251.)

"The basic substantive change in the law [brought about by the Family Law Act] is *the elimination of fault or guilt as grounds for* granting or denying divorce and for refusing alimony and *making unequal division of community property*. . . ." (Italics added; In re Marriage of McKim (1972) 6 Cal. 3d 673, 678 [100 Cal. Rptr. 140, 493 P.2d 868]; and see Civ. Code, §4800 [now Family Code §2550].) . . . The equal division of community property was one of the ways "of advancing [the Act's] primary no-fault philosophy." (In re Marriage of Juick (1971) 21 Cal. App. 3d 421, 427 [98 Cal. Rptr. 324].) So strong is the policy behind the Act that in family law proceedings relating to property rights, any pleading or proof relating to misconduct, or "guilt," or "innocence" of a party "*shall be improper* and inadmissible. . . ." (Italics added; see Civ. Code §4509 [now Family Code §2335].)

In a summary of the Act, and particularly its section 4800 [now Family Code section 2550] calling for equal property division, respected writers have said:

> The basic theory of the new law is that, in disposing of the property, a dissolution of marriage should be treated much like the dissolution of a business partnership. Regardless of the economic circumstances of business partners or of their moral conduct during the existence of the partnership, on dissolution the partners receive a portion of the assets commensurate with their respective partnership interests. (Attorney's Guide to Family Law Act Practice (Cont. Ed. Bar 2d ed. 1972) p.250.)

The Family Law Act applies not only to valid marriages. It expressly covers a family relationship based on a void or voidable marriage where "either party or both parties believed in good faith that the marriage was valid. . . ." (See Civ. Code, §4452 [now Family Code §2251].)[1]

An analysis of [Family Code] section [2251] discloses that where one party to a nonmarital family relationship in bad faith knew of the marriage's infirmity or nonexistence, and the other did not, the Act neither penalizes nor rewards the respective parties upon a judicial division of their accumulated property. The party who in bad faith brought about the pseudomarriage is not for that reason left where found by the court. Nor may any "guilt" or "innocence" of the parties in their relationship after entering the illegitimate union be considered by the court. Sections [2251], [2335] and [2550] assure that the parties, without "punishment" or "reward" to either, shall receive an equal division of that which would have been community property had they been validly married.

But in the case before us *both parties* appear "guilty"; each was aware of the lack of a marital ceremony. Paul urges that since the Act does not expressly cover such a situation, the pre-1970 notion that the law must leave the parties where it finds them is the applicable rule.

We disagree.

Giving effect to such an argument would lead to an unreasonable result and frustrate the obvious objective of the Act. We should be obliged to presume a legislative intent that a person, who by deceit leads another to believe a valid marriage exists between them, shall be legally guaranteed half of the property they acquire even though most, or all, may have resulted from the earnings of the blameless partner. At the same time we must infer an inconsistent legislative intent that two persons who, candidly with each other, enter upon an unmarried family relationship, shall be denied any judicial aid whatever in the assertion of otherwise valid property rights. . . .

By the Family Law Act the Legislature has announced it to be the public policy of this state that concepts of "guilt" (and punishment therefor) and "innocence" (and reward therefor) are no longer relevant in the determination of family property rights, whether there be a legal marriage or not, and if not, regardless of whether the deficiency is known to one, or both, or neither of the parties. . . .

It therefore becomes our duty to give expression to the public policy expressed by the Family Law Act. We hold, as to the issue before us, that the Act supersedes contrary pre-1970 judicial authority.

It follows that the trial court properly disregarded evidence of the "guilt" of the parties to the instant action. Having done so, it was obliged to divide their property evenly, according to the dictate of Civil Code section 4800 [Family Code section 2550].

It is argued that our holding would tend to discourage the unemployed family partner from entering into a marital union, since that party without marriage would nevertheless have the marriage's property benefits. But with equal or greater force the point might be made that the pre-1970 rule was calculated to cause the income-

---

1. Civil Code section 4452 [now Family Code section 2251]: "Whenever a determination is made that a marriage is void or voidable and the court finds that either party or both parties believed in good faith that the marriage was valid, the court shall declare such party or parties to have the status of a putative spouse, and, if the division of property is in issue, shall divide, in accordance with Section 4800, that property acquired during the union which would have been community property or quasi-community property if the union had not been void or voidable. Such property shall be termed 'quasi-marital property.' If the court expressly reserves jurisdiction, it may make the property division at a time subsequent to the judgment."

producing partner to avoid marriage and thus retain the benefit of all of his or her accumulated earnings. . . .

It should be pointed out that the criteria for application of the rule we apply to the case before us is much more than that of an unmarried living arrangement between a man and woman. The Family Law Act obviously requires that there be established not only an ostensible marital relationship but also an actual family relationship, with cohabitation and mutual recognition and assumption of the usual rights, duties, and obligations attending marriage. . . .

[T]he judgment is affirmed. The parties will bear their respective costs. MOLINARI, P.J., and SIMS, J., concurred.

Notes and Questions

1. Kay and Amyx report:

> Despite the court's statement that "[b]oth knew they were not married," Janet testified that she had believed common law marriages were valid and alleged that Paul had shared her belief. The case was briefed and argued on the theory that Janet claimed the status of a putative spouse. . . . [W]ith a minor extension of existing case law, she could have been found to be a putative spouse. [Marvin v. Marvin: Preserving the Options, 65 Cal. L. Rev. 937, 945-946, 960 (1977).]

The authors' remarks foreshadow Wagner v. County of Imperial, supra at page 439, decided six years later. Do you agree that Janet could have been treated as a putative spouse without effectively reviving a substantial portion of the doctrine of common law marriage in California?

2. Are you persuaded by the court's assertion that California Family Code section 2251 allows the "bad faith" putative spouse to share equally with the "good faith" putative spouse? Kay and Amyx examine the statute's legislative history and conclude that *Cary* is incorrect, supra Note 1 at 949-951. Is the court's interpretation of section 2251 necessary to its resolution of *Cary?*

3. To what extent does *Cary* effectively revive the doctrine of common law marriage in California? What sorts of relationships would be included and excluded by the *Cary* rubric? See Comment, In Re Cary: A Judicial Recognition of Illicit Cohabitation, 25 Hastings L.J. 1226 (1974); Comment, In Re Marriage of Carey [sic]: The End of the Putative-Meretricious Spouse Distinction in California, 12 San Diego L. Rev. 436 (1975).

4. Kay and Amyx criticize *Cary* on the ground that it relies on traditional sex-based spousal roles to find a Family Law Act relationship, supra Note 1 at 952. Do you agree? Assume the *Cary* facts, but that Janet and Paul were attorneys in the same Legal Services office and relied upon "flex-time," babysitters, and their local community center for child care. Would the court have reached a different conclusion? What facts are essential to the *Cary* finding? See also Estate of Atherley, 44 Cal. App. 3d 758, 119 Cal. Rptr. 41 (1975). Compare Beckman v. Mayhew, 49 Cal. App. 529, 122 Cal. Rptr. 604 (1975). Both cases are briefly discussed in the supreme court's *Marvin* opinion immediately infra.

5. Kay and Amyx ultimately conclude that *Cary* is a regressive development for

women, particularly those who would like to escape the constraints of traditional family life. *Cary* would:

> impose upon men and women who choose to live together in nonmarital cohabitation a lifestyle characterized by the restrictions formerly associated with traditional marriage. . . . The entry of women into the labor force and their rising expectations of equal pay and equal opportunity [have] meant that they, too, are coming to look upon themselves as primary individuals who need help from others to carry on their daily lives smoothly. If ambitious and goal-oriented persons find that marriage or family relationships have become a hindrance to their self-realization, then it is likely that such persons will be reluctant to commit themselves to long-term relationships. It is commonly thought, however, that the maintenance of stable intimate relationships is a necessary prerequisite for the mental and physical health of adults as well as the healthy development of children. Such relationships ought, therefore, to be encouraged. [Note 1, supra, at 953, 976.]

The authors conclude that the parties, and women especially, are best served by law that allows them to freely structure their relationships without running any risk that the legal rules of marriage will be imposed upon them, as they were in *Cary*, id. at 977.

MARVIN v. MARVIN
18 Cal. 3d 660, 557 P.2d 106, 134 Cal. Rptr. 815 (1976)

TOBRINER, J.—During the past 15 years, there has been a substantial increase in the number of couples living together without marrying.[1] Such nonmarital relationships lead to legal controversy when one partner dies or the couple separates. Courts of Appeal, faced with the task of determining property rights in such cases, have arrived at conflicting positions: two cases (In re Marriage of Cary (1973) 34 Cal. App. 3d 345 [109 Cal. Rptr. 862]; Estate of Atherley (1975) 44 Cal. App. 3d 758 [119 Cal. Rptr. 41]) have held that the Family Law Act (Civ. Code, §§4000 et seq.) [now the Family Code] requires division of the property according to community property principles, and one decision (Beckman v. Mayhew (1975) 49 Cal. App. 3d 529 [122 Cal. Rptr. 604]) has rejected that holding. We take this opportunity to resolve that controversy and to declare the principles which should govern distribution of property acquired in a nonmarital relationship.

We conclude: (1) The provisions of the Family Law Act [Family Code] do not govern the distribution of property acquired during a nonmarital relationship; such a relationship remains subject solely to judicial decision. (2) The courts should enforce express contracts between nonmarital partners except to the extent that the contract is explicitly founded on the consideration of meretricious sexual services. (3) In the absence of an express contract, the courts should inquire into the conduct of the parties to determine whether that conduct demonstrates an implied contract, agreement of partnership or joint venture, or some other tacit understand-

---

1. "The 1970 census figures indicate that today perhaps eight times as many couples are living together without being married as cohabited ten years ago." (Comment, In re Cary: A Judicial Recognition of Illicit Cohabitation (1974) 25 Hastings L.J. 1226.)

ing between the parties. The courts may also employ the doctrine of quantum meruit, or equitable remedies such as constructive or resulting trusts, when warranted by the facts of the case.

In the instant case plaintiff and defendant lived together for seven years without marrying; all property acquired during this period was taken in defendant's name. When plaintiff sued to enforce a contract under which she was entitled to half the property and to support payments, the trial court granted judgment on the pleadings for defendant, thus leaving him with all property accumulated by the couple during their relationship. Since the trial court denied plaintiff a trial on the merits of her claim, its decision conflicts with the principles stated above, and must be reversed.

1. THE FACTUAL SETTING OF THIS APPEAL

Since the trial court rendered judgment for defendant on the pleadings, we must accept the allegations of plaintiff's complaint as true, determining whether such allegations state, or can be amended to state, a cause of action. . . . We turn therefore to the specific allegations of the complaint.

Plaintiff avers that in October of 1964 she and defendant "entered into an oral agreement" that while "the parties lived together they would combine their efforts and earnings and would share equally any and all property accumulated as a result of their efforts whether individual or combined." Furthermore, they agreed to "hold themselves out to the general public as husband and wife" and that "plaintiff would further render her services as a companion, homemaker, housekeeper and cook to . . . defendant."

Shortly thereafter plaintiff agreed to "give up her lucrative career as an entertainer [and] singer" in order to "devote her full time to defendant . . . as a companion, homemaker, housekeeper and cook"; in return defendant agreed to "provide for all of plaintiff's financial support and needs for the rest of her life."

Plaintiff alleges that she lived with defendant from October of 1964 through May of 1970 and fulfilled her obligations under the agreement. During this period the parties as a result of their efforts and earnings acquired in defendant's name substantial real and personal property, including motion picture rights worth over $1 million. In May of 1970, however, defendant compelled plaintiff to leave his household. He continued to support plaintiff until November of 1971, but thereafter refused to provide further support.

On the basis of these allegations plaintiff asserts two causes of action. The first, for declaratory relief, asks the court to determine her contract and property rights; the second seeks to impose a constructive trust upon one half of the property acquired during the course of the relationship.

Defendant demurred unsuccessfully, and then answered the complaint. Following extensive discovery and pretrial proceedings, the case came to trial. Defendant renewed his attack on the complaint by a motion to dismiss. Since the parties had stipulated that defendant's marriage to Betty Marvin did not terminate until the filing of a final decree of divorce in January 1967, the trial court treated defendant's motion as one for judgment on the pleadings augmented by the stipulation.

After hearing argument the court granted defendant's motion and entered judgment for defendant. Plaintiff moved to set aside the judgment and asked leave to amend her complaint to allege that she and defendant reaffirmed their agreement after defendant's divorce was final. The trial court denied plaintiff's motion, and she appealed from the judgment.

2.   PLAINTIFF'S COMPLAINT STATES A CAUSE OF ACTION FOR BREACH OF AN EXPRESS CONTRACT

In Trutalli v. Meraviglia (1932) 215 Cal. 698 [12 P.2d 430] we established the principle that nonmarital partners may lawfully contract concerning the ownership of property acquired during the relationship. We reaffirmed this principle in Vallera v. Vallera (1943) 21 Cal. 2d 681, 685 [134 P.2d 761], stating that "If a man and woman [who are not married] live together as husband and wife under an agreement to pool their earnings and share equally in their joint accumulations, equity will protect the interests of each in such property."

In the case before us plaintiff, basing her cause of action in contract upon these precedents, maintains that the trial court erred in denying her a trial on the merits of her contention. Although that court did not specify the ground for its conclusion that plaintiff's contractual allegations stated no cause of action, defendant offers some four theories to sustain the ruling; we proceed to examine them.

Defendant first and principally relies on the contention that the alleged contract is so closely related to the supposed "immoral" character of the relationship between plaintiff and himself that the enforcement of the contract would violate public policy. He points to cases asserting that a contract between nonmarital partners is unenforceable if it is "involved in" an illicit relationship . . . or made in "contemplation" of such a relationship. . . . A review of the numerous California decisions concerning contracts between nonmarital partners, however, reveals that the courts have not employed such broad and uncertain standards to strike down contracts. The decisions instead disclose a narrower and more precise standard: a contract between nonmarital partners is unenforceable only *to the extent* that it *explicitly* rests upon the immoral and illicit consideration of meretricious sexual services. . . .

The principle that a contract between nonmarital partners will be enforced unless expressly and inseparably based upon an illicit consideration of sexual services not only represents the distillation of the decisional law, but also offers a far more precise and workable standard than that advocated by defendant. Our recent decision in In re Marriage of Dawley (1976) 17 Cal. 3d 342 [131 Cal. Rptr. 3, 551

---

4. Defendant also contends that the contract was illegal because it contemplated a violation of former Penal Code section 269a, which prohibited living "in a state of cohabitation and adultery." (§269a was repealed by Stats. 1975, ch. 71, eff. Jan. 1, 1976.) Defendant's standing to raise the issue is questionable because he alone was married and thus guilty of violating section 269a. Plaintiff, being unmarried could neither be convicted of adulterous cohabitation nor of aiding and abetting defendant's violation. (See In re Cooper (1912) 162 Cal. 81, 85-86 [121 P. 318].)

The numerous cases discussing the contractual rights of unmarried couples have drawn no distinction between illegal relationships and lawful nonmarital relationships. (Cf. Weak v. Weak (1962) 202 Cal. App. 2d 632, 639 [21 Cal. Rptr. 9] (bigamous marriage).) Moreover, even if we were to draw such a distinction—a largely academic endeavor in view of the repeal of section 269a—defendant probably would not benefit; his relationship with plaintiff continued long after his divorce became final, and plaintiff sought to amend her complaint to assert that the parties reaffirmed their contract after the divorce.

P.2d 323] offers a close analogy. Rejecting the contention that an antenuptial agreement is invalid if the parties contemplated a marriage of short duration, we pointed out in *Dawley* that a standard based upon the subjective contemplation of the parties is uncertain and unworkable; such a test, we stated, "might invalidate virtually all antenuptial agreements on the ground that the parties contemplated dissolution . . . but it provides no principled basis for determining which antenuptial agreements offend public policy and which do not." (17 Cal. 3d 342, 352.)

Similarly, in the present case a standard which inquires whether an agreement is "involved" in or "contemplates" a nonmarital relationship is vague and unworkable. Virtually all agreements between nonmarital partners can be said to be "involved" in some sense in the fact of their mutual sexual relationship, or to "contemplate" the existence of that relationship. Thus defendant's proposed standards, if taken literally, might invalidate all agreements between nonmarital partners, a result no one favors. Moreover, those standards offer no basis to distinguish between valid and invalid agreements. By looking not to such uncertain tests, but only to the consideration underlying the agreement, we provide the parties and the courts with a practical guide to determine when an agreement between nonmarital partners should be enforced.

(2) Defendant secondly relies upon the ground suggested by the trial court: that the 1964 contract violated public policy because it impaired the community property rights of Betty Marvin, defendant's lawful wife. . . .

In the present case Betty Marvin, the aggrieved spouse, had the opportunity to assert her community property rights in the divorce action. . . . The interlocutory and final decrees in that action fix and limit her interest. Enforcement of the contract between plaintiff and defendant against property awarded to defendant by the divorce decree will not impair any right of Betty's, and thus is not on that account violative of public policy.[8]

(3) Defendant's third contention is noteworthy for the lack of authority advanced in its support. He contends that enforcement of the oral agreement between plaintiff and himself is barred by Civil Code section 5134 [now Family Code section 1611], which provides that "All contracts for marriage settlements must be in writing. . . ." A marriage settlement, however, is an agreement in contemplation of marriage in which each party agrees to release or modify the property rights which would otherwise arise from the marriage. (See Corker v. Corker (1891) 87 Cal. 643, 648 [25 P. 922].) The contract at issue here does not conceivably fall within that definition, and thus is beyond the compass of section 5134.[9]

Defendant finally argues that enforcement of the contract is barred by Civil Code section 43.5, subdivision (d), which provides that "No cause of action arises

---

8. Defendant also contends that the contract is invalid as an agreement to promote or encourage divorce. (See 1 Witkin, Summary of Cal. Law (8th ed.) pp.390-392 and cases there cited.) The contract between plaintiff and defendant did not, however, by its terms require defendant to divorce Betty, nor reward him for so doing. Moreover, the principle on which defendant relies does not apply when the marriage in question is beyond redemption (Glickman v. Collins (1975) 13 Cal. 3d 852, 858-859 [120 Cal. Rptr. 76, 533 P.2d 204]); whether or not defendant's marriage to Betty was beyond redemption when defendant contracted with plaintiff is obviously a question of fact which cannot be resolved by judgment on the pleadings.

9. Our review of the many cases enforcing agreements between nonmarital partners reveals that the majority of such agreements were oral. In two cases (Ferguson v. Schuenemann, 167 Cal. App. 2d 413 [334 P.2d 668 (1959)]; Cline v. Festersen, 128 Cal. App. 2d 380 [275 P.2d 149 (1954)]), the court expressly rejected defenses grounded upon the statute of frauds.

for . . . breach of promise of marriage." This rather strained contention proceeds from the premise that a promise of marriage impliedly includes a promise to support and to pool property acquired after marriage (see Boyd v. Boyd (1964) 228 Cal. App. 2d 374 [39 Cal. Rptr. 400]) to the conclusion that pooling and support agreements not part of or accompanied by promise of marriage are barred by the section. We conclude that section 43.5 is not reasonably susceptible to the interpretation advanced by defendant. . . .

In summary, we base our opinion on the principle that adults who voluntarily live together and engage in sexual relations are nonetheless as competent as any other persons to contract respecting their earnings and property rights. Of course, they cannot lawfully contract to pay for the performance of sexual services, for such a contract is, in essence, an agreement for prostitution and unlawful for that reason. But they may agree to pool their earnings and to hold all property acquired during the relationship in accord with the law governing community property; conversely they may agree that each partner's earnings and the property acquired from those earnings remains the separate property of the earning partner.[10] So long as the agreement does not rest upon illicit meretricious consideration, the parties may order their economic affairs as they choose, and no policy precludes the courts from enforcing such agreements.

In the present instance, plaintiff alleges that the parties agreed to pool their earnings, that they contracted to share equally in all property acquired, and that defendant agreed to support plaintiff. The terms of the contract as alleged do not rest upon any unlawful consideration. We therefore conclude that the complaint furnishes a suitable basis upon which the trial court can render declaratory relief. (See 3 Witkin, Cal. Procedure (2d ed.) pp. 2335-2336.) The trial court consequently erred in granting defendant's motion for judgment on the pleadings.

3. PLAINTIFF'S COMPLAINT CAN BE AMENDED TO STATE A CAUSE OF ACTION FOUNDED UPON THEORIES OF IMPLIED CONTRACT OR EQUITABLE RELIEF

As we have noted, both causes of action in plaintiff's complaint allege an express contract; neither assert any basis for relief independent from the contract. In In re Marriage of Cary, supra, 34 Cal. App. 3d 345, however, the Court of Appeal held that, in view of the policy of the Family Law Act, property accumulated by nonmarital partners in an actual family relationship should be divided equally. Upon examining the *Cary* opinion, the parties to the present case realized that plaintiff's alleged relationship with defendant might arguably support a cause of action independent of any express contract between the parties. The parties have therefore briefed and discussed the issue of the property rights of a nonmarital partner in the absence of an express contract. Although our conclusion that plain-

10. A great variety of other arrangements are possible. The parties might keep their earnings and property separate, but agree to compensate one party for services which benefit the other. They may choose to pool only part of their earnings and property, to form a partnership or joint venture, or to hold property acquired as joint tenants or tenants in common, or agree to any other such arrangement. (See generally Weitzman, Legal Regulation of Marriage: Tradition and Change (1974) 62 Cal. L. Rev. 1169.)

tiff's complaint states a cause of action based on an express contract alone compels us to reverse the judgment for defendant, resolution of the *Cary* issue will serve both to guide the parties upon retrial and to resolve a conflict presently manifest in published Court of Appeal decisions.

Both plaintiff and defendant stand in broad agreement that the law should be fashioned to carry out the reasonable expectations of the parties. Plaintiff, however, presents the following contentions: that the decisions prior to *Cary* rest upon implicit and erroneous notions of punishing a party for his or her guilt in entering into a nonmarital relationship, that such decisions result in an inequitable distribution of property accumulated during the relationship, and that *Cary* correctly held that the enactment of the Family Law Act in 1970 overturned those prior decisions. Defendant in response maintains that the prior decisions merely applied common law principles of contract and property to persons who have deliberately elected to remain outside the bounds of the community property system.[11] *Cary*, defendant contends, erred in holding that the Family Law Act vitiated the force of the prior precedents.

. . . [T]he truth lies somewhere between the positions of plaintiff and defendant. . . .

[T]he cases prior to *Cary* exhibited a schizophrenic inconsistency. By enforcing an express contract between nonmarital partners unless it rested upon an unlawful consideration, the courts applied a common law principle as to contracts. Yet the courts disregarded the common law principle that holds that implied contracts can arise from the conduct of the parties.[16] Refusing to enforce such contracts, the courts spoke of leaving the parties "in the position in which they had placed themselves" (Oakley v. Oakley, supra, 82 Cal. App. 2d 188, 192), just as if they were guilty parties in pari delicto. . . .

Thus as of 1973, the time of the filing of In re Marriage of Cary, supra, 34 Cal. App. 3d 345, the cases apparently held that a nonmarital partner who rendered services in the absence of express contract could assert no right to property acquired during the relationship. The facts of *Cary* demonstrated the unfairness of that rule.

Janet and Paul Cary had lived together, unmarried, for more than eight years.

---

11. We note that a deliberate decision to avoid the strictures of the community property system is not the only reason that couples live together without marriage. Some couples may wish to avoid the permanent commitment that marriage implies, yet be willing to share equally any property acquired during the relationship; others may fear the loss of pension, welfare, or tax benefits resulting from marriage (see Beckman v. Mayhew, supra, 49 Cal. App. 3d 529). Others may engage in the relationship as a possible prelude to marriage. In lower socio-economic groups the difficulty and expense of dissolving a former marriage often leads couples to choose a nonmarital relationship; many unmarried couples may also incorrectly believe that the doctrine of common law marriage prevails in California, and thus that they are in fact married. Consequently we conclude that the mere fact that a couple have not participated in a valid marriage ceremony cannot serve as a basis for a court's inference that the couple intend to keep their earnings and property separate and independent; the parties' intention can only be ascertained by a more searching inquiry into the nature of their relationship.

16. "Contracts may be express or implied. These terms however do not denote different kinds of contracts, but have reference to the evidence by which the agreement between the parties is shown. If the agreement is shown by the direct words of the parties, spoken or written, the contract is said to be an express one. But if such agreement can only be shown by the acts and conduct of the parties, interpreted in the light of the subject matter and of the surrounding circumstances, then the contract is an implied one." (Skelly v. Bristol Sav. Bank (1893) 63 Conn. 83 [26 A. 474], quoted in 1 Corbin, Contracts (1963) p.41.) Thus, as Justice Schauer observed in Desny v. Wilder (1956) 46 Cal. 2d 715 [299 P.2d 257], in a sense all contracts made in fact, as distinguished from quasi-contractual obligations, are express contracts, differing only in the manner in which the assent of the parties is expressed and proved. (See 46 Cal. 2d at pp.735-736.)

They held themselves out to friends and family as husband and wife, reared four children, purchased a home and other property, obtained credit, filed joint income tax returns, and otherwise conducted themselves as though they were married. Paul worked outside the home, and Janet generally cared for the house and children.

In 1971 Paul petitioned for "nullity of the marriage."[17] Following a hearing on that petition, the trial court awarded Janet half the property acquired during the relationship, although all such property was traceable to Paul's earnings. The Court of Appeal affirmed the award.

Reviewing the prior decisions which had denied relief to the homemaking partner, the Court of Appeal reasoned that those decisions rested upon a policy of punishing persons guilty of cohabitation without marriage. The Family Law Act, the court observed, aimed to eliminate fault or guilt as a basis for dividing marital property. But once fault or guilt is excluded, the court reasoned, nothing distinguishes the property rights of a nonmarital "spouse" from those of a putative spouse. Since the latter is entitled to half the "'quasi marital property'" (Civ. Code, §4452 [Family Code §2251]), the Court of Appeal concluded that, giving effect to the policy of the Family Law Act, a nonmarital cohabitator should also be entitled to half the property accumulated during an "actual family relationship." (34 Cal. App. 3d at p.353.)[18]

Cary met with a mixed reception in other appellate districts. In Estate of Atherley, supra, 44 Cal. App. 3d 758, the Fourth District agreed with *Cary* that under the Family Law Act a nonmarital partner in an actual family relationship enjoys the same right to an equal division of property as a putative spouse. In Beckman v. Mayhew, supra, 49 Cal. App. 3d 529, however, the Third District rejected *Cary* on the ground that the Family Law Act was not intended to change California law dealing with nonmarital relationships.

---

17. The Court of Appeal opinion in In re Marriage of Cary, supra, does not explain why Paul Cary filed his action as a petition for nullity. Briefs filed with this court, however, suggest that Paul may have been seeking to assert rights as a putative spouse. In the present case, on the other hand, neither party claims the status of an actual or putative spouse. Under such circumstances an action to adjudge "the marriage" in the instant case a nullity would be pointless and could not serve as a device to adjudicate contract and property rights arising from the parties nonmarital relationship. Accordingly, plaintiff here correctly chose to assert her rights by means of an ordinary civil action.

18. The court in *Cary* also based its decision upon an analysis of Civil Code section 4452 [now Family Code section 2251], which specifies the property rights of a putative spouse. . . . *Cary* concluded, the "guilty spouse" (the spouse who knows the marriage is invalid) has the same right to half the property as does the "innocent" spouse.

Cary then reasoned that if the "guilty" spouse to a putative marriage is entitled to one-half the marital property, the "guilty" partner in a nonmarital relationship should also receive one-half of the property. . . .

This reasoning in *Cary* has been criticized by commentators. (Sec Note, op. cit., supra, 25 Hastings L.J. 1226, 1234-1235; Comment, In re Marriage of Carey [sic]: The End of the Putative-Meretricious Spouse Distinction in California (1975) 12 San Diego L. Rev. 436, 444-446.) The commentators note that [Family Code section 2254] provides that an "innocent" party to a putative marriage can recover spousal support, from which they infer that the Legislature intended to give only the "innocent" spouse a right to one-half of the quasi-marital property under section [2251].

We need not now resolve this dispute concerning the interpretation of [Family Code section 2251]. Even if *Cary* is correct in holding that a "guilty" putative spouse has a right to one-half of the marital property, it does not necessarily follow that a nonmarital partner has an identical right. In a putative marriage the parties will arrange their economic affairs with the expectation that upon dissolution the property will be divided equally. If a "guilty" putative spouse receives one-half of the property under section [2251], no expectation of the "innocent" spouse has been frustrated. In a nonmarital relationship, on the other hand, the parties may expressly or tacitly determine to order their economic relationship in some other manner, and to impose community property principles regardless of such understanding may frustrate the parties' expectations.

If *Cary* is interpreted as holding that the Family Law Act requires an equal division of property accumulated in nonmarital "actual family relationships," then we agree with Beckman v. Mayhew that *Cary* distends the act. No language in the Family Law Act addresses the property rights of nonmarital partners, and nothing in the legislative history of the act suggests that the Legislature considered that subject.[19] The delineation of the rights of nonmarital partners before 1970 had been fixed entirely by judicial decision; we see no reason to believe that the Legislature, by enacting the Family Law Act, intended to change that state of affairs.

But although we reject the reasoning of *Cary* and *Atherley*, we share the perception of the *Cary* and *Atherley* courts that the application of former precedent in the factual setting of those cases would work an unfair distribution of the property accumulated by the couple. . . . We should not, therefore, reject the authority of *Cary* and *Atherley* without also examining the deficiencies in the former law which led to those decisions.

The principal reason why the pre-*Cary* decisions result in an unfair distribution of property inheres in the court's refusal to permit a nonmarital partner to assert rights based upon accepted principles of implied contract or equity. We have examined the reasons advanced to justify this denial of relief, and find that none have merit.

First, we note that the cases denying relief do not rest their refusal upon any theory of "punishing" a "guilty" partner. Indeed, to the extent that denial of relief "punishes" one partner, it necessarily rewards the other by permitting him to retain a disproportionate amount of the property. Concepts of "guilt" thus cannot justify an unequal division of property between two equally "guilty" persons.[21]

Other reasons advanced in the decisions fare no better. The principal argument seems to be that "[e]quitable considerations arising from the reasonable expectation of . . . benefits attending the status of marriage . . . are not present [in a nonmarital relationship]." (Vallera v. Vallera, supra, 21 Cal. 2d at p.685.) But, although parties to a nonmarital relationship obviously cannot have based any expectations upon the belief that they were married, other expectations and equitable considerations remain. The parties may well expect that property will be divided in accord with the parties' own tacit understanding and that in the absence of such understanding the courts will fairly apportion property accumulated through mutual effort. We need not treat nonmarital partners as putatively married persons in

19. Despite the extensive material available on the legislative history of the Family Law Act neither *Cary* nor plaintiff cites any reference which suggests that the Legislature ever considered the issue of the property rights of nonmarital partners, and our independent examination has uncovered no such reference.

21. Justice Finley of the Washington Supreme Court explains: "Under such circumstances [the dissolution of a nonmarital relationship], this court and the courts of other jurisdictions have, in effect, sometimes said, 'We will wash our hands of such disputes. The parties should and must be left to their own devices, just where they find themselves.' To me, such pronouncements seem overly fastidious and a bit fatuous. They are unrealistic and, among other things, ignore the fact that an unannounced (but nevertheless effective and binding) rule of law is inherent in any such terminal statements by a court of law. The unannounced but inherent rule is simply that the party who has title, or in some instances who is in possession, will enjoy the rights of ownership of the property concerned. The rule often operates to the great advantage of the cunning and the shrewd, who wind up with possession of the property, or title to it in their names, at the end of a so-called meretricious relationship. So, although the courts proclaim that they will have nothing to do with such matters, the proclamation in itself establishes, as to the parties involved, an effective and binding rule of law which tends to operate purely by accident or perhaps by reason of the cunning, anticipatory designs of just one of the parties." (West v. Knowles (1957) 50 Wn. 2d 311 [311 P.2d 689, 692] (conc. opn.).)

order to apply principles of implied contract, or extend equitable remedies; we need to treat them only as we do any other unmarried persons.[22]

The remaining arguments advanced from time to time to deny remedies to the nonmarital partners are of less moment. There is no more reason to presume that services are contributed as a gift than to presume that funds are contributed as a gift; in any event the better approach is to presume, as Justice Peters suggested, "that the parties intend to deal fairly with each other." (Keene v. Keene, supra, 57 Cal. 2d 657, 674 (dissenting opn.); see Bruch, op. cit., supra, 10 Fam. L.Q. 101, 113.)

The argument that granting remedies to the nonmarital partners would discourage marriage must fail; as *Cary* pointed out, "with equal or greater force the point might be made that the pre-1970 rule was calculated to cause the income-producing partner to avoid marriage and thus retain the benefit of all of his or her accumulated earnings." (34 Cal. App. 3d at p.353.) Although we recognize the well-established public policy to foster and promote the institution of marriage (see Deyoe v. Superior Court (1903) 140 Cal. 476, 482 [74 P. 28]), perpetuation of judicial rules which result in an inequitable distribution of property accumulated during a nonmarital relationship is neither a just nor an effective way of carrying out that policy.

In summary, we believe that the prevalence of nonmarital relationships in modern society and the social acceptance of them, marks this as a time when our courts should by no means apply the doctrine of the unlawfulness of the so-called meretricious relationship to the instant case. As we have explained, the nonenforceability of agreements expressly providing for meretricious conduct rested upon the fact that such conduct, as the word suggests, pertained to and encompassed prostitution. To equate the nonmarital relationship of today to such a subject matter is to do violence to an accepted and wholly different practice.

We are aware that many young couples live together without the solemnization of marriage, in order to make sure that they can successfully later undertake marriage. This trial period,[23] preliminary to marriage, serves as some assurance that the marriage will not subsequently end in dissolution to the harm of both parties. We are aware, as we have stated, of the pervasiveness of nonmarital relationships in other situations.

The mores of the society have indeed changed so radically in regard to cohabitation that we cannot impose a standard based on alleged moral considerations that have apparently been so widely abandoned by so many. Lest we be misunderstood, however, we take this occasion to point out that the structure of society itself largely depends upon the institution of marriage, and nothing we have said in this opinion should be taken to derogate from that institution. The joining of the man and woman in marriage is at once the most socially productive and individually fulfilling relationship that one can enjoy in the course of a lifetime.

We conclude that the judicial barriers that may stand in the way of a policy based upon the fulfillment of the reasonable expectations of the parties to a nonmarital relationship should be removed. As we have explained, the courts now hold that express agreements will be enforced unless they rest on an unlawful meretricious consideration. We add that in the absence of an express agreement, the courts

---

22. In some instances a confidential relationship may arise between nonmarital partners, and economic transactions between them should be governed by the principles applicable to such relationships.

23. Toffler, Future Shock (Bantam Books, 1971) page 253.

may look to a variety of other remedies in order to protect the parties' lawful expectations.[24]

The courts may inquire into the conduct of the parties to determine whether that conduct demonstrates an implied contract or implied agreement of partnership or joint venture (see Estate of Thornton (1972) 81 Wn. 2d 72 [499 P.2d 864]), or some other tacit understanding between the parties. The courts may, when appropriate, employ principles of constructive trust (see Omer v. Omer (1974) 11 Wash. App. 386 [523 P.2d 957]) or resulting trust (see Hyman v. Hyman (Tex. Civ. App. 1954) 275 S.W.2d 149). Finally, a nonmarital partner may recover in quantum meruit for the reasonable value of household services rendered less the reasonable value of support received if he can show that he rendered services with the expectation of monetary reward. (See Hill v. Estate of Westbrook, 39 Cal. 2d 458, 462 [247 P.2d 19 (1952)].)[25]

Since we have determined that plaintiff's complaint states a cause of action for breach of an express contract, and, as we have explained, can be amended to state a cause of action independent of allegations of express contract,[26] we must conclude that the trial court erred in granting defendant a judgment on the pleadings.

The judgment is reversed and the cause remanded for further proceedings consistent with the views expressed herein.

WRIGHT, C.J., McCOMB, J., MOSK, J., SULLIVAN, J., and RICHARDSON, J., concurred.

Notes and Questions

1. Would Janet Cary have prevailed under any theory of recovery proposed by the supreme court in *Marvin?* See Alderson v. Alderson, 180 Cal. App. 3d 450, 181 Cal. App. 3d 462A, 225 Cal. Rptr. 610 (1986).

2. Not surprisingly, Kay and Amyx prefer *Marvin* to *Cary,* although they express concern about the boundlessness of the supreme court's opinion and suggest several ways to contain it. Marvin v. Marvin: Preserving the Options, 65 Cal. L. Rev. 937, 972 (1977).

3. Does *Marvin* posit an unduly unitary and static view of the parties' intent? Did Michelle "choose" not to marry Lee Marvin? (Janet and Paul Cary each wished to marry, but not, apparently, at the same time, id. at 946, n.60.) Assume an initially "liberated" cohabitation in which the woman's expectations change over the course of time as the parties assume traditional social roles or have a child. But cf.

---

24. We do not seek to resurrect the doctrine of common law marriage, which was abolished in California by statute in 1895. (See Norman v. Thomson (1898) 121 Cal. 620, 628 [54 P. 143]; Estate of Abate (1958) 166 Cal. App. 2d 282, 292 [333 P.2d 200].) Thus we do not hold that plaintiff and defendant were "married," nor do we extend to plaintiff the rights which the Family Law Act grants valid or putative spouses; we hold only that she has the same rights to enforce contracts and to assert her equitable interest in property acquired through her effort as does any other unmarried person.

25. Our opinion does not preclude the evolution of additional equitable remedies to protect the expectations of the parties to a nonmarital relationship in cases in which existing remedies prove inadequate; the suitability of such remedies may be determined in later cases in light of the factual setting in which they arise.

26. We do not pass upon the question whether, in the absence of an express or implied contractual obligation, a party to a nonmarital relationship is entitled to support payments from the other party after the relationship terminates.

id. at 970, 972. How might one interpret the couple's continuing failure to marry? How does contract law, upon which *Marvin* relies, generally treat situations in which there is no meeting of the minds, for example, where one party desires (and perhaps acts out as well) all the "togetherness" of legal marriage while the other wishes to retain all the prerogatives of personal autonomy (and perhaps acts them out as well)?

4. Ought a court presume that, absent evidence to the contrary, there is no sharing agreement between cohabitants? Or should a sharing agreement be presumed absent an agreement to the contrary? Professor Bruch takes the latter position, Property Rights of De Facto Spouses, Including Thoughts on the Value of Homemakers' Services, 10 Fam. L.Q. 101 (1976). Do you see why this is a significant issue? Does *Marvin* address it?

5. For the view that men and women are not equally situated with respect to marriage and cohabitation, and that contract law is generally inadequate to resolve the economic issues that may arise when a marriage-like cohabitation is terminated by permanent separation or death, see Blumberg, Cohabitation Without Marriage: A Different Perspective, 28 UCLA L. Rev. 1125 (1981).

6. Lawful marriage encompasses myriad "incidents," many of which involve legal rights or claims against the government and other third parties. These include, inter alia, survivors' and derivative spouses' claims under workers' compensation and social security; special treatment under federal and state income, estate, inheritance, and gift tax laws; and wrongful death and loss of consortium claims against tortfeasors who injure or kill one's spouse. As Estate of Leslie indicates, the putative spouse has generally been treated as a spouse for both inter se and third party claims. The *Marvin* contractual rubric, however, extends only to the claims one cohabitant may have against the other; it is inadequate to establish entitlements against third parties. Blumberg, supra Note 5, at 1137-1159. California courts have generally followed the *Marvin* theme that cohabitation does not establish any claim to the status-based incidents of marriage. See, for example, Elden v. Sheldon, 46 Cal. 3d 267, 758 P.2d 582, 250 Cal. Rptr. 254 (1988) (no recovery for loss of consortium when one's cohabitant is tortiously injured; marriage is a prerequisite for loss of consortium claims); Estate of Edgett, 111 Cal. App. 3d 230, 168 Cal. Rptr. 686 (1980) (surviving cohabitant is "unrelated" for purposes of state inheritance tax and pays greater tax than "surviving spouse"); Department of Industrial Relations v. Workers' Comp. App. Bd., 94 Cal. App. 3d 72, 156 Cal. Rptr. 183 (1979), disapproved on other grounds in Atlantic Richfield Co. v. Workers' Comp. App. Bd., 31 Cal. 3d 715, 727, 644 P.2d 1257, 182 Cal. Rptr. 778 (1982) (in view of *Marvin*, reverses old view that workers' compensation claims are absolutely barred by meretricious relationship, but classifies cohabitant as "other dependent," rather than higher-status "surviving spouse"). See also Hinman v. Department of Personnel Admin., 167 Cal. App. 3d 516, 213 Cal. Rptr. 410 (1985) (upholding state denial of "family member" dental benefits to "partners" of homosexual employees).

When a cohabitant asserts a claim that traditionally arises not only out of the marital relationship but also extends, for example, to "dependents" or the "closely related," cohabitants have fared somewhat better, although the results are still mixed. See, for example, Department of Industrial Relations v. Workers' Comp. App. Bd., supra. But see Elden v. Sheldon, supra, (man witnessing tortious injury and death of woman with whom he had a significant and stable cohabitation was not sufficiently "closely related" to victim to maintain an action for negligent infliction of emotional distress). See also the cases determining whether a worker has satisfied the good cause requirement when she leaves a job and claims unemployment insurance benefits. (Leaving a job to accompany a spouse to a new location is invariably good cause.) Compare MacGregor v. Unemployment Ins. App. Bd., 37 Cal. 3d 205, 689 P.2d 453, 207 Cal. Rptr. 823 (1984) (when a worker leaves her employment to accompany a nonmarital partner to another state in order to maintain the familial relationship they have established with their young child, the good cause requirement is satisfied), with Norman v. Unemployment Ins. App. Bd., 34 Cal. 3d 1, 663 P.2d 904, 192 Cal. Rptr. 134 (1983) (good cause requirement is not satisfied when a worker leaves her job in order to accompany cohabitant to a new location). Distinguishing *Norman, MacGregor* explains that there need not be a marriage, but there must be a "compelling" family relationship.

However, same-sex and certain elderly opposite-sex cohabitants may qualify for many of the incidents of lawful marriage by registering as "domestic partners" under Family Code sections 297-298.5 (see pages 450-451 supra).

7. *When cohabitation is followed by marriage.* California courts have declined to assimilate, or tack, premarital cohabitation to the parties' subsequent marriage. Marriage of Bufford, 155 Cal. App. 3d 74, 202 Cal. Rptr. 20 (1984), holds that premarital property claims may not be raised in a divorce proceeding and may only be brought in an independent *Marvin* action. (For further discussion of independent claims and their consolidation with a divorce proceeding, see pages 488-490 infra.) Marriage of Bukaty, 180 Cal. App. 3d 143, 225 Cal. Rptr. 492 (1986), considered whether a divorcing wife who had premaritally cohabited with her husband might tack on the period of cohabitation to show a "long marriage" for the purpose of obtaining spousal support. *Bukaty* held that premarital cohabitation may not be tacked onto marriage. See also Marriage of Hebbring at page 487 infra and discussion in note 3 at page 489 infra. Compare Marriage of Chapman, 191 Cal. App. 3d 1308, 237 Cal. Rptr. 84 (1987) (the spouses' initial marriage and subsequent remarriage may be tacked together to constitute a "long marriage" for purposes of spousal support).

California cases indicate a strong preference for bright-line drawing. Other states have taken a more relaxed approach. See, for example, Marriage of Burton, 92 Or. App. 287, 290, 758 P.2d 394 (1988) ("The period of cohabitation before the marriage is relevant to determining the length of the marriage. . . . The court should consider the entire length of the relationship, not simply the time during which the parties are legally married, in determining the value of the assets for the property division.")

<hr/>

MARVIN v. MARVIN (ON REMAND)
122 Cal. App. 3d 871, 176 Cal. Rptr. 555 (1981)

<hr/>

COBEY, J.—Defendant, Lee Marvin, appeals from that portion of a judgment ordering him to pay to plaintiff, Michelle Marvin, the sum of $104,000, to be used by her primarily for her economic rehabilitation.

Defendant contends, among other things, that the challenged award is outside the issues of the case as framed by the pleadings of the parties (see Code Civ. Proc., §588) and furthermore lacks any basis in equity or in law. We agree and will therefore modify the judgment by deleting therefrom the challenged award.

This statement of facts is taken wholly from the findings of the trial court, which tried the case without a jury. The parties met in June 1964 and started living together occasionally in October of that year. They lived together almost continuously (except for business absences of his) from the spring of 1965 to May or June of 1970, when their cohabitation was ended at his insistence. This cohabitation was the result of an initial agreement between them to live together as unmarried persons so long as they both enjoyed their mutual companionship and affection.

More specifically, the parties to this lawsuit never agreed during their cohabitation that they would combine their efforts and earnings or would share equally in any property accumulated as a result of their efforts, whether individual or combined. They also never agreed during this period that plaintiff would relinquish her professional career as an entertainer and singer in order to devote her efforts full time to defendant as his companion and homemaker generally. Defendant did not agree during this period of cohabitation that he would provide all of plaintiff's financial needs and support for the rest of her life.

Furthermore, the trial court specifically found that: (1) defendant has never had any obligation to pay to plaintiff a reasonable sum as and for her maintenance; (2) plaintiff suffered no damage resulting from her relationship with defendant, including its termination and thus defendant did not become monetarily liable to plaintiff at all; (3) plaintiff actually benefited economically and socially from the cohabitation of the parties, including payment by defendant for goods and services for plaintiff's sole benefit in the approximate amount of $72,900, payment by defendant of the living expenses of the two of them of approximately $221,400, and other substantial specified gifts;[3] (4) a confidential and fiduciary relationship never existed between the parties with respect to property; (5) defendant was never unjustly enriched as a result of the relationship of the parties or of the services performed by plaintiff for him or for them; (6) defendant never acquired any property or money from plaintiff by any wrongful act.

The trial court specifically found in support of its challenged rehabilitation award that the market value of defendant's property at the time the parties separated exceeded $1 million, that plaintiff at the time of the trial of this case had been recently receiving unemployment insurance benefits, that it was doubtful that plaintiff could return to the career that she had enjoyed before the relationship of the parties commenced, namely, that of singer, that plaintiff was in need of rehabilitation—i.e., to learn new employable skills, that she should be able to accomplish such rehabilitation in two years and that the sum of $104,000 was not only necessary primarily for such rehabilitation, but also for her living expenses (including her debts) during this period of rehabilitation, and that defendant had the ability to pay this sum forthwith.

Moreover, the trial court concluded as a matter of law that inasmuch as defendant had terminated the relationship of the parties and plaintiff had no visible means of support, "in equity," she had a right to assistance by defendant until she could become self-supporting. The trial court explained that it fixed the award at the highest salary that the plaintiff had ever earned, namely, $1,000 a week for two years, although plaintiff's salary had been at that level for only two weeks and she ordinarily had earned less than one-half that amount weekly.

---

3. The trial court also found that "Defendant made a substantial financial effort to launch Plaintiff's career as a recording singer and to continue her career as a nightclub singer."

This is a judgment roll appeal in the sense that we have no transcript of the evidence taken at the apparently lengthy trial below. The issues in a lawsuit are, aside from those added by a pretrial order, either those framed by the pleadings or as expanded at trial. (See 4 Witkin, Cal. Procedure (2d ed. 1971) Trial, §336, p.3138.) Here, however, since we do not have before us the evidence taken at trial and there was no pretrial order expanding the issues, we can look only to the pleadings to determine the issues between the parties.

Plaintiff's amended complaint, upon which this action went to trial, asks, with respect to the support of plaintiff by defendant, only that defendant be ordered to pay to plaintiff a reasonable sum per month as and for her support and maintenance. Plaintiff did not ask in this basic pleading for any limited rehabilitative support of the type the trial court apparently on its own initiative subsequently awarded her. Consequently, the special findings of fact and conclusions of law in support of this award must be disregarded as not being within the issues framed by the pleadings. . . . When this is done, the challenged portion of the judgment becomes devoid of any support whatsoever and therefore must be deleted.

The trial court apparently based its rehabilitative award upon two footnotes in the opinion of our Supreme Court in this case. (Marvin v. Marvin (1976) 18 Cal. 3d 660 [134 Cal. Rptr. 815, 557 P.2d 106].) These are footnotes 25 and 26, which respectively read as follows:

> Our opinion does not preclude the evolution of additional equitable remedies to protect the expectations of the parties to a nonmarital relationship in cases in which existing remedies prove inadequate; the suitability of such remedies may be determined in later cases in light of the factual setting in which they arise. (Id. at p.684.)
>
> We do not pass upon the question whether, in the absence of an express or implied contractual obligation, a party to a nonmarital relationship is entitled to support payments from the other party after the relationship terminates. (Id. at p.685.)

There is no doubt that footnote 26 opens the door to a support award in appropriate circumstances. Likewise, under footnote 25, equitable remedies should be devised "to protect the expectations of the parties to a nonmarital relationship." The difficulty in applying either of these footnotes in the manner in which the trial court has done in this case is that, as already pointed out, the challenged limited rehabilitative award of the trial court is not within the issues of the case as framed by the pleadings and there is nothing in the trial court's findings to suggest that such an award is warranted to protect the expectations of *both* parties.

Quite to the contrary, as already noted, the trial court expressly found that plaintiff benefited economically and socially from her relationship with defendant and suffered no damage therefrom, even with respect to its termination. Furthermore, the trial court also expressly found that defendant never had any obligation to pay plaintiff a reasonable sum as and for her maintenance and that defendant had not been unjustly enriched by reason of the relationship or its termination and that defendant had never acquired anything of value from plaintiff by any wrongful act.

Furthermore, the special findings in support of the challenged rehabilitative award merely established plaintiff's need therefor and defendant's ability to respond to that need. This is not enough. The award, being nonconsensual in nature, must be supported by some recognized underlying obligation in law or in equity. A court of equity admittedly has broad powers, but it may not create totally new substantive rights under the guise of doing equity. . . .

The trial court in its special conclusions of law addressed to this point attempted to state an underlying obligation by saying that plaintiff had a right to assistance from defendant until she became self-supporting. But this special conclusion obviously conflicts with the earlier, more general, finding of the court that defendant has never had and did not then have any obligation to provide plaintiff with a reasonable sum for her support and maintenance and, in view of the already-mentioned findings of no damage (but benefit instead), no unjust enrichment and no wrongful act on the part of defendant with respect to either the relationship or its termination, it is clear that no basis whatsoever, either in equity or in law, exists for the challenged rehabilitative award. It therefore must be deleted from the judgment.[4]

The judgment under appeal is modified by deleting therefrom the portion thereof under appeal, namely, the rehabilitative award of $104,000 to plaintiff, Michelle Marvin. As modified it is affirmed. Costs on appeal are awarded to defendant, Lee Marvin.

POTTER, J., concurred.

KLEIN, P.J.—I dissent.

. . . As "it is impossible to reconcile this judgment with the findings . . . , it is clearly the duty of this court to reverse this judgment and remand the case to the trial court for . . . correction . . . of the [inconsistencies] in its findings [and conclusions] or its judgment or both." (Machado v. Machado, 26 Cal. App. 16, 18 [145 P. 738 (1914)]; 6 Witkin, Cal. Procedure (2d ed. 1971) Appeal, §541, pp.4482-4483.)

I would reverse the judgment and remand for further proceedings consistent with this dissent.

Respondent's petition for a hearing by the Supreme Court was denied October 7, 1981.

Notes and Questions

1. Why would a trial judge make an award that "lacks any basis in equity or law"? What was the probable source of the judge's inspiration?

2. Review the trial court's findings. Do you find them surprising? The trial was largely a swearing contest in which Michelle testified to the contract alleged in her pleadings, and Marvin flatly denied any agreement. The trial court believed Marvin, an understandable tendency when the stakes are great and the claim is inherently implausible. After all, Lee wielded all the economic power and therefore probably the psychological power as well. Why should he have promised any more than he had to—which was nothing more than a share of his high standard of living while the parties lived together? Indeed, even if he seemed to promise more in tender moments ("everything I have is yours"), his words were entirely gratuitous, unsup-

---

4. We obviously disagree with our dissenting colleague regarding the clarity and consistency (with the judgment) of the trial court's special findings of fact and conclusions of law in support of the challenged rehabilitative award. There is no need to remand this case to the trial court for correction of these matters since the award itself is without support in either equity or law.

ported by any consideration, and not the stuff upon which enforceable contracts are based. If Lee had intended to create a sharing partnership with Michelle, he would have married her. He knew about community property. He had been married before and would later marry again.

Lee was "between marriages." Yet for Michelle, the relationship occupied five of the "better years" of her life, years in which she pretty much abandoned her not very successful efforts to be self-supporting and became an unmarried home-maker. (It is true that the court found the parties never made a quid pro quo agreement that Michelle do this. Nevertheless, this is what Michelle did.) How would you resolve Michelle's termination claims? Do you agree with the court of appeal that an award is warranted only when it will "protect the expectations of *both* parties"? How do you understand footnotes 25 and 26 in the supreme court's *Marvin* opinion?

3. In the years immediately following the California Supreme Court's 1976 *Marvin* decision, the principles developed in *Marvin* were, with a few notable exceptions, widely adopted by other state appellate courts. For a listing of cases, see Blumberg, Cohabitation Without Marriage: A Different Perspective, at 28 UCLA L. Rev. 1125, n.2 (1981). Nevertheless, since then there have been remarkably few reported cases. Absent a written, signed contract, attorneys consider *Marvin* cases difficult. Trial judges tend to be skeptical of and hostile to plaintiff's claims and may strongly pressure her attorney to accept extremely low settlement offers.

Consider the observations of Richard E. Denner, a judge of the Los Angeles County Superior Court.

RICHARD E. DENNER, NONMARITAL COHABITATION AFTER *MARVIN*: IN SEARCH OF A STANDARD*
2 Cal. Fam. L. Monthly 229-235 (1986)

On December 27, 1976, the Supreme Court decided Marvin v. Marvin (1976) 18 Cal. 3d 660, 134 Cal. Rptr. 815, 557 P.2d 106. The principles that govern distribu-tion of property in a nonmarital relationship had allegedly been declared. The Family Law Act [now the Family Code] would not be the legal vehicle that would establish the rights of unmarried cohabitants. Unmarried parties were free to con-tract with one another while they lived together and the courts were directed to inquire if there were implied contracts or tacit understandings. Even in the absence of these, remedies based on quantum meruit or other equitable doctrines could be used.

The law of nonmarital cohabitation appeared to have been expanded in a sin-gle case to parallel the law of marital cohabitation. The law appeared to be ex-panding to meet the needs of those who wished to live together but not marry. *Marvin* contained [suggestions] that further parallels to the law of marital cohabita-tion would be made in future cases.

In the nine years since *Marvin*, those cases have not materialized. Many appellate decisions have limited *Marvin*'s effect. These trends are likely to continue unless the Supreme Court or Legislature changes the direction of the law.

NONMARITAL AND MARITAL RIGHTS COMPARED

Those who are married may obtain orders for custody and visitation of their children, child and spousal support, attorney's fees, division of marital property, and certain injunctive orders regarding protection of property, person and emotional well-being in a single proceeding under the Family Law Act [now the Family Code]. Unmarried cohabitants, by contrast, have frequently found that their legal relief was either more complex or in many cases nonexistent. . . .

Before *Marvin*, there was no question that the rights of unmarried cohabitants with respect to property differed from those of their married friends. Married persons may contract with each other with respect to their property. . . . However, if the parties made no agreement, their property was divided according to the rules contained in the Family [Code]. . . .

Unmarried cohabitants were not usually entitled to the fruits of each other's efforts even if the property was acquired during the period of cohabitation [Hill v. Estate of Westbrook (1950) 95 Cal. App. 2d 599, 602, 213 P.2d 727]. Only in those situations in which each had contributed funds or services to the acquisition of property or had expressly agreed to provide services, such as housekeeping for compensation, was recovery allowed [Vallera v. Vallera (1943) 21 Cal. 2d 681, 685, 134 P.2d 761]. If part of the agreement to share property rights was an understanding to live in a so-called "illicit" relationship in which one party had kept house and the other earned the income, the nonincome earner got nothing for his or her efforts [Trutalli v. Meraviglia (1932) 215 Cal. 698, 701-702, 12 P.2d 430].

The *Marvin* court, by contrast, apparently ignored the previous decisions' concern with the morality of the living arrangements. In a sense, many earlier decisions seemed to be based on the theory that recognition of property divisions in marriage-like living arrangements somehow depreciated the institution of marriage and was contrary to public policy. However, in 1976, the morality of a living arrangement that had great public acceptance seemed to be a lesser consideration.

Spousal support has long been a potential issue between marital partners under [Family Code §4330]. No spousal support rights existed for unmarried cohabitants before *Marvin*.

Attorney's fees were also frequently a potential issue in a marital matter under [Family Code §270]. However, unless unmarried cohabitants had children, so that fees could be awarded . . . for matters such as child support and custody, no statutes or cases authorized such an award to them.

PROMISE OF *MARVIN*

No one case is likely to completely develop an area of law. *Marvin* is illustrative of this proposition. First, the trial courts were given authority to fashion "additional equitable remedies" as suitable factual situations appeared in the future [Marvin v. Marvin (1976) 18 Cal. 3d 660, 684 fn. 25, 134 Cal. Rptr. 815, 557 P.2d 106]. Just what additional equitable remedies the Court had in mind is not clear from the opinion. However, it is obvious the majority intended that courts should not hesitate to apply other equitable remedies even if they were not mentioned in the original decision.

Second, the Court left open the possibility that spousal support for an unmarried cohabitant might be authorized in the absence of an express or implied contract [Marvin v. Marvin (1976) 18 Cal. 3d 660, 685 fn. 26, 134 Cal. Rptr. 815, 557 P.2d 106]. Spousal support was not a part of the original *Marvin* pleadings and its inclusion in the opinion without authority suggested to many that in future cases the Court would decide the issue noted, but not ruled on, in the original decision.

Third, the doctrine of implied contract might well have been applied, with appropriate appellate guidance, to situations in which parties live together for significant periods in stable relationships. This implication has many practical applications. Most *Marvin* agreements are alleged to be oral and while the statute of frauds may not apply to them, they are notoriously difficult to prove [see Marvin v. Marvin (1976) 18 Cal. 3d 660, 674 fn. 9, 134 Cal. Rptr. 815, 557 P.2d 106; see also Civ. Code §1624]. Like most married persons, most unmarried cohabitants do not write down their understandings, much less go to an attorney so that the agreement may be prepared as precisely as possible. Agreements usually have to be proved from the mouths of the parties themselves because usually no witnesses are present when the contracts were allegedly made. Memories that may have faded over time and become biased with self-interest are the only source of the precise terms or proof of existence of an oral contract about property, which may be worth thousands or even millions of dollars. Obviously, implications drawn from the actions of the parties are a far more objective way of adjudicating property rights.

No appellate cases have considered the factual circumstances under which a contract might be implied between unmarried cohabitants. For example, if both parties work, put their funds into a common bank account, and one party makes investments in his or her own name from that account, a contract to share proceeds is likely to be implied. However, what of the situation in which only one party has income and the other keeps house? Is this a situation in which a contract will be implied if the relationship is significant and stable? No cases yet provide the answer.

MARVIN'S RESULTS

What has happened in the appellate courts with *Marvin* issues has been far different than what the original case seemed to portend. Those advocating pro-*Marvin* positions on issues have not had many victories. . . .

[Judge Denner reviews the generally unsuccessful attempt of cohabitants to claim the incidents of marriage in third party actions. See pages 466-467 supra.]

While *Marvinizers* met little success in attaining rights under laws aiding married persons, results of the second appeal in *Marvin* restricted the effect of the original *Marvin* decision [Marvin v. Marvin (1981) 122 Cal. App. 3d 871, 873, 176 Cal. Rptr. 555 (hg. den.)]. The trial court found no contracts, express or implied, were made between the parties. It further found that the plaintiff gained both economically and socially from the arrangement and that the defendant was not unjustly enriched. It then found a rehabilitative need for the plaintiff to receive spousal support and the defendant's ability to pay, and ordered support for two years. Such findings might have been enough if the parties had been married.

The court of appeal noted that the issue of spousal support had not been framed by the pleadings and the award did not protect the expectations of both parties [Marvin v. Marvin (1981) 122 Cal. App. 3d 871, 876, 176 Cal. Rptr. 555]. Spousal support was appropriate only if there was an existing substantive right and the court said that a new right could not be created. It was also suggested that one might need to show unjust enrichment or some wrongful act of the defendant with respect to the relationship or its termination [Marvin v. Marvin (1981) 122 Cal. App. 3d 871, 877, 176 Cal. Rptr. 555]. A party's wrongful acts or his or her fault is not material to an award of spousal support in a marriage [Family Code §2335], but it apparently forms one of the grounds for an award of spousal support in a *Marvin* action.

While the second *Marvin* appeal was a "two-to-one" decision and the dissent suggested that a substantive right could be created, the Supreme Court's refusal to hear or depublish the decision must leave a trial court wondering whether this is what the Court intended the law to be.

IS THERE A FUTURE FOR *MARVIN*?

The future for the doctrines enunciated in *Marvin* is very unclear. If the trend observed in the appellate courts for the past nine years continues it is likely that *Marvin* will become a legal curiosity with application to very few persons. Very difficult problems of proof now exist for the party asserting a contract. No less bothersome is the thought that a person can be deprived of much of his or her property based on the word of another person alone. The use of the implied contract doctrine might resolve this problem but no appellate cases provide clear authority for this practice.

Furthermore, little guidance has been given for the application of marriage-like rights, such as spousal support and attorney's fees. Potentially, these rights may exist but recent court of appeal decisions do not support their legal viability. *Marvin-izers* obtain few if any statutory benefits that marital partners enjoy nor are they generally favored under the tort laws of the state.

In short, the law of nonmarital cohabitation is confused and does not appear to be consistent nor have clear objectives. One cannot ascertain whether the current law seeks a comprehensive structure that basically parallels marriage or some other status. Unless the Legislature or the Supreme Court provides guidance, this confusion is likely to continue.

Notes

1. *What percentage of American couples, other-sex and same-sex, live in nonmarital cohabitation?* During the last third of the 20th century, the number of unmarried cohabiting couples increased greatly in most western countries. In the United States, in 1998 there were 8 unmarried opposite-sex couples for every 100 married couples, up from 1 per 100 in 1970. More than one-third of these couples had a child under the age of 15 in the household.

The change is shown in the following table, taken from Bureau of the Census, Current Population Reports, Series P-20-484, Marital Status and Living Arrangements: March 1994 (1996), as corrected and updated through 1998 based on data for "Male, Married, Spouse present" in the Current Population Survey for 1994-1998, available at http://www.census.gov/population/www/socdemo/ms-la.html.

Unmarried Couple Households, by Presence of Children:
1970-1994 (1998)

| Year | Total Married Couples | Unmarried Couples | | | Unmarried Couples per 100 Married Couples |
		Total	Without Children Under 15	With Children Under 15	
1998	55,303,000	4,236,000	2,716,000	1,520,000	8
1994	54,261,000	3,661,000	2,391,000	1,270,000	7
1990	53,256,000	2,856,000	1,966,000	891,000	5
1985	51,114,000	1,983,000	1,380,000	603,000	4
1980	49,714,000	1,589,000	1,159,000	431,000	3
1970	44,593,000	523,000	327,000	196,000	1

In 1990, the Census Bureau began collecting data on same-sex couples (as opposed to "roommates"). The data since 1994 show the following:

| Year | Total Married Couples | Unmarried Couples | | | Opposite-Sex Couples per 100 Married Couples | Same-Sex Couples per 100 Married Couples | Total Unmarried Couples per 100 Married Couples |
		Opposite Sex	Same Sex	Total			
1998	55,303,000	4,236,000	1,674,000	5,910,000	8	3	11
1996	54,667,000	3,958,000	1,684,000	5,642,000	7	3	10
1994	54,261,000	3,661,000	1,678,000	5,339,000	7	3	10

Same-sex couples are less than half as frequent as unmarried opposite-sex couples. In combination, in 1998 there were 11 unmarried couples for every 100 married couples.

2. *Exploring the path not taken.* Marriage of Cary, supra at page 451, represents the path not taken by California and most American jurisdictions. Instead, most states have followed the *Marvin* contract rubric. *Cary,* in contrast, effectively asked: "Does this nonmarital couple (or family) look like a family? If so, why not apply our already well-developed family law?" Washington state does follow *Cary* with respect to property division. It applies community property law to long-term stable nonmarital domestic relationships. Connell v. Francisco, 898 P.2d 831 (Wash. 1995). See also Shuraleff v. Donnelly, 817 P.2d 764 (Or. Ct. App. 1991), and Wilbur v. De Lapp, 850 P.2d 1151, 1153 (Or. Ct. App. 1993) (conceptually straddling the fence between Washington and California); and Pickens v. Pickens, 490 So. 2d 872 (Miss. 1986) (homemaker has equitable claim to property accumulated during long-term cohabiting relationship without regard to contract inquiry).

Ontario (Canada) includes cohabitants as well as lawfully married persons in its statutory definition of "spouse" for purposes of spousal support obligations. A "spouse" includes:

either of a man or a woman who are not married to each other and have cohabited,

> (a) continuously for a period of not less than three years, or
> (b) in a relationship of some permanence if they are the natural or adoptive parents of a child.

Ontario Family Law Reform Act of 1986, §§29 and 30, codified at R.S.O 1990, c. F.3, s. 29 and s. 30. An earlier version of the Act required, under subsection (a), continuous cohabitation for not less than five years. Ontario Family Law Reform Act of 1979, 1978 Ont. Stat. 5, ch. 2, §14(b).

In M and H [1999] 2 S.C.R. 3, a same-sex cohabitant challenged the Ontario statutory definition ("either of a man or a woman who are not married to each other and have cohabited") as violative of the equal protection guarantee of the Canadian Charter (equivalent to the United States Constitution). Reasoning that financial dependency and interdependency, to which the statute is designed to respond, are no less likely in same-sex cohabitation than in heterosexual cohabitation, the Supreme Court of Canada concluded that the exclusion of same-sex cohabitants is not rationally connected to the legislative objective of ensuring adequate economic provision for cohabitants at the termination of their relationship.

The British Columbia spousal support statute includes same-sex partners within its definition of spouses. See Family Relations Act of British Columbia [R.S.B.C. 1996, as amended October 1, 1998], ch. 128, §1 (for purposes of spousal support, a "spouse" includes a person who "lived with another person in a marriage-like relationship for a period of at least 2 years . . . and, for purposes of this Act, the marriage-like relationship may be between persons of the same gender").

The New South Wales (Australia) Property (Relationships) Act 1984 (NSW), as amended to include same-sex relationships by the Property (Relationships) Legislation Amendment Act 1999, defines a de facto relationship as a "relationship between two adult persons . . . who live together as a couple, and . . . who are not married to one another" §4(1). The legislation includes a list of criteria to determine whether a relationship constitutes a de facto relationship. De facto relationships give rise to support and property rights at the termination of the relationship by inter vivos separation, as well as by death. The law of New South Wales also creates quasi-marital rights against third parties and the state. See generally Study Paper 4, Recognizing Same-Sex Relationships, Law Commission of New Zealand (1999).

In 2000, the government of New Zealand rejected the Law Commission proposal (supra) that New Zealand create a special domestic partnership status for the one out of seven New Zealand couples, same-sex and opposite-sex, who live in nonmarital cohabitation. Instead, the government proposed and enacted legislation that treats long-term (more than three years) stable nonmarital cohabitation equally with marriage. The legislation brings such cohabitation, same-sex and opposite-sex, under the New Zealand Marital Property Act, which at dissolution requires an equal division of property acquired by either party during the relationship and prescribes continuing support obligations in appropriate cases. The Act, renamed the Property (Relationships) Act,[14] also treats marital and nonmarital couples equally with respect to death rights. Like married couples, New Zealand de facto couples have the contractual right to opt out of property division, provided that their contract is not "clearly unfair" to one of the parties at the termination of

---

14. Property (Relationships) Amendment Act, 2001 (N.Z.), available at http://www.brookers. co.nz/property_act/dfault.htm.

their relationship. The government's decision to treat nonmarital couples equally with married couples, rather than create a special status for them, was widely applauded by the New Zealand media. See, for example, New Property Law One Step Forward, The New Zealand Herald, April 4, 2000, at A10.

3. *The American Law Institute's treatment of nonmarital cohabitation.* Chapter 6 of the Principles of the Law of Marital Dissolution addresses nonmarital cohabitation. The ALI treatment begins with the premise that parties may always explicitly contract for the rules that will govern their relationship. And the ALI allows them to do so, within the formal and substantive limitations of Chapter 7. (See pages 104-105 supra.) Thus the quest in Chapter 6 is for a set of default rules to apply to parties who have not explicitly agreed otherwise. With respect to claims that one nonmarital partner may have against the other at the termination of their relationship (the Principles deal only with the obligations of the parties to each other), the Principles take the view that the equitable considerations that shape the rules governing at the end of a marriage apply equally at the end of a stable nonmarital cohabitation of substantial duration, whether same-sex or opposite-sex. Thus the Principles, with minor variation, apply at the termination of such nonmarital cohabitation the same rules that control property distribution and continuing obligations, if any, to share income after a marriage has ended. The Principles characterize couples subject to these rules as *domestic partners,* defined as "two persons of the same or opposite sex, not married to one another, who for a significant period of time share a primary residence and a life together as a couple." Despite the generality of this definition, few cases should require intrusive inquiry into the lives of the parties because the Principles use a per se rule and a presumption, which are triggered by objective indices, to identify most domestic partners. Principles of the Law of Family Dissolution: Analysis and Recommendations §6.03 (2002). Chapter 6 was presented to the ALI membership for final approval in May 2000. After contentious debate, it was approved by a substantial majority of the members. Nevertheless, Chapter 6 has attracted more criticism than any other chapter of the Principles. See, for example, David Westfall, Forcing Incidents of Marriage on Unmarried Cohabitants: The American Law Institute's Principles of Family Dissolution, 76 Notre Dame L. Rev. 1467 (2001); Lynne Marie Kohn, How Will the Proliferation and Recognition of Domestic Partnerships Affect Marriage?, 4 J.L. & Fam. Stud. 105 (2002); and articles collected in Symposium on the ALI Principles of the Law of Family Dissolution, 2001 BYU L. Rev. 857-1278. Of the 14 symposium articles on the seven chapters of the Principles, six articles are devoted to the ALI's treatment of domestic partners. See additionally Symposium on the ALI Principles of the Law of Family Dissolution, 4 J.L. & Fam. Stud. 1-228 (2002).

The black letter provisions of Chapter 6 are as follows:

§6.01 Scope

(1) This Chapter governs the financial claims of domestic partners against one another at the termination of their relationship. For the purpose of defining relationships to which this Chapter applies, domestic partners are two persons of the same or opposite sex, not married to one another, who for a significant period of time share a primary residence and a life together as a couple, as determined by §6.03.

(2) A contract between domestic partners that (i) waives or limits claims that would otherwise arise under this Chapter or (ii) provides remedies not provided

by this Chapter, is enforceable according to its terms and displaces any inconsistent claims under this Chapter, so long as it satisfies the requirements of Chapter 7 for the enforcement of agreements.

(3) Nothing in this Chapter forecloses contract claims between persons who have no claims under this Chapter, but who have formed a contract that is enforceable under applicable law.

(4) Claims for custodial and decisionmaking responsibilities, and for child support, are governed by Chapters 2 and 3, and not by this Chapter.

(5) Claims arise under this Chapter from any period during which one or both of the domestic partners were married to someone else only to the extent that they do not compromise the marital claims of a domestic partner's spouse.

§6.02   Objectives of the Rules Governing Termination of the Relationship of Domestic Partners

(1) The primary objective of Chapter 6 is fair distribution of the economic gains and losses incident to termination of the relationship of domestic partners by

(a) allocating property according to principles that respect both individual ownership rights and equitable claims that each partner has on the property in consequence of the relationship, and that are consistent and predictable in application; and

(b) allocating financial losses that arise at the termination of the relationship according to equitable principles that are consistent and predictable in application. Equitable principles of loss recognition and allocation should take into account

(i) loss of earning capacity arising from a partner's disproportionate share of caretaking responsibilities for children or other persons to whom the partners have a moral obligation;

(ii) losses that arise from the changes in life opportunities and expectations caused by the adjustments individuals ordinarily make over the course of a long relationship;

(iii) disparities in the financial impact of a short relationship on the partners' postseparation lives, as compared to their lives before the relationship; and

(iv) the primacy of the income earner's claim to benefit from the fruits of his own labor, as compared to the claims of a domestic partner.

(2) The secondary objective of Chapter 6 is protection of society from social-welfare burdens that should be borne, in whole or in part, by individuals.

§6.03   Determination That Persons Are Domestic Partners

(1) For the purpose of defining relationships to which this Chapter applies, domestic partners are two persons of the same or opposite sex, not married to one another, who for a significant period of time share a primary residence and a life together as a couple.

(2) Persons are domestic partners when they have maintained a common household, as defined in Paragraph (4), with their common child, as defined in Paragraph (5), for a continuous period that equals or exceeds a duration, called the *cohabitation parenting period,* set in a rule of statewide application.

(3) Persons not related by blood or adoption are presumed to be domestic partners when they have maintained a common household, as defined in Paragraph (4), for a continuous period that equals or exceeds a duration, called the *cohabitation period,* set in a rule of statewide application. The presumption is rebuttable by evidence that the parties did not share life together as a couple, as defined by Paragraph (7).

(4) Persons *maintain a common household* when they share a primary residence only with each other and family members; or when, if they share a household with other unrelated persons, they act jointly, rather than as individuals, with respect to management of the household.

(5) Persons have a *common child* when each is either the child's legal parent or parent by estoppel, as defined by §2.03.

(6) When the requirements of Paragraph (2) or (3) are not satisfied, a person asserting a claim under this Chapter bears the burden of proving that for a significant period of time the parties shared a primary residence and a life together as a couple, as defined in Paragraph (7). Whether a period of time is significant is determined in light of all the Paragraph (7) circumstances of the parties' relationship and, particularly, the extent to which those circumstances wrought change in the life of one or both parties.

(7) Whether persons share a life together as a couple is determined by reference to all the circumstances, including

(a) the oral or written statements or promises made to one another, or representations jointly made to third parties, regarding their relationship;

(b) the extent to which the parties intermingled their finances;

(c) the extent to which their relationship fostered the parties' economic interdependence, or the economic dependence of one party upon the other;

(d) the extent to which the parties engaged in conduct and assumed specialized or collaborative roles in furtherance of their life together;

(e) the extent to which the relationship wrought change in the life of either or both parties;

(f) the extent to which the parties acknowledged responsibilities to each other, as by naming the other the beneficiary of life insurance or of a testamentary instrument, or as eligible to receive benefits under an employee benefit plan;

(g) the extent to which the parties' relationship was treated by the parties as qualitatively distinct from the relationship either party had with any other person;

(h) the emotional or physical intimacy of the parties' relationship;

(i) the parties' community reputation as a couple;

(j) the parties' participation in a commitment ceremony or registration as a domestic partnership;

(k) the parties' participation in a void or voidable marriage that, under applicable law, does not give rise to the economic incidents of marriage;

(l) the parties' procreation of, adoption of, or joint assumption of parental functions toward a child; and

(m) the parties' maintenance of a common household, as defined by Paragraph (4).

§6.04 Domestic-Partnership Property Defined

(1) Except as provided in Paragraph (3) of this section, property is domestic-partnership property if it would be marital property . . . had the domestic partners been married to one another during the domestic-partnership period.

(2) The domestic-partnership period

(a) starts when the domestic partners began sharing a primary residence, unless either partner shows that the parties did not begin sharing life together as a couple until a later date, in which case the domestic-partnership period starts on that later date, and

(b) ends when the parties ceased sharing a primary residence.

For the purpose of this paragraph, parties who are the biological parents of a common child began sharing life together as a couple no later than the date on which their common child was conceived.

(3) Property that would be recharacterized as marital property under [the transmutation-over-time provisions] if the parties had been married, is not domestic-partnership property.

§6.05   Allocation of Domestic-Partnership Property

Domestic-partnership property should be divided according to the principles set forth for the division of marital property. . . .

§6.06   Compensatory Payments

(1) Except as otherwise provided in this section,

(a) a domestic partner is entitled to compensatory payments on the same basis as a spouse . . . , and

(b) wherever a rule implementing a [compensatory payment] principle makes the duration of the marriage a relevant factor, the application of that principle in this Chapter should instead employ the duration of the domestic partnership period, as defined in §6.04(2).

(2) No claim arises under this section against a domestic partner who is neither a legal parent nor a parent by estoppel . . . of a child whose care provides the basis of the claim.

F.   THE END OF THE ECONOMIC COMMUNITY

When marriage ends by death, the community ceases at the time of death. The survivor continues to own his or her interest in the community property; the decedent's share passes by will or intestacy.

When marriage ends before the death of either party, the choice of a point at which the economic community should be deemed to end is more problematic. Historically, California treated the husband's earnings as community property until there was a judicial termination of the marriage, that is, a judgment of legal separation or divorce. Yet the wife's earnings were her separate property after permanent physical separation. In 1971, the legislature made the governing statute sex-neutral by extending the treatment of the wife's earnings to those of the husband. California Family Code section 771 now provides:

> The earnings and accumulations of a spouse . . . , while living separate and apart from the other spouse, are the separate property of the spouse.

MARRIAGE OF BARAGRY
73 Cal. App. 3d 444, 140 Cal. Rptr. 779 (1977)

FLEMING, J.—Wife appeals that part of the interlocutory judgment of dissolution which fixes the date of the parties' separation as 4 August 1971, the date husband moved out of the family home. She contends the date should be 14 October 1975, the date husband filed his petition for dissolution, and, alternatively, that husband is estopped to contend the separation took place before 14 October 1975.

The facts are undisputed, and the issue is the legal conclusion that should flow from the facts. The parties were married in September 1956, and have two daughters, now 13 and 10. Husband is an eye physician and surgeon. After a quarrel with wife, husband moved out of the family residence on 4 August 1971 and stayed for a time on his boat. Thereafter he took an apartment, into which his 28-year-old girl-friend and employee, Karen Lucien, moved and in which both now live. Although not sleeping in the family residence, husband maintained continuous and frequent contacts with his family. He ate dinner at home with wife almost every night in 1971 and 1972 and thereafter ate at home at least three to five times a week. He maintained his mailing address at the home. In 1971 and 1972, he took wife and daughters to Yosemite and San Francisco. On Christmas Eve, 1971, he slept at home. Throughout 1972 and 1973, he took his family to all UCSB basketball games. In 1973, he went with his wife to Sun Valley for a week without the children. He frequently took wife to social occasions—parties at friends' homes, dinners for professional and academic groups, outings with other doctors and their wives. He sent wife numerous Christmas, birthday, and anniversary cards throughout the years 1971 to 1975, including a card stating, "I love you" in 1973, and an anniversary card with a huge box of flowers in September 1975. In 1974 he filed an enrollment card at their daughter's private school stating that she lived at home with both parents. The parties continued to file joint income tax returns, and husband maintained his voting registration at the home address. He paid all the household bills and supported his family. He regularly brought his laundry home to wife, who washed and ironed it twice a month.

The parties had no sexual relations after 4 August 1971. Wife knew husband was living with Karen but wife desired a reconciliation, and continued to hope husband would return. Husband did not tell her he was never coming back. Husband testified he took wife on outings in order to preserve social appearances and to keep in touch with his children, who otherwise would not come to see him. He delayed filing for divorce because his "solid mid-Western upbringing" made him reluctant to file for divorce. Both parties agree that their relationship was entirely amicable but nonsexual after August 1971 and that they maintained the habits and appearance of a married couple except that husband slept with Karen. For four years husband maintained the facade of a marital relationship, but he now claims to have been . . . separated from his wife. As proof he tenders his extra-marital activities.

What little law defines separation under Civil Code section 5118 [now Family Code section 771] holds that "living separate and apart" refers to "that condition when spouses have come to a parting of the ways with no present intention of resuming marital relations." (In re Marriage of Imperato (1975) 45 Cal. App. 3d 432, 435-436 [119 Cal. Rptr. 590].) That husband and wife may live in separate residences is not determinative. (Makeig v. United Security Bank & Trust Co. (1931) 112 Cal.

App. 138, 143 [296 P. 673]; Tobin v. Galvin (1874) 49 Cal. 34.) The question is whether the parties' conduct evidences a complete and final break in the marital relationship. Here the only evidence of such a break is the absence of an active sexual relationship between the parties and husband's cohabitation elsewhere with a girlfriend. In our view such evidence is not tantamount to . . . separation.

At bench the bone of contention is the community property character of husband's earnings from 1971 to 1975. To determine whether the conduct of the parties was such as to transmute the nature of that property from community to separate, we briefly recall the basic nature of the community property system. Property acquired during a legal marriage is strongly presumed to be community property. . . . That presumption is fundamental to the community property system . . . and stems from Mexican-Spanish law which likens the marital community to a partnership. Each partner contributes services of value to the whole, and with certain limitations and exceptions both share equally in the profits. . . . So long as wife is contributing her special services to the marital community she is entitled to share in its growth and prosperity. . . . "Under the principles of community property law, the wife, by virtue of her position as wife, made to that value the same contribution as does a wife to any of the husband's earnings and accumulations during marriage. She is as much entitled to be recompensed for that contribution as if it were represented by the increased value of stock in a family business." (Referring to valuation of goodwill.) (Golden v. Golden (1969) 270 Cal. App. 2d 401, 405 [75 Cal. Rptr. 735].)

At bench, husband was presumably enjoying a captain's paradise, savoring the best of two worlds, and capturing the benefits of both. Wife was furnishing all the normal wifely contributions to a marriage that husband was willing to accept and most of the services normally furnished in a 20-year-old marriage. Husband was reaping the advantages of those services and may be presumed to owe part of his professional success during that four-year period to wife's social and domestic efforts on his behalf. One who enjoys the benefit of a polygamous lifestyle must be prepared to accept its accompanying financial burdens. (Marvin v. Marvin (1976) 18 Cal. 3d 660 [134 Cal. Rptr. 815, 557 P.2d 106]; Civ. Code, §3521.) During the period that spouses preserve the appearance of marriage, they both reap its benefits, and their earnings remain community property. To hold otherwise would be tantamount to saying that because husband slept on the living room couch for four years, or because he regularly slept elsewhere with another woman, wife can be deprived of her share in the household earnings.

Because there is no sufficient evidence to rebut the presumptive status of a legal marriage continuing until 14 October 1975, the judgment is reversed, and the cause is remanded for further proceedings. Costs to wife.

ROTH, P.J., and BEACH, J., concurred.

A petition for a rehearing was denied October 14, 1977, and respondent's petition for a hearing by the Supreme Court was denied November 17, 1977.

Notes and Questions

1. *Separation or intent?* Did Dr. Baragry's separation argument fail because he neglected to tell Mrs. Baragry that he was never coming back? If he had told Mrs. Baragry that there was no hope for a full reconciliation, would he have effected a termination of the economic community? Supposing Mrs. Baragry were satisfied

with her husband's unusual domestic arrangements and did not desire a return to the status quo ante Karen, would the Baragry facts warrant a finding that the economic community had come to an end? In short, does Dr. Baragry's claim founder on "separation" or "intent"?

2. *Does reconciliation before a final divorce wipe out any prior "permanent separation"?* In Marriage of Jaschke, 43 Cal. App. 4th 408, 50 Cal. Rptr. 2d 658 (1996), the husband left the wife when he discovered her infidelity, and he promptly filed for divorce. An interlocutory default judgment was entered. A week later, the husband purchased property. The parties later reconciled and the divorce action was ultimately dismissed by stipulation of the parties. Six months after their reconciliation, the parties separated again, this time for good. At issue was the character of the property purchased by the husband during the. initial separation. The trial court held that it was the husband's separate property because, when the husband purchased it, he intended to terminate the marriage. The court of appeal reversed, holding that there cannot be a "complete and final break in the marital relationship" when the parties later reconcile. The California Supreme Court was not satisfied by this analysis. In denying a petition for review, it ordered that the opinion of the court of appeal not be officially published.

3. *The national landscape.* The California view that the economic community may be terminated by informal separation has been followed by few jurisdictions. (See Wash. Rev. Code §26.16.140 (2002) and Suter v. Suter, 97 Idaho 461, 546 P.2d 1169 (1976).) In most community property and equitable distribution jurisdictions, the economic community continues until the marriage comes to a legal conclusion, either by death, divorce, or a judicial decree of legal separation. A small but growing number look to the date on which the divorce complaint is filed. See, for example, Schanck v. Schanck, 717 P.2d 1 (Alaska 1986); Brandenburg v. Brandenburg, 83 N.J. 198, 206, 416 A.2d 327, 333 (1980); Jolis v. Jolis, 111 Misc. 2d 965, 968, 446 N.Y.S.2d 138, 140, aff'd., 98 A.D.2d 692, 470 N.Y.S.2d 584 (1983). The ALI Principles provide that the community ends on

> the filing and service of a petition for dissolution (if that petition ultimately results in a decree dissolving the marriage), unless there are facts, set forth in written findings of the trial court . . . , establishing that use of another date is necessary to avoid a substantial injustice.

The American Law Institute, Principles of the Law of Family Dissolution: Analysis and Recommendations §4.03 (5) (2002).

Professor Carol Bruch has strongly criticized the California view. She observes that almost one-third of separating couples later reconcile, that litigation-oriented behavior is not conducive to reconciliation, and that the California rule that the economic community ends on informal separation unnecessarily precipitates adversary and litigious behavior between spouses. Bruch, The Legal Import of Informal Marital Separations: A Survey of California Law and a Call for Change, 65 Cal. L. Rev. 1015 (1977).

IX

PROPERTY DISTRIBUTION AT DIVORCE

A.   THE JURISDICTION OF THE COURT

CALIFORNIA FAMILY CODE SECTION 2550

Equal division of community estate

Except upon the written agreement of the parties, or an oral stipulation of the parties in open court, or as otherwise provided in this division, in a proceeding for dissolution of marriage or for legal separation of the parties, the court shall, either in its judgment of dissolution of the marriage, in its judgment of legal separation of the parties, or at a later time if it expressly reserves jurisdiction to make such a property division, divide the community estate of the parties equally.

ROBINSON v. ROBINSON
65 Cal. App. 2d 118, 150 P.2d 7 (1944)

WOOD (W.J.), J.—In this action to quiet title plaintiff has appealed from a judgment awarding to defendant a life interest in the real property which is the subject of the litigation.

An interlocutory decree was awarded to Theresa Robinson, defendant herein, on June 10, 1942, she having theretofore commenced an action against plaintiff for separate maintenance in which she later changed her prayer to ask for a divorce. In the divorce action she listed various properties of the parties, some of which she alleged to be community property. She specifically alleged that the real estate which is the subject of the present litigation was the separate property of the plaintiff herein, Lewis Robinson. A cross-complaint was filed in the divorce action and the court in its interlocutory decree of divorce ordered the plaintiff herein to pay to defendant herein the sum of $12.50 per month until the further order of the court and also gave her "the right to remain in and to continue to reside and enjoy possession of the premises she now occupies at 1609 East 110th Street, Los Angeles." A part of the community property was awarded to each of the parties. In the final decree of divorce, which was entered on June 17, 1943, no reference was made to the real property involved in this action.

The present action was commenced on January 12, 1943. By its judgment entered on October 5, 1943, the court decreed that plaintiff is the owner in fee of the land described in the complaint, "subject however, to a life estate therein of defendant Theresa Robinson during her natural life to use the improvement thereon consisting of a dwelling known as 1609 East 110th Street, Los Angeles, California."

The power of the court in disposing of the property of the parties in a divorce action is limited to their community property. In such a proceeding the court has no power to dispose of the separate property of one of the parties, nor to carve out a life estate therein. (Roy v. Roy, 29 Cal. App. 2d 596 [85 P.2d 223].) In the divorce action of the parties to the present litigation no issue was made concerning the ownership of the real estate in question, for it was specifically alleged by the wife that the realty was the separate property of the husband. The court therefore was without jurisdiction to award to the wife a life estate therein.

The judgment is reversed. . . . MOORE, P.J., and McCOMB, J., concurred.

Notes and Questions

1. The court's jurisdiction is further limited when the respondent defaults. Even though the court may have personal jurisdiction over the respondent and perhaps in rem jurisdiction over the community property as well, when a respondent defaults there can be no property division unless it is specifically requested in the divorce petition. Burtnett v. King, 33 Cal. 2d 805, 205 P.2d 657 (1949), based this conclusion on California default judgment statutes; it is arguably also compelled by due process notice requirements.

2. The parties may join together to request the divorce court to resolve separate property ownership questions. When such issues have been pleaded and tried before the divorce court, it may dispose of them. See, e.g., Marriage of Dorris, 160 Cal. App. 3d 1208, 207 Cal. Rptr. 160 (1984); Crook v. Crook, 184 Cal. App. 2d 745, 7 Cal. Rptr. 892 (1960); Huber v. Huber, 27 Cal. 2d 784, 793, 167 P.2d 708 (1946). See also Marriage of Gagne, 225 Cal. App. 3d 277, 274 Cal. Rptr. 750 (1990).

3. In 1985, the legislature added California Civil Code section 4800.4, now Family Code section 2650:

> In a proceeding for division of the community estate, the court has jurisdiction, at the request of either party, to divide the separate property interests of the parties in real and personal property, wherever situated and whenever acquired, held by the parties as joint tenants or tenants in common. The property shall be divided together with, and in accordance with the same procedure for and limitations on, division of [the] community estate.

What sort of property remains beyond the divorce court's jurisdiction? How does Family Code section 2650 interact with sections 2581 and 2640? In light of the 1986 revision of section 2581, does section 2650 serve any purpose?

MARRIAGE OF HEBBRING
207 Cal. App. 3d 1260, 255 Cal. Rptr. 488 (1989)

KING, J. — In this case we hold that . . . the trial court possesses jurisdiction in a marital dissolution action to order reimbursement for separate property of one spouse which has been wilfully destroyed by the other from the community property share of the latter. . . .

Jess and Cindy Hebbring had been married for two years, two months, and had no children when they separated on January 2, 1984.[3] Cindy filed for dissolution on October 3, 1984. . . .

On February 21, 1985, Cindy obtained a temporary restraining order precluding Jess from disposing of her separate property jewelry, which he had taken. In response to an order to show cause to extend this order, Jess filed a declaration stating he had thrown Cindy's jewelry into the sea after separation, when it appeared no reconciliation would occur. Cindy asked the court to reimburse her for the jewelry. The trial court found the jewelry was Cindy's separate property and ordered Jess to reimburse her the stipulated value, $5,100, from his share of the community property. Jess contends the trial court lacked jurisdiction in a dissolution action to award Cindy what he claims were damages for the tort of conversion.

The Family Law Act limits the trial court's jurisdiction in a dissolution proceeding to characterizing property as separate or community, confirming separate property to a particular spouse, and dividing the community and quasi-community property. It lacks jurisdiction to dispose of either spouse's separate property. (In re Marriage of Buford (1984) 155 Cal. App. 3d 74, 78 [202 Cal. Rptr. 20]; In re Marriage of McNeill (1984) 160 Cal. App 3d 548, 565-566 [206 Cal. Rptr. 641].) Thus the trial court in a dissolution action may not impose a constructive trust on one spouse's separate property nor may it award damages for conversion. To obtain such relief, a spouse must file an independent civil action which may then be consolidated with the dissolution action. (In re Marriage of Buford, supra, 155 Cal. App. 3d at pp.78-79.)

In this case the trial court did not attempt to dispose of either spouse's separate property, nor did it award Cindy damages for the tort of conversion. Having found the destroyed jewelry to be Cindy's separate property, the court simply required Jess to reimburse her for its value from his share of the community property. Similarly, in In re Marriage of McNeill, supra, 160 Cal. App. 3d at page 566, the court held a trial court might impress a lien against the community proceeds of a wife

---

3. Although the parties lived together for seven and one-half years prior to their marriage, no "*Marvin*" action was filed. (Marvin v. Marvin (1976) 18 Cal. 3d 660 [134 Cal. Rptr. 815, 557 P.2d 106].) Thus there is no claim of property or support rights pursuant to an express or implied agreement. Spousal support rights are determined considering the factors set forth in section 4801, subdivision (a) [now Family Code section 4320]. The duration of the marriage under that section is limited to the period between the date of marriage and date of separation. The premarital cohabitation period cannot be tacked onto this period. (In re Marriage of Bukaty (1986) 180 Cal. App. 3d 143 [225 Cal. Rptr. 492].)

who refused to return furniture and furnishings confirmed as husband's separate property. Although the court in *McNeill* noted that husband had filed an independent civil action which had been consolidated with the dissolution (id. at p.567), it also relied on equitable principles. "Even prior to enactment of the Family Law Act, courts fashioned remedies to enforce their orders. . . . We find no error in the conditional order to return the property or be charged for its equivalent, as the court may fashion an order to effect its decree. (§4380 [now Family Code §290].)" (Id. at p.568.)

It is not in either spouse's interest to expend time and money to pursue this type of claim in a separate civil action, nor should the taxpayers be required to provide such a forum when the dispute can be easily, fairly and completely resolved within the dissolution action. (See Lossing v. Superior Court (1989) 207 Cal. App. 3d 635 [255 Cal. Rptr. 18]; Green v. Uccelli (1989) 207 Cal. App. 3d 1112 [255 Cal. Rptr. 315].) In any event, dissolution proceedings, despite our highly detailed statutory scheme, still retain some vestige of equity and the trial court properly relied upon equitable principles. Jess's wilful destruction of Cindy's jewelry certainly constitutes "unclean hands" and precludes his seeking judicial relief. He may not complain when his conduct was so egregious.

. . . [T]he judgment is affirmed. The parties shall each bear their own costs on appeal.

Low, P.J., and HANING, J., concurred.

Notes and Questions

1. Are you persuaded by Justice King that the divorce court did not award Cindy damages for the tort of conversion? Do you nevertheless agree with Justice King that reimbursement to Cindy should be within the divorce court's jurisdiction? If so, is the divorce court's jurisdiction too narrowly drawn? Ought the divorce court, for example, be empowered to settle all claims between the parties incident to the breakdown of their marriage?

2. As *Hebbring* indicates, an attorney must file independent civil actions in order to raise claims that exceed the *divorce* court's jurisdiction. Such civil claims may generally be consolidated with the dissolution action. For good discussion of divorce-related consolidation, see Marriage of McNeill, 160 Cal. App. 3d 548, 206 Cal. Rptr. 641 (1984). *McNeill* illustrates a variety of possibilities:

> Wife represented many material facts to husband during their six-year marriage. She told him she was an attorney, had a master's degree in accounting, and was suffering from cancer. Further she led him to believe there was an outstanding premarital judgment against her which she said could affect their assets. All were lies.
>
> Husband owned a residence before the marriage. Shortly thereafter, title was changed by grant deed from his name alone to "Samuel Blair McNeill III, and Jo B. McNeill, Husband and Wife." Two years later, husband, upon wife's urging and believing she needed complete rest and quiet because of alleged chemotherapy treatments, moved out of the home. The next year wife told husband she had only 90 days to live and encouraged him to execute documents she had prepared transferring their assets to a trust. Husband, relying on wife's legal and tax expertise and allegations of her imminent

death, signed all of the documents. In fact, wife had presented husband with a marital settlement agreement transferring almost all of his assets to her and a grant deed to the residence transferring title to her alone.

Husband did not learn the house had been put into wife's name until a year later. He filed suit claiming the house was his separate property but did not immediately serve her. Wife, still very much alive, filed a petition for dissolution, alleging all property, including the residence, had been divided by the property settlement agreement. Husband's response in the dissolution action pleaded the agreement was void and the residence was his separate property. He also amended his civil complaint to include four causes of action. In the first, he asked for cancellation of the deed and to quiet title to the residence. The second cause of action alleged fraud and sought a declaration that the deed and settlement agreement were void. He further requested compensatory and exemplary damages. Husband's third cause of action alleged constructive fraud resulting from wife's breach of her fiduciary duty and again sought cancellation of the deed and marital agreement, plus compensatory and exemplary damages. Husband pleaded rescission of the deed and marital settlement agreement in the fourth cause of action. . . . Husband's motion to consolidate his action and the dissolution was granted. The parties also stipulated to an advisory jury which heard the issue of fraud.

Id. at 555-556.

In a brief concurrence to *McNeill*, Justice Wallin expressed concern about consolidation:

> I concur in the result. The trial court's decision to consolidate the civil action with the dissolution petition is troubling because the former included requests for mental distress and punitive damages. These claims inevitably must be supported by testimony inimical to the no fault concept of the Family Law Act. Since the majority has stricken the mental distress damages and correctly concluded the punitive damages awarded are reasonable, consolidation in this case caused no harm.
>
> In general, however, consolidation of a civil action and a dissolution petition should only be allowed when claims other than intentional torts are at issue. *Marvin* claims, contract disputes or disagreements concerning the characterization of property can properly be addressed in a consolidated proceeding because they do not raise questions of fault or involve emotional fingerpointing.

Id. at 569. Do you agree with Justice Wallin's concerns? From your reading of post-1970 community property cases, to what extent does current law exclude consideration of fault? Assuming that Justice Wallin is expressing legitimate concerns, do you agree with his conclusion that "consolidation in this case caused no harm"?

3. The text of *Hebbring* outlines the *procedural* issues arising from the divorce court's limited subject matter jurisdiction. Footnote 3, in contrast, poses a substantive issue that cannot be resolved by satisfying procedural requirements. Both Jess and Cindy worked full-time. Jess earned $41,800 a year in the merchant marine while Cindy earned $20,000 a year as a law office manager. The trial court ordered that Jess pay Cindy $500 a month spousal support for six months, and the court reserved jurisdiction with respect to continued support. Jess appealed the court's reservation of continuing jurisdiction, arguing that the court should have relin-

quished jurisdiction to order further support in such a short marriage. Noting that the parties "had been married for two years, two months, and had no children when they separated," the court of appeal agreed with Jess and held "that under the facts of this case—a marriage of short duration where the spouse seeking reten- tion of jurisdiction is in good health and enjoys permanent employment providing income for self-support—it is reversible error to retain open-ended jurisdiction over spousal support." 207 Cal. App. 3d 1260, 1266-1267 (1989). Had the court tacked the seven-year premarital cohabitation to the marriage, it would have reached a different result. Cf. Family Code section 4336. (For further discussion of premarital cohabitation, see page 467 supra.)

B. THE EQUAL DIVISION REQUIREMENT

With the exception of personal injury recoveries (see page 273 supra), at di- vorce all community and quasi-community property must be divided equally be- tween the parties. The California norm is equal division of each asset. At death, the survivor is entitled, without exception, to a one-half interest in each community asset. (See pages 543-547 infra.) The statutory divorce provisions, however, allow an exception to the general section 2550 rule of in-kind division.

1. *Deviation from In-Kind Division*

California Family Code sections 2600 and 2601 provide:

§2600. Special rules for division of community estate

Notwithstanding Sections 2550 to 2552, inclusive, the court may divide the community estate as provided in this part.

**§2601. Awarding asset to one party to effect substantially
            equal division**

Where economic circumstances warrant, the court may award an asset of the community estate to one party on such conditions as the court deems proper to effect a substantially equal division of the community estate.

MARRIAGE OF BRIGDEN
80 Cal. App. 3d 380, 145 Cal. Rptr. 726 (1978)

COBEY, Acting P.J.—Ann L. Brigden (hereafter Wife) and John K. Brigden (hereafter Husband) are cross-appellants from an interlocutory judgment of disso- lution of marriage. . . .

Both parties urge that the major issue upon appeal concerns that portion of the judgment disposing of 66,304 community-owned shares of stock in Logicon, Inc. (hereafter Logicon). The entire block of Logicon stock was awarded to Husband as his separate property. But one-half of this award, the 33,152 shares which represent Wife's equal interest in the stock, was awarded to Husband subject to conditions which are summarized below.[1]

Wife contends that . . . under the facts of this case, an equal "in kind" division of the Logicon stock is required; and . . . the division of community property that was made is not substantially equal.

We agree with Wife. . . .

Wife and Husband were married June 17, 1953. Nineteen and a half years later, on December 2, 1972, they separated. The separation was permanent and on November 10, 1976, the judgment of dissolution of marriage under appeal was granted.[2]

In 1961 Husband was one of eight persons who formed a company named Logicon, Inc. At its inception Logicon's business was primarily systems engineering and work in the computer science field. But in recent years it has diversified and become involved in additional commercial activities such as manufacturing. Logicon has never lost money. It was founded with about $1,000 total capital and has "generally" grown "about 40 percent a year." Annual revenues at the time of trial had "grown to about 30 some million."

Husband has been on the board of directors of Logicon during its entire existence. He also is senior vice president of Logicon, a position which gives him responsibility for "the outside financial affairs of the corporation, with our liaison with our legal counsel, with corporate planning, long range planning, and in the general management of the corporation." All eight of the persons who founded Logicon were placed on its original board of directors, but only one other of the founders remains as a director.

Over the course of their marriage Wife and Husband acquired 66,304 shares of Logicon stock, which constitutes 7.6 percent of the 872,180 total shares of Logicon stock outstanding. This is not a sufficient number of shares to guarantee Husband's election to the board of directors of Logicon or to assure that his position

---

1. Husband must either purchase the shares representing Wife's interest or release them to her pursuant to a decreed schedule. The schedule provides for (1) disposition of 500 shares on or before December 31, 1976; (2) disposition of 1,500 shares on or before December 31, 1977; (3) disposition of 1,500 shares on or before December 31, 1978; (4) disposition of 1,500 shares on or before December 31, 1979; and (5) disposition of the remaining 28,152 shares on or before December 31, 1980.

The schedule, however, specifies only final dates upon which a minimum number of shares must be purchased or released. The order gives Husband the right to pay for or release to petitioner all or any part of these 33.152 shares at any time prior to the dates set forth in the schedule. The price to be paid for each share of stock is to be determined by the average market sales price during the month of November of the year of payment if the payment is made strictly according to schedule. If Husband elects to accelerate his payments to purchase shares ahead of schedule, the price to be paid is the average stock sales price on the date of accelerated payment. It is provided, however, that Husband shall pay at least $4 for each share of stock or, if he releases any shares to Wife when the average market price is less than $4 per share, he must make up the difference between $4 and the average market price. "No interest shall be paid by [Husband] on his obligation to pay [Wife] for her interest in the stock."

Unless and until Husband releases stock to Wife, Husband has complete control and voting power over all the Logicon stock, except that if he liquidates more than 33,152 of the shares of stock he must pay Wife for each share sold in excess of the said 33,152 shares. The judgment gives Wife no security for her interest in the stock.

2. The apparent reason that three and one-half years transpired between the separation of the parties and the dissolution of their marriage is that the parties were attempting to negotiate a property settlement during this time.

as senior vice president will not be terminated, but it is a useful power base. The community-owned shares have always been voted in favor of Husband's election to the board of directors of Logicon.

At the time of trial the Logicon stock was traded as an "over the counter" stock and had an approximate value of $4 a share. Logicon stock is now traded on the American Stock Exchange. Its value on March 1, 1978, was $13.75 per share. Its highest value over the 52 weeks prior to that date was $17.625 per share. Its lowest value over the 52 weeks prior to that date was $9 per share. As of the time of trial Logicon had never declared a dividend on its shares.

Wife requested at trial that the court award her one-half of the Logicon stock in kind. She testified that the primary reason she wants the stock is because she believes that it is a "valuable asset" which "should be more valuable in the future." She also indicated an interest in "possibly getting a place on the board of directors . . . to be able to participate and maybe help [her] investment grow." She said she thought her participation "would be an advantage to the company as well as an advantage to [herself]" due to the current absence of management level women at Logicon. But she was uncertain that she would become so involved.

Husband requested that all the stock be awarded to him. He testified that there were two reasons for his request. The first reason is that he had spent "virtually all [his] adult life" working for Logicon and felt as if Logicon was his company. It therefore is "important to [him] emotionally to own that stock." The second reason is that the stock gives him a power base. He testified, "I can't say this, that without the stock, if I didn't have the power base in the stock, it doesn't mean that I could get fired overnight nor if I have all the stock does that mean I will always keep my job. [¶] But it's very helpful and important to maintain the political power base that I need to stay in that company."

There were insufficient community assets to offset the value of the award of the entire block of stock to Husband. Husband did not have the ability to compensate Wife, by access to his separate property or other sources of funding, for the award to him of her interest in the stock.

The distinctive feature of California marital property law is that the marital community is viewed as a partnership in which the spouses are equal partners. It has long been recognized in California "that the marriage, in respect to property acquired during its existence, is a community of which each spouse is a member, equally contributing by his or her industry to its prosperity, and possessing an equal right to succeed to the property after dissolution." (Meyer v. Kinzer (1859) 12 Cal. 247, 251.) "The spouses are seen as contributing equally to acquisition regardless of the actual division of labor in the marriage and regardless of which spouse actually 'earned' the property." (Prager, The Persistence of Separate Property Concepts in California's Community Property System (1976) 24 UCLA L. Rev. 1, 6. . . .) Both spouses have "present, existing and equal" interests in community property [Family Code §751] and the spouses have the same rights of management and control. [Family Code §1100.]

The equal division of the community property of the spouses, upon dissolution of marriage, appears to be an implicit recognition of this equality in interest that prevailed during marriage. (See Prager, Sharing Principles and the Future of Marital Property Law (1977) 25 UCLA L. Rev. 1.) Equal division is certainly the fundamental objective of the Family Law Act [now Family Code] in this respect. (In re Marriage of Juick [(1971) 21 Cal. App. 3d 421, 427, 98 Cal. Rptr. 324]; In re Marriage of Tammen (1976) 63 Cal. App. 3d 927, 930 [134 Cal. Rptr. 161].) The theory behind such division is that "in disposing of the property, a dissolution of marriage should be treated much like the dissolution of a business partnership. Regardless of the economic circumstances of business partners or of their moral conduct during the existence of the partnership, on dissolution the partners receive a portion of the assets commensurate with their respective partnership interests." (Attorney's Guide to Family Law Act Practice (Cont. Ed. Bar 1972) §5.6, p.250.) Thus Civil Code section 4800, subdivision (a) [now Family Code section 2550], provides that upon the dissolution of marriage, the court shall "divide the community property . . . of the parties . . . equally."

This subdivision establishes equal division as the general rule both in terms of the method of division and the result to be achieved. For division by any method other than by partition into equal portions (equal in kind division) will result in the spouses receiving *different* property even though they receive property of mathematically equal value. Methods of division other than division in kind can achieve no more than "a substantially equal division of the property" and therefore are permitted under Civil Code section 4800, subdivision (b)(1) [now Family Code section 2601], only "[*w*] *here economic circumstances warrant.*" Pursuant to this subdivision, "the court may award *any asset* to *one party* on such conditions as it deems proper *to effect a substantially equal division* of the property." (Italics added.) Thus the trial court may divide the community property, where warranted, by methods such as awarding an asset to one spouse conditioned upon later payments or making offsetting awards of the community assets. But even when property is divided pursuant to this subdivision the spouses must receive property of at least substantially equal value. And this requirement has been construed to mean essentially equal in value. . . .

In the case at bench Wife contends that the economic circumstances do not warrant a substantially equal division pursuant to [Family] Code section [2601] and that even if the trial court was empowered to make such a division she did not receive property substantially equal in value to that received by Husband.

In evaluating these contentions the meaning of "[w]here economic circumstances warrant" must first be considered. Since this clause triggers an exception to the general rule of equal in kind division it should be strictly construed so that the exception does not become broader than the basic rule itself. . . . Moreover, a narrow construction of the clause is required because the award of an asset to one spouse alone involves the elimination of the other spouse's prior equal interest in that asset. . . .

There are other policy considerations, as well, which favor a narrow reading of the phrase "economic circumstances." Equal in kind division avoids valuation problems. It eliminates the need to place a disproportionate risk of loss on either party, is impervious to charges of favoritism, and apportions the risk of future tax liabilities equally. . . . It also accomplishes an immediate division of property and provides the parties with the most post-dissolution economic stability.

Finally, the legislative history of the Family Law Act in the form of the Assembly Committee Report thereon also supports a limited reading of the phrase "economic circumstances." The report indicates that the application of the exception is confined to situations where an asset cannot be divided *without impairment.* "The new act requires an equal division in all but two specific instances without regard to the reasons for the dissolution. The first exception [Family Code §2601] is that *if the nature of the property is such* that *an equal division is not possible without impairment of a principal asset,* then the court shall have discretion to establish conditions which will result in substantially equal division." (Italics added.) The report then goes on to give the example of an ongoing family business and to say "[I]t could well be destructive to award each spouse a half interest therein." (Assem. Com. Rep. on Assem. Bill No. 538 and Sen. Bill No. 252 (The Family Law Act), Com. on Judiciary, 4 Assem. J. (1969 Reg. Sess.) at p.8061.) A later Assembly Committee Report adds the example of the award of the family residence to the spouse with the custody of minor children as another situation where economic circumstances warrant the application of this exception to the equal division requirement. (1 Assem. J. (1970 Reg. Sess.) p.787.)

Thus [Family] Code section [2601] has been characterized as the "single asset proviso" (In re Marriage of Juick, supra, 21 Cal. App. 3d at p.428) and been said to apply "where a major item of community property" is "not reasonably subject to division." (In re Marriage of Tammen, supra, 63 Cal. App. 3d at p.930.) We construe this statement to mean that the "economic circumstances" which empower a court to award an asset to one spouse alone are limited to those circumstances where the asset is not subject to division without impairment and we so hold.

But the determination whether an asset is subject to division without such impairment must be flexibly made. (See 1 Assem. J. (1970 Reg. Sess.) p.786.) This is evident from the two examples given by the legislative committee report. In the first example impairment of the asset is found in the deadlock inherent in the award to former spouses of equal interests in an ongoing family business. The second example recognizes impairment where the asset satisfies a critical need of one of the spouses and there is no adequate replacement for it.

We regard the block of stock at issue as a single asset.[6] Though it is usually possible to divide such an asset in kind, it does not follow that it always can be done without impairment. Were the stock at issue here stock in a close corporation (Corp. Code, §158) or shown to be essential to Husband's ability to earn a living then economic circumstances would perhaps warrant the award of the entire block of stock to Husband upon conditions effecting a substantially equal division of property. A close corporation is the functional equivalent of a family business. An asset which is essential to a party's ability to earn a living satisfies a critical need which cannot be satisfactorily replaced.[7]

But where, as here, the stock is traded on a national exchange and its possession is merely "helpful," economic circumstances do *not* warrant the award of the entire block to one spouse. The stock is subject to division without impairment and both spouses have economic concerns which cause them to desire the stock. The concerns of each [are] worthy of the same consideration. . . . Under the circumstances of this case Wife has a right to an equal in kind award of her interest in the Logicon stock or, in other words, an equal partition of the block of stock. . . .

Even assuming arguendo that economic circumstances did warrant a division

6. We regard it as highly significant, however, that the shares of stock at issue are fungible and therefore the block of stock is easily divided in kind. There are many assets such as parcels of real property, automobiles, and jewelry which simply are not ordinarily subject to such division.

7. Award of stock upon dissolution where it is shown to be essential to earning a living is analogous to Civil Code section 5125, subdivision (d)'s grant during marriage of sole management and control to the spouse who is "operating or managing a business or an interest in a business which is community personal property." In both cases the need of the one spouse overrides recognition of the other spouse's equal interest in the asset. [For the current version of Civil Code section 5125(d), see Family Code section 1100(d).—Ed.]

devised pursuant to [Family] Code section [2601], the spouses did not receive property of substantially equal value as is required by this [section]. No award was made
as such to offset the award of the stock to Husband. Moreover, the judgment awarding the stock is inequitable in terms of the financial position in which it places the
parties, the security they are given, and their tax consequences. . . . If this award
had been made upon the dissolution of a business partnership its impropriety would
be beyond dispute. Its impropriety should be equally obvious in the marital context.

The most glaring inequity stems from the tremendous financial advantage that
accrues to Husband from the fact that under the judgment he alone decides
whether to advance the times of payment for or release of the stock. As already
noted, the value of Logicon stock is extremely variable. . . . Should Husband choose
to exercise his option to make an immediate payment for all of the 33,152 shares
representing Wife's interest, his timing could decrease the amount needed to pay
Wife by hundreds of thousands of dollars. In his position as senior vice president,
concerned with general corporate management and planning, he is the prototypic
corporate insider — privy to information that would allow him to maximize the
value of the timing of the exercise of his option.

The structure of the judgment also deprives Wife of control over decisions
affecting her financial future. She does not have an interest that she may sell, pledge
or hypothecate. Instead she can only wait to receive funds from Husband, payable
to her at least partially in his discretion. Although this scheme, especially the $4
floor on the value of her interest, is no doubt designed to give her the advantage
of any rise in the value of the stock, while protecting her interest, it is inconsistent
with the Legislature's stated objective that the woman's "approaching equality with
the male should be reflected in the law governing marriage dissolution and in the
decisions of courts with respect to matters incident to dissolution."[10] (Assem. Com.
Rep. on Assem. Bill No. 538 and Sen. Bill No. 252 (The Family Law Act), Com. on
Judiciary, 4 Assem. J. (1969 Reg. Sess.) p.8062; . . . Karst, Foreword: Equal Citizenship under the Fourteenth Amendment (1977) 91 Harv. L. Rev. 1, 53-59.)

Also, the unsecured nature of a compensatory award is recognized as a factor
to be considered in evaluating the value of the compensation given a party for his
or her interest in an asset upon dissolution of marriage. . . . Here the decree gives
Wife no security. Should Husband fall into financial difficulties, Wife stands in no
better position than any other general unsecured creditor. Husband, on the other
hand, has no security concerns as he is awarded the stock itself. . . .

DISPOSITION

The judgment is reversed and the case remanded for further proceedings consistent with the views expressed herein.

Allport, J., and Potter, J., concurred.

Notes and Questions

1. Why does Mr. Brigden resist his wife's claim to one-half of the Logicon stock?
What worries him?

---

10. While a promissory note would have deprived Wife of any rise in the stock's value, a court may
take into account the speculative value of an asset in fixing its valuation and a promissory note has the
advantage of being marketable at the time dissolution is granted. . . .

2. What should the trial court do on remand? Does the court of appeal require an in-kind Family Code section 2550 division or does it merely object to the manner in which the trial court made its section 2601 division? Asking the question in terms of the language of section 2601, does the *Brigden* trial court disposition founder on "where economic circumstances warrant [a deviation from in-kind division]" or "on such conditions as the court deems proper to effect a substantially equal division of the community estate"? Under the circumstances, could the trial court have made a section 2601 division that would have adequately taken into account the wife's interests?

3. In footnote 10, the court discusses the advantages of a promissory note. Since Logicon stock is publicly traded, would a marketable (at a discount) promissory note have obviated Mrs. Brigden's objections? How might Mr. Brigden feel about a promissory note that would be marketable at a price that would enable Mrs. Brigden to purchase sufficient Logicon stock to replace her half interest in the stock awarded to her husband? Ought a court inflate the amount due or interest rate on a promissory note in order to take into account the discount the recipient will experience if she sells it? See Marriage of Hopkins, 74 Cal. App. 3d 591, 141 Cal. Rptr. 597 (1977); Marriage of Tammen, 63 Cal. App. 3d 927, 134 Cal. Rptr. 161 (1976). See also Marriage of Herrmann, 84 Cal. App. 3d 361, 148 Cal. Rptr. 550 (1978). But see Marriage of Connolly, the next principal case.

4. "[We hold] . . . that the economic circumstances which empower a court to award an asset to one spouse alone are limited to those where the asset is not subject to division without impairment. . . ." What does this mean? Can the award of a home to a child's custodial parent, which was clearly contemplated by the statute's legislative history, be encompassed by the court's holding? How does the court meet this objection? Why is a particular home any more "critical" to a custodial parent than Mr. Brigden's control of his Logicon stock? See Marriage of Duke, 101 Cal. App. 3d 152, 155-156, 161 Cal. Rptr. 444 (1980):

> The value of a family home to its occupants cannot be measured solely by its value in the market place. The longer the occupancy, the more important these noneconomic factors become and the more traumatic and disruptive a move to a new environment is to children whose roots have become firmly entwined in the school and social milieu of their neighborhood. . . .

When it would be desirable to delay the sale of the family home and other community assets are insufficient to constitute an equal offsetting award to the other spouse, the trial court has several options. It may award the home to the parties as tenants in common but delay sale until, for example, the youngest child reaches majority or is otherwise emancipated. Marriage of Boseman, 31 Cal. App. 3d 372, 107 Cal. Rptr. 232 (1973). (A *Boseman* division is essentially unequal because the noncustodial parent loses his half interest in the home's occupancy value until it is sold. *Boseman* sanctions this inequality as an award of child support against a noncustodial parent whose income is inadequate to pay sufficient child support.) Or, a court may award the home to the custodial spouse but require her to refinance it in order to obtain funds with which to pay the other spouse his share of the equity, or require her to create a mortgage in his favor with periodic payments of interest and principal. Marriage of Juick, 21 Cal. App. 3d 421, 429, 98 Cal.

Rptr. 324 (1971). The offsetting note, frequently sanctioned to divide a community business, was disapproved as a method to effect an equal division of a community home in Marriage of Herrmann, 84 Cal. App. 3d 361, 148 Cal. Rptr. 550 (1978). The court of appeal instructed the trial court instead to place the home in tenancy in common and provide for later sale and division of the proceeds. Marriage of Herrmann points up the various problems raised by an offsetting note. But see Marriage of Bergman, 168 Cal. App. 3d 742, 214 Cal. Rptr. 661 (1985) (approving use of a secured short-term promissory note at the prevailing interest rate).

With respect to the postponed sale of a family home, see also California Family Code sections 3800-3810, which are reprinted in the Statutory Appendix. Enacted in 1988 and amended in 1990, sections 3800-3810 are the most recent of a series of statutes regulating "deferred sale of home orders."

MARRIAGE OF CONNOLLY
23 Cal. 3d 590, 591 P.2d 911, 153 Cal. Rptr. 423 (1979)

[The divorce court, with both parties' consent, awarded all the community property Amdahl stock to the husband, who executed a promissory note to the wife for the value of her share of the stock. Later, the value of the Amdahl stock rose dramatically. The wife moved to reopen the judgment of dissolution.]

RICHARDSON, J.—This case involves a contested marital dissolution proceeding in which, after trial, corporate stock conceded to be community property was awarded to husband, a director of the corporation. The issue presented is whether husband had a fiduciary obligation to inform wife of facts which might affect the stock's value even though such information was readily ascertainable by wife or her counsel upon reasonable inquiry. We conclude that under the circumstances of this case husband had no such duty. . . .

In further support of her application for . . . relief, wife, through other counsel on appeal, now contends that [Family Code sections 2550 and 2601] mandated an equal division in kind of the Amdahl stock and that it was a "mistake of law" for the trial court, counsel, and parties to believe that the stock could all be awarded to husband. . . .

In urging her interpretation of [Family Code sections 2550 and 2601] wife places considerable reliance on In re Marriage of Brigden (1978) 80 Cal. App. 3d 380 [145 Cal. Rptr. 716]. There, in a dissolution of marriage proceeding it was held to be reversible error for the trial court, where wife had specifically requested an equal division, to award the husband as his separate property all of the community-owned stock in a publicly held corporation, subject to conditions that the husband must either purchase the shares representing the wife's interest or release them to her pursuant to a decreed schedule. The Brigden court found the trial court judgment in equitable in terms of the financial position in which it placed the parties, the security they were given, and their tax consequences.

Brigden, however, is clearly distinguishable on its unique facts and should not be construed as uniformly applicable to all division of community-held stock. Unlike the wife in Brigden, plaintiff wife here did not request award of the stock either partially or in toto. Even if she believed, as she alleges, that she was not entitled to request an equal division of the stock, she could have requested that the entire stock be awarded to her. This she did not do. On the contrary, as noted above, with the advice of her own counsel, she suggested that it be awarded to husband.

In *Brigden,* the wife received no immediate financial compensation for her share of the community-held stock. In the present case wife received a promissory note for what then appeared to be the reasonable value of the stock as determined by the trial court and fixed as of the date which was stipulated by the parties. Regardless of any subsequent fluctuations in the stock value, up or down, wife would be entitled to the fixed sum due under the note.

Contrary to wife's assertions, [Family] Code section [2601] was intended to, and does, vest in the court considerable discretion in the division of community property in order to assure that an equitable settlement is reached. In particular cases, strict "in kind" divisions, such as wife now urges, may cause, rather than avoid, financial inequalities. A spouse with a high income may be able to afford to retain high-risk assets while an unemployed spouse wholly dependent upon spousal support may not. By dividing "in kind" high-risk assets such as the Amdahl stock, a court may, for purposes of fairness, divide the risk of loss disproportionately. The exercise of a trial court's sound discretion is best preserved by maintaining a maximum degree of allowable flexibility.

The record clearly establishes the volatile nature of the Amdahl stock. The prospectus for the stock, dated August 12, 1976, states "The Common Stock offered hereby involves a high degree of risk. Prospective investors should consider carefully the risk factors indicated under 'Introduction Statement-Risk Factors.'" The prospectus added that "the Company has never paid dividends on its Common Stock and presently plans to continue this policy in order to retain its earnings, if any, to finance the development of its business."

This uncertain, non-income-producing stock might be a valuable holding for an individual who was otherwise financially secure, but a court or counsel might well conclude that a less-risky, more assured income-producing investment such as an interest-bearing note with a fixed principal would more appropriately serve an unemployed woman with custody of two minor children.

From the financial status of Amdahl at the time of the trial and the interlocutory decree, a person evaluating Amdahl shares might reasonably conclude that if a public offering did not rescue Amdahl from its extreme deficit position, both in net worth and in current assets, the corporation could well face bankruptcy, making the stock wholly worthless. The fact that later events included a successful public offering which resulted in a financial bonanza must not divert us from our conclusion that at the time the trial court, counsel, and the parties made and accepted the property division before us its essential terms were fair and reasonable.

The trial court could properly infer that wife's trial counsel had complied with his obligations in advising her to seek a more secure asset. From that inference the trial court could well conclude that wife's decision to take the note instead of the stock was a knowing tactical decision rather than the product of fraud or mistake of law.

The order denying wife's motion to vacate the judgment of dissolution is affirmed. BIRD, C.J., TOBRINER, J., MOSK, J., CLARK, J., MANUEL, J., and NEWMAN, J., concurred.

Appellant's petition for a rehearing was denied April 12, 1979.

Notes and Questions

1. "*Brigden,* however, is clearly distinguishable on its unique facts. . . ." In what sense are the facts of *Brigden* unique?

2. In view of the "two bites at the apple" posture of *Connolly* as well as the wife's suggestion at trial that all the Amdahl stock be awarded to her husband, the supreme court's discussion of Family Code section 2601 should probably be treated as dictum. Nevertheless, supreme court dictum is noteworthy, and the court has since spoken, in obiter dictum, to the same effect in Marriage of Fink, 25 Cal. 3d 877, 885-886, 603 P.2d 881, 160 Cal. Rptr. 516 (1979).

3. According to the supreme court, when may "economic circumstances warrant" a deviation from in-kind division? How does its formulation differ from that of the court of appeal in *Brigden?*

4. *Connolly* approves disproportionate allocation of risk to the party better able to bear it. Is this fair? Does it satisfy the section 2601 requirement that any deviation from in-kind division still produce "a substantially equal division of the community estate"?

5. Is *Brigden* or *Connolly* more consistent with the principles that underlie current California community property law?

2. Deliberate Misappropriation of Community Property by One Spouse

Before you read the next two cases, review the fiduciary duty statutes at pages 413-415.

WILLIAMS v. WILLIAMS
14 Cal. App. 3d 560, 92 Cal. Rptr. 385 (1971)

GUSTAFSON, J.—Plaintiff wife and defendant husband were married May 8, 1955. Almost 13 years later the marriage had deteriorated to the point where divorce was imminent. The husband thereupon withdrew $39,251.50 from a savings and loan association account and received $73,237.76 from the dissolution of a stock account at the office of a stock broker. The failure of the trial court to make any findings with respect to this total sum of $110,489.26 is the principal point giving rise to this appeal. . . .

Since each party was awarded a divorce, the court was required under the law then applicable to equally divide the community property. (De Burgh v. De Burgh (1952) 39 Cal. 2d 858 [250 P.2d 598].) The wife's claim is that she was not awarded one-half of the community property since she was awarded no part of the $110,489.26 referred to above. . . .

The first question is whether, assuming that some or all of the $110,489.26 available to the husband immediately prior to the filing of this action was community property, any of it still existed as such at the time of the dissolution of the marriage. The second question is whether, if the community property portion of the cash was not shown to have been disposed of for community purposes, the wife should have a right to a judgment against the husband in this action for her share of it.

The first of these two questions is a question of fact which should have been resolved by the trial court. The evidence with respect to the $110,489.26 was that the accountant appointed by the court was able to trace $22,126 as having been spent by the husband on mortgage payments, taxes and other expenses on real property. Whether any of this amount was spent on the real property which was found to be the separate property of the husband is not clear from the record. The accountant further found that $39,000 was paid by the husband to five persons. The husband claimed that the payments were made to discharge debts created by loans from those individuals to him. The court did not find that the debts actually existed and, if they did, that they were community debts. The accountant was unable to find what happened to the remaining $49,363.26. The husband testified that he spent this amount in the year preceding trial for ordinary living expenses and that he had no money left. The trial court made no finding with respect to the disposition of this $49,363.26.

The question of what if anything remained of such portion of the $110,489.26 as was community property was clearly raised by the pleadings and the evidence. By submitting proposed findings to the court, the wife satisfied section 632 of the Code of Civil Procedure placing upon the party desiring findings the burden of requesting them. Failure of the trial court to make findings with respect to the $110,489.26 was error and we therefore remand with instructions to the trial court to make findings on the issue under discussion.

It may well be that the findings which we have instructed the trial court to make will obviate the necessity of resolving the second of the two questions we have posed above. If the court finds that all of the community portion of the $110,489.26 was expended for proper community purposes, and that the remainder was the husband's separate property, then the second question need never be reached. If, on the other hand, the court determines that all of the community property was not used for authorized purposes, the second issue will be squarely raised. On the possibility that the second issue will be reached, we think it proper to indicate our views on it.

As to the second question, the extent of a husband's duty to his wife with respect to community property has not been uniformly or satisfactorily defined by the cases. In Fields v. Michael (1949) 91 Cal. App. 2d 443 [205 P.2d 402], the wife was permitted to recover from the estate of her deceased husband half of the value of gifts of community personal property which the husband made without the consent of the wife while he was living. The community property was treated as though it were the corpus of a trust of which the husband was the trustee. In Vai v. Bank of America (1961) 56 Cal. 2d 329 [15 Cal. Rptr. 71, 364 P.2d 247] the husband was said to have the "duties of a fiduciary" with respect to community property. But the husband is the manager of the community property (Civ. Code, §5105) and, except as specifically prohibited by statute, he may do with the community personal property what he could do with his separate estate. (Civ. Code, §5125.) Although a trustee or a fiduciary might be personally liable for a loss sustained by virtue of an improvident investment in speculative stock, we question whether a husband is liable to his wife for a loss sustained under those circumstances.

In White v. White (1938) 26 Cal. App. 2d 524 [79 P.2d 759] the court rejected the husband's argument that the trial court had no jurisdiction to render a personal judgment in favor of the wife for community income disposed of by the husband "regardless of the fact that no satisfactory account has been made by him of such funds." The court stated: "Where the handling of the community funds is entrusted by law to the husband, a certain amount of precaution devolves upon him to keep an approximately accurate account of their disbursements . . . or to take the legal consequences of being unable to satisfactorily account therefor." (Accord: Pope v. Pope (1951) 102 Cal. App. 2d 353 [227 P.2d 867].) We suspect that it would be extremely rare to find a man who has been married for many years who can account for every cent of his income during the marriage. Again, we question the wisdom of requiring the husband at his peril to be a bookkeeper. . . .

[I]n Weinberg v. Weinberg (1967) 67 Cal. 2d 557 [63 Cal. Rptr. 13, 432 P.2d 709] . . . the husband's duties were described as "analogous to those of a partner; he cannot obtain an unfair advantage from the trust placed in him as a result of the marital relationship." It would seem that a husband's duty not to obtain an unfair advantage over his wife by reason of his control of the community property does not require that the husband be as prudent as a trustee or that he keep complete and accurate records of income received and disbursed.

But here we are not concerned with the disposition of community property many years prior to a divorce action. The $110,489.26 in dispute here was intact immediately prior to the filing of the action. Under these circumstances, the husband would obtain "an unfair advantage" over his wife if he is not required to account for that portion of the money which was community property and to reimburse the wife for her share of any of the community property not shown to have been used for community purposes. . . .

That portion of the judgment disposing of the community property is reversed and the cause is remanded for further proceedings in accordance with the views expressed herein. . . .

WOOD, P.J., concurred.

MARRIAGE OF ROSSI
90 Cal. App. 4th 34, 108 Cal. Rptr. 2d 270 (2001)

EPSTEIN, J.—Denise Rossi appeals from a postjudgment order . . . awarding all the lottery winnings concealed by Denise during the dissolution proceedings to her ex-husband, Thomas Rossi.[1] . . .

Denise and Thomas were married in 1971. In early November 1996, Bernadette Quercio formed a lottery pool with a group of her co-workers, including Denise. Each member of the pool contributed $5 per week. Denise contributed her $5 for a short time—three weeks—but, according to her papers, on December 1, 1996, or about that date, she withdrew from the pool.

In late December 1996, Ms. Quercio called Denise to say that their group had won the lottery jackpot. The jackpot prize was $6,680,000 and Denise's share was $1,336,000, to be paid in 20 equal annual installments of $66,800 less taxes, from

---

1. "We refer to the parties by their first names 'to humanize a decision resolving personal legal issues which seriously affect their lives,' and to make our opinion easier to understand. . . ." (In re Marriage of Hokanson (1998) 68 Cal. App. 4th 987, 990, fn. 2, 80 Cal. Rptr. 2d 699.) . . .

1996 through 2015. According to declarations by Denise and by Ms. Quercio, Ms. Quercio told her that she wanted to give Denise a share in the jackpot as a gift. Denise explained: "I was afraid to tell [Thomas] because I knew he would try to take the money away from me. I went to the Lottery Commission office and told them I was married but contemplating divorce. They told me to file before I got my first check, which I did. I believed that the lottery winnings were my separate property because they were a gift." In early January 1997, Denise filed a petition for dissolution of marriage in the Los Angeles Superior Court. She never told Thomas about the lottery jackpot. She used her mother's address to receive checks and other information from the California Lottery because it would be safer since Thomas would not see the lottery checks.

Thomas was served with the dissolution petition in January 1997. He and Denise talked about a settlement the same day. Thomas was not represented by counsel in the dissolution proceedings. He and Denise met with Denise's attorney. According to Thomas, he was given several papers to sign to finalize the dissolution. These included a marital settlement agreement and a judgment of dissolution. . . .

Denise filled out a schedule of assets and debts dated January 27, 1997; a final declaration of disclosure; and an income and expense declaration dated January 30, 1997. [See Family Code sections 2100-2122.] She did not reveal the lottery winnings in any of these documents, either as community or separate property. Because Thomas did not have an attorney, Denise also filled out Thomas's schedule of assets and debts.

The marital settlement agreement was approved as part of the judgment of dissolution . . . [that] was entered April 7, 1997. In 1998, Thomas filed for bankruptcy. In May 1999, a letter was sent to Thomas's home address, asking if Denise was interested in a lump-sum buy-out of her lottery winnings. This was the first Thomas knew about the lottery prize. . . . Thomas retained counsel, who contacted Denise's attorney. . . . Denise's attorney confirmed that she had won a share of a lottery prize; "however, his client was unwilling to share any 'meaningful' amount of the lottery proceeds. . . ." . . .

In July 1999, Thomas filed a motion to set aside the dissolution of marriage based on fraud, breach of fiduciary duty and failure to disclose; for adjudication of the lottery winnings as an omitted asset; and sought the award of 100 percent of the lottery winnings pursuant to Family Code section 1101, subdivision (h). Thomas sought ex parte orders for an accounting and a restraining order preventing the disposition of any of the lottery proceeds paid to Denise or of any assets obtained with lottery proceeds.

The trial court ordered an accounting of lottery proceeds received by Denise; restrained the disposition of lottery proceeds; and ordered that all lottery proceeds be placed in a money market account with no right of withdrawal without court order or joint consent of Thomas and Denise, except in the ordinary course of business or for necessities of life. . . .

The trial court found that Denise intentionally failed to disclose her lottery winnings in the marital settlement agreement, the judgment, and her declaration of disclosure. It found that Denise breached her fiduciary duties under sections 721, 1100, 2100, and 2101 by fraudulently failing to disclose the lottery winnings and that she intentionally breached her warranties and representations set forth in . . . the Marital Settlement Agreement. The court specifically found that Denise's failure to disclose the lottery winnings constituted fraud . . . within the meaning of

Civil Code section 3294 and section 1101, subdivision (h). The trial court awarded Thomas 100 percent of the lottery winnings pursuant to . . . section 1101, subdivisions (g) and (h).

The trial court found that Denise's evidence that her share of the lottery winnings was a gift was not credible, and concluded that the lottery winnings were community property. . . . Denise filed a timely notice of appeal.

We review factual findings of the family court for substantial evidence, examining the evidence in the light most favorable to the prevailing party. (In re Marriage of Hokanson, supra, 68 Cal. App. 4th at p.994, 80 Cal. Rptr. 2d 699.) . . . Because Civil Code section 3294 requires proof by "clear and convincing evidence" of fraud, oppression, or malice, we must inquire whether the record contains "substantial evidence to support a determination by clear and convincing evidence. . . ." (Shade Foods, Inc. v. Innovative Products Sales & Marketing, Inc. (2000) 78 Cal. App. 4th 847, 891, 93 Cal. Rptr. 2d 364.) . . .

Section 721, subdivision (b) imposes a fiduciary duty on spouses in transactions between themselves: "This confidential relationship imposes a duty of the highest good faith and fair dealing on each spouse, and neither shall take any unfair advantage of the other. This confidential relationship is a fiduciary relationship subject to the same rights and duties of nonmarital business partners. . . ."

Section 1101, subdivision (h) provides: "Remedies for the breach of the fiduciary duty by one spouse when the breach falls within the ambit of Section 3294 of the Civil Code shall include, but not be limited to, an award to the other spouse of 100 percent, or an amount equal to 100 percent, of any asset undisclosed or transferred in breach of the fiduciary duty."

Thomas argues that imposition of the 100 percent penalty under section 1101, subdivision (h) was mandatory, once the family court found that Denise acted with fraud . . . in concealing the lottery winnings during the dissolution proceedings.

The . . . family court's order awarding Thomas all of the lottery winnings was based on the finding that Denise's conduct constituted fraud within the meaning of Civil Code section 3294. Civil Code section 3294 provides in pertinent part: "(a) In an action for the breach of an obligation not arising from contract, where it is proven by clear and convincing evidence that the defendant has been guilty of oppression, fraud, or malice, the plaintiff, in addition to the actual damages, may recover damages for the sake of example and by way of punishing the defendant. . . . (c) As used in this section . . . 'fraud' means an intentional misrepresentation, deceit, or concealment of a material fact known to the defendant with the intention on the part of the defendant of thereby depriving a person of property or legal rights or otherwise causing injury. . . ."

Punitive damages

The evidence established that Denise filed for dissolution after learning that she had won a share of a substantial lottery jackpot; that she consulted the Lottery Commission personnel about ways in which she could avoid sharing the jackpot with her husband; that she used her mother's address for all communications with the Lottery Commission to avoid notifying Thomas of her winnings; and that she failed to disclose the winnings at any time during the dissolution proceedings, despite her warranties in the marital settlement agreement and the judgment that all assets had been disclosed. The family court expressly rejected her evidence that the winnings constituted a gift and, as such, were her separate property. The record supports the family court's conclusion that Denise intentionally concealed the lottery winnings and that they were community property. . . .

Denise argues she committed no fraud because the statutory definition of that term "denotes conduct much more malicious and vile in nature than the failure of a physically and emotionally abused woman to disclose an asset to her husband, whose gambling and money mismanagement problems detrimentally affected her life and caused her to file for bankruptcy and caused him to threaten to kill her. In not disclosing what Denise Rossi believed was her separate property, Denise Rossi did not intend to deprive Respondent of an asset that he was entitled to because she felt it belonged to her alone. Denise Rossi did not believe that she was misappropriating a community asset, and therefore did not have the requisite fraudulent intent to deprive Respondent of a community asset."

The problem with her argument is that the court expressly found her evidence was not credible. The record supports this finding. The court put it in the following clear terms: "I believe the funds used to purchase the ticket were community. I don't believe the story about the gift." The court expressly found that Denise intentionally failed to disclose her lottery winnings in the marital settlement agreement, the judgment and her declaration of disclosure. This case presents precisely the circumstance that section 1101, subdivision (h) is intended to address. Here, one spouse intentionally concealed a significant community property asset. . . . This supports a finding of fraud within the meaning of Civil Code section 3294. The family court properly concluded that under these circumstances, Thomas was entitled to 100 percent of the lottery winnings under section 1101, subdivision (h).

As we observed in In re Marriage of Hokanson, supra, 68 Cal. App. 4th at p. 993, 80 Cal. Rptr. 2d 699: "The clear import of the language in subdivision (h) is that an award of attorney fees is discretionary, over and above the mandatory award of the entire asset at issue." The strong language of section 1101, subdivision (h) serves an important purpose: full disclosure of marital assets is absolutely essential to the trial court in determining the proper dissolution of property and resolving support issues. The statutory scheme for dissolution depends on the parties' full disclosure of all assets so they may be taken into account by the trial court. A failure to make such disclosure is properly subject to the severe sanction of section 1101, subdivision (h). . . .

We find nothing in the language of the statute to justify an exception to the penalty provision of section 1101, subdivision (h) because of the supposed unclean hands of the spouse from whom the asset was concealed. Nor are we cited to legislative history which would suggest such an exception. None of the cases cited by Denise in support of her unclean hands defense is a family law case construing section 1101. This undercuts Denise's primary argument on appeal, that she was justified in concealing the lottery winnings because of Thomas's behavior. The plain meaning of section 1101, subdivision (h) disposes of Denise's argument that there should be a "downward departure in any remedy against Denise" because, as she claims, she was battered emotionally and physically by Thomas. She cites federal law to the effect that evidence of the battered woman's syndrome is a valid basis for a discretionary downward departure of criminal penalties otherwise applicable under federal criminal sentencing guidelines, and to California criminal cases addressing this syndrome. As we have discussed, no such exception is codified into section 1101. The cases cited are off point. The statute provides that, where a spouse conceals assets under circumstances satisfying the criteria for punitive damages under Civil Code section 3294, a penalty representing 100 percent of the concealed asset is warranted. The statute is unambiguous and no exception is provided. . . .

The order of the family court is affirmed. . . .

CHARLES S. VOGEL, P.J., HASTINGS, J., concur.

Notes and Questions

1. *Mitigating factors.* Suppose Denise Rossi had persuaded the trial court that her husband abused her physically, emotionally, and economically. Should that bear on the court's application of section 1100(h)? Do you agree with *Rossi* that whenever a spouse intentionally conceals a material fact with the intention of depriving the other of property rights, the language of section 1100(h) *requires* a 100 percent award of the asset to the other spouse?

2. In 1989, the legislature enacted Code of Civil Procedure section 412.21, now Family Code section 2040, which provides that a summons in an action for divorce or annulment shall contain a temporary restraining order.

§2040.   Temporary restraining order in summons

. . . [T]he summons shall contain a temporary restraining order:

(a) Restraining both parties from removing the minor child or children of the parties, if any, from the state without the prior written consent of the other party or an order of the court.

(b) Restraining both parties from transferring, encumbering, hypothecating, concealing, or in any way disposing of any property, real or personal, whether community, quasi-community, or separate, without the written consent of the other party or an order of the court, except in the usual course of business or for the necessities of life and requiring each party to notify the other party of any proposed extraordinary expenditures at least five business days before incurring those expenditures and to account to the court for all extraordinary expenditures made after service of the summons on that party.

Notwithstanding the foregoing, nothing in the restraining order shall preclude a party from using community property, quasi-community property, or the party's own separate property to pay reasonable attorney's fees and costs in order to retain legal counsel in the proceeding. . . .

(c) Restraining both parties from cashing, borrowing against, canceling, transferring, disposing of, or changing the beneficiaries of any insurance or other coverage including life, health, automobile, and disability held for the benefit of the parties and their minor child or children.

The restraining orders remain effective until modified by a court or until the decree is entered or the petition is dismissed. Orders are enforceable by law enforcement agencies, and willful violation of a restraining order is a misdemeanor, punishable by up to one year in the county jail. Family Code §233.

In Estate of Mitchell, 76 Cal. App. 4th 1378, 91 Cal. Rptr. 2d 192 (1999), a divorcing husband filed a declaration of severance of joint tenancy property held with his wife, for the purpose of destroying the joint tenancy right of survivorship and instead holding the property as tenants in common, without a right of survivorship. The husband subsequently died during the divorce proceedings. The wife took the position that the severance was void because it violated the section 2040 restraining order. *Mitchell* held that severance of a joint tenancy is not a "transfer" or "disposition" of property within the meaning of section 2040 and thus does not violate the temporary restraining order and injunction that prohibit the husband and wife from transferring or disposing of any property during the pendency of dissolution proceedings.

3. For further discussion of the managing spouse's fiduciary duties, see pages 413-423 supra and 520-542 infra.

3.   Division of Liabilities

Civil Code section 4800(a), initially enacted as part of the 1969 no-fault divorce law, directed the court to "divide the community property and the quasi-community property of the parties equally." It further provided: "For purposes of making this division, the court shall value the assets and *liabilities* as near as practicable to the time of trial. . . ." This section, now codified at Family Code sections 2550 and 2552, was understood to require that assets and liabilities be tallied and that the net division be equal. At divorce, the trial court assigned each debt to one or the other party.

During the next two decades, the legislature made three exceptions to the general requirement that outstanding liabilities incurred during marriage be divided equally at divorce. Education loans may be assigned, without offset, to the spouse receiving the education. Family Code §§2627 and 2641. When a spouse during marriage incurs tort liability that is "not based upon an act or omission which occurred while the married person was performing an activity for the benefit of the community," the liability is assigned to the tortfeasor spouse, without offset. Family Code §2627. The legislature also modified a case law exception (Marriage of Eastis, 47 Cal. App. 3d 459, 120 Cal. Rptr. 861 (1975)) for divorces in which liabilities exceed assets: "To the extent that community debts exceed total community and quasi-community assets, the excess of debt shall be assigned as the court deems just and equitable, taking into account factors such as the parties' relative ability to pay." Family Code §2622(b).

The statutory treatment of debt assignment did not, however, adequately instruct the trial court. Suppose, for example, that a divorcing couple's community assets are worth $200,000, and their entire debt consists of the wife's $50,000 premarital obligation. Should this debt be divided equally? Community property debtor-creditor rules do not provide an answer. As you have seen in Chapter 7, for debtor-creditor purposes, California has never adopted the notion that there are "community" debts and "separate" debts.[1] The community property is liable for

---

1. Other community property states have, for purposes of debtor-creditor liability, adopted a "community debt" system. See, e.g., discussion in Grolemund v. Cafferata at pages 425-426 supra. See generally W. Reppy, Jr., and C. Samuel, Community Property in the United States 17-8–17-20 (3d ed. 1990).

Prior to the 1986 revision of Civil Code section 4800, the only California statutory manifestation of the community debt concept appeared in the Civil Code section 5122, now Family Code section 1000, order of satisfaction for tort liabilities. (See page 431 supra.) Several cases had treated certain debts incurred during marriage as the separate obligations of one spouse *for purposes of interspousal debt apportionment at divorce.* See Marriage of Lister, 152 Cal. App. 3d 411, 199 Cal. Rptr. 321 (1984), and Marriage of Stitt, 147 Cal. App. 3d 579, 195 Cal. Rptr. 172 (1983). Neither these cases nor Family Code purport to affect creditors' rights. Like Family Code sections 2620-2626, they regulate only the parties inter se rights. See *Stitt*, supra, 147 Cal. App. 3d at 586-589.

the debts of both spouses contracted before or during marriage. (See pages 423-434 supra.)

In 1986, the legislature extensively amended Civil Code section 4800 to distinguish, *solely for purposes of debt allocation at divorce*, between debts that are allocable to the community and those that are allocable to each spouse as his or her separate obligation. 1986 Cal. Stat., ch. 215, now codified at Family Code sections 2551 and 2620-2626. The divorce court is directed to divide the community estate equally and, in confirming or assigning the liabilities of the parties for which the community estate is liable, to characterize liabilities as separate or community and confirm or assign them to the parties in accordance with the following rules:

CALIFORNIA FAMILY CODE SECTIONS 2551 and 2620-2626

§2551. Characterization of liabilities as separate or community and confirming or assigning them to parties

For the purposes of division and in confirming or assigning the liabilities of the parties for which the community estate is liable, the court shall characterize liabilities as separate or community and confirm or assign them to the parties in accordance with Part 6 (commencing with Section 2620).

PART 6. DEBTS AND LIABILITIES

§2620. Confirmation or division of community estate debts

The debts for which the community estate is liable which are unpaid at the time of trial, or for which the community estate becomes liable after trial, shall be confirmed or divided as provided in this part.

§2621. Debts incurred before marriage

Debts incurred by either spouse before the date of marriage shall be confirmed without offset to the spouse who incurred the debt.

§2622. Debts incurred after marriage but before separation

(a) Except as provided in subdivision (b), debts incurred by either spouse after the date of marriage but before the date of separation shall be divided as set forth in Sections 2550 to 2552, inclusive, and Sections 2601 to 2604, inclusive.

• (b) To the extent that community debts exceed total community and quasi-community assets, the excess of debt shall be assigned as the court deems just and equitable, taking into account factors such as the parties' relative ability to pay.

§2623. Debts incurred after separation but before judgment

Debts incurred by either spouse after the date of separation but before entry of a judgment of dissolution of marriage or legal separation of the parties shall be confirmed as follows:

(a) Debts incurred by either spouse for the common necessaries of life of either spouse or the necessaries of life of the minor children of the marriage, in the absence of a court order or written agreement for support or for the payment of these debts, shall be confirmed to either spouse according to the parties' respective needs and abilities to pay at the time the debt was incurred.

(b) Debts incurred by either spouse for nonnecessaries of that spouse or minor children of the marriage shall be confirmed without offset to the spouse who incurred the debt.

§2624. Debts incurred after entry of judgment

Debts incurred by either spouse after entry of a judgment of dissolution of marriage but before termination of the parties' marital status or after entry of a judgment of legal separation of the parties shall be confirmed without offset to the spouse who incurred the debt.

§2625. Separate debts

Notwithstanding Sections 2620 to 2624, inclusive, all separate debts, including those debts incurred by a spouse during marriage and before the date of separation that were not incurred for the benefit of the community, shall be confirmed without offset to the spouse who incurred the debt.

§2626. Reimbursement for debts paid after separation but before trial

The court has jurisdiction to order reimbursement in cases it deems appropriate for debts paid after separation but before trial.

Notes and Questions

1. For purposes of Family Code section 2625, what is a "separate" debt? What types of debts incurred during marriage are not "for the benefit of the community"? In Marriage of Cairo, 204 Cal. App. 3d 1255, 251 Cal. Rptr. 731 (1988), the court of appeal approved the assignment of a $1,100 credit card debt to the husband as his section 2625 "separate debt" because he used at least some of the money for gambling and did not give his wife any household money from these borrowed funds. Would the court have taken the same view if the husband had used the funds to buy himself clothing or art lessons or books? In other words, does "community benefit" include each spouse's personal consumption?

2. Until recently, there were various uncertainties regarding creditors' rights after assignment. Now, however, Family Code section 916 clearly defines the rights of creditors as well as the reimbursement claims one spouse may have against the

other for debts discharged. Other interspousal reimbursement claims may arise under sections 914 (necessaries), 915 (child and spousal support), and 2641 (education). See also section 920 (general reimbursement rules).

C. TIME OF VALUATION

CALIFORNIA FAMILY CODE SECTION 2552

Valuation date for assets and liabilities

(a) For the purpose of division of the community estate upon dissolution of marriage or legal separation of the parties, except as provided in subdivision (b), the court shall value the assets and liabilities as near as practicable to the time of trial.

(b) Upon 30 days' notice by the moving party to the other party, the court for good cause shown may value all or any portion of the assets and liabilities at a date after separation and before trial to accomplish an equal division of the community estate of the parties in an equitable manner.

MARRIAGE OF MARRON
170 Cal. App. 3d 151, 215 Cal. Rptr. 894 (1985)

[See text of *Marron* at pages 317-320 supra.]

Questions

Why should assets normally be valued at the date of trial? Under what general circumstances should assets be valued at the date of separation rather than the date of trial?

D. INCOME TAX CONSEQUENCES OF DIVISION

The Domestic Relations Tax Reform Act of 1984 eliminated some of the tax problems associated with community property practice. Transfers *between* husband and wife are no longer treated as taxable events. When, for example, a spouse uses a separate property promissory note to buy out the other spouse's community property interest in a business, the transaction is no longer treated as a taxable "sale or exchange." Hence the bought-out spouse is no longer subject to income taxation on gain from the sale, that is, the amount by which the value of the separate-property promissory note received in exchange for her one-half community property interest exceeds her basis in the business.

Nevertheless, divorce may occasion the sale of community property assets to *third parties*, in which case the usual rules of income taxation come into play. If, for example, the couple's chief asset is an income-producing apartment house, the court may order that it be sold so that each party can enjoy half the equity. Assume that the parties' equity in the apartment house is valued at $350,000 and the husband's pension, the couple's only other asset, is valued at $150,000. The court awards the husband his pension and a $2/7$ interest in the apartment house, awards the wife a $5/7$ interest in the apartment house, and orders that it be sold. The parties are taxable on the gain they receive from the sale. Taxable gain is net proceeds less adjusted basis. Adjusted basis is generally the price the couple paid for the apartment house plus the cost of any improvements, less any depreciation taken. If, for example, they purchased the apartment house for $100,000, added a pool for $10,000, depreciated the apartment house by $50,000, and sold it at divorce for $410,000, they would have to pay tax on $350,000 gain. How should the trial court treat the tax consequences? If, instead, a wife is awarded the community property business she manages and her husband is awarded the community property home of equal equity value, should the court consider the tax consequences of a possible future sale of either asset?

MARRIAGE OF FONSTEIN
17 Cal. 3d 738, 552 P.2d 1169, 131 Cal. Rptr. 873 (1976)

SULLIVAN, J.—In this action for dissolution of marriage, appellant Sarane Fonstein (Sarane) appeals from that portion of an interlocutory judgment of dissolution of marriage dividing the community property. Specifically, she challenges the trial court's valuation, as an item of community property, of cross-appellant Harold Fonstein's (Harold) interest in his law partnership. . . . In valuing Harold's interest in the law partnership on the basis of his contractual right to withdraw from the firm, did the trial court err by taking into account the tax consequences which he might incur *if* he did withdraw at some later time, and by reducing the value of his interest accordingly, even though Harold was not withdrawing and had no intention to withdraw?

We considered the converse of the instant situation in Weinberg v. Weinberg (1967) 67 Cal. 2d 557 [63 Cal. Rptr. 13, 432 P.2d 709]. There the trial court awarded the plaintiff wife a money judgment for half the full value of the community interest in defendant husband's wholly owned corporations. We upheld the monetary award to the plaintiff in lieu of a division of stock of the corporations and rejected the husband's contention that the award to the wife should have been reduced by the tax obligation which would have been incurred had the stock been sold. We reasoned:

> Although there will be tax consequences if defendant satisfies the judgment
> by withdrawing funds from the corporations or selling some of his stock, there
> is no indication that he must or intends to do either to satisfy the judgment.
> He may choose to borrow the money or make the payments out of other
> property. Of course, once the property is divided pursuant to the trial court's
> order, the future tax consequences may vary on further sale or liquidation
> from what they would have been had the property been divided differently.

> The trial court need not speculate on such possibilities, however, or consider tax consequences that may or may not arise after the division of the community property. . . . (67 Cal. 2d at p.566.)

We shall point out how the foregoing rationale is applicable to the case at bench and ultimately resolves the main issue on appeal. We first advert to some settled precepts. In dividing the community property equally under the mandate of [Family] Code section [2550], the court must distribute both the assets and the obligations of the community so that the residual assets awarded to each party after the deduction of the obligations are equal. . . . However as *Weinberg* makes clear, once having made such equal division, the court is not required to speculate about what either or both of the spouses may possibly do with his or her equal share and therefore to engraft on the division further adjustments reflecting situations based on theory rather than fact. The division, having been properly accomplished, is, as it were, functus officis; it is beside the point to conjure up other results, had it been done differently.[5]

Applying these principles to the case at bench, we first observe that the tax obligations which Harold contends should be charged against the community property of this marriage will be incurred, if at all, only after dissolution of the marriage and division of the community property. At that time, Harold's interest in his law partnership will be his separate property; it will be solely his decision to receive taxable withdrawal payments and the benefit of those payments will go to him alone. . . .

While the parties assumed that the partnership would be valued on the basis of a withdrawal value, the fact remains that Harold was *not* withdrawing and no tax liability was incurred during marriage. There is therefore no liability to be charged to Sarane or against her share of the community property. . . . Moreover, since there is no indication in the record that Harold is withdrawing, must withdraw, or intends to withdraw from his firm in order to obtain the cash with which to pay Sarane her share of the community property, there is no equitable reason for allocating to Sarane a portion of the tax liability which may be incurred if and when he does withdraw. . . . In short, to paraphrase *Weinberg*, although Harold conceivably may do a number of things concerning his law partnership which may create tax consequences, "there is no indication that he must or intends to do" any of them.

We recognize that when community assets are divided in kind the risk of future tax liabilities from the disposition or realization of the assets is apportioned equally, while such risks are not necessarily distributed evenly when the community property is divided according to its value. There will be some compensating distribution of the potential liabilities, however. For example, the award of the family residence to Sarane imposed upon her a burden of [income] tax should she choose to sell the house at some future time. Harold, on the other hand, will assume the risk of

---

5. We disagree with Harold's argument that *Weinberg* can be distinguished on the ground that there was no evidence of tax consequences presented in that case (67 Cal. 2d at p.566, fn. 1), while in the instant case, Harold presented the expert testimony of an accountant as to the tax consequences which would result from Harold's receipt of withdrawal payments. . . .

The failure of proof in *Weinberg*, however, was the lack of any showing of "*immediate* and *specific* tax liability." (67 Cal. 2d at p.567; italics added.) Regardless of the certainty that tax liability will be incurred if in the future an asset is sold, liquidated or otherwise reduced to cash, the trial court is not required to speculate on or consider such tax consequences in the absence of proof that a taxable event has occurred during the marriage or will occur in connection with the division of the community property. (67 Cal. 2d at p.566.) . . .

a tax liability upon his receipt of withdrawal payments. We do not believe that any hypothetical inequity in the distribution of these tax burdens or in disregarding tax consequences in valuing the community assets is adequate justification for introducing an unnecessarily complicated and speculative factor into the process of dividing the community property. The amount of taxes which Harold will incur if he ever withdraws from his firm will depend upon a number of variables, the variety of which makes impossible anything more than a speculative approximation of the potential tax liability. Since these variables are largely subject to Harold's control, it is appropriate to allocate to him the potential liability.

We reject Harold's contention that potential tax liability is one of those risks of nonrealization of an asset which we directed the courts to consider in valuing nonvested pension rights in In re Marriage of Brown, 15 Cal. 3d 838, 848 [544 P.2d 561, 126 Cal. Rptr. 633 (1976)]. We were concerned in that case with "the possibility that death or termination of employment may destroy [pension] rights before they mature." (Id.) Both parties obviously should bear the risk that a pension will not vest and contingent community property will not be realized at all. The tax obligations which we consider today are not contingencies to the realization of an asset of the community. They are merely potential debts associated with the use or disposition of an item properly chargeable to the person owning the property at the time the tax obligation is incurred. Since the trial court incorrectly charged these obligations against the community property of the marriage prior to division, that portion of its judgment dividing the community property must be reversed. . . .

WRIGHT, C.J., McCOMB, J., TOBRINER, J., MOSK, J., CLARK, J., and RICHARDSON, J., concurred.

Note

How broad is the holding of *Fonstein?* It would strain credulity to take into account the tax consequences of a partnership withdrawal that we never expect to take place. Yet, does *Fonstein* turn on the court's initial choice of a relatively indirect valuation technique, the price set by a buy-out agreement? Or does *Fonstein* apply broadly to all valuation, including that which directly measures a future stream of taxable income? Does *Fonstein,* for example, apply equally to goodwill capitalization and to pension valuation? See Marriage of Marx, 97 Cal. App. 3d 552, 159 Cal. Rptr. 215 (1979) (citing *Fonstein* for the proposition that future income taxation of pension benefits should be ignored in valuing a pension interest); accord, Marriage of Bergman, 168 Cal. App. 3d 742, 754, 214 Cal. Rptr. 661, 669 (1985). One might argue that valuation techniques directly measuring a stream of future income (see discussion of capitalization of goodwill at page 310 supra) should look only at after-tax income because that is all the earner will actually receive.

Despite the intuitive attractiveness of this argument, it is largely, although not entirely, incorrect. Capitalization of future earnings involves two steps: calculation of the stream of future income and discounting that income to present value. When we discount income to present value, we use prevailing rates of interest and do not take into account the tax consequences of generating that interest. If the discounted present value of a pension is invested at prevailing interest rates, and that interest is taxed, the yield will approximate the stream of after-tax income that the pensioner would have received from the pension. Suppose that, based on before-tax future benefits, the discounted present value of Wilma's vested pension is $100,000. Wilma is awarded her pension and Herman is awarded an offsetting award of a $100,000 community property savings account. Herman invests the $100,000 at prevailing interest rates so that he and Wilma will eventually enjoy similar yield from each person's community property award. Herman must pay taxes on the interest so that his yield will not match the discount rate projections. Wilma's yield will also fall short because pension payments will be taxed as she receives them. Thus, Herman and Wilma are similarly situated, and it would have been an error to initially consider Wilma's after-tax benefits instead of her before-tax benefits.

Nevertheless, Wilma and Herman are not identically situated. Insofar as future pension benefits embody the recovery of the $100,000 principal value awarded to Wilma at divorce, Wilma will have to pay income tax not only on the interest but also on the $100,000 itself if and when it is distributed in the form of pension benefits. Herman, in contrast, will never have to pay income tax on the $100,000 cash distributed to him at divorce. Thus the tax problem is generated not by the fact that a recipient is generally taxed on pension benefits or other future income but rather because some portion of future pension benefits represents a return of the principal, or discounted present value, that was distributed at divorce. For students who have already studied taxation, the problem is essentially a problem of basis inequality. Wilma has no basis in her pension. Herman has full basis in the $100,000 offsetting cash award. If Wilma had paid Herman off in highly appreciated community assets, say low-basis stock or a low-basis family home, the parties would be almost equally situated. See Walker, What Is Equal Division?, 7 Cal. Fam. L. Monthly 113 (1990) and Blumberg, Comment, id. at 119.

Even assuming extreme basis inequality, when a divorce distribution is made during the early years of pension accumulation, the tax unfairness to the employee spouse is likely to be slight because most of the ultimate pension payments will derive from postdivorce interest and accumulations. Moreover, the discounting to present value of any properly attributable future tax liability will make it sufficiently insignificant that it can be ignored. When, however, there have been many years of pension accumulation during marriage and taxes on benefits will begin to accrue in the near future, tax inequality may be substantial.

MARRIAGE OF EPSTEIN
24 Cal. 3d 76, 592 P.2d 1165, 154 Cal. Rptr. 413 (1979)

TOBRINER, J. — . . . The trial court ordered the family residence sold and the proceeds divided between the parties . . . in such a manner as to equalize the division of the community property. Since husband received personal property of substantially greater value than that awarded wife, she will receive the larger share of the proceeds from the sale of the house. . . .

The trial court's order does not mention the possibility that the parties might incur state and federal . . . tax liability as a result of the sale of the residence. Noting that equalization of community property shares before taxes may result in her receiving less than half of the net value of community property remaining after payment of taxes, wife contends the trial court erred by not expressly considering tax liability in its order. We agree with wife that the court's division of community property should take account of any taxes actually paid as a result of the court-ordered sale of the residence, but explain that this result can be achieved merely by construing the trial court's order, without need to posit error by the court below.

In In re Marriage of Fonstein (1976) 17 Cal. 3d 738 [131 Cal. Rptr. 873, 552 P.2d 1169], we held that the trial court, in assigning to husband the value of his interest in a law partnership, need not take into account the tax that might be incurred if husband at some uncertain future date sold that interest. We there declared that "Regardless of the certainty that tax liability will be incurred . . . the trial court is not required to speculate on or consider . . . tax consequences in the absence of proof that a taxable event has occurred during the marriage or *will occur in connection with the division of the community property.*" (17 Cal. 3d at p.749, fn. 5; see Weinberg v. Weinberg, 67 Cal. 2d 557, 566 [432 P.2d 709, 63 Cal. Rptr. 13 (1967)].) (Italics added.)

Unlike *Fonstein*, which involved a speculative future tax liability arising on the hypothetical sale of an asset, in the present case the taxable event, the sale of the residence, occurs as a result of the enforcement of the court's order dividing the community property. . . .

In cases such as the instant matter involving the sale of a family residence, the uncertainty concerning the amount of . . . tax liability stems from provisions in state and federal tax law which defer liability to the extent that the proceeds from the sale are reinvested in a new residence within one year of the sale. (Rev. & Tax. Code, §18091; Int. Rev. Code, §1034(a).)[9] That uncertainty, however, will be resolved within a year or two of the court's decree.[10] In the present case, the amount of the tax liability may have been fixed by events pending the decision of this appeal, so the trial court, upon the remand of this case . . . can recognize that liability in dividing the proceeds of the sale. If not, and in similar cases arising in the future, the court can take account of tax liability by providing that the liability incurred, if any, is owed equally by both spouses. In unusual cases, it could retain jurisdiction to supervise the payment of taxes and adjust the division of the community property. (See In re Marriage of Clark, 80 Cal. App. 3d 417, 424 [145 Cal. Rptr. 602 (1978)].)

The trial court's order states simply that, following reimbursement to husband, "the balance of said sale proceeds shall be divided between the parties in a fashion which will equalize the division of the parties' community property." We do not think it necessary to interpret that order as rejecting consideration of the tax consequences of the sale, and then to brand the order so construed as erroneous. The judgment is susceptible of a construction consistent with the principles declared in this opinion. . . . We therefore construe the judgment to provide that the balance of the proceeds be divided so as to equalize the division of the community property after payment of any . . . tax incurred upon the sale of the residence, and direct that the trial court, upon the remand of this case, so apply the judgment. . . .

9. Amendments enacted subsequent to the trial of this case extended the period for reinvestment of the proceeds to [two years].

10. If the parties use the proceeds to purchase a new residence, the resulting deferral of the . . . tax reduces the basis of the new residence. Depending upon future events, that reduction in basis may result in a higher tax when and if the new residence is sold. (Rev. & Tax. Code, §18095; Int. Rev. Code, §1034(c).) That possible future tax burden, however, is an example of the speculative and uncertain tax consequences which the trial court need not consider under In re Marriage of Fonstein, supra, 17 Cal. 3d 738, 749.)

BIRD, C.J., MOSK, J., CLARK, J., RICHARDSON, J., MANUEL, J., and NEWMAN, J., concurred.

Problem and Notes

1. *Differential basis.* Jason and Jill, who are seeking a divorce, separately manage two Family Code section 1100(d) community property businesses. The physical assets of each business are currently valued at $150,000 and the goodwill at $50,000.

Jason established his dry cleaning business in 1985, at which time he began depreciating the physical assets. Every year he takes a tax deduction for some fixed percentage of the original cost of the physical assets. For income tax purposes, his current adjusted basis in the physical assets is $50,000. Adjusted basis is the amount by which Jason may reduce the proceeds of the sale of his business in order to calculate his net taxable gain. If, for example, Jason were to sell the business for $200,000, he would have $150,000 taxable gain. (This problem assumes that Jason has no basis in his personal goodwill, that is, he did not purchase the goodwill but instead developed it himself.)

Jill did not open her pet boarding facility until 1991. Thus, her adjusted basis in the physical assets of her business is now $120,000. Looking ahead and assuming approximately equal gross receipts from each business, Jill will be in the more advantageous tax situation. She still has $120,000 to deduct from future income in order to reach net taxable income; Jason only has $50,000 to reduce future taxable income. Jason and Jill stipulate to division of the other insubstantial community assets and further stipulate that each should be awarded the community property business he or she manages. They disagree only on whether the adjusted basis difference should be taken into account. Jason invokes *Epstein* and argues that the parties should split the difference in tax liabilities arising from the $70,000 difference in adjusted basis. Jill replies that *Fonstein* controls: The tax liability is necessarily speculative because adjusted basis becomes significant only if the business is sold or, alternatively, a depreciation deduction is valuable only insofar as the business earns income in excess of its expenses. How should the trial court resolve this issue?

2. *Differential marginal tax rates. Epstein* requires that immediate nonspeculative tax consequences directly traceable to a court order be paid equally by the parties. In a system of progressive income taxation, this requirement may produce perverse results insofar as the parties have different marginal tax rates and the determinants of each party's marginal tax rate are unrelated to the marriage. If, for example, when the appreciated asset is sold, the wife has a high marginal tax rate because of income from separate property or because she has remarried a wealthy man with whom she files jointly, her poorer ex-spouse, who has a lower marginal rate, must subsidize her taxes.

3. *Gain from the sale of a principal residence.* In 1997, Congress changed the income tax treatment of "gain" from the sale of a taxpayer's principal residence. Gain is the proceeds from sale less the (undepreciated) purchase price of the home and the cost of improvements. Gain of up to $250,000 from the sale of a principal residence may be excluded from taxable income by a single taxpayer. Up to $500,000 may be excluded by a couple. The exclusion may be claimed as frequently as every two years. Taxpayer Relief Act of 1997, Pub. L. 105-34, §312, codified at I.R.C. §121 (2002).

E.   COMMUNITY ASSETS NOT LISTED IN
THE PLEADINGS

HENN v. HENN
26 Cal. 3d 323, 605 P.2d 10, 161 Cal. Rptr. 502 (1980)

BIRD, C.J. — This court must determine whether a former spouse may bring an action to establish her community property interest in her ex-husband's federal military pension which was not adjudicated or distributed in the final decree of dissolution.

Helen and Henry Henn were married in 1945. After 25 years, Henry petitioned for dissolution of their marriage in the Superior Court for the City and County of San Francisco. An interlocutory decree was granted on February 22, 1971, and a final judgment issued on May 19, 1971. The decree incorporated a property settlement which awarded the parties specific items of the marital community as their separate property. The decree also awarded Helen $500 monthly support payments until the death of either party or her remarriage.

Neither the pleadings nor the judgment made mention of the fully matured federal military retirement pension that Henry was receiving at the time of the interlocutory decree. The pension had been partially earned during the marriage, and its existence was known to Helen at the time of the dissolution proceedings. Henry concedes that the court made no determination with respect to the pension. . . .

[Some] years later, Helen filed the underlying complaint in the Superior Court of San Mateo County. Helen sought (1) a determination that Henry's military pension was community property to the extent earned by Henry during their marriage; (2) a full accounting of all pension payments received by Henry since March 1, 1971; and (3) a division of the community property portion of the pension. In his answer to the complaint, Henry raised the defense of res judicata based on the original decree of dissolution. . . . He also contended that these proceedings, together with Helen's recovery in settlement of a malpractice action against her former attorneys, estopped her from maintaining the present action.[1] After a separate trial on these affirmative defenses, the trial court entered judgment on Henry's behalf. Helen appealed. . . .

It is clear that Henry's entitlement to his federal military pension was fully vested and matured in 1971 at the time of the dissolution of the Henns' marriage. To the extent earned during the marriage, it was part of their community property. However, Henry argues that Helen is prevented from seeking a judicial division of her community property interest in this asset under the principles of res judicata and collateral estoppel. These defenses are grounded on the original decree of dissolution and property settlement. . . .

---

1. On November 8, 1974, Helen filed a malpractice action against the attorneys who represented her during the dissolution proceedings. She alleged that she had detrimentally relied upon their advice that Henry's pension was his separate property. That case was settled in April 1976. On appeal, Henry denied that he urged "the doctrine of election of remedies as an affirmative defense," and conceded "that a litigant may pursue more than one remedy against different persons." Since Henry has not argued on appeal that Helen's recovery from her former attorneys prevents her from maintaining the present action, or otherwise limits her rights against him, that issue is not before this court.

The doctrine of res judicata has long been recognized to have a dual aspect. . . . "In its primary aspect the doctrine of res judicata operates as a bar to the maintenance of a second suit between the same parties on the same cause of action." (Clark v. Lesher (1956) 46 Cal. 2d 874, 880 [299 P.2d 865].) Also, the doctrine comes into play in situations involving a second suit, not necessarily between the same parties, which is based upon a different cause of action. There "[t]he prior judgment is not a complete bar, but it 'operates [against the party against whom it was obtained] as an estoppel[4] or conclusive adjudication as to such issues in the second action as were actually litigated and determined in the first action.'" (Id., citations omitted.) Neither aspect is applicable to the original judgment of dissolution and property settlement in this case.

Under California law, a spouse's entitlement to a share of the community property arises at the time that the property is acquired. [Family Code §§751, 760.] That interest is not altered except by judicial decree or an agreement between the parties. Hence "under settled principles of California community property law, 'property which is not mentioned in the pleadings as community property is left unadjudicated by decree of divorce, and is subject to future litigation, the parties being tenants in common meanwhile.'" (In re Marriage of Brown, 15 Cal. 3d at pp.850-851 [544 P.2d 561, 126 Cal. Rptr. 633 (1976)], quoting In re Marriage of Elkins (1972) 28 Cal. App. 3d 899, 903 [105 Cal. Rptr. 59].) . . . This rule applies to partial divisions of community property as well as divorces unaccompanied by any property adjudication whatsoever.

Helen's interest in Henry's military pension arose independent of and predates the original decree of dissolution and property settlement. This interest was separate and distinct from her interest in the items of community property which were divided at the time of the dissolution. Since it is conceded that the issue of Henry's military pension was not before the court which issued the final decree, the judgment of that court cannot be said to have extinguished Helen's putative interest in that asset.

Further, Helen cannot be collaterally estopped from litigating her community property right in that pension. Henry has not asserted that Helen is relying upon some factual or legal theory which was adjudicated in the prior litigation or which would have had to have been adjudicated if it had been raised at the time. (E.g., Sutphin v. Speik (1940) 15 Cal. 2d 195, 202-205 [99 P.2d 652, 101 P.2d 497].) Rather, Henry argues that Helen's failure to assert her community property right in the pension, when there was an adjudication of her entitlement to other assets of the community, should preclude her from asserting her rights to the pension now.

The doctrine of collateral estoppel cannot be stretched to compel such a result. . . . As explained in Carroll v. Puritan Leasing Co. (1978) 77 Cal. App. 3d 481, 490 [143 Cal. Rptr. 772], the rule prohibiting the raising of any factual or legal contentions which were not actually asserted but which were within the scope of a prior action, "does not mean that issues not litigated and determined are binding in a subsequent proceeding on a new cause of action. Rather, it means that once an issue is litigated and determined, it is binding in a subsequent action notwithstanding that a party may have omitted to raise matters for or against it which if asserted

---

4. This second aspect is referred to as judgment by estoppel or, more commonly, collateral estoppel. (See Clark v. Lesher, supra, 46 Cal. 2d at p.880.)

may have produced a different outcome." Hence, the doctrine of collateral estoppel is not applicable here because Henry failed to demonstrate that Helen is relying upon some specific factual or legal contention which would have been relevant to the adjudication of the parties' rights to the property distributed in the 1971 decree if it had been raised.[6] . . .

The enforcement of Helen's rights in the pension payments received by Henry since the 1971 adjudication and distribution of the community assets does not present any substantial danger of unjust enrichment. On remand, Henry may seek to limit retrospective enforcement of Helen's claim on an equitable estoppel theory by demonstrating that she in fact received additional support payments in lieu of a share in the pension.[8] . . .

If Helen is allowed to recover her share of the pension payments received by Henry between 1971 and the initiation of the present action, a problem may arise. It may be substantially more burdensome for Henry to account for the pension payments he has received since the 1971 division of community assets than it would have been for him to have complied with a partition effected at that time. Henry is likely to have treated the asset as his separate property and disposed of it according to his needs. The court is confident that this problem may be adequately addressed under the defense of laches. The exercise of a court's authority to so limit equitable relief will provide litigants with an additional incentive to assert all tenable community property rights in assets known to exist at the time of the initial judicial distribution of the marital community.

The judgment is reversed. TOBRINER, J., MOSK, J., CLARK, J., RICHARDSON, J., MANUEL, J., and NEWMAN, J., concurred.

Notes and Questions

1. What is the content of the *issue* that the court finds has not been "actually litigated" in any prior proceeding and hence not barred by the doctrine of collateral estoppel? How did Henry define the *issue?*

In the adjudication of marital property rights, are there any special concerns that argue for either relaxed or stringent application of res judicata and collateral estoppel principles?.

2. May Mrs. Henn experience an economic windfall that she would not have received had the pension been divided in the initial divorce proceeding? With respect to the court's confident assertion in footnote 8, see California Family Code section 3651, which provides that "[a]n order for spousal support may not be modified or terminated to the extent that a written agreement, or, if there is no written agreement, an oral agreement entered into in open court between the parties, spe-

6. In support of his argument, Henry relies principally upon Kelly v. Kelly, 73 Cal. App. 3d 672 [141 Cal. Rptr. 33 (1977)]. That court, faced with a case similar to the instant one in all relevant considerations, ruled that the existence of a prior judicial division of community property precluded the plaintiff from litigating her entitlement to a pension which had not been adjudicated in the earlier proceeding. *Kelly* is disapproved to the extent that it stands for the proposition that any judicial division of community property necessarily precludes the subsequent litigation of community property rights in an asset known to exist at the time of the earlier proceedings, and which could have been adjudicated at that time.

8. Of course, the defendant spouse may seek a prospective modification of his or her support payments in light of any new partition of an asset not previously adjudicated.

cifically provides that the spousal support is not subject to modification or termination.''

With respect to Henry's *future* pension benefits, may a *Henn* division impose burdens on Henry that he would not have experienced had the pension been divided at divorce? What would you argue for Henry? What responses might you make for Helen?

3. Can a divorce attorney anticipate and foreclose the possibility of a subsequent *Henn* proceeding? What sort of separation agreement or divorce decree stipulations might suffice to accomplish this goal? Ought any provision be sufficient?

Suppose, for example, that the divorce decree incorporates an agreement that provides, inter alia, that the terms of the agreement represent a final settlement of all property claims arising from the marriage. Does this clause simply make explicit that which both parties normally understand at the signing of a separation agreement? If so, should the inclusion of such a clause be effective to bar a subsequent *Henn* proceeding? This analysis suggests either that *Henn* is incorrectly decided or that any attempted waiver of *Henn* rights should be deemed ineffective.

Compare Espy v. Espy, 191 Cal. App. 3d 1163, 236 Cal. Rptr. 771 (1987), review denied and depublished by the Supreme Court on September 3, 1987 (general release does bar subsequent *Henn* action), with Huddleson v. Huddleson, 187 Cal. App. 3d 1564, 232 Cal. Rptr. 722 (1986) (general release does not bar subsequent *Henn* proceeding).

4. In *Henn,* ''neither the pleadings nor the judgment made mention of the fully matured . . . pension that Henry was receiving at the time of the interlocutory decree [and] the court made no determination with respect to the pension.'' Is a *Henn* action barred if the pleadings or judgment merely mention the asset in question, or must ownership have actually been adjudicated? See Brunson v. Brunson, 168 Cal. App. 3d 786, 214 Cal. Rptr. 398 (1985) (1980 *Henn* action to divide a pension not barred by 1971 interlocutory divorce judgment that mentioned the pension in reference to spousal support payments but did not adjudicate the parties' property rights in the pension): accord, Miller v. Miller, 117 Cal. App. 3d 366, 172 Cal. Rptr. 747 (1981).

5. A divorced spouse in Helen's circumstances may, as Helen did, bring a malpractice action against her divorce attorney for negligent failure to identify a community asset. Even if pension law was uncertain when the Henns were divorced in 1971, by 1974 it was clear that Helen had an unrealized community property claim. Did Helen's divorce attorney have a continuing duty to follow her case and advise her that she might now bring a proceeding to divide the property? (But query whether the *Henn* issue was settled in 1974.)

6. In 1989, the legislature enacted California Civil Code section 4353, now Family Code section 2556.

§2556. Continuing jurisdiction to award community estate assets or liabilities

In a proceeding for dissolution of marriage, for nullity of marriage, or for legal separation of the parties, the court has continuing jurisdiction to award community estate assets or community estate liabilities to the parties that have not been previously adjudicated by a judgment in the proceeding. A party may file a postjudgment motion or order to show cause in the proceeding in order to obtain adjudication of any community estate asset or liability omitted or not adjudicated by the judgment. In these cases, the court shall equally divide the omitted or unadjudicated community estate asset or liability, unless the court finds upon good cause shown that the interests of justice require an unequal division of the asset or liability.

This statute simultaneously codifies the substantive holding of *Henn*, obviates the need for an independent *Henn* proceeding, and adds an unequal division proviso. The unequal division proviso may be intended merely to embody the laches discussion in *Henn* regarding benefits already received and spent before the initiation of the distribution proceeding. Or, it may open the door to broader claims for equitable, as opposed to equal, distribution. Should, for example, the relative needs of the parties be taken into account in making a section 2556 distribution?

F.   SETTING ASIDE A PROPERTY SETTLEMENT OR DECREE FOR MISTAKE, FRAUD, BREACH OF FIDUCIARY DUTY, BREACH OF CONFIDENTIAL DUTY, OR DURESS

One spouse may seek to avoid a property settlement or decree on the grounds of mistake, fraud, breach of fiduciary duty, breach of confidential duty, or duress. In each of the following cases, identify the precise ground or grounds invoked by the petitioner. These cases can profitably be read as preventive law. What ought to have been done that was not done? Are there instances of attorney malpractice?

In terms of procedural posture, the cases may be divided into three groups. Vai v. Vai involves no judgment at all. Mrs. Vai seeks merely to avoid a property settlement agreement. The other claimants seek to upset a judgment. Marriage of Connolly and Marriage of Brockman are brought within six months of entry of the judgment, a period dur ing which ostensibly more permissive rules apply. During the six-month period "the court may . . . relieve a party . . . from a judgment . . . taken against him or her through his or her mistake, inadvertence, surprise, or excusable neglect." Cal. Code of Civ. Pro. §473. In contrast, Kulchar v. Kulchar and Marriage of Alexander are brought after the expiration of the six-month period, when judgments may be understood to carry greater finality.

Yet most of the cases do not rely on procedural differences to distinguish other cases. (But see *Alexander*.) Instead the cases discuss and distinguish each other in terms of the spouses' behavior and the nature of their legal obligations to each other.

Pre-1991 case law must be read in light of the 1991 amendments to current California Family Code sections 721, 1100, and 1101. 1991 Cal. Stat., ch. 1026, §3. The amendments to sections 721 and 1100 were specifically intended to repeal aspects of recent California case law. You may find it helpful to review the 1991 and 2002 amendments, reprinted at pages 413-415 supra, before you read the following cases.

Additionally, in 1992 the legislature added two new chapters to the current Family Code. Chapter 9 (sections 2100-2109) further regulates divorce-related disclosure of assets and liabilities in proceedings commenced on or after January 1, 1993. Chapter 10 (sections 2120-2129) allows aggrieved spouses some relief from unfairly obtained judgments entered on or after January 1, 1993. The 1992 legislation is reprinted in the Statutory Appendix and should also be read before you consider the following cases.

KULCHAR v. KULCHAR
1 Cal. 3d 467, 462 P.2d 17, 82 Cal. Rptr. 489 (1969)

TRAYNOR, C.J. — Plaintiff appeals from an order of the Superior Court of San Mateo County modifying an interlocutory decree of divorce to relieve defendant of liability to pay federal income taxes assessed against the parties on income accruing to plaintiff in New Zealand.

Plaintiff secured an interlocutory decree of divorce from defendant on July 3, 1964. The decree included the disposition of the community and separate property of the parties.[1] The decree provided, in part: "Defendant shall indemnify and hold plaintiff free and harmless in the matter of any monies due any taxing agency, whether Federal, State or County, for the calendar years prior to 1964."

In 1966, following the divorce proceedings, defendant received a tax assessment of approximately $22,000 for federal income taxes based on theretofore undisclosed income accumulated during the marriage by a New Zealand corporation in plaintiff's name. Defendant moved to modify the divorce decree to relieve him of any liability for taxes on the New Zealand income on the grounds of extrinsic fraud and extrinsic mistake. After a hearing on defendant's motion, the trial court concluded that the tax provision in the decree "was included and approved by the parties as a result of the mutual mistake of the parties and further, that there was no intent of the parties that defendant should pay United States Federal income tax resulting from income to plaintiff in New Zealand." The court struck the tax provision from the decree "because of the mutual mistake of the parties."

Under certain circumstances a court, sitting in equity, can set aside or modify a valid final judgment. . . . This power, however, can only be exercised when the circumstances of the case are sufficient to overcome the strong policy favoring the finality of judgments.

> A basic requirement of an action which can lead to a valid judgment is that a procedure should be adopted which in the normal case will give to the parties an opportunity for a fair trial which is reasonable in view of the requirements of public policy in the particular type of case. If this requirement is met, a judgment awarded in an action is not void merely because the particular individual against whom it was rendered did not in fact have an opportunity to present his claim or defense before an impartial tribunal. . . . [P]ublic policy requires that only in exceptional circumstances should the consequences of res judicata be denied to a valid judgment. (Rest., Judgments, §118, com. a.)

Interlocutory divorce decrees are res judicata as to all questions determined therein, including the property rights of the parties. (In re Williams' Estate (1950)

---

1. There was no formal property settlement agreement. All provisions of the decree relating to the distribution of property were submitted to the court on the stipulation of the parties.

36 Cal. 2d 289, 292 [233 P.2d 248, 22 A.L.R.2d 716]; Adamson v. Adamson (1962) 209 Cal. App. 2d 492, 501 [26 Cal. Rptr. 236].) If a property settlement is incorporated in the divorce decree, the settlement is merged with the decree and becomes the final judicial determination of the property rights of the parties. (Broome v. Broome (1951) 104 Cal. App. 2d 148, 154-155 [231 P.2d 171].)

Thus, the rules governing extrinsic fraud and mistake apply to alimony awards and property settlements incorporated in divorce decrees. . . .

Extrinsic fraud usually arises when a party is denied a fair adversary hearing because he has been "deliberately kept in ignorance of the action or proceeding, or in some other way fraudulently prevented from presenting his claim or defense." (3 Witkin, Cal. Procedure, p.2124.)

> Where the unsuccessful party has been prevented from exhibiting fully his case, by fraud or deception practiced on him by his opponent, as by keeping him away from court, a false promise of a compromise; or where the defendant never had knowledge of the suit, being kept in ignorance by the acts of the plaintiff; or where an attorney fraudulently or without authority assumes to represent a party and connives at his defeat; or where the attorney regularly employed corruptly sells out his client's interest to the other side, — these, and similar cases which show that there has never been a real contest in the trial or hearing of the case, are reasons for which a new suit may be sustained to set aside and annul the former judgment or decree, and open the case for a new and a fair hearing. (United States v. Throckmorton (1878) 98 U.S. 61. 65-66 [25 L. Ed. 93, 95].)

The right to relief has also been extended to cases involving extrinsic mistake. (Bacon v. Bacon (1907) 150 Cal. 477, 491-492 [89 P. 317]; Olivera v. Grace, supra, at p.577.) "In some cases . . . the ground of relief is not so much the fraud or other misconduct of the defendant as it is the excusable neglect of the plaintiff to appear and present his claim or defense. If such neglect results in an unjust judgment, *without a fair adversary hearing*, the basis for equitable relief is present, and is often called 'extrinsic mistake.'" (3 Witkin, Cal. Procedure, p.2128.)

Extrinsic mistake is found when a party becomes incompetent but no guardian ad litem is appointed . . . ; when one party relies on another to defend . . . ; when there is reliance on an attorney who becomes incapacitated to act . . . ; when a mistake led a court to do what it never intended . . . ; when a mistaken belief of one party prevented proper notice of the action . . . ; or when the complaining party was disabled at the time the judgment was entered. . . . Relief has also been extended to cases involving negligence of a party's attorney in not properly filing an answer (Hallett v. Slaughter (1943) 22 Cal. 2d 552, 556-557 [140 P.2d 3] . . .); and mistaken belief as to immunity from suit (Bartell v. Johnson (1943) 60 Cal. App. 2d 432, 436-437 [140 P.2d 878]).[2]

Relief is denied, however, if a party has been given notice of an action and has not been prevented from participating therein. He has had an opportunity to present his case to the court and to protect himself from mistake or from any fraud

---

2. The decisions in both *Hallett* and *Bartell* have been criticized. (See Comment (1943) 31 Cal. L. Rev. 600.) "The cases on *intrinsic fraud*, involving perjury, false documents and other reprehensible conduct by the adverse party, are far more compelling, yet relief is uniformly denied for good reason. . . . The *Hallett* and *Bartell* cases involve no true extrinsic factors in the accepted sense, and they raise serious questions as to the practical finality of any default judgment." (3 Witkin, Cal. Procedure, p.2130.)

attempted by his adversary. (Jorgensen v. Jorgensen, [32 Cal. 2d 13, 18, 193 P.2d 728 (1948)]. . . .) Moreover, a mutual mistake that might be sufficient to set aside a contract is not sufficient to set aside a final judgment. The principles of res judicata demand that the parties present their entire case in one proceeding. "Public policy requires that pressure be brought upon litigants to use great care in preparing cases for trial and in ascertaining all the facts. A rule which would permit the re-opening of cases previously decided because of error or ignorance during the progress of the trial would in a large measure vitiate the effects of the rules of res judicata." (Rest., Judgments, §126, com. a.) Courts deny relief, therefore, when the fraud or mistake is "intrinsic"; that is, when it "goes to the merits of the prior proceedings, which should have been guarded against by the plaintiff at that time." (Comment, Equitable Relief From Judgments, Orders and Decrees Obtained by Fraud (1934) 23 Cal. L. Rev. 79, 83-84. . . .)

Relief is also denied when the complaining party has contributed to the fraud or mistake giving rise to the judgment thus obtained. . . . "If the complainant was guilty of negligence in permitting the fraud to be practiced or the mistake to occur equity will deny relief." (Wilson v. Wilson (1942) 55 Cal. App. 2d 421, 427 [130 P.2d 782].)

Whether the case involves intrinsic or extrinsic fraud or mistake is not determined abstractly. "It is necessary to examine the facts in the light of the policy that a party who failed to assemble all his evidence at the trial should not be privileged to relitigate a case, as well as the policy permitting a party to seek relief from a judgment entered in a proceeding in which he was deprived of a fair opportunity fully to present his case." (Jorgensen v. Jorgensen, supra, 32 Cal. 2d 13 at p.19.)

The evidence in the present case establishes that it is a case in which a party "failed to assemble all his evidence at the trial." Defendant testified that he knew of the New Zealand holdings prior to the divorce and that plaintiff was receiving $640 every four months from New Zealand. In defendant's divorce questionnaire, circulated to determine the extent of marital property holdings, expenses and income, he listed as plaintiff's separate property "50% stock interest in David Lloyd Co., Ltd.,—a New Zealand holding corporation for many subsidiary companies (cement, coal, paper) —exact worth unknown to defendant—estimated to run into millions of dollars." In a letter sent by defendant's attorney to plaintiff's attorney in which the principal points of the property settlement were summarized, defendant proposed to transfer to plaintiff "any interest he may have in her holdings in New Zealand." Plaintiff also knew of the holdings but did not know of their value or their tax consequences. In 1957 when preparing income tax returns, an attorney, who later represented defendant in the divorce action, made some inquiry into the nature of the New Zealand income at the request of defendant. The attorney abandoned further investigation after plaintiff stated that a law firm known to defendant's attorney had advised her that the New Zealand income was not taxable. The attorney knew that the New Zealand holdings were "sizable." Both parties testified that the tax provision was included in the decree because of an audit being conducted by the Internal Revenue Service with respect to an unrelated transaction by defendant.

Clearly the present case does not involve the failure of one spouse to disclose fully the assets to be divided upon separation. . . . The duty to disclose arises out of the fiduciary relationship between the husband and wife. . . .There is no evidence that the wife withheld any information relevant to the nature of her New Zealand income.

The factual situation in the present case is analogous to that in Jorgensen v. Jorgensen, supra. In *Jorgensen* the husband disclosed all known assets of the parties. The husband claimed certain assets as his separate property. The wife and her attorney accepted the husband's statements at face value without any independent investigation. Subsequent to the divorce decree, however, they learned that some of the assets the husband claimed as separate property were actually community property, in which the wife was entitled to a one-half interest. The wife was denied the right to set aside the property settlement agreement.

> If the wife and her attorney are satisfied with the husband's classification of the property as separate or community, the wife cannot reasonably contend that fraud was committed or that there was such mistake as to allow her to overcome the finality of a judgment. . . . Plaintiff is barred from obtaining equitable relief by her admission that she and her attorney did not investigate the facts, choosing instead to rely on the statements of the husband as to what part of the disclosed property was community property. (Jorgensen v. Jorgensen, supra, 32 Cal. 2d 13 at pp.22-23. . . .)

In the present case both parties knew of the New Zealand assets, but the husband and his attorney chose not to investigate their taxability. The property settlement agreement expressly covered unknown tax liability. Having had full opportunity to consider all income of the wife and its concurrent tax consequences, the husband cannot now complain of the added tax burden.

The order is reversed. PETERS, J., TOBRINER, J., BURKE, J., and SULLIVAN, J., concurred.

MCCOMB, J. — I dissent. I would affirm the order of the trial court.

Notes and Questions

1. Today, could Mrs. Jorgensen bring a Family Code section 2556 (*Henn*) action to divide the community assets that her husband erroneously or fraudulently identified as his separate property? (*Henn* is reprinted at page 516 supra.)

In any event, does *Jorgensen* survive the 1991 amendments to current Family Code section 1100(e) (page 414 supra)? If the *Jorgensen* divorce had been commenced on or after January 1, 1993, how would the results vary under Family Code sections 2100-2129?

2. Does *Kulchar* effectively involve an omitted liability, as opposed to an asset, that may be assigned in a subsequent section 2556 proceeding? Suppose that there had been no stipulation about tax liability, that the parties filed jointly during marriage, and that, after divorce, the Internal Revenue Service exacted the $22,000 in back taxes from Mr. Kulchar. Could he then bring a section 2556 proceeding to have liability for the debt apportioned according to Family Code sections 2625 and 916? Mr. Kulchar would, of course, attempt to have the debt apportioned entirely to his wife because it was a tax liability generated by her separate income. If he were successful, he would seek reimbursement pursuant to section 916(b). Mr. Kulchar's petition seems even more appealing than Mrs. Henn's claim. The Henn pension

was in existence at the time of the divorce; it was simply omitted from the pleadings. The Kulchar debt did not even exist at divorce: The Internal Revenue Service first claimed the back-tax liability two years later.

3. Does the stipulation in which Mr. Kulchar agreed to take care of all pre-1964 tax liabilities foreclose a section 2556 action? How should the stipulation have been drafted? Does Mr. Kulchar have a malpractice claim against his divorce attorney?

4. Are *Kulchar* and *Henn* conceptually consistent? *Henn* actions operate, effectively, to cure mistakes. Yet *Kulchar* holds the parties to their mistakes. If *Kulchar* is warranted by res judicata concerns, is *Henn* incorrect?

VAI v. BANK OF AMERICA
56 Cal. 2d 329, 364 P.2d 247, 15 Cal. Rptr. 71 (1961)

WHITE, J. — This is an appeal by Tranquilla Vai from a judgment for defendant Bank of America as coexecutor with Henry Bodkin of the estate of Giovanni Vai, deceased, in a suit brought to rescind a property settlement agreement on the ground of fraud, for recovery of part of the property received by the husband under the agreement, and for damages in the event recovery thereof cannot be had.

Plaintiff and Giovanni (John) Vai were married in Italy in 1907 and emigrated to this country and Los Angeles in 1912. John joined his brother James in operating a winery. He remained in this business and related operations continuously from 1912 until his death in February 1957, and plaintiff actively assisted him until their only child Madeline was born in 1925. Their daughter is mentally arrested and has required constant care and attention. Apparently the relations between plaintiff and her husband had been something less than harmonious for several years before January 1953, when she left their home in Alta Loma and moved to another residence they owned in Parkside, where she has since resided. She consulted with counsel, Mr. Hallam Mathews, on January 7, 1953. After plaintiff gave him a list of the property in which she believed John had an interest, Mr. Mathews secured a Dun and Bradstreet report on Padre Vineyard Company, owned jointly by John and his brother, and a combined report on Cucamonga Valley Wine Company and Rancho El Camino, John's individual businesses. Mr. Mathews also secured descriptions of real property in San Bernardino County and a description of the Parkside property, consisting of a 30-year-old residence with 15 apartments.

On February 6, 1953, plaintiff filed a separate maintenance action, and John was served with a "Subpoena In Re Deposition and Order to Show Cause for Support, etc. Pendente Lite." John and his attorney represented, and the trial court so found, that John's health was such that adversary proceedings would be highly detrimental; that it would not be necessary for Mr. Mathews to pursue his legal remedies of discovery; that plaintiff would be voluntarily supplied with full and complete information; and that John would negotiate a fair and equitable property settlement agreement. No further independent investigation was made by plaintiff except for an appraisal of the Parkside property which she was to receive in the property settlement agreement. Following execution of this agreement, on March

16, 1953, the action for separate maintenance was abandoned. The present action was instituted shortly after John's death. . . .

The complaint initiating this suit to rescind the property settlement agreement charged that in the negotiation of the property settlement, John Vai was guilty of actual fraud, consisting of allegedly false representations and intentional concealment of material facts, by which the plaintiff was deceived and defrauded. It also charged constructive fraud, consisting of breach of John Vai's duty as a fiduciary to make a free and full disclosure of all important and relevant facts. *The trial court ruled that John was not a fiduciary, that the parties dealt at arm's length, that there was no issue of constructive fraud and that there was no proof of actual fraud.*

Plaintiff contends that although the confidential relationship between herself and her husband, based on her confidence and trust in him, may have been terminated by her filing suit for separate maintenance, her husband remained in a fiduciary position in respect to her interest in the community property. He breached his fiduciary duty, she asserts, by concealing material facts and by falsely representing others.

Defendants contend that Collins v. Collins, 48 Cal. 2d 325 [309 P.2d 420], is directly applicable to the facts at bar as found by the trial court. In *Collins,* the wife sought recision of a property settlement agreement on the ground that her husband had concealed community property assets from her and thus breached his duty of full disclosure arising out of the confidential relationship. Her attorney in Nevada, where she had gone to establish residence for divorce, requested the defendant husband to furnish them with a full and accurate list of community property. This request was never complied with. Mrs. Collins returned to California and signed an agreement prepared by defendant's attorney, and against the advice of her own counsel. Some properties standing in defendant's name were not listed in the agreement, but no attempt had been made by the defendant to conceal these properties which he claimed to be his separate property, or to hinder in any way an investigation begun by Mrs. Collins and her attorney. Manifestly, Mrs. Collins was fully aware that her husband had not disclosed any information about their community property, and expressly waived any such disclosure in writing when she executed the agreement. She knowingly chose to deal at arm's length and to rely on her own investigation of community assets. Thus by her own act, Mrs. Collins terminated the fiduciary relationship in respect to her interest in the community property and the attendant duty to disclose.

Plaintiff in the instant case discontinued the adversary proceedings commenced by her at the request of the defendant who offered to supply full and complete information concerning the property all of which was conceded to be community, and who further stated that he was willing to negotiate a fair and equitable property settlement. It would seem that plaintiff chose not to terminate the fiduciary relationship nor to deal at arm's length, but instead to take the defendant's offer at face value. She signed the agreement believing that she was fully and accurately informed as to the Vai community financial position.

Manifestly, therefore, the facts in *Collins,* supra, are markedly dissimilar from those in the instant case except insofar as both wives were represented by counsel who commenced investigations.

Section 161a (Civ. Code) provides: "The respective interests of the husband and wife in community property during continuance of the marriage relation are present, existing and equal interests under the management and control of the husband as is provided in sections 172 and 172a. . . . This section shall be construed as defining the respective interests and rights of husband and wife in the community property."[1]

Because of his management and control over the community property, the husband occupies the position of trustee for his wife in respect to her one-half interest in the community assets. (Fields v. Michael, 91 Cal. App. 2d 443, 447-448 [205 P.2d 402].) Recognizing this principle, Justice Traynor, speaking for a unanimous court, stated in Jorgensen v. Jorgensen, 32 Cal. 2d 13, 21 [193 P.2d 728], "As the manager of the community property the husband occupies a position of trust . . . , which is not terminated as to assets remaining in his hands when the spouses separate. It is part of his fiduciary duties to account to the wife for the community property when the spouses are negotiating a property settlement agreement."

"Even divorce proceedings pending do not, in themselves, interrupt the husband's powers with respect to the management and control of community property, as the effect of such proceedings is not to take the property into the custody of the court. The husband continues to have control of it and full power to dispose of it." (Chance v. Kobsted, 66 Cal. App. 434, 437 [226 P. 632].) "When a divorce is pending the power of a husband over the community property exists until the entry of a final decree. (Lord v. Hough, 43 Cal. 581; Chance v. Kobsted, 66 Cal. App. 434, 437 [226 P. 632]; In re Cummings, 84 F. Supp. 65, 69.)" (Harrold v. Harrold, 43 Cal. 2d 77, 81 [271 P.2d 489].)

Since the husband's control of the community property continues until there has been a division of it by agreement or by court decree, it would follow that the husband would continue to remain a fiduciary in respect to his wife's interest in the community assets until such division was made. Of course, as was the case in Collins v. Collins, 48 Cal. 2d 325 [309 P.2d 420], the wife may choose not to rely on her husband and release him from the performance of his fiduciary duties.

This fiduciary relationship arises by virtue of the community property system which gives the husband management and control of such property in order that the assets be more efficiently handled, and exists only as to the community property over which the husband has control. It should be distinguished from the confidential relationship which is presumed to exist between spouses.

> A confidential relation exists between two persons when one has gained the confidence of the other and purports to act or advise with the other's interest in mind. A confidential relation may exist although there is no fiduciary relation; it is particularly likely to exist where there is a family relationship or one of friendship or such a relation of confidence as that which arises between physician and patient or priest and penitent. (Rest., Trusts 2d, §2, comment b.)

The confidential relationship and obligations arising out of it are, therefore, dependent upon the existence of confidence and trust, but the husband's fiduciary duties in respect to his wife's interest in the community property continue as long as his control of that property continues, notwithstanding the complete absence of confidence and trust, and the consequent termination of the confidential relationship.

---

1. Civil Code, §172: "The husband has the management and control of the community personal property. . . ." Civil Code, §172a: "The husband has the management and control of the community real property. . . ."

The prerequisite of a confidential relationship is the reposing of trust and confidence by one person in another who is cognizant of this fact. The key factor in the existence of a fiduciary relationship lies in control by a person over the property of another. It is evident that while these two relationships may exist simultaneously, they do not necessarily do so. For example, in Estate of Cover, 188 Cal. 133 [204 P. 583], where all of the property under the husband's control was his separate property, only a confidential relation existed. . . .

The simultaneous existence of a confidential relationship based on trust and confidence and a fiduciary relationship arising out of control of property of another is readily apparent in many common associations — principal and agent, attorney and client, business partners, to name a few. It is evident that although the confidential relationship may be terminated by either party, if an individual continues to control property of the other he is held to the duties of a fiduciary as long as he retains such control, notwithstanding the termination of the confidential relationship. . . .

The dissolution of a partnership and attendant agreements respecting partnership property appear to be remarkably similar to the dissolution of the conjugal relation and property settlement agreements. Briefly, "in all proceedings connected with the conduct of the partnership every partner is bound to act in the highest good faith to his copartner and may not obtain any advantage over him in the partnership affairs by the slightest misrepresentation, concealment, threat or adverse pressure of any kind. . . ." (Llewelyn v. Levi, 157 Cal. 31, 37 [106 P. 219]. . . .) In view of the nature of the relation, the necessity of exercising the highest good faith in it is especially marked between a managing partner and his copartners, and proof that one has waived his rights against the other must be clear. . . . In the course of negotiations for dissolution, each partner must deal fairly with his copartners and not conceal from them important matters within his own knowledge touching the business and property of the partnership. . . . Thus, one partner, in negotiating for the purchase of his copartner's interest in the partnership, owes the latter the duty of fair play and full disclosure, but once the sale is consummated, the relationship between them immediately ceases and the purchaser is justified in dealing *thereafter* with the other at arm's length. (Wise Realty Co. v. Stewart, 169 Cal. 176 [146 P. 534]; 120 A.L.R. 724.)

Manifestly, the fiduciary duties and rules governing their performance by a husband should be no fewer or less rigorous than those imposed upon business partners. To hold, as defendant urges, that if a wife employs able counsel upon whom she relies in negotiating a property settlement agreement in conjunction with her action for separate maintenance, that her husband is thereby released from any fiduciary duties in respect to her interest in the community property, would put a wife in a far less protected position than a partner whose partnership is being dissolved. It would

> permit the authority of the husband in controlling the community property, given him in the interest of greater freedom in its use and for its transfer for the benefit of both himself and his wife, to become a weapon to be used by him to rob her of every vestige of interest in the community property with which the law has expressly invested her. Such a conclusion would violate every sense of justice, and outrage every principle of fair dealing known to the law. (Provost v. Provost, 102 Cal. App. 775, 781 [283 P. 842].)

Plaintiff alleges that due to misrepresentations and concealments by the defendant, she was not informed as to the actual value of the community property and that she would not have executed the property settlement agreement in question had she been accurately and fully informed.

Specifically, plaintiff contends that the value of Rancho El Camino was misrepresented and concealed. The following findings in respect to Rancho El Camino were made by the trial court. Mr. Mathews, plaintiff's counsel, was shown a financial statement prepared by John showing the book value of the vineyard land at Rancho El Camino to be $200 per acre. Plaintiff's counsel was told of other vineyard land which sold for $400 to $450 an acre but that such land was closer to factories. He was not told of the price received by John ($566 per acre) for vineyard land immediately to the north of Rancho El Camino sold nine months previously. The trial court found that Mr. Mathews (plaintiff's attorney) was told that Rancho El Camino was of little market value as a vineyard and could hardly be sold when the wine market was depressed. However, on February 21, 1953, 23 days prior to the execution of the property settlement agreement, John Vai executed a sale deposit receipt for $25,000 with Donald Duncan, for the sale of Rancho El Camino, at a price of $525,000, or $814 an acre. Plaintiff was never informed of this fact. Escrow was opened four days after execution of the property settlement agreement with plaintiff, and the property duly sold to Duncan.

As additional breaches of John's fiduciary duty, plaintiff draws our attention to representations relating to the financial condition of Padre Vineyard which were made by John to his wife and her attorney. When consideration is given to representations found by the trial court to have been made to plaintiff and comparison is had with other findings as to the verity of such representations, it is readily apparent that many representations were either not true or at least only partially true. For instance, to cite a few: (1) Representation: Little would be realized if Padre were liquidated. Finding: Padre's assets at the time of the execution of the property settlement agreement exceeded its liabilities by approximately one million dollars; its net book value was in excess of $800,000. (2) Representation: Padre was in danger of insolvency. Finding: It was not in danger of immediate insolvency, but if its operations continued to lose money as it had in the past, a danger of insolvency existed. (3) Representation: Salaries due to John and his brother as officers of Padre had not been paid. Finding: Salaries of $300 to $500 a month had been and were currently being paid. (4) Representation: Padre owed John $80,000 to $90,000 and could not meet its obligations. Finding: Various payments, including $2,500 per month, on indebtedness owing to John had been made by Padre during the months previous to the execution of the property settlement agreement. (5) Representation: A grave danger existed that Mrs. Vai and John would be held liable on a continuing guaranty of Padre's liabilities up to $300,000 to the Bank of America. Finding: The indebtedness to the Bank was secured by the hypothecation of assets worth $1,320,729 including only a part of the wine inventory which could have been sold on the market for $435,000. . . .

Numerous other contentions relating to the existence of actual fraud are made by plaintiff, many of which appear to have merit. It does not seem necessary to discuss them, however, in view of our holding contrary to that of the trial court that a husband is under a fiduciary duty with respect to his wife's interest in the community property under his control and management. The failure of the husband in the instant case to disclose fully and fairly material facts relating to the value of community assets from which John gained an advantage constitutes a concealment of material facts and a breach of this fiduciary duty. This is constructive fraud, whether or not such failure to disclose was accompanied by an actual intent to defraud. . . . The facts as found by the trial court show the existence of a fiduciary relationship and constructive fraud as a matter of law. . . .

Defendants contend, however, that plaintiff is barred by laches and estoppel. The complaint in the instant action was not filed until March 18, 1957, although the agreement was signed by the parties on March 16, 1954. The trial court found that the plaintiff was told of the sale of Rancho El Camino by John and by one of his employees in the "Spring" of 1954, and consequently is barred by the equitable doctrine of laches: an unreasonable delay in commencing the action which has prejudiced the defendants.

There is no evidence in the record that plaintiff actually knew of the fraud before the death of her husband. However, "discovery is different from knowledge, [so] that where a party defrauded has received information of facts which should put him upon inquiry, and the inquiry if made would disclose the fraud, he will be charged with a discovery as of the time the inquiry would have given him knowledge." (Victor Oil Co. v. Drum, 184 Cal. 226, 240 [193 P. 243].)

"The circumstances must be such that the inquiry becomes a duty, and the failure to make it a negligent omission." (Tarke v. Bingham, 123 Cal. 163, 166 [55 P. 759].) "Where no duty is imposed by law upon a person to make inquiry, and where under the circumstances 'a prudent man' would not be put upon inquiry, the mere fact that means of knowledge are open to a plaintiff, and he has not availed himself of them, does not debar him from relief when thereafter he shall make actual discovery." (MacDonald v. Reich & Lievre, Inc., 100 Cal. App. 736, 740-741 [281 P. 106].)

Assuming that plaintiff could have discovered the fraud had she investigated, defendants have not pointed out any circumstances which should have put plaintiff upon inquiry until after John's death in 1957 when she was told that she had not been treated fairly by her husband.

Defendants argue that plaintiff is estopped and precluded from rescission by the stipulation in the agreement that it was entered into freely and voluntarily without promises or representations not contained therein, and the trial court so found. But, as plaintiff correctly points out, when the agreement itself is procured by fraud, none of its provisions have any legal or binding effect. . . .

It is manifest from the foregoing that plaintiff is neither estopped nor barred by laches from seeking to rescind the property settlement agreement, and that she is entitled to the relief sought because of the constructive fraud of her husband.

For the foregoing reasons the judgment is reversed. GIBSON, C.J., PETERS, J., DOOLING, J., AND FOURT, J. pro tem., concurred.

Respondents' petition for a rehearing was denied August 23, 1961. . . . TRAYNOR, J., and SCHAUER, J., were of the opinion that the petition should be granted.

Notes and Questions

1. What is the difference between a confidential relationship and a fiduciary relationship? What duties are imposed by each? How would you define each in our era of equal management?

2. In *Collins*, did Mr. Collins breach his fiduciary duty by failing to furnish Mrs. Collins with a full and accurate list of community property? What was Mrs. Collins supposed to do then? Why was she unable to rescind the agreement? How do you

distinguish *Collins* from *Vai*? Does *Collins* survive the 1991 amendments to current Family Code section 1100? The 1992 enactment of sections 2100-2129?

3. Is the dissolution of a business partnership an apt analog for the termination of a marriage? Should business partners be held to a higher or lower standard than conjugal partners?

4. *Vai* was an easy case on its facts, for there was actual fraud. The language of *Vai* is far more expansive than necessary to resolve the complaint before the court. The dictum of *Vai* has been largely ignored in appellate decisions. Marriage of Connolly, which follows, is illustrative.

MARRIAGE OF CONNOLLY
23 Cal. 3d 590, 591 P.2d 911, 153 Cal. Rptr. 423 (1979)

RICHARDSON, J.—This case involves a contested marital dissolution proceeding in which, after trial, corporate stock conceded to be community property was awarded to husband, a director of the corporation. The issue presented is whether husband had a fiduciary obligation to inform wife of facts which might affect the stock's value even though such information was readily ascertainable by wife or her counsel upon reasonable inquiry. We conclude that under the circumstances of this case husband had no such duty.

Wife and husband were married April 16, 1961, in Los Angeles and they have three minor children. The couple separated July 29, 1973. In August 1973 wife filed a marital dissolution action against husband. The relationship of the parties thereafter was adversary and we recite the ensuing significant chronology.

After two years and nine months of fruitless pretrial discovery and negotiation between the parties and counsel, trial on the disposition of the community property was conducted from May 17 to 20, 1976. Consistent with [Family] Code section [2552], the parties agreed that all securities owned by the community were to be valued as of May 17, 1976, for purposes of division.

One of the securities was 10,000 shares of the common stock of Amdahl Corporation (Amdahl), a computer company. Husband had become an "outside" director of Amdahl in 1972 and had been permitted to purchase these shares at 6 cents a share. Although at the time of trial the stock was not publicly traded, in 1973 Amdahl had unsuccessfully attempted a public offering of its stock. A second attempt in 1974 was also frustrated. In November 1975, seven months prior to trial, Amdahl publicly announced a third attempt at a public offering. An article in the November 3, 1975, issue of Electronic News under the headline *Amdahl Weighs Public Offering* indicated that "Amdahl hopes to make a stab at going public possibly early next year." A similar article in the March 8, 1976, issue of Business Week stated that "Amdahl Corp., another private computer company rumored to be going public soon, is also highly regarded by Wall Street analysts. The company has not yet turned a profit, but Hochfeld wouldn't be surprised if it earned $10 million in 1976." Each of three short articles in Investment Dealers Digest, dated April 20, 1976, April 27, 1976, and May 4, 1976, reported Amdahl's intended public sale.

At trial the court was obliged to set a value on the Amdahl stock and husband was questioned by court and counsel regarding this matter. However, he was neither asked about, nor volunteered, his views as to Amdahl's financial condition or future, including any prospective public issue of Amdahl stock. He testified accurately that recent private sales of Amdahl shares had been in the range of $5 to $10 per share and that the company itself had set a value of not more than $10 per share on the stock for the purpose of stock option plans for employees and directors. Husband requested that the 10,000 shares be awarded to him in the division of the community property in order to preserve his influence as a director.

On June 7, wife filed with the trial court a written "Petitioner's Closing Arguments," in which she valued the stock at "$100,000(?)" and suggested that it be awarded to husband. The June 14 issue of the Wall Street Journal contained an article on Amdahl which began, "Amdahl Corp., a Sunnyvale, Calif., maker of large computers, plans to go public with an initial offering of one million common shares." The court issued its original memorandum of intended decision June 29 indicating that it proposed to award the Amdahl stock to husband and to require him to execute and deliver an unsecured promissory note to wife for half the value of the stock, without designating the principal amount of the note. On July 7, after a meeting with counsel in chambers, the court filed its amended memorandum which again awarded the Amdahl stock to husband but which increased spousal support to wife.

In implementation of the court's memorandum, the interlocutory judgment of dissolution of marriage was entered July 19, 1976, without objection by wife or her counsel. Under the terms of the decree the 10,000 Amdahl shares, valued at $7.50 per share, were awarded to husband. In consideration for the award of the shares (and to otherwise equalize division of the community property) the note, bearing a principal sum of $37,500, was payable in 11 annual installments with interest at 7 percent. The judgment reflected that both parties had waived findings of fact, the right to appeal, and the right to move for a new trial. A final judgment of dissolution of marriage was entered on July 20.

In the early part of August the status of the public offering of Amdahl stock remained uncertain. An article in the August 6, 1976, issue of the Wall Street Journal, headlined *Amdahl Stock Issue Runs into Trouble; Release Is Delayed,* reported that the Securities and Exchange Commission had challenged a portion of Amdahl's financial statement. The article continued, "Yesterday morning, before the problems developed, First Boston [managing underwriter for the proposed issue] indicated the Amdahl issue would be priced at $30 a share, at the low end of the $30 to $35 range originally estimated." On August 12, 1976, the public offering was finally made and 1,062,500 shares of Amdahl stock were sold, representing 1 million shares held by the company and 62,500 shares owned by shareholders (not including husband). The opening price of the stock was $27.50 a share, translated into a value for 10,000 shares as of the date of the offering, of $275,000. (Since then the stock again has substantially increased in value.)

On January 12, 1977, wife filed a motion pursuant to Code of Civil Procedure section 473 seeking to reopen the interlocutory and final judgments of dissolution alleging fraud on the part of husband in failing to reveal voluntarily that Amdahl contemplated a public offering. Section 473 provides in relevant part that "The court may, upon such terms as may be just, relieve a party or his legal representative from a judgment, order, or other proceeding taken against him through his mistake, inadvertence, surprise or excusable neglect." Relief under this section is authorized where there is proof of fraud which results in excusable neglect or mistake. (Kulchar v. Kulchar (1969) 1 Cal. 3d 467 [82 Cal. Rptr. 489, 462 P.2d 17, 39 A.L.R.3d 1368]; In re Marriage of Carletti (1975) 53 Cal. App. 3d 989 [126 Cal. Rptr. 1]; see

5 Witkin, Cal. Procedure (2d ed. 1971) Attack on Judgment in Trial Court, §§126, 130.)

As part of her section 473 motion, wife requested one-half of the Amdahl stock. She alleged that husband owed her a fiduciary duty, as an Amdahl director, to disclose to her the proposed public sale of Amdahl stock and, further, that his failure to do so constituted a violation of Corporations Code section 25402 which in pertinent part reads:

> It is unlawful for an issuer or any person who is . . . [a] director . . . whose relationship to the issuer gives him access, directly or indirectly, to material information about the issuer not generally available to the public, to purchase . . . any security of the issuer in this state at a time when he knows material information about the issuer gained from such relationship which would significantly affect the market price of that security and which is not generally available to the public, and which he knows is not intended to be so available, unless he has reason to believe that the person selling to or buying from him is also in possession of the information.

More specifically alleging fraud, wife contended that husband knew at the time of trial that the Amdahl stock would be the subject of a public offering at a price of $25 to $30 a share, that he knowingly withheld such information from her permitting him to acquire her community interest in their shares at the price of $7.50 a share, and that she discovered the alleged fraud only when the announcement of public sale was made. Wife further asserted that had she and her counsel known of the impending public offering, they would have insisted that the Amdahl shares be divided equally.

On March 15, 1977, the trial court denied wife's motion to vacate the judgment on two grounds, after concluding that she had not established any basis for section 473 relief. The court determined, first, that there was no evidence that in his capacity as a corporate director husband had obtained or withheld information "not generally available to the public." The court concluded that the information regarding the proposed Amdahl public offering was neither confidential nor secret, had been published prior to trial, was reasonably available to wife and her counsel, and would have come to her knowledge, if in fact it did not, had she made even a most cursory examination of the financial background of the stock. Second, the court found that the value of the Amdahl stock on May 17, 1976, the stipulated valuation date, was reasonably determined to be $7.50, and that there was no substantial evidence otherwise.

In reviewing the evidence in support of a section 473 motion, we extend all legitimate and reasonable inferences to uphold the judgment. The disposition of such a motion rests largely in the discretion of the trial court, and its decision will not be disturbed on appeal unless there has been a clear abuse of discretion. . . . [W]hen two or more inferences can reasonably be deduced from the facts, a reviewing court lacks power to substitute its deductions for those of the trial court. . . .

Applying the foregoing well-established standards, we conclude that the determination of the trial court was supported by substantial evidence. The information which husband possessed regarding the proposed public offering was generally available to the public. The court had before it numerous news articles which had been published before trial which discussed the public offering. While some of these reports, perhaps, may have had limited circulation, an article published in the Wall Street Journal on June 14, 1976, during the period in which counsel and the court were negotiating a final settlement, even described the number of shares to be sold, and although wife's counsel admitted that at the time of trial he had heard "vague rumors" of a public offering, no further information was sought. Not only would the information about the public offering have been readily available to wife or her counsel had they read the financial papers, but even a cursory examination of the background of the stock would have revealed such information to them. Further, husband testified in his opposition to wife's section 473 motion that he had on occasion mentioned the proposed public sale to wife.

The value of the Amdahl stock was in issue at trial, and the court found it necessary to take evidence on the matter. It would not have been an unreasonable burden or difficult for wife or her counsel to have presented independent evidence at trial regarding the value of the stock through the testimony of a stock broker, a securities analyst, an accountant, banker or a fiscal officer of Amdahl. At trial, husband could have been cross-examined on the point.

The burden of discovery in a matter such as that before us does not seem onerous, and we note two recent analogous situations. In In re Marriage of Carter [19 Cal. App. 3d 479, 491, 97 Cal. Rptr. 274 (1971)] (in connection with a stipulated division of community property), wife contended that husband had concealed the value of certain community property assets including the husband's wholly owned corporation. The court, in rejecting wife's section 473 motion, noted that husband had not concealed the existence of any assets and that

> [wife's] complaint that she was not informed of the market value of the several items does not constitute concealment. . . . As to items not reflected at market value, most of the stocks and bonds were the separate property of the husband. With respect to the remaining bonds, it would appear that an examination of the stocks and bonds listed in the Wall Street Journal would have reflected current fair market value. . . . Similarly, investigation could have revealed the fair market value of the husband's corporations.

In Boeseke v. Boeseke (1974) 10 Cal. 3d 844 [112 Cal. Rptr. 401, 519 P.2d 161], husband failed to disclose all the facts in his possession relating to the value, nature and extent of the community property, but did give to wife and her counsel the property descriptions. Wife executed a property agreement without making her own independent investigation of the value of the property and later, after husband's death, attempted to rescind the agreement. In a unanimous opinion we held that there had been no fraud on the part of husband. We observed:

> It is true [husband] did not disclose all facts in his possession relating to the value, nature, and extent of the community property. However, [wife] and her counsel were fully advised of the property descriptions. They were also aware that some of the property was of substantial value, that there was substantial income — and substantial debt. As far as can be determined, neither she nor her counsel requested further *facts* relating to the value, the nature, or the extent of the marital assets. And rather than seeking the facts, she chose to accept her husband's offer of settlement even after being advised by counsel that she should investigate. She may not now complain. The trial court's finding of fraud predicated on [husband's] lack of disclosure fails. . . .

>Finally, during negotiation to settle marital property rights, fairness dictates the managing spouse be under no duty to *evaluate* the marital assets. And if the managing spouse does assert an opinion of value, he or she must be able to do so without warranty. Valuation, like designation of property as being either community or separate, is an issue on which reasonable views often differ, and in the absence of concealment of assets — or facts materially affecting their value — a property settlement agreement may not later be set aside solely on the basis of the managing spouse's inaccurate opinion of value or on his or her refusal to have rendered such opinion. (Italics in original, at pp.849-850.)

A similar situation is herein presented. Substantial evidence supports the trial court's conclusion that husband did not conceal material facts from wife. She had every opportunity to ascertain the complete status of the Amdahl stock. She made a tactical decision not to pursue further investigation. Husband made no attempt to hinder such an inquiry and while on the witness stand during trial was readily available to answer any and all questions put to him. The record does not disclose that he answered the questions that were put to him untruthfully. Given the evidence it had before it, the trial court did not abuse its discretion in determining that husband had not breached his general fiduciary duty as a director by omissions in his testimony.

The trial court also found that $7.50 was a reasonable price for the stock as of May 17, 1976, the date agreed upon for valuation. The record reflects abundant evidence to support this determination. During the period, March to May 1976, more than 25,000 shares of Amdahl stock had been traded in more than a dozen different transactions between parties fully cognizant of the prospective public sale, at prices ranging from $5 to $10 per share. On May 17, 1976, the company's board of directors unanimously adopted a resolution valuing the company's common stock at *not more than* $10 per share for purposes of stock options. The directors of the company clearly would have been aware of the intended offering. At the time of trial Amdahl had never shown a profit. Given the information that it had, the court could reasonably determine that $7.50 per share, the middle of the $5 to $10 per share range which had been established by the evidence, was the fair value of the stock.

Wife further contends that husband owed her a separate fiduciary duty arising from the marital relationship. We are unable to accept the argument. From the time that wife filed her petition seeking dissolution of the marriage in 1973 her relationship with her husband was an adversary one. Any obligation of trust between them was terminated. They were locked in litigation. They maintained separate residences. Each was represented by his or her own counsel. They pursued their individual and separate legal interests with enthusiasm. The trial court characterized the case as "an extremely well tried case with high but controlled emotions and a difficult legal problem."

We have repeatedly held that parties may elect to deal with each other at arms' length, and when they do so any fiduciary obligation otherwise owing is thereby terminated. (Boeseke v. Boeseke, supra, 10 Cal. 3d 844, 849; Collins v. Collins (1957) 48 Cal. 2d 325, 330-331 [309 P.2d 420]; Jorgensen v. Jorgensen (1948) 32 Cal. 2d 13, 23 [193 P.2d 728]; see also In re Marriage of Carter, supra, 19 Cal. App. 3d 479, 491.) The actions of the parties in the present case establish that husband and wife chose to deal with each other as legal adversaries and that at all times during the negotiations relative to the Amdahl stock wife never relied on any relationship of confidentiality or mutual trust.

Our holding in Vai v. Bank of America (1961) 56 Cal. 2d 329 [15 Cal. Rptr. 71, 364 P.2d 247], is not contrary. In *Vai* wife sued for separate maintenance, but discontinued the adversary proceeding at the request of husband, who told her that she would not have to pursue her legal remedies in order to obtain a reasonable division of property. He represented to her that she would be supplied with full and complete information about the community property and that he would negotiate a fair and equitable property settlement agreement. On the basis of these statements the wife made no further independent investigation of the value of the community property, and executed the agreement. Husband died and, upon learning of what she believed to be gross inequities in the values of the community property received by each of the parties, wife sued to rescind the agreement on the basis of fraud. . . .

The present case differs. Here, after the dissolution action was filed, wife was never led to believe that she could or should rely on husband. The dispute over the property lasted almost three years, during which time wife and her counsel pursued their own independent investigation of the community property, at least to the extent of submitting a proposed property division. The value of the Amdahl stock was far from certain. In her pleadings dated June 7, 1976, wife speculated that the Amdahl stock was worth "$100,000(?)." Parties in a civil adversary proceeding who bear no special relationship to each other bear the responsibility of using those reasonable means available to develop and ascertain factual information affecting their interests in the litigation. Wife had the means to do so, including the cross-examination of husband at trial. If she and her counsel chose not to investigate and were, as she alleges, ignorant of the proposed public offering, they may not be heard to complain if they fail to utilize those reasonable means of discovery readily at hand. As we observed in *Vai,* "Of course, as was the case in Collins v. Collins [supra], 48 Cal. 2d 325, the wife may choose not to rely on her husband and release him from the performance of his fiduciary duties." (56 Cal. 2d at p.337.) We are satisfied that this is what happened in the present case. . . .

The order denying wife's motion to vacate the judgment of dissolution is affirmed. BIRD, C.J., TOBRINER, J., MOSK, J., CLARK, J., MANUEL, J., and NEWMAN, J., concurred.

Appellant's petition for a rehearing was denied April 12, 1979.

Notes and Questions

1. *Connolly* stands on several legs, thus providing little in the way of solid holding. Nevertheless, its dictum indicates that the supreme court had substantially changed its views since *Vai*. After *Connolly* and *Boeseke* (discussed in *Connolly* at pages 534-535 supra), what was the bare minimum that would satisfy one divorcing spouse's fiduciary obligation to the other?

For further discussion of the pre-1991 content of the fiduciary duty after separation, see Marriage of Modnick, 33 Cal. 3d 897, 663 P.2d 187, 191 Cal. Rptr. 629 (1983); Miller v. Bechtel Corp., 33 Cal. 3d 868, 663 P.2d 177, 191 Cal. Rptr. 619 (1983); Marriage of Alexander, 212 Cal. App. 3d 677, 261 Cal. Rptr. 9 (1989); Marriage of Baltins, 212 Cal. App. 3d 66, 260 Cal. Rptr. 403 (1989); Resnick v. Superior Court, 185 Cal. App. 3d 634, 230 Cal. Rptr. 1 (1986); Marriage of Stevenot, 154

Cal. App. 3d 1051, 202 Cal. Rptr. 116 (1984); and Marriage of Munguia, 146 Cal. App. 3d 853, 859, 195 Cal. Rptr. 199 (1983).

2. *Vai* reflects the court's view of how divorcing spouses ought to act; *Connolly* probably reflects the court's view of how divorcing spouses do act. To what extent does the adoption of the *Vai* or *Connolly* perspective become a self-fulfilling prophecy? Compare the broad dicta of *Vai* and *Connolly* in terms of their implications for the parties, their attorneys, and the judicial system. Which do you prefer?

3. *Connolly* assumes a vigorous adversary setting, but some divorcing couples now reject adversary proceedings in favor of mediation. What fiduciary standard is appropriate in mediation?

4. What is left of *Kulchar, Connolly,* and *Boeseke* after the 1991 and 2002 amendments to current Family Code sections 721, 1100, and 1101 (pages 413-415 supra)? What acts or behavior, if any, would constitute a waiver of section 721 and 1100 rights?

With respect to post-1992 proceedings (sections 2100-2109) and post-1992 judgments (sections 2120-2129), what remains of *Kulchar, Connolly,* and *Boeseke?*

MARRIAGE OF ALEXANDER
212 Cal. App. 3d 677, 261 Cal. Rptr. 9 (1989)

KING, J. — In this case we [reaffirm] . . . the rule enunciated in In re Marriage of Stevenot (1984) 154 Cal. App. 3d 1051, 1068 [202 Cal. Rptr. 116], that "After relief is no longer available under Code of Civil Procedure section 473 for mistake, inadvertance [sic], surprise or excusable neglect, an otherwise valid and final judgment may only be set aside if it has been obtained through extrinsic, not intrinsic, fraud." An inequitable division of community property, by itself, is insufficient to set aside such a judgment and the marital settlement agreement of the parties incorporated therein.

Patrick Alexander appeals from an order setting aside a marital settlement agreement and the property settlement portions of a dissolution judgment. We reverse.

Patrick and Carolyn Alexander separated in January 1986 after 21 years of marriage. Carolyn left the family home in Pleasant Hill and moved to Barstow. She told Patrick she wanted a divorce and wanted nothing from the marriage.

Patrick consulted a divorce manual for nonlawyers and prepared a marital settlement agreement consisting of six individual agreements and an interspousal grant deed. A month after the separation, Carolyn returned to the family home to retrieve some personal belongings. She reviewed the settlement documents with Patrick for approximately 10 minutes, and told Patrick for the first time that she wanted half the equity in the home. He accordingly retyped the individual agreement pertaining to the home. The documents were then executed by the parties before a notary public.

The six agreements provided the following: (1) the current equity in the family home was $53,000, of which Carolyn would receive half upon sale of the property within 12 years, (2) Carolyn had already received $4,000 as partial payment for the equity in the home, (3) Carolyn waived all rights to all savings plans or accounts held jointly with or separately by Patrick, (4) Carolyn waived any interest she held in Patrick's pension plan, (5) all furnishings, personal property and motor vehicles in the respective parties' possession would be their separate property, and (6) Carolyn waived all rights to spousal support. The interspousal transfer grant deed conveyed Carolyn's interest in the family home to Patrick as his separate property.

Patrick then filed a petition for dissolution of marriage. Carolyn defaulted. On August 20, 1986, the court rendered a dissolution judgment incorporating the marital settlement agreement. Neither party had obtained legal counsel.

Fifteen months later, on November 24, 1987, Carolyn, now represented by counsel, filed a motion to set aside the judgment and marital settlement agreement on the ground of extrinsic fraud. She asserted that she had been suffering from severe emotional distress (due to her daughter's illness with cancer and the breakup of the marriage) when she signed the settlement documents and was not conscious of their nature or seriousness, and had relied on statements by Patrick that she did not need an attorney and they should remain friends.

The court granted the motion and set aside the marital settlement agreement and the property settlement portions of the dissolution judgment. The court found that Carolyn "has not carried her burden of establishing extrinsic fraud," but concluded that the marital settlement agreement should be set aside because it was inequitable and because Carolyn had not made a knowing waiver of her rights. The court relied on In re Marriage of Moore (1980) 113 Cal. App. 3d 22 [169 Cal. Rptr. 619], which cited inequity and the lack of a knowing waiver as grounds for setting aside a marital settlement agreement before the rendition of a dissolution judgment.

Patrick correctly contends the court's express finding of no extrinsic fraud precluded the setting aside of the marital settlement agreement and judgment. This is because Carolyn did not file her motion within the six-month period prescribed by Code of Civil Procedure section 473 (hereafter section 473) for obtaining relief from a judgment due to mistake, inadvertence, surprise or excusable neglect. Once this six-month period elapsed, as we have previously held, the *only* ground for relief was extrinsic fraud. (In re Marriage of Stevenot, supra, 154 Cal. App. 3d at p.1068.) The court having expressly found Carolyn had failed to establish extrinsic fraud, there was no basis for granting relief, and the court erred in doing so.

The decision upon which the court relied, In re Marriage of Moore, supra, 113 Cal. App. 3d 22, differs from the present case in a fundamental respect. In *Moore* the motion to set aside the marital settlement agreement was filed *before rendition of the dissolution judgment* (id. at p.26), and thus contract defenses such as mistake and unconscionability were applicable. Here, in contrast, the motion was not filed until after the marital settlement agreement was incorporated into a judgment and after the six-month period for relief under section 473. "Marital settlement agreements, once incorporated into a judgment, are no longer mere contracts and a showing of extrinsic fraud is required to set them aside. Thus, they become a hybrid, more like a judgment than a contract, and contract defenses such as mutual mistake are insufficient to set them aside." (In re Marriage of Stevenot, supra, 154 Cal. App. 3d at p.1071.) Once a marital settlement agreement is incorporated into a judgment and relief is unavailable under section 473, a strong showing of extrinsic fraud is required to set aside the agreement. (Ibid.)

Carolyn insists that notwithstanding the court's express finding, there had actually been extrinsic fraud, in that Patrick induced her not to retain counsel, concealed the effect of the settlement documents, and concealed an employee stock plan. She is entitled to appellate review on this point for the purpose of determining whether the order was ultimately correct despite the improper grounds asserted by the court. (Code Civ. Proc., §906.)

The court's express finding of no extrinsic fraud and the consequent implied rejection of these assertions by Carolyn are not subject to challenge, however, if supported by substantial evidence. (See generally 9 Witkin, Cal. Procedure (3d ed. 1985) Appeal, §278 et seq.) Such supporting evidence was present in Patrick's testimony and his declaration in opposition to the motion. The implied finding of no inducement to forego counsel was supported by Patrick's assertions that he merely suggested it would be less expensive and traumatic to proceed without counsel and did not threaten Carolyn or make any false representations to induce her not to see an attorney. Carolyn herself testified that Patrick never told her not to go to an attorney and she knew she had a right to see one. The implied finding of no concealment of the effect of the settlement documents was supported by Patrick's assertions that he spent 10 minutes going over the documents with her (Carolyn conceded this fact), asked if she had any questions concerning them, and advised her to get a copy of the divorce manual he had used to draft them. The implied finding of no fraudulent concealment of the employee stock plan (which Patrick admitted he did not "specifically" disclose to Carolyn, although it was included in a yearly summary sent to their home) was supported by Patrick's assertion that Carolyn said she wanted no community property arising from his employment.

Thus, notwithstanding Carolyn's contrary testimony, the court's finding of no extrinsic fraud was supported by substantial evidence, consisting of Patrick's testimony and declaration. (See In re Marriage of Mix (1975) 14 Cal. 3d 604, 614 [122 Cal. Rptr. 79, 536 P.2d 479] [testimony of a single witness, even a party, may constitute substantial evidence].) That finding is therefore not subject to challenge. . . .

Thus, the general rule we established in *Stevenot* is [determinative]. . . . "After relief is no longer available under Code of Civil Procedure section 473 for mistake, inadvertance [*sic*], surprise or excusable neglect, an otherwise valid and final judgment may only be set aside if it has been obtained through extrinsic, not intrinsic, fraud." (In re Marriage of Stevenot, supra, 154 Cal. App. 3d at p.1068.) The trial court's finding of no extrinsic fraud was determinative that Carolyn's motion should have been denied. Extrinsic fraud was required. Once the six-month period prescribed by Code of Civil Procedure section 473 has passed, an inequitable division of the community property, by itself, is insufficient to set aside a marital dissolution judgment and the marital settlement agreement of the parties incorporated therein.

Changing the names, we repeat the final paragraph from *Stevenot:* "In sum, we conclude that the record does not disclose that [Carolyn] was either deliberately kept in ignorance of the proceeding or fraudulently prevented by [Patrick] from presenting her claims. Any failure was due to her own failure to act diligently. Absent extrinsic fraud, it was error to set aside the default and interlocutory judgment of dissolution of marriage. As Justice Traynor stated, 'Relief is denied, however, if a party has been given notice of an action and has not been prevented from participating therein. He has had an opportunity to present his case to the court and to protect himself from mistake or from any fraud attempted by his adversary.' (Kulchar v. Kulchar [1969] 1 Cal. 3d [467], 472 [82 Cal. Rptr. 489, 462 P.2d 16, 39 A.L.R.3d 1368].) [Carolyn] had her opportunity and failed to exercise diligence and take advantage of it." (In re Marriage of Stevenot, supra, 154 Cal. App. 3d at pp.1075-1076, citation omitted.)

The order is reversed, Patrick shall recover costs on appeal.

Low, P.J., and Hanning, J., concurred.

Note

Do you approve the result in *Alexander*? Do the 1991 and 2002 amendments to Family Code sections 721(b) and 1100(e) (see pages 413-415 supra) allow or compel a different result in *Alexander*? Do the 1991 amendments alter the meaning of "extrinsic fraud"?

If the *Alexander* proceedings had been begun on or after January 1, 1993 (Family Code sections 2100-2109), or the judgment had been entered on or after January 1, 1993 (sections 2120-2129), would a different result have been allowable or required?

MARRIAGE OF BROCKMAN
194 Cal. App. 3d 1035, 240 Cal. Rptr. 96 (1987)

KINGSLEY, Acting P.J. — Wife appeals the denial of her motion to vacate following a judgment of dissolution. We reverse.

The issue on appeal is whether wife can set aside a property and custody settlement agreement that she signed to end the parties' bitter custody dispute. The facts are as follows: In 1984, wife filed for divorce in Pasadena seeking to terminate her five-year marriage to respondent. At the same time, she obtained an ex parte order restraining husband from approaching within 100 yards of herself, the couple's young son, and appellant's 14-year-old daughter. Respondent stated that this action was never served on him, however, and shortly thereafter he filed his own petition for dissolution in Burbank. In spite of the restraining order, appellant allowed respondent to take the children away for the weekend. Respondent flew the children from Sacramento, where they were staying with appellant, to Los Angeles, and refused to return them. He then applied for, and was granted, his own ex parte order in Burbank awarding him custody of the children.

After some weeks with the children, however, respondent reconsidered and offered to return custody to appellant. Appellant stated that respondent promised to relinquish custody to her at an upcoming order to show cause. According to appellant, however, at the time of the hearing, respondent presented lengthy demands and threatened to keep custody of the children unless appellant agreed. Respondent's attorney wrote out a settlement agreement by hand, in a hallway of the courthouse, which appellant signed. Essentially, appellant gave up all claims to the couple's estimated $400,000 to $800,000 in community property in exchange for sole physical custody of the children. She was allowed to keep $10,000 and a Camaro automobile, and was awarded $500 a month in child support and $300 a month spousal support for 10 years. Husband agreed to forfeit a $100,000 note if he should ever contest the custody or support order.

Eight months later, the judgment of dissolution was signed and entered by the court incorporating the above terms. Appellant moved to vacate the judgment, however, as it contained several provisions which were not a part of the agreement. Respondent indicated that he had no opposition to this motion.

In the meantime, however, appellant changed attorneys. Four months after the judgment was entered, she moved to vacate it in its entirety on the ground that the settlement agreement was coerced. The motion to vacate was denied and this appeal follows. . . .

Having determined that appellant can appeal the denial of her motion to vacate, we now reach the merits of the case.[3] As one would expect, the question whether respondent coerced appellant into signing the settlement agreement by threatening to deprive her of her children is closely contested by the parties. On the one hand, the manifest inequality of the settlement agreement, the hurried circumstances of its drafting, and husband's history of violent behavior all contribute strongly to the conclusion that appellant was under duress. Moreover, as the court noted in In re Marriage of Gonzalez (1976) 57 Cal. App. 3d 736, 747-748 [129 Cal. Rptr. 566]: "The involvement of the children that automatically raises the issue of their welfare places this type of litigation in an arena of its own. The emotions and fears of the parties are more intense and are not comparable to litigants [sic] in a normal civil action. If threatened use of a custody hearing can cause so much fear in the mind of the responding parent that contractual volition is destroyed, the court is not required to legally recognize the agreement when equity demands otherwise." On the other hand, supporting respondent's position is the fact that appellant waited more than a year to raise the issue of coercion and was undeniably represented by counsel throughout all the proceedings. No finding on the issue of duress, however, was made by the trial court.[4] Rather, the court relied on In re Marriage of Stevenot (1984) 154 Cal. App. 3d 1051 [202 Cal. Rptr. 116], for the proposition that once a settlement agreement is incorporated into a judgment, it may only be set aside for extrinsic fraud. . . .

The trial court evidently concluded that . . . [extrinsic fraud] encompassed the entire universe of grounds on which a judgment might be set aside. It does not. The briefest scrutiny demonstrates that there are many conditions that cannot be characterized as either extrinsic or intrinsic fraud, even with resort to the most procrustean measures. This is because the distinction between intrinsic and extrinsic fraud refers only to claims of fraud — that is mistake or misrepresentation by the opposing party. Grounds other than fraud have long been recognized as also permitting a judgment to be set aside. As the court observed in Zastrow v. Zastrow (1976) 61 Cal. App. 3d 710, 716 [132 Cal. Rptr. 536]: "Fraud and mistake are the usual but not the only grounds for equitable relief from a judgment. The leading California case in this area (Olivera v. Grace, supra, [(1942) 19 Cal. 2d 570]) involved an attack upon a judgment allegedly procured through the mental incompetence of the plaintiff's decedent. The decedent had suffered a head injury which resulted in unadjudicated mental incompetence, was served with papers in a deed reformation action and suffered a default at the hands of the plaintiff in that action. The Supreme Court sustained the claim as one justifying relief; spoke of equity's power 'to relieve incompetent defendants from judgments taken under circumstances of unfairness and injustice'; mentioned extrinsic fraud and extrinsic mistake as 'typical of the situations' in which equity interferes with final judgments; quoted from an authoritative text which posits accident (as well as fraud and mistake) as a ground of relief; finally voiced the following general rule: 'One who has been prevented by extrinsic factors from presenting his case to the court may bring an independent action in equity to secure relief from the judgment entered against

---

3. Appellant also requests that her motion to vacate be construed as a request for relief under Code of Civil Procedure section 473. This we cannot do, however, as the issue is raised for the first time on appeal.

4. The closest the court comes is saying that appellant "participated" in the settlement agreement. This does not reflect, however, whether her participation was or was not coerced.

him.' [Citation.] [¶]. The quintessential basis for equitable relief from the judgment is not that the wife was defrauded or mistaken; rather, that some kind of disability deprived her of 'a fair opportunity fully to submit her case to the court.' [Citation.] *Olivera* demonstrates that fraud or mistake are not the exclusive grounds; that equity, indeed, does not limit the kinds of disability which justify relief."

Stevenot itself recognizes that duress is neither intrinsic or extrinsic fraud, but is still a ground for setting a judgment aside. *Stevenot* states: "It appears from Pamela's declaration in support of her motion that she is torn between whether to allege her failure to seek an attorney sooner was due to duress by Richard or because of extrinsic fraud committed by him. Duress is to be distinguished from extrinsic fraud, although, if proven, it is a valid ground to set aside a judgment and marital settlement agreement." (In re Marriage of Stevenot, supra, 154 Cal. App. 3d at p.1073, fn.6.)

Accordingly we conclude that the trial court was in error by failing to determine whether appellant's consent to the settlement was coerced. If the trial court should so decide, it must vacate the judgment and settlement agreement. The instant order denying the motion to vacate is therefore reversed and remanded to the trial court for further proceedings. Appellant to recover costs.

McCLOSKY, J., and MUNOZ, J., concurred.

A petition for a rehearing was denied October 15, 1987. . . . Respondent's petition for review by the Supreme Court was denied December 3, 1987.

Note

For illustration of spousal overreaching and good discussion of fraud and duress, see Marriage of Baltins, 212 Cal. App. 3d 66, 260 Cal. Rptr. 403 (1989).

X

PROPERTY DISTRIBUTION
AT DEATH

A. RECAPTURE OF UNAUTHORIZED INTER VIVOS GIFTS AFTER THE DONOR'S DEATH AND THE ITEM THEORY OF COMMUNITY PROPERTY DISTRIBUTION AT DEATH

DARGIE v. PATTERSON
176 Cal. 714, 169 P. 360 (1917)

[In 1910, Mr. Dargie, without his wife's knowledge, made a gift of community realty to a third party. At that time, community property law did not require that a wife join in a conveyance of realty, but Civil Code section 172 (now Family Code section 1100(b)) did require a wife's written consent to any gift of community property. After Mr. Dargie's death, his widow sought to void the conveyance. The trial court granted the widow's petition and the donee appealed.]

SLOSS, J. . . . May the wife avoid the deed in its entirety, or only so far as is necessary to protect her rights? . . . [T]he only logical conclusion is that the wife's right to assail the conveyance where, as here, the action is brought after the husband's death, is limited to an undivided half of the property. . . .

If he had made no conveyance, the widow would, upon his death, have been entitled to one-half of the property in question, as of all other community property. The other half would have passed to his heirs or devisees, and the widow, as such, would have had no interest in it. His heirs or devisees are bound, as he himself was bound, by the conveyance made. Why, then, should the widow's claim extend to any more than the one-half which would pass to her as survivor of the community. The privilege of avoiding the gift is conferred upon her as a means of protecting her interest in the community property. We see no reason why, in assailing the gift, she should enjoy greater rights than she would have had if the gift had never been made. Furthermore, if the deed should be set aside in its entirety, and the property

543

restored to the community, the one-half not passing to the widow would be distributed as a part of the husband's estate. His representatives and successors would,
therefore, be in the very position which they would occupy if they were entitled,
in their own right, to disaffirm the conveyance—a thing which, as we have seen,
they cannot do. It is not necessary to the widow's protection that she attack the
transfer, except as to one-half, and she should not be allowed to attack it for the
benefit of others who are bound by it. . . .

It follows that the judgment declaring the conveyance void and decreeing that
the grantee has no interest in the property cannot stand.

. . . It was agreed and found that the value of the estate of W. E. Dargie subject
to distribution exceeds five hundred thousand dollars; that the value of the land
involved in this action does not exceed one hundred thousand dollars. All of this
was community property. It appearing, therefore, that the amount of the estate
which passed into the hands of the executors was sufficient to satisfy the claim of
the widow to one-half of all the community property, including the lot conveyed
without her consent, she must, it is argued, seek satisfaction of her demand for
one-half of the community estate out of the property retained by the testator until
his death, instead of proceeding against his grantee. We may assume, for the purposes of this discussion, that the record shows that the debts of the estate and the
expenses of administration are not sufficient to reduce the balance in the hands
of the executors beyond the amount necessary to meet such claim of the widow.

The appellant's position is based upon the suggestion made by Chief Justice
Beatty in his concurring opinion in the first *Spreckels* case. The late chief justice
thus expressed his view (116 Cal. 350, [48 Pac. 232]):

> Upon the dissolution of the community by the death of the husband, or by
> divorce, I think that in estimating her share of the community property she
> would be entitled to have any property given away by the husband subsequent
> to the act of 1891 reckoned as a part of the community assets, and that she
> would be entitled to reclaim from the donee enough to make up her half of
> the whole, if less than one-half remained undisposed of. In all ordinary cases
> this would be a proper and sufficient remedy for any infringement of her
> rights. . . . If the wife survives her husband, she will get her full share of the
> community property out of that which remains. If the husband survives the
> wife, he will get everything that he has not voluntarily parted with. . . .

[W]e are not disposed to adopt the suggested rule. The widow, upon showing
the existence of the facts bringing a conveyance within the terms of the proviso of
section 172, is entitled, so far as her rights are concerned, to treat that conveyance
as a nullity. She has the right to avoid the conveyance so far as is necessary for the
protection of her interest in the property conveyed. As to her, the case must be
regarded as if there had been no conveyance, and the property had, accordingly,
remained a portion of the community estate, of which the husband had died seised.
Upon his death, she succeeded to one-half of such community estate. . . .

Her right . . . goes to every part and parcel of the community estate. Immediately upon his death she became the owner of an undivided one-half interest in
every item of property owned by him, including the parcel of land which he had
conveyed, but which, as against her objection, must be treated as still a part of the
community property. Since, however, the conveyance made by him is binding upon
those who claim under his will, and she cannot pursue her rights through the me-

dium of any action instituted by the executors, she must have the right to proceed directly against the grantee claiming to hold the land in opposition to her right. If, then, she, upon the death of the husband, is the legal owner of one-half of the land, on what ground can it be said that she should be divested of this legal ownership, and be required to resort to a proceeding against the other heirs of the husband for reimbursement to the extent of the value of the property of which she is thus deprived? Ordinarily, the owner of an interest in specific real or personal property cannot be compelled against his will to surrender title to the specific property, and take in exchange therefor other property of like value, or the money equivalent of such value. The only reason for requiring the widow to seek recourse out of the other property of the estate is that thereby the gift in its entirety will be enforced against the grantor and his devisees, as to all of whom it was valid. But we are not, in this proceeding, passing upon the relative equities of the devisees and the grantee named in the deed. If any such equity exists in favor of a grantee who has given no valuable consideration for the conveyance, the widow is in no way affected thereby. Taking, as a volunteer, a conveyance declared by the law to be voidable at the option of the nonconsenting wife, the grantee knowingly runs the risk that the wife may elect to avoid the transfer. Such rights as may exist in favor of the grantee against those claiming under the husband's will cannot be worked out through the wife, but should be sought in an action brought directly against the parties concerned.

We conclude, therefore, that upon the death of a husband who has attempted to convey community property contrary to the provisions of section 172 [now Family Code section 1100], his nonconsenting wife may recover an undivided one-half of such property in an action brought against the grantee, and this without regard to the amount or condition of the estate remaining in his hands at the time of his death. . . .

The judgment is reversed, with directions to the trial court to enter judgment that the plaintiff is the owner of an undivided one-half interest in the property in question, and that the defendant is the owner of the other undivided one-half thereof. The rents, issues, and profits which have accrued during the pendency of the litigation should, by the terms of the judgment, be divided in accordance with this conclusion.

SHAW, J., MELVIN, J., HENSHAW, J., and ANGELLOTTI, C.J., concurred.
Rehearing denied.

Notes and Questions

1. Dargie v. Patterson settled two important issues in California community property law. First, *Dargie* establishes that an inter vivos gift of community property made without the consent of the other spouse shall be treated as a testamentary transfer of the donor's one-half interest if the gift is not judicially challenged before the donor's death. Second, *Dargie* rejects the "aggregate" theory proposed by former Chief Justice Beatty and adopts instead the "item" theory of community property distribution at death: A surviving spouse owns a one-half interest in *every* item of community property. Hence the decedent may transfer, by will or testamentary substitute, no more than his one-half interest in each asset.

2. Does the item theory misunderstand the wisdom of Solomon: "And the king said, Divide the living child in two, and give half to the one, and half to the other"? 1 Kings 3. What considerations, if any, argue for allowing aggregate division

at divorce (see pages 490-509 supra) but insisting on item division when death dissolves a marriage? Which approach is more efficient in terms of judicial administration? In terms of total transaction costs for all the parties? Which is more just for the decedent? For the surviving spouse?

How would you draft a will for a client who married early and happily, has accumulated substantial community wealth, including a large home in Beverly Hills and several vacation residences, and wishes to provide adequately for both her husband and her developmentally disabled brother? She would like to exercise fully her power to dispose of her half of the community property in favor of her disabled brother, but also wishes to respect scrupulously her devoted husband's one-half interest in the community property. She rejects your suggestion that she leave all to her husband and allow him to take care of her brother. She explains that her husband does not share her sense of duty and love for her brother. Do you see the problem posed by the item theory? (Some relief is provided by the "survivor's election" doctrine, which is the subject of the next two principal cases.)

3. Of the community property states that have considered the issue, only Arizona has adopted the aggregate approach to community property distribution at death. Gaethje v. Gaethje, 8 Ariz. App. 47, 442 P.2d 870, 875 (1968). Louisiana, Texas, and Washington have, like California, chosen the item theory. Demoruelle v. Allen, 218 La. 603, 50 So. 2d 208, 213 (1950); Wright v. Wright, 154 Tex. 138, 274 S.W.2d 670, 675-676 (1955); Estate of Patton, 6 Wash. App. 464, 494 P.2d 238, 245 (1978). Yet the distribution of various will substitutes, such as life insurance and "in trust for" bank accounts, varies among those states espousing the item theory. Some treat certain will substitutes as testamentary transfers that invoke the item theory. Others treat them as inter vivos gifts that call into play a different set of rules. Such variation in the treatment of life insurance proceeds is discussed in the following note.

4. California classifies as community property the proceeds of a community-funded life insurance policy. When the insured spouse has named a beneficiary other than his spouse, California treats the beneficiary designation as a testamentary transfer of the insured's one-half interest. His surviving spouse is entitled to the remaining half as her share of the community property proceeds. Travelers Ins. Co. v. Fancher, 219 Cal. 351, 26 P.2d 482 (1933). Idaho and Washington also take this view. Travelers Ins. Co. v. Johnson, 97 Idaho 336, 544 P.2d 294, 298 (1976); Francis v. Francis, 89 Wash. 2d 511, 573 P.2d 369, 373 (1978). In contrast, Nevada and Texas treat the beneficiary designation as an inter vivos gift and give full effect to the third party beneficiary designation so long as the resulting gift of community property is "reasonable." Jones v. Jones, 146 S.W. 265 (Tex. Civ. App. 1912); Christensen v. Christensen, 91 Nev. 4, 530 P.2d 754, 755 (1975). (See generally the discussion of the Spanish law "reasonable gift" approach to inter vivos gifts of community property at page 400 supra.) Arizona treats the beneficiary designation as a testamentary transfer, but uses the aggregate theory of distribution and hence honors the beneficiary designation so long as the survivor has received at least one-half of the aggregate community property. Gaethje v. Gaethje, 8 Ariz. App. 47, 442 P.2d 870 (1968). Louisiana takes the anomalous view that life insurance proceeds may never be part of the community estate, effectively enabling the insured spouse to make a gift of the entire proceeds. T. L. James & Co. v. Montgomery, 332 So. 2d 834, 847 (La. 1976). The California approach seems doctrinally sound but makes it difficult to use life insurance as an estate-planning device. Suppose that you are preparing a will for your Los Angeles accountant, a woman now in her second

marriage. In the course of estimating her total assets, she tells you that she relies on life insurance to discharge her postmortem support obligations. Since her second marriage 10 years ago, she has purchased three large paid-up policies of the sort she has always urged you to buy because of their favorable income tax consequences. The first, with a face value of $200,000, names her aged dependent father as beneficiary; the second, also for $200,000, names as beneficiary her 13-year-old daughter from her first marriage, who primarily resides with her father; and the third, for $400,000, names as primary beneficiary her current husband and, in the event her husband does not survive her, the children of their marriage. What problems do you foresee? What do you advise?

5. It is useful to review the context in which *Dargie* chose between the item and aggregate theories of community property distribution at death. In 1917, the wife had no testamentary power over her interest in the community property: It all went to her husband if she predeceased him. (That is why Chief Justice Beatty observed, "If the wife survives her husband, she will get her full share of the community property. . . . If the husband survives the wife, he will get everything that he has not voluntarily parted with.") Thus the issue in *Dargie* was the extent to which the husband's management power included dead-hand control of the community property. *Dargie* may thus be seen as a progressive choice: A husband could not choose which of the community assets would go to his surviving wife; instead she had a right to one-half of each community asset. (Query what rule the court might have chosen if a predeceased wife had testamentary control over her half of the community property. Would the court have been satisfied with a rule that left the surviving husband with one-half of each community asset?)

From the perspective of equal testamentary capacity and equal management powers, the choices posited by *Dargie* may seem unduly confining. Why not, for example, permit the *survivor* to select those assets that will constitute his or her one-half of the community property? As between the deceased and surviving member of the community, why not favor the survivor? The decedent would lose little testamentary freedom because *Dargie* already cripples his capacity to will a particular community asset to a third party. All he would lose is his capacity to will one-half of a particular asset to a third party. What administrative and transaction costs would this proposal entail?

B. THE SURVIVING SPOUSE'S OBLIGATION TO ELECT

ESTATE OF PRAGER
166 Cal. 450, 137 P. 37 (1913)

SLOSS, J. — Fannie Prager Cohn, one of the devisees under the will of Charles Prager, deceased, appeals from a decree of settlement of final account and of distribution.

The will, so far as its terms are material here, provides as follows:

"Second. I direct that all of the real property owned by me at the time of my death, situate without the corporate limits of the city of Los Angeles, be distributed to the following named persons, share and share alike, to wit: My brother, Morris Prager; my nephews Lesser, Michael and Harry Prager; and my nieces, Eva and Bella Prager, and Regina Feintuch, Fannie Cohn, Celia Cohn, and Rosa Eppstein. . . ." . . . Then follows this provision: "All the rest, residue and remainder of my estate, of every kind and character, including all real property owned by me within the corporate limits of the city of Los Angeles, and mortgages, notes, bonds and other personal property of every description, I give, devise and bequeath unto my wife, Mary J. Prager, absolutely." . . .

Charles Prager died on the fourteenth day of September, 1911. The total value of the estate, as shown by the appraisement, was $630,321.67. The real property situate outside of the city of Los Angeles, covered by paragraph second of the will, was appraised at $179,928.50. All of this was community property. There was other community property consisting, principally, of a note secured by mortgage and two bonds, said note and bonds, together, being of the appraised value of sixteen thousand dollars; also two parcels of land in the city of Los Angeles, appraised at fifty-four thousand dollars. The separate property of the decedent consisted of land in the city of Los Angeles, appraised at three hundred and eighty thousand dollars.

Very shortly after the testator's death, the widow, Mary J. Prager, through her attorney and coexecutor, Mr. Lawler, informed the devisees named in the second paragraph that she claimed the right to succeed to one-half of the community property, in addition to taking what was given her by the will. Most of the said devisees at once conceded the validity of this claim. For a considerable period during the administration, two of them, Mrs. Fannie Prager Cohn and Mrs. Celia Prager Cohn, opposed the position of the widow, contending that she was put to her election to take under the will or as survivor of the community. Mrs. Celia Cohn finally abandoned her opposition, and Mrs. Fannie Cohn, the appellant, remains as the only one of the devisees now contesting the widow's claim.

By a decree of partial distribution, the real property outside the city of Los Angeles was distributed as follows: one-half thereof to Mary J. Prager, as surviving widow of the decedent; and the other one-half in equal shares of an undivided one-twentieth each, to the ten persons named in paragraph second, or their assigns. Thereafter, . . . the court made the decree here appealed from, by which the residue of the estate . . . was distributed to the widow. The claim of the appellant, Fannie Cohn, is that the widow, by taking under the decree of partial distribution one-half of the community property not devised to her, had manifested her election to forego the benefits given her by the will.

Reading the will by itself or in the light of the circumstances shown by the record, we find no ground for holding that the widow was called upon to surrender either her interest in the community property or the devises and bequests given her. The rules of law governing the question of election in cases like the present have been declared in numerous decisions of this court. The testator is presumed to have made his will with knowledge that his power of testamentary disposition did not extend to the surviving wife's interest in the community property. The presumption is, further, that he did not intend to devise or bequeath the one-half of the community property which, upon his death, would vest in his widow irrespective of any attempt that he might make to dispose of it by will. In the absence of anything in the instrument to indicate a contrary intent, the testamentary dispositions must, accordingly, be understood as intended to cover only the property which the testator had the right to devise or bequeath, i.e., his separate property and an undivided half of the community property. The mere fact that provision, however liberal, is made in the will for the wife, is not enough to justify the conclusion that such provision was intended to be in lieu of her interest as survivor of the community. . . .

The widow's obligation to elect arises only where the testator has, by the terms of the will, clearly manifested the intention to make the testamentary gift to her stand in lieu of her interest in the community property. The provision may be "declared in terms to be given in lieu of" the right as survivor of the community (Morrison v. Bowman, 29 Cal. 337), or the language of the will may be such as to show clearly an intent to dispose of the whole of the community property in such manner that "the widow cannot take the moiety given her by law without, to that extent, defeating the plain intent of the testator." . . .

The will before us does not declare that the gifts to the widow shall be in lieu of her community right. Neither do its provisions show an intention which would be frustrated by permitting the widow to take both her moiety of the community property and the residue given to her. The property given to the widow included both separate and community estate. Some of the community property, i.e., the land outside the city of Los Angeles, was devised to the persons named in paragraph second. There is nothing to indicate that the latter provision was intended to operate as a gift of more than the share which was subject to the decedent's testamentary disposition. Applying the presumptions of which mention has been made, the will discloses a simple and consistent scheme, which may be carried out in every respect without affecting the widow's right to claim her lawful interest in the community property. In every case in which the widow has been held to be put to her election, the will contained language which, when read in the light of the circumstances, showed plainly that the testator was undertaking to dispose of the entire community property, and that his intention could not be given effect if one-half of such property were withdrawn from the operation of the will. This case presents no such features. On the contrary, it is in every material respect like a number of those . . . in which this court concluded that no duty of election arose. . . .

The decree is affirmed. ANGELLOTTI, J., and Shaw, J., concurred.

ESTATE OF WOLFE
48 Cal. 2d 570, 311 P.2d 476 (1957)

SHENK, J.—Leanore L. Wolfe, the sister of the decedent, Merland J. Wolfe, appeals from a judgment in a proceeding to determine heirship. The court held that Troi C. Wolfe, the surviving wife, was not required to elect between the interests conferred upon her by her deceased husband's will and her rights as the surviving member of the community. The sister contends that this was error and that the surviving wife should have been required to make an election.

Merland and Troi Wolfe were married in 1935. In 1937 Mrs. Wolfe filed a complaint for divorce against her husband. The action did not go to trial and was dismissed in 1940 upon the filing, by Mrs. Wolfe, of a second complaint for divorce. Upon the trial of the second action, an interlocutory decree was entered in favor of Mrs. Wolfe. Shortly thereafter, she left California on a trip to New York. Upon her return, three weeks later, the parties agreed to a reconciliation. Thereupon, Mrs. Wolfe resumed living with her husband and continued to do so until he died on November 24, 1952. In 1943, the second divorce action was dismissed without the entry of a final decree.

In conjunction with the second divorce action two property settlement agreements were entered into between the parties. The first, which divided the community property, contained releases of after-acquired property. . . .

In 1941, the husband purchased certain real property, title to which was taken in the name of "Merland J. Wolfe, a married man." The property was purchased from the earnings of the garage business. It was subsequently sold and the husband took back a deed of trust in his own name. The proceeds of the sale were used to purchase ranch property in Northridge which is the principal asset of the estate. Title to the Northridge property was taken in the name of "Merland J. Wolfe, a married man." A deed of trust was executed by the husband and wife on the ranch property. The balance of the purchase price was paid from the earnings of the garage business. . . .

In 1951, Mr. Wolfe brought an action for declaratory relief against Mrs. Wolfe in which he sought a judgment to determine the Northridge property to be his separate property. The action was dismissed in 1952 by mutual consent.

The will of the deceased husband contained the following provisions: "Third: All property in which at this date I have an interest is my separate property, pursuant to the provisions of a certain property settlement agreement heretofore entered into between my said wife and me. It is my intention to dispose of all property over which I have the power of testamentary disposition." Paragraph Fourth made specific bequests of ". . . my Cadillac automobile, jewelry, silver, books, pictures, paintings, works of art, household furniture and furnishings, clothing and other personal effects . . ." to Mrs. Wolfe. . . . Paragraph Sixth provided: "I give, devise and bequeath all of the residue of my estate, real and personal, wherever situated, including all failed and lapsed gifts . . . in trust . . ." for the benefit of Leanore L. Wolfe, and Troi Wolfe, to terminate upon the death of the survivor, the remainder to be distributed to designated charities. . . .

The trial court found and concluded on sufficient evidence, that the property settlement agreement was abrogated upon the subsequent reconciliation of the parties and that all of the property in which the decedent had an interest at the time of his death was the community property of the spouses.

If the will expressly requires the wife to make an election, no substantial problem is presented. (Estate of Dunphy, 147 Cal. 95 [81 P. 315].) The testator may, however, so frame his will as to present the problem whether an election is required. If the testator purported to dispose of both his and his spouse's share of the community property, and it appears that the intent of the testator will be thwarted by giving literal effect to the will while recognizing the community property rights of the surviving spouse, an election should be required. The purpose of the election is to adjust the distribution of the property under the will to conform to the express or implied intention of the testator. Thus, it becomes necessary to examine the will for an expression of that intention, and if it cannot be readily determined from the face of the will, or if the will is ambiguous, rules of construction must be invoked to assist in the determination of that intent.

If the respondent be required to make an election, she may repudiate the will and claim her statutory share of the community property or she may reject her interest under the law and claim under the will. She cannot take under both. If no election be required, one-half of the property found by the trial court to be community property would belong to the surviving spouse (Prob. Code, §201) and she would be entitled to the additional interests conferred upon her by the will. . . .

Where an interpretation is required, that construction which leads to the conclusion that the testator was disposing only of his interest in the community property will be adopted. (Estate of Moore, 62 Cal. App. 265, 271 [216 P. 981].) The last sentence of the third paragraph of the will recites "It is my intention to dispose of all property over which I have the power of testamentary disposition." When read in the light of the constructional preference stated in the Moore case, this sentence supports the conclusion that the testator did not intend to dispose of any property over which he did not have the power of testamentary disposition.

In settling the testamentary trust upon his sister and widow, the testator described the corpus of the trust in general terms. It was a gift of the residue of his estate and the property which composed the corpus was not designated. Where the testator describes his property in general terms, that is, "all of my property," or "all of my estate," he will be presumed to have intended to dispose of only that interest which was subject to his power of testamentary disposition. . . .

Although the testator's declaration that he intended to dispose of all of the property over which he had the power of testamentary disposition and his description of the estate in general terms support the trial court's construction, it becomes clear, from a reading of the will in its entirety, that an election is required.

The testator, in the third paragraph of the will, recited that the whole of the property in which he had an interest was his separate property. Obviously he believed that the property settlement agreement was still in force and that all of the property disposed of by the will, including the property conveyed in trust, was his separate property. This belief is supported by his references to the Northridge property as "my ranch property." Although the trial court was not bound to give effect to the testator's declarations that the property was his separate property, those declarations were entitled to consideration in determining the intended scheme of distribution.

In Estate of Vogt, 154 Cal. 508 [98 P. 265], the testator expressly provided that all of the property in his estate except property of the value of $8,000 was his separate property. The will contained numerous references to the property as "my property." The testator's wife was a beneficiary under the will. The testator sought to dispose of the whole of the property as his estate, and without regard to his wife's community interest. This court held that his will must be construed to have disposed of the property accordingly, while protecting the testator's wife's community property interest. An election was required in order to carry out the legal effect of the terms of the will.

The respondent widow contends that the rules of construction enunciated in La Tourette v. La Tourette, 15 Ariz. 200 [137 P. 426] apply here. In that case, the testator described the estate in general terms. The will did not show a mistaken belief as to the character of the property. The court correctly applied the rule that where the testator describes the estate in general terms such as "all of the property of which I may die possessed," the will is deemed to dispose only of that part of the property in which the testator in fact had an interest at the time of his death and no election should be required. The Arizona Supreme Court distinguished Estate of Vogt, supra, 154 Cal. 508, by reference to language in the Vogt will in which the testator declared that his estate consisted in part of separate property.

The language of the will in the present case, considered in the light of the cases construing similar provisions, would indicate that the trial court should have required Mrs. Wolfe to make an election. . . .

An intention on the part of the testator to dispose of his wife's interest in the community property will not be implied where another construction is permissible.

The third paragraph of the will purported to dispose of his own and his wife's share of the community property as his separate property and . . . to divide the residue equally between his sister and his wife. Under the circumstances, the assertion by the wife of her rights under the will and at the same time of her interest in the community property under Probate Code, section 201, are inconsistent. A required election is clearly indicated.

The judgment is reversed. GIBSON, C.J., CARTER, J., TRAYNOR, J., SCHAUER, J., and SPENCE, J., concurred.

McCOMB, J., dissented.

Respondent's petition for a rehearing was denied June 19, 1957. McCOMB, J., was of the opinion that the petition should be granted.

Notes and Questions

1. Estate of Prager appears an easier case today than it did in 1913. The second clause of Charles Prager's will devised "all of the real property [outside of Los Angeles] owned by me at the time of my death." In 1913, the accepted view was that Charles, during his lifetime, owned *all* the community property and that his wife Mary's one-half interest was a "mere expectancy" that would vest only if she divorced or survived Charles. See, for example, Roberts v. Wehmeyer, 191 Cal. 601, 612, 218 P. 22 (1923), and Spreckels v. Spreckels, 172 Cal. 775, 782, 158 P.2d 537 (1916). Does the phrase "at . . . my death" offer some support for the court's conclusion? Since 1927, when the legislature declared that the "interests of husband and wife in community property during continuance of the marriage relation are present, existing and equal interests," the "all my property" language of the sort used by Charles Prager more readily supports an inference that the testator was referring only to his one-half interest in the community property.

Do you think that the court's holding effectuates the testamentary intentions of Charles Prager? How do you think Charles might have explained the organization of his testamentary plan?

2. As *Prager* and *Wolfe* indicate, California courts will enforce an explicit clause requiring the survivor to elect between her community rights and her benefits under the decedent spouse's will. Other community property states do likewise. See, for example, Reed v. Nevins, 77 N.M. 587, 425 P.2d 813, 815 (1967), and Davis v. East Texas Savings & Loan Assn., 354 S.W.2d 926, 932 (Tex. 1962). Nevertheless, the practice has been strongly criticized on the ground that an attempt to convey property belonging to another (the survivor) is a legal nullity and should not be enforced through the device of an election clause. W. de Funiak and M. Vaughn, Principles of Community Property 496-498 (2d ed. 1971). Do you agree?

3. Cases in which a testator has not explicitly called for an election, but is nevertheless found to have implicitly required one, frequently involve, as in Estate of Wolfe, an apparently good faith, though erroneous, conclusion by the testator regarding the classification of particular property. In *Wolfe,* the husband believed the Northridge realty was his separate property because of a lapsed property settlement. See also In re Stewart, 74 Cal. 98, 103, 15 P.445 (1887); Estate of Kennedy, 135 Cal. App. 3d 676, 681, 185 Cal. Rptr. 540 (1982); Estate of Moore, 62 Cal. App. 265, 268-269, 216 P. 981 (1923). In these cases, how would the testators have behaved had they not been mistaken? Do testators start out with a fixed property or dollar amount for each devisee (in which case an implied election is plausible)

or does a testamentary plan reflect in part a spouse's understanding of pre-existing property interests? For example, if a testator intends to make a generous devise to his wife, we would expect him to leave her more than one-half the community property, which is hers in any event. If he believes that all the community property is his separate property, he may consider a devise of one-half a generous gift. Yet, if he knew the true character of the property when making his will, he might well have left her more. If we suspect that knowledge of the true state of property owner-ship might have altered a mistaken testator's will plan, the *Wolfe* practice of inferring an election requirement from a mistaken belief seems questionable. *Wolfe* effectively enforces the testator's mistake. Washington takes a different view. See, for example, In re Cooper's Estate, 32 Wash. 2d 444, 202 P.2d 439, 441 (1949):

> The appellants urge that the respondent, by the terms of the will, was put to her election whether she would take that portion of the testator's estate bequeathed and devised to her or claim an award and set off of a homestead; and that, by offering the will for probate and affirmatively demanding her half share of the residuum, she has elected to renounce her homestead and accept merely her one-half of such residuum.
>
> The doctrine of election as pronounced by this court finds frequent ex-pression in those cases where a testator husband in his will gave specific prop-erty in which his wife had an interest and over which he had no testamentary disposition to some other person and gave to her in lieu thereof property over which he had complete testamentary disposition, with the intention that his wife surrender a right she had in exchange for such bequest or devise. Lewis v. Lichty, 3 Wash. 213, 28 P. 356, 28 Am. St. Rep. 25; Herrick v. Miller, 69 Wash. 456, 125 P. 974; Collins v. Collins, 152 Wash. 499, 278 P. 186; Ta-coma Savings & Loan Ass'n v. Nadham, 14 Wash. 2d 576, 128 P.2d 982.
>
> An essential element of the doctrine of election is that the testator clearly and unmistakably intended to dispose of property which was in fact not his own and was not within his power of disposition. In his will Mr. Cooper spe-cifically declared that Lot 16, Block 12 of East Park Addition to Seattle was his separate property. Such a declaration on the part of a testator is of no effect if it is not factually or legally true or correct, but it is to be given consid-eration by the court when the question of his intention is involved. It will thus be seen from that which is now before us that the doctrine of elec-tion can have no application because Mr. Cooper did not intend to devise away from his wife property in which she had any interest, as he believed he was devising his separate property over which he would have testamentary disposition.

4. Review the client problems in Notes 2 and 4 following *Dargie*, at pages 545-547 supra. What assistance do *Prager* and *Wolfe* offer?

5. The survivor is not required to make an election between her community property rights and her intestacy rights, Estate of King, 19 Cal. 2d 354, 357, 121 P.2d 716 (1942). Thus, if the surviving spouse is also the sole residual legatee, her election to assert her community property rights may be costless. The residual leg-acy will fail and all the residual community property will pass to the surviving spouse under the community property intestacy provision, Prob. Code §6401(a).

Suppose, for example, that decedent's estate largely consists of Blackacre and Whiteacre, both of which are community property. Decedent wills Whiteacre to his wife and Blackacre to his brother. The will explicitly puts the wife to an election and also makes her the residual legatee, that is, the person who takes any property that is not otherwise passed by the will. The wife elects to take her one-half community property interest in both Blackacre and Whiteacre. The brother takes a one-half interest in Blackacre under the will. The remaining one-half interest in Whiteacre becomes part of the residue, which the wife cannot take under the will because she elected to assert her community property rights instead. The residuary clause fails and the residue passes to the wife in intestacy. However, if the residual estate includes separate property, the surviving spouse will receive no more than one-half of the separate property if the decedent is also survived by issue, parents, siblings, or siblings' issue. Prob. Code §6401(c).

6. Thus far we have considered arguably inconsistent claims that arise from decedent's will and the survivor's community property rights. May an election also be required when a spouse attempts to take under decedent's will and simultaneously asserts a 100 percent survivorship interest in a joint tenancy of which decedent attempted to will "her half" to a third party? (Decedent erroneously believed that the joint tenancy was community property.) See Estate of Kennedy, 135 Cal. App. 3d 676, 681, 185 Cal. Rptr. 540 (1982) (surviving husband required to elect between will provisions and survivorship right in joint tenancy). See also Estate of Waters, 24 Cal. App. 3d 81, 100 Cal. Rptr. 775 (1972) (accord). May an election be required when the surviving spouse takes under the will and also asserts a 50 percent community property interest in insurance proceeds for which decedent designated a third party as beneficiary? See Estate of Roach, 176 Cal. App. 2d 547, 554 1 Cal. Rptr. 454 (1959) (election required).

The preceding discussion considers instances in which a surviving spouse tries to take under decedent's will and assert her community property or other ownership rights as well. In such cases, decedent's will may expressly or implicitly put the survivor to an election between her two claims. Does the same election doctrine apply to will substitutes, such as life insurance and gifts causa mortis (inter vivos gifts made in contemplation of death), when the survivor asserts both her 50 percent community ownership in the will substitute and an additional claim arising from the decedent's beneficiary designation or donative transfer? *Tyre* and *Trimble*, discussed below, are illustrative.

7. A spouse may insure his life with community funds, name his spouse as the policy beneficiary, and effectively exercise dead-hand control by providing that, at his death, his spouse shall receive periodic annuity payments instead of lump-sum policy proceeds. In Tyre v. Aetna Life Ins., 54 Cal. 2d 399, 353 P.2d 725, 6 Cal. Rptr. 13 (1960), Mr. Tyre struck a bad bargain for his wife. His life insurance policy had a face value of $20,000. Without his wife's knowledge or approval, he selected an annuity option that would, after his death, make payments to his wife based upon her life expectancy at his death, but in no event for fewer than 10 years. If she died within 10 years, their three daughters would receive the benefits during the remaining portion of the 10-year period. At Mr. Tyre's death, Mrs. Tyre's poor health made it unlikely that she would enjoy the 14 years of life generally predicted by standard mortality tables for persons of her age. Moreover, even if she did, the annuity payments would total only $20,664. (Aetna presumably would pocket most of the interest.) Mrs. Tyre sought to avoid her husband's agreement with Aetna by arguing that her husband was not simply acting as the lawful community manager during his lifetime but had effectively made a testamentary disposition of her half of the community policy by choosing the annuity option. Accepting this characterization, the court held that Mrs. Tyre, by insisting on her community property right to one-half the face value of the policy, gave up her claim to possession of the other

half under her husband's (also testamentary) beneficiary designation. Thus, Mrs. Tyre was entitled to a lump sum of $10,000 as her share of the community policy proceeds, and annuity payments, now halved, went to the Tyre daughters, whom Mr. Tyre had named as beneficiaries in the event that Mrs. Tyre did not survive for 10 years. (The Tyre daughters were entitled to payments for 10 years or until Mrs. Tyre's death, whichever occurred later.)

Do you approve the result? Is it consistent with the rubric set out by Estate of Wolfe? In what respect does it carry out Mr. Tyre's intent? The *Tyre* scenario seems even more likely in our era of equal management. Ought a court reach the same result under equal management? Assuming *Tyre* is correct, does it have any bearing on your accountant's estate planning problem (Note 4 at page 546 supra)? Recall that her estate plan largely consists of three community-funded life insurance policies: $200,000 for her aged father; $200,000 for her daughter from a first marriage; and $400,000 for her current husband, or if he does not survive her, for the children of the current marriage.

But compare Trimble v. Trimble, 219 Cal. 340, 347-348, 26 P.2d 477 (1933). Mr. Trimble made a deathbed conveyance of two parcels of community property to his children, reserving a life estate in favor of his wife. After his death, Mrs. Trimble moved to set aside the conveyances, which she successfully did to the extent of her one-half community property interest: "[O]nly one-half of the Fruitvale property should have been adjudged to belong to the [children], *subject, of course, to the life estate of their mother*" (emphasis added). It does not appear that the Trimble children argued that Mrs. Trimble should have been put to an election between her community property one-half fee interest and the life estate in both halves reserved for her in Mr. Trimble's conveyance. Ought she have been put to such an election? Does *Trimble* present a more or less forceful case than *Tyre* for putting the widow to an election? Are *Trimble* and *Tyre* doctrinally reconcilable by treating *Trimble* as an inter vivos gift case and *Tyre,* contradistinctively, as a testamentary transfer case? In any event, when a surviving spouse seeks to void (to the extent of her one-half interest) an inter vivos gift decedent made without her consent, should she be allowed to take some other interest, as Mrs. Trimble did, under the very same conveyance she now seeks to avoid? Should she be allowed to retain *any* gift made by decedent to her during marriage when she seeks to void decedent's inter vivos gift of community property to a third party?

C.   APPORTIONMENT OF DEBTS

In the administration of a decedent's estate, debts are paid before the net estate is distributed. The community property system and, more recently, equal management provisions add complexity to an otherwise straightforward process. Which debts are taken into account? Only the debts contracted by decedent, or those contracted by the survivor as well? From which property should they be paid: decedent's separate property, the survivor's separate property, decedent's one-half of the community property, or all the community property? To help you think about these questions, assume an elderly, recently married couple, the Hansens, whose entire community property consists of a $10,000 bank account. Each has a separate property bank account: Dorothy's contains $4,000 and Samuel's $7,000. Dorothy dies, leaving "all my property to my sister Elaine." Dorothy has two debts: a $1,000 debt she brought into marriage and an $8,000 debt for dental treatment during marriage. Her surviving husband Samuel brought $6,000 of debt into marriage and contracted $4,000 of debt during marriage. How should the various debts be treated in the administration of Dorothy's estate? If Dorothy's debts are satisfied from her property alone (her separate property and one-half the community property), will her sister Elaine receive anything? Would this result be appropriate? Suppose instead that the community bank account alone is applied to satisfy Dorothy's debts, and all Dorothy's separate property passes to her sister. What about Samuel's interests as well as those of his creditors, who were relying, in part, on the community property for repayment of his debts? He would now have $10,000 of outstanding debt and only $8,000 left to pay it. Yet before Dorothy's death, the couple's resources ($21,000) were both sufficient and available to repay all their debts ($19,000).

In 1938, the court of appeal, in dictum, first recognized the possibility that some debts might appropriately be apportioned to the community property while others might more suitably be apportioned to the decedent's separate property. Estate of Haselbud, 26 Cal. App. 2d 375, 383, 79 P.2d 443. Several years later, the supreme court, also in dictum, took a different approach to the apportionment of debts between the community property and decedent's separate property. As you read the following excerpts from Estate of Coffee, also note the court's response to the question, "*Whose* debts are apportioned in the administration of a married person's estate?"

ESTATE OF COFFEE
19 Cal. 2d 248, 120 P.2d 661 (1941)

EDMONDS, J. — The Controller has appealed from an order fixing the inheritance tax in the estate of Harry Coffee, deceased, which, in effect, allows his widow to take one-half of their community property without deduction for debts, expenses of administration or inheritance taxes. . . .

The Controller contends that the entire community property, proportionately with the husband's separate property, is subject to his debts and the expenses of administration, and that the widow is only entitled to take one-half of the community property remaining after the payment of these charges. . . .

[In 1923, the legislature amended Civil Code sections 1401 and 1402.] Section 1401 became: "Upon the death of either husband or wife, one-half of the community property belongs to the surviving spouse; the other half is subject to the testamentary disposition of the decedent, and in the absence thereof, goes to the surviving spouse, subject to the provisions of section . . . [1402] of this code." The following section [1402] was amended to read: "Community property passing from the control of the husband, either by reason of his death or by virtue of testamentary disposition by the wife, is subject to administration, his debts, family allowance and the charges and expense of administration. . . ." In 1931, these were enacted without substantial change of language as sections 201 and 202, respectively, of the Probate Code. . . .

For many years, the rule in this state has been that during the lifetime of a husband, the community property is liable for his debts. (Grolemund v. Cafferata,

17 Cal. (2d) 679 [111 Pac. (2d) 641]; Spreckels v. Spreckels, 116 Cal. 339 [48 Pac. 228, 58 Am. St. Rep. 170, 36 L.R.A. 497].) And section 202 of the Probate Code, said the United States District Court in a recent case,

> subjects all community property passing from the control of the husband, by his death or otherwise, to administration, to his debts, and to certain other charges. This is a provision more or less typical of the law in all community property states and should be construed as correlative to the principle that during the husband's life the community property is subject to his debts. Both are apparently corollaries to his right of management and control. (Sampson v. Welch, 23 Fed. Supp. 271.)

It is clear, therefore, that the portion of the community property which belongs to the wife is the one-half which remains after the payment of the husband's debts and the expenses of administration apportioned between the community and separate property in accordance with the value thereof, and this is true even when the husband's share of the community, together with his separate property, is ample to pay those debts and expenses. . . .

The judgment is reversed with directions to the probate court to compute the inheritance tax in accordance with the conclusions which have been stated.

GIBSON, C.J., SHENK, J., and TRAYNOR, J., concurred.

Notes and Questions

1. *Coffee* would apportion "the payments of the husband's debts and the expenses of administration . . . between the community and separate property in accordance with the value thereof. . . ." How does this differ from the *Haselbud* suggestion that debts be allocated according to the nature of the debt?

In 1986, the California Law Revision Commission, observing that California law was not providing adequate instruction for spousal debt allocation, recommended legislation that was enacted as Probate Code section 11444:

> In the absence of an agreement, each debt of the decedent shall be apportioned on the basis of all the property of the spouses liable for the debt at the date of death. . . , in the proportion determined by the value of the property. . . , adjusted to take into account any right of reimbursement that would have been available if the property were applied to the debt at the date of the death, and the debt shall be allocated accordingly.

1987 Cal. Stat., ch. 923, §93. "[P]roperty . . . liable for the debt" and "right of reimbursement" were intended to incorporate by reference Family Code sections 900-1000, which had recently been drafted by the Law Revision Commission and enacted by the legislature to amend and codify liability and reimbursement rules. Law Revision Comm'n com. to §11444 ("This section makes clear that allocation of liability is to be based on rules applicable to liability of marital property for debts during marriage").

In 2001, the legislature repealed section 11444 and replaced it with a different approach, based on rules enacted in 1986 to regulate the assignment of outstanding debt at divorce, that is, Family Code Sections 2551 and 2620-2626. Current section 11444 provides:

> In the absence of an agreement, each debt subject to allocation shall first be characterized by the court as separate or community, in accordance with the laws of the state applicable to marital dissolution proceedings [Family Code §§2551 and 2620-2626].

2001 Cal. Stat., ch. 72 (S.B. 668), §1. Once a debt has been characterized as separate or community, section 11444 provides explicit instructions for its allocation. Section 11444 is reprinted in its entirety in the Statutory Appendix.

2. *Coffee,* decided during the period of male management but after the 1923 reform that gave the wife the right to will away her one-half of the community property, held that at the husband's death *all* the community property as well as his separate property is applied to *his* debts. Confining inquiry to *his* debts seems unexceptionable because the wife was not legally capable of indebting either the community property or the husband's separate property. (Presumably, any debt she incurred for "necessaries" (see current Family Code section 914) was treated as *his* debt.) As *Coffee* indicates, the same process ensued when the wife predeceased the husband and left her half of the community property to persons other than her surviving husband. Before the property passed to third parties, it was subject to the claims of her surviving husband's creditors. (Was his half considered as well? Ought it have been? Would any other result have been consistent with *Coffee?* Yet the statute included only "community property passing from the control of the husband.")

This discussion points up the necessity under equal management of subjecting the couple's property to debts contracted by *both* spouses when one of them dies and either community or separate property will pass by will or intestacy to third parties. Accordingly, current Probate Code section 11440 allows the surviving spouse to petition for allocation of a debt *of the surviving spouse* that is "payable in whole or in part from property in the decedent's estate." If material, the petition must include an inventory of the separate property of the surviving spouse and of any community and quasi-community property that is not administered in the decedent's estate. Cal. Prob. Code §11442.

3. Since 1976, most property passing at death from a married person to his surviving spouse need not pass through formal administration (probate). The current version of the Set-Aside Law, Probate Code sections 13550-13660, provides that all the property that passes by will or intestacy from a decedent to his surviving spouse may pass without administration unless it is held in trust or the survivor takes less than a fee interest. If the survivor or decedent's estate does not affirmatively elect formal administration, the set-aside provisions control. In such case, sections 13550 and 13551 provide that:

§13550. Personal liability for debts chargeable against property

Except as provided in Section 11446[1] . . . , upon the death of a married person, the surviving spouse is personally liable[2] for the debts of the deceased spouse

---

1. Section 11446 states: "Notwithstanding any other statute, funeral expenses and expenses of last illness shall be charged against the estate of the decedent, and shall not be allocated to, or charged against the community share of, the surviving spouse, whether or not the surviving spouse is financially able to pay such expenses and whether or not the surviving spouse or any other person is also liable for the expenses." — ED.

2. What is the meaning of "personal liability" in a statutory scheme that limits recovery to the value of certain property? Do the statutes contemplate something more than in rem liability yet less than full personal liability? — ED.

chargeable against the property described in Section 13551 to the extent provided in Section 13551.

§13551.   Limitation of liability

The liability imposed by Section 13550 shall not exceed the fair market value at the date of the decedent's death, less the amount of any liens and encumbrances, of the total of the following:

(a) The portion of the one-half of the community and quasi-community property belonging to the surviving spouse under Sections 100 and 101 that is not exempt from enforcement of a money judgment and is not administered in the estate of the deceased spouse.

(b) The portion of the one-half of the community and quasi-community property belonging to the decedent under Sections 100 and 101 that passes to the surviving spouse without administration.

(c) The separate property of the decedent that passes to the surviving spouse without administration.

Initially, the set-aside provisions applied only to community and quasi-community property. Now they apply as well to separate property passing from decedent to the surviving spouse. Any property passing by will or intestacy to third parties remains subject to administration.

Under some circumstances, it may be preferable for a surviving spouse to choose the more lengthy administration over the informal set-aside provisions. If decedent has willed a substantial portion of his property to third parties, the surviving spouse's interest in fair debt apportionment may be best served by a unified proceeding. This may be true whether the estate is composed entirely of community property or of both community and separate property. If, instead, the survivor uses the set-aside law, all the community property she holds (her half and whatever the decedent has left her) as well as decedent's separate property that passes to her is subject to the decedent's debts. Even if decedent's entire estate passes to the surviving spouse, administration should still be considered because it provides an early closure on debt claims against decedent's estate. This may be of particular value to the survivor of a professional spouse, whose estate may be vulnerable to posthumous malpractice claims.

D.   THE ANCESTRAL PROPERTY SUCCESSION STATUTE

Assume that a surviving spouse dies intestate (without a will) and leaves no spouse or issue. In such circumstances, the surviving spouse-decedent has named no person to receive her property and there is no surviving relative who presents a compelling intestate claim to her property, that is, there is no living spouse or issue. At this juncture, the intestacy law generally orders the claims of the decedent's other surviving relatives. See Probate Code sections 6402(a)-(d) and (f). Yet, in the case of certain property that came to decedent from a predeceased spouse, the law takes a different tack.

CALIFORNIA PROBATE CODE
SECTION 6402.5

§6402.5. **Predeceased spouse; portion of decedent's**
estate attributable to decedent's predeceased
spouse

(a) For purposes of distributing real property under this section if the decedent had a predeceased spouse who died not more than 15 years before the decedent and there is no surviving spouse or issue of the decedent, the portion of the decedent's estate attributable to the decedent's predeceased spouse passes as follows:

(1) If the decedent is survived by issue of the predeceased spouse, to the surviving issue of the predeceased spouse. . . .

(2) If there is no surviving issue of the predeceased spouse but the decedent is survived by a parent or parents of the predeceased spouse, to the predeceased spouse's surviving parent or parents equally.

(3) If there is no surviving issue or parent of the predeceased spouse but the decedent is survived by issue of a parent of the predeceased spouse, to the surviving issue of the parents of the predeceased spouse or either of them. . . .

(4) If the decedent is not survived by issue, parent, or issue of a parent of the predeceased spouse, to the next of kin of the decedent in the manner provided in Section 6402.

(5) If the portion of the decedent's estate attributable to the decedent's predeceased spouse would otherwise escheat to the state because there is no kin of the decedent to take under Section 6402, the portion of the decedent's estate attributable to the predeceased spouse passes to the next of kin of the predeceased spouse who shall take in the same manner as the next of kin of the decedent take under Section 6402.

(b) For purposes of distributing personal property under this section if the decedent had a predeceased spouse who died not more than five years before the decedent, and there is no surviving spouse or issue of the decedent, the portion of the decedent's estate attributable to the decedent's predeceased spouse passes as follows: [same as (a) (1)-(5)]. . . .

(f) For the purposes of this section, the "portion of the decedent's estate attributable to the decedent's predeceased spouse" means all of the following property in the decedent's estate:

(1) One-half of the community property in existence at the time of the death of the predeceased spouse.

(2) One-half of any community property, in existence at the time of death of the predeceased spouse, which was given to the decedent by the predeceased spouse by way of gift, descent, or devise.

(3) That portion of any community property in which the predeceased spouse had any incident of ownership and which vested in the decedent upon the death of the predeceased spouse by right of survivorship.

(4) Any separate property of the predeceased spouse which came to the decedent by gift, descent, or devise of the predeceased spouse or which vested in the decedent upon the death of the predeceased spouse by right of survivorship.

(g) For the purposes of this section, quasi-community property shall be treated the same as community property.

(h) For the purposes of this section:

(1) Relatives of the predeceased spouse conceived before the decedent's death but born thereafter inherit as if they had been born in the lifetime of the decedent.

(2) A person who is related to the predeceased spouse through two lines of relationship is entitled to only a single share based on the relationship which would entitle the person to the larger share.

Notes and Problems

1. This 1986 reformulation of the ancestral property provision is, in some respects, a simplification and contraction of the ancestral property concept. The predecessor sections to 6402.5 applied no matter how long the period between the deaths of the spouses and prescribed somewhat different intestacy distribution depending on whether the property decedent derived from her predeceased spouse had been their community property or his separate property. See Estate of McInnis, 182 Cal. App. 3d 949, 227 Cal. Rptr. 604 (1986); Reppy and Wright, California Probate Code §229: Making Sense of a Badly Drafted Provision for Inheritance by a Community Property Decedent's Former Inlaws, 8 Community Prop. J. 107 (1981).

2. The issue of a predeceased spouse may also take under subsections (e) and (g) of the general intestacy statute, Probate Code section 6402:

Except as provided in Section 6402.5, the part of the intestate estate not passing to the surviving spouse under Section 6401, or the entire intestate estate if there is no surviving spouse, passes as follows:

(a) To the issue of the decedent, the issue taking equally if they are all of the same degree of kinship to the decedent, but if of unequal degree those of more remote degree take [by representation].

(b) If there is no surviving issue, to the decedent's parent or parents equally.

(c) If there is no surviving issue, parent or issue of a parent, to the issue of the parents or either of them, the issue taking equally if they are all of the same degree of kinship to the decedent, but if of unequal degree those of more remote degree take [by representation].

(d) If there is no surviving issue, parent or issue of a parent, but the decedent is survived by one or more grandparents or issue of grandparents, to the grandparent or grandparents equally, or to the issue of such grandparents if there is no surviving grandparent, the issue taking equally if they are all of the same degree of kinship to the decedent, but if of unequal degree those of more remote degree take [by representation].

(e) If there is no surviving issue, parent or issue of a parent, grandparent or issue of a grandparent, but the decedent is survived by the issue of a predeceased spouse, to such issue, the issue taking equally if they are all of the same degree of kinship to the predeceased spouse, but if of unequal degree those of more remote degree take [by representation].

(f) If there is no surviving issue, parent or issue of a parent, grandparent or issue of a grandparent, or issue of a predeceased spouse, but the decedent is survived by next of kin, to the next of kin in equal degree, but where there are two or more collateral kindred in equal degree who claim through different ancestors, those who claim through the nearest ancestor are preferred to those claiming through an ancestor more remote.

(g) If there is no surviving next of kin of the decedent and no surviving issue of a predeceased spouse of the decedent, but the decedent is survived by the parents of a predeceased spouse or the issue of such parents, to the parent or parents equally, or to the issue of such parents if both are deceased, the issue taking equally if they are all of the same degree of kinship to the predeceased spouse, but if of unequal degree those of more remote degree take [by representation].

Note that subsections (e) and (g) pass *all* intestate property that is not passed by section 6402.5 or prior subsections of 6402.

3. The content of sections 6402.5 and 6402 can most readily be grasped by application to specific situations. The following problems will guide you through the statutes and point up their ambiguities.

(a) Mrs. Sarah Guth, a 93-year-old widow, recently died intestate in Palo Alto. Her estate consists of her home in Palo Alto; an antique diamond ring valued at $20,000 left to her by her mother; an interest-bearing checking account containing almost $20,000 from annuity payments derived from insurance policies on her pre-deceased husband's life; and a summer home near Yosemite National Park. The Palo Alto home was purchased by Mrs. Guth and her late husband, Solomon, and held as community property. The Yosemite summer home was brought into the marriage by Mr. Guth. Several years before his death, he transferred it into joint tenancy, naming himself and Sarah as joint tenants. Mr. Guth died in 1988, leaving all his property to his wife Sarah.

Sarah and Solomon married in 1960. Both were previously married and wid-owed. Not surprisingly, no children were born to Sarah and Solomon. Sarah's first marriage was also childless. Solomon had three grown children from his first mar-riage, Ann, Robert, and Rose, none of whom survived Sarah. Ann is survived by her son, Arthur, and Robert is survived by his daughter, Rachel. Sarah's nearest living relative is Regina Brown, a descendant of her grandmother's brother Max. To whom should the Palo Alto house, the Yosemite summer house, the ring, and the checking account be distributed?

The answer is amazingly simple, isn't it? Rachel and Arthur take the entire estate equally. (Section 6402.5 passes some portion of Sarah's estate to Rachel and Arthur. Precise identification of this portion is unnecessary because section 6402(e) passes whatever remains to Rachel and Arthur.) Why should the predeceased spouse's issue take precedence over the decedent's more distant kin even with re-spect to the decedent's separate property?

(b) Assume all the same facts, but suppose that Sarah's administrator has dis-covered another living relative, Benjamin Stone, whose great-great-grandfather was Sarah's grandfather. (Benjamin and Sarah are first cousins twice-removed. In some parts of the United States, they may be called "third cousins.") Now the distribution is more complex, isn't it? Start with Probate Code section 6402.5 because section 6402 distributes only property that is not already distributed by section 6402.5. What property is covered by section 6402.5(f)(3)? (Is a joint tenancy "community prop-erty"?) Do subsections (f)(1) and (2) both apply to the Palo Alto home? If so, how much of the Palo Alto home is encompassed by subsection (f)? Of the Yosemite summer house?

The legislative history of section 6402.5(f), which was derived from a 1979 amendment, indicates that the legislature intended section 6402.5 to encompass only property that, in general property ownership terms, can be said to derive from the predeceased spouse — that is, any interest of the predeceased spouse that passed to the decedent by gift, will, or descent. Section 6402.5 was not intended to include, for example, the decedent's one-half interest in the community property. See generally sources cited in Note 1 supra.

(c) Assume all the facts given in situation (b), but also suppose that one year before her death, Mrs. Guth sold the Yosemite summer home and put the entire $85,000 proceeds in a new term bank account. With accumulated interest, the account now contains $93,742. To whom should the contents be distributed? Early cases permit tracing under prior versions of the ancestral property statute. See Simonton v. Los Angeles Trust & Sav. Bank, 205 Cal. 252, 270 P. 672 (1928), and Estate of Brady, 171 Cal. 1, 4-5, 151 P. 275 (1915). But those versions did not distinguish between realty and personalty. Under current section 6402.5, should it matter that the proceeds have not been reinvested in real property?

4. To simplify matters, the problem and variations proposed above involve readily classifiable property. The character of property held by decedent at her death may not always be clear. Who should bear the burden of showing that property in decedent's estate is or is not section 6402.5 property? Should the usual presumptions apply? See Estate of Adams, 132 Cal. App. 2d 190, 203, 282 P.2d 190 (1955): "[W]hen the surviving spouse dies intestate, the presumption is that all property in his estate is his sole and separate property, and the one claiming it to be community must assume the burden of proving what portion of that estate was in fact the community property of the two parties at the time of the death of the predeceased spouse." Compare Cal. Family Code §802.

5. What general theory or view of community property underlies the ancestral property provision? Is it consistent with the post-1927 notion that each spouse has a "present, existing and equal interest" in the community property during marriage?

XI

CHOICE OF LAW AT DIVORCE
AND DEATH

A. INTRODUCTION

A choice of law question arises when the forum court could apply the law of more than one jurisdiction to the issue before it, *and* choosing the law of one jurisdiction instead of another would make a difference in the outcome. The forum court applies the forum state's choice of law principles to select the jurisdiction whose law the forum will apply to resolve a particular issue. Sometimes legislatures explicitly or implicitly formulate choice of law rules. California quasi-community property law, discussed at pages 571-578 infra, is illustrative. More frequently, choice of law principles are fashioned by case law. Historically, courts generally used lex locus rules, choosing the law of the place of the transaction — for example, the law of the place where the contract was made, the law of the place where the tortious injury occurred or, to determine personal property rights, the law of the place where the spouses were domiciled at the time the personalty was acquired. See generally Restatement, Conflict of Laws (1934). While not abandoning lex locus rules, the Restatement, Second (1971) additionally proposes that the forum court may choose the law of the jurisdiction having the most significant relation to the issue before the court. To compare lex locus and significant relation analysis, reread section 283 of the Restatement, Second reprinted at page 445 supra. Section 283 proposes alternative validating measures for marriage. Subsection (2) expresses the traditional lex locus rule; subsection (1) embodies significant relation analysis.

Choice of law issues frequently arise at death or divorce because Americans are an unusually mobile people. In California divorce and estate practice, the community property lawyer frequently finds that his clients have significant choice of law connections with sister states and foreign countries. He may also be consulted as an expert on California law in out-of-state proceedings involving property acquired by parties when they were previously domiciled[1] in California.

---

1. Two factors are necessary to establish "domicile": physical presence in the jurisdiction *and* lack of intent to maintain or make one's home elsewhere. The terms "residence" and "domicile" are often carelessly interchanged. Residence denotes only physical presence. Domicile includes physical presence

A husband and wife domiciled in New York may, for example, remove their domicile to California, where their marriage is subsequently terminated by divorce or death. What law should regulate the distribution of property acquired when the couple was domiciled in New York? What law should regulate the distribution of property acquired in California? Similarly, a couple married in Nevada but domiciled in California may make a permanent move to New York, where death or divorce ends the marriage. What law should control the distribution of property accumulated in California? Of property acquired in New York?

Depending on the jurisdictions involved, the questions posed may present two discrete choice of law issues: Which law determines title, and which law determines the nature of distribution at divorce or death? Californians may miss this nuance because, with the exception of property passing by intestacy, California distribution rules are now identical to California community property ownership rules. Consider, in contrast, the choices inherent in a New York divorce court distribution of the property of New York domiciliaries, some of which was acquired when the couple was previously domiciled in California. Even if the judge looks to California law to determine title to property acquired there and concludes that it is owned equally by the parties, she must still decide whether to apply New York equitable distribution law or California 50-50 division law to that property at divorce. (This point is further discussed in Section E of this chapter.)

In determining either or both the title and distribution issues, a court might look to the law of the place where the marriage took place and ignore subsequent moves on the theory that the parties at marriage contracted for whatever statutory scheme the jurisdiction provides.[2] Or, the court might look to the law of the jurisdiction in which the asset is located. Alternatively, the court might look to the law of the jurisdiction in which the parties were domiciled at the time that the particular asset was acquired. Finally, the court might look to the law of the jurisdiction in which the parties were domiciled at the dissolution of the marriage. Each of the four divergent approaches seems to satisfy due process requirements because each is based on a substantial rational connection between the parties and the jurisdiction whose law the court chooses to apply. Does any one of the choices seem clearly correct or incorrect to you? Courts and legislatures have, at various times and in differing contexts, taken all four approaches, but, as you shall see in this chapter, the last three views have predominated in American divorce and probate law.[3]

Finally, choice of law problems may arise even for the marriage firmly rooted

---

and intent to remain or, more precisely, lack of intent to depart. Thus, a visiting professor from New York University remains domiciled in New York though he may reside in Los Angeles for the year that he spends at UCLA.

2. See, e.g., De Nicols v. Curlier, [1900] A.C. 21, and In re De Nicols, [1900] 2 Ch. 410, two English cases applying French law to personalty and land acquired in England by English nationals who had previously been French citizens when they married in France. The parties, who had no express contract, were deemed to have entered at marriage an implied contract, the terms of which were French marital property law applicable to persons who marry without an express contract. This view has not been adopted in the United States. See Leflar, Community Property and Conflict of Laws, 21 Cal. L. Rev. 221, 223, 230-238 (1933).

3. American courts frequently choose the law of the situs (the place where the property is located) to define property interests in *realty* (see next section), but rarely take the same approach to personalty, title to which is generally held to be determined by the law of the domicile of the spouse at the time he acquired the personalty. Leflar, supra note 2. Some community property states, including California, effectively take the fourth view and apply their own law to divorce and death distribution of property owned by persons domiciled within their borders.

in one, and only one, state. When a marriage of California domiciliaries is dissolved by divorce or death, the distribution of out-of-state realty raises jurisdictional, full faith and credit, and choice of law issues.

B. OUT-OF-STATE REAL PROPERTY ACQUIRED BY SPOUSES DOMICILED IN CALIFORNIA AT ALL RELEVANT TIMES

1. Introduction

Several strains of law converge to protect a jurisdiction's power to regulate real property within its borders. A court of one state lacks jurisdiction to alter title to land located in another state; in rem jurisdiction is required.[4] Divorce courts having in personam jurisdiction over both parties have sought to avoid this impasse by exercising their equitable power to order one party to convey an interest in out-of-state realty to the other. The success of this approach is certain only when the title-holding party actually makes the conveyance in the divorce forum. In such case, the conveyance must be recognized by the jurisdiction in which the realty is located, even if the conveyance was made "under the threat of contempt proceedings, or after duress by imprisonment."[5] If, however, the respondent defaults or leaves the forum jurisdiction before the decree is rendered, conveyance in the forum jurisdiction will not be possible and the party seeking enforcement may encounter difficulties elsewhere. The decree cannot constitutionally command full faith and credit in sister-state courts because the forum lacked in rem jurisdiction over the realty.[6] (Nor is a conveyance executed by an official of the forum court entitled to full faith and credit in sister states.[7]) Nevertheless, today most states do grant full faith and credit or comity (discretionary recognition) to such in personam decrees.[8] But the in personam approach is not available in death cases; in rem relief is required, apparently because no mortal court can exercise in personam jurisdiction over the person of the decedent. Thus, administration of a decedent's assets takes place in each state in which the assets are located.

Concern about state sovereignty over land within its borders also underlies the traditional choice of law principle that issues involving real property are to be resolved by the law (as well as the courts) of the jurisdiction in which the property is located.[9] The traditional choice of law principle persists today, although it may

4. Carpenter v. Strange, 141 U.S. 87, 105-106 (1891).
5. Fall v. Eastin, 215 U.S. 1, 6 (1909) (dictum).
6. Id. at 7.
7. Id. at 6.
8. See generally cases collected in Annot., 34 A.L.R. 3d 962 (1970 and Supp. 1986). But see, e.g., Rozan v. Rozan, 129 N.W.2d 694 (N.D. 1964) (declining to grant full faith and credit to a portion of a California decree purporting to alter title to North Dakota realty).
9. See generally R. Weintraub. Commentary on the Conflict of Laws 398 (2d ed. 1980); R. Leflar, American Conflicts Law 341-343 (3d cd. 1977); Hancock, Conceptual Devices for Avoiding the Land Taboo in Conflict of Laws, 20 Stan. L. Rev. 1 (1967).

Neither constitutional law nor choice of law has evidenced similar concern about *personal* property located within a state's borders. An in personam decree adjudicating title to out-of-state personal property is granted full faith and credit in all sister states, including the one in which the property is located. This appears to be less a matter of constitutional compulsion than a reflection of the choice of law rules generally applied to personalty.

yield to a competing *significant relationship,* or *interest,* analysis. Suppose, for example, that a California spouse has used community property to purchase Maine real property and has taken title in her name alone. At her death, there will be ancillary administration in Maine for the Maine realty. Maine may apply its own ownership rules and elective share legislation to property owned by domiciliaries of a community property jurisdiction that has different ownership rules and no elective share legislation. Alternatively, Maine may, as a matter of choice of law, apply California law to either or both the title and distribution issues.[10] In so doing, Maine would reject the traditional choice of law principle that the law of the site of realty is controlling and use instead an *interest,* or *significant relation,* analysis that takes into account California's as well as Maine's concerns in the adjudication and death disposition of the Maine real property interests of California domiciliaries.

2.   At Death

A decedent's assets may be subject to judicially supervised administration in as many states as they are located. Domiciliary administration occurs in the state in which the decedent was domiciled at death. Ancillary administration takes place in states that were not decedent's domicile at death.[11]

That the decedent's assets may be distributed in a nondomiciliary forum does not necessarily mean that the forum will apply its own substantive rules of distribution. The forum must choose which law to apply to a nondomiciliary's property located within its borders. Traditionally, the law of the situs has been applied to *realty,* and the law of the decedent's domicile at death has been applied to *personalty.* These broad, divergent rules have been criticized and are subject to numerous exceptions.[12] Nevertheless, when a California decedent owns out-of-state property that would be treated as community property if it were located in California, how it will be treated in ancillary administration may turn on whether it is characterized as realty or personalty (immovables or movables). If it is personalty, it is likely to be treated as California community property. If it is realty, the substantive laws of the situs may be applied. Thus, under traditional choice of law principles, the California community property system may not reach out-of-state realty owned by Californians at death.

This traditional choice of law constraint on community property law has been rejected by the Uniform Disposition of Community Property Rights at Death Act (reprinted and discussed at pages 605-606 infra), which has been adopted by Alaska,

---

[Where] there was no express contract between the parties, . . . the law of matrimonial domicile governed, not only as to all the rights of the parties to their property in that place, but also as to all personal property everywhere, upon the principle that movables have no situs, or rather that they accompany the person everywhere, while as to immovable property the law *rei sitae* prevails. [Story on Conflict of Laws (8th ed. 1883) 267.]

(But query which domicile, that at acquisition or dissolution?)

10. Maine might, for example, apply California ownership rules and Maine elective share legislation. Do you see why the surviving spouse would prefer this approach? See Quintana v. Ordono, at page 601 infra. Compare the Uniform Disposition of Community Property Rights at Death Act, reprinted at pages 605-606 infra.

11. R. Leflar, American Conflicts of Law 413 (3d ed. 1977).

12. See generally J. Schoenblum, I Multistate and Multinational Estate Planning 268-282, 309-320 (1982).

Arkansas, Colorado, Connecticut, Hawaii, Kentucky, Michigan, Montana, New York (in a modified version), Oregon, Virginia, and Wyoming. In domiciliary and ancillary administration, for both ownership and distribution purposes, the Act treats as community property all real property located within the state (and all personalty wherever located) that is traceable to community property sources.

3.   At Divorce

Historically, California Civil Code section 5110 defined community property as "all real property situated in this state and all personal property wherever situated" acquired by married Californians. The statute might have been read to suggest that, as a matter of choice of law, out-of-state real property acquired by married Californians was not California community property. In other words, the statute might have been understood as a legislative adoption of the lex locus choice of law rule for realty and the resulting conclusion that out-of-state realty was not therefore California community property. Alternatively, the statute might have been interpreted simply as legislative acknowledgment of the jurisdictional, full faith and credit, and choice of law issues attending California community property classification of out-of-state realty. Consistent with this second reading, the California Supreme Court repeatedly held that section 5110 did not exclude out-of-state realty from the California community property system, but instead that out-of-state realty acquired with community funds by married Californians was California community property. See, for example, Marriage of Fink, 25 Cal. 3d 877, 884, 603 P.2d 881, 160 Cal. Rptr. 516 (1979). The Family Code recodification of Civil Code section 5110 incorporates this principle.

§760.   Community property

Except as otherwise provided by statute, all property, real or personal, wherever situated, acquired by a married person during the marriage while domiciled in this state is community property.

Family Code section 2660 authorizes divorce courts to divide out-of-state community realty and suggests decretal techniques for doing so effectively, that is, for avoiding full faith and credit problems and, indeed, for avoiding even the appearance of adjudicating title to out-of-state realty.

CALIFORNIA FAMILY CODE SECTION 2660

Division where community estate includes real property located in another state

(a) Except as provided in subdivision (b), if the property subject to division includes real property situated in another state, the court shall, if possible, divide the community property and quasi-community property as provided for in this division in such a manner that it is not necessary to change the nature of the interests held in the real property situated in the other state.

(b) If it is not possible to divide the property in the manner provided for in subdivision (a), the court may do any of the following in order to effect a division of the property as provided for in this division:

(1) Require the parties to execute such conveyances or take other actions with respect to the real property situated in the other state as are necessary.

(2) Award to the party who would have been benefited by the conveyances or other actions the money value of the interest in the property that the party would have received if the conveyances had been executed or other actions taken.

Notes and Questions

1. How might a court evenly divide the community and quasi-community property so that "it is not necessary to change the nature of the interests held in the real property situated in the other state"? Does section 2660 effectively create an additional exception to the norm of in-kind division generally prescribed by section 2550? (See generally discussion of section 2601 at pages 490-491 supra.)

Subsection (b)(1) avoids the full faith and credit problem when both parties are before the court and hence subject to its contempt power. Suppose, however, that the person in whose name the out-of-state community realty is titled has defaulted. Subsection (b)(1) instructs the trial court to frame an in personam rather than an in rem decree. As such, it is more likely to be accorded full faith and credit or comity in sister-state courts. Under what circumstances might a court use subsection (b)(2)? If all else fails, does section 2660 allow a California court to directly adjudicate title to out-of-state community realty and hope for the best, that is, that the out-of-state court will extend comity to the California decree?

2. The preceding discussion assumes that husband and wife were *both* California domiciliaries at all relevant periods of time. It does not address the possibility that only one spouse has been domiciled in California. Section 760 defines community property as that "acquired by a married *person* during the marriage while domiciled in this state." Whether property acquired during marriage is community property would thus seem to turn on whether the *acquiring* spouse was the California domiciliary. The result in a long marriage might be anomalous. Assets earned by a California domiciliary would be divisible community property, but those earned by his nondomiciliary spouse would be subject to some other state law marital property regime, most of which still do not require equal division. Commissioner v. Cavanagh, 125 F.2d 366 (9th Cir. 1942) (interpreting California law); Beemer v. Roher, 137 Cal. App. 293, 30 P.2d 547 (1934). See generally Note, Marital Property Rights of Separately Domiciled Spouses and Conflicts of Law, 22 J. Fam. L. 311 (1984). This possibility is not remote in our era of bicoastal marriages. It is not only the rich and famous who may be domiciled in different states. Academic, business, and professional couples may find themselves employed in distant states for long periods of time.

More frequently, out-of-state spouses effect a permanent physical separation, and one of them moves to California, establishes domicile here, and initiates a divorce proceeding. The couple's preseparation property cannot be considered community property because it was acquired before *either* spouse was domiciled here, and property acquired after separation is separate property. Yet the property acquired before separation may be *quasi-community* property, which is also subject to division at divorce. This possibility will be discussed at pages 584-601 infra.

3. Do you agree that the inclusion of out-of-state realty within the California community property system effectively represents a California choice of law rule? If so, what law would you expect California courts to apply to California realty owned by out-of-state domiciliaries?

C. CALIFORNIA REAL PROPERTY OWNED BY MARRIED COUPLES DOMICILED OUTSIDE CALIFORNIA AT ALL RELEVANT TIMES

The California legislature has been evenhanded in its choice of law legislation. Just as it wishes to include within the California community property system all property, wherever located, acquired by California domiciliaries, it does not wish to apply the California system to California realty owned at death by out-of-state domiciliaries. Probate Code section 120 instructs California courts to apply the elective share legislation of the decedent's domicile:

CALIFORNIA PROBATE CODE SECTION 120

§120. Nondomiciliary decedent; real property within state; surviving spouse's right; effect of will

If a married person dies not domiciled in this state and leaves a valid will disposing of real property in this state which is not the community property of the decedent and the surviving spouse, the surviving spouse has the same right to elect to take a portion of or interest in such property against the will of the decedent as though the property were located in the decedent's domicile at death.[13]

By analogy, a California court should grant full recognition to a sister-state decree divorcing sister-state domiciliaries and distributing, inter alia, their California realty.

D. PROPERTY ACQUIRED BY OUT-OF-STATE COUPLES WHO LATER BECOME CALIFORNIA DOMICILIARIES

1. The Quasi-Community Property Statutes

This section addresses the most frequent choice of law issue encountered by California community property practitioners: How does California treat property that was

---

13. To the same effect, see Uniform Probate Code section 2-201(b), 8 U.L.A. 74 (1983):

> If a married person not domiciled in this state dies, the right, if any, of the surviving spouse to take an elective share in property in this state is governed by the law of the decedent's domicile at death.

acquired by California couples *before* they became domiciled in California? The choice of law issue arises predominantly at divorce and probate proceedings in which one spouse is making a claim to certain assets acquired during marriage but titled in the other's name alone. To appreciate the problems posed by this issue, it is useful to plot the result if California were to apply traditional choice of law rules. Suppose that a New York couple retires and moves to California with substantial personal property earned during marriage and titled in the husband's name alone. If California were to follow the traditional lex locus choice of law rule that title to personal property is determined by the law of the jurisdiction in which the parties were domiciled at the time the property was acquired, California would conclude that the New York assets were the husband's property. When the marriage is terminated by divorce or the husband's death, if California were to follow the traditional choice of law rule that the law of current domicile (California) controls divorce and death distribution, the wife would have no claim to the property acquired in New York because, with the exception of property that passes by intestacy, California law does not distribute the property of one spouse to the other spouse. (Note that the California predicament arises from the tie-in of its marital property system, on the one hand, and its divorce and death distribution law, on the other. Contrast the common law systems described in Chapter 1. The surviving spouse's elective share, for example, reaches *all* the decedent's property.) At this juncture, as a matter of choice of law, California might look instead to the death or divorce distribution laws of the jurisdiction in which the parties were domiciled at acquisition, in this case New York. When California initially considered this issue, most other American jurisdictions had entirely undeveloped or, by current standards, less-than-adequately developed marital property and elective share systems. California would have been reluctant to apply sister-state law to current California domiciliaries at the divorce or death of a spouse if the application of sister-state law might impoverish them and make them public charges of the state of California. Thus, in 1917, the legislature boldly extended the community property system to include assets earned elsewhere during marriage and brought into California by new domiciliaries. This provision was constitutionally challenged in Estate of Thornton, 1 Cal. 2d 1, 33 P.2d 1 (1934). Decided in the heyday of economic substantive due process doctrine, *Thornton* held that the legislation violated two clauses of the Fourteenth Amendment.

ESTATE OF THORNTON
1 Cal. 2d 1, 33 P.2d 1 (1934)

PRESTON, J. . . . The basic question is that of the constitutionality of so much of section 164 of the Civil Code as provides that all other property (than separate property as defined by sections 162 and 163 of said code) "acquired after marriage by either husband or wife, or both, including . . . personal property wherever situated, heretofore or hereafter acquired while domiciling elsewhere, which would not have been the separate property of either if acquired while domiciled in this state is community property. . . ." . . .

Further reflection upon the question presented convinces us that under the compulsion of well-understood constitutional provisions, as well as settled pronouncements of this court, no alternative remains but to declare the above-quoted provision unconstitutional and void.

Since the statute of 1891 (Stats. 1891, p.425, sec. 172, Civ. Code), enlarging the right of the wife in the community property, it has been consistently and repeatedly held that any interference with the right of ownership or dominion over the common property is a disturbance of a vested right of the husband. (Spreckels v. Spreckels, 116 Cal. 339 [48 Pac. 228, 58 Am. St. Rep. 170, 36 L.R.A. 497].) Each step taken in recognition of the wife's increasing claims upon said property has been met by express holdings of this court that such statutes are inapplicable to existing community property and could only apply to subsequent acquisitions of the marital union. (Spreckels v. Spreckels, 172 Cal. 775 [158 Pac. 537]; Roberts v. Wehmeyer, 191 Cal. 601 [218 Pac. 22]; Stewart v. Stewart, 199 Cal. 318 [249 Pac. 197]; McKay v. Lauriston, 204 Cal. 557 [269 Pac. 519].)

If this be true as to the common property, how much plainer must the application of the same principle be to the separate property of either spouse. We then must consider whether separate property acquired by either spouse in a common-law state can be converted to common property by the mere act of bringing it into a community property state and establishing a domicile therein. . . .

So long as we are bound by the holding that to limit the right of one spouse by increasing the right of the other in property acquired by their united labors, is the disturbance of a vested right, we entertain no doubt of the application of at least two provisions of the 14th amendment to the Constitution of the United States. If the right of a husband, a citizen of California, as to his separate property, is a vested one and may not be impaired or taken by California law, then to disturb in the same manner the same property right of a citizen of another state, who chances to transfer his domicile to this state, bringing his property with him, is clearly to abridge the privileges and immunities of the citizen. Again, to take the property of A and transfer it to B because of his citizenship and domicile, is also to take his property without due process of law. This is true regardless of the place of acquisition or the state of his residence.

The doctrine that a change of domicile to this state, accompanied by an importation of the personalty is an implied consent to a submission to requirements of this statute, cannot be sustained, for to do so would be to give effect to a restriction prohibited by the Constitution. . . .

Neither can we hurdle these barriers by holding the amendments in question to be part of our succession laws and hence valid as a statute of succession. For we are met with plain holdings of our own court that such is not the effect of said statute. . . .

The judgment is affirmed. WASTE, C.J., SHENK, J., and SEAWELL, J., concurred.

LANGDON, J., Dissenting.—. . . To make such deprivation or impairment of a vested property right a condition of entrance into this state is undoubtedly unconstitutional, as the majority opinion points out. This question has been fully considered in the law reviews, and the principles and cases will be found fully discussed therein. (See 20 Cal. L. Rev. 201; 5 So. Cal. L. Rev. 309; 21 Cal. L. Rev. 221.) But the conclusion that the section under consideration is unconstitutional in so far as it attempts to diminish the husband's property rights during his lifetime does not solve the problem of the instant case. William Thornton is dead and has no property rights. No claim of rights was made by his wife before his death. The parties before the court all have claims arising after death, and the only rights conceivably involved are those of succession and testamentary disposition.

This is made clearer by an examination of the relevant statutes. Section 164 defines community property; sections 162 and 163 define separate property; section 201 of the Probate Code provides that upon the death of either husband or wife, "one-half of the community property belongs to the surviving spouse; the other half is subject to the testamentary disposition of the decedent." Now, to say that the widow here claims under section 164, and that she must fail because that section is unconstitutional, is unsound. Section 164 is not a statute of succession and the widow cannot claim rights under that section alone. Section 164 declares none of the interests of the spouses in community property, and hence it affects no rights. It is a definition, nothing more. To declare it void by itself is meaningless. It is only invalid when, taken together with some other statutory provision for the incidents of community property as defined in section 164, a violation of a constitutional right appears. . . .

[H]ere, the widow claims under section 201 of the Probate Code, and the constitutionality of that section, as broadened by the definition of section 164, is the only question on this appeal. The issue is whether the state of California may require that upon the death of a decedent, certain property owned by him and brought into this state shall be subject to the same rules of testamentary disposition and succession as community property acquired in this state. There can be no doubt as to the answer. It is a rule of almost universal acceptance that the rights of testamentary disposition and of succession are wholly subject to statutory control, and may be enlarged, limited or abolished without infringing upon the constitutional guaranty of due process of law. . . .

Taking its cue from Justice Langdon's dissent, the California legislature promptly enacted the predecessor provisions to current Probate Code sections 101 and 66:

CALIFORNIA PROBATE CODE SECTIONS 101 AND 66

§101. Quasi-community property

Upon the death of a married person domiciled in this state, one-half of the decedent's quasi-community property belongs to the surviving spouse and the other half belongs to the decedent.

§66. Quasi-community property

"Quasi-community property" means the following property, other than community property as defined in Section 28:

(a) All personal property wherever situated, and all real property situated in this state, heretofore or hereafter acquired by a decedent while domiciled elsewhere that would have been the community property of the decedent and the surviving spouse if the decedent had been domiciled in this state at the time of its acquisition.

(b) All personal property wherever situated, and all real property situated in this state, heretofore or hereafter acquired in exchange for real or personal property, wherever situated, that would have been the community property of the decedent and the surviving spouse if the decedent had been domiciled in this state at the time the property so exchanged was acquired.

Later, the legislature extended the quasi-community principle to property division at divorce:

CALIFORNIA FAMILY CODE SECTIONS 125, 63, AND 2550

§125. "Quasi-community property"

"Quasi-community property" means all real or personal property, wherever situated, acquired before or after the operative date of this code in any of the following ways:

(a) By either spouse while domiciled elsewhere which would have been community property if the spouse who acquired the property had been domiciled in this state at the time of its acquisition.

(b) In exchange for real or personal property, wherever situated, which would have been community property if the spouse who acquired the property so exchanged had been domiciled in this state at the time of its acquisition.

§63. "Community estate"

"Community estate" includes both community property and quasi-community property.

§2550. Equal division of community estate

Except upon the written agreement of the parties, or on oral stipulation of the parties in open court, or as otherwise provided in this division, in a proceeding for dissolution of marriage or for legal separation of the parties, the court shall, either in its judgment of dissolution of the marriage, in its judgment of legal separation of the parties, or at a later time if it expressly reserves jurisdiction to make such a property division, divide the community estate of the parties equally.

Problem

Assume that John and Mary Green, who had been Massachusetts domiciliaries since their marriage 30 years ago, moved to California after John retired. John was a physician and Mary has been a homemaker. All their current wealth is personal property traceable to John's earnings during marriage. It is all held in John's name alone and is located in California.

1. What happens if John predeceases Mary? With a will in which John leaves "all my property to my brother Frank"? Without a will?
2. If Mary predeceases John? With a will in which she leaves "all my property to my sister Ethel"? Without a will? (Compare Probate Code sections 100 and 101.)
3. If they are divorced?
4. Who has management and control during marriage?
5. During marriage, may a creditor reach the property to satisfy a debt contracted by Mary? (See California Family Code sections 63, 910, and 912.) Is this result conceptually consistent with your answer to question 4? Is it constitutional? See Note 2 at page 583 infra.

NOTE: CALIFORNIA DEATH RECAPTURE LEGISLATION FOR QUASI-COMMUNITY PROPERTY

Because quasi-community designation has no effect until divorce, death, or a creditor's effort to reach the property for debts incurred by either spouse, a spouse may avoid quasi-community property treatment by inter vivos gift to third parties. A spouse would be unlikely to do so before divorce because he would be giving away his one-half interest as well as his wife's. But persons do occasionally attempt to disinherit a spouse by pre-death transfers. Probate Code section 102 allows the surviving spouse to recapture certain pre-death transfers of a decedent's quasi-community property.

CALIFORNIA PROBATE CODE SECTION 102

§102. Transfer of quasi-community property; restoration of decedent's estate; requirements

(a) The decedent's surviving spouse may require the transferee of property in which the surviving spouse had an expectancy under Section 101 at the time of the transfer to restore to the decedent's estate one-half of the property if the transferee retains the property or, if not, one-half of its proceeds or, if none, one-half of its value at the time of transfer, if all of the following requirements are satisfied:

(1) The decedent died domiciled in this state.

(2) The decedent made a transfer of the property to a person other than the surviving spouse without receiving in exchange a consideration of substantial value and without the written consent or joinder of the surviving spouse.

(3) The transfer is any of the following types:

(A) A transfer under which the decedent retained at the time of death the possession or enjoyment of, or the right to income from, the property.

(B) A transfer to the extent that the decedent retained at the time of death a power, either alone or in conjunction with any other person, to revoke or to consume, invade, or dispose of the principal for the decedent's own benefit.

(C) A transfer whereby property is held at the time of the decedent's death by the decedent and another with right of survivorship.

(b) Nothing in this section requires a transferee to restore to the decedent's estate any life insurance, accident insurance, joint annuity, or pension payable to a person other than the surviving spouse.

(c) All property restored to the decedent's estate under this section belongs to the surviving spouse pursuant to Section 101 as though the transfer had not been made.

Notes and Questions

1. Consider the following questions:

a. Does section 102 recapture all pre-death transfers?

b. What kind does it recapture? Why did the legislature specify these three types of transfer?

c. Can John Green, during his marriage to Mary, make an effective pre-death gift of all his quasi-community property to his godson John?

2. How should California treat assets earned during marriage by residents of other *community property* states who subsequently become domiciled in California? The legislature addressed this question in Probate Code section 28:

§28. Community property

"Community property" means:

(a) Community property heretofore or hereafter acquired during marriage by a married person while domiciled in this state.

(b) All personal property wherever situated, and all real property situated in this state, heretofore or hereafter acquired during the marriage by a married person while domiciled elsewhere, that is community property, or a substantially equivalent type of marital property, under the laws of the place where the acquiring spouse was domiciled at the time of its acquisition.

(c) All personal property wherever situated, and all real property situated in this state, heretofore or hereafter acquired during the marriage by a married person in exchange for real or personal property, wherever situated, that is community property, or a substantially equivalent type of marital property, under the laws of the place where the acquiring spouse was domiciled at the time the property so exchanged was acquired.

3. Texas and Arizona have also enacted quasi-community property legislation, but it applies only when a marriage is dissolved by divorce. Tex. Fam. Code §3.63(b) (Supp. 1992) and Ariz. Rev. Stat. Ann. §25-318 (1991). See also Estate of Hanau v. Hanau, 730 S.W.2d 663 (Tex. 1987) (Texas quasi-community property rules applicable at divorce have no application at death). In contrast, Idaho and Washington have adopted quasi-community property for dissolution by death, but not by divorce. Idaho Code §§15-2-201 to 15-2-209 (1989) and Wash. Rev. Code Ann.

§§26.16.220 to 26.16.250 (Supp. 1992). In the absence of such legislation, recent decisions in community property states have generally determined ownership and distribution of an asset according to the law of the parties' domicile at the time the property was acquired. See, for example, Hughes v. Hughes, 91 N.M. 339, 573 P.2d 1194, 1198-1202 (1978) (in divorce of New Mexico domiciliaries, Iowa title and equitable jurisdiction law applied to property acquired in Iowa when parties were formerly domiciled there). Accord, Berle v. Berle, 97 Idaho 452, 546 P.2d 407 (1976); Braddock v. Braddock, 91 Nev. 735, 542 P.2d 1060 (1975). See generally Marriage of Landry, 103 Wash. 2d 807, 699 P.2d 214 (1985) (en banc).

2.   *The Constitutional and Statutory Limits of Quasi-Community Property*

Shortly after its enactment, the California quasi-community divorce statute was constitutionally challenged in Addison v. Addison, 62 Cal. 2d 558, 399 P.2d 897 (1965). Portions of *Addison* are reproduced below in order to help you evaluate the issues presented by *Roesch, Jacobson, Fransen,* and *Ben-Yehoshua.*

ADDISON v. ADDISON
62 Cal. 2d 558, 399 P.2d 897 (1965)

PETERS, J.—Plaintiff Leona Addison (hereafter referred to as Leona) was granted an interlocutory decree of divorce from defendant Morton Addison (hereafter referred to as Morton) on the ground of his adultery. As part of that judgment the trial court held, inter alia, that the only community property was the household furniture and furnishings. . . . Both parties have appealed, Leona on the question of the extent of the community property. . . .

At the time of their marriage in Illinois in 1939, Morton, having previously engaged in the used car business, had a net worth which he estimated as being between $15,000 and $20,000. Leona, however, testified that her husband's net worth was almost nothing at the time of their marriage. In 1949 the Addisons moved to California bringing with them cash and other personal property valued at $143,000 which had been accumulated as a result of Morton's various Illinois business enterprises. Since that time Morton has participated in several California businesses.

On February 20, 1961, Leona filed for divorce and requested . . . division of the marital property. On trial, . . . Leona attempted to apply the recently enacted quasi-community property legislation by contending that the property presently held in Morton's name was acquired by the use of property brought from Illinois and that that property would have been community property had it been originally acquired while the parties were domiciled in California.

The trial court . . . held the quasi-community property legislation to be unconstitutional. . . .

The sociological problem to which the quasi-community property legislation addresses itself has been an area of considerable legislative and judicial activity in this state. One commentator has expressed this thought as follows: "Among the perennial problems in the field of community property in California, the status of marital personal property acquired while domiciled in another State has been particularly troublesome. Attempts of the Legislature to designate such personalty as community property uniformly have been thwarted by court decisions." (Comment (1935) 8 So. Cal. L. Rev. 221, 222.)

The problem arises as a result of California's attempts to apply community property concepts to the foreign, and radically different (in hypotheses) common-law theory of matrimonial rights. In fitting the common-law system into our community property scheme the process is of two steps. First, property acquired by a spouse while domiciled in a common-law state is characterized as separate property. (Estate of O'Connor, 218 Cal. 518 [23 P.2d 1031, 88 A.L.R. 856].) Second, the rule of tracing is invoked so that all property later acquired in exchange for the common-law separate property is likewise deemed separate property. (Kraemer v. Kraemer, 52 Cal. 302.) Thus, the original property, and all property subsequently acquired through use of the original property is classified as the separate property of the acquiring spouse.

One attempt to solve the problem was the 1917 amendment to Civil Code section 164, which had the effect of classifying all personal property wherever situated and all real property located in California into California community property if that property would not have been the separate property of one of the spouses had that property been acquired while the parties were domiciled in California. Insofar as the amendment attempted to affect personal property brought to California which was the separate property of one of the spouses while domiciled outside this state, Estate of Thornton, 1 Cal. 2d 1 [33 P.2d 1, 92 A.L.R. 1343], held the section was unconstitutional. . . .

Another major attempt to alter the rights in property acquired prior to California domicile was the passage of Probate Code section 201.5 [now sections 66 and 101]. This section gave to the surviving spouse one half of all the personal property wherever situated and the real property located in California which would not have been the separate property of the acquiring spouse had it been acquired while domiciled in California. As a succession statute, its constitutionality was upheld on the theory that the state of domicile of the decedent at the time of his death has full power to control rights of succession. (In re Miller, 31 Cal. 2d 191, 196 [187 P.2d 722].) In other words, no one has a vested right to succeed to another's property rights, and no one has a vested right in the distribution of his estate upon his death. Hence succession rights may be constitutionally altered. This theory was a basis of the dissent in *Thornton*.

In the present case, it is contended that Estate of Thornton, supra, 1 Cal. 2d 1, is controlling and that the current legislation, by authority of *Thornton,* must be held to be unconstitutional. *Thornton* involved a situation of a husband and wife moving to California and bringing with them property acquired during their former domicile in Montana. Upon the husband's death, his widow sought to establish her community property rights in his estate as provided by the then recent amendment to Civil Code section 164. The majority held the section unconstitutional on the theory that upon acquisition of the property the husband obtained vested rights which could not be altered without violation of his privileges and immunities as a citizen and also that "to take the property of *A* and transfer it to *B* because of his citizenship and domicile, is also to take his property without due process of law. This is true regardless of the place of acquisition or the state of his residence." (Estate of Thornton, supra, 1 Cal. 2d 1, 5.)

The underlying rationale of the majority was the same in *Thornton* as it had been since Spreckels v. Spreckels, 116 Cal. 339 [48 P. 228, 58 Am. St. Rep. 170, 36 L.R.A. 497], which established, by a concession of counsel, that changes in the community property system which affected "vested interests" could not constitutionally be applied retroactively but must be limited to prospective application.

Langdon, J., in his dissent in *Thornton,* conceded the correctness of the vested right theory but argued that the statute was merely definitional, giving no rights to anyone except as provided by other legislation. Therefore, the widow would only be acquiring rights pursuant to a right of succession as granted by statute. As to the constitutionality of this application of amended Civil Code section 164 he declared: "It is a rule of almost universal acceptance that the rights of testamentary disposition and of succession are wholly subject to statutory control, and may be enlarged, limited or abolished without infringing upon the constitutional guaranty of due process of law." (Estate of Thornton, supra, 1 Cal. 2d 1, 7.) The majority refused to construe amended Civil Code section 164 in this limited fashion.

The constitutional doctrine announced in Estate of Thornton, supra, has been questioned. Justice (now Chief Justice) Traynor in his concurring opinion in Boyd v. Oser, 23 Cal. 2d 613 [145 P.2d 312], had the following to say (at p.623):

> The decisions that existing statutes changing the rights of husbands and wives in community property can have no retroactive application have become a rule of property in this state and should not now be overruled. It is my opinion, however, that the constitutional theory on which they are based is unsound. . . . That theory has not become a rule of property and should not invalidate future legislation in this field intended by the Legislature to operate retroactively.

The underlying theory of *Thornton* has also been questioned by several legal authorities in this field. (Armstrong, "Prospective" Application of Changes in Community Property Control — Rule of Property or Constitutional Necessity? (1945) 33 Cal. L. Rev. 476; Schreter, "Quasi-Community Property" in the Conflict of Laws (1962) 50 Cal. L. Rev. 206; Comment, Community and Separate Property: Constitutionality of Legislation Decreasing Husband's Power of Control Over Property Already Acquired (1938) 27 Cal. L. Rev. 49, 51-55; see also Comment (1927) 15 Cal. L. Rev. 399.)

Thus, the correctness of the rule of *Thornton* is open to challenge. But even if the rule of that case be accepted as sound, it is not here controlling. This is so because former section 164 of the Civil Code has an entirely different impact from the legislation presently before us. The legislation under discussion, unlike old section 164, makes no attempt to alter property rights merely upon crossing the boundary into California. It does not purport to disturb vested rights "of a citizen of another state, who chances to transfer his domicile to this state, bringing his property with him. . . ." (Estate of Thornton, supra, 1 Cal. 2d 1, at p.5.) Instead, the concept of quasi-community property is applicable only if a divorce or separate maintenance action is filed here after the parties have become domiciled in California. Thus, the concept is applicable only if, after acquisition of domicile in this state, certain acts or events occur which give rise to an action for divorce or separate maintenance. These acts or events are not necessarily connected with a change of domicile at all.

It cannot be successfully argued that the quasi-community property legislation is unconstitutional because of a violation of the due process clause of the federal

Constitution. Morton has not been deprived of a vested right without due process. As Professor Armstrong has correctly pointed out in her article, supra:

> Vested rights, of course, may be impaired "with due process of law" under many circumstances. The state's inherent sovereign power includes the so called "police power" right to interfere with vested property rights whenever reasonably necessary to the protection of the health, safety, morals, and general well being of the people. The annals of constitutional law are replete with decisions approving, as constitutionally proper, the impairing of, and even the complete confiscation of, property rights when compelling public interest justified it.
>
> The constitutional question, on principle, therefore, would seem to be, not whether a vested right is impaired by a marital property law change, but whether such a change reasonably could be believed to be sufficiently necessary to the public welfare as to justify the impairment. (Armstrong, "Prospective" Application of Changes in Community Property Control—Rule of Property or Constitutional Necessity? (1945) supra, 33 Cal. L. Rev. 476, 495-496.)

Clearly the interest of the state of the current domicile in the matrimonial property of the parties is substantial upon the dissolution of the marriage relationship. This was expressly recognized by the United States Supreme Court in Williams v. North Carolina, 317 U.S. 287 [63 S. Ct. 207, 87 L. Ed. 279, 143 A.L.R. 1273], where it was said (at p.298):

> Each state as a sovereign has a rightful and legitimate concern in the marital status of persons domiciled within its borders. The marriage relation creates problems of large social importance. Protection of offspring, property interests, and the enforcement of marital responsibilities are but a few of commanding problems in the field of domestic relations with which the state must deal.

In recognition of much the same interest as that advanced by the quasi-community property legislation, many common-law jurisdictions have provided for the division of the separate property of the respective spouses in a manner which is "just and reasonable" and none of these statutes have been overturned on a constitutional basis.[11]

In the case at bar it was Leona who was granted a divorce from Morton on the ground of the latter's adultery and hence it is the spouse guilty of the marital infidelity from whom the otherwise separate property is sought by the operation of the quasi-community property legislation. We are of the opinion that where the innocent party would otherwise be left unprotected the state has a very substantial inter-

---

11. Because of the experience of the common-law jurisdictions it is the position of the California Law Revision Commission, whose recommendations formed the basis of the 1961 legislation, that where, as here, the divorce is granted on the ground of adultery, and it is the property of the adulterous spouse that is being divided as the court deems just, no valid constitutional objection can be raised. (See Marsh, A Study Relating to Inter Vivos Rights in Property Acquired by Spouse While Domiciled Elsewhere (1961) 3 Cal. Law Revision Com. Rep., Rec. & Studies I-21, I-26, attached to the commission's report.)

Illinois, the former domicile of the Addisons, has no specific statutory authority granting a spouse a share in the other spouse's separate property upon divorce. However, in 1949 it enacted legislation authorizing a settlement of property in lieu of alimony (Ill. Rev. Stat. ch. 40, §19 (1959)) and this statute has been frequently utilized in situations analogous to the instant case. (See Schwarz v. Schwarz, 27 Ill. 2d 140 [188 N.E.2d 673]; Smothers v. Smothers, 25 Ill. 2d 86 [182 N.E.2d 758]: Savich v. Savich, 12 Ill. 2d 454 [147 N.E.2d 85].)

est and one sufficient to provide for a fair and equitable distribution of the marital property without running afoul of the due process clause of the Fourteenth Amendment. For the same reasons sections 1 and 13 of article I of the California Constitution, substantially similar in language, are not here applicable.

Morton also asserts that there is an abridgment of the privileges and immunities clause of the Fourteenth Amendment citing Estate of Thornton, supra, 1 Cal. 2d 1. As has been observed "The 'privileges and immunities' protected are only those that belong to citizens of the United States as distinguished from citizens of the States—those that arise from the Constitution and laws of the United States as contrasted with those that spring from other sources." (Hamilton v. Regents of the University of California, 293 U.S. 245, 261 [55 S. Ct. 197, 79 L. Ed. 343], rehg. den. 293 U.S. 633 [55 S. Ct. 345, 79 L. Ed. 717].) Aside from the due process clause, already held not to be applicable, Thornton may be read as holding that the legislation there in question impinged upon the right of a citizen of the United States to maintain a domicile in any state of his choosing without the loss of valuable property rights. As to this contention, this distinction we have already noted between former Civil Code section 164 and quasi-community property legislation is relevant.

Unlike the legislation in Thornton, the quasi-community property legislation does not cause a loss of valuable rights through change of domicile. The concept is applicable only in case of a decree of divorce or separate maintenance.

It is also argued that the legislation here under discussion may be unconstitutional under the privileges and immunities clause of section 2 of article IV of the United States Constitution. It is there provided that "The Citizens of each State shall be entitled to all Privileges and Immunities of Citizens in the several states." The argument is that under the doctrine of Spreckels v. Spreckels, supra, 116 Cal. 339, California has refused to tamper with vested marital property rights of its own citizens and must therefore accord the same treatment to citizens of other states. As the United States Supreme Court has observed,

> Like many other constitutional provisions, the privileges and immunities clause is not an absolute. It does bar discrimination against citizens of other States where there is no substantial reason for the discrimination beyond the mere fact that they are citizens of other States. But it does not preclude disparity of treatment in the many situations where there are perfectly valid independent reasons for it. Thus the inquiry in each case must be concerned with whether such reasons do exist and whether the degree of discrimination bears a close relation to them. The inquiry must also, of course, be conducted with due regard for the principle that the States should have considerable leeway in analyzing local evils and in prescribing appropriate cures. (Toomer v. Witsell, 334 U.S. 385, 396 [68 S. Ct. 1157, 92 L. Ed. 1460], rehg. den. 335 U.S. 837 [69 S. Ct. 12, 93 L. Ed. 389].)

In the case at bar, Leona, as a former nondomiciliary of California, is a member of a class of people who lost the protection afforded them in Illinois had they sought a divorce there before leaving that state. (See Marsh, Marital Property in Conflict of Laws (1st ed. 1952) pp.233-234 and cases cited in fn. 22.) She has lost that protection, and is thus in need of protection from California. Hence, the discrimination, if there be such, is reasonable and not of the type article IV of the federal Constitution seeks to enjoin.

Additionally, it is urged that the quasi-community property legislation is not applicable to Morton because the legislation was enacted subsequent to the filing of the cause of action but prior to the judgment. This position is untenable. (See Peabody v. City of Vallejo, 2 Cal. 2d 351, 363-364 [40 P.2d 486] (the law at the time of judgment is controlling); see also Tulare Dist. v. Lindsay-Strathmore Dist., 3 Cal. 2d 489, 526-528 [45 P.2d 972].)

Nor is the statute being applied retroactively. That is so because the legislation here involved neither creates nor alters rights except upon divorce or separate maintenance. The judgment of divorce was granted after the effective date of the legislation. Hence the statute is being applied prospectively.

It follows that the trial court was in error in refusing to apply the quasi-community property legislation to the case at bar. . . .

TRAYNOR, C.J., TOBRINER, J., PEEK, J., BURKE, J., and SCHAUER, J., concurred.

Notes and Questions

1. Do *Miller* and *Addison* approve California quasi-community property distribution at death and divorce because it essentially parallels the equitable distribution and elective share legislation of common law states? If so, the "quasi-community" designation unnecessarily raises constitutional issues. The legislature would have done better to avoid any property label and simply to have provided, for example, that at divorce "the court shall divide all community property and all property acquired elsewhere which would have been community property had the parties been domiciled in California." How, if at all, would this provision differ from an equitable distribution statute requiring the court to "equitably distribute all property acquired by the spouses during marriage"?

2. If you agree with this reading of *Miller* and *Addison,* what bearing, if any, do they have on the constitutionality of the 1984 California enactment that subjects a spouse's quasi-community property to liability "for a debt incurred by either spouse before or during marriage, regardless of which spouse has the management and control of the property and regardless of whether one or both spouses are parties to the debt or to a judgment for the debt"? Family Code §§63 and 910. If you were representing a wife whose quasi-community property was being sought by a creditor on account of a debt incurred solely by her husband, what arguments would you make?

On the other hand, does *Addison* set the constitutional *limits* of quasi-community property doctrine? Could the legislature, for example, constitutionally grant both spouses management rights in quasi-community property? See generally Schreter [Kay], "Quasi-Community Property" in the Conflict of Laws, 50 Cal. L. Rev. 206, 230-240 (1962) and the excerpts from Phillips Petroleum Co. v. Shutts, reprinted at page 591 infra. But compare Brilmayer, Interest Analysis and the Myth of Legislative Intent, 78 Mich. L. Rev. 392 (1980).

3. *Thornton* and *Addison* consider the extent to which the legislature may constitutionally impair pre-existing interests by enacting community property legislation that applies retrospectively as well as prospectively. *Thornton* recounts the California Supreme Court's restrictive response to early legislative efforts to increase married women's control and ownership of community property. In the series of cases cited in *Thornton,* the court held that the reform legislation was constitutional only insofar as its application was confined to property *acquired* after the effective date of the statute. *Addison* indicates that by 1965 the court was dissatisfied with blanket prohibition of retroactive application. The court was not yet obliged to confront the venera-

ble proscription because it concluded that *Addison* did not pose any issue of retroactive application: The Addisons were *divorced* after the statute's effective date. It was not until Marriage of Bouquet, 16 Cal. 3d 583, 546 P.2d 1371, 128 Cal. Rptr. 427 (1976), that the California Supreme Court rejected the blanket prohibition of retroactivity and prescribed instead the case-by-case constitutional adjudication suggested in *Addison*. *Bouquet* approved retroactive application of an amendment to current Family Code section 771, which provides that after separation the earnings of *both* spouses are separate property. Previously, the wife's earnings during separation were her separate property, but the husband's earnings belonged to the community. *Bouquet* recasts *Addison* as a retroactive application case: The property divided in *Addison* was *acquired* before the statute's effective date.

Bouquet should not be understood to announce blanket acceptance of retroactive application of new community property rules. That it instead prescribes case-by-case adjudication is demonstrated by the supreme court's subsequent holdings in such cases as Marriage of Buol, page 192 supra, and Marriage of Heikes, page 199 supra. (Note that *Heikes* adopts the *Bouquet* view that a statute determining property rights at divorce operates retroactively when it is applied to property *acquired* before its effective date. *Addison* should be considered disapproved insofar as it looked instead to the date of divorce to determine whether the statute had been applied retroactively.)

Thus current law does not always control the classification of property owned by married persons. The date of acquisition may be critical. Several questions must be asked:

    a. What was the law when the asset was acquired?

    b. Do subsequent enactments purport to alter ownership or management rights in the asset? In other words, do subsequent enactments operate retroactively? Statutes are frequently unclear on this point, and it may be necessary to look to legislative history and judicial interpretation.

    c. If so, is such retroactive application constitutional?

4. In order to invoke California divorce jurisdiction, at least one party must be domiciled in California. Family Code §2320. The Addisons were both domiciled in California when Leona filed for divorce. *Addison* states, in dictum, that "the concept of quasi-community property is applicable only if a divorce or separate maintenance action is filed here after the *parties* have become domiciled in California" (emphasis added). Reread sections 125 and 2550 at page 575 supra. Do they require that *both* parties be domiciled in California? Should the quasi-community property statutes be understood to require that both parties be domiciled in California before quasi-community property principles become operative? As a matter of statutory interpretation? Choice of law? Constitutional due process? The next group of cases presents these questions.

MARRIAGE OF ROESCH
83 Cal. App. 3d 96, 147 Cal. Rptr. 586 (1978), cert. denied, 440 U.S. 915 (1979)

CHRISTIAN, J.—The marriage of Helen F. Roesch and William R. Roesch was dissolved by an interlocutory judgment. Wife appeals from certain portions of the judgment.

The parties were married in Brownsville, Pennsylvania, on April 17, 1947, when both were aged 21; they separated in Pittsburgh, Pennsylvania, on December 28, 1973. The parties have two children, a daughter who is of age, and a minor son, David, born April 2, 1959. Before the birth of the first child in July 1948, wife was briefly employed in an unskilled job. Since that time, however, she has been occupied exclusively as a homemaker.

Except for a brief period early in the marriage, the marital domicile was Pennsylvania, a common law state. When husband left the household he established his residence in California. Wife and the parties' son, David, have remained in Pennsylvania.

During virtually the entire period of the marriage, husband was employed by Jones & Laughlin Steel Corporation in Pittsburgh, Pennsylvania. He began as a coal miner, and gradually rose through the ranks of that corporation until on October 1, 1970, he was elected to the position of president and chief executive officer. His total gross earnings in that position were $163,000 in 1971. On January 1, 1972, husband was elected chairman of the board of directors and president at a base annual salary of $200,000.

In 1973, husband entered negotiations for employment with Kaiser Industries Corporation of Oakland, California. On November 12, 1973, prior to the separation and while he was still employed by Jones & Laughlin Steel Corporation, husband entered into an employment agreement with Kaiser. Under the terms of the agreement, husband was to assume the position of president and chief executive officer commencing January 1, 1974, for a term ending December 31, 1980, with a right of extension to May 31, 1990. The agreement set a base annual salary of $225,000 plus bonuses and other benefits. . . .

When the parties separated, husband moved his domicile to California; on January 1, 1974, he began performance of his employment agreement with Kaiser. In July 1974, husband commenced the present action for marital dissolution in Alameda County.

There was evidence that during the marriage the parties acquired as tenants by the entireties, as provided by Pennsylvania law, the family home and its furnishings, an automobile, and certain other property.

Other assets acquired by husband during the marriage were, under Pennsylvania law, the separate property of husband. These assets included:

1. Interest in Conoco Exploration Ltd.
2. Interest in Eastgate Shopping Center at Garden City, Kansas.
3. The insurance trust held by Mellon Bank. . . .
4. Pennsylvania funds (liquid assets which, at the time of separation, totaled $275,413.86).

The trial court characterized all of the above assets as quasi-community property, and divided them between the parties. . . .

Wife contends that the trial court's division of certain assets which it characterized as quasi-community property was improper. Specifically, she challenges the propriety of the trial court's order with respect to retirement benefits from Jones & Laughlin, certain insurance policies on respondent's life acquired by the parties during marriage, and certain income-producing assets.

In the absence of a statute to the contrary, personal property acquired by a spouse during marriage while domiciled in a common law state does not lose its character as the separate property of the acquiring spouse upon a change of domicile to a community property state. (Addison v. Addison (1965) 62 Cal. 2d 558, 563 [43 Cal. Rptr. 97, 399 P.2d 897, 14 A.L.R.3d 391]; see Annot. 14 A.L.R.3d 404, 411-416.) Furthermore, the rule of tracing is invoked so that all property later acquired in exchange for the common law separate property is likewise deemed separate property. (Id.)

The Legislature has twice attempted to alter the "domicile of acquisition" principle. A former statutory provision (Civ. Code, §164 as amended in 1917 . . .) attempted to treat as community property all personal property acquired during marriage by either husband or wife, or both, while domiciled elsewhere, which property would have been community property if acquired while domiciled in this state. In Estate of Thornton (1934) 1 Cal. 2d 1 [33 P.2d 1, 92 A.L.R. 1343], this provision was held ineffective, on the basis that changes in the community property system which would impair "vested interests" could not constitutionally be applied retrospectively.

The constitutional foundation of *Thornton,* supra, has arguably been undermined by subsequent decisions holding that vested property rights can be diminished by retrospective application of changes in marital property law if such application is demanded by a sufficiently important state interest. (In re Marriage of Bouquet (1976) 16 Cal. 3d 583, 592 [128 Cal. Rptr. 427, 546 P.2d 1371]; Addison v. Addison, supra, 62 Cal. 2d 558, 567-569; see generally Boyd v. Oser (1944) 23 Cal. 2d 613, 623 [145 P.2d 312].) Thus, in Addison v. Addison, supra, 62 Cal. 2d 558, the court held that a 1961 enactment expanding the definition of community property could constitutionally be applied in cases meeting two prerequisite conditions: (1) both parties have changed their domicile to California, and (2) subsequent to the change of domicile the spouses sought in a California court legal alteration of their marital status. Unless both of these conditions exist, the interest of the State of California in the status of the property of the spouses is insufficient to justify reclassification without violating the due process clause of the Fourteenth Amendment and the privileges and immunities clause of article IV, section 2, of the federal Constitution. . . .

In the present case the parties lived in Pennsylvania for virtually their entire married life. *After* their separation, husband transferred his domicile to California; wife and the parties' minor son remained in Pennsylvania. Under these facts, the interest of California in the marital property of the parties is minimal, while that of Pennsylvania is substantial. Moreover, as a domiciliary of Pennsylvania, wife is entitled to the protection of the laws of that state. Application of California's quasi-community property statute was therefore improper. While no modification of the judgment is called for in the absence of an appeal by husband, wife cannot be heard to complain that the apportionment to her was insufficient, from assets which under governing Pennsylvania law were not subject to apportionment at all.[14] . . .

RATTIGAN, Acting P.J., and PAIK, J., concurred.

A petition for a rehearing was denied August 17, 1978, and appellant's petition for a hearing by the Supreme Court was denied September 27, 1978. BIRD, C.J., was of the opinion that the petition should be granted.

Notes and Questions

1. Is *Roesch* a choice of law or a due process case? Can these two usually discrete questions be fully separated in *Roesch*?

---

14. Pennsylvania was a "title" state (see Chapter 1) until 1980, when it enacted equitable distribution provisions, now codified at 23 Pa. Cons. Stat. Ann. §3501-3503 (West 1991). — ED.

2. Assuming, for purposes of discussion, that *Roesch* is essentially a choice of law case, how should a court respond when neither party pleads sister-state law? Compare Louknitsky v. Louknitsky, at page 169 supra.

3. Whose due process rights are violated by the application of California quasi-community property law when William, a California domiciliary, sues Helen, a Pennsylvania domiciliary, for divorce in a California court? At first glance, one might think that Helen may have a due process claim, but she is not asserting it. (Why not?) On the contrary, she clearly consents to the application of California quasi-community property law; she challenges only the particular results. Could William plausibly argue (he has not, in fact, even filed an appeal) that Helen's lack of California domicile renders the court's property division violative of *his* due process?

MARRIAGE OF MARTIN
156 Ariz. 440, 752 P.2d 1026 (App. 1986)

Brooks, Judge.

This is an appeal from a decree of dissolution distributing various marital assets between husband, a California resident, and wife, a resident of Arizona. The relevant facts are as follows.

Richard Martin (husband) and Mary Martin (wife) were married in Wyoming in 1950. Due to the nature of husband's work, the parties travelled extensively throughout the United States and the world. In August 1979, the parties returned to the United States from Singapore, where husband had worked for Union Oil Company of California. The parties became domiciled in California, where husband's job was located. Shortly thereafter, they bought a townhouse in Prescott, Arizona as a planned retirement home. Wife moved into the Prescott townhouse in December, 1979, taking with her a substantial portion of the furnishings from the couple's California home. Husband remained in California, intending to join his wife in Prescott upon his planned retirement. During the period they remained separated, husband gave wife money for living expenses and payments on the townhouse mortgage. Things did not bode well for the marriage, however, and wife filed this action seeking dissolution of the marriage in 1982.

During the parties' three year separation prior to the action for dissolution, husband lived in California and worked for Union Oil Company. He maintained almost total control over the parties' extensive marital assets, sending only a fixed and relatively small monthly sum to his wife in Arizona. At no time has husband ever resided in Arizona. . . .

The trial court . . . ruled that, under Arizona law, husband's post separation earnings in California were community property.

Husband now appeals. . . .

Husband . . . contends that the trial court erred by applying Arizona rather than California law to the issue of whether his post-separation earnings were separate or community property. Under A.R.S. §§25-211 and 25-213, post-separation earnings are community property in Arizona until a final decree of dissolution is entered. Jurek v. Jurek, 124 Ariz. 596, 606 P.2d 812 (1980); Matter of Estate of Messer, 118 Ariz. 291, 576 P.2d 150 (App. 1978). Under California law, however, such earnings are considered the separate property of the spouse who acquires them. Cal. Civ.

Code §5118 (West 1983) [now Family Code §771]. We are thus confronted with a conflict of law question.

Husband contends that where parties are domiciled in different states when marital property is acquired, the law of the state where the acquiring spouse is domiciled at the time applies to determine the property's disposition upon dissolution. Restatement (Second) of Conflict of Laws, §258, comment c (1971). He claims that since wife was domiciled in Arizona and he was domiciled in California when the post-separation earnings were acquired, California law should be applied to characterize these earnings as his separate property.

While husband agrees that Arizona's quasi-community property law, A.R.S. §25-318(A),[1] would normally supersede the *Restatement*'s choice of law rule and convert his earnings into community property, Woodward v. Woodward, 117 Ariz. 148, 571 P.2d 294 (App. 1977), he argues that Arizona law should not apply where only one of the parties is domiciled in this state. In support of this argument, he relies on In re Marriage of Roesch, 83 Cal. App. 3d 96, 147 Cal. Rptr. 586 (App. 1978). In *Roesch,* the California Court of Appeals refused to apply California's quasi-community property law to a situation where only one of the parties was domiciled in that state. The court held that California law was applicable only where *both* spouses are domiciled in California. *Roesch,* 83 Cal. App. 3d at 107, 147 Cal. Rptr. at 593.

Husband contends that since California's quasi-community property law is so similar to our own,[2] see Sample v. Sample, 135 Ariz. 599, 602, 663 P.2d 591, 594 (App. 1983), we should, by analogy, adopt California's view. Wife counters by arguing that this issue has already been decided against husband in Woodward v. Woodward, supra.

We begin our analysis by noting that Arizona has not decided the issue of whether our quasi-community property law supersedes the usual choice of law rule stated in comment c to the Restatement (Second) of Conflict of Laws §258 in cases such as the one at hand. Contrary to wife's claim, *Woodward* did not decide the issue. *Woodward* held only that *where* §25-318(A) applies, it *necessarily* supersedes the *Restatement*'s choice of law rule. However, the issue of whether the statute applies where only one spouse is domiciled in Arizona was not addressed. The issue is thus one of first impression in this jurisdiction.

We are not persuaded that we should follow California's lead on this issue. It seems clear from our reading of *Roesch* that the court's refusal in that case to apply California's quasi-community property law to cases where only one spouse is domiciled there rests upon a misinterpretation of past California case law. The *Roesch* court refused to invoke California law where only one spouse was domiciled in that state because it was confronted with what it perceived to be constitutional limita-

---

1. A.R.S. §25-318(A) states in pertinent part:

   In a proceeding for dissolution of the marriage . . . property acquired by either spouse outside this state shall be deemed to be community property if the property would have been community property if acquired in this state.

2. California's quasi-community property law is embodied in Cal. Civ. Code §4803 (now Family Code §125), which reads:

   As used in this part, "quasi-community property" means all real or personal property, wherever situated, heretofore or hereafter acquired in any of the following ways:
   (a) By either spouse while domiciled elsewhere which would have been community property if the spouse who acquired the property had been domiciled in this state at the time of its acquisition.

tions imposed in Addison v. Addison, 43 Cal. Rptr. 97, 399 P.2d 897 (1965). In *Addison,* the California Supreme Court addressed a constitutional challenge to California's quasi-community property statute. In upholding the statute's constitutionality, the *Addison* court simply interpreted the statute to mean that the concept of quasi-community property did not apply until a divorce action was filed in the California courts after *both* parties became domiciled there. Id. at 102, 399 P.2d at 902. The court then held that since something more than merely moving into California was required for the statute to apply — namely, that a divorce action be filed in the state court — the statute did not violate the federal privileges and immunities clause by disturbing the vested rights of other state's citizens. The court went on to hold that the statute did not violate federal due process because California had a compelling interest in the marital relationship and disposition of the marital property upon divorce. The California Court of Appeals in *Roesch,* however, broadly interpreted *Addison* as creating two *constitutional* prerequisites to the application of California's quasi-community property statute: 1) that *both* spouses be domiciled in California, and 2) that they seek a dissolution there. In refusing to invoke California's quasi-community property statute, the *Roesch* court declared:

> Unless both of these conditions exist, the interest of the State of California in the status of the property of the spouses is insufficient to justify reclassification [by application of the quasi-community property statute] without violating the due process clause of the Fourteenth Amendment and the privileges and immunities clause . . . of the federal Constitution.

83 Cal. App. 3d at 107, 147 Cal. Rptr. at 593.

We do not find *Roesch* to be a proper interpretation of *Addison* and we decline to follow it. *Addison* did not seek to place constitutional restraints on the exercise of California's quasi-community property statute; rather, it only gave a statutory interpretation of what the court thought the statute *itself* required before the quasi-community property concept could be invoked. The court simply held that this interpretation of the statute's meaning would unquestionably pass constitutional muster. Nowhere did the court imply that the statute would be unconstitutional unless given such an interpretation. The court did not even address the issue of whether other interpretations of the statute were constitutionally permissible. To say, therefore, as *Roesch* does, that *Addison* created a two-pronged test for the constitutionality of applying the concept of quasi-community property misconstrues *Addison* and inflates its holding.

Moreover, while we note that the language of California's quasi-community property statute is very similar to our own, we decline to interpret our statute, as was done in *Addison,* to require both spouses to be domiciled here before the statute may be invoked. Indeed, no rationale was given by the *Addison* court as to why it interpreted California's statute in such a restrictive manner. It does not appear that the *Addison* court felt such an interpretation was necessary to uphold the statute's constitutionality since the court itself cast doubt upon the validity of the petitioner's constitutional challenge from the beginning. Such an interpretation is at odds with the broad language of both statutes. For instance, Arizona's statute, A.R.S. §25-318(A), provides that "property acquired by *either* spouse outside of this state" is subject to being treated as quasi-community property. This broad language clearly encompasses the facts of the instant case.

Furthermore, apart from the lack of any rationale in *Addison* for restricting the application of A.R.S. §25-318(A), we find that factors such as uniformity of result and judicial economy favor application of our quasi-community property law to all dissolution actions filed in this state. The alternative would be to apply the traditional *Restatement* choice of law rule to cases such as this. However, the *Restatement* rule has been criticized as "anachronistic" and "unworkable in modern mobile America." Ismail v. Ismail, 702 S.W.2d 216, 222 (Tex. App. 1985); Sampson, Interstate Spouses, Interstate Property, and Divorce, 13 Tex. Tech. L. Rev. 1285, 1344 (1982). Under the *Restatement,* a court may find itself with the task of applying various rules of disposition to different marital assets depending upon where each spouse was domiciled when the particular asset was acquired. For example, in the instant case, it is conceivable that husband could have been transferred to other states or countries—as he so often was in the past—after the parties separated. His post-separation earnings and any property acquired with them would thus be subject not only to California law (to the extent they were earned while he resided in California), but also to the law of the other jurisdictions. The problems that would confront a trial court in reaching a proper and equitable disposition of the marital estate in such a case can be readily appreciated. We believe that the trial court's task is sufficiently complicated without adding unnecessary burdens. From a choice of law standpoint, we therefore find that application of Arizona's quasi-community property law is the better approach in cases such as this. We hold, therefore, that A.R.S. §25-318(A) applies to this case and, under *Woodward,* supra, supersedes the usual choice of law rule stated in comment c to §258 of the Restatement (Second) of Conflict of Laws.

Without offering any particular legal analysis, husband next argues that such a blanket application of A.R.S. §25-318(A) may well give rise to constitutional problems. However, we believe that any question concerning the constitutionality of applying Arizona's quasi-community property law to a spouse who has never been domiciled here is subsumed by the issue of whether Arizona may acquire personal jurisdiction over such spouse.

The rule is well established that where Arizona has personal jurisdiction over both parties to a dissolution proceeding, it may apply its substantive law in dividing the marital property between the parties—even if that property is located in another state. Auman v. Auman, 134 Ariz. 40, 653 P.2d 688 (1982); Bowart v. Bowart, 128 Ariz. 331, 625 P.2d 920 (App. 1980). Whether Arizona courts may constitutionally exercise such personal jurisdiction over a non-resident spouse depends upon whether the spouse has sufficient minimum contacts with the state to justify being haled before an Arizona court. Schilz v. Superior Court, 144 Ariz. 65, 695 P.2d 1103 (1985); Meyers v. Hamilton Corp., 143 Ariz. 249, 693, P.2d 904 (1984); Rodriguez v. Rodriguez, 8 Ariz. App. 5, 442 P.2d 169 (1968). In the case at hand, however, we need not address whether husband's contacts with Arizona were sufficient to properly subject him to personal jurisdiction in an Arizona court since he voluntarily submitted himself to such jurisdiction. As husband has consented to the Arizona court's jurisdiction, he cannot now claim that he is being treated unfairly by having Arizona's substantive law applied to the facts of this case. We find, therefore, that there is no constitutional infirmity in applying Arizona's quasi-community property law to the husband in this case. Consequently, we affirm the trial court's application of Arizona law to the issue of whether husband's post-separation earnings were community or separate property. Under Arizona law, they are clearly community property subject to division upon dissolution. . . .

FROEB, J., concurs.

Note

Although *Martin* is more soundly reasoned than *Roesch*, *Martin*'s concluding dictum is misleading. That Arizona has personal jurisdiction over both parties does not give the Arizona forum constitutional carte blanche with respect to choice of law. In Phillips Petroleum Co. v. Shutts, 472 U.S. 797, 86 L. Ed. 2d 628, 105 S. Ct. 2965 (1985), the United States Supreme Court held that although a Kansas trial court properly asserted personal jurisdiction over absent plaintiff class members, nevertheless the Kansas court was not constitutionally free to apply Kansas substantive law to claimants and claims that had no relation to Kansas. Nor could a class member's consent to the Kansas court's exercise of jurisdiction be deemed a consent to its application of Kansas substantive law.

> Kansas must have a "significant contact or significant aggregation of contacts" to the claims asserted by each member of the plaintiff class, contacts "creating state interests," in order to ensure that the choice of Kansas law is not arbitrary or unfair. *Allstate* [Insurance Co. v. Hague], 449 U.S. [302], at 312-313. Given Kansas' lack of "interest" in claims unrelated to that State, and the substantive conflict with jurisdictions such as Texas, we conclude that application of Kansas law to every claim in this case is sufficiently arbitrary and unfair as to exceed constitutional limits.
>
> When considering fairness in this context, an important element is the expectation of the parties. See *Allstate*, supra, at 333 (opinion of POWELL, J.). There is no indication that when the leases involving land and royalty owners outside of Kansas were executed, the parties had any idea that Kansas law would control. Neither the Due Process Clause nor the Full Faith and Credit Clause requires Kansas "to substitute for its own [laws], applicable to persons and events within it, the conflicting statute of another state," Pacific Employees Ins. Co. v. Industrial Accident Commn., 306 U.S. 493, 502 (1989), but Kansas "may not abrogate the rights of parties beyond its borders having no relation to anything done or to be done within them." Home Ins. Co. v. Dick, [281 U.S. 397], 410 [1930].
>
> Here the Supreme Court of Kansas took the view that in a nationwide class action where procedural due process guarantees of notice and adequate representation were met, "the law of the forum should be applied unless compelling reasons exist for applying a different law." 235 Kan., at 221, 679 P.2d, at 1181. Whatever practical reasons may have commended this rule to the Supreme Court of Kansas, for the reasons already stated we do not believe that it is consistent with the decisions of this Court. We make no effort to determine for ourselves which law must apply to the various transactions involved in this lawsuit, and we reaffirm our observation in *Allstate* that in many situations a state court may be free to apply one of several choices of law. But the constitutional limitations laid down in cases such as *Allstate* and Home Ins. Co. v. Dick, supra, must be respected even in a nationwide class action.
>
> We therefore affirm the judgment of the Supreme Court of Kansas insofar as it upheld the jurisdiction of the Kansas courts over the plaintiff class members in this case, and reverse its judgment insofar as it held that Kansas law was applicable to all of the transactions which it sought to adjudicate. We remand the case to that court for further proceedings not inconsistent with this opinion.

Id. at 821-823. See also Sun Oil Co. v. Wortman, 486 U.S. 717, 100 L. Ed. 2d 743, 108 S. Ct. 2117 (1988). Does California's *interest* in *Roesch* constitutionally warrant application of California quasi-community property law? Does Arizona's *interest* in *Martin* constitutionally warrant Arizona's application of Arizona quasi-community property law? Are the state interests identical in *Roesch* and *Martin*? As you rethink *Roesch* and *Martin,* and as you study the next three cases, consider the possibility that *Phillips Petroleum* not only sets out a constitutional standard but also offers a coherent rationalization for *all* the post-*Addison* cases in this section.

MARRIAGE OF JACOBSON
161 Cal. App. 3d 465, 207 Cal. Rptr. 512 (1984)

STONE, P.J.—Herbert Adolph Jacobson (husband) appeals from a judgment on [an issue] bifurcated from the dissolution of marriage trial—his military retirement benefits. . . .

Husband contends that: (1) the trial court did not have jurisdiction to apply California law to military retirement benefits; (2) the military retirement plan should retain its character as separate property under Iowa state law. . . .

We find no error and affirm the judgment.

June 11, 1980, wife filed a petition for legal separation and order to show cause for temporary spousal, child support and injunctive relief. The parties, married 15 years, had 2 minor children.

June 30, 1980, husband filed a responsive declaration to the order to show cause and also a notice of motion to dismiss the California proceeding based on forum non conveniens and lack of consent to the request for legal separation. [Family Code §2345.]

July 1, 1980, the parties signed a handwritten stipulation and order on the order to show cause, signed by a commissioner and filed that date, which provided: "Petitioner agrees to accept her % interest in Respondent's Pension, as opposed to a cash out, when Respondent first becomes eligible to retire from U.S. Navy [20 years] in exchange Respondent will forthwith dismiss with Prejudice Iowa dissolution proceeding and further agrees to have case resolved under Calif(ornia) law & here." Husband's response to the request for legal separation listed his United States Navy pension to be divided by the court. On November 24, 1980, at trial on the dissolution of marriage, husband, through different counsel, moved that the court terminate the action and find that Iowa had subject matter jurisdiction. The court denied the motion. Upon stipulation by the parties, the court amended the petition from legal separation to dissolution of marriage.

November 25, 1980, prior to conclusion of trial the parties stipulated in writing as follows: "The court to reserve jurisdiction over respondent's retirement rights through U.S. Navy, reservation to include all aspects, including whether [they] are separate or community, their value and parties' rights to distribution thereof." Said stipulation was accepted by the court and incorporated into the interlocutory judgment. The court entered final judgment of dissolution December 10, 1981. . . .

January 26, 1983, husband became eligible to but did not retire from the Navy. His pension as of that date was $1,579.85 per month.

March 11, 1983, wife filed notice of motion to divide husband's pension rights. . . . The instant appeal follows the trial court's August 19, 1983 judgment.

It is undisputed that husband is a domiciliary of Iowa, and a resident of California only through military assignment. Title 10 United States Code section 1408(c)(4) sets forth the jurisdictional bases for a California court to apply California law to military retirement benefits: "(4) A court may not treat the disposable retired or retainer pay of a member in the manner described in paragraph (1) unless the court has jurisdiction over the member by reason of (A) his residence, other than because of military assignment, in the territorial jurisdiction of the court, (B) his domicile in the territorial jurisdiction of the court, or (C) his consent to the jurisdiction of the court."

The trial court found husband consented to the court's jurisdiction by signing the July 1980 stipulation and by filing a response to the petition for legal separation in which he listed the naval pension as community or quasi-community property. Husband contends that the trial court erred because the November 25, 1980, stipulation superseded and abrogated that of July 1, the effect of which was to leave open for later determination whether the property was separate or community and the question of which state's substantive law should be applied. According to husband, FUSFSPA [the Federal Uniformed Services Former Spouses' Protection Act] creates a "new express protection for the service member" — the right to have his military retirement benefits determined by his home or domiciliary state — and California, although it has in personam jurisdiction to hear the matter, must apply the law of Iowa.

Husband's interpretation of FUSFSPA is broader than ours. We find nothing in the statutory scheme to indicate that it means other than what it says, e.g., that a court may treat disposable retired pay either as property solely of the member or as property of the member and his spouse in accordance with the law of the jurisdiction of such court (10 U.S.C. §1408(c)(1)) and that a court may have jurisdiction over the member by his consent to that court's jurisdiction. (10 U.S.C. §1408(c)(4)(C).) Even if the November 25, 1980, stipulation abrogated the July 1, 1980, stipulation, husband, by his election to respond to the petition and forego his motion to dismiss on forum non conveniens grounds, made a general appearance and thereby consented to the jurisdiction of the court and the application of the substantive law of California. (1 Witkin, Cal. Procedure (2d ed. 1970) Jurisdiction, §118, pp.646-647.) Consequently, California's jurisdiction under FUSFSPA was clear. (§1408(c)(4)(C).) "Once a party has generally consented to a court's jurisdiction, it may not be attacked later." (In re Marriage of Sarles (1983) 143 Cal. App. 3d 24, 29 [191 Cal. Rptr. 514].) . . .

FUSFSPA . . . gave him no greater rights than he had before. As a nondomiciliary he could have moved to dismiss proceedings on forum non conveniens grounds or consent to the jurisdiction. He chose the latter. . . .

Husband next contends that even if he consented to California's jurisdiction, the military retirement plan should retain its character as separate property under Iowa law because the interest of the State of California is insufficient to justify its reclassification without violating the due process clause of the Fourteenth Amendment (U.S. Const., 14th Amend.) and the privileges and immunities clause of article IV, section 2 of the federal Constitution.

In re Marriage of Roesch (1978) 83 Cal. App. 3d 96 [147 Cal. Rptr. 586] upon which husband relies is distinguishable however. In *Roesch,* the parties had no connection with California until the husband moved to the state and filed for dissolution. Wife, child and real property were in Pennsylvania, their domicile. The appellate court held that wife was entitled to protection of Pennsylvania laws and that California's quasi-community property statute could not be applied unless both parties had changed their domicile to California and subsequent thereto sought legal alteration of their marital status in California courts. (83 Cal. App. 3d at p.107.) *Roesch* did not address consent to jurisdiction. . . . FUSFSPA provides consent as an alternative to domicile for jurisdiction. Therefore, the criteria of *Roesch* . . . are met — wife's domicile, husband's consent (as an alternative to domicile) and wife's request to alter the marital status. Even assuming, arguendo, that the November 25 stipulation abrogated that of July 1, if the parties meant to reserve to husband the right to have the substantive law of Iowa applied to the military pension, they should have so indicated in the November 24, 1980, stipulation which reads "whether assets are separate or community." Iowa law does not recognize community property but mandates that division of property is based on each marital partner's right to a just and equitable share of the property accumulated as the result of their joint efforts. (In re Marriage of Hitchcock (Iowa 1981) 309 N.W.2d 432, 437; see Iowa Code Annotated, vol. 39 Domestic Relations, §598.21.) Since we find that husband consented to have the substantive law of California apply to his military retirement, it is unnecessary to speculate whether Iowa law would have achieved the same result. . . .

Notes and Questions

1. Examine the July 1 and November 25 stipulations. Are they inconsistent? If you were representing Marilyn, how would you have responded to Herbert's assertion that the November 25 stipulation abrogated the earlier agreement and "left open the question of which state's substantive law should be applied"?

On the other hand, assuming that the November 25 stipulation abrogated the July 1 stipulation, are you persuaded by the court's interpretation of the November 25 stipulation? Does the stipulation express the husband's consent to the application of California community property law? Can you give "whether [the pension rights] are separate or community" a different interpretation?

2. Does *Jacobson* treat the pension earned by the husband, an Iowa domiciliary, as quasi-community property because he consented to the California divorce court's jurisdiction by making a general appearance *or* because he specifically consented in the stipulations to the application of California community property law? Should the answer make a difference? See the note following *Martin* at page 591 supra.

When, in the language of FUSFSPA, "a court may treat disposable retired pay . . . in accordance with *the laws* of the jurisdiction of such court," what portions of its law should the forum court consider? Only its marital property law or its (constitutionally adequate) choice of law principles as well?

MARRIAGE OF FRANSEN
142 Cal. App. 3d 419, 190 Cal. Rptr. 885 (1983)

STEPHENS, Acting P.J. — This is an appeal from an interlocutory dissolution of marriage order awarding Alwayne Fransen (wife and appellant) . . . a 5 percent share of her husband's military pension. . . . Cross-appellant and husband, Arnold

Fransen, also appeals from this order insisting that portion of the order awarding wife Alwayne a 5 percent share of his military pension rights must be reversed.[1]

We find the trial court did err in . . . its award of 5 percent of Arnold's military pension to Alwayne. We therefore remand to the trial court . . . for reconsideration in accordance with this opinion.

Alwayne and Arnold were married on August 13, 1943, in San Jose, California. From this marriage, the Fransens have two children who have since reached their majority. At the time of their marriage Arnold was in the third year of a 25-year naval career. He retired from the Navy in 1966 after attaining the rank of Commander. Arnold began receiving a retainer payment (pension) upon his retirement.

In 1966, the Fransens moved from his California duty station to Oregon. There they purchased a home and lived together until their separation on November 27, 1966.

Alwayne was in California visiting their daughter when Arnold notified her of his desire to separate. Arnold later informed her that he wished a divorce and advised her not to return to Oregon. As a result, she remained in California.

In March 1967, Arnold moved to Idaho and filed for divorce on April 25, 1967. Alwayne retained California counsel in an attempt to obtain support benefits.

In the Idaho divorce petition, Arnold alleged that only a Ford pickup truck was within the jurisdiction of the court for the court to dispense in a settlement. Alwayne failed to appear upon her counsel's advice that Idaho could not adjudicate her property or support rights without her consent. A default was entered and the truck was awarded to Arnold. No provision for support was requested or granted. Three days later Arnold and Alwayne entered into an agreement whereby Alwayne accepted title to the Oregon house plus its furnishings.[2]

On June 6, 1967, Arnold remarried. In September of that year, Arnold and his new wife moved to Ohio. Arnold took a job with Ohio University. In May of 1970, Arnold and his wife moved to Texas.[3] There, too, Arnold engaged in new employment. In 1974, Arnold again relocated, this time in California, and engaged in new employment.

On September 24, 1974, Alwayne commenced a proceeding in Ventura County Superior Court for dissolution of marriage. Included in her petition for dissolution was a request for spousal support in the amount of $500 per month, a community share in Arnold's vested military pension, attorney fees, and costs.

Arnold answered the petition by alleging that no property was subject to disposition by the court because the Idaho decree of divorce "settled all issues in the matter." The court found the Idaho decree was valid and did effectively dissolve the marriage of the parties as of May 26, 1967. However, the court noted that other than the Ford pickup truck, the Idaho decree did not divide, allocate or mention any of the other property of the parties. The court therefore concluded Alwayne had not waived her claims to spousal support or Arnold's pension rights and that it had sufficient jurisdiction over the residue of the couple's property interests to make a disposition.

---

1. In an air of brevity, the remainder of Arnold's argument on appeal is limited to the insistence that "[A]n appellate court will not disturb a trial court's implied fact findings supporting an order appealed from." (Citing Bailey v. County of Los Angeles (1956) 46 Cal. 2d 132 [293 P.2d 449].)

2. The house was later sold by Alwayne for a net earning of $10,900.

3. Alwayne had originated actions in both Ohio and Texas in an attempt to gain support benefits. Both actions were dismissed for lack of personal jurisdiction over Arnold.

An interlocutory judgment of dissolution of marriage was granted to Alwayne on December 5, 1979.[4] The court ordered Arnold to pay Alwayne 5 percent of his military pension rights, spousal support in the sum of $70 per month, and attorney fees and costs in the sum of $1,585.10. From this decision, both Alwayne and Arnold appeal. . . .

The California trial court concluded that the Idaho decree had "no effect on the rights of the parties to spousal support or to the military pension."

While the Idaho decree did dissolve the marriage of the Fransens, it failed to adjudicate questions regarding the parties community or quasi-community property rights. The California decree from which both Alwayne and Arnold appeal attempted to adjudge Arnold's military pension. A judgment was entered awarding Alwayne 5 percent of Arnold's military pension. . . .

Section 1408(c)(1) [of FUSFSPA] holds that "a court may treat disposable retired or retainer pay payable to a member . . . either as property solely of the member or as property of the member and his spouse *in accordance with the laws of the jurisdiction of such court.*" (Italics added.)

The trial court's award of five percent of Arnold's military pension failed to dispense the pension in accordance with established California community property/quasi-community property law. . . .

The court noted that from the date of marriage until September 1966, the Fransens lived in various states and foreign countries including California. For some 2½ years, or 10 percent of the 23-year marriage, the Fransens were domiciled in California exclusively. Based substantially upon these facts, it awarded Alwayne one-half (5 percent) of the 10 percent of Arnold's military pension it found to have been earned entirely in California. For purposes of dispensing with that portion of the pension earned exclusively in California as Alwayne's community property share, we are in accord. However, if 10 percent of the pension is community property, then the remaining 79.9 percent[11] of the pension earned during the marriage but outside of California was arguably subject to an equal division under California's quasi-community property law.

Civil Code section 4803, subdivision (a), [now Family Code section 125] states in pertinent part that "[A]ll real or personal property, wherever situated, heretofore or hereafter acquired . . . [¶] by either spouse while domiciled elsewhere which would have been community property if the spouse who acquired the property had been domiciled in this state at the time of its acquisition" is quasi-community property. The trial court concluded that

> Under In Re Marriage of Roesch, [(1978) 83 Cal. App. 3d 96 (147 Cal. Rptr. 586)] [the] benefits could not have been *entirely* quasi-community property. Had both parties been in California seeking a marriage dissolution in California at that time, retirement benefits could have been quasi-community property and been subject to disposition by the court.
>
> [F]or retirement benefits under California law to be community or quasi-community property, there must be some significant connection with California during the course of the marriage. Personal property acquired by a spouse during the marriage while domiciled in a common law state does not lose its

---

4. The effect of the second declaration of dissolution is questionable since the California court specifically found the 1967 Idaho divorce was valid.

11. Eighty-nine and nine-tenths percent of the total pension had accrued during the Fransens' marriage.

character as separate property of the acquiring spouse on a change of domicile to a community property state. However, a concept of quasi-community property on retirement benefits in a marriage dissolution could be asserted if two conditions existed:

1. Both parties changed their domicile to California; and,
2. Subsequent to the change of domicile, the spouses sought in a California court a legal alteration of their marital status. Absent these facts, the retirement personal property must be determined by the law of the state in which it accrued. [See In re Marriage of Roesch, supra, 83 Cal. App. 3d at p.107; italics added.]

In In re Marriage of Roesch, supra, 83 Cal. App. 3d 96, a 26-year marriage, most of which was spent in Pennsylvania, ended in separation. Husband came to California immediately after separation and approximately seven months later, filed for dissolution. The trial court treated certain property still remaining in Pennsylvania as quasi-community property. The appellate court . . . found that both parties lived in Pennsylvania for virtually their entire married life, and seven months of residency by the husband was insufficient to afford California a greater interest in protecting the marital property of the parties than Pennsylvania's interest. That property in question was adjudicated husband's separate property.

Turning to the mechanics of *Roesch* as applied by the trial court, we find the court's application less than acceptable.

The first criterion of *Roesch* (83 Cal. App. 3d at p.107), relied upon by the trial court, was the requirement of finding that both parties had changed their domicile to California. Unlike *Roesch*, where the husband alone established his domicile in California, the trial court here made a specific finding that both parties were domiciled in California.[12] Thus, the nonresidency which barred Mrs. Roesch's claim to a quasi-community property share is not present here.[13]

The second criterion of *Roesch*, supra, 83 Cal. App. 3d at page 107, relied upon by the trial court, was whether the parties had sought any legal alteration of their marital status in a California court. The trial court apparently concluded they did not and thus declared that the property acquired by Arnold while domiciled outside of California was not subject to a quasi-community property division.

Roesch reiterated the requirement that "subsequent to the change of domicile the *spouses* [must have] sought in a California court legal alteration of their marital status." (Italics added.) (83 Cal. App. 3d at p.107.) We declare that this criterion of *Roesch* is satisfied when *either* spouse initiates a legal proceeding to alter the marital status. To require otherwise would enable one spouse to defeat a quasi-community property claim of the other spouse by merely refusing to seek a dissolution, annulment or legal separation.

12. Alwayne has been domiciled in California since 1967; Arnold has been domiciled in California since 1974.

13. The Fransens' contacts with California were much more than incidental. The Fransens were married in California. Arnold's home at that time was in California. During a portion of Arnold's military service, the couple resided in California for a period of four years. While Arnold was overseas, Alwayne and the children remained in California for approximately two and one-half years. At the time Arnold moved to Idaho to seek a divorce, Alwayne remained in California. These are significant factors distinguishing the present facts from those of *Roesch*. Furthermore, this represents substantial support for the argument that California has much more than a minimum interest in protecting the parties' marital property.

Therefore, Alwayne has complied with the two requirements of *Roesch*.[14] The additional 79.9 percent of Arnold's pension earned during marriage but outside of California is subject to an equal division between the parties. . . .

ASHBY, J., and HASTINGS, J., concurred.

A petition for a rehearing was denied May 25, 1983. . . . The petition of appellant Husband for a hearing by the Supreme Court was denied July 20, 1983.

Notes and Questions

1. *Fransen* illustrates the "divisible divorce." Either spouse may obtain a divorce, that is, a change of legal status from married to unmarried, in his current domicile. The divorce court need not have personal jurisdiction over the other spouse. So long as the petitioner has established bona fide domicile, which is the basis for the court's divorce jurisdiction, the resulting ex parte decree is entitled to full faith and credit in every sister state. Williams v. North Carolina (I), 317 U.S. 287, 87 L. Ed. 279, 63 S. Ct. 207 (1942); Williams v. North Carolina (II), 325 U.S. 226, 89 L. Ed. 1577, 65 S. Ct. 1092 (1945). See also Sherrer v. Sherrer, 334 U.S. 343, 92 L. Ed. 1429, 68 S. Ct. 1087 (1948) (full faith and credit requirements with respect to bilateral divorces).

Yet the court must have personal jurisdiction over both spouses in order to determine *support* rights. To determine *property* rights, the court must have either personal jurisdiction over both parties or constitutionally adequate in rem jurisdiction over the property in issue. (Note that the *Fransen* Idaho ex parte decree distributed only property subject to the court's in rem jurisdiction, namely the Ford pickup truck.) If a divorce court granting an ex parte divorce does purport to adjudicate the parties' support and property rights without adequate jurisdictional basis, this portion of the judgment does not command full faith and credit in sister-state courts. Thus, despite a valid ex parte divorce, a sister-state court having personal jurisdiction over both parties may subsequently adjudicate the parties' support and property rights. The United States Supreme Court approved the doctrine of divisible divorce in Vanderbilt v. Vanderbilt, 354 U.S. 416, 1 L. Ed. 2d 1456, 77 S. Ct. 1360 (1957). (But cf. Simons v. Miami Beach First Natl. Bank, 381 U.S. 81, 14 L. Ed. 2d 232, 85 S. Ct. 1315 (1965).) As a constitutional matter, the doctrine is simply permissive. California may, as a matter of its substantive family law, adjudicate the economic incidents of a marriage after it has been dissolved elsewhere by a valid ex parte decree. In fact, California and a majority of other states have chosen to follow the doctrine of divisible divorce. Hudson v. Hudson, 52 Cal. 2d 735, 344 P.2d 295 (1959); H. Clark, Law of Domestic Relations 314-319, 436-439 (1968). See also Uniform Marriage and Divorce Act, §307, 9A U.L.A. 238 (1987). See generally Currie, Suitcase Divorce in the Conflicts of Laws, 34 U. Chi. L. Rev. 26 (1966); Comment, Divorce Ex Parte Style, 33 U. Chi. L. Rev. 837 (1966).

Thus, in Marriage of Fransen, Alwayne's counsel properly advised her to stay at home in California when Arnold sued her for divorce in Idaho. The Idaho divorce was effective to terminate the marriage, but not to conclude Alwayne's support and property rights.

---

14. The California court determined that the Idaho termination of marital status was valid. There had been no disposition of property in the Idaho determination, however, and California had jurisdiction.

2. Alwayne pursued Arnold to Ohio and Texas to assert her support claims (footnote 3), but Arnold moved to another state before Alwayne could subject him to the local court's personal jurisdiction. Then Arnold, like so many Americans before and since, could not resist the lure of California even if it meant a final reckoning of Alwayne's claims. The California trial court had personal jurisdiction over both parties and was an appropriate forum in which to finally settle the economic aspects of the parties' divorce. Yet, does Arnold's establishment of California domicile years *after* his valid 1967 Idaho divorce constitute an adequate basis for applying California quasi-community property law to that portion of his pension earned when he was not domiciled in California? If Arnold had not moved to California in 1974 but had instead remained in Texas and gallantly consented to make a general appearance in Alwayne's 1974 California action, would application of California quasi-community property law have been appropriate? Does Arnold's 1974 move to California alter your analysis?

3. Are you satisfied by the court's treatment of the Marriage of Roesch requirement that "subsequent to the change of domicile the spouses [must have] sought in a California court legal alteration of their marital status"? Even if you accept the court's substitution of "one spouse" for "the spouses," is the condition fulfilled? Specifically, can one refer to Alwayne as a "spouse" in 1974, when she brought her California action? Stated differently, is it sufficient to seek dissolution of a marriage that has already been terminated by divorce? Should the *Roesch* requirement be expanded to include California initiation of postdivorce "divisible divorce" proceedings for property division and support?

4. Why does the court of appeal stretch so far to apply California quasi-community property law to Arnold's military retirement pay? Does *Fransen* reach a just result? As a matter of choice of law, is *Fransen* reconcilable with *Roesch*?

MARRIAGE OF BEN-YEHOSHUA
91 Cal. App. 3d 259, 154 Cal. Rptr. 80 (1979)

BROWN (G.A.), P.J. — Shimshon Ben-Yehoshua, husband, appeals from an interlocutory decree of dissolution . . . dividing certain property located in Israel. We . . . affirm. . . .

Wife is a United States citizen. Husband is a citizen of Israel. They were married in Israel on April 10, 1962. Three children were born of the marriage: Eyal, born August 15, 1964, Liat, born June 20, 1967, and Amit, born August 16, 1972. Husband and wife, together with their children, were domiciled in Israel from the time of their marriage for 13 years. On June 25, 1975, wife came to Hanford, Kings County, California, with the three children to visit her mother. She testified that when she initially came here she did not have in mind separating or divorcing her husband or remaining in California. However, 14 days after her arrival, on July 9, 1975, she filed a petition for separation in Kings County. The court issued an ex parte pendente lite order awarding custody of the children to the wife and prohibiting the husband from removing them from California. She has not returned to Israel since that time.

Husband followed the wife to California. He accepted service of process, employed counsel and appeared personally at the order to show cause hearing. At that hearing the parties stipulated that the wife have custody pendente lite with certain limited visitation rights in the husband. . . .The husband was enjoined from removing the children from the jurisdiction of the court.

Near the end of July or early August 1975, without the wife's consent, the husband surreptitiously removed the children, took them to Israel, and has not returned. While the husband did not personally appear at subsequent proceedings in Kings County, he did appear through counsel at all subsequent proceedings. . . .

On January 16, 1976, the wife filed an amended petition for dissolution of the marriage and the interlocutory decree from which this appeal was taken was entered on December 17, 1976. That decree awarded . . . an undivided one-half interest in certain real and personal property situated in Israel to the wife.

Upon returning to Israel with the children the husband instituted divorce proceedings in which on June 23, 1976, he was awarded temporary custody of the children and on February 23, 1977, was awarded a decree of divorce and custody of the children by the Israel court. The wife was served with process in those proceedings but did not appear in person or through counsel. . . .

The [California] decree appealed from states in part:

> 5. The quasi-community property of the parties is awarded as follows:
> Petitioner and Respondent are each awarded an undivided one-half (1/2) interest in and to the following real and personal property:
>> a. Real Property and improvements situated at No. 17 Gluskin Blvd., City of Rehovot, State of Israel.
>> b. One (1) acre of property situate in Sitriya, State of Israel.

Appellant contends the award is improper and contrary to law because the California court lacks jurisdiction to award quasi-community real property located in Israel. . . .

Under [Family Code] section [125], quasi-community property includes real property acquired by either spouse while domiciled elsewhere which would have been community property if acquired while domiciled in this state. . . .

It is recognized that California cannot enter a decree directly affecting title or interest in real property outside its borders. (Rozan v. Rozan (1957) 49 Cal. 2d 322, 330 [317 P.2d 11].) It may, however, establish and declare the interests in such property and enter orders in aid of such declaration requiring the parties to execute conveyances in compliance therewith. (§[2660], subd. (b)(1); Rozan v. Rozan, supra, 49 Cal. 2d 322, 330.) In support of the judgment we interpret the decree entered as a mere declaration of entitlement to the property which has no direct effect on the title to the property in Israel.

. . . [T]he judgment is affirmed. Each party to bear his or her own costs.

FRANSON, J., and BEST, J., concurred.

Notes and Questions

1. As a matter of choice of law, are the results in *Roesch, Miller, Fransen,* and *Ben-Yehoshua* reconcilable?

2. If you had been advising Mr. Ben-Yehoshua when he first received the shocking news in Israel, would you have counseled him to appear in the California proceeding? Why do you think he did appear? If you had been representing Mr. Ben-

Yehoshua at trial, how would you have approached the property issues? In terms of constitutional law, are *Roesch, Miller, Fransen,* and *Ben-Yehoshua* reconcilable?

3. If you were representing Mr. Ben-Yehoshua when his former wife came to Israel to seek enforcement of her California decree, what arguments would you make?

E.   COMMUNITY PROPERTY ACQUIRED BY CALIFORNIANS WHO SUBSEQUENTLY BECOME DOMICILED IN ANOTHER JURISDICTION (PREACQUIRED COMMUNITY PROPERTY)

This subject is likely to arise infrequently in California practice, although the California community property practitioner may be called upon as a consultant or expert witness in an out-of-state divorce or probate proceeding. That expert witness testimony on California law may be required in out-of-state proceedings implies that other states generally characterize preacquired community property as community property or a close equivalent, even though the couple subsequently establishes domicile in a noncommunity property state where the marriage is dissolved by divorce or death. This is in fact the prevailing view, and it is expressed in a Uniform Act as well as in case law.

To help you think about the issues that commonly arise, consider the following problems as you read this section:

1. Jake and Cindy are married Californians. Their only assets are $500,000 of community property savings and Jake's separate property savings of $100,000. They move to New York, taking all their savings with them. After becoming domiciled in New York, they file for divorce. Assume that you are the New York judge hearing their divorce. How are you going to treat the savings they brought with them from California? As you consider this question, you may find it helpful to think about property characterization and property distribution as discrete, although possibly related, issues.

2. Assume the same facts, but that the marriage of Jake and Cindy endures until Jake's death. Jake's duly executed will leaves "all my property to my disabled brother Sam." Assume that you are the New York probate judge. How are you going to treat the savings Jake and Cindy brought with them from California?

When you finish this section, you should be able to resolve both problems.

QUINTANA v. ORDONO
195 So. 2d 577 (Fla. Dist. Ct. App. 1967)

HENDRY, Chief Judge. — Plaintiffs, children of the deceased by a prior marriage, sought a declaratory decree to determine the rights of the defendant widow, and the estate of the deceased in certain property. The chancellor granted the plaintiffs' motion for summary decree and found that the property was solely owned by the deceased at the time of his death. He therefore decreed that the estate of the deceased is now the owner of the property and the widow, Carmen Camps de Quintana, has no right, title or interest in the property except such interest as may be set off to her by the County Judge's Court of Dade County, Florida, under the probate laws of Florida.

There is no substantial conflict as to the material facts. The defendant and the deceased were married on September 10, 1936, in Oriente Province in Cuba. Both parties were Cuban Nationals. Under the then existing laws of Cuba the marriage was under the regime of "Sociedad de Gananciales," a form of community property marriage. The deceased had no assets at the time of his marriage. The husband and wife were domiciled in Cuba until 1960. A Florida domicile was established when the couple moved here in 1960. They remained in Florida up to the time of the husband's death on September 1, 1963. The husband died intestate.

On or about June 12, 1952, the husband purchased for $50,000.00, five thousand shares of Okeelanta Sugar Refinery, Inc. stock, a Florida corporation. An additional five thousand shares was acquired for $50,000.00 on October 30, 1958. On December 29, 1961, as a result of a ten-for-one stock split, these shares were exchanged for one hundred thousand shares.

[In] 1963, the husband received the promissory note of Stewart Macfarlane, then President of Okeelanta Sugar Refinery, Inc., payable to the husband in the amount of $810,000.00 and a contract for additional monies from Macfarlane for the alleged sale of the one hundred thousand shares.

The interest of the estate of the deceased and the widow in the promissory note and contract are the subject of this action. . . .

Paragraph 1401, Civil Code of Cuba provides:

> 1401. To the Society of gains belong:
> 1. Property acquired by onerous title,[1] during the marriage, at the expense of community property, whether the acquisition is made for the community or for only one of the consorts.
> 2. That obtained by the industry, salaries or work of the consorts or of either of them.
> 3. The fruits, rents, interests collected or accrued during the marriage, and which came from the community property, or from that which belongs to either one of the consorts.

Paragraph 1407, Civil Code of Cuba provides:

> 1407. All the property of the marriage shall be considered as community property until it is proven that it belongs exclusively to the husband or to the wife.

Initially, it must be determined what interest, if any, the widow had in the one hundred thousand shares of Okeelanta Sugar Refinery, Inc. stock.

The plaintiffs submitted an affidavit of a friend of the family, N. H. Tomayo,

---

1. Blood v. Hunt, 97 Fla. 551, 121 So. 886 (1929). "'By onerous cause or title,' viz. by purchase or for value paid."

in opposition to defendant's motion for summary decree. It is alleged therein that the husband came to Florida in 1951 to act as plant manager and supervise the operation of the Okeelanta Sugar Refinery, Inc. Further, that from 1951 until the time of his death in 1963, almost all of the husband's income and assets were acquired in Florida. It is also alleged that as an inducement to continue working in Florida, the husband was given an opportunity to buy stock in Okeelanta Sugar Refinery, Inc.; and, that while he was employed in Florida, the husband returned to Cuba for weekends and other occasional visits.

The defendant submitted an affidavit which indicated that the source of the purchase price of the stock was from profits and salaries of enterprises within Cuba, and a loan on an estate in Cuba.

Whether the source of the purchase price of the stock was from enterprises within Cuba or Florida is not material. What is material and not in conflict is that the husband and wife were domiciled in Cuba at the time of the acquisition of the stock.

As plaintiffs contend, the law of the situs has primary control over property within its borders. However, by the almost unanimous authority in America, the "Interests of one spouse in movables acquired by the other during the marriage are determined by the law of the domicile of the parties when the movables are acquired."[2] This rule is applicable where the money used to purchase the movables is earned from services performed in a place other than the place of the domicile.[3] We accept this rule, founded on convenience, as the only logical method of determining marital interest in movables.

Section 1407 of the Civil Code of Cuba, the place of the domicile at the time of the acquisition of the stock, provides that all property of the marriage shall be considered as community property until proven to be separate property of the husband or wife. The plaintiffs presented no evidence which would tend to prove that the stock was the separate property of the husband or purchased from proceeds of his separate property. The uncontradicted evidence does show that the husband brought no assets to the marriage.

Therefore, under the laws of Cuba the stock did not vest in the husband but in the "Sociedad de Gananciales."[4] Thus the wife had a vested interest in the stock equal to that of her husband.[5]

The interest which vested in the wife was not affected by the subsequent change of domicile from Cuba to Florida in 1960.[6]

While domiciled in Florida, the husband allegedly sold the stock and received in exchange therefor the promissory note and contract with which we are concerned. The wife denied that the stock was in fact sold, alleging that it was merely transferred to Stewart Macfarlane, as trustee. Whether or not the stock was sold is not material to the determination of the ownership of the assets in question.

Since the promissory note and contract were acquired while the husband and wife were domiciled in Florida, this transaction is controlled by our law.

2. Restatement, Conflict of Law §290 (1934); Leflar, Conflict of Laws §176 at 336 (1959); Stumberg, Conflict of Laws 313 (2d ed. 1951); 2 American Law of Property §7.18 at 163 (Casner ed. 1952).

3. Shilkret v. Helvering, 78 U.S. App. D.C. 178, 138 F.2d 925, 929 (1943).

4. See Sanchez v. Bowers, 70 F.2d 715 (2d Cir. 1934).

5. 2 Tiffany, Real Property §438 (3d cd. 1939); 4 Powell, Real Property pt. 3 §627 at 688 (1954).

6. In re Thornton's Estate, 1 Cal. 2d 1, 33 P.2d 1, 92 A.L.R. 1343 (1934); Depas v. Mayo, 11 Mo. 314, 49 Am. Dec. 88 (1848); Restatement, supra note 2 §292; Leflar, supra note 2 §177 footnote 56; Stumberg, supra note 2 at 314; 2 American Law of Property §7.18 at 165 (Casner ed. 1952).

Under Florida law, if a portion of the consideration belongs to the wife and title is taken in the husband's name alone, a resulting trust arises in her favor by implication of law to the extent that consideration furnished by her is used.[7] A resulting trust is generally found to exist in transactions affecting community property in noncommunity property states where a husband buys property in his own name.[8] Therefore, while the husband held legal title to the note and contract, he held a one-half interest in trust for his wife. . . .

The chancellor was correct in his determination that there exist no material issues of fact. However, the applicable law was misapplied in granting the plaintiffs' motion for summary decree and in denying defendant's motion.

Therefore, the decree appealed is reversed and the cause remanded with directions to enter a decree in accordance with this opinion.

Reversed and remanded.

Notes and Questions

1. Did the Florida appellate court treat the promissory note and contract as Cuban community property? Do you think it mattered to the widow whether her interest was called community property or a resulting trust? Why do you think the Florida court chose a resulting trust?

2. Some noncommunity property states purport to treat preacquired community property strictly as community property even though this form of ownership is otherwise unknown in the jurisdiction. See, for example, People v. Berjarano, 145 Colo. 304, 358 P.2d 866 (1961); In re Kessler's Estate, 177 Ohio St. 136, 203 N.E.2d 221 (1964).

3. Quintana v. Ordono resolves a title issue. Does it, however, conclude all the wife's claims? Suppose that decedent husband had left a will leaving all his property to his children. May Mrs. Camps de Quintana now claim a surviving spouse's one-third elective share in all of decedent's remaining property, that is, all property other than her resulting trust?[15] Similarly, in a divorce case, assume that a common law jurisdiction fully honors the community property inception of the parties' property and holds that during marriage each party owns a one-half interest in property acquired while domiciled in a community property jurisdiction. The jurisdiction also follows the majority common law view that, at divorce, title is not controlling and the parties' marital property should be equitably divided according to various case law or statutorily prescribed factors. Does the court's community property finding mandate an equal distribution? Would a finding that the spouses were common law joint tenants mandate an equal division of a joint tenancy?

Should community property be more immune from equitable distribution at divorce than common law equal ownership interests? Robert Leflar, a choice of law authority, takes the view that only the title issue should be resolved by community property law; divorce distribution should be controlled instead by the law of the

---

7. Foster v. Thornton, 131 Fla. 277, 179 So. 882, 883, 887 (1938).

8. Rozan v. Rozan, N.D. 1964, 129 N.W.2d 694, 701; Stone v. Sample, 216 Miss. 287, 62 So. 2d 307, 63 So. 2d 555 (1953); Depas v. Mayo, supra note 6; Stumberg, supra note 2 at 315; Bogert, Trusts & Trustees §26 at 221, §454 at 516 (2d ed. 1964).

15. The application of traditional choice of law rules would produce this result. See pages 567-568 supra and J. Schoenblum, 1 Multistate and Multinational Estate Planning 320 (1982).

forum, which is also generally that of the parties' current domicile. In such case, title would be only one of many factors the divorce court would consider. Leflar, Conflicts of Laws: Dividing Property When Marriage Ends, 1 Fairshare 9 (1981).

When a court follows Leflar's view, it is still worthwhile for the nontitled owner to assert community ownership at divorce in an equitable distribution jurisdiction. The court is more likely to divide equally an asset owned jointly during marriage.

4. The Uniform Disposition of Community Property Rights at Death Act, which has been adopted in Alaska, Arkansas, Colorado, Connecticut, Hawaii, Kentucky, Michigan, Montana, New York (in a modified version), Oregon, Virginia, and Wyoming, addresses both the Quintana v. Ordono title issue and the elective share question posed in the preceding note:

§1. [Application]

This Act applies to the disposition at death of the following property acquired by a married person:

(1) all personal property, wherever situated:

(i) which was acquired as or became, and remained, community property under the laws of another jurisdiction; or,

(ii) all or the proportionate part of that property acquired with the rents, issues, or income of, or the proceeds from, or in exchange for, that community property; or

(iii) traceable to that community property;

(2) all or the proportionate part of any real property situated in this state which was acquired with the rents, issues or income of, the proceeds from, or in exchange for, property acquired as or which became, and remained, community property under the laws of another jurisdiction, or property traceable to that community property.

§2. [Rebuttable presumptions]

In determining whether this Act applies to specific property the following rebuttable presumptions apply:

(1) property acquired during marriage by a spouse of that marriage while domiciled in a jurisdiction under whose laws property could then be acquired as community property is presumed to have been acquired as or to have become, and remained, property to which this Act applies; and

(2) real property situated in this State and personal property wherever situated acquired by a married person while domiciled in a jurisdiction under whose laws property could not then be acquired as community property, title to which was taken in a form which created rights of survivorship, is presumed not to be property to which this Act applies.

§3. [Disposition upon death]

Upon death of a married person, one-half of the property to which this Act applies is the property of the surviving spouse and is not subject to testamentary disposition by the decedent or distribution under the laws of succession of this State. One-half of that property is the property of the decedent and is subject to testamentary disposition or distribution under the laws of succession of this State. With respect to property to which this Act applies, the one-half of the property which is the property of the decedent is not

subject to the surviving spouse's right to elect against the will [and no estate
of dower or curtesy exists in the property of the decedent].

(Uniform Disposition of Community Property Rights at Death Act, 8A U.L.A. 121
(1983 and 1992 Supp.).)

5. The Uniform Disposition of Community Property Rights at Death Act recognizes that the community property and common law marital property systems are asynchronous. (Stated differently, community property title law does the work of common law divorce and death distribution law.) Thus, a forum court cannot "mix and match" elements from each without reaching extreme results that were contemplated by neither jurisdiction. If Florida, for example, after applying Cuban community property law to determine title, takes the traditional choice of law view that death distribution is regulated by the law of the decedent's domicile at death, it may apply its elective share legislation to give Mrs. Camps de Quintana a one-third share of decedent's estate. Thus, she will take two-thirds of the Cuban community property and one-third of all other property owned by decedent at his death. When common law domiciliaries move to community property states, application of traditional choice of law principles yields similarly distorted results. In this case, there effectively is no divorce or death distribution of preacquired property because the title law of the common law jurisdiction applies to produce a "separate property" classification and, intestacy aside, a community property state gives a divorcing or surviving spouse no claim to the other spouse's separate property. Thus, a result-focused choice of law analysis for couples who move from a common law to a community property jurisdiction, or vice versa, should generally look to the law of only one jurisdiction to resolve both the title and distribution issues.[16] This unitary choice of law analysis is reflected in the Uniform Disposition Act and California law.

6. The deferential posture that many noncommunity property states take toward preacquired community property is not matched by an equally deferential California attitude toward sister-state law (see quasi-community property legislation at pages 571-578 supra) insofar as it might affect persons currently domiciled in California. The difference can be explained by doctrinal and state interest considerations. From a common law perspective, the most striking feature of community property is the creation of *present* equal interests in property acquired during marriage. To deny community property ownership rights that vested before the couple became domiciled in a noncommunity property jurisdiction would violate basic notions of property rights. When a married couple moves in the other direction, that is, away from a noncommunity property state, neither spouse has yet acquired any vested interest in property titled in the other's name. California disregard of the noncommunity property state's divorce and death distribution laws only deprives the spouses of inchoate expectancies that, unlike a present community property interest, may never come into being. The husband who predeceases his wife, for example, will never enjoy an equitable distribution or elective share of her property. Is this difference between the inchoate interests of common law states and the present equal interests of community property states a distinction of constitutional magnitude? Does California, for example, have more constitutional latitude to ig-

---

16. The only instance in which "mix and match" produces arguably acceptable results is the situation contemplated by Leflar in Note 3 supra, in which community property is brought into a common law jurisdiction, treated by the forum as community property for title purposes, but, as such, subject to the forum's equitable distribution powers at divorce.

nore preacquired common law inchoate interests than New York has to ignore pre-acquired California community property rights? The Prefatory Note to the Uniform Disposition of Community Property Rights at Death Act assumes that constitutional limitations are nationally uniform: If California can constitutionally impose quasi-community property treatment on preacquired property at divorce and death, common law states may constitutionally disregard community property rights at death and divorce. Do you agree?

Historically, the legal content of community property and common law treatment of the property interests of married persons was widely diverse. Essentially, community property provided a marital property system operative at divorce or death, and common law did not. Thus, the consequences of deference to the laws of another jurisdiction were entirely different. If California did not treat preacquired property as quasi-community property, one of its domiciliaries might be left impoverished, might even become a public charge. If a noncommunity property state, in contrast, deferred to California community property law, it was not compromising any state interest in the welfare of its domiciliaries. Although the jurisdiction might prefer not to adopt the exotic community property system, no harm was done to its interests by applying community property rules to preacquired property held by former domiciliaries of a community property state.

The historical explanation loses much of its force today when common law states have developed elaborate systems of equitable distribution at divorce and elective share rights for the surviving spouse. Nevertheless, it does tend to explain why California initially adopted different choice of law rules for preacquired property. The doctrinal explanation, which relies on the much-criticized but still vital distinction between vested and inchoate property interests, still retains considerable force.

7. In summary: California's statutory choice of law rules for out-of-state realty and preacquired property have one goal: to ensure that California community property law regulates the property relations of current California domiciliaries. Consistent with this emphasis on current domicile is California's deferral to sister-state elective share legislation in order to determine title to California realty owned by sister-state domiciliaries. California has, effectively, abandoned traditional choice of law principles that determine title, in the case of personalty, according to the law of the parties' domicile at the time of acquisition and, in the case of realty, according to the jurisdiction in which the property is located. California has selected instead an approach that emphasizes the welfare concerns of the parties' current domicile.

XII

FEDERAL PREEMPTION OF STATE
MARITAL PROPERTY LAW

Historically, regulation of domestic relations has been left to the states.[1] Congress has refrained from legislating in this area and only in rare circumstances has the Supreme Court, invoking the supremacy clause of the Constitution, held that federal law preempts state family law. While instances of federal preemption have been relatively infrequent, issues of federal-state conflict are of current concern. In recent years, federally created and federally regulated benefits, such as military pensions and private sector ERISA-regulated pensions, have played an increasingly important role in state law marital dissolution proceedings. This trend has enlarged the opportunities for conflict between particular congressional goals and the general policies of state marital property law.

BOGGS v. BOGGS
520 U.S. 833, 117 S. Ct. 1754, 138 L. Ed. 2d 45 (1997)

Justice KENNEDY delivered the opinion of the Court.

We consider whether the Employee Retirement Income Security Act of 1974 (ERISA), 88 Stat. 832, as amended, 29 U.S.C. §1001 et seq., pre-empts a state law allowing a nonparticipant spouse to transfer by testamentary instrument an interest in undistributed pension plan benefits. Given the pervasive significance of pension plans in the national economy, the congressional mandate for their uniform and comprehensive regulation, and the fundamental importance of community property law in defining the marital partnership in a number of States, the question is of undoubted importance. We hold that ERISA pre-empts the state law.

I

Isaac Boggs worked for South Central Bell from 1949 until his retirement in 1985. Isaac and Dorothy, his first wife, were married when he began working for

---

1. United States v. Yazell, 382 U.S. 341, 15 L. Ed. 2d 404, 86 S. Ct. 500 (1966); In re Burrus, 136 U.S. 586, 593-594 (1890).

the company, and they remained husband and wife until Dorothy's death in 1979. They had three sons. Within a year of Dorothy's death, Isaac married Sandra, and they remained married until his death in 1989.

Upon retirement, Isaac received various benefits from his employer's retirement plans. One was a lump-sum distribution from the Bell System Savings Plan for Salaried Employees (Savings Plan) of $151,628.94, which he rolled over into an Individual Retirement Account (IRA). He made no withdrawals and the account was worth $180,778.05 when he died. He also received 96 shares of AT & T stock from the Bell South Employee Stock Ownership Plan (ESOP). In addition, Isaac enjoyed a monthly annuity payment during his retirement of $1,777.67 from the Bell South Service Retirement Program.

The instant dispute over ownership of the benefits is between Sandra (the surviving wife) and the sons of the first marriage. The sons' claim to a portion of the benefits is based on Dorothy's will. Dorothy bequeathed to Isaac one-third of her estate, and a lifetime usufruct in the remaining two-thirds. A lifetime usufruct is the rough equivalent of a common-law life estate. See La. Civ. Code Ann., Art. 535 (West 1980). She bequeathed to her sons the naked ownership in the remaining two-thirds, subject to Isaac's usufruct. All agree that, absent pre-emption, Louisiana law controls and that under it Dorothy's will would dispose of her community property interest in Isaac's undistributed pension plan benefits. A Louisiana state court, in a 1980 order entitled "Judgment of Possession," ascribed to Dorothy's estate a community property interest in Isaac's Savings Plan account valued at the time at $21,194.29.

Sandra contests the validity of Dorothy's 1980 testamentary transfer, basing her claim to those benefits on her interest under Isaac's will and 29 U.S.C. §1055. Isaac bequeathed to Sandra outright certain real property including the family home. His will also gave Sandra a lifetime usufruct in the remainder of his estate, with the naked ownership interest being held by the sons. Sandra argues that the sons' competing claim, since it is based on Dorothy's 1980 purported testamentary transfer of her community property interest in undistributed pension plan benefits, is pre-empted by ERISA. The Bell South Service Retirement Program monthly annuity is now paid to Sandra as the surviving spouse.

After Isaac's death, two of the sons filed an action in state court requesting the appointment of an expert to compute the percentage of the retirement benefits they would be entitled to as a result of Dorothy's attempted testamentary transfer. They further sought a judgment awarding them a portion of: the IRA; the ESOP shares of AT & T stock; the monthly annuity payments received by Isaac during his retirement; and Sandra's survivor annuity payments, both received and payable.

In response, Sandra Boggs filed a complaint in the United States District Court for the Eastern District of Louisiana, seeking a declaratory judgment that ERISA pre-empts the application of Louisiana's community property and succession laws to the extent they recognize the sons' claim to an interest in the disputed retirement benefits. The District Court granted summary judgment against Sandra Boggs. 849 F.Supp. 462 (1994). It found that, under Louisiana community property law, Dorothy had an ownership interest in her husband's pension plan benefits built up during their marriage. The creation of this interest, the court explained, does not violate 29 U.S.C. §1056(d)(1), which prohibits pension plan benefits from being "assigned" or "alienated," since Congress did not intend to alter traditional familial and support obligations. In the court's view, there was no assignment or alienation because Dorothy's rights in the benefits were acquired by operation of community property law and not by transfer from Isaac. Turning to Dorothy's testamentary transfer, the court found it effective because "[ERISA] does not display any particular interest in preserving maximum benefits to any particular beneficiary." 849 F. Supp., at 465.

A divided panel of the Fifth Circuit affirmed. 82 F.3d 90 (1996). The court stressed that Louisiana law affects only what a plan participant may do with his or her benefits after they are received and not the relationship between the pension plan administrator and the plan beneficiary. Id., at 96. For the reasons given by the District Court, it found ERISA's pension plan anti-alienation provision, §1056(d)(1), inapplicable to Louisiana's creation of Dorothy Boggs' community property interest in the pension plan benefits. It concluded that the transfer of the interest from Dorothy to her sons was not a prohibited assignment or alienation, as this transfer was "two steps removed from the disbursement of benefits." Id., at 97.

Six members of the Court of Appeals dissented from the failure to grant rehearing en banc. 89 F.3d 1169 (1996). In their view, a testamentary transfer of an interest in undistributed retirement benefits frustrates ERISA's goals of securing national uniformity in pension plan administration and of ensuring that retirees, and their dependents, are the actual recipients of retirement income. They believed that Congress' creation of the qualified domestic relations order (QDRO) mechanism in §1056(d)(3), whose requirements were not met by the 1980 judgment of possession, further supported their position. (A QDRO is a limited exception to the pension plan anti-alienation provision and allows courts to recognize a nonparticipant spouse's community property interest in pension plans under specific circumstances.)

The reasoning and holding of the Fifth Circuit's decision is in substantial conflict with the decision of the Court of Appeals for the Ninth Circuit in Ablamis v. Roper, 937 F.2d 1450 (1991), which held that ERISA pre-empts a testamentary transfer by a nonparticipant spouse of her community property interest in undistributed pension plan benefits. The division between the Circuits is significant, for the Fifth Circuit has jurisdiction over the community property States of Louisiana and Texas, while the Ninth Circuit includes the community property States of Arizona, California, Idaho, Nevada, and Washington. Having granted certiorari to resolve the issue, 519 U.S. — —, 117 S. Ct. 379, 136 L. Ed. 2d 297 (1996), we now reverse.

II

ERISA pre-emption questions are recurrent, two other cases on the subject having come before the Court in the current Term alone. . . . In large part the number of ERISA pre-emption cases reflects the comprehensive nature of the statute, the centrality of pension and welfare plans in the national economy, and their importance to the financial security of the Nation's work force. ERISA is designed to ensure the proper administration of pension and welfare plans, both during the years of the employee's active service and in his or her retirement years.

This case lies at the intersection of ERISA pension law and state community property law. None can dispute the central role community property laws play in the nine community property States. It is more than a property regime. It is a commitment to the equality of husband and wife and reflects the real partnership inherent in the marital relationship. State community property laws, many of ancient lineage, "must have continued to exist through such lengths of time because of their manifold excellences and are not lightly to be abrogated or tossed aside." 1 W. de Funiak, Principles of Community Property 11 (1943). The community property regime in Louisiana dates from 1808 when the territorial legislature of Orleans drafted a civil code which adopted Spanish principles of community property. Id., at 85-89. Louisiana's community property laws, and the community property regimes enacted in other States, implement policies and values lying within the traditional domain of the States. These considerations inform our pre-emption analysis. See Hisquierdo v. Hisquierdo, 439 U.S. 572, 581, 99 S. Ct. 802, 808, 59 L. Ed. 2d 1 (1979).

The nine community property States have some 80 million residents, with perhaps $1 trillion in retirement plans. See Brief for Estate Planning, Trust and Probate Law Section of the State Bar of California as Amicus Curiae 1. This case involves a community property claim, but our ruling will affect as well the right to make claims or assert interests based on the law of any State, whether or not it recognizes community property. Our ruling must be consistent with the congressional scheme to assure the security of plan participants and their families in every State. In enacting ERISA, Congress noted the importance of pension plans in its findings and declaration of policy, explaining:

> [T]he growth in size, scope, and numbers of employee benefit plans in recent years has been rapid and substantial; . . . the continued well-being and security of millions of employees and their dependents are directly affected by these plans; . . . they are affected with a national public interest [and] they have become an important factor affecting the stability of employment and the successful development of industrial relations. . . ." 29 U.S.C. §1001(a).

ERISA is an intricate, comprehensive statute. Its federal regulatory scheme governs employee benefit plans, which include both pension and welfare plans. All employee benefit plans must conform to various reporting, disclosure and fiduciary requirements, see §§1021-1031, 1101-1114, while pension plans must also comply with participation, vesting, and funding requirements, see §§1051-1086. The surviving spouse annuity and QDRO provisions, central to the dispute here, are part of the statute's mandatory participation and vesting requirements. These provisions provide detailed protections to spouses of plan participants which, in some cases, exceed what their rights would be were community property law the sole measure.

ERISA's express pre-emption clause states that the Act "shall supersede any and all State laws insofar as they may now or hereafter relate to any employee benefit plan. . . ." §1144(a). We can begin, and in this case end, the analysis by simply asking if state law conflicts with the provisions of ERISA or operates to frustrate its objects. We hold that there is a conflict, which suffices to resolve the case. . . .

We first address the survivor's annuity and then turn to the other pension benefits.

III

Sandra Boggs, as we have observed, asserts that federal law pre-empts and supersedes state law and requires the surviving spouse annuity to be paid to her as the sole beneficiary. We agree.

The annuity at issue is a qualified joint and survivor annuity mandated by ERISA. Section 1055(a) provides:

> Each pension plan to which this section applies shall provide that —
>   (1) in the case of a vested participant who does not die before the annuity starting date, the accrued benefit payable to such participant shall be provided in the form of a qualified joint and survivor annuity.

ERISA requires that every qualified joint and survivor annuity include an annuity payable to a nonparticipant surviving spouse. The survivor's annuity may not be less than 50% of the amount of the annuity which is payable during the joint lives of the participant and spouse. §1055(d)(1). Provision of the survivor's annuity may not be waived by the participant, absent certain limited circumstances, unless the spouse consents in writing to the designation of another beneficiary, which designation also cannot be changed without further spousal consent, witnessed by a plan representative or notary public. §1055(c)(2). Sandra Boggs, as the surviving spouse, is entitled to a survivor's annuity under these provisions. She has not waived her right to the survivor's annuity, let alone consented to having the sons designated as the beneficiaries.

Respondents say their state-law claims are consistent with these provisions. Their claims, they argue, affect only the disposition of plan proceeds after they have been disbursed by the Bell South Service Retirement Program, and thus nothing is required of the plan. ERISA's concern for securing national uniformity in the administration of employee benefit plans, in their view, is not implicated. They argue Sandra's community property obligations, after she receives the survivor annuity payments, "fai[l] to implicate the regulatory concerns of ERISA." Fort Halifax Packing Co. v. Coyne, 482 U.S. 1, 15, 107 S. Ct. 2211, 2219, 96 L. Ed. 2d 1 (1987).

We disagree. The statutory object of the qualified joint and survivor annuity provisions, along with the rest of §1055, is to ensure a stream of income to surviving spouses. Section 1055 mandates a survivor's annuity not only where a participant dies after the annuity starting date but also guarantees one if the participant dies before then. See §§1055(a)(2), (e). These provisions, enacted as part of the Retirement Equity Act of 1984 (REA), Pub. L. 98-397, 98 Stat. 1426, enlarged ERISA's protection of surviving spouses in significant respects. Before REA, ERISA only required that pension plans, if they provided for the payment of benefits in the form of an annuity, offer a qualified joint and survivor annuity as an option entirely within a participant's discretion. 29 U.S.C. §§1055(a), (e) (1982 ed.). REA modified ERISA to permit participants to designate a beneficiary for the survivor's annuity, other than the nonparticipant spouse, only when the spouse agrees. §1055(c)(2). Congress' concern for surviving spouses is also evident from the expansive coverage of §1055, as amended by REA. Section 1055's requirements, as a general matter, apply to all "individual account plans" and "defined benefit plans." §1055(b)(1). The terms are defined, for §1055 purposes, so that all pension plans fall within those two categories. See §1002(35). While some individual account plans escape §1055's surviving spouse annuity requirements under certain conditions, Congress still protects the interests of the surviving spouse by requiring those plans to pay the spouse the nonforfeitable accrued benefits, reduced by certain security interests, in a lump-sum payment. §1055(b)(1)(C).

ERISA's solicitude for the economic security of surviving spouses would be undermined by allowing a predeceasing spouse's heirs and legatees to have a community property interest in the survivor's annuity. Even a plan participant cannot defeat a nonparticipant surviving spouse's statutory entitlement to an annuity. It would be odd, to say the least, if Congress permitted a predeceasing nonparticipant spouse to do so. Nothing in the language of ERISA supports concluding that Congress made such an inexplicable decision. Testamentary transfers could reduce a surviving spouse's guaranteed annuity below the minimum set by ERISA (defined as 50% of the annuity payable during the joint lives of the participant and spouse). In this case, Sandra's annuity would be reduced by approximately 20%, according to the calculations contained in the sons' state-court filings. There is no reason why testamentary transfers could not reduce a survivor's annuity by an even greater amount. Perhaps even more troubling, the recipient of the testamentary transfer need not be a family member. For instance, a surviving spouse's §1055 annuity might be substantially reduced so that funds could be diverted to support an unrelated stranger.

In the face of this direct clash between state law and the provisions and objectives of ERISA, the state law cannot stand. Conventional conflict pre-emption principles require pre-emption "where compliance with both federal and state regulations is a physical impossibility, . . . or where state law stands as an obstacle to the accomplishment and execution of the full purposes and objectives of Congress." Gade v. National Solid Wastes Management Assn., 505 U.S. 88, 98, 112 S. Ct. 2374, 2383, 120 L. Ed. 2d 73 (1992). . . . It would undermine the purpose of ERISA's mandated survivor's annuity to allow Dorothy, the predeceasing spouse, by her testamentary transfer to defeat in part Sandra's entitlement to the annuity §1055 guarantees her as the surviving spouse. This cannot be. States are not free to change ERISA's structure and balance.

Louisiana law, to the extent it provides the sons with a right to a portion of Sandra Boggs' §1055 survivor's annuity, is pre-empted.

IV

Beyond seeking a portion of the survivor's annuity, respondents claim a percentage of: the monthly annuity payments made to Isaac Boggs during his retirement; the IRA; and the ESOP shares of AT & T stock. As before, the claim is based on Dorothy Boggs' attempted testamentary transfer to the sons of her community interest in Isaac's undistributed pension plan benefits. . . .

A brief overview of ERISA's design is necessary to put respondents' contentions in the proper context. The principal object of the statute is to protect plan participants and beneficiaries. . . . Section 1001(b) states that the policy of ERISA is "to protect . . . the interests of participants in employee benefit plans and their beneficiaries." Section 1001(c) explains that ERISA contains certain safeguards and protections which help guarantee the "equitable character and the soundness of [private pension] plans" in order to protect "the interests of participants in private pension plans and their beneficiaries." The general policy is implemented by ERISA's specific provisions. Apart from a few enumerated exceptions, a plan fiduciary must "discharge his duties with respect to a plan solely in the interest of the participants and beneficiaries." §1104(a)(1). The assets of a plan, again with certain exceptions, are "held for the exclusive purposes of providing benefits to participants in the plan and their beneficiaries and defraying reasonable expenses of administering the plan." §1103(c)(1). The Secretary of Labor has authority to create exemptions to ERISA's prohibition on certain plan holdings, acquisitions, and transactions, but only if doing so is in the interests of the plan's "participants and beneficiaries." §1108(a)(2). Persons with an interest in a pension plan may bring a civil suit under ERISA's enforcement provisions only if they are either a participant or beneficiary. . . .

ERISA confers beneficiary status on a nonparticipant spouse or dependent in only narrow circumstances delineated by its provisions. For example, as we have discussed, §1055(a) requires provision of a surviving spouse annuity in covered pension plans, and, as a consequence the spouse is a beneficiary to this extent. Section 1056's QDRO provisions likewise recognize certain pension plan community property interests of nonparticipant spouses and dependents. A QDRO is a type of domestic relations order which creates or recognizes an alternate payee's right to, or assigns to an alternate payee the right to, a portion of the benefits payable with respect to a participant under a plan. §1056(d)(3)(B)(i). A domestic relations order, in turn, is any judgment, decree, or order that concerns "the provision of child support, alimony payments, or marital property rights to a spouse, former spouse, child, or other dependent of a participant" and is "made pursuant to a State domestic relations law (including a community property law)." §1056(d)(3)(B)(ii). A domestic relations order must meet certain requirements to qualify as a QDRO. See §§1056(d)(3)(C)-(E). QDRO's, unlike domestic relations orders in general, are exempt from both the pension plan anti-alienation provision, §1056(d)(3)(A), and ERISA's general pre-emption clause, §1144(b)(7). In creating the QDRO mechanism Congress was careful to provide that the alternate payee, the "spouse, former spouse, child, or other dependent of a participant," is to be considered a plan beneficiary. §§1056(d)(3)(K), (J). These provisions are essential to one of REA's central purposes, which is to give enhanced protection to the spouse and dependent children in the event of divorce or separation, and in the event of death of the surviving spouse. Apart from these detailed provisions, ERISA does not confer beneficiary status on nonparticipants by reason of their marital or dependent status. . . .

The surviving spouse annuity and QDRO provisions, which acknowledge and protect specific pension plan community property interests, give rise to the strong implication that other community property claims are not consistent with the statutory scheme. ERISA's silence with respect to the right of a nonparticipant spouse to control pension plan benefits by testamentary transfer provides powerful support for the conclusion that the right does not exist. . . .

We conclude the sons have no claim under ERISA to a share of the retirement benefits. To begin with, the sons are neither participants nor beneficiaries. A "participant" is defined as an "employee or former employee of an employer, or any member or former member of an employee organization, who is or may become eligible to receive a benefit." §1002(7). A "beneficiary" is a "person designated by a participant, or by the terms of an employee benefit plan, who is or may become entitled to a benefit thereunder." §1002(8). Respondents' claims are based on Dorothy Boggs' attempted testamentary transfer, not on a designation by Isaac Boggs or under the terms of the retirement plans. . . .

Respondents . . . in effect ask us to ignore §1002(8)'s definition of "beneficiary" and, through case law, create a new class of persons for whom plan assets are to be held and administered. The statute is not amenable to this sweeping extratextual extension. . . .

The conclusion that Congress intended to pre-empt respondents' nonbeneficiary, nonparticipant interests in the retirement plans is given specific and powerful reinforcement by the pension plan anti-alienation provision. Section 1056(d)(1) provides that "[e]ach pension plan shall provide that benefits provided under the plan may not be assigned or alienated." Statutory anti-alienation provisions are potent mechanisms to prevent the dissipation of funds. In Hisquierdo we interpreted an anti-alienation provision to bar a divorced spouse's interest in her husband's retirement benefits. See 439 U.S. [572], at 583-590, 99 S. Ct. [802], at 809-813. ERISA's pension plan anti-alienation provision is mandatory and contains only two explicit exceptions, see §§1056(d)(2), (d)(3)(A), which are not subject to judicial expansion. See Guidry v. Sheet Metal Workers Nat. Pension Fund, 493 U.S. 365, 376, 110 S. Ct. 680, 687, 107 L. Ed. 2d 782 (1990). The anti-alienation provision can "be seen to bespeak a pension law protective policy of special intensity: Retirement funds shall remain inviolate until retirement." J. Langbein & B. Wolk, Pension and Employee Benefit Law 547 (2d ed. 1995).

Dorothy's 1980 testamentary transfer, which is the source of respondents' claimed ownership interest, is a prohibited "assignment or alienation." An "assignment or alienation" has been defined by regulation, with certain exceptions not at issue here, as "[a]ny direct or indirect arrangement whereby a party acquires from a participant or beneficiary" an interest enforceable against a plan to "all or any part of a plan benefit payment which is, or may become, payable to the participant or beneficiary." 26 CFR §1.401(a)-13(c)(1)(ii). Those requirements are met. Under Louisiana law community property interests are enforceable against a plan. See Eskine v. Eskine, 518 So. 2d 505, 508 (La. 1988). If respondents' claims were allowed to succeed they would have acquired, as of 1980, an interest in Isaac's pension plan at the expense of plan participants and beneficiaries.

As was true with survivors' annuities, it would be inimical to ERISA's purposes to permit testamentary recipients to acquire a competing interest in undistributed pension benefits, which are intended to provide a stream of income to participants and their beneficiaries. . . . Pension benefits support participants and beneficiaries in their retirement years, and ERISA's pension plan safeguards are designed to further this end. . . . Under respondents' approach, retirees could find their retirement benefits reduced by substantial sums because they have been diverted to testamentary recipients. Retirement benefits and the income stream provided for by ERISA-regulated plans would be disrupted in the name of protecting a nonparticipant spouses' successors over plan participants and beneficiaries. Respondents' logic would even permit a spouse to transfer an interest in a pension plan to creditors, a result incompatible with a spendthrift provision such as §1056(d)(1).

Community property laws have, in the past, been pre-empted in order to ensure the implementation of a federal statutory scheme. See, e.g., McCune v. Essig, 199 U.S. 382, 26 S. Ct. 78, 50 L. Ed. 237 (1905); Wissner v. Wissner, 338 U.S. 655, 70 S. Ct. 398, 94 L. Ed. 424 (1950); Free v. Bland, 369 U.S. 663, 82 S. Ct. 1089, 8 L. Ed. 2d 180 (1962); Hisquierdo v. Hisquierdo, 439 U.S. 572, 99 S. Ct. 802, 59 L. Ed. 2d 1 (1979); McCarty v. McCarty, 453 U.S. 210, 101 S. Ct. 2728, 69 L. Ed. 2d 589 (1981); Mansell v. Mansell, 490 U.S. 581, 109 S. Ct. 2023, 104 L. Ed. 2d 675 (1989); cf. Ridgway v. Ridgway, 454 U.S. 46, 102 S. Ct. 49, 70 L. Ed. 2d 39 (1981). Free v. Bland, supra, is of particular relevance here. A husband had purchased United States savings bonds with community funds in the name of both spouses. Under Treasury regulations then in effect, when a co-owner of the bonds died, the surviving co-owner received the entire interest in the bonds. After the wife died, her son — the principal beneficiary of her will — demanded either one-half of the bonds or reimbursement for loss of the community property interest. The Court held that the regulations pre-empted the community property claim, explaining:

> One of the inducements selected by the Treasury is the survivorship provision, a convenient method of avoiding complicated probate proceedings. Notwithstanding this provision, the State awarded full title to the co-owner but required him to account for half of the value of the bonds to the decedent's estate. Viewed realistically, the State has rendered the award of title meaningless. Id., at 669, 82 S. Ct., at 1093.

The same reasoning applies here. If state law is not pre-empted, the diversion of retirement benefits will occur regardless of whether the interest in the pension plan is enforced against the plan or the recipient of the pension benefit. The obligation to provide an accounting, moreover, as with the probate proceedings referred to in *Free*, is itself a burden of significant proportions. Under respondents' view, a pension plan participant could be forced to make an accounting of a deceased spouse's community property interest years after the date of death. If the couple had lived in several States, the accounting could entail complex, expensive, and time-consuming litigation. Congress could not have intended that pension benefits from pension plans would be given to accountants and attorneys for this purpose.

Respondents contend it is anomalous and unfair that a divorced spouse, as a result of a QDRO, will have more control over a portion of his or her spouse's pension benefits than a predeceasing spouse. Congress thought otherwise. The QDRO provisions, as well as the surviving spouse annuity provisions, reinforce the conclusion that ERISA is concerned with providing for the living. The QDRO provisions protect those persons who, often as a result of divorce, might not receive the benefits they otherwise would have had available during their retirement as a means of income. In the case of a predeceased spouse, this concern is not implicated. The fairness of the distinction might be debated, but Congress has decided to favor the living over the dead and we must respect its policy.

The axis around which ERISA's protections revolve is the concepts of participant and beneficiary. When Congress has chosen to depart from this framework, it has done so in a careful and limited manner. Respondents' claims, if allowed to succeed, would depart from this framework, upsetting the deliberate balance central to ERISA. It does not matter that respondents have sought to enforce their rights only after the retirement benefits have been distributed since their asserted rights are based on the theory that they had an interest in the undistributed pension plan benefits. Their state-law claims are pre-empted. The judgment of the Fifth Circuit is

Reversed.

Justice BREYER, with whom Justice O'CONNOR joins, and with whom THE CHIEF JUSTICE and Justice GINSBURG join . . . , dissenting. . . .

Notes and Questions

1. *The pension benefits. Boggs* involves three distinct assets earned as part of Isaac's company retirement plans during the marriage of Isaac and Dorothy: Sandra's lifetime pension benefits, as Isaac's surviving spouse, under Isaac's ERISA-

regulated pension; Isaac's Individual Retirement Account (IRA), which contained funds rolled over from a lump-sum savings plan distribution; and shares of stock from the company's employee stock ownership plan (ESOP).

The Court's treatment of Sandra's surviving spouse's pension claim is unexceptionable. Congress intended to protect the surviving spouses of deceased workers when it provided, in the Retirement Equity Act of 1984, that every ERISA-regulated pension must be provided in "joint and survivor" form, and that the survivor's benefit may only be waived in favor of a higher lifetime benefit for the employee when both spouses join together to consent to the waiver. In view of this history, community property law allowing a surviving spouse's benefit to be willed away to a third party clearly would undermine the congressional purpose to provide for surviving spouses.

2. *The IRA and the ESOP.* Yet the Court goes further and also includes within the preemptive umbrella the contents of an employee savings plan (IRA) and an employee stock plan (ESOP). Are these two assets distinguishable from the pension? Why, exactly, does federal preemption extend to assets that are essentially savings accounts? What does this do to state community property law? In any given death case, what facts are likely to be dispositive in determining whether an asset is subject to state community property law or preemptive ERISA regulation?

3. *Divorce implications of Boggs.* In Marriage of Shelstead, 66 Cal. App. 4th 893, 78 Cal. Rptr. 2d 365 (1998), the trial court framed an ERISA-required qualified domestic relations order (QDRO) that directed the pension plan to pay the nonparticipant divorcing wife her community property share of the participant's pension and, should the wife predecease the participant, to pay the wife's share to a successor in interest designated by the wife. After the wife's death, her former husband claimed that the QDRO was unenforceable because ERISA does not permit a participant's spouse to designate a successor in interest to her community property portion of the pension. Following the logic of *Boggs, Shelstead* held for the husband on the ground that a QDRO may designate as a beneficiary only a participant or an alternate payee (defined by ERISA as "a spouse, former spouse, child, or other dependent").

Several years later, the Ninth Circuit Court of Appeals reached the same conclusion. Interpreting *Boggs,* Branco v. UFCW–Northern California Employers Joint Pension Plan, 279 F.3d 1154 (9th Cir. 2002), held that ERISA preempts a California divorce court distribution of a community property pension insofar as it purports to enable a divorced wife to leave her share of a community property pension earned by her former husband to her heirs at her death. Under *Branco,* the interest of a former spouse who is an alternate payee under an ERISA QDRO expires at his or her death and reverts to the surviving employee spouse. *Shelstead* and *Branco* thus revive the *Waite* arm of the terminable interest rule for pensions distributed at divorce. (For discussion of ERISA QDROs and *Waite,* see pages 296-297 and 348-350 supra.)

4. *Employee group life insurance regulated by ERISA.* In Kimble v. Metropolitan Life Ins., 969 F. Supp. 599 (E.D. Cal. 1997), a California husband named his wife, his mother, and his daughter as equal beneficiaries of his community property ERISA-regulated employee life insurance. When the husband died, his surviving wife claimed her community property one-half interest in the proceeds. The U.S. District Court for the Eastern District of California held that ERISA preempts community property treatment of the proceeds, and that ERISA gives full effect to the employee's beneficiary designation.

Plaintiff next apparently argues that California community property law entitles her to one-half of the insurance proceeds as community property, and that she is entitled to one-third of the remaining half pursuant to Kimble's designation of beneficiaries. To the extent plaintiff argues that the plan administrator must recognize her community property rights and accordingly pay her one-half of the proceeds under the plan, such claim is preempted by ERISA.

ERISA preempts all state law claims that "relate to" any employee benefit plan. 29 U.S.C. §1144(a); Pilot Life Ins. Co. v. Dedeaux, 481 U.S. 41, 47-48, 107 S. Ct. 1549, 1552-53, 95 L. Ed. 2d 39 (1987). ERISA regulates employee welfare benefit plans that "through the purchase of insurance or otherwise" provide benefits in the event of death, 29 U.S.C. §1002(1), and therefore preempts state law to the extent the state law purports to impose obligations on the plan administrator that are inconsistent with those obligations imposed by ERISA. See Metropolitan Life Ins. Co. v. Pressley, 82 F.3d 126, 129 (6th Cir. 1996) (listing the various circuit court decisions holding that ERISA preempts state laws dealing with designation of beneficiaries).

ERISA requires MetLife to pay proceeds in accordance with Kimble's designation of beneficiaries. . . . In contrast, California community property law entitles plaintiff to at least one-half of the proceeds. See Polk v. Polk, 228 Cal. App. 2d 763, 39 Cal. Rptr. 824 (1964). Because MetLife's obligations as plan administrator under ERISA do not necessarily satisfy plaintiff's ultimate rights under California community property law, ERISA preempts the application of the community property law insofar as it would require MetLife to pay benefits in accordance with plaintiff's community property rights. See Boggs v. Boggs, 520 U.S. 833, 117 S. Ct. 1754, 1761, 138 L. Ed. 2d 45 (1997); Ingersoll-Rand Co. v. McClendon, 498 U.S. 133, 142, 111 S. Ct. 478, 484-85, 112 L. Ed. 2d 474 (1990).

Id. at 603.

Kimble is particularly troubling on its facts, because extrinsic evidence indicated that Mr. Kimble intended to name his mother and daughter as contingent beneficiaries who would take only if Mrs. Kimble failed to survive him. Otherwise, he intended the proceeds to go entirely to Mrs. Kimble. However, Mr. Kimble erroneously inserted the names of his mother and daughter in the box for co-beneficiaries, instead of the box for contingent beneficiaries. Under state law, such evidence would have been taken into account. It was ignored by the ERISA-regulated insurance provider. The court held that not only does ERISA preempt state law regulation, but also that ERISA does not require an insurance provider to look beyond the four corners of the beneficiary designation form.

Kimble was not mentioned by the Ninth Circuit Court of Appeals three-judge panel that subsequently decided Emard v. Hughes Aircraft Co., 153 F.3d 949 (9th Cir. 1998). Although every other circuit addressing the matter has adopted the *Kimble* position, *Emard* holds that a participant's beneficiary designation in an ERISA-regulated life insurance policy does not trump a surviving spouse's community property interest in the policy proceeds.

5. *A hundred years of federal preemption.* As *Boggs* indicates, the United States Supreme Court has held that federal law preempts state community property distribution of many federally regulated assets. Despite sharp dissents by justices from the western states, the Court has concluded that federal law preempts the operation of state community property law in every case that it has ever reviewed. The first case, McCune v. Essig, 199 U.S. 382 (1905), held that federal homestead law pre-

empted community property distribution of federal homestead land acquired by a spouse during marriage.

Half a century later, the Supreme Court addressed Armed Forces life insurance benefits. Federal law states that a service person may name any person as the beneficiary of an Armed Forces life insurance policy. State community property law provides that proceeds from a life insurance policy earned during marriage are the community property of the spouses. In Wissner v. Wissner, 338 U.S. 655 (1950), the Court held that the federal beneficiary provision preempts state law distribution of one-half the proceeds to the service person's spouse.

United States Treasury regulations state that when either co-owner of a U.S. savings bond dies, the survivor is the sole and exclusive owner of the bond. When a spouse uses community property funds to purchase a savings bond and takes title with someone other than his spouse, a conflict may arise between the operation of the federal provision and the state community property rights of the purchaser's surviving spouse. In Free v. Bland, 369 U.S. 663 (1962), the Court held that the Treasury regulations preempt the operation of state community property law, effectively cutting off the surviving spouse's community property interest in the bond proceeds. Free v. Bland is quoted with approval in *Boggs*.

Pension benefits of railway workers are regulated by the Federal Railroad Retirement Act (FRRA). In Hisquierdo v. Hisquierdo, 439 U.S. 572 (1979), the Court held that the FRAA provision making the retired worker the owner of his pension preempts state law community property division of benefits earned during marriage. In 1983 Congress limited *Hisquierdo* to benefits intended to replace social security benefits. All other benefits provided under the FRRA, called "supplemental benefits," are subject to state law community property distribution. 45 U.S.C. §231m(b)(2) (2002).

In McCarty v. McCarty, 453 U.S. 210 (1981), the Court concluded that state community property distribution of federal military benefits ("retired pay") earned during marriage was implicitly preempted by federal law. In 1982, Congress enacted the Uniformed Services Former Spouses' Protection Act (USFSPA), which permits a state court to treat retired pay as either separate or community property, in accordance with state law. 10 U.S.C. §1408(c)(1) (2002).

Although California treats disability pay received after permanent separation as the separate property of the disabled spouse, nevertheless when a retired worker takes disability pay instead of community property retirement benefits he would otherwise receive, California treats the disability pay as community property to the extent of the displaced community property retirement benefits. This so-called *Stenquist* treatment is discussed at pages 353-357 supra. In Mansell v. Mansell, 490 U.S. 581 (1989), the Court held that USFSPA preempts *Stenquist* treatment of military disability pay elected instead of retirement benefits because USFSPA does not authorize state law distribution of military disability pay.

The United States Supreme Court's willingness to find federal preemption contrasts sharply with the posture of California state courts, which usually hold that Congress did not intend to preempt California community property law. However, most of these state rulings have ultimately been reversed by the United States Supreme Court.

The Supreme Court has not yet addressed a marital property case involving federal copyrights or patents. Marriage of Worth, 195 Cal. App. 3d 768 (1987), holds that federal copyright law does not preempt California community property distribution of copyright proceeds, but it is uncertain whether the holding of *Worth* would survive United States Supreme Court review. Nor has the Supreme Court ever considered whether state law distribution of social security benefits is preempted by federal law. Nevertheless, it has been obvious to most state courts that the federal Social Security Act is preemptive. The Act provides separate social security benefits for spouses, dependents, widows, and divorced spouses, clearly evincing federal intent to occupy the entire field and displace state law. Marriage of Hillerman, 109 Cal. App. 3d 334 (1980).

CALIFORNIA STATUTORY APPENDIX

THE FAMILY CODE

Chapter 2. Relation of Husband and Wife

Chapter 3. Property Rights During Marriage

PART 2. CHARACTERIZATION OF MARITAL PROPERTY

Chapter 1. Community Property

Chapter 2. Separate Property

Chapter 3. Damages for Injuries to Married Person

Chapter 4. Presumptions Concerning Nature of Property

Chapter 5. Transmutation of Property

PART 3.   LIABILITY OF MARITAL PROPERTY

Chapter 1.   Definitions

Chapter 2.   General Rules of Liability

Chapter 3.   Reimbursement

Chapter 4.   Transitional Provisions

Chapter 5.   Liability for Death or Injury

PART 4.   MANAGEMENT AND CONTROL
OF MARITAL PROPERTY

PART 5.   MARITAL AGREEMENTS

Chapter 1.   General Provisions

Chapter 9.   Disclosure of Assets and Liabilities

Chapter 10.   Relief from Judgment

PART 2.   JUDICIAL DETERMINATION OF VOID
OR VOIDABLE MARRIAGE

Chapter 1.   Void Marriage

Chapter 2.   Voidable Marriage

Chapter 3.   Procedural Provisions

PART 3.   DISSOLUTION OF MARRIAGE AND LEGAL
SEPARATION

Chapter 1.   Effect of Dissolution

DIVISION 1. PRELIMINARY PROVISIONS AND DEFINITIONS

PART 1. PRELIMINARY PROVISIONS

§1. Title of code

This code shall be known as the Family Code.

Comment—Law Revision Commission

. . . The operative date of this code is January 1, 1994.

§2. Continuation of existing law

A provision of this code, insofar as it is substantially the same as a previously existing provision relating to the same subject matter, shall be considered as a restatement and continuation thereof and not as a new enactment. . . .

§11. Reference to married person includes formerly married person

A reference to "husband" and "wife," "spouses," or "married persons," or a comparable term, includes persons who are lawfully married to each other and persons who were previously lawfully married to each other, as is appropriate under the circumstances of the particular case.

§12. Meaning of shall, may, shall not, and may not

"Shall" is mandatory and "may" is permissive. "Shall not" and "may not" are prohibitory.

PART 2. DEFINITIONS

§63. "Community estate"

"Community estate" includes both community property and quasi-community property.

§80. "Employee benefit plan"

"Employee benefit plan" includes public and private retirement, pension, annuity, savings, profit sharing, stock bonus, stock option, thrift, vacation pay, and similar plans of deferred or fringe benefit compensation, whether of the defined contribution or defined benefit type whether or not such plan is qualified under the Employee Retirement Income Security Act of 1974 (P.L. 93-406) (ERISA), as amended. . . .

§92. "Family support"

"Family support" means an agreement between the parents, or an order or judgment, that combines child support and spousal support without designating the amount to be paid for child support and the amount to be paid for spousal support.

§125. "Quasi-community property"

"Quasi-community property" means all real or personal property, wherever situated, acquired before or after the operative date of this code in any of the following ways:

(a) By either spouse while domiciled elsewhere which would have been community property if the spouse who acquired the property had been domiciled in this state at the time of its acquisition.

(b) In exchange for real or personal property, wherever situated, which would have been community property if the spouse who acquired the property so exchanged had been domiciled in this state at the time of its acquisition.

DIVISION 2.　GENERAL PROVISIONS

PART 1.　JURISDICTION

§200.　Jurisdiction in superior court

The superior court has jurisdiction in proceedings under this code.

PART 5.　ATTORNEY'S FEES AND COSTS

§270.　Determination that party has ability to pay

If a court orders a party to pay attorney's fees or costs under this code, the court shall first determine that the party has or is reasonably likely to have the ability to pay.

§271.　Award of attorney's fees and costs based on conduct of party or attorney

(a) Notwithstanding any other provision of this code, the court may base an award of attorney's fees and costs on the extent to which the conduct of each party or attorney furthers or frustrates the policy of the law to promote settlement of litigation and, where possible, to reduce the costs of litigation by encouraging cooperation between the parties and attorneys. An award of attorney's fees and costs pursuant to this section is in the nature of a sanction. In making an award pursuant to this section, the court shall take into consideration all evidence concerning the parties' incomes, assets, and liabilities. The court shall not impose a sanction pursuant to this section that imposes an unreasonable financial burden upon the party against whom the sanction is imposed. In order to obtain an award under this section, the party requesting an award of attorney's fees and costs is not required to demonstrate any financial need for the award.

(b) An award of attorney's fees and costs as a sanction pursuant to this section shall be imposed only after notice to the party against whom the sanction is proposed to be imposed and opportunity for that party to be heard.

(c) An award of fees and costs as a sanction pursuant to this section shall be payable only from the property or income of the party against whom the sanction is imposed, except that the award may be against the sanctioned party's share of the community property.

§272.　Order for direct payment to attorney

(a) Where the court orders one of the parties to pay attorney's fees and costs for the benefit of the other party, the fees and costs may, in the discretion of the court, be made payable in whole or in part to the attorney entitled thereto. . . .

PART 6.   ENFORCEMENT OF JUDGMENTS
AND ORDERS

§290.   Methods of enforcement

. . . [A] judgment or order made or entered pursuant to this code may be enforced by the court by execution, the appointment of a receiver, or contempt, or by such other order as the court in its discretion determines from time to time to be necessary.

DIVISION 2.5.   DOMESTIC PARTNER REGISTRATION

PART 1.   DEFINITIONS

§297.   Requirements for domestic partnership

(a) Domestic partners are two adults who have chosen to share one another's lives in an intimate and committed relationship of mutual caring.

(b) A domestic partnership shall be established in California when all of the following requirements are met:

(1) Both persons have a common residence.

(2) Both persons agree to be jointly responsible for each other's basic living expenses incurred during the domestic partnership.

(3) Neither person is married or a member of another domestic partnership.

(4) The two persons are not related by blood in a way that would prevent them from being married to each other in this state.

(5) Both persons are at least 18 years of age.

(6) Either of the following:

(A) Both persons are members of the same sex.

(B) One or both of the persons meet the eligibility criteria under Title II of the Social Security Act as defined in 42 U.S.C. Section 402(a) for old-age insurance benefits or Title XVI of the Social Security Act as defined in 42 U.S.C. Section 1381 for aged individuals. Notwithstanding any other provision of this section, persons of opposite sexes may not constitute a domestic partnership unless one or both of the persons are over the age of 62.

(7) Both persons are capable of consenting to the domestic partnership.

(8) Neither person has previously filed a Declaration of Domestic Partnership with the Secretary of State pursuant to this division that has not been terminated under Section 299.

(9) Both file a Declaration of Domestic Partnership with the Secretary of State pursuant to this division.

(c) "Have a common residence" means that both domestic partners share the same residence. It is not necessary that the legal right to possess the common residence be in both of their names. Two people have a common residence even if one or both have additional residences. Domestic partners do not cease to have a common residence if one leaves the common residence but intends to return.

(d) "Basic living expenses" means shelter, utilities, and all other costs directly related to the maintenance of the common household of the common residence of the domestic partners. It also means any other cost, such as medical care, if some or all of the cost is paid as a benefit because a person is another person's domestic partner.

(e) "Joint responsibility" means that each partner agrees to provide for the other partner's basic living expenses if the partner is unable to provide for herself or himself. Persons to whom these expenses are owed may enforce this responsibility if, in extending credit or providing goods or services, they relied on the existence of the domestic partnership and the agreement of both partners to be jointly responsible for those specific expenses.

PART 2.   REGISTRATION

§298.   Declaration of domestic partnership

(a) The Secretary of State shall prepare forms entitled "Declaration of Domestic Partnership" and "Notice of Termination of Domestic Partnership" to meet the requirements of this division. These forms shall require the signature and seal of an acknowledgment by a notary public to be binding and valid.

(b)(1) The Secretary of State shall distribute these forms to each county clerk. These forms shall be available to the public at the office of the Secretary of State and each county clerk.

(2) The Secretary of State shall, by regulation, establish fees for the actual costs of processing each of these forms, and shall charge these fees to persons filing the forms.

(c) The Declaration of Domestic Partnership shall require each person who wants to become a domestic partner to (1) state that he or she meets the requirements of Section 297 at the time the form is signed, (2) provide a mailing address, (3) sign the form with a declaration that representations made therein are true, correct, and contain no material omissions of fact to the best knowledge and belief of the applicant, and (4) have a notary public acknowledge his or her signature. Both partners' signatures shall be affixed to one Declaration of Domestic Partnership form, which form shall then be transmitted to the Secretary of State according to the instructions provided on the form. Violations of this subdivision are punishable as a misdemeanor.

§298.5.   Registration of domestic partnership

(a) Two persons desiring to become domestic partners may complete and file a Declaration of Domestic Partnership with the Secretary of State.

(b) The Secretary of State shall register the Declaration of Domestic Partnership in a registry for those partnerships, and shall return a copy of the registered form to the domestic partners at the address provided by the domestic partners as their common residence.

(c) No person who has filed a Declaration of Domestic Partnership may file a new Declaration of Domestic Partnership until at least six months after the date that a Notice of Termination of Domestic Partnership was filed with the Secretary of State pursuant to subdivision (b) of Section 299 in connection with the termination of the most recent domestic partnership. This prohibition does not apply if the previous domestic partnership ended because one of the partners died or married.

PART 3. TERMINATION

§299. Termination of domestic partnership

(a) A domestic partnership is terminated when any one of the following occurs:

(1) One partner gives or sends to the other partner a written notice by certified mail that he or she is terminating the partnership.

(2) One of the domestic partners dies.

(3) One of the domestic partners marries.

(4) The domestic partners no longer have a common residence.

(b) Upon termination of a domestic partnership, at least one former partner shall file a Notice of Termination of Domestic Partnership with the Secretary of State by mailing a completed form to the Secretary of State by certified mail. The date on which the Notice of Termination of Domestic Partnership is received by the Secretary of State shall be deemed the actual termination date of the domestic partnership, unless termination is caused by the death or marriage of a domestic partner, in which case the actual termination date shall be the date indicated on the Notice of Termination of Domestic Partnership form. The partner who files the Notice of Termination of Domestic Partnership shall send a copy of the notice to the last known address of the other partner.

(c) A former domestic partner who has given a copy of a Declaration of Domestic Partnership to any third party in order to qualify for any benefit or right shall, within 60 days of termination of the domestic partnership, give or send to the third party, at the last known address of the third party, written notification that the domestic partnership has been terminated. A third party who suffers a loss as a result of failure by the domestic partner to send this notice shall be entitled to seek recovery from the partner who was obligated to send it for any actual loss resulting thereby.

(d) Failure to provide the third-party notice required in subdivision (c) shall not delay or prevent the termination of the domestic partnership.

PART 4. LEGAL EFFECT

§299.5. Effect of domestic partnership

(a) The obligations that two people have to each other as a result of creating a domestic partnership are those described in Section 297. Registration as a domestic partner under this division shall not be evidence of, or establish, any rights existing under law other than those expressly provided to domestic partners in this division and any provision of law specifically referring to domestic partners.

The provisions relating to domestic partners provided in this division and any provision of law specifically referring to domestic partners shall not diminish any right under any other provision of law.

(b) Upon the termination of a domestic partnership, the partners, from that time forward, shall incur none of the obligations to each other as domestic partners that are created by this division and any other provision of law specifically referring to domestic partners.

(c) The filing of a Declaration of Domestic Partnership pursuant to this division shall not, in and of itself, change the character of property, real or personal, or any interest in any real or personal property owned by either domestic partner or both of them prior to the date of filing of the declaration.

(d) The filing of a Declaration of Domestic Partnership pursuant to this division shall not, in and of itself, create any interest in, or rights to, any property, real or personal, owned by one partner in the other partner, including, but not limited to, rights similar to community property or quasi-community property.

(e) Any property or interest acquired by the partners during the domestic partnership where title is shared shall be held by the partners in proportion of interest assigned to each partner at the time the property or interest was acquired unless otherwise expressly agreed in writing by both parties. Upon termination of the domestic partnership, this subdivision shall govern the division of any property jointly acquired by the partners.

(f) The formation of a domestic partnership under this division shall not change the individual income or estate tax liability of each domestic partner prior to and during the partnership, unless otherwise provided under another state or federal law or regulation.

DIVISION 3.   MARRIAGE

PART 1.   VALIDITY OF MARRIAGE

§300.   Marriage relation; consent, license, and solemnization

Marriage is a personal relation arising out of a civil contract between a man and a woman, to which the consent of the parties capable of making that contract is necessary. Consent alone does not constitute marriage. Consent must be followed by the issuance of a license and solemnization as authorized by this division. . . .

§301.   Capacity of adult to consent to and consummate marriage

An unmarried male of the age of 18 years or older, and an unmarried female of the age of 18 years or older, and not otherwise disqualified, are capable of consenting to and consummating marriage.

§302.   Capacity of minor to consent to and consummate marriage

An unmarried male or female under the age of 18 years is capable of consenting to and consummating marriage if each of the following documents is filed with the county clerk issuing the marriage license:

(a) The written consent of the parents of each underage person, or of one of the parents or the guardian of each underage person.

(b) A court order granting permission to the underage person to marry, obtained on the showing the court requires.

§306. Procedural requirements; effect of noncompliance

. . . [A] marriage shall be licensed, solemnized, and authenticated, and the certificate of registry of marriage shall be returned as provided in this part. Noncompliance with this part by a nonparty to the marriage does not invalidate the marriage.

§308. Validity of foreign marriages

A marriage contracted outside this state that would be valid by the laws of the jurisdiction in which the marriage was contracted is valid in this state.

§308.5. Marriage limited to a man and a woman

Only marriage between a man and a woman is valid or recognized in California.

§310. Methods of dissolution

Marriage is dissolved only by one of the following:

(a) The death of one of the parties.
(b) A judgment of dissolution of marriage.
(c) A judgment of nullity of marriage.

PART 3. SOLEMNIZATION OF MARRIAGE

Chapter 2. Solemnization of Marriage

§420. Essential element of solemnization

(a) No particular form for the ceremony of marriage is required for solemnization of the marriage, but the parties shall declare, in the presence of the person solemnizing the marriage and necessary witnesses, that they take each other as husband and wife. . . .

DIVISION 4. RIGHTS AND OBLIGATIONS DURING MARRIAGE

PART 1. GENERAL PROVISIONS

Chapter 1. Definitions

§700. Leasehold interest in real property defined

For the purposes of this division, a leasehold interest in real property is real property, not personal property.

Chapter 2.   Relation of Husband and Wife

§720.   Mutual obligations

Husband and wife contract toward each other obligations of mutual respect, fidelity, and support.

§721.   Transactions with each other and third parties; fiduciary relationship of husband and wife

(a) Subject to subdivision (b), either husband or wife may enter into any transaction with the other, or with any other person, respecting property, which either might if unmarried.

(b) Except as provided in Sections 143, 144, 146, 16040, and 16047 of the Probate Code [which requires a trustee to invest and manage trust assets as would a prudent investor], in transactions between themselves, a husband and wife are subject to the general rules governing fiduciary relationships which control the actions of persons occupying confidential relations with each other. This confidential relationship imposes a duty of the highest good faith and fair dealing on each spouse, and neither shall take any unfair advantage of the other. This confidential relationship is a fiduciary relationship subject to the same rights and duties of nonmarital business partners, as provided in Sections 16403, 16404, and 16503 of the Corporations Code,* including, but not limited to, the following:

(1) Providing each spouse access at all times to any books kept regarding a transaction for the purposes of inspection and copying.

(2) Rendering upon request, true and full information of all things affecting any transaction which concerns the community property. Nothing in this

---

* Section 16403 gives partners access to the partnership books and records. Section 16503 regulates transfers of partnership interests. Section 16404, which is reprinted below, sets out the fiduciary duties that a partner owes to the partnership and the other partners.

§16404.   Fiduciary duties

(a) The fiduciary duties a partner owes to the partnership and the other partners are the duty of loyalty and the duty of care set forth in subdivisions (b) and (c).

(b) A partner's duty of loyalty to the partnership and other partners includes all of the following:

(1) To account to the partnership and hold as trustee for it any property, profit, or benefit derived by the partner in the conduct and winding up of the partnership business or derived from a use by the partner of partnership property or information, including the appropriation of a partnership opportunity.

(2) To refrain from dealing with the partnership in the conduct or winding up of the partnership business as or on behalf of a party having an interest adverse to the partnership.

(3) To refrain from competing with the partnership in the conduct of the partnership business before the dissolution of the partnership.

(c) A partner's duty of care to the partnership and the other partners in the conduct and winding up of the partnership business is limited to refraining from engaging in grossly negligent or reckless conduct, intentional misconduct, or a knowing violation of law.

(d) A partner shall discharge the duties to the partnership and the other partners under this chapter or under the partnership agreement and exercise any rights consistently with the obligation of good faith and fair dealing.

(e) A partner does not violate a duty or obligation under this chapter or under the partnership agreement merely because the partner's conduct furthers the partner's own interest.

(f) A partner may lend money to and transact other business with the partnership, and as to each loan or transaction, the rights and obligations of the partner regarding performance or enforcement are the same as those of a person who is not a partner, subject to other applicable law.

(g) This section applies to a person winding up the partnership business as the personal or legal representative of the last surviving partner as if the person were a partner.

section is intended to impose a duty for either spouse to keep detailed books and records of community property transactions.

(3) Accounting to the spouse, and holding as a trustee, any benefit or profit derived from any transaction by one spouse without the consent of the other spouse which concerns the community property.

Chapter 3.   Property Rights During Marriage

§750.   Methods of holding property

A husband and wife may hold property as joint tenants or tenants in common, or as community property, or as community property with a right of survivorship.

§751.   Interests of spouses in community property

The respective interests of the husband and wife in community property during continuance of the marriage relation are present, existing, and equal interests.

§752.   Interest of spouses in separate property

Except as otherwise provided by statute, neither husband nor wife has any interest in the separate property of the other.

PART 2.   CHARACTERIZATION OF MARITAL PROPERTY

Chapter 1.   Community Property

§760.   Community property

Except as otherwise provided by statute, all property, real or personal, wherever situated, acquired by a married person during the marriage while domiciled in this state is community property.

§761.   Property in certain revocable trusts as community property

(a) Unless the trust instrument or the instrument of transfer expressly provides otherwise, community property that is transferred in trust remains community property during the marriage, regardless of the identity of the trustee, if the trust, originally or as amended before or after the transfer, provides that the trust is revocable as to that property during the marriage and the power, if any, to modify the trust as to the rights and interests in that property during the marriage may be exercised only with the joinder or consent of both spouses.

(b) Unless the trust instrument expressly provides otherwise, a power to revoke as to community property may be exercised by either spouse acting alone. Community property, including any income or appreciation, that is distributed or withdrawn from a trust by revocation, power of withdrawal, or otherwise, remains community property unless there is a valid transmutation of the property at the time of distribution or withdrawal.

(c) The trustee may convey and otherwise manage and control the trust property in accordance with the provisions of the trust without the joinder or consent of the husband or wife unless the trust expressly requires the joinder or consent of one or both spouses.

(d) This section applies to a transfer made before, on, or after July 1, 1987.

(e) Nothing in this section affects the community character of property that is transferred before, on, or after July 1, 1987, in any manner or to a trust other than described in this section.

Chapter 2.   Separate Property

§770.   Separate property of married person

(a) Separate property of a married person includes all of the following:

(1) All property owned by the person before marriage.

(2) All property acquired by the person after marriage by gift, bequest, devise, or descent.

(3) The rents, issues, and profits of the property described in this section.

(b) A married person may, without the consent of the person's spouse, convey the person's separate property.

§771.   Earnings and accumulations while living separate and apart

(a) The earnings and accumulations of a spouse and the minor children living with, or in the custody of, the spouse, while living separate and apart from the other spouse, are the separate property of the spouse. . . .

§772.   Earnings and accumulations after judgment of legal separation

After entry of a judgment of legal separation of the parties, the earnings or accumulations of each party are the separate property of the party acquiring the earnings or accumulations.

Chapter 3.   Damages for Injuries to Married Person

§780.   Damages for personal injury to married person as community property

Except as provided in Section 781 and subject to the rules of allocation set forth in Section 2603, money and other property received or to be received by a married person in satisfaction of a judgment for damages for personal injuries, or pursuant to an agreement for the settlement or compromise of a claim for such damages, is community property if the cause of action for the damages arose during the marriage.

§781. Cases where damages for personal injury are separate property

(a) Money or other property received or to be received by a married person in satisfaction of a judgment for damages for personal injuries, or pursuant to an agreement for the settlement or compromise of a claim for those damages, is the separate property of the injured person if the cause of action for the damages arose as follows:

(1) After the entry of a judgment of dissolution of a marriage or legal separation of the parties.

(2) While either spouse, if he or she is the injured person, is living separate from the other spouse.

(b) Notwithstanding subdivision (a), if the spouse of the injured person has paid expenses by reason of the personal injuries from separate property or from the community property, the spouse is entitled to reimbursement of the separate property or the community property for those expenses from the separate property received by the injured person under subdivision (a).

(c) Notwithstanding subdivision (a), if one spouse has a cause of action against the other spouse which arose during the marriage of the parties, money or property paid or to be paid by or on behalf of a party to the party's spouse of that marriage in satisfaction of a judgment for damages for personal injuries to that spouse, or pursuant to an agreement for the settlement or compromise of a claim for the damages, is the separate property of the injured spouse.

§782. Injuries to married person by spouse

(a) Where an injury to a married person is caused in whole or in party by the negligent or wrongful act or omission of the person's spouse, the community property may not be used to discharge the liability of the tortfeasor spouse to the injured spouse or the liability to make contribution to a joint tortfeasor until the separate property of the tortfeasor spouse, not exempt from enforcement of a money judgment, is exhausted.

(b) This section does not prevent the use of community property to discharge a liability referred to in subdivision (a) if the injured spouse gives written consent thereto after the occurrence of the injury.

(c) This section does not affect the right to indemnity provided by an insurance or other contract to discharge the tortfeasor spouse's liability, whether or not the consideration given for the contract consisted of community property.

§783. Injuries to married person by third party; extent concurring negligence of spouse allowable as defense

If a married person is injured by the negligent or wrongful act or omission of a person other than the married person's spouse, the fact that the negligent or wrongful act or omission of the spouse of the injured person was a concurring cause of the injury is not a defense in an action brought by the injured person to recover damages for the injury except in cases where the concurring negligent or wrongful act or omission would be a defense if the married did not exist.

Chapter 4. Presumptions Concerning Nature of Property

§802. Presumption not applicable where marriage terminated by dissolution more than four years before death

The presumption that property acquired during marriage is community property does not apply to any property to which legal or equitable title is held by a person at the time of the person's death if the marriage during which the property was acquired was terminated by dissolution of marriage more than four years before the death.

§803. Property acquired by married woman before January 1, 1975

Notwithstanding any other provision of this part, whenever any real or personal property, or any interest therein or encumbrance thereon, was acquired before January 1, 1975, by a married woman by an instrument in writing, the following presumptions apply, and are conclusive in favor of any person dealing in good faith and for a valuable consideration with the married woman or her legal representatives or successors in interest, regardless of any change in her marital status after acquisition of the property:

(a) If acquired by the married woman, the presumption is that the property is the married woman's separate property.

(b) If acquired by the married woman and any other person, the presumption is that the married woman takes the part acquired by her as tenant in common, unless a different intention is expressed in the instrument.

(c) If acquired by husband and wife by an instrument in which they are described as husband and wife, the presumption is that the property is the community property of the husband and wife, unless a different intention is expressed in the instrument.

Chapter 5. Transmutation of Property

§850. Transmutation of property by agreement or transfer

Subject to Sections 851 to 853, inclusive, married persons may by agreement or transfer, with or without consideration, do any of the following:

(a) Transmute community property to separate property of either spouse.

(b) Transmute separate property of either spouse to community property.

(c) Transmute separate property of one spouse to separate property of the other spouse.

§851. Fraudulent transfers laws apply

A transmutation is subject to the laws governing fraudulent transfers.

§852. Form of transmutation

(a) A transmutation of real or personal property is not valid unless made in writing by an express declaration that is made, joined in, consented to, or accepted by the spouse whose interest in the property is adversely affected.

(b) A transmutation of real property is not effective as to third parties without notice thereof unless recorded.

(c) This section does not apply to a gift between the spouses of clothing, wearing apparel, jewelry, or other tangible articles of a personal nature that is used solely or principally by the spouse to whom the gift is made and that is not substantial in value taking into account the circumstances of the marriage.

(d) Nothing in this section affects the law governing characterization of property in which separate property and community property are commingled or otherwise combined.

(e) This section does not apply to or affect a transmutation of property made before January 1, 1985, and the law that would otherwise be applicable to that transmutation shall continue to apply.

§853. Effect of will

(a) A statement in a will of the character of property is not admissible as evidence of a transmutation of the property in a proceeding commenced before the death of the person who made the will.

(b) A waiver of a right to a joint and survivor annuity or survivor's benefits under the federal Retirement Equity Act of 1984 (Public Law 98-397) is not a transmutation of the community property rights of the person executing the waiver.

(c) A written joinder or written consent to a nonprobate transfer of community property on death that satisfies Section 852 is a transmutation and is governed by the law applicable to transmutations and not by Chapter 2 (commencing with Section 5010) of Part 1 of Division 5 of the Probate Code.

PART 3.   LIABILITY OF MARITAL PROPERTY

Chapter 1.   Definitions

§900. Application of definitions

Unless the provision or context otherwise requires, the definitions in this chapter govern the construction of this part.

§902. "Debt"

"Debt" means an obligation incurred by a married person before or during marriage, whether based on contract, tort, or otherwise.

§903. Time debt "incurred"

A debt is "incurred" at the following time:
  (a) In the case of a contract, at the time the contract is made.
  (b) In the case of a tort, at the time the tort occurs.
  (c) In other cases, at the time the obligation arises.

Chapter 2.   General Rules of Liability

§910. Community estate liable for debt of either spouse

(a) Except as otherwise expressly provided by statute, the community estate is liable for a debt incurred by either spouse before or during marriage, regardless of which spouse has the management and control of the property and regardless of whether one or both spouses are parties to the debt or to a judgment for the debt.

(b) "During marriage" for purposes of this section does not include the period during which the spouses are living separate and apart before a judgment of dissolution of marriage or legal separation of the parties.

§911. Liability of married person's earnings for premarital debt of spouse

(a) The earnings of a married person during marriage are not liable for a debt incurred by the person's spouse before marriage. After the earnings of the married person are paid, they remain not liable so long as they are held in a deposit account in which the person's spouse has no right of withdrawal and are uncommingled with other property in the community estate, except property insignificant in amount.

(b) As used in this section:
  (1) "Deposit account" has the meaning prescribed in paragraph (29) of subdivision (a) of Section 9102 of the Commercial Code.*
  (2) "Earnings" means compensation for personal services performed, whether as an employee or otherwise.

§912. Liability of quasi-community property

For the purposes of this part, quasi-community property is liable to the same extent, and shall be treated the same in all other respects, as community property.

§913. Liability of separate property

(a) The separate property of a married person is liable for a debt incurred by the person before or during marriage.

(b) Except as otherwise provided by statute:

---

* See footnote 3 on page 428.—ED.

(1) The separate property of a married person is not liable for a debt incurred by the person's spouse before or during marriage.

(2) The joinder or consent of a married person to an encumbrance of community estate property to secure payment of a debt incurred by the person's spouse does not subject the person's separate property to liability for the debt unless the person also incurred the debt.

§914.   Liability for necessaries

(a) Notwithstanding Section 913, a married person is personally liable for the following debts incurred by the person's spouse during marriage:

(1) A debt incurred for necessaries of life of the person's spouse while the spouses are living together.

(2) Except as provided in Section 4302, a debt incurred for common necessaries of life of the person's spouse while the spouses are living separately.

(b) The separate property of a married person may be applied to the satisfaction of a debt for which the person is personally liable pursuant to this section. If separate property is so applied at a time when nonexempt property in the community estate or separate property of the person's spouse is available but is not applied to the satisfaction of the debt, the married person is entitled to reimbursement to the extent such property was available. . . .

§915.   Liability for support obligation

(a) For the purpose of this part, a child or spousal support obligation of a married person that does not arise out of the marriage shall be treated as a debt incurred before marriage, regardless of whether a court order for support is made or modified before or during marriage and regardless of whether any installment payment on the obligation accrues before or during marriage.

(b) If property in the community estate is applied to the satisfaction of a child or spousal support obligation of a married person that does not arise out of the marriage, at a time when nonexempt separate income of the person is available but is not applied to the satisfaction of the obligation, the community estate is entitled to reimbursement from the person in the amount of the separate income, not exceeding the property in the community estate so applied.

(c) Nothing in this section limits the matters a court may take into consideration in determining or modifying the amount of a support order, including, but not limited to, the earnings of the spouses of the parties.

§916.   Liability after property division

(a) Notwithstanding any other provision of this chapter, after division of community and quasi-community property pursuant to Division 7 (commencing with Section 2500):

(1) The separate property owned by a married person at the time of the division and the property received by the person in the division is liable for a debt incurred by the person before or during marriage and the person is personally liable for the debt, whether or not the debt was assigned for payment by the person's spouse in the division.

(2) The separate property owned by a married person at the time of the

division and the property received by the person in the division is not liable for a debt incurred by the person's spouse before or during marriage, and the person is not personally liable for the debt, unless the debt was assigned for payment by the person in the division of the property. Nothing in this paragraph affects the liability of property for the satisfaction of a lien on the property.

(3) The separate property owned by a married person at the time of the division and the property received by the person in the division is liable for a debt incurred by the person's spouse before or during marriage, and the person is personally liable for the debt, if the debt was assigned for payment by the person in the division of the property. If a money judgment for the debt is entered after the division, the property is not subject to enforcement of the judgment and the judgment may not be enforced against the married person, unless the person is made a party to the judgment for the purpose of this paragraph.

(b) If property of a married person is applied to the satisfaction of a money judgment pursuant to subdivision (a) for a debt incurred by the person that is assigned for payment by the person's spouse, the person has a right of reimbursement from the person's spouse to the extent of the property applied, with interest at the legal rate, and may recover reasonable attorney's fees incurred in enforcing the right of reimbursement.

Chapter 3. Reimbursement

§920. General provisions

A right of reimbursement provided by this part is subject to the following provisions:

(a) The right arises regardless of which spouse applies the property to the satisfaction of the debt, regardless of whether the property is applied to the satisfaction of the debt voluntarily or involuntarily, and regardless of whether the debt to which the property is applied is satisfied in whole or in part. The right is subject to an express written waiver of the right by the spouse in whose favor the right arises.

(b) The measure of reimbursement is the value of the property or interest in property at the time the right arises.

(c) The right shall be exercised not later than the earlier of the following times:

(1) Within three years after the spouse in whose favor the right arises has actual knowledge of the application of the property to the satisfaction of the debt.

(2) In proceedings for division of community and quasi-community property pursuant to Division 7 (commencing with Section 2500) or in proceedings upon the death of a spouse.

Chapter 4. Transitional Provisions

§930. Enforcement of debts

Except as otherwise provided by statute, this part governs the liability of separate property and property in the community estate and the personal liability of a married person for a debt enforced on or after January 1, 1985, regardless of whether the debt was incurred before, on, or after that date.

§931. Reimbursement rights

The provisions of this part that govern reimbursement apply to all debts, regardless of whether satisfied before, on, or after January 1, 1985.

Chapter 5.   Liability for Death or Injury

§1000.   Liability for death or injury

(a) A married person is not liable for any injury or damage caused by the other spouse except in cases where the married person would be liable therefor if the marriage did not exist.

(b) The liability of a married person for death or injury to person or property shall be satisfied as follows:

(1) If the liability of the married person is based upon an act or omission which occurred while the married person was performing an activity for the benefit of the community, the liability shall first be satisfied from the community estate and second from the separate property of the married person.

(2) If the liability of the married person is not based upon an act or omission which occurred while the married person was performing an activity for the benefit of the community, the liability shall first be satisfied from the separate property of the married person and second from the community estate.

(c) This section does not apply to the extent the liability is satisfied out of proceeds of insurance for the liability, whether the proceeds are from property in the community estate or from separate property. Notwithstanding Section 920, no right of reimbursement under this section shall be exercised more than seven years after the spouse in whose favor the right arises has actual knowledge of the application of the property to the satisfaction of the debt.

PART 4.   MANAGEMENT AND CONTROL OF MARITAL PROPERTY

§1100.   Management and control of community personal property: fiduciary duty

(a) Except as provided in subdivisions (b), (c), and (d) and Sections 761 and 1103, either spouse has the management and control of the community personal property, whether acquired prior to or on or after January 1, 1975, with like absolute power of disposition, other than testamentary, as the spouse has of the separate estate of the spouse.

(b) A spouse may not make a gift of community personal property, or dispose of community personal property for less than fair and reasonable value, without the written consent of the other spouse. This subdivision does not apply to gifts mutually given by both spouses to third parties and to gifts given by one spouse to the other spouse.

(c) A spouse may not sell, convey, or encumber community personal property used as the family dwelling, or the furniture, furnishings, or fittings of the home, or the clothing or wearing apparel of the other spouse or minor children which is community personal property, without the written consent of the other spouse.

(d) Except as provided in subdivisions (b) and (c), and in Section 1102, a spouse who is operating or managing a business or an interest in a business that is all or substantially all community personal property has the primary management and control of the business or interest. Primary management and control means that the managing spouse may act alone in all transactions but shall give prior written notice to the other spouse of any sale, lease, exchange, encumbrance, or other disposition of all or substantially all of the personal property used in the operation of the business (including personal property used for agricultural purposes), whether or not title to that property is held in the name of only one spouse. Written notice is not, however, required when prohibited by the law otherwise applicable to the transaction.

Remedies for the failure by a managing spouse to give prior written notice as required by this subdivision are only as specified in Section 1101. A failure to give prior written notice shall not adversely affect the validity of a transaction nor of any interest transferred.

(e) Each spouse shall act with respect to the other spouse in the management and control of the community assets and liabilities in accordance with the general rules governing fiduciary relationships which control the actions of persons having relationships of personal confidence as specified in Section 721, until such time as the assets and liabilities have been divided by the parties or by a court. This duty includes the obligation to make full disclosure to the other spouse of all material facts and information regarding the existence, characterization, and valuation of all assets in which the community has or may have an interest and debts for which the community is or may be liable, and to provide equal access to all information, records, and books that pertain to the value and character of those assets and debts, upon request.

§1101. Remedies for breach of fiduciary duty between spouses

(a) A spouse has a claim against the other spouse for any breach of the fiduciary duty that results in impairment to the claimant spouse's present undivided one-half interest in the community estate, including, but not limited to, a single transaction or a pattern or series of transactions, which transaction or transactions have caused or will cause a detrimental impact to the claimant spouse's undivided one-half interest in the community estate.

(b) A court may order an accounting of the property and obligations of the parties to a marriage and may determine the rights of ownership in, the beneficial enjoyment of, or access to, community property, and the classification of all property of the parties to a marriage.

(c) A court may order that the name of a spouse shall be added to community property held in the name of the other spouse alone or that the title of community property held in some other title form shall be reformed to reflect its community character, except with respect to any of the following:

(1) A partnership interest held by the other spouse as a general partner.

(2) An interest in a professional corporation or professional association.

(3) An asset of an unincorporated business if the other spouse is the only spouse involved in operating and managing the business.

(4) Any other property, if the revision would adversely affect the rights of a third person.

(d)(1) Except as provided in paragraph (2), any action under subdivision (a) shall be commenced within three years of the date a petitioning spouse had actual knowledge that the transaction or event for which the remedy is being sought occurred.

(2) An action may be commenced under this section upon the death of a spouse or in conjunction with an action for legal separation, dissolution of marriage, or nullity without regard to the time limitations set forth in paragraph (1).

(3) The defense of laches may be raised in any action brought under this section.

(4) Except as to actions authorized by paragraph (2), remedies under subdivision (a) apply only to transactions or events occurring on or after July 1, 1987.

(e) In any transaction affecting community property in which the consent of both spouses is required, the court may, upon the motion of a spouse, dispense with the requirement of the other spouse's consent if both of the following requirements are met:

(1) The proposed transaction is in the best interest of the community.

(2) Consent has been arbitrarily refused or cannot be obtained due to the physical incapacity, mental incapacity, or prolonged absence of the non-consenting spouse.

(f) Any action may be brought under this section without filing an action for dissolution of marriage, legal separation, or nullity, or may be brought in conjunction with the action or upon the death of a spouse.

(g) Remedies for breach of the fiduciary duty by one spouse including those set out in Sections 721 and 1100, shall include, but not be limited to, an award to the other spouse of 50 percent, or an amount equal to 50 percent, of any asset undisclosed or transferred in breach of the fiduciary duty plus attorney's fees and court costs. The value of the asset shall be determined to be its highest value at the date of the breach of the fiduciary duty, the date of the sale or disposition of the asset, or the date of the award by the court.

(h) Remedies for the breach of the fiduciary duty by one spouse, as set forth in Sections 721 and 1100, when the breach falls within the ambit of Section 3294 of the Civil Code* shall include, but not be limited to, an award to the other spouse of 100 percent, or an amount equal to 100 percent, of any asset undisclosed or transferred in breach of the fiduciary duty.

§1102. Management and control of community real property

(a) Except as provided in Sections 761 and 1103, either spouse has the management and control of the community real property, whether acquired prior to or on or after January 1, 1975, but both spouses, either personally or by a duly

---

* Civil Code section 3294 provides:

§3294. Exemplary damages; when allowable; definitions

(a) In an action for the breach of an obligation not arising from contract, where it is proven by clear and convincing evidence that the defendant has been guilty of oppression, fraud, or malice, the plaintiff, in addition to the actual damages, may recover damages for the sake of example and by way of punishing the defendant. . . .

(c) As used in this section, the following definitions shall apply:

(1) "Malice" means conduct which is intended by the defendant to cause injury to the plaintiff or despicable conduct which is carried on by the defendant with a willful and conscious disregard of the rights or safety of others.

(2) "Oppression" means despicable conduct that subjects a person to cruel and unjust hardship in conscious disregard of that person's rights.

authorized agent, must join in executing any instrument by which that community real property or any interest therein is leased for a longer period than one year, or is sold, conveyed, or encumbered.

(b) Nothing in this section shall be construed to apply to a lease, mortgage, conveyance, or transfer of real property or of any interest in real property between husband and wife.

(c) Notwithstanding subdivision (b):

(1) The sole lease, contract, mortgage, or deed of the husband, holding the record title to community real property, to a lessee, purchaser, or encumbrancer, in good faith without knowledge of the marriage relation, shall be presumed to be valid if executed prior to January 1, 1975.

(2) The sole lease, contract, mortgage, or deed of either spouse, holding the record title to community real property to a lessee, purchaser, or encumbrancer, in good faith without knowledge of the marriage relation, shall be presumed to be valid if executed on or after January 1, 1975.

(d) No action to avoid any instrument mentioned in this section, affecting any property standing of record in the name of either spouse alone, executed by the spouse alone, shall be commenced after the expiration of one year from the filing for record of that instrument in the recorder's office in the county in which the land is situated.

(e) Nothing in this section precludes either spouse from encumbering his or her interest in community real property as provided in Section 2033, to pay reasonable attorney's fees in order to retain or maintain legal counsel in a proceeding for dissolution of marriage, for nullity of marriage, or for legal separation of the parties.

§1103. Management and control where spouse has conservator or lacks legal capacity

(a) Where one or both of the spouses either has a conservator of the estate or lacks legal capacity to manage and control community property, the procedure for management and control (which includes disposition) of the community property is that prescribed in Part 6 (commencing with Section 3000) of Division 4 of the Probate Code.

(b) Where one or both spouses either has a conservator of the estate or lacks legal capacity to give consent to a gift of community personal property or a disposition of community personal property without a valuable consideration as required by Section 1100 or to a sale, conveyance, or encumbrance of community personal property for which a consent is required by Section 1100, the procedure for that gift, disposition, sale, conveyance, or encumbrance is that prescribed in Part 6 (commencing with Section 3000) of Division 4 of the Probate Code.

(c) Where one or both spouses either has a conservator of the estate or lacks legal capacity to join in executing a lease, sale, conveyance, or encumbrance of community real property or any interest therein as required by Section 1102, the procedure for that lease, sale, conveyance, or encumbrance is that prescribed in Part 6 (commencing with Section 3000) of Division 4 of the Probate Code.

---

(3) "Fraud" means an intentional misrepresentation, deceit, or concealment of a material fact known to the defendant with the intention on the part of the defendant of thereby depriving a person of property or legal rights or otherwise causing injury. . . .

PART 5.   MARITAL AGREEMENTS

Chapter 1.   General Provisions

§1500.   Effect of premarital and other marital property agreements

The property rights of husband and wife prescribed by statute may be altered by a premarital agreement or other marital property agreement.

§1501.   Agreements by minors

A minor may make a valid premarital agreement or other marital property agreement if the minor is emancipated or is otherwise capable of contracting marriage.

§1502.   Recording of agreements

(a) A premarital agreement or other marital property agreement that is executed and acknowledged or proved in the manner that a grant of real property is required to be executed and acknowledged or proved may be recorded in the office of the recorder of each county in which real property affected by the agreement is situated.

(b) Recording or nonrecording of a premarital agreement or other marital property agreement has the same effect as recording or nonrecording of a grant of real property.

§1503.   Law applicable to premarital agreements made before January 1, 1986

Nothing in this chapter affects the validity or effect of premarital agreements made before January 1, 1986, and the validity and effect of those agreements shall continue to be determined by the law applicable to the agreements before January 1, 1986.

Chapter 2.   Uniform Premarital Agreement Act

Article 1.   Preliminary Provisions

§1600.   Short title

This chapter may be cited as the Uniform Premarital Agreement Act.

§1601.   Application of chapter

This chapter is effective on and after January 1, 1986, and applies to any premarital agreement executed on or after that date.

Article 2.   Premarital Agreements

§1610.   Definitions

As used in this chapter:

(a) "Premarital agreement" means an agreement between prospective spouses made in contemplation of marriage and to be effective upon marriage.

(b) "Property" means an interest, present or future, legal or equitable, vested or contingent, in real or personal property, including income and earnings.

§1611. Formalities; consideration

A premarital agreement shall be in writing and signed by both parties. It is enforceable without consideration.

§1612. Subject matter of premarital agreement

(a) Parties to a premarital agreement may contract with respect to all of the following:

(1) The rights and obligations of each of the parties in any of the property of either or both of them whenever and wherever acquired or located.

(2) The right to buy, sell, use, transfer, exchange, abandon, lease, consume, expend, assign, create a security interest in, mortgage, encumber, dispose of, or otherwise manage and control property.

(3) The disposition of property upon separation, marital dissolution, death, or the occurrence or nonoccurrence of any other event.

(4) The making of a will, trust, or other arrangement to carry out the provisions of the agreement.

(5) The ownership rights in and disposition of the death benefit from a life insurance policy.

(6) The choice of law governing the construction of the agreement.

(7) Any other matter, including their personal rights and obligations, not in violation of public policy or a statute imposing a criminal penalty.

(b) The right of a child to support may not be adversely affected by a premarital agreement.

(c) Any provision in a premarital agreement regarding spousal support, including, but not limited to, a waiver of it, is not enforceable if the party against whom enforcement of the spousal support provision is sought was not represented by independent counsel at the time the agreement containing the provision was signed, or if the provision regarding spousal support is unconscionable at the time of enforcement. An otherwise unenforceable provision in a premarital agreement regarding spousal support may not become enforceable solely because the party against whom enforcement is sought was represented by independent counsel.

§1613. Agreement becomes effective upon marriage

A premarital agreement becomes effective upon marriage.

§1614. Amendment; revocation

After marriage, a premarital agreement may be amended or revoked only by a written agreement signed by the parties. The amended agreement or the revocation is enforceable without consideration.

§1615. Enforcement

(a) A premarital agreement is not enforceable if the party against whom enforcement is sought proves either of the following:

(1) That party did not execute the agreement voluntarily.

(2) The agreement was unconscionable when it was executed and, before execution of the agreement, all of the following applied to that party:

(A) That party was not provided a fair, reasonable, and full disclosure of the property or financial obligations of the other party.

(B) That party did not voluntarily and expressly waive, in writing, any right to disclosure of the property or financial obligations of the other party beyond the disclosure provided.

(C) That party did not have, or reasonably could not have had, an adequate knowledge of the property or financial obligations of the other party.

(b) An issue of unconscionability of a premarital agreement shall be decided by the court as a matter of law.

(c) For the purposes of subdivision (a), it shall be deemed that a premarital agreement was not executed voluntarily unless the court finds in writing or on the record all of the following:

(1) The party against whom enforcement is sought was represented by independent legal counsel at the time of signing the agreement or, after being advised to seek independent legal counsel, expressly waived, in a separate writing, representation by independent legal counsel.

(2) The party against whom enforcement is sought had not less than seven calendar days between the time that party was first presented with the agreement and advised to seek independent legal counsel and the time the agreement was signed.

(3) The party against whom enforcement is sought, if unrepresented by legal counsel, was fully informed of the terms and basic effect of the agreement as well as the rights and obligations he or she was giving up by signing the agreement, and was proficient in the language in which the explanation of the party's rights was conducted and in which the agreement was written. The explanation of the rights and obligations relinquished shall be memorialized in writing and delivered to the party prior to signing the agreement. The unrepresented party shall, on or before the signing of the premarital agreement, execute a document declaring that he or she received the information required by this paragraph and indicating who provided that information.

(4) The agreement and the writings executed pursuant to paragraphs (1) and (3) were not executed under duress, fraud, or undue influence, and the parties did not lack capacity to enter into the agreement.

(5) Any other factors the court deems relevant.

§1616. Effect of void marriage

If a marriage is determined to be void, an agreement that would otherwise have been a premarital agreement is enforceable only to the extent necessary to avoid an inequitable result.

§1617. Limitation of actions

Any statute of limitations applicable to an action asserting a claim for relief under a premarital agreement is tolled during the marriage of the parties to the agreement. However, equitable defenses limiting the time for enforcement, including laches and estoppel, are available to either party.

Chapter 3. Agreements Between Husband and Wife

§1620. Restrictions on contract altering spouses' legal relations

Except as otherwise provided by law, a husband and wife cannot, by a contract with each other, alter their legal relations, except as to property.

DIVISION 6. NULLITY, DISSOLUTION, AND LEGAL SEPARATION

PART 1. GENERAL PROVISIONS

Chapter 1. Application of Part

§2000. Application to dissolution, nullity, and legal separation proceedings

This part applies to a proceeding for dissolution of marriage, for nullity of marriage, or for legal separation of the parties.

Chapter 2. Jurisdiction

§2010. Authority of court

In a proceeding for dissolution of marriage, for nullity of marriage, or for legal separation of the parties, the court has jurisdiction to inquire into and render any judgment and make such orders that are appropriate concerning the following:

(a) The status of the marriage.

(b) The custody of minor children of the marriage.

(c) The support of children for whom support may be ordered, including children born after the filing of the initial petition or the final decree of dissolution.

(d) The support of either party.

(e) The settlement of the property rights of the parties.

(f) The award of attorney's fees and costs.

Chapter 3.5. Attorney's Fees and Costs

§2030. Costs and attorney's fees during pendency of proceeding

(a) During the pendency of a proceeding for dissolution of marriage, for nullity of marriage, or for legal separation of the parties, the court may, upon (1) determining an ability to pay and (2) consideration of the respective incomes and needs of the parties in order to ensure that each party has access to legal representation to preserve all of the party's rights, order any part, except a governmental entity, to pay the amount reasonably necessary for attorney's fees and for the cost of maintaining or defending the proceeding. From time to time and before entry of judgment, the court may augment or modify the original award for attorney's fees and costs as may be reasonably necessary for the prosecution or defense of the proceeding or any proceeding related thereto, including after any appeal has been concluded.

(b) Attorney's fees and costs within this section may be awarded for legal services rendered or costs incurred before or after the commencement of the proceeding.

(c) For services rendered or costs incurred after entry of judgment, the court may award the attorney's fees and costs reasonably necessary to maintain or defend any subsequent proceeding, and may augment or modify an award so made, including after an appeal has been concluded.

(d) Any order requiring a party who is not the spouse of another party to the proceedings to pay attorney's fees or costs shall be limited to an amount reasonably necessary to maintain or defend the action on the issues relating to that party.

§2032. Award of attorney's fees and costs to be just and reasonable under relative circumstances of parties

(a) The court may make an award of attorney's fees and costs under Section 2030 . . . where the making the award, and the amount of the award, are just and reasonable under the relative circumstances of the respective parties.

(b) In determining what is just and reasonable under the relative circumstances, the court shall take into consideration the need for the award to enable each party, to the extent practical, to have sufficient financial resources to present the party's case adequately, taking into consideration, to the extent relevant, the circumstances of the respective parties described in Section 4320. The fact that the party requesting an award of attorney's fees and costs has resources from which the party could pay the party's own attorney's fees and costs is not itself a bar to an order that the other party pay part or all of the fees and costs requested. Financial resources are only one factor for the court to consider in determining how to apportion the overall cost of the litigation equitably between the parties under their relative circumstances.

(c) The court may order payment of an award of attorney's fees and costs from any type of property, whether community or separate, principal or income.

(d) Either party may, at any time prior to the hearing of the cause on the merits, on noticed motion, request the court to make a finding that the case involves complex or substantial issues of fact or law related to property rights, visitation, custody, or support. Upon that finding, the court may in its discretion direct the implementation of a case management plan for the purpose of allocating attorney's fees, court costs, expert fees, and consultant fees equitably between the parties. The case management plan shall focus on specific, designated issues. The plan may provide for the allocation of separate or community assets, security against these assets, and for payments from income or anticipated income of either party for the purpose described in this subdivision and for the benefit of one or both parties. Payments shall be authorized only upon agreement of the parties or, in the absence thereof, by court order. The court may order that a referee be appointed . . . to oversee the case management plan.

§2033. Encumbrance to pay family law attorney's fees

(a) Either party may encumter his or her interest in community real property to pay reasonable attorney's fees in order to retain or maintain legal counsel in a proceeding for dissolution of marriage, for nullity of marriage, or for legal separation of the parties. This encumbrance shall be known as a "family law attorney's real property lien" and attaches only to the encumbering party's interest in the community real property.

(b) Notice of a family law attorney's real property lien shall be served either personally or on the other party's attorney of record at least 15 days before the encumbrance is recorded. . . .

§2034. Objection to family law attorney's real property lien

(a) On application of either party, the court may deny the family law attorney's real property lien described in Section 2033 based on a finding that the encumbrance would likely result in an unequal division of property because it would impair the encumbering party's ability to meet his or her fair share of the community obligations or would otherwise be unjust under the circumstances of the case. The court may also for good cause limit the amount of the family law attorney's real property lien. A limitation by the court is not to be construed as a determination of reasonable attorney's fees. . . .

Chapter 4. Protective and Restraining Orders

Article 1. Orders in Summons

§2040. Temporary restraining order in summons

(a) . . . [T]he summons shall contain a temporary restraining order:

(1) Restraining both parties from removing the minor child or children of the parties, if any, from the state without the prior written consent of the other party or an order of the court.

(2) Restraining both parties from transferring, encumbering, hypothecating, concealing, or in any way disposing of any property, real or personal, whether community, quasi-community, or separate, without the written consent of the other party or an order of the court, except in the usual course of business or for the necessities of life and requiring each party to notify the other party of any proposed extraordinary expenditures at least five business days before incurring those expenditures and to account to the court for all extraordinary expenditures made after service of the summons on that party.

Notwithstanding the foregoing, nothing in the restraining order shall preclude a party from using community property, quasi-community property, or the party's own separate property to pay reasonable attorney's fees and costs in order to retain legal counsel in the proceedings. . . .

(3) Restraining both parties from cashing, borrowing against, canceling, transferring, disposing of, or changing the beneficiaries of any insurance or other coverage, including life, health, automobile, and disability held for the benefit of the parties and their child or children for whom support may be ordered. . . .

§2041. Rights, title, and interest of purchaser for value

Nothing in Section 2040 adversely affects the rights, title, and interest of a purchaser for value, encumbrancer for value, or lessee for value who is without actual knowledge of the restraining order.

Chapter 6. Employee Benefit Plan as Party

Article 1. Joinder of Plan

§2060. Application and order for joinder of plan

(a) Upon written application by a party, the clerk shall enter an order joining as a party to the proceeding any employee benefit plan in which either party to the proceeding claims an interest that is or may be subject to disposition by the court.

(b) An order or judgment in the proceeding is not enforceable against an employee benefit plan unless the plan has been joined as a party to the proceeding.

Chapter 9. Disclosure of Assets and Liabilities

§2100. Legislative intent

The Legislature finds and declares the following:

(a) It is the policy of the State of California (1) to marshal, preserve, and protect community and quasi-community assets and liabilities that exist at the date of separation so as to avoid dissipation of the community estate before distribution, (2) to ensure fair and sufficient child and spousal support awards, and (3) to achieve a division of community and quasi-community assets and liabilities on the dissolution of marriage or legal separation of the parties as provided under California law.

(b) Sound public policy further favors the reduction of the adversarial nature of marital dissolution and the attendant costs by fostering full disclosure and cooperative discovery.

(c) In order to promote this public policy, a full and accurate disclosure of all assets and liabilities in which one or both parties have or may have an interest must be made in the early stages of a proceeding for dissolution of marriage or legal separation of the parties, regardless of the characterization as community or separate, together with a disclosure of all income and expenses of the parties. Moreover, each party has a continuing duty to immediately, fully, and accurately update and augment that disclosure to the extent there have been any material changes so that at the time the parties enter into an agreement for the resolution of any of these issues, or at the time of trial on these issues, each party will have as full and complete knowledge of the relevant underlying facts as is reasonably possible under the circumstances of the case.

§2101. Definitions

Unless the provision or context otherwise requires, the following definitions apply to this chapter:

(a) "Asset" includes, but is not limited to, any real or personal property of any nature, whether tangible or intangible, and whether currently existing or contingent.

(b) "Default judgment" does not include a stipulated judgment or any judgment pursuant to a marital settlement agreement.

(c) "Earnings and accumulations" includes income from whatever source derived, as provided in Section 4058.

(d) "Expenses" includes, but is not limited to, all personal living expenses, but does not include business related expenses. . . .

(f) "Liability" includes, but is not limited to, any debt or obligation, whether currently existing or contingent.

§2102. Fiduciary relationship; length and scope of duty; termination

(a) From the date of separation to the date of the distribution of the community or quasi-community asset or liability in question, each party is subject to the standards provided in Section 721, as to all activities that affect the assets and liabilities of the other party, including, but not limited to, the following activities:

(1) The accurate and complete disclosure of all assets and liabilities in which the party has or may have an interest or obligation and all current earnings, accumulations, and expenses, including an immediate, full, and accurate update or augmentation to the extent there have been any material changes.

(2) The accurate and complete written disclosure of any investment opportunity, business opportunity, or other income-producing opportunity that presents itself after the date of separation, but that results from any investment, significant business activity outside the ordinary course of business, or other income-producing opportunity of either spouse from the date of marriage to the date of separation, inclusive. The written disclosure shall be made in sufficient time for the other spouse to make an informed decision as to whether he or she desires to participate in the investment opportunity, business, or other potential income-producing opportunity, and for the court to resolve any dispute regarding the right of the other spouse to participate in the opportunity. In the event of nondisclosure of an investment opportunity, the division of any gain resulting from that opportunity is governed by the standard provided in Section 2556.

(3) The operation or management of a business or an interest in a business in which the community may have an interest.

(b) From the date that a valid, enforceable, and binding resolution of the disposition of the asset or liability in question is reached, until the asset or liability has actually been distributed, each party is subject to the standards provided in Section 721 as to all activities that affect the assets or liabilities of the other party. Once a particular asset or liability has been distributed, the duties and standards set forth in Section 721 shall end as to that asset or liability.

(c) From the date of separation to the date of a valid, enforceable, and binding resolution of all issues relating to child or spousal support and professional fees, each party is subject to the standards provided in Section 721 as to all issues relating to the support and fees, including immediate, full, and accurate disclosure of all material facts and information regarding the income or expenses of the party.

§2103. Declarations of disclosure; requirements

In order to provide full and accurate disclosure of all assets and liabilities in which one or both parties may have an interest, each party to a proceeding for dissolution of the marriage or legal separation of the parties shall serve on the other party a preliminary declaration of disclosure under Section 2104 and a final declaration of disclosure under Section 2105, unless service of the final declaration of disclosure is waived pursuant to Section 2105 or 2110, and shall file proof of service of each with the court.

§2104. Preliminary declaration of disclosure

(a) After or concurrently with service of the petition for dissolution or nullity of marriage or legal separation of the parties, each party shall serve on the other party a preliminary declaration of disclosure, executed under penalty of perjury on a form prescribed by the Judicial Council. The commission of perjury on the preliminary declaration of disclosure may be grounds for setting aside the judgment, or any part or parts thereof, pursuant to Chapter 10 (commencing with Section 2120), in addition to any and all other remedies, civil or criminal, that otherwise are available under law for the commission of perjury.

(b) The preliminary declaration of disclosure shall not be filed with the court, except on court order; however, the parties shall file proof of service of the preliminary declaration of disclosure with the court.

(c) The preliminary declaration of disclosure shall set forth with sufficient particularity, that a person of reasonable and ordinary intelligence can ascertain, all of the following:

(1) The identity of all assets in which the declarant has or may have an interest and all liabilities for which the declarant is or may be liable, regardless of the characterization of the asset or liability as community, quasi-community, or separate.

(2) The declarant's percentage of ownership in each asset and percentage of obligation for each liability where property is not solely owned by one or both of the parties. The preliminary declaration may also set forth the declarant's characterization of each asset or liability.

(d) A declarant may amend his or her preliminary declaration of disclosure without leave of the court. Proof of service of any amendment shall be filed with the court.

(e) Along with the preliminary declaration of disclosure, each party shall provide the other party with a completed income and expense declaration unless an income and expense declaration has already been provided and is current and valid.

§2105. Final declaration of disclosure of current income and expenses; execution and service; contents; waiver; perjury or noncompliance with chapter

(a) Except by court order for good cause, before or at the time the parties enter into an agreement for the resolution of property or support issues other than pendente lite support, or, if the case goes to trial, no later than 45 days before the first assigned trial date, each party, or the attorney for the party in this matter, shall serve on the other party a final declaration of disclosure and a current income and expense declaration, executed under penalty of perjury on a form prescribed by the Judicial Council, unless the parties mutually waive the final declaration of disclosure. The commission of perjury on the final declaration of disclosure by a party may be grounds for setting aside the judgment, or any part or parts thereof, pursuant to Chapter 10 (commencing with Section 2120), in addition to any and all other remedies, civil or criminal, that otherwise are available under law for the commission of perjury.

(b) The final declaration of disclosure shall include all of the following information:

(1) All material facts and information regarding the characterization of all assets and liabilities.

(2) All material facts and information regarding the valuation of all assets that are contended to be community property or in which it is contended the community has an interest.

(3) All material facts and information regarding the amounts of all obligations that are contended to be community obligations or for which it is contended the community has liability.

(4) All material facts and information regarding the earnings, accumulations, and expenses of each party that have been set forth in the income and expense declaration.

(c) In making an order setting aside a judgment for failure to comply with this section, the court may limit the set-aside to those portions of the judgment materially affected by the nondisclosure.

(d) The parties may stipulate to a mutual waiver of the requirements of subdivision (a) concerning the final declaration of disclosure, by execution of a waiver under penalty of perjury entered into in open court or by separate stipulation. The waiver shall include all of the following representations:

(1) Both parties have complied with Section 2104 and the preliminary declarations of disclosure have been completed and exchanged.

(2) Both parties have completed and exchanged a current income and expense declaration, that includes all material facts and information regarding that party's earnings, accumulations, and expenses.

(3) Both parties have fully complied with Section 2102 and have fully augmented the preliminary declarations of disclosure, including disclosure of all material facts and information regarding the characterization of all assets and liabilities, the valuation of all assets that are contended to be community property or in which it is contended the community has an interest, and the amounts of all obligations that are contended to be community obligations or for which it is contended the community has liability.

(4) The waiver is knowingly, intelligently, and voluntarily entered into by each of the parties.

(5) Each party understands that this waiver does not limit the legal disclosure obligations of the parties, but rather is a statement under penalty of perjury that those obligations have been fulfilled. Each party further understands that noncompliance with those obligations will result in the court setting aside the judgment.

§2106. Entry of judgment; requirement of execution and service of declarations; exceptions; execution and filing of declaration of execution and service or of waiver

Except as provided in subdivision (d) of Section 2105 or in Section 2110, absent good cause, no judgment shall be entered with respect to the parties' property rights without each party, or the attorney for that party in this matter, having executed and served a copy of the final declaration of disclosure and current income and expense declaration. Each party shall execute and file with the court a declaration signed under penalty of perjury stating that service of the final declaration of disclosure and current income and expense declaration was made on the other party or that service of the final declaration of disclosure has been waived pursuant to subdivision (d) of Section 2105. . . .

§2107. Noncomplying declarations; requests to comply; remedies

(a) If one party fails to serve on the other party a preliminary declaration of disclosure under Section 2104 or a final declaration of disclosure under Section 2105, or fails to provide the information required in the respective declarations with sufficient particularity, and if the other party has served the respective declaration of disclosure on the noncomplying party, the complying party may, within a reasonable time, request preparation of the appropriate declaration of disclosure or further particularity.

(b) If the noncomplying party fails to comply with a request under subdivision (a), the complying party may do either or both of the following:

(1) File a motion to compel a further response.

(2) File a motion for an order preventing the noncomplying party from presenting evidence on issues that should have been covered in the declaration of disclosure.

(c) If a party fails to comply with any provision of this chapter, the court shall, in addition to any other remedy provided by law, impose money sanctions against the noncomplying party. Sanctions shall be in an amount sufficient to deter repetition of the conduct or comparable conduct, and shall include reasonable attorney's fees, costs incurred, or both, unless the court finds that the noncomplying party acted with substantial justification or that other circumstances make the imposition of the sanction unjust.

(d) If a court enters a judgment when the parties have failed to comply with all disclosure requirements of this chapter, the court shall set aside the judgment. The failure to comply with the disclosure requirements does not constitute harmless error.

(e) Upon the motion to set aside judgment, the court may order the parties to provide the preliminary and final declarations of disclosure that were exchanged between them. Absent a court order to the contrary, the disclosure declarations shall not be filed with the court and shall be returned to the parties.

§2108. Court authority to liquidate assets

At any time during the proceeding, the court has the authority, on application of a party and for good cause, to order the liquidation of community or quasi-community assets so as to avoid unreasonable market or investment risks, given the relative nature, scope, and extent of the community estate. However, in no event shall the court grant the application unless, as provided in this chapter, the appropriate declaration of disclosure has been served by the moving party.

§2109.   Application of chapter

The provisions of this chapter requiring a final declaration of disclosure do not apply to a summary dissolution of marriage, but a preliminary declaration of disclosure is required.

§2110.   Default judgments; declarations of disclosure

In the case of a default judgment, the petitioner may waive the final declaration of disclosure requirements provided in this chapter, and shall not be required to serve a final declaration of disclosure on the respondent nor receive a final declaration of disclosure from the respondent. However, a preliminary declaration of disclosure by the petitioner is required.

Chapter 10.   Relief from Judgment

§2120.   Legislative intent

The Legislature finds and declares the following:

(a) The State of California has a strong policy of ensuring the division of community and quasi-community property in the dissolution of a marriage as set forth in Division 7 (commencing with Section 2500), and of providing for fair and sufficient child and spousal support awards. These policy goals can only be implemented with full disclosure of community, quasi-community, and separate assets, liabilities, income, and expenses, as provided in Chapter 9 (commencing with Section 2100), and decisions freely and knowingly made.

(b) It occasionally happens that the division of property or the award of support, whether made as a result of agreement or trial, are inequitable when made due to the nondisclosure or other misconduct of one of the parties.

(c) The public policy of assuring finality of judgments must be balanced against the public interest in ensuring proper division of marital property, in ensuring sufficient support awards, and in deterring misconduct.

(d) The law governing the circumstances under which a judgment can be set aside, after the time for relief under Section 473 of the Code of Civil Procedure has passed, has been the subject of considerable confusion which has led to increased litigation and unpredictable and inconsistent decisions at the trial and appellate levels.

§2121.   Relief from adjudication of support or property
division

(a) In proceedings for dissolution of marriage, for nullity of marriage, or for legal separation of the parties, the court may, on such terms as may be just, relieve a spouse from a judgment, or any part or parts thereof, adjudicating support or division of property, after the six-month time limit of Section 473 of the

Code of Civil Procedure has run, based on the grounds, and within the time limits, provided in this chapter.

(b) In all proceedings under this chapter, before granting relief, the court shall find that the facts alleged as the grounds for relief materially affected the original outcome and that the moving party would materially benefit from the granting of the relief.

§2122. Grounds for relief; limitation of actions

The grounds and time limits for a motion to set aside a judgment, or any part or parts thereof, are governed by this section and shall be one of the following:

(a) Actual fraud where the defrauded party was kept in ignorance or in some other manner was fraudulently prevented from fully participating in the proceeding. An action or motion based on fraud shall be brought within one year after the date on which the complaining party either did discover, or should have discovered, the fraud.

(b) Perjury. An action or motion based on perjury in the preliminary or final declaration of disclosure, the waiver of the final declaration of disclosure, or in the current income and expense statement shall be brought within one year after the date on which the complaining party either did discover, or should have discovered, the perjury.

(c) Duress. An action or motion based upon duress shall be brought within two years after the date of entry of judgment.

(d) Mental incapacity. An action or motion based on mental incapacity shall be brought within two years after the date of entry of judgment.

(e) As to stipulated or uncontested judgments or that part of a judgment stipulated to by the parties, mistake, either mutual or unilateral, whether mistake of law or mistake of fact. An action or motion based on mistake shall be brought within one year after the date of entry of judgment.

(f) Failure to comply with the disclosure requirements of Chapter 9 (commencing with Section 2100). An action or motion based on failure to comply with the disclosure requirements shall be brought within one year after the date on which the complaining party either discovered, or should have discovered, the failure to comply.

§2123. Restriction on grounds for relief

Notwithstanding any other provision of this chapter, or any other law, a judgment may not be set aside simply because the court finds that it was inequitable when made, nor simply because subsequent circumstances caused the division of assets or liabilities to become inequitable, or the support to become inadequate.

§2124. Negligence of attorney

The negligence of an attorney shall not be imputed to a client to bar an order setting aside a judgment, unless the court finds that the client knew, or should have known, of the attorney's negligence and unreasonably failed to protect himself or herself.

§2125. Scope of relief

When ruling on an action or motion to set aside a judgment, the court shall set aside only those provisions materially affected by the circumstances leading to the court's decision to grant relief. However, the court has discretion to set aside the entire judgment, if necessary, for equitable considerations.

§2126. Date of valuation

As to assets or liabilities for which a judgment or part of a judgment is set aside, the date of valuation shall be subject to equitable considerations. The court shall equally divide the asset or liability, unless the court finds upon good cause shown that the interests of justice require an unequal division.

§2127. Statement of decision

As to actions or motions filed under this chapter, if a timely request is made, the court shall render a statement of decision where the court has resolved controverted factual evidence.

§2128. Effect on other law

(a) Nothing in this chapter prohibits a party from seeking relief under Section 2556.

(b) Nothing in this chapter changes existing law with respect to contract remedies where the contract has not been merged or incorporated into a judgment.

(c) Nothing in this chapter is intended to restrict a family law court from acting as a court of equity.

(d) Nothing in this chapter is intended to limit existing law with respect to the modification or enforcement of support orders.

(e) Nothing in this chapter affects the rights of a bona fide lessee, purchaser, or encumbrancer for value of real property.

§2129. Application of chapter

This chapter applies to judgments entered on or after January 1, 1993.

PART 2. JUDICIAL DETERMINATION OF VOID OR VOIDABLE MARRIAGE

Chapter 1. Void Marriage

§2200. Incestuous marriages

Marriages between parents and children, ancestors and descendants of every degree, and between brothers and sisters of the half as well as the whole blood, and between uncles and nieces or aunts and nephews, are incestuous, and void from the beginning, whether the relationship is legitimate or illegitimate.

§2201. Bigamous and polygamous marriages

(a) A subsequent marriage contracted by a person during the life of a former husband or wife of the person, with a person other than the former husband or wife, is illegal and void from the beginning, unless:

(1) The former marriage has been dissolved or adjudged a nullity before the date of the subsequent marriage.

(2) The former husband or wife (i) is absent, and not known to the person to be living for the period of five successive years immediately preceding the subsequent marriage, or (ii) is generally reputed or believed by the person to be dead at the time the subsequent marriage was contracted.

(b) In either of the cases described in paragraph (2) of subdivision (a), the subsequent marriage is valid until its nullity is adjudged pursuant to subdivision (b) of Section 2210.

Chapter 2. Voidable Marriage

§2210. Grounds for nullity

A marriage is voidable and may be adjudged a nullity if any of the following conditions existed at the time of the marriage:

(a) The party who commences the proceeding or on whose behalf the proceeding is commenced was without the capability of consenting to the marriage as provided in Section 301 or 302, unless, after attaining the age of consent, the party for any time freely cohabited with the other as husband and wife.

(b) The husband or wife of either party was living and the marriage with that husband or wife was then in force and that husband or wife (1) was absent and not known to the party commencing the proceeding to be living for a period of five successive years immediately preceding the subsequent marriage for which the judgment of nullity is sought or (2) was generally reputed or believed by the party commencing the proceeding to be dead at the time the subsequent marriage was contracted.

(c) Either party was of unsound mind, unless the party of unsound mind, after coming to reason, freely cohabited with the other as husband and wife.

(d) The consent of either party was obtained by fraud, unless the party whose consent was obtained by fraud afterwards, with full knowledge of the facts constituting the fraud, freely cohabited with the other as husband or wife.

(e) The consent of either party was obtained by force, unless the party whose consent was obtained by force afterwards freely cohabited with the other as husband or wife.

(f) Either party was, at the time of marriage, physically incapable of entering into the marriage state, and that incapacity continues, and appears to be incurable.

§2212. Effect of judgment of nullity of marriage

(a) The effect of a judgment of nullity of marriage is to restore the parties to the status of unmarried persons.

(b) A judgment of nullity of marriage is conclusive only as to the parties to the proceeding and those claiming under them.

Chapter 3. Procedural Provisions

§2250. Petition for judgment of nullity

(a) A proceeding based on void or voidable marriage is commenced by filing a petition entitled "In re the marriage of _____ and _____" which shall state that it is a petition for a judgment of nullity of the marriage. . . .

§2251. Status of putative spouse; division of quasi-marital property

(a) If a determination is made that a marriage is void or voidable and the court finds that either party or both parties believed in good faith that the marriage was valid, the court shall:

(1) Declare the party or parties to have the status of a putative spouse.

(2) If the division of property is in issue, divide, in accordance with Division 7 (commencing with Section 2500), that property acquired during the union which would have been community property or quasi-community property if the union had not been void or voidable. This property is known as "quasi-marital property."

(b) If the court expressly reserves jurisdiction, it may make the property division at a time after the judgment.

§2252. Liability of quasi-marital property for debts

The property divided pursuant to Section 2251 is liable for debts of the parties to the same extent as if the property had been community property or quasi-community property.

§2254. Support of putative spouse

The court may, during the pendency of a proceeding for nullity of marriage or upon judgment of nullity of marriage, order a party to pay for the support of the other party in the same manner as if the marriage had not been void or voidable if the party for whose benefit the order is made is found to be a putative spouse.

§2255. Attorney's fees and costs

The court may grant attorney's fees and costs in accordance with Chapter 3.5 (commencing with Section 2030) of Part 1 in proceedings to have the marriage adjudged void and in those proceedings based upon voidable marriage in which the party applying for attorney's fees and costs is found to be innocent of fraud or wrongdoing in inducing or entering into the marriage, and free from knowledge of the then existence of any prior marriage or other impediment to the contracting of the marriage for which a judgment of nullity is sought.

PART 3.   DISSOLUTION OF MARRIAGE
AND LEGAL SEPARATION

Chapter 1.   Effect of Dissolution

§2300.   Effect of dissolution

The effect of a judgment of dissolution of marriage when it becomes final is to restore the parties to the state of unmarried persons.

Chapter 2.   Grounds for Dissolution or Legal Separation

§2310.   Grounds for dissolution or legal separation

Dissolution of the marriage or legal separation of the parties may be based on either of the following grounds, which shall be pleaded generally:

(a) Irreconcilable differences, which have caused the irremediable break-down of the marriage.

(b) Incurable insanity.

§2311.   Irreconcilable differences

Irreconcilable differences are those grounds which are determined by the court to be substantial reasons for not continuing the marriage and which make it appear that the marriage should be dissolved.

Chapter 3.   Residence Requirements

§2320.   Residence requirement for dissolution judgment

A judgment of dissolution of marriage may not be entered unless one of the parties to the marriage has been a resident of this state for six months and of the county in which the proceeding is filed for three months next preceding the filing of the petition.

§2322.   Separate domicile or residence

For the purpose of a proceeding for dissolution of marriage, the husband and wife each may have a separate domicile or residence depending upon proof of the fact and not upon legal presumptions.

Chapter 4.   General Procedural Provisions

§2330.   Petition for dissolution or legal separation

(a) A proceeding for dissolution of marriage or for legal separation of the parties is commenced by filing a petition entitled "In re the marriage of _____ and _____" which shall state whether it is a petition for dissolution of the marriage or for legal separation of the parties. . . .

§2333. Court finding and order where ground is irreconcilable differences

Subject to Section 2334, if from the evidence at the hearing the court finds that there are irreconcilable differences which have caused the irremediable breakdown of the marriage, the court shall order the dissolution of the marriage or a legal separation of the parties.

§2334. Continuance for reconciliation

(a) If it appears that there is a reasonable possibility of reconciliation, the court shall continue the proceeding the dissolution of the marriage or for a legal separation of the parties for a period not to exceed 30 days.

(b) During the period of the continuance, the court make make orders for the support and maintenance of the parties, the custody of the minor children of the marriage, the support of children for whom support may be ordered, attorney's fees, and for the preservation of the property of the parties.

(c) At any time after the termination of the period of the continuance, either party may move for the dissolution of the marriage or a legal separation of the parties, and the court may enter a judgment of dissolution of the marriage or legal separation of the parties.

§2335. Evidence of specific acts of misconduct

Except as otherwise provided by statute, in a pleading or proceeding for dissolution of marriage or legal separation of the parties, including depositions and discovery proceedings, evidence of specific acts of misconduct is improper and inadmissible.

§2339. Waiting period before dissolution judgment becomes final

. . . [N]o judgment of dissolution is final for the purpose of terminating the marriage relationship of the parties until six months have expired from the date of service of a copy of summons and petition or the date of appearance of the respondent, whichever occurs first.

§2340. Statement in judgment of date marriage terminates

A judgment of dissolution of marriage shall specify the date on which the judgment becomes finally effective for the purpose of terminating the marriage relationship of the parties.

§2341. Effect of appeal or motion for new trial

. . . (b) Notwithstanding any other provision of law, the filing of an appeal or of a motion for a new trial does not stay the effect of a judgment insofar as it relates to the dissolution of the marriage status and restoring the parties to the status of unmarried persons, unless the appealing or moving party specifies in the notice of appeal or motion for new trial an objection to the termination of the marriage status. No party may make such an objection to the termination of the marriage status unless such an objection was also made at the time of trial.

§2344. Death of party after entry of judgment

(a) The death of either party after entry of the judgment does not prevent the judgment from becoming a final judgment under Sections 2339 to 2343, inclusive.

(b) Subdivision (a) does not validate a marriage by either party before the judgment becomes final, nor does it constitute a defense in a criminal prosecution against either party.

§2345. Consent to legal separation

The court may not render a judgment of the legal separation of the parties without the consent of both parties unless one party has not made a general appearance and the petition is one for legal separation.

§2346. Judgments; nunc pro tunc entry; rights to judgment

(a) If the court determines that a judgment of dissolution of the marriage should be granted, but by mistake, negligence, or inadvertence, the judgment has not been signed, filed, and entered, the court may cause the judgment to be signed, dated, filed, and entered in the proceeding as of the date when the judgment could have been signed, dated, filed, and entered originally, if it appears to the satisfaction of the court that no appeal is to be taken in the proceeding or motion made for a new trial, to annul or set aside the judgment, or for relief under Chapter 8 (commencing with Section 469) of Title 6 of Part 2 of the Code of Civil Procedure.

(b) The court may act under subdivision (a) on its own motion or upon the motion of either party to the proceeding. In contested cases, the motion of a party shall be with notice to the other party.

(c) The court may cause the judgment to be entered nunc pro tunc as provided in this section, even though the judgment may have been previously entered, where through mistake, negligence, or inadvertence the judgment was not entered as soon as it could have been entered under the law if applied for.

(d) The court shall not cause a judgment to be entered nunc pro tunc as provided in this section as of a date before trial in the matter, before the date of an uncontested judgment hearing in the matter, or before the date of submission to the court of an application for judgment on affidavit pursuant to Section 2336. Upon the entry of the judgment, the parties have the same rights with regard to the dissolution of marriage becoming final on the date that it would have become final had the judgment been entered upon the date when it could have been originally entered.

**§2347. Legal separation judgment does not bar
subsequent dissolution judgment**

A judgment of legal separation of the parties does not bar a subsequent judgment of dissolution of the marriage granted pursuant to a petition for dissolution filed by either party.

DIVISION 7.   DIVISION OF PROPERTY

PART 1.   DEFINITIONS

§2500. Application of definitions

Unless the provision or context otherwise requires, the definitions in this part govern the construction of this division.

§2502. "Separate property"

"Separate property" does not include quasi-community property.

PART 2.   GENERAL PROVISIONS

§2550. Equal division of community estate

Except upon the written agreement of the parties, or on oral stipulation of the parties in open court, or as otherwise provided in this division, in a proceeding for dissolution of marriage or for legal separation of the parties, the court shall, either in its judgment of dissolution of the marriage, in its judgment of legal separation of the parties, or at a later time if it expressly reserves jurisdiction to make such a property division, divide the community estate of the parties equally.

**§2551. Characterization of liabilities as separate or
community and confirming or assigning them
to parties**

For the purposes of division and in confirming or assigning the liabilities of the parties for which the community estate is liable, the court shall characterize liabilities as separate or community and confirm or assign them to the parties in accordance with Part 6 (commencing with Section 2620).

§2552. Valuation date for assets and liabilities

(a) For the purpose of division of the community estate upon dissolution of marriage or legal separation of the parties, except as provided in subdivision (b), the court shall value the assets and liabilities as near as practicable to the time of trial.

(b) Upon 30 days' notice by the moving party to the other party, the court for good cause shown may value all or any portion of the assets and liabilities at a date after separation and before trial to accomplish an equal division of the community estate of the parties in an equitable manner.

§2553. Orders necessary to carry out purposes of this division

The court may make any orders the court considers necessary to carry out the purposes of this division.

§2554. Arbitration where parties do not voluntarily agree to division

(a) Notwithstanding any other provision of this division, in any case in which the parties do not agree in writing to a voluntary division of the community estate of the parties, the issue of the character, the value, and the division of the community estate may be submitted by the court to arbitration for resolution pursuant to Chapter 2.5 (commencing with Section 1141.10) of Title 3 of Part 3 of the Code of Civil Procedure, if the total value of the community and quasi-community property in controversy in the opinion of the court does not exceed fifty thousand dollars ($50,000). The decision of the court regarding the value of the community and quasi-community property for purposes of this section is not appealable.

(b) The court may submit the matter to arbitration at any time it believes the parties are unable to agree upon a division of the property.

§2555. Revision of property disposition on appeal

The disposition of the community estate, as provided in this division, is subject to revision on appeal in all particulars, including those which are stated to be in the discretion of the court.

§2556. Continuing jurisdiction to award community estate assets or liabilities

In a proceeding for dissolution of marriage, for nullity of marriage, or for legal separation of the parties, the court has continuing jurisdiction to award community estate assets or community estate liabilities to the parties that have not been previously adjudicated by a judgment in the proceeding. A party may file a postjudgment motion or order to show cause in the proceeding in order to obtain adjudication of any community estate asset or liability omitted or not adjudicated by the judgment. In these cases, the court shall equally divide the omitted or unadjudicated community estate asset or liability, unless the court finds upon good cause shown that the interests of justice require an unequal division of the asset or liability.

PART 3.   PRESUMPTION CONCERNING PROPERTY HELD IN JOINT FORM

§2580.   Legislative findings and declarations

The Legislature hereby finds and declares as follows:

(a) It is the public policy of this state to provide uniformly and consistently for the standard of proof in establishing the character of property acquired by spouses during marriage in joint title form, and for the all allocation of community and separate interests in that property between the spouses.

(b) The methods provided by case and statutory law have not resulted in consistency in the treatment of spouses' interests in property they hold in joint title, but rather, have created confusion as to which law applies to property at a particular point in time, depending on the form of title, and, as a result, spouses cannot have reliable expectations as to the characterization of their property and the allocation of the interests therein, and attorneys cannot reliably advise their clients regarding applicable law.

(c) Therefore, a compelling state interest exists to provide for uniform treatment of property; thus, former Sections 4800.1 and 4800.2 of the Civil Code, as operative on January 1, 1987, and as continued in Sections 2581 and 2640 of this code, apply to all property held in joint title regardless of the date of acquisition of the property or the date of any agreement affecting the character of the property, and those sections apply in all proceedings commenced on or after January 1, 1984. However, those sections do not apply to property settlement agreements executed before January 1, 1987, or proceedings in which judgments were rendered before January 1, 1987, regardless of whether those judgments have become final.

§2581.   Community property presumption for property held in joint form

For the purpose of division of property on dissolution of marriage or legal separation of the parties, property acquired by the parties during marriage in joint form, including property held in tenancy in common, joint tenancy, or tenancy by the entirety, or as community property, is presumed to be community property. This presumption is a presumption affecting the burden of proof and may be rebutted by either of the following:

(a) A clear statement in the deed or other documentary evidence of title by which the property is acquired that the property is separate property and not community property.

(b) Proof that the parties have made a written agreement that the property is separate property.

PART 4.   SPECIAL RULES FOR DIVISION OF COMMUNITY ESTATE

§2600.   Special rules for division of community estate

Notwithstanding Sections 2550 to 2552, inclusive, the court may divide the community estate as provided in this part.

§2601. Awarding asset to one party to effect substantially equal division

Where economic circumstances warrant, the court may award an asset of the community estate to one party on such conditions as the court deems proper to effect a substantially equal division of the community estate.

§2602. Award or offset of amount deliberately misappropriated by party

As an additional award or offset against existing property, the court may award, from a party's share, the amount the court determines to have been deliberately misappropriated by the party to the exclusion of the interest of the other party in the community estate.

§2603. Community estate personal injury damages

(a) "Community estate personal injury damages" as used in this section means all money or other property received or to be received by a person in satisfaction of a judgment for damages for the person's personal injuries or pursuant to an agreement for the settlement or compromise of a claim for the damages, if the cause of action for the damages arose during the marriage but is not separate property as described in Section 781, unless the money or other property has been commingled with other assets of the community estate.

(b) Community estate personal injury damages shall be assigned to the party who suffered the injuries unless the court, after taking into account the economic condition and needs of each party, the time that has elapsed since the recovery of the damages or the accrual of the cause of action, and all other facts of the case, determines that the interests of justice require another disposition. In such a case, the community estate personal injury damages shall be assigned to the respective parties in such proportions as the court determines to be just, except that at least one-half of the damages shall be assigned to the party who suffered the injuries.

§2604. Award where community estate less than $5,000 and one party cannot be located

If the net value of the community estate is less than five thousand dollars ($5,000) and one party cannot be located through the exercise of reasonable diligence, the court may award all the community estate to the other party on conditions the court deems proper in its judgment of dissolution of marriage or legal separation of the parties.

PART 5. RETIREMENT PLAN BENEFITS

§2610. Retirement plans; orders to ensure benefits

(a) Except as provided in subdivision (b), the court shall make whatever orders are necessary or appropriate to ensure that each party receives the party's full community property share in any retirement plan, whether public or private, including all survivor and death benefits, including, but not limited to, any of the following:

(1) Order the disposition of any retirement benefits payable upon or after the death of either party in a manner consistent with Section 2550.

(2) Order a party to elect a survivor benefit annuity or other similar election for the benefit of the other party, as specified by the court, in any case in which a retirement plan provides for such an election, provided that no court shall order a retirement plan to provide increased benefits determined on the basis of actuarial value.

(3) Upon the agreement of the nonemployee spouse, order the division of accumulated community property contributions and service credit as provided in the following or similar enactments:

(A) Article 1.2 (commencing with Section 21215) of Chapter 9 of Part 3 of Division 5 of Title 2 of the Government Code.

(B) Chapter 12 (commencing with Section 22650) of Part 13 of the Education Code.

(C) Article 8.4 (commencing with Section 31685) of Chapter 3 of Part 3 of Division 4 of Title 3 of the Government Code.

(D) Article 2.5 (commencing with Section 75050) of Chapter 11 of Title 8 of the Government Code.

(E) Chapter 15 (commencing with Section 27400) of Part 14 of the Education Code.

(4) Order a retirement plan to make payments directly to a nonmember party of his or her community property interest in retirement benefits.

(b) A court shall not make any order that requires a retirement plan to do either of the following:

(1) Make payments in any manner that will result in an increase in the amount of benefits provided by the plan.

(2) Make the payment of benefits to any party at any time before the member retires, except as provided in paragraph (3) of subdivision (a), unless the plan so provides. . . .

PART 6.   DEBTS AND LIABILITIES

§2620.   Confirmation or division of community estate debts

The debts for which the community estate is liable which are unpaid at the time of trial, or for which the community estate becomes liable after trial, shall be confirmed or divided as provided in this part.

§2621.   Debts incurred before marriage

Debts incurred by either spouse before the date of marriage shall be confirmed without offset to the spouse who incurred the debt.

§2622. Debts incurred after marriage but before separation

(a) Except as provided in subdivision (b), debts incurred by either spouse after the date of marriage but before the date of separation shall be divided as set forth in Sections 2550 to 2552, inclusive, and Sections 2601 to 2604, inclusive.

(b) To the extent that community debts exceed total community and quasi-community assets, the excess of debt shall be assigned as the court deems just and equitable, taking into account factors such as the parties' relative ability to pay.

§2623. Debts incurred after separation but before judgment

Debts incurred by either spouse after the date of separation but before entry of a judgment of dissolution of marriage or legal separation of the parties shall be confirmed as follows:

(a) Debts incurred by either spouse for the common necessaries of life of either spouse or the necessaries of life of the children of the marriage for whom support may be ordered, in the absence of a court order or written agreement for support or for the payment of these debts, shall be confirmed to either spouse according to the parties' respective needs and abilities to pay at the time the debt was incurred.

(b) Debts incurred by either spouse for nonnecessaries of that spouse or children of the marriage for whom support may be ordered shall be confirmed without offset to the spouse who incurred the debt.

§2624. Debts incurred after entry of judgment

Debts incurred by either spouse after entry of a judgment of dissolution of marriage but before termination of the parties' marital status or after entry of a judgment of legal separation of the parties shall be confirmed without offset to the spouse who incurred the debt.

§2625. Separate debts

Notwithstanding Sections 2620 to 2624, inclusive, all separate debts, including whose debts incurred by a spouse during marriage and before the date of separation that were not incurred for the benefit of the community, shall be confirmed without offset to the spouse who incurred the debt.

§2626. Reimbursement for debts paid after separation but before trial

The court has jurisdiction to order reimbursement in cases it deems appropriate for debts paid after separation but before trial.

§2627. Educational loans and tort liability

Notwithstanding Sections 2550 to 2552, inclusive, and Sections 2620 to 2624, inclusive, educational loans shall be assigned pursuant to Section 2641 and liabilities subject to paragraph (2) of subdivision (b) of Section 1000 shall be assigned to the spouse whose act or omission provided the basis for the liability, without offset.

PART 7.   REIMBURSEMENTS

§2640. Separate property contributions to community estate property acquisition

(a) "Contributions to the acquisition of the property," as used in this section, include downpayments, payments for improvements, and payments that reduce the principal of a loan used to finance the purchase or improvement of the property but do not include payments of interest on the loan or payments made for maintenance, insurance, or taxation of the property.

(b) In the division of the community estate, under this division, unless a party has made a written waiver of the right to reimbursement or has signed a writing that has the effect of a waiver, the party shall be reimbursed for the party's contributions to the acquisition of the property to the extent the party traces the contributions to a separate property source. The amount reimbursed shall be without interest or adjustment for change in monetary values and shall not exceed the net value of the property at the time of the division.

§2641. Community contributions to education or training

(a) "Community contributions to education or training" as used in this section means payments made with community or quasi-community property for education or training or for the repayment of a loan incurred for education or training, whether the payments were made while the parties were resident in this state or resident outside this state.

(b) Subject to the limitations provided in this section, upon dissolution of marriage or legal separation of the parties:

(1) The community shall be reimbursed for community contributions to education or training of a party that substantially enhances the earning capacity of the party. The amount reimbursed shall be with interest at the legal rate, accruing from the end of the calendar year in which the contributions were made.

(2) A loan incurred during marriage for the education or training of a party shall not be included among the liabilities of the community for the purpose of division pursuant to this division but shall be assigned for payment by the party.

(c) The reimbursement and assignment required by this section shall be reduced or modified to the extent circumstances render such a disposition unjust, including, but not limited to, any of the following:

(1) The community has substantially benefited from the education, training, or loan incurred for the education or training of the party. There is a rebuttable presumption, affecting the burden of proof, that the community

has not substantially benefited from community contributions to the education or training made less than 10 years before the commencement of the proceeding, and that the community has substantially benefited from community contributions to the education or training made more than 10 years before the commencement of the proceeding.

(2) The education or training received by the party is offset by the education or training received by the other party for which community contributions have been made.

(3) The education or training enables the party receiving the education or training to engage in gainful employment that substantially reduces the need of the party for support that would otherwise be required.

(d) Reimbursement for community contributions and assignment of loans pursuant to this section is the exclusive remedy of the community or a party for the education or training and any resulting enhancement of the earning capacity of a party. However, nothing in this subdivision limits consideration of the effect of the education, training, or enhancement, or the amount reimbursed pursuant to this section, on the circumstances of the parties for the purpose of an order for support pursuant to Section 4320.

(e) This section is subject to an express written agreement of the parties to the contrary.

PART 8.   JOINTLY HELD SEPARATE PROPERTY

§2650.   Division of jointly held separate property

In a proceeding for division of the community estate, the court has jurisdiction, at the request of either party, to divide the separate property interests of the parties in real and personal property, wherever situated and whenever acquired, held by the parties as joint tenants or tenants in common. The property shall be divided together with, and in accordance with the same procedure for and limitations on, division of community estate.

PART 9.   REAL PROPERTY LOCATED IN ANOTHER STATE

§2660.   Division where community estate includes real property located in another state

(a) Except as provided in subdivision (b), if the property subject to division includes real property situated in another state, the court shall, if possible, divide the community property and quasi-community property as provided for in this division in such a manner that it is not necessary to change the nature of the interests held in the real property situated in the other state.

(b) If it is not possible to divide the property in the manner provided for in subdivision (a), the court may do any of the following in order to effect a division of the property as provided for in this division:

(1) Require the parties to execute conveyances or take other actions with respect to the real property situated in the other state as are necessary.

(2) Award to the party who would have been benefited by the conveyances or other actions the money value of the interest in the property that the party would have received if the conveyances had been executed or other actions taken.

DIVISION 9.   SUPPORT

PART 1.   DEFINITIONS AND GENERAL PROVISIONS

Chapter 1.   Definitions

§3500.   Application of definitions

Unless the provision or context otherwise requires, the definitions in this chapter govern the construction of this division.

§3515.   Separate property

"Separate property" does not include quasi-community property.

Chapter 3.   Support Agreements

Article 1.   General Provisions

§3580.   Provisions for spousal and child support in separation agreement

Subject to this chapter and to Section 3651, a husband and wife may agree, in writing, to an immediate separation, and may provide in the agreement for the support of either of them and of their children during the separation or upon the dissolution of their marriage. The mutual consent of the parties is sufficient consideration for the agreement.

Article 3.   Spousal Support

§3590.   Support agreement severable and enforceable by court

The provisions of an agreement for support of either party shall be deemed to be separate and severable from the provisions of the agreement relating to property. An order for support of either party based on the agreement shall be law-imposed and shall be made under the power of the court to order spousal support.

§3591. Authority to modify or terminate spousal support agreement

(a) Except as provided in subdivisions (b) and (c), the provisions of an agreement for the support of either party are subject to subsequent modification or termination by court order.

(b) An agreement may not be modified or terminated as to an amount that accrued before the date of the filing of the notice of motion or order to show cause to modify or terminate.

(c) An agreement for spousal support may not be modified or revoked to the extent that a written agreement, or, if there is no written agreement, an oral agreement entered into in open court between the parties, specifically provides that the spousal support is not subject to modification or termination.

§3592. Agreement discharged in bankruptcy

If an obligation under an agreement for settlement of property to a spouse or for support of a spouse is discharged in bankruptcy, the court may make all proper orders for the support of the spouse, as the court determines are just, having regard for the circumstances of the parties and the amount of the obligations under the agreement that are discharged.

Chapter 6.   Modification or Termination of Support

Article 1.   General Provisions

§3650. "Support order" defined

Unless the provision or context otherwise requires, as used in this chapter, "support order" means a child, family, or spousal support order.

§3651. Authority to modify or terminate

(a) Except as provided in subdivisions (c) and (d) . . . , a support order may be modified or terminated at any time as the court determines to be necessary. . . .

(c) . . . [A] support order may not be modified or terminated as to an amount that accrued before the date of the filing of the notice of motion or order to show cause to modify or terminate.

(d) An order for spousal support may not be modified or terminated to the extent that a written agreement, or, if there is no written agreement, an oral agreement entered into in open court between the parties, specifically provides that the spousal support is not subject to modification or termination.

(e) This section applies whether or not the support order is based upon an agreement between the parties. . . .

Chapter 8.   Deferred Sale of Home Order

§3800. Definitions

As used in this chapter:

(a) "Custodial parent" means a party awarded physical custody of a child.

(b) "Deferred sale of home order" means an order that temporarily delays the sale and awards the temporary exclusive use and possession of the family home to a custodial parent of a minor child . . . whether or not the custodial parent has sole or joint custody, in order to minimize the adverse impact of dissolution of marriage or legal separation of the parties on the welfare of the child.

(c) "Resident parent" means a party who has requested or who has already been awarded a deferred sale of home order.

§3801. Determination of economic feasibility

(a) If one of the parties has requested a deferred sale of home order pursuant to this chapter, the court shall first determine whether it is economically feasible to maintain the payments of any note secured by a deed of trust, property taxes, insurance for the home during the period the sale of the home is deferred, and the condition of the home comparable to that at the time of trial.

(b) In making this determination, the court shall consider all of the following:

(1) The resident parent's income.

(2) The availability of spousal support, child support, or both spousal and child support.

(3) Any other sources of funds available to make those payments.

(c) It is the intent of the Legislature, by requiring the determination under this section, to do all of the following:

(1) Avoid the likelihood of possible defaults on the payments of notes and resulting foreclosures.

(2) Avoid inadequate insurance coverage.

(3) Prevent deterioration of the condition of the family home.

(4) Prevent any other circumstance which would jeopardize both parents' equity in the home.

§3802. Matters to be considered by court in determining whether to grant order

(a) If the court determines pursuant to Section 3801 that it is economically feasible to consider ordering a deferred sale of the family home, the court may grant a deferred sale of home order to a custodial parent if the court determines that the order is necessary in order to minimize the adverse impact of dissolution of marriage or legal separation of the parties on the child.

(b) In exercising its discretion to grant or deny a deferred sale of home order, the court shall consider all of the following:

(1) The length of time the child has resided in the home.

(2) The child's placement or grade in school.

(3) The accessibility and convenience of the home to the child's school and other services or facilities used by and available to the child, including child care.

(4) Whether the home has been adapted or modified to accommodate any physical disabilities of a child or a resident parent in a manner that a change in residence may adversely affect the ability of the resident parent to meet the needs of the child.

(5) The emotional detriment to the child associated with a change in residence.

(6) The extent to which the location of the home permits the resident parent to continue employment.

(7) The financial ability of each parent to obtain suitable housing.

(8) The tax consequences to the parents.

(9) The economic detriment to the nonresident parent in the event of a deferred sale of home order.

(10) Any other factors the court deems just and equitable.

§3806. Order concerning maintenance and capital improvements

The court may make an order specifying the parties' respective responsibilities for the payment of the costs of routine maintenance and capital improvements.

§3807. Modification or termination of order

Except as otherwise agreed to by the parties in writing, a deferred sale of home order may be modified or terminated at any time at the discretion of the court.

§3808. Presumption arising upon remarriage or other change in circumstances

Except as otherwise agreed to by the parties in writing, if the party awarded the deferred sale of home order remarries, or if there is otherwise a change in circumstances affecting the determinations made pursuant to Section 3801 or 3802 or affecting the economic status of the parties or the children on which the award is based, a rebuttable presumption, affecting the burden of proof, is created that further deferral of the sale is no longer an equitable method of minimizing the adverse impact of the dissolution of marriage or legal separation of the parties on the children.

§3809. Reservation of jurisdiction by court

In making an order pursuant to this chapter, the court shall reserve jurisdiction to determine any issues that arise with respect to the deferred sale of home order including, but not limited to, the maintenance of the home and the tax consequences to each party.

PART 2.   CHILD SUPPORT

Chapter 1.   Duty of Parent to Support Child

Article 1.   Support of Minor Child

§3900. Duty of parents

Subject to this division, the father and mother of a minor child have an equal responsibility to support their child in the manner suitable to the child's circumstances.

Chapter 2.   Court-Ordered Child Support

Article 1.   General Provisions

§4000.   Civil action to enforce parent's duty to support

If a parent has the duty to provide for the support of the parent's child and willfully fails to so provide, the other parent, or the child by a guardian ad litem, may bring an action against the parent to enforce the duty.

Article 2.   Statewide Uniform Guideline

§4050.   Legislative intent

In adopting the statewide uniform guideline provided in this article, it is the intention of the Legislature to ensure that this state remains in compliance with federal regulations for child support guidelines.

§4052.   Mandatory adherence to guideline

The court shall adhere to the statewide uniform guideline and may depart from the guideline only in the special circumstances set forth in this article.

§4053.   Mandatory adherence to principles

In implementing the statewide uniform guideline, the courts shall adhere to the following principles:

(a) A parent's first and principal obligation is to support his or her minor children according to the parent's circumstances and station in life.

(b) Both parents are mutually responsible for the support of their children.

(c) The guideline takes into account each parent's actual income and level of responsibility for the children.

(d) Each parent should pay for the support of the children according to his or her ability.

(e) The guideline seeks to place the interests of children as the state's top priority.

(f) Children should share in the standard of living of both parents. Child support may therefore appropriately improve the standard of living of the custodial household to improve the lives of the children.

(g) Child support orders in cases in which both parents have high levels of responsibility for the children should reflect the increased costs of raising the children in two homes and should minimize significant disparities in the children's living standards in the two homes.

(h) The financial needs of the children should be met through private financial resources as much as possible.

(i) It is presumed that a parent having primary physical responsibility for the children contributes a significant portion of available resources for the support of the children.

(j) The guideline seeks to encourage fair and efficient settlements of conflicts between parents and seeks to minimize the need for litigation.

(k) The guideline is intended to be presumptively correct in all cases, and only under special circumstances should child support orders fall below the child support mandated by the guideline formula.

(l) Child support orders must ensure that children actually receive fair, timely, and sufficient support reflecting the state's high standard of living and high costs of raising children compared to other states.

§4054. Periodic review by Judicial Council

(a) The Judicial Council shall periodically review the statewide uniform guideline to recommend to the Legislature appropriate revisions.

(b) The review shall include economic data on the cost of raising children and analysis of case data, gathered through sampling or other methods, on the actual application of the guideline after the guideline's operative date. The review shall also include an analysis of guidelines and studies from other states, and other research and studies available to or undertaken by the Judicial Council.

(c) Any recommendations for revisions to the guideline shall be made to ensure that the guideline results in appropriate child support orders, to limit deviations from the guideline, or otherwise to help ensure that the guideline is in compliance with federal law. . . .

(f) In developing its recommendations, the Judicial Council shall consult with a broad cross-section of groups involved in child support issues, including, but not limited to, the following:

(1) Custodial and noncustodial parents.

(2) Representatives of established women's rights and fathers' rights groups.

(3) Representatives of established organizations that advocate for the economic well-being of children.

(4) Members of the judiciary, district attorney's offices, the Attorney General's office, and the Department of Child Support.

(5) Certified family law specialists.

(6) Academicians specializing in family law.

(7) Persons representing low-income parents.

(8) Persons representing recipients of assistance under the CalWORKS program seeking child support services.

(g) In developing its recommendations, the Judicial Council shall seek public comment and shall be guided by the legislative intent that children share in the standard of living of both of their parents.

§4055. Formula for statewide uniform guideline for determining child support

(a) The statewide uniform guideline for determining child support orders is as follows: $CS = K[HN - (H\%)(TN)]$.

(b)(1) The components of the formula are as follows:

(A) CS = child support amount.

(B) K = amount of income to be allocated for child support as set forth in paragraph (3).

(C) HN = high earner's net monthly disposable income.

(D) $H\%$ = approximate percentage of time that high earner has or will have primary physical responsibility for the children compared to the other parent. In cases in which parents have different time-sharing arrangements for different children, H% equals the average of the approximate percentages of time the high earner parent spends with each child.

(E) TN = total net monthly disposable income of both parties.

(2) To compute net disposable income, see Section 4059.

(3) K (amount of income allocated for child support) equals one plus H% (if H% is less than or equal to 50 percent) or two minus H% (if H% is greater than 50 percent) times the following fraction:

Total Net Disposable Income per Month	K
$0-800	0.20 + TN/16,000
$801-6,666	0.25
$6,667-10,000	0.10 + 1,000/TN
Over $10,000	0.12 + 800/TN

For example, if H% equals 20% and the total monthly net disposable income of the parents is $1,000, K = (1 + 0.20) × 0.25, or 0.30. If H% equals 80% and the total monthly net disposable income of the parents is $1,000, K = (2 − 0.80) × 0.25, or 0.30.

(4) For more than one child, multiply CS by:

2 children	1.6
3 children	2
4 children	2.3
5 children	2.5
6 children	2.625
7 children	2.75
8 children	2.813
9 children	2.844
10 children	2.86

(5) If the amount calculated under the formula results in a positive number, the higher earner shall pay that amount to the lower earner. If the amount calculated under the formula results in a negative number, the lower earner shall pay the absolute value of that amount to the higher earner. . . .

§4056. Amount differing from guideline formula; information used in determining statewide uniform guideline amount

(a) To comply with federal law, the court shall state, in writing or on the record, the following information whenever the court is ordering an amount for support that differs from the statewide uniform guideline formula amount under this article:

(1) The amount of support that would have been ordered under the guideline formula.

(2) The reasons the amount of support ordered differs from the guideline formula amount.

(3) The reasons the amount of support ordered is consistent with the best interests of the children.

(b) At the request of any party, the court shall state in writing or on the record the following information used in determining the guideline amount under this article:

(1) The net monthly disposable income of each parent.

(2) The actual federal income tax filing status of each parent (for example, single, married, married filing separately, or head of household and number of exemptions).

(3) Deductions from gross income for each parent.

(4) The approximate percentage of time pursuant to paragraph (1) of subdivision (b) of Section 4055 that each parent has primary physical responsibility for the children compared to the other parent.

§4057. Presumption that child support established by guideline is correct; rebuttal of presumption

(a) The amount of child support established by the formula provided in subdivision (a) of Section 4055 is presumed to be the correct amount of child support to be ordered.

(b) The presumption of subdivision (a) is a rebuttable presumption affecting the burden of proof and may be rebutted by admissible evidence showing that application of the formula would be unjust or inappropriate in the particular case, consistent with the principles set forth in Section 4053, because one or more of the following factors is found to be applicable by a preponderance of the evidence, and the court states in writing or on the record the information required in subdivision (a) of Section 4056:

(1) The parties have stipulated to a different amount of child support under subdivision (a) of Section 4065.

(2) The sale of the family residence is deferred pursuant to Chapter 8 (commencing with Section 3800) of Part 1 and the rental value of the family residence in which the children reside exceeds the mortgage payments, homeowner's insurance, and property taxes. The amount of any adjustment pursuant to this paragraph shall not be greater than the excess amount.

(3) The parent being ordered to pay child support has an extraordinarily high income and the amount determined under the formula would exceed the needs of the children.

(4) A party is not contributing to the needs of the children at a level commensurate with that party's custodial time.

(5) Application of the formula would be unjust or inappropriate due to special circumstances in the particular case. These special circumstances include, but are not limited to, the following:

(A) Cases in which the parents have different time-sharing arrangements for different children.

(B) Cases in which both parents have substantially equal time-sharing of the children and one parent has a much lower or higher percentage of income used for housing than the other parent.

(C) Cases in which the children have special medical or other needs that could require child support that would be greater than the formula amount.

§4058. Annual gross income

(a) The annual gross income of each parent means income from whatever source derived, except as specified in paragraph (c) and includes, but is not limited to, all of the following:

(1) Income such as commissions, salaries, royalties, wages, bonuses, rents, dividends, pensions, interest, trust income, annuities, workers' compensation benefits, unemployment insurance benefits, disability insurance benefits, social security benefits, and spousal support actually received from a person not a party to the proceeding to establish a child support order under this article.

(2) Income from the proprietorship of a business, such as gross receipts from the business reduced by expenditures required for the operation of the business.

(3) In the discretion of the court, employee benefits or self-employment benefits, taking into consideration the benefit to the employee, any corresponding reduction in living expenses, and other relevant facts.

(b) The court may, in its discretion, consider the earning capacity of a parent in lieu of the parent's income, consistent with the best interests of the children.

(c) Annual gross income does not include any income derived from child support payments actually received, and income derived from any public assistance program, eligibility for which is based on a determination of need. Child support received by a party for children from another relationship shall not be included as part of that party's gross or net income.

§4059. Annual net disposable income

The annual net disposable income of each parent shall be computed by deducting from his or her annual gross income the actual amounts attributable to the following items or other items permitted under this article:

(a) The state and federal income tax liability resulting from the parties' taxable income. . . . State and federal income taxes shall be those actually payable (not necessarily current withholding) after considering appropriate filing status, all available exclusions, deductions, and credits. . . .

(b) Deductions attributed to the employee's contribution or the self-employed worker's contribution pursuant to the Federal Insurance Contributions Act (FICA), or an amount not to exceed that allowed under FICA for persons not subject to FICA, provided that the deducted amount is used to secure retirement or disability benefits for the parent.

(c) Deductions for mandatory union dues and retirement benefits, provided that they are required as a condition of employment.

(d) Deductions for health insurance or health plan premiums for the parent and for any children the parent has an obligation to support and deductions for state disability insurance premiums.

(e) Any child or spousal support actually being paid by the parent pursuant to a court order, to or for the benefit of any person who is not a subject of the order to be established by the court. In the absence of a court order, any child support actually being paid, not to exceed the amount established by the guideline, for natural or adopted children of the parent not residing in that parent's home, who are not the subject of the order to be established by the court, and of whom the parent has a duty of support. Unless the parent proves payment of the support, no deduction shall be allowed under this subdivision.

(f) Job-related expenses, if allowed by the court after consideration of whether the expenses are necessary, the benefit to the employee, and any other relevant facts.

(g) A deduction for hardship, as defined by Sections 4070 to 4073, inclusive, and applicable published appellate court decisions. The amount of the hardship shall not be deducted from the amount of child support, but shall be deducted from the income of the party to whom it applies. In applying any hardship under paragraph (2) of subdivision (a) of Section 4071, the court shall seek to provide equity between competing child support orders. . . .

§4060. Monthly net disposable income

The monthly net disposable income shall be computed by dividing the annual net disposable income by 12. If the monthly net disposable income figure does not accurately reflect the actual or prospective earnings of the parties at the time the determination of support is made, the court may adjust the amount appropriately.

§4061. Allocation of additional child support;
adjusted net disposable income

The amounts in Section 4062, if ordered to be paid, shall be considered additional support for the children and shall be computed in accordance with the following:

(a) If there needs to be an apportionment of expenses pursuant to Section 4062, the expenses shall be divided one-half to each parent, unless either parent requests a different apportionment pursuant to subdivision (b) and presents documentation which demonstrates that a different apportionment would be more appropriate.

(b) If requested by either parent, and the court determines it is appropriate to apportion expenses under Section 4062 other than one-half to each parent, the apportionment shall be as follows:

(1) The basic child support obligation shall first be computed using the formula set forth in subdivision (a) of Section 4055, as adjusted for any appropriate rebuttal factors in subdivision (b) of Section 4057.

(2) Any additional child support required for expenses pursuant to Section 4062 shall thereafter be ordered to be paid by the parents in proportion to their net disposable incomes as adjusted pursuant to subdivisions (c) and (d).

(c) In cases where spousal support is or has been ordered to be paid by one parent to the other, for purposes of allocating additional expenses pursuant to Section 4062, the gross income of the parent paying spousal support shall be decreased by the amount of the spousal support paid and the gross income of the parent receiving the spousal support shall be increased by the amount of the spousal support received for so long as the spousal support order is in effect and is paid.

(d) For purposes of computing the adjusted net disposable income of the parent paying child support for allocating any additional expenses pursuant to Section 4062, the net disposable income of the parent paying child support shall be reduced by the amount of any basic child support ordered to be paid under subdivision (a) of Section 4055. However, the net disposable income of the parent receiving child support shall not be increased by any amount of child support received.

§4062. Additional child support

(a) The court shall order the following as additional child support:

(1) Child care costs related to employment or to reasonably necessary education or training for employment skills.

(2) The reasonable uninsured health care costs for the children as provided in Section 4063. . . .

(b) The court may order the following as additional child support:

(1) Costs related to the educational or other special needs of the children.

(2) Travel expenses for visitation.

§4064. Adjustment for seasonal or fluctuating income

The court may adjust the child support order as appropriate to accommodate seasonal or fluctuating income of either parent.

§4065. Stipulated child support agreement

(a) Unless prohibited by applicable federal law, the parties may stipulate to a child support amount subject to approval of the court. However, the court shall not approve a stipulated agreement unless the parties declare all of the following:

(1) They are fully informed of their rights concerning child support.

(2) The order is being agreed to without coercion or duress.

(3) The agreement is in the best interests of the children involved.

(4) The needs of the children will be adequately met by the stipulated amount. . . .

(d) If the parties to a stipulated agreement stipulate to a child support order below the amount established by the statewide uniform guideline, no change of circumstances need be demonstrated to obtain a modification of the child support order to the applicable guideline level or above.

§4066. Order or stipulation designating family support

Orders and stipulations otherwise in compliance with the statewide uniform guideline may designate as "family support" an unallocated total sum for support of the spouse and any children without specifically labeling all or any portion as "child support" so long as the amount is adjusted to reflect the effect of additional deductibility. The amount of the order shall be adjusted to maximize the tax benefits for both parents.

§4070. Financial hardship deductions

If a parent is experiencing extreme financial hardship due to justifiable expenses resulting from the circumstances enumerated in Sections 4071 and 4072, on the request of a party, the court may allow the income deductions under Section 4059 that may be necessary to accommodate those circumstances.

§4071. Circumstances evidencing hardship

(a) Circumstances evidencing hardship include the following:

(1) Extraordinary health expenses for which the parent is financially responsible, and uninsured catastrophic losses.

(2) The minimum basic living expenses of either parent's natural or adopted children for whom the parent has the obligation to support from other marriages or relationships who reside with the parent. The court, on its own motion or on the request of a party, may allow such income deductions as necessary to accommodate these expenses after making the deductions allowable under paragraph (1).

(b) The maximum hardship deduction under paragraph (2) of subdivision (a) for each child who resides with the parent may be equal to, but shall not exceed, the support awarded each child subject to the order. For purposes of calculating this deduction, the amount of support per child established by the statewide uniform guideline shall be the total amount ordered divided by the number of children and not the amount established under paragraph (8) of subdivision (b) of Section 4055.

(c) The Judicial Council may develop tables in accordance with this section to reflect the maximum hardship deduction, taking into consideration the parent's net disposable income before the hardship deduction, the number of children for whom the deduction is being given, and the number of children for whom the support award is being made.

§4072. Statement of reasons for and duration of hardship deductions

(a) If a deduction for hardship expenses is allowed, the court shall do both of the following:

(1) State the reasons supporting the deduction in writing or on the record.

(2) Document the amount of the deduction and the underlying facts and circumstances.

(b) Whenever possible, the court shall specify the duration of the deduction.

§4073. Court to consider legislative goals when ordering hardship deduction

The court shall be guided by the goals set forth in this article when considering whether or not to allow a financial hardship deduction, and, if allowed, when determining the amount of the deduction.

PART 3.   SPOUSAL SUPPORT

Chapter 1.   Duty to Support Spouse

§4300.   Duty to support spouse

Subject to this division, a person shall support the person's spouse.

§4301.   Use of separate property for support while living together

Subject to Section 914, a person shall support the person's spouse while they are living together out of the separate property of the person when there is no community property or quasi-community property.

§4302.   Spouse living separate by agreement

A person is not liable for support of the person's spouse when the person is living separate from the spouse by agreement unless support is stipulated in the agreement.

Chapter 2.   Factors to Be Considered in Ordering Support

§4320.   Determination of amount due for support; considerations

In ordering spousal support under this part, the court shall consider all of the following circumstances:

(a) The extent to which the earning capacity of each party is sufficient to maintain the standard of living established during the marriage, taking into account all of the following:

(1) The marketable skills of the supported party; the job market for those skills; the time and expenses required for the supported party to acquire the appropriate education or training to develop those skills; and the possible need for retraining or education to acquire other, more marketable skills or employment.

(2) The extent to which the supported party's present or future earning capacity is impaired by periods of unemployment that were incurred during the marriage to permit the supported party to devote time to domestic duties.

(b) The extent to which the supported party contributed to the attainment of an education, training, a career position, or a license by the supporting party.

(c) The ability of the supporting party to pay spousal support, taking into account the supporting party's earning capacity, earned and unearned income, assets, and standard of living.

(d) The needs of each party based on the standard of living established during the marriage.

(e) The obligations and assets, including the separate property, of each party.

(f) The duration of the marriage.

(g) The ability of the supported party to engage in gainful employment without unduly interfering with the interests of dependent children in the custody of the party.

(h) The age and health of the parties.

(i) Documented evidence of any history of domestic violence, as defined in Section 6211, between the parties, including, but not limited to, consideration of emotional distress resulting from domestic violence perpetrated against the supported party by the supporting party, and consideration of any history of violence against the supporting party by the supported party.

(j) The immediate and specific tax consequences to each party.

(k) The balance of the hardships to each party.

(l) The goal that the supported party shall be self-supporting within a reasonable period of time. Except in the case of a marriage of long duration as described in Section 4336, a "reasonable period of time" for purposes of this section generally shall be one-half the length of the marriage. However, nothing in this section is intended to limit the court's discretion to order support for a greater or lesser length of time, based on any of the other factors listed in this section, Section 4336, and the circumstances of the parties.

(m) The criminal conviction of an abusive spouse and the elimination of the award in accordance with Section 4325.

(n) Any other factors the court determines are just and equitable.

§4323. Effect of cohabitation on support

(a)(1) Except as otherwise agreed to by the parties in writing, there is a rebuttable presumption, affecting the burden of proof, of decreased need for spousal support if the supported party is cohabiting with a person of the opposite sex. Upon a determination that circumstances have changed, the court may modify or terminate the spousal support as provided for in Chapter 6 (commencing with Section 3650) of Part 1.

(2) Holding oneself out to be the husband or wife of the person with whom one is cohabiting is not necessary to constitute cohabitation as the term is used in this section.

(b) The income of a supporting spouse's subsequent spouse or nonmarital partner shall not be considered when determining or modifying spousal support.

(c) Nothing in this section precludes later modification or termination of spousal support on proof of change of circumstances.

§4324. Attempted murder of spouse; prohibited awards

In addition to any other remedy authorized by law, when a spouse is convicted of attempting to murder the other spouse . . . , the injured spouse shall be entitled to a prohibition of any temporary or permanent award for spousal support or medical, life, or other insurance benefits or payments from the injured spouse to the other spouse.

As used in this section, "injured spouse" means the spouse who has been the subject of the attempted murder for which the other spouse was convicted, whether or not actual physical injury occurred.

§4325. Temporary or permanent support to abusive spouse; rebuttable presumption disfavoring award; evidence

(a) In any proceeding for dissolution of marriage where there is a criminal conviction for an act of domestic violence perpetrated by one spouse against the other spouse entered by the court within five years prior to the filing of the dissolution proceeding, or at any time thereafter, there shall be a rebuttable presumption affecting the burden of proof that any award of temporary or permanent spousal support to the abusive spouse otherwise awardable pursuant to the standards of this part should not be made.

(b) The court may consider documented evidence of a convicted spouse's history as a victim of domestic violence . . . perpetrated by the other spouse, or any other factors the court deems just and equitable, as conditions for rebutting this presumption.

(c) The rebuttable presumption created in this section may be rebutted by a preponderance of the evidence.

Chapter 3. Spousal Support upon Dissolution or Legal Separation

§4330. Order for spousal support in dissolution or legal separation proceeding

(a) In a judgment of dissolution of marriage or legal separation of the parties, the court may order a party to pay for the support of the other party an amount, for a period of time, that the court determines is just and reasonable, based on the standard of living established during the marriage, taking into consideration the circumstances as provided in Chapter 2 (commencing with Section 4320). . . .

§4331. Examination by vocational training consultant

(a) In a proceeding for dissolution of marriage or for legal separation of the parties, the court may order a party to submit to an examination by a vocational training counselor. The examination shall include an assessment of the party's ability to obtain employment based upon the party's age, health, education, marketable skills, employment history, and the current availability of employment opportunities. The focus of the examination shall be on an assessment of the party's ability to obtain employment that would allow the party to maintain herself or himself at the marital standard of living. . . .

(f) The court may order the supporting spouse to pay, in addition to spousal support, the necessary expenses and costs of the counseling, retraining, or education.

§4332. Court findings concerning circumstances

In a proceeding for dissolution of marriage or for legal separation of the parties, the court shall make specific factual findings with respect to the standard of living during the marriage, and, at the request of either party, the court shall make appropriate factual determinations with respect to other circumstances.

§4333. Retroactivity of order

An order for spousal support in a proceeding for dissolution of marriage or for legal separation of the parties may be made retroactive to the date of filing the notice of motion or order to show cause, or to any subsequent date.

§4334. Support for contingent period of time

(a) If a court orders spousal support for a contingent period of time, the obligation of the supporting party terminates on the happening of the contingency. The court may, in the order, order the supported party to notify the supporting party, or the supporting party's attorney of record, of the happening of the contingency.

(b) If the supported party fails to notify the supporting party, or the attorney of record of the supporting party, of the happening of the contingency and continues to accept spousal support payments, the supported party shall refund payments received that accrued after the happening of the contingency, except that the overpayments shall first be applied to spousal support payments that are then in default.

§4335. Support for fixed period of time

An order for spousal support terminates at the end of the period provided in the order and shall not be extended unless the court retains jurisdiction in the order or under Section 4336.

§4336. Retention of jurisdiction

(a) Except on written agreement of the parties to the contrary or a court order terminating spousal support, the court retains jurisdiction indefinitely in a proceeding for dissolution of marriage or for legal separation of the parties where the marriage is of long duration.

(b) For the purpose of retaining jurisdiction, there is a presumption affecting the burden of producing evidence that a marriage of 10 years or more, from the date of marriage to the date of separation, is a marriage of long duration. However, the court may consider periods of separation during the marriage in determining whether the marriage is in fact of long duration. Nothing in this subdivision precludes a court from determining that a marriage of less than 10 years is a marriage of long duration.

(c) Nothing in this section limits the court's discretion to terminate spousal support in later proceedings on a showing of changed circumstances.

(d) This section applies to the following:

(1) A proceeding filed on or after January 1, 1988.

(2) A proceeding pending on January 1, 1988, in which the court has not entered a permanent spousal support order or in which the court order is subject to modification.

§4337. Effect of death or remarriage

Except as otherwise agreed by the parties in writing, the obligation of a party under an order for the support of the other party terminates upon the death of either party or the remarriage of the other party.

§4338. Order of resort to property for payment of spousal support

In the enforcement of an order for spousal support, the court shall resort to the property described below in the order indicated:

(a) The earnings, income, or accumulations of either spouse, while living separate and apart from the other spouse, which would have been community property if the spouse had not been living separate and apart from the other spouse.

(b) The community property.

(c) The quasi-community property.

(d) The other separate property of the party required to make the support payments.

§4339. Security for payment

The court may order the supporting party to give reasonable security for payment of spousal support.

Chapter 5. Provision for Support after Death of Supporting Party

§4360. Annuity, life insurance, or trust for support

(a) For the purpose of Section 4320, where it is just and reasonable in view of the circumstances of the parties, the court, in determining the needs of a supported spouse, may include an amount sufficient to purchase an annuity for the supported spouse or to maintain insurance for the benefit of the supported spouse on the life of the spouse required to make the payment of support, or may require the spouse required to make the payment of support to establish a trust to provide for the support of the supported spouse, so that the supported spouse will not be left without means of support in the event that the spousal support is terminated by the death of the party required to make the payment of support.

(b) Except as otherwise agreed to by the parties in writing, an order made under this section may be modified or terminated at the discretion of the court at any time before the death of the party required to make the payment of support.

SELECTED PROVISIONS FROM CALIFORNIA
PROBATE CODE
West 1992

§28. Community property

"Community property" means:

(a) Community property heretofore or hereafter acquired during marriage by a married person while domiciled in this state.

(b) All personal property wherever situated, and all real property situated in this state, heretofore or hereafter acquired during the marriage by a married person while domiciled elsewhere, that is community property, or a substantially equivalent type of marital property, under the laws of the place where the acquiring spouse was domiciled at the time of its acquisition.

(c) All personal property wherever situated, and all real property situated in this state, heretofore or hereafter acquired during the marriage by a married person in exchange for real or personal property, wherever situated, that is community property, or a substantially equivalent type of marital property, under the laws of the place where the acquiring spouse was domiciled at the time the property so exchanged was acquired.

§32. Devise

"Devise," when used as a noun, means a disposition of real or personal property by will, and, when used as a verb, means to dispose of real or personal property by will.

§44. Heir

"Heir" means any person, including the surviving spouse, who is entitled to take property of the decedent by intestate succession under this code.

§50. Issue

"Issue" of a person means all his or her lineal descendants of all generations, with the relationship of parent and child at each generation being determined by the definitions of child and parent.

§59. Predeceased spouse

"Predeceased spouse" means a person who died before the decedent while married to the decedent, except that the term does not include any of the following:

(a) A person who obtains or consents to a final decree or judgment of dissolution of marriage from the decedent or a final decree or judgment of annulment of their marriage, which decree or judgment is not recognized as valid in this state, unless they (1) subsequently participate in a marriage ceremony purporting to marry each to the other or (2) subsequently live together as husband and wife.

(b) A person who, following a decree or judgment of dissolution or annulment of marriage obtained by the decedent, participates in a marriage ceremony to a third person.

(c) A person who was a party to a valid proceeding concluded by an order purporting to terminate all marital property rights.

§66. Quasi-community property

"Quasi-community property" means the following property, other than community property as defined in Section 28:

(a) All personal property wherever situated, and all real property situated in this state, heretofore or hereafter acquired by a decedent while domiciled elsewhere that would have been the community property of the decedent and the surviving spouse if the decedent had been domiciled in this state at the time of its acquisition.

(b) All personal property wherever situated, and all real property situated in this state, heretofore or hereafter acquired in exchange for real or personal property, wherever situated, that would have been the community property of the decedent and the surviving spouse if the decedent had been domiciled in this state at the time the property so exchanged was acquired.

§78. Surviving spouse

"Surviving spouse" does not include any of the following:

(a) A person whose marriage to the decedent has been dissolved or annulled, unless, by virtue of a subsequent marriage, the person is married to the decedent at the time of death.

(b) A person who obtains or consents to a final decree or judgment of dissolution of marriage from the decedent or a final decree or judgment of annulment of their marriage, which decree or judgment is not recognized as valid in this state, unless they (1) subsequently participate in a marriage ceremony purporting to marry each to the other or (2) subsequently live together as husband and wife.

(c) A person who, following a decree or judgment of dissolution or annulment of marriage obtained by the decedent, participates in a marriage ceremony with a third person.

(d) A person who was a party to a valid proceeding concluded by an order purporting to terminate all marital property rights.

§100. Community property

(a) Upon the death of a married person, one-half of the community property belongs to the surviving spouse and the other half belongs to the decedent.

(b) Notwithstanding subdivision (a), a husband and wife may agree in writing to divide their community property on the basis of a non pro rata division of the aggregate value of the community property or on the basis of a division of each individual item or asset of community property, or partly on each basis. Nothing in this subdivision shall be construed to require this written agreement in order to permit or recognize a non pro rata division of community property.

§101. Quasi-community property

(a) Upon the death of a married person domiciled in this state, one-half of the decedent's quasi-community property belongs to the surviving spouse and the other half belongs to the decedent.

(b) Notwithstanding subdivision (a), a husband and wife may agree in writing to divide their quasi-community property on the basis of a non pro rata division of the aggregate value of the quasi-community property, or on the basis of a division of each individual item or asset of quasi-community property, or partly on each basis. Nothing in this subdivision shall be construed to require this written agreement in order to permit or recognize a non pro rata division of quasi-community property.

§102. Transfer of quasi-community property; restoration to decedent's estate; requirements

(a) The decedent's surviving spouse may require the transferee of property in which the surviving spouse had an expectancy under Section 101 at the time of the transfer to restore to the decedent's estate one-half of the property if the transferee retains the property or, if not, one-half of its proceeds or, if none, one-half of its value at the time of transfer, if all of the following requirements are satisfied:

(1) The decedent died domiciled in this state.

(2) The decedent made a transfer of the property to a person other than the surviving spouse without receiving in exchange a consideration of substantial value and without the written consent or joinder of the surviving spouse.

(3) The transfer is any of the following types:

(A) A transfer under which the decedent retained at the time of death the possession or enjoyment of, or the right to income from, the property.

(B) A transfer to the extent that the decedent retained at the time of death a power, either alone or in conjunction with any other person, to revoke or to consume, invade, or dispose of the principal for the decedent's own benefit.

(C) A transfer whereby property is held at the time of the decedent's death by the decedent and another with right of survivorship.

(b) Nothing in this section requires a transferee to restore to the decedent's estate any life insurance, accident insurance, joint annuity, or pension payable to a person other than the surviving spouse.

(c) All property restored to the decedent's estate under this section belongs to the surviving spouse pursuant to Section 101 as though the transfer had not been made.

§103. Simultaneous death; community or quasi-community property

Except as provided by Section 224 [regulating life and accident insurance proceeds], if a husband and wife die leaving community or quasi-community property and it cannot be established by clear and convincing evidence that one spouse survived the other:

(a) One-half of the community property and one-half of the quasi-community property shall be administered or distributed, or otherwise dealt with, as if one spouse had survived and as if that half belonged to that spouse.

(b) The other half of the community property and the other half of the quasi-community property shall be administered or distributed, or otherwise dealt with, as if the other spouse had survived and as if that half belonged to that spouse.

§120. Nondomiciliary decedent; real property within state; surviving spouse's right; effect of will

If a married person dies not domiciled in this state and leaves a valid will disposing of real property in this state which is not the community property of the decedent and the surviving spouse, the surviving spouse has the same right to elect to take a portion of or interest in such property against the will of the decedent as though the property were located in the decedent's domicile at death.

§5130. Joint account

"Joint account" means an account payable on request to one or more of two or more parties whether or not mention is made of any right of survivorship.

§5302. Sums remaining upon death of party

Subject to Section 5600:

(a) Sums remaining on deposit at the death of a party to a joint account belong to the surviving party or parties as against the estate of the decedent unless there is clear and convincing evidence of a different intent. . . .

§5305. Married parties; community property; presumption; rebuttal; change of survivorship right, beneficiary, or payee by will

(a) . . . [I]f parties to [a bank] account are married to each other, whether or not they are so described in the deposit agreement, their net contribution to the account is presumed to be and remain their community property.

(b) Notwithstanding Sections 2581 and 2640 of the Family Code, the presumption established by this section is a presumption affecting the burden of proof and may be rebutted by proof of either of the following:

(1) The sums on deposit that are claimed to be separate property can be traced from separate property unless it is proved that the married persons made a written agreement that expressed their clear intent that such sums be their community property.

(2) The married persons made a written agreement, separate from the deposit agreement, that expressly provided that the sums on deposit, claimed not to be community property, were not to be community property.

(c) Except as provided in Section 5307, a right of survivorship arising from the express terms of the account or under Section 5302, a beneficiary designation in a Totten trust account, or a P.O.D. [payable on death] payee designation, may not be changed by will.

(d) Except as provided in subdivisions (b) and (c), a multiple-party account created with community property funds does not in any way alter community property rights.

§5307. Community property account

For the purposes of this chapter, except to the extent the terms of the account or deposit agreement expressly provide otherwise, if the parties to an account are married to each other and the account is expressly described in the account agreement as a "community property" account, the ownership of the account during lifetime and after the death of a spouse is governed by the law governing community property generally.

§5600. Nonprobate transfer to former spouse executed before or during marriage; failure of transfer due to dissolution or annulment of marriage; situations that do not cause a nonprobate transfer to fail; rights of subsequent purchaser

(a) Except as provided in subdivision (b), a nonprobate transfer to the transferor's former spouse, in an instrument executed by the transferor before or during the marriage, fails if, at the time of the transferor's death, the former spouse is not the transferor's surviving spouse as defined in Section 78, as a result of the dissolution or annulment of the marriage. A judgment of legal separation that does not terminate the status of husband and wife is not a dissolution for purposes of this section.

(b) Subdivision (a) does not cause a nonprobate transfer to fail in any of the following cases:

(1) The nonprobate transfer is not subject to revocation by the transferor at the time of the transferor's death.

(2) There is clear and convincing evidence that the transferor intended to preserve the nonprobate transfer to the former spouse.

(3) A court order that the nonprobate transfer be maintained on behalf of the former spouse is in effect at the time of the transferor's death.

(c) Where a nonprobate transfer fails by operation of this section, the instrument making the nonprobate transfer shall be treated as it would if the former spouse failed to survive the transferor.

(d) Nothing in this section affects the rights of a subsequent purchaser or encumbrancer for value in good faith who relies on the apparent failure of a nonprobate transfer under this section or who lacks knowledge of the failure of a nonprobate transfer under this section. . . .

§5601. Joint tenancy created before or during marriage severed if former spouse not decedent's surviving spouse; situations where joint tenancy is not severed

(a) Except as provided in subdivision (b), a joint tenancy between the decedent and the decedent's former spouse, created before or during the marriage, is severed as to the decedent's interest if, at the time of the decedent's death, the former spouse is not the decedent's surviving spouse as defined in Section 78, as a result of the dissolution or annulment of the marriage. A judgment of legal separation that does not terminate the status of husband and wife is not a dissolution for purposes of this section.

(b) Subdivision (a) does not sever a joint tenancy in either of the following cases:

(1) The joint tenancy is not subject to severance by the decedent at the time of the decedent's death.

(2) There is clear and convincing evidence that the decedent intended to preserve the joint tenancy in favor of the former spouse.

(c) Nothing in this section affects the rights of a subsequent purchaser or encumbrancer for value in good faith who relies on an apparent severance under this section or who lacks knowledge of a severance under this section.

(d) For purposes of this section, property held in "joint tenancy" includes property held as community property with right of survivorship, as described in Section 682.1 of the Civil Code.

§6400. Property subject to intestacy provisions

Any part of the estate of a decedent not effectively disposed of by will passes to the decedent's heirs as prescribed in this part.

§6401. Surviving spouse; intestate share;
community or quasi-community property;
separate property

(a) As to community property, the intestate share of the surviving spouse is the one-half of the community property that belongs to the decedent under Section 100.

(b) As to quasi-community property, the intestate share of the surviving spouse is the one-half of the quasi-community property that belongs to the decedent under Section 101.

(c) As to separate property, the intestate share of the surviving spouse or surviving domestic partner . . . is as follows:

(1) The entire intestate estate if the decedent did not leave any surviving issue, parent, brother, sister, or issue of a deceased brother or sister.

(2) One-half of the intestate estate in the following cases:

(A) Where the decedent leaves only one child or the issue of one deceased child.

(B) Where the decedent leaves no issue but leaves a parent or parents or their issue or the issue of either of them.

(3) One-third of the intestate estate in the following cases:

(A) Where the decedent leaves more than one child.

(B) Where the decedent leaves one child and the issue of one or more deceased children.

(C) Where the decedent leaves issue of two or more deceased children.

§6402. Intestate estate not passing to surviving spouse

Except as provided in Section 6402.5, the part of the intestate estate not passing to the surviving spouse or surviving domestic partner . . . under Section 6401, or the entire intestate estate if there is no surviving spouse or domestic partner, passes as follows:

(a) To the issue of the decedent, the issue taking equally if they are all of the same degree of kinship to the decedent, but if of unequal degree, those of more remote degree take [by representation].

(b) If there is no surviving issue, to the decedent's parent or parents equally.

(c) If there is no surviving issue or parent, to the issue of the parents or either of them, the issue taking equally if they are all of the same degree of kinship to the decedent, but if of unequal degree those of more remote degree take [by representation].

(d) If there is no surviving issue, parent or issue of a parent, but the decedent is survived by one or more grandparents or issue of grandparents, to the grandparent or grandparents equally, or to the issue of those grandparents if there is no surviving grandparent, the issue taking equally if they are all of the same degree of kinship to the decedent, but if of unequal degree those of more remote degree take [by representation].

(e) If there is no surviving issue, parent or issue of a parent, grandparent or issue of a grandparent, but the decedent is survived by the issue of a predeceased spouse, to that issue, the issue taking equally if they are all of the same degree of kinship to the predeceased spouse, but if of unequal degree those of more remote degree take [by representation].

(f) If there is no surviving issue, parent or issue of a parent, grandparent or issue of a grandparent, or issue of a predeceased spouse, but the decedent is survived by next of kin, to the next of kin in equal degree, but when there are two or more collateral kindred in equal degree who claim through different ancestors, those who claim through the nearest ancestor are preferred to those claiming through an ancestor more remote.

(g) If there is no surviving next of kin of the decedent and no surviving issue of a predeceased spouse of the decedent, but the decedent is survived by the parents of a predeceased spouse or the issue of those parents, to the parent or parents equally, or to the issue of those parents if both are deceased, the issue taking equally if they are all of the same degree of kinship to the predeceased spouse, but if of unequal degree those of more remote degree take [by representation].

§6402.5 Predeceased spouse; portion of decedent's estate attributable to decedent's predeceased spouse

(a) For purposes of distributing real property under this section if the decedent had a predeceased spouse who died not more than 15 years before the decedent and there is no surviving spouse or issue of the decedent, the portion of the decedent's estate attributable to the decedent's predeceased spouse passes as follows:

(1) If the decedent is survived by issue of the predeceased spouse, to the surviving issue of the predeceased spouse. . . .

(2) If there is no surviving issue of the predeceased spouse but the decedent is survived by a parent or parents of the predeceased spouse, to the predeceased spouse's surviving parent or parents equally.

(3) If there is no surviving issue or parent of the predeceased spouse but the decedent is survived by issue of a parent of the predeceased spouse, to

the surviving issue of the parents of the predeceased spouse or either of them. . . .

(4) If the decedent is not survived by issue, parent, or issue of a parent of the predeceased spouse, to the next of kin of the decedent in the manner provided in Section 6402.

(5) If the portion of the decedent's estate attributable to the decedent's predeceased spouse would otherwise escheat to the state because there is no kin of the decedent to take under Section 6402, the portion of the decedent's estate attributable to the predeceased spouse passes to the next of kin of the predeceased spouse who shall take in the same manner as the next of kin of the decedent take under Section 6402.

(b) For purposes of distributing personal property under this section if the decedent had a predeceased spouse who died not more than five years before the decedent, and there is no surviving spouse or issue of the decedent, the portion of the decedent's estate attributable to the decedent's predeceased spouse passes as follows:

(1) If the decedent is survived by issue of the predeceased spouse, to the surviving issue of the predeceased spouse. . . .

(2) If there is no surviving issue of the predeceased spouse but the decedent is survived by a parent or parents of the predeceased spouse, to the predeceased spouse's surviving parent or parents equally.

(3) If there is no surviving issue or parent of the predeceased spouse but the decedent is survived by issue of a parent of the predeceased spouse, to the surviving issue of the parents of the predeceased spouse or either of them. . . .

(4) If the decedent is not survived by issue, parent, or issue of a parent of the predeceased spouse, to the next of kin of the decedent in the manner provided in Section 6402.

(5) If the portion of the decedent's estate attributable to the decedent's predeceased spouse would otherwise escheat to the state because there is no kin of the decedent to take under Section 6402, the portion of the decedent's estate attributable to the predeceased spouse passes to the next of kin of the predeceased spouse who shall take in the same manner as the next of kin of the decedent take under Section 6402. . . .

(f) For the purposes of this section, the "portion of the decedent's estate attributable to the decedent's predeceased spouse" means all of the following property in the decedent's estate:

(1) One-half of the community property in existence at the time of the death of the predeceased spouse.

(2) One-half of any community property, in existence at the time of death of the predeceased spouse, which was given to the decedent by the predeceased spouse by way of gift, descent, or devise.

(3) That portion of any community property in which the predeceased spouse had any incident of ownership and which vested in the decedent upon the death of the predeceased spouse by right of survivorship.

(4) Any separate property of the predeceased spouse which came to the decedent by gift, descent, or devise of the predeceased spouse or which vested in the decedent upon the death of the predeceased spouse by right of survivorship.

(g) For the purposes of this section, quasi-community property shall be treated the same as community property.

(h) For the purposes of this section:

(1) Relatives of the predeceased spouse conceived before decedent's death but born thereafter inherit as if they had been born in the lifetime of the decedent.

(2) A person who is related to the predeceased spouse through two lines of relationship is entitled to only a single share based on the relationship which would entitle the person to the larger share.

§6412. Dower and curtesy; nonrecognition

Except to the extent provided in Section 120, the estates of dower and curtesy are not recognized.

§7000. Passage to devisee or intestate heirs

Subject to Section 7001, title to a decedent's property passes on the decedent's death to the person to whom it is devised in the decedent's last will or, in the absence of such a devise, to the decedent's heirs as prescribed in the laws governing intestate succession.

§7001. Administration of decedent's property; rights of beneficiaries and creditors

The decedent's property is subject to administration under this code, except as otherwise provided by law, and is subject to the rights of beneficiaries, creditors, and other persons as provided by law.

§11440. Petition to allocate debt

If it appears that a debt of the decedent has been paid or is payable in whole or in part by the surviving spouse, or that a debt of the surviving spouse has been paid or is payable in whole or in part from property in the decedent's estate, the personal representative, the surviving spouse, or a beneficiary may, at any time before an order for final distribution is made, petition for an order to allocate the debt.

§11441. Contents of petitions

The petition shall include a statement of all of the following:

(a) All debts of the decedent and surviving spouse known to the petitioner that are alleged to be subject to allocation and whether paid in whole or part or unpaid.

(b) The reason why the debts should be allocated.

(c) The proposed allocation and the basis for allocation alleged by the petitioner.

§11442. **Value of separate and community property affecting allocation where no inventory and appraisal provided; show cause order**

If it appears from the petition that allocation would be affected by the value of the separate property of the surviving spouse and any community property and quasi-community property not administered in the estate and if an inventory and appraisal of the property has not been provided by the surviving spouse, the court shall make an order to show cause why the information should not be provided.

§11444. **Allocation of debt**

(a) The personal representative and the surviving spouse may provide for allocation by agreement and, on a determination by the court that the agreement substantially protects the rights of interested persons, the allocation provided in the agreement shall be ordered by the court.

(b) In the absence of an agreement, each debt subject to allocation shall first be characterized by the court as separate or community, in accordance with the laws of the state applicable to marital dissolution proceedings. Following that characterization, the debt or debts shall be allocated as follows:

(1) Separate debts of either spouse shall be allocated to that spouse's separate property assets, and community debts shall be allocated to the spouses' community property assets.

(2) If a separate property asset of either spouse is subject to a secured debt that is characterized as that spouse's separate debt, and the net equity in that asset available to satisfy that secured debt is less than that secured debt, the unsatisfied portion of that secured debt shall be treated as an unsecured separate debt of that spouse and allocated to the net value of that spouse's other separate property assets.

(3) If the net value of either spouse's separate property assets is less than that spouse's unsecured separate debt or debts, the unsatisfied portion of the debt or debts shall be allocated to the net value of that spouse's one-half share of the community property assets. If the net value of that spouse's one-half share of the community property assets is less than that spouse's unsatisfied unsecured separate debt or debts, the remaining unsatisfied portion of the debt or debts shall be allocated to the net value of the other spouse's one-half share of the community property assets.

(4) If a community property asset is subject to a secured debt that is characterized as a community debt, and the net equity in that asset available to satisfy that secured debt is less than that secured debt, the unsatisfied portion of that secured debt shall be treated as an unsecured community debt and allocated to the net value of the other community property assets.

(5) If the net value of the community property assets is less than the unsecured community debt or debts, the unsatisfied portion of the debt or debts shall be allocated equally between the separate property assets of the decedent and the surviving spouse. If the net value of either spouse's separate property assets is less than that spouse's share of the unsatisfied portion of the unsecured community debt or debts, the remaining unsatisfied portion of the debt or debts shall be allocated to the net value of the other spouse's separate property assets.

(c) For purposes of this section:

(1) The net value of either spouse's separate property asset shall refer to its fair market value as of the date of the decedent's death, minus the date- of-death balance of any liens and encumbrances on that asset that have been characterized as that spouse's separate debts.

(2) The net value of a community property asset shall refer to its fair market value as of the date of the decedent's death, minus the date-of-death balance of any liens and encumbrances on that asset that have been characterized as community debts.

(3) In the case of a nonrecourse debt, the amount of that debt shall be limited to the net equity in the collateral, based on the fair market value of the collateral as of the date of the decedent's death, that is available to satisfy that debt. For the purposes of this paragraph, "nonrecourse debt" means a debt for which the debtor's obligation to repay is limited to the collateral securing the debt, and for which a deficiency judgment against the debtor is not permitted by law.

(d) Notwithstanding the foregoing provisions of this section, the court may order a different allocation of debts between the decedent's estate and the surviving spouse if the court finds a different allocation to be equitable under the circumstances.

(e) Nothing contained in this section is intended to impair or affect the rights of third parties. If a personal representative or the surviving spouse incurs any damages or expense, including attorney's fees, on account of the nonpayment of a debt that was allocated to the other party pursuant to subdivision (b), or as the result of a debt being misallocated due to fraud or intentional misrepresentation by the other party, the party incurring damages shall be entitled to recover from the other party for damages or expense deemed reasonable by the court that made the allocation.

§11446. Last illness and funeral expenses

Notwithstanding any other statute, funeral expenses and expenses of last illness shall be charged against the estate of the decedent and shall not be allocated to, or charged against the community share of the surviving spouse, whether or not the surviving spouse is financially able to pay the expenses and whether or not the surviving spouse or any other person is also liable for the expenses.

§13500. Husband and wife dying intestate or testate; surviving spouse; administration not necessary

Except as provided in this chapter, when a husband or wife dies intestate leaving property that passes to the surviving spouse under Section 6401, or dies testate and by his or her will devises all or a part of his or her property to the surviving spouse, the property passes to the survivor subject to the provisions of Chapter 2 (commencing with Section 13540) and Chapter 3 (commencing with Section 13550), and no administration is necessary.

§13501. Property subject to administration

. . . [T]he following property of the decedent is subject to administration under this code:

(a) Property passing to someone other than the surviving spouse under the decedent's will or by intestate succession.

(b) Property disposed of in trust under the decedent's will.

(c) Property in which the decedent's will limits the surviving spouse to a qualified ownership. . . .

§13502. Property subject to administration upon election of surviving spouse

(a) Upon the election of the surviving spouse or the personal representative, guardian of the estate, or conservator of the estate of the surviving spouse, all or a portion of the following property may be administered under this code:

(1) The one-half of the community property that belongs to the decedent under Section 100, the one-half of the quasi-community property that belongs to the decedent under Section 101, and the separate property of the decedent.

(2) The one-half of the community property that belongs to the surviving spouse under Section 100 and the one-half of the quasi-community property that belongs to the surviving spouse under Section 101. . . .

§13550. Personal liability for debts chargeable against property

. . . [U]pon the death of a married person, the surviving spouse is personally liable for the debts of the deceased spouse chargeable against the property described in Section 13551 to the extent provided in Section 13551.

§13551. Limitation of liability

The liability imposed by Section 13550 shall not exceed the fair market value at the date of the decedent's death, less the amount of any liens and encumbrances, of the total of the following:

(a) The portion of the one-half of the community and quasi-community property belonging to the surviving spouse under Sections 100 and 101 that is not exempt from enforcement of a money judgment and is not administered in the estate of the deceased spouse.

(b) The portion of the one-half of the community and quasi-community property belonging to the decedent under Sections 100 and 101 that passes to the surviving spouse without administration.

(c) The separate property of the decedent that passes to the surviving spouse without administration.

§21610. Share of omitted spouse

Except as provided in Section 21611, if a decedent fails to provide in a testamentary instrument for the decedent's surviving spouse who married the decedent after the execution of all the decedent's testamentary instruments, the omitted spouse shall receive a share in the decedent's estate consisting of the following property in said estate:

(a) The one-half of the community property that belongs to the decedent under Section 100.

(b) The one-half of the quasi-community property that belongs to the decedent under Section 101.

(c) A share of the separate property of the decedent equal in value to that which the spouse would have received if the decedent had died without having executed a testamentary instrument, but in no event is the share to be more than one-half the value of the separate property in the estate.

§21611. Spouse not receiving share; circumstances

The spouse shall not receive a share of the estate under Section 21610 if any of the following is established:

(a) The decedent's failure to provide for the spouse in the decedent's testamentary instruments was intentional and that intention appears from the testamentary instruments.

(b) The testator provided for the spouse by transfer outside the estate passing by the decedent's testamentary instruments and the intention that the transfer be in lieu of a provision in such instruments is shown by statements of the decedent or from the amount of the transfer or by other evidence.

(c) The spouse made a valid agreement waiving the right to share in the decedent's estate.

§21612. Manner of satisfying share of omitted spouse

(a) Except as provided in subdivision (b), in satisfying a share provided by this chapter:

(1) The share shall first be taken from the decedent's estate not disposed of by will or trust, if any.

(2) If that is not sufficient, so much as may be necessary to satisfy the share shall be taken from all beneficiaries of decedent's testamentary instruments in proportion to the value they may respectively receive. Such value shall be determined as of the date of the decedent's death.

(b) If the obvious intention of the decedent in relation to some specific devise or other provision of a testamentary instrument would be defeated by the application of subdivision (a), the specific devise or gift or provision may be exempted from the apportionment under subdivision (a), and a different apportionment, consistent with the intention of the decedent, may be adopted.

CALIFORNIA FINANCIAL CODE

§851. Married persons

A bank account by or in the name of a married person shall be held for the exclusive right and benefit of the person, shall be free from the control or lien of any other person except a creditor, and shall be paid to the person or to the order of the person, and payment so made is a valid and sufficient release and discharge to the bank for the deposit or any part thereof.

TABLE OF CASES

INDEX